D1238143

GERMANY

IN WESTERN CIVILIZATION

GERMANY
IN
WESTERN
CIVILIZATION

WILLIAM HARVEY MAEHL

THE UNIVERSITY OF ALABAMA PRESS
University, Alabama

SECOND PRINTING 1981

Library of Congress Cataloging in Publication Data
Maehl, William Harvey, 1915–
  Germany in Western civilization.

  Bibliography: p.
  Includes index.
  1. Germany—History. I. Title.
DD89.M23   943   77-1394
ISBN 0-8173-5707-6

Copyright © 1979 by
The University of Alabama Press
ALL RIGHTS RESERVED
Manufactured in the United States of America

CONTENTS

PREFACE

For a decade after World War II the study of German history was in disrepute. It was the uninformed view of an angry world that Hitler had in fact been the culmination of militaristic and authoritarian tendencies that had lurked in the German mentality from time immemorial. For the victor peoples the fall of the Reich was to be compared with Lucifer's fall into hell.

Feeling that heaven had to be on the winning side, the youth of Germany shared this view. They repudiated their national heritage. They believed that a failure of such titanic proportions as represented by the two German wars of the century must in some occult way be attributable to the inheritance of undesirable national characteristics from the past. They therefore wanted to hear no more about the glorious deeds of Germany's heroes and statesmen from the Middle Ages to modern times. They did not even care to hear much about the cultural contributions of their forefathers. Never had a generation so resolutely lowered the portcullis upon its history. Rejecting all things, including their parents, that had brought the Reich to catastrophe, German youth, like the fool in the Roman proverb *(malo accepto stultus sapit),* having suffered great evil, now became improbably wise.

The total destruction of the balance of power in the Europe of 1945 provoked the post-Nazi generation into turning away from the whole idea of nationalism because it was subversive of German interests. The state could be interred, but the German people must be rescued. The one hope for resurrection lay in merging Germany with old Europe. The fact that as a result of the war the continental states had been reduced to a family of dwarfs beside the Russian colossus encouraged the belief that this could be done. After all, misery likes company. For the sake of reviving a balance of power against the USSR, the other states might very well welcome the integration of German industry, technology, manpower, and military potential with a new, supranational continental polity. Manifestly, in such an intellectual climate the study of German history almost died on the vine.

In the first postwar decade journalistic historians, who had little regard for the scientific method and who catered to the emotions, saw the entire history of Germany through the alembic of the Third Reich. Postulating that the whole national development had been but the prolegomenon to Nazism, they laid the objective study of the German past under an interdict. Fortunately such pontifical dicta did not long prevail. They were gradually but firmly pushed aside. In the late 1950s honest efforts, if not quite Rankean or Burkean in their objectivity, were made to reconstruct the history of Germany, less in the light of the changing fashions of the day than from the standpoint of the role of Germany in each period of European civilization. The renaissance of German historical studies was at the same time aided by swift publication of secret documents from German foreign office and governmental archives, as well as by introduction of new American sociological, economic, and statistical methods of examining history.

The revival of the scientific study of German history has engendered bitter controversy between champions of differing perspectives. Thus, Meinecke, Schnabel, Eyck, Dehio, Iggers, and Pflanze all have stressed the political immaturity of the Germans in recent history and charted the aberration of German political institutions and philosophy from the mainstream of European democratic development. Some, like Iggers, have tried to trace Hitlerism to defects in the national character and have maligned the baleful influence of historicism upon it. Other scholars, among them Rothfels, Ritter, Bühler, Bussmann, A. O. Becker, Zechlin, Muralt, Rein, Golo Mann, Schieder, and Reiners, have rejected such theses as gross distortions of fact. Some of these scholars have stressed nonrecurrent accidental factors as the key to the fate of recent Germany, whereas others have pointed to the overriding significance of the requirements generated by Germany's historically central geographic location *(Staat der Mitte)*.

Although Germany shared with several other countries a heritage of internecine and external wars and military occupation, these handicaps did not, of course, transmogrify the German mind. During the Middle Ages Germany did not cease to embody the ennobling ideal of a Holy Empire, the ruler and dominant estates of which were theoretically and often practically dedicated to the proposition that Europe should be a Christian corporative community governed by statutes that harmonized with divine law and satisfied the conscience. The emperor, who was usually a German, was supposed to espouse this exalted concept. When in the twilight of the medieval era the territorial states system in Germany came to substitute for the *sacrum imperium,* a majority of German rulers still held fast to the notion of the sanctity of divine and natural law. Accordingly, this, more often than not, provided an effective restraint to princely cupidity and aggressiveness even when customary or statutory law did not. The German system of pluralistic sovereignty therefore never degenerated into a Hobbesian war of all against all, for the whole system was suffused by a conservative, religious, and, later, rationalist *Weltanschauung*. This outlook permitted only nicely delimited changes in the existing territorial configuration.

The endemically conservative Germanic bias was exemplified not only in the policies of Frederick II (after 1743), Stein, Hardenberg, Frederick William III, Frederick William IV, and William I, but also by the rulers of many secondary German states. The natural disposition of these rulers was to resist drastic alterations in the existing Central European states system. When they accommodated themselves to revolutionary changes, as during the Thirty Years' War and the epoch of the French Revolution and the Napoleonic wars, it was because they were forced to by external circumstances.

Bismarck, too, was arguably (Muralt) an ethical conservative who was guided by strong religious convictions as well as by respect for tradition. His basic conservatism, which was the antithesis of Hitler's demoniacal radicalism, led him to build a house of compromises, for that is what the Second Empire was in most respects. After 1871 no one championed the preservation of the status quo more stoutly than he did. It has been cogently argued by Ritter, Steglich, Herzfeld, Bussmann, W. Mommsen, von Vietsch, and many others, in opposition to the Fritz Fischer school, that the same moderation and restraint characterized the foreign policy of Chancellor Bethmann-Hollweg in the years 1914–17. It has been affirmed that he, no less than Stein and Bismarck, wished to preserve the old order but with modifications and that he toiled to insure the survival of an independent European states system.

Enough has been said to indicate that, as is the case with all world-historic peoples, there have always been saints as well as devils in Germany. Its political, constitutional, and intellectual development has been a complex phenomenon conditioned by many factors. High among them have been geography, fragmentation, religious schism, the impact of the technological and industrial revolution, a capacity for work, and an inferiority complex that derived from having been for so long the object of the divisive diplomacy and aggression of stronger neighbors.

A generation has elapsed since the Second German War. It ought now to be possible to eliminate most of the ethnic and nationalist bias that has poisoned assessments of the German contribution to Western civilization. Because this has become possible, there is increasing need for a variety of objective reconstructions of the record of a people who have always been the hub of Europe and whose blood and creativity, in league with Christianity and the Greco-Roman cultural heritage, have been, as James W. Thompson contended, one of the three main components of European civilization.

It is the more appropriate to offer a new abridgement of German history because the civilization of which the old Germany was the heart has now manifestly come to an end. The cities of that country, as with all others of the world, are now greatly changed in appearance. Urban structure, technology, industry, communications, and transportation, and the role and attitudes of the masses in both present-day Germanies would be unintelligible, if not unrecognizable, to past generations. As Europeans make the agonizing transition from one civilization to another it is imperative that they reappraise their heritage. They must perpetuate a knowledge of historic accomplishments in many fields, even as the Romans did for the total Greek bequest. Such knowledge may help keep alive the conviction that the Germans are *one* people who by right and reason ought to be united in a single state, even though it may one day become a federated component of a United States of Europe.

I have virtually omitted footnotes, not merely for brevity's sake but because a general work such as this ought not to be freighted with scholarly paraphernalia. Were I to have indicated all the myriad streets of literature I threaded in the writing of this work, I would unavoidably have wearied the reader and fallen wide of the target.

My work on this book was begun more than a decade ago and is informed by the experience of a generation of teaching German history classes. The completion of this book was made possible by a series of grants-in-aid, which were awarded by Auburn University. Although a number of people have read and commented on parts of this work, my special gratitude is due to Professor Emeritus of the University of Chicago, S. William Halperin, and Professor Bernard C. Weber of The

University of Alabama for having read the whole manuscript and having made cogent suggestions for its improvement. Frequent visits to Germany during a quarter of a century have probably enhanced my understanding of certain aspects of the perennial German problem. At the very least they have led me away from the morass of myth to the firmer ground of fact. Long ago I concluded that if a survey of German history is to have any merit, it must be inspired by a resolve to think objectively and justly about the grand controversial issues in the German record. If I have failed at times to do this, good intentions notwithstanding, the fault is mine alone. Similarly, errors of fact and opinion in this book must be ascribed to me and none other.

I dedicate this book to my loyal wife, Josephine, who read the manuscript for grammar and style. Throughout the years of my writing it she exhibited a patience and forbearance that I, confessedly, did not deserve. She has been of greater material and spiritual aid to me than I care to say. It does not reflect upon her vigilance to admit that I am to a certain extent dissatisfied with the product of my labors. However, I console myself with the thought that dissatisfaction with our work and our world is a habit common to all men.

WILLIAM HARVEY MAEHL

December, 1978   Auburn, Alabama

GERMANY

IN WESTERN CIVILIZATION

PART I

BELOW THE HORIZON

OF HISTORY

Chapter 1

THE ANCIENT GERMANS

Introduction

The political history of the Germans does not begin until nine centuries after Julius Caesar's death. Rome had joined Egypt in the mausoleum of civilizations and the Forum was being used as a quarry when in Carolingian times the Salian Franks welded together Gauls, Bavarians, Saxons, Alemanni, Thuringians, and East Franks into an "Empire of the West." Two more centuries passed before the first independent, almost wholly German state stood forth from the ruins of Charlemagne's empire. All that precedes this natal period is German prehistory. The period of genesis fills a span as long as that which has elapsed since the establishment of the first kingdom of Germany.

Like the rude Slavic tribes to the east of them, the inhabitants of ancient Germany worked out their destinies in the penumbra of Mediterranean civilization. During all the centuries when Babylon and Memphis were storied cities, when Greece was laying the foundation of Western thought, and Rome was teaching the world the craft of imperial administration, the peoples of Germany remained divided and were without written literature, towns, polity, or any of the higher amenities of life. Celts, Illyrians, and Germans for the most part, they stretched out thinly, tribe beyond tribe, through central Europe, dwelling in primeval forest clearings, by sand dunes against the sea, and along the river valleys.

A majority of the motley assortment of predominantly Indo-European inhabitants of central Europe were Germans. The word *German* would appear to be of Celtic origin and was used by the Celts in western Europe and the British Isles to designate Angles and Saxons as well as Suevi, Cimbri, Marcomanni, Bructi, and the other Teutonic tribes. The Romans borrowed the name after Caesar's wars against the Cimbri, and reference is made to the "Germani" in the sixth book of Caesar's *Commentaries on the Gallic Wars*. Although the Germani were really a specific tribe, the word was soon used to apply without distinction to all of the non-Celtic tribes that occupied the space from the Baltic Sea to the Danube and from the Rhine to the Oder River. From Roman usage the term *German* passed into the languages of many people. The word *Deutsch* and the Latin *theodisca* (Italian—*tedesco*) do not seem to have been widely current before the eighth century, and the country itself is not called Deutschland or Tyskland until the eleventh or twelfth century, and until the latter century the Germans themselves had no common term by which to designate themselves as a nation. Far from being a homogeneous blonde, fair-skinned people, the ancient Germans were mainly brunette in the south, blonde in the center, and not infrequently red-headed in the north and northwest. Scientifically there was no such thing as a German type, but there was a common culture embracing all tribes.

The Land and Its People
in Prehistoric Times

Since the emergence of the Baltic shores from under the last glacier about 14,000 to 12,000 years ago, Germany has been divided into two broad zones: plains and uplands. In the north the country forms part of the European northern lowlands, a vast plain curving like a postillion's horn from the Pyrenees to Russia, with trumpet facing east. In the midlands and south there is a triangle of uplands and Alpine forelands *(Mittelgebirge),* whose base rests in the Rhineland and whose apex is in Austria. The plains zone comprises dunes, Baltic terminal moraines, alluvial deposits, and loess. The uplands range from sandy ridges along the tributaries of the Weser and Elbe, over plateaus, to the mountains, vales, and spinel-green lakes of Swabia, Bavaria, and Austria.

Not till the sixth millennium B.C. did the long prevalence of the hunting and food-gathering way of life—associated successively with the Neanderthaloid and Cro-Magnon *(Homo sapiens)* residents of Germany—come to an end. The Mesolithic was joining the upper Paleolithic cultural era in oblivion when in the dawning Neolithic or new stone age the advent of agriculture inaugurated the greatest revolution in prehistory. Spreading along the Danube Valley from the Near East, the new modes of subsistence did not replace but supplemented the older ones. Pursuit of dry farming and animal husbandry promoted the development of semifixed communities. A host of polished stone implements, among them hoes, scythes, sickles, and (we must surmise, for none have survived) wooden plows, ultimately radically increased the food supply and population of the country. It is known that Neolithic inhabitants of Germany raised cattle, sheep, goats, and pigs and cultivated barley, millet, and three varieties of wheat. They also ground grain with querns, stored it in pots, and roasted it.

As pasturage, fertility of soil, and proximity of water permitted, Neolithic men—heirs of the Magdalenian, Ahrensburger, Swiderian, and Kirchdorfer cultures of the Mesolithic era—settled down permanently and consolidated into tribes. They began to accumulate possessions and build rectangular or oblong houses of wattled roofs and wickerwork walls caked with lime. A variety of furniture and utensils filled them. Handmade pottery (but not the potter's wheel) appeared, funnel beaker vessels being manufactured in north Germany and banded pottery being the vogue in much of the rest of the country. The weaving of flax and wool was widespread, but hemp was unknown. About 2000 B.C. simple wheeled wagons were invented, and banded pottery culture gave way to cord or string pottery. The upper Neolithic peoples of Germany seem to have possessed shamans or wise men, practiced fertility rites, and propitiated the world of malign spirits with human sacrifices.

By the second millennium B.C. the belt of moisture-bearing westerlies that had settled over Germany had given rise to dense rain forests, which everywhere encroached upon the clearings earlier made by human communities. Though these woods were neither as impenetrable as in the tropics nor so impoverished in animal life as the Russo-Siberian taiga, they gave Germany an unenviable reputation.

Nine hundred years before the end of the Roman republic, Homer, writing on the bright Ionian shore, located his Kingdom of the Dead in Germany. When eight hundred years later Poseidonius described the land, it seemed no less somber. Covered with a high, dense canopy of leaves, except in the winding river valleys and along the sandy dunes, Germany was not inviting. Precipitation from the westerlies was fairly high the year round, even if temperatures were seldom extreme. Snow was more common than in Britain but less than in Poland and Russia. Summers were mild to warm with relatively clear skies. Conditions were most suitable for the development of culture in the west and south. It is not surprising, therefore, that the first towns in Germany were built by the Romans precisely in the valleys of the Rhine, Isar, Neckar, Inn, and Danube.

From protohistoric to Christian times the configuration of the rivers of Germany long obstructed its unification. Unlike those of France and Russia, they divided rather than united the country. Either like the Weser, Elbe, Oder, and Rhine, the rivers flowed in a northerly or northwesterly direction, or, like the Danube and its tributaries, their currents set eastward. Germany was destined to develop culturally along two main corridors, the Danubian and Rhenish, and to possess no hub of political activity. Throughout the Roman and European ages geography was to favor German particularism.

The Bronze Age Germans

Modern philological and ethnological research has not been able to solve the problem of the origins of the Germans. It has, however, discredited the older theory that they were pure descendants of an homogeneous stock—the Indo-Europeans or Indo-Germans, themselves a branch of *Homo sapiens diluvialis,* who came from the Asiatic steppe and settled northern and eastern Europe in Neolithic times. It now seems unlikely that such diverse racial types and languages as Germanic, Indo-Iranian, Baltic, Slavic, Italic, Greek, Celtic, Armenoid, and Albanian could have derived from the same Neolithic root stock and speech. But if evidence now inclines against the once-popular theory of descent from a single root stock, there is good reason to believe that Germanic culture as we find it on both sides of the Baltic in the Bronze Age (1800–750 B.C.) evolved from a fairly uniform Indo-European, agrarian culture that in Neolithic times had extended from Spain to Russia. The latter culture resembled that of the banded and cord pottery peoples. Evidence as to the seat of origin of this pattern of life places it in a temperate and plains habitat, such as is found in the north European lowlands or the Eurasian steppe area, probably the latter.

In the Bronze Age the Germans were most thickly clustered in the dune and heather region between the estuaries of the Weser and Oder rivers. These people had domesticated the horse, and they cultivated crops in the vicinity of fixed villages. But the Germans supplemented agriculture with fishing, piracy, and trade in amber and furs. These primordial "Northmen" did not break out of the Baltic circle until the close of the Bronze Age when the onslaught of much colder weather forced them to move southward.

Below the German world in Bronze Age times lay the domain of the Celts, who were part of a chain of tribes that extended from Gaul to Russia. The Celts of south Germany appear to have been very anciently domiciled in enclaves there. During the Bronze age they extended their sway over all the country south of the Harz Mountains and the Main River. Their linguistic bequest was not inconsiderable: the Rhine, Neckar, Lippe, Main, Lau, Donau, Lech, Inn, and Isar rivers are all Celtic names, and the Taunus and Sudeten mountains were also named by this people.

With the coming of cooler, damper climate and the spread of parkland between 800 and 500 B.C. the lot of the people east of the Rhine grew harder. The Celts began to trek toward Gaul and Italy. Their migration accelerated once the battle with the Germans was joined. Although the Celts were largely expelled from Germany by the fourth century B.C., many remained behind south of the Main River. They transmitted facial traits, pigmentation, stature, and brachycephalic skulls to their German conquerors. Meanwhile in the seventh century B.C. the Vandals and Goths drove another non-Germanic people, the Illyrians or Veneti, as the Romans called them, from lands between the Oder and Vistula. A culturally advanced people who were known for their delicate red and light-colored pottery, the Illyrians finally settled at the head of the Adriatic (Venice) and along its eastern shore.

Early in the first millennium B.C. the economic picture of the future German land area was complex but more peasant than nomad. Fields were tilled by men using plows pulled by yoked oxen. Bronze Age crops were, except for oats and flax, what they had been in Neolithic times. Plowshares had not much improved, and fertilizer was not used. The remedy for soil exhaustion was to move on to virgin acres. Wealth was reckoned principally in cattle, and fines were paid in that medium. Where permanent villages existed, they were located on the banks or at the confluence of rivers or at the intersection of roads in forest clearings. Trade was conducted along the chief rivers of Germany and across the North and Baltic seas. Imports of gold, tin, and copper were paid for by the Germans with furs, slaves, fine metal weapons and tools, and amber ("transparent gold").

Although a primitive religious writing, known as *runic* (meaning "secret"), was widely used among the northern tribes, most other tribes had not advanced beyond the pictographic stage or evolved an alphabet of any kind. But writing was little missed in a society that had no history, records, or calendars. Characteristically associated with coastal Germanic religion was the graceful S-shaped horn, called the *lure* (pl. *lurer*), which was capable of a wide range of notes and was as fine a musical instrument as antiquity can boast.

The First German Advance

As a result of increase of population due to the agricultural revolution, land hunger among the larger tribes became intense after 500 B.C. Shortage of arable was aggravated by reason of the encroachments of the spreading rain forest. Failure to drain bogs and marshy soil only made the situation of the Germans worse. Henceforth the Celts were subjected to steady pressure.

On the eve of the contest for mastery of Germany, the Germans comprised three main groupings: northern, eastern, and western. From the first were to spring the Norse, Danes, and Swedes. From the eastern tribes, who had taken up abandoned lands from the middle Oder to the Vistula, were to emerge such great protonations as the East and West Goths, Vandals, Burgundians, and Langobards (Lombards). The western Germans, who were to furnish the shock troops in the first skirmishes with Rome, comprised the Ingaevoni of Jutland, Schleswig-Holstein, and Hanover, the Herminoni of north-central Germany, and the Istvaeoni, who inhabited the Rhine Valley and were geographically closest to the civilized peoples and included Chatti, Bructi, Chattuari, Batavians, Teutons, Marsi, Cimbrians, and Chauki.

All efforts to block the German advance availed nothing. At some time in the course of the third century B.C. the backbone of Celtic resistance was broken, and this people for the most part evacuated central and western Germany, fleeing to the east, south, and west. Many Celts, of course, were captured and enslaved or even remained behind as allies or free subjects of the Germans. The vacated areas were filled by Quadi, Marcomanni, Suebi, and other western Germans. As the second century B.C. dawned, Germany was under the domination of one race at last. However, that race could no longer claim to be pure, for the conquest of middle Europe had involved racial admixture with the conquered.

Toward the end of the second century B.C. the Germans at last came up along the Rhine against the Roman armies that had conquered Celtic Gaul. An interlude of consolidation and appraisal ensued. Roman and German sized each other up. Astonished Germans beheld their first cities and marveled at the disciplined drill of Roman legionaries. Irritated Romans abruptly awakened to the unpleasant fact that behind the Celts stood the Germans and that all previous reports from beyond the Rhine, which had confused Celt with German, were worthless. The haughty Roman eye, contemptuously sweeping the motley German barbarians, could not catch a vision of that moral fiber and vigor that centuries later, commingled with the Mediterranean inheritance, were to build the brilliant civilization of the "European Age."

After four hundred years of southward migration the German vanguard finally found its way down to the north Italian plain, where in 222 B.C. it was annihilated by Roman legions. Neither these invaders nor the Cimbri and Teutons who followed a century later were motivated primarily by lust for booty or love of war. It was land hunger and a desire for a place in the milder south that drove them on. Groping their way along the fabled "amber trail" up the Elbe River into Bohemia and the Danubian regions, thence up the Inn and Rhine into Rhaetia (Switzerland) and northern Italy—they traded and fought as they marched.

Fighting between the attacking Cimbri and Teutons and the Roman defenders of Gaul filled the years 120–101 B.C. Four Roman legions were cut to pieces in 107 B.C., an event that called forth the Marian reforms abolishing property qualifications for service in the Roman army. Then in 102 B.C. Marius himself, with a democratized army, struck the Teutons near Aquae Sextiae (Aix-en-Provence) and destroyed them. In 101 B.C. he caught up with the Cimbri who had by then crossed the Maritime Alps into Italy. Rejecting their third request for lands, Marius with 55,000 soldiers smote the Cimbri near Vercellae in northern Italy. Thousands of male survivors were taken to Rome in bondage, but of women none was enslaved. For at Vercellae, as at Aix, the Romans were treated to a blood-curdling spectacle of incredible devotion. As the tide of battle turned against the Germans, the women, singing battle songs, entered the fray. Then when all their exertions had failed, they requested of the victors that they might become vestal virgins. When this was scornfully rejected, the women slew their children, then themselves.

The migration of the Cimbri and Teutons made straight the paths for the last major territorial expansion of the Germans within their homeland. By driving the Helvetii south of the Rhine and north of the Alps, the Cimbri and Teutons cleared all Baden, Swabia, and Bavaria for themselves.

German military operations were devoid of all plan and invited defeat in detail. Had the tribes achieved a national organization under the leadership of one of their able chieftains, such as Ariovistus, Maroboduus, or Arminius, Western Europe might have been Germanized by the first century A.D. Gaul would have become the antechamber of Germany or, in the event the tribes completely forsook central Europe, the seat of a new hybrid culture. The opportunity for a world-historic German victory would have been present because at each crucial juncture in the first century B.C. Rome had also to fight on other fronts.

As it was, the hopeless defect in the German order of battle was conclusively demonstrated in the war between Ariovistus and Caesar in 58 B.C. For the Germans, loss of this campaign meant the end of their dream of empire in Gaul; for the Romans it provided incentive to conquer Germany.

The Rhenish Roadblock

Between 58 and 55 B.C. Caesar carried everything before him along the Rhine. Yet, the Roman victories were not immediately followed by a full-scale attempt to subdue all Germany. For this, Rome's resources were spread too thin. After defeating Ariovistus, who had only been the *Heerbahn* "(chieftain") of seven tribes, the Romans established a buffer zone between the Empire and Inner Germany. A number of tribes, such as the Ubi, Sugambri, and Batavians, were given land on the left bank of the Rhine, where there gradually developed a rich, hybrid Germano-Roman culture. After 55 B.C. a large number of Germans were brought into the Roman administrative pale, so that the Rhineland gradually assimilated Latin speech, manners, culture, and religion. For some centuries Rome's German provinces stood as a roadblock against further migrations from Inner Germany.

Character of the Germans

The Germans were devoted to their freedom *(Freiheit),* but this was little more than an anarchic individualism that bred endless intertribal war. The German's endemic attachment to personal freedom long obstructed the unification of his country, but it also postponed the destruction of the Roman Empire, which might otherwise have succumbed to concerted German assault centuries before it did.

In a land that possessed only rudimentary legal notions, the oath of personal allegiance *(Treupflicht)* to a leader assumed disproportionate importance. Dearer to the German warrior than his life was this oath of service and fidelity. He clove to it through thick and thin, often carrying loyalty to a point where it altogether compromised the interests of his nation, which, being formally nonexistent, meant next to nothing to him.

The *Treupflicht* found its most common expression in connection with the body-guard *(Gefolgswesen* or *Gefolgschaft;* Latin, *comitatus).* This was an elite corps of warriors, usually of noble status, who attached themselves to a leader of military prowess. The followers pledged fidelity in return for protection, food, shelter, and booty. In wartime the bodyguard fought by the side of its leader unto victory or death. "On the battlefield," wrote Tacitus, ". . . it is disgraceful for the chief to be surpassed in valor and disgraceful for his companions not to equal him; but it is reproach and infamy for a lifetime to retreat from the field surviving him. . . . The chief fights for victory, the entourage for the chieftain."*

Active outdoor life in an exhilarating climate molded the German frequently into a physical paragon who excited the admiration of the Romans. The contrast between the two ethnic types must have been heightened by the fact that the ancient Germans were, on the average, taller and fairer, and the Romans shorter and darker than their modern counterparts. Hailed by a sophisticated Roman patriciate as "children of nature," over whom there was much sentimentalizing, the Germans invited emulation. In their efforts to copy such statuesque apparitions as Thusnelda and Bissula, Roman ladies affected German hair, dress, rosy cheeks, and manner. They dyed their hair blonde or purchased switches of genuine German tresses, in which shopkeepers in Italy did a land-office business.

Society

The family was the oldest and most cohesive unit in ancient German society. All persons of close consanguinity were embraced in the family. To lose a kinsman was thought to be a little less than loss of part of oneself. Great respect was shown the head of the household, always a male. He exercised ultimate authority over all its members. Theoretically, at least, he could for just cause slay wife or child or sell them into slavery. Above family stood the clan *(Sippe).* This was a community of more distantly related persons living in the same district. In wartime the clan was the cell of the tribal army, fighting as one man. Similarly, for work in field or forest it was an economic unit. The fraternal spirit that inspired the *Sippe* was reflected in the fact that all of its members bore a common name, usually ending in the patronymic suffix *ingen* or *ungen.*

---

*Tacitus, "Germany," in *Agricola, Germany, Dialogue on Orators* (Indianapolis: Library of Liberal Art, 1967), p. 47.

Women enjoyed no independent status in this patrilineal society. They were confined to house and garden, yet their position was not unenviable. Although they played no role in public affairs, they elicited respect. The German mother was the light of the family, whose devotion to her man and children was her surest title to authority. Her moral influence injected a stability into German society that helps explain its historic conservatism and sentimentality.

Marriage rested upon a sales contract. A German tribesman bought his bride for a fixed sum of money *(Mitgift)*. This remained the property of the wife after marriage, affording her a small measure of independence. Only rarely might the *Mitgift* be confiscated by the husband. At the marriage ceremony a ring and sword were solemnly exchanged: " . . . she is reminded," wrote Tacitus, "by the very first ceremonies with which her marriage begins that she comes as a partner in labors and dangers, who will suffer and dare the same thing as her husband in peace, the same thing in war. . . ."* German women lived fenced around with chastity, and adultery was very rare. Its punishment was dire and at the wish of the husband. He might strip her in the presence of her relations and drive her with lashes through the village. In Saxony an adulteress was usually driven to hang herself, after which her corpse was burned and her seducer hanged above her ashes. Little wonder that monogamy and lifelong marriages were the rule among the Germans!

It is a myth that social democracy ever existed among the primitive Germans. Society was divided into four classes: nobles *(Adel)*, common freemen *(Gemein-freie)*, semifree *(Haushörige)*, and slaves *(Knechte)*. In Roman times a fifth class, the clergy, developed. Nobles, who were privileged as to property and person, never comprised more than 3 percent of any tribe. Free men always constituted the majority and were the backbone of the fighting force and the sovereign popular assembly *(Landesding)*. The semifree had legal status but were excluded from all privileges, restricted in their movements and obliged to render stipulated services and payments to noblemen or to the tribe. The semifree originated either through emancipation or voluntary surrender of rights that marked one free. Slaves, whose status usually could be traced back to capture in war or nonpayment of debts, were chattel property, had no legal standing, and were obligated to service and payments that were more onerous than those imposed upon the semifree. Earlier, many slaves, being Germans, could hope for eventual emancipation, but after the fifth century A.D. whole populations were reduced to permanent bondage.

Political Organization

In ancient times the Germans never built a state. Their largest political entity was a confederation of tribes *(Völkerschaft)*. The basic political unit was the individual tribe *(Stamm)*. Fundamentally military, it defended the *Mark,* which was the aggregate of all lands owned by the tribe. Political institutions were basically

---

*Ibid., p. 49.

democratic. The tribal assembly *(Landesding)* was the oracle of the sovereign will of the free community except where a confederate assembly *(Bundesversammlung)* handed down military decisions that were binding on several peoples. Normally all qualified warriors were required to attend assembly meetings with their weapons. Decisions were reached by clang of arms.

Tribal organization was military and relatively democratic. All subdivisions—"thousands," "five hundreds," "hundreds," and clans—were based on the number of fighting men in a given unit. The basic one was the "hundred" *(Hundertschaft),* which embraced two to four times the fifty families normally grouped into a clan. The domicile of the "hundred" was the district *(Gau),* whose assembly of warriors was called the *Thingversammlung.* A prince or, after the third century A.D., a king *(Kuning)* led the tribe. Monarchy by 500 A.D. was universal among the tribes but seldom hereditary and never absolute. The king, by grace of the tribal assembly, was commander-in-chief and supreme judge. The domain belonged to the tribe, and the baleful concept of the realm as royal property did not come to prevail before Merovingian times.

Warfare

War was the prime concern of German men. Battle was almost a religious rite, waged for acquisition of land, cattle, food, and slaves. The tribal army was sheer mass. Strategy, grand tactics, and logistics, properly speaking, were unknown to the Germans. Infantry was the strength of the army, and attack its only tactic. What earned the admiration of the Romans was the raw fighting quality of the German. In combat he was thought to be unexcelled. Nor were German women simply spectators of battle. If the fortunes of war turned against their tribe, they might even take the field. They encouraged their men otherwise by cheers, shouts, songs, and the display of their bodies. In all respects women were the chief deterrent to retreat.

Despite use of iron among Germans, stone- and bone-tipped wooden weapons long prevailed. Spears were highly prized, being a mark of free status, but a good sword and sheath often brought as many as seven cows in trade. Bows and arrows were uncommon before the coming of the Northmen. Rather, the mainstay of the German warrior was the missile—hatchet, battle axe, sling, or spiked club, when not the spear, used either at close quarters or hurled. Among the Franks the favored weapon was the battle axe, the so-called *Francisca* (whence the tribal name); among the Saxons, it was the single-edged sword *(Saxe)* of bronze or iron; and among the Angles, it was the *Angon (Hanion),* a harpoon-like javelin.

Settlements and Farming

In their native state the free German tribes did not progress beyond village economy, for only in Roman-administered parts of Germany were there cities. Villages were grouped into districts, and several of the latter formed the tribal domain. Areas between tribes were uninhabited march *(Mark)* land. Most houses were of wood, unpainted, and of plain construction. They were chiefly square, single-storied, and averaged 150–250 square feet of floor space.

The arable was tribally owned and divided into strips or blocks, long and narrow in south Germany and irregular in the north. Farming was supervised by officials appointed by district assemblies. The officials annually allotted varying amounts of land, which was then cultivated as it was owned—collectively, except where the land belonged to a nobleman. On the other hand, houses and garden plots, cattle, horses, and wagons were owned in severalty. When by the fourth century A.D. the population came to exceed five million, tribal gave way to clan ownership of land. In the seventh century individual proprietorship became the rule. Thereafter common ownership persisted only in the case of woods and meadows.

A gradual increase in the number of livestock had two results for the Germans. Continued heavy cropping of meadow caused soil exhaustion and impelled the tribes to migrate in search of virgin soil; or cropping together with mounting fuel and building requirements led tribesmen to clear away ever more of the forest primeval.

Religion

By the first century A.D. the Germans had arrived at the stage of personalized polytheism. They believed in an indeterminate afterlife but not in a resurrection. Whereas some tribes still worshiped demons, most had passed over to the veneration of a host of shining spirits. These were associated with natural phenomena—sunshine, moonlight, rain, wind, lightning, snow, ice, and fire. Ancient German mythological notions were probably akin to those of other primitive peoples who worshiped forces that they could not control but were decisive for them. Ultimately, not much before A.D. 400, German legends were refined to a point where they invited comparison with Helladic myths.

Tribal religious concepts mirrored the romanticism of the German mind. It was thought that after death and the usual cremation the soul came to invest a lower animal organism or dwell in some mountain, river, lake, or tree. The German found it easy to believe in incorporealism. He peopled his environment with races of good and evil geniuses—heavenly deities, giants, demons, elves, nymphs, and water sprites. Even after the advent of Christianity, animism long persisted alongside the new faith. Vestiges of the ancient German affinity for the sylvan and the occult survive to this day in Grimm's *Fairy Tales* and in the typical German's sentimental fondness for nature.

Besides the sun and moon and fire, which were universally worshiped, there was an immense gallery of radiant divinities. Among them were Time or Saturn (Saturday), sower of the earth and tireless continuator of the work of Heaven; Woden (Wednesday), creator of men and lord of the gold-mailed centuries of Valkyries, hosts of the air; Easter, wife to Woden, dispenser of rainfall and queen of Heaven; Hertha, incarnation of the earth's bounty; Thor or Donar (Thursday—

Donnerstag), god of thunder and defender of Heaven; Yule, king of Elfland and patron of hunters and the Yuletide season; Nerthus, lord of the shore and the sea's loud thundering surges; Frija or Friga (Friday), goddess of love and marriage; and Tieu (Tuesday), god of war. There were giants, who were foes of men, elves who rifled gold from the earth, and demons. For every natural phenomenon there was a spirit who had to be propitiated.

Scenes of worship were woodland glades or spring sites. The naturalistic, mystical ritual was accompanied by fire, choral singing, dancing, and burning of incense. There does not seem to have been any profound moral content to this religion, yet it was long until the rigors of German mythology receded before the milder concepts of Christian charity.

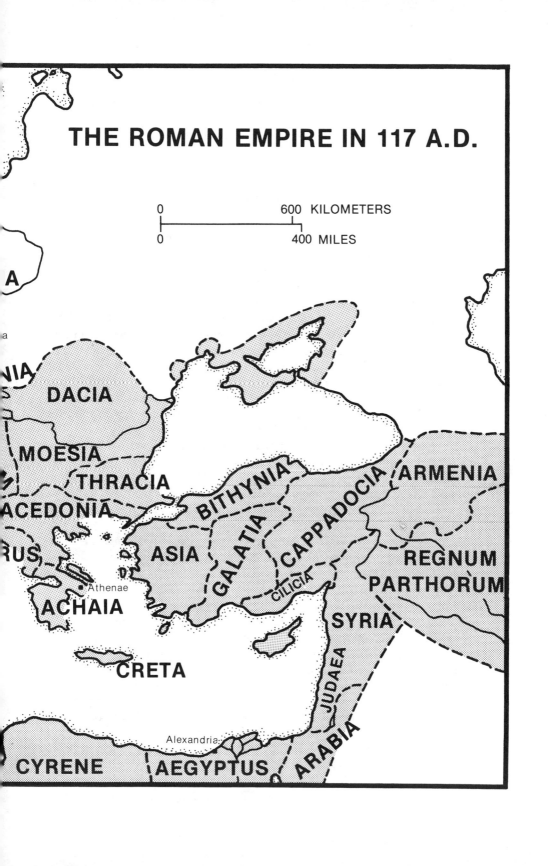

THE ROMAN EMPIRE IN 117 A.D.

0   600 KILOMETERS

0   400 MILES

A

DACIA

MOESIA

THRACIA

ACEDONIA

BITHYNIA

ARMENIA

RUS

ASIA

GALATIA

CAPPADOCIA

CILICIA

REGNUM
PARTHORUM

Athenae

ACHAIA

SYRIA

CRETA

JUDAEA

Alexandria

CYRENE   AEGYPTUS

ARABIA

Chapter 2

THE CONQUEST OF

THE ROMAN EMPIRE

Stalemate

In the reign of Emperor Augustus (27 B.C.–A.D. 14) support developed for the view that Germany could and must be added to the Empire. The Romans found their pretext for resuming hostilities when the Sugambri in 17 B.C. destroyed an entire legion near Aachen. Drusus, stepson of Augustus, was entrusted with supreme command of an army of six legions that had been transferred to the German provinces for the coming offensive. He was also given a fleet with which he managed to establish strong points at the mouths of the Ems, Weser, and Elbe. His aim was to block egress to the Germans and provide the Romans with easy access to the interior. After three years of preparation, Drusus (Germanicus) crossed the Rhine in 12 B.C. in force and commenced a campaign that carried the Roman armies to their deepest penetration of Germany.

The Roman counteroffensive had forced many tribes to trek eastward. Encouraged by the evacuation of the area between the Main and Neckar rivers, the Romans established the Province of Germany, which was later divided into Upper and Lower Germany. This initial province, whose capital was Colonia Agrippina (Cologne, Köln), was intended to embrace all the depopulated lands to the middle Elbe. Unfortunately, however, the formidable strength of the Cheruscans had not been broken, and beyond them to the east of the Elbe there was forming a large federation of tribes under Maroboduus, or Marbod, the *Heerbahn* of the Marcomanni and Quadi.

Tiberius, backed by twelve superbly trained and equipped legions, was in the act of closing a pincers upon the foe's Bohemian stronghold when suddenly Pannonia, Illyria, and Dalmatia went up in smoke, and he had to pull back in all haste in 6 B.C. to protect Italy. Never again was Rome strong enough to mount so great an offensive against the Germans.

Like Ariovistus, Maroboduus neglected in 6 B.C. to take advantage of the embarrassment of the Romans to drive them out of Germany. Instead he made peace with Tiberius on the basis of the status quo. Maroboduus' timidity then and later, when Arminius sorely needed his help against the Romans on the Rhine, betrayed the national cause and postponed for centuries the founding of a kingdom of Germany. The subjects and allies of Maroboduus, finding his policy pusillanimous, fell away from him. Defeated by Arminius in A.D. 17, Maroboduus was unable to check the ensuing swift dissolution of his empire.

In A.D. 9 the bell tolled for Germany a second time. Rome's military supremacy was successfully challenged by Arminius, *Heerbahn* of the Cheruscans. Although he had served under Tiberius, was a Roman citizen, was versed in Latin, and might have made a brilliant future in Italy, Arminius returned to

Germany to defend its freedom. He banded together Chatti, Ubi, Chattuari, Brukteri, and Cheruscans and in the difficult terrain of the Teutoburg Forest virtually destroyed three Roman legions in September, A.D. 9. Unfortunately the battle had not been part of a plan to destroy the Roman provinces of Germany, and so the annihilation of 20,000 Romans was, in a sense, bootless. Teutoburg Forest was no Cannae, and Arminius, no Hannibal. Nevertheless, Arminius' name lived on in song and legend.

As was customary among the Germans, their victory was followed by an orgy of revenge upon the vanquished. Varus, the Roman commander, escaped indignities only by falling upon his sword. Many hundreds of his tribunes and centurions met a less honorable death, being hanged from trees like tinsel or savagely sacrificed on woodland altars to the gods. Arminius lived to destroy the power of Maroboduus but not to unite Germany. He perished ingloriously in a minor civil war in A.D. 21, leaving the Germans as disunited as he had found them.

Although a new Germanicus, nephew to Tiberius, avenged the defeat of Varus with three victorious campaigns in Germany, Teutoburg Forest confirmed the emperor in his decision to stand in the future on the defensive along the Rhine and Danube and consolidate what had been won. Beset with manifold problems, the Romans were compelled to choose a permanently defensive posture, which ultimately proved to be their undoing. Until well into the third century A.D. the barbarians were held east of the Rhine and north of the Danube, along which line the Romans concentrated a defensive force of fourteen of their grand total of thirty-one legions. Only in the valleys of the Lahn, Lippe, and Main did they hold bridgeheads that gave them command of corridors to Inner Germany.

In keeping with the concept of strategic defense, the Romans shortened their front in Germany. They abandoned earlier conquests along the German (North) Sea coast from the Waal to Jutland. In this way the Frisians recovered their independence. Thereafter, the Roman line remained anchored in the Netherlands and at Vindobona (Vienna). Between Xanten and Vindobona the frontier dished in a shallow crescent from the Rhine to the Danube. Almost all fortresses and garrison towns were behind that line. Each town supported a garrison of from 50,000 to 70,000 regular and auxiliary troops. Many of these strong points became cities: in the Rhine-Moselle area—Castra Vetera (Xanten), Colonia Agrippina (Köln), Castra Bonnensia (Bonn), Confluentes (Koblenz), Augusta Treverorum (Trèves or Trier), Mogontiacum (Mainz); east of the Vosges—Argentoratum (Strassburg) and Wormatia (Worms); in northern Rhaetia—Augusta Vindelicorum (Augsburg), Castra Regina (Regensburg), and Castra Betava (Passau); in Noricum—Lauriacum (Lorch); and in Pannonia—Vindobona.

The *Limes*

By the end of the first century in the reign of Domitian the Romans had greatly shortened the German frontier by connecting the Rhine and Danube with a fortified line called the *Limes*. This was Rome's Maginot line, an artificial barrier raised where river defenses were lacking. It denied to the barbarians a corridor of invasion between the upper Rhine and Danube. By cutting off this deep salient, the *Limes* permitted reduction in troop strength. More than a hundred square or trapezoidal fortresses fronted by slopes, palisades, or stone walls and connected by excellent roads guarded the 350-mile length of the line. From 15-foot-high wooden towers at regular intervals sentries stood watch, warning of the foe's approach by trumpet if by day and fire if by night.

The Tithe Lands

Behind the *Limes* lay the fair provinces of Upper Germany and Rhaetia, embracing the upper Rhine, Danube, Inn, Main, and Neckar-Kinzig river valleys. Here lay the imperial Tithe Lands *(Agri decumates),* where retired veterans and reliable farmers, chiefly Germans and Celts, dwelt on small tracts that had been leased to them by the state at low rentals amounting to a tenth of the annual revenue from the holding. Though this tenancy arrangement was unknown elsewhere in the Empire, it served two useful purposes here: it denied the wedge between Rhine and Danube to hostile tribes, and it insured the garrisons of a certain amount of indigenous logistic support.

With the influx of infantrymen, first villages *(vici)* and then towns *(civitates)* sprang up near the fortresses. Local craftsmen and merchants catered to the needs of the Roman army. In walled towns, such as Nida, Ladenburg, Wimpfen, and Baden-Baden, a commingling of Romans, Celts, and Germans developed a rich, hybrid culture. In the course of time the Tithe Lands became an immense cantilever over which Mediterranean civilization marched into central Europe.

When all is said, however, the cultural policies of Rome compromised her position in Germany. The grant of land to aliens ultimately undermined the Roman establishment in Upper Germany and along the middle Rhine. Similarly, the award of the privilege to Tithe Land residents to elect their own municipal councils was a mistake. It had to be retracted in the fourth century when imperial administrative appointees were again instituted. Rome compounded her blunders by developing an increasing dependence upon German federated troops to contain the restive tribes east of the Rhine.

Provincial Culture

Rome brought security, civilization, and prosperity to the German border lands. The natives were left in undisturbed possession of their farms, cottages, religion, language, and customs, and in Upper and Lower Germany the Pax Romana put an end to internecine warfare. Self-government was accorded the local populace, and private enterprise soon came to replace public ownership of industry and resources. The provisioning and servicing of thousands of soldiers and administrators created opportunities for enriching the natives. In exchange for food, goods, services, and weapons, the Romans poured gold and silver into the provinces. Later, in the fluid conditions of the Great Migrations this immense treasure was often buried, possibly giving rise to the legend of the Rhinegold, the hoard of the Nibelungs. In the sunshine of the provincial hothouse an orchidaceous culture flourished. Large towns cropped up. The public buildings of Mogontiacum and Colonia Agrippina, two of the biggest cities of the Roman world, were among the finest in Germany. Gates of impressive majesty, like the Porta Nigra of Augusta Treverorum, were built. Canals were dug, new life throbbed in the arteries of the Rhineland, and gradually the German-Celtic mixed population came to view the Roman order not as a cross but a crown.

Incontrovertibly the five hundred years of Roman rule in provincial Germany had more lasting influence than the four centuries of Roman presence in Britain. Yet Latin never replaced the west German dialects in the provinces. For this the relative sprinkling of soldiers and administrators was too light to permeate the ethnic subsoil. Even in imperial Treverorum (Trier) the mob, crowding into the amphitheater to enjoy the gladiatorial games, babbled in German. The natives became cultural retreads, but never Romans.

When in the late third century the emperor occasionally held court in Treverorum and brought with him a retinue of poets, artists, musicians, and savants, the Indian summer of provincial culture commenced. From this period date some of the choicest specimens of Greco-Roman art, which are preserved in the museums of Trier, Speyer, Bonn, Mainz, Worms, and Cologne. The Roman schools at Treverorum and Colonia Agrippina, though small, were famous. They lightened the darkness of central Europe, stirring new visions in barbarian minds. Finally, by the late fourth century Christian missionaries had built the first true churches in the Rhineland, such as St. Gereon's in Colonia Agrippina and St. Matthias in Augusta Treverorum.

The Alemanni and the Crumbling of the *Limes*

A factor of enormous importance in the ultimate ruin of the Empire was the abandonment by the Roman legions of the strategic salient between the Rhine and the Danube. This was done under pressure of a grand offensive conducted in stages by a new, confederated German people, the Alemanni. Their conquest of the *Limes,* which pushed the Roman defense line back to the Alps, must rank with the Visigothic victory at Adrianople in 378 as one of the two decisive military events in the disintegration of the Empire. The Alemannic victory may be ascribed to the failure of the Roman high command to garrison and colonize the middle Elbe area, which could have been done from Bohemia, if not from the Rhineland. Neglect to divide Germany permanently enabled the tribes to coalesce into regional confederacies and generate strength for the grand offensive that overwhelmed the Roman frontier positions.

Barbarian pressure on the *Limes* became critical by A.D. 161. By then the tribes had begun to consolidate into the powerful protonations of the fourth century— Vandals, Franks, Goths, Saxons, Thuringians, and Alemanni (later Swabians).

For long the anarchy that reigned among the barbarians was worse than within the Empire. But by the reign of Marcus Aurelius (A.D. 161–80) the first major displacements of German peoples began, leading eventually to the Great Migrations.

After A.D. 161 the Chatti broke through the defenses of Upper Germany, and the Burgundians occupied Upper Silesia. The Goths, meanwhile, stabbed to the Black Sea. All along the frontier from the Rhine to Dacia the Romans were hard-pressed. They were compelled to withdraw practically all regulars from the area between Strassburg and Vienna and entrust the defense solely to German auxiliaries. In the winter of A.D. 166–67 the Langobards, Quadi, and Marcomanni got wind of this and crossed the Danube unopposed, driving all the way to Aquileia on the Adriatic (A.D. 169). It took three years for Marcus Aurelius to roll back the invaders and recover Noricum and Pannonia. Rome had been rocked to its foundations.

The annihilation of the mortally wounded Marcomanni in A.D. 179 afforded Marcus Aurelius an unrivaled opportunity to reorganize the northern defense system. For obvious reasons he decided to annex the enemy's base of operations, Bohemia and Moravia. That this was not done must be blamed on his gladiator son and successor Commodus, who neglected to devise a program that must have split Germany in two but instead reverted to a policy of patches and expedients. He abandoned his father's project in favor of client subsidy treaties, while continuing his humane but mistaken program of settling myriads of German peasants in the war-ravaged Danubian provinces. In this way Commodus snatched defeat from the jaws of victory.

Between 179 and 253 the Romans increasingly entrusted the defense of the Empire to German warriors. The process, begun in the age of Augustus, abandoned for a time, taken up again by Hadrian, and molded into a system by Gallienus (A.D. 260–68) and Aurelian (A.D. 270–75) had by mid third century just about wrought the ruin of the regular army: barbarians had been individually integrated in the cohorts, and many German units, led by their chieftains, had been accepted as auxiliary troops (*brucellari* or *foederati*) of the border constabulary. Also, the increased prestige of barbarian contingents enabled many Germans to gain admission to the Roman officers corps, from which in the first and second centuries they had been excluded. With such a weapon it is hard to see how the Roman authorities could expect to repulse a general German offensive.

While velleity was creeping over the Roman army a young and formidable confederation of tribes was pushing southward from the Main Valley. The coalition, called Alemanni or Swabians (from the Suebi), becoming prominent in the third century A.D., was destined to conquer all the lands between Lake Constance (Bodensee) and the Taunus Mountains. In A.D. 253, after preliminary skirmishing, the Alemanni went over to a concerted push, and the *Limes* broke like a pie crust on a 100-mile front. The great fortress of Niederbieber fell in 260, and the floodgates to Rhaetia were thrown open. The frontier was forced back to the right angle of the Rhine and Danube as in Augustus' day. Shortly thereafter the foe spilled over the Rhine to the foot of the Vosges, and in 271 he passed through the Alps. The Aurelian wall was then erected around Rome.

The winds of chance that had set the Alemanni and Franks in motion also drove Goths, Vandals, Marcomanni, Burgundians, and Sarmatians down upon the sagging Roman frontier. At this juncture the Persians, heirs of the Parthians, struck the Empire's Mesopotamian flank, and by 260–70 the long border blazed from end to end.

Somehow the Empire survived, but enfeebled for the rest of its life. With Herculean efforts, Claudius (268–70), Aurelian (270–75), and Probus (276) managed to retake Cologne and Strassburg and force back the Germans. The Tithe Lands were again substantially in Roman hands. However, toward the end of Diocletian's reign the *Limes* was tacitly allowed to slip into enemy hands, because it was too costly to defend; and the feared Alemanni soon found themselves again in possession of the Black Forest, Wetterau, the Kinzig and Lech valleys, and the Allgäu. By mid-fourth century even the Rhine had ceased to be the frontier between the Empire and Inner Germany. By then the Alemanni had crossed that stream for good, taken Mulhouse, Sélestat, Colmar, and Strassburg and traversed the Swiss plain to Lakes Brienz and Thun. From this time forth the Tithe Lands were called Alemannia or Swabia.

The "Watch on the Rhine"
Against the Franks

It was not the Alemanni but the Salian Franks who were destined to conquer Gaul. No confederation, unless it be of the Angles and Saxons, was fated for a greater future than the Franks. They were destined to build a kingdom whose span, vaulting the Rhine and Moselle, rested on piers in Gaul and Germany. Their achievement lives on in the German word for France—*Frankreich,* "kingdom of the Franks."

Like the Alemanni, their southern neighbors, the Franks were at first a confederation of turbulent tribes that had seen their heyday in Caesar's time. The Franks dwelt along the middle Rhine, Ruhr, Lippe, and upper Ems. By the late third century the confederation had split into two major groups: a northern, dwelling close to the German sea and along the Ijssel River valley in Belgica; and a southern, along the right bank of the Rhine opposite Cologne, Bonn, and Koblenz. Because the northern Franks lived in the valley of the Sala (Ijssel) and near the salt sea, they were called the Salian Franks. Their southern cousins were called Riverine or Ripuarian Franks, because they dwelt by the Rhine.

The Romans were long able to hold off the Ripuarians, but the Salians methodically rolled up the Roman flank in Belgica. They found the Roman hold on heavily walled Tongeren and Traiectum (Utrecht) so weak that they were soon able to occupy the lands of the Batavians from Noviomagus (Nijmegen) to the isles of Zeeland. About 350, after a tranquil period, the Ripuarian Franks temporarily forced the river at several points but in hard fighting were again slammed back across the Rhine. However, the Roman authorities were at last convinced of the frailty of a defense that rested only upon military preparedness. Thereafter more trust was put in bribes than bulwarks, a policy that was transformed into a system by Julian, the "Apostate" (361–63). In 358 he tried to buy off the Salian Franks by ceding to them Toxandria (northern Brabant) and Campine. This involved final abandonment of the strategic bottleneck of the lower Rhine, Waal, and Scheldt, forcing the Romans to withdraw to a point where, geographically speaking, every step backward must lengthen the already perilously thin defense line.

By A.D. 430 the "watch on the Rhine" had become a farce, entrusted as it was to the kin of the foe, and the war, a phony. The will to fight was gone, for the issues had become blurred. Not only was the provincial army now mainly German, but the very commanders commissioned to defend the Empire were German chieftains. Stilicho, Silvanus, Athaulf, Mallobaudes, Aspar, and Arbogast were high Roman "brass" who thought German thoughts and lived surrounded by their *Gefolgschaften.*

Even though Stilicho won the Franks to temporary alliance, the Alans, Vandals, and Suebi could not be prevented from streaming into Gaul in 407. In the confusion caused by the arrival of the fierce Asiatic Huns in Gaul in 451, the Ripuarian Franks, who meanwhile had abandoned the Romans, seized Cologne (455) and Trier (465). After the death of Aetius (454), who had beaten Attila and his Hunnic invaders of Gaul on the Catalaunian Field near Troyes (451), the last shreds of Roman rule were blown away. A decade later (476) the fiction of de jure imperial sovereignty, which for fifty years had been a travesty, was destroyed by an obscure East Gothic prince, Odovakar, when he deposed the child-emperor Romulus Augustulus. The event passed almost unnoticed in Germany and Gaul, where the heirs of Rome had long been enjoying their loot.

Inner Germany in Ferment

With the migrations of the many German tribes who forsook their homeland never to return, this narrative has little to do. It is concerned mainly with the tribes that remained behind or, migrating, retained contact with Germany. Of these, the Saxons, Thuringians, Bavarians, Swabians (Suebi or Alemanni), Ripuarian and Salian Franks, and Frisians were the most notable.

As the Franks pressed the Romans back in the Low Countries, much of the land between the Weser and lower Rhine became vacant, only to be filled by inrushing Frisians and Saxons. The Saxons were a confederation of many tribes indigenous to the area extending from the Ems to the Lüneburg Heath and the mouth of the Elbe. Until the mid-fifth century the Saxons were crowded by Lombards, Angles, Jutes, and Frisians to the north, and by Warni, Rugi, and Thuringians to the east. Then the Angles, Jutes, and Maritime Saxons sailed for England, and the Lombards began their trek to Silesia and the valley of the Morava. From then on, the Saxons had more elbow room and they spread to the southeast. Identified by their red shields, single-edged swords, and phlegmatic nature, this people, who came to occupy all the land between the Mulda and the North Sea, were valorous, energetic, and creative. They were destined to be the principal element in the future conquest of Slavic lands.

The Thuringian nation comprised elements of the northern Hermunduri, Angles, and Warni. Numerically weak, the Thuringians dwelt south and southeast of the Saxons before the latter expanded. Occupying the Harz and Thuringian forest, an elevated region of cliffs and thick pine and fir forests, the Thuringians were never conquered or corrupted by Rome. They were as knotty as the conifers of their native woods, and they transmitted as pure a culture as medieval Germany could boast. They, too, played a major role in the later offensive against the Slavs.

The Bavarians or Baiovari were a derivative, like the Hermunduri, from a Herminoni people—the Marcomanni in this case. In the fourth century the Bavarians dwelt in Bohemia but by the late fifth had begun to enter the area between the Enns and Lech rivers. The Ziller and Inn rivers formed the southern boundaries of this nation, for whom the duchy of Bavaria was to be named. More conservative than the Saxons and inspired with romantic love of nature and song, the self-satisfied Bavarians were destined later to become a rallying point for particularism. They were also the great southern pipeline for transmission of German culture down the Danube to future Austria and Hungary.

The Burgundians, a tall, fair-haired people who followed in the traces of the Vandals, reached and crossed the middle Rhine shortly after 406. They captured Worms, which became their first capital. Their history, when for thirty years they bestrode the river as *foederati* of the Romans, is told in the *Nibelungenlied*. About 430 the fugacious realm of the Burgundians began to wither, blighted by the appearance of the Huns (Hsiung-nu). Fleeing for their lives, the Burgundians slipped into Gaul. Attila (Etzel of the *Nibelungenlied*) fell upon their flank and destroyed more than half the race as well as the entire royal family before the Burgundians found imperial sanctuary near Swiss Geneva. After his death, following the battle of the Catalaunian Fields (451), the Burgundians seized Lyons (Lugdunum), which became their second capital. Thereafter in the course of fighting the West Goths (Visigoths) and the Alemanni, the Burgundians extended their sway over Provence and the Nevers region and as far eastward as Solothurn, where their domain marched with that of the Alemanni. Eventually the Burgundians were conquered by the Salian Franks. Today the last romantic relics of the caducous Burgundian race are the mountaineers of the French and Savoyard Alps, among the tallest humans in Europe.

The Frisians, like the Thuringians, are today among the most homogeneous of German stocks. Ponderous as the heavy Dutch of whom they are an ancestor, conservative to the core, and intrepid as they are industrious, the Frisians lived in the valley of the Ems and in Groningen. A seafaring people, they spoke a low Saxon dialect, called *overlandisch* by their southern neighbors. Their culture, replete with gruesome customs, such as execution by submergence in a marsh, was primitive. Too few to become one of the great prehistoric German peoples, the Frisians could only infiltrate the offshore islands near Leeuwarden and Emden after the decline of the Batavians and the disappearance of Roman authority. At their farthest penetration southward, the Frisians reached the Scheldt estuary, where they abutted on the Salian Franks. The dividing line between the two nations became the Calais-Tongeren-Aachen road. This highway, in fact, became the permanent boundary between lands where German stock and language heavily predominated and lands where these were never more than a veneer over a Gallo-Roman base. The Frisians, too, eventually fell under the sway of the Franks.

The Hessians are the descendants of the Chatti. By A.D. 260 they had come into possession of the lands north of the confluence of the Nidda and the Nidder, the southern part of modern Hesse-Darmstadt. Not until the eighth century did the Hessians, hemmed in by powerful neighbors—Franks, Burgundians, and Saxons—petition for union with the Frankish Empire.

The Great Migration of Peoples
(*Völkerwanderung*)

In the late fourth and fifth centuries the Visigoths, Vandals, Angles, Saxons, Jutes, Langobards (Lombards), Burgundians, Salian Franks, and other proto-nations entered the Roman Empire in force, mostly never to return to the homeland. After having been condemned for centuries to sterile wanderings in Germany, Poland, or southern Russia, as in the case of Ostrogoths, or to pressing vainly on Rome's defenses, the tribes were at last able to effect penetrations into the moribund Empire in great depth. Generally the Germans were motivated by land hunger. The fair fields of Gaul, Pannonia, Noricum, northern Italy, and the bread baskets of Sicily and Africa excited their cupidity. For a people whose population was increasing more rapidly than its food supply, the rich, arable lands of Gaul and the Po Valley, which enjoyed a longer frost-free growing season and more sunshine, were an irresistible fata morgana.

Barbarian occupation of the Roman provinces and Italy was achieved at small cost of life. Yet the conquest was not carried off as part of any grand operational plan to destroy the Empire. The whole movement, which was only halfheartedly resisted, was sporadic and uncoordinated. By the early sixth century it had spent itself, when Roman dominion no longer survived anywhere in the west.

It has often been asserted that the Germans brought an admixture of new, virile blood to the Mediterranean peoples. Although this may be conceded, the fact remains that the overriding consequence of the *Völkerwanderung* was the destruction of one of the very greatest civilizations in world history. The quartering of almost two million Germans in the western wing of the Roman mansion ruptured it from within. For the summum bonum of political unity, which the Germans could not appreciate never having enjoyed it, they substituted fragmentation; for the Pax Romana and the rule of universal law, the ultima ratio of war amongst competing sovereignties; for the rich urban culture of Gaul and Italy, an austere, agrarian-military regime; and for the Roman acropolis of the muses, the pit of ignorance.

The tribes varied in their receptivity to Roman influence, the Burgundians being perhaps the most impressionable, the Vandals least. But all German peoples endeavored to conserve some features of Mediterranean law, institutions, language, religion, and social usages. More often borrowers than raffish wreckers, the German kings toiled at the salvage of the Roman craft, striving with clumsy hands and feeble understanding to preserve what, in the last analysis, they could not.

It is true that Roman civilization was in full decline before the invasions. Yet the Germans pushed it into its grave. In place of the grand old Empire, the Germans substituted a collection of sovereign states that owed their power not to a law of nations but to mere personalities who recognized no higher terrestrial authority. Furthermore, the custom among most tribes, especially the Franks, of dividing a realm in nearly equal shares among all surviving male heirs in the direct line promoted regional reduction-division of territory and led to the rise of a host of petty, unstable, quarrelsome principalities. Thus, no German prince was ever able to put Humpty Dumpty together again.

Because the Germans vaguely respected the Roman achievement, they made concessions to Mediterranean traditions. This gave rise to the principle of the "personality of the law." Each people residing in a mixed jurisdiction was judged in accordance with its own laws. Alongside the Salian, Visigothic, and Burgundian tribal laws, applicable to Germans, was established, with the aid of Gallo-Roman jurists, a number of Roman codes: in Gaul, the *lex Salica;* in the realm of Burgundy, the *lex Burgundiorum;* and in Visigothic Spain and south France, the *lex Visigothorum* ("Breviary of Alaric"), which for centuries remained the written law of the Midi. From the mid-seventh century, when tribal law was suppressed, until the eleventh these codes almost alone perpetuated knowledge of Roman law.

The very conception of the state was debased as a result of the conquest. German kings regarded their realms not as a public trust (res publica) but as personal property *(Hausmacht)*. On the other hand, credit must be given the Germans for at least creating a system of fairly large states. They checked the centrifugal forces to which their kingdoms were naturally prey. German kings initially adopted Roman administrative units and officials. These existed for decades alongside the tribal system of hundreds and thousands until both were replaced by novel authorities vested with broad powers—on the provincial level, dukes (sing., *Herzog, Dux, duc*), and on the county and municipal, counts (sing., *Graf, comes, compte*). These agents of central government helped arrest the general dissolution, that is, the kind of unlimited fragmentation that was to be the lot of Europe after the breakup of the Carolingian Empire.

Chapter 3

GERMANY UNDER THE FRANKS

The Rise of the Franks

After the death of Attila (453), the empire of the Huns vanished, freeing the German tribes to resume their occupation of Roman provinces. The Ripuarian Franks now spread rapidly through the Rhineland and Moselle Valley. By 490 they had interdicted Lower Germany to the Alemanni and had gained control of both sides of the Rhine from the Ruhr to the Neckar. Their domain embraced almost all fortress towns in Lower Germany and extended westward to Metz, Toul, and Verdun. To the north and east their realm abutted upon that of the Salian Franks and to the south, upon the lands of the Alemanni.

The death of Aetius left Gaul without a Roman buckler. Consequently, by 480 the Salian Franks had enveloped all Artois and reached the Somme. They were led by Clovis or Chlodwig (466?–511), a man of rugged strength, keen intelligence, and ruthless ambition. The founder of the Salian Frankish empire, Clovis reversed the disintegrative tendencies operative in western Europe and set in motion regenerative processes that promoted the creation of a grand political system that later came to embrace Gaul, Germany, and northern Italy.

In 486 the Salians brushed aside the cardboard kingdom of Syagrius, a Celtic prince of northern Gaul, who had pretentiously styled himself "king of the Romans." Clovis then moved his government to Paris, which became the capital of the Merovingian* realm. By 491 the Franks had absorbed Aetius' old bastion between the Seine and Loire but made no attempt to colonize lands to the south.

Meanwhile, between 455 and 470 the Alemanni, foes of the Franks and Burgundians, had expanded. In contrast with the latter, the Alemanni had resisted Romanization. By 495 they had Germanized Alsace and northern Rhaetia from Salodurum (Solothurn) to Curiae (Chur). Clovis planned a decisive campaign against the Alemanni. He finally beat them at Tolbiac or Zülpich in 496 and expelled them from Alsace but not Switzerland or Swabia. Although they dwelt thereafter under suzerainty of the Salians, the Alemanni exercised paramount influence over northern Switzerland. The ethnological division they imposed on that country has endured to this day.

The Battle of Zülpich had other important results. It led to the fairly rapid conversion of the Franks to Roman orthodoxy and marked the initiation of a policy of alliance between Gaul, "the eldest daughter of the Church," and the papacy that was to endure for centuries. The defeat of the Alemanni sounded the knell of Arianism** north of the Alps. More important, the valves of Germany were shut

---

*The Franks claimed descent from a mythical hero whom they called Meroveus or Merovech, whose name was given to the first Frankish dynasty.

**A heretical belief entertained by many Germans, Arianism had originated with Arius (d. 336), a priest of Alexandria, who maintained that Jesus was not consubstantial with God.

to further westward migrations. Except for the Lombards the rest of the German tribes were henceforth confined to central Europe. Further expansion of the German nation had to be at the expense of the Slavs, to whom the heart of Europe was permanently interdicted. Secure on the Rhine, Clovis had now only to expel the Visigoths from Gaul. This, also, he accomplished (494–507). By 508 his fame had spread so far that it reached the Golden Horn, where the Emperor Anastasius bestowed on him the unsolicited title of honorary consul.

During the last three years of his life the restless monarch again looked avidly toward the east. Possessed of violent hidden drives, Clovis arranged the assassination of the Ripuarian King Sigibert and his son. Then Clovis had himself crowned in Cologne as lord of the East Franks, and he incorporated all their German dependencies into his kingdom. More than any other leader, it was he, as Erich Zöllner and Ludwig Schmidt have made clear, who elevated the Franks to supreme importance in Europe.

None of the Merovingian dynasts, with the possible exception of Theudebert I (534–48), measured up to Clovis. So well did he lay the foundation of the Salian Frankish kingdom that it survived Lombard and Avar invasions, internal strife, and the rule of a string of vicious and worthless monarchs until the eighth century, when great organizing geniuses, such as Pepin the Short and Charlemagne, emerged to lead the Franks.

Frankish Expansion Following Clovis

After Clovis, Gaul, in accordance with Salic law, was divided into four parts among his surviving sons. An attack by three of them upon the Romanized Burgundians led to the subjugation of that nation and by 537 a breakthrough to the Maritime Alps and the Mediterranean. Where the Romans had failed, the Franks succeeded, too, in conquering much of Germany. A fourth son of Clovis beat the Thuringians on the Unstrut near Erfurt in 531 and put an end to their independence. In 537 Theudebert I, the last Merovingian dynast worthy of the royal mantle, united the feuding Frankish clans and led them in a campaign against south Germany. He brought the broken-down remnants of the Alemanni and Alpine Romans (Romansch) of Graubünden into the Frankish house, occupied Baiovaria (Bavaria) to the borders of Pannonia, and conquered northern Italy.

After Theudebert I, who died in 548, Merovingian power declined. Ineptitude was enthroned, and the Frankish realm developed fissures. Upper Italy had to be relinquished, and the Germans beyond the Rhine became restive. The Alemanni resumed their penetration of Rhaetia, while the Bavarians, swollen by accretions of Suebi, Skirians, and some Alemanni, achieved a degree of autonomy under the Agilolfinger dukes. The Franks managed to crush a Thuringian uprising in mid-sixth century, it is true, but the fiercely pagan Saxons succeeded in breaking away and for a time even compelled the Franks to pay tribute. East of the Elbe and Saale the Slavic Warns, Wends, and Sorbs, no longer fearful of the Franks, pushed westward in large numbers. On top of all this, the Frankish empire was after 548 wracked by civil wars for a century and a quarter. Public morals steadily declined until by mid-seventh century corruption, treason, murder, and savagery had become the Frankish way of life.

Decline of the Kingdom of the Franks

In the sixth century the Frankish kingdom was divided into three parts: Austrasia, which was inhabited by the bulk of the Salians and Ripuarians, comprising all the lands and towns between the Lippe and the Somme rivers; Neustria, or the "new land," which stretched from the Marne and the Somme to Armorica (Brittany) and the Loire River; and Burgundy, which lay in southeast Gaul, watered by the Saône, Doubs, Isère, and Rhone. Aquitaine was subject to Neustria. Over each subkingdom, in keeping with Salic law, had been set a Merovingian kinglet. By the seventh century the centralizing work of Clovis had largely unraveled. Political unity had all but vanished. Crown lands had been alienated on a lavish scale to Church and nobility, and the royal treasury (fisc) had been emptied. Subkingdoms multiplied on the ruins of the Frankish realm. Bavaria, Alemannia, Thuringia, and Saxony reverted to complete independence. The progress of dissolution was only temporarily checked in the reign of Dagobert (629–39), but decrepitude held sway after his death.

Absence of effective central authority promoted anarchy and military weakness in the face of impending invasions from Northmen and Saracens. A recognition of this impotence called into being the feudal system as Europe's last hope of defense. At the same time the decentralization of security and sovereignty thrust Europe back into a turbulent and retrograde agrarian era, the so-called Dark Ages.

The Rise of the Arnulfinger
Mayors of the Palace

Till 687 Frankish history had been one of creeping paralysis. But in that year the Arnulfinger duke of Austrasia, Pepin II Herestal (680–714), an extremely wealthy nobleman, defeated his powerful rivals in a pitched battle at Tertry (near St. Quentin) on the Somme. He thereby secured recognition of the hereditary rights of his family to the key post of mayor of the palace of Austrasia. From that position his descendants came to dominate the throne and state the policies of the central government.

Pepin Herestal's son and immediate successor was Charles Martel (715–41). Charles, whose name is imperishably linked to his great victory over the Saracens in the Battle of Tours (732), was able to check, but not reverse, the disintegration of the kingdom. In his time the Franks subjugated Frisia and secured Thuringia upon the death of its last native monarch. On the other hand, Bavaria and Alemannia were as far away as ever from bowing their proud necks to Frankish sovereignty, and the Saxons still raged unconverted. Before perishing, Charles Martel divided his kingdom among his sons. The eldest son, who had been assigned Austrasia, Alemannia, and Thuringia, abdicated after a few years and retired to a monastery.

He left as sole ruler of the Frankish realm his brother, Pepin III, the Short (mayor of the palace, 741–51; king, 751–68).

During his momentous reign Pepin the Short subdued part of Saxony, ground the Alemanni into submission, expropriated their nobility, and suppressed the ducal office in Swabia. After 746 that duchy itself was broken into counties and administered by Frankish counts. Swabia, Switzerland, Alsace, Frisia, Westphalia, Thuringia, and part of Saxony were at last all firmly in Pepin's hands. Seemingly, even Bavarian resistance was crushed when in 748–49 Duke Odilo's army was defeated. However no sooner had his son Tassilo been given a diminished Bavaria as a benefice than he broke away from Frankish suzerainty.

Establishment of the
Carolingian Monarchy

Friction between the papacy and Lombards gave Pepin his chance for a crown. Abandoned by the Byzantine emperor and defenseless against the militant Lombards, the pope implored the Franks for aid. In return, Pepin was encouraged to depose the Merovingian puppet and usurp the East Frankish throne. This Pepin did in 751 with the support of the Frankish assembly. Then he led an army into Italy and was annointed king of the Franks by the pope. After two campaigns, Pepin the Short forced the Lombards to accept the second Treaty of Pavia (756) which, while guaranteeing their independence, obliged them to cede important territories to the papacy. Pavia established in central Italy the Patrimony of St. Peter, later known as the Papal States. This so-called Donation of Pepin conferred upon the papacy the wealthy duchy of Rome, the exarchate of Ravenna (Umbria and the Romagna), and the duchies of Spoleto and Benevento. With Italy now pacified and the Holy See reduced to a French footstool, the way was open for the architectonic work of Pepin's great son.

Charlemagne

On Pepin's death in 768 his kingdom was divided between his two sons, Carloman and Charles. When the former died in 771 the latter, known to history as Charles the Great or Charlemagne (also Carolus Magnus and Karl der Grosse, 771–814), seized the entire kingdom. Although the empire he built was indeed modest compared with the contemporary Caliphate of Baghdad or T'ang China, it was the largest and most stable in the West at the time. Neither an administrator nor soldier of genius, Charlemagne was nonetheless the architect of a new world culture. His contributions to Western civilization were of such an order that to this day Frenchmen and Germans vie with each other in claiming him as the founder of their national glory.

A man of huge frame, Charlemagne stood nearly seven feet tall. His appearance, sitting or standing, was most impressive. He was a superb athlete, heavy eater, and an insatiable lover of women, including his own daughters. He could express himself fluently in Latin and could understand Greek but was unable to

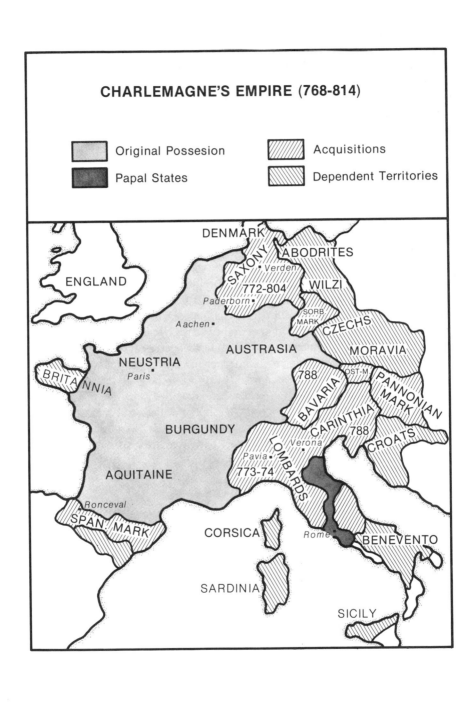

CHARLEMAGNE'S EMPIRE (768-814)

Original Possesion

Papal States

Acquisitions

Dependent Territories

DENMARK

ENGLAND

ABODRITES

SAXONY

Verden

772-804

WILZI

Paderborn

SORB. MARK

CZECHS

AUSTRASIA

MORAVIA

NEUSTRIA

Paris

OST-M

PANNONIAN MARK

BRITANNIA

788

BAVARIA

CARINTHIA

BURGUNDY

Verona

788

CROATS

Pavia

LOMBARDS

AQUITAINE

773-74

Ronceval

SPAN. MARK

CORSICA

Rome

BENEVENTO

SARDINIA

SICILY

speak it. Though he took grammar lessons and practiced his letters at night on a slate that he always kept under his pillow, he never learned to write. Nevertheless, his literary intimates sententiously addressed him as "David," and he called them "Horace," "Flaccus," "Homer," and "Pindar." An indefatigable builder, Charlemagne strove to make his capital, Aachen (Aix-la-Chapelle), a northern Rome. Although pious, he could be ruthless; for, like Alexander the Great, he was a puzzle of contradictions. In Charlemagne creative and destructive forces were always at war for possession of his soul.

Founding the Empire of the West

Charlemagne added substantially to the realm, while maintaining and strengthening contact with the Germanic homeland and orienting his policy toward the east. In his time he subdued the adamant Bavarians, destroyed the Lombard kingdom (774), repelled the Moslems of Spain (778), bound the papacy to him by defending it and enlarging its patrimony, conquered the Saxons, smashed the Avars, and injected new vitality into the moribund ideal of European unity. Although in the end Charles the Great failed to fulfill extravagant hopes for the restoration of an all-European, Christian empire, he did manage to establish Frankish suzerainty over much of Germany and Italy. His accomplishments were recognized by the pope when on Christmas day, 800, in St. Peter's basilica Leo III crowned him "Emperor of the West."

The Conquest of Saxony

Until Charlemagne's time, the Saxons had been a stumbling block to Frankish universal dominion. They had defied efforts of many missionaries—Swibert, Ewalden, and St. Boniface among them—to destroy their heathen faith. The Saxons harried the Frisians and terrorized the people of the lower Rhine Valley. The Saxons were also a strategic threat to the left flank of the Frankish army in any undertaking to subjugate the Bavarians and had to be eliminated. Charlemagne found the Saxons as tough as hickory. He warred against them intermittently for more than thirty years. While preaching the Gospel "with an iron tongue," he methodically reduced resistance, literally from *Gau* to *Gau*.

The tenacity of the Saxons was matched only by the determination of the Franks to break it. The conflict was marred by unspeakable atrocities, as when in 783 at Verden Charlemagne put 4,500 captives to the sword; or when the desperate foe, being pulled down into the quicksands of disaster, allied with the Danes and retaliated by hanging and mutilating Christians, burning churches, spitting missionaries, and lighting all the land between the Rhine and the Elbe with the faggots of their revenge. Although their leader, Widukind, was in 785 persuaded to lay down his arms, it was really not till the end of the century that the shattered Saxons finally bowed to the yoke. The harsh Carolingian Capitulary for the Saxons (797) decreed, among other abominations, that one out of every three enemy warriors, together with their immediate families (about 7,000 persons in all), be carried off as hostages to Austrasia. In 802 all Saxons residing east of the Elbe were reset-tled west of that stream in order that a militarized march might be established against the Danes. As a consequence of the evacuation of the trans-Elbean terri-tory, Slavic Abodrites poured into the Dane Mark and western Mecklenburg. By 810 virtually all lands east of the Elbe and Saale, which had once been occupied by Germans, were in possession of Slavic Sorbs, Wilzi, Wends, and Abodrites.

The Integration of Bavaria

During the eighth century Tassilo III, duke of Bavaria, revived the power of the Bavarian nation and made it an anti-Frankish factor in the international combi-nations of the times. By 770 he had established an infirm dominion over a large area between the Enns and Carpathians and between Thuringia and the Adriatic, embracing not only Germans but Asiatic Avars and many Slavic tribes. Tassilo III, no less than Charlemagne, fought the battle of civilization against the heathen. One of his major services was to introduce Christianity to Bohemia, Carinthia, and Carniola. Between 772 and 777 the Bavarians converted the Carinthians and established the monastery of Innichen at the gateway to Carniola and the great abbey of Kremsmünster at the mouth of the Enns. Yet Tassilo was to be the author of his own ruin. When he leagued with the main force of the Avars, the foe of the German people, his own vassals deserted him in horror. This gave Charlemagne a golden opportunity to put an end to Bavarian independence. The ensuing conquest concluded a chapter that saw all Germany incorporated into the Empire of the West.

It was of the greatest significance that the cross went along with the sword into subjugated Bavaria. Vast stretches of park, woodland, field, and meadow were confiscated and, when not given to Frankish or allied lords, subinfeudated to eccle-siastical foundations. Princely benefices were awarded the bishoprics of Salzburg, Passau, Freising, Regensburg, Ingolstadt, and the abbeys of Wessobrunn, Krems-münster, Tegernsee, Innichen, Herrenwörth, Frauenwörth, St. Florian, Maninseo, Mondsee, and Benediktbeuren. At the same time, non-Bavarian Germans came to settle in the conquered land. Yet nowhere did this movement take on the character, as was to be the case with the later trans-Elbean migrations, of a mass colonization involving all strata of German society.

Carolingian Rule in Germany

Frankish rule was not tyrannical or even highly centralized. Rather it was suffused, as Walter Ullmann has made clear, with a theocratic perspective that eventually by the ninth century was to express itself in the subordination of the ruler to the law. Charlemagne's empire was also basically Frankish, not German: a polyglot creation discreetly dominated by an overlord people. Frankish sway manifested itself everywhere in Germany. The ducal tribal governments were systematically eradicated. Native dukes and tribal assemblies were abolished, as were most evidences of national independence. However, Charlemagne did not try legally and linguistically to assimilate the "stem" peoples *(Stämme):* Swabians, Saxons, Thuringians, Frisians, Bavarians, and Ripuarian Franks. Rather, he showed respect for their unique characters as long as their laws did not conflict with royal ordinances (capitularies). From this fundamentally tolerant relationship derived the peculiar dualism of the Carolingian system, the joining of centralism and localism. From the apex of the governmental pyramid descended a unifying imperial influence, operating through emperor, chancellor, public assembly of nobles *(placitum)*, rudimentary ministries, itinerant royal agents, and appointive regional administrators (the counts). From the bottom welled up the usages and customs of the tribes, expressed by the representative assemblies of the "hundreds."

Persistence of Tribal Institutions

Charlemagne did not organize the stem duchies into a genuine federation because he feared that would tip the balance in favor of the Germans within his empire. Yet he could not ignore their tribal heritage. He deemed it wise to build his military on a tribal basis, draw diocesan boundaries that only rarely spanned two stem duchies, and leave administration of justice largely in the hands of the "hundred" courts.

The central problem of Carolingian government was the absence of intermediate administrative machinery in Germany. The ducal governments had been destroyed, and no indigenous institutions above the hundreds remained. The job of building a governing superstructure in Transrhenia was assigned to counts *(Grafen)* and counts of the march or margraves *(Markgrafen)*. Appointed by the emperor from the native or Frankish nobility, these unsalaried dignitaries supervised implementation of royal capitularies and presided over the hundred courts.

The county *(Grafschaft)* was the most important unit of Carolingian administration, but it was less effective in Germany than in Gaul. Because the emperor or his justiciar, the count palatine *(Pfalzgraf)*, could not always personally check on the counts and margraves, itinerant noble administrators called *missi dominici* (German, *Sendboten*) were commissioned to travel over the wretched German roads from county to county. Their function was to insure compliance with military duties, review judgments, collect imperial revenues, hear appeals from hundred courts, and summon provincial assemblies. Notwithstanding surveillance by the *missi*, however, the tendency was for the greatest imperial bailiffs, remote from Aachen and possessed of vast benefices, to become nearly autonomous hereditary lords whose jurisdictions not infrequently overlapped. To further complicate administration, the tribes lived under a bewildering variety of customary laws and local authority, and even the church had its own law and independent structure of lay administrators *(Kirchenvögte)*.

Primitive Conditions
of Judicial Procedure

In spite of the Church and the humane traditions of the Theodosian Code, German procedural law was barbarous, impoverished, inequitable, and suffused with superstition. Almost no attempt had been made to superimpose uniform standards upon the tribal courts, judges, or jurors *(Schöffen)*. Yet German law was the expression of the will of the people of the locality and was not thought to be the business of the crown.

Criminal law was more developed than civil because of the backward state of commerce. Criminal trials were by compurgation, combat, or ordeal, and the accused was considered guilty until proved to be innocent. In case of compurgation, trial evidence consisted not of sworn testimony of witnesses but of friends or relatives of the defendant, a procedure that favored a popular or powerful man. Trial by combat, in the course of which God's judgment was supposedly revealed, was not normally between plaintiff and defendant but hired champions, whom only the wealthy could afford. By the eighth entury, however, trial by ordeal—either by variants of fire or water—had come to be the principal judicial procedure in Germany.

After "divine judgment" had established the guilt of the defendant, the hundred court imposed sentence. Penalties ranged from payment of compensation *(Wergeld)* to the plaintiff or next of kin to forefeiture of all property or hanging (which was an original German method of execution).

The Spread of Christianity

It is an old error, often repeated by modern historians, to contend that the work of converting those Germans who had not yet forsaken the mythology of their fathers was exclusively the achievement of the Gaels and Anglo-Saxons. It is, of course, true that in the early seventh century a number of Gaelic apostles swept all the northern, western, and southern corridors of Germany, putting the natives under a spell. Thus Gaelic St. Columban and twelve disciples who arrived in Gaul in 590 founded the monastery of Luxeuil on the western slopes of the Vosges Mountains and preached to the Alemanni with success. Gallo or St. Gallus, who was St. Columban's most distinguished pupil and companion, founded the first great monastery on German soil—St. Gall, in eastern Switzerland. St. Kilian missionized at Würzburg and was beheaded in 689 by the Ripuarian Franks, an event that is still remembered in the symbolism of the churches of that city. St. Fridolin founded the monasteries of Säckingen and Primin. St. Corbinian founded the cloister at Freising. Eventually, the Gaelic monks founded more than forty religious houses. However, the reluctant German tribesmen, who were just emerging from the nature-worship stage, led the Irish missionaries many a weary, spiritual chase through the dense woods, like Puck in Oberon's forest.

Despite all Gaelic successes, it remains a fact that the most active bearers of the banners of Christianity in the seventh century were men from the Gallo-Roman south, especially the monastery of Solignac near Limoges. In the Roman counteroffensive against the Gaels there figured Bishop Kunibert, the Ripuarian Frank, who founded the first missionary hub in Frisia, and Bishop Haimhram, another Frank, who in 660 established the episcopal see of Regensburg (Ratisbon). The Roman Catholic Hrodbert (Rupert) converted many thousands in Bavaria. Gradually the Gallo-Roman missionaries, who far outnumbered the Gaels, recovered the field from them. Contiguity, wealth, and sheer numbers were the decisive factors in regaining Germany for Rome. Important, too, was the example of the Gaelic foundations, which although individually autonomous, repelled people by their exceptionally rigorous and austere rule.

St. Boniface,
Apostle to the Germans

In the eighth century the Anglo-Saxons gave a decisive impetus to the Roman counteroffensive by bringing both Frisia and Saxony into the fold. In 690 St. Willibrord (657?–739), later consecrated archbishop of Utrecht, and eleven English monks gained a foothold in eastern Frisia. Protected by the Merovingian government, he nonetheless met a martyr's death in Frisia. Winfried of Exeter (680–755) carried the gospel to Inner Germany, notably to Hesse and Thuringia. He founded many churches and monasteries, among them Fritzlar in Hesse, Orthorpf in Thuringia, and Hersfeld, and the convents at Kitzingen, Ochsenfurt, and Taubersbischofsheim. Made an archbishop by the pope, Winfried consecrated many bishops and laid Germany out into a diocesan gridwork. The bishoprics of Würzburg, Erfurt, Marburg, and Eichstädt were wholly his creations. Others— Salzburg, Freising, Lorch (later Passau), and Regensburg—owed much to his help. After being appointed primate in 743 by the synod of Germany, Winfried brought the German prelacy under practical domination of the Frankish crown and into close attendance on Rome. Through his appointments he drowned Celtic notions of autonomy in the heavy wine of Roman authoritarianism.

At length Winfried turned his rare abilities toward Saxony, where he founded the monasteries of Fritzlar and "Golden Fulda" on the rim of the Vogelsberg. Known to history as St. Boniface, Apostle of Germany, he was one of the four or five greatest men of his time. Later martyred by the Frisians (755), to whom he had returned to complete Willibrord's work, he was interred at Fulda. Boniface's disciple, Sturm, and his archepiscopal successor, Lullus, continued his centralizing work and also founded the Saxon bishoprics of Paderborn, Halberstadt, Osnabrück, and Münster.

Consequences of the Conversion
of the Germans

The fact that almost all Germans had by the time of Charlemagne's death been converted gave to Western civilization a Teutonic flavor. It also facilitated later the conversion of Poland, Bohemia, Hungary, Carinthia, Carniola, and Dalmatia to the Roman faith, denying these regions to Orthodox Christianity and Islam. The conquest of Germany so fortified the Roman Church as to enable it to counterpose to ninth-century disintegrative tendencies a culturally unifying and constructive influence. Also, Christianity benefited from conversion of the Germans in that it was supplied with new wellsprings of zeal, vigor, and youth from which ever and again were to bubble up movements of elemental regenerative force.

Church and Upper Clergy
in Carolingian Times

Boniface's organizational religious work was continued by Charlemagne. The emperor, who willed his entire personal fortune to the Church, completed the division of Germany into archbishoprics, bishoprics, and parishes. By 814, there were four of the first (as compared with twelve in France and five in Italy), twenty-two of the second, and hundreds of the third. Royal control over the clergy was achieved through domination of episcopal elections, firm support of the episcopacy, and the grant of endowments and vast fiefs. These fiefs sometimes, as in the case of Tegernsee, Fulda, and Gandersheim, embraced thousands of manors.

The wealth of the bishops continued to wax. In the tenth century all of them were elevated to princely rank. By then the most affluent prelates had come, as respects revenues and holdings, to surpass all but a few secular lords. It is no wonder that the Church became the auxiliary of royal policy. The practical expression of the feudal relationship between ecclesiastical vassal and imperial overlord was the armored and helmeted prelate astride his mighty war horse; his hands were as used to the sword as to the crozier.

The False Renaissance and Germany

During Charlemagne's reign a modest revival of learning took place at the palace school at Aachen under the aegis of such men as Alcuin of York, Paul the Deacon of Lombardy, Einhard (the emperor's biographer), Peter of Pisa, and Theodulf, Bishop of Orléans. The literary output of these men, despite Alcuin's popularity, was defective, imitative of a dead style, and written in a land where style was not even appreciated. By contrast with the effervescent outpourings of Roman authors, the product of their Carolingian epigones was only a trickle of vinegar.

Immature Germany was wholly incapable of supporting a true renaissance. Neither the requisite knowledge nor the literary tradition was present. For the Germans, the Carolingian renaissance was never anything more than the feeblest gegenschein of the distant Italian sun. This is not to say that men such as the aforementioned were wholly lacking in influence upon Germany. They transplanted some cultural shoots there. Thus, Alcuin's pupil Hrabanus Maurus (776–856) founded an important monastic school at Fulda. Others, too, were founded, with the encouragement of Aachen, at Cologne, Freising, St. Gall, Reichenau, and Salzburg. In these schools the palace output served as models in historical writing, miniature painting, and exegesis. Year after year German monks recorded in terse, unimaginative prose pedestrian notes on the events of their times. Half-fact, half-fiction, these "seasonal books" or annals were modeled after Bede's Anglo-Saxon *Ecclesiastical History of England*. Examples are the *Moselle Annals, Great Laurisse Annals,* and the *Annals of the Alemanni.* When all is said for the literary and historical renaissance, however, it must be insisted that Charlemagne was less interested in this sort of thing than in the spiritual regeneration of Frankish society.

As for art, Charles rejected Byzantine and Moslem canons in favor of Roman. He encouraged the spread of Celtic calligraphy and illumination of manuscripts. As a result, German monastic art attained a distinction that was denied German literature in this epoch. Celtic and Roman currents merged to produce admirable examples of handwritten bibliogony. Half-uncial or, more often, Frankish minuscule lettering, sometimes penned in golden ink and usually ornamented with sumptuous, polychrome capitals, stood forth on parchment pages that were occasionally bordered with intricate and sinuous floral tracery. Illuminated manuscripts were prepared especially at Strassburg, Reichenau, Kremsmünster, and Freising, but among the finest jewels of Carolingian writing are the Bibles of Metz (Bishop Drago's), Aachen, Strahower, Nuremberg, and Munich. Most magnificent of all, rivaling Dublin's *Book of Kells,* was Godescalk's *Evangelarium* (781), which was written on purple parchment in exquisite half-uncial letters of gold and silver and illustrated lavishly with miniature paintings.

Alcuin's disquisition on the Trinity *(De fide trinitatis)* had a great vogue in Germany and inaugurated a trend toward religious literature that intensified with the decades. To the *Hildebrandslied* (copied circa 800), that sole surviving example of Old High German epic poetry, now succeeded the biblical commentaries of Walafrid Strabo, the visions of Hincmar of Reims, the martyrologies of Wandalbert of Prüm, and the predestinarian tracts of the Benedictine monk Gottschalk. The best piece of real literature of the ninth century, written in German, would seem to have been *Das Heliand* or *Heiland* [The Savior], an heroic, alliterative poem by an unknown author (circa 830), depicting Christ as a knightly messiah.

Charlemagne's Significance

Charles the Great was a man whose dream was too big for his hoop. Much inferior in learning and refinement to his contemporary, Harun-al-Rashid, Caliph of Baghdad, Charlemagne ruled over a realm that was mean and small by comparison with the Caliphate and enjoyed only a wretched fraction of what annually accrued in revenues to Harun. Yet these things were not the measure of the Frank's importance. Charlemagne was the first Western ruler in three centuries to bear an imperial title. His coronation in St. Peter's demonstrated that the Roman unifying concept had never died. It may be that, as C. Delisle Burns has contended, Charles had himself crowned emperor out of personal ambition, or that, as Karl Heldemann, Werner Ohnsorge, and Walter Ullmann have cogently argued, the papacy engineered the coronation for Italian political considerations. But it is more likely that it was, as James W. Thompson, Geoffrey Barraclough, and Ferdinand Lot have maintained, a combination of mighty forces that drove Charlemagne. In any case, his labors enabled the first independent civilization north of the Alps to rise. This was the new Christo-Germanic-Roman civilization, which we call Western or European civilization. As yet unleavened by international commercial or fermentative additives from the Mediterranean or Hellenistic East, this civilization was destined eventually to conquer all continents except Asia.

Disintegration of the Empire of the West

After Charlemagne's death, the imperial edifice was undermined as a result of the absence of a strong ruler, the spread of lawlessness, and the coming of invasions. In the hands of Louis the Pious (814–40), the incompetent son of Charlemagne, the Empire verged on ruin. Louis had luckily inherited the realm intact but, like his father in 806, had divided it among his four sons. One of them died, but the other three fought among themselves and against Louis. In a very bloody battle at Fontenoy (Auxerre) on June 25, 841 Charles and Ludwig combined to defeat their older brother, Lothaire. In this battle the flower of Carolingian chivalry perished with disastrous results for the defense of Europe against the Northmen. The following year at Strassburg, Charles and Ludwig allied again against Lothaire and took an oath of mutual support, written in *theodisk* (the father of Old High German) and Gallo-Frankish (primal medieval French).

Unable to ignore Lothaire, who after Fontenoy was still powerful, the younger brothers agreed to the Treaty of Verdun in 843. This treaty commenced the partitioning of the Empire. Most of the western counties (France) were assigned to Charles the Bald. The lands east of the Rhine went to Ludwig the German. In spite of his defeat. Lothaire received the imperial title and a rich block of Austrasian and north Italian lands. Nevertheless, since genuine national consciousness did not yet exist in Europe, it would be a mistake to see in the Treaty of Verdun the beginnings of the nation-states of France and Germany. In 870 by the Treaty of Mersen Lothaire's kingdom (*Lotharii regnum*) was divided between Charles and Ludwig, the bulk of the realm, subsequently known as the duchy of Lorraine (Lothringen), being awarded to the latter.

The last years of the Carolingian Empire were ones of dolorous decay. Imperial revenues had been pawned, and the crown had well-nigh pauperized itself by alienating lands to enlist the military support of powerful nobles. For a brief hour, Charles III, the Fat (884–87), gave the illusion of checking the disintegration, but being afflicted with obesity and epilepsy, he was unequal to the task of an emperor. Under him the imperial office fell into disrepute. By contrast, the pope rose to preeminence, and Frankish kings had to be confirmed by him.

Arnulf of Carinthia (887–99), a powerful margrave and nephew of Charles III, kept up pretenses a while longer, but on his death the unstable realm crumbled forever. Its place was taken not by relatively large Germanic kingdoms, as after the Roman Empire, but by a dust cloud of feudal particles. Arnulf's son, Louis the Child (899–911), was a minor whose feeble authority did not extend beyond Germany. During his time imperial pretenders followed each other thick and fast— formless shadows in the penumbra of Carolingian history. When Louis died, the Germans, dimly conscious of their peculiar interests, elected Duke Conrad of Franconia king of an independent Germany on November 10, 911. With this act the political history of Germany began.

PART II

GERMANY'S FIRST AGE

OF ASCENDANCY

(911–1254)

Chapter 4

ESTABLISHING THE

FIRST GERMAN EMPIRE

The Stem Duchies

Germany's future turned upon the fact that the Carolingian Empire had disintegrated before the old tribal configuration could be erased. The ruin of the ducal dynasties had not entailed the suppression of the old stem loyalties, nor had the basic political geography of the country changed. During the ninth century the counts and margraves, who were usually Franks from Gaul, endeavored to keep alive the fiction of imperial authority in Germany. However, by the early tenth century they realized that they alone could offer adequate military protection to their vassals and the common people. With *de facto* power came a novel spirit of independence. The descendants of the alien counts then went about reviving the stem duchies. As dukes *(Herzöge)*, these rulers became the embodiments of regional authority.

The position of the dukes was strengthened during the short reign of Conrad I (911–19), the first king of Germany. Inasmuch as he owed his coronation to the hierarchy, he was at pains richly to reward the prelates. This angered the disquieted lay nobility. Incited by Duke Henry of Saxony, the temporal lords rose in rebellion. Finally, when it had become clear that the arrant Conrad I was unable to check the Hungarian invaders, territorial assemblies, loyal above all to their dukes, remembered their duty in time of danger and conferred upon them almost regal powers.

Eight duchies took shape: Saxony, Frisia, Thuringia, Franconia, Lorraine, Swabia, Bavaria, and Rhaetia. Of these, the political boundaries of Bavaria, Swabia, Saxony, and Thuringia corresponded most closely with ethnic realities; those of Frisia and Rhaetia less so; and those of Franconia and Lorraine, because they were often altered by Frankish kings, not at all. Saxony, Thuringia, and Bavaria, which were shield or march provinces that bore the brunt of fighting invaders, were fairly easily consolidated under ducal control, which in time became hereditary. Thus the ducal state was restored to Bavaria and Thuringia in 908, and to Saxony in 913. Franconia, Swabia, and Lorraine, protected by the marches, only slowly achieved ducal organization. Political disintegration was at a maximum in Lorraine, where the process was aided by episcopal influence. German attempts to hold on to Lorraine failed, and it temporarily fell to France. Frisia, dominated by the bishops of Utrecht, Bremen, and Münster, did not emerge as a duchy until the turn of the eleventh century.

Ducal Functions

In theory the dukes were the viceroys of the king and exercised appropriate powers. Actually their authority rested upon performance of military services, possession of numerous fortresses and strong points, and identity with the interest of their stem. Decomposition of the Carolingian Empire and mounting threats from the Slavs and Hungarians led to a decentralization of authority in favor of the dukes. The latter, in addition to the duty of external defense, had also to guard internal peace, dispense justice, govern, and even conduct foreign policy. Their judicial responsibilities were very important. After the disappearance of the *missi dominici,* the dukes became, under customary law, the supreme appellate authorities in the duchies. To them came appeals from the county and baronial courts, matters involving state security, and disputes between major vassals, but seldom cases from courts ecclesiastic, which enjoyed special privileges. While all ordinary or "low" judicial competence rested with the counts and their deputies *(Zehntgraf, Gograf,* and *Schultheiss),* "high" or "blood" justice, which often involved sentences of mutilation or death, was reserved for the dukes. Between the tenth and twelfth centuries ducal power steadily augmented until it came to embrace practically all internal territorial affairs. By 1200 the dukes might with right claim to be the real government of Germany.

Saxon Dynastic Achievements

With the accession of the Saxon dynasty to the throne in 919, Germany embarked upon a period of rapid growth and expansion. In the tenth century, unutterably bright in retrospect, the manifold undertakings of the Germans were like the rush of flowers in the spring. From Henry I to Otto III, a vigorous dynasty established the primacy of Germany in Europe. An overambitious program embraced the following royal aims: (1) subjugation of the stem duchies; (2) augmentation of monarchical authority; (3) reduction of church and papacy to the condition of servile coadjutors of the king; (4) repulse of the Danes and Hungarians; (5) conquest and conversion of the trans-Elbean Slavs; (6) eastward expansion and colonization; (7) seizure of the Lombard crown and hegemony over Italy; (8) incorporation of Lorraine and Burgundy into the Holy Roman Empire; (9) expulsion of the Saracens from southern Italy; and (10) restoration of a loosely knit western empire, this time under German rule. Of all these objectives the loftiest was the impossible dream of Otto III of renovating the Roman *imperium;* the most heroic was the destruction of the armed might of the Hungarians and their domestication; and the most enduring was the extension of Germanic, Christian, and Roman civilization into east-central Europe. If the Saxon arrow really was aimed too high, it nevertheless sped further than that of any other European people.

Henry the Fowler (919–36)

The efforts of Henry I, duke of Saxony and king (919–36), to reverse the drift toward decentralization and establish Saxon hegemony over all of Germany encountered stout resistance from the dukes, especially those of Swabia and Bavaria. The rest of Germany resented the determination of the only recently civilized Saxons to rule regions that had been in contact with Greco-Roman culture for a thousand years. Nevertheless, Henry I constructed castles and fortifications, strengthened his feudal levies, bound the clergy to himself with landed fiefs and endowments, and established a corps of royal administrators exempt from surveillance by the stem dukes. He also built a powerful *Hausmacht* upon extensive crown lands in Saxony and Franconia. While abolishing the ducal authority in both of these areas, Henry I also dismissed the dukes of rebellious Swabia (926) and Bavaria (935).

Henry's military successes took the heart out of the ducal Fronde in the south. In 925 he regained Lorraine, the old core of the Carolingian Empire and the kingdom of Lothaire. In Lorraine, Germany not only acquired a duchy with a concentration of wealthy towns and the reformist monastery of Gorze but a western border protected by difficult terrain. The frontier at this point was to remain unchanged for three centuries. This accession also freed the Saxon dynasty for the tasks of driving back the Slavs and establishing German sway over northern Italy. A series of victories over the pagan Slavs (Hevelli, Doleminzi, Wilzi, Sorbs, and Abodrites) in 928–29 intimidated them for the rest of the reign. The push also brought the Germans control of the town of Branibor, the future Brandenburg, and paved the way for the establishment of new sees between the Saale and Elbe. In 934 Henry I beat back the Danes and founded the Schleswig March against them. The trading town of Haithabu was annexed, and suffragan bishops were appointed to sees that were opened in Schleswig, Aarhus, and Ripen. New heathen lands were thus brought into the German-Christian pale. The expulsion of Danes and Slavs from portions of the south Baltic shore made possible establishment of two great march provinces, the Billung (Mecklenburg) and Brandenburg, which in the future served as bases of operation against the Slavic tribes.

Most celebrated of all Henry's victories was that on the Unstrut River on March 15, 933, over the fierce Magyars. The blow dealt them resounded throughout Europe. The supremacy of German heavy, armored cavalry was established, and the stem dukes were cowed. By detaching Magyar lands, Henry augmented his *Hausmacht*. After Unstrut, Henry I was regarded as the paradigm of European monarchs. In June, 935, King Rudolf of Burgundy solemnly presented him at Ivois with the Holy Lance, which was thought to confer upon him imperial power and the overlordship of Upper Burgundy and Italy.

In reality it was Henry who founded the German monarchy. He had built a centralized power, encroached upon the rights of the stem duchies, and soldered the prelates to the royal cause. His deeds, which made him the paladin of Christendom, conjured up a vision of the conquest of fabled Italy and the restoration of the *sacrum romanum imperium*. But Henry I died before he could take the step from monarchy to empire.

Otto I, the "Great" (936–73)

Henry's most famous son, Otto I, the only German medieval king to bear the name "Great," was a deeply religious man endowed with amazing vigor and keen intelligence. No monarch of the tenth century came closer than he to elevating his office to a national magistracy.

A precondition to founding the sacred empire was the weakening of ducal power. In his campaign to accomplish this, Otto was aided by the submission of the king of Burgundy. When Duke Eberhard of Bavaria defied Otto in respect of Italy, the king deposed him and in 938 appointed a new duke of Bavaria who renounced the right of episcopal investiture in favor of the crown. In 939 Duke Eberhard of Franconia conspired with Duke Giselbert of Lorraine and Otto's brother, Henry, against the king, but they were defeated by him. Franconia was then put under royal administration and transformed into the very plinth of Saxon dyanstic power. In Lorraine Giselbert was deposed and a son-in-law of Otto was appointed duke. Later the Bavarian East March *(Ostmark)* was also subordinated to a count designated by Otto.

Although Otto I did not succeed in reducing all duchies to royal appanages, he inaugurated the centralization of administrative authority. Absolute monarchy was beyond his reach, but he drove the dukes from the commanding position they had occupied at the outset of the tenth century.

Otto I energetically pursued a two-pronged program to convert the Slavs and colonize their lands as far as the Oder River and to shatter the Magyars. While securing the north by strengthening the growing sees, he also established the Lusatian, Meissen, and Billung marches, and the see of Magdeburg. In driving the Slavs back, Margrave Hermann Billung and Count Gero of Thuringia played leading roles. They founded the bishoprics of Havelberg and Brandenburg (Branibor) and in 963 forced Miesko, king of an emerging Poland, to recognize German overlordship for his holdings between the Oder and Warthe rivers. Meanwhile, the great victory that Otto I won over the Hungarians on August 10, 955, on the Lechfeld near Augsburg forever exorcised the Magyar menace and foreshadowed assimilation of Hungary by Europe.

While Otto's eyes were on the east, Berengar of Ivrea was striving to gain control over northern Italy. In 961 an incensed Otto marched into the peninsula, thrust aside Berengar, and caused the iron crown of Lombardy to be put on his own head. Then, proceeding to Rome, Otto I extended his protection to the young Pope John XII (whom he was to depose in 963 for conspiring against him) and on February 2, 962, received an imperial crown at his hands.

In accepting the title *Imperator augustus romanorum et francorum* ("Emperor of the Romans and Franks"), Otto did not covet universal dominion. He aimed at no more than primacy and the creation of a Germanic Empire, to include northern Italy, Burgundy, and Lorraine, but not France.

In accepting the crown Otto was motivated by certain considerations: (1) firm leadership of the restive Germans required that he proclaim himself emperor; (2) Swabian and Bavarian ambitions respecting Italy had to be forestalled if the unity of Germany were to be preserved; (3) subordination of the papacy to German monarchical authority would aid Otto's designs in the Slavic east; (4) conquest of Italy, a vital link in the modest trade with Byzantium and the Caliphate of Baghdad, would enrich the culture of Germany and augment her prosperity; and (5) Lorraine and Burgundy could be permanently attached to Germany only if her king wore the crown of Lombardy.

In joining Germany and Italy, Otto I forced a union of incompatibles, achieving not so much holy wedlock as unholy deadlock. Marriage with the dark-eyed madonna engendered impossible tensions and cost Germany oceans of blood and treasure. The enormity of Otto's error in diverting manpower, energy, and wealth from genuinely German historical missions is compounded when it is considered that in 962 Germany was not yet consolidated and royal power was not firmly entrenched. What Otto I did could have been ventured only when papal strength was still negligible.

The End of the Saxon Dynasty

When Otto I died in his sixtieth year, he was succeeded by an eighteen-year-old son, Otto II (973–83), the offspring of his able Lombard wife, Adelheid. Before Otto I died, he had arranged a marriage between his son and Theophano, a daughter of the Byzantine emperor. This marriage encouraged the introduction of Byzantine art, manners, and refinement into Germany.

The reign of Otto II, a red-complexioned, stunted, homely youth, brought further growth of royal power. Yet Germany's international prestige declined. Otto II tried to substitute the spiritual for the lay nobility as the principal pillar of the state. While favoring the Church, he brought it under direct royal control by granting ecclesiastical foundations immunities from all except royal surveillance. This put limits to the avarice of the nobility, who for long had been sequestrating Church property. At the same time the counts were replaced by itinerant bishops and abbots as agents of royal authority and the main source of miliary levies. The close union between Church and state in Otto II's reign was confirmed by the foundation of the important bishoprics of Prague, Odensee (Fynn), and Röskilde (Seeland) and by the cardinal role that was assigned in the central government to Willigis, archbishop of Mainz.

Until the penultimate year of his reign Otto II gave the impression of success in foreign affairs. He held the Danes and Norwegians in fealty, subdued a revolt in Bavaria (976), maintained good relations with Miesko, king of Poland, forced the king of France to recognize the permanent cession of Lorraine (980), and had himself crowned king of the Romans. Yet his triumphs were etched in water. In 982 he suffered a disastrous defeat in Italy at the hands of Greeks and Saracens, and in 983 German armies were battered along the Elbe by the forces of the Hevelli, Redari, Abodrites, and Liutizi. The latter defeat was the graver. The Slavs crossed the Elbe in force and drove as far as Hamburg, butchering as they went, before they were slammed back by troops led by the archbishop of Magdeburg and the bishop of Halberstadt. Thereafter Boleslav Chrobry (992–1025), king of an emerging Poland, blocked further German penetration toward the east for a century. Meanwhile, the nation digested the recently colonized lands between the Saale and Elbe.

GERMANY IN THE 10TH AND 11TH CENTURIES

When Otto II died in Italy, he was succeeded by his son, Otto III (983–1002), a minor. Until 995 Queens Theophano (d. 991) and Adelheid were the regents, aided by Archbishop Willigis of Mainz. Before Otto III could seize the reins, well-nigh irreparable harm had been done. Denmark had fallen away from imperial surveillance and reverted to paganism; Poland had crystallized into a stable monarchy; the Lusatian march (Lausitz) and eastern Meissen had been lost to the Slavs; and Hungary had begun to consolidate under Stephen I, who was crowned by Otto III. To the Billunger and North marches near the Baltic, the East March centering at Halberstadt, Mark Meissen, and the Zeitz March on the Elster had been added, but at this late date most of these provinces were insecure or partly occupied by the enemy.

Under Otto III the Empire became more Roman than German. He transferred the center of his interests to Italy and neglected German affairs. In 998 he asserted his equality with the Byzantine emperor and built a magnificent palace on the Avantine hill in Rome, where he surrounded himself with a sumptuous court. On the other hand, he filled most of the higher administrative and episcopal posts, whether in Germany or Italy, with Germans and advanced his tutor, Gerbert of Aurillac, to the papacy as Sylvester II. None of the main councilors (Gerbert, Abbot Odilo of Cluny, Notger of Liège, and Bernward of Hildesheim) of this brilliant monarch was an Italian.

In jangling all the keys of the piano simultaneously, Otto III incurred the hostility of the Byzantine emperor and antagonzied Italians of all classes and orders. Nor did he win the affection of the German temporal lords. It profited him nothing to be called the "wonder of the world" *(stupor mundi)*. As a stranger in Italy and almost one in Germany, Otto accomplished little. Had he lived much longer than 1002 he must have encountered serious rebellion. In seeking to transform the German into a Western Roman Empire, he had abandoned the logical fundament of his power for Mediterranean castles in the air.

Henry II (1002–24)

With Otto III the direct Saxon line died out. The new king, Henry II of Bavaria, who was Otto's legal heir, pursued lowlier aims. In place of his predecessor's ambitious *Renovatio imperii romanorum,* the bull of Henry II bore the modest inscription *Renovatio regni francorum* ("restoration of the kingdom of the Franks").

Except with respect to Italy, to which he made only short visits and where he relied upon concessions and an imperial party, Henry II continued the policies of Otto III. He strove to strengthen royal control over the Church, while his pious wife (St.) Kunigunde encouraged clerical reform. He labored to break the hold of temporal lords upon episcopal offices and at the same time free the crown from excessive dependence upon the lay nobility. To this end he founded the key bishoprics of Bamberg (Nordgau) and Würzburg and substituted prelates for dukes and counts in the duchy of Franconia.

In the Slavic east, where the threat to Germany was growing, Henry battled

Boleslav Chrobry, who had joined Poland and Bohemia together. Although Henry shattered the fugacious union between the Slavic states in 1004, the best he could do was wrest from Boleslav (1018) suzerainty over certain fiefs east of the Warthe River.

From Conrad II to Henry III

The first Salian king, Conrad II (1024–39), was a wise statesman and prudent diplomat. He seems to have made fewer mistakes than any other medieval German monarch. His reign was generally peaceful and prosperous. He retained the Polish king as vassal for specific territories, allied the Empire with Canute of Scandinavia, and bequeathed his successor a stable realm that stretched from Rome to Denmark and from the Rhone to the Oder. His chief accessions were Burgundy (1032) and Lusatia.

Conrad II further hobbled the power of the temporal lords by creating a system of lowborn royal functionaries, lay and ecclesiastical, called ministerials *(ministeriales)*. They resembled the lay advocates *(Kirchenvögte)* of the great estates of the Church in that the ministerials were completely beholden to their master. Gradually these ministerials grew in numbers and expertise until they superseded the prelates and counts as main struts of the central government. With this new bureaucracy Conrad II was able to circumvent feudal ties, because there was much alodial land and very few fortresses *(Burgen)* at that time in Germany, making anything more than economic feudalism still impractical. Conrad II sapped the prestige of the ancient nobility even more by raising many lesser aristocrats to high office. He also augmented the royal *Hausmacht* by bringing the duchies of Franconia, Swabia, Bavaria, and Carinthia under the firm control of the crown.

The second Salian king, Henry III, called ''the Black'' (1039–56), was the most pious and charitable of all German medieval kings. Although contemporaries believed that conscience was his only yardstick, the newer historical scholarship sees Henry III as a calculating exponent of monarchical authority. His aim was to transform Germany into a unitary theocracy.

The main weapon that Henry III used to contain the power of the nobility was the Cluniac movement. This religious reform radiating from the monasteries of Cluny (Burgundy), Gorze (Lorraine), Brogne (Namur), and Hirsau (Swabia), aided the king both to regenerate German spiritual life and curb the rapacity of the high nobility. By supporting the demands of the Cluniac monks for clerical celibacy and exemption of monastic foundations from episcopal visitation, the king was able to arrest secularization of Church lands, retard the progression of the great lords toward independence, and shatter the growing power of the episcopacy.

Henry's wish that only champions of reform occupy the Holy See was in the future to have dire consequences for the Empire. It led him to compel Gregory VI, who owed his tiara to purchase, to abdicate (1046), and it influenced the accession to the pontificate of a series of high-minded bishops. However, these championed the interest of the Church with such zeal that they were able not only to establish their sovereignty over it but to develop claims to a plenipotence that ultimately brought the popes into deadly conflict with the emperors. The fact is that Henry III's concern for reform raised the pope to an eminence from which every succeeding emperor tried to dislodge him.

Although Henry III ruled over a very large area, his policy of exalting the crown alienated the nobility and brought to naught his hopes of further expanding the Empire. During his reign Poland, Hungary, and Bohemia all temporarily sank to the level of vassal states of Germany, but not for long.

On the other hand, the king's last years were troubled by formidable opposition in half his Empire. In the east his efforts to check fragmentation finally foundered on the obduracy of the margraves as well as upon his inconsistent policies. While Henry III enveloped March Meissen in his *Hausmacht,* he transferred the duchy of Bavaria in 1042 to Henry von Luxemburg and the duchy of Carinthia in 1047 to Count Welf III, the progenitor of a mighty family. Styria, too, was alienated to the Margrave von Steyer (whence *Steiermark*), and Carniola, which Henry detached from Styria, was given to another lord. Finally, the king prepared unnecessary trouble in Saxony for himself. He strove there to enclose forest lands at the expense of free peasants and substitute royal authority for that of the haughty Billunger dukes. This he attempted through Archbishop Adalbert of Bremen, who became his viceroy for Saxony. These actions provoked rebellion in northern Germany.

The Papal Revolution

In the eleventh century the papacy set out to establish its hegemony over Europe. Rome found a champion in the ascetic but resolute genius of the Cluniac reform movement, the monk Hildebrand. As Gregory VII (1073–85), he led the Church back to a more pristine ideal and guided the papacy to supremacy over prelacy, and the Church to near-supremacy over the state. Relying upon scripture, canon law, and the forged "Donation of Constantine" (by which a fourth-century bishop of Rome was allegedly given the overlordship of the Western Roman Empire by Constantine), Gregory VII advanced claims whose acceptance would have reduced the kingdoms of Christendom to papal satrapies and arrested development of the sovereign states system. But since his claims were successfully combatted, it is probable, as Gerd Tellenbach and other modern historians have pointed out, that the pope's assault upon the theory of divine right of kings facilitated later efforts to give a secular theoretical foundation to the state.

In the 1050s the pope began to break the imperial shackles that had hobbled the Holy See. In 1054 selection of the popes was transferred from the emperor to a college of cardinals. Then, during the nine-year minority of young Henry IV (1056–65), two strong non-German pontiffs were elected: Nicholas II (1059–61) and Alexander II (1061–73). Heavily influenced by Hildebrand, they methodically elaborated a theory of Petrine power that was to bring war with the Empire as soon as Henry attained his majority.

Henry IV (1056–1106)
and the Decline of Royal Power

Before Henry IV was fifteen, the high feudality of Germany had thoroughly plundered the royal fisc. The monarch would have been reduced to a figurehead had it not been for the able services of Archbishop Adalbert of Bremen (1000?–1072), one of medieval Germany's most celebrated statemen. A scion of the powerful Wettin family, Adalbert was Henry IV's chief adviser until 1066. The archbishop fought like a tiger against the rebellious nobility, especially in Saxony and the Billung March. He also aspired to subordinate the Church in Scandinavia to the see of Bremen, and the fragments of Canute's northern empire to the German monarchy. Unfortunately for his centralizing policies and his dream of a northern patriarchate, Adalbert was toppled from favor by the nobility, who subsequently despoiled his archdiocese.

In 1073 broad segments of the German nobility, hostile to the centralizing, pro-ministerial policies of the crown and bitter over the favor Henry IV had shown the Church, rose in rebellion. The regency of the queen-mother Agnes having terminated, Henry now devised his own policy for paralyzing the nobility. He entrusted many of the fortresses and castles which guarded the crown lands, like Goslar and the mighty Wartburg, to the ministerials. In doing this, his confidence was not misplaced. As respects material wealth and power, the ministeriality was wholly indebted to the king and sedulously furthered his aims. After the twelfth century, it is true, they were less useful to the crown, because by then they had become powerful and affluent lords in their own right and had converted their limited tenures into hereditary holdings. But in the eleventh century they were not yet a privileged, legal estate. Therefore, the king committed to their custody a network of castles, hundreds of strongholds, and other properties. Gradually the ministerials, who at that time could still be relied on not to sequestrate royal lands, replaced the counts and bishops as agents of the crown.

In 1075 Henry IV came close to decisive victory over the feudality. At Langesalz on the Unstrut he crushed the long-smoldering Saxon rebellion led by Magnus and Hermann Billung and Otto of Nordheim, duke of Bavaria. The Saxons were deprived of their autonomy, and Otto, a main figure in the history of particularism, lost his duchy to the Welfs, who a century later were to lead an even more calamitous states' rights offensive. Just then, when prospects of centralized monarchy were good, the pope struck Henry from the rear and ruined everything.

Gregory VII possessed a lofty character unsullied by generosity. Three months after his uncanonical coronation he had revealed his pitiless temperament in flaming words: "Cursed be he that keepeth back his sword from blood." In his resolve, reflected in the pretentious *Dictatus Papae* (1075), to assert the supremacy of the papacy over Church and states, he emptied the vials of his wrath upon the king of France and the emperor. He deposed the former on grounds of turpitude and publicly assailed Henry IV for the practice of lay investiture.

Gregory demanded that Henry dismiss his whole crown council on grounds the investitures had been acts of simony. Henry responded at the synod of Worms in January, 1076, by accusing the pope of depravity and by questioning the validity of his election. Supported by most German bishops, Henry demanded that Gregory abdicate. He responded by deposing the king and absolving his subjects from allegiance to him. By shattering the keystone, the pope thought to bring down the whole arch of the independent states system. His deliberate incitation to rebellion was subversive of all temporal government.

It profited Henry IV not that the bulk of the episcopate, led by the now excommunicated Siegfried, archbishop of Mainz, and Archbishop Thedald of Milan, stood by him in defense of the monarchical principle. The high nobility, captained by Otto von Nordheim, leagued with the papal camp against the centralizing policies of the Salians. When the enormity of this alliance became clear to Henry, he knew the game was up unless he could split his foes. He therefore pretended to capitulate to the princes at the Diet of Tribur in October, 1076. He promised to make peace with the pope and secure the removal of the ban. He made the transit of the Alps in mid-winter and intercepted Gregory VII at Canossa in Tuscany, as he was en route to Germany to try him and receive the country as a fief from the princes. For three days toward the end of January, 1077, the courageous monarch stood barefoot and in scant attire before the castle of the Countess Mathilda, beseeching her pontifical guest to extend him the forgiveness that he knew a pope must grant to a penitent sinner. Henry's trip to Canossa, though unprecedentedly mortifying, temporarily detached the pope from the antimonarchical alliance and dispelled the anathema.

Furious at the success of Henry's stratagem, the princes convened in Forcheim in March and declared him deposed. They proclaimed Rudolf, duke of Swabia, king in his stead. This was the first time in German history that the nobility had acted as a vested interest to remove a monarch and assert the constitutional principle of elective succession to the throne.

In the ensuing civil war, which raged in Germany intermittently for twenty-five-years, Rudolf was repeatedly defeated before being slain in 1080. An anti-pope (Clement III) was elevated by Henry's supporters, but the three popes who succeeded Gregory VII in Rome reaffirmed Henry's excommunication. Wounds of such gravity were inflicted on Germany by this strife as to make her unification impossible for centuries.

Provoked by Gregory's declaration for Rudolf, Henry IV invaded Italy, took Rome, and bottled up the pope in Castel Sant' Angelo. In 1084, the year of his imperial coronation by the anti-pope, the king laughed while Rome burned. He withdrew his troops to the hills of Latium when Robert Guiscard's Sicilian levies came up to aid the pope. He knew what to expect. Guiscard's men on May 28 sacked and put the torch to the eternal city and carried off their ally, Gregory VII, into exile where a year later he died, a broken and confused man.

Meanwhile, Henry lost his grip on north Italy, which practically rid itself of German suzerainty for almost two generations. The German episcopate abandoned the anti-pope Clement III and began to leave Henry, as rats would a sinking ship. Urban II (1088–99) accentuated Henry's misery by proclaiming in 1095 a crusade against the Seljuk Turks. Whatever the larger justification for this brilliant move, there can be no doubt that at one stroke the pope raised the papacy to European leadership. Supremacy passed from Henry to Urban, who thenceforth toiled successfully to turn the king's allies and own family against him.

The young Salian princes, Conrad and Henry, now allied with the grand seigneurs against their father, the emperor. Henry IV's earlier successes were forgotten by a nation that of a sudden perceived in him only a formerly unrecognized ineptitude. He died on August 7, 1106, still manfully striving to hold on to his kingdom. He had failed in his efforts to block the unifying, papal imperial program and rescue direct monarchical government. Against the program of the ablest of the Salians had risen all the elements of a swiftly maturing feudal society. Chaos, famine, and disintegration were all he could bequeath his unnatural son.

Henry V (1106–25) and
the Rise of Feudalism

In a supreme effort to quell the strife that was tearing down the whole royal bureaucracy, Henry V turned his back on absolutism and made peace with the princes. He confirmed them in the constitutional rights they had won at Forcheim in 1077. He now substituted for strong, central government a feudal and particularist society in which the paramount figure was no longer the king-constable but the castled prince whose authority derived less from titles and property than from the armed support of his vassals.

Henry was also ready to make peace with the pope. Although German kings had long insisted upon virtually complete control over investiture, Henry V now asked Pope Paschal II for just one of two things: either recognition of the royal right to enfeoff bishops and abbots with feudal lands and temporal offices and regalia on condition of fealty to the king, or assent to the forfeiture to the crown of all feudal episcopal and abbatial properties. In the latter case prelates would retain only alodial lands, be exempt from secular investiture, and be eliminated as a major factor in civil government.

Paschal II accepted the second proposition in 1109, but the outraged German and Italian prelates, who were faced with loss of most of their lands and revenues, forced him to retract. When the pope hedged, Henry V, now backed by a nobility covetous of the Church lands, marched into Italy. On February 9, 1111, at Sutri he forced the pope to enjoin all prelates of the Empire to relinquish their feudal lands and offices. In April Paschal even conceded prior lay investiture to Henry.

Outraged by the pope's pusillanimity, the prelates gathered in synod and excommunicated the emperor. Henry V then blundered by trying to confiscate almost all the technically vacant Church fiefs in north Germany. This caused the jealous nobles to ally with the prelates against him. The king's action met with particularly bitter opposition from the powerful Supplinburg and Ascanian families in the north. In this crisis Henry rallied the Rhenish towns and refurbished his father's reputation by having his remains transferred in pomp to Speyer cathedral. Nevertheless, in 1119 the hydra-headed opposition was about to overwhelm him when he abruptly initiated a policy of appeasement. A royal charter of that year confirmed the princes in enjoyment of their property and rights and assured the prelates that their temporal interests would be protected in the coming settlement with the papacy. Taken together, the concessions of 1077 and 1119 constitute the Magna Carta of German history.

In 1122 Henry V and Pope Calixtus II signed the compromise Concordat of Worms, which ended the First War of Investiture. The French and English precedent—double investiture—was adopted. The pope reserved the right to invest with ring and crozier, leaving lay investiture to the crown. Although the scales favored the king, Worms was a milestone in aggrandizement of the power of the papacy. Never before had the claim of ecclesiastical investiture been recognized by an emperor. Royal control over the prelates was gravely weakened. Absolute monarchy seemingly had fallen to the earth and been devoured by Worms.

The Constitutional Revolution of 1125

The death of Henry V, last of the Salians, in 1125 provoked a constitutional crisis. He had devised all his possessions to Frederick, the One-Eyed, Hohenstaufen duke of Swabia. However, the latter, as lord of Swabia and most of Saxony, Franconia, and the Rhineland, posed a formidable menace to the nobility. The fact that Frederick had espoused Judith, the daughter of Henry the Black, the Welf duke of Bavaria, put the son of that marriage (Barbarossa) in a position of intolerable strength. Therefore, the diet of princes rejected Frederick. Asserting the elective principle, it enthroned the sixty-five-year-old, less powerful Lothar II (1125–38) von Supplingen, for a price, of course. Lothar, who had once been a Gregorian partisan and a leader of the revolt against Henry V, was so pious that he was virtually tempted to sacrifice the gains of the Saxon kings for the sake of his pusillanimous devotion to the great St. Bernard of Clairvaux.

Apart from an attempted conquest of Sicily, the main importance of Lothar's reign lay in the fact that he summoned the east to life. He founded the bishopric of Havelberg, opened up Pomerania, and laid the cornerstones of a new duchy of Saxony by enfeoffing Conrad von Wettin with Lusatia and Meissen, and of the margraviate of Brandenburg by transferring the Ostmark to Albert von Ballenstedt (the Bear) of Ascanian. In other respects, however, Lothar's reign was overshadowed by the might of Henry the Proud, his son-in-law and son of Henry the Black, to whom he also gave Saxony.

Guelphs and Ghibellines

Upon Lothar's death Henry the Proud was passed over in favor of Conrad von Hohenstaufen of Waiblingen (Italian-Ghibelline), who signed another compact reaffirming the elective and federative nature of the monarchy.

Conrad III (1138–52), a huge, raw-boned man, commenced his reign with a staggering blow at Henry, who had refused to do him homage. Henry's duchies of Saxony and Bavaria were confiscated. Albert the Bear received the former but exchanged it in 1142 for the Nordmark, to which he shortly added Prigniz, Ruppin Land, and the bishoprics of Havelberg and Brandenburg to forge the structure of the margraviate of Brandenburg (1150). Bavaria went to Heinrich Jasomirgott (1114–77) of the Babenberg family, who in 1141 also became margrave of Austria (duke in 1156).

After Henry the Proud died in 1139, Welf, who was seeking compensation for the losses of his family by penetrating Mecklenburg, led a rebellion against the king. In bringing him down, Conrad III had fancied himself a Caesar reaching out for empire over the fallen body of Pompey, whereas he was nothing of the sort. In reality, the king was not strong enough to destroy the Welfs (Guelphs). Belatedly realizing this, Conrad in 1146, as Henry the Lion entered his majority, allowed the royal fisc to be taxed beyond the breaking point by heeding Pope Eugene III's appeal for aid against his vassal, Roger II, king of Sicily. Conrad was preparing to come to the pope's rescue and take the Sicilian crown from the Normans, when the fiery St. Bernard of Clairvaux crossed his plans by preaching a Second Crusade for the reconquest of Edessa from the Turks.

The Second Crusade (1147–49) was another fiasco for Conrad III, who had docilely allowed himself to be enlisted by St. Bernard in a venture that could only destroy the king's last claims to respect. Such of his troops as escaped being hacked to pieces by the Turks were further reduced by disease and exposure. Meanwhile, behind his back young Henry the Lion (the Proud's son) and his uncle Welf rebelled and overwhelmed the king's forces at Goslar. Conrad was faced with certain ruin when he died on February 15, 1152—a failure in all his works.

During the reign of Conrad III the monarchy had careered toward the precipice. Weaker than the Welfs in northern Germany and at their mercy in the south, inferior in *Hausmacht* to the Swabian Zähringer and the Bavarian-Austrian Babenberger, the king was obliged to play second fiddle in every chamber of his house. Refusing to husband his resources, he fought the Welfs all over Germany, chased the will-o'-the-wisp in the Holy Land, and sank up to his neck in the Italian bog. He spread his fertilizer so thin that he reaped a harvest in no field of his labors.

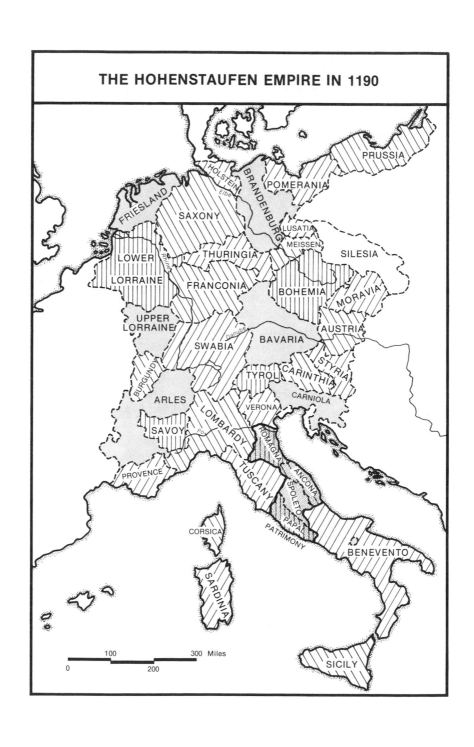

THE HOHENSTAUFEN EMPIRE IN 1190

PRUSSIA

HOLSTEIN

BRANDENBURG

POMERANIA

FRIESLAND

SAXONY

Elbe

LUSATIA

MEISSEN

SILESIA

LOWER

LORRAINE

Rhine

THURINGIA

FRANCONIA

BOHEMIA

MORAVIA

UPPER

LORRAINE

Danube

AUSTRIA

SWABIA

BAVARIA

STYRIA

BURGUNDY

TYROL

CARINTHIA

ARLES

CARNIOLA

VERONA

SAVOY

LOMBARDY

Po

ROMAGNA

PROVENCE

TUSCANY

ANCONA

SPOLETO

CORSICA

PAPAL

PATRIMONY

BENEVENTO

SARDINIA

100   300 Miles

0   200

SICILY

Chapter 5

HOHENSTAUFEN GLORY

The Reputation of
Frederick I Barbarossa (1152–90)

On his deathbed, Conrad III, knowing the nobility would not accept his minor son, recommended his brother's heir, Frederick the Red Bearded (Barbarossa; *Rotbart*), for the crown. Barbarossa was the son of Frederick the One-Eyed and Judith the Welf, sister of Henry the Proud. The blood of both Welfs and Hohenstaufens flowed in the veins of Prince Frederick. In his thirties when he came to the throne, Barbarossa was of medium height, broad frame, and noble visage. Extolled for his valor, justice, and charity, he was destined to found the most brilliant of all medieval dynasties.

Frederick Barbarossa is said to have accomplished great things. He markedly broadened the base of Hohenstaufen dynastic power by sequestrating large parts of Burgundy and Lombardy. Through marriage, he arranged the eventual acquisition of Sicily. He asserted royal authority over his formidable cousin, Henry the Lion, head of the House of Welf, to whom, however, he restored Bavaria and Saxony. Frederick I successfully asserted the primacy of the Germans and their *sacrum imperium* among all the peoples of Europe and reestablished imperial suzerainty over Bohemia, Poland, and Hungary. Within the Empire he proclaimed the equality of its three constituent kingdoms—Germany, Italy, and Burgundy. Finding the apparatus of central government in decrepitude when he mounted the throne, he transformed and integrated it to support, not absolute monarchy, but the structure of a feudal state. Against the pernicious elective principle he revived that of hereditary monarchy, winning the approval of the Reichstag for the coronation of his son in 1167 as king and in 1184 as co-emperor. Finally, he made peace after years of combat with the papacy. Then, taking the cross at seventy, Frederick Barbarossa lost his life in Turkey during the ill-starred Third Crusade (1189).

The heroic dimensions of his career, his sense of duty, chivalry, charity, piety, profound sense of honor, and perfect self-control even in moments of terrible anger, combined with the mystery of his death in the Salef River in Asia Minor have all conspired to draw the veil of romance about Barbarossa. Popular opinion has come to see in him some of the fabulous strength and nobility of Siegfried. In modern times the Kyffhäuser legend, long associated with his grandson, was rewoven around Frederick I. It was whispered that he lay asleep in the bowels of the Kyffhäuser Mountain in Thuringia, where he would remain until the day when the German people, divided and under the conqueror's heel, would summon him forth to free them and revive their glory.

Although a number of modern historians have sustained the popular estimate of Frederick I, among them Rassow, Krammer, Schmeidler, and Barraclough, it is the view of this writer that from the standpoint of the ultimate consequences of his policies, Barbarossa was the most successful failure of the medieval era. Ostensibly his share in the restoration of the Empire was great, but actually his policies prepared the way for its demise. For the sake of domestic peace, he paid the highest possible price in lands and privileges. Because nonalodial lands were usually swiftly transformed into hereditary patrimony, the emperor's generosity accelerated the drift toward a territorial states system. To compound his errors, the headstrong Frederick charged his cousin, Henry the Lion, with contumacy and in 1181 confiscated the great Welf fiefs of Saxony and Bavaria. The surgery Barbarossa performed on these duchies, especially the former, demolished the fundament on which some kind of federated German state might have been perpetuated. The prospect of a monarchical federation resting upon a free association of tribal duchies now went the way of the earlier dream of a unitary, absolutist state. The blow dealt to the House of Welf also compromised its great colonizing work in the east. On the other hand, refusal to appreciate the enduring importance of the Lion's work in Trans-Elbea caused such trouble at home as to reduce military commitments to the Italian theater. The concessions Barbarossa made to the Lombard towns merely encouraged them to enter into hostile alliances, which frustrated his most vigorous efforts to digest any part of Italy.

Frederick's Territorial
Changes in Germany

From the outset of his reign Frederick I tried to buy the support of a few powerful feudal tenants-in-chief. He enfeoffed Conrad III's son with the better part of Swabia and eastern Franconia and restored to Henry the Lion, his cousin, nearly all his lands and power. From 1155 to 1177 a veritable Welf-Hohenstaufen duumvirate dominated Germany. The allies cooperated in the work of winning the east and reestablishing Germanic hegemony in Europe. Henry ruled the north and southeast of the country and the marches along the Bremen-Munich axis. Frederick held sway in western Franconia, the middle Rhine Valley, and part of Swabia. To insure that the Welfs would keep the peace, the Austrian march was permanently severed from Henry's duchy of Bavaria and was given in perpetuity to the Babenberg Duke Henry Jasomirgott. Thenceforth Bavaria's southeastern boundary was fixed. However, the Welfs were given a small consolation prize: Welf VI received the duchies of Tuscany and Spoleto as imperial fiefs. At the same time, Frederick built up a very powerful ally in the Zähringer. To them he gave many Swabian fiefs and lands in Geneva, Lausanne, and the Valais (Wallis) and also promised the reversion of Upper Burgundy and Provence, which had again fallen under his suzerainty owing to the marriage in 1156 of Frederick to Beatrice of Burgundy. Contemplating these major concessions to princes in the southeast and southwest, it is impossible to resist the conclusion that Frederick I was manufacturing new calamities for Germany.

The Conquest of Italy

Italy, which had always played an ancillary role in and never dictated the policies of the Saxon and Salian kings, now became the "golden fleece" of the Hohenstaufen. The deaths of Pope Eugenius III in (1153) and Roger (1154), the last Norman king of Sicily, presented a singular chance for the realization of Hohenstaufen ambitions in Italy. Frederick bore down upon Rome with an army, hoping to gratify the pope by suppressing a communal revolution against him. The king seized Arnold of Brescia, hanged him, demolished his regime in Rome, and restored the recently elected Pope Hadrian IV to his throne. Although the English pontiff was obliged to crown Frederick emperor (June 18, 1155), the Roman populace almost immediately rose up against him. While he was on his way back to Germany, the pope allied himself with William, "the bad," of Sicily. Hadrian's reversion to the old alliance with Sicily was the gauntlet thrown at the emperor's feet. Frederick's response was to reject papal suzerainty, which all strong pontiffs since Gregory VII had stubbornly reaffirmed, and to launch the Second War of Investiture.

Before he could strike at Rome, Frederick I felt the need to establish a strong base in Lombardy and Tuscany, where the communes, thriving on the revival of Mediterranean trade, had everywhere come to replace feudal lords as the dominant force. To revive his dwindling *Hausmacht* the emperor attacked the Lombard towns. His first blow was delivered against the greatest of them, Milan. Its resistance having been broken, a diet was convened at Roncaglia on the Po in 1158 with the purpose of filling the royal fisc. Besides prohibiting town leagues, the Roncaglia decrees stipulated that wherever a charter conferring regal rights could not be produced, prerogatives and revenues deriving from it must revert to the crown. All communes now lost their political and judicial privileges, while Frederick peddled regalia and replenished his empty treasure.

The Roncaglia decrees were so badly kept that war was shortly resumed. Cremona, Milan, and Brescia rose against the emperor, the Cremonese on one occasion massacring German troops on the ramparts of the besieged city. When victory finally perched on Frederick's standards, he caused Cremona, Lodi, and Milan to be burned to the ground. By 1163 Frederick I had seemingly achieved the first of three strategic objectives: subjugation of the Lombard towns. The enslavement of the papacy and conquest of Sicily were his other goals.

After the death of Hadrian IV in 1159, division over his successor gave the emperor an opportunity to secure his second aim. He supported the claims of Cardinal Monticello, who was elected Victor IV by a part of the College of Cardinals. Since the bulk of the upper clergy had meantime secured the consecration of Roland Bandinelli as Pope Alexander III, two pontiffs thenceforth competed for the allegiance of Christendom. Alexander soon sought asylum in France, where he built a vast anti-imperial coalition. Subsequently his English ally left the coalition in indignation at the papal stand in the Thomas à Beckett episode. This facilitated the consummation of a marriage between Henry the Lion and Mathilda, daughter of King Henry II of England, which was the basis for the later alliance between Guelph and Plantagenet against Capetian and Hohenstaufen.

In 1163 and again in 1166 Frederick I invaded Italy. In 1166 he drove Alexander II out of Rome and enthroned a new anti-pope, Alexander III. The "eternal city" lay at Frederick's feet, when suddenly the German army was hit by a pestilence. Retreat to Pavia became imperative. Many Italians regarded this calamity as a scourge of God to punish Frederick I for his sins. It was, moreover, interpreted by all parties to the conflict as a catastrophe for Frederick's Italian policy.

The Victory of the Lombard League

Meanwhile the opportunity was given Frederick to consolidate royal control over a spacious block of lands from the borders of Saxony to Provence and Tuscany. In 1168 Swabia and eastern Franconia reverted to the crown as a result of the death of the son of Conrad III, their overlord. At this time the Hohenstaufen also possessed Pleissen and Eger, which extended their *Hausmacht* to the Elbe. It only remained to add the populous commercial centers of Lombardy to these possessions to restore the king to a semblance of the commanding position the Salian kings had once enjoyed. However, before this could be achieved, the League of Lombard towns, organized in 1167, had to be overcome. The Lombard League, which proved to be a more formidable antagonist than the pope, embodied two principles that the emperor consistently underestimated: bourgeois individualism, which was the antithesis of the feudal spirit, and the city-state, which was the reverse of empire.

When the emperor descended in 1174–75 into the peninsula for the fifth time and laid siege to the new fortress of Alexandria for six months, he was rebuffed. He was obliged to abandon the position struck at Roncaglia and recognize the municipal liberties of the Lombard towns.

In dire need of reenforcements, Frederick I now summoned his chief vassal, Henry the Lion, to come to his aid. But Henry, whose fortress had been sequestrated in 1168 by the emperor and who sharply disagreed with his policy toward the Lombard towns, refused to honor the feudal contract. The resulting rift between the cousins insured the decisive Lombard victory at Legnano on May 29, 1176. In consequence, Frederick had to recognize Alexander III and disavow the antipope. Alexander was confirmed in his temporal rights in northern Italy and in possession of the papal patrimony, including the Mathildan Tuscan lands. In the final Treaty of Venice of July 21, 1177, Frederick was obliged to recognize William as king of Sicily and beg the pontiff's forgiveness.

Fall of the House of Welf

Convinced that Henry had been responsible for his humiliation, Frederick resolved to avenge himself on the Lion, cost what it might. For twenty-six years, Henry, who was richer than the emperor himself, had been given a free hand in his duchies and the east. Undoubtedly Henry had grown intolerably ambitious, and Gottfried von Viterbo was right when he wrote: "Though only a turtle, Henry wanted to fly."*

---

*Quoted in Theodor Mayer, K. Heilig and C. Erdmann, *Kaisertum and Herzogsgewalt im Zeitalter Friedrichs I* (Stuttgart, 1952), p. 338.

Masterful and resourceful, the Welf had almost unaided restored Germany's sway beyond the Elbe. In 1156 Henry the Lion had even been empowered by the emperor to invest bishops and found churches and monasteries, an authority that was the foundation of his virtual sovereignty in the march lands. Henry the Lion was mainly responsible for the subjugation and the missionizing of many Slavic tribes, the exploitation of their lands, and the spread of Germanic culture to Poland, Bohemia, and Moravia. He belongs among the great empire builders of history. Nevertheless, when all is said on his behalf, it remains a fact that Henry, who was the grim Hagen of this epic, had treasonably taken part in the conspiracy of Swabian nobles to overthrow Frederick I.

In a sensational trial, held from 1179 to 1180 at Worms and Magdeburg, Henry, who refused to appear, was prosecuted, not for breach of feudal contract, but for high treason. It was alleged against him that he had plotted with foreign powers, notably Sicily and England, to depose the emperor. Inasmuch as neither of these countries came to his aid, and his Saxon vassals rose against him, there was nothing for Henry to do but capitulate. It probably helped the cause of Frederick I that he had rallied the major princes of the Empire *(Reichsfürsten)* to his side in 1180 by raising them to virtually autonomous status and by granting them extensive privileges over their vassals.

At Erfurt in 1181 the outmaneuvered Henry the Lion accepted the verdict the Reichstag had handed down at Gelnhausen the previous year. The proud Lion's lands were declared forfeit and his ducal power suppressed. Saxony was partitioned—the western part going to Philip, archbishop of Cologne, and the eastern, with the ducal title, to Bernard of Anhalt, youngest son of Albert Ascanian, "the Bear." Bavaria, from which two new duchies (Styria and Andechs-Meran) were sliced, was given to Otto of the faithful Wittelsbach family, which held it until 1918. Henry himself was allowed to retain tiny Brunswick (Braunschweig) but was exiled for three years.

If Frederick had hoped by the Gelnhausen Edict to obtain more elbow room for the monarchy, he was in for a disappointment. The privileges conferred upon the *Reichsfürsten,* taken in context with the confiscations and partitions of 1181, rather helped the rise of territorial princes, over whom the king exercised less control than ever. More than the popes, Frederick Barbarossa caused the explosion that produced the cloud of feudal dust that was to hover over late medieval Germany. Beyond that, the emperor destroyed the best part of the Lion's work in that the *Drang nach Osten* was set back by decades. Last, in the north, the partition of Saxony brought down the whole Scandinavian position of Germany.

The Peace of Constance (1183)

After the emperor's amazingly successful Lion hunt, his prestige soared with the German princes, and he was able to pacify Italy. By the Treaty of Constance of June 25, 1183, with the Lombard League, the northern communes—Lodi, Verona, Vercelli, Novara, Milano, Bergamo, Brescia, Mantova, Vicenza, Padua, Treviso, Bologna, Faenza, Modena, Parma, Reggio, and Piacenza—were accorded self-government and sovereign jurisdiction within their walls. The Lombard League was recognized, as were the liberties of its members, on condition that a compensatory royal authority be established in the countryside of Tuscany and Spoleto. After the communes accepted, the emperor was able to subdue rural areas south of Lombardy and recover the imperial lands that had been sequestrated by the Tuscan and Romagnese towns.

By 1185 Frederick I was well on the way to securing new fulcra for his Italian ambitions. He had secured feudal revenue from the Lombard towns, achieved direct rule over the Tuscan and Romagnese countryside, and had married his son Henry to Constance, daughter of Roger II of Sicily. Of all his blunders, however, the Sicilian marriage was the worst. It led the emperors further than ever from the realization of specifically national German purposes. The marital contract stipulated that upon the death of Sicilian King William II, Constance and Hohenstaufen Henry would inherit the Fortunate Isle and its mainland dependencies.

Frederick's triumphs caused his compatriots to forget that he had compromised the whole imperial position in Italy by failing either to eliminate the wedge of the Lombard League or compel the papacy to abandon its feudal claims in the peninsula. The circumstances of Frederick's death, while on crusade against the great Saladin, blinded contemporaries to the reality that Barbarossa had dealt the Empire mortal wounds.

The Short Reign of Henry VI (1190–97)

Henry VI, regent of Germany and king of Italy since 1184, was a hardheaded, overbearing man. Yet, learned in the law, he exemplified valor with fidelity.

Almost his first move upon mounting the German throne was to eliminate Sicily from the circle of his foes. He had urged his wife's claims to the Fortunate Isle when William II died but was unable to subdue the population until 1194. Two years later Henry VI swooped down on Italy again. this time subjugating it from end to end and completely alienating Celestine III. When the Sicilians rose once more in 1197, he put them down with such ferocity that for generations they reviled the Germans.

In Germany Henry VI sought to attach the high feudality to the crown. He conferred Thuringia in 1191 upon an imperial prince and Styria upon the already powerful Duke Leopold of Austria. In 1196 Henry even offered to convert the fiefs of princes into hereditary alodial lands if they would only accept the principle of hereditary Hohenstaufen succession to the throne, but the princes demurred.

Henry was then at the peak of his power. His brain throbbed with grandiose dreams of dominion. Suzerain of England, lord of Armenia, Cyprus, Antioch, Italy, and Sicily, the emperor was blinded by the Byzantine east, where he aspired to fill the shoes of Justinian. However, just as Henry VI was about to take the cross, disease took him at age thirty-two. He left behind him a three-year-old son, Frederick (crowned in 1196), and a testament of insoluble problems. Thereafter the Empire fell prey to division, and Henry's work was utterly unraveled.

Innocent III and Germany's "Time of Troubles"

The initiative in grand politics now passed to France and the papacy. In 1198 the thirty-seven-year-old Lothario di Segni was crowned Pope Innocent III (1198–1216). He displayed a diplomatic and administrative genius which, sustained by an indomitable will, was to raise the papacy to suzerainty over Europe. At first all things favored Innocent—the minority of Frederick of Sicily, the outbreak of civil strife in Germany, the ineptitude of John of England and his struggle with Philip Augustus of France, and the fact that Queen-regent Constance of Sicily had acknowledged papal overlordship. In Germany, where young Frederick's claims were ignored, a disastrous double election took place. One camp of nobles proclaimed Henry's brother, the chivalrous and refined Philip of Swabia, king. The other camp chose the youngest son of Henry the Lion, the base and avaricious Frenchman, Otto, count of Poitou and duke of Brunswick.

Philip offended the pope by threatening his position in Italy and by asserting the right of the princes to elect a monarch without papal interference. Innocent responded by pitting the Welfs and English against the Hohenstaufen and undermining what was left of the German monarchy. At the same time princes, nobles, and prelates seized the opportunity to usurp royal regalia and expropriate Hohenstaufen lands in Swabia.

In 1200 the pope recognized Otto, who was allied with King John. However, the French king's confiscation of English fiefs in France in 1204 not only sapped John's position but discredited Otto IV. He had to flee to England for reinforcements. While German prestige declined, that of France and the imperial princes rose. The pontiff gained control of much of Italy, and the German Church and state sank lamely into prolonged tutelage to the papacy.

When Otto IV fled to England, the pope, who hated John like sin, felt compelled to embrace Philip of Swabia. But unfortunately Philip was assassinated in 1208, and Otto was restored to the throne. To buy the pope's support he was now obliged to issue the Edict of Speyer (March 22, 1209), by which he surrendered to him all disputed properties in Italy and renounced interference with episcopal elections in Germany or ecclesiastical appeals to the Holy Curia. This was tantamount to surrender of all the rights which the Concordat of Worms had conferred upon the German crown. The Edict of Speyer, reaffirmed by Otto's successor, pointed the way to resubmission of the German Church to Roman domination. It marked a great moment in the life of Innocent III. Otto soon disappointed him, however, causing him to drop the Welf in favor of the young and unembittered son of Henry VI, Frederick, who was crowned king of Germany in December, 1212.

The End of Otto IV (1198/1208–15)

In return for papal recognition, Frederick II accepted vassalage to Innocent III for the fief of Sicily, reaffirmed the Treaty of Constance, and in the Golden Bull of Eger (July 12, 1213) approved the concessions of the Edict of Speyer. Then all south and middle Germany rallied to Frederick's banner against Otto IV, as did France, which was embattled with England. The shattering French victory in the Battle of Bouvines (near Lille) on August 27, 1214, over an allied army of Britons, Flemings, and German Welfs, put the tombstone over Otto's hopes. The following year, the fourth Lateran Council deposed Otto IV (the unhappy ally of King John) and recognized Frederick II (1215–50) as emperor. It was the first time that a Church council had presumed to decide the fate of Germany. Otto died in 1218 deserted by all. He was the last German ruler to assert the authority of the monarchy against papacy and princes.

Frederick II, Stupor Mundi (1215–50)

Born in 1194, Frederick II was an ethnic admixture of German, Norman, and Sicilian, but he was by training and temperament most of all Sicilian. He is reported to have said of his beloved island: ''It is impossible that the God of the Jews would have so praised the land that he gave his chosen people had he only known the kingdom of Sicily.''*

Refined, superbly educated product of the exotic court at Palermo, Frederick developed such talents and interests as to astonish even Walter von der Vogelweide and Dante. In Frederick was apparent the marvelous succession of influences— Greek, Judaic, Carthaginian, Roman, Norman, Saracenic, and German—that had formed the Sicilian mentality. Small of stature but sturdy and athletic, he possessed great skill with sword and bow. From his handsome countenance shone majestic grace. If there was one defect in this paragon it was cynicism. He distilled everything through the alembic of incredulity. Born before his time, Frederick II exemplified the viewpoint of the secular future rather than of an Age of Faith.

Frederick II accepted the imperial crown almost reluctantly. To the end of his life he remained above all a Sicilian *grand signore,* and his whole imperial policy aimed at expanding the Sicilian kingdom into Italy rather than the German kingdom southward. If Innocent III considered this less dangerous than the designs of Henry VI and Otto IV, it was merely because Sicily was a smaller base of operations and the union between it and Germany was to be purely personal. Papal suspicions were further allayed when at Frederick's imperial coronation in 1220 he promised to keep the Fortunate Isle permanently separated from the Empire— a pledge on which he never reneged. To achieve the consent of the ruling classes to this arrangement, however, Frederick was obliged to empty a whole bag of pretty gifts into the laps of the spiritual and temporal lords.

As respects the Church, Frederick II in 1220 gave it increased freedom from all imperial controls, firm protection of ecclesiastical property against sequestration, royal support of clerical efforts to eradicate heresy, and assurances that with-

---

*Quoted in Karl Hampe, *Deutsche Kaisergeschichte in der Zeit der Salier und Staufer* (Leipzig, 1929), p. 217.

out abbatial or episcopal approval no more fortresses would be built on church lands. Frederick even made the *beau geste* of appointing archbishop Engelbert of Cologne regent of Germany during Prince Henry's minority. The emperor had to pay an especially high price for support of the lay nobility for the crowning of Henry as king of Germany (May, 1222). Frederick at that time so augmented the power of the German princes as to efface the last traces of central government in Germany.

One of the weakest kings in three centuries, Henry had all he could do to husband the scraps of power left to him. Even in this he was thwarted by his implacable father, the emperor. Despite the fact that after 1220 Frederick II did not visit Germany for fifteen years, he had no intention of turning over the Empire to anyone else. He felt he needed the regalian revenues, the primacy the imperial crown conferred, and the guarantee it afforded against the rise of a German competitor for control of Italy. Clearly, his attitude diminished the importance of the German monarch. Thus, when the brilliant victory at Bornhöved (July 22, 1227) was won over the king of Denmark, Henry had no hand in it. The duchies and the north German towns were solely responsible for a success that broke the Danish hold on Lübeck and Reval and made possible German mercantile dominion over the Baltic Sea.

Gregory IX (1227–41), who became pope at eighty, had two passions in life: love of the Church and hatred of Frederick II. The emperor had scandalized Gregory by declaring: "The world has permitted itself to be duped by three deceivers—Jesus Christ, Moses and Mohammed."* When in 1228 Frederick defied the pope by leading the Fifth Crusade to the Holy Land, Gregory IX put him under the ban. While the emperor was absent in the Levant, the pope tried to overthrow him in southern Italy. Frederick, meanwhile, had negotiated an astonishing peace with the sultan in 1129, which won the emperor the crown of Jerusalem, a ten-year truce, Bethlehem, Nazareth, and Jerusalem, and the key port cities. However, Frederick only managed to save his Palermitan throne by returning to Sicily posthaste and patching up the truce of Ceperano on August 28, 1230. This recognized the territorial status quo in Italy, conserved the papal patrimony, and made extensive concessions to the Sicilian prelates.

After Ceperano Frederick privately resolved upon the establishment of his absolutist rule over all of Italy. With every year the file of Sicilian castles crept farther up along the Neapolitan coast. Meanwhile, in the Constitutions of Melfi (1231) Frederick gave the nobility of Italy a preview of what to expect should he realize his design. This recodification of Roman and Sicilian laws stressed the public rather than feudal character of the state and deprived clergy and aristocracy of most of their power, fiscal exemptions, and privilege of waging private wars.

The final round in the contest between pope and emperor was postponed because

---

*Quoted in Johannes Bühler, *Deutsche Geschichte* (Berlin, 1935), II, 166.

of the spread of heresy in Lombardy and Germany. The pope could not afford to ignore this danger, even though it was less acute than in Languedoc and Toulouse. He grudgingly took the advice of Hermann von Salza, who had become imperial chancellor, that state and Church must stand together against heresy.

This diversion gave Frederick another chance to carry out his plan of subjugating all Italy to the Sicilian monarchy. If, to this end, the German princes had to be bought, Frederick was a man of the world. In May, 1232, at the Diet of Cividale (Friuli) the emperor issued the Constitution in Favor of the Spiritual and Temporal Princes, which confirmed all customary concessions and laws of the past century as respects the high nobility of Germany. It was a terrible defeat for Henry that he was obliged to agree to this statute, for it introduced a new concept into public law, that of territorial sovereignty vested in a shoal of imperial princes.

His pride humbled, Henry rebelled against his father. Practically all Germans, save the Rhenish towns and some Swabian ministerials, rallied to Frederick. Even the pope stood by as Henry was deposed and imprisoned in 1235. After the princes in 1237 proclaimed Conrad IV, a nine-year-old son of Frederick, king of Germany, they no longer had to fear the growth of imperial *Hausmacht*. It was also unlikely that the crown would ever again do anything analogous to Frederick's confiscation of the duchies of Austria, Styria, and Carinthia from the Babenbergers.

Now that he had shelved the German problem, Frederick proceeded to chastize the rebellious Lombard towns. He won a brilliant victory over them at Cortenuova (November 23, 1237), which almost wiped out the shame of Legnano.

The European Crisis of 1239–1241

Frederick's success at Cortenuova, coupled with the elevation of his natural son Enzio (*"falconello"*) to the throne of Sardinia, caused the pope's slumbering hatred to revive. On Palm Sunday, 1239, in an hour of grave crisis when Europe was being stormed by the Tartars from Asia, Gregory IX again hurled the ban of the Church against Frederick. After having long mulled over the emperor's crimes, the pope thundered his verdict: "His body we consign to Satan that his soul may be saved for God's day!"

Meanwhile, the Tartars, pouring into Hungary, Bohemia, and Silesia, enountered only a badly divided Europe—a continent in which the Swedes and the Teutonic Knights were battling orthodox and schismatic Russians at the behest of a pope whose logic, if persuasive, was wrong. At Wahlstaat in Silesia in 1241 the German and Polish levies, hastily assembled by Conrad IV to stem the unrushing Mongols, were ignominiously beaten by them. Only the recall of the Tartaric field commanders to assist at the coronation of the successor to the deceased Khan Ogodai saved all central Europe from the Asiatic scourge. Incredibly, while Hungary was being ravaged and the marches of Germany menaced, Frederick II was bogged down in Italy waging the endlessly vexing struggle against the papal Guelphs.

Destruction of the Hohenstaufen Empire

Frederick II lived to toast the death of Gregory IX. Each had lived against the day of the other's doom. It is possible that Frederick wrote the following lines of verse that were sent to the pope just before his death:

I am Frederick, the Hammer, the Doom of the World. Rome tottering long since, to confusion is hurled, Shall shiver to atoms and never again be Lord of the World.*

At the time of Gregory's death in 1241 the emperor controlled most of Italy. But the new pope, Innocent IV (1243–54), was as devoted as his predecessor to the Sisyphean task of "wiping out the whole nest of Hohenstaufen vipers." At the Council of Lyons in the summer of 1245 Innocent IV delivered a philippic against Frederick II, pulling out all the emotional stops like a master organist. He excommunicated the emperor anew and laid Sicily under interdict.

Although opinions will always differ on the subject, it would seem that the guilt for this last round in a deadly conflict was divided. Whereas the pope would brook no such rival as the mighty Hohenstaufen, Frederick was a victim of his own vanity. He had done nothing to dissuade his admirers from apotheosizing him or to dispel a new variety of emperor worship. He let the idea grow that the charismatic imperial race was a breed apart, akin to the angels. In his youth he had been called *stupor mundi;* in his middle years he was called *dominus mundi*—"lord of the world." No German emperor had ever so completely regarded himself as in all things heir and peer of the Caesars.

The scales that had formerly tipped in favor of the emperor now began to weigh slowly against him. The pope was now beyond the emperor's grasp and remained so until the latter's death. Innocent IV preferred to live in the safety of Lyons, France. From his sanctuary the pope stirred up nobles, townsmen, and prelates against the tyrant. The Anti-Christ's coming had been predicted for the year 1260, and the Guelphs spread the report that Frederick II was he. Cardinal Rainer of Viterbo, the pope's right-hand man, depicted the emperor as the lord of darkness. Nor was it hard in a superstitious century for contemporaries to perceive in the bizarre Frederick II, seated on a dun horse, the symbol of death followed by a retinue of owls, monkeys, leopards, and Ethiopians. In Germany, too, the pope turned most of the episcopacy and many monks against the Hohenstaufen.

After 1245, perfidy, betrayal, libel, and attempted assassinations (his own physician tried to poison him) made of Frederick II in fact a despot. More and more he was wont to impale his foes on a trident of tyranny, terror, and torture. During these years Frederick's hatchet man was his son-in-law, Eccelino of Romano, the so-called "Devil of Treviso," who, possessed of an unslaked thirst for power,

---

*Ernst Kantorowicz, *Frederick II, 1194–1250* (New York, 1957), p. 519.

enforced the imperial decrees in northern Italy with almost Borgian cruelty. Frederick himself personally supervised the hanging of three hundred Mantovans along the banks of the Po and the beheading of one hundred burghers of Reggio. In this fight to the finish the German towns and peasants and some of the regular clergy supported the emperor; the nobility were neutral, and only the German episcopacy was uniformly hostile. He was on the verge of subjugating at least all of Italy when he suddenly died of gastritis on December 13, 1250. When his son Conrad IV died in 1254, there was left as the last of the legitimate Hohenstaufen only his two-year-old son Conradino.

In Germany, where the Interregnum began in 1254, all was turmoil, dissolution, and brigandage. Symptomatic of the times was the coalescence of the towns into protective leagues, such as the Rhenish, which was formed in the same year. When the counter-king, William of Holland, was killed in battle in 1256, Germany was plunged back again into the misery of a double election. Richard of Cornwall, brother of English Henry III, and Alphonse of Castile, Spanish grandson of Philip of Swabia, were both elected, but neither showed much inclination to come to Germany. This circumstance promoted the political decomposition of the country. Not till Richard's death in 1272 was an end put to the charade.

In Italy Frederick's natural son, the gifted Manfred, assumed the regency of Sicily, but his power did not extend to Germany. The French Pope Clement IV (1265–68) preached against him and in 1265 invited Charles of Anjou, brother of King Louis IX, to accept the Sicilian fief. Manfred was forced to battle the French and fell on the field of Benevento on February 26, 1266. Thereafter, Clement IV refused to recognize the claims of Conradino to either the Sicilian or German throne. Accordingly, Sicily passed under the French Angevins until 1282. Conradino, the last of the Hohenstaufen, was captured in July 1268 and executed in October in Naples.

Nothing had contributed so much to the collapse of the German monarchy and the triumph of localism in both Germany and Italy as the Hohenstaufen endeavor to join the fortunes of the two countries. Even worse was the decision to transfer the court from the north to Sicily. Imperial policy in Italy, contradicting that of the papacy, lamed cooperation between the pope and emperor to the misfortune of all Christendom and of unifying tendencies north and south of the Alps. In Germany the effect of the emperor's inordinate ambition was to encourage the princes to assert their autonomy and enable the electors to dominate the crown. Beyond this, the later Hohenstaufen rulers, by putting Germany's wealth in the service of their Italian ambitions, neglected German interests. In the thirteenth century Germany was the thriving foyer of an emerging mercantile capitalist economy. She possessed vastly more wealth than she had in the eleventh century. Had that affluence, productive capacity, and enterprise been geared to national, rather foreign or territorial objectives, Germany could have entered the commercial era as the foremost European power. As it was, however, torn by vendettas, she crumbled into city-states and toy principalities which, with the passing of time, lost practically all larger importance and any capacity for reunion.

Chapter 6

THE GERMANS FACE EAST

The Course of Conquest

It was under Charlemagne that the drive began that was to carry the German people across the Elbe into lands they had lost to the Slavs during the era of migrations. However, the advance eastward and southeastward proceeded only slowly during the next two centuries because the Slavs and a new people, the Hungarians, offered fierce resistance.

Germany's *Drang nach Osten* was obstructed by heavily forested terrain, slow transportation, poor communications, the strength and resourcefulness of the foe, and the necessity of fortifying every square mile of ground recovered from him. Both the Slavs and Hungarians speedily learned how to imitate almost every Germany military, technological, or managerial development and used this new knowledge to slow down the invader.

In the ninth and tenth centuries the Slavs dealt a series of stiff jolts to the Germans. The latter were so dismayed that they virtually abandoned attempts to conquer the trans-Elbean and trans-Leitha regions until the mid-twelfth century. When again the Germans averted their gaze from Italy, they discovered that new kingdoms had arisen in Poland and Hungary and that the whole eastern horizon glistened with Slavic armor and bristled with fortifications. By then the task of conquest was too heavy for Germany with its limited means, and it was too late to allay the hatred of the Poles, Czechs, and Hungarians.

In the twelfth century German colonists and missionaries, backed by strong military support, again inched forward, occupying all the lands between Lübeck and Stettin, as well as Berlin, Dresden, and the valley of the middle and upper Oder. The next century saw German occupation of the Oder River valley and much of Further Pomerania. The fourteenth century witnessed the palmy days of the Hanseatic League when the German lava flow crept over all of Pomerania to the Stolpe. Beyond that point, however, lay a strongly fortified Polish corridor along the lower Vistula, which the Germans infiltrated but could not take. Further eastward, East Prussia was becoming German, while in southern Galicia, Slovakia, and Siebenbürgen (Transylvania) other remote patches of German settlement were taking shape. After the fourteenth century, which opened with the Slavic victory of Tannenberg (1410) over the Teutonic Knights, conditions did not favor any further German advances.

The Building of Austria

The defeat of the Magyars on the Lechfeld (955) by Otto the Great cleared the way for the founding of the duchies of Austria and Carinthia. Efforts by the Hungarians and Slavs to recover them were in 1040 definitely repulsed. However, in 1058 the emperor recognized the independence of Hungary, which ever afterward blocked any farther German advances in that quarter. Meanwhile, a new march duchy, Styria *(Steiermark),* which was to protect Germany from the Magyars, was carved out of Carinthia.

The spontaneous flow of monks, settlers, gentry, and German culture into the lands beyond the Inn River—called *osterrichi* (''land in the east''), later Osterrich, Österreich, or Austria—came mainly from Bavaria. Although the movement was partly organized and directed by the Babenberg rulers of Osterrich, the main initiative came from the enthusiastic Bavarian nobles and the bishops of Salzburg, Bamberg, Freising, Eichstätt, and Passau. Bavaria figuratively emptied her jewel box over Austria, if we may judge from the many beautifully decorated abbey churches that were built beyond the Inn: Kremsmünster, Mondsee, Heiligenkreuz, Klosterneuburg, Tegernsee, St. Peter, Altenburg, Michelbeuern, St. Emmeran, St. Florian, Seckau, and Baumgartenberg.

Expansion beyond the Elbe
in Saxon and Salian Times

In the age of the German migrations the northern Slavs—Abodrites, Wilzi, Wends, Hevelli, and Sorbs—had moved westward on the traces of the Germans. By the ninth century when they were separated from their south Slav Byzantine Christian brothers by the Magyar invasion, the northern Slavs had come to occupy Bohemia and all the lands south and west of the Balts from the middle Vistula to the middle Elbe. By the early tenth century they had penetrated to the Saale, the upper Main River, the middle Danube, and had even sent long fingers into the valleys of the Alpine forelands. Mainly food-producing people rather than hunters, the northern Slavs had only a rudimentary knowledge of agriculture and did not possess the heavy iron mold board plow. They were not as good farmers as the Germans, but it was nevertheless to their credit that they were the first people to make a beginning with the cultivation of the soil and the clearing of the forest on the Polish and trans-Elbean plain. If the northern Slavs were culturally backward, it was because they had never had the advantage of prolonged contact with either the Latin or Byzantine civilizations.

In the tenth century the Saxons took the lead in colonizing the Slavic lands beyond the Saale and Elbe. As they did so, their political and demographic focus shifted to the loess lands bordering the Harz Mountains. From this base the Saxons penetrated the precincts of the Slavs with sword, saw, and sacrament. While Brennaburg and Prague were taken in the reign of Henry I and Bohemia had acknowledged the overlordship of the king of Germany, it was not until the reign of Otto I that the most determined and ruthless phase of German aggrandizement set in. Since available arable existed in abundance in Germany and population pressure was negligible, the drive against the Slavs lacked the merit of necessity.

Following the earlier conversion of Bohemian Duke Wenceslas, king Mieszko (962–92) of Poland led his people into the Roman Christian Church, presumably with the aim of appeasing the pillaging Germans, for Otto I had inaugurated the forcible and systematic Christianization of Slavic lands. After the great Slavic uprisings of 983 and 1018, which had been the Polish answer to gruesome plundering campaigns of Otto I's henchmen Hermann Billung and Gero, the entire German position east of the Elbe lay in ruins. The achievements of two generations of pioneers had been swept away in a twinkling. The Germans pulled back to the Elbe and did not resume the advance for a generation. Then in the eleventh century Conrad II launched a successful campaign of reconquest in Meissen and Lower Lusatia, the aim of which was no longer to slay, grab booty, and devastate the villages, but rather to transform the Slavic inhabitants into peaceful subjects of the German king and establish orderly relations in the occupied lands.

However, in mid-eleventh century the stubborn Slavs utterly demolished the German colonial position along the Baltic shore. In 1066 the Abodrites, incensed at the harsh policies of the Billunger dukes of Mecklenburg in the Billunger March, staged the worst rebellion of all. They overran every *Burgward* all the way to Wismar, burned the monasteries, and destroyed the episcopal churches at Ratzeburg and Mecklenburg. The entire march felt the sting of their lash. Even Schleswig was laid waste. Hamburg was sacked and its garrison crucified. Once again the night of paganism descended over all the south shore of the Baltic. The uprising provoked the overthrow of the right-hand man of Henry IV, the zealous Archbishop Adalbert of Bremen-Hamburg, by the Diet of Tribur (1066). These two events spelled the temporary eclipse of German influence in the Baltic area. For two generations thereafter the Slavs of Mecklenburg were virtually free, while superintendence of the Scandinavian Church was transferred in 1104 by the pope to the archbishop of Lund in Sweden. Meanwhile, the first Piast king of Poland, Boleslav III, had grasped at all the Wendish lands between the Oder and Elbe, defeated the Prussians and Pomeranians and incorporated their lands east of the Oder estuary into his Christian kingdom, and defended Silesia against Henry V in 1109.

When shortly afterward the Germans resumed their *Drang nach Osten,* the drive was spearheaded by Lothar II von Supplinburg, whose family in 1106 had succeeded to the lands of the Billung dynasty. But Lothar failed to break Boleslav's grip on the disputed eastern lands, and it was not until his death (1138), when his realm was divided among his five contentious sons, that conditions were favorable for a resumption of the German advance. Disregarding Adolph von Holstein's advice peacefully to infiltrate the coveted lands east of the Elbe, the Welf, Ascanian, and Wettin (Henry the Lion, 1139–95; Albert the Bear, 1100?–1170; and Conrad the Great, 1124–56), launched a "crusade." Participants in the campaign against the Wends were promised plenary indulgences and material rewards. Within a few years Mecklenburg and Pomerania were subdued. After the fall of Rügen (1168) to the Danes, the whole coastline up to the mouth of the Vistula was opened to German colonization. In 1170 the Cistercian monastery of Oliva was founded near Danzig. Farther south Frederick Barbarossa with Bohemian aid drove the Poles from their Silesian villages in 1157 and pushed them back to the Warthe. The king of Bohemia was rewarded with Upper Lusatia, and ever afterward he favored German immigration into the region between Meissen and the upper Oder. By 1175 Slavic opposition in the zone south of Mecklenburg and north of the Sudetes Mountains had collapsed, and it was safe for the Germans to move as far as the Oder Valley.

The Settlement of the Eastern Lands

Hot on the heels of the knights came land-hungry peasants and hymn-singing monks. Among the missionaries the Premonstratensians and gray-clad Cistercians, mostly from the Rhineland, were in the vanguard. They figured prominently in planning and colonizing settlements along the entire Oder and, because of their knowledge of agronomy, horticulture, apiculture, and husbandry, were much in demand. In their work the missionaries received more support from both Slavic and German temporal lords than from the emperor. It was mainly the Welf, Ascanian, and Wettin dukes, and to lesser extent the Přzemyslid kings of Bohemia and their Slavic vassals, who transplanted the many Flemish, Walloon, Frisian, and Westphalian peasants who were induced to make the long trek to settle the new east. In the end a territory two-fifths the compass of the Empire in the tenth century was added to Germany.

Before 1200 there were still very few German villages east of the Oder, Most of the colonizing had been achieved in Mecklenburg, West Pomerania, the Uckermark, the Nordmark, Lusatia, and Meissen. But thereafter the really grand phase of the migrations set in. It was to continue with undiminished force until the late thirteenth century. Within a hundred years a huge new granary was added to the kingdom of Germany, and with it, a hybrid blend of Slavs, Franconians, Flemings, Saxons, Mecklenburgers, Rhinelanders, and others domiciled in the new lands.

By 1225 the old Billung March, the Altmark, Hither Pomerania, the Nordmark, the middle Brandenburg lands, Zeitz, Lusatia, and Meissen had become corporate parts of Germany. They were to remain so until 1945. The tide of settlement was also by the third decade of the thirteenth century surging smoothly forward into Further Pomerania, the Neumark, Posen, and Silesia and was lapping at the forelands of the Bohemian enceinte. Czechish and Polish landlords were competing to induce German colonists to settle on their domains. Of course, the farther east the pioneers went, the more formidable was the ethnocultural resistance they encountered. A point was finally reached where the newcomers were less an onrushing wave than diverse streams emptying into a Slavic sea. Distant German communities consolidated at Riga (founded in 1201), in the silver and copper mining areas of the High Tatra Mountains between Slovakia and Galicia (Zips area), in Moravia, and in Transylvania (Siebenbürgen). These remote blocks of Germans had no hope of ever being rejoined to the fatherland or receiving its military protection.

The main result of the colonization movement was not the corrosion of the feudal-manorial system or the acquisition of new territories, as some historians have suggested, but the dissemination of German knowledge, methods, and culture through regions that lay far beyond the pale of German sovereignty. German influence was the main factor in integrating with the western cultural community all the colonial lands east of the Elbe, Saale, and Regnitz, as well as Austria, Styria, Carinthia, and Carniola.

The Teutonic Knights and
the Eastern Baltic Lands

About 1200 the Knights of the Sword *(Schwertbrüder)* of Livonia, a German crusading order, began to operate around the new see of Riga at the mouth of the western Dvina in support of missionaries and colonists. The order suffered several sharp defeats by the native Lithuanians. However, in 1226 Duke Conrad of Masovia summoned to its aid a second military order, the Teutonic Knights *(Deutschordensritter),* under the capable Grand Master Hermann von Salza. Founded in 1190 during the siege of Acre, the Ritterorden was merged in 1237 with the Knights of the Sword.

The defeat of the Knights on the frozen waters of Lake Peipus (April 5, 1242) by Alexander Nevsky and the Russians slowed but did not stop the tide of colonization of the Baltic lands. By 1260 East Prussia and Samland had been conquered by the Knights, while Courland, Livonia, and Esthonia, with varying hybrid populations, were brought under the diocesan authority of the German archbishop of Riga. Marienburg, in the Danzig area, became the seat of the Ritterorden in 1309. The Knights achieved their high point under Grand Master Winrich von Kniprode (1351–82). By that time or shortly afterward they had founded about 1,400 villages and 93 towns, including Kölln-Berlin, Frankfurt on the Oder, and Königsberg. Thus the Knights came to rival the Hanse in extending German influence to the eastern Baltic.

The Knights' efforts in the Baltic area were not always crowned with success. Opposition of the Lithuanians, Letts, Estonians, and Slavs increased the farther eastward the crusaders stormed. Thus, Lithuania managed to retain a power-wedge between German East Prussia and German-dominated Livonia. Moreover, northeast of the Western Dvina, German settlements, largely confined to the purlieus of Dünaburg, Dorpat, and Reval, were insufficient to change the ethnography of the area.

In East Prussia so thorough were the conversion and assimilation of the conquered Prussians that a century after 1260 their language was no longer spoken there. The last holdouts had fled northeastward in 1283. Nevertheless, the conquest was incomplete. Southern Prussia was never completely Germanized, for the Poles soon seeped back into the Mazurian Lakes region where, though culturally under German tutelage, they remained an indestructible ethnic block. They also drove their own wedge of colonization into Pomerelia between Further Pomerania and East Prussia, creating in West Prussia a permanent "Polish Corridor."

After the great Slavic victory at Tannenberg in 1410 the Knights, unsupported by any strong German central authority, faced their sunset. Tannenberg, taken in context with the dynastic Jagellon Union (1387) of Poland and Lithuania and the outbreak of the protracted Hussite wars in 1419, shut all eastern doors in the German face.

Strife, treachery, and velleity laid hands on the Teutonic Knights. By the mid-fifteenth century the membership of the order had fallen by two-thirds and was then only three hundred. In 1456 the Ritterorden's unpaid mercenary German and Slavic troops sold the Polish king a number of Prussian strongholds. A decade later almost all the key centers of East Prussia were in Polish hands. By that date too Poland had come to exercise suzerainty over West Prussia. Obviously the German colonizing wave had spent its force. Thereafter much of its substance was to disappear into the Slavic and Lithuanian strand.

Bohemia and the Eastern Lands

During the better part of the period 1253–1411 Bohemia bulked large in the development and settlement of Silesia, Upper and Lower Lusatia, and eastern Brandenburg. The very ambitious and Germanophile king of Bohemia, Ottokar II (1253–78), who at one time (1251–69) held the entire inheritance of the extinct Babenberg line, did everything to encourage the settlement of Germans on his domains, even extending to them the rights of German law. But after his death fighting Rudolf von Habsburg in 1278, Bohemia's fortunes plummeted. She lost all her imperial fiefs, including Austria, Styria, Carinthia, and Slovenia-Carniola, to the Habsburg Emperor Rudolf (1273–91). Then under the Luxemburg Emperor Charles IV (1347–78), whose capital was Prague, Bohemia revived. From 1373–1411 it was she who mainly directed the development and settlement of Silesia and Lusatia. Habsburg expansionism was forced to seek an outlet to the southeast. However, in the fifteenth century the Hussite Wars (1419–33) undermined Bohemia's brilliant position, and she lost further influence upon German expansion.

Factors Discouraging Later Expansion

When Saxony and Bavaria had led the colonizing movement, it was diversified and vigorous because it depended heavily upon local enterprise. After the elimination of the Přemyslid and Luxemburg dynasties of Bohemia, however, the movement came to depend almost exclusively upon the Hohenzollern margraves (electors after 1415) of Brandenburg and the Habsburg archdukes of Austria. This development discouraged individual colonial enterprise, so that the old freedom and challenge linked with the frontier vanished.

Nevertheless, it was no single factor that dried up the influx of settlers into the trans-Elbean and southeastern lands. To the effects of the rise of territorial dynasties in newer Germany, the Battle of Tannenberg, and the union of Poland-Lithuania, must be added the deterrent of the Hussite Wars, the Mohammedan Turkish advance into the Balkans in the late fourteenth and the fiteenth centuries, and the fact that the Black Plague (1348–49) and its recurrences entailed improvement in the economic position of peasants and laborers in older Germany. Finally, the growth of towns and the grant of new privileges to their inhabitants tended to make the residents of west and south Germany more satisfied with their lot.

The New Villages in the East

Management of the costly and difficult colonizing ventures was entrusted by the local lord to an entrepeneur *(Vogt)* on a contract basis. He received a large tract of land on which he was to settle pioneers. He engaged professional "locators" or promoters from the merchant class to plan the operation. The immigrants, who came by wagon-train with all their worldly possessions into the promised land, hailed from all over Germany and from the Low Countries. They came from strife-torn lands where the manorial system had become insufferable; where dues, rents, and debts had become backbreaking; and socage *(Frondienst),* a major thief of time. They came in search of equitable justice, broader freedom and mobility, economic improvement, and more food. The settlers gave as good as they took. Long-robed Cistercian and Premonstratensian monks and laymen brought to the new lands a superior knowledge of agriculture, plows with wheels and mold-boards, better seed, and a three-field system of rotating grain and stubble.

The more than two thousand towns and villages founded in the east between 1200 and 1348 took their names from natural features or nearby fortresses. Name suffixes were commonly descriptive, such as *-bühel* ("hill"), *-au* ("meadow"), *-bach* ("brook"), *-berg* ("hill"), or *-burg* ("fortress"). Villages and towns were laid out in the form of a gridiron with a market square in the center and a single street, the highway, running through them. The village was surrounded by crude defense works, while the town was ringed with a stout stone wall. Around the settlement was the arable *(Flur),* which was laid out in three fields and grouped in blocks of tenures *(Gewannen).* While at first there were very few restrictions upon the frontiersmen, a long-term deterioration in their status set in in the fifteenth century. This was due to agricultural depression and the rise of great Junker *(Jung-Herr,* or "young lord") domains *(Rittergüter).* The Junkers and a parvenu landed gentry of dubious origins acquired such a grip upon the formerly free peasants that they slowly sank into tenancy and bondage. By 1500 serfdom was more common on the great eastern estates than in economically diversified older Germany, where an embattled peasantry had acquired unprecedented rights and proprietary titles.

PART III
MEDIEVAL LIFE

Chapter 7

MEDIEVAL LIFE

IN TOWN

AND VILLAGE

Carolingian Economy

In a celebrated passage in his *Medieval Cities* the Belgian historian Henri Pirenne maintained that it is a great mistake to blame the German invasions rather than the Moslem conquest of the Mediterranean for the rise of a purely agricultural economy and stagnation of international trade. Whatever the applicability of this thesis to the Mediterranean area, it simply does not accord with the facts when applied to trans-Alpine Europe. Since World War II Pirenne's concept has been rejected by most historians, and the tendency has been to agree with P. Courcelle *(Literary History of the Germanic Invasions)* that the German penetration of the Empire had a traumatic effect upon anything more than local trade.

Following the invasions there was a very sharp contraction in the volume of commerce. It was worst where the migratory tide rolled heaviest. In northeastern Gaul, the Rhineland, the Tithe Lands, and Rhaetia the damage wrought to town life and trade was almost immediate and crushing. This was not because the Germans had any deep-seated aversion to towns but because these were the chief centers of resistance and the invaders had only rudimentary understanding of administration and intercourse. Nowhere was the disruption of political unity and the decline of the classical Roman economy so pronounced as in Outer Germany.

Long before the Moslem sweep through Spain, the towns of west and south Germany, which had born the brunt of the *Völkerwanderung,* had ceased to resemble the once-proud Roman centers whose names they perpetuated. Abandoned by middle class and legionaries, battered and burned many times, and cut off from the civilizing fountain of life that still bubbled feebly in Italy, the German towns had by the early eighth century forfeited three-quarters of their population. The entire monetary, banking, and credit structure had collapsed, and traffic along the rivers had virtually come to a halt. Germany had to pay in the hard coin of stagnation for the thrill of having clipped the Roman eagle's wings. Pepin the Short's time saw agriculture as the only occupation of any real importance. By then, a drastically reduced population was cultivating an arable that had noticeably diminished since the third century, and all but the most easily plowed and productive soils had been abandoned to the red deer, boar, woodsman, and hermit. As in Neolithic times, once again much of Germany was silently reconquered by the forest, by a thick cover of pine, spruce, fir, hemlock, and beech.

Charlemagne's Empire promoted a very modest increase in population and an analogous revival of town life in Germany. With some exaggeration some Medievalists, such as de Roover, Lane, Packard, Lopez, and Adelson, have even spoken of the coming of a commercial revolution in high Carolingian times. A reawakened interest in commerce and communications was exemplified in the construction of the east-west Hellweg highway from Duisburg to Paderborn. Nevertheless, it is easy to exaggerate this economic renewal. Specie continued in very short supply, and what there was was often debased. Credit was still nonexistent, and capitalism figured only as a chapter in ancient history. By the late century, however, the subjugation of the trans-Elbean Slavs, colonization of their lands, and the foundation of the Holy Roman Empire stimulated a sharp increase in trade. Commercial treaties with foreign powers promoted German prosperity, while the exploitation of the Rammelsberg silver and copper mines near Goslar augmented the volume of coins.

Farming and Herding

From the ninth through the twelfth centuries Germany's income was largely derived from agriculture. By comparison with it, other pursuits, such as viniculture, herding, and stock-raising, were unimportant. Dairy and feed cattle and flocks of sheep required considerable capital outlay. They were therefore to be found almost exclusively on the estates of the Church, secular lords, or crown, and then principally on uplands pasturage. The vine was sovereign only in the Rhine, Moselle, and Neckar valleys, where it absorbed much labor power. As for large orchards, free peasants did not often care to assume their risks.

Almost everywhere oats were the chief staple, being in demand for fodder and for making bread and cereal. In the ninth century wheat began its triumphant invasion of Germany from the west but was sown only on the best soils. The Rhenish gentry set the style of eating wheaten bread, whose finer texture they preferred to oaten loaves. Rye was not widely grown until Hohenstaufen times. Barley and hops were the third and fourth most popular crops, because beer was the poor man's daily drink. Much acreage was also sown to flax and hemp, whose fibers were woven into a variety of linen and other cloths. Organic waste was the only fertilizer, and a compost heap stood before every cottage.

The Rise of Manors

Manors were the building blocks of the pyramid of feudalism. They were the aggregate of land belonging to a noble landlord in a given district. Several scores or hundreds of manors, sometimes involving as many as 200,000 acres, constituted the "fief" *(Lehen)* that a vassal held from one or more overlords. Manorial arable was chiefly worked by serfs and other immobile labor. Although in Carolingian times numerous small proprietary holdings (alods) existed in Germany, and free men *(Gemeinfreie)* persisted throughout the Middle Ages in at least Frisia, Ditmarsch, Saxony, and the Alpine forelands, it was servile labor and the manorial system that by the tenth century were paramount.

In the turbulent times of the Norse and Magyar raids unobligated land, subject to neither rents nor services, had tended to grow ever scarcer. Feeling that individualism was becoming too risky, many freemen had voluntarily commended themselves and their land to some strong seigneur. In keeping with the unwritten feudal constitution *(Fronhofverfassung)* that came almost everywhere to prevail, they received back a share of strips or tenures in the manor's *(Fronhof)* arable together with the right to the use of wood, meadow, and waste *(Allmende)* belonging to the manorial community. The condition was payment of rent in kind and of a capitation tax *(Leibzins)*, as well as the performance of manual, nonmilitary, socage services *(Frondienst* or *corvée)*. The acreages allotted to individual householders on the manor were all roughly equal and were about as much as a family could cultivate. Tenures and rights to the common lands awarded to an individual were collectively called a *Hufe* (Lat. *mansus)*.

Organized along semimilitary lines, the manor served many social, economic, administrative, judicial, and defensive purposes. In the almost total absence of agrarian capitalism in early medieval Germany, peasants formed productive and defensive associations. Such groupings stood under surveillance of the seigneur *(Lehnsherr)*. They enjoyed a modicum of self-government, a relatively dependable subsistence, and collective security.

The Manorial Population

To appreciate the "joint stock" aspect of the manor we must keep in mind that there were very few slaves left in medieval Germany. This class, which in Merovingian times had composed the bulk of the rural labor force, was vanishing because it was too costly to maintain slaves and their productive output was low. A slave's condition was hereditary, and hard work held little promise of improvement in his lot. By the ninth century the slaves as a class were being assimilated by the lowest serfs. Their condition, to be sure, was also hereditary, and they were bound to the soil *(Scholle)*, but they were not chattel property.

While conditions of dependence among peasants on the manor varied, serfdom *(Hörigkeit)*, which carried with it economic and legal disabilities, was the most common. Serfs were differentiated in accordance with the terms of their bondage. But whether classified as *Liten, Aldien, Barschalke*, or *Lasven*, they were all nailed to the manor *(praedium*, whence "predial" serf*)*. They were taxable without limit and regarded by the upper classes as almost subhuman. Villeins *(Leibeigene)* were higher dependent peasants who were not subject to sale with the land, were tenants in perpetuity, and were liable only to limited and prescribed socage rent and renders.

Serfs and villeins held shares in the collective manorial enterprise, but cotters *(Kötter)* normally did not. The first two categories of peasant occupied fixed tenures *(Hufen)* equal to a fraction or a full share of the communal enterprise and were paid in proportion to their investment in land and labor. They had the use of the *Allmende* and, against payment of a fee, might use the lord's mill, bake-oven, brewery, or wine press. Cotters, who became fairly numerous in the high Middle Ages, were a class of agricultural proletarians. They owned or leased less than five acres of alodial land and were obliged to supplement their wretched earnings by work at low wages on the lord's demesne.

Tenures

Cultivation of manorial arable was collective responsibility. Tenures were allotted annually among the serfs and villeins. The most common type of allotment was a long, narrow plowland *(Langstreifenflur)* of variable size, but usually of 4 by 40 rods. The shares of any given peasant family were not consolidated but dispersed throught two or three open fields of the manor.

The three-field system of crop rotation *(Drei-Felder Wirtschaft)* was introduced into medieval Germany along with tenures. Contiguous strips of several peasant families were grouped into arable blocks *(Gewannen)*. A family might own shares in several *Gewannen* in each of the three fields. The aggregate of all *Gewannen* and common lands belonging to a village was called the *Dorfmark,* and it might embrace from ten to one hundred or more households.

In keeping with the manor's master plan for joint farming, the arable was planted to wheat, barley, oats, or rye by the bulk of the village labor force. Similarly in seeding and harvesting the peasants worked collectively and were shifted from one *Gewanne* to another without regard to tenancy. In the trans-Elbean lands the *Blockflur,* rather than the scattered strip *Langstreifenflur,* was the rule. In the former system irregular blocks of arable in a single field were assigned to a householder.

Manorial Obligations

In time the village or manor came to be regarded as a semicorporative body with its own laws *(Dorfrecht)* drafted and applied by the village communal assembly *(Dorfding)*. During four hundred years, from A.D. 800 to 1200, despite a threefold increase of population and growing differentiation of the population of the manors, customs, obligations, and rights under *Dorfrecht* remained substantially unchanged. *Dorfrecht* was geared to an economy that was largely, but certainly not exclusively, self-sufficient. In the village community everyone was more or less equal in poverty with his neighbor. Tenants enjoyed the entire income from their investment, subject to contributions to the lord in kind and labor. The extent of obligation was governed by the type of tenure and terms of the manorial contract and differed for men and women. The latter were expected to furnish handicraft products, spun wool, cloth, dyes, flaxen thread, and wood.

Obligatory payments or contributions were supervised by an *Amtmann* or bailiff. Under *Dorfrecht* the lord was entitled to: (1) a fixed percentage of the gross yield from the serf's contractual share; (2) the capitation tax; and (3) in the case of villeins and cotters, rent. In addition, the bondsman had to pay inheritance taxes upon his tenures, which were always devised in accord with primogeniture, and a fee when he took a wife or when his lord's son was knighted or daughter married, and to make contributions of handicraft products, which were usually achieved during the winter months. The lord also claimed a fixed number of days of unremunerated manual work from every bonded peasant on the manor. In time of siege or assault all peasants bore arms.

Other Aspects of the Manor

Besides tenures and common lands there were on the manor tithe lands that were set aside to support the parish priest, and the lords' own private property called *Herrengut* or *Salland*. This land was divided into the demesne proper and the close. The former was sometimes tended by cotters, but more often by serfs, who were obligated to do this, and was administered by ministerials of unfree origin. The demesne, which usually comprised the most favorably located and fertile arable on the manor, often surrounded the lord's great house and generally amounted to a fourth or more of the whole manorial tillage. The close was leased out on special terms to ambitious villagers who wished to increase their income. Together, the demesne and close, both of which were usually at least partly enclosed, occupied a third to two-fifths of the major.

In the center of the manor nestled the village, consisting of houses of varying construction. Most often, dwellings were of half-timber *(Fachwerk)* of a style that varied with the region. Looming above the village was the church spire and the multistoried manor house—of timber until the late twelfth century and of stone thereafter. Villages were generally one of three types: the old irregular but consolidated *Haufendorf* situated in the lee of the manor house and surrounded by strip tenures; the middle German and Rhenish linear village *(Gereihtedorf)* bordering a highway or stream; and the colonial *Angerdorf,* which was a compact, huddled settlement in the east, surrounded by rough-shaped, block tenures. Villages built in Carolingian times bore the identifying suffixes of *hausen, weiler,* and *dorf.* Later settlements, and especially those established in the new, eastern lands, were given endings such as *burg, bach, heim, feld, fels, bronn, thal,* and *berg,* in consonance with some prominent feature of the landscape.

The Three-Field System

Romans and ancient Germans had known only a two-field system of farming. One field had been sown to crop while the other had been allowed to lie fallow until the following year, and there was little appreciation of the regenerative role of legumes. The three-field system was the innovation of the early European Age. This arrangement, inaugurated no earlier than Carolingian times, was made possible by the discovery that certain crops might be planted in the autumn as well as in the spring, thus permitting a triple rotation of crops and allowing each field to recuperate once in every three years. The division of the entire manorial arable into three irregular fields that were rotated annually was more economical and more profitable than the old, two-course system, because on a 1,200-acre manor, 800 acres could be sown to crop as compared with only 600 under the two-field plan. The new system to a degree rationalized farming, conserved labor, raised the communal standard of living, and encouraged a greater variety of crops because of the larger acreage under cultivation at any one time.

Justification of the Manorial System

It is beside the point to argue the practicality of the manorial system. Something like it was unavoidable in the absence of strong central government. The manorial system was the only hindrance to social anarchy in the ninth and tenth centuries. If the burdens laid upon the peasant's brutish back were onerous, they tended, at least in the older parts of Germany, to diminish as opportunities to flee to the towns increased, as the leasehold system spread, and as labor shortage occasioned by plagues became acute. Furthermore, it was for long possible for peasants to escape oppression by migrating to the new lands beyond the Elbe and the Inn.

Likewise many objections to the serf's obligations are irrelevant. Their harshness is an aspect of the low national product and the relative scarcity of labor-saving devices. Only on the basis of the toil of the many, moreover, could the few be freed for defense. The merciless ravages of the Norse, Magyars, and Slavs, resulting in the wholesale slaughter or enslavement of entire populations, revealed what the alternative to military security was. To free the fighting aristocracy for its prime function in an era when cavalry was king and equipment costly, when there were no mercenary armies, the masses had to toil. Perhaps too many prelates had also to be supported in affluent indolence, but it should be remembered that medieval man laid cardinal store by the mediatory functions of the priesthood. There was the economic justification too that as part of a cooperative enterprise the peasant stood a better chance of improving his lot, for he benefited from access to the lord's courts, village shops, mills, brewery, bake-oven, and bridges and from other manorial facilities that lightened his load. In contributing to the satisfaction of the mounting needs of the lord, moreover, the serfs derived at least a modest benefit from the material economic progress that those requirements generated. In almost every way, except as respects personal freedom with all of its physical hazards, life on the nearly self-sufficient manor had advantages over that on the isolated individual farm. Finally, it may be noted that German serfs as a class were materially better off than the predominantly free Slavic peasants of eastern Europe.

Type of Carolingian Towns

No generalizations regarding the continuity of Roman towns into the Middle Ages can be ventured except to say that the mortality rate of towns was high and those that survived the impact of the *Völkerwanderung* were, like Xanten, Trier, Metz, Cologne, Worms, Andernach, Bonn, Mainz, Lauracum, Koblenz, and Strassburg, doomed to a starveling existence for centuries. Even when town records resumed with Carolingian times, the urban revival was again set back by the forays of the Norse and Hungarians in the ninth and early tenth centuries. In 882 Trier, for example, was subjected to three days of pillage, fire, and massacre by the Danes, who in 845 had already destroyed Hamburg. The ravages of the Northmen in the northwest and of the Hungarians in the southeast so emptied the towns that by the mid-ninth century it was rare to find one with more than two thousand souls. As late as the twelfth century, German towns continued very small, none of them equaling Palermo, Cordova, or Kiev. Till the end of the Middle Ages only a small percentage of the German population of from ten to twelve million lived in towns.

A very few towns, like Aachen and Frankfurt am Main, began their careers as royal or imperial residences. More owed their start to trade. But by far the largest number of towns before the year 1200 owed their origins to the clergy. This circumstance was in part due to the fact that the German lay nobility were forbidden, except by special permission, to build castles or fortified centers for their own use. In Carolingian times the typical *civitas* or *vicus,* as towns were generally called, was founded by the high clergy on abbatial or episcopal lands. It grew up around cloister, church, or fortress *(Burg).* Probably no one in early Carolingian times did more toward establishing towns in Germany than did the great St. Boniface, who found it necessary to establish many of them in connection with his subdivision of Germany into dioceses. Others, of older vintage, such as Metz, Trier, Würzburg, Fritzlar, and Salzburg, benefited greatly from having been selected as episcopal sees and residences. These Church-controlled towns were wholly exempt from royal surveillance, since administrative, fiscal, and judicial immunities were customarily stipulated in infeudation contracts between crown and prelates.

After the towns of ecclesiastical origin those spawned by trade and transportation, though few in number, were the next most important. In this category the coastal towns, although menaced by the Vikings, were older and more flourishing than those of the interior. Surviving into Carolingian times from the earlier Merovingian was a necklace of commercial settlements strung out along the Baltic coast and the North Sea from Libau (Liepaja) in Latvia to Flanders, all connected by intercourse with each other. Brugge, Ghent, Tiel, Deventer, Douai, Dorestad, and Ypres were the cynosures of trade in the northwest, while in the Baltic circle it was Birka and the island of Lillö (both near modern Stockholm), Kaupang i Skiringsaal on the west side of Oslo Fjord, Grobin (near Liepaja), and Truso (near Danzig). But Haithabu at the base of Jutland was the brightest jewel in the whole necklace. Because east-west traffic did not flow through the Skaggerak and Kattegat in those days, but forded the Jutland peninsula, between the Schlei and the Treene, Haithabu prospered.

The Baltic circle towns initiated the trade between the Flemish and Dutch centers in the west and the Russian in the east, which was to become one of the long sides of the European medieval commercial rectangle. Wares coming from Persia, Byzantium, and inner Russia were shipped through Novgorod and Pskov, thence westward to Sweden and to Haithabu, where they were transshipped to the Low Countries, north Germany, or points in Scandinavia, The Baltic water route retained its importance all through the era of the Norse invasions because the Danes and Swedes (Varangians) wanted to maintain commercial contacts with the east and south. In an age when water-borne commerce was of capital importance, the towns of northern Germany acquired a headstart on those of the interior.

Growth of the Towns

The town was conceived in the manorial womb. Townspeople were at first just so many peasants, usually serfs, who sallied forth every morning to tend the surrounding fields or pasture their livestock on the common. Towns were virtually self-sufficient and existed mainly to satisfy local needs or, at most, those of some nearby abbey or episcopal court. Only gradually did division of labor set in, as here and there a peasant, freed by his lord, abandoned his fields to become an artisan or tradesman.

Towns grew only very slowly. Until the ninth century there were not more than 40 of them in all Germany. In the eleventh century there were at most 120 towns; and in the twelfth, 250. Their great era hardly commenced before A.D. 1250, but by the beginning of the fourteenth century there were more than 3,000 towns. Of this total, only about 50, with populations in excess of 10,000, were called cities. In A.D. 1300 the vast majority of so-called town dwellers still lived in settlements of less than 500 persons.

Town growth was stimulated by the holding of fairs *(Messen),* brief ones on holy days and much longer ones at certain seasons. The repetition of seasonal fairs *(Markttage)* was always the occasion for lively trading, money changing, and an influx into the larger fair cities, such as Metz, Magdeburg, Leipzig, and Frankfurt am Main, of a motley horde of merchants, peasants, priests, artisans, scribes, peddlers, strolling minstrels, jugglers, thieves, and idle lazzaroni. All of this aided the growth of a commercial and manufacturing element. Towns were also soon recognized to be the best answer to the problem of regional defense. When palisades and walls were built around them in the turbulent ninth and tenth centuries, the promise of military protection attracted population from the countryside for miles around. Furthermore, the custom of automatic emancipation of any serf who took refuge in a town and managed to dwell in it continuously for a year and a day *(Stadtluft macht frei*—"city air makes one free") also magnetized the rural population. Finally, for many the town was the wheel of fortune. Merchants, craftsmen, and money lenders, tempted by the prospect of fat profits, settled there to supply the mounting needs of the municipal lord or bishop for cloth, plate, jewelry, wrought iron, furniture, and luxury goods.

Merchants

Wandering traders or peddlers from distant parts were the earliest capitalists to take up residence in the towns. The merchants were at first accorded individual liberties, but by the tenth century the crown was conferring special rights upon groups of them who could prove a fixed place of business. While such collective privileges were first conferred upon the merchants of Magdeburg, those of Regensburg (Ratisbon), Würzburg, Bamberg, Passau, and Metz all received royal diplomas before A.D. 1063. By the twelfth century a nationally recognized mercantile law *(jus mercatorum)* had come to govern all business transactions.

Initially alien to the aristocratic-peasant order, the merchant class was grafted on to the agrarian and administrative stalk of town life. The emerging capitalist element lived in a compound adjacent to the village, known as the *pagus meratorum* or *Wik*. The *Wik*—a low German suffix meaning "merchants' quarter" and ostensibly linked with the word Viking—comprised a cluster of tax-free houses occupied by a social cohort that at first had no right of self-administration but was subordinate to either a burgrave or an episcopal intendant. Mayors and municipal councils were, of course, still centuries away. In time, artisans and handicraft workers were also domiciled in the *Wik*. Then, at the end of generations of evolution, hardly before the thirteenth century, the merchant class became the dominant stratum in the towns.

For long, the merchants were attached to the feudal system. They were both traders and warriors. Not till the fourteenth century were they able, by pleading special privilege under mercantile law, to escape military service. By then the wealthy burghers had evolved into a distinct class, with corporative interests and litigant rights, exempt from all feudal oaths and obligations.

Charters

In the struggle for municipal self-government, each town at first entered the lists alone against its seigneur. Only later did the burghers find an ally in the king, whose campaign to crush the provincial power of the aristocracy and establish administrative centralism paralleled that of the rising bourgeoisie. Among the first towns to win charters from their overlords were Worms (1073), Cologne (1106), and Goslar (1107). The charter for Worms, granted by its bishop, became the envied model for many other towns, but not all of them were able to secure the same degree of autonomy. There came to be, in fact, a variety of codes of civic rights *(Burgrechte):* like those of Worms, Lübeck, Mageburg, Nuremberg, Leobschütz, and Iglau. While some centers, such as Strassburg, Worms, Speier, Basel, Bremen, Nuremberg, Wetzlar, Frankfurt, Schletstadt, Aachen, Rothweil, Memmingen, and Überlingen, completely rid themselves of the seigneurial yoke, becoming towns under direct supervision of the emperor, many others reached the end of the Middle Ages without having completely freed themselves from feudal tutelage. This was true of Salzburg but more especially of the great sees of northern and central Germany: Münster, Magdeburg, Hildesheim, Paderborn, and Würzburg. By contrast, episcopal control of towns was weaker in the southwest, where by 1400 a majority of them had fallen under the tutelage of the emperor.

Trade Routes

Many of the larger towns owed their prosperity more to location than to produce. Soest in the Ruhr, more important then than now, owed its prominence less to salt exports than to the fact that she was the main station on the Hellweg, the great highway from the Rhine to the Weser. Magdeburg, astride the middle Elbe, was a point of distribution of goods to all lands eastward to the Oder Valley. Leipzig was a site for big regional fairs and a market for Meissen, Lusatia, and the Elster Valley lands. Brugge (Bruges) on the Zwinn in Flanders was *the* emporium for exchange of Mediterranean and northern merchandise, a rendezvous where the galleys of Genoa and Venice met regularly with the Hanseatic fleet carrying staples from the Baltic. Augsburg and Ulm controlled commerce in the upper Danubian basin, while Basle, at the bend of the upper Rhine, was for long the chief competitor of Innsbruck for overland Italian imports. Zurich owed its competitive position in the Italian trade to the opening in the thirteenth century of the St. Gotthard pass through the Schoellenen gorge in the Alps. Cologne, destined to become Germany's largest inland port, was admirably situated for trade with the Netherlands and England, while Strassburg was on a major east-west highway.

It is one of the striking ironies of history that whereas in Roman times the bulk of Mediterranean goods went through Germany, in early medieval times it flowed around her. From the ninth through the twelfth centuries commerce showed a preference for sea lanes. Comparatively speaking, only a thin stream of merchandise reached central Europe by way of the Alpine, Rhine-Moselle, and Danubian river routes. This helps explain the relative smallness and poverty of interior German towns in the early Middle Ages.

Town Leagues

In the thirteenth century German imperial authority sharply declined. Chaotic conditions encouraged myriad robber barons to confiscate or levy exorbitant tolls upon merchandise passing through their domains. This greatly increased ultimate costs to consumers and discouraged risk capital. The towns were finally driven to league together to defend their interests. An example was provided by the success the Lombard town league in Italy had attained in its struggles against lords and emperor. The characteristic thing about the German town leagues was that member communes retained their juridical and political personalities, while pledging themselves to united action for economic or political ends.

The first major league of German towns was the Rhenish, organized in 1254. It spread up and down the Rhine Valley like wildfire, absorbing seventy communes and many bishoprics within the first two years of its existence. All important towns in the zone from Zurich to the North Sea and from Aachen to Regensburg were full or associate members of the Rhenish League. It worked for the abolition of illegal tolls, protection of goods in transit, apprehension of robbers and pirates, recognition of municipal and mercantile law, and the security of rights of all social classes *(Stände)*. Even the king came to regard the Rhenish League as an arm of royal justice for the pacification of the country.

The second great town league, the Swabian League, which was like the first, reached its zenith in the fourteenth century. It embraced most towns of southwest Germany.

Greater than either of these was the Hanseatic League or Hanse. It had its remote origins in an association of German Baltic towns, called the Society of Gotland

Traders, Among its members were Lübeck, Soest, Dortmund, Cologne, Riga, and Bremen. Its headquarters were at Visby on the Swedish isle of Gotland. The society, which attained its zenith in the twelfth century and was dissolved in 1299, was primarily concerned with middle and western Baltic trade, but it spun a commercial and cultural web of silver all the way from London to Novgorod, and Riga, Mitau, Dorpat, and Reval were all ensnared in it. Especially significant was the society's influence upon the development of Pskov, Novgorod, and all northwestern Russia. There German merchants with their culture were long able to block the ascendancy of xenophobe, Muscovite forces.

The Hanseatic League

The Hanseatic League was the heir of the Society of Gotland Traders. Taking shape shortly after 1240, when Lübeck, Hamburg, Rostock, Stralsund, Wismar, and many Wendish towns entered into commercial pacts with each other and established a trading association, the Hanseatic League had by 1270 secured special trading privileges in London. Recognized by the English king as the Hanse Alamaniae, it was accorded a trading compound in London, which was at first called the German Guild Hall and later the Steelyard (Staalhof). By the close of the thirteenth century the Hanse had established entrepôts at Brugge and in almost all the larger Baltic towns. In the subsequent growth of the great German league, Lübeck took the leading role. Under guidance of strong mayors, such as the Pleskow brothers, Heinrich Westhof, and Heinrich Rapesulver, Lübeck preempted the mantle of Visby.

At the height of its power the Hanse embraced more than eighty member cities and scores of associated towns. In Germany the member cities were thickly clustered in the north and to the west of the Oder. Hamburg, Danzig, Stettin, Bremen, Brunswick, Münster, Paderborn, Cologne, Frankfurt am Oder, and Stralsund were among them. In the Low Countries the member list was headed by Amsterdam, Nijmegen, and Dordrecht, while east of the Vistula it included Elbing, Königsberg, Windau, Riga, Reval, and Dorpat. Aside from Lübeck, the most important roles in the league were played by Stralsund, which for a time coveted the captaincy of the Hanse, and Danzig. There were no full-fledged members in Denmark, Norway, or Sweden. Nevertheless, Stockholm maintained close ties with the Hanse, and Norway was dependent upon the Hanseatic merchants of the German Bridge (Deutsche Brücke) at Bergen for grain imports. Beyond the inner circle of towns was an outer ring in Scandinavia, the Netherlands, south Germany, and northwestern Russia, which enjoyed associate status. The principal piers of the immense suspension by which the German merchants joined west and east were the Steelyard in London and the Petershof in Novgorod.

Affluence and Decline of the Hanse

In the later Middle Ages the Hanse was the controlling factor in the economic life of the northern world. Hanseatic ships transported grain, Irish linen, German

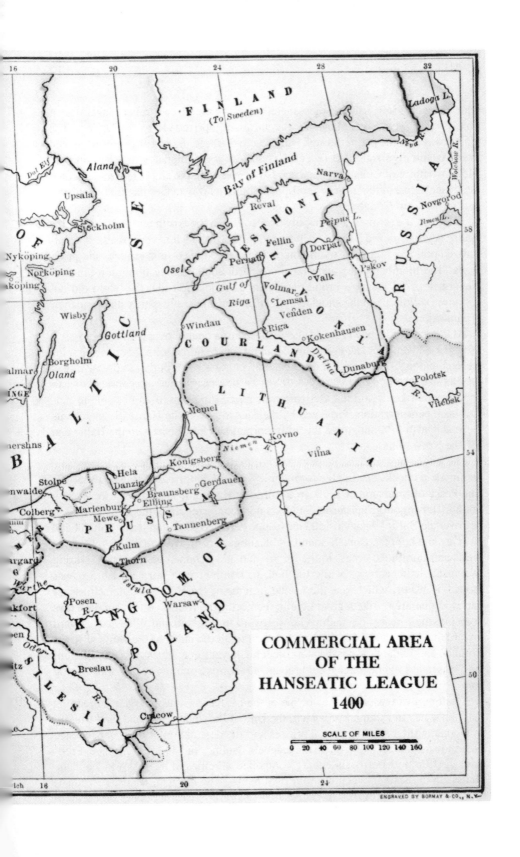

COMMERCIAL AREA
OF THE
HANSEATIC LEAGUE
1400

SCALE OF MILES

0 20 40 60 80 100 120 140 160

ENGRAVED BY BORMAY & CO., N.Y.

beer and wine, salt, fish, needles, metal wares, wax, silver, timber, naval stores, flax, English wool, and, above all, the universally prized cloths of Flanders. The Hanse was also the prism through which were diffused the colors of European and even Asiatic civilization. It received rays from the Caliphates of Islam and the Mongol empire of China, for Riga and Novgorod were the emporia through which the merchandise of the Eastern hemisphere found its way to German Baltic wharves and to the Low Countries.

Although it exercised a monopoly over traffic in the North and Baltic seas, the Hanse never achieved a highly galvanized organization. It never possessed a centralized political character, common treasury, or enjoyed uniform law and privileges. The member cities were far more particularistic than dominion-minded. Nevertheless the league's proud merchants doubtless felt that the world did not rest more solidly upon the shoulders of Atlas than Baltic prosperity did upon their organization.

At the apex of its power the Hanse disposed of a fleet of over a thousand vessels *(Koggen)*. The typical *Kogge* weighed about one hundred tons, but heavier ships were common in the fifteenth and sixteenth centuries. With this impressive fleet the Hanse controlled Baltic and North Sea traffic, intimidated the politically weak Scandinavian kings and the German princes, and interposed an obstacle to monarchical centralization. Protected by their naval power the Hanseatic merchants were able also to monopolize the all-important herring fisheries in the Baltic and off the Norwegian coast.

The league aggrandized its power to no small degree through war. It long held Denmark in check, beating the formidable King Waldemar Atterdag in 1366–67. The Peace of Stralsund of 1370, in confirming Hanseatic control over the Danish Sound, Helsingborg, Falsterbø, and Skannör, conferred upon the league supremacy over the Baltic. Again in 1522 the league defeated Christian II of Denmark and Norway and kept the Danish Sound and Kattegat open, while insuring to German merchants continued access to the Norwegian and Schonen herring beds. During two and a half centuries while the bulk of commerce in northern Europe was moved by water, which was the league's element, the Hanse maintained ascendancy in that area. Like a great light in the north, the Hanse cast its lambent rays deep into the forests of Scandinavia, westward to England and Wales, southward toward the Alps and Bohemia, and eastward to all the lands of the Gulfs of Riga, Bothnia, and Finland. More than any other medieval force, unless it be the Church, the Hanseatic League made a cultural and economic community out of the Baltic zone.

The foremost reason for the decline of the league was the emergence of strong national states in Denmark, Sweden, the United Provinces, England, and Russia. In Germany the rise of territorial princes and the destruction of the independence of the towns played a key role in the league's decline. In 1442, for instance, Frederick II (Irontooth) of Brandenburg compelled all cities in his realm to leave the Hanse. In the sixteenth century four rival fleets—the English, Danish, Swedish, and Dutch—finally broke the Hanse's two-hundred-year monopoly on northern water-borne trade. Denmark gained a stranglehold on all commerce passing through the Sound and imposed stiff tolls that hit the German merchants hard. Meanwhile, the Protestant Reformation, by dividing Germany, crippled the Hanseatic towns. By mid-sixteenth century more than three times the number of Dutch, as German, ships were passing through the Sound. When Brugge was ruined by the silting up of the Zwin, Antwerp usurped her place in international trade and refused to allow the Hanse the privileges it had enjoyed at Brugge. After the Dutch War for Independence ended in 1609, the Westphalian towns were exposed to remorseless, cutthroat competition from Dutch rivals. In England the league lost its special trading rights, and Elizabeth closed the Steelyard in 1589. In Russia Ivan III, who had captured Novgorod in 1478, showed increasing hostility toward the Hanseatic merchants, and in 1499 the Petershof was temporarily shut down. Around Lake Constance, trading companies with improved business techniques arose in the sixteenth century, while families of finance-capitalists, such as the Fugger, Höchstetter, Imhof, and Welser, siphoned off contracts that might have gone to Hanseatic traders. Their conservatism, inadequacy of capital, and superannuated forms of business organization repelled customers. In the end, even the herring deserted the Hanse, moving from the Baltic to the North Sea, where they were to become the foundation of Amsterdam's glory.

Chapter 8

NOBILITY AND CLERGY

Feudalism

By the ninth century a new aristocracy had come to the fore in Germany, entirely replacing the old tribal military leaders of the Frankish Empire. The new nobility pledged fealty directly to the emperor, was both lay and ecclesiastical, and owed its position to a monopoly over weapons and the possession of land. The marked shortage of investment capital in early medieval Germany, as in all Christian Europe, made land more important than money. The result was that the fief *(feodum, Lehen),* which was a nexus of manors and abbeys collectively held by a seigneur, became the most significant feature of early and high medieval peasant-aristocratic economy.

The Germans, who remained heavily influenced by tribal concepts of the pater-familias, *Gefolgschaft,* and *Hausmacht,* were inclined to personalize all services and rewards. Thus, in Charlemagne's day the feudal compact was one of personal fealty and protection, in which transfer of land was only incidental. Against an act of commendation or homage by which a vassal *(vassus)* solemnly promised to be the lord's man, the seigneur or overlord solemnly agreed to protect him and his family in the enjoyment of life, liberty, and property. In its more mature form the feudal compact evolved into a commercial contract. Against a pledge of military service, subject to encashment on notice and often honored in the vassal's blood, the overlord *(Lehnsherr)* conferred the use of a benefice upon him. In the final form it attained, the contract stipulated a fief, rather than a *beneficium.* The fief differed from the benefice solely in the degree of precision with which the obligations of vassal and overlord were defined. The central considerations, however, remained land and aid. The vassal *(Lehnsempfänger)* was bound to offer his *Lehnsherr* military aid and counsel *(Pflicht zur Hilfe mit Rat und Tat).* Etymologically the word "feudal" clearly reveals that this was the essence of the contract, for "feudal" is derived from a joining of the Roman word *fides* ("faith") and the Old German words *Odal* ("land") or *Ot* ("property").*

Since the development of feudalism was, above all, determined by military necessity, the failure of a vassal to answer his lord's summons to armed support was a capital felony. It was customarily punished with all the severity of which the Middle Ages was capable. Infidelity might result in forfeiture of fiefs. Often the offender was also imprisoned, outlawed, or condemned to death. Similar penalties were meted out for cowardice in battle. If the overlord himself should be convicted of felony, which was unlikely, the vassal was entitled to convert his fief into an alod or free possession.

---

*The German word for nobleman—*Adel*—also derives from *Odal* and means "land-holding class." Similarly the word *alod* or *alodium,* signifying absolute title to property, comes from the joining of the words *alle* ("everything") and *Odal.*

The Medieval Notion of Social Service

The advent of feudalism ushered in a more responsible attitude of the ruling class toward the peasantry. The cultivated owner of a Roman *latifundium* had been haughtily unmindful of the plight of the lowly *coloni* on his villa lands. In the early European Age, however, the Germanic nobility, with its unsophisticated attachment to the countryside and its notions of fidelity and Christian ethics, generally acknowledged, even when it did not always implement, a moral obligation to extend at least minimal protection to the army of dependents committed to its care.

While it is in retrospect easy to idealize the medieval German lord's sense of social responsibility, it is nonetheless true that it usually marked an advance over that of the owner of a Roman *latifundium*. The feudal landlord could not often afford blatantly to ignore the central teaching of the Church that salvation was not to be won by faith alone but also by performance of good works, the finest of which was charity. Without it, claims to virtue and grace were hollow pretenses. As they hoped for eternal life, the lords had to be concerned for at least the minimal well-being of their peasants. On the other hand, torts, felonies, misprision, and other offenses against persons or property, Church or *Dorfrecht,* committed or allegedly committed by serfs afforded many a seigneur the opportunity to indulge a savage strain in his nature. However, it is safe to say that the great majority of noblemen evinced the requisite social concern. This was of particular importance where the greater lords had been granted "immunity" from royal surveillance and themselves exercised the high justice and the low on their manors without fear of external interference.

Feudalism and the German Constitution

The rush for protection in the insecure ninth century augmented the importance of the feudal nobility. Consequently fiefs were often converted into hereditary alodial holdings. This trend was only partly offset by the ruse of enfeoffing clergymen, who were forbidden to devise their holdings to heirs of their blood and so might be expected to befriend the crown. Furthermore, in the ninth and tenth centuries nobles were able to acquire much forested and frontier land on their own initiative. This circumstance conferred upon them a strength and independence that surpassed that of the French aristocracy. Enjoyment of *forestis* rights (legal authority over lands reclaimed from the forest or colonized by the nobility) so fortified the German lords that the king could never subdue them.

The corrosive features of feudalism were never as serious in Germany as in France and Italy. This was because the stem dukes were really cornerstones of a pluralistic or federated German monarchy. On the other hand, the fact that Germany was little more than a federation of stem duchies obstructed national consolidation. The special relationship between king and dukes underlay the constitutional system of the First German Empire from start to finish, making it impossible for the German kings, unlike the French, to transform their rights as suzerains into monarchical prerogatives. Immemorial tribal, federal, and feudal impedimenta combined to frustrate their best efforts. The stem dukes served till almost the end of the fifteenth century as bulwarks of local custom and particularism.

Noble Status

In medieval Christendom the nobility possessed the only real military power. In an age when cavalry dominated the battlefield, only the lay and spiritual lords could afford or, for that matter, cared to cultivate fighting as a surpassing accomplishment. The exigencies of armored and equestrian combat required that the military caste be relieved of the obligation to produce, in order that it might protect. Conversely, the great mass of the peasantry, who were shielded against robber lords and foreign invaders, were obliged to toil all the harder to compensate for the critical social loss resulting from the alienation of the labor of the best and bravest segment of society.

Noble status was the reward of valor and fidelity, qualities that were thought to be best demonstrated on the battlefield. The red badge of courage opened the gates to privilege and preferment. Bishops and abbots, who also belonged to the warrior class *(Ritterstand)*, made no serious attempt to alter the popular idolatry of the knight *(Ritter)* in shining armor. That noblemen truly sought their justification in combat and in deeds of heroism is confirmed by the high mortality rates that prevailed among the sons of Germany's leading families, a fact that to an actuary would have made the knight a poor risk. In the War of the Investiture, for example, many aristocratic families died out entirely in the male line as a result of the sanguinary fighting. The reward of the surviving noblemen was that they not infrequently became the founders of princely dynasties.

Finally, it was thought that only a nobleman could be endowed with a noble spirit. Although charity was regarded as a virtue in a knight, it was not thought to be indispensable to his calling. Conversely, cruelty did not seriously impair the functional worth of a nobleman as long as he was brave and loyal.

The Nobility and High Office

In militarized, feudal society function and authority were the preconditions of property-holding. High office or paramount responsibility was the basic fief. Lands and tenements were merely the endowment of authority. The main offices of state and Church, with rare exceptions, were reserved for the aristocrats (who might depute them to advocates or wardens, called *Vögte*), because they alone possessed the virtue and *esprit* appropriate to the exercise of broad responsibility. This blind preconception explains why it was that almost all royal ministers, crown chatelains, prelates, and abbesses were drawn from the hereditary nobility. A small percentage came from the ministerial nobility; and a minuscule number, from the common people. While, toward the beginning of the fifteenth century, an opposing and competing image of bourgeois virtues emerged, the aristocracy continued to play the prima donna in all capital offices of authority. Furthermore, it may be affirmed that, despite a certain late medieval deterioration in upper-class morals, the seigneurs were usually mindful of their social and contractual duties and strove to discharge them in such wise that noble purpose and behavior would always merit the general esteem.

Feudal Trammels on Royal Power

From the viewpoint of public law, medieval Germany was unique in that the entire realm was for long regarded, as it had been among the ancient tribes, the proprietary possession *(Hausmacht)* of the king. Although this was a serious obstacle to the evolution of a rational theory of monarchy, there were others almost as bad. For instance, up until the mid-twelfth century prelates often denied the right of the crown to sit in judgment on them, and many were even reluctant to serve the king. Fortunately the latter attitude did not represent the prevailing one among the bishops and abbots, because if it had the feudal system would have been subverted. Nevertheless, it was not until the harsh example of the confiscation of the fiefs of Henry the Lion (1180) that the proud prelates all bowed their necks to the king.

Another obstacle to the growth of monarchical power was the existence, parallel to decretal law, of a body of older, customary or "folk" law, the ineradicable bequest from tribal times. Folk law for centuries put limits to the ambitions of German kings, because it endowed royal vassals with a legal competence which the monarch might not infringe without running the risk of armed rebellion for violating imprescriptible rights. The extensive powers of royal vassals in western and southern Germany invited imitation, furthermore, in the new lands of the east. Counterpart prerogatives evolved in the newer colonial area, where the great lords of the marches, practically obliged to govern by themselves the huge domains wrested from the Slavs, preempted plenary *forestis* rights.

In consequence there persisted throughout the Middle Ages a dichotomy between regional and public law in Germany. Besides this, the variations in feudal relations were a source of immense confusion, gave rise to endless litigation, and frustrated the most determined efforts at political and juridical consolidation. The conflict in laws generated so many uncertainties respecting feudal-contractual relationships that both monarch and seigneurs sought palliatives in the ministerial system. The ministerials, being originally of non-noble lineage, possessed no autochthonous rights or personal immunities. They were bound to serve just one overlord. Their rise to importance counterbalanced some of the deficiencies of the feudal polity.

Decline of Feudalism

Between 1200 and 1250 the feudal system and courtly culture entered upon decline. Peasants and burghers, armed with bow or lance, would soon topple armored cavalry from the commanding position it had occupied since the Battle of Tours. The employment of artillery in the fifteenth century completed the absolute ruin of knighthood. The increased efficiency of the infantry in the mercenary armies of the Renaissance era promoted broader freedom and recognition for the common man. In the declining Middle Ages the worker in field and town possessed a greater social importance than he had ever known in the history of the West. The emancipatory process was aided by the critical attitude of the lower clergy and the cathedral chapters toward the lord bishops. Gradually but surely the feudal ties unraveled.

Peasant demands for reform, which intensified as the economic status of the agricultural element improved, helped to destroy the tiny feudal principalities and clear the way for the rising territorial princes. Peasant uprisings occurred at Worms in 1431, the Allgäu in 1461, Würzburg in 1476, Hamburg in 1483, Osnabrück in 1488, and Augsburg in 1491. In many areas during the fifteenth century peasants broke the seigneurial monopoly over hunting and park preserves, mills, breweries, bake-ovens, wine presses, and bridges and defiantly refused to pay the traditional fees for their use. From all this ferment and accelerating change the lesser nobility especially suffered. Its plight worsened as a result of the effects of the Great Plague, the rise of tenant farming, and the development of industry, international trade, and a money economy. The steadily increasing demands of the burghers for agricultural produce brought a novel influx of coins into the countryside. This had a revolutionary effect upon the agricultural economy. On the dissolving manors leasehold arrangements came to substitute for socage copyhold, which in former ages had determined a plowman's dependent status. But the advent of cash in the countryside was no boon to most noble landlords. Because of the growing disparity between the value of the urban and agrarian social product, the landed aristocrats tended to fall behind in competition with the urban patricians and capitalists. Unfamiliar with the mysterious workings of a money economy, the lords were at a disadvantage. They prepared to abandon the *Fronhof* system and rent their lands for cash. But still they were ever less able to maintain costly class pretenses and stay out of debt. Gradually, as they sank into a state of genteel poverty, the gap between them and their peasant tenants narrowed. As respects the latter, the drift toward leasehold prepared the way for the coming of rural capitalism and the attendant development of an agrarian proletariat, neither of which had had a place in the cooperative manorial system of the peasant-aristocratic age.

The rise of plural territorial sovereignty greatly accelerated the decline of feudalism. During the fourteenth century the dukes of Austria, Saxony, and Bavaria, the margrave of Brandenburg, and the bishop of Bremen, for example, managed to establish direct authority over all persons within their principalities. In 1356 the emperor was obliged to grant to the electoral princes *(Kurfürsten)* and later in the century to all imperial cities *(Reichsstädte)* and princes *(Fürsten)* immunity from royal judicial summons. By the Civil Peace of Eger (1389), finally, the emperor conferred practical judicial autonomy upon princes and cities.

In the competition between old and new economic systems, the big winner was the antifeudal and anti-imperial estate of territorial princes. The rulers of the principalities, served by reliable ministerials and impoverished lesser nobles, were the legatees of feudal government.

The Medieval Scale of Values

Unquestionably, faith in God was the foundation stone of the medieval German's life. The countless spacious town churches and the picturesque abbeys that adorned his countryside are proof of this. All the current of that remote, peasant-aristocratic age set toward those stone symphonies to the Creator. Of course, this is not to deny the existence of abuses or of moral lapses, which occasionally cast a tenebrous pall over the reputation of the religious community, but it is to insist that the sins of the few do not sharply alter the general picture. In medieval Germany the best in society and culture was most often to be found in the Church.

If the medieval German mind exhibited conceptual unity, this was due to the common conviction that the material order was inferior to the spiritual and that all social elements must be coordinated to implement divine purposes on earth. Individual goals were disparaged. All human efforts must be put in the service of higher ends and glorify God. Through example, preachments, homilies, administration of the sacraments, art and literature, and even confession and punishment, the Church strove to extend its values to all men. In the popular mind it stood like an immense rock that barred the way to hell. The mediatory priesthood, which derived its enormous influence from the general conviction that salvation could only be achieved with the aid of the sacraments, which the clergy alone might administer, used its position to remind all stations of men of their Christian and corporative duties. The Church preached—admittedly often to deaf ears—that to be good was better than to be powerful and that heaven opens equally to prince and pauper.

German monarchs generally refrained from tyrannizing the clergy. The government never struck at the Church per se, only at clerical wrongdoers. Church and state were believed to be one and inseparable, the two faces of the Common Corps of Christendom.

Power of the High Clergy

From the outset of the Middle Ages bishops and abbots stood in the closest relationship to the civil power. In every century the prelates figured as formative influences in the political life of Germany. For many generations only carefully trained progeny of the first families were eligible for the highest Church offices. Some sees did not have during the entire Middle Ages a single prelate who was not a nobleman. The fact is, the German episcopacy was unabashedly more aristocratic than that of any other country. The greatest churchmen were often also dukes and counts, immediate vassals of the king, not infrequently even overlords of the monarch for certain fiefs. After 1168 when the bishop of Würzburg and 1180 when the bishop of Cologne were elevated to the status of princes of the Empire *(Reichsfürsten),* owing fealty directly to the emperor, increasing numbers of prelates were raised to the *Reichsfürstentum.* Vast was the wealth of some prelates. Enormous *latifundia* with legions of serfs were enfeoffed or granted in perpetuity to episcopal sees and monasteries. Among the latter, for example, the abbey of Benedictbeuren possessed 8,700 manors, Hildesheim more than 11,000, and golden Fulda, the last resting place of St. Boniface, 15,000.

The consideration for fiefs, revenues, immunities, princely residences, and special minting, customs, and judicial rights which prelates enjoyed was unfaltering support of the crown. By the time of Otto I, who was very generous toward the prelacy, the episcopal, when not the abbatial, hierarchy had been substantially feudalized. High churchmen were for the king a source of counsel, revenue, and military levies. The bulk of the spiritual lords served the king in peace or war, and that was their surest title to power.

If the influence of the upper clergy had been great in Saxon and Franconian times, it was greater still in the thirteenth century. In 1220 Frederick II alienated important regalia to abbots and bishops. All ecclesiastical, no less than temporal, seigneurs acquired full sovereignty as respects justice, constabulary, military affairs, customs, minting, taxation, and the construction of fortresses within their own domains. Toward the close of that century the pope further augmented the power of the abbots and bishops. Late medieval decentralizing tendencies in German political life contributed to still more growth of the power and responsibilities of prelates. The adoption of finance-capitalist techniques by prelates who controlled enormous funds still further strengthened the secular power of the German Church. The result was that the German prelates became by 1550 less spiritual-minded than those of almost any other country. The might of the German Church was by then such that it altogether compromised its cardinal purpose.

The Contributions of the Church

No medieval institution contributed more than the Church to the improvement of public morals. Its services were most conspicuous in times of great popular reform movements, but generation in, generation out, the Church helped to make men more civilized. In the tenth century the clergy instituted the Peace of God (*pax Dei*) and the Truce of God (*treuga Dei*). The purpose of the former was to exempt Church lands from military operations and protect noncombatants; of the latter, to restrict feudal warfare to Monday through Thursday as well as to the most unpleasant months of the year. Unfortunately, after the end of the eleventh century, neither truce was well observed. The Church also strove to abolish the death penalty (except for witchcraft), suppress mutilation, mitigate torture, stamp out slavery, improve the status of bondmen, and make usurious interest rates illegal. Many types of eleemosynary work were undertaken by the Church. Benedictines, Antonites, Premonstratensians, Brethren of the Holy Ghost, and Cistercians distributed alms to the needy, cared for the sick and infirm, and succored the oppressed. Annually the Church fed and clothed an army of derelicts. Upon it devolved almost the entire bill for providing medical, pharmaceutical, and hospital services to the nation. The clergy or clerical support accounted for most medieval advances in medicine and surgery in the German land area.

Productive processes in many industries and crafts were likewise improved as a result of the labors of the clergy. Monks lent themselves well to such collective projects as colonizing, irrigating and draining swamps, clearing woodland, major construction, and large-scale staple crop farming. They introduced such comestibles as salad plants, cabbage, oil hops, and fine wines and liqueurs. The disciplined and toilsome lives of the monks (most orders were obligated to a minimum of seven hours of manual labor six days a week) were a major factor in the enviable production records of abbatial domains. Until the fourteenth century virtually exclusive responsibility for education at all levels rested on the clergy. This monopoly was not challenged in the field of higher education until 1347, when the first German university (Prague) was founded, and in the field of preparatory education not until the fifteenth century, when the first municipal schools were opened.

At first, schools run by religious foundations accepted only the sons of the aristocracy, who were destined for high temporal office or for holy orders. In the tenth century, however, schools for the education of the daughters of the aristocracy opened. It was not until the eleventh century that the ministerials and low-born boys began to infiltrate these bastions of the nobility. The influx from below had the effect of lowering standards of education, which after the eleventh century did not again regain their earlier level.

The opulence of many cloisters and the laxity of morals that sometimes prevailed within them did not undermine cultural standards, but the democratization of the religious did. The invasion of persons of peasant and bourgeois origin into formerly exclusively noble regular houses, such as those of Fritzlar, Corvey, Ellwangen, Lorsch, Einsiedeln, St. Gall, Maria Lach, Reichenau, Kremsmünster, and Fulda, dimmed the lamp of learning that had burned there intensely in the Ottonian era.

Educational Qualifications
of the Regular Clergy

The felicitous combination of versatility and virtuosity, which the Italian Renaissance called *virtù*, distinguished many Ottonian monks. Their multiple talents, moreover, magnified not so much the glory of the individual as of God. The monks were not the reputed ascetic, contemplative souls whose lives were a round of paternosters and whose minds lay fallow. On the contrary, the Benedictines, Carthusians (founded in 1084 by Bruno of Cologne), Cistercians (founded in 1098 by Robert of Molesme), and Premonstratensians (founded in 1121 by St. Norbert of Xanten) not only engaged in a broad spectrum of practical pursuits but also did praiseworthy work in the cultural sphere.

Although library facilities in the cloisters were not very good (there was an unwholesome preponderance of antiphonaries, homilies, liturgical tracts, catechisms, and hagiographical works), the necessary stimulus to creative thought was there. Alongside the dross were priceless manuscripts from Periclean Greece and the golden and silver ages of Roman literature. The monastic teachers who instructed in the fundamentals of the lower form or *trivium,* which comprised dialectic, grammar, and rhetoric, or of the upper form or *quadrivium,* which embraced arithmetic, geometry, astronomy, and music, often discovered that the curriculum was a mere starting point for exciting explorations into unchartered areas. In any case, the schoolmaster was often called upon to demonstrate publicly his knowledge or talents in some tangible, significant fashion. As late as the thirteenth century the clergy still wrote most of the poetry, plain chant, antiphony, instrumental music, chronicles, and biographies, did most of the manuscript-copying and illumination, excelled in architectural design, metal work, lapidary, and all manner of plastic arts, painted most of the murals, manufactured the bulk of the stained glass, and carved the choir stalls and sculptured the statuary that filled the churches, which they often literally built with their own hands.

This cascade of creativity began to diminish sharply in the late thirteenth century. In the next century the educated and many-sided monk, who had earlier been the garden variety of society, became the exception. The assault of the low-born and of the mystics upon the monasteries and nunneries produced a hyperbolic renunciation of things worldly. This had as depressing an effect upon artistic exuberance as Banquo's empty chair at Macbeth's feast.

The Hirsau Reform

Admittedly the price of the cultural progress in Saxon and Salian times was not a bagatelle in terms of moral decay. Temporal princes conferred many prebends upon undeserving favorites; episcopal property was not infrequently alienated to the nephews or bastard sons of prelates; high churchmen were occasionally maintaining concubines with revenues from religious foundations; and the lower clergy often only wept that they could not sin on the grand scale of their superiors.

An initial impulse to monastic reform came from the house of Gorze near Metz but appears to have affected only a handful of German monasteries: Tegernsee, St. Emmeran, and Altaich. Burgundian Cluny was to have immeasurably greater influence upon the German clergy. Founded in 910 and governed by a line of long-lived, able abbots, Cluny became a kind of archabbey with which in time several hundred subordinate monasteries (priories) were affiliated. The abbots of Cluny, by championing congregational solidarity and a monarchically organized monastic government, virtually put an end to autonomous houses and to those that were dependent upon secular authorities. By insisting upon clerical celibacy, Cluny also effectively combatted the spoliation of monastic property.

In the eleventh century the Cluniac movement spread to Germany. Cluny's chief disciple there was the monastery of Hirsau near Kalv in the Black Forest. Hirsau, now a ruin, rose to prominence under Abbot Wilhelm (1069–91). The Cluniac-Hirsau rule, which he devised, was adopted by scores of abbeys which affiliated themselves with the archmonastery in the Black Forest. By the end of the century there was no area in Germany that had escaped the edifying influence of this reform movement. Sin and license were hounded out of the cloisters, and their lands and tenements were protected from the avarice of lay nobility and crown. The Hirsau reform raised the regular clergy to new heights of prestige in the public eye by making celibacy and piety mandatory for the clergy. A shower of gifts recompensed the monks and nuns for their sacrifices. It became a downpour when in 1095 the First Crusade was proclaimed against the Seljuk Turks, who had smashed the Byzantines at Manzikert (1071) and occupied the Holy Land. By the beginning of the twelfth century, which was an age of penitence, the German regular clergy had reached the zenith of its influence.

Spread of Reformism

In emulation of the Cluniac-Hirsau houses, ever stricter religious orders were founded in the late eleventh and in the twelfth centuries: the Carthusians (originating at Grand Chartreuse), the white-robed Cistercians (originating at Cîteau), and the semi-apostolic Premonstratensians (originating at Prémontré in 1121). Reverting to the rigors of early Benedictine rule, the new reforming orders tried to eliminate all luxuries from monastic life, encourage abstention and fasting, and shackle their religious to unremitting toil and prayer. These reforms lapped also at the cathedral chapters. There, as a result of a papal order of 1139, all canons, who were usually sons of noblemen and holders of rich prebends or recipients of episcopal revenues, were, without distinction, obliged to accept a moral and communal rule that in its rigors resembled the Augustinian.

In the twelfth century the universal disposition toward piety and charity, strongly stimulated by the sacrificial example of the Crusaders, encouraged many new donations to the religious orders, which as a consequence were less able to resist materialist temptations. However, in the thirteenth century another regeneration took place. In Italy and Spain two great mendicant orders were founded: in the former the democratic Franciscan Minor Brothers *(Ordo fratrum minorum* or O.F.M.), who were summoned into being by St. Francis of Assisi (1182–1226) and who ministered mainly to the poor, halt, and sick of the towns; in the latter the Dominican Order of Preachers *(Ordo praedicatorum* or O.P.), which was founded by St. Dominic of Castile (1175–1221) and devoted itself mainly to preaching, teaching the children of the upper classes, and the detection of heresy. Both orders of friars eschewed the cloistered existence and went out into the world to fight sin. Both accepted female affiliates. As a consequence many auxiliary nunneries were established throughout western and southern Germany.

The Rise of Mysticism

In the fourteenth century the Franciscans, grown affluent, split into the Observantine and Conventual Friars. The former, who adhered strictly to the ideals of poverty and spirituality and regarded their wayward brethren, the Conventuals, as floating on a sea of alcohol covered by a rich scum of temptation, were responsible for an upsurge of religious radicalism in Germany. Partly or wholly heretical groups of religious arose—Flagellants, Luciferans, Beguines, Beghards, Dolcinists, Brethren of the Cross, which in the vigor of their attacks against authority and immorality surpassed all previous reform movements. Most of these religious fall into the category of mystics, who dwelt in a kind of twilight zone between orthodoxy and heresy, closer to the former than to the latter.

Mysticism was an irrational, popular movement. It derived not only from a whole line of visionaries—Hugo and Adam of St. Victor, St. Bernard, Hildegard of Bingen, St. Francis of Assisi, St. Mechtild of Magdeburg, St. Elizabeth of Thuringia, St. Dominic, St. Bonaventura, and Jacopone da Todi—but also from the distinguished nominalist theologian, William of Occam. Occam's postulation of a twofold path to truth encouraged the mystics in their faith in revelation and illumination and a belief in a immanent force that holds the soul in orbit around its Maker.

Following the mid-fourteenth-century Great Plague, mysticism made enormous strides in the older parts of Germany. The movement also benefited from developments external to the Empire. Among these the most stimulating were the decline of the papacy, vigorous Dominican support of mysticism, the Conciliar Reform (which strengthened democratic tendencies in the Church), the preaching of the Brethren of the Common Life, and the Turkish conquest of the Balkans.

Cistercians, such as Mechtild of Magdeburg and Mechtild of the Saxon Hefta convent, had given a strong impetus to German mysticism, but more important were the Dominicans, who were to produce most of the literature of mysticism. The chief German mystics—Meister (Master) Eckhart (1260–1327) of Hochheim, Johannes Tauler (1290–1361) of Strassburg, and Heinrich Suso or Seuse (1300–66) of Swabia—were all Dominicans.

The Dutch Brethren of the Common Life, with schools at Deventer and Zwolle in the Netherlands, set a shining example for northwestern Germany. The Brethren graduated the influential mystics Thomas à Kempis (Thomas Hemerken von Kempen, 1380–1471), who later wrote the phenomenally successful *Imitation of Christ,* Wessel Gansfort (1420?–89), and Nicholas of Cusa (1401–64). The ideas of the Brethren entered into the thinking of Eckhart, who was a magister in theology and the Dominican provincial for Saxony, and he in turn imparted their message to his principal pupils, Suso and Tauler. The three men left cells wherever they taught or preached, even in Prague, where Eckhart was after 1307 Dominican vicar general for Bohemia and where Mathias of Janou and John Hus fell under his spell. Eckhart's *Booklet of Eternal Wisdom* was widely read, while Suso's *German Theology* was destined to enjoy an even greater impact, especially on Luther.

Mysticism was basically pantheist in that it held that the only reality is that which proceeds from the Holy Spirit and that anything that alienated the individual from God is sinful. For most mystics, externalities, sacraments, icons, vestments, institutionalized religion, and hierarchical authority were of small account compared with grace shed by the divine inner light. This perspective tended to diminish the importance of the episcopacy, priesthood, mass, and sacraments. It had an extraordinary appeal for the masses. An offspring of the gloomy fourteenth century, mysticism developed into the last great popular religious movement of the Middle Ages.

Late Medieval Religious Decay

All during the last two centuries before Luther there was an unraveling of religious authority in the Empire. The whole land, politically defenseless against the exactions of the opulent Renaissance papacy, rumbled to the echo of a mounting chorus of attacks upon the institutionalized Church. The peasants, suffering from the effects of the long agricultural depression of the closing Middle Ages, joined the burghers in their strident criticisms of the Church. The sharpest strictures were directed against the wretched scramble for prebends, ecclesiastical dignities, and personal wealth. To many people, the Church had come to symbolize a monstrous system of exactions. It seemed that while the masses were sweating to feed the sacred cow at one end, the prelates were milking her at the other. What made the position of the German nation intolerable, however, was that after the bull *Execrabilis* in 1460 had reestablished papal absolutism, Rome had managed to block every avenue of escape from the extortions of the hierarchy.

Chapter 9

CULTURAL ACHIEVEMENTS

Survey

It was an impressive ascent from Carolingian to Hohenstaufen culture, only less steep than that from the Helladic Greek to the lofty harmonies of the Periclean age. In the four centuries that separated Charlemagne from Frederick II there was a prodigious intensification of creative activity. The Carolingian period was still only an early thaw, but the Ottonian ushered in the real spring. From then on, the waters of a hundred cultural streams came rushing from all the uplands of thought and art to form the shimmering river of the thirteenth century.

By the twelfth century in certain lines, such as religious architecture, Germany had come to surpass the achievements of every other European country. Although with the advent of the Gothic style she lost that primacy, her thirteenth-century contributions to epic poetry were the most remarkable before Dante's *Divine Comedy,* unless we except the Welsh-Breton Arthurian legends. Even so, it is doubtful whether any single piece of epic poetry of another country equalled either the *Parzival* of Wolfram von Eschenbach or the *Tristan und Isolde* of Gottfried von Strassburg.

In the twelfth-century springtime of culture, German sculptors and woodcarvers sensitively portrayed not only the Holy Family and the saints, but the magic of nature and that menagerie of birds and animals that formed an intimate part of medieval man's world. In architecture, fortesses like the Wartburg, Markstein, Hohenzollern, Marienburg, Hoch Königsberg, and the imperial castle of the Kaiserpfalz at Goslar in the Harz were built. Crowning wooded hills or clinging to rocky eminences above some river valley, these reliquaries of chivalry still evoke admiration for the medieval German architect's feeling for proportion and dramatic effect. To these things must be added the many marvelous Romanesque churches that were built in the twelfth century, such as at Bamberg, Regensburg, Soest, Speyer, Worms, Corvey, Trier, Würzburg, Cologne, and Maria-Lach.

Literature in Saxon and Franconian Times

With relatively few exceptions, tenth-century German literature was dreary and monotonous. Most of it, written by clergymen, was freighted with homilies and hagiographical narrative or was exegetic and didactic. While written, as Carolingian literature had been, mainly in rough-hewn vernacular, these works hardly mirrored the life of the masses.

Among the significant exceptions to the rule was the lay *Walter of the Strong Hand (Waltharius manu fortis),* a hexametric Latin epic revolving about the old Germanic theme of the remorseless fight of Gunther and Hagen. Noteworthy, too, were the narratives, such as the *Deeds of Otto the Great,* and the salacious closet comedies of the nun Roswitha (Hrotsvitha, 932?–1001), canoness of the secular convent of Gandersheim. Roswitha, who was the first to narrate the Faust theme *(The Fall and Salvation of Theophilus),* was the first illustrious authoress in German history.

Chivalrous and courtly notions, coming from France and England, began to blow like warming zephyrs over Germany at the close of the Saxon era. They caused the sap to rush into all the branches of the literary tree, releasing dormant energies and causing the whole to burst into the sweetest green that Christian Europe had ever seen. The first harbinger was the gay, knightly *Ruodlieb,* which was written in Latin around 1030 by an unknown monk of Tegernsee. The *Ruodlieb* was not only the first novel in German history, it was the initial tableau of medieval life, and its author was Germany's Chaucer.

But one swallow does not make a spring. During the troubled times of Henry IV the stern, ascetic spirit of Cluny and Hirsau descended briefly upon German literature, and the indecorous sallies of the *Ruodlieb* were not repeated. Typical of the chill religious reaction associated with the First Crusade was the *Ezzoleich (Lay of Ezzo),* which was written around 1060 by a monk. At the same time the partisan spirit engendered by the War of the Investiture was reflected in political tracts by Gebhard von Salzburg, Walram von Naumburg, and Peter Damian.

Because during the War of the Investiture the best pens were put in the political service of either the Church or the Empire, German literature of Salian times offered many didactic or polemical tracts and very little else. Among the few exceptions were Lamprecht's translation from the French of the *Song of Alexander (Alexanderlied,* c. 1130), which contained the exquisite story of the mysterious encounter of Alexander the Great and his officers with the flower maidens in a sylvan woods. Beyond this there was really only the impoverished genre called minstrel poetry *(Spielmannsdichtung).* This type was not as yet very rich in lyric quality because the wandering troubadours who composed these works were neither well-educated nor original in their approach. They, therefore, turned out mainly sensational and bizarre figments.

Germany's Literary Apogee

Regenerative forces were stimulated in the Hohenstaufen period of the Middle High German era when about 1131 Duke Henry the Proud of Bavaria returned from a trip to France with a copy of the *Chanson de Roland* in his saddle pouch. He gave it to a priest named Konrad von Regensburg, who translated it as the *Rolandslied (Lay of Roland).* In Konrad's version of the heroic exploits of Charlemagne's count of the Breton march the sign of the Cross was unmistakably stamped on the translation. The action was subordinate to the Christian message. On the other hand, the *Rolandslied* was only partly in harmony with the spirit of the age because, although religious in tone, it lacked love interest. Other French and British *chansons de geste,* such as the amorous tales of Chrestien de Troyes and

Guillaume de Lorris and the Arthurian romances of Geoffrey of Monmouth and Marie de France, exercised more influence upon German literature.

German medieval literature at last flowered between approximately 1180 and 1250 in the mighty age of Gothic cathedral building. In this golden age of Middle High German writing the three most important types of poetry were the popular or folk epic *(Volksepos).* the chivalrous or court epic *(Höfischesepos),* and lyric verse *(Minnesang).* All three forms were closely associated with the ruling nobility and reflected its domination of taste and style. However, the picture of the feudal aristocracy that was presented in this literature was not of a class at its social zenith but in its decline. Notwithstanding, thirteenth-century German literature—satirical, sportive, sensuous, and bold—was one of the most radiant blooms ever to open in Europe's garden.

Folk or heroic epics, such as the *Nibelungenlied (Song of the Nibelungen), Gudrunslied (Song of Gudrun), Der Rosengarten (The Rose Garden), Die Rabenschlacht (Battle of the Ravens), Walthari, Ortnit, Wolfdietrich,* and *Dietrich von Bern,* were all chiselled from the hard diorite of tribal legend. Admittedly, efforts to hang civilized drapery over the rugged contours of barbarian chieftains often led to the sacrifice of congruity and dramatic unity. Yet in the case of the *Nibelungenlied* neither the unreality of the tale nor its historical implausibilities detract from the fundamental strength of this virile and majestic masterpiece by an unknown Austrian genius of the late twelfth century. Based upon older and sometimes unrelated sagas from northern and central Europe, the epic commences with a genuflection to the knightly ideals of the twelfth century and then proceeds to the stark tragedy resulting from the foul murder of Siegfried by Hagen von Tronje. The ensuing struggle between Hagen and Siegfried's yellow-haired wife, Kriemhilde, queen of the Saxons, displays the author's remarkable insight into the psyche of a woman transformed by treachery from a gentle maiden into the Lady Macbeth of German literature. The *Gudrunslied,* too, is an epic treasure. Less grandiose but more realistic than the *Nibelungenlied,* it contains thirty-two tales of high adventure, the central theme of which is the unflagging loyalty of Gudrun to her lover, Herwig. The *Gudrunslied* not only extolls feminine virtues but is also a hymn to the Viking love of the sea and adventure. It has often been compared with the *Odyssey,* whereas the *Nibelungenlied* recalls the sterner *Iliad.*

The court or chivalrous epic was less transparently Germanic than the heroic epic. The former was written in stilted, erotic language and was both composed and sung by high-born poets, called minnesingers *(Minnesänger,* from *Minne,* "love"). The rise of a French-type chivalrous love epic contributed to the alienation of the German nobility from the lower classes to whom its language was largely incomprehensible.

After a brief transitional period during which German authors tried valiantly but unsuccessfully to capture, as in Eilhard von Oberge's *Tristan und Isolde* and Heinrich von Veldeke's *Eneit,* the cadences and elegant symmetry of medieval French court poetry, there at length emerged three incomparable German masters of the genre.

Hartmann von Aue (1170–1212/1220?), a Swabian ministerial of good education, wrote two Arthurian lays, *Erec* and *Iwein,* the latter being based on Chrestien de Troye's epic of the same name. However, Hartmann's reputation rests upon his imperishable *Poor Henry (Der arme Heinrich).* This is a sentimental and introspective tale, simply told, of a proud and knightly figure who is punished for his sins with leprosy but is eventually saved by the sacrificial love of an innocent girl.

Wolfram von Eschenbach (1170?–1220) was the foremost bard of Germany. This penurious, lesser nobleman from Ansbach was the Hegel of medieval literature. He conceived highly personalized, abstruse verse of elemental power. Yet he could neither read nor write. Perfectly fluent in conversational French, as were most German noblemen at that time, he used to have the *Conte de Graal* of Chrestien de Troyes read to him. Then in dynamic, original cadences he would dictate his own version. Neither as melodious nor as uncomplicated as Hartmann nor as elegiac as Gottfried von Strassburg, Wolfram von Eschenbach is adjudged by many to be the most profound analyst of character before Goethe. Wolfram's works include the *Titurel* and *Willehalm,* but the 25,000 rhymed verses of *Parzival* constitute his masterpiece. In *Parzival,* an Arthurian story of a knight's quest for grace through recovery of the Holy Grail, which symbolizes man's love of God, Wolfram achieved a Plutonian, inexpressibly gripping tale of sin and atonement. Although the epic is incidentally concerned with *Minne,* the focus is always on the character of Parzival, his sinking into a morass of bitterness, his catharsis, and subsequent steadfast quest for redemption.

Gottfried von Strassburg (late twelfth and early thirteenth centuries), the third member of the Middle High Germanic poetic trinity, was of bourgeois origin. Yet he was a master of the iridescent French style. His tremulous, uncompleted masterpiece, *Tristan und Isolde,* dealt with not a religious but an erotic problem, the adulterous, ravaging love of Tristan for the fair Isolde, wife of the aged King Mark of Cornwall:

Ein man, ein wip; ein wip, ein man;
Tristan, Isolt; Isolt, Tristan.

Tristan und Isolde, elegant in style and opulent in vocabulary, ranks not merely as a chief monument of Middle High German literature but as one of the world's immortal love tales.

Much of the literary talent of the aristocracy went into composing love lyrics or minnesongs. These Sapphic outpourings of a knight's sublimated or adulterous love for some wedded lady were a rebellion against the sacrament of marriage and Christian sexual mores. Minnesongs extolled the type of illicit relationships that the Church had always condemned and in Germany, more than in France, were frequently grossly salacious, blasphemous, and gruesome. Some of the most objectionable in this last respect were written by Konrad von Würzburg (1230–1287), notably his *Story of a Heart.*

With few exceptions, minnesingers were noblemen, often of the highest social station, and their lyrics, which were not committed to paper, were often couched in elegant language. Every minnesong was supposed to express the composer's unique style and spirit, even though structurally the lyrics were imitative of those of the Provençal *trouvères*. Among the finest minnesingers were Neidhart von Reuntal, Reinmar the Elder of Hagenau, Heinrich von Morungen, Ulrich von Lichtenstein, Heinrich von Meissen, and, above all, the Tirolean aristocrat Walter von der Vogelweide (1165/1170–1230). A great patriot, the impoverished Walter was the ablest and sweetest German lyricist before Goethe.

The Age of Bourgeois Poetry and Drama

After the age of gold came one of dross. Beginning around 1250, the slowly developing social revolution that was to usher in an era of bourgeois significance produced a deterioration in every branch of German literature. This was probably less because the middle class was uninterested in *Minne* than because the burghers, lacking the education of the minnesingers and epicists, could not emulate their achievement. They therefore burlesqued or parodied them in bad verse. In tedious works, such as Wernher Gardener's *Meier Helmbrecht* and Heinrich von Wittenweiler's *Der Ring,* bourgeois poetasters emptied vials of scorn upon nobles and knights. The sum aesthetic value of middle class didactic verse was small. Length substituted for beauty, and bombast masqueraded as style.

By 1350 poetry had come to be dominated by plebeian tradesmen and artisans, who pretended to write it but were as flightless as kiwis. These men were called meistersingers *(Meistersänger).* In place of a Walter von der Vogelweide competing against a Wolfram von Eschenbach at the cultivated court of the duke of Thuringia, we now have a late medieval cobbler competing in brittle, inelegant verse against a stone mason on the market square. The best-remembered of this ungainly variety is Hans Sachs (1492–1576), a Nuremberg shoemaker who wrote, besides verse, more than two hundred miracle plays and secular dramas. Regarded by many as the father of early modern German drama, Sachs was immortalized in the nineteenth century in Wagner's opera, *Die Meistersinger von Nürnberg.* Among the other middle-class men who by 1500 had come to monopolize the writing of secular plays, which at long last had evolved out of the medieval religious tableaux, two more of the least tedious playwrights of the fifteenth century were Hans Schnepperer and Hans Fels, both guildmasters.

Church Architecture:
Advent of the Romanesque Style

For centuries Germanized Europe, having no indigenous architecture of its own to contribute and nothing but Roman models to copy, could do little more than borrow from the provincial and metropolitan civilization whose ruins it had inherited. Dilapidated Greco-Roman temples and some later Roman basilica-type churches were in certain cases still around. Crumbling Roman edifices that had survived the invasions were often used as quarries. Their dressed stones, bricks, collonades, porches, and decorations were put together again by the Germans into buildings not very different in conception from the old. The Carolingian period witnessed the building of the imitative first and second abbey churches at Fulda, the monasteries of St. Gall, Reichcnau, and Lorch, the cathedral of Hildesheim, and a new cathedral at Cologne. Thereafter, a decline set in until Salian and Franconian times. Then, from the early eleventh through the early thirteenth centuries, Germany celebrated its grand Romanesque epoch.

The revolutionary change that set the Romanesque churches off from the temples of antiquity was that the former had become places of mass worship, whereas the latter had been essentially shrines, inviting individual prayer and offerings. Early medieval churches were therefore larger than most ancient temples. Moreover, the Romanesque style made other important modifications: a transept of equal breadth with the nave; elongation of the sanctuary area and addition of a choir; division of the nave into side bays housing altars or sarcophagi; elaborate use of the barrel or wagon cross-vaulting often supplemented by intersecting vaults; construction of semicircular or polygonal, domed or vaulted apses at the east end of the chancel or even at both ends of the church; and the replacement of antique columns with massive piers linked in arcades of semicircular vaults.

In the later Romanesque period lavish stained glass windows were set in church walls, and a great rose window was introduced above the main portal. Also rib and panel groin-vaulting replaced earlier simple cross vaults. Although the interior of a Romanesque church was naturally gloomy because of a dearth of windows, the high, massive walls were covered with frescoes and decorated moldings. The outside walls were buttressed by shallow pilasters, while below the roof was often an arcade of blind or compound arches. Unlike the churches of France, German Romanesque often had both western and eastern apses, each surmounted by dual towers.

The finest examples of mature Romanesque, unsurpassed elsewhere, were achieved in Germany during the eleventh and twelfth centuries. To this period belong the cathedrals of Bamberg, St. Michael's in Hildesheim, the second cathedral of Regensburg, Speyer with its majestic west façade, Trier, Worms with its circular and octagonal turreted towers, Limburg-an-der Lahn with its cluster towers, and Mainz, which was perhaps the noblest jewel in the Romanesque casket. These and other stately edifices gave Germany an architectural primacy which she was not again to enjoy until the early eighteenth century.

Church Architecture: Gothic

In the thirteenth century, Romanesque architecture gradually receded before the ogival or Gothic style. This was imported from France where it originated with the cathedrals of St. Denis, Sens, Noyon, Laon, Soissons, and Chartres. A luscious, exuberant, soaring style, Gothic incorporated the heavenly aspirations of the age more perfectly than had the staid Romanesque. The greater ethereal beauty of the Gothic cathedral derived from a number of calculated devices, principally the pointed arch, ogival traceried windows with exquisite stained glass, walls which were but a frame for the windows, roof of exceptionally high vaulting whose weight was distributed along diagonal, cross, and transverse ribs of masonry to heavy piers within the church and to delicately arched flying buttresses external to the aisle and nave walls, and a forest of lacy pinnacles and gargoyles surmounting buttresses and towers. The organic unity of the Gothic church harmonized with the Thomistic synthesis of reason and faith. An orchestration of sinuous masonry and colored glass, the Gothic church, its interior bathed in mystic, mosaic light and its exterior scraping the sky, was perhaps the most original architectural conception in all history.

As compared with French Gothic, German is imperfect. Perhaps this is due to the German vogue of east and west apses and a multiplicity of towers or to the simple fact that German Gothic only achieved maturity in the late thirteenth century when the style was already degenerating in France. This, however, is not to disparage the magnificent stone wedding cake that is Cologne cathedral, the unprecedentedly high 527-foot spire of Ulm cathedral, the tower of Strassburg, the arches of St. Lawrence in Nuremberg, the fabulous open-traceried spire of Freiburg in Breisgau, or the beauty of Regensburg cathedral, but it is to say that there is more to criticize in the mathematical relationships of a German than of a French Gothic church.

Toward the end of the thirteenth century a characteristically German, late variant of Gothic put in its appearance. This was the ''hall'' church *(Hallenkirche* or *Dreischiffigekirche)*. Much heavier in aspect than the high Gothic edifice, the hall church had stouter walls, which were designed to carry most of the weight of the roof, and sacrificed the principle of transparency—the glass cage effect—that had been the marvel of high Gothic. Hall churches, which were apt to be vast and possessed side aisles that were as high as the nave, were to be found mainly in northern Germany. They were most often of brick and seemed not so much to soar as to cling to the ground under their enormous weight.

Sculpture and Wood Carving
Romanesque and Gothic

German medieval sculpture was closely associated with the Church. Romanesque stone figures were covered with armor or heavy drapery that hid the human form. The sculptor, constrained to allow no carnal suggestion to interfere with his prayerful message, was obliged to restrict individuality to expression and physiognomy. Though endowed with extraordinary vitality, statuary was subordinated to architecture, frozen to its niche or embedded in the walls, and deliberately elongated. The plastic mobility of the face often stood in contrast with the rigidity and formalism of the body. Only a few of the greatest works of German Romanesque have survived. Among them are the tympanum groups above the portals of Worms, Speier, and Bamberg cathedrals; the equestrian knight of Bamberg—one of the most sensitive achievements of the epoch; and the figures above the south portals of the cathedrals of Paderborn and Münster.

The earliest attempt to imitate the liquefaction of French Gothic sculpture was the Last Judgment group in the tympanum of the west portal of Magdeburg cathedral. Later, at Bamberg advances were achieved with the statues of Henry II and Queen Kunigunde and the nude figures of Adam and Eve. At the zenith of High Gothic the svelte females representing the "true church" and the "false synagogue" were added to the Last Judgment group above the Prince's Portal at Magdeburg. There, too, were carved the fickle, flowing figures of the ten wise and foolish virgins, whose hair ripples over undulating robes to achieve an enchanting linear effect. The cathedral of Mainz, the parish church at Bassenheim near Coblenz, and Cologne cathedral also exhibit noteworthy Gothic statuary. Very possibly, however, the new style never achieved greater success than in the cathedral of Naumburg, where an unknown master (the same who worked at Bassenheim) conceived the realistic statues of Uta, marchioness of Meissen, whose face is of rare beauty, and of her worldly-minded consort, Eckhart.

Under the influence of the middle class and the mystics German sculpture slowly declined in the fourteenth century. Late medieval sculpture was mainly without grace or vigor. Most of the statues were commonplace efforts to commemorate some founder or bishop and are chiefly of interest to genealogists. Exceptions to this rule are: the tomb of Conrad III at Mainz cathedral; Christ carrying the Cross on the tomb of Dean Burgmann at Speyer cathedral; the marvelous "head with binding" by Westlettner at Mainz; the fountain standing before the *Frauenkirche* of Nuremberg; and the holy well at Ratisbon cathedral.

Unquestionably it was in wood rather than in stone that the plastic genius of late medieval Germany was best expressed. Wooden statues, altars, and reredoes from the hands of her carvers were in demand everywhere in northern Europe. Among the best extant examples of this genre are: the altar by Stephan Lochner (1400–51) in Cologne cathedral; the Neustädter altar in St. Stephan's in Vienna; the realistic heads on the Ulm cathedral choir stalls by Jörg Syrlin (1425?–91); Tilmen Riemenschneider's (1460–1531) Adam and Eve in Würzburg cathedral; Peter Vischer's (1460–1529) King Arthur and Theodoric for the tomb of Emperor Maximilian; Veit Stoss's (1440–1533) altarpieces at Bamberg and Schwabach; and the stations of the cross in St. Lawrence's in Nuremberg done by Adam Kraft (1460?–1508).

Illuminated Manuscripts

After the use of papyrus for manuscripts disappeared in the fifth century, a book came to be a codex of bound sheets of durable parchment, or vellum. Much more than a vessel of ideas, a book was the triumphant and cooperative expression of early European art.

In Germany, where there were many mediocre imitators of a few masterpieces of chirography, marginal tracery, or polychrome miniature painting, the illumination of codices was for long inferior to Gaelic and French prototypes. However, by the end of the thirteenth century German manuscripts had attained a high level of artistic excellence. By then miniaturists were achieving beautiful embellishment not only of bibles, psalters, and breviaries, but of grammars, bestiaries, secular song books, and Latin classics. Such exquisite masterpieces had appeared as the *Carmina Burana,* the *Heidelberger Liederhandschrift (Heidelberg Song Book),* and the *Manesse Codex.* One of the most lavishly illustrated of all German medieval manuscripts, the secular *Manesse Codex,* prepared by Rüdiger Manesse and his son Johann of Zurich, was an anthology of minnesongs and was dedicated to the Emperor Henry VI.

The fine vellum, ivory, enamel, or other rich exteriors of medieval parchment manuscripts were matched by the elegant script of the text. In Carolingian times Frankish minuscule writing largely came to replace the older majuscule or uncial characters (consisting mainly of capital letters) and was eventually employed for all official records and most serious writing during the Middle Ages. By the fourteenth century a Gothic, stylized variant, called *Fraktur,* was developed in the German monasteries. It exhibited pointed tips, conceits, and curly tails. From this more angular type of lettering developed Gothic print.

Not till the end of the fourteenth century was painting emancipated from the text, where it had been inserted between the lines or alongside the text. When pictures came to fill whole pages, the artist soon exchanged the book for the easel.

Late Medieval Painting

In the fifteenth century Flemish influences, stemming from Jan and Hubert van Eyck, Rogier van der Weyden, Hans Memling, Hugo van der Goes, and Hieronymus Bosch, were the main inspiration for German painters and paved the way for the coming of canvas painting. Among the foremost German exponents of the rising Flemish style of easel portraiture in oils were two Rhenish masters of the first half of the century—Meister Francke, about whom little is known, but who was active in Cologne and Hamburg, and Stephan Lochner (d. 1451), a south German who studied in the Netherlands and whose masterpiece was the three-paneled altar in Cologne. The Cologne school, to which these men belonged, pioneered the way for the giants of German Renaissance art—Martin Schongauer (1445?–91) of Colmar, Matthias Grünewald (1470–1528) of Isenheim altar fame, and Albrecht Dürer (1471–1528), the universal genius of Nuremberg.

Castles

The noble castles *(Burgen)* of Germany are almost as romantic a part of the medieval mosaic as are her stained glass churches. Indeed, these fortresses were the cynosure of aristocratic culture. It is as hard to imagine a knight without his castle as a bishop without a cathedral. The castle, answering the need for defense in an age of localism and turbulence, stood constant watch on its shaggy crag, offering asylum to the surrounding population in time of war. By Barbarossa's time, scores of stone castles, which in the twelfth century had come to replace the flammable wooden strongholds, were rising throughout the country. The new fireproof fortified structures became the fundament of the defense system of both the principalities and the Empire.

Almost all of the ten thousand castles that towered over Germany by the late thirteenth century have crumbled away. Among the four hundred castled ruins that are all that are left today are such stately monuments along the Rhine as Gutenfels, Drachenfels, Markburg, Rheinstein, and the restored Hochkönigsburg in Alsace. Elsewhere are the Heidelberg castle complex, Hohen Neuffen near Beuren, Marienburg in Würzburg, Hohenzollern-Hechingen in Württemberg, and the massive strongholds of the princes: Goslar, Gelnhausen, Henry the Lion's Dankwarderode in Brunswick, the Thuringian Wartburg, and Hohensalzburg in Salzburg.

By the thirteenth century almost all the nobles had shut themselves up in these giant mausoleums. In some parts of Germany, notably Frisia, a relatively safe area, there were very few castles. The reverse was true of Austria and trans-Elbea, where *Burgen* bristled like palisades. Because of the formidable nature of the defenses, these water fortresses *(Wasserburgen)* or mountain strongholds *(Höheburgen)* were the objects of protracted siege operations in which the chief hope of the assailant lay in starving the garrison into submission.

Most castle interiors, however romantic their exteriors, were lacking in comfort and were somber, cold, dank, drafty, and primitively furnished. Life within their walls must often have been tedious. Enforced confinement and inactivity must have led to ennui and claustrophobia. This furnished an excuse for tournaments, jousting, immoderate hunting, knight errantry, and private warfare and explains in part addiction to excessive eating, drinking, and gambling.

In all fairness, it should be remembered that the purpose of the castle was to provide protection, rather than a luxurious and cultured existence. The castle fulfilled its purpose well. Until the mid-fifteenth century those piles of stone and mortar were all but impregnable. Not until the employment of cannon and gunpowder in siege operations did the attacker again, as in antiquity, gain the advantage over the defender. Then the castle's military capabilities became incommensurably less than its liabilities.

Chapter 10

SCHOLARSHIP AND SCIENCE

Carolingian and Salian Thought

The intellectual contributions of Germany in the ninth and tenth centuries were mediocre and inferior to those of Britain. German savants were mostly theologians, commonly ponderous, prolix, and unimaginative. Generally they were content to extoll authority and disparage reason. They were typified by the Saxon theologian Gottschalk (d. 869), who was content simply to rework St. Augustine's teachings on grace, free will, and predestination and spend his energies rolling the rock of dogma up the mountain of reality. Although a large number of works from Greek and Roman times had survived in monastic libraries, this treasure of ideas, scarcely tapped by narrow doctrinaires, gathered dust on library shelves until the twelfth century.

Unless it be in Ch'in China, history records no such flight from the accumulated knowledge of the past as was staged in early medieval Europe. In time, the flight became a rout, and havoc raged through higher thought. Exact thinking was at a ruinous discount, especially in Germany, where intellectual stagnation was accentuated by the turbulence in which the country was long held by Magyar forays and where a morbid preoccupation with dialectics, which is characteristic of all closed systems of thought, consumed a scholar's best years.

Apart from theology, the only considerable learned writing done in Germany before the day of Otto I was of two kinds: chronicles and biographies. Both were generally arid, distorted, and based upon fragmentary or unreliable sources. Chronicles, which were unadorned records of events, bulked large in the writings of those days. Among the better early chronicles were the Annals of Lorch (741–901), the *Chronicon* of Regino of Prum (843–906), and those of the abbeys of Reichenau, Altaich, and St. Gall. The monks of Fulda and St. Gall wrote some of the best biographies of saints and rulers, which contain rich source material and vignettes of German medieval life.

The reign of Otto I encouraged the writing of political apologia, such as the review of the relations of Otto I with Saxony by Widukind of Corvey and the *Antipodosis* by the Lombard Bishop Liutprand of Cremona, which was a piquant examination of relations between Italy and Germany for the period 887–950. Of the many diocesan chronicles that were compiled also in the Saxon dynastic period the most interesting were those of Bishop Theitmar von Walbeck of Merseburg and Adam of Bremen.

Historical Writing and the *Spiegel*

With the coming of the Cluniac-Hirsau reform and the War of Investiture, polemical writing experienced a boom. Most German clergymen, subscribing as they did to the Gelasian theory that God had assigned only spiritual power to the pope but temporal to the emperor, rallied to the cause of Henry IV. They were exemplified by bishops Walram von Naumburg and Wenrich of Trier, both impassioned opponents of Pope Gregory VII. A minority of clergymen followed the line of Cardinal Humbert, an archfoe of the king and the whole Saxon dynasty, or of the Alsatian priest Manegold von Lautenbach, who justified deposition of Henry IV on grounds of breach of a social contract.

Less contentious than the foregoing were the numerous narratives about the reigns of Henry IV, Henry V, and Conrad II, which were mainly compiled in the abbeys of Hersfeld, St. Blasien, and Fulda—the *Annals of Hersfeld,* the *Cologne Chronicle of Kings,* the *Saxon Analist,* and the *Ratisbon Chronicle of Emperors.* The best biography was that of Conrad II by the royal chaplain Wipo.

The most significant German historian of the Middle Ages was Bishop Otto von Freising (1114?–58), a grandson of Emperor Henry IV and a half-brother of Conrad III. Otto employed a method that did not basically differ from that of early chroniclers but wrote more and better history than any predecessors. He penned a qualified defense of his nephew, Frederick I, in the *Gesta Friderici Imperatoris,* but his chief work was the *De duabus civitatibus (The Two Cities).* In this lengthy philosophical-historical disquisition on world history Otto insisted upon the superiority of ecclesiastical over secular authority. He represented the "City of Man" as in full moral decline and fast approaching a cataclysm, which he identified as the probable destruction of the Holy Roman Empire by the papacy.

After Otto von Freising the bulk of historical writing increased, but quality deteriorated. Writing not only became more voluminous and less factual but was commonly in German and by statesmen, counselors, and magistrates. A vogue for verse seized upon narrators. In the late thirteenth century history became more like poetry, and poems like histories. Excursions into literature, however, did not save historiography. The breakup of the Hohenstaufen Empire took the heart out of German historians. The best talent no longer had the will to recount the national tragedy. Historical letters, typified by the Strassburg and Limburg chronicles, passed into a long decline from which they did not emerge until the early nineteenth century.

Another type of medieval nonfictional writing was the *Specula* or *Spiegel* ("mirror"). This was a vast, uncritical compendium of information upon a wide range of pseudo-scientific, philosophical, and, in particular, juridical matters. As a compilation of laws, the *Spiegel* was a source for the study of the evolution of German constitutional forms and an arbiter in litigation. The oldest of the legal treatises dates from the reign of Frederick II and is called the *Sachsenspiegel* (1215–1235). It was chiefly the work of a jurist named Eike von Repgow. In no sense a commentary, such as was written by Bracton, the *Sachsenspiegel* nevertheless committed to paper for the first time an enormous body of customary law. Other regional and national imitations were the *Schwabenspiegel* and *Deutschenspiegel.*

Germany and the Scholastic Revival

Except in literature, German thought had long to labor under the heavy handicap of the country's immaturity. This was especially apparent as respects higher education. Germany's cathedral schools were inferior, except for Cologne, to those of York, Utrecht, Tour, Chartres, Paris, Reims, and Liège, a circumstance that caused Germany's most promising scholars to emigrate. No change for the better set in until the late twelfth century when the impact of Moslem thought, resulting from Latin translations from the Arabic, enormously broadened German horizons. When, finally, the bulk of Aristotle's works were translated for the first time, they produced a ferment throughout Europe and an impact upon Christendom which was not to be surpassed till Newton's time.

From the late twelfth-century intellectual ferment emerged one of the four or five greatest systematic intellects of all time—Albertus Magnus (1193?–1280), the "universal doctor" and the only scholar in Western history to be called "the great." In him Germany possessed the finest intellect of his age. A Swabian count (Albrecht von Bollstädt), he forsook secular concerns to become a Dominican and eventually provincial of that order. He taught at Cologne and then went to the University of Paris, where he acquired a doctorate and lectured for many years. Finally, he was appointed bishop of Regensburg. Albertus Magnus was the author of what amounts to thirty-eight quarto volumes in the most recent edition of his works. No one since Aristotle had summarized and systematized so much knowledge as Albert did. Many of his judgments, like those of the great Stagirite, were jejune, but he nonetheless did important spade work in biology, botany, physics, astronomy, and mathematics. By demonstrating the sphericity of the earth, he implied the incongruity of the Ptolemaic system and paved the way for Copernicus. Albert's mastery of the entire corpus of Aristotle's works was accomplished in defiance of the papal bans of 1215 and 1231 on the study of his *Metaphysics*. Albert's compelling interest in the reconciliation of Aristotelian naturalism and Christian dogma was transmitted to his great Italian pupil, "the angelic doctor," St. Thomas Aquinas (1225–74) of Rocca Secca, who was destined to achieve it. In spite of Albertus Magnus, who, in any case spent the years 1252–80 in France, the general level of philosophic and scientific output in Germany remained comparatively low even in the great thirteenth century.

The Rise of Universities

The situation might have been helped had Germany possessed universities to promote scholarship and research. But until the fourteenth century it had few schools of higher learning that enjoyed an international reputation. The best of them were the order schools *(Ordenschulen),* which were operated in important towns by religious communities, mainly Dominican and Franciscan. Germany's first true universities—Prague (1347), Erfurt (1379), Heidelberg (1385), Cologne (1388), and Leipzig (1409)—were established one hundred and fifty years or more after those of Paris, Padua, Bologna, Oxford, and Cambridge.

The transition from order school to university was facilitated by the ambitions of the aspiring territorial princes, many of whom believed institutions of higher learning in their principalities would augment their prestige. As the states entered the field of higher education with charters and financial aid, the monopoly formerly exercised by the religious over advanced instruction was forever broken.

It was the German universities, all of which had faculties of jurisprudence, that opened the sluice gates to Roman law. An import from Bologna, Roman law with its chiselled logic and universality promised to aid the princes in cutting through the tanglewood of inherited tribal and customary law. The universities, especially those founded by the princes in the fifteenth century—Rostock (1419), Greifswald (1456), Freiburg im Breisgau (1457), Trier (1457), Ingolstadt (1472), Tübingen (1477), and Mainz (1477)—contributed to the rise of novel theories of sovereignty and of sanctions that served developing secular authority.

More and Cheaper Books

Movable type, a Chinese Sung invention, which was first adopted in the West by the Alsatian printer Johannes Gutenberg (d. 1488), did more to fructify scholarship than anything else in history. Paper, a Chinese invention of Eastern Han times, which was cheaper to manufacture than parchment, entered Germany in the fourteenth century. By the early fifteenth century, paper books containing mainly pictures and a few lines of print were being block-printed. Gutenberg's adaptation of the Sung invention enormously aided commerce, education, and the emergence of the middle class. Beginning with the fragment of "The Last Judgment," the Gutenberg Bibles (both of 1454), and the Psalter of 1457, books poured from the German presses. By the close of the century there were fifty-one printing presses operating in Germany, which was far more than in any other country.

Thought on the Empire and Papacy

Growing senescence of the Holy Roman Empire in the thirteenth century encouraged the rise not only of German national consciousness but of pluralistic political theory. Until the mid-fourteenth century a line of powerful thinkers—Albertus Magnus, Alexander of Roes, Conrad of Megenburg, and Lupold of Bebenburg—affirmed the merits of imperial supremacy. At the same time Albertus affirmed that the Empire was, as all monarchies ought to be, a *Rechtsstaat,* i.e., a state rule not by the king's fiat but in accordance with laws.

By the end of the fifteenth century the tide had definitely turned against the Empire. Those who saw in the territorial and national states the most promising factors of the future had come to prevail. Presaging this development were the writings of Engelbert, the able late thirteenth-century abbot of Benedictine Admont in Styria. He concluded that while universal empire was indeed the best form of government, it had been in protracted decline and was beyond hope of rehabilitation. Engelbert reasoned further that the origins of the state were legalistic rather than divine and were to be sought in a hypothetical social compact that was binding on all estates.

Notwithstanding this, the imperial cause died hard. The "invisible doctor," the English Franciscan William of Occam (1300?–49), broke a lance on its behalf.

Having taken refuge at the court of Louis of Bavaria from the wrath of John XXII (1316–34), William joined forces with Dante and Marsiglio of Padua in extolling monarchy and denouncing papal suzerainty. In the fifteenth century a number of brilliant German polemicists—Conrad of Megenburg, Lupold of Bebenburg, Heinrich of Langenstein, Dietrich of Niem, Conrad of Gelnhausen, and Nicholas of Cusa—helped erode the prestige of the papacy. Of these critics, the most mordant was Nicholas (1401–64), who was born near Trier and had been educated at Dutch Deventer and at Padua. Nicholas achieved a European reputation as a champion of conciliar supremacy by writing the *De concordantia catholica* (1431–36) and the *De docta ignorantia* (1440). He argued that sovereignty in the Church lay with the congregation of the faithful who were virtually represented in ecumenical councils such as those of Constance (1414–18) and Basel (1431–49). While contending for a strong emperor, Nicholas also recognized the need for strong estates and averred that common consent, rather than individual authority, is the source of all law and the basis of good government. From the proposition that government must enjoy the approval of the governed, Nicholas deduced the conclusion that popes could be deposed for just cause by general councils. In all fairness, however, it must be mentioned that shortly after the end of the Council of Basel, Nicholas experienced his "Damascus." Fearful that the reformers had opened Pandora's box, he deserted the conciliar cause, became an advocate of papal absolutism, and was eventually rewarded with the see of Brixen and a cardinal's hat (1448).

German Science to the
Thirteenth Century

The German contribution to science during the Middle Ages was conspicuously inferior to that of the Italians, Spanish, or French. It has been estimated that of the 121 most eminent Christian scientists of the late thirteenth century, only 7 were Germans. The absence of universities and medical schools in Germany was an important factor discouraging the growth of a corps of savants who were interested in observing, diagnosing, dissecting, and experimenting. Also hindering scientific progress was the crudity of the German language, which still lacked precision and a rich vocabulary.

Early European German thought was rarely exclusively scientific. It was befogged by superstition and weird misconceptions. Science was, moreover, little more than a department of philosophy, which itself was under public suspicion. Before 1200 the sole German thinker of scientific importance was a nun, the Benedictine Hildegard of Bingen (d. 1179). Despite preoccupation with religion, she is thought to have been the only German naturalist and medical authority of note in the twelfth century. Of less importance were Herrad, abbess of Alsatian Hohenburg, who compiled the encyclopedic *Hortus deliciarum* for plants; Honorarius of Autun (d. 1150), not a Frenchman but a German residing in Ratisbon, who wrote the geographic treatise *Imago mundi;* and Theophilus Presbyter, who composed studies on the properties of dyes, ink, oil, glues, and regents. However, until the late twelfth-century influx of translations from Arabic and Greek from Toledo and Palermo, German science continued to be absorbed with the compilation of herbals, bestiaries, lapidaries, and encyclopedias.

The stimulus to broader and deeper research came from the Low Countries and Italy. Following the lead of Henry Bate of Maline and William of Moerbeke, the general of the Dominican order, Jordanus the Saxon (d. 1237), also known as Jordanus Nemorarius, attained unusual originality in mathematics and mechanics. He improved upon the theory of numbers of the ancients, substituting alphabetic letters for digits in equations. Jordanus also pushed kinematics and mechanics beyond Hellenistic limits, computed the component of gravity along a trajectory, and investigated static moment and the displacement of bodies.

In geology and natural history the brightest luminary of the thirteenth century was Albertus Magnus. Possessed of true scientific curiosity for even the trivial, he compiled data on all the fauna and flora in his little world. He assembled more new material of value in botany and zoology than any Christian since antiquity. Although not an innovator of the first magnitude, Albert had many genial insights. For example, he inferred the embryological development of plants, identified fossils as the remains of animals and plants from remote times, and expressed the belief that certain lands had once been submerged beneath the sea. He also studied the phenomena of erosion, glaciation, vulcanism, mineral springs and geysers, the tides, origins of clouds and rain, and the flow of terrestrial waters.

Late Medieval Science

The notions of Albertus Magnus inspired many later German scientists who, standing on his broad shoulders, were able to see further than he could. For example, Conrad of Megenburg (1309–74) established the fact that all terrestrial waters derive solely from rain. Dietrich of Freiburg (d. 1311), an optics student, demonstrated the nature of the spectrum by passing light through a crystal and argued that the primary rainbow is created when light is refracted within billions of water droplets and then reflected out from their inner, concave surfaces. Also Heinrich of Hesse, taking his cue from Albert, did valuable spade work in plant pathology and speculated on the origin of species.

Although the fourteenth century had surpassed the thirteenth in the volume of scientific work done in Germany, it was only with the fifteenth century that she achieved a transient leadership in Europe in the fields of mathematics, optics, geology, mechanics, natural history, and cartography. Some of the most impressive work was done in the Nuremberg area, where a number of scientists were patronized by the wealthy Pirckheimer family. In that city the chief luminary was Regiomontanus (Johannes Müller, 1436–76), the foremost scientist of the century. He founded trigonometry, improved existing astronomical tables, and accurately predicted all eclipses for half a century to come. His pupil, Bernard Walter (1430–1504), was the first to devise a precision clock driven by hanging weights. Georg Peuerbach (1423–61) of Vienna contributed to a revision of the thirteenth-century Alfonsine Tables of astrological and nautical information. Last, Nicholas of Cusa, the most perceptive thinker of the age, suggested fruitful lines of investigation in mechanics and astronomy. Specifically he anticipated the notion of uniform building blocks (elements) of the universe and the heliocentric theory of the planetary system.

Technological Progress

As everywhere else in late medieval Europe, technological progress in Germany was slow and unimpressive. There was very little improvement upon the machines and production techniques known to ancient Rome. Most of Germany's machines in the fourteenth century were still of wood, lacking strength or durability. However, there were some hydraulically powered mechanical hammers, crushers, and flour mills, and draw plates for the manufacture of wire.

Some technological advances were made in the twelfth and thirteenth centuries, but the era of the Black Death was for Germany one of industrial stagnation. Not till the fifteenth century did a new surge forward occur. Then improvements in production techniques and concentration and mechanization were achieved above all in the south German towns, Rhineland and Ruhr. Whereas in the early Middle Ages such technological and managerial advances as had been registered were the work mainly of the monasteries, in the fifteenth century they were engineered by private joint stock companies.

In the vanguard of mechanization and concentration was the metallurgical industry. Bloomeries and smelting furnaces dotted Germany, and important smelting centers for producing pig iron and steel had grown up in Chemnitz, Iglau, Graz, the Harz towns, Solingen, and parts of Westphalia. Goslar, which possessed rich silver mines, also led Europe, until the opening of the Swedish Stora Kopparberg mines, in production of copper, lead, and zinc. A considerable German literature was devoted to all aspects of the metallurgical industry, but especially to methods of extracting ore, building smelting hearths, and decarbonizing iron. A great impetus was given to the processing of ferrous metals in the fifteenth century as a result of the development of artillery and firearms and of a revived demand for armor. Coupled with these factors was the exhaustion of the mines of Bohemia, Alsace, Saxony, and the Harz, which forced the German hearth and forge masters to effect industrial combinations and rationalization to augment output. The result was the construction of super-smelting plants *(Saigerhütten)* and the reorganization of the metallurgical industry along vertical lines for the control of virtually every step of production from extraction of the ore to the sale of ferrous end-items.

PART IV
RENAISSANCE AND
REFORMATION

Chapter 11

THE TWILIGHT OF

THE FIRST REICH

Development of a Power Vacuum

During the Interregnum (1254–72) the German solar system exploded: Italy tore away from the Empire, Flanders courted France, the Burgundies shot out from the German field of gravitation, Austria and Styria were invaded by the Bohemians, and the Hanseatic cities embarked upon an independent Baltic policy. Yet nothing was devised that could have reversed the thousand disruptive tendencies that were tearing the Empire asunder. While a formless nebula hovered over central Europe, great new states—Denmark, Norway, Sweden, Poland, and Bohemia—swiftly took shape in neighboring areas.

The power vacuum in Germany led the princes to ally with France against the emperor. This not only frustrated lingering hopes of reunification but encouraged French aggrandizement. France could now embark with impunity upon that line of encroachment—the single most productive cause of European wars in modern history—that was one day to carry her to the Rhine from Basel to the sea. The rising might of France was matched by the consolidation of Poland, which destroyed all prospects of building a new east-west axis of German power, and by the renewal of the Turkish assault upon Hungary.

Milling purposelessly, the German people lost their olden political predominance in Europe. Henceforth, until Bismarck's day, political power in Germany was decentralized. It was now to be found in the ducal capitals. The plans of the Habsburg, Ascanian, Wittelsbach, Wettin, Hohenzollern, and Luxemburg dynasts loomed larger than those of the emperors. Even when a powerful prince happened to occupy the imperial throne too, he evinced more concern for his own domain than for the moribund Empire.

Influence of the German People

Ignominious as the fragmentation of post-Hohenstaufen Germany was, the nation itself did not lack strong influence upon the development of late medieval European culture. Political pluralism engendered a marvelous cultural diversity within the Empire and promoted greater individual freedom than almost anywhere else on the continent. The presence of a frontier in the east and the ravages of the Black Plague helped diminish the harshness of serfdom. The strength of the town leagues, the proliferation of systems of urban law, and the success of the Swiss cantonal independence movement were some of the factors aiding the growth of individual and corporate rights in an increasingly complex society.

In the later Middle Ages the German people, who were to be the true authors of the Reformation indictment of the papacy, came to exert a revolutionary influence over religious matters. For their lost political hegemony, the German people came to substitute a moral leadership of Christendom. All those who cherished freedom hailed this development just as enthusiastically as they did the parallel gravitation toward juridical *Freiheit,* which was the result of the spread of town leagues, territorial and cantonal sovereignty, and the free competitive market, and of the increase in the number of imperial cities.

The Eastward Shift of Political Power

During the later medieval period the historic exodus of German peasants and artisans from the older, congested areas toward the new lands in the east brought vast, formerly Slavic-held territories under German law for the first time. This entailed an eastward displacement of political and military power from the Rhine and upper Danube. So large did the "legend of the east" bulk in the popular imagination that the lords of the new principalities in that quarter were able to establish their ascendancy over the whole German galaxy of states. So greatly did the power and wealth of such eastern dynasties as the Hohenzollerns, Luxemburgs, and Habsburgs come to outweigh the *Hausmacht* of their west German peers that the eastern princes from Rudolf to Maximilian were virtually able to monopolize the royal throne. Between 1273 and 1519 Brandenburg, Bohemia, and Austria were the foci of the Empire.

Rudolf von Habsburg (1273–91)

During the Interregnum the First Reich almost expired. The crown of Germany was worn by a succession of foreign shadow kings: William of Holland (till 1256), Alfonse of Castile (1257–72), and Richard of Cornwall (1257–72). In 1273, however, the chivalrous but impoverished Count Rudolf von Habsburg was elected king. His family had originated in the Swiss Aargau at the Habichtsburg ("hawk's fortress"), but he had his sights on Austria, whose Babenberger ducal line had become extinct in 1246. Rudolf's election was, as had been customary since 1220, by the "college" of electoral princes. This comprised three prelates—the archbishops of Mainz, Trier, and Cologne, who were respectively the imperial chancellors for Germany, Burgundy, and Italy—and three lay electors—the duke of Saxony, margrave of Brandenburg and count palatine of the Rhine. A vote was not accorded Bavaria because the Wittelsbachs already had one for the Rhenish Palatinate, which in 1250 had been devised by Duke Otto of Bavaria to one of his two sons. After Rudolf's accession the electoral system, manipulated by the territorial princes, superseded the defunct principle of hereditary succession to the throne.

Rudolf's reign saw the beginning of the crumbling of the Empire's western wall. French Philip III (1270–85), lured by Germany's weakness, had just embarked upon a course of eastward expansion. Rudolf, evincing a passive lassitude, yielded extensive fiefs in Flanders, Lorraine, and Burgundy to Philip. However, in Rudolf's defense it should be said that even had he strongly opposed this development, he could not have prevented these lands from gravitating toward France since it was clearly in their economic interest to do so.

A more serious threat emanated from Bohemia. The decline of the Empire and the influx of colonists and wealth into that predominantly Slavic area conferred upon it a novel dominance in central Europe. Ottokar II Přemyslid (1253–78), a grandson of Philip of Swabia, had managed through alliance with Poland and marriage to the widow of the last Babenberg duke to acquire Austria in 1251 and Carinthia, Carniola, Istria, and Slovenia in 1269. But Ottokar's ambition was too big for his hoop. He was defeated by Rudolf von Habsburg and slain on August 26, 1278, in the decisive battle at Dürnkrut on the Marchfeld. The Přemyslids were forced to relinquish Austria and all its dependencies to the Habsburgs and swear fealty to Rudolf for Bohemia and Moravia. Rudolf's new accessions, added to those already in his hands—Aargau, Zurich-Land, Thurgau, and the Sundgau—vastly strengthened the Habsburg dynasty, whose cause was further promoted by a double marriage with the Přemyslids.

Significantly, the new crown lands were in the east, not old Germany. Rudolf, who needed French support against his princes and Bohemia, found it expedient not to resist the encroachments of Philip III and Philip IV (1285–1314). Accordingly, by the end of his reign the Empire had been plucked of all its Gallic feathers. The dynasty that moved to Vienna with Rudolf wisely abandoned Barbarossa's policy, which had rested upon a tripod of Burgundy, Swabia, and Italy and had wrought the ruin of the Hohenstaufen. By orienting themselves toward the east, the Habsburgs were able to build a powerful dynastic state that insured them indirect domination of Germany.

French Aggression

Until the French were beaten by the English at Crécy (1346), France waxed at the expense of Germany. Despite efforts of King Adolf of Nassau (1292–98) to forge an Anglo-German alliance against France, she managed between 1305 and 1310 to extend her sway over the Free County of Burgundy (Franche Comté, Freie Grafschaft), the Vivarais, and the Lyonnais. Also the French penetrated deeper into Lorraine (1301) and pushed their frontier northeastward toward the Scheldt (1292). By 1314 France had reached, and in places passed, the line of the Scheldt-Meuse-Saône-Rhone. Louis X (1314–16) took the Metz area (pays Messin) and the counties of Diois and Valentinois, which brought France closer to the Savoyard Alps. The Valois monarch Philip VI (1328–50) lopped Belgian Cambrai and its hinterland from the Empire in 1339, and the kingdom of Arles in 1349. Arles gave France control over the western Alpine passes, putting her in position to deny the Germans access to Italy.

The Second Bohemian Offensive

In the reign of Albert von Habsburg (1298–1308), successor to the deposed Adolf of Nassau, the Bohemian threat revived. While Philip IV was nibbling at the Empire in the west, King Wenceslas II was trying to reestablish dominion over Poland, Upper Silesia, the Egerland, Pleissnerland, Meissen, Bohemia, and Moravia. However, an irritated Boniface VIII deprived him of his Polish fief and kept Hungary from his grasp. Thereupon Albert counterattacked and forced Wenceslas III, the last of his line, to renounce the Egerland and Meissen.

The Swiss Confederation

In the fourteenth century the Swiss cantons smashed the east-west axis the Habsburgs were toiling to build between their lands in the Sundgau and Aargau and those along the middle Danube. Already on August 1, 1291, the three forest cantons *(Waldstätte)* of Uri, Schwyz, and Unterwalden had united on Rütli field by the *Vierwaldstätte* lake to defend themselves against the Habsburgs and the hardly less powerful Zähringer family. This Rütli oath was the first step toward Swiss independence.

A generation later the Habsburg levies were beaten by the Swiss peasants at Morgarten on November 15, 1315. Meanwhile Swiss merchants established a new trade route from Zurich to Milan through the Schoellenen gorge and the Gotthard Pass. This persuaded thriving towns such as Zurich and Lucerne that their economic interests lay with not the Empire but the emerging Swiss Confederation (Schweizerische Eidgenossenschaft). This decision promoted a bourgeois-peasant alliance. By themselves, the poor farmers of the forest cantons could not have prevailed against emperor and Zähringer, and the legends of William Tell and Arnold von Winkelried would have died on the vine. But with the aid of the towns, Swiss independence was feasible. When affluent Zurich joined the Confederation in 1351, she drew Glarus and Zug (1352) and Bern (1353) after her. Then the eight rebel cantons rushed on to the famous victories of Sempach (1386) and Näfels (1388) and the substance of sovereignty.

The Turbulent Reign of
Ludwig the Bavarian (1314–47)

During the brief reign of French-trained Henry VII (1308–13) von Luxemburg, Germany had another dance with Italy. The circumstance that Pope Clement V was dwelling at Avignon under the thumb of the French invited Henry's invasion of the peninsula. However, despite enthusiastic support from Dante and the Ghibellines, a coalition of the pope, France, Naples, and the north Italian towns frustrated the king. He did manage to storm Rome and force his coronation as emperor, but it was a hollow victory. Siena and the Guelphs defied him. There ensued the disastrous Battle of Tagliacozzo (August 23, 1313) and on the same day the death of Henry VII, who in the meantime had fallen ill. To counteract the Italian fiasco, however, was the acquisition of Bohemia. Henry had married his son John to Elizabeth Přemyslid of Bohemia, and when John became king (1313–48) of that realm it became the plinth of Luxemburg *Hausmacht*.

In 1313 a majority of German princes backed the Bavarian Duke Ludwig von

Wittelsbach (1282–1347) for the throne against the Habsburg Frederick the Fair (1314–22; 1325–26). There was a double election followed by civil strife. Finally, at Erharting near Mühldorf in 1322 Frederick was beaten and captured by Ludwig. Then the latter was excommunicated by the anti-German Avignonese Pope John XXII (1316–34) on the thin pretext of his having encouraged heresy in Lombardy. Once again Germany was plunged into turmoil.

Ludwig's academic champions now launched a formidable counterattack upon the papacy. The theory of papal supremacy was challenged by William of Occam and his Franciscan brothers, Michael of Cesena (general of the order) and Bonagratia of Bergamo, as well as the Ghibelline Marsiglio of Padua, author of the *Defensor Pacis*. These men were sheltered by Ludwig in Munich or in Pisa. The ensuing vendetta strengthened the territorial states of Germany. So far from reversing the slow erosion of the Empire, the European policy of Ludwig, as Max Spindler and Dieter Albrecht have recently shown, promoted territorialism and enabled him to acquire new dynastic lands and rationalize Bavaria's government.

Upon extinction of the Ascanian line in 1320 Ludwig had acquired for the Wittelsbachs control of Brandenburg, certain Dutch provinces, and the Tirol. The growth in Wittelsbach *Hausmacht* excited the jealousy of other German princes. Ultimately they took advantage of his diplomatic failures, especially as respects the English alliance and the purchase of the support of Pope Benedict XII (1334–42). The accession of the French Pope Clement VI (1342–52), who was an adamant foe of Ludwig, was the signal for the formation of a *fronde* against him. Suspicious of his growing power and arrogance and sick of the strife he had brought, the princes moved in 1345 to depose him. However, before they could consummate their plans, he died while on the hunt. Ludwig had alienated the Luxemburgers by coveting the Tirol, and now nobody seriously thought of putting his son on the throne.

Bohemian Ascendancy: Charles IV (1347–78)

The electors chose Charles von Luxemburg or Lützelburg (1316–78), the son of King John of Bohemia. Charles was culturally more a product of France than of Bohemia or Germany, even though his *Hausmacht* lay mainly in the land of the Czechs. With his coronation an era of Bohemian hegemony dawned.

If Germanized Prague enjoyed for centuries thereafter a reputation for magnificence, this was chiefly due to the treasure that Charles IV lavished on the jewel of the Moldau (Vltava). To the old city, he added a new one, laid out Italian botanical gardens, constructed the Charles' Bridge (Karlsbrücke, Karlovy Most), built churches, mansions, and the new palace in the kremlin *(Hrádschany)*, commissioned Mathias of Arras and Peter Parler of Schwäbisch-Gmünd to construct the beautiful St. Veit's cathedral in the *Hrádschany*, and altogether transformed Prague from a Czechish into a cosmopolitan city. He patronized wood-carvers, miniaturists, metalsmiths, and the Bohemian glass industry. He encouraged the efforts of Wurmser of Strassburg, the best artist of the new school of painting in

Prague. A benefactor of learning, Charles IV founded the first university in the Empire, Prague (1348), and spared no pains to obtain an eminent faculty for it. Indeed, the emperor was a munificent patron of humane letters and so zealously supported scholarship that he elicited the praise of Petrarch. Charles ended by making Prague the chief cultural center of central Europe. In doing so, he raised the prestige of Bohemia to such degree that its possession came to be regarded thenceforth as a necessary precondition to election to the imperial throne.

Appreciating the vigor of the vernacular, the emperor instructed his chancellor, Johann Neumarkt, a distinguished classicist, to use the Middle German Frankish and Thuringian dialects in the conduct of affairs of state and German script on chancellery documents. Charles also approved Neumarkt's efforts to introduce Roman civil law, sanctioned the use of Slavonic instead of Latin in church services, and encouraged freedom of thought at the university. All of this contributed markedly to generating in Bohemia an attitude of criticism that paved the way for the Hussite heresy.

Constitutional Reforms of Charles IV

When Charles became king royal power was effective only in areas where he was also proprietary lord. For the rest of the country the authority of the crown had sifted away, a development that was accelerated by the terrible loss of population occasioned by the ravages of the Black Death (bubonic plague) in 1348–49. The king possessed neither standing army nor reliable feudal levies. Theoretically he was still feudal suzerain, but in practice the princes sabotaged his requests for military service by his vassals. All the bonds holding the tenants-in-chief to the throne had greatly loosened, for feudalism was dying.

Both as respects legislation and administration of justice the pendentives of royal authority were in 1347 too weak to support the dome of empire. The royal council had evolved into an inchoate Reichstag, it is true, but it had no precise composition or statute of procedure. Roughly, the Reichstag comprised representatives from three estates *(Stände)*: the princes, who constituted the First Estate and dominated the diet; the temporal and ecclesiastical lords, who constituted the Second Estate; and the burgesses and patricians from the larger towns, who made up the third. Under Charles IV the Reichstag, unsupported by an army, possessed less power than the English parliament. The supreme court of the Empire *(Reichsgericht* or *Reichshofgericht)* had no fixed seat, no set composition, and no corpus of judge-made law to guide it. Lower imperial courts dispensed somewhat better and faster justice but were not exempt from serious abuses.

Charles IV realized that although he was strong as king of Bohemia, monarchical absolutism was an impossibility in Germany. After his experience with the refractory diets of Rhens (1338) and Frankfurt (1344), he saw clearly that Germany could not be ruled in defiance of the princes. He understood his task as merely soliciting the cooperation of the First Estate in the governance of the kingdom. Meanwhile, as a territorial prince in his own right, he strengthened his

Hausmacht by annexing Lower Silesia and Lusatia to Bohemia and temporarily confiscating Brandenburg.

In the Golden Bull of Nuremberg of January 10, 1356, named after its golden seal or *bulla,* Charles IV sought to prevent further territorial fragmentation. Electoral principalities, at least, were made indivisible, and this was widely copied by the lesser states. The strong tenor of the clauses underlining German independence reflected the rising tide of German nationalism as also the impotence of France, which had just been beaten by the British and was in no position to impose the sway of her papal puppet on the Reich. The Bull assigned certain powers to the emperor but gave the princes prerogatives that actually put the governance of Germany in their hands. Seven rulers were designated electoral princes, the king of Bohemia being added to those who in 1273 had elected Rudolf. Careful regulations were devised to preclude double elections. Because Charles was contemptuous of the growing middle class, the Bull forbade town leagues as being conspiracies against the peace. Only confederations for the maintenance of regional peace *(Landfrieden),* in which princes were also members, would be tolerated.

Benevolent Effects of the
Policies of Charles IV

Bold innovations were not to the liking of Charles IV. All his reforms aimed at making the existing aristocratic-peasant order operative under changed conditions. Yet for all of these paltry concessions, Germany had to assume a mortgage of political retardation. Charles neither comprehended the lesson of nationalist political consolidation exemplified by France nor the revolutionary implications of the popular movements engendered by the Great Plague.

Sweeping in from Asia and Constantinople in 1348, the Black Death, in both the pneumonic and less lethal bubonic forms, struck Europe with such fury that available physicians simply could not cope with it. Perhaps a fourth of Germany's population died within a year. The countryside was depopulated, and in the towns craftsmen perished like flies. The gross national product fell precipitously. In the wake of the disaster came higher wages but also depression and destitution. The plague also gave rise to popular movements to free the serfs, democratize society, and substitute mysticism for institutionalized religion. Diminishing population pressure also entailed loss of interest in colonizing eastern lands.

Confronted with this severe challenge, Charles IV reacted unimaginatively. He did almost nothing to harness the mighty winds of change. The few reforms that this conservative initiated were mostly insincere and did not survive him by more than a decade. He left Germany without psychological or economic armor against external attack, and had it not been for the fact that France was bogged down in the Hundred Years' War and the papacy hobbled by its Avignonese captivity, Germany might have fared very badly at the hands of her neighbors. Also, Charles left the German bourgeoisie handicapped in all the marts of trade. Merchants lived in dread of the capricious policies of a hundred territorial princes who imposed tolls and taxes upon goods passing through their domains. If the growth of the middle class was checked for a century, Charles was partly to blame.

The Do-Nothing Successors
of Charles IV

After 1378 the Empire was a rope of sand. The central government in the hands of inept or venal rulers, for whom Germany was no longer uppermost in their minds, was incapable of defending the realm, harnessing the energies of the warring estates, or putting limits to the greed of the high clergy. The reality of power in late medieval times was with the dynasts, who were springing up like weeds in the east and south. Yet no territorial principality could fill the void left by the slow decomposition of the Reich. No dynast could develop the requisite lofty political sanction or national perspective that alone could revive the German state. Until the fifteenth century none could even rise above outworn feudal notions, such as that the state was private property.

Wenzel (Wenceslas, 1378–1400), the first of the sons of Charles IV to succeed to the throne, devoted most of his life to strengthening his *Hausmacht* in the east, where the Ottoman Turks were just then winning historic victories, such as Kossovo (1389) and Nikopolis (1396). If there was one commendable objective for which Wenzel strove it was to establish an imperial peace. For years the goal eluded him, but finally he did manage at Eger in 1339 to secure the Reichstag's acceptance of the idea, only to see the peace melt under the fierce displeasure of the princes and the defiance of the town leagues and the Swiss Confederation. In 1400 the estates, alleging Wenzel's failure to protect German territory against France and his shocking intemperance, deposed him.

In a forlorn effort to return the center of power to the west, the supreme lords made Rupert, who was Count Palatine of the Rhine, king (1400–10). The power play was a failure and was never repeated. Rupert's ten years on the throne were largely dissipated in counteracting Wenzel, who would not be reconciled to his loss. While the rivals were gesturing ridiculously against a backdrop of unreality, the Poles in resurrected might dealt the Germans the worst defeat since 983.

Tannenberg and the Decline
of the Teutonic Knights

When the Piast line of Polish kings died out in 1370, German power in the Baltic area stood near its zenith. From the Danish Sound to Reval the sea was dominated by the Hanse. The Danes were kept in check by an alliance between it and the Teutonic Knights, to whom in 1346 Denmark was forced to cede Estonia. Under the last grand master of consequence of the *Ritterorden,* Winrich von Kniprode (1351–82), who ruled his lands from his East Prussian Marienburg castle like a Turkish sultan, the Knights experienced their Indian summer. The Germanization of the Polish majority in Pomerelia was progressing, baronial feuds had been suppressed, government was relatively just and efficient, and the cost of living in Prussia was low. Six great cities had risen under protection of the order—Thorn,

Kulm, Elbing, Braunsberg, Königsberg, and, lately, the port of Danzig. While conditions in this colonial march land were still too harsh to admit a high degree of culture, important educational advances were being made on every level.

In 1386 the Polish Queen Jadwig married Jagiello, grand duke of Lithuania. The resulting kingdom of Poland-Lithuania fell under the Teutonic Order's mortal foe, Lithuania. This proved disastrous for the Knights. Not only did Poland-Lithuania turn out to be an impassable roadblock to German expansion, but the conversion of the Lithuanians to Roman Catholicism even deprived the order of an honest mission. After the well-nigh ruinous defeat of the Poles and Lithuanians on the Vorskla in 1399 by Tamerlane, Jagiello's army combined with the Czechs, Hungarians, and Tartars, and this motley horde then dealt Grand Master Heinrich von Jungingen's *Ritterorden* a staggering blow on July 15, 1410, at Tannenberg, or Grünewald, in East Prussia. After Jungingen's death on the battlefield the Knights were driven back to the great fortress of Marienburg, where they held out for many months before making peace.

Although the Peace of Thorn (1411) was fairly lenient, a heavy war indemnity was laid upon the order, which also had to cede Samogitia to Poland. The Knights, who earlier had brought prosperity, through wise administration, to all classes of Prussia, now had no alternative but to levy contributions upon them. Even so, the Teutonic Order was unable to repel new assaults by Bohemia and Poland in 1414, 1422, and 1431. In the general strife that enveloped Samland, Ermland, Culmland, Omesania, and Danzig, town life fell into ruin. Depopulation laid its wasting hand on all the territories of the order. The Prussian population came to regard it as an incubus, something that stubbornly refused to die. The estates formed a Prussian Federation in 1440 and leagued with Poland-Lithuania against the Knights. They were again defeated and forced to sign the humiliating Second Treaty of Thorn (1466). The order had to surrender Culmland, Pomerelia, Ermland, Elbing, and Marienburg, in fact all of its western lands, which were then joined in personal union with the Polish crown.

Cut off from Germany by a "Polish corridor" and obliged to accept Poles up to 50 percent of its membership, the *Ritterorden* was marked for extinction. In 1525 Albert von Hohenzollern of Brandenburg-Ansbach, the last grand master of the order, secularized its remaining lands and agreed to hold them as the duchy of East Prussia from the king of Poland. The Knights of the Sword of Livonia did not long survive the *Ritterorden*. In 1558–61 Livonia and Esthonia were lost to Sweden, and the isles of Ösel and Dagö (Bay of Riga) to Denmark. Thereupon, Gotthard Ketteler, the last grand master, decided to accept the duchy of Courland and Semgallen, all that remained to the Knights of the Sword, as a fief from Poland.

A Century Too Late: Sigmund (1411–37)

The lordly, talented third son of Charles IV, Sigmund, was chosen king of Germany in 1411. He wore his crown under a cloud of military failure. He had been beaten in 1396 at Nikopolis by Sultan Bajazet I. Thereafter Sigmund had lived against the day when he could lead a crusade against the Turks. He convened the Council of Constance not simply to end the Schism but to galvanize the Church behind a grand crusade. What he got, however, was one directed against the Hussites rather than the Turks. Sigmund's betrayal of his pledge of safe conduct to John Hus, who, notwithstanding, was burned in 1415 by order of the council, provoked the nationalistic Hussite Wars, in the course of which the German armies staggered from defeat to defeat at the hands of the Czechs. At the same time, Habsburg aggression, Polish-Lithuanian advances, a rift with the Hohenzollerns, and French hostility all plagued Sigmund. An ever higher screen rose between him and his paramount goal until it was obscured entirely.

The indecisive Hussite Wars were finally ended in July, 1436, by the Compacts of Prague, which were signed by the moderate Czechs (Utraquists) and the Empire. Bohemia and Moravia acknowledged Sigmund as king, but he conceded that the laity in those areas should receive both bread and wine in the Holy Eucharist and that priests should have the right to elect their own prelates.

The main results of the wars from the German standpoint were an increased susceptibility to heresy and an acceleration of the flow toward particularism. The emperor had failed all down the line, and the chief beneficiaries of the wars had been the princes, who controlled the military power and into whose contentious hands the future of Germany was consigned.

The Contradiction of
Pluralism and Nationalism

The fifteenth century was one of grave political disappointments for the Germans. The brief reign of Albert II (1438–39) was followed by a long and disastrous one under Frederick III (1440–93), during which all the divisive forces that rent the country were aggravated. Frustration drove the population to seek refuge in mysticism and occultism. Under conditions where there was no supreme challenge that might have trumpeted forth a charismatic leader around whom the nation could unite, autonomy waxed so luxuriantly that plural sovereignty became the hallmark of the national polity.

Nevertheless, there was general recognition by mid-fifteenth century that at long last a German nation had materialized. This concept, while not identified with the "state," was manifested in intangibles: the writings of patriotic men of letters; the fact that the German language had conquered court, council, and chancellery; and an increasing uniformity of law and standardization of governmental institutions and practices everywhere. In the provincial diets, municipal councils, and the world of business the vernacular had all but elbowed Latin out. The Council of Constance had already recognized the existence of a *natio teutonica,* which it considered to be coextensive with the German language area in central Europe, while in the Acceptance of Mainz (1439) and the Vienna Concordat (1448) the term *nostre Germanice nacioni* ("our German nation") was employed. As the emperor lost control over Burgundy, Provence, Italy, Switzerland, and Lorraine, the Church councils ceased to speak of the *sacrum imperium* and spoke only of the "Roman Empire of the German nation" *(Römisches Reich Deutscher Nation)*.

Fragmentation

In A.D. 1500 the German principalities, both secular and ecclesiastic, embraced more than 12 million people. From Luxemburg to Silesia and from Mecklenburg to Styria there were far more than the oft-stated figure of 350 territorial states. However, most of them were minuscule. There were imperial cities, such as Frankfurt, Bremen, Lübeck, Hamburg, and forty others; and there were large temporal states, such as the kingdom of Bohemia, archduchy of Austria, margravate of Brandenburg, Rhenish Palatinate, landgraviate of Hesse-Darmstadt, the two duchies of Saxony, and the duchies of Mecklenburg, Württemberg, and Bavaria. Two-thirds of the country and probably a proportionate amount of its wealth lay in the hands of these and the middling secular princes. The remainder was mostly under the control of the Church. Rivaling some of the big temporal states were the bishoprics of Mainz, Trier, Cologne, Paderborn, Münster, Würzburg, Magdeburg, Passau, and Bremen.

Imperial Government

Part of the weakness of the German monarchy may be ascribed to the fact that it had developed no true imperial organs and no system of universal fiscal controls that could have replaced the vanishing authority which German kings had once as feudal suzerains exercised over their vassals. Unlike the kings of England and France, the German monarch was still reliant in the fifteenth century upon the largesse and good pleasure of the high nobility, and he wandered like a beggar with outstretched hand from court to court.

What was potentially the most important institution of "central" government—the Reichstag or imperial diet—was controlled by the princes and was, in any case, not a true national legislature. The emperor might ignore its resolutions, and so might the princes. The Reichstag, obligated neither to regular sessions nor to any rules of procedure, was not a serious factor in the formulation of national policy. Deputies did not think of themselves, moreover, as representatives of the nation but as plenipotentiaries from the principalities, who had periodically to request voting instructions.

Although the princes might personally attend the Reichstag as members of the First or Second Estates, the lesser noblemen were only "virtually" represented. The same was true of prelates who were not princes. Only those who were invited might attend a given session of the Reichstag. Episcopal or abbatial towns were accorded no direct representation, nor were the peasants, even though the latter constituted more than 85 percent of the population.

What gave the Reichstag its all-German character was the inclusion of deputies from some fifty imperial cities. Here was a development of great constitutional potentiality. German burghers had not been able to wrest from the crown those critical fiscal concessions that had been won by their English cousins, nor was there in Germany any comparable definition of the parliamentary rights of the Third Estate. Nevertheless by 1255 representatives of select towns were being invited by the king to sit at crown council meetings that in remote times had been attended only by temporal and spiritual lords. From then onward the German crown council rapidly evolved into a Reichstag. By the early fourteenth century the burghers had come to be recognized as one of the constitutional estates of the Empire, a status that (unlike the situation in France) was never accorded to the German clergy. No imperial diet of the late fourteenth or fifteenth century sat without the presence of town deputies.

Dualism in the Principalities

If pluralism was the Empire's "shirt of Nessus," dualism—the conflict between the princes and their own estates in each principality—was the chief obstacle to territorial absolutism. In an age when feudal responsibilities and royal power were both on the point of vanishing, the princes strove to gather into their hands prerogatives earlier exercised by suzerain or king. Princes acquired the right to levy tolls, construct fortresses, administer Church lands and properties, mint coins, and mine salt and silver. They also came to exercise appellate jurisdiction that had formerly been reserved to the crown. Important, too, was the fact that the princes were, through the device of securing the election of their younger sons to bishoprics, steadily coming to replace the crown as protector of the Church and its property. With the growth of territorial sovereignty *(Landesherrschaft)*, the princes developed a fierce appetite for money. Their efforts to wheedle or wring it from their estates evoked stiff opposition and demands for a share in control of finances. From this contest emerged the political dualism that marked late medieval Germany.

In the fifteenth century domainal resources no longer sufficed to defray mounting governmental expenses, whose sharp increases were due to costlier wars and the assumption of new, nonfeudal duties by the princes. They thought to find a way out of their distress by summoning territorial diets *(Landtage)*, which were superior to provincial diets and had a broader grasp of the needs of the whole principality. The habit of consulting the territorial estates ultimately forced the princes into dependence upon them, especially in an emergency. For their part, the estates used their power of taxation to obstruct the rise of absolutism.

The *Landtag* estates in almost all principalities represented only three social elements: nobles of the blood or by patent, urban patricians, and prelates. The territorial estates did not so much champion narrow sectional interests, which were the concern of the provincial diets, as the collective liberties of the whole population against the prince. This was exemplified by the opposition of the *Stände* to the subdivision of states. No corporative interest fought harder for political unity.

If the struggle did not end in complete checkmate for the princes, it was because of three things. First, primogeniture and dynastic continuity, wherever operative, favored their cause. Second, the prince split the opposition by absorbing marginal nobles into army, bureaucracy, and council, where they shone again as in days when their purses were full and their mortgaged castles had not yet tumbled into ruin. Last, the bourgeoisie soon came to see that its interest lay in developing uniform laws and administration, ordered finances, and an effective territorial defense.

Efforts by the emperors to halt the drift toward territorial sovereignty by playing the *Landtage* off against the princes usually failed. The estates generally understood the need for larger unity and better government. They came to limit their criticism to attacks upon incompetence, corruption, or extravagance and seldom assailed the system as such. The diets all aimed at collegial government—rule by the prince with their consent. Beginning in 1471 in Silesia, they commonly speedily achieved the suppression of arbitrary impositions and won the right to assess taxes and to grant or withhold funds. Thus the German states system of the closing Middle Ages was characterized not by despotism, as in the Italian city-states, but by dualism and constitutionalism. Innumerable contracts between rulers and diets had conferred significant rights upon the German people.

Other Checks to Absolutism

Other major obstacles to territorial despotism were: frequent peasant rebellions, except in the Tirol, Vorarlberg, and East Frisia, where the peasants were recognized as an estate; the absence of fixed princely residences and adequate facilities for public administration; stubborn persistence of local, peasant rights and customs *(Dorfrecht),* which obstructed the centralizing tendencies of Roman law; class warfare between the knights and burghers; removal of the imperial cities from princely control; and the lack of a statute of primogeniture and entail, which led to the division of many a state (e.g., Thuringia, Braunschweig, Saxony, and Württemberg). These impediments gave the German states system its characteristic dualism and blocked the development of territorial absolutism.

Brandenburg and the Gordian Knot

The first German state to reverse the current toward dualism was Brandenburg. Frederick I, Hohenzollern burgrave of Nuremberg, to whom the emperor had in 1411 given the margravate and in 1415 the electoral title *(Kurfürst),* and Frederick II (1440–70) Irontooth had with bulldog tenacity worn down the independence of the nobility. Albert Achilles (1471–86) further consolidated princely power when in 1473 in the celebrated *Dispositio Achilles* he split his Ansbach, Franconian, and Brandenburgian holdings among his three sons but bound them thenceforth to the rule of primogeniture and entail. At the same time the Hohenzollern margraves in hard fighting humbled the towns of Brandenburg, which were forced to lower staple tolls and were forbidden to combine into leagues. Brandenburg's towns during the fifteenth century were broken by warfare, ruinous exactions, and the suppression of local autonomy. The result was the transfer of essential control over the public purse to the margrave.

Trier, Clèves, the Rhenish Palatinate, Bavaria, and Saxony also faced offensives by ambitious princes. However, their efforts were as yet only indifferently successful. In many states, such as Württemberg and the Vorarlberg, the *Stände* were too firmly allied for the prince to prevail. At very least, however, the rulers succeeded in attaching the nobles more securely to themselves, exploiting the centralizing legacy of Roman law, and strengthening their armies, administration, and judiciary.

Failure of Imperial Reform

Although several plans for renovating imperial government had been proposed, among them the "Reformation of the Emperor Sigmund," none had ever been accepted by the Reichstag. This was due to the uncooperative attitude of the princes of the north and east, who dominated it. On the other hand, the western and southwestern princes, whose principalities were often no bigger than postage stamps, and the imperial cities believed that constitutional reform held for them either the promise of equality with the grand seigneurs of Trans-Elbea or, at least, of survival.

In 1481–82 Duke Eberhard of Württemberg took the first step by renouncing arbitrary taxation and proposing substitution of a fixed annual impost on all property and the abolition of existing levies and tolls. Had this plan been adopted at the national level, imperial finances would have been put on a dependable basis.

The leading champions of imperial reform came from southwestern Germany and the Rhineland. Their leader was Berthold von Henneberg, archbishop of Mainz (1484–1504) and a great patriot. He wished to transform national offices into genuine departments of state and reknit the country. However, Frederick III was averse to the primate's proposal to establish a supreme imperial council in which public policy would be framed by the emperor with the assent of the electors.

Emperor Maximilian (king of the Romans, 1486; emperor, 1493) took a more vigorous line than his predecessor had. Maximilian wanted to reform the military and increase taxes to finance its needs. The diets of Worms (1495) and Augsburg (1500) discussed these and other reform proposals. At Augsburg it was decided, in spite of the emperor's personal opposition, to create an Imperial Regency Council (Reichsregiment or Reichsrat) with permanent seat at Nuremberg. Members were to be nominated by the Reichstag. No representation in this council was to be accorded the peasantry, and the combined votes of electors and princes were to outweigh those of the towns. Since, however, the Reichsregiment was given considerable consultative and appointive powers, Archbishop Henneberg's proposal was basically realized. It was also decided at Augsburg that the Reichstag was to meet at least one month in every year and be consulted in all important matters of public policy; that a new supreme tribunal or *Reichskammergericht* with a fixed seat was to be established as a primary court for princes and estates and an appellate court for other litigants; that the Empire was to be divided for administrative, judicial, and military purposes into six provinces called circles or *Reichskreise* (four more were added in 1512); and that costs of defense were to be raised through a uniform tax called the "Turkish" or "Common" Penny.

Most of these reforms soon ran into the sand. Maximilian sabotaged all organs that might reduce his prerogatives. The princes and burghers were, it is true, mildly interested in buttressing the Reichstag and Reichsregiment but showed no enthusiasm for the Common Penny, an imperial army, or the supreme court. The lesser princes especially feared the tax and troop levies because they might antagonize the turbulent peasants. The *Reichskammergericht,* moreover, seldom met, possessed no military sanction that might have compelled compliance with its verdicts, and was ridiculed by most princes. The Common Penny was abandoned after only a year. The Reichsregiment, having no assured operational funds, was crippled from birth and shortly fell into desuetude. Nevertheless, the reforms had not been in vain. As one authority expressed it: "While the new order of 1495 left much to be desired, one service must be acknowledged: despite inadequacies, it withstood the test of dismemberment and the tremendous convulsion of German life occasioned by the Reformation."*

----

*Willy Andreas, *Deutschland vor der Reformation: Eine Zeitwende,* 6th ed. (Stuttgart, 1959), p. 218.

Chapter 12

THE HABSBURG BID

FOR ASCENDANCY

IN EUROPE

The Pragmatic Sanction of Mainz

Sigmund's successor, Albert II (1436–39) von Habsburg, was energetic and intelligent. Within a year he had acquired the Hungarian, German, Bohemian, and Holy Roman crowns, something nobody had ever done before. Unfortunately, filled with the urgency of winning decisive victory over the Turks, he threw his life away in a poorly thought-out campaign against them.

The most important event of Albert's brief reign was the promulgation of the Pragmatic Sanction of Mainz (1439). The pious emperor was influenced by the example of the French Pragmatic Sanction of Bourges (1438). The "acceptation" of Mainz endorsed the anti-papal decrees of the councils of Constance and Basel and established control over the German Church by territorial governments and native clergy. The Mainz reforms promised to suppress the papacy's right to appoint to vacant benefices or collect annates and to provide for election of bishops and archbishops by cathedral chapters. If these provisions had remained in force, it is improbable that a critical estrangement with the Holy See would have developed, and the Lutheran Reformation would almost certainly have been avoided. As it was, the disunity of Germany destroyed the bright promise of the Acceptation. The princes were unable to make common front against a resourceful and never-flagging papal diplomacy, which carried the popes swiftly to victory over the conciliar movement and, in the pontificate of Pius II, to papal supremacy over the Church (1460).

Reign of a Thousand Misfortunes:
Frederick III

During the long, disastrous reign of the humane Frederick III (1440–93) von Habsburg the prestige of the Empire and of the *regnum Teutonicum* sank to an all-time low. Frederick was filled more with the glory of Austria than of Germany. In 1462, for example, he had signed a privilegium that conferred a preferential position in the Empire upon Austria and the hereditary rank of archduke upon its rulers. Even while not yet emperor he had divined a charismatic mission for his beloved Austria from the vowels *a, e, i, o, u—Austriae est imperare orbi universo* or *Alles Erdreich ist Oesterreich unterthan* ("the whole world is subject to Austria").

Almost from the outset of his imperial reign Frederick III exhibited a great, unrecognized ineptitude. In 1448 he negotiated the Concordat of Vienna (or

Aschaffenburg), which, while authoritative for Church-state relations in Austria until 1806, practically rescinded the Acceptation of Mainz. The Concordat conceded Frederick, as duke of Austria, Styria, Carinthia, and Carniola, extensive power over episcopal elections, Church revenues, and monasteries within his dynastic lands but virtually ignored his interest in imperial Church-state relations. In return for minor concessions to the weak emperor, the pope was almost everywhere, except in Austria, restored to his former far-reaching control over benefices and investitures.

In military affairs the emperor cut no valorous figure. Not Frederick III, but new kings of Poland and Hungary, personally defended central Europe against the Turks. Against the ambitions of his brother Albert, Frederick was similarly ineffectual. Only the proverbial luck of the Habsburgs saved his crown lands from dissolution. After the division of the Habsburg lands in 1379 the senior branch of the house had retained only the archduchy of Austria. From 1446–57 even this residuum had to be divided. Only Albert's death restored all Austria to Frederick in 1463, while the Tirol again fell to him by chance in 1490. Fate also drew a veil over the passivity of Frederick's policy in the east, where he was rescued from the cupidity of Wladislaw III of Poland and Hungary when he was slain in battle with the Turks. Frederick was similarly spared the nightmare of a resurrected Bohemian empire when the bellicose Taborite Georg Kunstadt von Poděbrad, king of Bohemia (1459–71), suddenly died, and his realm was divided between Poland and Hungary. Frederick's one clever move in the east was to negotiate in 1465 a treaty with King Matthias Corvinus (1458–90), providing that in the event of his death without issue, Hungary and its dependencies should pass to the Habsburgs.

In the west, both Burgundy and France chewed at the Empire. Charles the Bold, then at the summit of his power, seized Hainault, Liège, and Luxemburg. Meanwhile, the French drove into Metz and Upper Alsace, Breisach, and Basel, lands Charles needed to link his northern and southern possessions. To all these challenges Frederick III made no serious response. He would have made a good abbot of Melk, but as emperor he was a national calamity.

The Burgundian Windfall

From the struggle of the Swiss against Charles the Bold, the last male of his line, were to derive three rich dividends for the Habsburgs: abatement of Swiss hostility, destruction of the dangerously mushrooming duchy of Burgundy, and Austrian inheritance of much of Charles's domain. When he died in the slaughter at Nancy on January 5, 1477, Burgundy's southern lands were divided between France and Switzerland. The duchy proper went to France, Franche Comté to the Swiss. Because Frederick's son Maximilian had in 1477 married Charles's daughter and sole heir, Mary, Burgundy's northern territories (the Netherlands, Artois, and Piccardy) now passed to the Habsburgs. In 1493 by the Treaty of Senlis even Franche Comté was transferred to Austria.

The fabulous gains from the Burgundian marriage far outweighed all the losses of Frederick's reign. The venture also demonstrated the superiority of diplomacy over war: *Bella gerant alii; tu felix Austria nube* ("Let others make war; you, happy Austria, marry").

It is less easy to strike a balance between the remote results of this marriage. By blocking France's advance to the east, the Burgundian bequest accentuated rivalry between the Valois and Habsburgs. The double-headed imperial eagle now faced as much to the west as to the east. Habsburg acquisition of the Burgundian Circle raised a rampart against further French aggression at the expense of Germany and forced a detour through Italy. The imperative of the "watch on the Rhine" *(Die Wacht am Rhein)* henceforth dissuaded the Habsburgs from concentrating on penetrating the Balkans or consolidating their hold on Germany. Contrariwise, the Burgundian windfall enabled the Habsburgs permanently to monopolize the imperial throne. Suspicion that the Habsburgs were following a purely dynastic policy also impelled the German princes to oppose royal encroachments by allying themselves with foreign powers. In this dogged contest the territorial rulers fought with steadily increasing success because all social classes came eventually to feel that a dynasty whose interests lay mainly outside the country would always be tempted to divert Germany's wealth and manpower to non-national ends.

The "Last Knight"

The reign of Maximilian (1493–1519) bears the ruby red seal of humanism. At the court of this chivalrous monarch gathered some of the foremost humanists of the day. Men such as Johann Reuchlin (1455–1522), Conrad Celtis (1459–1508), Sebastian Brandt (1457–1521), Ulrich von Hutten (1488–1525), Johann Wimpheling (1450–1528), Willibald Pirckheimer (1470–1528), and Mutianus Rufus (1471–1528) were sanguine that Maximilian, revered for his intellect and resolution, would be able to weld Germany into a whole and restore it to European preeminence.

While the humanists strongly supported Maximilian's Italian policy, which was the inescapable sequel to the Burgundian marriage, they did not understand that this made impossible complete victory in the east against the mounting threat from King Matthias of Bohemia and Hungary. Nor did the humanists even realize that Maximilian's forward policy in Italy would drive the imperial dynasty back into the same morass that had swallowed the Hohenstaufen. The emperor, therefore, went his way with their blessing. He married a Sforza of Milan in 1482 upon the death of his first wife, Mary, and then scooped up some Tirolian towns. These things opened Italy to him. He next allied himself with the Holy League (Milan, Venice, the pope, England, and Aragon) against the French. This raised the curtain on an Italian adventure that yielded only shattered illusions for the emperor, dissipated German energies, and blurred the national purpose.

After France in the Treaty of Senlis (1493) had lost most of the Burgundian lands (Franche Comté, Luxemburg, and the Low Countries), Charles VIII (1483–

94) sought to repair his fortunes by conquering Italy. In 1494 he advanced long dormant French claims to the Neapolitan throne and invaded the peninsula, where he swept things before him and took Naples. Eventually, however, the hostility of the Neapolitans and the emperor forced the king of France to withdraw from Italy.

Shortly afterward, French fears of Maximilian's motives brought Charles's successor Louis XII (1498–1515) into the field against the Habsburgs. The double marriage in 1496 of Maximilian's son Philip to Joanna of Castile and of the emperor's daughter Margaret to the Spanish Infante John suddenly conjured up a nightmare for the French government. It was feared in Paris that France might be caught in a vice between a Habsburg Germany and a Habsburg Spain. The Swiss cantons, whose suspicions were similar, joined Louis XII in 1499 in war against Maximilian. In this "Swiss" or Swabian War, the emperor hurled the ban of the Empire against the Swiss and revived all the old claims of dynastic suzerainty, but the latter beat the imperial armies on every battlefield, and Maximilian had to sign the unfavorable peace of Basel before the year was out. The Swiss were relieved of obligations of homage and obedience to the emperor and to imperial law. Graubünden (Grisons, Grigioni), the Gotthard pass, and Ticinese Bellinzona were secured to the Swiss Confederation, which attained de facto independence. Schaffhausen and Basel followed Graubünden into the Confederation until by 1515 it comprised thirteen freely associated cantons with different types of governments.

Maximilian's Italian policy, to which he subordinated German interests, was a fiasco. This "last knight" of a dying epoch was not strong enough to prevent the Milanese from slipping under the hand of Louis XII. The latter, laying claim to the duchy through his grandmother (Valentina Visconti), had invaded Italy in 1498, overrun Milan, taken Ludovico il Moro (Sforza) prisoner, and had himself proclaimed duke. Try as he might, Maximilian could not rid himself of the French incubus. His policy stumbled into a marsh of contradictions. In 1508 the emperor blundered into an alliance with France, England, and the papacy (League of Cambrai) to strip Venice of her territories. Then in 1511 Maximilian did a volte face and joined the Holy League, organized by Julius II (1503–13), to drive out the French (1512). When finally the Sforza family was restored to the duchy of Milan, it looked as if Maximilian's peninsular policy had at long last been vindicated. But at this juncture Louis XII died, and his successor, Francis I (1515–47), swiftly flung together another army and swooped down upon Italy again. This inaugurated four wars that absorbed the attention of the emperor for the rest of his reign. Francis inflicted a terrible defeat upon the Swiss at Marignano (1515), pricking the bubble of Austrian ascendancy over northern Italy. At Cambrai (1517) Pope Leo X (1513–22) recognized Aragonese primacy in the south of Italy and French in the north, an action that thrust into garish light the utter collapse of Maximilian's foreign policy and provoked a wave of indignation in Germany against the papacy.

In 1515 Maximilian tried to win with the aid of Venus the laurels Mars had denied him. He arranged a double marriage only slightly less portentous than his own had been with Mary of Burgundy. His granddaughter was wedded to Louis II, son of Ladislas, king of Hungary and Bohemia, while Ladislas' daughter Anna was married to Ferdinand, the emperor's grandson. When in 1526 Louis fell fighting the Turks at Mohács, Hungary, the gateway to the Balkans, fell under the claws of the double eagle.

Lord of the One-Half World

By 1519 the storm winds of Lutheranism were driving across Germany, uprooting and scattering old loyalties and obscuring the goals of national consolidation and constitutional reform. Many who saw how rapidly Lutheran doctrines were spreading believed that the Empire, simultaneously menaced by the French and Turks, would now disintegrate. Indeed, the treaties of Brussels (1522) and Worms (1525) appeared to be the prolegomenon to this ending. By these pacts all the old Austrian crown lands were awarded to Spanish-trained Ferdinand, a younger son of Philip I of Spain and Joanna, while the western accessions of the Habsburgs (Spain, Burgundy, and the Low Countries) and the imperial title were to be retained by their elder son, Charles. These treaties established the independence of Austria and in later generations disposed many people to regard it as external to Germany.

Flemish Charles (1500–58), who was nineteen when he became emperor (1519–56), had ruled over Burgundy and the Netherlands since 1506 and the Spanish Empire (as Charles I, 1516–56) since 1516. The financial backing of the Welser and Fugger bankers secured him the imperial crown in the competition with Henry VIII of England (1509–47) and Francis I of France (1515–47).

The new emperor was cosmopolitan and something of a humanist. He was far from being a religious reactionary. Unfortunately, however, Charles did not think like a German. He was too good a European for that and demonstrated it by appointing as his first lord chancellor the Italian jurist Mercurio Gattinara. When Charles addressed his first Reichstag at Worms he spoke in French. It hardly diminished the consternation of his audience, to whom he had been billed as a ruler of ''noble German blood,'' that he could just as easily have addressed them in Italian, Flemish, or Latin.

Charles and Great Power Politics

Suspicion of the dynastic ambitions of Charles V gnawed at the lashings of the Empire. Coupled with the failures of Maximilian, they help explain the success of the Reformation. The old Habsburg lust for territory manifested itself in Charles's annexations in the Low Countries, Friesland, Burgundy, and northern Italy. The operating expenditures for the vast imperial establishment were so great that they kept the emperor in constant debt and fanned popular complaint. The several wars with France over northern Italy and Burgundy transformed suspicion into widespread hostility to him. In the end, on the eve of his abdication, he was exhausted, cynical, and prematurely old—''broken with the storms of state,'' like Shakespeare's Henry VIII. It is thus that we behold Charles in Titian's third portrait of him, hanging in the Madrid Prado gallery—tired, melancholy, with shovel-chinned, sensitive face, chained to the seat of a war horse, where, against his will, he had been most of his life.

In his wars against France Charles V was motivated not so much by desire to repel French aggression and restore Milanese independence as to acquire the duchy of Burgundy and perhaps hegemony over Italy and Europe.

As a result of his meeting with Henry VIII on the famous "Field of the Cloth of Gold" in May, 1520, the emperor laid the framework of an alliance to expel the French from Italy and restore the Sforzas. To win the support of the German princes for the projected war, Charles convened the Diet of Worms (January, 1521) and gave Luther a national hearing. The Italian campaign was delayed when Suleiman the Magnificent stormed Belgrade in August, 1521, but finally got under way in 1522. The Habsburg military effort was hobbled by the changing attitudes of popes Adrian VI (1522–23) and Clement VII (1523–34), as well as by the outbreak of the German peasants' revolt. Victory over Francis I was achieved in the end only by dangling the apple of a general Church council on German soil before the princes. Francis I was captured in the Battle of Pavia (February 24, 1525), and the ensuing Treaty of Madrid (January 14, 1526) set him free only on consideration of the cession of the duchy of Burgundy to the Empire and recognition of Habsburg sovereignty over Artois and Flanders.

Between the first and second wars with France the emperor's position in Germany deteriorated. There the Catholic princes formed a league to extirpate Protestantism, and the Protestants replied in 1526 with their own Torgau-Gotha league under the leadership of the young Landgrave Philip of Hesse. In May, 1526, Francis I tore up the Treaty of Madrid, formed the League of Cognac (Florence, Venice, Clement VII, and Francesco Sforza) against the emperor, and incited the Poles, Bohemians, and Turks to fall upon the Habsburg flank. The Turks at once dealt the imperial armies a mighty blow at Mohács in August, 1526. In the fray King Louis II of Hungary fell, and Ferdinand, in keeping with the treaty of 1515, became ruler of Bohemia and Hungary, where he encountered stiff opposition from the voyvode of Siebenbürgen, John Zápolya, an ally of the Turks.

In 1529 it was not the support of Ferdinand by the Protestant princes but lack of supplies and bad weather that compelled the Turks to lift their siege of Vienna. Meanwhile, Francis I made peace with Charles V at Cambrai on August 5, 1529, leaving him in control of southern Italy and Milan in return for Burgundy. Similarly, amicable relations between Empire and papacy, which had been strained by the sack of Rome (May, 1527) by undisciplined and unpaid imperial troops, were restored. With the pope smiling and Francis I appeased, Charles V hoped to be able to reunite Germany.

All the emperor's attempts to find the amulet of conciliation in Germany failed. Instead, the anti-imperial Schmalkaldic League took shape late in 1530. This confederation was another milestone in the direction of a sovereign states system within the Empire. Purportedly organized to protect the Lutheran faith and the material interests of its members, the Schmalkaldic League banded together a number of Protestant princes and south German cities. Among its leaders were Landgrave Philip of Hesse, the Ernestine Wettin Elector John of Saxony, and Margrave George of Brandenburg.

The league offered France an unrivaled opportunity to drive a wedge into Germany. By the Treaty of Scheyern (1532) Francis I contracted with the Protestant princes to become not only *their* protector but also of those Catholic princes who, like the duke of Bavaria, feared the lengthening Habsburg shadow. Francis also tried to sick the Turks upon the emperor, but this failed because many Protestant princes still loathed the Ottoman infidel and therefore put troops under the command of Ferdinand, who in 1531 had been elected king. As a result, the Austrians were able to relieve the siege of Guns in August, 1532, and administer setbacks to the Turks in Hungary (1535), the total effect of which hardly altered the fact that most of Hungary had now fallen under Turkish sway and was to remain so for one hundred and fifty years. As for Francis, he allied with Pope Clement VII, who opposed the emperor's plan to convene a general Church council.

The death of Francesco II Sforza, last of his line, led to a third war between Francis I and Charles V. The French king signed a military pact with the Sublime Porte. Then buttressed with German Protestant, papal, and Turkish support, he attacked Milan and Savoy in 1536. The emperor was beaten all over Italy and forced to sign the adverse Treaty of Nice (June, 1538), which was a ten-year truce.

Francis exhibited his disregard for treaties by launching a fourth war within five years. The occasion for it was a deterioration of the Habsburg position in Hungary, where in 1540 the magnates had risen against Ferdinand and summoned Suleiman the Magnificent to their aid. The Turks had again stormed over the Hungarian plains and in 1541 had taken Ofen (Budapest). When Charles V and Francis I went to war in 1543 the former had the support of the Reichstag as well as England. The odds arrayed against Francis I soon persuaded him to accept the, for him, unfavorable Treaty of Créspy (September, 1544). By it Charles V was acknowledged lord of the Low Countries, Naples, and the Free County of Burgundy, while the emperor renounced the duchy of Burgundy, whose acquisition had been the grand goal of his foreign policy.

Though it appeared that the king of France was at last giving the emperor a green light to settle accounts with the Protestants, it is impossible to exaggerate the damage done to the cause of unity by the four wars between Francis I and Charles V. French diplomacy had pricked the bubble of religious reconciliation in Germany and set a fell precedent for a continuing French policy of subsidies to and alliances with German princes against the emperor. Furthermore, loss of the duchy of Burgundy deprived the Habsburgs of a glacis from which they could have resisted a French drive to the east. The only long-term gain that conceivably accrued to the Habsburgs from Créspy was the decline of French power in Italy.

Civil War

The truces with the Protestants to which Charles had time and again been driven by the Franco-Turkish combination now gave way to a resolve to smash the

Schmalkaldic League once and for all. Charles V had been inordinately patient, even though he realized that while his hands had been tied the Schmalkaldic League had been growing in strength. Since its formation in 1531 it had come to embrace almost all German towns and states that rejected Catholicism. Every important secular principality had been won over. Württemberg, Ulm, and Augsburg, moreover, had defected to the league. Only Bavaria, the Habsburg dominions extending from Silesia to Carniola, and the sees of Mainz, Würzburg, Salzburg, Constance, Bamberg, Münster, Halberstadt, and Magdeburg still held tenaciously to the Catholic cause. Furthermore, the league possessed more and better fighting men than the emperor did. Protestant forces could also be concentrated, while Charles V had difficulty gathering his from all corners of Europe.

The failure of the Diet of Regensburg (April, 1541) and the announcement of a Protestant boycott of the Church council that Pope Paul (1534–49) had convened at Trent (March 15, 1545) decided Charles V to impose religious unity upon the Empire. Philip of Hesse and John Frederick of Saxony were put under the ban, but this only provoked them to rebel. In the ensuing Schmalkaldic War of 1546–47 Charles counted on divisions in the enemy camp. He knew that John Frederick and Philip could not cooperate, whereas he himself had just arranged a state marriage that had ended the rift between Wittelsbach and Habsburg. In addition, Charles had bribed Duke Maurice of Albertine Saxony to remain neutral in return for the electoral title that was then held by the Ernestine Wettins.

Allegedly Charles pursued dynastic aims in connection with the civil war, but the truth is that for once they rose above personal purposes. He fought for the restoration of the unity of the German Church and the maintenance of the German constitution in face of rebellion. Charles V was the last paladin of Christian solidarity and the last to aspire to exercise a European magistracy. Unfortunately, he had little understanding of the fact that the fight was, from the German standpoint, one against foreign servitude.

What advantages the Protestants had they managed to fling away in the first months of the war. Thereafter, military reverses robbed them of further financial support from urban money-lenders. Before long, Spanish troops carried the war into the Protestant camp, and on April 24, 1547, Charles's general, the duke of Alva, in a daring attack on the field of Mühlberg on the Elbe, inflicted a major defeat on the Schmalkaldic League. Elector John Frederick was taken prisoner. His lands were confiscated, and the electoral dignity was transferred to Duke Maurice of Saxony. A month later Philip of Hesse threw himself upon the emperor's mercy.

The Augsburg Interim

Charles V now stood at the summit of his power. Yet he was lenient toward the foe, who, after all, was German. Perhaps, too, suspension of the Council of Trent by Pope Paul III made Charles realize that the final reform decrees were still distant and that in the meantime he could not hope to impose a religious settlement upon Germany. Never doctrinaire and always willing to revoke ill-considered measures, the victorious Charles V pursued a pragmatic course at the Diet of Augsburg in 1547–48. Although he completely dominated it, he played pianissimo. He persuaded the Protestants to accept the compromise religious formula known as the Augsburg Interim. This instrument, which was predominantly Catholic in tone, made some surprising concessions, including communion with both bread and wine, justification by faith, and conditional marriage of priests. By omitting to mention secularized Church lands, the Interim made another overture to the Lutherans. In a codicil the emperor also promised the princes to suppress annates, cumulation of benefices, and simony and to insure that Church reforms would be carried out in a national synod.

A roar arose in Germany over the Augsburg Interim, but the protest was not universal. The followers of Philip Melanchthon and other moderate German Lutherans, such as Camerarius of Bavaria, Bugenhagen, and Major of Wittenberg, were not so sure that the Interim was not a step in the right direction. The conciliatory Melanchthon was just then rejoicing in his liberation from "truly odious slavery" to Luther, who had died in 1546. Melanchthon helped draft an additional, mildly Lutheran document that received the endorsement of the Diet of Leipzig in 1548. The Leipzig Interim was approved by the elector of Saxony, the margrave of Brandenburg, and the pope.

Although the Augsburg and Leipzig interims were the law of the land, there was hardly a principality or city in north Germany that did not, mainly out of territorial interests, flout them openly. Irreconcilable firebrands as Bishop Nicholaus Amsdorf of Naumberg and the young Vlachich (Flacius Illyricus) of Wittenberg hurled bombs of wrath at the "traitor" Melanchthon. They stung the Lutherans to defy Charles V.

Toward "Canossa"

From the pinnacle of power at Mühlberg, the emperor's fortunes declined. He was embarrassed by quarrels with his brother Ferdinand over the succession, with Maurice of Saxony, with Pope Paul III over suspension of the Council of Trent, and with Julius III (1550–55) over the dominant role of Catholic extremists in the council when it reconvened in March, 1551. Charles was also handicapped by the secret alliance of Chambord (or Friedwald), which Henry II of France (1547–59) had contracted with the Protestant princes in January, 1552, making him a "vicar of the Empire" for Toul, Verdun, and Metz in Lorraine.

For many months Charles V was unaware of the trap his enemies were laying. When in March, 1552, Henry II suddenly attacked Cambrai and the Lorraine towns, the emperor was caught off guard. Everywhere his armies were forced to retreat. The renegade Maurice of Saxony drove deep into south Germany and took Augsburg and Innsbruck. Ferdinand of Austria was strangely inactive during the crisis, possibly because the Turks, encouraged by the French, were again on the offensive.

For Charles V nothing halted the march of disaster. In the end, he and Ferdinand were compelled to accept the humiliating Peace of Passau (August 2, 1552), which annulled both the Augsburg and Leipzig interims. The signatories pledged permanent internal peace, promised settlement of the religious controversy by a diet to be called within six months (which never met), and left the secularized Church properties in the hands of their expropriators.

The Religious Peace of Augsburg

After Passau Charles V passed forever out of the ill-starred German orbit. Leaving Maurice of Saxony and Ferdinand, now allies, to stem the Turks, he laid siege to Metz, failed there, drew into a shell, and renounced all his crowns. He retired, a broken man, to a monastery in Estremadura, where he died in 1558. His bequest of strife was the marriage between his son Philip II of Spain (1556–98) and Mary Tudor of England.

Meanwhile Ferdinand finally opened the Diet of Augsburg on February 5, 1555. From its deliberations issued the Act of Religious Pacification the same year. The Peace of Augsburg was not so much a triumph of Lutheranism over Catholicism as of the princes in the long struggle against the emperors.

The aim of the Peace of Augsburg was not individual but territorial religious freedom in keeping with the principle *cuius regio, eius religio* ("he who rules determines the religion of the state"). The parity of Catholicism and Lutheranism within the Empire was recognized, but Calvinists, Zwinglians, and Anabaptists were banned. The declining power of the towns was illustrated by their treaty obligation to accord freedom of worship within their walls to both Lutherans and Catholics. Although the act was ambiguous as to the rights of princes to secularize bishoprics and abbeys, it affirmed that such secularization of ecclesiastical property as had occurred prior to 1552 was irrevocable. The Habsburgs' one important victory was the famous "ecclesiastical reservation." This stipulated for prelates who had secularized their lands deprivation of all clerical and temporal dignities, privileges, lands, prebends and emoluments; and, in respect of episcopal vacancies created, it authorized new elections. By withholding property and income, the ecclesiastical reservation removed the main motives for the wholesale apostasy of prelates and insured the long-term survival of the ecclesiastical states and, consequently, of the Empire itself.

Importance of the Habsburg Failure

Charles V succeeded only in demonstrating the impracticality of trying to maintain the critical mass of his colossal empire. He had toiled in vain to achieve many goals: smash French aggression in Italy; regain Burgundy; reestablish imperial dominion over Lombardy; reorganize Germany; hold Austria, Hungary, Bohemia, Spain, and the Low Countries in the same span; repel the Turks; block French acquisition of Metz, Toul, and Verdun; convene a general Church council on German soil; impose compromise upon the Protestants; and force the Reichstag to acknowledge the supremacy of the crown. In the completeness of his failure

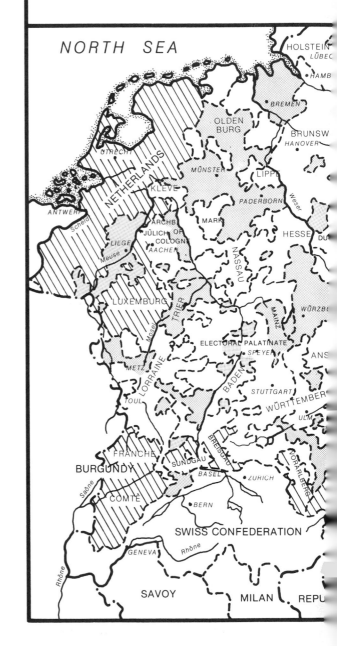

GERMA

—·— BOUNDARY OF THE HOLY ROMAN EMPIR

— — — BOUNDARY OF THE STATES OF THE EMP

NORTH SEA

HOLSTEIN
LÜBEC
•*HAMB*
•*BREMEN*
OLDEN
BURG
BRUNSW
HANOVER
LIPP
MÜNSTER
PADERBORN
Weser
UTRECHT
NETHERLANDS
KLEVE
MARK
HESSE
DU
NASSAU
ARCHB
JÜLICH OF
COLOGN
AACHEN
LIEGE
Scheld
ANTWER
Meuse
LUXEMBURG
TRIER
WÜRZB
MAINZ
Mosel
ELECTORAL PALATINATE
•*SPEYE*
ANS
METZ
LORRAINE
BADEN
STUTTGART
WÜRTTEMBER
TOUL
ULM
FRANCHE
BREISG
VORARLBERG
BURGUNDY
SUNDGAU
BASEL
•*ZURICH*
COMTÉ
Saône
•*BERN*
SWISS CONFEDERATION
Rhône
GENEVA
Rhône
Rhône
SAVOY
MILAN
REPU

N 1547

⧄	HAPSBURG TERRITORIES
▨	ECCLESIASTICAL PRINCIPALITIES

BALTIC SEA

PRUSSIA

Vistula

POMERANIA

STETTIN

NBURG

Netze

ELECTORATE OF
BRANDENBURG

POLAND

• BERLIN

POSEN •

Warthe

ELECTORATE

Oder

PZIG

OF

• *BRESLAU*

• *DRESDEN*

SILESIA

SAXONY

PRAGUE •

PER

BOHEMIA

G

MORAVIA

NATE

EGENSBURG

VARIA

Inn

Danube

VIENNA •

AUSTRIA

• *SALZBURG*

STYRIA

GRAZ

CARINTHIA

20   100 MILES

CARNIOLA

0   40

E

VENICE

he recalls Conrad III. Nevertheless, it must be admitted that the purposes of Charles V had, in the main, been exalted, and the honorable and sincere pattern of his behavior had not been in disharmony with them. Europe was not to see his like again.

Upon the breakup of Charles's empire, his son Philip was given the Netherlands, Sicily, and Spain, while in 1558 Charles's brother Ferdinand became emperor.

As a consequence of the division, the kings of Germany were again given an opportunity to devote themselves to Central European tasks. The fears of German princes that their interests would be perpetually subordinated to Spanish imperial ambitions were banished. The political center of gravity within the Empire now shifted once more to the east, with Bohemia the hub of the emperor's grand policy as in the days of Charles IV. Having shortened his lines, Ferdinand could now snap his fingers at threats of secession. All was by no means lost. From the chaos of thought and passion at least the structural unity of the Holy Empire, though enfeebled, had been saved.

Chapter 13

WINDS OF REVOLUTION:

THE AGE OF LUTHER

Causes of the Reformation

In a sense, all German medieval history was the prolegomenon to the Reformation, and the temptation exists to accept every kind of popular unrest as a contributing cause. While historians continue to differ as to emphasis, they now at least agree on two obvious points: no one cause, be it clerical corruption or the rise of capitalism, can be stressed to the exclusion of others; and, except for the impact of many nonreligious forces upon the German mind, there would have been no Protestant upheaval.

Of major importance in explaining the break with Rome was a complex of political factors. The rise of strong national monarchies elsewhere in Europe had left Germany the only ring, except for Italy, where government was pluralistic and the people had no shield against the extortions of prelates or popes. Also, territorial rulers of Germany coveted the lands and revenues of the high clergy and aimed at absolute control of the Church by the state. The drive for territorial sovereignty involved the princes in an offensive against the papacy no less than against the emperor. In that compaign, which was basically directed against external controls of any kind, a rising German national consciousness brought the princes welcome support. Their campaign against Charles V derived added force from the facts that he was a foreigner, most of his advisers were aliens, and that he strove for reforms the attainment of which would reverse the drift toward territorial sovereignty. Beyond these things, the nobility was gravely divided on religious policy, while differences between emperor and pope paralyzed the Catholic defense. As for the cities, they were dissatisfied with their lowly role in the Reichstag and had embarked upon a struggle for full equality with the electors and the princes.

Emerging capitalism did its bit to undermine the immemorial foundations of the Church. Corporative Christian values were rapidly giving way to aggressive, capitalistic drives. The landed nobles were put at a disadvantage by the rise of a money economy and the steady shift of wealth from agriculture to commerce. As a result, they were obliged to turn the screws tighter upon their peasants to keep up with the affluent bourgeoisie.

The whole fifteenth century had been one of prolonged depression and hardship for the lower classes. The emergence of a capitalist economy, discovery of gold and silver mines in America, imports of bullion, and the resulting inflation of the European price structure had all entailed a sharp rise in the cost of living for the toilers. As a result, the class conflict everywhere intensified. This was especially so in the south German Renaissance cities, where, as Peter Eitel has shown, the essentials of political power continued to be in the hands of the mercantile and financial patricians. At the same time, another conflict developed between free enterprise and monopoly. The ramifying interests of such grand financiers as the Paumgartner, Welser, Höchstetter, Gossenbrot, Herwart, and Fugger, whose capital far surpassed that of the older Ravensburg Trading Society of Lake Constance, gave them incomparable advantages over the guild masters. All urban and rural classes united in denouncing the monopolists as a main factor in the spiraling cost of living.

A significant social cause of the Reformation was the insecurity of the imperial knights. The economic basis of chivalry had vanished, and the flower of knighthood had lost its petals. Changes in weaponry had again put infantry in the commanding position from which it had been dislodged in Carolingian times by cavalry and that had destroyed the prestige of the knights. The advent of artillery, too, which could be fired by common soldiers, further reduced the knights' importance. When they could not take service in the officers' corps of a prince, they had to seek solvency in the mortgage or sale of their estates. Those who managed to hang on to their tiny holdings during the long agricultural depression often lived in penury and were ripe for every kind of conspiracy and brigandage. Robber barons, such as Franz von Sickingen or Götz von Berlichingen, attacked towns and sometimes sacked them. In their frenzied resistance to the economic revolution the imperial knights occasionally posed as champions of the oppressed peasantry but actually were no more capable of implementing the reform program of another class than of formulating one of their own. Rather, like the spindrift of turbulent waves, the knights were blown with stinging force by winds they were powerless to control.

To these heaps of tinder add the spark of peasant unrest. By 1500 peasant initiative, sapped by economic distress, was exhausted. It registered no further grand achievements on the scale of the colonization of Trans-Elbea. The peasants now resisted change and sought to husband the little they had. They extolled the virtues of a dying order, championed traditional rights, and battled all attempts to increase the fees, renders, and services for which they were liable. Occasionally they forcibly resisted efforts of the aristocracy to raise ground rents, taxes, death dues, emigration fees, tithes, and crop taxes. They denounced infringements upon their domiciliary immunities, and all restrictions on freedom of movement, marriage, and the use of common woodland, pasture, and meadow. The peasants of Baden, Württemberg, and the Rhineland, who farmed unduly small farms, and those of Thuringia and Franconia were particularly vociferous in their complaints. This was so despite the fact that they were far better off than the serfs on the great Junker estates of the east; furthermore, the rulers of the small western states were weak.

The great Peasants' Rebellion of 1524–25 was preceded by seventy-five years of agricultural depression and social vulcanism. In 1458, 1462, 1476, 1478, and 1500–1502 peasant uprisings occurred in various parts of Germany. An extremely contagious and violently destructive movement, the Bundschuh, which originated in Alsace and Baden and flaunted a blue and white flag with half-laced peasant's shoe, caused the lords to tremble. After years of rumbling, the Bundschuh under

Joss Fritz erupted in bloody class war in 1517. However, the Bundschuh and the similar Poor Conrad (Armer Konrad) uprisings were ruthlessly suppressed and their leaders beheaded.

Theological differences were not an important cause of the Reformation. Doctrinal subtleties were lost upon the unlettered masses, who accepted unorthodox dogma only where it reinforced some social, economic, political, or moral complaint.

Too much stress has been put upon the Reformation as a reaction against the impiety and corruption of the clergy. The fact is that for three generations prior to 1517 there had been progressive improvement in the probity and morals of the lesser clergy. The reform, so fervently propagandized by foes of the Church, had already commenced.

More important than doctrine or clerical morals was the weakness of the papacy. During the fourteenth and fifteenth centuries a thousand things had tarnished its image and obscured the ideals for which it stood. Not least of its mistakes had been involvement in the cesspool of Italian politics and tacit acquiescence in finance capitalist practices and ethics. The vast revenues of the Holy See and the profligacy with which Renaissance popes dispensed their favors had encouraged venality and corruption in high ecclesiastical office. Simony, nepotism, pluralism of sees, and scandalously high annates, contributions, and ecclesiastical fees had undermined the prestige of the episcopacy and conjured up in the poor German's mind a sinfulness that suggested rather the kingdom of Lucifer than of God.

Mysticism heightened the emotional overtones of the gravamina of the German nation against papal injustice. Although no longer as luxuriant a growth as in the early fifteenth century, mysticism continued to have a certain appeal to people who deplored the materialism of the prelates and dreaded the loss of personal salvation. The movement produced no more figures of the stature of Tauler, Eckhart, Suso, Kempis, or even John of Wesel (Johannes Ruchrath, d. about 1481), but, as practiced by the Brethren of the Common Life, it still represented a vital way of life. The schools of this order, dotting the Netherlands, north Germany, and the Rhineland, disseminated a teaching known as the "new devotion" *(devotio moderna),* which stressed faith, direct communion between the believer and God, and the supremacy of the divine word as revealed in the Bible.

It is worth mentioning, too, that the natural contempt of most clergymen for sin was intensified by the conviction, so eloquently expressed by John of Wesel, that it was mainly committed by the upper clergy, whose incomes were one hundred to a thousand times that of priests. Instinctively the impoverished lower clergy sympathized with the reformers.

Intellectual Causes

A tiny coterie of academic reformers, called "Christian humanists," aspired to a scientific restoration of the texts of the Bible. Their aim was thereby to combat error in the Church and the long tyranny which the *devotio antiqua* had exercised over theology. All of them hoped by humanizing religion to make of it something more than a cult of amulets, statues, and sacraments to which, in their opinion, the ignorance of the masses had reduced it. In long and bitter struggle against the old guard the humanistic *devotio moderna,* which aspired to conquer the Church from within, captured academic chairs at the universities of Heidelberg, Vienna, Erfurt (est. 1392), Basel (est. 1460), Ingolstadt (est. 1472), Tübingen (est. 1477), Wittenberg (est. 1502), and Frankfurt am Oder (est. 1506). Nevertheless, their successes were almost wholly confined to the schools, for the humanists, whose language was classical, were without a mass following.

Among the most celebrated German humanists were Rudolf Agricola (1443–85) of Heidelberg, who was hailed as the "educator of Germany" and who influenced Philipp Melanchthon; Conrad Celtis (1459–1508) of Ingolstadt and Vienna, whose geographical treatise *Germania illustrata* fanned fires of nationalism; Konrad Muth or Mutianus Rufus (1471–1526), who had studied humanism in Italy; Jakob Wimpheling (1450–1528), who spread the new learning through the Rhine Valley from Strassburg; the aristocratic and passionately patriotic Ulrich von Hutten (1488–1523), one of the few Germans who knew Greek, who had translated Lorenzo da Valla's epochal "Forged Donation of Constantine" and attacked the papacy; Willibald Pirckheimer (1470–1530), the Nuremberg burgher who, by reason of his broad interests and versatility, qualified as a German *uomo universale;* and, most important of all, the Swabian "transalpine Greek," Johannes Reuchlin (1455–1522), and the Dutch "prince of humanists," Desiderius Erasmus of Rotterdam (1466?–1536). Reuchlin, who had acquired a greater knowledge of ancient Greek and Hebrew than any German before his time, was a caustic critic of the *via antiqua* and a defender of the value of the Talmud, Kabbala, and other Judaic scriptures against obscurantists, such as those of the University of Cologne, who preferred to see them burned. Erasmus, a doctor of theology from Paris and a true "citizen of the world," was conceptually an eclectic nominalist who skirted the brink of heresy. His chief contributions to the Reformation were his questioning attitude toward authority, which encouraged the masses to disrespect the hierarchy, and a scrupulously annotated edition of the New Testament in Greek with a Latin translation (1516), which was to be the basis of Luther's German version.

The Emergence of the Leader

Martin Luther (1483–1546) was destined temporarily to concentrate all the chaotic forces of national revolt. The most successful heretic in a millennium and one of the three or four most-written-about personages of all time, Luther was a charismatic leader with a sense of divine mission. Yet he had no political instinct, which explains his failure to realize the national dream and impart to Germany either independence or unity of any kind. Endowed with abundant energy, unflagging zeal, lucid intellect, and the courage of martyrs, Luther was also overbearing, intolerant of error in others, and capable of uncontrollable fits of temper and vituperation. Able to synthesize the most dynamic ideas of the recent past, he inspired plain people with a new appreciation for the dignity of the Christian individual and revealed to them, through the formula *sola fides* (''faith alone''), an uncomplicated road to salvation.

Martin Luther was born in Eisleben, Thuringia, on November 10, 1483. Although his ancestors had been of lowly peasant stock, his frugal father had risen to become an entrepreneur with interests in a number of smelting and mining firms. Martin went to school at Magdeburg, where he fell under the influence of the Brethren of the Common Life. Later, at the University of Erfurt, a bastion of the *via moderna,* he received a thorough training in Latin and formed the Occamist conviction that the truths of religion are not susceptible of rational demonstration but must be accepted on faith. In 1505 Luther was awarded the master's degree. He was about to enter a school of law when in the midst of a terrifying lightning storm on the high road from Mansfeld to Erfurt he experienced his ''Damascus'' (July 2, 1505). He vowed to enter a monastery if only he were spared. He honored his oath by becoming a novice in the Erfurt house of the Observantine Eremites of St. Augustine. In 1507 Luther was ordained and celebrated his first Mass. In 1510 he was sent on a mission to Rome, where he contemplated with revulsion the sloth and splendor of the Eternal City under the mighty Julius II. Back in Germany again, Luther was appointed sub-prior of his order's Wittenberg house in 1511, received his doctorate in theology in 1512, and from 1513–16 lectured on theology and the Bible at the University of Wittenberg.

During these years he hammered out his basic views on salvation, which were to lead to his apostasy from the Church. In contrast to the older Catholic scholarship (Heinrich Denifle), which discovered the explanation of Luther's doctrines in grave character defects, in the moral turpitude and failures of the Wittenberg theologian, modern Catholic historians such as Joseph Lortz have sought the answer in Luther's alleged psychological abnormalities. This perspective has found no support among twentieth-century Protestant students of the Reformation (Ernest Rupp, Karl Holl, Roland H. Bainton, and Gerhard Ritter). Both Holl and Ritter placed much stress upon the novel ethical content of Luther's thinking, and Ritter believed that the key to his ethics was submission to the supremacy of the law of a merciful God.

Obsessed with a haunting fear that he was damned because of his carnal sins, Luther groped along all the galleries of religion for solace. He prayed often, followed an austere rule, took frequent communion, performed severe penance, indulged charity, and plugged up all the chinks in the armor of his faith, while waiting all the while for an apocalyptic sign. At length he came to dwell less upon the utter inability of man through good works and sacraments to achieve salvation and focused upon the sufficient mercy of God. In Saints Augustine and Paul he discovered the ''true light'': man was justified not by the law or by charity but by faith alone in the redemptive sacrifice of Christ. The fruits of Luther's travail by candlelight were revealed to the students of Wittenberg and the burghers in masterly lectures and sermons. The effect of the exalted pietism he preached was enhanced by his strictures against Rome and his pleas for reform of a corrupt Church.

Luther Throws Down the Gauntlet

It was a little thing that sent the magma of revolution hurtling out of the German crater. In 1517 into the tiny world of the Augustinian preacher came the Dominican prior Johannes Tetzel to peddle plenary indulgences for the remission of temporal or purgatorial punishment *(pena)* exacted for sins *(culpa)*. Julius II and Leo X had authorized preachment of this indulgence to obtain funds for the reconstruction of St. Peter's Cathedral in Rome and (secretly) to defray the huge indebtedness of Albert von Hohenzollern to the House of Fugger, which had financed his purchase of a dispensation that had permitted him before canonical age (he was only twenty-three) to become archbishop of Mainz and Brandenburg and bishop of Halberstadt. The vexed Luther did not know of the triangular bargain among Albert of Brandenburg, the Fuggers, and the pope, but, in any case, the whole theory of indulgences was offensive to him.

Luther's reply to Tetzel was to nail ninety-five theses to the church door in Wittenberg on October 31, 1517. Couched in Latin and unintelligible to the masses, the theses attacked only indulgences. Luther had no intention of fomenting rebellion against Church or papacy but was merely pressing for reforms long promised but still unfulfilled. Nevertheless, the attempt to limit the prerogatives of the pope in the matter of indulgences and the asseveration that the contrite sinner should seek forgiveness without expecting remission of punishment provoked hot denunciation. In a little while a German translation of the theses appeared that sorely disturbed the people and heightened the anger of the old guard.

When Luther had his popular *Sermon on Indulgence and Grace* printed, he set foot upon a road of no return. In the dispute this tract occasioned, most of the people of Wittenberg and a number of theologians—Martin Bucer (Butzer) of Alsace, Philipp Melanchthon, and Andrew Bodenstein (Carlstadt)—endorsed his views. When Pope Leo X summoned Martin Luther on August 7, 1518, to appear before the Holy Curia within sixty days, Luther appealed for protection to Duke Frederick, the wise elector of Saxony. Therewith the sluice gates were opened, and Luther's bridge of retreat was swept away.

The Break with Rome

Inasmuch as Leo X wanted to avoid any act that might antagonize Frederick the Wise, who was one of his last remaining supporters in central Europe, the pope had to agree that Luther merely be summoned before the Diet of Augsburg for interrogation by the papal legate, Cardinal Tommaso Cajetan. The gentle Thomist Cajetan toiled at Augsburg in October, 1518, to convince Luther, but he would not budge. Basically concerned with the question of salvation rather than reform, Luther insisted upon justification by faith alone, affirmed that popes could err, that some papal bulls were false, and appealed to the Bible as alone infallible.

While Leo X (1513–21) was postponing action against Luther, Carlstadt, his colleague at Wittenberg, had in 1519 been defeated in debate at Leipzig by John Eck, a cunning professor of theology at Catholic Ingolstadt. Luther had been obliged to take up the cudgels against Eck, but the Wittenberg champion had been maneuvered by his adversary into a canonically untenable and in some ways heretical position.

From the papal standpoint, the Leipzig disputations were a calamity. They focused popular attention upon Luther as the advocate of a whole range of national and special interests. Before the year was out he was joined by the humanists Crotus Rubeanus and Willibald Pirckheimer, the nationalist Ulrich von Hutten, guildmaster Hans Sachs, artist Albert Dürer, and imperial knight Franz von Sickingen. Above all, Frederick the Wise befriended Luther, but even the Czechs were urging him to unfurl the banner of Hus.

Events now rushed to a climax. On June 15, 1520, the pope anathematized Luther in the bull *Exsurge domine* (''Arise, O Lord''), giving him sixty days in which to recant or be excommunicated. Luther, meanwhile, had written a revolutionary tract, *An Open Letter to the Christian Nobility of the German Nation,* which was to be the cornerstone of the Evangelical Church. In this disquisition Luther for the first time attacked clerical celibacy, sanctioned the marriage of religious, affirmed the ''priesthood of all believers,'' denounced the pope as anti-Christ, and trumpeted the German people forth to rise up under Charles V or, failing him, their princes.

In August, 1520, Luther in a Latin tract, the *Babylonian Captivity of the Church,* rejected five of the seven sacraments. He was prepared to retain only baptism and the Holy Eucharist, for which he believed there was scriptural authority. He rejected the doctrine of transubstantiation and the sacrificial nature of the Mass. In November Luther answered the papal bull in a third great pamphlet, *On the Freedom of a Christian Man*. Appearing in Latin and German, it contained such dynamite as: ''A Christian individual is a free man and . . . is subject to none.'' Luther held that faith alone made men free, and that while good works will not save him, a free man will naturally follow God's law and indulge charity. In December, Luther, still an emaciated monk consumed by a fire that raged within him and not yet the bull-necked, phlegmatic apparition of Cranach's portrait, burned the bull *Exsurge domine* on the church square at Wittenberg before an applauding crowd. Leo X countered in January, 1521, by excommunicating him.

The Edict of Worms

Anxious to banish the terrible tension that gripped Germany, young Charles V gave Luther another chance. He was summoned to appear before the papal nuncio and the estates at the Reichstag of Worms, which had opened in January, 1521. With an imperial safe conduct, Luther went to Worms, acclaimed all along the route by a delirious public. On April 17 he stood for questioning by the nuncio Cardinal Jerome Aleander at the diet. Throughout the interrogation Luther insisted that he would recant his theses only if by reference to the Bible they were proved to be in error. Since this posited the abject error of all the doctors of the Church, ecumenical councils, and popes, many delegates were scandalized. The emperor felt no sympathy for the professor, who seemed to have no scruples about plunging Germany into civil war. Luther concluded his defense by drawing himself up proudly and declaring: "I cannot and I will not recant anything, for it is neither safe nor right to ignore one's conscience. So help me, God! Amen."

After Luther departed, the diet dissolved. On May 26 Charles V issued the Edict of Worms, which castigated Luther as being far worse than Hus and put the Wittenberger under ban of the Empire. However, Luther was already out of harm's way, for he had been conducted by Duke Frederick's agents to the castle of Wartburg near Eisenach.

The Wartburg "Idyll'

Disguised as an imperial knight called George, a bearded Luther with a thick crop of hair on his previously tonsured head dwelt for many months in the storybook castle in the Thuringian forest. He experienced difficult months. Ill with bleeding hemorrhoids and unable to sleep nights, Luther became depressed and uncertain as to whether he had not sinned in rejecting martyrdom. At times he imagined the devil was his roommate.

Meanwhile Carlstadt had written a treatise slandering monks and nuns who refused to marry and have children. Even Luther pretended to be ruffled. "Good God," he wrote, "our Wittenbergers will give wives even to the monks! But they will not thrust a wife on me!"* Basically, however, Luther sympathized with Carlstadt. Luther's tract *On Monastic Vows,* written at this time, condemned the cloistered life and had the effect that within two years every monk in the Augustinian house at Wittenberg, save the prior, left it, many to marry. In November, 1521, still at Wartburg, Luther wrote *On the Abrogation of the Private Mass,* in which he advocated giving the cup to the laity and rejected the teaching that the Holy Ghost had ordained a mediatory priesthood which, by administering the sacraments, could help the faithful to salvation. In this tract he formulated the doctrine of consubstantiation.** Luther next collected his Wittenberg sermons and published them as the *Kirchenpostille*. It strengthened the argument that there was no essential difference between layman and priest, except as to function, and it greatly influenced all Protestant thought. Luther said that a minister was simply to preach the Gospel. This was a new idea in the history of Christianity.

Luther's greatest achievement at Wartburg was his translation of Erasmus' edition of the New Testament into polished Saxon German. Prefaced by a scathing philippic against the papacy, this monumental version, completed in 1522, was

---

*James Mackinnon, *Luther and the Reformation* (New York and London, 1929), III, 20.

**Consubstantiation, while insisting that the body and blood of Christ are really present among the sacramental elements, denies that communion is an essential wellspring of divine grace. It maintains that sharing the Lord's Supper is simply an outward sign of the believer's faith in God's promise to forgive contrite sinners.

not only a major contribution to Protestant evangelism but a milestone in the evolution of the German language. After Luther, the Saxon dialect eventually became the vehicle for all higher forms of expression in German.

The Champion in the Lists Again

Back in Wittenberg "reforms" were proceeding at a frantic tempo under direction of the radicals (Carlstadt, Amsdorf, Zwilling, Jonas, and Stübner). Marriage of monks and nuns and the grant of the cup to the laity were only the beginning. Next, altars were removed from Churches and chapels, and riotous mobs, in the worst iconoclastic outburst since the eighth century, slashed religious pictures and demolished statues in the churches. Even wilder radicals from Zwickau, Saxony, popularly dubbed the "Zwickau Prophets," led by Thomas Münzer, were roving the countryside preaching that they alone were divinely enlightened and that all churches, being institutions of the devil, must be abolished. They understood by Luther's "priesthood of all believers" the right of every believer to interpret the Bible according to his own conscience.

Early in 1522 Frederick the Wise became alarmed. He at last saw that the gust of reform of 1519 had become a gale. Aware that as yet only a small minority of princes had apostasized, he condemned the Wittenburg "reforms." Fearful lest his electoral title be transferred by an angry emperor to Duke George of Saxony, Frederick ordered, much too late, the restoration of Catholicism in his duchy.

On urgent appeal from the gentler and more moderate Philipp Melanchthon (1497–1560), the humanist scholar and author of the *Loci Communes* [Commonplaces] (1521), which was almost a systematic Lutheran encyclopedia, Luther now repudiated some of his most disturbing utterances. In the *Faithful Exhortation to all Christians to Guard against Revolt* and *On Civil Authority* he now advised respect for secular authority and censured social revolution, affirming the competence of lay government over the bodies, property, and external relations of all subjects. These tracts of 1522 sounded the knell of social radicalism in Lutheranism and were the requiem of both unified Protestantism and an all-German purpose. The radical pietists abandoned Luther now, and the disheartening process of reduction-division set in among the defectors from Rome.

When Luther returned to Wittenberg in 1522 it was to chastise his foes on the right and left and to build an independent church. Polemics, treatises, correspondence, and pronunciamentos poured from the great man's pen. To the years 1522–24 belong his *Against the Falsely Designated Spiritual Estate of Pope and Bishops* and a revised edition (with Melanchthon's aid) of the New Testament. In the spring of 1523 he issued the *Reformed Service of the Mass,* which urged congregations to form spiritually democratic fellowships and hold divine services without regard for priests or prelates.

To the Four Winds

On the wings of the press and the vernacular, Lutheran teachings raced across Germany, Switzerland, Bohemia, and Hungary and within a decade had come to

penetrate every corner of Europe. Luther soon won over a majority of the Augustinian and Franciscan monks and many religious from all orders. He attracted some
of the princes, especially in Hesse and eastern Westphalia, but it was in the cities
that he reaped his biggest harvest. The message of reform travelled over the trade
routes and found a ready car with the restive artisans and bourgeoisie.

The conquest was not always easy. Brandenburg was interdicted to Lutheranism
by Joachim I (1499–1535), and the margraviate was only cautiously opened to
the new teachings after the accession of Joachim II (1535–71). In Westphalia the
fight was protracted and the Lutheran victory incomplete. The greater part of the
area was firmly in the hands of ecclesiastical princes. In Osnabrück, Paderborn,
Münster, and Minden the struggle was punctuated by uprisings, suppressions, and
executions.

Lutheran teachings made very rapid progress in many areas, especially in
Strassburg, Ulm, Magdeburg, Schwäbisch-Hall, Göttingen, Frankfurt am Main,
Heidelberg, Kassel, Darmstadt, Hamburg, and Bremen. East of the Vistula in
1523 the Hohenzollern grand master of the Teutonic Order introduced Lutheranism into East Prussia with a view to transforming (1525) his possessions into an
hereditary ducal fief, which he henceforth held from the king of Poland.

The same abuses existed in the Austrian crown lands as were found in the Rhine
Valley or Saxony. Therefore, Luther's writings found favor in Linz, Vienna,
Salzburg, Innsbruck, the Tirol, and in all Lower Austria. Furthermore, by 1525
Christian socialist doctrines, too, had taken root in Austria. Preached by Balthasar
Hübmaier, the knight errant of south German Anabaptism, they found a reception
with all those who condemned the exploitation of the toiling masses.

The sheer magnitude and diversity of the reform movement, representing the
complaints of all but the richest economic strata, made it a dangerous thing to
suppress. Franz von Sickingen and the imperial knights demonstrated the explosive democratic potentialities of the movement when in 1523 they expropriated
Church lands and plundered several towns in northwestern Germany. The maraud-
ers were finally trapped in Sickingen's castle at Landstuhl by the electors of Trier
and the Palatinate and the armed forces of the Swabian League. Sickingen was
slain and Ulrich von Hutten, his confederate, forced to flee to Switzerland. Thereafter the knights were finished as a factor in German politics, and the peasants
were deprived of their military support.

In view of the dimensions and savage zeal of the reforming movement, it is
no wonder that the German *Stände* drew back in dismay from a determined enforcement of the Edict of Worms. The decision of the diet of Nuremberg (1524) to do
nothing to suppress Lutheranism gave it new impetus and adumbrated victory for
Protestantism in many parts of Europe.

Lutheranism's Deeper Failure

Too strong to be suppressed, Lutheranism nonetheless was unable to galvanize
Germany into a new unity. It had not occurred to Luther that his doctrines of free-

dom of the Christian man and priesthood of all believers might lead to sectarianism. The Lutheran interpretation of the Bible encountered powerful critics in south Germany and Switzerland: Martin Butzer of Strassburg, Ulrich Zwingli in Zurich, and Johannes Oecolampadius in Basel. Similarly, Luther failed to win over the sacramentarian and humanist eclectics or to stem the defection of the radical Anabaptists from the main reform movement. On the other hand, Catholic princes, including the duke of Bavaria, were beginning to band together under Archduke Ferdinand of Habsburg, who after 1524 (Regensburg Reichstag) was resolved to prevent establishment of an independent church. The Lutheran movement, unable to retain the united loyalties of all reformers, opposed by an organization of Catholic princes led by the formidable Habsburg dynasty, and shortly to be forsaken by thousands of embittered peasants, ceased by 1525 to be an all-German cause. The reasons for this are many, but high on the list was Luther's inability to sit on two stools at once—the masses and the princes. His efforts to do so only alienated elements of both.

Renaissance Culture

Germany's brief Renaissance was in almost all respects inferior to that of Italy. Lacking the Italian genius, a numerous leisure class that could have indulged munificent patronage, and distracted by religious controversy, almost all of Germany's output in literature and fine arts were to those of Italy as grape juice compared with wine.

Strictly speaking, Germany produced no original secular literature in this period. We may merely note in passing *The Ship of Fools (Narrenschiff, 1494)* of Sebastian Brandt (1457?–1521) and the *Conspiracy of Fools (Narrenbeschwörung, 1512)* and *The Great Lutheran Fool (Von dem grossen Lutherischen Narren, 1522)* of Thomas Murner (1475–1537), which were all humorous satires. Of some importance was Conrad Celtis' edition of the plays of the medieval nun Roswitha. However, for the most part, German humanists, such as Jacob Wimpheling, Ulrich von Hutten, Heinrich Steinhöwel, Patrus Litichius, and Albert von Eyb, scribbled stilted, imitative poems in Latin or Greek, translated foreign works, or wrote treatises for a rarified intelligentsia. In any case, literature was but an oxbow of the main stream, which in Germany was religious and nationalist.

In the plastic arts and painting Germany made significant contributions, although in most cases on a level distinctly below that of Italy.

In painting and engraving Germany produced a genius in Albert Dürer (1471–1528) of Nuremberg. He excelled as an artist, woodcutter, and engraver. His works, notably the somber engravings *The Knight, Death and the Devil, Melancholia I,* and *St. Jerome in His Study,* exhibit an attention to sinuous line, perspective, and an absorption with the riddle of the soul that have won him the accolade among all German artists. However, Hans Holbein, the younger (1497?–1543), of Augsburg, who spent many years painting at the court of Henry VIII, was accounted by contemporaries a better portraitist. Lucas Cranach (1472–1533) was Germany's chief exponent of voluptuous, secular themes and an indefatigable student of Luther's physiognomy. While all of these men were pro-Lutheran, there was one great artist of the period who lay almost wholly under medieval religious influences. This was Matthias Grünewald (1500–30), resident of Strassburg and court painter to the elector of Mainz. Grünewald was endowed with original, Gothic talent which resisted Renaissance Italian pressures. Among his spiritualized paintings, many of which dealt with Christ's Passion, the most famous is the altar polyptych in the monastery chapel at Isenheim, Alsace. Other contemporary painters of lesser stature were Hans Baldung (1480–1553) and Albert Altdorfer (1480–1538).

In sculpture and wood carving Germany boasted, as has been noted earlier, an able cohort, including Adam Kraft (1460–1508), Peter Vischer (1460?–1529), Tilman Riemenschneider (1468–1531), and Veit Stoss (1440–1553). Of lesser fame were Simon Leinberger, Nicolaus Gerhart, and Hans Backhoffen.

Chapter 14

PROTESTANT DIVISION

AND CATHOLIC REFORM

The Rise of Anabaptism

As early as 1521 Anabaptism was to be found both in the canton of Zurich and in Saxon Zwickau and Wittenberg, where from the first it exercised powerful attraction upon simple-minded, underprivileged peasants. The Anabaptists *(Wiedertaüfer)* believed infant baptism was invalid in God's eyes and that adult rebaptism (Greek *anabaptismos*) was necessary. More than the Lutheran or Swiss Zwinglians they emphasized the virtues of "brotherly love" and the ideal behavior of Christians in Roman times. They accepted Luther's concepts of justification by faith and supremacy of the scriptures but parted company with him in that they believed in free ecclesiastical organization and a Catharist dualism of good and evil, Christ and Satan. They also resented Luther's allegedly equivocal attitude toward Catholicism, his leniency toward the high-born and rich, and his ineradicable social conservatism. To Anabaptist leader Thomas Münzer (1489?–1525), who was later beheaded, Luther was a "sensual person," the "Pope of Wittenburg," who "led a soft life."

Had the Swiss Anabaptists been able to win over Ulrich Zwingli, the Swiss reformer, they might have built a strong central European church rivaling the Lutheran. As it was, the leadership of the southern Anabaptists descended upon the scholarly but less capable Felix Manz and Conrad Grebel, both of prosperous bourgeois Zurich families. They made numerous converts, among them Balthasar Hübmaier, but were unable to convert the municipal council of Zurich.

Supported in those days chiefly by the lowly and downtrodden, often by the lunatic fringe of society, the Anabaptist leaders were savagely persecuted, and their mortality rate was very high. Nevertheless "brethren" such as Münzer, Grebel, Manz, Hübmaier, Melchior Hoffmann, Johannes Brötli, and Hans Hut in Anabaptism's most successful years (1523–34) cultivated a broad vineyard of the Lord, stretching from the Vosges and Jura to Bratislava and from the Alps to Saxony.

After Archduke Ferdinand of Habsburg became margrave of Moravia, the tide turned against the Anabaptists. Hübmaier and his wife were convicted in Vienna of heresy. He was burned at the stake (March, 1528), and she was put to death by drowning. Manz was drowned in the Limmat, while Hoffman was imprisoned in Strassburg in 1533 and never released. Incensed at the results of Anabaptist social teachings, as demonstrated in the horrors of the Peasants' Rebellion of 1524–25, authorities everywhere girded themselves to stamp out Anabaptism.

The "brethren" were forced to retreat to Westphalia, where under leadership of petulant zealots Anabaptism entered its most radical phase. This culminated in the tragedy of Münster in 1534–35. The Anabaptists had managed to gain control of the city, drive out bishop and council, and establish a patriarchal communism whose main features were abolition of private property and dissolution of marital bonds. A dictatorship, which inflicted inhuman torture upon dissenters, was set up under a Dutch tailor, Jan Beuckelsz (Bokelson), who styled himself King John of Leyden. The bubble burst when after a siege, forces led by Bishop Franz von Waldeck and Prince Philip of Hesse stormed and retook Münster in June, 1535. Anabaptist leaders were beheaded or tortured to death and their remains hoisted in iron baskets to the top of St. Lambert's, where they stayed until 1881. The recapture of Münster and its restoration to Catholicism dealt a blow to Westphalian Protestantism.

After the Münster orgy, leadership of Anabaptism devolved upon moderate men, such as Menno Simons (1492–1559), and the movement was largely confined to the Dutch Netherlands. In Germany the left wing of Protestantism was thenceforth represented by mild-mannered mystics, such as Caspar Schwenckfeld (1489–1561) and Sebastian Franck (1499–1542), leaders of groups but not masses of men.

Zwingli's Evangelical Reformed Church

Of all the early Protestant leaders, Huldrych (Ulrich) Zwingli (1484–1531) possessed the most refined intellect. Born at Wildhaus, Toggenburg, he studied at Basel, Bern, and Vienna, at which last university he received a master's degree in 1506. In the same year he was ordained a priest. By 1516 he had attained a thorough knowledge of Latin and Greek and had learned some Hebrew. Between 1516 and 1519 he arrived independently at unorthodox conclusions respecting the exclusive redemptive power of faith in Jesus and the need for an evangelist approach to religion. On January 1, 1519, he was invited by the council of Zurich to speak in the Grossmünster on the Limmat. From then until his death in the Second Battle of Kappel in 1531 he preached in the great church at Zurich every Sunday on a different book of the Bible. Meanwhile, Zwingli carried on a campaign that ended with the suppression of monasticism, clerical celibacy, confession, and the Mass, not only in Zurich but in other cantons.

The most challenging affirmation of Zwingli was that Christ, who had revealed himself to man in the New Testament, was, without the intercession of any other person or agency, our one road to God and immortality. The legal training of the Swiss reformer led him to talk as much about God's will and eternal laws as Luther did about the sufficiency of divine grace and faith. Zwingli hypothecated not merely the predestination of exceptionally virtuous individuals but a universal compulsion to obey God's commandments and sufficient strength to do so. So imperative was this concept with Zwingli that justification by faith tended to recede into the background of his theological schema.

Zwingli believed that Christ was spiritually present in the Eucharist but rejected the miraculous corporal presence of the Lord, either in the Lutheran form of consubstantiation or the Catholic of transubstantiation. He emphasized the collective approach to the Lord's Supper, because of supreme importance to him was not so much the purification of the individual worshiper as the sanctification of the congregation.

Disputations were held in Zurich in January and October, 1523, on Zwingli's views, and the following year the municipal council decreed acceptance of the Reformation. Altars thereafter were replaced with tables, choirs were suppressed, church organs removed, murals and wall decorations in churches plastered over, images demolished, and monasteries and convents dissolved. On April 16, 1525, the Mass was suppressed in Zurich, and simple readings from the scriptures were substituted.

The Spread of Swiss Protestantism

Zwingli yearned to see his Reformed Church triumph in all Switzerland. He had powerful sympathizers in several cantons: in Glarus, Valentin Tschudi; in Basel, Oecolampadius (Johannes Häushagen); in Solothurn, Melchior Macrinus; and in Bern, Berchtold Haller and the playwright Niklaus Manuel. In Strassburg Butzer entertained views analogous to Zwingli's. In Appenzell canton a historically important decision was taken in 1524 to allow each community to decide for itself what liturgy and confession it preferred. Schaffhausen embraced the Reformation in 1529, and the same iconoclastic excesses were enacted there as in Zurich, Basel, and Bern. Even Schaffhausen's marvelous minster organ was hacked to pieces. In Glarus there was a stiff struggle with the Catholics, and in the end it was deemed wise to adopt the Appenzell formula there. In St. Gall Joachim von Watt (Vadian) and Johannes Kessler encountered strong opposition, not so much from the Catholics as from the Anabaptists. However, by 1528 the Reformed Church had triumphed in the old monastic city, and images and altars were burned. In Graubünden, where there was no strong central power, a string of communities broke away from Catholicism as early as 1521 and 1522. Chur, the largest town of the canton, went Zwinglian by 1523. However, in 1526 the diet at Davos decided to apply the Appenzell formula to Graubünden too. Thus several Swiss cantons took the first steps toward qualified religious freedom long before the Dutch provinces or France did.

The Failure to Win Switzerland

Zwinglianism was no more able to unite Switzerland than Lutheranism was Germany. Considerably before the coming of the French reformer, John Calvin, the Swiss population was split three ways. The peasantry and most poor artisans, who hoped that an Anabaptist victory would lead to an improvement in their social condition, flocked to the pulpits where Manz, Grebel, Jurg the Blueshirt, and Hübmaier spoke. In some cantons, notably St. Gall and Basel, the Anabaptist movement generated alarming support. Nevertheless, the old faith continued to have many devotees in Rheinthal, Sargens, Graubünden, Thorgau, and Appenzell, while Lucerne and the four forest cantons held solidly to Catholicism.

It was not long before the Zwinglians had to defend themselves against the Christian Union Alliance, which the Catholic cantons had formed with Austria in 1529. When the forces of Zurich and Bern met the Catholics for a second time on the battlefield near Kappel on October 11, 1531, Zwingli fell in the fray. The ensuing peace of Kappel (November 16–20, 1531) established the parity of Catholicism and Zwinglianism in Switzerland. No new element was introduced until John Calvin launched a second reformation a decade later in Geneva.

The Reformation in Alsace

In Alsace the tide did not turn decisively in favor of Protestantism until after 1523. Then a series of remarkable evangelists, heavily influenced by Dutch sacramentarianism, set about their work. Wolfgang Capito (1478–1541), Martin Butzer (1491–1551) of Schletstadt (Sélestat), and Gaspard Heyd (Heidion, 1494–1552) drew the population away from sacramentarianism, which merely denied the efficacy of the Eucharist in the hands of unworthy priests, and founded the Alsatian Protestant church. The Alsatian evangelists were of the opinion that the Lord's Supper was purely symbolic and rejected the adoration of the Host as idolatrous. Such views earned them the scathing condemnation of Luther.

In general, the religious evolution of Alsace was peaceful. The Protestants there repudiated Anabaptism, took up a theoretical position between Luther and Zwingli, and even tried, howsoever unsuccessfully, to reconcile them at the Marburg Disputation in 1529. Eventually, despite belated concessions to the Lutheran conception of the Lord's Supper, the Alsatian Protestants, who had won out in almost all the towns of the province by 1531, found their brackish way into the great sea of Calvinism.

The Peasants' Revolt

In 1524 the *Bundschuh* flag was again unfurled. The peasants, led by their own kind or by petty nobles, rose up against the lords, towns, and territorial governments. The initial centers of the rebellion were to the northeast of Schaffhausen and at Stühlingen in the Black Forest *(Schwarzwald)*. Soon all Baden, Württemburg, the Allgäu, the archbishopric of Salzburg, Lower Austria, the Tirol, Carinthia, and Styria took flame. Then Thuringia and Franconia were engulfed, and by early 1525 a third of Germany was caught up in the worst social conflagration in European history. The rebels had been excited by Luther's teachings respecting Christian freedom and social justice, but to an even greater extent the uprising fed on the militant exhortations of Grebel, Manz, and Münzer.

Under direction of the blacksmith Ulrich Schmidt and the furrier Sebastian Lotzer, the peasants of the southwest formulated at Memmingen the famous "Twelve Articles of the Swabian Peasants." Except for the first article, which demanded revocation of all measures contrary to the word of God, this manifesto repeated the aims of earlier Bundschuh uprisings: reduction of tithes, feudal dues, and rents; the grant of access to common fields, woodlands, and streams; and the abolition of serfdom, forced labor, and inheritance taxes. After the Battle of Pavia (February 24, 1525), German soldiers, returning from Italy, made it possible to suppress the rebellion. The peasants than passed into the climactic phase of their uprising. In April, at the height of the sacking of monasteries, sequestration of noble and ecclesiastical property, and murdering of lords, Luther wrote his *Exhortation to Peace in Response to the Twelve Articles of the Swabian Peasants and in Opposition to the Spirit of Murder and Brigandage of other Rioting Peasants*. This was followed by a second broadside, *Against the Murdering and Thieving Hordes of Peasants*. The English Methodist ecclesiastical historian, Ernest Gordon Rupp, has argued that the intemperance of these diatribes derived from the fear that the peasants' rebellion might destroy the whole work of the Reformation. In any case, the tracts showed that Luther clearly sympathized with the established social order and deplored revolt under any circumstances. His earlier demand for religious freedom and individualism was compromised by his exhortation to rulers ruthlessly to combat false doctrines.

The suppression of the insurrection was exceptionally bloody. Thousands died in the carnage. A broken peasantry, which could look forward to worse servitude than ever, now denounced Luther as a false prophet and fell away from him in droves. Many went over to Anabaptism or Zwinglianism; others, totally disillusioned with Protestant preachments, returned to the Catholic fold. After 1525 Luther could no longer represent the national purpose. Protestantism had become sectarian. On the other hand, by siding with the authorities against the rebels, Luther rescued his church.

When next Lutheranism stood on the summit, as was the case in Germany between 1538 and 1546, the movement was led by princes, not pastors. Luther himself moved with the current, adducing arguments in support of princely absolutism and urging the masses to obey Protestant rulers, who had been instituted by God. Having succeeded in subverting the power of pope and bishop, Luther ended by exalting that of temporal government.

The Diet of Augsburg, 1530

A politically motivated attempt to reunite Sacramentarians, Zwinglians, and Lutherans failed in discussions held October 1–3, 1529, at Hessian Marburg. Zwingli's obdurate republican spirit differed from that of the authoritarian-minded Luther, whose aristocratic outlook scandalized the democratic Swiss and Alsatian reformers. Beyond this, Zwingli would not accept either the Lutheran conception of faith or baptism, and he rejected the view that salvation depended upon assimilation of the corporal body of Christ by a believing communicant. Luther,* on the other hand, could not see how any parabolic construction of the Lord's Supper as a commemorative manducation of bread (the view of Capito and Butzer) could

---

*In 1525 Luther had married the former nun, Katarina von Bora, by whom he was to have five children.

be made to harmonize with the clear statement in the Bible: *Hoc est enim corpus meum* ("This is my body"). A deeper reason for failure of the Marburg Conference was that many Lutherans (Osiander, Agricola, Melanchthon, Jonas, Dietrich, Brenz, and Myconius among them) wished to keep the line of retreat open for possible reunion with reformed Catholicism.

The emperor nurtured such hopes when he invited both Lutherans and Catholics to present their views before the Diet of Augsburg in 1530. Instead of Luther, who was still under the ban of the Empire, the Evangelical Church sent Melanchthon as one who had both written the first systematic exposition of Lutheran teachings and worked for Christian reunion. His reputation was enormous. Melanchthon came armed with recent statements of the Lutheran position, which he summarized in the so-called Augsburg Confession *(Confessio Augustana)*. Comprising twenty-eight articles, to twenty-one of which Catholics could not object, the confession was intended to magnify the differences between Catholics and Lutherans, on the one hand, and Zwinglians, on the other. Yet all of Melanchthon's tact could not hide the fact that beyond a certain point Luther would not yield to the Catholics. Besides this, more was at stake than doctrine. There were the secularized church properties, which no amount of casuistry would persuade the Protestant princes to disgorge. As for the Zwinglians, who had not been invited to the diet, their *Confessio Tetrapolitana,* which was submitted in July, 1530, on behalf of the four towns of Strassburg, Constance, Lindau, and Memmingen *in absentia,* was accorded no attention whatever.

Very possibly Charles V would have accepted the Augsburg Confession as a basis for further discussion had it not been for the uncompromising attitude of Catholic theologians such as Eck, Cochlaeus, and Faber. In the end the emperor accepted a watered-down version of their Catholic Refutation *(Confutatio),* and he now pronounced the *Augustana* heretical. Thereupon, the chief Protestant princes bolted the diet. On November 15 Charles V decreed immediate enforcement of the Edict of Worms, and on the nineteenth the Reichskammergericht brought suit against all princes and towns that refused to restore sequestrated church properties. The Lutherans responded by forming the Schmalkaldic League.

Revival of Protestant Fortunes

In the 1530s the scales again tipped in favor of Protestantism. Lutheranism triumphed in all Scandinavia, Finland, Iceland, Hungary, and Transylvania, the Baltic states, and parts of Poland. It made deep inroads, too, into Bohemia and Moravia, while in Switzerland Heinrich Bullinger (1504–75), Zwingli's successor in Zurich and the most prolific Protestant pen of the century, had restored the flagging confidence of Swiss Protestants after their defeat at Kappel.

In the revival of Protestant fortunes four factors were paramount: the resumption of the wars of Charles V in 1532; the decision of certain key princes to introduce reformed doctrine into their principalities; the establishment of a working alliance between the Strassburg and the Lutheran reformers; and the development of a Lutheran-Catholic schism.

The revival of Protestant fortunes in the 1530s was mainly due to the princes. Between 1533 and 1534 the rulers of Hanover, Pomerania, Anhalt, and Mecklenburg, moved by expectations of material gain, took steps to introduce Lutheranism in their territories. By 1538 all northern Germany, except for some ecclesiastical states and Brunswick, had gone Lutheran. Also, a lodgement had been effected in Westphalia and the Rhineland, where Bishop Franz von Waldeck of Münster, Minden, and Osnabrück, and Archbishop Hermann von Wied of Cologne at last invited evangelists to preach in their principalities. In Augsburg the Protestant liturgy was adopted in 1537, whereupon all Württemberg followed suit. Hesse, Baden, and the Rhenish Palatinate all defected from Catholicism so that by 1539 the southwestern Protestant block was nearly solid. By then Butzer, Capito, and Luther had reached the Wittenberg Agreement, by which Alsace, too, accepted the Lutheran doctrine of consubstantiation. German religious solidarity again seemed within reach.

The Second Check to Protestantism

While four-fifths of Germany had gone Lutheran by 1544, Calvinism was fortifying the Protestant position in Switzerland. John Calvin (1509–64), French student of law and theology, had already strengthened the anti-Catholic camp when in 1536 he published his *Institutes of the Christian Religion,* the era's most systematic exposition of Protestant principles. In 1541 Calvin returned to Geneva, from which he had earlier been exiled. While catering to the city's bourgeois economic philosophy, he organized a rigidly dogmatic church, characterized by severe discipline, predestinarian doctrine, and the theocratic power to expel heretics from congregation and city.

Calvin, no more than Zwingli or Luther, was able to amalgamate all German Protestant confessions. It is true that by 1549 Calvin won over the Zwinglians to his conception of the spiritual presence of Christ at communion. However, his bitter controversy with the Wittenberg leaders over the Lord's Supper dimmed hopes for a greater union. Not even the tactful successor of Calvin, Theodor Beza (1519–1605), cared to withdraw the sword that Calvin had thrust into the Protestant corpus. The Swiss *Confessio Helvetica* of 1566 forever lowered the portcullis to Lutheranism.

By contrast with the Protestant movement, which was fractured, the Catholic by the mid 1540s began to regroup and galvanize. A beginning was made with the renovation of the papacy during the pontificate of Paul III (1534–49). A host of new religious orders, more for than against something, were founded, and a new inspirational example was furnished by the Spanish Carmelite nun Theresa of Avila (1515–82) and the Spanish soldier Ignatius Loyola (1491–1556), the author of the popular *Spiritual Exercises*.

Meanwhile the prestige of Protestantism, jeopardized by the caprice of hundreds of rulers, was tarnished by the news that its main secular leader, Landgrave Philip of Hesse (1509–67), was a bigamist. His indiscretion hurt the Protestant cause and decided the primate of Germany to remain with the old faith. While some new Protestant gains, such as the secularization in 1543 of the bishoprics of Minden, Osnabrück, and Münster by Bishop Franz Waldeck of Hildesheim, were registered, the big Lutheran push was grinding to a halt in the 1540s. Resistance was developing in Münster and northern Westphalia to Waldeck's ambitions, and in Cologne to Archbishop Herman von Wied, who had apostasized from Catholicism. Finally, Luther's increasing conservatism alienated Protestant democrats, who concluded that he was much too subservient to the princes.

After the signing of the Treaty of Créspy, Charles V attacked the Protestants. In the Schmalkaldic War (1546–47), which Luther did not live to see (he died February 17, 1546), the emperor won a resounding victory at Mühlberg in 1547. Hermann von Wied was, as a result, deposed. With him went the last chance to build a Protestant causeway from Hesse to Holland.

Catholicism's Second Springtime

The forelopers of the Catholic Reformation in Germany were the Jesuits, members of Loyola's Company of Jesus (f. 1540). They began the campaign for the reconquest of Germany from the Rhine Valley, the so-called priests' lane *(Pfaffengasse),* and specifically from Cologne in 1540. Although the Jesuit counter-offensive failed of its maximum goal, it achieved lasting penetrations of Protestant positions.

In 1543 the first and greatest non-Romance figure was inducted into the Society of Jesus: a Dutchman named Pieter de Hondt, known to history as St. Peter Canisius (1521–97), the ''Second Apostle to Germany.'' When Canisius was ordained a priest in 1546 he found the Catholic clergy morally soiled and spiritually in rags. Priests were often uneducated, ignorant of theology, and foggy about the differences between Catholicism and Lutheranism. There were very few seminaries for training the religious, and many parishes were without priests.

Catholicism's task was, of course, made somewhat easier by the circumstance that Lutheranism, deprived of the iron hand of its founder, was sinking into a morass of incontinence. Not only were many Protestants scandalized by the doctrinal vendetta that had arisen among Calvinists, Anabaptists, and Lutherans, but they were sorely depressed by the spectacle of the drunkenness, debauchery, and impiety that were spreading in the non-Catholic sections of Germany.

The revival of German catholicism did not depend, as has often been maintained, solely upon the support of a few south German princes and the papacy. The revival was encouraged by the deplorable example set by many Protestants.

The Work of Peter Canisius

Although luxury-loving and cultivated, Canisius, founder of the first Jesuit colony in Germany, was pious, zealous, and able. In the course of a long life he won recognition as the indomitable generalissimo of the reform forces of Catholic Germany. His influence radiated over all central Europe, and his name was known in the hovels of Polish peasants and the châteaux of Hungarian magnates. Invited in 1549 by William V (1579–97) of Bavaria to come to the moribund University of Ingolstadt, where since Eck's death theology was dying on the vine, he assisted Claude Le Jay and Salmerón to restore the institution. In 1555 Canisius published his *Summary of Christian Doctrine,* not the first, but the most successful Latin catechism to be prepared in Germany. For thirteen years after 1556, Canisius was the first provincial of the Jesuit Order in Germany. Betwen 1559–66 he preached, at the invitation of Bishop Truchsess, at Augsburg with success. Canisius dexterously drove a deeper wedge too between Melanchthon's moderate supporters and the Lutheran extremists under Flacius Illyricus. Above all, Canisius' influence was felt in education, where he helped found many colleges and higher institutions of Catholic learning, notably the archducal college at Vienna and colleges at Cologne, Nymwegen, Fribourg, Innsbruck, and Prague.

Canons of the Council of Trent

The many decrees on dogma and abuses of canon law which were adopted during the three periods of the Council of Trent (1545–49, 1551–52, 1562–63) had a profound influence upon the Catholic reform. Despite some initial hostility from German cathedral schools, an increasing number of Catholics came to appreciate the larger advantages of the Tridentine decrees. They clearly drew the line between Catholic and Protestant doctrine so that all might understand, and they offered the best chance of reform and revival of confidence in the Roman church.

One of the most important decrees was that of October, 1551, which tackled abuses of the episcopal office, reminding bishops of their residential duties and exhorting them to use their authority not to crush their subjects but lovingly to guide them into the paths of righteousness, tempering punishment, where necessary, with mercy. Associated with this decree were eleven canons that formulated the official position of the Roman Church on the Eucharist. It was averred that Christ is totally—physically and spiritually—present in the sacrament of the Eucharist and that to receive him properly faith alone will not suffice because a recipient must be in a state of grace.

Doctrinal decisions of 1563 touched on indulgences, intercession of saints for the mitigation of punishment of souls in purgatory, and the efficacy of prayer. At the final session of the council disciplinary reforms were adopted, which aided in the rehabilitation of Catholicism. These were designed to eliminate abuses that had evoked the widest condemnation, renovate the morals of the clergy, and establish schools and seminaries to give systematic religious and theological training to youths for the purpose of staffing the immense bureaucracy of the Church.

In Germany the effect of the Tridentine decisions was to wash away the accumulated scum from the lamp of the Roman pharos so that it could once more send its beam into the farthest recesses of Europe. Although there was more of a tendency among German prelates to ignore the disciplinary than the doctrinal decisions of Trent, by 1570 all the religious orders at least, except for the strife-torn Franciscans, had endorsed the reforms. Needless to say, millions of plain people also gratefully hailed the decrees. On the other hand, the princes, more than the prelates, viewed the Tridentine platform as a new device for centralizing power in the hands of the pope. Many princes now felt free either not to apply the decrees or to procrastinate with those respecting concubinage, residential obligations of bishops, and cumulation of benefices.

The Educational Counteroffensive

Set in motion by giant hands beyond the borders of Germany, the episcopal reform gathered momentum during the 1560s. Encouraged by Carlo Borromeo (1538–84), the great archbishop of Milan, and by a line of far-sighted popes— Pius IV (1559–65), Pius V (1566–72), Gregory XIII (1572–85) and Sixtus V (1585–90)—the Catholic counteroffensive advanced from Louvain, Douai, Trier, Cologne, Münster, Osnabrück, and Paderborn in the north; from Mainz, Freiburg i. Br., Mülheim, Luzern, and Fribourg in the southwest; from Würzburg in the center; and from Augsburg, Dillingen, Ingolstadt, Salzburg, Munich, Passau, and Vienna in the south and southeast. At the same time a new devotion to the Church of Rome was inspired by an exuberant religious architecture—the arabesque, fantastically ornamented baroque churches that were springing up all over southern and western Germany. Finally, the people were gladdened by the decision that the Bible, as interpreted by Catholic authority, was to be put in everyone's hands to aid salvation.

Among the scholars and prelates who helped found colleges and universities to train a new Catholic intelligentsia were P. Claude Le Jay, Alphonse Salmerón, Abbot Joachim Buchauer of St. Peter's in Salzburg, Cardinal Archbishop Melchior Khlesl of Vienna (1552–1630), Cardinal Bishop Otto Truchsess von Waldburg of Augsburg (1543–73), Archbishop Jean von der Leyden of Trier (1556–67), Bishop Jules Echter von Mespelbrunn of Würzburg (1573–1617), Bishop Heinrich von Knöringen of Augsburg (1598–1646), and Bishop Urban von Trennbach of Passau (d. 1598).

Newly established or recaptured institutions of higher learning, such as Münster, Bamberg, Heidelberg, Mülheim, Paderborn, Osnabrück, Trier, Cologne, Mainz, Würzburg, Innsbruck, Prague, and Freiburg i. Br., made successful front against Protestant educational foundations at Leyden, Marburg, Wittenberg, Erfurt, Jena, Rostock, and Frankfurt am Oder, all of which had been enriched by spoliations. In Styria the University of Graz was founded in 1586, filling a lacuna in Austrian higher education until Khlesl's renovation of the University of Vienna. Yet, when all is said, it took Catholic education more than a half-century after 1555 to get back on its feet. In the arduous task of training teachers, however, Germany's Catholic institutions were aided by Pope Gregory XIII, who in 1573 founded what came to be known as the German College *(Collegium Germanicum)*. This seminary graduated many a religious leader of the German Catholic Reformation.

Catholic Dynastic Leadership

It might be supposed that the bastion of the Catholic Reformation would have been the Austrian crown lands, but this was not so. The emperor's dynastic ambi-

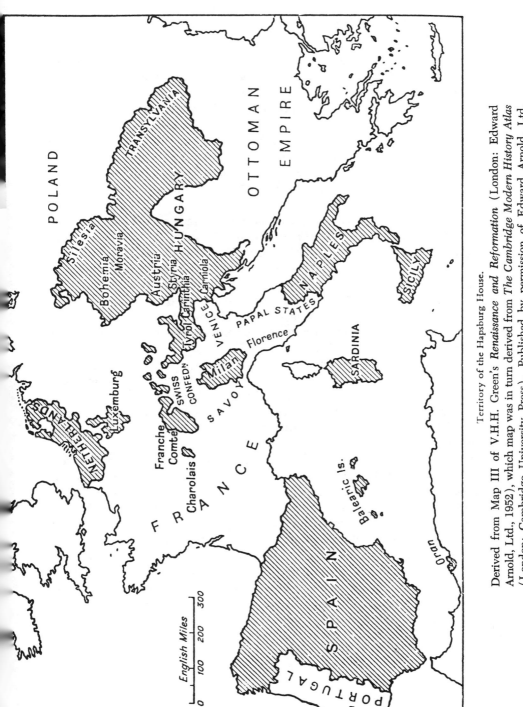

Territory of the Hapsburg House.

Derived from Map III of V.H.H. Green's *Renaissance and Reformation* (London: Edward Arnold, Ltd., 1952), which map was in turn derived from *The Cambridge Modern History Atlas* (London: Cambridge University Press). Published by permission of Edward Arnold, Ltd. and Cambridge University Press.

R.C.

tions and the fact that Maximilian II (1564–76) was secretly a Protestant not only prevented the Habsburgs from assuming leadership of the militant Catholic counteroffensive until very late but even obstructed its triumph in the crown lands.

Failing the Habsburgs, Bavaria became the Catholic redoubt of the sixteenth century. The cultivated dukes Albert V (1550–79) and William V (1579–97) moved energetically to compel the *Landtag* to accept the Tridentine decrees. The Wittelsbach dukes also engaged the Jesuits to revive the fame of Ingolstadt and encouraged Cardinal Truchsess to found a new university at Dillingen. After 1570 the dukes also put an inquisitorial Spiritual Council in the service of the Catholic reform.

Eventually also a close working alliance was formed between the Habsburgs and the apostolic Church. The Emperor Rudolf II (1576–1612) resolutely broke with the policy of concessions that had been pursued by his predecessors. He instituted reformation commissions, comparable to the Lutheran consistories, for the recatholicization of the Austrian crown lands. He also prevailed upon the Reichstag in 1582 to refuse representation to the scores of self-appointed, materialistic "administrators" who, in violation of the ecclesiastical reservation of the Treaty of Augsburg, had since usurped abbatial and episcopal seats and sequestrated Church property and revenues.

Rudolf also aided in recatholicizing territories that had never been under Habsburg sovereignty—the Rhenish Jülich-Berg and the Westphalian country, Bamberg, Ermland, Poland, and Pomerelia. Finally, no less than the dukes of Bavaria and the bishops of Würzburg and Salzburg, Rudolf donated lavishly to religious foundations and financed the construction of many a church or chapel in the new baroque style.

Catholicism had not only survived the worst hours of the Protestant Revolution but had been able to regroup, revive its flagging energies, and reconquer a large number of positions in Germany. The territorial gains of Catholicism in the later sixteenth century more than offset the victory of Calvinism in the Rhenish Palatinate during the reign of Frederick III (1559–76) and the final loss of Brandenburg in the reign of Margrave John George (1571–98). The south German Protestants were actually in danger of being cut off from their northern brothers. If the Catholic princes could cut a swathe from Bohemia through Catholic Würzburg to Cologne and Westphalia, it is plain that Strassburg, the Calvinist Palatinate, and Lutheran Württemberg and Baden would eventually subside beneath rising French and German Catholic waters.

PART V

WAR AND CULTURE
IN THE BAROQUE ERA

Chapter 15

THE THIRTY YEARS' WAR

Town and Country About 1600

On the eve of the Thirty Years' War, the Empire, with the largest population of any European political entity, was still overwhelmingly agrarian. Of its 21 million inhabitants, only approximately 15 percent lived in towns. Few urban centers had more than 10,000 inhabitants. Perhaps twenty ranked as big cities *(Grossstädte)*. Of these, Nuremberg, Lübeck, Augsburg, and Vienna each had more than 50,000 souls. Perhaps twenty-five other towns had from 2,000 to 10,000. Below these may have been six hundred towns and villages with populations of from 500 to 2,000, and at the bottom of the pyramid were four or five thousand villages with less than 500 people.

In general it may be affirmed that the "golden age" of the German towns lay behind them. In contrast with demographic trends in the Low Countries, England, and France, the drift of people toward the towns had ceased by the end of the first quarter of the sixteenth century. Thereafter until 1618 the ratio of urban to rural population remained constant at 15 to 85. Among the factors responsible for stunting urban growth were: the Schmalkaldic wars; the loss of the Hanseatic League's monopoly over Baltic trade and favorable competitive positions in England, the Low Countries, and Russia; hostility of the princes toward town leagues; the rise of the Dutch and English merchant marines; internal territorial fragmentation; establishment of powerful nation-states around Germany, transfer of international trade routes; establishment of overseas trading monopolies by Portugal, Spain, and England; and, from the fourth quarter of the sixteenth century onward, increasing, crippling state controls over business. The evidences of an urban slowdown were more apparent in the south German towns, remote from the ocean, where to the above factors must be added the decline in importance of the Italian towns and overland trade routes and the diminution of capital reserves.

In the light of recent research, however, older notions that the failure of the finance-capitalist houses—the Fuggers, Welsers, Imhofs, Klebergers, and Höchstetters—wrecked the south German economy must be discarded. True, Augsburg and Nuremberg were jolted when the Spanish Habsburgs, to whom the Fuggers had advanced 20 million ducats, repudiated their debts in 1557–59 and when the Valois similarly defaulted. However, the finance-capitalists were not the decisive factor in the prosperity of the region. The far more important and numerous merchants and industrialists were saved by an uninterrupted flow of income from real estate and profits from many sources. Actually, free enterprise benefited from the ruin of the finance-capitalists, who had exercised monopolies over the mining and sale of silver, salt, iron, amber, and copper. Princes and nobles thenceforth were more inclined to transfer their investment capital from land to trade and industry. After some hesitation, the south German economy, aided by increased volume of currency, proliferation of credit facilities, and improved operational techniques, began to move sluggishly forward again.

North Germany's towns did much better. The Hanse may have been in full decline, but some of its member cities were not. Lübeck, Hamburg, and Bremen continued to be important maritime trading centers. Between 1500 and 1600 German merchants even managed to augment their share in greatly increased traffic through the Danish Sound from 20 percent to 25 percent. As late as the middle of the century Germany's merchant marine, though far behind the Spanish and Dutch and about to slip behind the English, was still third in the world. Furthermore, Germany may not have participated directly in the growing volume of oceanic trade in the late sixteenth century, but north German exporters, especially of Cologne and Hamburg (which were proximate to Antwerp and Amsterdam), established contacts with those who did.

After 1550 there was a modest improvement in the standard of living of the peasantry, who were better off than at any time since the Black Plague. On the whole, despite fluctuations, grain prices rose for a century after 1550. The arable expanded, agricultural production increased, and peasant gross income rose. Nevertheless, the standard of living in the countryside remained low and stationary. In the late sixteenth century, prices of manufactured articles began to outrun those of farm produce, and the peasants were put at a disadvantage in competition with other classes. The peasant's diet was deficient in proteins and vitamins, leaving him subject to many malnutritional diseases. His farming methods were primitive, and soil chemistry was unknown to him. His work was long and backbreaking and no lighter for the failure of his great revolt in 1524–25. His life expectancy, if he survived the first grim year of infancy, was 35 compared to a burgher's 45 or 50. Disease and starvation cut the peasant down, for villages were more vulnerable than towns to cholera, typhus, smallpox, and famine. Finally, the Thirty Years' War was figuratively a "valley of death" for the peasants. Only at its close did the princes come to their aid with import tariffs on grain, tax concessions, and subsidies. Then the realization that the German princes were adopting state paternalism at a time when other monarchs were abandoning their peasants brought new hope to the countryside.

The Financial and Speculative Community

Capitalism opened more speculative opportunities than the world had ever known. What were originally simple associations of German merchants or family partnerships grew into great banking, capital, and credit houses (*Kapitalgesellschaften*) with ramifying interests. These capital associations in the sixteenth century were to be found mostly in south Germany, where they took the form of partnerships, companies, family-type firms (Fuggers, Klebergers, Imhofs, Welsers, Höchstadters) or syndicates. Their liquid capital came from hundreds and thousands of small investors, who, exercising no directive control over the association, received payment in the form of interest or profit on the money they loaned at rates varying from 10 to 15 percent.

With the emergence of high finance there opened a new, hazardous way of life for many thousands of people. Betting and trafficking in paper certificates or specie became the rage. Some speculators hoarded goods or crops until they could be marketed at fancy profits; some dealt in letters of exchange, selling them at exhorbitant prices to merchants who wished to avoid sending specie to distant correspondents; some profited from discrepancies in paper values by regularly transporting stock certificates from one locality to another; and still others speculated on the price of gold, silver, or other metals. Some persons and firms trafficked in "futures"—buying or selling commodities under agreements for delivery at a future date when the price might be substantially higher.

Because the cry for speedier transfers of capital was insatiable, credit banks and clearinghouses sprang up. The earliest banks in Germany were of this type and were modeled on the Neapolitan Monté de Pietà (est. 1539). Disposing of the pooled capital of a consortium of financiers, these banks lent money to businesses for undertakings or for industrial development and expansion. By the seventeenth century many credit banks had collaborated to found giro banks, which provided dependable transfer and clearinghouse services for the exchange of coins, commercial paper, and securities and the balancing of payments. The first giro bank was the Amsterdamsche Wisselbank (est. 1609); the earliest German examples were founded in Hamburg (1619) and Nuremberg (1621). By contrast, the first bank of deposit (Berlin) was not established in Germany until 1717.

At the same time the first stock exchanges opened their doors, inaugurating the era of grand speculation. Those of Lübeck, Augsburg, Nuremberg, Frankfurt, Cologne, and Hamburg were modeled after the prototype established in Antwerp in 1531. Although German stock exchanges never attained the international importance of those of Antwerp, London, and Copenhagen, they nonetheless facilitated buying and selling of commodities without the cost and inconvenience of physical shipments, encouraged industrial enterprise and development, and made possible the swift accumulation of large fortunes.

The Onslaught of "Cold War"

All this relative prosperity was insecure because force and blackmail had become the language employed by Protestant and Catholic Germany in dealings with each other. Militant Catholicism revoked privileges and immunities that, during the reign of the privately Lutheran Emperor Maximilian II (1564–67), had been granted to Protestant princes and towns in Austria, Styria, Carinthia, Carniola, Bohemia, and Bavaria. Conversely, the manifold advantages of the Bohemian and Hungarian geographic positions emboldened Czechs and Magyars to capitalize on them by extorting heavy concessions from the emperor. In Hungary, for instance, the king enforced his will during periods of peace, but whenever war resumed with

Turkey the Austrian archdukes had to buy back the support of the Magyar estates with grants of liberties and immunities. This constant alternation between persecution and bribery surcharged the early seventeenth century political atmosphere with electricity. Bohemia, like Thor's hammer, was to bring it flashing down upon Germany.

In his time Maximilian II sought to reconcile the Catholic and Lutheran positions. While secretly Protestant, he publicly declared for Catholicism because he realized that the hopes of his family to inherit the Spanish succession depended upon his profession of the older faith. While waiting for the elusive doctrinal reconciliation to materialize, Maximilian's guiding principle was to preserve the Religious Peace of Augsburg. He encouraged German Catholics to look upon the king of Spain as their natural ally but conceded far-reaching liberties to his non-urban Protestant estates, especially in Bohemia (1567) and Upper Austria (1568). On the other hand, Maximilian II abided by a promise made to the pope to maintain Catholicism as the paramount faith in the Habsburg dominions. In turn the emperor required of Protestant nobles' subjects that they respect Catholicism as the dominant religion in his dynastic lands and refrain from sequestrating further Catholic properties, diverting Church revenues, expelling priests, or imposing civil disabilities upon old believers. In 1571 Maximilian II in a "Religious Assurance" conferred religious freedom upon the entire Austrian nobility, thus legalizing an unrecognized secret concession Emperor Ferdinand I had made at Augsburg in 1555. Ultimately Maximilian was even able to confer religious liberty upon a few Austrian towns, but such concessions were impermanent since they lacked systematic fundament and depended entirely upon the caprice of future rulers.

During the long and disastrous reign of Rudolf II the truce came to an end. It was feared that the young sovereign, who was a strict Catholic and was known to be excessively pious, indiscreet, and wedded to a bigoted queen, would discard tolerance for persecution. These fears lacked foundation to the extent that they attributed to Rudolf II an energy, zeal, and singleness of purpose which he did not, in fact, possess. Time and again Rudolf was to amaze friend and foe alike by his indifference to political and religious issues and by his preference for women, horses, alchemists, astrologers, and other curiosities.

The web drew closer when Rudolf II imposed a host of annoying restrictions upon Protestant residents of his crown lands. All prebends, benefices, and vacancies in church, administration, courts, and schools were reserved to Catholics. In Lutheran Germany, meanwhile, a Formula of Concord had been adopted on June 28, 1580, which systematized and rigidly defined Protestant dogma. The concord received the endorsement of the electors of Brandenburg and Saxony, twenty-two other princes, and thirty-five imperial cities. The Calvinists, who rejected it, adopted their own confessional statement in the same year. It was accepted by the counts palatine of the Rhine and Lautern, the landgrave of Hesse-Cassel, certain towns in Brandenburg, and the Swiss Protestant cantons.

These dogmatic formularies heightened Catholic resentment. With the accession of the able and determined Duke William V (1579–97) to the Bavarian throne, the Catholic political counteroffensive began in earnest. Catholic lodgements were soon effected in Durlach, Freiburg, Württemberg, and elsewhere. Lutheranism was repulsed in the archbishopric of Mainz. Cologne was recovered for Catholicism through a coup and a war (1584–86) shortly after that principality had defected in 1582, and Catholic doctrine regained domination in Württemberg, Jülich, Berg, Münster, Hildesheim, and Fulda. As a result, much of Westphalia was opened to Catholic operations, and Osnabrück, Minden, and Paderborn were soon restored. A broad salient was driven between the Calvinist Dutch Netherlands and the Protestant states of Hesse-Nassau and Brunswick. In this wedge Catholicism was again everywhere ensconced.

While the English and Dutch were blunting the counteroffensive of the Spanish Habsburgs in the west, Catholicism was swinging like a scythe through most of the lands around Germany. In 1598 Aachen fell to the Catholics. In Poland, King Sigmund III stamped out Lutheranism and aided Catholic penetration of his Prussian and Livonian fiefs. In Hungary, Catholicism regained control in the western districts, while the magnates allied themselves with the emperor against the Protestants of Transylvania. After 1583 Alsace began to slide back into the Roman camp, partly due to the labors of Cardinal Charles of Lorraine and partly to the conversion in 1593 of King Henry IV of France. In Switzerland in 1586 the cantons of Lucerne, Uri, Schwyz, Unterwalden, and Wallis formed the Golden League of Carlo Borromeo and put the Protestant cantons back on the defensive. Finally, in Lower Austria the fiery and uncompromising Duke Ferdinand II was persecuting the disorganized Protestant communities. In south and southwest Germany by 1600 an improved Catholic position clearly adumbrated the disappearance of the dwindling islands of Protestantism.

Preliminary Skirmishes

Two opposing confederacies now took shape in Germany. In 1603 a political Protestant Union founded in 1594 was transformed into a military alliance linked with Henry IV. Led by the Calvinist Elector Frederick IV of the Rhenish Palatinate and Maurice of Hesse-Cassel (1592–1627), the union came by 1607 to embrace the vast majority of Lutheran and Calvinist principalities.* The Catholics countered by forming the militant Catholic League,** which was led by the crafty but religiously uncompromising Duke Maximilian I the Great (1597–1651) of Bavaria. Both sides courted foreign aid: the union from the French, Dutch, and English; and the league from Spain and Austria.

---

*Lutheran members: Mecklenburg, Baden, Neuberg, Saxe-Lauenburg, Brunswick-Lüneburg, Brunswick-Wolfenbüttel, Holstein, East Friesland, and parts of Württemberg. Calvinist states: Hesse-Cassel, Rhenish Palatinate, Anhalt, Nassau, Ansbach, Pomerania, Zweibrücken, Bayreuth, and the Calvinist margrave of the otherwise Lutheran Brandenburg.

**Catholic members: Bavaria, Hesse-Darmstadt, Alsace, Berg, Jülich, Mainz, Cologne, Trier, Bamberg, Constance, Münster, Paderborn, Osnabrück, Würzburg, Speier, Salzburg, Hildesheim, Minden, Carniola, and parts of Württemberg.

The Catholic League was hamstrung from the outset by reason of the fact that Austria, which was not a member, was the theater of a vendetta between Habsburg brothers. The politically latitudinarian Matthias, the brother of the emperor, had waited impatiently for years at the foot of the throne. Matthias conspired to force Rudolf's abdication. He purchased the neutrality of the Turks and offered broad liberties to the Hungarians, Bohemians, and Austrians in return for their support. The emperor, too, tried to broaden his political base. In 1608 he convened the diet in Prague and issued a Letter of Majesty, which abolished the Compacts of Prague and granted civil liberties and religious toleration to the Czechs. In the end, however, Rudolf was obliged to buy off Matthias with the cession of Upper and Lower Austria and Moravia and the promise of Hungary.

Meanwhile, an opportunity opened in northwest Germany for the Catholic cause. At stake were the industrially and minerally important duchies of Jülich, Clèves, and Berg and the counties of Mark and Ravensberg, whose thrones became vacant in 1609. In Protestant hands these states would block the Spanish overland route from Italy to Belgium; in Catholic, they would isolate the Calvinist Palatinate. The two strongest claimants to the whole inheritance were Lutheran Wolfgang William of Pfalz-Neuburg, who soon concluded that the prize was "worth a mass," and John Sigmund, the aging Calvinist margrave of Brandenburg (1608–19), who had been the first German prince to abjure the *cuius regio eius religio* formula. The conversion of Wolfgang William almost set off the great war, which had long been threatening. Only the assassination in 1610 of Henry IV, the archfoe of the Habsburgs and the banker of German Protestantism, averted it.

Eventually the Clèves-Jülich dispute was peacefully settled by the Treaty of Xanten (November 12, 1614). Berg and Jülich were assigned to Catholic Wolfgang William, thus widening the Catholic corridor in northwestern Germany. Clèves, Mark, and Ravensberg were provisionally awarded to Brandenburg, which made it a west German power and strengthened John Sigmund's commitment to religious liberty enshrined in his great Edict of Toleration of February 24, 1614.

The Bohemian Phase of the Thirty Years' War

In 1612 Matthias had been unanimously elected emperor (1612–17). The new sovereign, in whom major and minor notes were mixed, espoused toleration but, being infirm with gout and without a son, he was obliged to transfer the responsibility of governing to his cousin, Archduke Ferdinand of Styria. Even before Matthias' death in 1617, Ferdinand was crowned king of Bohemia, and the following year king of Hungary.

It was Germany's tragedy that Ferdinand was wholly devoted to the militant Catholic cause. True, he had instituted many economically beneficial measures in Austria, and he was both amiable and kind-hearted to a fault. Fatherly and patient with all save heretics, Ferdinand had a ready smile and mild manner that belied the iron in his veins. His unoriginal ideas possessed an inner harmony that inspired confidence in those who agreed with them and desperate fears in those who did not. His fixed idea was that the vast weight of the traditional faith must one day smother all the works of Protestantism. However, it would be unfair to ascribe Ferdinand's policies toward the Protestants entirely to religious conviction. He was also convinced that the main obstacle to his centralizing measures was the estates of the crown lands. Since all of them were heavily infiltrated with Protestants, Ferdinand concluded that the road to benevolent despotism lay through the cemetery of heresy.

For the Bohemians, Moravians, Silesians, and Lusatians Ferdinand's coronation foreshadowed reduction of their homelands to satrapies of Austria. Only recently the capital of the Empire had been transferred from Prague to Vienna, and the concessions made in the Letter of Majesty had been whittled away. The Bohemians now counterattacked by excluding all but Czech-speaking citizens from enjoyment of civil rights and ownership of real property in Bohemia and Moravia. Then, on May 23, 1618, a murderous mob, led by Count Thurn, forced its way into the Hradschin palace, seized two Jesuit royal councilors, and in old Bohemian style tossed them out of a window (defenestration). Although a dung pile broke their fall, this act of defiance was answered with war.

The Thurn faction in the Bohemian diet deposed Ferdinand and offered the throne to the foppish war hawk, the Calvinist elector of the Rhenish Palatinate, Frederick V (1587–1632), who was a son-in-law of James I of England. On August 26, 1619, Frederick was elected king by the Bohemian diet. Unaware of this, the Reichstag at Frankfurt on September 9, 1619, elected Ferdinand II (1619–37) Holy Roman Emperor.

Except for the prince of Transylvania, of all the powers that might have sent aid to Frederick, none did. By contrast, Ferdinand II displayed energy and resourcefulness, swiftly spinning a web of diplomacy that enmeshed his rival. Within a little more than a year he had won Spanish financial and military backing, the alliance of the battle-tested Maximilian the Great (on condition that Frederick's electoral title and lands be transferred to him), and the neutrality of England, France, Hesse, and some other German princes and cities. Ferdinand reached an understanding with the Lutheran Elector John George of Saxony and even persuaded the Protestant Union to abstain from supporting Frederick V in return for a guarantee by the Catholic League (but not Spain) not to invade the Palatinate or other union territories. Having isolated Frederick, the emperor sealed Bohemia's fate in the Battle of White Hill (Weissenberg), fought on November 8, 1620. After this contretemps, Frederick had to flee Prague, which surrendered without a shot. Ever afterward, Frederick was mocked as the "Winter King," because he had been able to hold his throne for only a single season.

Because the Bohemian nobility had refused to make the economic concessions that might have rallied the peasants to the cause of national independence, resistance swiftly collapsed. Separatist elements were now imprisoned, exiled, or executed. All Church properties that had been sequestrated in either Bohemia or

Moravia since 1552 were restored to the clergy, which now received an immense accession of wealth and power. Furthermore, Ferdinand II caused thousands of native-owned estates and farms to be confiscated and redistributed mainly among his German supporters. From this time date some of the great foreign-name families of Bohemia—the Galles, Liechtenstein, Wallis, Dietrichstein, and Piccolomini. The principal individual beneficiary was the harsh and saturnine Albert Wenzel von Wallenstein (1583–1634), a Catholic courtier of Gratz and a wealthy widower, who scooped up nine Bohemian towns and three-score villages, while contriving to buy for a song additional confiscated properties. Taken in aggregate, Ferdinand's expropriations and distribution of the spoils recall those of William after the conquest of England.

In what had been the richest domain of the Empire, three-fourths of all estates were transferred, usually without indemnification, to Catholics. Not only all churches and schools, but the Utraquist University of Prague, were seized by the invaders, and the Protestant clergy were outlawed. One-third of all the land in the country passed into German Catholic hands, where it remained until World War II. Many rebel nationalists were executed, and scores of thousands of Czechish Protestants fled the country. Expropriations also took place in rebellious Hungary, even though many magnates affected Catholic conversion to forestall loss of property. In Slovakia it was the same, but in Lusatia and Silesia the landlords were spared. A prostrate Bohemia was compelled, moreover, to furnish troops for the imperial armies during the Thirty Years' War. Deprived of its most talented sons, shackled with political and economic chains, and obliged to accord parity to the German language in schools, councils, diets, and courts, Bohemia withered on the vine. It was two centuries before she bore good fruit again.

The last act in this Sophoclean tragedy was the Renewed Land Ordinance of 1627 for Bohemia and Moravia. It transferred all law-making authority from the diets to the emperor. Catholicism was declared to be the sole permissible faith; the German language was accorded legal parity with Czech; and the crown of St. Vacslav (Wenceslas) was made hereditary in either the male or female lines of the Habsburg dynasty.

After the Battle of White Hill and Spanish Ambrosius Spinola's initial victories in the Rhenish Palatinate, the Protestant Union was dissolved (April 12, 1621). Thereafter, the two remaining major obstacles to peace were the cupidity of the ruthless General Ernst von Mansfeld (1580–1626) and the dynastic ambitions of Duke Maximilian of Bavaria. Mansfeld solicited half the princes of Europe for further military employment, which could very well make his fortune. Maximilian, for his part, demanded the pound of flesh the emperor had imprudently promised him. The duke's efforts to secure the Rhenish Palatinate, whose ruler had not been deposed, and a second electoral title, ultimately sucked the major powers into the German whirlpool. His chances brightened when Spinola and the Catholic Flemish condottiere John T'serclaes, count of Tilly (1559–1632), occupied the remainder of the Palatinate in September, 1622. On February 23, 1623, the Diet of Regensburg at length awarded the duke of Bavaria Frederick's electoral title and lands. By September further Catholic victories forced the Winter King to sign an armistice and go into exile in the Dutch Netherlands.

The Danish Phase, 1625–29

When handsome Christian IV (1577–1648) of Denmark cast his hat in the ring, the zone of war widened to embrace most of north Germany. From his decision flowed four noteworthy consequences: (1) for the first time in history the armies of a Habsburg monarch reached the Baltic; (2) the complicated clash of dynastic aims changed the character of the war from a mainly Czechish nationalist and religious struggle into one of conquest; (3) the mounting frequency of battles, the cruel methods of conscription and logistics, and the depredations and reprisals entailed a fearful decline in morals; and (4) before 1630 the fortunes of German Protestantism sank to their lowest point since 1547.

Christian IV sought to establish Danish control over the Lower Saxon Circle in an effort to anticipate the schemes of Sweden's king, Gustavus Adolphus, who was just then mired in Poland. However, Christian had no luck. Tilly got the drop on him repeatedly, and Wallenstein arrived in northern Germany to close in for the kill.

Albert Wenzel von Wallenstein, the last major condottiere in history, was a brilliant improvisor and a military organizer of genius. But he was an unprincipled rogue and only a second-rate field commander. For him religious aims were completely subordinate to personal. No general must bear heavier blame for making this war the most savage in European history. Wallenstein had whipped together a motley horde of 60,000 Protestant and Catholic levies, mostly from Bohemia. With this force he penetrated northern Germany and stripped it of everything of value. His armies left behind them gutted houses, barren fields, and violated women. As Wallenstein approached the Baltic, he accumulated lands and titles as a Sioux warrior did scalps. The emperor made him duke of Sagan, Mecklenburg, and Friedland, and also admiral of the Baltic and Oceanic seas. At Dessau Bridge (Elbe) on April 25, 1626, he met and, by sheer weight of numbers, repulsed Mansfeld, a better man than he. Then Wallenstein joined up with Tilly, who meantime had carried everything before him from Fulda to Minden, and together they humbled King Christian IV at Lütter on August 27, 1626.

By 1629 Protestant fortunes were nearing low tide. Hungary had been subjugated by the imperial General Pappenheim; the fearful Mansfeld had died of fever; and Denmark had been beaten. All Lower Germany, save the key Rhenish-Wesel area, which the Dutch had occupied, and Brandenburg, which had clung to neutrality, was under Catholic occupation. Christian IV had no choice but to accept the Treaty of Lübeck, which left him his German fiefs on condition that he abandon schemes of aggrandizement within the Empire and affirm his loyalty to the emperor. Evidently Wallenstein had been lenient because the alternative might have been a Danish-Swedish alliance, which would have frustrated his vaulting Baltic ambitions.

Catholic Ascendancy

In 1629 Ferdinand II stood at the peak of power. In addition to his victories he had secured a foothold in north Germany for his son Leopold William, bishop of Strassburg and Passau, who was now given the secularized bishoprics of Bremen, Halberstadt, and Magdeburg. Hungary had been subdued, while within both Bavaria and the Habsburg crown lands Protestantism had been crushed in all the rural areas. In Austria there had been many executions, and even the Protestant nobles had been intimidated by dire threats when not seduced by bribes.

Ferdinand II promulgated the Edict of Restitution in 1629. The most audacious assault upon the property of Protestant princes, this edict ordered restoration of all Church properties that had been secularized since 1552. Two archbishoprics, twelve bishoprics, and no fewer than five hundred abbeys were faced with seizure and return to the Catholic Church. However, the obstacles in the way of enforcement of the edict prevented anything more than token implementation.

Meantime the numerous enemies of Wallenstein, who objected to his avarice, egotism, and officiousness, conspired to force his dismissal. Ferdinand II was warned that only by dropping the condottiere could he prevent the defection of Saxony and Bavaria from the Catholic camp and Bavaria's alliance with France and Sweden. On April 12, 1630, the emperor gave in to the demand of the Reichstag at Regensburg that Wallenstein be dismissed. Behind this demand hid the diplomacy of Cardinal Richelieu, who had already driven a wedge between Maximilian and Ferdinand II. Wallenstein's release was a serious check to the emperor and, at the same time, the first in a string of clear-cut Protestant victories that were to fill the next three years.

The Swedish Phase, 1630–35

By the autumn of 1630 a typhoon was on the emperor's horizon. The French had made peace with the English and the Huguenots in 1629. On July 4, 1630, King Gustavus Adolphus of Sweden (1594–1632), hot from his triumph over Poland (Truce at Altmark, 1629), had landed on the German north coast at Usedom. On January 23, 1631, Richelieu concluded the Treaty of Bärwalde with Sweden, guaranteeing French subsidies for five years or for as long as Gustavus Adolphus should keep an army of at least 30,000 men on German soil.

Sweden's entrance into the central European dogfight internationalized the conflict, which would otherwise swiftly have died down, and it inflicted eighteen more years of massacre, pillage, pestilence, and famine upon unlucky Germany. From the standpoint of that nation the continuation of the war was without real purpose or ultimate gain. A general peace in 1630 or 1631 would have had much to recommend it. Apart from the preservation of German culture or what was left of it, it would have put Protestantism and Catholicism in a state of balance with victory going to neither side, and it would have confirmed the "German liberties" for which constitutionalists on both sides were really fighting. The emperor would have been left stronger and more respected than in generations.

When Gustavus Adolphus set foot at Usedom he was in his prime. Thirty-six years old, handsome, huge of frame and chivalrous, he was already celebrated far and wide for his military exploits, statesmanship, administrative achievements, linguistic accomplishments, and devotion to Lutheranism. Endowed with a rugged strength and capable of exceptional stamina, the king of Sweden tolerated weakness in others, but not in himself. His troops loved him past understanding, while for Wallenstein it was only possible to display crocodile affection.

No more than Christian IV did Gustavus Adolphus come to Germany simply as a liberator. Descended from the landgraves of Hesse and married to a sister of the elector George William of Brandenburg, the king of Sweden was not the man to be paid off with expressions of gratitude. He aspired to territorial gains that would give his country effective control over the estuaries of the rivers of north Germany and, together with recent acquisitions from Poland, make the Baltic a Swedish lake. Beyond this, he dreamt of making Sweden the buckler of Protestant Europe.

Gustavus Adolphus overcame nearly every obstacle on the north German plains. Alone, the armed neutrality of Brandenburg prevented him from coming to the timely relief of Magdeburg when it was besieged by Tilly and Pappenheim. That city fell on May 20, 1631, and was given over, without Tilly's express approval, to slaughter and the torch. It is thought that 25,000 out of a total of 30,000 inhabitants perished in the orgy. Tilly ordered their corpses thrown into the Elbe to avoid pestilence, and the river, red with blood, was choked with flesh for miles.

Gustavus now moved like an avenging angel through Brandenburg and Saxony, forcing Margrave George William and Duke John George to abandon their neutrality. By the time the "Lion of the North" caught up with the main imperial army under the gaunt and grizzly Tilly, the whole German plains area had been "coordinated" with Swedish purposes. Even Bavaria had forsaken the emperor and signed a secret treaty with France. The Battle of Breitenfeld, four miles from Leipzig, was the most glorious in the annals of the Swedish army. Fought on September 18, 1631, Breitenfeld brought the Catholic counteroffensive in central Europe to an end. The Habsburgs had to abandon all hope of reestablishing Catholic sway in Europe. Coming on the heels of the Dutch victories, this battle gave the Protestants mastery of the continent from Middle Germany to Lapland. "God of a sudden had become a Lutheran."

While Gustavus' lieutenant von Arnim occupied Prague, the "Golden King" himself wheeled westward with his main force toward the *Pfaffengasse* and Frankfurt am Main, the administrative heart of the Empire. En route, city after city fell to the Swedes, who burned many of them. In Würzburg the whole garrison and scores of monks were slain. On November 27, finally, Gustavus arrived in Frankfurt to superintend the foundation of his new order. By the close of 1631 the whole Rhineland, including the Palatinate, and Swabia were in Protestant hands.

At this juncture Maximilian of Bavaria, who feared that Sweden's king was too ambitious, decided to play Brutus to Gustavus' Caesar. Maximilian's army attacked the Swedes. At the same time Ferdinand II recalled Wallenstein as supreme commander on his own terms (April, 1632), which, though shrouded in conjecture, probably involved vast gifts in land, titles, and gold and the grant of autonomy in areas under his sway. Meanwhile, Tilly, who had fallen on the Swedish flank, had been slain on April 14 at Rain on the Lech. This blow to Catholicism brought Bavaria back to Austria's side.

Gustavus Adolphus now hastened northward to prevent Maximilian from joining up with Wallenstein's army in Saxony. The tournament of giants occurred on November 16, 1632, at Lützen, southwest of Leipzig. In the course of the battle, fought for the most part in mist and fog, both Pappenheim and Gustavus Adolphus died. Wallenstein's front had broken like thin ice, and the Protestants had won a pyrrhic victory. But Sweden's sun was extinguished forever.

Henceforth, the Swedish army in Germany was a body without a brain. Under the divided command of Gustavus Horn and John Banér it stumbled stolidly from one misfortune to another, dragging with it two uncoordinated German armies under Duke Bernhard (1604–39) of Saxe-Weimar and Landgrave William (1627–37) of Hesse-Cassel. On the home front the regent Oxenstierna (for the seven-year-old Christina) had to tack to meet a threatening invasion of Sweden by the Vasa king of Poland, who claimed the throne of Gustavus Adolphus. Richelieu, for whom peace in Central Europe spelled Habsburg supremacy, now renewed the Bärwalde subsidies to Sweden, and a new confederation of German princes, the League of Heilbronn, was organized. It embraced middle and southwestern German Protestant towns and princes as well as the margrave of Brandenburg.

Still, the Protestant position would probably have crumbled more rapidly than it did if Wallenstein had been dependable. But so haughty, cruel, and unscrupulous did the great condottiere become in the winter of 1633–34 that he was an insufferable bone of contention in the Catholic camp. Since Wallenstein's bubble reputation had been pricked by his disastrous campaign in Saxony, the emperor decided to throw him to the wolves. Dismissed on charges of treason, Wallenstein was assassinated, as were also his chief aids, on the night of February 24, 1634, by officers who were probably seeking to curry favor with Ferdinand II.

With Wallenstein's passing, the "heroic" phase of the war ended. All the other illustrious field commanders—Christian of Brunswick, Mansfeld, Tilly, Gustavus Adolphus, and Pappenheim—were in their graves. Henceforth the war dragged on without even the saving interests of Pompeys and Caesars.

The League of Heilbronn rapidly disintegrated when the combined armies of the emperor, Bavaria, Lorraine, and Spain, commanded by Matthias Gallas, won a bloody but decisive victory over the Protestant armies of Bernard of Saxe-Weimar and Horn at Nördlingen on September 6, 1634. In one fell swoop the Habsburgs recovered more than half of their losses. After Nördlingen the imperial armies burst like cannister in all directions—Franconia, the Upper Palatinate, Baden, Württemberg, Würzburg, and Heilbronn. Despite the offer of greater French subsidies, the League of Heilbronn could not be revived. Saxony forsook it and made peace on May 30, 1635, in return for Lusatia. The other belligerents signed a general truce at Prague (1635). This peace treaty rescinded the Edict of Restitution in that it established 1627 as the year for determining proprietorship over secularized Church property and it dissolved all leagues.

The Franco-Swedish Phase, 1635–48

In 1635 France reopened the war, but at an inopportune time. Only conclusion of peace between Poland and Sweden rescued Richelieu's chestnuts. Shortly after the death of Ferdinand II in 1637 Sweden's army under Lennart Torstenson was transferred from Poland to reenforce Banér's in Germany. This increment of strength to the Bourbon-Vasa-German Protestant alliance prolonged the war till 1648.

After 1637 came eight years of imperial setbacks, marked by Bernard's capture of Freiburg in 1638 and Torstenson's astonishing victories in 1642–45 in Silesia, Moravia, Bohemia (Jankau), Saxony (Breitenfeld and Leipzig), and at Vienna (the *Wolfschanze*). Following the deaths of Richelieu (1642) and Louis XIII (1643), the French armies under Turenne and Prince de Condé (Duc d'Enghien) performed indifferently in south Germany, but the latter won a great victory over Spain at Belgian Rocroi (1643). The uncertainties of a regency and the development of new Swedish-Polish tensions decided Cardinal Mazarin, Richelieu's successor, to open peace negotiations. The Emperor Ferdinand III (1637–57) was also urged to make peace by his minister Maximilian von Trautmannsdorff. Beginning in 1642, the lengthy negotiations finally culminated in 1648 in the treaties of Osnabrück (for Sweden) and Münster (for France), collectively known as the Peace of Westphalia.

The Treaty of Westphalia

From the peace settlement emerged many victors but only one loser—Germany. Both France and Sweden, strong national states, acquired broad footholds on German soil. France gained sovereignty, nonetheless lasting for being semantically ambiguous, over Alsace, together with the imperial vicarship over its ten principal towns. France also acquired bridgeheads across the Rhine, giving her access to south Germany. Sweden received an indemnity and West Pomerania with Stralsund and Stettin, the offshore islands of Rügen and Wollin, the port city of Wismar, and the secularized bishoprics of Bremen and Verden, which entitled her to representation in the Reichstag. Henceforth Sweden could levy tolls on goods passing down the Weser, Elbe, and Oder rivers and strangle the commerce of upstream principalities.

All princes and imperial cities were restored to such rights, immunities, and properties as they had held in 1619. The dukes of Mecklenburg were awarded the secularized bishoprics of Ratzeburg and Schwerin; Saxony received Lusatia; the Rhenish Palatinate was restored together with an eighth electoral dignity; Bavaria got the Upper Palatinate plus the electoral vote conceded earlier, which left the imperial college with five Catholics and three Protestants; and Branden-

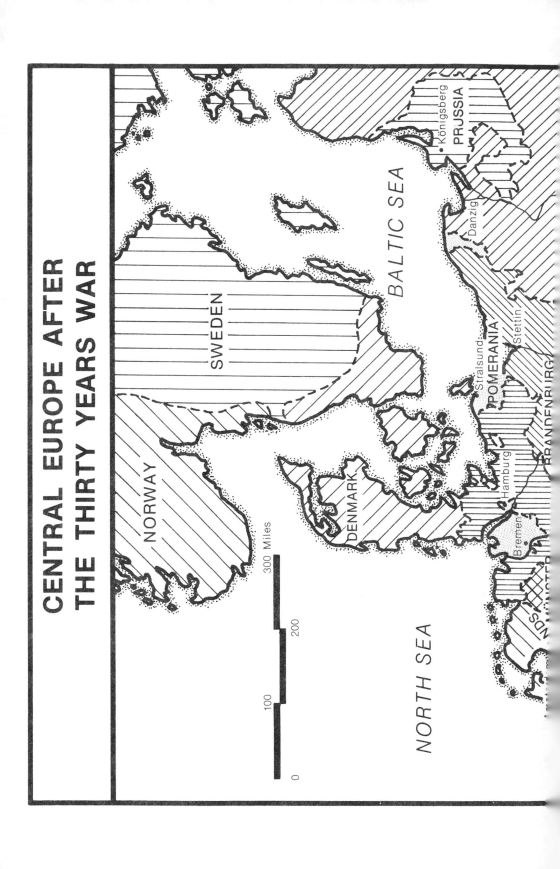

CENTRAL EUROPE AFTER
THE THIRTY YEARS WAR

NORWAY

SWEDEN

DENMARK

NORTH SEA

BALTIC SEA

PRUSSIA

Königsberg

Danzig

POMERANIA

Stralsund

Stettin

BRANDENBURG

Hamburg

Bremen

NDS

0   100   200   300 Miles

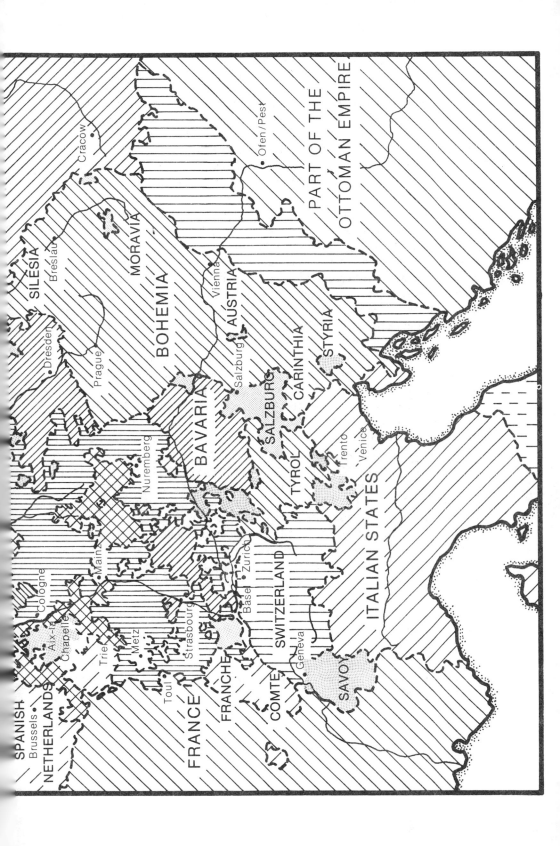

SPANISH
NETHERLANDS

Brussels •

Aix-la-
Chapelle

• Cologne

• Cracow

SILESIA

Breslau •

• Dresden

MORAVIA

BOHEMIA

• Prague

Nuremberg

Mainz

Trier

Metz •

Toul

Strasbourg

FRANCE

FRANCHE
COMTÉ

Basel •

Zurich •

SWITZERLAND

Geneva •

SAVOY

Salzburg •

AUSTRIA

• Vienna

• Ofen/Pest

PART OF THE

OTTOMAN EMPIRE

BAVARIA

SALZBURG

TYROL

CARINTHIA

STYRIA

Trento •

Venice •

ITALIAN STATES

burg received the bishoprics of Halberstadt, Minden, Kammin, the reversion of the new duchy of Magdeburg, and eastern Pomerania with the port of Kolberg. These accessions, added to those of Xanten (1614), made the margrave of Brandenburg the foremost Protestant prince in the Empire.

Westphalia reduced the emperor to a lustrous cypher. De facto sovereignty henceforth reposed with the territorial princes and imperial cities, which could make laws, mint money, levy tolls and imposts, dispense justice, conduct diplomacy, and make war or peace on the sole condition that they did not violate imperial law and the interests of the German "nation."

Religiously, the treaty buried any hope that Germany might become a confessional unit. The Reformed (Calvinist) faith received full recognition at public law and was guaranteed representation in all the organs of the Empire. In all respects Calvinism was to enjoy equal rights with Lutheranism or Catholicism. It may be true that these confessional provisions accelerated the drift toward religious freedom, but from Germany's standpoint, they undoubtedly sapped the little remaining vigor of the Empire.

The widespread secularization of Church property that had occurred during the Swedish and French phases of the war was for the most part made retroactive to January 1, 1624. Benefices and other ecclesiastical properties were to be restored to those who had owned them on that date, except as respects the Rhenish Palatinate, Baden, and Württemberg, where 1618 was to be the governing date due to the drastic changes that had taken place in those areas at the outset of the war.

The principle *cuius regio, eius religio* was reaffirmed but so hedged with exceptions as to further the cause of toleration in Germany. As a general rule, any subjects who before 1624 (or 1618 in the cases noted) had embraced a religion differing from that of their sovereign were confirmed in their liberty, while persons who had only done so after the definitive year of restoration were given options of abjuring their new faith, obeying their ruler, or emigrating within five years.

Beyond a doubt, the Treaty of Westphalia made Germany the anvil of European diplomacy. The nebulous religious freedom guaranteed by the convention was only interpreted abroad as a sign of senility. As protectors of the peace settlement, France and Sweden were put in a position to intervene almost at will in German affairs on the pretext of maintaining the status quo, whereas actually they used their prerogative to consolidate or extend their liens on German soil. The task of defending German interests and territorial integrity, meanwhile, devolved basically upon a legion of captious princes. The fact was, however, that plural sovereignty and divided military command made any effective defense of the Empire illusory.

Chapter 16

BAROQUE CULTURE

AND THOUGHT

Evolution of the Baroque Style

About 1580 a new art style, called baroque, meaning "unsymmetrical," began its triumphal procession from Spain and Italy through all Europe. The word "baroque" later came to be used by the Age of the Enlightenment in a disparaging sense, to mean effusive, eccentric, extravagant, rapturous, bombastic, fantastic, and grotesque. If more than a kernel of truth lay in this indictment, it was because the seventeenth-century artist strove mainly, in defiance of classical norms, to transform the static and tranquil art of the Renaissance into something that was dynamic, powerful, uninhibited, and aerial. To him form was less important than space; horizontals and verticals less than diagonals and curves; the symmetrical less than the askew; the earthbound less than the upward-rushing; the practical less than the fanciful.

Down to 1660 the successes of the baroque were identified with the Catholic Reformation and the Second Age of Faith. Baroque poetry, literature, painting, and architecture reflected the awful fears, doubts, superstitions, orgiastic dreams—in a word, the spiritual torment that gripped the popular mind in a macabre era. Cupola murals tried to compensate for the poverty of existence by investing heaven with every solace that would have delighted a Mohammedan voluptuary. While affecting to parade in sackcloth and ashes, much of the writing of this time was mordantly preoccupied with carnal concupiscence, crime, and deformity. It was felt in some perverse way that portraits of human depravity would magnify the perfection of heaven.

After 1650 the tumorous, bombastic, and rapturous features of the baroque slowly faded away. The fortunes of the style in Germany were then hitched to the interests of hedonistic princes and their courts at Dresden, Munich, Würzburg, Berlin, Heidelberg, Salzburg, and Vienna. The fine arts flourished, but literature, which received only scant subsidies, sank deeper into the well of tedium. Pretentious poetry, stiffly corseted in French Alexandrine stays, held sway. Interminable epics, freighted with adjectives, were frosted with mounds of lofty titles.

Whereas earlier in the century Dutch bourgeois standards had offered Spanish court styles competition on the German market, after 1660 the arts, if not literature, followed the fashions set by the French or Italian aristocracy. The more precise French canons came to prevail in every department of fine arts except music, where Italian influences dominated. In architecture, the majestic conceptions of Perrault, Le Veau, and Mansart were emulated; in painting, the elegant murals and canvasses of Le Brun, Poussin, Lorrain, and Champaigne; in formal landscape gardening, the geometrical wizardry of Le Nôtre; and in drama and literary criticism, the works of Corneille, Racine, Molière, and Boileau belatedly came to evoke imitation. Similarly Cartesian rationalism invaded Germany as the century drew to a close, tempering Teutonic mysticism and idealism with logic and mathematical precision. German ladies and gentlemen dressed in the French manner and indulged extravagantly polite forms of address and a preciosity of speech and wit that lay like an incongruous veneer upon the coarseness of the national temperament.

About 1725 the baroque passed into the gladsome rococo. The majestic and overpowering gave way to the frivolous and intimate. A whipped-cream exuberance revealed itself in the gorgeous, new princely residences and gilt churches of Germany, as well as in florid operas in the Italian style and polychromatic concerti. Under the wands of France and Italy, Germany advanced into the brilliant foyer of the rococo.

Literature: Poetry

In a certain sense German literature was founded in this era. Yet no German baroque writer scaled the heights reached by the great literary masters of Spain's *siglo de oro,* France's *grand siècle,* or England's Elizabethan and Stuart age. The fact is, lack of originality, form, and style characterized the German literary works of this era. Ciceronian and Virgilian standards loomed so large that they overshadowed and stultified most of the unique native plantings. The German baroque preferred to ignore the relevant in life.

Early baroque poetry imitated foreign verse forms such as the madrigal, villanella, canzone, and Alexandrine. The last-named, a French verse form of twelve syllables, vied with the English iambic for supremacy over German poetry about 1600. The first major effort to adapt the Alexandrine to German was made by Abraham von Dohna (1579–1631), who left behind him 2,600 such verses. The crude labors of other poets, such as Johann Brandmüller of Basle (1593–1664), to adapt Latin hexameters, strophes, and dactyls to the disjointed native idiom were even more ludicrous and only proved that German poets of this era were quite mad.

The high priest of the German poetic temple was Martin Opitz (1597–1639), poet laureate of the Empire after 1625. His *Buch von der deutschen Poeterey* (1624) was the most influential work on poetics produced in Germany in the era. It was Opitz's hope that German verse might be purified and elevated to the heights attained by the Greeks. No German poet for three generations after him dared to write verse without an eye to Opitz's straightjacket rules of prosody. So great was the hypnotism of his brief for stilted French Alexandrines and English iambics that after him there was no place at all for simple poetry with popular appeal.

Literature: Drama and Novels

Biblical and morality plays, most of which were didactic, tedious, and in Latin, engaged the talents of many Catholic playwrights of the baroque. Of the more popular secular drama, the chief exponent was the Pomeranian Kaspar Brülow (1585–1627), while the most successful writer of court plays was Jakob Ayrer of Nuremberg (1543–1605), who wrote some seventy plays in the English manner. Many secular dramas were staged before 1617 at the famous Strassburg Academy Theater and at ducal theaters, the first of which was opened by Landgrave Maurice of Hesse-Cassel at his capital in 1604. Spanish, Dutch, and English models long dominated German drama. Even after 1650 the preference continued to be for the Italian *commedia dell' arte* and the fiery extravagance of the Spanish theater. The elegant French manner only slowly after 1694 conquered Germany.

After Johann Fischart (1546–90) German prose fell on evil days. The era of the Thirty Years' War produced only gloomy or ghastly literature, the main examples of which are the novels of Jakob C. von Grimmelshausen (1621?–76) and the plays of Andreas Gryphius (1616–64). The former wrote a despondent but gripping tale of the war, the *Simplicius Simplicissimus* (1669), a work that not only suggests Wolfram's *Parzival* but also Picaro, the swaggering hero of Aleman and Guevara and of most Spanish contemporary romances. Grimmelshausen's absorption with the struggle of the human spirit against an overpowering environment was matched only by his affinity for the picaresque, as exemplified in a series of novels, the best of which were *Der seltsame Springinsfeld* [The Strange Whippersnapper], 1670, and *Das wunderbarliche Vogelnest* [The Curious Bird's Nest], 1673.

The fame of the somber Gryphius rests upon his tragedies. All of these—particularly his *Cardenio and Celinde* (1647), *Charles Stuart* (1657), and *The Dying Papinian* (1659)—closely resemble in form and content the plays of the popular Dutch contemporary playwright Joost van den Vondel (1587–1679). Gryphius cried for blood as a babe cries for its mother's milk. His insatiable appetite for the sanguinary put its mark upon his florid plays, in which action was sacrificed to fustian and declamation.

Well past 1675, when the gilded word and impeccable classicism of Corneille, Racine, Molière, and Boileau had triumphed in France, bombast thundered down the galleries of German literature. Better than French influences, Spanish Gongorism (an emotional and tumultuous type of prose imitative of the writings of Luis des Gongora y Argote) and Italian Marinism (from the blustering, declamatory works of Gianbattista Marion) synchronized with the frequently explosive cadence of the German language. Gongorism finally strangled itself with a tumorous tour de force of 3,000 pages—Lohenstein's novel *Arminius* (1689).

When the translation of Molière's work appeared in Germany in 1694, Gongorism and Marinism began to recede before the shimmering French style. Then German literature, paradoxically, became not so much elegant as vapid. Ponderous German prose had now to learn to trip with fairy feet. Writers such as Johann von Besser (1664–1729) and Ulrich von König (1688–1744) made valiant attempts to slough off the Faustian coil and imitate the nonchalance, refinement, and glitter of the French manner, but their efforts were ludicrous. The best of the imitators was probably Christian Weise (1641–1708), the author of more than fifty forgotten plays.

Early Baroque Music

Both of the major styles of European music—the *stile antico* (traditional harmony originating with Palestrina) and the *stile moderno* had been cradled in Italy. The latter, which had been developed in Venice by Giovanni Gabrieli, C. Monteverdi, and G. Frescobaldi, recognized the close consanguinity of music with other arts and conceded that it should support them.

Under Italian influence German music tended after 1600 to become increasingly chromatic, sensuous, and sonorous. Voice reigned supreme on stage and in orchestra, as was demonstrated in the evolution of monody or homophony, which assigned predominance to a single part or voice, and in the development of opera from the Renaissance intermezzo. The craze for cantatas and *bel canto* arias, which were often sung by male sopranos *(castrati),* was paralleled by similar emphasis upon voice and vibrant instrumental pyrotechnics, which encouraged an unprecedented exploration of the capabilities of stringed instruments. Not till the coming of Bach and Händel did Europe tire of the solo.

Among the early baroque Lutheran composers of religious music Michael Praetorious (1571–1621), Johann Hermann Schein (1586–1630), Samuel Scheidt (1587–1654), and, greatest of them all, Heinrich Schütz (1585–1672), stand out. While Calvinism was opposed to any devotional music other than the psalms, the Lutherans borrowed hymns and motets from Catholicism and lavished energy upon the writing of chorales, which remained until the late baroque the most important avenue of Protestant devotional expression. In the hands of Andreas Hammerschmidt (1639–75), Paul Gerhard (1607–76), and Schütz, the northern chorale evolved from Germanic rigidity to Italian plasticity. It developed from traditional congregational singing to the instrumental concertato, of which Schütz was the greatest expositor. The end product of this evolution was the chorale cantata, which told a story through vocal solos.

Heinrich Schütz was the best German composer of the century. He wrote much religious music, including the dramatic "Sacred Symphonies" (1629, 1647, and 1650), the monodic vocal concertati called *Kleine geistliche Konzerte* (1636–39), vocal masterpieces such as *The Seven Words upon the Cross,* and the Passions according to Saints Matthew, Luke, and John.

Catholic Germany before 1648 achieved nothing comparable in music. In Vienna, Munich, and Salzburg the Italian style and Italian-born composers and musicians (Bertali, Valentini, Bernardi, and the two Bernabeis) held unchallenged sway.

Germany's most significant baroque secular composer was J. H. Schein, who adapted with skill the short madrigal poem to the contrapuntal song form. Much more popular with Germans was the so-called strophic continuo lied, the great-grandfather of the nineteenth-century lied (song). Heinrich Albert (1604–51) was the most successful composer of the former. The first noteworthy works for harpsichord and clavichord, which were in their infancy before 1660, were composed by Johann Froberger (1616–67), while organ music found its most eminent exponent in Samuel Scheidt. Much more in demand than keyboard music, however, was that for the vielle, viola de braccia, viola da gamba, and violin, especially the last. Nikolaus Strungk, Johann Schmelzer, and—ablest of them all— Heinrich Biber of Salzburg (1644–1704), improved on the range, positions, and bowing of the violin, practically exhausting the possibilities of that instrument.

Later Baroque Music

Under the influence of Pallavicino, Stradella, and Scarlatti, the theaters of Hanover, Dresden, Munich, Prague, and Heidelberg catered almost exclusively to the works of Italian operatic composers and librettists or to Germans who worked in the Italian manner. Nowhere was the Italian style so much the rage, however, as at the court of Charles VI in Vienna, where Italian was even the polite language of conversation. All Vienna was a stage on which the world's greatest prima donnas and castrati sang *bel canto* opera against gorgeous backdrops. The most rhapsodic German composer in the capital was Johann Josef Fux (1660–1741). Under him Viennese opera developed the luxuriant qualities for which it became world-famous—choral prominence, opulent staging, orchestral depth, and contrapuntal majesty.

That German instrumental music in the high baroque was not swamped by the tides from France and Italy but could preserve and extend its own harmonic, polyphonic, and contrapuntal idiom was due to Johann Kuhnau of Leipzig (1660– 1722), Johann Pachelbel of Nuremberg (1653–1706), Georg Böhm of Lüneberg (1661–1733), and the Swedish-born Dietrich Buxtehude of Lübeck (1637–1707). Most of all, the eventual ascendancy of German instrumental music was established by the surpassing musical genius of the whole baroque, Johann Sebastian Bach (1685–1750).

Bach, in whose family music ran like salmon in the Columbia, was an accomplished violinist and organist and the harassed father of twenty children. A student of Buxtehude, Bach served as cantor of St. Thomas' in Leipzig and, after 1736, composer to the elector of Saxony. A scrupulous and enormously productive craftsman who went blind from eye strain shortly before his death, Bach stands like a glorietta at the end of the baroque vista. More than two hundred compositions demonstrated his intricate mastery of church chorales and the cantata form. His capacity for combining independent melodies into rich, harmonic, contrapuntal textures was revealed in his *Brandenburg Concerti*; and his mastery of the keyboard prelude and fugue, in the *Well-tempered Clavichord*. His pietism is enshrined in the great passions according to John and Matthew. By the debut of the ensuing rococo era Bach had achieved a perfect balance between harmony and polyphony.

Another titan of the closing baroque was Georg F. Händel of Halle (1685–1759), who, while still resident in Germany, wrote concerti and seria-style operas, but who went to England in 1711, where he composed his masterpieces.

Early Baroque Architecture

The Jesuit priests employed architecture and sculpture as auxiliaries of the Catholic reform. Their Italianate churches were in fact the pictures that illustrated their tracts and sermons. They borrowed the baroque style from Italy, where Alessi, Sansovino, Longhens, and da Vignola were in revolt against the static mass and horizontal severity of Renaissance style and were embellishing the palaces they designed with columnar and sculpturesque effects, supporting their awesome domes with scroll buttresses and volutes, and enobling interiors with celestial staircases and ceiling murals. The Italian vogue substituted music for mathematics in construction. Exemplified initially by Il Gesu church in Rome, the new style did not sweep Germany until the masterpieces of the great Italian baroque masters—Carlo Maderna (1556–1629), Lorenzo Bernini (1589–1680), and Francesco Borromini (1599–1667)—had been built. Then central Europe yielded to this libertine style. However, it should not be thought that baroque architecture was accepted in Germany without reservation. Many people, especially Protestants, believed the alarming conflicts of the new style were a sign of decadence, and they rejected as indigestible the excessively lavish interiors, writhing columns, massive staircases, elysian cupolas, florid façades, roof statuary, and bulbous towers.

The first phase of the German baroque, from 1580–1630, yielded no religious architectural masterpieces, unless we except the stately cathedral of Salzburg (1611–34) by Vincenzo Scamozzi. However, the relative prosperity of Germany after 1555 encouraged secular building. Indulging the craving for a more luxurious life, princes, nobles, and burghers built mansions *(Residenzen),* costly guild halls *(Zunfthäuser),* and town halls *(Rathäuser)* in the new manner. Among the important early baroque palaces were the Summer House in Stuttgart by Georg Beer (1580–1593) and Duke Maximilian's residence at Munich (1611–19). Commercial baroque was best represented in the town halls of Danzig (1587), Bremen (1612), and Augsburg (1615–20), as well as in the Drapers' Hall (Gewandhaus) (1592) at Danzig.

High Baroque Architecture

Not since the thirteenth century had Germany enjoyed such a wonderful architectural age as she did in the high baroque. The new style at its apogee was the idiom of perhaps a larger number of first-rate architects than in any other country. Austria in particular, because of her shining military victories, became the Mecca of all the building and plastic arts. She was adorned with the masterpieces of Johann B. Fischer von Erlach (1656–1723), Jakob Prandtauer (1660–1726), Lukas von

Hildebrandt (1668–1745), and, in the rococo era, Johann Balthasar Neumann (1687–1753).

J. B. Fischer von Erlach, the imperial superintendent of building, designed many beautiful baroque edifices: the Bohemian chancellery in Vienna, the Palais Trautson, and the Clam Gallas in Prague. His surpassing masterpiece, however, was the Carlo Borromeo church (Karlskirche, 1715–37) in Vienna, completed after his death by his son, Josef Emanuel (1693–1742). J. B. Fischer von Erlach also designed, and his capable son completed, in the Austrian capital the Imperial Academy and Library, the Hofburg palace, and the hospital. Hildebrandt, who was born in Genoa, designed, among many other fine structures, the Upper and Lower Belvedere Palaces in Vienna for Prince Eugene of Savoy, thought to be unsurpassed for the charm of their interior arrangements. In Salzburg Hildebrandt rebuilt the Mirabelle Palace, and in Würzburg he designed the magnificent grand staircase of the *Residenz*. Prandtauer did his best secular work in St. Florian and Linz but built many fine churches, too, such as at Waidhofen on the Ybbs and at St. Pölten and Melk on the Danube.

The foremost architects at the court of Duke Max Emmanuel of Bavaria (d. 1736), where refined Italian taste reigned, were Enrico Zucalli (1642–1724) and Josef Effner (1687–1745), both of whom improved the Nymphenburg palace and built pavilions in its park. In church architecture the most esteemed masters in Bavaria were the Asam brothers (Cosmas Damian, 1686–1742; and Egid Quirin, 1692–1750). They built and decorated churches, such as those at Weingarten, Waltenburg, Rohr, and Schäftlarn, synthesizing many art forms.

In Bohemia and Moravia Italian masters long held sway. Their monopoly over architecture was first broken by the Dientzenhofer family (Christoph, Kilian, Georg, and Johann). Christoph (1655–1722), employing Italian techniques, constructed the façade and interior of St. Nicholas in Mala Straná in Prague (1703–11). A generation later his son Kilian (1689–1751) built the church of St. John of Nepomuk in the Hradčany, while in the city itself he erected the lofty domed church of St. Nikolaus auf der Kleinseite (1732–37).

Enchanting examples of the high baroque may be seen in many other parts of Germany: at Rastatt, Ludwigsburg, Stuttgart, and in the "fan city" of Karlsruhe. In Westphalia the beautiful castle of Brühl (1725–28) was designed by Johann Conrad Schlaun. In central and northern Germany noteworthy period palaces were designed by Andreas Schlüter (1660?–1714), Georg Bähr (1666–1738), and Matthäus Daniel Pöppelmann (1662–1736). Under the gallant Duke Frederick Augustus I, the Strong (1694–1733), who became king of Poland in 1697, Saxony became a cynosure of artists. While Johann Böttger of Dresden was rediscovering in 1709 the Chinese process of manufacturing fine, glazed, translucent porcelain ("white gold"), the city itself was garlanded with such an abundance of splendid buildings that Dresden came to be called the "northern Florence." Among the most famous to be constructed were the Japanese Palace (1727–33), the French Moritzburg hunting lodge (1723–33), the *Marienkirche* and the *Frauenkirche,* and, above all, Pöppelmann's lusciously frosted Zwinger (completed only in 1820). Destroyed in World War II, the Zwinger was subsequently rebuilt.

Sculpture

Early baroque sculpture was dominated by Flemish influences, but after 1648 the Italian style supplanted it. As it infiltrated Germany, sculpture lost its independence and once again, as in medieval times, sank back to the level of an auxiliary of architecture. Among the later leading practitioners of the art were Andreas II Faistenberger (1647–1736), who did noteworthy work in Munich, and Meinrad Guggenbichler (1649–1723), who was active in Vienna and Salzburg. In Dresden the most celebrated sculptor was undoubtedly Balthasar Permoser (1651–1732), who achieved the vigorous figures of the church fathers in the *Hofkirche* and the statuary in the Zwinger. Egid Quirin Asam conceived a number of spectacular altars (e.g., at Osterhofen and Rohr). However, the preeminent baroque sculptor was the versatile Andreas Schlüter, the royal architect in Berlin, who is best remembered for his tomb of Frederick I and his queen and for the equestrian statue of the Great Elector.

Painting

Neither in the seventeenth nor the eighteenth century were Germany's accomplishments in painting outstanding. She produced no world-historic frescoist or portraitist. German painting was marked by an emphasis upon curves, motion, chromatic effects, and apocalypses. However, in north Germany, where exhilarating Dutch and Flemish influences still prevailed, consequential work was done by Jürgen Ovens (1623–78), who was a pupil of Rembrandt, and by Matthias Schets (1625–1700). In Berlin the typical portraitist was Johann Kupetsky (1667–1740), while in Silesia the best brush was the colorist Michael Willmann (1630–1706). South of the Main River, of course, Italian influences predominated. In Bavaria the Asam brothers were the leading painters. Hans Georg, Egid Quirin, and Cosmas Damian Asam decorated many churches with frescoes in the exquisitely delicate Venetian style of Tiepolo.

Sorcery and Witchcraft

In the late sixteenth century Europe stood tremulously in the first shafts of a scientific sunrise. Yet to the masses it was a cold, false dawn. Their lives were not noticeably affected by the harvest of reason and experiment. Everywhere the popular mind was still warped by superstition, passion, and fear.

In Germany the governing criminal law in the sixteenth and seventeenth centuries was the *lex Carolina,* the criminal code of Charles V. Unlike Roman law, which had died out in the later Middle Ages, the *lex Carolina* authorized torture to extract confessions of guilt. Not only did the civil authorities exact the death penalty in most jurisdictions for any one or more of a hundred crimes, but every respectable town in Germany had its gibbet on the hill or road outside the walls. Most communities had their torture wheels often draped admonishingly with the broken body of some offender. Every town had its chamber of horrors, equipped with an arsenal of persuasive devices: cauldrons of boiling oil, lead, or vitriol— for bathing; chains, racks, thumb-screws, and strappados; knives for exploring parts of the anatomy; and "iron ladies" for embracing and impaling impenitents. Once charges were brought against a defendant, he was usually lost. The victim had then to be tortured until he confessed, when he was remanded for mutilation or death.

After 1486, when religious sects were not hacking at each other, they were engaged in frenzied witch hunts. Rivulets of evidence sent seas of old women to their deaths. Of course, many were mentally deranged, malicious, evil, or contentious. Some were heretics. Commonly cited charges were inflicting a plague, famine, hail storm, or flood on a community; hexing an army; striking livestock dead; causing cows to give no milk and bear no calves; inducing sterility in women; administering adulterous love potions; or cursing with the "evil eye." It was widely supposed that witches had signed a compact with the devil and that this could be proven by some mole, wen, or birthmark on their bodies. Everyone knew that witches could fly on a broom or a cat and that they assembled annually on Walpurgis night (May 1) to dance the "sabbat" on the Blocksberg to revive their infernal powers.

Almost universal by the beginning of the baroque era was the belief in witchcraft, demonism, and magic. Only a very few executions for witchcraft had taken place during the Middle Ages, and Roman law frowned on such measures. However, in 1484 Innocent VIII issued a bull, which, while making special reference to Germany, formally sanctioned the destruction of witches and sorcerers. To help implement it, the German inquisitors Heinrich Institor (Krämer) and Jacob Sprenger in 1486 published the *Malleus Maleficarum* [Witch's Hammer], an encyclopedia of occult rites and incantations. This work was for a long time a guide for prosecutors in witch trials.

Almost nobody was brave enough to denounce the barbarous tortures that swiftly broke most suspects, causing them to confess the most implausible crimes. Even Luther, William Harvey, Jean Bodin, and Johann Kepler believed in witchcraft. In Germany in the seventeenth century alone 100,000 witches and wizards, not a few of them children, were exterminated. In 1590 the Germans burned 1,500 witches. Between 1615 and 1635 some 5,000 were burned at Strassburg. In Würzburg 900 were sent to the stake between 1623 and 1631. In 1629 at Mittenberg 178 out of a population of 3,000 were burned. In Protestant Silesia at Zuckmantel 152 were destroyed as late as 1651. In his time the distinguished jurist and professor of law at Leipzig, Benedikt Carpzov (1595–1666), in his capacity as supreme court judge at Leipzig, sentenced 20,000 witches and sorcerers to death. These figures diminished by 1700, but it was not until 1783 that the last bonfire was lit in Switzerland.

German Science before Kepler

Despite widespread belief in sorcery and occult arts (chiromancy, astrology, and alchemy), Germany led the world in this era in astronomical research. Copernicus (1473–1543) of Cracow and Breslau returned to the heliocentric theory of Aristarchus of Samos and overthrew Ptolemy's system. Tycho Brahe (1546–1601), a Danish nobleman who had studied at Leipzig and Wittenberg and worked at the observatory on the isle of Hveen, rejected Copernicus' view that the orbits of the planets were circular. Brahe's assistant Kepler (1571–1630), hypothecated elliptical orbits and discovered that the planes of all planets pass through the center of the sun. Kepler then went on to state the mighty laws that govern theii motion.

In medicine, anatomy, and chemistry the lines all led from either the Italian Andreas Vesalius of Padua (1514–64) or the German Theophrastus von Hohenheim (Paracelsus, 1493–1541) of Villach. Paracelsus improved methods of treating diseases, introduced mineral baths as therapy, and improved on the medicaments of his time. After him the most noteworthy contributors to the aforementioned fields were Thurneiser, Wurz, Glauber, Braunschweig, Schenk von Grafenburg, Andreas Libavius, and Andreas of Coburg. Coburg (1540–1616) wrote an *Alchymia* (1597) which, despite faults, was the most important treatise on chemistry before Robert Boyle's *Skeptical Chymist* (1661).

In botany, where more important progress was made than in zoology, the tradition of Albertus Magnus was continued in Luther's day by Georg Bauer (Agricola, 1494–1555), Conrad Gesner (1516–65), and to lesser extent by Braunfels, Bock, and Fuchs. In the late sixteenth century the most important botanist was Clusius of Leiden (1525–1609), while in the first half of the next century it was Joachim Jung (1587–1657).

Noteworthy advances were also made in metallurgy, mineralogy, geology, cartography, hydraulics, and mathematics. Agricola laid the foundations of the first three with a series of capital publications after 1546. In geography the best contributions were made by Sebastian Münster (1489–1552) of Basel and the Fleming Gerhard Kraemer (Mercator) of Duisburg (1512–94). Kraemer worked out the famous "Mercator projection" (1569) and gave Germany its most comprehensive collection of geographic charts (the *Atlas,* 1585–95). In mathematics the chief name before Kepler was Joost Bürgi (1552–1632), who devised a system of antilogarithms (replaced by Napier's) and built the first precise pendulum clock (1560).

From Kepler to Leibniz

The Swabian Johannes Kepler inaugurated a new era of science, liberating it from its long bondage to philosophy. In his *Epitome astronomiae* (1618–21) he brilliantly confirmed the central hypothesis of Copernicus. Kepler also published in 1627, on the basis of the notations bequeathed him by Brahe, his master, the famous Rudolphine Tables (named for the emperor) of heavenly bodies. Mathematics, the sleeping beauty of the sixteenth century, was awakened by his kiss. He made contributions to geometry and set forth methods for measuring curves and the volumes of solids in revolution. Above all, his claim to lasting fame rests upon his formulation of the laws of planetary motions. The first two were set forth in his *New Astronomy* (1609), and the third appeared in his *Harmony of the Spheres* (1619).

Only a few of Kepler's German scientific contemporaries can be mentioned here. Paul Guldin of Vienna (1577–1643) contributed important studies on the centers of gravity of curves, surfaces, and solids. The Jesuit Father Athanasius Kircher (1602–80), building on Gilbert's discoveries, advanced knowledge of magnetism, constructed more precise optical instruments, and discovered the origins of volcanoes. He also hypothesized that the earth's internal temperature increases with the distance from the surface. The Jesuit Father Kaspar Schott (1608–66) made important contributions to mechanics and hydraulics, but the most important scientist in those fields was Otto von Guericke (1602–86). Guericke's most famous invention was the air pump, whose power he demonstrated in 1654 in his experiment of the Magdeburg hemispheres. He proved that once his pump had withdrawn the air from two hollow bronze hemispheres fitted rim to rim, two teams of eight horses could not pull them apart. In botany Kaspar Bauhin (1560–1624) of Basel classified more than 6,000 plants by their shape, stem, leaves, fruit, and roots. Bauhin anticipated Linnaeus by employing a binomial nomenclature of genus and species. Also in botany Joachim Jung of Lübeck greatly enlarged contemporary understanding of plant morphology and physiology. While no German chemist attained the standing of a van Helmont or a Boyle, Johann Rudolf Glauber (1604–68) of Karlstadt was the best of a weak field. He discovered the properties of the four main reagents of inorganic chemistry and urged the notion that certain chemicals possess affinities for others.

The dissemination of scientific and technological knowledge was furthered by the establishment of professional societies and scholarly publications. The first German academy devoted exclusively to physical science was established by Jung in Rostock in 1672. The first successful scientific journal, the *Acta Eruditorum,* was founded by Leibniz about 1680. With Hohenzollern support Leibniz also founded in 1700 the Berlin Academy, which proved to be a major stimulus to German research.

Leibniz

In Gottfried Leibniz (1646–1716), Germany's most distinguished mathematician and philosopher of the era, the currents of rationalism and idealism converged to form a river of exceptional breadth. Born in Leipzig and educated in Paris, Leibniz had in 1675, when he was twenty-nine (thirteen years before publication of Newton's *Mathematical Principles*), worked out the infinitesimal calculus. His contributions in that direction inspired not only Newton but the Swiss mathematician Johann Bernouilli (1667–1748). In 1684 Leibniz published in the *Acta Eruditorum* his principles of differential calculus, treating the relations of differentials to constants on which they depend. He also systematically worked out the differentiation and integration of mathematical entities and contrived a new mathematical symbolism for use in connection with calculus.

Among contemporary German scientists of this later era the most eminent was

Gabriel Fahrenheit (1686–1736), the inventor of the thermometric scale. He also devised high precision meteorological instruments and discovered that pure liquids always boil at constant temperatures.

Philosophy

Whatever Germany's contributions may have been to mathematics and science, her work in pure philosophy before Leibniz was inconsiderable. No figure of the Empire merits comparison with Pierre Gassendi (1592–1655), René Descartes (1596–1650), or Baruch Spinoza (1632–77). After 1650 a number of German savants—Clauberg, Jung, Weigel, and J. C. Strum—introduced Cartesian rationalism to the Empire. Philosophies of pure reason and of empiricism were constructed by antimetaphysicists, the chief of whom was Christian Thomasius (1655–1728), the author of *Introduction to the Science of Reason* and the *Exposition of Rationalism* (both 1691).

In Leibniz, a man of lofty culture and humanity, Platonic idealism and German Christian mysticism lived on, but disciplined by rigorous method. His great aim was to reconcile the religious with the mechanistic interpretation of causation. Although he never wrote a comprehensive exposition of his system, he sought in a number of disquisitions to prove the teleological origins of the universe. He suggested that it is composed of an infinite number of independent psychic units of spiritual force, which he called "monads." These mirrored in microcosm the cosmos or the revelation of the will of God, who was the super-monad, the source and end of all others.

Political Theory

During the baroque era the central problem of German political theory was sovereignty. Whereas Catholics and Calvinists favored limited monarchy and corporative rights, Lutherans held that princes received authority from heaven and were responsible only to God for governance of their subjects.

German Catholic theorists, influenced by Francisco Suarez (1548–1617) and Cardinal Bellarmine (1542–1621), embraced ideas of limitations upon absolutism. More radical were the Calvinists Dominicus Arumaeus of Jena (1579–1637) and Johannes Althus (Althusius, 1557–1638), who argued on behalf of a corporate sovereignty that was vested not in the prince but democratically in the estates.

After 1648 limited sovereignty (except for the emperor's powers) came under heavy attack. The victory of the princes in the Thirty Years' War encouraged a reaction in each principality in favor of a strong executive. This tendency received external support from the eminent theorists Hugo Grotius of Delft (1583–1645) and Thomas Hobbes (1588–1679).

After 1648 the prime German champions of absolutism were Veit Ludwig von Seckendorff (1626–92) and Samuel Pufendorf (1632–94). Seckendorff's influential *German Princely State* (1656) and *Christian State* (1685) expounded the divine right theory and defended enlightened despotism. Pufendorf, a Saxon professor at the University of Heidelberg, provided a moral fundament for German public law.

In his immensely important *Status of the German Empire (De statu rei publicae Germanicae*, 1667) and *On Natural Law and the Law of Nations (De jure naturae et gentium*, 1672) he vindicated divine right and princely absolutism but contended that the cardinal aim of rulers must be, in harmony with natural law, to promote the security and well-being of their people.

Chapter 17

TOWARDS AN AUSTRO-PRUSSIAN

POLARIZATION

Decay of Imperial Institutions

After 1648 the Roman Empire of the German nation was a glittering anachronism, a polity with a glorious past but no future. The Treaty of Westphalia condemned it to protracted invalidism during which its pulse beat ever more feebly. By mid-eighteenth century the Empire was to slip into a long coma from which it never emerged. In 1806 it was unceremoniously dumped into the grave by Napoleon.

In the century following Westphalia there was no sharp break in the continuity of imperial ritual and government. The old usages, formalities, and institutions, although cracking in every joint, continued to operate, but they carried with them a steadily diminishing show of vitality. The coronation ceremonies at Frankfurt am Main, when the sumptuously attired emperor seemed to be the reincarnation of the Caesars, continued to evoke delusions of grandeur, but nobody was really deceived as to the realities of power. Everyone realized that the one-time paradigm among monarchs had by the late seventeenth century become a lustrous nonentity. His power was so paralyzed by tight constitutional and contractual controls that the bediamonded scepter was in constant danger of falling from his nerveless fingers. All the sanctions of true sovereignty lay with the territorial princes, the emperor having neither armies nor universal tax revenues at his disposal. Nor was there any really effective imperial judiciary endowed with competence to review state laws for harmony with German public law, or any strong or well-trained bureaucracy. Under the circumstances, it was impossible to speak of the emperor as governing; he only mediated between the princes of his realm. The one thing that sustained the prestige of the imperial office was royal patronage. By continuously making conditional gifts of escheated lands and offices to nobles, the emperor was able to assert an uncertain claim to leadership of the German nation.

Notwithstanding this, all the agencies of imperial power gradually atrophied after 1648. The defense of the Empire was, moreover, all but rendered impossible when in 1681 military authority was divided among the ten circles. Similarly, the most consequential decisions after 1648 were no longer taken by Reichstag, supreme court, or imperial chancellery, but by the governments of approximately 200 out of about 1,800 political entities of the Empire.

The Reichstag had become nothing more than a council of plenipotentiaries of sovereign states. Cumbersome in procedure and antediluvian in organization, it was often ignored by the princes. Normally half-empty, the Reichstag was divided into three chambers—electors, princes, and imperial cities. Neither the villages (in which the bulk of the population dwelt) nor the knights and barons (of whom there were about 1,500) were accorded representation. In the first chamber or curia sat eight prince-electors (three spiritual and five temporal) until 1693, when a ninth elector (for Hanover) was added. Each possessed only one vote. In the second curia, which was divided into two colleges, sat all other princes and nobles entitled to membership. The upper college comprised the greater temporal and spiritual lords, totaling about one hundred, of whom about thirty were ecclesiastics. Here also sat the emissaries of foreign rulers who held land within the Empire: Sweden for Bremen and Verden; Denmark for Holstein; France for Alsace; and England, after 1714, for Hanover. The lower college comprised the lesser prelates, totaling about one hundred, and the counts. In the upper college voting proceeded by head, but in the lower by ''benches,'' of which there were six, including two for the clergy. In the third curia sat the delegates of some fifty-one ''free,'' old, imperial cities, but none from the newer princely capitals. Likewise split into two colleges, a Rhenish headed by Cologne, and a south German by Regensburg, the third chamber of the Reichstag had two votes, to be cast only if the other two chambers disagreed. In practice princes and prelates made common cause against the cities. In all three chambers of the Reichstag the Catholics had a majority, although the Protestants predominated in the empire.

Even the creation in 1555 of a smaller standing committee, the *Reichsdeputation,* consisting of all electors, save the king of Bohemia, and a curia or council *(Fürstenrat)* of princes and imperial cities, could not revive the prestige of the Reichstag. At times attendance fell to less than twenty-five emissaries. Although the diet of Regensburg sat continuously after 1663 as the ''eternal Reichstag'' until its extinction in 1806, the sole important act passed by it in that interval was the Imperial Constitution of 1681. This subdivided the empire into ten military circles, exclusive of Bohemia and Moravia, and authorized a German army of 40,000 to defend the nation against Louis XIV of France.

Although reorganized in 1654, the Imperial Cameral Tribunal *(Reichskammergericht)* retained anachronistic forms, and judicial procedures remained incredibly complicated. Sitting at Speier until 1693 and then at Wetzlar until 1806, the court exercised only dubious competence. In view of the disesteem in which it was held, it is not surprising that its deliberations were interminable and trivial. In 1806 the court ended its career with a backlog of more than 20,000 cases pending. Neither the jurisdiction of the tribunal nor the supremacy of public law was recognized in the larger principalities. Their rulers insisted upon the sovereign purview of territorial courts and law. In view of the difficulties of obtaining justice from Speier, many litigants preferred to bring suit before eminent professors of law, who swiftly handed down verdicts when the *Reichskammergericht* could not.

Princes and Polycentrism

By 1700 the salient feature of the German political landscape was a myriad of ant-hill absolutisms. Polycentrist despotism was encouraged by several things: the success of the French prototype; the rationalizations of absolutism that had been undertaken by such political scientists as Hobbes, Harrington, King James I,

Spinoza, Bossuet, and Bodin; the decisive political failure of the aristocracy in the French Fronde (1648–52); the grant of almost unlimited powers to ecclesiastical rulers after 1698; increasing acceptance by princes of primogeniture and entail;* the emergence of standing armies dependent upon the prince; and subsidies paid German rulers by France.

The creation of a service nobility and the general ruin wrought by the Thirty Years' War helped the evolution toward pluralistic despotism by reducing the gesturings of the provincial diets to opéra bouffe. Impoverished noblemen sold their services to the territorial prince, who employed them in chancellery, treasury *(Kamera)*, diplomatic service, or officers' corps. The grant to them of sinecures, pensions, and sweeping controls over the peasantry reinforced the bonds that held the aristocracy to the prince and at the same time isolated the bourgeoisie in their opposition to despotism. The decay of towns and reduction of population in the years 1618–48 further strengthened princely authority. As a result of the war, production had been sharply curtailed, capital had vanished, and the great majority of German towns—among them Leipzig, Augsburg, Prague, Magdeburg, Göttingen, and Heidelberg—had been ruined. The Swedes alone had destroyed 1,500 of them. Modern scholarship has reduced older estimates of loss of life due to the Thirty Years' War; even so, the population of the Empire declined from 21 million to 13 million, mainly due to pestilence rather than slaughter. Livestock was reduced by two-thirds. Since imperial authority was impotent, the princes had to intervene to save their people and insure the survival of their principalities.

From the middle of the great war onward, the economic sector of society fell swiftly under the control of a host of sovereign princes. Commerce, finance, industry, and agriculture were all subject to polycentrist controls and harnessed to territorial ends. Cameralist (from *Kamera*, "treasury") views rationalized the drift toward autarchy and complemented the theory of divine right of kings. The founder of the science of political economy *(Kameralwissenschaft)* was Pufendorf, but other cameralist enthusiasts of the time were Ludwig von Seckendorff (1626–92), Johann J. Becher (1625–85), and Philip Wilhelm von Hornick (1638–1712). These writers all took the view that the German principalities were organic units, whose managing directors, the princes, had the mission of rehabilitating the German economy. Cameralists recommended the establishment of comprehensive controls over trade, industry, and agriculture. They advocated subsidies to attract foreign laborers, improvement and extension of education, development of native industries, suppression of guild and other private monopolies, increased consumption of native products, abolition of usury, establishment of a stable currency and a rational tax system, foundation of state factories, augmentation of commodity exports, reduction of imports except for bullion, and

---

*Adopted by Franconia and Brandenburg in 1473, Bavaria in 1545, the Habsburg lands in 1621, Hesse-Cassel in 1648, and the Mecklenburg duchies in 1701.

accumulation of reserves of specie. Because in devastated Germany there was urgent need to protect the weak from predators, the cameralists stressed the paternalistic responsibilities of the sovereign.

In implementing cameralist theories, the Protestant, especially Calvinist, princes went much further than the Catholic. Protestant rulers more energetically and systematically developed the resources of their states and increased the territorial product while freeing industry from vestigial medieval encumbrances.

The Decline of the Diets

Germany in 1555 had been well along the road to developing a system of constitutional states. The strength of the representative estates *(Stände)* in the territorial diets *(Landtage)* was due to the marked influence of an affluent burgher element. The typical prince, who was usually up to his ears in debt, had periodically to be bailed out by his estates, which voted him special grants or taxes. In payment, the diets had usually extorted their pound of flesh. Where the *Stände* had been strong, as in Jülich, Berg, Mark, Cleves, Saxony, Württemberg, Austria, and Brandenburg, the *Landtage* had been able to check the growth of a territorial bureaucracy and nurture the illusion of dawning representative government. By 1600 in most states (but not Bavaria, Hesse-Cassel, or Hesse-Darmstadt) the diets had won rights to superintend collection of taxes and customs and to disburse funds and audit public accounts. In 1606 the cardinal principle of no taxation without the assent of the diet was formally recognized in Brandenburg by the Elector Joachim Frederick (1598–1608).

Thereafter the tide turned against the estates. This was due mainly to the financial independence that secularization of Church property conferred upon the princes. But it was also due to the occupation by Catholic forces of Protestant territories after the Battle of Nördlingen (1634), which had the effect of crippling many a diet that had met until then with some regularity. The absolutist counteroffensive began in Brandenburg, where in 1604 the elector established a secret or privy council *(Geheimer Staatsrath)*. This body was destined for wide imitation and was to play a cardinal role in the progression toward benevolent despotism. With the Privy Council's support the elector soon felt strong enough to reject the diet's petitions of grievances. However, the *Landtag* continued to be a political factor during the weak rule of Sigismund (1608–18) and the reign of the grossly incompetent George William (1618–40), and it was not really until the accession of Frederick William (1640–88), an absolutist of indomitable will, that the diet of Brandenburg sank into the quiet desperation that comes with impotence.

As the national economy was torn apart in the final phases of the Thirty Years' War, the heart of the diets almost ceased to beat. In Bavaria, Austria, and Brandenburg, they scarcely met at all between 1640 and 1648. Yet they survived the ordeal by fire, but so weakened as to be unable to resist the demands of princes and generals for ever more money. The establishment of standing armies, which put the ultimate sanction of force in the hands of the rulers, ultimately obliged the diets to kowtow to the princes. Where in the later seventeenth century the estates still met they had to content themselves with mere efforts to curb the extravagance of the court and the size of the armies. In other words, instead of fighting a constitutional struggle for limited monarchy, the diets had now to restrict themselves to a campaign merely for economy.

It was no longer possible for a gravely weakened middle class to do anything but dance attendance upon the princes. Foreign control of the principal river estuaries virtually excluded German merchants from world commerce and arrested accumulation of capital. English and French subsidies, meanwhile, injected iron into the backbones of the princes, enabling them to maintain permanent armies and achieve independence from the diets. In the end, many of them had no alternative but to capitulate. They commonly acknowledged the ruler's sovereign competence for functions the *Landtage* had formerly exercised and agreed to assemble only by order of the prince. Although they carried on the uphill struggle until the Napoleonic era, it was with diminishing vigor. With each succeeding decade the frost of despotism lay a little heavier on the field of liberty.

The Price and Dividends of Polycentrism

All but the larger German states were nonviable. The toy states system *(Kleinstaaterei)* was wasteful and vicious. Peasants and townsmen were heavily taxed to support government, gingerbread army, and profligate court with its palace, topiary gardens, and wild-life park. Rulers expended an enormous treasure in these senseless duplications in vain attempts to create the illusion of power. Although this offered employment to an impoverished gentry and a fawning middle class, their labor was squandered upon tasks without larger national objective. The masses, who footed the bill for all this vainglory, were obliged to invest in an enterprise that could neither profit nor protect them.

Strangely enough, the system of *Kleinstaaterei* was, from the standpoint of cultural output, marvelously productive. Political fragmentation in post-Westphalian Germany, as in Attic Greece and Renaissance Italy, fostered creative competition. Many a prince fancied himself a Maecenas. He subsidized large numbers of artists, writers, musicians, and scientists, who imparted luster to his court. All this cultural activity had a civilizing effect upon the leisure class and helped elevate standards of German taste.

Good and Bad Rulers

Administration was the substitute that the age of despots invented for politics. Acquiescence in loss of liberty was purchased with the promise of enlightened rule.

There were not a few conscientious, able, and cultivated German princes, secular and ecclesiastical, who regarded service to the state their métier. Among them were: Louis VI (1758–90) of Hesse-Darmstadt and his cultivated wife Henrietta Caroline, who counted among her friends Klopstock, Herder, Goethe, and Grimm; Charles Theodore (1724–99), count palatine of the Rhine, whose enlightened rule must rank as the most prosperous in the history of the Palatinate; Charles (1670–1730) and William VIII (1682–1760) of electoral Hesse-Cassel; Charles Augustus (1757–1828) of Saxe-Weimar-Eisenach, one of the noblest intellects of his time, who attracted to his mini-court of Weimar Herder, Wieland, Schiller, and Goethe; and Charles Frederick (1738–1811) of Baden, who did much to elevate his margraviate.

Of course, there were also many profligate and debased princes. Others were like palimpsests in that their fundamentally tyrannical natures showed through all pretenses like imperfectly erased writing. Among the worst were: Ernst Louis of Hesse-Darmstadt, who in 1739 bequeathed the duchy a mountain of debt; Eberhard IV (1676–1733) of Württemberg, who sacrificed everything to the caprice of his mistress, Christina Wilhelmina von Grävenitz; and Francis Josiah and his son Ernst, who completely ruined the finances of the 764-square-mile Thuringian duchy of Saxe-Altenburg. Similarly, religious obscurantism sometimes led a ruler to inflict grave economic injury upon his state, as in the case of Archbishop Anton von Firmian (d. 1744), who expelled 30,000 Protestants out of a total population of 190,000 from Salzburg.

While primogeniture and entail governed the succession to many German thrones, some rulers divided their territories among their sons, thus adding to the confusion that made Germany a target of encroachment by more unified neighbors. Ernestine Saxony, totaling only 1,397 square miles, was, for example, divided in 1554 into four tiny duchies—Saxe-Weimar, Saxe-Meiningen, Saxe-Gotha, and Saxe-Altenburg—and was not reunited until 1758; the duchy of Mecklenburg, after an initial division in 1611, was repartitioned in 1702 into the duchies of Mecklenburg-Schwerin and Mecklenburg-Strelitz; and the landgraviate of Hesse was in 1567 broken into four duchies—Hesse-Cassel, Hesse-Darmstadt, Hesse-Marburg, and Hesse-Rheinfels, but in 1604 consolidated into two states.

Saxony and Bavaria

Apart from Prussia and Austria, there were two other states—Saxony and Bavaria—that might conceivably have entered the finals for the crown of Germany.

After the Wettins had partitioned their lands in 1554, only Albertine Saxony possessed a future, for Ernestine Saxony lay pulverized. For half a century after 1648 Albertine Saxony was the fourth most powerful German state. She was rich in resources, had a thriving linen industry, and dominated the north German overland trade with the Slavic countries, a fact that promoted the accession in 1697 of Duke Frederick Augustus I, the Strong (1694–1733) to the Polish throne. With the invention of "white gold" in 1709, Saxony became the "porcelain kingdom," richer than ever. At that time she boasted three universities (Jena, Wittenberg, and Leipzig) and was hailed as the "school of Europe." In Leipzig Saxony possessed the publishing center of the continent, while Dresden, the ducal capital, was extolled as the "Florence on the Elbe."

The joining of the thrones of Saxony and Poland in the hands of a Catholic convert was the ruin of Saxony. It brought war with Sweden (1701–21), the occupation of both Poland and Saxony by the armies of Charles XII, crushing debts, and the alienation of the Saxons themselves, who were Lutherans. Saxony's decline was accelerated by her participation in the War of the Polish Succession (1733–38) and the fact that in the War of the Austrian Succession (1740–48) and Seven Years' War (1756–63) she was on the losing (Austrian) side. Saved from extinction by the Treaty of Hubertusburg (1763), Saxony, which had had to pay the bulk of the Prussian war costs, had all she could do thereafter to keep from being devoured by the Hohenzollerns.

Catholic Bavaria had been brought to the apogee by Duke Maximilian I, the Great. He had added to its territories, acquired the electoral title, and given Bavaria an absolutist structure that enabled it to hold its own for another generation against Austria and Brandenburg. However, by 1700 Bavaria, which was overwhelmingly agrarian, had fallen behind in the race economically and militarily. The duchy's prevailing opposition to Austria gradually wore down the Wittelsbach state. In the War of the Austrian Succession (1740–48) Bavaria was the ally of France and Prussia against Austria. Charles Albert (1726–45), the luckless Wittelsbach duke, hoped for extensive annexations and the imperial crown. Although he was unanimously elected as Charles VII on January 24, 1742, the first non-Habsburg emperor in three hundred years, his house of cards suddenly collapsed when an Austrian army invaded Bavaria. Charles's successor, Maximilian III Joseph (1745–77), was obliged to support the imperial ambitions of Francis Stephen of Lorraine and abandon all designs on the Habsburg lands.

After 1777, when the Bavarian Wittelsbachs became extinct, the independence of the duchy was preserved on two occasions, in 1778 and 1785, only by intervention of the king of Prussia. If Bavaria still survived, it was because a balance of power in south Germany was needed.

The Great Elector of Brandenburg

Above all other German states of the baroque era, Brandenburg-Prussia illustrated the rich dividends that could come from centralization. Yet in 1640 the margraviate, due to the incompetence of George William (1619–40), the caprice of his minister Count von Schwarzenberg, and the mismanagement of territorial finances, had been on the verge of dissolution.

With the accession of Frederick William (1640–88) a new day dawned for Brandenburg. When he mounted the throne the income of his state was only 440,000 thalers, and its population 325,000. In 1648, however, he secured annexations totaling nearly 20,000 square miles, and in 1680 the promised reversion of the great secularized ˙archbishopric of Magdeburg. While Brandenburg's Rhenish and central dynastic possessions were not as yet woven together, sprawling as they did like an archipelago over northern Germany, they were lucratively situated astride the Rhine, Weser, Elbe, Oder, and Vistula, which was the making of the state's fortune.

Frederick William was the first German ruler to raise his principality above the throng of comic opera states within the Empire. Born in 1620 in Berlin, he had received a good education and had learned to speak Dutch, French, and Polish fluently. Himself a son of a princess of Orange, he married Louise Henriette of that house, the eldest daughter of the Dutch stadtholder. This union gave cover to Brandenburg's exposed Westphalian territories.

While no genius, Frederick William was sagacious and practical. He compensated for slight intellectual shortcomings by amazing industry. He thought that rulers should consume themselves, like candles, for the good of their subjects. His motto might well have been: "Work is the soul of luck." He had a feeling for what was feasible and the crowning virtue of a statesman—the knack of success.

War and military strength figured prominently in Frederick William's policies. The army was for him what it was to be for Bismarck—the main tool with which the power of the state was to be fashioned. During the first Northern War (1655–60) he extorted in succession from Sweden (Treaty of Labiau, 1656), from Poland (Treaty of Wehlau, September 19, 1657), and from all belligerents (final Treaty of Oliva, May 3, 1660) recognition of his full sovereignty in East Prussia.

In the interests of Brandenburg Frederick William could be calculating, even ruthless. He knew no permanent friends, only pawns in the chess game of power politics, and he changed allies with the caprice of a woman changing styles. On the other hand, he, a strict Calvinist, never put his religion in the service of personal ambition, and he was averse to frivolous or unjust wars. Always paramount in his state, he exercised both ultimate military and civil authority and made all final decisions. If Frederick William was able to a surprising degree to further the grand goals of a rational public policy, it was because he believed strongly in the primacy of the civilian over the military. A vaulting ambition for Brandenburg was joined with a moral appreciation that law, propriety, and a lasting international comity at all times interdicted the pursuit of vulgar martial ends.

Although Frederick William confirmed the seignorial authority of the Junkers over their peasants and did little to promote the formal education of the common people, the bulk of whom were serfs, he did inculcate all classes with a sense of identity with the Hohenzollern state. He enlarged governmental control over the economy, founded an ill-fated African Trading Corporation (1682) that established colonies on the Guinea Coast (1684); and built the Friedrich Wilhelm Canal (1662–68), connecting the Oder with the Spree and making Berlin a major inland port. When the Edict of Nantes was revoked in 1685 by France, he opened sparsely populated Brandenburg to 20,000 Huguenots. He engineered the economic recovery of Brandenburg and Prussia from the Thirty Years' War and raised their respective populations by the time of his death to approximately 400,000 and 270,000, the total population of the realm being at that time a little more than a 1 million. Frederick William increased what came in his time to be a permanent standing army from a strength of 4,000 men and officers to a little more than 30,000 by 1688. He built an integrated state that was cemented by the mortar of the army and civil service. In his progression toward the organic, total state

(Gesamtstaat), the Great Elector coordinated his scattered territories, instituted a system of direct taxes which financed the needs of army and government, centralized the administration, and reduced diets and selfish interests to docility.

A great lover of nature, Frederick William founded the royal botanical gardens and encouraged the reforestation of his sandbox principality. He also founded museums and the Royal Library in Berlin. Although Frederick William did not mitigate the worst features of serfdom but even extended it in 1653, he was tolerant and won the support of all sects and classes. The continuation of his main programs by his three successors during long reigns of respectively twenty-five, twenty-seven, and forty-six years made Brandenburg-Prussia the lintel of the north.

Centralization

In 1641 Frederick William rescued the Privy Council *(Geheimer Staatsrath)* from the obscurity into which it had fallen. Influenced by Count George Frederick von Waldeck, he began in December, 1651, the thoroughgoing reorganization of the council along departmental-geographic lines and made it, at least for a generation, the sheet anchor of the central government.

Although the provincial diets continued to exist, the Brandenburg *Landtag* fought its last battle in 1652 against despotism when it granted the margrave a large sum of money for six years. In return, the extensive rights of the nobility over peasants and smaller towns were confirmed. Frederick William was now able to wage the First Northern War (1655–60) without having to convene the diet. The final Peace of Oliva (1660) so strengthened his hand that he never again had to summon the estates of Brandenburg. Thus the only organ that had any chance of evolving into a representative limitation on autocracy perished in exile. After 1660 the Privy Council gathered into its hands control over every aspect of official business. Even the opposition of the Prussian estates was broken in 1661–63, when their leaders were imprisoned and the diet was deprived of control over taxation.

In his predatory drive to break the estates and establish the supreme power of the prince, Frederick William appreciated that the key to despotism was the financial independence of the chief executive. Accordingly, he devised two lines of attack: he levied new excise taxes in the towns and he established a general war office *(Generalkriegskommissariat)* alongside a general staff. Both reforms were rendered imperative by the emergence of a standing army, which was destined to become the vertebral column with which all other state agencies were articulated.

The new taxes were levied in the towns upon a variety of comestibles, beer, and liquors, as well as upon all artisans. Called consumers' excises *(Konsumptionsaksizen),* the imposts were to be paid in silver and to be collected by fiscal agents directly responsible to the central government. In rural areas the old feudal, local capitation, and land taxes *(Kontributionen),* for which only commoners were liable, remained in force and, like consumers' excise proceeds, were allocated to the army. Civil governmental expenses were largely covered by other forms of revenue, such as from the rental of electoral domains, taxes on Jews, revenues from tolls, coinage, and fines. Although state revenues were originally paid into a variety of treasuries, by 1683 civil receipts had all been concentrated in a general treasury, while military revenues had come to be put in a war treasury. Allocation of civil receipts was superintended thenceforward by the General Directory of Finances, while military tax and budgetary matters were controlled by the General War Office.

The First Northern War and mounting military tax receipts promoted rapid growth of the General War Office's administrative empire. By 1688 the War Office had come to surpass the Privy Council in importance, a development that was in consonance with the increasing power of the army in the margraviate. Although in 1686 some of the responsibilities of the War Office were transferred to a permanent general staff *(Generalstab)*, the former had indubitably become the great wheel that moved all others, including the Privy Council, in the inchoate absolutist state.

Continued Progress under Frederick I

When on May 9, 1688, Frederick William died after two years of suffering, he was succeeded by Frederick III (1688–1713), the second son of Frederick William's first wife. Although Frederick III was not endowed with much vigor or administrative talent, Brandenburg neither broke up nor retrogressed under him. In 1710 and 1713 he solemnly reaffirmed the Disposition of Achilles and the indivisibility of his realm. His able minister Eberhard von Danckelmann (1643–1722) fashioned a bureaucratic, rather than a monarchical, absolutism. Neither corruption, malfeasance, royal extravagance, nor three wars (War of the League of Augsburg, War of the Spanish Succession, and Great Northern War) undermined the Hohenzollern edifice. Even the notorious financial mismanagement under Danckelmann's successor, Count von Wartenburg, did not seriously impair the credit or stability of the state.

If Frederick's image continued reputable throughout his life, this was due to Danckelmann's foreign policy, which consistently subordinated everything to Brandenburg's alliance with Austria and the Maritime Powers. That policy won Frederick generous subsidies from the latter, some territorial bagatelles (Mörs, Lingen, Guelderland, Orange, and Neuchâtel), and a kingdom in East Prussia. The subsidies financed his magnificent court and his cultural projects. The Dutch territories strengthened Brandenburg's hold on the lower Rhine.

Minor reforms strengthened the margraviate. The consolidation of the offices of rural tax collector and war commissar in a single new office of noble country counselor *(Landrat)* effected substantial economies. The fact that after 1700 the War Office acted through the *Landräte* in the countryside and the tax counselors *(Steuerräte)* in the towns to collect military contributions injected more symmetry and efficiency into the system. At the end of twenty-five years of rule, the reputedly profligate Frederick had augmented governmental receipts from 2½ million to 4 million thalers per year, while the peacetime army was increased from 30,000 to 40,000.

Had Frederick III pursued a more aggressive foreign policy, such as allying with France against Austria, he might have alienated the very powers whose support he needed to acquire a royal crown. Instead, his caution and good sense allayed the suspicions of their governments, and he was rewarded by being recognized king (Frederick I) *in* Prussia (January, 1701). His successor was confirmed in this title by the treaties of Utrecht (1713), Rastatt, and Baden (1714). Frederick I prudently contented himself with territorial crumbs from the banquet table of the great powers. He was too canny to jeopardize his newly won crown for the sake of Swedish Pomerania, and so he did not enter the Great Northern War (1700–21), which would have merged the two theaters. Moreover, his leisurely participation in the war against Louis XIV allowed time to Frederick and his noble wife, Sophie Charlotte (1668–1705), vigorously to promote art and thought in Brandenburg.

The Cast-Iron King: Frederick William I

Brandenburg-Prussia first acquired a harsher cast under Frederick William I (1713–40). Although physically corpulent, the new king was a stern martinet. His passion in life was the army, and his watchwords were "austerity" and "economy." He deplored the refined tastes of his royal parents and despised pomp and display. His one extravagance was the army. During his reign he raised its peacetime strength from 40,000 to 76,000. The surest way to curry favor with him was to send him a gift of a uniformed giant for his beloved Potsdam Grenadiers. In other respects, he had the heart of a miser and the eye of an auditor. He turned the spacious gardens before the palace into a parade ground and his residence into an administrative building.

An absolutist to the core, Frederick William I treated his family like subjects and his subjects like bondsmen. His civil service was the hardest working and the poorest paid corps of officials in Europe. It is said that he was a pious Lutheran, unlike his Calvinist father, but the truth is that he saw in the church less the ladder to heaven than a stepping-stone to power. He declared that while salvation might be the affair of God, everything else belonged to the king. When he was thwarted he was capable of insane fits of temper. In a fury of anger over the flight of his recreant son, Frederick, he came within an ace of slaying him.

The king looked like a lout. Although the beneficiary of a good education, his manners were those of a swineherd. When not reviewing his Potsdam giants or on the hunt, he sought relaxation in the company of beer-drinking, foul-mouthed cronies, whom the public derided as his "tobacco cabinet." Puritanical in other respects and pious as to outward appearances, he was contemptuous of everything that passed as culture. Frederick William I was ostentatiously German in speech and dress when it was fashionable to imitate the French in both. Vulgar, irascible, despotic, and disagreeable, he was a boor who made his home a penitentiary, his court a stable, and his kingdom a barracks. Fortunately his spirit did not triumph in Prussia.

Contributions of Frederick William I

Despite serious character defects, Frederick William I achieved big things. He began by making a capital territorial gain. He exploited Sweden's involvement in the Second Northern War to ally himself with Russia, forcing Stockholm to buy his neutrality (Treaty of Stockholm, 1720) by ceding him the islands of Wollin and Usedom and western Pomerania from the Oder to the Peene, together with Stettin. Although the extreme western tip of Pomerania was retained by Sweden, which did not relinquish Stralsund until 1815 and Wismar until 1903, she was never again in a position to menace German liberties. Hanover had been enlarged, too, by Sweden's cession of Bremen and Verden in 1719, so that now Prussia's gains of 1720 sounded the knell of Sweden as a Baltic power.

In internal affairs the Potsdam autocrat left his realm stronger and more centralized. An excellent judge of men, who could extract work from them as one squeezes juice from a lemon, the king was shrewd and tenacious. Under his adept management the financial position of Prussia improved to the point where in 1739 the treasury bulged with 8 million thalers, and the government was free of debt, besides which, the kingdom was unprecedentedly prosperous. It is thought that the gross territorial product almost tripled during his reign. He increased profits from the operation of the royal domains to a point where by 1739 they were yielding half the annual revenue of the government. Although Frederick William I was hostile to higher education and besmirched his name by driving the philosopher Christian Wolff from the University of Halle, the king was the first ruler of modern times to institute mandatory, primary education. In 1717 he decreed that all boys and girls must attend school till their twelfth year.

The decisive achievement of Frederick William's life was the development of a first-class army. Yet he was loath to use it, for he was fundamentally a man of peace. The king strengthened the Prussian officers corps and recruited it mainly from the landed nobility. He established a military academy in Berlin. In 1733 he instituted universal conscription on a district quota basis, with the result that the army came to be filled with crude, peasant, part-time levies rather than full-time, dependable regulars. Frederick William improved quartermaster and transport facilities and ordnance. He also caused new, oblique assault tactics to be adopted and substantially augmented the size and budget of the army. By 1739 the army had become everybody's concern. It absorbed two-thirds of the annual royal income, had increased to 76,000 men out of a population of 2,500,000 and had come to influence the policies of the state and to a profound degree transform the social values of the citizenry.

The cornerstone of the king's avowedly militarily oriented reforms was the law of 1723, which established the Central General Directory *(General Ober-*

finanz-,Kriegs-, und Domänendirektorium). This capstone agency was organized into four departments, and it fused the treasury, war office, and office of the royal demesne. Each of the four departments superintended one of the four geographic areas into which the kingdom was divided and exercised duplicate functions. Subordinate to the central general director were the finance office (civil revenue) and war treasury. Strict audit of both was conducted after 1723 by a general accounting office. Comparable consolidation was achieved on the provincial and communal levels. There was no room in this autocratic administrative system for corruption or local initiative. Vice, class interests, and liberty were all more or less crushed beneath the vast weight of the Central General Directory.

Chapter 18

AUSTRIA AT ITS ZENITH

Obstacles to Centralization

After 1648 circumstances seemed to favor consolidation of the Habsburg crown lands. Primogeniture and entail had been adopted by the dynasty in 1621, and the Grand Monarchy had, except for Bohemia, achieved a rapid recovery from the war. Ferdinand III (1637–57) had broken the power of the estates, forged a decisive alliance with the aristocracy, imposed religious conformity, kept the peasantry servile and the middle class weak, and had managed to create the illusion of military victory. Last, the intelligence and ability of the Emperor Leopold I (1657–1705) argued for the success of the aims of the powerful Habsburg dynasty.

Nevertheless, the forces of particularism proved to be stronger than despotism. The crown lands were polyglot and, as respects law and custom, variegated. The empire embraced two kingdoms—Bohemia (including the Silesian and Moravian dependencies), where the crown was hereditary, and Hungary, where it was elective and royal authority extended to only a quarter of the realm—and the archduchy of Austria, to which Styria, Carniola, and Carinthia were subordinate. To the latter dependencies were subsequently added the Tirol in 1665 and Croatia and the Banat of Temesvar in 1718. Inner, Lower, and Upper Austria, and each crown land had its own diet. Although earlier in the century the several estates had been deprived of control over major state policies, they met with fair regularity and continued to be responsible for collecting land taxes and military contributions and for local administration. The diets remained the foci of particularism.

War affords the chief explanation for the persistence of states' rights within the Habsburg empire. Perennial strife with the Turks put the survival of the realm into question. The dynasty was forever constrained to temporize with and persuade the subject nations of the empire to cooperate for defense of the Balkan frontier. This suppliant policy became the more exigent when Louis XIV confronted Austria with war on two fronts.

Like other seventeenth-century rulers, Leopold I harbored despotic dreams. The ethnic heterogeneity of his empire, of course, made them slightly ludicrous. But besides this, the gray threads that had been woven into his birthweb disqualified him as a despot. Humane, well-educated, a lover of all culture, and endowed with a lofty sense of duty, he was also morbidly pious, bookish, worrisome, and indecisive. Fortunately, after much vacillation he usually made the right choice. This facility, plus the ability to recognize talent and enlist it in his service, transformed the reign of this spade-faced, diminutive, simply attired but extravagantly wigged Habsburg into one of momentous achievements. Yet absolute monarchy was not among them.

The Turkish Challenge

From 1648 to 1740 the Turkish problem figured prominently in Austrian grand politics. To beat back the massive assaults of the still fearsome Ottomans was the constant study of the emperors. To do this, Leopold I had need of every resource and skill. His problem was more political and diplomatic than military, for it was basically to retain the allegiance of Austria's polyglot dependencies. However, Turkey had also to be deprived of the support of France, and Poland had to be detached from the list of Bourbon pensionaries. The adroitness with which Leopold made the necessary gambits outclassed the diplomacy of the Sun King and constitutes Leopold's chief claim to being the architect of Austria's Balkan empire.

Success against the Turks hinged upon whether the crown would arrange a *modus vivendi* with the diets and the nobles. Leopold decided to conciliate the former by giving them petty administrative and fiscal authority, and the latter with posts in the army, bureaucracy, and ministry, as well as extensive jurisdiction over the peasantry. The primacy of foreign policy in the capital city on the Danube explains why the appearance of a standing army, the aulic council *(Hofkanzlei)*, and an imperial privy council *(Geheime Konferenz*, 1669), and even the appointment of absolutist-minded counselors such as Lobkowitz, Montecuccoli, and Bishop Kollontish were, as respects the prospects of despotism, all initiatives without issue.

Montecuccoli's defeat of Ahmed II Küprüli's Turkish army at St. Gotthard a.d. Raab (August 1, 1664) led to the Treaty of Vasvar (August 20, 1664), by which the emperor purchased a twenty-year truce at the price of abandoning most of Hungary to the Ottomans and recognizing Apafy, a vassal of the sultan, as lord of Transylvania. During the recent fighting certain Magyar magnates, among them Nádasdy, Frangepan, Rákoczy, Zriny, Vesselenyi, and Tököli, had collaborated with the foe. In 1671 Nádasdy, Frangepan, and Zriny were executed for treason. However, when in 1681 a war with France threatened, Leopold found it expedient to buy off the Magyar magnates by granting them religious freedom and dissolving every centralizing agency that had been established in Hungary since 1606.

During two months in 1683 Grand Vizier Kara Mustapha Basa Küprüli led 200,000 troops in a last great siege of Vienna. He was defeated in a three-day battle from September 12 to 14 on the Kahlenberg heights above the Danube. This decisive victory was won by the king of Poland, John III Sobieski (1674–96), commanding the allied armies of Poland, Russia, Lorraine, Venice, and Austria and is commemorated by a vast painting that glows and kindles half of one hall away in the Vatican palace museum. A second crushing victory at Mohács in 1687 cleared the Turks from all of Hungary and Transylvania.

At the Diet of Pressburg in October, 1687, Leopold was at last able to impose his will on the rebellious Magyar nobles. The Hungarian estates were obliged to forfeit immemorial rights, the national crown was declared to be no longer elective in Hungary but hereditary in the male Habsburg line, and Hungary was in all respects securely hitched to the Austrian chariot. In 1689 a charter confirmed Austrian control over the Hungarian church, courts, army, administration, schools, and hospitals, while limiting the power of the magnates. The charter also confirmed the rights of the peasants, reduced obligatory labor *(Robot)* to three days per week, and, by authorizing a number of steps for the revival of trade and industry, also strengthened the bourgeoisie against the magnates. The charter facilitated the gradual Germanization of Hungarian culture. When, after the victory of Prince Eugene of Savoy (1663–1736) over the Ottoman armies at Zenta (1697), all Hungary, together with suzerainty over Transylvania *(Siebenbürgen)*, was ceded to the Habsburgs by the Treaty of Karlowitz (1699), and the 1689 Constitution was extended to the reconquered territories.

The Confederation of the Rhine

It was imperfectly understood by the German princes after 1648 that the main goal of the Habsburgs had become the creation of a Danubian-Balkan Grand Monarchy that could not menace them. Conversely the princes scarcely realized that Cardinal Mazarin's grand policy aimed at securing for France the Rhine frontier from Basel to the sea, an aim that would involve the conquest of Franche-Comté, Lorraine, Alsace, the Spanish Netherlands, and a part of the Lower Rhenish Westphalian Circle. Instead, scores of princes (especially the Great Elector) allowed themselves to become pensionaries of the clever cardinal in his studied efforts to divide Germany into three parts—Austria, Brandenburg, and a French-controlled league.

Misguided fears of Austrian expansionist schemes led the princes to form between 1654 and 1657 an alliance of both Catholic and Protestant rulers, which by 1658 evolved into the Confederation of the Rhine (Rheinbund). Its founders were the arch-chancellor of the Empire, John Philip von Schönborn (1605–73), archbishop of Mainz and bishop of Worms, and his astute chancellor, Count John Christian Boyneburg. Although Schönborn was no mere fugleman of the French government, pressure and subsidies from France and the support of Brandenburg determined that the Rheinbund would be aimed at the Habsburgs. Animated by resentment over his failure in 1659 to acquire Jülich and Berg by sneak attack, Frederick William took the advice of his minister, Count George von Waldeck, who had been arguing the material advantages of joining the Rheinbund.

It was, however, Austria's marital connections with the Spanish Habsburgs that engendered lively fears that for some years nourished the Confederation of the Rhine. Margaret Theresa, younger daughter of Philip IV of Spain, had been promised to Leopold Ignatius (king of Hungary since 1655), second son of Emperor Ferdinand III. The danger therefore existed that all Habsburg possessions, on which "the sun never set," would once again be concentrated in one ruler's hands. The Rhineland would become a Habsburg corridor to the Low Countries, and France would be nearly encircled. For this, Austria could be expected to risk much; to prevent it, France would risk more. To block the Habsburgs, Charles X was admitted as duke of Bremen and Verden to the Rhenish Confederation, even as France had been for her Alsatian vicarship, both with a view to guarding against the emperor's breach of faith.

After 1659 the Rheinbund passed its apogee. The Franco-Spanish Treaty of the Pyrenees (1659) enabled Louis XIV to turn his attention to expanding the eastern and northeastern frontiers of France. Her successes caused the German princes to review their commitments. Frederick William of Brandenburg, for example, now blamed Louis XIV for Brandenburg's failure to expel the Swedes from Stettin and western Pomerania. When in 1663 the Turks resumed the offensive against the Habsburg empire, most German princes refused to stab Leopold I in the back. They had no alternative but to support him. By the time the Great Elector formally joined the Rheinbund in 1664, it had ceased to be directed mainly against the emperor. Beset with confusion, it expired when Louis XIV, its patron, commenced his War of Devolution (1667–68) against Spain's possessions of Franche-Comté and Belgium.

Austrian Policy toward France, 1667–78

Leopold I was intimidated by the initial victories of the French generals, Turenne and Condé. Against the advice of Austria's best diplomat, Franz Paul von Lisola (1613–74), Leopold refused to join the Triple Alliance (England, Sweden, and the Netherlands) but secretly compacted with Louis XIV to partition the Spanish Empire in anticipation of the death of Spanish King Charles II. Spain and her American possessions were to go to Leopold, while Franche-Comté, the Netherlands, Luxemburg, Milan, and Naples were to be the French share. For the emperor the strategy of partition proved to be a contretemps, which only encouraged Bourbon aggression.

Not till the War of the Dutch Invasion (1672–78) did Leopold I and Europe perceive the true scope of the French menace to the sovereign states system. Then at last the eastern alliance system which the French monarch had carefully constructed utterly disintegrated, while the devastation of the Rhenish Palatinate by Marshal Turenne and the French occupation of Alsace were deeds that sent a surge of anger through all Germany. By 1674 the Coalition of the Hague took shape. This vast alliance embraced Austria, Brandenburg, Saxony, the Palatinate, Brunswick, the electors of Mainz and Trier, Lorraine, Denmark, and Spain.

Lisola's arguments now carried the day in Vienna. Under pressure from Leopold I, the German Reichstag on May 24, 1674, formally declared an "imperial war" against France. Prince Montecuccoli was dispatched with an army to the Rhine, and thereafter the French position in Germany rapidly crumbled. Some months later Montecuccoli's old foe, Turenne, fell in 1675 on the battlefield of Sassbach, and the Great Elector's troops beat the Swedes at Fehrbellin (June 28, 1675) in Pomerania. The Swedes, allies of France, were expelled from Bremen, Verden, and Hanover. At the same time Charles II of England abandoned the secret Treaty of Dover of 1670, by which he had disgracefully agreed to become the pensionary of Louis XIV. By 1677 Louis' position had become untenable, and he had to sue for peace.

The Treaty of Nijmegen (1678) transferred a few towns in the Spanish Netherlands and full sovereignty over Franche-Comté to France. France also obtained a right of transit through the duchy of Lorraine, which, except for the towns of Metz, Toul, Verdun, Nancy, and Longwy, was restored to its lawful duke. Freiburg remained in French hands as a bridgehead into south Germany. In the north, Brandenburg was left to paddle its own canoe. The Great Elector had to make peace as best he could with Sweden at St. Germain-en-Laye (June 29, 1679), restoring to her western Pomerania, save a small strip on the right bank of the Oder. Sweden, sustained by France, also recovered Bremen and Verden. These treaties were a grievous disappointment to German public opinion, for it was plain that the Coalition of the Hague had not been able to translate its crushing superiority into decisive victory. Nijmegen (Nymwegen) was derided as the *Nym-weg* ("take away") peace.

A disillusioned Frederick William now defected from the Grand Alliance and contracted to become the hireling of Louis XIV for 100,000 livres a year. The example was calamitous, for Bavaria, Saxony, Mainz, Trier, and Cologne all jumped back on the French bandwagon. Once more Louis XIV had demonstrated that German solidarity was a rope of sand.

The Chambers of Reunion and the League of Vienna

Louis XIV, whose armies had occupied Lorraine as early as 1662, now moved to annex middle Rhenish territory. He convened special law courts, called chambers of reunion, to sit in Breisach, Besançon, Metz, and Doornick, and they were ordered to determine which territories of the Empire were by feudal law dependent upon lands that had been granted France by the treaties of Westphalia and Nijmegen and, having decided this, to declare such dependencies part of France. The judges found that her sovereignty ought to be extended to parts of the principalities of Speyer and Trier, all of Alsace, and key cities in the mineral-rich Saarland. In 1681, accordingly, Louis XIV forced a French garrison on Strassburg.

After the chambers of reunion, the emperor reluctantly organized the Alliance of Laxenburg, which embraced several Franconian rulers, the new dukes of Bavaria and Saxony, as well as Hanover and Spain. The Reichstag authorized an imperial army of 40,000 men. At this juncture, unfortunately, the reliable Turks launched a large-scale diversion in the east. Encouraged by Louis XIV, whose contempt for international law was notorious, the sultan had in 1682 ordered an attack upon Vienna. The consideration was the partition of the Habsburg possessions: Bohemia, Moravia, and Silesia to be reserved for the dauphin, who would also be Holy Roman emperor; and Transylvania, Hungary, and Austria to fall to the Ottoman Empire.

On September 1, 1683, Louis XIV sent his armies into the Spanish Netherlands, and from September 12 to 14 Kara Mustapha's Turkish army was fighting the decisive battle for Vienna against Sobieski and Charles of Lorraine. Enraged at the French king's cynical betrayal of the Christian cause, Leopold I refurbished the Laxenburg alliance in 1684, admitting Sweden, Brunswick, and the Netherlands to it. It then came to be renamed the League of Vienna. Nevertheless, Leopold I hesitated to attack in the west because the Turkish danger was still present. To secure his rear while he cleared the Turks from Hungary, Leopold bribed Louis XIV in the Treaty of Regensburg (August 15, 1684): in return for a twenty-year truce, Leopold recognized the French seizures in Alsace and the Saar.

The Turn of the Tide (1688–97)

In the years before the War of the League of Augsburg France was progressively isolated. Poland, having slipped the French snare in 1683, was not to be recaptured for love or money. The Turks were driven from Hungary. Revocation of the Edict of Nantes (1685) alienated Frederick William and caused him to conclude an alliance for the defense of the Empire. In July, 1686, the League of Augsburg was organized, embracing the emperor, Spain, Sweden, Bavaria, and other German states. When in 1688 William III of Orange became king of England, Britain's huge resources were put at the disposal of the coalition. Louis's only hope was to strike before the foe could concentrate his forces. So the French invaded Germany in the fall.

The emperor, filled with the glory of recent victories over the Turks at Mohács, Szlankamen, and Zenta, and the capture of Ofen (Budapest) and Belgrade, decided to meet the French challenge, even though a peace treaty had not yet been signed with the Turks. Before Leopold could move, however, Frederick III of Brandenburg, who had been crowned in May, 1688, had formed the Concert of Magdeburg with John George III of Saxony, Charles of Hesse-Kassel, and Ernest Augustus of Hanover and had mobilized the armed forces of all north Germany against France. In 1690 Spain and Savoy joined the grand alliance.

Angered by initial setbacks that drove the French armies under Luxembourg and Villars from most of Germany, Louis XIV ordered a merciless devastation of the Palatinate. During the winter of 1688–89 not only its fortresses, but villages, farmsteads, and the very grain in the fields were burned or bombarded so thoroughly that even a crow passing over the Palatinate "would have had to carry his own provisions." This atrocious deed, so out of harmony with the concepts of "cabinet war," enraged the Germans and long poisoned relations with France.

The cumbersome grand alliance that finally took shape in 1690 lost its best commander when Charles of Lorraine died in that year. Thereafter the combination was unable to bring its superior weight to bear effectively. Consequently, with the exception of Tourville's sharp defeat at the hands of the Anglo-Dutch navy at Cape La Hogue in May, 1692, and Marshal Luxembourg's great victory over the Germans and Dutch at Neerwinden in May, 1693, the war gradually degenerated into a series of sluggish maneuvers. Even the French burning of Heidelberg and the blowing up of its castle in the same year failed to whip Germany into a fury again. Louis' fortunes only slowly ebbed, and it was not till May, 1697, that he was ready for peace.

The Treaty of Ryswick of October 30, 1697, terminated the third war against

France. The convention was signed in expectation of the imminent demise of the ailing Charles II. Another disappointment for Germany, the treaty was dubbed the *Reiss-weg* ("tear away") treaty in spite of the fact that it marked a decline in French fortunes. Louis secured, to be sure, recognition of his sovereignty over the lands he had annexed at the suggestion of the chambers of reunion, but the French frontier was pushed back slightly in the northeast, while along the upper Rhine Breisach, Freiburg, Kehl, and Philippsburg were restored to the Empire, and Lorraine to its duke.

The Treaty of Karlowitz (1699)

Austria could have wrested half the Balkan peninsula from the sultan if Prince Eugene had continued his spectacular drive south of the Save and the Danube. However, after his victory at Zenta (September 11, 1697) he halted before Belgrade on orders from the emperor, who believed that Charles II, the valetudinarian king of Spain, was about to die and that the partition of the Spanish Empire was the order of the day. The Turks, left in the lurch by France and physically exhausted, had to accept the peace Treaty of Karlowitz (January 26, 1699). Hungary and Transylvania, and all the lands north of the Save, west of the Theiss (Tisza), and north of the Maros River, were ceded to the emperor, but Belgrade and the Banat of Temesvar were left to the Turks. For the first time in generations the Hungarian plain was almost completely under Habsburg control. Although a quarrelsome assortment of Magyars, Croats, Slovakians, Serbs, Rumanians, and Bulgars were brought under Austrian sovereignty, the lands and resources won proved to be greater and more enduring assets than those Louis XIV had acquired by his wars. Fearing further deterioration of the European position from the French standpoint, Louis XIV now resolved to accept the calculated risk of general war, which would surely result from the implementation of the last testament of Charles II.

The War of the Spanish Succession (1702–13/14)

By 1700 all efforts to settle the Spanish succession without war had foundered. Two partition treaties had already come to grief. That of February 6, 1699, in particular, had been frustrated by Leopold because he had demanded as his share not only Spain, the Spanish Netherlands, and overseas colonies, but Italy too. The final will (of October 7, 1700) of Charles II had affirmed the indivisibility of his empire and devised it intact to the duke of Anjou, second grandson of Louis XIV who was himself a son of a daughter of Philip III and whose first wife was the eldest daughter of Philip IV. If, however, France rejected the Spanish inheritance, it would, under the terms of the will, pass to Austrian Charles, second son of Leopold I who was himself descended from Philip III and was wed to a younger daughter of Philip IV. Obviously Louis XIV hoped that a Bourbon on the Spanish throne would secure the borders of France and establish Bourbon ascendancy in Italy as well.

When Louis XIV accepted the last testament of Charles II, Austria, Britain, the United Netherlands, and most German states and cities banded together in the Grand Alliance of the Hague (September 7, 1701). Only the Wittelsbach rulers, the electors of Bavaria and Cologne, decided to cast for France. After the Empire declared war on September 30, 1702, Louis XIV sought ultimate victory by fusing the war in the west with the Great Northern War. However, Brandenburg acted as a wall between the theaters. Sweden was blocked from ingress to Germany, blighting France's one hope of beating the coalition.

The decisive engagement in Germany was fought on August 13, 1704, at Bavarian Blenheim (Höchstädt), when Prince Eugene overwhelmed the Bavarians and the duke of Marlborough stormed the French positions. Blenheim was the first major military catastrophe sustained by Louis XIV, and it sent a wave of rejoicing throughout the Empire, where Marlborough was made a prince. Before the year was out the allies had retaken Ulm, Trier, and Landau. Eugene fought an indecisive battle against Vendôme at Cassano, Italy, but Marlborough retrieved the situation by smashing Villeroi's armies on May 23, 1706, at Ramillies near Tongeren. In September, finally, Eugene won a great battle at Turin, and by the beginning of 1708 French positions in Italy, Germany, and Belgium were a shambles.

Meanwhile, love of independence died hard with the Magyars. Although the magnates had in 1689 foresworn the right of armed resistance *(ius resistendi)* to an unjust king, they rose again in 1703. Francis II Rákóczy, Károlyi, and Palffy threw down the gauntlet to Leopold, only to be beaten at Trentschin in 1708 by the armies of Emperor Joseph I (1705–11), Leopold's successor. On April 29, 1711, the Magyars were persuaded to sign the Peace of Szátmar, a generous settlement that confirmed the liberties of 1689 on condition of an oath of allegiance to the emperor. When Charles VI (Charles III of Hungary, 1711–40) succceded his brother Joseph on the Habsburg throne, Vienna turned an even more conciliatory face toward Budapest. Charles's wisdom in bartering the Hungarian peasantry to the rapacious Hungarian magnates in return for support of his daughter's claims to the crown was questionable, but it ultimately yielded a gladsome harvest of loyalty during the Silesian Wars with Frederick the Great.

After 1705, old age, rigidity, and ineptitude took command of the French war effort. Louis XIV, past seventy, had outlived his popularity and, what was worse, his best statesmen and generals. While Swedish Charles XII was going down to an epochal defeat at Poltava, Russia (June, 1709), his French allies were being chastised at Oudenarde (July 11, 1708) and Malplaquet (September 11, 1709) in the Netherlands. In March, 1710, Louis XIV, despondent over these defeats and the deaths of successive heirs to the throne, sued for peace, but his offer was rejected. Then, of a sudden the blind God Loki smiled on him again. Vendôme's troops restored Philip V to the Spanish throne from which he had been driven. Queen Anne had set about undermining the position of the duke of Marlborough, whose policy was war to the bitter end. But it was the death of young Emperor Joseph on April 17, 1711, that was the miracle that saved the Bourbons, for all of his titles and claims were now inherited by his brother Charles, who was the Allied candidate for the Spanish succession. Since it would have been absurd to continue the war for the sake of creating a Habsburg predominance in Europe, the English dropped Marlborough and Godolphin with a thud and opened negotiations for a separate peace. The unexpected victory of Villars over the Dutch at Denain, Belgium, on July 24, 1712, France's one important victory in six years, made it possible for Louis to make peace with honor in 1713.

The Treaties of Utrecht, Rastatt, and Baden

The seven treaties of April 11, 1713, collectively called the Treaty of Utrecht, left the Bourbon dynasty on the Spanish throne and subtracted small border strips from France toward Savoy and Belgium. Pending restoration of the Bavarian Wittelsbach to his hereditary possessions, Luxemburg and the counties of Namur and Charleroi were assigned to Bavaria.

It was not until March 6, 1714, that the emperor could bring himself to concede that the Habsburg remedy for Spain was worse than the Bourbon disease and to sign the Treaty of Rastatt. The Latin Treaty of Baden between France and the imperial princes was signed on September 7, 1714. The peace settlement restored the rulers of Cologne and Bavaria, wartime allies of the French, to their possessions and rights, thus demonstrating the profound attachment of Germans for law. Confirmation of the cessions of Landau, Alsace, and Franche-Comté to France advertised that Louis XIV's campaigns, though costly, had not been in vain, for the French frontier with Germany had been strengthened by these accessions. By the peace treaty, Austria recovered Breisach, Freiburg, and Kehl—the Rhenish approaches to southern Germany. In Italy Austrian ascendancy was secured by award of the Milanese, Mantua, the Tuscan ports, Naples, and Sardinia. Finally, Austria was given the Spanish Netherlands, subject to the right of the Dutch to garrison "barrier fortresses" along the French frontier.

Government of the Grand Monarchy about 1700

If the Habsburg dynasty had an historic mission, it was to bestow cultural, economic, and judicial unity upon the peoples of the Moldau-Theiss-Danubian area. To accomplish this, the Grand Monarchy had to stand as a bulwark against the Mohammedan Turkish and Russian Orthodox civilizations, and the Habsburg emperor had to form a loftier conception of his responsibilities. He had to be less concerned with centralization, which had become impracticable as a result of the heavy increase of Slavs, Magyars, and Dacians within the Grand Monarchy, and more concerned with the development of a cooperative community of component nations.

Charles VI, being without male heir, had to tread lightly lest he offend the nobility. His determination to have his daughter Maria Theresa (1717–80) succeed him, which was without precedent in Austrian history, was to fill his reign with an intricate diplomatic problem. After he had promulgated the Pragmatic Sanction

(1713), affirming that the hereditary Bohemian, Hungarian, and German lands constituted a collective monarchy (*Gesamtstaat*) which might also be devised indivisibly, the survival of the Danubian empire took precedence over centralization. Charles VI had to buy the assent of all the diets by promising that their ancient liberties would be respected and that decentralization would be preserved.

Habsburg governmental machinery had grown up haphazardly. The Pragmatic Sanction could not supply the cement that geography and nationality had denied the Grand Monarchy. Heinrich Ritter von Srbik was right to say that the constitution of the monarchy was oriented to the protection of the limbs at the expense of the body, so that it was foolish to speak of the existence of a supreme and unifying political will. Charles VI did not confuse his several crowns but deduced his sovereign prerogatives from the juridical and constitutional complex peculiar to each realm. Consequently government proceeded less by directive from Vienna than by negotiation between the parts of the Habsburg empire.

There was in the Grand Monarchy a shortage of central institutions. There existed, to be sure, an imperial privy council (*Geheime Konferenz*) on which sat, among others, Prince Eugene, Prince Trautson, and Count Zinzendorff, but there was no chancellor, and the council was in no sense a supreme executive authority. Other councils and ministries included those for defense (*Hofkriegsrat*), finance (*Hofkammer*), and foreign affairs (*Hofkanzlei*). The *Hofkanzlei*, also called the aulic council, in addition exercised an uncertain supreme appellate jurisdiction. Bohemia and Hungary each had its own chancellery, and the Austrian Netherlands and Italy had their high administrative councils, but there was little liaison among all these top echelon agencies.

In this melee of conflicting and overlapping governments, the *Hofkanzlei* launched a campaign to bring all capital councils and chancelleries under its control. However, except as respects Bohemia, the initiative failed. As a result, duplication of functions, rivalry, secrecy of operations, and uncertainty in policy-framing persisted in the governance of the Habsburg empire. The only institution whose purview extended to the whole empire was the college of commerce, a cameralist body, headed by Zinzendorff, devoted to the rationalization of production. On the other hand, the continuing heterogeneity and personality of laws and customs were fortified by the vigor of the territorial and provincial diets. These, which were the palladia of individual and corporative liberties, never fully relinquished control over taxes, allocation of money, recruitment of troops, or a range of eleemosynary, educational, and sanitary functions.

The Turkish War (1716–18)

After the Peace of Rastatt, Austria tore up the Treaty of Karlowitz that had been signed with Turkey and renewed her offensive in the southeast. In the years 1716–18 Prince Eugene inflicted serious defeats upon the Turks in the battles of Peterwardein (1716), Temesvar (1716), and Belgrade (1717). With the capture of Belgrade, the Austrians were able to consolidate their control over the Banat and the Save, Drave, and middle Danube rivers. Taken in context with the Austrian victories at Blenheim, Turin, and Malplaquet, these battles brought the Habsburgs greater military glory in shorter time than ever before in history.

Charles VI had hoped to demolish the Turkish position in the Balkans, but before this could be done the great powers imposed their mediation. Nonetheless, the Treaty of Passarowtiz of July 21, 1718, conferred upon Austria commercial privileges within the Ottoman Empire and sovereignty over northern Serbia and Belgrade, the Banat, and part of Wallachia to the Aluta River. Hundreds of thousands of new subjects—mainly Hungarians, Rumanians, and Mohammedan Serbs—passed under Viennese rule. Passarowitz marked the apogee of Habsburg power in the Balkans.

The Beginning of an Austro-Prussian Confrontation

Until 1725 Austria's chief headache in western Europe was Spain, whose designs upon Italy gravely worried Vienna. In that year, however, Charles VI did a volte-face and signed an "unnatural" alliance with Bourbon Spain, which immediately provoked a great counteralliance, the League of Hanover (September, 1725), embracing Britain, France, Prussia, Sweden, the Dutch Netherlands, and Denmark. Austria then countered with an entente with Russia in 1726. At this point, Prussia's switch of alliances saved the peace.

Frederick William I entertained only the fuzziest ideas on foreign policy and was, moreover, dangerously impetuous. His gambits conferred no security on Prussia but were as unpredictable as frog leaps. As compensation for expected Austrian expansion in Italy sanctioned by the First Treaty of Vienna (1725), Frederick William I hoped to get the lands of the aging, childless Charles Philip of Neuburg, duke of Jülich and Berg. To this end the king signed the Treaties of Wusterhausen (October 17, 1726) and Berlin (December 23, 1728), by which Prussia promised to recognize the Pragmatic Sanction and come to Austria's aid in the event of war with the League of Hanover, while Austria agreed to support Prussian annexation of the Rhenish duchies. Feeling more secure in Germany now, Charles VI soon abandoned the Spanish connection and gravitated back toward France and England. Meanwhile, however, he deceived the Prussian king, for in 1726 he secretly promised the duchy of Berg to another. When the elector found this out, he was enraged and thundered that his son, Frederick, would avenge him.

The War of the Polish Succession (1733–35)

An Austro-Prussian showdown was only postponed because the Polish problem revived the old Habsburg-Bourbon rivalry. In 1733 Austria, Saxony, and Russia caused the Wettin Augustus III to be crowned king of Poland, setting aside the diet's choice, Stanislas Leszczyński (father-in-law of Louis XV). France found in this a pretext for war against the emperor, although her real aim was acquisition of Lorraine, whose duke, Francis Stephan, was betrothed to Maria Theresa. The Reichstag and even Frederick William I of Prussia rallied to Charles VI and sent him troops.

A string of reverses in Italy caused the emperor to sue for peace in 1735. Eventually on November 18, 1738, the Third Treaty of Vienna was signed, which, to the peril of Austria's hold on Sicily (acquired in 1720 from Savoy in exchange for Sardinia), awarded the Spanish infante, Don Carlos, the throne of Naples. In compensation, Austria was appeased with Parma and Piacenza, while Francis Stephan, who had married Maria Theresa in 1736, was made duke of Tuscany. Augustus III was allowed to remain on the Polish throne, but Stanislas Leszczyński was placated with Lorraine on condition that on his death is would revert to the French king, who was his son-in-law.

The Germ of Austro-Prussian Dualism

Seeing himself dismissed without pay, the Prussian king in 1738 made a desperate grab at Jülich and Berg, whose senile duke stubbornly refused to die. However, France, England, the Netherlands, and Austria conspired to compel the Prussians to retire. Meanwhile, the French had sold the Prussian king short. Desirous to protect his rear in case of war with England, which might arise out of the Anglo-Spanish ''War of Jenkins' Ear'' that had broken out in 1739, Louis XV compacted with the emperor to back the claims of the ruler of Sulzbach-Pfalz to the entire Jülich-Berg area.

The Austro-French convention of 1739 was not the main cause of the First Silesian War. Rather, it was the growing weakness of the Danubian monarchy. When Eugene of Savoy died in 1736, the Turks struck hard (1736–39) and beat the Habsburg armies on every battlefield. By the humiliating Treaty of Belgrade (1739), Austria was obliged to retrocede Belgrade, Serbia, Orsova, and western Wallachia. The southern boundary of the Habsburg dominions was set back to the Save-Danubian line, where it had been in 1700. Ottoman sway in the Balkans had been given a new, long lease on life. Conversely, all the centrifugal forces of the Grand Monarchy were now intensified. Its very survival was put in question when an inexperienced young woman ascended the throne of Ferdinand II.

PART VI
DEATH OF THE OLD STATES SYSTEM

Chapter 19

THE AGE OF FREDERICK THE GREAT

The Purposes of Frederick II (1740–86)

Historians call the half-century of the reign of Frederick II the age of dualism, because for the first time power within the Holy Roman Empire was divided between Prussia and Austria, both of which were much stronger than any other principality. During this epoch the king of Prussia evinced no ambition to establish absolute ascendancy over the Germanies. By no means merely a "crowned robber," as Gooch labeled him, or a "militarist," as many Western historians believe, Frederick II pursued grand policy aims that were fundamentally moral. Animated by a lofty sense of responsibility, as Koser, Heyer, Ritter, and Rainer have maintained, Frederick II privately detested the alarms and horror of war and sincerely strove to promote the welfare of his subjects. Able to detect the often obscure boundary between reasons of state and sheer personal ambition, he pursued only nicely delimited, dynastic aims. He was content, where Napoleon, Louis XIV, and Charles XII were not, with the acquisition of a few specific patches of territory which he thought were necessary to the attainment of Prussian great power status.

Bismarck once said that because of Prussia's exposed position, where she was vulnerable to attack from all sides, she had to be either a pike or a carp; conscience was irrelevant, even a hindrance. Resolved not to be a carp, Frederick II concentrated all his energies upon acquiring, by fair means or foul, two strategically placed territories—Silesia and West Prussia—which would qualify Brandenburg-Prussia to be a major power. But once these aims had been achieved, he regarded his realm as a satiated state whose interests would be jeopardized by the ingestion of more territory. Certainly after 1773 Frederick II was a consistent champion of the status quo and a conservative foreign policy.

Character of Frederick II

For the sake of the state, Frederick II drove everybody relentlessly, himself most of all. He took as his motto the device: "The king is the first servant of the state." Throughout his reign, whether on the field, in council, at court, or in his office perforating stacks of official papers, Frederick II exemplified fidelity to that precept. His Spartan habits, which set the tone for the entire population, were at first disliked; by comparison, his father was thought to have been a spendthrift. But pride was not in Frederick II. As the years passed and Prussia was buffeted by one calamity after another, the king shed his few remaining vanities, even preferring to attire himself in a threadbare army uniform. The masses of his people came eventually to revere him, for they saw that virtue, like a rare stone, is best plain-set. He, for his part, held the vulgar, fickle mob in ineffable contempt, even though he freely conceded the basic equality of all men and the silliness of social distinctions based on rank and privilege.

A philosopher king of the cast of Marcus Aurelius, Frederick II was wholly free of fear of death and proved it on a score of battlefields. That he was, in spite of ostensible austerity and heroic cast, of a fundamentally pleasure-loving disposition, being buoyant to the point of effervescence, epicurean in his private tastes, musically and intellectually gifted, a lover of all that was refined and beautiful, made it exceedingly difficult for him to bend himself to the yoke of unremitting duty. So far from exemplifying intellect without rectitude, Frederick II embodied the triumph of character over temptation. He was one of a very few world-historic statesmen who have put devotion to the state above all love of self.

Services of Frederick II

In his reign Frederick II developed the army into a superb instrument of power politics, so that at his death it was rated the first in Europe. He streamlined but did not fundamentally change the central administrative apparatus he had inherited from his father. In the field of communal administration Frederick accomplished very little, but despite his wars he strengthened the Prussian economy, imparted high standards of probity to the bureaucracy, increased the population of his kingdom, and filled its treasury. Inspired by the writings of Beccaria, Frederick II reformed the penal code and abolished torture. Evincing the typical concern of an enlightened despot for culture, he made education a national industry. More than his father or the Great Elector, he succeeded in galvanizing aristocracy, army, bourgeoisie, intelligentsia, bureaucracy, artisanate, and peasantry into a patriotic whole. The most brilliant monarch of his age—and it was a great age— he conferred upon the Prussian absolutist system, which under his father had become tarnished, a nimbus that derived from the lofty principles with which the son endowed it. When he died in 1786 Prussia had become one of the five major powers. But since nothing great in statecraft is ever achieved without cost, the people of Prussia had to pay to the breaking point for the opportunity he proffered them. Despite this, the example of "Old Fritz" has never failed to inform the lives and mentality of the best of his countrymen down to the present.

Crown Prince Frederick

For a decade prior to Frederick's accession to the throne in 1740, he had been in open or smoldering rebellion against his martinet father. The recipient of a well-rounded education, Frederick early came to admire every facet of the French rococo—its rationalism, refinement, delicacy, balance, and *fêtes galantes*. He dabbled in poetry, music, and art and was in a fair way to break his unsympathetic father's heart. The latter feared that the crown prince would end by dissipating the work of a lifetime. When in 1730 Frederick was allegedly caught conspiring with the English against his father, the latter was furious. Frederick and an accomplice named Katte tried to flee to England but were apprehended. Katte was sentenced to death by a military tribunal and executed, whereas Frederick got off with a brief imprisonment in the fortress of Küstrin.

After this personal crisis the crown prince decided to do his father's bidding. Frederick took part in military campaigns, not without relish, and complied with the paternal order to marry a drab and homely princess of Brunswick. Ever afterward Frederick regarded this marriage as a personal calamity and his luckless spouse as a creature who might expect from him frigid courtesy but nothing more. In August, 1736, he was permitted to establish his own ménage at the rococo palace of Rheinsberg, where he spent the happiest years of his life, because for once he had the opportunity to indulge his cultural and literary interests. At the same time, being ambitious, he immersed himself in finance, administration, and military affairs. Gradually blood, tradition, and personal ambition combined to exert as much influence upon this dynamic little man as did the Enlightenment.

In the last five years of his life the king relented and again focused his hopes on his son. Much later, when the heavy weight of a crown had tamed the crown prince, he expressed admiration for much of his father's achievements.

During his Rheinsberg years Frederick read omnivorously and mastered a vast fund of the kind of knowledge that intelligently informs the decisions of a chief of state. At the same time he composed for the flute and was accounted one of the finest flautists in the kingdom. One of the most cultivated men of his age, Frederick regularly corresponded with savants, including Christian von Wolff and Voltaire. From the Rheinsberg period, too, date Frederick's youthful publications on political philosophy, the enlightened and ethical *Anti-Machiavell* and the *Considerations upon the State of the European Political System*.

The War of the Austrian Succession, 1740–48

When Maria Theresa succeeded to the Habsburg throne in 1740, the European powers ransacked their archives for claims upon her lands, for it was believed she would be a weak ruler. Maria had been reared at an emphatically feminine court. Although imbued with a love of music and art, she had been given no special training in administration, history, government, or military affairs. Of a frank, ingenuous, and morally upright nature, she was fair to behold and seemed designed by Providence for kissing, children, and cooking. Indeed, little more was expected of Maria Theresa than a queenly demeanor, a robust piety, and a drove of children (she accommodated by giving birth to seventeen). The heavy tasks of state were to devolve upon an experienced statesman, such as her father's indispensable aid, the Alsatian jurist, Johann Christoph Bartenstein (1689–1767).

Although the twenty-eight-year-old Frederick II lacked the experience that a Stein or Bismarck possessed when they came to power, he was able to cut through a screen of irrelevancies and discover what was really in the interests of Prussia. In 1740 Frederick II reasoned that Catholic principalities might very well join Protestant in plucking leaves from the Habsburg artichoke, and that Silesia could be detached without lethal injury to Austria's omnibus empire.

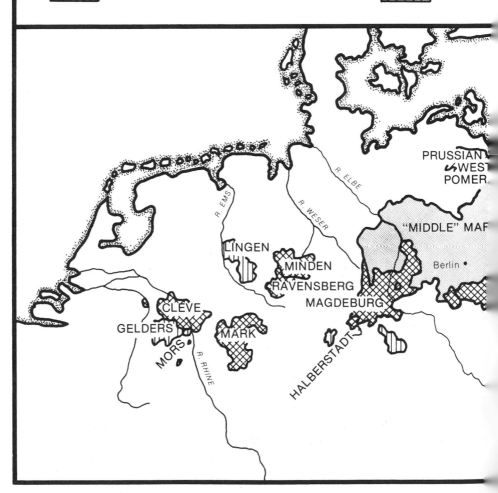

THE GROWTH OF BRAI

TERRITORIES GAINED BY 1455

TERRITORIES GAINED 1618-1648

TERRI

TERRIT

R. EMS

R. ELBE

R. WESER

PRUSSIAN
WEST
POMER

"MIDDLE" MAI

Berlin •

LINGEN

MINDEN

RAVENSBERG

MAGDEBURG

CLEVE

GELDERS

MORS

R. RHINE

MARK

HALBERSTADT

BURG-PRUSSIA TO 1795

GAINED IN 1660 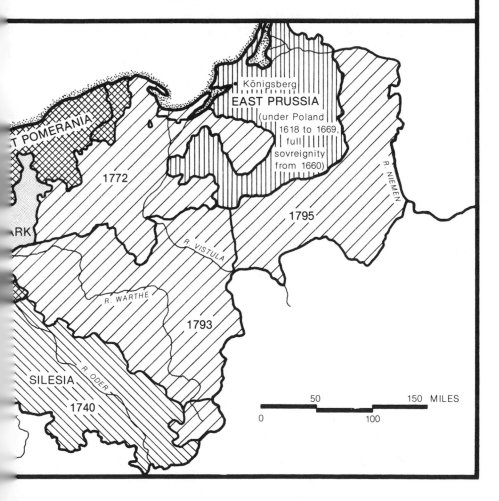 ACQUISITION OF SILESIA, 1740

AINED IN 1721 PRUSSIAN SHARE OF THE PARTITIONS OF POLAND

Königsberg

EAST PRUSSIA

(under Poland 1618 to 1669, full sovreignty from 1660)

T POMERANIA

1772

ARK

R. NIEMEN

1795

R. VISTULA

R. WARTHE

1793

R. ODER

SILESIA

1740

50   150 MILES

0   100

In reaching for Silesia, the Prussian fox was motivated by a number of considerations. With that acquisition Prussia would acquire a rich land along the middle Oder, containing 1,200,000 people and possessing factories, mines, a flourishing linen industry, and the big city of Breslau. Silesia would not only strengthen Prussia's economy, but would also give her a defensible frontier to the southeast and put both Saxony and Posen in a vise. Finally, loss of Silesia would probably exclude Austria from Polish and north German affairs.

Since England was involved in the War of Jenkins' Ear with Spain and could not aid Austria, Frederick II struck while the iron was hot. The First Silesian War was undertaken, in part, to break the developing entente between Bourbon and Habsburg. The attack, which Frederick launched against the advice of his generals, without benefit of an operational plan, or support from other powers, was an improvisation. It almost collapsed before it succeeded. Notwithstanding, the occupation was completed by December, 1741, at small cost. It proved decisive for Frederick's whole career. Silesia set Prussia's foot on the ladder of continental power. Austria's worry was now that Prussia might reach out for hegemony over Germany.

The First Silesian War was dominated by the battle of Mollwitz (April 10, 1741), a narrow victory for Prussia ensured by the timely aid of General von Schwerin. Mollwitz encouraged the German princes to support the election of Charles Albert, duke of Bavaria, to the imperial throne. The slim victory also brought France into a calamitous war.

By the end of 1741 Bavaria, Saxony, and Spain had joined the Anti-Pragmatic Alliance, while England's concern for her Hanoverian duchy insured her neutrality. Maria Theresa only evaded ruin by making a dramatic personal appearance on September 11, 1741, in Budapest, where she enlisted the aid of the Hungarian magnates. However, the election of Charles Albert on January 24, 1742, as Charles VII by a vote of eight to one badly frightened the archduchess. To the three-months truce of Klein Schnellendorf (October, 1741) between the Austrians and Prussians now succeeded in June of 1742 the separate Treaty of Breslau. By this convention Frederick left the dilatory French in the lurch. He acquired Silesia and Bohemian Glatz on condition that Prussia leave the war, pay a 1,700,000 crown indemnity to England, and that he vote for Francis Stephen at the next imperial election.

Despite Breslau, the war widened in 1743. England, Hanover, and Piedmont-Sardinia declared war on France, and Habsburg hopes revived. Maria Theresa dreamed of annexing Bavaria and Alsace-Lorraine, which Frederick could not allow. He therefore tore up the Treaty of Breslau, joined the inchoate Frankfurt Union (France, Hesse, Bavaria, and the Palatinate) on June 5, 1744, and then launched the Second Silesian War.

Frederick II began operations with 140,000 troops and a full treasury, but shortly after he took Prague, epidemic hit his army and his war chest was rapidly emptied. Charles VII died on January 20, 1745, and Maria Theresa's husband was elected Emperor Francis I (1745–65). Austrian troops occupied Munich, and

Saxony found it expedient to switch sides. Then in a flash Prussia won three resounding victories—Hohenfriedburg (June 4, 1745), Soor (September 30), and the decisive battle of Kesseldorf (November 30). The Prussians occupied all Saxony, and Austria, who had gone out for wool and come back shorn, concluded the Treaty of Dresden on December 25, 1745, with Prussia. By it, the cession of Silesia was confirmed on condition that the integrity of Austria's remaining possessions in Germany be respected.

Meanwhile, following the great French victory at Fontenoy (1745), Louis XV also made peace. The Treaty of Aix-la-Chapelle (1748) restored the European status quo, except for Silesia, whose possession by Prussia was guaranteed. Austria, despite minor losses in Italy, remained the strongest power in central Europe. Nevertheless, Austria's failure to conquer Bavaria or regain Alsace forced the Habsburgs to dismiss hopes of controlling south Germany and drove them remorselessly toward the Balkans. Consequently the old Habsburg-Bourbon feud gradually became unreal.

The Diplomatic Revolution, 1755–56

After the death of the French minister Cardinal Fleury (1743) there was only one statesman in Europe who realized that the old system of alignments was anachronistic. Count Wenzel Anton von Kaunitz-Rietberg (1711–94), a tall, well-built valetudinarian, who was Austrian state chancellor and foreign minister for almost forty years, held it to be a popular error to think that the Habsburgs needed the alliance of England and Holland to regain Silesia. Instead, he urged the practicability of a triple combination of France, Russia, and Austria, to which Saxony would naturally adhere out of fear that Prussia might one day devour her.

During eight years Kaunitz labored to weave this revolutionary alliance. His first victory was to persuade Louis XV to remain neutral in the event of an Austro-Prussian war. The way was then clear for Sweden to attack Prussia to regain Pomerania and for Denmark to reconquer Holstein. Before a combination of Austria, Saxony, Sweden, Denmark, and Russia, with France neutral, it seemed Frederick II would have to capitulate. It had been Kaunitz's most delicate task to link the inevitable colonial conflict between England and France with the Austro-Prussian contest in such a way as not to involve England in continental military operations. Success crowned his efforts when an Anglo-Russian subsidy treaty was signed on September 30, 1755, obligating the Russians to dispatch 50,000 troops to protect Hanover against Prussia.

Frederick II, who refused to believe that Bourbon-Habsburg rivalry was a thing of the past, sustained a rude shock when he learned of the subsidy agreement. He immediately sued at the English counter, concluding on January 16, 1756, the famous Convention of Westminster, by which Prussia substituted for the more remote Russia as protector of Hanover. Failing English subsidies for Russia, it seemed that Kaunitz's design had been frustrated, peace would be preserved, and Elizabeth Petrovna's hunger for East Prussia would go unslaked.

Unfortunately the Treaty of Westminster did not avert war, because on May 1, 1756, Kaunitz spirited the ace of trumps from the deck by signing a defensive alliance at Versailles with the French. By this pact the allies put their armies in the service of a strategy that aimed not at the detachment of territory from Prussia but her annihilation, for such was the real goal of Kaunitz. Nor did the Convention of Westminster even put the Russian bear on a chain, for Elizabeth, expecting the French would now substitute for the English paymaster, impatiently urged the Austrians to attack Prussia no later than the summer of 1756. Even after Frederick had irrefutable proof of the First Treaty of Versailles, he refused to believe in the imminence of war and would not recognize the true character of Russian troop movements in Livonia. Yet Kaunitz planned to attack Prussia in the spring of 1757, when all the armies of the coalition would have concentrated against her. "With God's help," said he, "we shall set so many enemies around the neck of that arrogant king that he will crumble under their weight . . . as once upon a time in our history it befell the famous Henry the Lion."*

On June 22 Frederick finally learned from bartered documents originating with the Saxon ambassador to Vienna that Russia was planning an early attack with 240,000 men. Not a moment was to be lost if Prussia was to be saved. Frederick's treasury was full, his army ready, and, inasmuch as Britain and France had already begun a global war against each other (May 17), financial aid from England could be expected. Frederick did not want war and was not even sure that in case of victory he could make any permanent gains, but his hand was being forced. If he now precipitated the inevitable general war, he would at least have the advantage of the initiative.

The Seven Years' War (1756–63)

The charge that Frederick was planning the conquest of Saxony is not supported by a shred of evidence. He had no hope in 1756 of duplicating his spectacular success in the Austro-Prussian and Silesian wars. He knew that both Elizabeth of Russia and Maria Theresa regarded him with the same aversion as the devil would holy water. He knew, too, that invasion of Saxony must set off such a war that Prussia would be lucky to survive it. Only fear that in 1757 the odds against him would be even worse drove Frederick on August 28 to invade Saxony. His immediate war aims were defensive in nature. They were to preserve his own kingdom and prevent the conquest of East Prussia by Russia.

In the Seven Years' War Frederick enjoyed the military aid of only Hanover, Hesse-Kassel, Brunswick-Wolffenbüttel, Schaumburg-Lippe, and Gotha. English financial aid was at first only modest. However, Frederick had the advantage of operating on interior lines and was fortunate in having the services of a second in field command who was a military genius—his brother Henry. The Prussian

---

*Reinhold Koser, *Friedrich der Grosse* (Stuttgart and Berlin, 1904), I, 611.

tactic was the traditional one employed by numerically inferior armies—rapid marches, surprise attacks, lightning thrusts at supply lines, and efforts to keep the foe continuously off balance.

Although Saxony was immediately knocked out, the Reichstag voted all military and financial support to Emperor Francis I in his just war against the "aggressor," and France subsidized Württemberg and Bavaria. Frederick II strove to maintain the offensive in the first half of 1757, but the scales slowly tipped against him. The unequal contest sucked his kingdom dry. Not even the conversion on January 11, 1757, of the Treaty of Westminister into an Anglo-Prussian military alliance could dissipate the clouds. In January, 1757, an Austro-Russian military alliance was formed; in March Sweden declared war on Prussia; and on May 1 the French promised to put 105,000 men on German soil.

Frederick sustained his first great defeat when the Austrian General Daun beat him at Kolin on June 18, 1757. Simultaneously the Duke of Cumberland signed the convention of Kloster Zeven with France, by which England surrendered Hanover and agreed to leave the continental war. By the summer of 1757 Frederick's prospects were so dark that he refused to accept a new offer of subsidies from Britain. The British ambassador to Berlin wrote to his foreign office: "I was pleased but not surprised with the noble dignity of his answer; for I have seen the king of Prussia great in prosperity but greater still in adversity."*

Autumn brought unexpected sunshine. Prussia's General Seydlitz won a great victory at Rossbach on November 5, while Frederick himself triumphed at Leuthen (near Breslau) on December 5. Within a month Frederick's reputation was restored. The English repudiated Kloster Zeven, dispatched 55,000 troops to the continent, and offered large subsidies to the king of Prussia. However, until the British funds arrived in October, 1758, Prussia's treasury was empty and exactions had to be levied on Saxony.

Many of Frederick's victories were Cadmean. He only narrowly beat the Russians in the bitter battle of Zorndorf (near Küstrin) on August 24, 1758, but lost a third of his effectives. From Zorndorf onward the road was even rockier. The Prussians were defeated at Hochkirch October 13–14, 1758, and almost annihilated by the Russians at Kunersdorf on August 12, 1759. Coming on the heels of the closely spaced deaths of three loved ones—his sister (the marchioness of Bayreuth), brother (Prince William), and mother, the battle of Kunersdorf plucked out the king's heart. He ran about the battlefield like a madman. determined not to survive his mortification. Fortunately for him, the Russian field commanders were undecided as to what to do and neglected to administer the coup de grace to his army, which slipped away to fight another day.

After Kunersdorf Frederick's luck was all bad. The new king of England, George III, and his circus master, Lord Bute, repudiated Pitt's continental policy.

---

*Chester Easum, *Prince Henry of Prussia, Brother of Frederick the Great* (Madison, Wis., 1942), p. 34.

Despite Frederick's incredible exertions in the battles of Liegnitz (August 15, 1760) and Torgau (November 3), the English figuratively threw him to the wolves. By December, 1761, his ruin seemed near.

At this juncture fortune changed her address again. Elizabeth of Russia died on January 5, 1762, and was succeeded by Peter III, an insipid but fervent admirer of Frederick. The tsar allowed the king to write his own peace, which was concluded on May 5 on the basis of the status quo ante bellum. Then Peter III turned around and even allied himself with Prussia against Austria! Although he was assassinated on June 28, 1762, and succeeded by his scheming German wife Catherine II (1762–96) of Anhalt Zerbst, Russia did not reenter the war on either side.

At that moment Austria was also approaching exhaustion. Prussia's tardy victories at Burkersdorf in July and Freiburg in October, 1762, made it plain even to the simple Maria Theresa that her pious prayers had not prevailed. When, therefore, Sweden left the war and England and Spain composed their differences, the Austrians decided to leave things before things left them. On February 15, 1763, they signed peace with the Prussians at Hubertusburg. This treaty restored to Prussia and Saxony all of their respective territories but offered no compensation to Dresden for the extraordinary contributions Frederick had levied on the duchy during the war. The king also promised to cast his vote at the next imperial election for Maria Theresa's son, Joseph.

Results of the Conflict

Emerging from the long war like a spent shell, Frederick had successfully defended his state and retained Silesia. Prussia was now a kingdom of great expectations. On Frederick fell the mantle of the duke of Saxony as head of the *Corpus reformatorum* and the leadership of north Germany. Prussia might now expect to become the main beneficiary of the secularization of the Westphalian bishoprics of Münster, Paderborn, Osnabrück, and Hildesheim.

A new eastern orientation of Prussian policy issued from the Seven Years' War. During the fighting Frederick had villified the Russian soldiery as "barbarians" and "half-Tartars," especially when they occupied Berlin for three days in 1760. Yet he learned from his mistakes. In his second *Political Testament* (1768) he recommended to his successor that in view of Austria's flirtations with France he cultivate the Russian connection and under no circumstance allow Prussia to be caught in a cross-fire between France and Russia. Demonstrably, Frederick was the true author of that eastern policy which sustained Prussia in the era of Stein and Hardenberg and was the pledge of Bismarck's triumph over Austria.

The Polish Question

In 1763 a mortally stricken Poland, torn by dissension and hobbled by a crippling constitution, was staggering toward the grave. The constant worry of old allies and the temptation of voracious neighbors, Poland had become the migraine of Europe. Permanently on the defensive, she had been proscribed by Russia, the reaper of expiring states. Upon the death of the last Wettin king in 1763 Catherine II had induced the Polish diet (Sejm) to crown one of her discarded lovers, Stanislas Poniatowski. As insurance against any Austro-Prussian combination against her, she inveigled Frederick II into signing a mutual defense assistance pact on April 11, 1764, and a supplemental convention (May 4, 1767). Intended to run for only eight years, the alliance remained operative until 1780.

In the civil war that began in 1768 between the Lutheran-Calvinist, pro-Russian Confederation of Radom and the pro-Austrian, Roman Catholic Confederation of Bar, Catherine's army attacked the latter, thereby provoking Turkish intervention and a six-year Russo-Turkish war.

The Russo-Turkish war threatened to widen into a general one when in 1771 Austria and Turkey buried the hatchet and concluded a secret alliance. Austria, fearing the rising might of Russia, admonished Catherine II that unless she withdrew her troops from Moldavia and Wallachia by the end of the year, she could expect the Habsburg empire to attack. Frederick II, fearful that he might have to honor his promises to Russia, strongly urged the tsarina to substitute compensations in Poland for contingent conquests in the Balkans. Catherine was obliged to give in. Yet it was not she but Maria Theresa who took the initial step toward the partition of Poland. Austrian occupation in 1769 of the Polish county of Zips led in 1772 to the first amputation. By tripartite agreement Russia seized all the Polish lands east of the western Dvina and Dnieper rivers; Prussia absorbed West Prussia and Ermland; while Maria Theresa, reconciling her morality with the imperialism of her son Joseph (co-regent, 1765–80), mournfully sorted out Galicia, Lodomeria, Wieliczka (with its rich salt mines), and Zips—areas inhabited by 2 million people. "I am ashamed to show my face . . . ," she wrote to Kaunitz,* but Frederick II did not for a minute believe her. "She is always in tears," he wrote, "yet she is always ready to take her share."**

Thereafter, without implicating Austria or Prussia, the Russo-Turkish war continued until 1774. The king of Prussia was able to retain his Russian shield against the Austrian threat, while Austria's reward for remaining neutral was the cession in 1775 of Turkish Bukovina (Buchenland).

The "Potato" War

The last decade of Frederick's reign saw a revival of Austro-Prussian antagonism. Emperor Joseph II (1765–90) felt that the steady thrust of Austria into Slavic lands was alienating her from the Reich. He dreamt of a rejuvenated Germany under Austrian control and hoped to be able to enlarge Habsburg holdings south of the Main River. His opportunity came when on December 30, 1777, the childless Duke Maximilian III Joseph of Bavaria died. Kaunitz immediately

*Alfred von Arneth, *Die Geschichte Maria Theresias* (Vienna, 1863–79), VIII, 366.
**C. L. Morris, *Maria Theresa, the Last Conservative* (New York, 1937), p. 317.

negotiated a treaty with the Wittelsbach heir, Karl Theodor, elector of the Palatinate, which recognized him as duke of Bavaria on condition that he cede lower Bavaria to Austria. In mid-January, 1778, Joseph II sought to frame the treaty with iron by sending an army into Bavaria. At this juncture Frederick II championed the dualist balance of power, despite the fact that few princes supported him. In the last "cabinet war" of the century the sixty-eight-year-old king and his brother Henry marched against Bohemia. When, however, Catherine II warned that if peace were not made at once, she would attack Austria, the tempest in a teapot instantly subsided. The ensuing Treaty of Teschen (May 13, 1779) awarded all of Bavaria to Karl Theodor, who thereafter held two electoral titles, while to Austria were given minor territories along the right bank of the Inn from Passau to Salzburg. Prussia's rights in Ansbach and Bayreuth were confirmed.

Austria's Second Try at Ascendancy

After the death of Maria Theresa on November 29, 1780, Joseph II turned back toward the Balkans and made a major effort to revive the defunct Russian connection. His aim was to partition European Turkey. He succeeded in negotiating an alliance with Catherine the Great at Moghilev in the spring of 1781. But when the sultan declared war on Russia in 1787, Joseph was caught napping. He had just signed a treaty that mired him in German affairs. He had contracted with Duke Karl Theodor of Bavaria for the transfer of his duchy to Austria in return for the Belgian Netherlands. This gave Prussia the chance to twist Kaunitz's arm again.

On the brink of the grave Frederick II blew the bugle once more. This time the princes responded. Saxony, Hanover, and fourteen other states joined him in 1785 in the League of Princes *(Fürstenbund)* to defend the imperial constitution. When Frederick died at Sans-Souci on August 17, 1786, it was in the consoling knowledge that the states' rights policies he had championed would be vindicated by his successor, Frederick William II (1786–97), and his minister Hertzberg.

Although the German fat was in the fire, Joseph paid little mind but imprudently averted his gaze toward the Balkans. Taking the long chance that Prussia would not stir, he joined Russia in 1788 in war against the Turks. Prussia, however, countered by allying with the Sublime Porte on January 30, 1790, and by trying to stir up rebellion in Hungary, Bohemia, and the Netherlands.

Everywhere the hand of Prussia intervened with success to frustrate Austrian imperialism and preserve the traditional German states' system. Austria's French ally, paralyzed by revolution, could not help her. On the other hand, a coalition of Prussia, some German states, Sweden, and Turkey was in the making. Therefore, when Joseph II died on February 20, 1790, his successor, Leopold II (1790–92), moved swiftly to liquidate the rash Balkan and Bavarian ventures.

The Long Truce

It would not have taken much in 1790 to uproot the Habsburg empire. It was still flowering at the top but rotting at the bottom. It was the merit of Leopold II to understand this. He had but one idea, but it was right: Austria must, above all, avert dissolution. Shunning the advice of the old war horse Kaunitz, Leopold signed the Truce of Reichenbach with Prussia on July 27, 1790. The omission of Frederick William II to deal the Habsburgs the coup de grace was, of course, a waiver of claim to the leadership of Germany. His action has ever since been vilified by German nationalist historians.

The Convention of Reichenbach pledged the Emperor to terminate the war with Turkey, which he willingly did at Sistova on August 4, 1791, on the basis of the *status quo ante*. By the Pact of Reichenbach the Prussian king agreed to forsake the Hungarian, Galician, and Belgian rebels, thus enabling Austria to master the dark forces that were tearing her asunder. However, it was not the specific provisions of the treaty that were so significant; it was the fact that it adjourned for almost sixty years the struggle between Austria and Prussia for supremacy over Germany. In the desperate situation in which Austria had found herself the convention was like a gift horse. Furthermore the way was now open for a concerted defense of Europe's Old Regime against the demonism of the French Revolution. In sacrificing an emerging nationalism to the Austro-Prussian entente, with which Russia also was linked, and in postponing the solution of the German problem, Reichenbach stands forth as the last wise achievement of eighteenth-century diplomacy.

Chapter 20

DESPOTISM'S GILDED HOUR

Development of the Theory of Absolutism

In the Age of Reason, apologists of monarchical absolutism—Thomas Hobbes, Samuel von Pufendorf, Bishop Bossuet, and Jean Bodin—had made available to Germany's rulers an elaborate justification of centralized administration. These theorists had espied in the leveling policies of the French state the prologue to a new chapter in the annals of government. By the close of the seventeenth century the academicians may have been divided as to the distinctions between natural and positive law and the origins of sovereignty, but they were agreed on two points: sovereignty was *sui generis* absolute; and a centralized polity directed by a prince whose power was limited only by supernal law was best for mankind. They believed that sovereignty had to be both incontestible and indivisible, because concentrated authority was the latent force in the social order that accounted for the security and organic symmetry of the state.

The Age of Enlightenment (Aufklärung) trusted not so much in God as humanity. Central European savants vigorously espoused the view that monarchy was charged with an ethical-social mission and should assume many eudemonic responsibilities. Among those who maintained this were the German jurist and philosopher Christian Thomasius (1655–1728), the author of *The Fundaments of Natural Law and the Law of Nations (Fundamenta juris naturae et gentium*, 1765), and Christian von Wolff (1679–1754), professor of philosophy at Halle and author of *Institutions of Natural Law and the Law of Nations (Institutiones juris naturae et gentium*, 1749). They hypothecated a delegation of responsibility to the prince, originating in an actual or an imaginary social contract. An honest discharge of this commission by the prince was thought to harmonize with the dictates of reason and the basic goodness of human nature. Enlightened despotism was also endorsed by the bourgeoisie, who wished for uniform laws and the abolition of impediments to trade and intercourse.

Virtually all the great figures of the *Aufklärung*—Lessing, Schiller, Klopstock, and Goethe among them—supported concentration of administrative, judicial, economic, and military authority in the hands of an absolutist prince. Because the German idealist tradition conceived of the functions of central government in positive ethical and utilitarian terms, the traditional view of eighteenth-century German government as reactionary and obscurantist is fallacious. The fiduciary concept of political responsibility also explains why laissez-faire restrictions on the power of the state never achieved much of a following in central Europe. Noninterference with the economy would have been considered tantamount to dereliction of duties that the government had contracted to discharge and would have vitiated the moral principle that underlies civic society. The flood of sumptuary, regulatory, social, and cameralist decrees that issued from the chancelleries was rationalized in numerous apologies for absolutism. Diverging from the British emphasis upon local initiative and limited executive authority and from the stress of the French philosophes upon the rights of man, German political philosophy came increasingly to regard the centralized state as a kind of great shade tree that benignly spreads its branches over all conditions of subjects.

The Fortunes of Absolutism in the Secondary States

In hundreds of Lilliputian principalities absolutism foundered on the rocks of corporative rights. It was often impossible—as in Cleves, Hanover, Mecklenburg, Württemberg, and Saxony—for the ruler to cut his way through the feudal juridical jungle. In ecclesiastical states the prince was frequently curbed by mortmain, the cathedral chapters, and the electoral character of the episcopal office. Only in the larger states, where sovereignty was backed by adequate force, could princely ambitions be realized.

By the late seventeenth century the territorial and provincial estates of the majority of states in the Reich were undeniably in decline. Even imperial cities such as Magdeburg, Braunschweig, Erfurt, and Bremen had lost much of their autonomy. At the same time, these old strongholds of self-government were being economically undercut by competition from cameralist-directed principalities. By the late eighteenth century the absolutist offensive had achieved a number of praiseworthy things: improvement of public administration; bureaucratic probity; heightened territorial security; standardization of law and legal procedures; fiscal efficiency; abolition of internal tolls; establishment of uniform weights, measures, and coinage; inauguration of postal and other public services; and establishment of elementary educational systems.

Despite all attacks by benevolent despots upon the "constitutional liberties" of their principalities, the banner of progress certainly flew over the camp of absolutism. It must be remembered that the strongest and best of the German despots were among the most highly cultivated men of their time. Furthermore, the multiplicity of vigorous provincial diets, committees, and free cities, which in the past had lent texture to German public life, was not really a pledge of the security of the state or of civic freedom.

In some major principalities strong diets survived. This was the case in Saxony, where Duke Augustus II, the Strong (1670–1733) had become both king of Poland and a Catholic in 1697. As a result, the position of the Saxon estates was strengthened because the population feared a papist reconquest of the duchy. Also impeding the progress of absolutism in Saxony were the inept defense of Poland by Augustus II during the Great Northern War and the duchy's involvement in three more disastrous wars during the reign of Augustus III (1733–63). The Saxon debacle in the Seven Years' War especially discredited the Wettin dynasty and strengthened the *Stände*. The Saxon estates survived the century as a vital financial and political force—one of the strongest in Germany.

In Württemberg the dukes for almost forty years ignored the turbulent diets and tried to suppress particularist and *Stände* rights. The situation reached a crisis in the reign of Charles Alexander (1733–37), a Catholic and a bigot, who sought to destroy the Lutheran faith of the vast majority of his subjects, while arbitrarily levying heavy taxes upon them. Not till after his death and the execution of his detested minister, ''Jew Süss'' Oppenheimer, did the diet of Württemberg again convene. Its fortunes revived during the long minority of Duke Charles Eugene II and as a result of his later defeats in the Seven Years' War. In a protracted struggle to reduce taxes, governmental monopolies, and the size of the army, the *Landtag* triumphed. By 1770 the duke had been forced to exercise restraint in financial matters and confirm the ancient corporative and civil liberties of the people of Württemberg.

In Mecklenburg the *Landtag* achieved a great success in battle against the duke. An exceedingly reactionary nobility succeeded in hamstringing every effort to subject its enormous wealth in lands to just taxation. Similarly the aristocracy blocked every effort at administrative and judicial reform. When the *Reichsgericht,* at their suit, endorsed the deposition of Duke Karl Leopold in 1755, the *Landtag* imposed a compact favorable to it upon his successor. This gave the nobility control over the duchy until 1918. Similarly, in Hanover the reality of power after 1714 lay, in the absence of the duke (who was king of England), with the aristocracy and upper bourgeoisie, who controlled the diet.

By contrast, Baden, Hesse, and the Rhenish Palatinate exemplified the drift toward princely absolutism. In Baden the margraves were aided by French gold and a comparatively successful foreign policy. They forced the estates to advance huge sums of money for the construction of the great palace in Karlsruhe and gradually preempted almost all administrative, financial, and economic authority. In Hesse the estates had never regained the power they had lost during the Thirty Years' War. In any case, by the eighteenth century the landgraves were largely living off revenues from the rental of mercenary soldiers to Britain. Diets were held with fair frequency until close to the end of the century, but their gestures were purely theatrical since they lacked the one indispensable sanction—control over the public purse. Finally, the absolutist Landgrave William IX made bold to rule for eleven years without a diet. When the *Landtag* in 1797 was again permitted to assemble, it appeared with its tail between its legs. In the Rhenish Palatinate, too, evolution toward despotism set in after the Thirty Years' War and continued apace throughout the eighteenth century until the will of the prince was supreme.

Prussia Under Frederick II:
The Structure of Government

The successes of Frederick II in war and diplomacy were the principal reason why no radical innovations were made in administration during his reign. The king was satisfied with the relative efficiency of the apparatus he had inherited and was content to extract as much as possible from it.

In Frederick's time Prussian administration was activated by three big interlocking gears. These were: the Cabinet Ministry *(Kabinettsministerium)*, which handled foreign affairs; the Supreme Judicial Council *(Justizstaatsrat)*, which supervised a hierarchy of courts from the domainal, noble, and municipal up through the provincial and superior courts to the high tribunals of Berlin for Brandenburg and Königsberg for East Prussia; and the Central General Directory, which had been established in 1723 and took jealous care of almost everything else. To the directory, too, were subordinated the provincial military and domainal treasuries *(Kiregs- und Domänenkammern)* and whatever new ministries Frederick II established. After Silesia was annexed, a special ministry was set up for it and made directly responsible to the *Kabinettsministerium*. Until 1766 all receipts of the *Generalfinanzkasse* (civil) and the *Generalkriegskasse* (military) were controlled by the Accounting Office *(Oberrechenkammer)*. Thereafter, receipts from state monopolies were deposited in a separate treasury *(Dispositionskasse)*, belonging to the king alone.

As the reign progressed, the royal ministers came to possess steadily diminishing knowledge of the state's fiscal operations. Only Frederick had a comprehensive understanding of the financial condition of the realm. Ministers were seldom granted personal audiences with him, and their contacts with their master were mainly limited to correspondence. Only the king's marvelous memory, intellectual acumen, and unflagging industry—the real bases of his personal regime *(Kabinettsregierung)*—served to hide the fact that the Prussian government was as poorly integrated as its territories and increasingly at variance with newer European administrative concepts.

The main criticism that can be leveled against Frederick's government is that it trained no new statesmen, only functionaries. The officials who ran the government were commonly persons of probity and considerable ability—as, for example, Bodenkatt, Finckenstein, Podewils, Hertzberg, and Zedlitz. Yet ministerial initiative was at a sharp discount in Potsdam. The department heads made a virtue of unquestioning obedience to the king, knowing that insubordination or presumption, like corruption, were swiftly and harshly punished.

The king's versatility, industry, marvelous abilities, and incredible luck simply overawed everybody. He communicated his driving will and austere patriotism to his bureaucracy, which was celebrated throughout Europe for its rectitude and diligence. On the other hand, the Prussian system, while theoretically stressing limits upon princely authority, in practice magnified it to a point where it stultified all initiative. The penalty for personal rule was that when the reins slipped from Frederick's fingers in 1786, no one could be found who had been educated to assume his functions.

Prussia under Frederick II:
Limitations on Absolutism

Despite broad royal prerogatives, the government of Prussia was only imperfectly absolutist. To be sure, Frederick's realm exhibited pronounced centralization of power, administrative uniformity in the middle and upper echelons of the apparatus, rigorous discipline, a system of royal *fiscals* who spied into every operation of the fastidious bureaucracy, a nobility that had been deprived of an independent political role, estates that were moribund where they existed at all, and a *roi-connêtable* who let it be known that he was commander-in-chief in both the civil and military spheres. Yet for all this, strong social corporations protected by customary law still existed in Frederician Prussia. Towns and cities still enjoyed considerable self-government and even the peasantry possessed hoary, imprescriptible rights. The king himself exhorted the *Kammergericht,* the highest court of the kingdom, never to proceed or to impose sentence except in accordance with the immemorial law of the land and the conscience of the judges; where necessary, the court was even to ignore the king's own orders! The king wished that the state should be put above himself. The aristocracy also constituted a complex of rights and immunities which militated against the development of a Chinese despotism in Prussia. Nobles were required to discharge on their estates a broad range of administrative, judicial, economic, and supervisory functions which the central government, hampered by limited means, distance, and poor communications, was unable to assume. Frederick's Prussia may not have been exactly a *Rechtsstaat*, but in it customary and natural law circumscribed monarchical caprice.

Prussia under Frederick II:
Class Character of the Regime

Under the Old Regime in Prussia the three estates—nobility, bourgeoisie, and peasantry—continued till the Napoleonic period to exercise their respective responsibilities. The aristocracy led the armies, controlled the ministries, filled the principal civil offices, and superintended the peasantry; the bourgeoisie labored to expand the industrial base of the realm, increase general prosperity, and fill the royal treasury; and the peasantry furnished sons for the army and, through unremitting menial toil, food for all. It was the monarch's paternalist mission to hold the balance among the elements of this *Ständestaat*. His was the responsibility to prevent any order from shattering the carefully fitted, interlocking system of corporative rights and duties which, in the absence of a parliament, was the guarantor of the liberties of everybody.

Supported by customary and imperial law, the king of Prussia restrained the high-born nobles from running roughshod over the rights of the other orders, but the hereditary aristocracy was nonetheless the plinth of the monarchy. He assigned it commanding positions in the central and provincial governments, diplomatic corps, and army. By letting the noble landlords elect the rural councillors *(Landräte)* from among their own ranks, the king confirmed the nobiilty's ancient jurisdiction over the peasantry. Furthermore, he discontinued the practice, still so common in both France and Spain, of selling patents of nobility to the bourgeoisie.

Frederick's civil masterpiece was to terminate forever the political opposition of the nobility to the state and convert that order into the main wheel of his government. The king kept the nobles usefully employed. He never permitted them, as was the case in France, to be uprooted from the soil and attached to the court as ornaments. Perhaps this restricted the opportunities the Prussian aristocrats had for cultivating wit, charm, and letters. However, when the era of the French Revolution came, it probably saved their heads. Not only did the utilitarian Prussian aristocracy survive the Revolution, but the people accepted aristocratic leadership in the War of Liberation against Napoleon.

Prussia under Frederick II: Economic Recovery

Aided by a continental prosperity that prevailed in the 1770s and by the influx of investment capital from England, the Netherlands, and France into Rhenish enterprises, Prussia at last recovered from the ravages of the Seven Years' War. A period of rapidly growing national product succeeded upon one of hard times, tight money, and low income. The Prussian revival was helped by the active intervention of the government, in harmony with cameralist ideas, in the economic life of the realm. Encouragement to industry and trade and a well-thought-out, unified financial system were among the major contributions of government to the emerging euphoria. The central government granted subsidies; directed lucrative state monopolies (in metallurgy, textiles, silk, sugar, salt, coffee, tobacco, porcelain, insurance, and trade with Russia and the Levant); reduced or eliminated internal tolls; established a central bank of credit and issue (1763); built roads, dug canals, and drained the lower Oder and the Warthe and Netze rivers; developed an all-water route connecting Hamburg, Berlin, and Breslau; reclaimed land and financed its colonization; inaugurated soil and forest conservation programs; aided landlords and peasants with advice as to husbandry and breeding; stabilized grain (and hence bread) prices through a judicious program of import-export controls and storage of surpluses in times of good harvest; and accorded relief to the indigent.

For the fiscal year immediately preceding the death of Frederick II the revenue of the Prussian government was more than two-and-one-half times that of 1740, and treasury reserves six times as great. The Prussian surplus was more impressive when it is remembered that in France large budgetary deficits were hardy perennials and that in 1789 the French national debt was about 300 million livres. By contrast, in Prussia, despite the fact that half the royal revenue was invested in the armed forces, Frederick II still left behind him a personal treasury *(Dispositionsfonds)* of almost 55 million thalers in bullion, which was quadruple his private reserve of 1763.

An important aid to economic progress was the codification of Prussian law. In 1748 the *Codex Fredericianus* was completed by a corps of jurists directed by the celebrated minister of justice Samuel von Cocceji (1679–1755). The code standardized legal proceedings, centralized the judiciary, and made judges salaried officials whose tenure depended solely upon merit. Later in the reign the grand chancellor, Johann H. von Carmer (1721–1801), was assigned the task, with the aid of Karl Suarez (1746–98), of codifying and standardizing all civil and criminal law. Known as the General Common Law of Prussia *(Allgemeines preussische Landrecht)*, this code was not published until 1794, more than a decade before the Code Napoléon. Yet the Frederician Code remained in force until 1900. These great codes took the Hohenzollern kingdom a long way toward the *Rechtsstaat*, while not relinquishing the *Ständestaat* concept.

The fact that the aging Frederick II became an ever harder taskmaster, cynical and sardonic, cannot negate his achievements. These centered not merely in the additions he made to the territory of Prussia but in his contributions to the strengthening of its government and economy. By character and personal example he molded the thought of a people. Among contemporary European monarchs there was not his equal, and only in the Orient was there, perhaps, a ruler, the Manchu Emperor Ch'ien Lung (1736–95), who could bear comparison with Frederick the Great.

The Austrian Experiment: Governmental Reform under Maria Theresa

In the Habsburgs' polyglot empire needed structural reforms were obstructed by powerful aristocratic families. These proud entities, unlike the Prussian Junkers, could still work effectively through the provincial estates to block drastic centralization. An imperial declaration of 1741 brought the nobility a further accession of strength: out of concern for the succession of the first female to the Habsburg throne, the crown confirmed all Pragmatic Sanction agreements that had been negotiated between 1723 and 1732, recognizing ancient constitutional liberties and privileges of the component states of the Grand Monarchy.

No one rocked the boat until Austria had flagrantly failed to retrieve Silesia from Frederick II. After 1745 Vienna resolutely embarked upon the suppression of all opposition to at least those administrative reforms that were considered vital to survival of the Danubian Monarchy. Austrian reforms down to 1790 were greater in scope than those of Prussia and contemplated a radical alteration of the social and legal structure of the empire. Yet Habsburg reforms, being incapable of eradicating the ethnographic reticulation of the empire, were fundamentally failures. They did not significantly improve the international position of the Grand Monarchy and were largely revoked after the death of their principal protagonist, the impractical Joseph II.

In 1746 the energetic but not especially brilliant Friedrich Wilhelm Count von Haugwitz (1702–65) was summoned to overhaul the administration. However, since the Diet of Pressburg (1741) had promised Hungary autonomy, the most Haugwitz could accomplish was the fusion of the administrative machines of Austria and Bohemia and the suppression of their estates. He brought Bohemia under more direct administrative and fiscal control from Vienna, abolished the separate Bohemian court chancellery, and transferred its functions to a number of joint Austro-Bohemian ministries. He also assigned most of the powers of Bohemia's provincial estates, still appreciable as respects administration, finances, and recruiting, to district offices *(Kreisämter)*, which were subordinate to provincial "representations and chambers," renamed *Gubernia* after 1763. These in turn were made responsible to the joint ministries.

In 1754 the joint Bohemian-Austrian ministries were lumped together in a capstone body, the Public and Central Cameral Directory *(Directorium in publicis et cameralibus)*, which after 1761 was renamed the United Austro-Bohemian Chancellery. The latter differed from the Prussian Central General Directory in that administrative responsibility was not assigned by area, and in that town and country in each district were superintended by a single agent of the directory, the district captain *(Kreishauptmann)*.

Paralleling the Bohemian-Austrian administrative hierarchy was a judicial pyramid capped by a supreme court *(Justizstelle)*. There was also a central commercial directory with authority over Austria, Bohemia, and Moravia. Meanwhile, the older aulic council, with indeterminate purview for the entire Habsburg empire, and the royal war council *(Hofkriegsrat)* continued to function. In addition, a new office of foreign affairs, the so-called House, Court, and State Chancellery *(Geheime Haus-, Hof-, und Staatskanzlei)*, was put under the direction of the foreign minister, Prince Wenzel von Kaunitz-Rietberg, and housed at the Ballhausplatz in Vienna.

The most important governmental creation of the reign was the Council of State *(Staatsrat)*. Founded in 1762, it was the foreloper of a legion of imitators, including Napoleon's Council of State. In time the *Staatsrat* became the *deus ex machina* of the Viennese government, even as the council's strongest personality, Prince von Kaunitz, was unquestionably the *largo factotum* of the House of Austria. Consisting of seven personages of high rank, the council had no legislative or executive functions but nonetheless formulated almost all grand policy.

The Austrian Experiment: Josephism

When Joseph II (sole sovereign, 1780–90) became co-ruler upon the death of the Emperor Francis in 1765, a new phase of reformism opened. Until then, emphasis had been almost exclusively upon administrative renovation with the aim of centralizing operations and achieving more efficiency. After 1765, the year in which Haugwitz died, Joseph's humanitarianism and egalitarian ideals became the leitmotif of the whole reform movement. This was not apparent to everyone, because the joint regency had been a period of one long tug-of-war between the clever, energetic son and the doting but determined mother, but Joseph's driving role in the movement became plain to all after Maria Theresa died.

After 1780 the Josephist-Kaunitz partnership carried through so many basic reforms that the imperial corporative edifice was radically altered. Through it all, however, Joseph was very careful not to undercut the dominant social and economic position of the great landed aristocrats, whom he, no less than Frederick II, regarded as the dais of the throne. Consequently, Joseph made no attempt to create a large proprietary peasant class or revolutionize agrarian conditions in the Slavic, Hungarian, or Rumanian lands. Nevertheless Joseph's edict of November 1, 1781, emancipated the serfs, whose status in Habsburg territories commonly stemmed from hereditary attachment to the soil *(Erbunteränigkeit)* but seldom from corporal bondage *(Leibeigenschaft)*. Abolishing *Erbuntertänigkeit*, Joseph transformed the serfs into tenant farmers but neither gave them land of their own nor suppressed their obligation to perform compulsory labor *(Robot)* on their noble landlord's soil or property. Beyond this, the haughty, despotic, and insufferably arrogant emperor substituted free competitive enterprise for a cameralist and guild-oriented economy, dissolved governmental monopolies, instituted military conscription, converted universities into institutions, helped suppress the Jesuit order, put secondary schools under state supervision, replaced the provinces with *Gubernia*, finished off the provincial diets, granted the peasants freedom of movement and vocation, put an end to the autonomy of towns and cities, mitigated the censorship, nationalized the judiciary, granted religious toleration but not equality, established a short-lived free trade area that included the German and Slavic imperial territories, and decreed the equal liability of all to pay taxes.

One of Joseph's finest humanitarian efforts was in the field of law. Whereas the earlier penal code of Maria Theresa *(Nemesis Theresiana*, 1768–70*)* had not really brought Austrian criminal law into line with modern practices, Joseph's codes represented a great departure. His penal code, completed in 1787, in harmony with the views of the Marchese di Beccaria, the Italian jurist and author of the *Tratto dei Delitti e delle Pene*, abolished torture and confiscation of the property of convicted criminals as well as the death penalty in almost all cases except high treason. A part of the vast civil code was promulgated in 1786, but the bulk of it did not appear until 1811 in more conservative times.

Not all of Joseph's reforms were popular or even very tolerant. If, as Charles H. O'Brien has recently pointed out, enlightened Catholic clergymen such as Bishop Leopold von Hay and Joseph von Auersperg supported Joseph's Edict of Toleration of 1781, many humanists such as Joseph von Sonnenfels and J. B. Alxinger found it inadequate. Most people were shocked when the emperor severed the last bonds between Church and papacy, arbitrarily closed more than 800 monasteries, and suppressed the rights and immunities of the clergy. In subjecting the Church and clergy to rigid secular controls, Joseph also interfered with the liturgy and reduced the number of holy days.

After 1780 bureaucratic authoritarianism in the Habsburg empire gave way to a Prussian-type *Obrigkeitsstaat*. Joseph II, who was, as Paul P. Bernard has emphasized, as arrogant as he was superficial, suppressed the Council of State and solicited advice, as the spirit moved him, from individual ministers—Kaunitz and Sonnenfels for grand policy, the two Cobenzls for foreign policy, Kessel, Zinzendorf, and Gebler for financial and economic matters. The powers of the Austro-Bohemian Chancellery, renamed the United Court Chancellery, were strengthened and extended to judicial matters, while the system of district captains *(Kreishauptmänner)* and *Gubernia* was extended to Hungary. In the last years of his reign Joseph II gnawed resolutely at the ancient liberties of the kingdom of Hungary, while neglecting to institute desperately needed agrarian reforms there. Similarly he tried without success to crush the liberties of Lombardy and the Netherlands. In the end, all the grand territorial divisions of the Habsburg empire felt his despotic yoke.

Few of Joseph's precipitate reforms survived him. This was because they were generally premature, intemperate, and uncompromising. Nothing contributed so much to engulf the rest of his program in ruin or alienate large segments of the population as his decision to make the Church a department of the government. Although the abolition of *Erbuntertänigkeit* throughout the realm and of mandatory *Robot* upon royal domainal lands, as well as the grant to crown peasants of proprietary title to small tracts of arable were all permanent gains, the peasantry in other respects slipped back into dependency upon the nobility after his death. In Slovakia, Galicia, Ruthenia, Hungary, Transylvania, and Croatia the plight of the peasantry remained deplorable, as a consequence, throughout most of the nineteenth century.

Leopold II (1790–92), the third son of Maria Theresa and Francis, pursued a more liberal policy toward at least the Hungarian peasants because the emperor hoped to curb the power of the great magnates. On the other hand, Leopold thought it prudent to restore the provincial diets to a starveling existence. He also decided that the grand design of galvanizing the kingdoms of the Habsburg empire into one administrative corpus was impracticable. Hungary and the Netherlands had shown themselves to be as pliable as steel, and in 1790 their olden constitutions had to be restored.

Chapter 21

THE ENLIGHTENMENT

Nature of the German Enlightenment

Like the French Enlightenment, the German counterpart, *Die Aufklärung*, was sired by English thought. In the eighteenth century, central Europe stood under the spell of Hobbes, Locke, Boyle, Harvey, Newton, and Hume, but their seminal ideas generally reached Germany through French alembics. Fontenelle, Bayle, Voltaire, La Mettrie, D'Alembert, Helvétius, D'Holbach, Diderot, and Condillac distilled English empirical philosophy so that Germans could appreciate it.

The *Aufklärung* never developed the exquisite cultural sheen it had in France but was in Germany more a practical formula for improving and rationalizing social institutions. Germany was the executor of her historic legacy, especially of the Reformation and Thirty Years' War. She was impelled along channels cut by their consequences. Basing themselves on the paternalist tradition, the German public expected the territorial governments, that is, the ruling establishment, to be the instrument of social regeneration. Moreover, utopian schemes were not popular in Germany. West of the Rhine there may have been much rhapsodizing about social journeys to Cytherea, but in practical-minded Germany the ideas of the philosophes were much more than an intellectual divertissement; they were an invitation to contemporary governmental action.

Assiduously nourished by monarchical paternalism, the tree of the *Aufklärung* in time bore the good fruit of reforms. Because of this, it was not chopped down by revolution. Progressive suggestions by a Voltaire or a Baron Melchior von Grimm* not infrequently carried weight with such noble-minded rulers as Frederick the Great, Frederick August III of Saxony, Karl Frederick of Baden, Karl August of Weimar, Maximilian Joseph of Bavaria, Ernst of Gotha, and Joseph II of Austria, as well as the prelates of Cologne, Munich, Mainz, and Bamberg, who were far from indifferent to modern thinking.

Unlike England, where parliamentary government was equated with socially responsible government, or France, where entrenched corporative interests prevented realization of the program of the philosophes, Germany experimented with a practical approach to social problems. Many princes affirmed that all men are born equal and believed, too, with Immanuel Kant that the central purpose of the Enlightenment was to encourage the establishment of a rational political order that would nurture respect for human dignity. This philosophy spawned many ameliorative decrees and laws. The aggregate of this kind of concerned state action may not greatly have advanced personal liberty in Germany, but it forestalled a French-type mob tyranny and dictatorship.

---

*Grimm (1723–1807), of Ratisbon, was a naturalized French citizen, a friend of Diderot, d'Alembert, and Mme. d'Épinay, and the chief German source of information on happenings in European intellectual circles. His correspondence with European nobles fills seventeen volumes.

The Aristocracy and the Enlightenment

The chief exponents of the Enlightenment were the aristocrats. As a class they were the most cosmopolitan element in European society. While German noblemen often lacked the savoir-faire of their French cousins, who didn't care what they said as long as they said it elegantly, they were nonetheless accepted members of a European confraternity that ignored frontiers. In the last quarter of the seventeenth century the tone of the German nobility was, in any case, elevated as a result in part of the advent of the drinking of coffee, tea, and cocoa, and in part of the concomitant spread of smoking or snuffing tobacco (indulged by women too). These social habits stimulated group conversation in coffee houses and salons.

Much like their English, French, and Italian counterparts, German aristocrats lived in lavishly decorated, rococo mansions that were like gilded aviaries. The German nobles thought similar thoughts, listened to the same music, admired the same spectacular *fêtes galantes*, followed the same styles in dress and coiffure, and even spoke the same language (French) as did the *haute noblesse* of Versailles. German aristocrats not only often possessed excelling taste but the wealth to indulge it. Where they themselves were unable to make original cultural contributions, they patronized those who could.

The Feminine Touch

German upper-class women, who in the baroque era had still been accounted citizens second class, in the rococo broke the ancient masculine monopoly over letters. This harmonized with the trend toward the gracious, intimate life of which women had always been the soul. The fair sex became by the late rococo the vessel of all ennobling thought; and the boudoir, the cynosure of polite society. This circumstance, not surprisingly, helped make the nobility unprecedentedly effete.

The cultivated German woman *(das galante Frauenzimmer)* not infrequently possessed broad education. This, for example, was the case with Anna Maria Schurmann—a marvelous linguist, fluent in ten languages, including Hebrew. Women revelled in their emancipation, took a lively interest in chemical retorts, microscopes, and even skeletons, and oftentime the initiative in contracting adulterous and illicit sexual relations. As in the salons of France, so in those of Germany, gorgeously attired ladies pretended to be the arbiters of all manners and exalted conversation. It was to these Sapphos and Hebes that the Klopstocks and Gellerts wrote their odes, Goethe his *Sorrows of Young Werther*, and the Haydns and Mozarts their *kleine Nacht-musik*. And truly, feminine influence was something amazing. In the late rococo, for example, it was the custom for men, who in former times had greeted each other soberly, to embrace and kiss in public. Even tears in a man's eyes were thought to be a sign of sensibility.

Although Germany boasted no woman who was in a creative class with the French authoress Mme. de Staël (1766–1817), there was many a *hoch- and wohl gelehrtes Teutsches Frauenzimmer* ("noble and well-educated German lady") who attained regional or even national fame. The tradition set by the Hanoverian Queen Sophia Charlotte (1668–1705) of Prussia, who had been a friend to Leibniz and Spinoza, was carried on by the belletrist Lise Lotte von der Pfalz (Elizabeth Charlotte of Orléans, 1652–1722). Sophie von Braunschweig, Antonia von Württemberg, Louise Amöne von Anhalt, Charlotte von Stein (the beloved of Goethe), Anna Amelia of Weimar, Marie von Thurn und Taxis, Charlotte von Kalb (the mistress of Schiller), and Anna Marie Schurmann all enriched literature and the fine arts and helped fructify German culture.

Although rationalism for a time captured the fancy of the educated *Frauenzimmer*, her basic nature disposed her more toward emotionalism. Unquestionably the drift toward excessive sensibility and religion, noticeable in the transition from Christian Wolff and Gottsched to Gellert and unmistakable by the third quarter of the century, was strengthened by the mounting influence of German ladies upon culture.

The Universities

Characteristic of the German orientation, the main centers of the *Aufklärung* were not the salons, as in France, or the academies or coffee houses, as in England, but the universities. Most of these had lost their former corporative freedoms and had become state institutions catering to the nobility. The lively concern of the princes to make higher education more relevant was expressed not only in the favoritism shown to instruction in the vernacular in rational philosophy, political economy, law, and science, but in unprecedentedly large appropriations for education.

By 1725 the new *Weltanschauung* had the universities in its grip. A rationalist, secular influence had largely come to supersede the curricular stress upon religion and Latin. This trend was strengthened by the foundation of the University of Göttingen in 1737, which swiftly became famous for its freedom of thought and the excellence of its work in law and humane letters. By the second half of the century most German professors no longer accepted God, the trinity, redemption, or an afterlife. To the Leibnizs, Spinozas, and Pufendorffs, who had still clung to a revealed faith, succeeded a generation of deists who preferred empirical and rational perspectives or experimentally demonstrable solutions. While it would be an error to attribute to the masses the corrosive, anti-Christian skepticism of the intelligentsia, the latter certainly, in the main, followed in the traces of D'Holbach, Voltaire, and Hume.

The Importance of Christian von Wolff

This whole ferment was distilled in the mentality of Christian von Wolff (1679–1754), the first systematic philosopher in German history. Wolff was the most indefatigable champion of rationalism in the Holy Roman Empire. His way had been smoothed by Christian Thomasius (1655–1728), the author of trail-blazing rationalist disquisitions. However, it was Wolff who insured the triumph of neo-Cartesianism over Aristotelianism in the universities.

The son of a baker of Breslau, Wolff became a distinguished professor of mathematics and philosophy at the University of Jena. Although driven from this post in 1723 by Frederick William I, he was recalled by Frederick the Great in 1740 and promoted to the vice-chancellorship of Halle and was later made rector of Jena, where he was till his death the pharos of the *Aufklärung*. Possessed in rich measure of Germanic thoroughness, Wolff, though not so original as Leibniz, was regarded as the German Aristotle in the sense that he wrote vernacular treatises on about as many fields of knowledge as had the great Stagirite.

Wolff's rationalist philosophy, an insensitive and mathematical approach to basic questions, featured the empirical and psychological methods that had been introduced by John Locke. Through Wolff's efforts, the new approach to truth gradually pushed the metaphysical into the background in Germany. It was not surprising, therefore, that deism, as expounded by Samuel Reimarus (1694–1768), Johann Semler (1725–91), and Gotthold Ephraim Lessing (1729–81), discovered its most cogent arguments in Wolff's philosophy.

Whereas Leibniz had endowed individualism with a novel nimbus and subordinated method to message, Wolff buried the former's humane monodology under a mountain of dialectical ash. Weighing like an incubus upon the German spirit, Wolff's system was rendered even more insufferable by his disciples. Fortunately for his reputation, however, he was a dedicated teacher who demonstrated a profound love of education, and no man in his time did more than he to bind state and school together. To some extent the substructure of Wolff's thought was sapped by the speculative idealist Christian Crusius (1712–75), but it was Kant who first plucked German philosophy from the dustbin where Wolff had left it.

German Deism

German rationalism, unlike French rationalism, was never quite able to overshadow faith. Nevertheless, reason brought strong support to German deism, which flatly averred that God's influence over mankind had ceased with creation.

In the vanguard of those who assailed Christian dogma and its hierarchical superstructure was the eclectic Jewish philosopher Moses Mendelssohn (1729–86). Conceptually he was unexceptional, but it is to be noted that he heavily influenced the Jewish community of central Europe to embrace Germanization and secularization of its culture. Mendelssohn won numerous disciples for deism and toleration. Among them were the radical thinker Friedrich Nicolai (1733–81), literary critic and editor of the *Bibliothek der schönen Wissenschaften und der freien Künste*; August Schlözer (1735–1809), revolutionary political theorist and editor of the rationalist *Staatsanzeiger.;* and S. Reimarus, the theologian and naturalist philosopher, who in his *Wolfenbüttel Fragments* sharply assailed the Bible.

Science

Except in biology and mathematics Germany slipped far behind England and France in science during the eighteenth century. After the death of the Danzig physicist Gabriel Fahrenheit (1686–1736), the two most esteemed German scientists were perhaps the anatomist Kaspar Friedrich Wolff (1733–94) and the Swiss humanist Albrecht von Haller (1708–77). The former founded embryology. In his epigenetic *Theory of Generation* (1759) K. F. Wolff refuted the popularly held notion that all specialized parts of an embryo are present in miniature in the fertilized egg. Haller's chief service was that he wrote an eight-volume work on the *Elements of Physiology* (1757–65), which systematized all knowledge about the human body. He described the mechanics of nervous impulses, muscular reaction, and respiration and the role of the medulla as the control center of movement and sensation.

Germany's only other important scientific contributions were made by George W. Krafft (1701–54) in the medicinal aspects of chemistry (iatrochemistry) and by Friedrich Hoffmann (1660–1742) in connection with mineral waters. On the other hand, the false theory of phlogiston, proposed by Georg Ernst Stahl (1660–1734), impeded the advance of chemistry until demolished by Black, Cavendish, Priestley, and Lavoisier.

In mathematics the brothers Bernoulli (Jakob, 1654–1705; and Johann, 1667–1748), both professors at Basel, pioneered in the development of exponential and integral calculus, while Leonhard Euler (1707–83), for twenty-five years professor of mathematics at the Berlin Academy of Sciences, did basic work in calculus, imaginary numbers, determinate and indeterminate algebra, and astronomy.

Advent of the Second Golden Age of Literature

Not since the thirteenth century had Germany produced a literary figure of world-historic importance. In the last half of the eighteenth she spawned at least seven—Lessing, Klopstock, Wieland, Winckelmann, Herder, Schiller, and Goethe, as well as a preeminent philosopher in Kant.

Gotthold Ephraim Lessing (1729–81) was the first distinguished pen of the eighteenth-century literary renaissance. More than any predecessor, he honed the German language and created a national poetry and drama. The foremost critic of his day, he was cofounder of the *Briefe, die neueste Literatur betreffend (Letters concerning Modern Literature*, 24 vols., 1759–67). Lessing's tolerant, deist views are reflected in his dramatic poem *Nathan the Wise* (1779). He encouraged the revival of interest in classical and Shakespearean tragedy, stressed the paramountcy of character delineation over dramatic unities, and combatted French theatrical influence, which to him was only an apology for the aristocratic order that he despised. His best tragedy was the fatalistic *Emilia Galotti* (1772), but his single finest play was *Minna von Barnhelm* (1767), in which he sought to lash the middle class into consciousness of its revolutionary mission.

The growing infatuation with classical art forms was exemplified in the lives of Johann Joachim Winckelmann (1717–68) and Johann Christoph Wieland (1733–1813). The former was basically a renaissance type. He did more in his time than anyone else to substitute the humanistic canons of Greek sculpture and architecture for those of France. Winckelmann went to Italy in 1755 where he wrote works on ancient art, among them *Thoughts on the Imitation of Greek Works* (1754) and *A History of the Art of Antiquity* (1764). With his chiseled rhetoric he accomplished for the "noble simplicity and quiet grandeur" of Hellas something analogous to what Piranesi was doing for Augustan Italy with his engravings. In arguing that spirit and senses were the true divining rods of art, Winckelmann aided the reaction against the rationalist school. In extolling line and grace as the proper media of beauty he suggested that the brilliant fantasies and exaggerations of the French rococo had only blurred the Greek ideal and ignored the intimate connection between great art and the ethos of a people.

While Wieland also rejoiced in the "eternal summer" of Greek art, his heart was a battleground on which French and Attic literary canons warred for supremacy. His passion for Greece, which he never saw, and his strong affinity for French literature determined that his prose and poetry would be a blending of antique themes and Gallic style. Between 1762 and 1766 Wieland also devoted much time to studying Shakespeare, translating no less than twenty-two of his dramas into German. With his *Oberon* (1780), which was written under the sensuous spell of the *Midsummer Night's Dream*, Wieland crossed the border into the next epoch of German literary history.

Persistence of the Emotional, Religious Tradition

Rationalism and scientific method mounted a heavy assault upon the German mind but never stormed it. The ways of centuries were not to be changed in a single generation. The continuing popularity of clairvoyants, wizards, and charlatans, such as Lavater, Jung-Stilling, Gassner, Cagliostro, Schuppach, and Mesmer, only illustrated the heterogeneity of German thought patterns. The Catholic states, with some exceptions, likewise constituted an environment that was often hostile to rationalism and the experimental method. The *Aufklärung*, to be sure, sent its rays into some very dark corners of Catholic Germany; yet the church of St. Peter Canisius did not on that account strike its colors. Lastly, the revolutionary shibboleths of the Age of Reason had never evoked widespread sympathy among the German masses, who were commonly content with benevolent despotism and were pious and parochial.

Before the Catholic counteroffensive against the reign of reason began, the masses often sought to cope with it by embracing pietism. A movement aiming at a devotional revival within the framework of the Lutheran church, pietism strongly resembled the personalized, medieval mystical approach to religion. Pietists were indifferent to philosophy, because they were all feeling and no mind. For them, as for the English Methodists, the Bible, prayerfully followed, was the perfect guide for behavior; and the inner light, the sign of grace.

After the death of the Alsatian Philipp J. Spener (1635–1705), the chief court chaplain at Dresden and founder of German pietism, his mantle fell upon August

H. Francke (1663–1727). The pietists were expelled from Saxony when in 1697 Elector Frederick Augustus I became a Catholic convert. They then took refuge in Giessen, Erfurt, Halle, and Berlin. From Halle and Berlin, which were their main centers, Francke's followers missionized in the Scandinavian countries, India, and America.

By 1727 pietism had passed its acme, although continuing to spread into the Low Countries and Württemberg. Meanwhile, its teachings had led to the revival of the Moravian Brethren in Bohemia and had won the heart of Count Nicolaus Ludwig von Zinzendorf (1700–60), who permitted the brethren to settle on his estate in Saxony, from whence they eventually spread to Prussia. The finest service of the Moravian Brethren was to rescue pietism when it was faltering in its efforts to keep the flame of religious feeling burning in a skeptical age.

Early Sentimental Literature

Among the numerous "apostles of the heart" who prepared the way for the sentimental, idealist creations of the Storm and Stress (Sturm und Drang) period that followed rationalism, the two most important transitional figures were Christian Fürchtegott Gellert (1715–69) and Friedrich Gottlieb Klopstock (1724–1803).

Gellert, a professor at Leipzig, evinced pietist influences in his *Religious Odes and Songs* (1757). Gellert, who seems to have synthesized the general revulsion against the pomp and ostentation of the baroque era, also wrote lachrymose comedies, which were imitative of the style of Nivelle de La Chaussée, the creator of the French sentimental comedy. Among Gellert's plays were *Die Betschwester (The Hypocrite)* and *Die zärtlichen Schwestern (The Affectionate Sisters)*.

The transition from rationalism to what the Germans call *Empfindsamkeit* ("sentimentality or sentience") was promoted by Klopstock, a devotee of the creative force of individualism. Acclaimed as the "German Milton," Klopstock wrote the finest epic of the mid-eighteenth century, *The Messiah* (4 vols., 1751–73), a pietistic tale of the Christ. As a composer of odes, Klopstock was superior to Gellert or to any other German poet of the age. A great patriot who never tired of upbraiding his countrymen for their abject imitation of French masters, Klopstock pioneered the romantic nationalist revival with his Arminius or Hermann trilogy of heroic dramas—*Die Hermannschlacht (The Battle of Arminius,* 1769), *Hermann und die Fürsten (Arminius and the Princes,* 1784), and *Hermanns Tod (The Death of Arminius,* 1787). Fortified by a wide familiarity with the Eddas, the Scaldic epics, and medieval literature, Klopstock helped found a national school of letters.

The literary output of German rationalism, which was only an import, was modest compared with that of German idealism. The steep ascent to the summit of the world of letters, meanwhile, lay over the foothills represented by Salomon Gessner, Johann J. Bodmer, Albrecht von Haller, Gellert, Hammann, Klopstock, and Justus Möser.

The Rococo

The elegant, superbly balanced art style that dominated the Age of the Enlightenment between approximately 1725 and 1770 is called the "rococo." The word derives from the French *rocaille*, which described the naturalistic rock work in certain parts of the royal park at Versailles.

Rococo art aimed at the pleasurable and sensuous. Because it played like sunlight on the surface of things, it has been called an art without depth or sincerity. Devoted as it was to portraying the carefree, aristocratic life, it was, to be sure, epicurean and refined, but shallow it was not. Some rococo architects and painters rank among the most creative in the history of the West. The style was embodied in many elegant *Lustschlösser* ("pleasure palaces") that mushroomed in Germany, notably in such summer residences as the Schönbrunn (Vienna), Schloss Favorite in Baden, and Sans Souci at Potsdam; in the curvilinear stucco ornamentation that made untiring use of a linkage of the "C" and "S" in continuing flourishes on the façades and interior walls of churches and mansions; in the imported Gobelin and Beauvais tapestries; in the gilded, graceful furniture of Risenburgh and Oeben; in the collections of china and porcelain that were the pride of every noble family, in the extravagant, courtly entertainments embellished with fireworks, illuminations, and dancing; and in the numerous stilted plays and florid operas that illustrated not so much the canons of timeless art as the urbane taste of the upper orders.

About the middle of the century the European-wide rococo style passed into a final phase in which emphasis was given to things that had been slighted by the preceding generation. Splendor and ostentation were less esteemed after 1750 than the intimate, simple, or bucolic.

Architecture

To the pompous edifices of the baroque era succeeded others of infinite grace. The new style exhausted every curvilinear and rhythmic possibility. Expressed in stone and stucco, rococo art suggested the music of Mozart. Princes and prelates competed in commissioning the construction of festal residences and churches that conjured up visions of Elysium. Especially in the period churches was there collaboration between the fine and the plastic arts. There, voluptuous stucco decorations, luminous ceiling frescoes, exuberant altars, overpowering organ consoles, rhapsodic grill work, fenestration, and ingenious spatial arrangements were integrated into a radiant whole.

In the Bavaria of Elector Max Emmanuel (1662–1726), Joseph Effner (1687–1745) continued work upon the older Nymphenburg palace, but the paramount influence at the Wittelsbach court was the Walloon François Cuvilliés (1698–1767). He built the Cuvilliés Theater and the façade of the Theatine Church in Munich, as well as the Amalienburg hunting lodge (1734–39), which was erected for Maria Amalia, wife of the enlightened Elector Karl Albrecht (1726–45).

The rococo left its imprint upon all Bavaria, particularly during the reign of

Duke Maximilian III Joseph. Dominikus Zimmermann, the brother of the stucco master Johann Baptist (1680–1758), built the church at Günzburg (1735–40) and the peerless Wieskirche (Church of the Meadows, 1745–54), often referred to as the "miracle of the German rococo." Cosmos Damian and Egid Quirin Asam figured prominently in the construction and embellishment of many churches, among them that of St. John Nepomuk near Munich. At Benediktbeuren the baroque monastery was supplemented with the beautiful Anastasia chapel (1751–52), a masterpiece of Johann Michael Fischer (1692–1766). Fischer also built the Benedictine cloister church at Zwiefalten (1738–65), which possessed one of the most gorgeous interiors of the times, and the churches at Berg am Lain (1738–63), Ottobeuren (1744ff), and Rott am Inn (1759ff).

From a range of architects and auxiliary artists working in south Germany, it is possible to select one who surpassed all others. This was Johann Balthasar Neumann (1687–1753). On his shoulders descended the mantle of J. B. Fischer von Erlach. Neumann's works are scattered like lilacs through much of Germany, but especially in Würzburg and the Rhineland. In the latter region he built the high altar of Worms cathedral and the Jesuit church at Mainz (1742), the Schönbornslust palace near Koblenz (1748–52), the palace of the margraves of Baden at Bruchsal, and the elegant French staircase of Brühl palace. In Würzburg, where he was professor and the bishop's superintendent of public buildings, Neumann achieved his supreme masterpiece, the princely *Residenz* (1719–44) and its incomparable chapel. The prototype of contemporary German palaces, the episcopal residence, with its balustraded marble staircase and decorative façade and rear, was the noblest mansion of the German rococo.

Dresden's architectural importance did not decline during this period. Matthäus Daniel Pöppelmann (1662–1736) continued his work on the Zwinger, while Balthasar Permoser (1651–1732) adorned the Zwinger pavilions in harmony with the prevailing taste. Zacharias Onguelune (1669–1748) collaborated with Pöppelmann to complete the porcelain Japanese palace in the Saxon capital. The Palais de Saxe was built by Georg Bähr (1666–1738), who also drafted the plans for the Fraumünster of Dresden (1725–43), the finest Lutheran church of the age.

Silesia and Poland reflected the Saxon rococo, while in Prague the Dientzenhofer family completed the St. Nicholas church in Malá Strana and St. John of Nepomuk in the Hradčany.

In Prussia it was not until the accession of Frederick II that the tradition of Frederick I was resumed. Then commissions were given to the outstanding architect-painter Georg Wenzeslau von Knobelsdorff (1699–1753) and the stucco-master Johann August Nahl (1710–81). They collaborated in building the golden gallery of the royal Charlottenburg Palace (1740–43). Knobelsdorff, the best architect of northern Germany after Pöppelmann, also built the revolutionary Berlin opera (1741–43), the Potsdam City Palace (1745–51), and then crowned his distinguished career with the construction of Sans Souci (1744–47), the lusciously frosted summer palace of Frederick the Great at Potsdam.

Sculpture and Painting

In the rococo, sculpture was chiefly an auxiliary to religious architecture. Once again as in the twelfth and thirteenth centuries the best work of German sculptors was on pietàs, tabernacles, pulpits, baptismal fonts, figures of saints, cherubs, altars, and church façades. Among the most patronized carvers in wood and marble were Joachim Dietrich (1690–1753), Joseph Anton Feuchtmayr (1696–1770), Ferdinand Dietz (1709–1777), Christian Wenzinger (1710–97), and, in Bohemia, Ferdinand Brockoff (1688–1731) and Matthias Braun (d. 1738). Probably superior to these were: Egid Quirin Asam; Permoser, court sculptor at Dresden, who also did the marble apotheosis of Prince Eugene in the art museum in Vienna; Paul Egell (1691–1752), court sculptor at Mannheim; Georg Raphael Donner (1693–1741), who was chiefly active in Pressburg (Bratislava); Johann Baptist Straub (1704–84), whose artistic bequests adorn Bavaria and Swabia; and Nahl.

Whereas Germany was widely celebrated for the incomparable porcelain masterpieces manufactured by Joachim Kändler (1706–75) of Meissen and Franz Anton Bustelli (1704–63) of Nymphenburg, her painting in this age was only mediocre. Her canvases were largely slavishly imitative of the florid, opulent style and the lustrous taffeta elegance that typified the paintings of Boucher, La Tour, Le Brun, Fragonard, and Gainsborough. Perhaps the best of an unimpressive field of German artists were: Johann Kupetsky (1667–1740), Antoine Pesne (1683–1757), who was a Parisian active at the court of Frederick II, and Anton Raphael Mengs (1728–79), an art critic who painted mainly in Dresden. After 1750 a more individualistic, simpler, and intimate treatment of themes was introduced by Franz Messerschmidt (1736–83) and Georg Edlinger (1741–1819) of Munich, Anton Maulbertsch (1724–96) of Austria, the Tischbein family (especially Friedrich August, 1750–1802) of Hesse, and the prolific Swiss portraitist Anton Graff (1736–1813), who was mainly active in Dresden.

In decorative fresco work, where the level of achievement was higher, the unsurpassed archetype was the Italian Giovanni Tiepolo, who had decorated ceilings in the Würzburg episcopal mansion. His most significant German imitators were Cosmas Damian Asam, Johann B. Göz (1708–74), Januarius Zick (1732–97), Giovanni D. Maulbertsch (1727–1804), and, in Austria, Daniel Gran (1697–1757) and Paul Troger (1698–1777).

Music

In the late eighteenth century, music achieved a variety and richness never known before. This was due not only to the exceptional refinement of the nobility and the perfection of instruments but also to the emancipation of music from religion. Enduring changes overtook song, oratorios, opera, and compositions for violin and orchestra. The oratorios of J. S. Bach sustained bourgeois, Protestant piety in an increasingly secular age. The lied, or true song, was divorced from polyphonic and contrapuntal hymns and was sung to the accompaniment of lute, violin, or keyboard. Richly textured, intensely Italian concerti, divertimenti, sonatas for violin, harpsichord, or clavier, chamber music, and symphonies were much in demand. Opera, still under the wand of Italy, commenced in the closing rococo to display national characteristics. After the modern technique of keyboard playing had been developed by Domenico Scarlatti, German rococo composers wrote thousands of sonatas of great precision and clarity for harpsichord and clavier. The newer sonata and symphonic forms were especially promoted by the Mannheim school of composers, headed by the Bohemian Johann Stamitz (1717–57).

In the rococo era, Germany produced three more composers of world-historic importance—Gluck, Haydn, and Mozart.

Willibald Gluck (1714–87), a Bavarian-born resident of Vienna, first broke with the Venetian and Neapolitan *bel canto* style opera. He pioneered with a new operatic form which stressed the plot and dynamic potentialities of the musical score rather than the sheer proficiency of vocalists. Among his emotionally expressive operas were *Alceste* (1767), *Paris and Helen* (1769), and *Iphigenia in Taurus* (1779).

Franz Joseph Haydn (1732–1809, the "father of symphony orchestra," was an Austrian of lowly birth. At the palace of the Prince Miklós Esterházy in the Burgenland, where Haydn spent most of his adult life in the prince's employ, he composed five masses, eleven operas, sixty symphonies, forty string quartets, thirty sonatas, and innumerable concertos. Eventually the composer of a grand total of 104 symphonies, including twelve he wrote in London in 1791 and 1794–95, Haydn, more than any predecessor, perfected the symphonic form, gave a new emphasis to the melodic role of violins, and afforded ample scope to dramatic orchestral effects.

Wolfgang Amadeus Mozart (1756–91) was, as is well known, phenomenally precocious as a boy composer and virtuoso, a *Wunderkind*. During his brief life, its last sixteen years passed in dire poverty, he wrote more than 600 musical pieces, most of them distinguished by their balance, symmetry, and marvelous clarity. They included 50 concertos, 53 sonatas, 41 symphonies, 29 orchestral sets, 15 masses (among them the unfinished *Requiem*), cantatas, divertimenti, chamber music, and such operettas and operas as the *Singspiel* (containing spoken dialogue and arias), *Die Entführung aus dem Serail (The Abduction from the Seraglio,* 1782*), Le Nozze di Figaro (The Marriage of Figaro,* 1786*), Don Giovanni* (1787), and *Die Zauberflöte (The Magic Flute,* 1791*).* Mozart revolutionized the *Singspiel,* achieved in his operas a more perfect fusion of vocal and instrumental music, and enormously enriched the sonata, symphonic, and mass forms. Yet Mozart died almost friendless, leaving most of his music unpublished.

Chapter 22

UNDER THE FRENCH HAMMER

The Nemesis of the French Revolution

As the eighteenth century drew to a close, most of Germany was once again arrayed against France. In that contest the latter appeared to many outsiders as the apocalypse of the future and Germany the champion of the existing order. France seemed to embody the dreams, impatience, and pugnacity of youth; Germany, the realism, practicality, and timidity of old age.

However, the twenty-three-year tournament upon which the fate of Europe was to depend was certainly much more than a confrontation between the future and the past. It was an epochal struggle between wholly different concepts of right and morality. We now know that France was not wholly concerned with human dignity and inalienable personal rights, as her propagandists represented her to be. Nor were the Germanies mere protagonists of superannuated notions of government and privilege that deserved to be relegated to the attic of history.

The real truth lies in another direction: the French Revolution ushered in an era of mass preponderance. It repudiated the idealist and paternalist Christo-Germanic conception of statesmanship which for eight hundred years had affirmed that political power was a magistracy held from God and that rulers were not privileged to pursue limitless objectives. Total tyranny and total war date only from the French Revolution.

It is ironical that the Red Terror, which was actuated by a vision of a republic of virtue, ended by arousing a demonism that had for centuries lain dormant in the masses. From the furnace of the Terror, too, emerged "the nation in arms," destined to be the progenitor of modern militarism. The Revolution suppressed the ancient estates and a network of corporative and prescriptive rights, replacing them with vague Rights of Man and Citizen. The revolutionary idealists believed they were ushering in an age of egalitarian democracy, whereas, in reality, the infallible general will *(volunté générale)* was soon shown to be a very thin skin hiding the sharp claws of demagogy. By recognizing neither objective legal norms nor a Kantian distinction between mere law and morality, the Revolution paved the way for the charismatic leader, the fierce spirit who panders to the ribald mob. Popular caprice, more often than the precepts of statesmanship, was before very long to become the arbiter of grand policy, and thus the French Revolution set mankind on a road one fork of which was to lead to the modern, totalitarian "people's state."

Initial German Reaction to the Revolution

There was never any real danger that Germany would follow France down the chute. It is true that Rhenish peasants, momentarily excited by an alien example, not infrequently refused to pay seignorial dues and sometimes burned title deeds.

But insurrection was discouraged by the facts that Germany was still overwhelmingly peasant-aristocratic, lacked a strong, class-conscious bourgeoisie, was politically fragmentized and confessionally split, and possessed no centrally located capital from which the masses could be systematically propagandized and "politicized." The German middle class entertained no thought of abolishing privilege and establishing parliamentary government by other means than those of gradual reform. Having never recovered from the crippling effects of the Thirty Years' War, they were, in any case, incapable of seizing power. Nor were the nobles sufficiently strong or independent to raise the standard of rebellion. The masses were lamed by pietism and still in a leaderless, prepolitical condition. The proletariat was as yet almost nonexistent, and the peasantry was averse to risking another knockout blow such as had been dealt to it in 1525. Finally, most Germans were fairly content with the existing order, flattering themselves that they were already in enjoyment of rights that the French were only about to win.

While German reaction to the French Revolution was from the first mainly hostile, Herder, Klopstock, Wieland, Kant, Humboldt, and Reimarus hailed the Revolution in 1789. They seem to have regarded it as a legalistic protest of the upper classes against despotism. A succession of sanguinary episodes in France soon chilled the enthusiasm of the German literati. Kant, Schiller, and Goethe were among the first to grow skeptical. Conversely, the radical Fichte was slow in discarding his illusions. Under the mounting influence of Edmund Burke's antirevolutionary *Reflections on the Revolution in France* (1790), numerous German thinkers reverted to the view, endemic to the national mentality, that the great ends of civic society—morality and liberty—could not be secured by violent revolution, which corrupts them, but are the products of constitutional evolution in keeping with natural and divine law. By the time war broke out in 1792 most German men of letters had come round to agreeing with Wieland that the French Revolution was the antithesis of reason and the nemesis of liberty.

The Coming of the War

Guilt for the outbreak of the Revolutionary Wars was divided. If the French government was inspired by crusading aims that posed a mortal threat to the conservative monarchical order, successive Holy Roman emperors (Leopold II, 1790–92, and Francis II, 1792–1806) were actively hostile to the Revolution, lent aid to the Bourbons, gave asylum to émigré nobles, and winked at the organization of counterrevolutionary armies on German soil. If behind the program of the French Constituent Assembly to spread "liberty, equality and fraternity" lurked the sinister aim of attaining the "natural frontiers" from Basel to the sea, it is also true that the Austro-Prussian alliance, which was presently concluded, confronted France with her worst nightmare since King William's Grand Alliance in the War of the Spanish Succession. Probably the expansionist goals of the French bourgeoisie would have rendered war inevitable even had there been no revolutionary assault upon the European social order, but so likewise would the aims of King Frederick William II (1786–97) of Prussia, who tried to exploit the alliance with Austria to acquire more territory in Luxemburg and the Rhineland. The Habsburgs, for their part, were searching for territorial compensation for recent Russian gains in Poland and for disappointments in the late war against Turkey.

Leopold II himself was little minded to lead a counterrevolutionary war against France. The awkward Polish problem, the war with Turkey (which ended in 1791), the demands of the Hungarian magnates for complete political autonomy, and the Dutch rebellion left the emperor little leisure for new military adventures. While he could not completely ignore the pleas of his sister, Marie Antoinette, that the count of Provence be allowed to establish a court at Koblenz, Leopold II hesitated till the end of his life to send his armies against France.

The initiative in the organization of a monarchical coalition against the Jacobins came from the emotional and proudly Germanic Frederick William II. Pretending to be scandalized by insults inflicted upon the Bourbons, he engineered the anti-revolutionary Agreement of Mantua (May 20, 1791) among Prussia, Austria, Spain, and some German states. Strongly influenced by his minister Hertzberg and the favorites Bischoffswerder and Wöllner, the king of Prussia also urged that an Austro-Prussian defensive alliance be concluded. Signed on February 7, 1792, it not only insured against possibility of a French attack upon the Germanies, but, as modified by the Austrian ministers Cobenzl and Spielmann, gave Frederick William II a free hand in Poland.

In March, 1792, the bellicose Francis II (1792–1835) ascended the Habsburg throne. By taunting France he not only played into war-minded Girondin hands but also into those of the aristocratic Feuillant faction, which wanted to stage a phony war leading to the voluntary surrender of the French armies and generals. The upshot was that when the emperor rejected an ultimatum to expel the count of Provence from Germany, dissolve the émigré army, and repudiate the alliance with Prussia, Louis XVI hypocritically declared war on April 20, 1792, against the "king of Bohemia and Hungary." Prussia perceived the intention of driving a wedge between her and Austria and responded by sending an army to invade France.

With these events a war of twenty-three years' duration, involving all the great and most of the smaller powers of Europe, began. In its course the Holy Roman Empire and all of the German ecclesiastical principalities were erased from the map. The protracted character of the struggle may not only be attributed to the renovation of France but to the friction between Austria and Prussia, which obstructed the development of joint operational plans and establishment of a unified command. Furthermore, the cupidity of the German princes and the absence of any sense of larger national purpose led the main German governments to barter away the nation's territorial patrimony and accommodate themselves to partition and a revolutionary restructuring imposed by a foreign tyrant.

The Prussian Phase

The war commenced with a Prussian thrust against France's eastern frontier. However, the Prussian commander, Karl Ferdinand, duke of Brunswick, soon committed a classic blunder that undermined his early victories and guaranteed a long war. In his manifesto of July 24, 1792, he proclaimed the intention to take "ever memorable" vengeance upon Paris if the French public did not submit to the "legitimate authority" of Louis XVI or if the slightest harm befell him. The Brunswick Manifesto galvanized all the bickering patriotic French factions behind the war effort and contributed to the overthrow of the Bourbon monarchy on August 10, 1792.

The Prussians, who took Longwy on August 28 and Verdun on September 2, were suddenly faced on September 20 with a tatterdemalion militia under General François A. Kellermann, at Valmy. Brunswick's army, already ravaged by dysentery, was repulsed by Kellermann's militia. The Prussian army was no longer that of Rossbach and Leuthen, and the sun was swiftly setting on its legendary glory. The victory of the canaille over the Prussian regulars inaugurated a new chapter in military history.

After Valmy the Germans retreated to Verdun and the Rhineland. The French broke into the Palatinate and Rhineland and took Landau, Speier, Worms, and Mainz by October, and Frankfurt on December 2, 1792. General François Dumouriez, meanwhile, was winning the biggest victory of the immediate counteroffensive. He smote the Austrians at Jemappes on November 6 and brought all Belgium under French control.

Jemappes struck fear into the hesitant English and Dutch. When the Convention on November 19 and December 15, 1792, announced that France would aid and protect all peoples who would accept her revolutionary dictatorship and rise up against their governments, Britain and the United Provinces declared war on February 1, 1793, and Spain followed suit on March 7.

The French armies sustained their first major disaster at Neerwinden on the Geete on the sixteenth. They were driven out of Belgium at the same time that they were defeated in the Rhineland. At this juncture the Committee of Public Safety discovered the talisman of success: a decree of August 23 instituted a mass levy and put the entire manpower and material of France at the disposal of the central government. Able, new appointees to the Committee of Public Safety—Carnot and Prieur de la Côte d'Or—implemented the levy in mass and reorganized the army. By September a new, though hastily trained, conscript force of 650,000 men, led by daring young republican generals, was ready to take the field.

Within less than a year the Spaniards were driven beyond the Pyrenees, Savoy was reoccupied, Belgium was conquered, and the whole left bank of the Rhine was in French hands. Even Amsterdam was obliged to open its gates to the invaders, and in January, 1795, the Dutch Batavian puppet republic was proclaimed.

Meanwhile, with the Austrians refusing to underwrite Frederick William's rapidly mounting war expenditures, Prussia's appetite for battle was waning.

Endangered from the Netherlands and the Rhine, where the French had taken Bonn, Koblenz, and Cologne, the Prussian army was pulled back. Part of it was concentrated in Westphalia, and part was sent to Poland where it could do more good. England and Holland offered subsidies to Prussia if she would continue in the coalition, but Brunswick's successor, the aging General Joachim von Möllendorff, would not cooperate. When the Prussian commander refused to transfer his troops from Alsace to rescue the Austro-English chestnuts in Belgium, the subsidy treaty was allowed to lapse. At the end of her tether financially and profoundly preoccupied with an impending final partition of Poland, Prussia prepared to make separate peace.

Influenced by Christian von Haugwitz and the Marchese Girolamo Lucchesini, the king of Prussia on April 5, 1795, signed the Treaty of Basel, terminating Prussian participation in the war. By secret articles French annexation of the whole left bank of the Rhine was recognized on condition that Prussia be appropriately compensated for the loss of Cleves, Mörs, and Upper Gelders. Saxony, Hanover, Saxe-Weimar, Hesse-Cassel, and other states followed the Prussian lead, while Holland also ceded the left bank of the Dutch Rhine to France. When on July 22 Spain also signed peace at Basel, only Austria and England were left in the First Coalition.

It has often been said that inasmuch as the war was a *Reichskrieg* Prussia's action was dishonorable and it cost her the leadership of Protestant Germany. The former charge is true, and it is also true that in a larger sense the decision of Frederick William II, as W. M. Freiherr von Bissing has insisted, confirmed Prussian isolation in international politics. But it is a specious argument that capitulation in the west cost Prussia her paramountcy in Protestant Germany. Basel was simply the price Prussia had to pay for sharing in the Third Partition of Poland. Prussia's military luster may have been tarnished by defeats, but the kingdom was enlarged and consolidated by adroit diplomacy. The territorial gains Prussia made in Poland left the Hohenzollern kingdom more powerful, if ethnically less homogeneous, than ever. Finally, it should be noted, virtually all north German states followed Prussia out of the war, relying on the French promise to recognize the neutrality of the area north of the Main. The states of that region could now turn to commerce and reconstruction.

The Partition of Poland

News of the Austro-Russian entente of January, 1795, had alarmed Berlin. The pact, it was learned, was aimed at Poland, Venice, and the Ottoman Empire. To forestall a huge and, for Prussia, intolerable extension of Habsburg dominion, Frederick William II turned from France and rushed to upset the plans of Vienna and St. Petersburg.

When the Polish nobility *(szlachta)* refused to accept the liberal constitution of 1791, they had appealed to the Tsarina Catherine II for aid. She had sent the *szlachta* 100,000 troops, but the Prussians, who backed the constitutionalists, had countered by dispatching an army to western Poland. A confrontation was avoided only when Hohenzollern and Romanov agreed to the Second Partition (January, 1793). On that occasion Russia acquired Podolia, Volhynia, and the remainder of Lithuania. Prussia got Danzig, Thorn, Posen, and the Wartheland, whose southern reaches were reorganized as "South Prussia." Austria got nothing. Her exclusion from the partition unseated her foreign minister, Count Philip Cobenzl, who was succeeded by Baron Franz de Paula Thugut (1736–1818), a bitter Prussophobe.

Frederick William II entered the dangerous poker game of the Third Partition of Poland at a disadvantage. He brought no laurels—only defeat and humiliation— from the Rhine. He was confronted with an Austro-Russian working agreement to oppose any large territorial concessions to Prussia and arrived in Poland only to find that the Russian army was already in occupation of all her eastern lands and acting as if they were an integral part of Russia. By the Third Partition of Poland, Austria acquired 2 million new Slavic subjects in the area between the northern Bug, Vistula, and Pilitza rivers, as well as Crakow. Prussia was fortunate to be given Warsaw, a part of Podlackia, Masovia, Białystok, and some land around Crakow—territories inhabited by a total of 1 million Slavs. Russia received what was left—a block of lands twice as large as that awarded Prussia. Liquidation of the Polish buffer state complicated the nationality problems for both Austria and Prussia and brought them into contiguity with Russia. This development inaugurated a new era in military rivalries.

The Peace of Campo Formio

After the Treaty of Basel, France launched a new offensive against her remaining continental adversary, Austria. Early successes were erased by the close of 1795 by German counteroffensives led by Count Carl Clerfait and General Wurmser. In 1796 the French tried to close a pincers on Vienna. Three armies—those of the middle and the upper Rhine and Italy—took part in the campaign. The French refused neutral status to the south German states and even violated the sanctuary north of the demarcation line. However, when the Austrians repulsed Jourdan at Wetzlar on June 15, the French signed an armistice.

Thereafter, Thugut's hope for decisive victory died on the vine. He failed to persuade Prussia to reenter the fray, and, instead, she signed the Treaty of Berlin (August 5, 1796) with France, again accepting the loss of the left bank of the Rhine in return for assurance of compensation in inner Germany and respect for the neutrality of north Germany. Austria's Russian card was also outtrumped by fate. Catherine II, who was about to go to war against France, died on November 17 and was succeeded by her son Paul, who, detesting all his mother's works, allowed the Russo-Austrian alliance of January, 1795, to lapse. Last, a new French commander of genius, Napoleon Bonaparte, dealt the Austrian and Piedmontese armies such staggering blows at Lodi, Castiglione, Arcole, and Rivoli in 1796–97 in Italy that they all but collapsed into worthless wreckage.

If Austria held out as long as she did, it was because of transient successes won in Germany by the successor of Clerfait, the twenty-five-year-old Archduke Karl von Habsburg (1771–1847), brother to the emperor, and one of the best generals Austria ever had. When Jourdan crossed the Rhine and pushed through Franconia to northern Bavaria and Moreau drove eastward across Baden and Württemberg, Archduke Karl prevented them from joining. He defeated Jourdan first at Wetzlar, then at Würzburg on September 3, 1796. After September 19 both Jourdan and Moreau were forced to flee westward to the Rhine, and Baden and Württemberg were obliged to conclude an armistice. However, the whole military picture was decisively changed by Napoleon's aforementioned victories at Arcole (November 15–17, 1796) and Rivoli (January 14–15, 1797). The south German states crept cautiously out of the cellar and reentered the fray. Then after Mantua capitulated on February 2 and Karl was beaten by Bonaparte on the Isonzo, the French armies pushed to the vicinity of Leoben, where they stood only one hundred miles from Vienna. The erstwhile hawk Thugut had no alternative but to coo with the doves, and so a preliminary peace was signed at Leoben on April 18, 1797.

The final peace of Camp Formio (Julian Alps), which was signed on October 17–18, 1797, embodied the substance of the preliminary terms. Austria ceded Belgium to France and agreed to the extinction of most of the independent north Italian states and their transformation into French satellites. Thugut acknowledged French sovereignty over the left bank of the Rhine on condition that the expropriated princes be indemnified at a later time with right bank territory. In secret clauses Prussia's left bank lands were retroceded, and she was to be denied a share in the redistribution of inner German territories, doubtless to avert any Hohenzollern threat to Habsburg paramountcy in south Germany. The immediate compensation of the Habsburgs was to be all the possessions of Venice as far as the Adige River and Lake Garda, together with Istria, Dalmatia, and some Adriatic islands.

By alienating the left bank of the Rhine, the cession of which was reluctantly confirmed on March 9, 1798, at a meeting of the lesser German princes at Rastatt, Campo Formio rendered illusory the independence of Germany, while making its defense impossible. Not surprisingly, the treaty undermined Austrian prestige and drove the last nails into the coffin of the Holy Roman Empire. The secret clauses foreshadowed the extinction of the ecclesiastical principalities, which had for centuries been the piers of the Empire and of Austrian domination over Germany. Furthermore, the French were accorded a primacy in Italy such as they had not enjoyed since the first half of the fifteenth century. For Austria, the acquisition of the Dalmatian coast was a lure that promised only to draw her deeper into dangerous south Slav waters.

The War of the Second Coalition

A series of French actions in 1798–1799 that violated treaties and sapped the old European order made war inevitable. Of these the most flagrant were committed in Switzerland and Italy. In March, 1798, the French invaded the former and by August forced all the cantons to ally with them. In 1799 Pope Pius VI was captured and brought to France, while the papal states were reorganized into the Roman and Parthenopian republics.

The French challenge was taken up by British Prime Minister William Pitt. He forged a new grand alliance, embracing Russia, Turkey, Austria, and the south German states. However, Pitt failed to budge the new king of Prussia, Frederick William III (1797–1840), from neutrality. Meanwhile, Austria provided the pretext for resumption of hostilities. She had mobilized 233,000 troops scattered from southern Germany to northern Italy and had granted transit rights to a Russian expeditionary force under General Korsakov. At the same time, Austria awaited the prearranged landing in Italy of General Suvorov and another Russian army. When, finally, Austria rejected a French ultimatum to withdraw her troops beyond the Inn, France declared war on March 1, 1799.

At the outset of the War of the Second Coalition the French were beaten by Archduke Karl in several minor battles. Meanwhile, Suvorov had landed in Italy, joined Austrian General Melas, humbled the armies of Joubert and Moreau in the battles of Cassano, the Trebbia, and Novi, and then drove the French out of upper Italy altogether. French setbacks provoked the dissolution of the Roman, Cisalpine, and Parthenopian satellite republics.

Initial French reverses produced havoc in Switzerland. Early Swiss fears that an Austro-Russian victory might wipe out French-inspired reforms and restore a range of defunct class privileges and vassal relationships that had disappeared in 1798 along with the *Eidgenossenschaft* were replaced by mounting antipathy for France and its puppet, the oppressive Helvetic Directory. A large number of uncoordinated and unsuccessful uprisings occurred in 1799 in at least seven cantons. Meanwhile, the arrival of an Austrian army in eastern Switzerland and of Suvorov and an Austro-Russian army in Graubünden forced the French to fall back to the north Swiss plain. For a time Switzerland was split in two between the rival forces. By September, 1799, about 150,000 soldiers were sucking the blood from the country, reducing its towns and villages to ruins, seizing its livestock, and requisitioning its cheese, bread, and wine. Intolerable conditions ultimately entailed a parliamentary coup against the Helvetic Directory on January 7, 1800. This brought about the collapse of all lawful government. Then in May, 1801, when the French star was again in the ascendancy and French pressure paramount in Switzerland, a new federative constitution was imposed upon the Swiss, and the Valais was surrendered to Napoleon.

Dissolution of the Second Coalition

Meanwhile Masséna destroyed the better part of Korsakov's army in the Second Battle of Zurich (September 25–26, 1799), and the English failure to reconquer the Dutch Netherlands evoked the tsar's bitter recriminations. Tsar Paul was disenchanted with his Austrian and British allies. When finally Suvorov, having crossed the Gotthard to come to Korsakov's rescue, was allowed by the Austrians to walk into a French trap from which he only narrowly extricated his half-starved troops, Russia bolted the coalition.

When Napoleon on November 9–10, 1799, became first consul of the French Republic, his first thought was to buttress his shaky regime with a decisive victory over the crumbling coalition. This lured him into Italy again. With the help of General Desaix he inflicted a crushing defeat on the Austrians at Marengo (June 14, 1800). Six months earlier Moreau had also beaten the Germans at Hohenlinden in Bavaria (December 3). These victories opened the road to Vienna and forced replacement of the implacable Thugut with the conciliatory Cobenzl.

After Marengo the heart went out of the Second Coalition. General peace was made in a series of treaties, in particular Lunéville (February 9, 1801) and Amiens (March 27, 1802). By the former settlement, which involved Austria, the Empire, and France, the territorial provisions of Campo Formio were confirmed, but the House of Habsburg-Lorraine now lost Tuscany too. The German princes were obliged to recognize French annexations of Belgium and the left bank of the Rhine but were assured of early compensation with lands east of the river, an arrangement that was endorsed by the Reichstag on March 7. In the face of overwhelming opposition from its inhabitants, the Rhineland was thereafter thrust under French government and law, and the last vestiges of feudalism were suppressed on the left bank. The sharp decline of Austria now brought the question of the survival of the ecclesiastical states into the limelight. Having attained her "natural frontiers" along the Rhine, France was on the verge of displacing Austria as the arbiter of German affairs. Under the circumstances there was now no more logic in perpetuating the Holy Roman Empire.

The Imperial Rescript of 1803

The last obstacle to French hegemony over southern and central Europe was removed when the British signed the Treaty of Amiens, by far the most dangerous peace England ever made. Bonaparte then entrusted the planning of a comprehensive territorial reorganization of Germany to his foreign minister, Maurice de Talleyrand. The first consul intended to isolate Austria from all allies, simplify the map of Germany, and reduce the more important secular principalities, including Prussia, to client states of France. Napoleon expected to win the assent of the German temporal princes to these dispositions by indemnifying most of them with ecclesiastical lands east of the Rhine.

Secularization of church property was not new in Germany. In recent years Bavaria and Joseph II had sequestrated monastic lands and hereditaments. However, the changes contemplated by Napoleon were of such magnitude as to inaugurate a new era in German history. They utterly destroyed the network of ecclesiastical states and free cities upon which the Austrian position in Germany depended. They stimulated a naked struggle for survival in which the larger states devoured their weaker neighbors, and the changes made straight the path of Prussian domination over central Europe.

Napoleon's campaign against Austria's position was aided by several things. As a result of French annexation of the electorates of Cologne, Trier, and Mainz, the Protestants had acquired a majority upon the electoral college. This spelled the end of the Habsburg monopoly upon the imperial crown. Also, the French pacts with Bavaria on August 24, 1801, and with St. Petersburg on June 3, 1802, strengthened Napoleon's hand. Austria's isolation was completed when France signed individual treaties with Prussia, Württemberg, Bavaria, Basel, Hesse-Cassel, and Frankfurt, specifying precise territorial indemnification for each signatory. With half of Germany dangling from his belt and Russia benign, Napoleon could proceed with impunity to the recasting of Germany.

The Reichstag, notorious for delay, now hastened to arrange its own burial. In August, 1802, it appointed an ad hoc committee (the *Reichsdeputation*) to handle all territorial indemnities. Its report was adopted on February 25, 1803, as an Imperial Recess, or *Reichsdeputationshauptschluss*.

The 'Recess' embodied provisions of a secret Franco-Russian plan that went far beyond any territorial changes envisaged at the time of Campo Formio or Lunéville. The Catholic Church, the plinth of Austrian hegemony, sustained the worst seismic shock since the Lutheran revolt. All ecclesiastical principalities were forever liquidated and annexed to favored secular states. Of all regnant prelates of Germany only Karl Theodor Dalberg, the prince primate, was spared because of his Francophile sympathies, but was transferred to the see of Regensburg. Clerical strength in the College of Princes declined from 34 to 2 votes. Of 314 principalities, 112 were eradicated, and of 51 free cities, only 6—Frankfurt, Hamburg, Bremen, Lübeck, Augsburg, and Nuremberg—survived mediatization. One-sixth of Germany and more than 4 million people were involved in these transfers.

No attempt was made to achieve an equitable distribution of plunder or indemnify in proportion to losses sustained on the left bank of the Rhine. Baden received about eight times and Württemberg five times the areas they had lost. Bavaria received only one-third more land than she had ceded to France, Baden, and Hesse but obtained by compensation very valuable lands in return—the bishoprics of Würzburg, Bamberg, Augsburg, Freising, parts of Eichstätt and Passau, as well as twelve abbeys and fifteen free cities. Prussia was interdicted from south Germany, but in return for the 48 square miles and 137,000 subjects she had surrendered she received 235 square miles of land and 600,000 new subjects. She thereby acquired the bishoprics of Hildesheim, Paderborn, Münster, Erfurt, Eichsfeld, part of Mainz, and the imperial cities of Mülhausen, Goslar, and Nordhausen. Unquestionably this discard of the ecclesiastical pieces from the German jigsaw puzzle promoted consolidation. It also facilitated economies and led to improvements in administration, education, and justice.

Perceiving that a discouraged Austria had abandoned opposition to his grand design, Napoleon approved Habsburg acquisition of the bishoprics of Trent and Brixen as indemnity for loss of the Breisgau and Ortenau. To the emperor's brother, Ferdinand of Tuscany, went the bishopric of Salzburg. For such petty coin Austria had to accept all the revolutionary changes that France had effected in Europe and agree to strengthening all of Austria's old rivals in Germany.

The Rheinbund and the End
of the Sacrum Imperium

In 1806 after Austria had been expelled from Germany, Napoleon dramatically reconstituted that country. He based all arrangements on the premise that the major south German states, all of which were historically particularist and steeled in a long struggle against the Habsburgs, could be brought into alliance with France. The bait would be annexations and unqualified independence for those states. Napoleon had to prepare this contemplated "revolution from above" with consummate skill. He encouraged the German client states to appropriate the lands of the imperial knights *(Reichsritter)*, whose separate existence no longer made sense. He contracted a series of marriages that linked the old, ruling families of the three south German states to the parvenu Bonaparte clan.* He also promised to make the dukes of Bavaria and Württemberg kings, and the rulers of Baden and Hesse and Archchancellor Dalberg grand dukes. Simultaneously Napoleon built a base of operations in north Germany by creating the Grand Duchy of Berg and Cleves, which he assigned to his brother-in-law, General Murat.

After the German princes had been bribed, Napoleon confidently arranged a series of treaties (July 13–16, 1806) which embodied Dalberg's suggestions that the Holy Roman Empire be dissolved and a Third Germany, a new Confederation of the Rhine (Rheinbund), be organized under French protection.

For Napoleon, the division of Germany into three parts—Austria, Prussia, and the Rheinbund—had become a strategic necessity from the moment Berlin leagued with the Third Coalition. If Napoleon could now induce Bavaria, Württemberg, and Baden to sign iron-clad alliances with France, it would mean that in any new war the initial fighting would be done hundreds of miles to the east of the Rhine. To this consideration was added the need to exclude Austria from Germany proper so that the south German allies of France might become beneficiaries of a further redistribution of territories.

Initially the Rheinbund embraced sixteen German rulers, but more joined in 1807.** All signatories had to secede from the Holy Roman Empire. Napoleon

---

*Eugène de Beauharnais to Amalie Auguste von Wittelsbach, daughter of Maximilian of Bavaria; Stephanie Tascher de Beauharnais to Grand Duke Charles Frederick of Baden; and Jerome Bonaparte to Catherine, daughter of Frederick of Württemberg.

**Original signatories were the kings of Bavaria and Württemberg, the grand dukes of Baden, Hesse-Darmstadt, and Berg, the dukes of Nassau, the duke of Aramberg, and the princes of Sigmaringen and Hechingen, Salm, Isenburg-Birstein, Liechtenstein, and von der Leyen. Joining later were the dukes of Saxony, Anhalt, Mecklenburg, and Oldenburg, the king of Westphalia, and some lesser princes.

withdrew recognition from that millenary invalid, which now sank unmourned into its grave. On August 6, 1806, Francis II abdicated the sacred throne but consoled himself with the title Francis I (1804–35), emperor of Austria.

No one could honestly say that this was Germany's finest hour. Every land-hungry member of the Rhenish Confederation had promised to furnish Napoleon troops in case of general war, regardless of how it arose. Not a single government of central Europe, except the Prussian and Austrian, against which the alliance was aimed, had the courage to condemn it, although the Rheinbund made Germany Napoleon's doormat.

In the scramble for annexations that attended the second arbitrary revision of the map of Germany, about 550 square miles and 1,300,000 persons were gobbled up by Bonaparte's client states. The three south German states and Hesse were the main beneficiaries. Among the territories absorbed were three more free cities—Augsburg, Nuremberg, and Frankfurt—and almost seventy tiny, secular principalities which till then had been spared the French guillotine. The smaller secular states thus followed the ecclesiastical into the museum of history.

Culturally and constitutionally the Confederation of the Rhine drove a deep wedge between the northern and southern parts of Germany. The Napoleonic Code and French administrative centralization were widely copied in the major client states—in Baden and Württemberg more, in Bavaria less—while, as in the days of Johann Christoph Gottsched, France once again became the arbiter of style and thought in Munich, Augsburg, Stuttgart, Frankfurt, Karlsruhe, and Darmstadt.

The massive hammer blows that shattered the complicated old structure and forged a simpler Germany elicited a wide range of reactions—jubilation, indifference, or dismay, depending upon material interests involved. On August 7, the day following the abdication of the Holy Roman Emperor, the politically otiose Goethe entered in his diary that a fight between his servant and coachman had aroused more interest in him than the news of the end of the Empire. Conversely, on August 26 the cause of liberation found its first martyr when the Nuremberg bookdealer Palm, publisher of the anonymous passionate denunciation "Germany in its Deepest Humiliation," was executed at Braunau by the French. Somehow Napoleon's German symphony had finished on a blatantly sour note in the bass.

PART VII

REGENERATION AND REACTION

Chapter 23

THE DARKNESS BEFORE DAWN

Preconditions of Liberation

In the annals of every people its most heroic hour is preceded by an agonizing ideological catharsis in which the national purpose is redefined. Before Germany could be finally victorious she had to make a reappraisal of her social and political forms to determine whether they might still serve the national interest. The ties that held German thought and letters in bondage to France had also to be cut. But, on the other hand, the lessons of the Revolution had to be studied. In full recognition of the fact that France had discovered ways of utilizing hitherto untapped resources, certain Gallic innovations had to be transplanted that might augment the strength of the German states system without undermining authority or legitimacy.

The "Storm and Stress" Movement

The period 1770–1786 was intellectually one of turbulent and confused winds of "Storm and Stress" (Sturm und Drang). In this period thought was iconoclastic and rebellious but did not pose a serious threat to the ruling classes. Consequently German authors were left surprisingly free to explore all the avenues of thought with vastly stimulating results.

The output of the Storm and Stress writers—Leisewitz, Klinger, Hamann, Müller, Wagner, Lenz, Johann Wolfgang Goethe (1749–1832), and Friedrich Schiller (1759–1805)—was commonly characterized by revelations of spiritual torment, extravagantly sentimental language, improbable plots, and an aesthetic animus against the existing social order because it inhibited the full and harmonious development of the individual's personality. It was this thoroughgoing idealistic, humanistic concern for the freedom of the spirit that inspired Goethe's first novel, *Die Leiden des jungen Werthers (The Sorrows of Young Werther 1774)*, a work that ended French literary ascendancy.

A Time of Cultural Achievements

In the quarter of a century following publication of Goethe's *Werther* Germany moved for the second time in history into the foremost files of culture. In the years 1775–1800 no other country produced a dramatist of the rank of Schiller, a poet of the stature of Goethe, a composer of operas and symphonies in a class with Mozart, a symphonic and piano composer comparable to Beethoven, a philosopher of history (unles it be Vico) of the influence of Herder, or a pure philosopher of the profundity of Kant. Between 1773 and the end of the century appeared such great works as Goethe's *Götz von Berlichingen* (1773), *Egmont* (1788), and *Wilhelm Meister* (1796); the tragic poet Hölderlin's Plutonian novel *Hyperion* (1797); Schiller's *Die Räuber (The Robbers,* 1781); *Wallenstein* (1796), *Mary*

Stuart (1800), and *William Tell* (1804); Lessing's *Nathan der Weise (Nathan, the Wise,* 1779*)*; Herder's *Ideen zur Philosophie der Geschichte der Menschheit (Ideas on the Philosophy of the History of Mankind,* 1784–91*)*; Klopstock's dramatic *Arminius* trilogy (1769–87); Mozart's *Le Nozze di Figaro (Marriage of Figaro,* 1786*), Don Giovanni* (1787), and *Die Zauberflöte (The Magic Flute,* 1791*)*; Kant's *Kritik der reinen Vernunft (Critique of Pure Reason,* 1781; rev. ed., 1787*), Kritik der praktischen Vernunft (Critique of Practical Reason,* 1788*),* and *Kritik der Urteilskraft (Critique of Judgment,* 1790*)*; and Johann Fichte's *Versuch einer Kritik aller Offenbarung (An Assay at a Critique of all Revelation,* 1792*)*.

The "Storm and Stress" and classical writers of the late eighteenth century started the rebellion against Gallomania. They shamed the German nobility on account of their insipid infatuation with French Old Regime models. The writers of this second "golden age" of German literature contributed an originality, dynamism, individuality, and sensibility to thought that brought down the skyscraper of rationalism.

That the first generation of rebels did not make the transition from cosmopolitanism to nationalism may be the secret of their lasting appeal. They were too individualistic and impractical to translate aesthetic apostasy into political action. Only the traumatic experience of war gradually disabused most of them (but not Beethoven or Goethe) of the illusion that French revolutionary experiments would realize their ideal of the harmonization of the individual with society.

The Threshold of National Consciousness

In the 1790s a struggle developed between the champions of world citizenship *(Weltbürgertum)* and those of a national cultural spirit *(Volksgeist)*. Both camps, however, joined to overthrow French domination of German letters. The concepts of *Weltbürgertum* were systematically developed by Immanuel Kant (1724–1804), a philosopher of Königsberg, but best incarnated in the life of Goethe. The ideas of the *Volksgeist*, which imparted a nationalist accent to nineteenth-century thought, were developed by the Latvian-German man of letters Johann Gottfried Herder (1744–1803).

Kant was the first to establish the limits of rationalism. With him we stand suddenly on the summit of European speculative thought. His *Critique of Pure Reason* rejected the concepts of Locke, Voltaire, and the philosophes. It was Kant's virtue that he saw that experience and reason did not go far enough in divining the hidden wells of human nature and altogether failed to accommodate the poetic and religious instincts of the soul. The dichotomy of knowledge that he hypothecated is seen in his distinction between the phenomenal world of appearance and the "noumenal," or the reality of the thing-in-itself *(Ding-an-sich)*. In later works Kant contended that it is the law of nature that rules in the former, the law of morality in the latter. He asserted the primacy of moral law, arguing that virtue and social progress are to be attained in battle against natural law whenever it contradicts moral or divine prescriptions. He implied that the individual can find meaning in existence only through ethical commitment and not, as Rousseau had thought, through mere physical improvement in his status. Kant also rejected the Anglo-French concept of freedom. While insisting that the state must respect fundamental law and the corporative and personal structure of society, he argued that freedom *(Freiheit)* is to be achieved only by cultivating civic virtues in obedience to law.

In Herder the shape of nineteenth-century thought is already limned. Like Kant and Klopstock, he rejected the notion that natural law determines the development of peoples or that politics can be reduced to an exact science. Herder established the theoretical foundations of a distinct German culture. Possessed of a surer historic instinct than Bolingbroke, Hume, or Voltaire, he was the foreloper of historicism, a school that viewed history as a continuum in which each nation's past is a spectral band of unique intensity and extension.

For Herder, the true guarantor of individualism lay not in general rights but in the *Volksgeist* or genius of a people. He did not believe that a country could be legislated into being by an act of the general will. Rather, a nation is the gift of history, the product of a protracted ethnic amalgamation and a unique institutional and organic growth.

Herder's preoccupation with the public mind was exhibited in works such as *Songs of Ancient Peoples* (1773) and *Voices of the Nations in Songs* (1778). Although he powerfully stimulated Germany's pulse, he had no vision of a politically unified nation. What he did was to invest history with communalism, and nations with the arcanum of an ethos *(Volksgeist)*.

The Veil of Romanticism

Extremely slow in their evolution toward political nationalism, the Germans nevertheless felt their spiritual and cultural oneness. They were more aware of their national individuality *(Volkstum)* than they were of any French-type universal rights. Echoing this gospel of European heterogeneity, August Wilhelm von Schlegel (1767–1845) averred that art is rooted in a country's soil and that every national speech, religion, and poetry can only be understood as a manifestation of the peculiar *Volksgeist*.

German intellectuals of the Napoleonic era found the origins of this ethos in the matrix of the high Middle Ages, when the Holy Roman Empire had enjoyed primacy among continental polities. A neo-Gothic, predominantly Catholic movement gradually took shape, to which Baron Friedrich von Hardenberg (Novalis, 1772–1801) gave the name "romanticism," after the French word *roman*. In its inception romanticism was unpolitical. It was, moreover, a mosaic of many colors. The main pieces derived from the "Storm and Stress" movement and the works of Goethe, Herder, and the so-called Magus of the North, Johann Hamann (1730–88). A lesser element came from the highland Scot James Macpherson and his translations (later believed to be spurious) of old Gaelic poems (e.g., *The Poems of Ossian*), which sent Goethe into raptures. The German romantic movement emerged in the late nineties as a result of the wanderings through Germany of two young men—Ludwig Tieck (1773–1853) and Wilhelm Heinrich Wackenroder (1773–98)—and their reflections upon medieval monuments and treasures they saw along the way. Wackenroder's *Outpourings of an Art-loving Monastic* (1797) contributed to the spread of neomedievalism, the rise of patriotism, and the development of an artistic, national symbolism. Tieck's *Popular Fairy Tales* (1797) were a foreloper of the better-known collections by the Grimm brothers and Hans Christian Andersen. Wackenroder and Tieck also collaborated to write the highly influential *Fancies about Art* (1799), which revived appreciation for the grand artistic creations of the German past.

Novalis gave a further impetus to the movement in 1799 when he published his *Heinrich von Ofterdingen*, the story of an eternal search for the Blue Flower, a timeless yearning for perfection which is in reality unattainable. In his *Christianity and Europe* (1799) Novalis, too, extolled the Christo-Germanic medieval ideal.

By the turn of the century the romantic stream had become a river. Visionaries, dreamers, irrationalists, and mountebanks came forth to confer on the movement an iridescence that beguiled the mind, as the Enlightenment and classicism had failed to do. German romanticism developed into something that was not merely paradigmatic but also unfathomable. A people who drank deeply of nationalist wine from a consecrated chalice were apt to believe in the political relevancy of Germany's great medieval folk epics and embrace the conviction that their country was about to awaken, like some sleeping giant, from the long stupor into which it had fallen since the day of Frederick Barbarossa.

At the turn of the century Jena and Heidelberg became seats of the romantic movement. At Jena August W. Schlegel and his brother Friedrich (1772–1829), the Catholic convert and orientalist of later times, resided. Together they founded the *Athenaeum* in 1798, the first central organ of the movement. At the University of Heidelberg a coterie of romantic writers was also to be found. Among them were Achim von Arnim (1781–1831), the historian and future editor of the anti-Napoleonic *Rheinische Merkur* Joseph Görres (1776–1848), Clemens Brentano (1778–1842), and Joseph von Eichendorff (1788–1822). These and other members of the Heidelberg circle labored to revive the memory of German medieval cultural accomplishments.

While the romanticists could not wholly abjure reason, they offered a corrective to the dictatorship of mechanistic determinism and natural law. To their way of thinking, rationalism had erred in trying to discover some single principle that underlay what was really an impossibly wide spectrum of national affinities. Rationalism had also ignored the need for religion, which wells from the deepest recesses of the soul. By contrast with the calm and stilted symmetry of French classicism, the German romanticists trafficked in spontaneity, imagination, and emotions, which for them resembled the thundering surges of the formless sea. Taking a joyous delight in the fickle, flowing dress of nature, the romanticists wore their hearts on their sleeves. They exhaustively charted the anatomy of the subjective. Always imaginative and lyric, often sad, endlessly yearning for the "blue flower," and seldom attaining the finish and elegance of German writers of the late eighteenth century, the romanticists dissipated much energy in a maudlin crusade for the "eternal rights" of the personality. Noble spirits often discussed the implications of this quest in salons, such as those held weekly in the Berlin mansions of those highly intelligent and refined Jewish converts, Henriette Herz and Rachael Levin.

Exhausted by ecstatic flights, German romanticism ran its course within about twenty years and was on the road to dormancy when E. T. A. Hoffmann (1776–1822), the wizard of the horror tales *(Märchen)* died. Goethe had said that romanticism was basically unhealthy. While romanticism undoubtedly laid the foundation for lasting achievements in the social sciences and law, Goethe's remark, as applied to literature and music, was certainly true. Too many romantic novels, poems, and musical compositions exuded torment and travail. Too often the labors of authors and composers ended in suicide (Kleist), insanity (Friedrich Hölderlin, 1770–1843), or premature death from strain (Wackenroder, Novalis, Wilhelm Müller, Wilhelm Hauff, Karl Maria von Weber, Franz Schubert, Felix Mendelssohn-Bartholdy).

Nevertheless, the romantic school continued to produce progeny until the end of the 1820s and to influence the subliminal mentality of Germany till the end of the century. Creative thinkers from many walks of life, who had even only transiently fallen under the occult spell of the romantic mystique—political economists like Adam H. Müller (1779–1829), lyric poets like Eduard Mörike (1804–75), philosophers like Arthur Schopenhauer (1788–1860) and Friedrich Nietzsche (1844–1900), and composers who were fascinated by old German myths and medieval *Minne*, like Richard Wagner (1813–83)—gave evidence that an affinity for the romance of nature, the supernatural, and the subconscious is one of the enduring traits of the German mentality.

Political Metamorphosis

By the time of the Battle of Jena (1806) a minority of intellectuals had managed to negotiate the transit from cultural to political nationalism. A reevaluation of the history of the Holy Roman Empire had convinced them that Germany was entitled to a place among the powers commensurate with her superior achievements. Almost all romantic thinkers had come to approve the crusade to drive the French out of Germany, because only thus could it breathe the air of freedom which was the precondition of a national Kultur.

German intellectuals increasingly heeded the conservative message of French émigré theorists, such as Vicomte François de Chateaubriand, Count Joseph de Maistre, and Vicomte Louis de Bonald. These thinkers strengthened the idealist and legalist indictments of the French Revolution that had already been drawn up by Burke, Haller, and Herder and imparted European sanction to German nation-

alist philosophy. De Maistre's views, in particular, that that which is most fundamental and essentially constitutional in the laws of a nation is precisely what
cannot be written and that humanity did not advance by revolutionary mutations
but rather with riverine continuity, harmonized perfectly with the conclusions of
Herder.

Among those who were encouraged by the French counterrevolutionary example to change from invertebrate aesthetes into political vertebrates were some
of Germany's most illustrious figures of the epoch: Wilhelm von Humboldt
(1767–1835), diplomat and future minister of education in Prussia; Ernst Moritz
Arndt (1769–1860), for a time professor at the University of Greifswald and the
author of *Geist der Zeit (Spirit of the Times*, 1806ff); Heinrich von Kleist (1777–
1811), who with Franz Grillparzer (1791–1872) was one of the two leading German dramatists of the day and who wrote the chauvinistic *Die Hermannsschlacht
(The Battle of Arminius*, posthumously published in 1821) in an effort to improve on Klopstock's tale; and Adam Müller (1779–1829), political economist and author of *Elemente der Staatskunst (Elements of Statecraft*, 3 vols.,
1810–11). Also Friedrich Eichhorn (1781–1854) and Friedrich Karl von Savigny
(1779–1861), the brilliant cofounders of the romantic-historical school of jurisprudence, contributed to the nationalist revolt. Both opposed French legalistic
rationalism and defended the idea of the organic growth of law as an expression
of the *Volksgeist*. Friedrich and August von Schlegel and Friedrich Schleiermacher (1768–1834), theologian and pastor of Berlin's Trinity Church, also denounced French tyranny. Of all these patriots, Müller was the most militant. He
averred that the military virtues were normal to the German character and that his
countrymen were God's chosen people, destined to rule subject races. Müller's
pernicious notions, to some extent shared by Arndt and Fichte, appeared vain and
absurd to most German intellectuals.

Of all the champions of political nationalism none was more fiery than Johann
Gottlieb Fichte (1762–1814), professor of philosophy at Jena. Initially a rationalist and a disciple of Kant, Fichte taught that the ideal polity was a supervisory
state *(Aufsichtsstaat)*, which should ultimately be responsible for the education
and cultural integration of its citizens. In 1807–8 in Berlin, then under French
occupation, Fichte had the audacity to deliver a series of thinly veiled philippics
against Napoleon (''Addresses to the German Nation,'' *Reden an die deutsche
Nation*), which had an elemental impact upon the restive youth of the country.
Probably of more importance in preparing them physically for the ordeal of liberation was *Turnvater* Friedrich Ludwig Jahn (1778–1852), who drilled young
people in gymnastics *(Turnen)*, thereby strengthening their bodies while steeling
their souls for insurrection.

When all is said, the problem of liberation was not to be solved by philosophers,
preachers, or gymnasts. The tiny minority of intellectuals who were political
activists could at best only state the problem and clamor for an answer. The solution itself had to be supplied by statesmen and generals, supported not so much by
elite patriotic associations (such as the Deutscher Bund, the Masonic Tugend-

bund, and the Fechtbodengesellschaft) as by the politicized masses, and then only on condition of Austro-Prussian collaboration. Even so, it is doubtful whether the independence of Germany could have been restored without aid from Russia and the "miracle" of Moscow in 1812.

A Time of Deep Travail

Napoleon's greed and cynicism provoked the formation of a third, and then a fourth coalition. His destruction of both bore him to the summit of fortune. Yet among his actions were irretrievable blunders that would ultimately confound all his hopes of pacifying Europe. New French encroachments upon northern Italy antagonized Francis II and drove him into a defensive alliance with Russia on November 6, 1804. The pact committed Austria and Russia to oppose further French aggression in Italy or Germany. At the same time, Napoleon himself sapped the vital neutrality of Prussia by occupying the electorate of Hanover, which he then used, to the chagrin of Frederick William III, as a pawn in negotiations with England. The suspicion that the French were playing a double game alienated the king of Prussia, to whom Bonaparte had promised Hanover.

A further turn of the French screw in Italy—the grant of Lucca and Piombino to Napoleon's sister, Princess Maria Eliza Bacciocchi, and the proclamation of the French satellite kingdom of Italy (March 1805)—afforded the Austrians and Russians pretexts for signing the militant Convention of St. Petersburg (April 11, 1805). Austria then secured a promise of British subsidies and mobilized against Emperor Napoleon,* who responded by signing comprehensive alliances with Baden, Württemberg, and Bavaria and by rapidly wheeling 150,000 troops that he had been concentrating at the Channel to the valleys of the Main and Neckar. On September 3, 1805, Austria declared war.

Once again the Austrian genius for arriving "one day late" was illustrated. General Mack advanced into Bavaria in early September prematurely, without Russian support, only to fall into a trap at Ulm between Marshal Ney's forces to the west, and Napoleon's, which had sprung up behind him at Donauwörth and Augsburg. On October 20, the day before Lord Nelson destroyed the combined French and Spanish fleets off Cape Trafalgar, Mack surrendered 29,000 men at Ulm. The rest of the Austrian army escaped northeastward, seeking to effect a junction with the Russians, who had obtained permission to advance through Prussia to Bohemia.

Meanwhile Napoleon's shady handling of the Hanover matter and the transit of Prussian Ansbach by French troops persuaded Frederick William III to enter the solemn military Convention of Potsdam with tsar Alexander I on November 3. At this juncture Talleyrand, the mist of ruin upon his crafty eyes, advised his master to arrange an immediate reversal of alliances before the armies of the Russian General Kutusov and Archduke Charles (hastening up from Italy) joined.

---

*In France the Empire had replaced the Republic in May, 1804.

But Napoleon went his way, rejecting all such counsel as well as Francis II's request for an armistice. On November 13 the Corsican entered Vienna as a conqueror.

When the impulsive tsar ordered Kutusov prematurely to attack the French near the Moravian village of Austerlitz on December 2, the "battle of the three emperors" was fought. When the wintry mists lifted from over the plateau of Pratzen and the icy swamps of the nearby Goldbach, Soult and Bernadotte proceeded to smash the Russian center on the plateau, while the French cavalry, under Lannes and Murat, overwhelmed Bagratian's forces. By the time the wan sun set over the field of Austerlitz the Third Coalition had been shattered and the fate of the Holy Roman Empire sealed.

After Austerlitz the German states jumped like fish into the French frying pan. Even Prussia seemed to do so when on December 15 she signed the pact of Schönbrunn, which allied her with France and obliged Prussia to cede Ansbach to Bavaria and Neuchâtel to the French. Frederick William received in return Hanover as his "shirt of Nessus."

The Treaty of Pressburg of December 26, 1805, between France and Austria facilitated the reorganization of Germany. Francis II was also obliged to cede Istria, except for Trieste, and the Dalmatian coast, including Ragusa, to France, and the Trentino and Vorarlberg to Bavaria in return for Salzburg. Württemberg and Bavaria were recognized as kingdoms, while Baden was elevated to a grand duchy. Napoleon summed it all up in one of his felicitous apothegms: "Fortune has changed her address!"

Frederick William III and his minister Haugwitz had no intention of allowing themselves to be intimidated by Napoleon's homilies, and they sabotaged the Treaty of Schönbrunn. When Napoleon got wind of this, he threatened war and imposed upon Prussia the even more objectionable Treaty of Paris (February 15, 1806). Prussia was required to close her ports to English imports, implement at once the annexation of Hanover, and guarantee the integrity of the Ottoman Empire against Russia.

Mistaking rivulets of intrigue for a stream of courage, Frederick William III had managed, without losing a battle, to bring his country to its knees. When in April England declared war on Prussia the Hohenzollern monarchy had seemingly reached the antipode of glory.

From this abject plight the king of Prussia was rescued by Napoleon's blunders. His creation of the Rheinbund, which shunted to a side track Prussian ambitions in north Germany and his treacherous promise to restore Hanover to England in return for Sicily infuriated Frederick William III. There now moved into the ascendancy in Berlin a patriotic party, including Prince Louis Ferdinand, General Blücher, Freiherr vom Stein, and the new foreign minister, Prince Karl August von Hardenberg (1750–1822). This camarilla succeeded in persuading the king to contract a secret entente (July 12, 1806) with Alexander I, which pledged Prussian neutrality in the event of a Franco-Russian war but bound the tsar to military support in case of a French attack upon Prussia.

Shortly afterward the Prussian army was again mobilized, and north German public opinion was fanned to white heat by news of French execution of the publisher Palm. On September 26 Frederick William III dispatched an ultimatum to Paris, demanding withdrawal of French troops from south German soil. At this moment when Prussia threw away the olive branch, she was still at war with England, unallied with Austria, opposed by Bavaria, Württemberg, and Baden, and, although supported by Saxony, Saxe-Weimar, and Brunswick, militarily hopelessly outclassed by France. Nevertheless, by her great act Prussia redeemed herself in the eyes of the world.

The war of the so-called Fourth Coalition (Russia, Prussia, Saxony, Brunswick, and Saxe-Weimar) was short and, for Napoleon, sweet. Its outcome turned upon two battles, those of Jena and Auerstädt, both fought on October 14 and both crushing defeats for Prussia. Prince Hohenlohe's forces were broken at Jena by Napoleon personally, while the aging duke of Brunswick's army was routed at Auerstädt by Davout's force. With lightning speed, meanwhile, the French occupied all key points in Prussia. Resistance to Napoleon collapsed everywhere. The Hohenzollern royal family fled to the tsar's side at Memel. At Berlin in November Bonaparte proceeded to organize a continental boycott of England and to liquidate Brunswick and Hesse-Cassel and elevate Prince Friedrich August of Saxony to a royal throne.

Following the indecisive and bloody battle of Preussisch-Eylau in East Prussia against the Russians (February 7–8, 1807), Napoleon tried unsuccessfully to detach Frederick William III from the tsar, but they only drew closer by signing the Alliance of Bartenstein (April 26), which pledged them to free Germany. Then, on June 14 the earth-shaker hurled his thunderbolt again, utterly destroying the Russian army on the East Prussian battlefield of Friedland. With a faithlessness born of despair, the tsar now abandoned Prussia.

The Treaty of Tilsit

In the historic encounter of July 7–9, 1807, between Alexander I and Napoleon, on a raft in the middle of the Niemen near Tilsit, Bonaparte's fury fell not upon the tsar but Frederick William III. All the beauty, tears, and entreaties of Queen Louise of Prussia could not dissuade the Corsican from clipping the wings and blunting the sharp bill of the Prussian eagle.

For Prussia, the Treaty of Tilsit represented not merely a military collapse but a moral one as well. Prussia was obliged to surrender all her territory west of the Elbe as well as that gained in the second and third partitions of Poland. Prussia was reduced to five provinces: Brandenburg, Pomerania, Silesia, West Prussia, and East Prussia. The very survival of the kingdom was only managed through the intercession of Alexander I. Prussia's west German territories were integrated with Hanover, while Brunswick and the northern Hessian lands were lumped together to form the new kingdom of Westphalia, whose ruler was to be Napoleon's brother Jerome. Prussia's Polish territories went to build the Grand Duchy of Warsaw, over which the king of Saxony was to reign. Danzig was declared a free port under French administration. Beyond these losses, Prussia was obliged to adhere without reservation to Napoleon's continental system against England, submit to French military occupation until an indefinite war indemnity had been discharged, pay the costs of the foreign occupation, and reduce her army to only 42,000 men. By this Treaty of Tilsit, Prussia was reduced to a negligible quantity among the European powers.

Chapter 24

REFORM AND LIBERATION

Napoleonic Reforms and the Rheinbund

By 1807–08 there had been introduced almost everywhere in Germany, in varying degree, administrative organs and rights that had been forged in the French crucible. The princes of south and west Germany for ulterior reasons adopted the Code Napoléon, introduced loophole systems of manhood conscription, reformed finances, reorganized the courts, established the liability of all to pay taxes, confiscated ecclesiastical properties, insured religious toleration, abolished feudal privileges, and subjugated church more firmly to state. The Rheinbund states copied the centralized French administrative system as far as possible. The imitative process was most pronounced in Hesse and the Rhenish provinces, especially in Baden and the kingdom of Westphalia. In the latter, King Jerome Bonaparte had, in the face of the handicap of heavy taxation (which ultimately produced "fiscal disaster") introduced numerous reforms. Württemberg and Bavaria, particularly the latter under King Maximilian I Joseph (1799–1825) and his minister Maximilian von Montgelas (1759–1838), also went over to constitutional government and were receptive to French influence. However, neither in Hesse, Württemberg, nor Bavaria was the peasantry freed from any more than personal servitude; juridical and domainal controls remained with the seigneurs.

We may castigate the princes of the Rheinbund, as did Herder for their unedifying imitation of French models, but it would be a mistake to conclude from this that the German rulers were only cowards intimidated by Napoleon's sword. More than anything else, it was cupidity and lust for power that motivated the princes. An immense booty was at hand in the lands of the ecclesiastical states and mediatized imperial knights. It was this that decisively influenced the policies of the sovereigns of Nassau, Hesse-Darmstadt, Baden, Württemberg, and Bavaria. Beyond this consideration, the Rheinbund rulers saw in the Napoleonic system a device for establishing in Germany highly centralized, powerful governments, unencumbered by diets or assemblies, something that had not been possible even in the Age of Despots.

The German princes showed no real interest in the liberal or egalitarian examples of the Revolution. Consequently, when the burdens and exactions of the French Grand Empire came to outweigh its largely illusory benefits, the German masses fell away from it like leaves from a blighted tree.

Purpose of the Prussian Reforms

By contrast with the French-model Rhenish and south German reforms, those inaugurated in Prussia after 1807 were in general consonance with national custom and the unwritten constitution. Born of the patriotic union of people and state, the Prussian reforms were oriented not to despotic centralization but the liberation of Germany. The reforms were introduced mainly from above, illustrating Kant's judgment that the German people were endemically inclined to obedience.

Actually Jena, Auerstädt, and Tilsit had not ruined Prussia. Therefore, no wholesale repudiation of the aristocracy had occurred. It is true that immediate hopes had been dashed, heavy losses sustained, and the public deeply vexed. Yet, almost everyone instinctively felt that time and numbers were on the side of Napoleon's foes. The outbreak of civil war in Spain supported this. The tyrant might win every battle save the last, but in the final encounter the continent would be rid of his incubus. This prospect of ultimate success preserved for the Prussian nobility a big residuum of power, which would not have been so if Prussia's defeat had been final.

Moderation was the string running through the necklace of Prussian reforms. They were aimed not at the destruction of the patrimonial and administrative authority of the aristocracy but at the liberalization of existing institutions. The purpose was not to set in train a social revolution but to make of the nobility and all classes more effective weapons against Bonaparte. Shortly after having accepted the chief post in the Prussian government in August, 1807, Baron Heinrich Karl vom und zum Stein (1757–1831), who was to be the motive power of the renovation, expressed this overriding aim: "The main idea is to arouse a moral, religious and patriotic spirit in the nation, to instill into the people once more courage, confidence, and a readiness to make any sacrifice to achieve independence from foreign domination and for the sake of national honor, and to begin the dangerous, bloody struggle when the first opportunity comes along."[*]

Stein was first and foremost a German patriot and only secondly a reformer. Stein's supreme objective was the liberation of Germany. Neither he nor any of his reformist colleagues had any intention of opening the sluice gates to the French revolutionary spirit. Stein would not even have countenanced the wholesale transfer of English liberal institutions to Prussia. He was prepared to compromise with the future only where the past had wretchedly failed.

His immediate purpose was to identify all classes of Prussian society with the great national task which the romanticists had already defined. All of Stein's proposed reforms—the emancipation of the peasants, the reorganization of the army, the elaboration of municipal self-government, the ministerial and constitutional innovations—were designed to demolish the image of the Prussian state as the private precinct of the aristocracy. They envisioned the creation of a corporative polity in which all citizens would be stockholders.

The Successful Failure

Queen Louise of Prussia spoke of Stein as "a great heart" and "an all-embrac-

---

[*]*H. K. vom Stein, Briefwechsel, Denkschriften und Aufzeichnungen,* ed. by Erich Botzenhart (Berlin, 1931–37), VI, 167.

ing spirit and intellect.'' The truth is, however, that Stein was too stormy and sardonic, too devoid of a saving sense of humor, to conciliate the opposition. He pressed his reforms with more zeal than prudence, and in this he recalls Martin Luther and Joseph II. He antagonized so many powerful people that his great reform program was doomed to remain a fragment. All of his designs were discarded or modified by either Frederick Wiliam III or by Stein's more cautious and adroit successors in office. Of all Stein's vaulting plans only that which touched municipal administration was substantially implemented. Thus it was that Stein, like Moses, came within sight of the promised land but never entered it. The reforming movement achieved its grand goal of liberation by 1814. It did not, however, succeed in the lesser aim of permanently liberalizing Prussia or, by example, any other German state.

It is not even clear that Stein, more than others, must be credited with the successful conclusion of the War of Liberation. He did not, in any case, achieve the unification of Germany, for which he alone among contemporaries campaigned. However, despite his immediate failure, Stein has always been one of the shining idols of German youths. He incorporated the ideal of fortitude combined with rectitude. His unselfishness was exceeded only by his masculine sense of civic duty. For all of his personality defects and conceptual limitations, Stein was a man for all seasons and all parties. The broad masses have always held him in esteem, because the politicization and democratization of the German people dates from him. Likewise all those convinced that class stratification is in the natural order of things have found kind words for Stein. He never ceased to regard the aristocracy as the great shield of liberty against the sort of despotism and militarism that had leveled France. Proponents of unity and centralization have also found him to their liking, because he, alone in his day, was prepared to sacrifice particularist interests for the sake of political unity.

Born of a respected but undistinguished family of imperial knights of Nassau, Stein was a thoroughgoing child of the Old Regime. He received a nobleman's education, attended the University of Göttingen, married a countess, and became a sturdy fixture in the supreme Prussian Central Directory. At the university he had, to the detriment of his health, immersed himself in the heavy waters of the history of German public law. This gave him a lifelong interest in medieval institutions, which later prompted him to aid in founding the *Monumenta Germaniae Historica*, a vast collection of medieval sources.

After twenty-four years in the service of Prussia, ''a land where hearts are colder than the climate,'' Stein on October 27, 1804, was made minister of finance in the Central Directory. There he identified himself with the emancipation of the crown peasants from servile obligations and inaugurated a series of minor fiscal and commercial reforms. When in the summer of 1807 Karl August von Hardenberg (1750–1822) incurred the enmity of Napoleon and was on that account dismissed, Stein, who had but lately resigned because of minor differences with his sovereign, was recalled to head the ministry. For fourteen months (October, 1807–November, 1808) Stein was the *deus ex machina* of the Prussian reforms.

Administrative and Ministerial Reform

Stein's ideas on governmental reform were set forth in the Nassau Memorandum of April–June, 1807, the substance of which was incorporated in the edict of November 28, 1808. Although Stein's dismissal made it impossible fully to implement his proposals, it is instructive to note that they advocated setting limits to absolutism. At the summit of his edifice was to be a cabinet *(Staatsrat)* of five ministers appointed by the king, who were to be responsible for all grand policy decisions. Each cabinet minister was to head a separate department of the Central General Directory. The president of the *Staatsrat* was not to be responsible to a parliament but, like his colleagues, was to hold office only as long as he enjoyed the monarch's confidence. On the other hand, the *Staatsrat* was to be endowed with broad autonomy and expected to govern Prussia. Stein hoped his corporative policy-making body would be a first step toward constitutional government. This would be more popular than the unofficial camarilla *(Kabinettsregierung)*, of whimsical composition and abject servility, which had been completely dominated by the crown since Frederick II.

The Central General Directory, that awkwardly articulated brontosaur, was also reorganized. Stein reconstituted it along functional rather than the olden geographic lines and reduced its departments to five—foreign affairs, war, interior, finance, and justice. Each departmental head was also assigned a seat in the *Staatsrat*. Delimitation of departmental responsibilities was long preserved. Indeed, the allocation of functions to responsible ministers survived the General Directory itself, which after 1810 was abolished by the Hardenberg ministry.

Under the ministry of Baron von Altenstein and Count von Dohna, which succeeded that of Stein, absolutist opposition to the policy-making cabinet and a chief minister was so strong that these schemes had to be dropped. When the Altenstein-Dohna ministry was in turn forced to resign in 1810, Hardenberg again moved into the ascendancy. He activated a new supreme organ of government, the ministry of state *(Staatsministerium)*. It bore only superficial resemblance to Stein's conception. The *Staatsministerium* was little more than a bureaucratic collegium of experts, wholly consultative and possessing no policy-making prerogatives. On the other hand, Hardenberg, who was more modern and less medieval than Stein, was able to persuade the king to create the post of chancellor. This office, tailored for Hardenberg, was to be one to which all five ministers of the council were to be subordinate. However, Hardenberg's radicalism, as much as his interpretation of the chancellor's powers, were to elicit stiff opposition from the nobility.

Tax Reform

There was little need for a drastic overhauling of the fiscal administration in Prussia. The management of public finances had been characterized by both a greater frugality and probity than the finances of France under her last three kings. Nevertheless, French demands in the summer of 1808 for an increase in the war indemnity from 73 million to 154 million francs, plus costs of supporting an occupation army of 150,000 men, necessitated new taxes. On October 27, 1810, Hardenberg promulgated an edict which for the first time subjected the nobility to a real property tax. Reminiscent of the Territorial Subsidy proposed in 1786 by the French minister Calonne, this measure evoked analogous resistance from the landholding class, which was led by the uncompromising Friedrich Ludwig von der Marwitz (1777–1837) of Brandenburg. The opposition was convinced the ministry was trying to ruin the Prussian nobility. In the end Marwitz prevailed, and a supplemental edict of September, 1811, exempted aristocrats from payment of the land tax. The contest revealed the weakness of the bourgeoisie and underlined the fact that the seignorial character of the Prussian state had not fundamentally changed.

Lower-Echelon Reforms

Of all of Stein's measures aimed at renovating Prussia, the most enduring was the Prussian Municipal Ordinance *(Städteordnung)* of November, 1808. It aimed at restoring self-government to the cities. Provision was made for the free election of municipal councils and mayors by town-dwellers and for the transfer to the councils of supervision of all communal and church property, tax collections, and eleemosynary services. The councils were also empowered to approve municipal budgets. The awakening of a sense of citizenship and communal responsibility by drawing the middle class into the law-making process was a popular ideal worthy of a statesman. In time, the Prussian Municipal Ordinance, which inspired imitation all over Germany, came to be regarded as the Magna Carta of urban liberties.

At the county level Stein in 1808 abolished the War and Domainal Chambers and substituted "governments" of even broader competence but without judicial and eleemosynary responsibilities. On the provincial level he tried to democratize the collegial administrative boards *(Kammercollegien)*. He also envisioned elective county diets and hoped to breathe life again into the virtually defunct provincial diets. Finally, Stein dreamed of establishing a national legislature that should transform Prussia into a limited monarchy.

In pressing for grass-roots reforms, Stein aimed at two things: (1) the liberalization of local government by means of the rehabilitation of bourgeois political power and the regeneration of the spirit of aristocratic responsibility, and (2) the establishment of self-governing counterweights to autocratic centralism. Unlike Napoleon's program, Stein's was directed to the preservation of town and country autonomy against encroachments by the leviathan. In harmony with this conception, the bourgeoisie and the aristocracy were to be the two shields of liberty.

When Hardenberg returned to office in 1810, it appeared he would introduce measures that would complement Stein's lower-echelon reform efforts. However, when Hardenberg abolished the superannuated system of *Landräte*, the noble rural appointees of the crown, he replaced them (law of July 30, 1813) with appointive district directors *(Kreisdirektoren)* with powers greater than those of the old county counselors. Hardenberg undoubtedly aimed at further extension of central governmental controls over the whole state. As in the case of tax reform, however, organized aristocratic opposition succeeded in sabotaging the implementation of this law.

Emancipation of the Serfs

Apart from political considerations, there were real humanitarian motives behind Stein's Emancipation Edict of October 6, 1807. The condition of the peasantry in eastern Prussia and in Mecklenburg had become scandalous. Many hereditary tenants in the past fifty years had been deprived of their lands by noblemen, whose estates had tended to grow ever larger. By contrast with the peasants in the western provinces, where there was far more personal mobility and bondsmen discharged their obligations in cash payments, the peasants in the east and north (like Russian serfs) usually had to perform compulsory labor *(Robot)*. Furthermore, the number of days in the week on which they were required to work for their lords tended to increase to a point where it compromised the standard of living of the peasantry.

The Edict of 1807 did not, perhaps, go as far in the direction of cleaning the feudal rubbish from the Augean stables as radicals, such as Schrötter and Schön, had wanted. It did not accommodate the demands of the disciples of Adam Smith and the bourgeois liberals for the creation of a completely free and unprotected reservoir of labor. Nor did it remove all impediments to the sale and alienation of peasant land. Stein was too much the traditionalist to wish, for the sake of promoting agrarian capitalism, to deprive a liberated peasantry of all protection. He firmly believed that the weak and poor must be protected against the strong and that this custodial task must still devolve upon the masters.

The edict of 1807 abolished serfdom *(Leibeigenschaft)* throughout the kingdom. Theoretically, but not actually, the lords' patrimonial rights were ended, and all former bondsmen became full-fledged citizens. All except the poorest peasants were now empowered to acquire land in fee simple with unrestricted rights of disposition. Seigneurs were required to make available to peasants, against cash redemption, between a third and a half of the acreage they had tilled as serfs. Also all surviving feudal services and renders were abolished on condition of arranged indemnification to the lords.

The participation of the peasantry in the political life of Prussia, a thing that had not been possible since 1525, was now invited. However, the scheme for redeeming servile land through purchase did not benefit tenants as much as might be supposed. The plots available after partition were usually too small to support a family. Moreover, no banks were established to extend credits to peasants.

Under the ministries of Altenstein and Dohna and of Hardenberg the landed nobility improved its position at the expense of the freedmen. The former, led by Marwitz, persuaded the government to abandon its traditional policy of protecting peasant holdings *(Bauernschutz)*. It was decreed that peasants might now redeem their obligations to former masters by alienating a further third to one-half of the land the peasants held. This was to substitute for monetary indemnification. However, the Prussian nobles, like those of Hesse, Württemberg, and Bavaria, were confirmed in the continued exercise of police and judicial supervision over the peasantry.

As a result of these decrees, three far-reaching developments overtook Prussian agriculture: (1) a large class of nonhereditary, tenant farms and a landless agricultural proletariat came into being; (2) the more than 2,200,000 acres of land lost by the peasantry, through division, alienation, and sale, largely gravitated into the hands of the gentry and bourgeoisie; and (3) the termination of *Bauernschutz* enabled the aristocracy to expropriate the peasantry and consolidate the lands acquired from it into great estates, principally east of the Elbe and aided by a big reservoir of agricultural wage labor, to effect the transition from feudal manor to capitalist *latifundium*.

Military Reform

Many Prussian officers preferred to put the blame for the debacles of Jena and Auerstädt upon incompetent field commanders or simply ascribe the defeats to French military superiority. However, a minority of officers felt that the lesson pointed to the need for reform. On the theory that the reverses amounted to an indictment of the narrow, class character of the army inherited from Frederick the Great, a cohort of able generals, including Gerhard von Scharnhorst (1755–1813), A. Neithardt von Gneisenau (1760–1831), Karl von Grolman (1777–1843), and Hermann von Boyen (1771–1841), were resolved to overhaul the military.

The emancipation of the serfs did more than any other measure to undermine the exclusive, aristocratic character of the old Prussian officers corps and open it to commoners of ability. An order of August 6, 1808, reminiscent of the Russian ukases of 1721 and 1722, made knowledge, achievement, and experience the sole bases for military promotion in peacetime, and added conspicuous bravery and initiative as further criteria in wartime. Popular appeal of military service was heightened when on August 3, 1808, new Articles of War were adopted, abolishing corporal punishment and conferring upon enlisted men new protection against inhumane treatment.

During the years 1807–13 the military reformers succeeded in injecting new vigor into the old military establishment, but they were unable to transform it completely. Neither Altenstein, Dohna, nor Hardenberg showed much enthusiasm for either a conscript trained army or a militia. Logistics and quartermaster services were improved, however, and armaments were modernized, ammunition reserves increased, and new arsenals established. Officer training schools were founded in Berlin, Breslau, and Königsberg, and a general staff school in Berlin. Finally, a ministry of war, designed to be one of the five ministries represented on the State Council, was established. On the other hand, a minister of war was not actually appointed until 1814. Since it was understood that his work would be subject to scrutiny by the king, unity of political and military policy was envisioned in Prussia at the outset.

The *Krümpersystem*, a method which had been instituted after 1808 for circumventing the limitations imposed on the size of the Prussian army, had yielded only a small number of additional recruits—half-baked trainees *(Krümper*, from *krumm*, meaning "crooked" or "misshapen") from each canton. Collectively the *Krümper* did not amount to more than 70,000 auxiliary forces by 1813. No levy in mass, eliminating all exemptions from military service and all substitutes, was authorized until February, 1813, hardly in time to impart consequential training against the imminent battle for Germany. Thus the Battle of Leipzig, the decisive engagement in the War of Liberation, had largely to be fought with the old regular army, which was selectively recruited in each canton, supplemented by poorly trained *Krümper* and by the forces of the National Guard *(Landwehr)* that was instituted in early 1813. This heterogeneous force, the core of which was narrowly professional—serving more the government than the people—numbered somewhat more than 275,000 men. It was but a poor substitute for an intensively trained military establishment based on universal service.

After Bonaparte had been beaten at Leipzig and Boyen had been appointed minister of war (1814–19), a victorious Prussian nobility at last allowed universal conscription to be implemented. The officers corps began to listen to the youthful theorist, Karl von Clausewitz (1780–1831), the later author of the three-volume *On War* (1833), who cogently argued that the demonism of the masses should be mobilized for defense.

Humboldt and Education

The hopes that Stein, Boyen, and Scharnhorst pinned on a democratized army could not be realized unless the people were educated to become citizens. This required a reform of the curriculum of the Prussian secondary schools. Here the initiative proceeded not from Stein but from Wilhelm von Humbolt (1767–1835), the undersecretary for culture and education (1808–10) in the ministry of the interior. Imbued with the cosmopolitan spirit of Weimar, where he had cultivated the friendship of Schiller and Goethe, Humboldt unified the curricular programs of the Prussian secondary schools and infused them with the ideal of academic excellence. Although devoting relatively little attention to primary schools or trade and technical schools *(Realschulen)*, he radically modernized the structure and curriculum of the liberal arts preparatory schools *(Gymnasien)*, transforming the narrow program of classical studies into one including also history, geography, music, mathematics, and modern languages.

Humboldt's most illustrious achievement was in higher education. He set about founding a university in Berlin (1810), which is now called, after its founder, the Humboldt University. To its faculty were summoned a number of Germany's leading scholars: the historian Barthold Niebuhr, philologist Friedrich Wolf, theologist Friedrich Schleiermacher, philosopher Fichte, economist Johann Hoffmann, physician Christian Hufeland, and jurists Friedrich Karl von Savigny and Karl F. Eichhorn, all national patriots and adherents of reform. Humboldt's achievements are the more impressive when it is considered that by 1810 many of Stein's reforms had been sapped or smothered and that the efforts of the too theoretically oriented Hardenberg were frequently destined to run into the sand.

The Austrian Phoenix: 1809

Decidedly, Prussia had no monopoly on the idea of liberation. Austria prefaced her participation in the War of the Fifth Coalition, in which England was to be her main ally, by summoning up all the popular passions. Unfortunately, the Habsburg effort was not so effective as it might have been had it been buttressed by comprehensive reforms or had Prussia lent her military support to Austria. Reforms preceding the battles of 1809 were almost wholly military in nature and cannot be compared in scope with the Prussian. The primary explanation of the modest nature of Austrian reforms lies in the circumstance that the Habsburg crown lands had not been militarily occupied or territorially sharply reduced and Austria was not under excruciating French pressure. Such reforms as were endorsed by the reactionary Francis I were piloted through by Count Johann Philipp von Stadion (1763–1824) of Mainz, the chancellor and foreign minister (1805–09). They embraced establishment of a ministry of war, improvement in officers' training in tactics and weaponry, and the institution of conscription and organization of a territorial reserve *(Landwehr)*.

Vienna was moved to declare war on France on February 8, 1809, out of consideration of French reverses in Spain, growing ferment in Germany, the promise of English subsidies, and the pressure of the Austrian war hawks supported by the bellicose Empress Marie Louise d'Este. Archduke Charles frittered away his one chance of victory when he inexplicably procrastinated taking the offensive. When fighting finally commenced, his forces were mauled by the armies of France and the Rheinbund on the fields of Tengen, Abensberg, Landshut, Eckmühl, and Ebersberg in April and early May. On May 13 Napoleon entered Vienna, and Charles had to withdraw the bulk of his army to the left bank of the Danube. The French (under Napoleon, Masséna, and Lannes) pursued him and engaged his forces at Essling and Aspern on May 20–21. In the stiff fighting Essling changed hands thirteen times, and the French were barely able to extricate themselves from a trap by retreating to the isle of Lobau.

From this point, Austria's prospects declined. Archduke Joseph was beaten on the Raab, while various uprisings upon which Vienna had been counting—Major Ferdinand von Schill's to liberate Magdeburg and Stralsund and Andreas Hofer's in the Tirol against Bavaria—were suppressed by French, Bavarian, Saxon, and Württemberg troops, and Hofer was executed.

On July 5, 1809, Napoleon sallied forth from Lobau in the Danube. With 50,000 men he attacked the foe on the left bank near the village of Wagram, where he wrested a victory of sorts over Charles. Despairing of foreign assistance by then, Austria concluded the armistice of Znaim (July 11, 1809) by which she agreed to pay a stiff indemnity and submit to partial occupation. In October the luckless Stadion was replaced at the chancellery by Count Klemens von Metternich (1773–1859), a much better diplomat who was destined for great things.

The Treaty of Schönbrunn of October 14, 1809, reduced Austria, despite its 20-million population, to a secondary power. She lost access to the Adriatic and had to cede to the French satellite of Illyria the provinces of Carinthia, Trieste, Fiume, and Istria, and to Russia part of eastern Galicia. Western Galicia was transferred to the French-dominated Grand Duchy of Warsaw. Bavaria obtained Salzburg, Berchtesgaden, the Inn and Hausruck areas, and northern South Tirol, while the kingdom of Italy acquired the rest of it.

Shortly afterward, Metternich tried to detach Russia from France, whose relations, he knew, were deteriorating. Also, when the tsar procrastinated in the matter of Napoleon's suit for the hand of Anne Romanov, Metternich persuaded Francis I on April 1, 1810, to grant his own eighteen-year-old daughter, Marie Louise, in wedlock to the Corsican. The chancellor's reasoning was that with this marriage Austria would be able to buy time in which to initiate whatever reforms would guarantee success in the next war against Bonaparte.

Hardenberg's Diplomacy

Meanwhile, Hardenberg was conducting Prussian diplomacy as if the hour of liberation were years away. He had practically been forced to crawl, while smiling, on all fours to overcome Napoleon's opposition to his reappointment (June 4, 1810). Privately the cautious Hardenberg was certain the tide had turned. Russia, he knew, had cut her French moorings. Millions of European Catholics were outraged by Napoleon's crass treatment of the pope and the Papal States. The English were making headway in the Iberian peninsula. Conspiracy was raising its head even in France, while in Germany and Italy the conqueror's system of fiscal exactions and military impressment had alienated the people, who had gradually come to realize that with Napoleon they were marching into a bottomless bog.

To far greater degree than the impulsive Stein, Hardenberg had always had a healthy respect for the rationalist achievements of revolutionary France. He favored copying the Code Napoléon and, where feasible, the centralizing administrative and tax reforms associated with the Grand Empire.

In spite of mounting conservative opposition to his reforms, Hardenberg persevered. He encouraged the liberalizing political efforts of the first elected All-Prussian Consultative Assembly of *Stände*, which met in Berlin from April, 1812, to July, 1815, and he supported the *Krümper* system, Humboldt's attempt to unify the secondary school system, establishment of the University of Berlin, equalization of tax burdens, civil equality for the Jews (decree of March 11, 1812), and the military innovations of Gneisenau and Scharnhorst (until Napoleon forced their dismissal) and later of Boyen and Grolman. Conversely, Hardenberg winked at the activities and publications of thinly disguised patriotic organizations, such as the Tugendbund (League of Virtue) and the Christlich-deutsche Tischgesellschaft (Christian-German Round Table).

When Scharnhorst and Gneisenau, both out of favor, advocated in 1811 that Prussia should instigate a Spanish-style popular rebellion, Hardenberg refused to be compromised. He thought more was to be gained for the time being by an alliance with Napoleon. Only when the French, who had opted for Austria, curtly rejected his offer did Hardenberg advise the king to risk approaching Tsar Alexander I. However, despite unmistakable signs of a Franco-Russian estrangement, Frederick William III moved but sluggishly in that direction, and in the meantime Prussia had to promise in February, 1812, to aid Napoleon with 40,000 men— 20,000 for his impending invasion of Russia and another 20,000 to do garrison duty as directed. Prussia also pledged to provide supplies and free transit to the Grand Army passing through her territories, because for Frederick William the French army of occupation was the towering feature of his landscape. Hardenberg, however, was subjected to a hail of recrimination, and many administrators resigned in disgust. The war hawks anathematized him for having again thrust Prussia under Napoleon's reaper.

Not until the eve of the Battle of Berezina in the late fall of 1812, after the Grand Army had been all but completely destroyed, was Hardenberg given the chance to redeem himself. He then courted Russia. Happily for him, Alexander I had decided, in keeping with the advice of his Rhenish Chancellor Nesselrode and of Freiherr vom Stein (who had taken service with the tsar), to reject Napoleon's peace overtures and instead hammer his army back to France.

While Hardenberg was preparing for a Russo-Prussian convention, a Prussian general, Hans David von Yorck (1759–1830), lit the fuse of the War of Liberation *(Befreiungskrieg)*. Yorck, the patriotic commander of the Prussian auxiliary forces of French Marshal MacDonald's Tenth Army, concluded on his own responsibility the Convention of Tauroggen (December 30, 1812) with the Russians. By it he pledged the neutrality of his army. Tauroggen, which was later approved by the timid Frederick William, threw open the gates of Prussia to the Russian army and provoked the rupture of Franco-Prussian relations. Prince Karl Philipp von Schwarzenberg (1771–1820), who had commanded the Austrian contingent of Bonaparte's Grand Army, concluded on January 30, 1813, on orders from Metternich a similar armistice at Zeycs with Russia.

Moved by a mighty ground swell of patriotism, the Prussian government on February 9 decreed universal conscription, although it did not energetically implement the decree. Three days later the regular army was mobilized. On March 28 the Russians and Prussians concluded formal articles of alliance at Kalisch. With this convention, the cornerstone of the last and greatest coalition against Napoleon was laid. Prussia and Russia each pledged 80,000 troops to fight for the liberation of Europe. On March 15 Prussia declared war on France, and on the seventeenth the king sought to join hands with his people by issuing a stirring appeal:

> You know what you have suffered during the past seven years. You know what your sad fate will be if we do not win victory in the struggle which is now beginning . . . Think of your ancestors . . . The great sacrifices that all will be called upon to make do not compare with the sacred blessings for the attainment of which we must now fight if we do not want to cease being Prussians and Germans!*

Metternich Squares the Circle

Shortly after the signing of the Treaty of Kalisch, other states—Denmark, Sweden, and Mecklenburg-Schwerin—rallied to the grand alliance. Many a Prussian town and village was moved by tremors of patriotism; yet, strangely enough the rest of Germany remained immobile. By way of compensation, Austria advanced closer to the coalition when on April 11 Metternich slyly proffered his services as an armed mediator prepared to support lenient Allied terms to France. However, Napoleon's outnumbered forces, sustained by his superior generalship, beat the Allies on the bloody field of Lützen on May 2. The Allied armies were pressed back to the right bank of the Oder; Napoleon triumphantly entered Dresden on May 8 and was greeted by his ally, the king of Saxony; further French victories at Bautzen and Wurschen (May 20–22) brought the occupation of all Saxony and half of Silesia. With these victories behind him, Napoleon, commanding 440,000 troops in Germany, snapped his fingers at Metternich, who presumably had opened an escape route for him.

Metternich, who has been the subject of a very great amount of research by historians from Heinrich Ritter von Srbik to Alan Palmer, is thought by many scholars (among them Helmuth Rössler, Éduard Driault, Louis Madelin, Henry Kissinger, Victor Bibl, and Edward Gulick) to have deceived Napoleon from beginning to end while ostensibly temporizing with him to win the Allies for Austrian war aims and obstruct the dream of German unity. However this may be, Metternich's next move, a consummately sly one, was to propose a twenty-four-day armistice, which must strengthen the Allies more than the French. Napoleon acceded on June 4, though for what purpose is not very clear, since delay further undermined his prospects for a decisive victory. Meanwhile, England joined the coalition on the fifteenth, and on the twenty-seventh Austria agreed secretly to do so too. When Bonaparte refused to evacuate all conquered lands, Austria declared war on August 11.

The Grand Alliance of Teplitz of September 9 bound Austria, Prussia, and Russia to secure the unconditional independence of the German states. In early October England and even Bavaria underwrote these obligations, and the iron ring closed around the Corsican.

---

*Quoted in Louis Villat, *La Révolution et l'Empire* (Paris, 1947), II, 202–3.

From Leipzig to Paris

Faced with a total of 300,000 troops in the converging armies of the Austrian Schwarzenberg, the Prussian General Gebhard von Blücher (1742–1819), the Russian General Kutusov, and King Bernadotte of Sweden, Napoleon, with only 160,000 men, was unable to prevent them from joining. Rather than wait any longer, the Corsican gambled on the great victory that could alone forestall desertion by his remaining German allies. For three days (October 16–19, 1813), in a "Battle of Nations," nearly half a million men were pitted in combat near Leipzig. In the end, the Allies achieved a tremendous strategic victory, and only Napoleon's rare skill prevented the battle from turning into a Cannae.

Following Leipzig, Napoleon's last German client states—Saxony, Württemberg, Brunswick, Oldenburg, Hesse-Darmstadt, Weimar, Nassau, and Frankfurt—went over to the coalition. Leipzig lit all the tinder that lay scattered about Germany. The war became of a sudden, as Erich Marcks once said, "a national crusade."

Bonaparte's minor tactical successes along the Rhine in the autumn of 1813 could not hide the fact that the old prestidigitator had lost his wand. Metternich, who had no wish to reduce France to the rank of a second-rate power, again reached out a hand to save Napoleon, for the Austrian was possessed of a farsightedness and flexibility that was denied Napoleon. Without consulting Prussia, the chancellor now offered peace on the basis of the "natural frontiers," i.e., the Alps, Pyrenees, and the Rhine, including perhaps Belgium. Castlereagh, the British foreign secretary, thought November was no time for such midsummer madness and opposed leaving either the Rhineland or Belgium in French hands. On March 9, 1814, the Treaty of Chaumont set the seal to a quadruple alliance among England, Prussia, Austria, and Russia, which was to be the cornerstone of the postwar Concert of Europe. As respects central Europe, the convention pledged the restoration of Prussia, Austria, and Switzerland and the establishment of a confederation of sovereign German states. Napoleon's capitulation shortly followed.

The first Treaty of Paris (May 30), which concluded twenty-two years of war, was more generous to France than the Teutonic patriots could have wished: France retained Alsace and the Saar (with Saarlouis, Saarbrücken, the mines, and Landau). But the main thing was that Germany, including the Rhineland, was free once more.

Chapter 25

THE REACTION, 1815–1833

The Meaning of Victory

On March 31, 1814, the tsar and the king of Prussia entered Paris in triumph. A terribly war-weary Europe had come to the end of an epoch. The shibboleths of liberty, equality, and fraternity had evoked a crusade such as had not been seen since the Middle Ages. For twenty-two years French armies had carried subversive ideas all over the continent. Into many lands the French system of highly centralized government, civic and legal equality, sequestration of church lands, expropriation of the nobility, plebiscitary democracy, conscription, and emancipation of the serfs had been introduced. In the end, however, that system, narrowly authoritarian, inspired by might rather than law or equity, and rendered abominable by incessant requisitions, ended by making Napoleon detested everywhere. After 1808 Europeans had come to view him as an incubus, and by 1814 there was hardly anyone who did not rejoice at the destruction of the Grand Empire.

The states of Europe had made war on Bonaparte for many reasons, but for none so much as that his new order had meant permanent upheaval. If he had been permitted to remain on the French throne, there could not logically have been a concerted effort to restore the legitimate monarchs and governments of the pre-revolutionary era.

During the War of Liberation many German princes had popularized the idea of legitimate monarchy. This they had done by plucking on the strings of national patriotism and promising their subjects charters or constitutions after the tyrant should be overthrown. However, for many Germans this was totally unnecessary. Revulsion against the ensnaring ideas of enlightenment and revolution was universal. An exhausted nation that looked back nostalgically to the comparative tranquillity of the eighteenth century was willing to tolerate monarchical restoration for the sake of peace. Believing that absence of war was in fact the summum bonum of civic society, the German people faced the future no longer in the spirit of zeal and reform but in that of a nameless weariness.

The Congress of Vienna

The Congress of Vienna (September, 1814–June, 1815) was a wonderfully lavish spectacle of revelry and divertissement that almost bankrupted the Austrian finance ministry. In a situation where many capital decisions were reached at Metternich's mansion, in private conversations in the foyers of ballrooms, or over coffee cups in Castlereagh's apartment, the hopes of the idealists were bound to be bitterly disappointed.

The choice of Vienna as the seat of the congress was felicitous. Not only was the city centrally located in Europe, but it was clear that Austria, which had been beaten to her knees four times in the late wars, was not the most bitter antagonist of France or even of Napoleon. Austria's level-headed attitude was guided by the wise resolve to leave France strong enough to insure equilibrium among the major powers.

Napoleon once said that "Metternich mistook intrigue for diplomacy." But if the measure of a policy is its success, that of the Austrian was astute. It gave Vienna an artificial hegemony over European affairs and was a principal factor in preserving the peace of the continent for a century. A contrary policy favoring nationalism and liberalism would have raised serious doubts about Metternich's loyalty and promoted the early dissolution of the Danubian empire.

Mainly because of Metternich, Austria emerged from the congress the dominant power in central Europe from the Baltic to Sicily. True, the Habsburgs had to surrender Belgium to the Dutch Netherlands and, contrary to Metternich's wishes, relinquish enclaves in the Breisgau, Swabia, and near Lake Constance. On the other hand, Austria now stood forth as a heterogeneous but compact block stretching uninterruptedly from Galicia to Tuscany and from Switzerland to the Carpathians. This conferred on Austria the advantage of being able to operate on interior lines in wartime, while politically it husbanded her energies, consolidated her economy, and accelerated the shift of Habsburg interests eastward and southward.

After years of playing the fox, Austria got the lion's share at the peace conference. She emerged with Polish Galicia, the Vorarlberg, upper Austria, Salzburg, the Tirol, Carinthia, Carniola, Istria, Trieste, Friuli, the Dalmatian coast, Lombardy, Venetia, and the fortresses of the quadrilateral—Mantua, Legnano, Peschiera, and Verona. In addition, Parma, Guastalla, and Piacenza were given to Marie Louise, the daughter of Emperor Francis, while Tuscany and Modena were transferred to Habsburg archdukes, who were required to sign alliances with Vienna. These dispositions raised a barricade against any possible Russian penetration of the west. Furthermore, the Adriatic was reduced to a mere Habsburg lake, and Italy, where the policies of the Papal States and the kingdom of the Two Sicilies were made to harmonize with those of the Hofburg, sank back into the status of a Habsburg "protectorate." By making Austria the balance wheel of Europe, the diplomats had artfully contrived to hold both France and Russia in check.

The decisions taken with respect to Germany must be viewed in the light of the intention of the peacemakers to restore a balance of power among the major states and to prevent the outbreak of another general war. Prussia was given much, but not so much that she could afford to repudiate the Reichenbach Convention (1790) and challenge Austria for the mastery of Germany. Prussia had wanted to devour all of Saxony, but that would have menaced Thuringia and Bavaria. In its avarice, however, Berlin was supported by St. Petersburg, which in turn received Prussian backing for the Romanov dynasty's maximum claims in defunct Poland. This working agreement evoked extreme tension in the Quadruple Alliance and led briefly in January, 1815, to the formation of a triple alliance of Austria, England, and France against Russia and Prussia. European war over the Saxon and Polish booty was averted only when Russia agreed to the retrocession of Galicia to Austria and the establishment of the tiny republic of Crackow, and when Prussia relinquished all the land she had acquired in the Third Partition of Poland to Russia and abandoned claims to the whole of Saxony.

By way of compensation for these renunciations and the cession of East Friesland and the port of Emden to Hanover, Prussia was permitted to retain Posen (Poznania) and West Prussia, together with Danzig and Thorn, and was awarded the northern half of Saxony with two-fifths of its population, western Pomerania *(Vorpommern)*, northern Thuringia, together with Erfurt, Upper and Lower Lusatia, most of the defunct kingdom of Westphalia, and the entire left bank of the Rhine (Rhineland) from north of Saarbrücken to Cleves and beyond the Wesel River. These dispositions proved to be very beneficial to Prussia, for she had been transformed into a preponderantly German rather than a hyphenated German-Polish state. This had the effect of reorienting Berlin's grand policy toward Germany and scotching impractical dreams of a new *Drang nach Osten*. All hopes of the congress to the contrary, Prussian gains foreshadowed an eventual resumption of the historic duel with Austria for dominion over Germany.

Professions of devotion to the principle of legitimacy were belied in the case of Germany. The olden ecclesiastical and the lesser secular principalities were not restored. However, Sweden was stripped of her German territories, Wismar going to the Grand Duchy of Mecklenburg, and Western Pomerania to Prussia. The Grand Duchy of Baden was enlarged with the right bank of the Rhenish Palatinate. Bavaria, which was strengthened along the upper Danube and Main rivers, received not only the left bank Rhenish Palatinate but the whole Grand Duchy of Würzburg.

As for the rest of Germany, Hesse and Württemberg retained approximately the frontiers they had acquired by 1806, and Hanover was enlarged by the addition of East Frisia and Paderborn. Ominously for the future, a corridor of Hanoverian and Hessian lands was made to separate Westphalia and the Rhineland from Brandenburg. The only other regional dispositions of importance taken were those that recognized five kingdoms in Germany—Prussia, Bavaria, Württemberg, Saxony, and Hanover—and established three new grand duchies—Saxe-Weimar, Mecklenburg, and Oldenburg.

The All-German Problem

Patriotic hopes that Germany might be unified were bitterly disappointed. Baron von Stein, who attended the congress as the tsar's referent for German affairs, formulated fuzzy plans for solving the perennial German problem, but his views were not adopted, because to have done so would have been to give the kiss of death to the whole painstakingly constructed peace system.

Stein allowed his disillusionment with Prussia to becloud his judgment. His ideas on unification were set forth in two memoranda to the tsar. One, dated September 17, 1812, proposed a division of power at the Main River between Catholic Austria and predominantly Protestant Prussia. The second memorandum, which contradicted the first, was written in August, 1813. It advocated establishment of a new federal empire, exclusive of Prussia, in which thirty-six quasi-sovereign states would be subject to a strong central government controlled by Austria. Neither memorandum was practical in view of the augmentation of Prussian power.

By contrast with Stein, Metternich knew exactly what he wanted and how to get it. An enlightened man of the salon rather than a romantic idealist, Metternich was the model of a grand seigneur—wise, winning, and benign. The Austrian chancellor, then forty-two and at the height of his powers, was handsome of face and figure with fine, regular features. Of middle height, he had a noble forehead and clear blue Sèvres eyes. His voice was nasal but not unpleasant, and his conversation was as elegant as his attire. A mild-mannered individual, he radiated dignity, charm, and an indefinable magic. Even when he was eighty-one and his voice was broken and inaudible, his hearing weak, and the world he had helped build had tumbled around him, he still stood erect and preserved his Mephistophelian magnetism.

Metternich viewed the German problem not from the nationalist or Habsburg perspective, but from the European. His central idea was that the composition of Germany must be a confederation that would express the ideal of unity in severalty and function as a component of the continental balance of power. The German confederation was to be linked through Austria with an Italian confederation. In both complexes Austria was to be the tutor, but the sovereignty of the German and Italian states was not to be impaired. This middle-European plan was designed not so much to insure Austrian hegemony as to build against France a defense line from the Baltic to Sicily.

The Act of Confederation that the congress adopted on June 8 sanctioned establishment of a loose German Confederation (Deutscher Bund), comprising thirty-nine sovereign entities, including the kings of England (for Hanover), Holland (for Luxemburg), and Denmark (for Holstein). The confederation possessed a permanent president in the Austrian emperor but had neither cabinet, administration, flag, nor (until 1820) even an army.

The lower chamber of the confederation was the Bundestag, which sat in Frankfurt a. M. Consisting of deputies appointed by the state governments, the Bundestag, like the old Polish diet, was hamstrung from the outset by the rule that all major measures required unanimity for adoption. In the upper house, or Bundesrat, the eleven largest states, each of which had a single vote, dominated. The twenty-eight smaller states were grouped into six curias, each with only one vote. Since a capital proposal required a two-thirds majority, the six biggest states (disposing of eleven out of a total of seventeen votes) could block the will of the other thirty-three, which represented a majority of the nation's population. In this monstrous travesty of a nation-state, parts of Prussia, inhabited by Germans, were excluded from membership, while Bohemia and Moravia were included.

Kleindeutsch historians from Treitschke to Erich Eyck and Gerhard Ritter have always insisted that the German Confederation was endemically incapable of banishing the rivalry between Austria and the mature Prussia, and that this had to lead to the mastery of Germany by one of them. On the other hand, foes of the *kleindeutsch* solution, from Konstantin Frantz and Wilhelm Liebknecht to Heinrich Ritter von Srbik and Franz Schnabel, have stressed that the Deutscher Bund made positive contributions in that it adjourned for almost half a century a naked power struggle between Prussia and Austria and was an impediment to the extension of Prussian authoritarianism over all of Germany. For the apologists of the *Bund*, it was the paladin of olden freedoms and the harbinger of the future *Rechtsstaat*. This was so because the liberal, constitutional regimes of south Germany were shielded by the confederation from Prussian and Austrian reactionary forces, which feared to violate the internationally guaranteed sovereignty of the middle states.

The Second Treaty of Paris

While the Congress of Vienna was still in session, Napoleon escaped from Elba, landed at Fréjus on March 1, 1815, and overthrew the Bourbon government in Paris. From June 16 to 18 the combined forces of Wellington and Blücher crushed his army of 120,000 at Waterloo. After the Bourbons were restored and Bonaparte was sent into exile for a second and last time, the second Treaty of Paris was signed on November 20, 1815. The terms, despite Blücher's demand for punitive demolitions in Paris, were surprisingly lenient. Saarbrücken, Saarlouis, and Landau were ceded to Prussia. An indemnity of 700 million francs was exacted and an army of occupation was to be stationed in the eastern departments until it was paid. While a France that had been forced back to the frontiers of 1790 was, to use Talleyrand's words, "no longer colossal," she was still well able to take a hand in the balance of power game.

The German Constitutions

In the period 1814–20 an impressive number of German states turned their backs upon the corporative-feudal past and ended for good the system of representation by estates *(Stände)*. Article XIII of the Act of Confederation guaranteed a constitution *(Landständische Verfassung)* to each member of the Deutscher Bund. Unfortunately the wording of the article conveyed the impression that the old provincial estates would be preserved and that parliamentary government for the principalities was not contemplated. Certainly this was the conclusion drawn by Austria, Prussia, Württemberg, and Hanover.

Metternich deplored representative government and popular elections as an assault upon the monarchical principle to which he was devoted. While he was not absolutely determinative for German affairs, he managed to impart a sable hue to the political complexion of central Europe. Because of Metternich, attempts of the diet, in conformity with Article X of the Act of Confederation and of the Final Act of Vienna of May 15, 1815, to organize national institutions of government and to codify German law remained fragmentary. Because of him the confederation was never able to play an independent role in international relations but had to act as a coadjutor of Austrian grand policy. In every corner of Germany and in every larger crisis the greatest statesman of his time intervened with success to defend conservatism and the status quo.

Of tragic consequence for the cause of constitutional monarchy was the gradual defection of Prussia from the reformist camp. In the flush of military victory Frederick William III had issued a decree on May 22, 1815, which authorized the drafting of a constitution with the aim of eventually establishing something Prussia had never had—a limited, representative monarchy. However, this concession to liberalism was vitiated by the politically dominant landed nobility. The Prussian conservatives, who were led by Duke Karl von Mecklenburg, General Ludwig von der Marwitz, Minister of Police Prince Georg von Wittgenstein, and Minister of the Interior Kaspar F. von Schuckmann, were fearful that representative government would aggravate antagonisms between the different regions of the realm. By 1823 the conservatives succeeded in driving almost all progressive ministers from the administration.

In this period the main Prussian progress was registered in the area of administration, not government. Under the waning influence of the mildly progressive Hardenberg and of administrators such as Ludwig von Vincke of Westphalia, Johann von Sack in the Rhineland, and Theodor von Schön in West Prussia, a more effective organization of the provincial bureaucracy was achieved. Furthermore, the Council of State *(Staatsrat)* was in 1817 transformed into a supreme administrative organ. Yet it was no more a cabinet than had been the *Staatsministerium* of 1810.

After 1819 Prussia's internal policy drew closer to Austria's. On August 1, 1819, Hardenberg and Metternich signed the Agreement of Teplitz, which pledged Prussia not to establish a legislature. Instead she was to preserve the corporative-estates system. Obviously Hardenberg was becoming more conservative. His defeat and death in November, 1822, was decisive for the parliamentary contest. The law of June 5, 1823, concerning the provincial estates was the tombstone of the Prussian constitutional movement and an accolade to conservatism. Each of Prussia's eight provinces was accorded a diet as of old, but it was to be elected only by the *Stände*. In the diets the nobility was, in effect, to predominate. In most major matters the diets were to possess only consultative competence. The district diets *(Kreistage)*, which were reorganized between 1825 and 1828, had even less power. For the Prussian bureaucracy, until a new reign, scope was left for progressive initiatives only in the economic sphere.

In south and west Germany the political climate was more favorable to constitutionalism. A number of states there between 1814 and 1820 made the transition from authoritarian to limited, constitutional government. Constitutions usually came as royal grants analogous to the Charter of Louis XVIII. In all of them primary responsibility for interpreting fundamental law and framing policy was left in the hands of the chief executive. Although all constitutional states came to have a bicameral legislature in which the lower chamber was elected by property owners, the regnant prince remained the nexus of power. For him the fundamental law was like a universal joint that he could turn and twist anyway he liked provided he gave it plenty of grease in the form of bribes and honors.

Constitutions were most readily adopted in states that had been integrated with the Napoleonic Order or in which the middle class was most numerous. The first principality to receive a constitution was Nassau (1814). Bavaria, Württemberg, Hesse-Darmstadt, and Baden received theirs before the end of 1820. By 1829 many smaller principalities had followed suit. On the other hand, apart from Prussia and Austria, a number of other states retained their old corporative diets: Saxe-Gotha, Oldenburg, Reuss, Mecklenburg-Schwerin, Mecklenburg-Strelitz, Schaumburg-Lippe, and the kingdom of Saxony.

The Theory of Conservatism

The stereotype of Metternich as an unprincipled reactionary is a fiction of liberal and nationalist historiography.

It is true that for him there could be no compromise with revolution in any of its guises. Objectively viewed, the revolutionary movement, he was convinced, was directed against both throne and people. However, left to itself, that "great nincompoop which is called the public" would work peacefully, rear its families, and be indifferent to constitutions and insurrection.*

Although Metternich certainly set himself against nationalism, democracy, liberalism, and individualism—all forces that might subvert the Grand Monarchy, he did not oppose reform as such. An offshoot of the Enlightenment, Metternich refused to equate reform with constitutionalism. Axiomatic to his thinking, however, was that Austria was a polyglot "monarchical union of corporative states," which needed stability and peace in order to serve the continent. He sincerely believed that initiative for reform should be left with the crown and not transferred to a representative legislature. Unfortunately he was sabotaged in his advocacy of monarchical benevolence by Emperor Francis I.

In his world outlook Metternich was supported by a great many European political theorists. While most German universities and men of letters also endorsed his *Weltanschauung,* the strongest artillery support for his conservatism was furnished by five men: Joseph Görres, Karl Ludwig Haller (1768–1854), Friedrich Julius Stahl (1802–61), Friedrich Karl von Savigny (1779–1861), and Georg Wilhelm Hegel (1770–1831). Görres, a former liberal, was a Catholic convert and for long the editor of the *Berliner Politische Wochenblatt*, which became the chief journal of the conservatives. The Swiss aristocrat and Catholic convert, Haller, interpreted political science in authoritarian terms. In his six-volume *Restauration der Staatswissenschaft (Restoration of Political Science, 1816–34)* he affirmed that the will of the prince was law. Stahl, who was both a lawyer and

---

*Heinrich Ritter von Srbik, *Metternich; Der Staatsmann und der Mensch*, 2nd ed. (Munich, 1957), I, 381.

philosopher, inveighed against the worthlessness of constitutions and extolled the corporative, paternalistic state. His influence was greatest toward the close of the era of Metternich. Savigny, professor of law at Berlin and founder of the historical school of jurisprudence, placed public law in symbiotic relationship to political evolution.

In many ways Hegel's philosophy also harmonized with the spirit of Metternich. Hegel's comprehensive system was set forth in some of the most abstruse works in any language. The most significant of his books in the present context was *The Philosophy of Law* (1821). Successively professor of philosophy at Heidelberg (1816–18) and Berlin (1818–31), he formulated a Christian and moral political philosophy. Idealist and antirevolutionary, his thinking exuded faith in the perfectibility of institutions and in eternal progress toward ever broader freedom. Hegel also exalted the state as the fulfillment, through a complicated dialectical process, of the divine will.

Hegel believed, as did Herder, Savigny, Haller, and Burke, that the state is the natural custodian of freedom and the embodiment of the ethos of a nation. Every government was for him the end product of a long evolution with which it is criminal to tamper. A natural inference from Hegel's philosophy, eagerly drawn by the apologists of legitimacy, was that the authoritarian-type German states conformed better to the *Volksgeist* than did governments created by fiat of constitutional assemblies.

The Bases of Conservatism's Success

If political reaction was the prevailing climate of postwar Germany, this was principally due to the absence of a power struggle between Austria and Prussia and to the incompleteness of the conservative victory.

In respect of the first factor, most important decisions in the German Confederation were taken jointly by Prussia and Austria, both of which had renounced expansion. For the first time dualism could operate without a duel. Besides this, Austria and Prussia were linked with Russia in a "Holy Alliance," which was merely a pious association for the vindication of conservative principles, and in the more concrete Quadruple Alliance (after 1818 Quintuple) in defense of legitimist ideas.

Metternich was the driver who held the Austrian and Prussian steeds in the same span. He was surprisingly successful in winning Berlin's confidence. This was doubtless because he was more a principle than a politician. No exponent of naked *Machtpolitik*, Metternich was an old-fashioned rationalist who unsentimentally regarded the "Austrian system" as in no way oriented to the benefit of any single state but to impersonal, supranational, timeless ends. The great constructive idea of Metternich lay in the federative principle, both in the Austrian empire as a federation of historic nationalities and in the heart of Europe as a conservative federation of sovereign German states. On this platform legitimist Prussia was ready to join Austria in resisting popular sovereignty and constitutionalism.

With respect to the second factor it was still possible after 1815 for the liberals to win victories without insurrection. This had been proven by the continuation of the Napoleonic Code in the Rhineland, the establishment of parliaments in some German states, and the adoption of constitutions in more. Furthermore, reformist concepts continued to inform the work of the bureaucracy in many principalities, not least of all in Prussia. To illustrate, in 1817 Humboldt secured the promulgation of a charter for the public school system of Prussia, which made primary schools *(Volksschulen)* free and compulsory for both sexes and subjected the schools through provincial authorities to a newly created ministry of Public Instruction and Ecclesiastical Affairs. Also, the Prussian minister of education, Baron Karl von Altenstein (1817–40), an exponent of freedom of thought, supervised the establishment of numerous preparatory schools *(Gymnasien)* for students between the ages of sixteen and nineteen. His reorganization of the classical secondary schools laid the basis for the superior quality of the German *Gymnasien* after 1819. Similarly in Bavaria, Württemberg, and Saxony exclusive state control over education was established. Almost everywhere, too, liberals could applaud the fact that both Protestant and Catholic churches were subject to state control.

With respect to the peasantry, the Prussian government moved from paternalism and protectionism toward a modern system of individual rights and ownership in severalty, which found approval with the bourgeoisie. While Hardenberg's land decrees of 1811 and 1816 did not by any means abolish the patrimonial jurisdiction of lord over peasant, they had the effect of leaving a large class of freedmen with inadequate protection against a new type of exploitation. The law of 1816, by interposing obstacles to becoming freeholders, made inevitable an exodus of discouraged, marginal tenants to the towns. Also, many small proprietors could neither discharge their commutation payments to former lords nor eke out a satisfactory existence on their tiny plots and were therefore forced to sell out to big landlords or bourgeois speculators and move to the cities. This influx of cheap labor was welcomed by the industrial bourgeoisie.

The conservative victory in Austria was also incomplete. Metternich, as Robert A. Kann has argued cogently, never equated the good of the Habsburg empire with the status quo and, as a son of the Enlightenment, did not oppose slow evolutionary reform per se. He was aware of the pedantry, officiousness, and inelasticity of the Habsburg bureaucracy and deplored the laming divisiveness of the territorial diets. He proposed to diminish these handicaps to efficient government by simply strengthening the Crown Council *(Staatsrat)* and transforming it into a central committee of delegates appointed by the crown from all the kingdoms and dominions of the empire. In spite of the fact that Emperor Francis I rejected this suggestion and notwithstanding the paramountcy of the true-blue reactionary Count Franz Kolowrat-Liebsteinsky (1778–1861) in internal affairs after 1826, the grand monarchy made sluggish progress toward social improvements.

Austria achieved commendable things for almost all her children in the field of education. Everyone was gratified at the remarkable progress that was made in establishing thousands of primary and secondary schools and in pushing the campaign against illiteracy. Similarly the common people were generally pleased with the continuation of a Prussian-type egalitarian military system and French-type taxation. Progress was registered in respect of the adoption of municipal constitutions, improvement of sanitation, and enactment of social welfare legislation. The great public hospital in Vienna, subsidized by the government, became a model for high medical standards and was widely imitated in Europe. Under Francis I, too, the system of criminal law was further humanized. While a strangling censorship and ubiquitous state police of Austria weighed heavily upon all groups and activities that posed a political threat to the regime, broad freedom was the rule in all nonpolitical intellectual and artistic pursuits. The universities flourished, and the Austrian archives and court library made their rich resources available to European scholarship.

Important segments of the Austrian middle class were reconciled by government-engineered programs for the promotion of trade and industry and by the abolition of internal tariffs. The bourgeoisie were persuaded to accept the defects of the Metternichian system for the sake of the material blessings it conferred. The intelligentsia were placated by the remarkable educational, scientific, and cultural opportunities that were made available under the existing order. Thus progress and opportunity split the revolutionary middle class. The bulk of it was not prepared to risk what it had gained under the Habsburg autocracy by seeking to overthrow it. The division, which persisted throughout the revolutions of 1848, helped the conservatives to retain the reins of power throughout the rest of the century. The danger to conservative control, of course, was that the populace might be lashed onward by the middle class to destroy the existing order. The aristocracy and the bureaucrats felt, however, that an ounce of prevention was worth a pound of cure: if the state governments only honestly discharged their responsibilities toward the workers and peasants, the lower classes would leave politics to the well-born and experienced.

The Reign of Repression

Metternich's principled German policy enjoyed the support of the major powers until 1820. These included France, which had joined the Concert of Europe (replacing the Quadruple Alliance) by the Treaty of Aix-la-Chapelle on October 9, 1818. The chancellor's whole external program was secured by the sanction of armed intervention in the affairs of any state where there existed a threat to the entire system, as in the Kingdom of the Two Sicilies in 1820. However, to this principle of intervention England demurred at the Conference of Troppau (1820), and even France displayed disquieting indifference. The same disunity marked the ensuing meeting of the concert held at Laibach in January, 1821. Notwithstanding, Austria dispatched an army to southern Italy and also aided in suppressing a revolution that had broken out in March against the king of Sardinia.

There was no organized opposition to the Metternichian system in Germany. Hostility was largely confined to a handful of professors and to students. Their

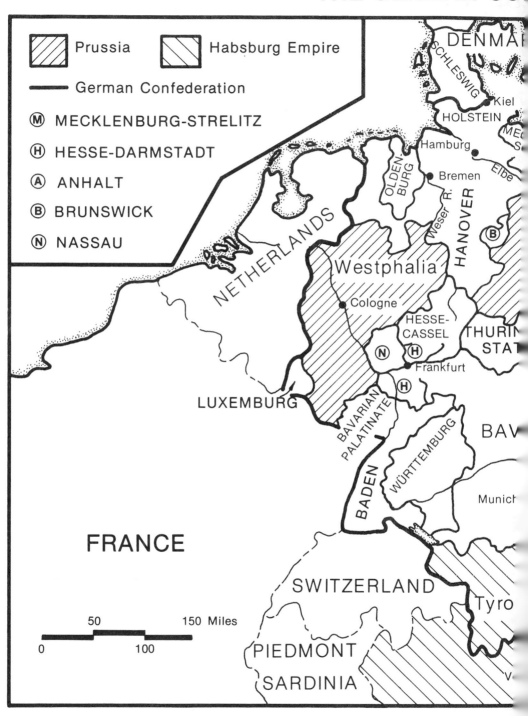

Prussia   Habsburg Empire

——— German Confederation

Ⓜ MECKLENBURG-STRELITZ

Ⓗ HESSE-DARMSTADT

Ⓐ ANHALT

Ⓑ BRUNSWICK

Ⓝ NASSAU

DENMA

SCHLESWIG

Kiel

HOLSTEIN

MEC
S

Hamburg

Elbe

OLDEN-BURG

Bremen

Weser R.

HANOVER

Ⓑ

NETHERLANDS

Westphalia

Cologne

HESSE-CASSEL

THURIN
STAT

Ⓝ Ⓗ

Frankfurt

LUXEMBURG

Ⓗ

BAVARIAN PALATINATE

WÜRTTEMBURG

BAV

BADEN

Munich

FRANCE

SWITZERLAND

Tyro

50   150 Miles

0   100

PIEDMONT

SARDINIA

views were expressed in journals such as *Isis, Merkur,* and *Patriot*, none of which had a large circulation or exerted much influence on public opinion. The intelligentsia, as a whole, having burned its fingers in the flame of the Enlightenment, had turned away from politics.

To the conservative governments, scandalized by a wave of assassinations and insurrections in Europe, the German student societies *(Burschenschaften)* were less a menace than an annoyance. The first society was founded at the University of Jena in June, 1815. Inspired by the catchwords "honor, freedom and fatherland," the *Burschenschaften* echoed the noble sentiments of Ernst Moritz Arndt and the historian Heinrich Luden (1780–1847). The societies adopted as their colors black, red, and gold, which happened also to have been those of the Holy Roman Empire. A group of students, headed by Karl Follen (1795–1840), poet, lecturer, and clergyman, soon gave a lead to political discussions at the University of Giessen.

On October 18, 1817, representatives of various student societies convened at Eisenach to celebrate the fourth anniversary of the Battle of Leipzig and, on the thirty-first, at historic Wartburg Castle for the tercentenary of Luther's great initial act at Wittenberg. These meetings featured incendiary speeches and burning of reactionary books. On October 16–18, 1818, the General Union of the German Student Societies was formed.

The revolutionary wing of the *Burschenschaften*, led by Follen, was prepared to employ terrorist tactics to overthrow the monarchy and found a unitary, bourgeois German republic. The immediate result of Follen's agitation was the fatal stabbing on March 23, 1819, in Mannheim of the Russian conservative journalist Kotzebue by Karl Sand, a theological student, who was caught and executed.

In Sand's deed Metternich discovered a pretext for initiating a program of repression. A conference of the larger German states was convened at Carlsbad (Karlovy Vary) August 6–31, 1819, to concert methods to cope with terrorism and insurrection. The conference decreed dissolution of the *Burschenschaften* and *Turnvater*—Jahn's athletic associations. The Carlsbad Decrees also instituted a system of inspectors to supervise universities and press and authorized intervention in any German state threatened with subversion. Beyond this, Metternich did not care to go. He made no effort to force the abrogation of the territorial constitutions that had already been granted, for this would have violated the principle of sovereignty.

The decade following the Carlsbad Decrees saw the floodtide of German reaction. The conservative counteroffensive was strengthened by vague fears provoked by the assassination in 1820 of the French heir presumptive to the throne, by the Cato Street conspiracy against the British government, and by revolutions in Italy and Spain. The reaction overwhelmed the "unconditional" radicals, consolidated Austrian ascendancy over central Europe, and compelled almost all the diets to endorse the Metternichian program. Even the Confederate army, or *Bundesheer*, which was formed in 1821 (comprising ten army corps, of which Austria and Prussia each contributed three), was not so much a shield against external aggression as a hammer in the hands of conservatism.

The upsurge of reaction also stiffened the Prussian government in its fight against constitutionalism. Thus, a law of 1823, which assigned the landed nobility the largest representation in the provincial diets, sharply limited the competence of the latter and reserved everything of capital importance to the crown. Succeeding Prussian laws of 1825 and 1828 established a system of grossly unequal representation, virtually disenfranchising the bourgeoisie and peasantry. In Bavaria the pro-Austrian Ludwig I (1825–48), who was sympathetic to Catholicism, was inclined to trail along in the wake of the Habsburg dreadnought, provided nobody interfered with his pleasures.

Impact of the Revolutions of 1830

The revolutions of 1830, which began in France in late July with the overthrow of the Bourbons and the advent of the bourgeois Orléanist monarchy, found the German liberals still disorganized and impotent. Although revolutionary sparks ignited Italy, Belgium, and Poland, those that were carried to Germany were easily extinguished. The radical ideologues were deceived in their expectation that the French revolution would also entail the deposition of the German princes. The democratic Hambach castle festival of late May, 1832, and the brush between students and police in Frankfurt a. M. on April 3, 1833, started no fire in Germany.

If the revolutions of 1830 hardly excited the German public, they nevertheless did give a new impetus to the German constitutional movement. In 1831 the Saxon bureaucracy persuaded the king to grant a constitution, in 1832 both Brunswick and electoral Hesse followed suit, and in 1833 the king of Hanover did likewise. However, in none of these or in any previously granted constitutions, with the exception of that of Hesse, whose basic law had been drafted under the influence of the liberal Karl Von Rotteck, was the diet given sovereign competence over legislation or taxation.

Although Germany had been all but immune to revolution in 1830, Metternich's scale of values—"order, authority, freedom"—had been sharply challenged in many parts of Europe. It was evident that internal repression alone had not succeeded in destroying the European underground movement that was marching toward the goal of the middle-class state.

There was convincing evidence that the bell had tolled for the aristocratic-peasant order in the west. Nonintervention, the Monroe Doctrine, the British Reform Act of 1832, the French and Belgian revolutions, and the chronic turmoil in the Iberian peninsula were all proof of that. By compensation, the conservatives strove to strengthen and consolidate their position east of the Rhine. The desirability of closer collaboration among Austria, Prussia, and Russia was suggested by the Italian and Polish uprisings of 1830. Berlin and St. Petersburg strongly supported the suppression of the revolutions in Italy, while Prussia stationed troops along the border of Posen to aid, if need be, in smothering the blaze in Poland.

After the conflagration had been put out, the three eastern powers, in 1833, entered into two separate conventions at Münchengrätz and Berlin. These pledged the signatories to pursue commonly endorsed policies toward partitioned Poland

and cooperate on a European scale in the fight against liberalism, individualism, and nationalism. The Treaty of Berlin, signed on October 15, further pledged the signatories to mutual and reciprocal aid in the event of any "external threat" to the security of one or more of the contracting parties. Although not supplemented by a military convention and lacking the precise phraseology of a genuine alliance, the Treaty of Berlin was an entente for the defense of the expiring order. It was decisive for the outcome of the Hungarian rebellion in 1848 and proved to be, in one form or other, the best device of the century to prevent the outbreak of general war.

PART VIII
NEW WINE IN OLD BOTTLES

Chapter 26

LIBERALISM AND RADICALISM

Limitations of German Liberalism

It has often been said that nothing was so important to European liberals as the individual's right to complete freedom of development. Applied to Germany this is not true, unless by that right is understood a purely aesthetic and theoretical freedom. In that country only a tiny band of radical ideologues preached irreconcilable struggle for political liberty. Except for insignificant numbers of workers, very few persons were prepared to countenance a class war for the forcible overthrow of the existing order. Since intellectual extremists were usually of common or humble origin, their rejection of the traditional synthesis of corporative and contractual liberties had little appeal for the solid bourgeoisie. The prevailing attitude in German liberalism, which was represented by the merchants and industrialists and their spokesmen in the diets, was fundamentally moderate. Most capitalists were not unmindful of the freedoms embodied in the unwritten territorial constitutions. They were convinced, too, that their economic aims, of paramount importance to them, could be achieved within the established social order. The bourgeoisie would naturally have preferred that a political extension be given to the olden concept of *Libertät*. However, in any iron choice between democratic institutions and national unification the bulk of the middle class was prepared to forego the former.

The nationalist outlook of the rising bourgeoisie is the main reason for the eccentric history of the German states system in the nineteenth century. It is in the economic and political practice of that class that we must seek the genesis of what Friedrich Meinecke, Franz Schnabel, Ernst Troeltsch, and Ludwig Dehio rightly or wrongly termed "Germany's astonishing deviation from the main line of European development."

The German middle-class outlook was governed by several major factors. To begin with, there had been in German history, unlike English or French, a total absence of successful social revolutions. Second, the fact that German industry and commerce limped very far behind their English competitors and even behind their French, Dutch, and Flemish had hobbled the German middle class with a backwardness that sharply arrested its ideological development and critically limited the influence of that class upon society. In the third place, the expulsion of the French armies from all lands east of the Rhine had had as an ineluctable consequence a rude setback for all continental liberal and egalitarian ideas. Last, the overthrow of the Bonapartist order had been the work mainly of the princes and nobles. The record of the bourgeoisie in war and diplomacy was, by contrast, inglorious. Thus, from every standpoint it was a class with an inferiority complex. This psychological handicap deprived it of the requisite courage to challenge the ruling establishment. This is the key to a century of German political history.

It is a fact that the industrial and mercantile capitalists basically revered the state as the fount of liberty. They were quite unwilling to jeopardize the rights of private property by repudiating the coercive prerogatives of the government. Accordingly, they were simply not available for anything other than moderate reformist tactics. Moreover, no responsible captain of industry argued that the erection of an all-German state should be achieved on a democratic-republican foundation, because it was clear to the upper bourgeoisie that unification could not be engineered without aid from either authoritarian Prussia or Austria. The middle class, therefore, looked forward to unification as to a cornucopia but believed that the horn of plenty could very well pour forth its blessings within the existing order.

The denatured German bourgeoisie was a class with great expectations. In the years before 1850 the prime instruments of production were concentrated so rapidly in its hands that the nobility at length came to realize that it could not much longer avoid compromising with the rising capitalists. When finally in the age of Bismarck the National Liberal party defected to him, liberalism became politically fashionable because by that time it had been thoroughly domesticated. It had become in fact a main strut of the Bismarckian and Wilhelmine empire.

Roots of German Liberalism

Many roots fed the tree of early nineteenth-century German liberalism: Swiss, Dutch, American, French, English, even the classical humanist tradition of Kant and Goethe. Of special importance were the French and English contributions. The French had appeal for ideologues and bourgeoisie of south and west Germany in particular. The idea of checks and balances and the division of powers in government, which were integral to the German philosophy of the *Rechtsstaat*, were derived from Montesquieu and his distorted understanding of the structure of English government *(Spirit of Laws,* 1748). Other concepts, such as the social contract, the rights of man and citizen, restricted franchise, economic individualism, and the inviolability of property, were drawn from the philosophes, Rousseau, the physiocrats, and especially from concrete revolutionary experiences in the years 1789–91, 1795–99, and during the Consulate. All of these ideas were sifted and refined in the Restoration era by a group of French rationalist political leaders who called themselves "Doctrinaires" (e.g., Pierre Royer-Collard, Victor Cousin, Benjamin Constant, and François Guizot). The Doctrinaires refused to acknowledge the absolute authority of either king or people and advocated a latitudinarian political philosophy centering on constitutional monarchy and limited franchise.

Of even greater importance for German liberalism was the English experience. Beginning with the Glorious Revolution of 1688 and Locke's *Two Treatises of Government* (1690), the English example had never ceased to find warm admirers in Germany. After the accession of the Hanoverian dynasty to the English throne in 1714, Hanover with its University of Göttingen (established 1727) became a center for disseminating principles of limited monarchy. In the early nineteenth century the attractions of British parliamentarism were reinforced by the pull of classical political economy. A school of laissez faire thought which embraced Adam Smith, Thomas Malthus, David Ricardo, J. B. Say, Nassau Senior, and James Mill, supplied a systematic apologia for the basic economic practices of the bourgeoisie. It was the central notion of classical economics that complete freedom of enterprise untrammeled by government interference would result in the augmentation of production, the improvement of methods of trade and manufacture, the lowering of costs and ultimately of prices to the consumer, and the general prosperity of the country. After the passage of the electoral Reform Act of 1832 and the repeal of the Corn Laws in 1846, which were great successes of the English capitalist class, it seemed to the German liberals that the English had shown the way by which bourgeois political and economic principles could be realized by reformist means.

Such was the esteem in which by 1815 the north German liberals held Britain that they were in danger of becoming the dupes of her virtues. Even Frederician style progressives, like Stein and Baron Ludwig von Vincke (1778–1844) of Westphalia, discovered in English political patterns much that was worthy of emulation. Gradually almost all German liberals came to agree that only a unified constitutional monarchy along English lines could guarantee the liberty they prized. Not till after 1848 did they perceive there was something in the German milieu that made limited monarchy incompatible with unification. Because the bourgeoisie were pushed ever more narrowly to choose between these two goals, liberalism, compelled to opt for unification by autocratic means, lost its humaneness and became cynical, harsh, insupportably materialistic and, in the end, contemptuous of the rights of man. But this was all in the future.

The main effect of classical political economy on Germany was to convert an originally Kantian preoccupation with the free development of personality into a paramount concern for the freedom of the economic man. Smith's doctrine that "every man is committed by nature to his own care" challenged the charitable and paternalist legacy of the German church and state. Malthus' *Essay on Population* (1789) presented German liberalism with the bitter draft of eternal social struggle for survival. Ricardo in his *Principles of Political Economy and Taxation* (1817) expounded the "iron law of wages," which affirmed that wages are always just enough to reproduce the labor power of a worker and that since they will not fall below the subsistence level, any interference with the laws, such as through government regulation of the conditions of labor, would be "useless" and "pernicious."

It may be imagined that the German liberals, with their memories of benevolent despotism, were never really at ease in the harsh milieu of laissez faire. Germany's leading political economist, Friedrich List (1789–1846), indubitably preferred the economic paternalist philosophy of Adam Müller to British individualism, because the latter was alien to the German tradition.

However, a war scare in 1840, which fanned suspicions that Paris was again reaching out for the Rhine boundary, dismayed German advocates of French governmental forms and produced a prestigious rise in British influence. This was abetted in 1846 when the English middle class demonstrated through repeal of the Corn Laws its capability of achieving basic class objectives in cooperation with the nobility. This vindicated the argument that the aims of the German bourgeoisie could be attained without proletarian support. The Revolutions of 1848 hardly shook this thesis. Deprived of the alliance of the bourgeoisie, the leaderless working class was in no position to seize power. To the irreconcilable revolutionary minority it must have seemed that Germany, like all the people in the palace of the Sleeping Beauty, had fallen into a century-long sleep.

Spokesmen of the Liberals

Predominantly nationalist and prosaic in its outlook, German liberalism never produced apologists of seminal genius, such as Smith, Locke, Bentham, Malthus, Mill, or Ricardo. German liberal academicians may have mastered all there was to know about constitutional and legal history, but their books only fed the intellect while starving the soul. Their idealistic political philosophy was little more than a supervenient graft upon eighteenth-century humanism. The leaders of the liberals stemmed mainly from middle-class bureaucratic or academic circles, but there were many aristocrats among them. By vocation they were apt to be lawyers, journalists, officials, or professors, and they often sat in the state diets.

Bureaucratic liberalism *(Geheimrathsliberalismus)* originated in eighteenth-century Germany but had been strongly influenced in the Restoration era by French examples. Stein was the finest prototype of the school, but Wilhelm von Humboldt was also an exponent of *Geheimratsliberalismus*. Both believed that the cardinal responsibility of government was to promote the liberty of individuals. Although in Prussia bureaucratic liberalism survived the Napoleonic wars, it subsequently led a sickly existence. The Vinckes, Sacks, and Schöns fought courageously against mounting odds. After 1819, when leading reformers such as General von Grolman, Field Marshal von Boyen, Humboldt, and Count Karl Friedrich von Beyme left the ministry in protest against the reactionary Carlsbad Decrees, the conservatives acquired a monopoly over the bureaucracy. Thereafter liberal administrators had scope for their philosophy only in the educational and economic spheres.

Bavaria, where the political climate was conditioned by a frozen constitution, was fundamentally hostile to liberal ideas. Nevertheless, there were still progressive bureaucrats, such as Georg von Zehnter and Baron Alexander von Lerchenfeld, who strove to patch together the aristocratic-bourgeois alliance of the *Befreiungskrieg* era. In Saxony, too, a number of administrators sympathized with the liberals. However, no state bureaucracy after 1820 could match the progressive record of the Grand Duchy of Baden. There, Archduke Charles (1811–18) had modified the polity along popular lines; a coterie of ministers, including Wilhelm Reinhard, Ludwig Winter, Ludwig von Liebenstein, and Karl F. Nebenius, cooperated with academic liberals in the *Landtag* to maintain an impressive tempo of reform.

Among the liberal political professors were men of distinction, such as the Grimm brothers, Karl Theodor Welcker (1790–1869), Karl von Rotteck (1775–1840), Robert von Mohl (1799–1875), Friedrich Christian Dahlmann (1785–1860), Theodor von Schön (1772–1836), Baron Heinrich von Gagern (1799–1880), Friedrich Hecker (1811–81), Carlo Salomo Zachariä von Lingenthal (1759–1843), and Johann Bluntschli (1808–81).

In the vanguard of the south German cohort of professorial liberals were Welcker and Rotteck, both of the University of Freiburg and deputies in the Badenser diet in Karlsruhe. They collaborated on the fifteen-volume *Staatslexikon (Encyclopedia of the Political Sciences,* 1834–43), which became the Bible of south German liberalism. Rotteck, in his magisterial *Universal History* (10 vols., 1812–18), had established the orientation of Badenser liberalism toward a conservative French rationalism rather than English economism. Zachariä von Lingenthal lectured at the University of Heidelberg and was a sometime member of both the upper and lower chambers of the diet. His chief claim to fame was his *Forty Books on the State* (5 vols., 1820–32).

In Württemberg the historian von Mohl was the leading academic liberal. He was proud of the tradition of Württemberg's diet, which, dominated by commoners and lower clergy, had never capitulated to the prince. His *History of the Constitutional Law of Württemberg* (1829) established him as the principal south German champion of the *Rechtsstaat*. Like most political professors, Mohl stood closer to the conservative than the radical camp: he was convinced that a state of law could best be achieved under leadership of an enlightened aristocracy within the old social order. To this view the eminent Swiss student of international law, J. K. Bluntschli, who was successively professor at Zurich, Munich, and Heidelberg, also subscribed.

In north Germany the immensely erudite historian Barthold Niebuhr (1776–1831), of the University of Berlin, admired the British political model but refused to take sides. Of greater influence upon north German liberalism was Dahlmann, the founder of the Prussian school of history, who was successively professor at Göttingen and Bonn. "A man of granite and bronze," he led seven Göttingen professors in 1837 in defiance of King Ernst August of Hanover (who had just mounted the throne after Hanover had been separated from Britain), asserting that they would refuse to tolerate any kind of authoritarian government.

The Legislative Offensive

The French Revolution of July, 1830, emboldened German liberal academicians and deputies to strike a more refractory posture. The expulsion of Duke Karl from Brunswick (September 7, 1830), the convocation on September 30 of Hesse-Cassel's long-awaited diet, and the grant of a militia by Hesse's William II heralded a decade of ascendancy of the bourgeois theorists over the whole reform movement. When the death of Emperor Francis I of Austria (March 2, 1835) removed one of the key piers of the Metternichian system, the liberal intelligentsia became sanguine. However, the accession of the spineless Ferdinand I (1835–48) failed to effect any essential modification to the Metternichian system. By the end of the 1830s the leadership of the German reform movement had passed from the intelligentsia to the liberal deputies in the diets.

Politically the most advanced *Landtage* were those of Württemberg and Baden. In the former, Professor Ludwig Uhland of Tübingen (the poet) and the bureaucrats Friedrich von Römer and Paul A. Pfizer spearheaded the attack upon authoritarianism. In Baden, where for some time Duke Leopold von Hochberg was passably sympathetic to reforms, Johann von Itzstein, Daniel Bassermann, Rotteck, Welcker, and Karl Mathy (in the lower chamber) and Prince Egon von Fürstenberg (in the upper) campaigned for a representative national assembly. The appointment of the conservative Friedrich Karl von Blittersdorf to the chancellorship in 1838 reversed the trend and inaugurated a feud between duke and diet that lasted until 1842, when Blittersdorf was overthrown. Thereafter, Duke Leopold, repenting of his earlier flirtation with liberalism, fought the diet and succeeded ultimately in dissolving it in 1846.

The new Badenser diet was more obdurate than the old but contained a divided left. The moderates on the left were dubbed "halves," while their radical colleagues were labeled "wholes." The latter, led by Hecker and Gustav von Struve (1805–70), the editor of the Mannheim *Deutscher Zuschauer,* being averse to cooperation with the "halves," convened independently at Offenburg in September, 1847. They invoked the French and Swiss republican legacy and demanded universal rights and freedom for all Germans, a militia instead of a standing army, graduated income taxes, a unitary republic, and a democratic national assembly. The "halves," who outnumbered the "wholes," feared the masses. At the moderates' convention at Rhein-Heppenheim in October they adopted a program calling for national unification, a constitution, and a national parliament. Among the leaders of the "halves" were Heinrich von Gagern, David J. L. Hansemann, Georg von Mevissen, and Ludolph Camphausen, all men of solid economic status.

In Hesse-Cassel earlier liberal gains were threatened when the regent Frederick William appointed the reactionary Hans von Hassenpflug first minister. Although the diet sent him packing in 1837, the regent continued to sap the constitutional concessions his father had made to the people. The tendency toward an increasing conservatism on the part of south and west German rulers was also illustrated in the case of King Ludwig I of Bavaria (1825–48). After 1828 he severed relations with the liberals, whom he had earlier aided in overthrowing Montgelas, an opponent of constitutionalism. Nine years later Ludwig summoned the conservative Karl von Abel to head the ministry, which was tantamount to a declaration of hostilities against the left. In 1847 a controversy with the diet over the royal mistress, the Irish dancer and adventuress, Lola Montez (Marie Dolores Gilbert), forced the king to dismiss Abel.

In Saxony the honeymoon between king and diet, inaugurated by the conservative constitution of 1831, proved to be very ephemeral, and the following fourteen years were filled with mutual acrimony. The long duel culminated in public protest meetings held in 1845 in Leipzig, where demonstrators were fired upon by royal troops. In Austria, where dissemination of radical ideas was punishable by stiff sentences, including death, the new emperor, Ferdinand I (1835–48), was a disappointment, for he showed no desire to oppose Metternich. However, by 1847 the diet summoned the courage to demand the abolition of all special rights for prelates and nobles and recognition of the principle of the equality of everyone before the law. A false dawn broke in Prussia when the Lutheran Pietist, Frederick William IV (1840–61), came to the throne. He clove to ancient notions of divine right and the mystic will of God and was the enemy of all constitutional movements because they substituted the powers of man for those of God. The liberals ought not to have seen in the king's initiative anything more than a meretricious exhibition of medieval paternalism when in 1842 he authorized the long-promised assembly of provincial diets of the kingdom, which von Schön and Johannes Jacoby and the East Prussian politicians had been demanding. All Frederick William IV was prepared to tolerate was a territorial estates general whose mission would be to revive the olden, corporative character of his realm. When the United Prussian *Landtag*, representing the eight provinces of the kingdom, finally did meet in 1847, it was found that half the lower chamber comprised noblemen and no less than seventy princes sat in the upper chamber. It can categorically be affirmed that the Revolution of 1848 was not made by this fundamentally conservative "estates general" but was merely thrust upon the liberal element in it.

Verdict on Pre-March Political Liberalism

Basically a movement of the intelligentsia, pre-1848 liberalism never enjoyed any large support among the German masses or military. Liberalism's cardinal class aims were to break the monopoly that the patriciate enjoyed over the diets and governments, win for the middle class a more important role in the formulation of public policy, and broaden the power of the legislature. These objectives were often sabotaged by big businessmen, who were more interested in economic gains and German unification than they were in representative institutions that might augment the power of the workers.

Indubitably the state constitutions were liberalism's most melodramatic achievement, but these were sapped by the reaction after 1819 and again after 1830. In any case, before 1848 representative government was only a grand illusion. The *Landtage* had only narrowly circumscribed powers, members were unpaid and enjoyed no immunity from arrest or judicial process, and no publicity was given to the deliberations of the diets. Parliamentarism was doomed to remain a chimera until the scales of economic power tipped unmistakably against the aristocracy.

The Zollverein

Liberal political gains were less impressive than economic. Outranking all other initiatives was the establishment of free trade in Germany. The bourgeoisie and their spokesmen in universities and diets fervently urged i., but the chief credit for establishing the German Customs Union (Zollverein) belongs to the bureaucrats.

The prime initiative toward free trade was taken and sustained over a period of fifteen years by the Prussian bureaucracy. Its drive for a common market must be regarded as the capital factor in the regeneration of Germany and its preparation for ultimate unification. The first milestone was the Prussian law of May 26, 1818, which established the principle of free trade throughout the Hohenzollern kingdom, levied low duties averaging 10 percent on manufactured imports, and repudiated mercantilist controls. This law was drafted by Karl Georg von Maassen (1759–1834), director general of customs, who meant it to be a first step toward a German Zollverein.

Between 1815 and 1826 Austria also took steps, but more hesitantly than Prussia, to eliminate internal tariff barriers. While they were dismantled as respects Salzburg, the Inn and Hausrück quarter, Tirol, Vorarlberg, and the Italian possessions, it was not until 1838, four years after the creation of the German Customs Union, that the Austrian Empire was finally brought under one universal tariff statute. This achievement was the work of the Habsburg state bureaucracy.

An earlier initiative than the Austrian was taken in 1820 by Bavaria, Württemberg, Baden, and the two Hessen. They formed a tariff union primarily designed to serve the interests of the secondary German states. However, the Bavarian-led union was crippled from birth. After 1823 Hesse-Darmstadt moved into the Prussian orbit and Baden into the French. Meanwhile, Saxe-Weimar and the kingdom of Saxony collaborated to form in 1822 a fourth free-trade area. It eventually came to embrace Thuringia, Brunswick, Hanover, Oldenburg, Nassau, Hesse-Cassel, and Frankfurt.

When Hesse-Darmstadt joined the Prussian free-trade area in 1828, permitting Berlin to build a continuous north German common market, the secondary states became convinced of the futility of trying to maintain an independent economic existence. Thereafter, Prussia closed swiftly upon her rivals. Under the aegis of Friedrich von Motz (1775–1830), negotiations were opened with Bavaria in 1829. The decisive Prussian-Bavarian trade treaty, by which Motz hoped to pry Germany loose from Austria, was ratified on July 12.

The Zollverein, aided by List's *Zollvereinblatt*, now rapidly took shape. In February, 1831, Saxe-Weimar promised to enter the Prussian union within four years, and in August electoral Hesse joined the mushrooming Prussian trade union, thereby completing the bridge between the Rhine and the Vistula. Before the year was out, Gotha and Meiningen had been induced to permit construction of a road to join the Prussian and Bavarian customs systems. Threatened by the sprawling Prussian union, which was now in position to squeeze the economic life out of them, Saxony (1831) and Thuringia (1833) capitulated and joined. A last gesture of defiance was struck by Hanover, which on May 1, 1834, organized still another short-lived customs union.

In 1834 the Deutscher Zollverein, comprising eighteen states with a combined population of 23 million, came into being. Externally, import duties were low, while within the union area there was a common market that covered three-fourths of Germany. Each member state received a share in customs receipts in proportion to its population.

Thereafter the Zollverein acted like a great whirlpool into whose vortex almost all the independent principalities were drawn. After Hanover finally joined on September 11, 1851, on exceptionally favorable terms, the customs union had uninterrupted access to the North Sea on a broad front. By 1854 only Liechtenstein, Holstein, Lauenburg, Mecklenburg, Hamburg, and Austria were still outside.

In summary, it may be said that nothing in the period 1815–64 so greatly advanced the cause of political unification as did the Zollverein. The great majority of the German states were obliged to work together harmoniously in the elaboration of trade treaties. The permanent customs union also contributed more than anything, unless it be the Prussian law of January 17, 1845, dismantling the monopolistic guilds and proclaiming the principle of free enterprise, to promote German industry. The Zollverein injected a greater dynamism into the economy and facilitated the transition of Germany from an agricultural to an industrial capitalist base. The union put at the disposal of German manufacturers, mine operators, and merchants a much bigger market than ever before and enabled them to enjoy, through the device of collective negotiation, more favorable commercial treaties.

The Revolutionaries

To the left of the liberals stood a small coterie of poets, journalists, and agitators who championed the urban masses and whose spirit was closer to that of the Jacobins than of the political professors. The aims of the tribunes of the rising "fourth estate" were conflicting. A majority, however, awaited a mass revolution that would destroy the nobility, subject business to state controls, and establish not merely a *Rechtsstaat*, but a republic based upon social democracy. These leftists were hated like sin by the bourgeoisie.

As with liberalism, radicalism received a strong impulse from the French Revolution of 1830. It inspired a spate of utopian and radical publications by German émigrés living in Paris, and by democrats in the Fatherland. Thus, in Paris Heinrich Heine (1799–1856) wrote poetry indicting despotism; and Ludwig Börne (1786–1837), diatribes against the old order. Inside Germany the themes of utopian socialists such as Charles Fourier and Count Saint Simon were echoed by Georg Büchner (1813–37). In the Breisgau the jurist Philip Siebenpfeiffer of Lahr spoke in similar tones, while in Munich Georg August Wirth, a jurist and historian, denounced in his *Deutsche Tribüne* the police state and inveighed against censorship of the press.

At the same time the trend toward political action received an impetus from two societies, the one political, the other mainly literary, but both named Junges Deutschland (Young Germany). An imitation of Mazzini's famous Young Italy, the Young Germany societies embraced such figures as: Heinrich Laube (1806–

40), author of the stirring tract *Das junge Europa (Young Europe);* Arnold Ruge (1802–80), editor of the radical *Hallische Jahrbücher* and later collaborator with Karl Marx; Georg Herwegh (1817–75), who wrote the *Aufruf (Summons)* against all tyrants; the celebrated lyricist Ferdinand Freiligrath (1810–76); Ferdinand Gutzkow (1811–78), author of the Areopagitica-type work, *Wally die Zweiflerin (Wally the Doubter*, 1833*)*; Ferdinand Kühne (1806–88), literary critic, novelist, and future editor of the radical *Europa* (1846–59); and Ludwig Börne (1786–1837), an arrant revolutionary ideologue famous for his *Briefe aus Paris (Letters from Paris)*.

Young Germany was born to tragedy. The movement had no foreign foe to drive out of the country as had Young Italy and was even constrained to turn its guns upon a German power—Austria. The great dream of the movement was, moreover, ambivalent. It was to found a unified, small German *(kleindeutsch)*, democratic republic, an aim that ignored the basic truth that at that time nationalism and democracy were incompatible in Germany. Yet, because the radicals, no less than the liberals, assigned top priority to unification, they had no love for polyglot, obstructionist Austria. Consequently, the Young Germans were eventually obliged to seek alliance with the Prussian conservatives who, after 1848, held the key to unification. With that, they ran directly onto the spear that authoritarian Prussia held out to them. Considering the strength of the nobility and weakness of the bourgeoisie, it is clear that Young Germany's democratic dreams were only "castles of the foam."

Toward the end of the 1830s utopian radicalism receded before the quickening force of a fighting, working-class philosophy. Year by year, aggressive, anti-capitalistic attitudes won more ground among the revolutionary ideologues and workers. Louis Blanc's influential writings made Jacobinism fashionable again and nurtured the hope that through universal, democratic suffrage and "national workshops" socialism would be ushered in. Pierre-Joseph Proudhon's *What is Property?* (1841) repudiated Blanc's gradualism and in the old spirit of Gracchus Babeuf flatly advocated the forcible seizure of power in the state by the workers. Louis August Blanqui was the first advocate of the dictatorship of the proletariat. French extremist views influenced the intellectual development of Joseph Moll, Moses Hess, Karl Schlapper, Arnold Ruge, Wilhelm Wolff, Karl Heinzen, and Karl Marx, all of whom were linked at one time or another either with the revolutionary Bund der Gerechten (Federation of the Just), an organization founded by the tailor's apprentice Wilhelm Weitling (1808–71), the Allgemeine deutsche Arbeiterverbrüderung (the General German Workers' Brotherhood), or the Kommunistenbund (Communist League).

Meanwhile, in the late 1830s an antireligious bias was imparted to the whole radical movement as a result of the emergence of a school of Biblical criticism founded by the Swabian Jew, David Friedrich Strauss (1808–74). His *Leben Jesu, kritisch bearbeitet (Life of Jesus*, 2 vols., 1835–36*)*, while not actually assailing organized religion, nevertheless opened up wide the sluice gates of atheism by rejecting the divine origin of the Bible. Ruge's *Hallische Jahrbücher*, taking its cue from Strauss, imbued the German radical movement with the conviction that the ecclesiastical hierarchy was merely another talon of the bird of prey that held the lower classes in its grasp.

The Young Hegelians

Among the inchoate, milling radical forces was one of extraordinary promise— the Young Hegelian movement. It was to be the last milestone on the road to "scientific socialism." Students of the philosophy and dialectical method of G. F. W. Hegel (1770–1831), the young Hegelians were led by Bruno Bauer (1809–82), a rationalist theologian and the author of the *Kritik der Evangelischen Synoptiker (Critique of the Synoptic Gospels*, 1840*)*, and Ludwig Feuerbach (1804–72), a materialist who viewed God as an anthropomorphism and had attacked antinomialism and immortality in his influential *Das Wesen des Christentums (The Essence of Christianity*, 1840*)*. However, the mainspring of the movement was undoubtedly Ruge, whose *Jahrbücher für deutsche Wissenschaft und Kunst (Annals for German Science and Art*, 1838–43*)* served as its oracle.

Hegel, Germany's greatest metaphysician since Kant, expounded a philosophy that derived all history from the will of the World Spirit. His conviction that behind the flux of human affairs was an arcane plan precluded any view of the world as chaotic or of human existence as aimless or accidental. Hegel's neopredestinarianism became the point of departure for all nineteenth-century determinist systems, for historicism, scientific history, and Marxist historical materialism.

Even more than his message, Hegel's method fascinated the radicals. He held that the dialectical process of abstract motion was the heart of history, and he employed it to chart the development of society from the beginning. By emphasizing the generative, evolutionary approach to history, as opposed to static or cyclical concepts, Hegel marched with the younger generation, for whom life was movement. The Young Hegelians simply discarded the master's Lutheran postulates and adopted his evolutionary determinism.

The Emergence of Communism

Hegel exercised great influence upon Karl Marx (1818–93), the brother-in-law of the Prussian minister of the interior, Count Ferdinand von Westphalen. A student of philosophy, Marx had sought to found a metaphysical system upon Hegel's thought, which was the dominant system of his day, but found the task frustrating. What most infuriated Marx in Hegel was that he consigned man to impotence. Marx believed that Hegel had missed the crucial point: social relations are not the expression of an idea, much less a religious idea, but are the issue of the interaction of man and his environment. Hegel transformed the history of man into "an abstraction," whereas, for Marx, history was basically the concrete activity of man in pursuit of his ambitions. It followed from this that the only worthwhile philosophical attitude is one of criticism with a view to action. Said Marx: "The philosophers have only interpreted the world differently; the point, however, is to change it.'' Under the influence of Young Hegelians (Bruno Bauer, Max Stirner, and Ruge) and of Friedrich Engels, Marx was soon to discover the ''demiurge'' of the historical process in the ''class.''

After receiving his doctorate from Jena in 1841, Marx became the editor of the radical *Rheinische Zeitung* of Cologne. There he evolved into a socialist and parted ways with the Young Hegelians, who never afterward amounted to much. Subsequent to the suppression of his journal (1843), Marx left Germany for Paris and Brussels and did not return until the outbreak of the Revolution of 1848. While abroad he wrote several philosophical works and in 1844 in Paris met Engels (1820–95), the son of an Elberfeld industrialist and the author of the *Condition of the English Working Class in 1844*. Under the influence of Engels and Moses Hess, Marx proceeded to fuse German philosophical radicalism with French proletarian socialism to form ''communism.'' He arrived at the view that radical thought must be fructified by revolutionary action. In his *Poverty of Philosophy* (1847), whose title was an inversion of Proudhon's book, Marx adopted the latter's view that property was the strongest force in history and that all states had a class character. He theorized that the whole character of a given era is determined by the existing level of the forces and modes of production and the social relationships they engender. He also averred that history is accompanied by an unremitting struggle between social classes, the overthrow of the ruling one being the precondition for the establishment of a new order. For his Fatherland, the so-called ''Red Prussian'' envisioned for the near future only a bourgeois-liberal revolution followed by an indefinite and perhaps prolonged period of proletarian organization and agitation. The immediate battle order for the German workers was to support bourgeoisie against nobility.

Although the heterogeneity of German socialism gradually diminished under verbal drubbing of the Marxists, communism enjoyed only scant influence before 1848. The publication of the *Communist Manifesto* by Marx and Engels in January, 1848, came too late to give direction to the gale that a few weeks later hit the ramshackle states systems of central Europe.

Chapter 27

THE CULTURAL AND INTELLECTUAL CLIMATE

Literature and Drama:
Romanticism and Flood Tide

The most extravagant period of German romanticism was ushered in with the publication of the first volume of *Des Knaben Wunderhorn (The Boy's Magic Horn*, 3 vols., 1805–08*)*. An anthology of enchanting folk songs collected by von Arnim and C. Brentano, the *Wunderhorn* had an impact upon the reading public comparable to that of the superb translation of Shakespeare's plays (1798ff) by August Wilhelm von Schlegel and Ludwig Tieck, or of the first part of Goethe's peerless philosophic poem *Faust* (1808).

Eventually the romantic movement burst its national confines. Aided by Joseph Görres' *Chapbooks* and by Madame de Staël's *De l'Allemagne (Germany*, 1813*)*, the sentient, emotional style swept all Europe. Of tremendous importance in popularizing romanticism was the appearance of the *Kinder- und Hausmärchen (Grimm's Fairy Tales*, 3 vols., 1812–23*)* by the philologists Jakob (1785–1863) and Wilhelm Grimm (1786–1859). Further aiding the spread of romanticism was the Restoration itself, which engendered among despondent men of letters a mood of subjectivism and escapism. Many frustrated spirits, no less than sober nationalist historians like Raumer, Pertz, Savigny, Luden, and Eichhorn, looked to the vanished past for answers to the riddle of life. This wistful longing for a Gothic past was immensely stimulated by the research of the philologists into German medieval folklore, legend, and song.

In full tide, German romanticism bore along as much mediocrity as genius. Many romantic vehicles were, from the dramatic and structural standpoints, inferior. Not infrequently the style degenerated into a passion for the funereal, morbid, or grotesque. This was true of Brentano's works, especially his *Rheinmärchen (Rhenish Tales)*, which teem with yarns about rats, such as "The Pied Piper of Hamelin" and the wicked bishop of Mainz who was devoured in his tower (the Mouse Tower) at Bingen by rodents. Similarly some of the tales in Brentano's epic poem *Stories of the Rosary*, written between 1803–12 but not published until 1852, are reminiscent of second-rate medieval miracle plays. In the crassly fantastic vein were some of von Arnim's works too. These often exuded the odor of the grave, as in the cases of *Die tolle Invalide (The Mad Invalid*, 1818*)* and the macabre *Die Majoratsherren (Heirs in Entail*, 1820*)*.

On the other hand, many works of striking originality and rhapsodic beauty were written not merely by the great triad of the movement—Goethe, Eichendorff, and Heine—but by secondary talents. One thinks of Brentano's poetic rendition of the tale of the Lorelei and of his poignant tragedy, *The Story of Honest Caspar and Beautiful Annie* (1817). Moreover, few dramas of the Napoleonic era compare for gripping interest and artistry with Kleist's *Die Hermannsschlacht* or his *Prinz Friedrich von Homburg* (written in 1808, published in 1821). Kleist's prose narrative *Michael Kohlhaas* was one of the more profound character portraits of the first half of the century. Likewise impressive in their spontaneity and freedom of dramatic treatment were many fine plays by Zacharias Werner (1768–1823). Friedrich de la Motte Fouqué (1777–1843), scion of a French émigré family, who excelled at fairy tales, explored a world of Norse sagas and wonderful nature myths in his *Der Held des Nordens (Hero of the North,* 1808–10*)*, while in his *Undine, eine Erzählung (Undine, A Tale)* he created the irresistible sylph who was to inspire Lortzing's opera *Undine*.

Immediately following the Napoleonic wars one of the best lyric writers of the century emerged—the Silesian Joseph Baron von Eichendorff (1788–1857). Nature and God were his unfailing inspirations. Among his chief works were *Ahnung und Gegenwart (Presentiment and the Present,* 1815*)*, which was a Stygian novel about the disillusionments of urban life, and his exquisitely melodic *Das zerbrochene Ringlein (The Little, Broken Ring)*, which inspired Franz Schubert's song of the same name.

Nobody better exemplified the contemporary appetite for the weird, magical, and occult than did the highly imaginative short story writer E. T. A. Hoffmann (1776–1822). His *Phantasiestücke (Tales of Fantasy,* 1814*)* are a mosaic of horror and supernaturalism. A precursor of Edgar Allen Poe, to whom, however, he was inferior, Hoffmann is remembered for many a grisly thriller (e.g., *The Devil's Elixir,* 1816, *Nocturnes,* 1817, and *The Mysterious Guest,* 1819), but also for the poignant *Märchen*, which were to inspire Jacques Offenbach's operetta *The Tales of Hoffmann*.

Literature and Drama:
The Indian Summer of Romanticism

Following Hoffmann's death in 1822, the last and, in some ways, loveliest roses of romanticism bloomed. High on the list of the latter-day devotees of the fading fairy world was Ludwig Uhland (1787–1862). A poet of the Swabian school to which Johann P. Hebel (1760–1826) belonged, Uhland was the most popular ballad writer of the pre-Biedermeier period. Among his best-known works were an anthology of *Old High and Low German Folk Songs* and such widely recited poems as ''Des Sängers Fluch'' (''The Curse of the Minstrel'') and ''Der gute Kamerad'' (''The Good Comrade''). Nearly as popular was Wilhelm Müller (1794–1827), who wrote such far-famed ballads *(Lieder)* as ''Die schöne Müllerin'' (''The Fair Maid of the Mill'') and ''Das Wandern ist des Müllers Lust'' (''To Wander is the Miller's Joy'').

In this Indian summer of romanticism Eichendorff also wrote his finest work, *Aus dem Leben eines Taugenichts (Life of a Ne'er-do-well,* 1826). This was the improbable tale of a happy-go-lucky lout who had been born with a golden spoon in his mouth.

The Swabian Eduard Mörike (1804–75), thought by some critics to be superior to Uhland, and the Austrian playwright Franz Grillparzer (1791–1872) also wrote some sentimental, erotic works in this final phase of romanticism. Of greater significance was the Jewish lyric poet Heinrich Heine (1797–1856), probably the second-finest German poet of the century. Like Uhland and the Hungarian-born Nikolaus Lenau (1802–50), Heine was a transitional figure. He was torn between the world of dreams and that of reality. As was true of Grillparzer, only his earlier career reveals a strong affinity for romanticism, exemplified by his *Die Harzreise (The Harz Journey*, 1826) and his widely admired *Buch der Lieder (Book of Songs*, 1827), which contained his finest poems, many of which were set to music for all posterity by Schubert, Mendelssohn, Schumann, and Rubenstein. After 1827, however, Heine passed into his journalistic and polemical phase, visiting England and Italy and settling down in France in 1831 for the next twenty-five years, where as the so-called "German Voltaire" he satirized in verse the reactionary German states system. As he became progressively more disillusioned with an unjust, materialistic society and increasingly came to lament human bondage and poverty, he made the transition from *Märchen* to Marxism.

Literature and Drama:
Romanticists in an Alien Age

The French July Revolution of 1830 heralded the close of an age of sentimentality. The completion in 1832 of the second part of Goethe's *Faust*, the supreme poetic masterpiece of modern times, rang the curtain down upon romanticism. By this time, however, important contributions had been made toward reviving interest in German medieval culture. Friedrich Rückert (1788–1866), a professor of oriental languages at Erlangen, had composed poems and historical dramas that gilded the memory of the Holy Roman Empire. Wilhelm Grimm had compiled a collection of forgotten ballads, *Die deutsche Heldensage (German Heroic Sagas*, 1829). Continuing into the ensuing materialistic Biedermeier age, the eminent philologist Karl Simrock (1802–76) made an admirable critical translation of the *Nibelungenlied* as well as a modernization of the *Heiland, Eddas,* and some of the epic poems of Gottfried von Strassburg and Walter von der Vogelweide. Beyond this, Simrock published six volumes of medieval tales *(Heldenbuch*, 1843–49) and thirteen volumes of *Chapbooks* (1845–66). Along similar lines another eminent philologist, Karl Konrad Lachmann (1793–1851), published highly scholarly editions of the *Nibelungenlied* and the works of Wolfram von Eschenbach, Hartmann von Aue, and Walter von der Vogelweide. With such wine-red pigments the romantic literati hoped to relieve the drab colors in the landscape painted by the rising realist school.

The Social Sciences: Philology

During the brief span between 1815 and 1830 romanticism set in motion the machinery of research that put social studies on a scientific basis.

In comparative philology Baron Wilhelm von Humboldt did the most important spade work. His penetrating treatises on the Basques, the language of Java, and the relationship of the differences in language structure to the ethos of a people were milestones in the development of linguistics. Wilhelm Grimm and August von Schlegel likewise helped found comparative philology by their research into Oriental linguistic origins, especially as respects Sanskrit.

In German philology the achievement was even more impressive. Here the most noteworthy scholars were: Konrad Lachmann, who practically founded the study of the variants of medieval German as well as modern philological criticism, Friedrich Beneke (1798–1854) of the universities of Göttingen and Berlin, Friedrich Creuzer (1771–1858), of the universities of Marburg and Heidelberg, and Johann Christian Heyse (1764–1829). But more distinguished than any of the foregoing was Jakob Grimm, Germany's most famous philologist of the century. His *Deutsche Grammatik (German Grammar*, 4 vols., 1819–37*)* exhaustively investigated the origins and evolution of the German language. He also wrote a *History of the German Language* (1848) in two volumes and a great, uncompleted *German Dictionary of Literature*.

The Social Sciences: History

In the forging of a scientific method in the field of history, students of classical civilizations vied with those of the Germanic past. Barthold G. Niebuhr (1776–1831), of the University of Berlin, wrote the first scientific history of Rome (1811–12; rev. ed., 1827–32), a work that was not to be superseded until publication of the equally scholarly but more artistic *Roman History* (1854–56) by Theodor Mommsen (1817–1902). Niebuhr also founded the *Corpus Scriptorum Historiae Byzantinae*, a collection of source materials on later Roman and Byzantine history. At the same time August Böck (1785–1867), professor of Greek philology at Heidelberg, did for Greece what Niebuhr had assayed for Rome. Böck also created the *Corpus Inscriptionum Graecarum*, a collection of more than 10,000 Greek epigraphs and documents. This project, financed by the Prussian Academy, put Hellenic studies on a solid basis. Karl Otfried Müller (1797–1840), a professor at Göttingen, wrote extensively upon Greek, Macedonian, and Etruscan history.

The great revival in German medieval studies was preceded by studies of the evolution of law. The founder of the historical school of law was a young conservative who taught at Göttingen, Karl Friedrich Eichhorn (1781–1854). He pioneered at the age of twenty-seven with a *History of German Law and Institutions* (1808), which presented law as the product of the interaction of cultural, economic, and political factors in a nation's life. Perhaps of even more importance was the work of the erudite Friedrich Karl von Savigny (1779–1861), a Prussian jurist and professor at Berlin. In his *The History of Roman Law in the Middle Ages* (6 vols., 1815–31) he established the relationship of public law to the political evolution of Germany. In a work of his mature years, *The System of Contemporary Roman Law* (8 vols., 1840–49), Savigny meticulously explored the persistence of elements of medieval customary and Roman law in modern corporative and public law.

The reconstruction of medieval German history was aided by Stein, who in collaboration with Heinrich Pertz (1795–1876), founded the *Monumenta Germaniae Historica* (1823–73), the most ambitious historical undertaking ever to be attempted in Germany. Stein's "finest legacy to the German people," the *Monumenta* was carried to completion by Pertz after the statesman-historian's death. Source materials from the Holy Roman imperial chancellery were also assembled and published as the *Regesta* by J. F. Böhmer (1795–1863).

The labors of Stein, Pertz, and Böhmer made possible the writing of systematic histories of medieval Germany by other historians. Friedrich Ludwig von Raumer (1781–1873), a progressive nationalist, achieved what was for long the definitive, integrated history of the Hohenstaufen dynasty, *The History of the Hohenstaufen and their Times* (6 vols., 1823–25). Adolf Harald Stenzel (1792–1854) wrote *A History of Germany under the Franconian Emperors* (1827–28). Heinrich Luden, a professor at Jena, who sought the genesis of the contemporary German mind in the medieval past, is best remembered for his nationalistic but syncretized *History of the German People* (12 vols., 1825–27). Luden's achievement was narrowly outtrumped by Friedrich Christoph Schlosser (1776–1861), a professor at Heidelberg, who wrote a mighty nineteen-volume, romantic-scientific *Universal History for the German Nation*, 1843–57).

Applying the newly devised, rigorous methods of his profession to early modern history, Ludwig Häusser (1818–67), a student of Schlosser and like him a professor at Heidelberg, systematically explored the age of Luther in the *History of the Era of the Reformation, 1517–1648*, which was posthumously published in 1868. This study laid the foundations for the greater work by Ranke. Häusser also contributed an important study on recent history, *A History of Germany from the Death of Frederick the Great to the Foundation of the German Confederation* (1845–57), which evaluated the impact of French revolutionary influences upon German life.

The Social Sciences: Ranke

While it is impossible for an historian to achieve absolute objectivity, even if this were desirable, it is a fact that no man in the nineteenth century did more to propagate the critical, heuristic method of Niebuhr and Böck than Leopold von Ranke (1795–1886). Universally esteemed as the foremost German historian of modern times, Ranke wrote more than fifty volumes of history and made many important contributions to historiography. A conservative monarchist who at first firmly believed in the polycentrist and corporative constitution of Germany and was suspicious of all schemes to unify it, Ranke gradually evolved toward a more realistic nationalism. An admirer of Prussian efficiency, he was rewarded in 1841 with the appointment as royal Prussian historiographer.

Despite his conservative political views, Ranke greatly aided in the emancipation of German historical writing from the sirupy chauvinism it had acquired in the era of the *Befreiungskrieg*. Equipped with an admirable knowledge of Hebrew, Latin, Greek, and several modern languages, Ranke meticulously scrutinized the credibility of sources. Internal criticism of documents virtually dates from him. A prodigious scholar with a broad perspective, Ranke wrote multivolume histories of France, England, and the world. However, it was his *History of the Popes in the Sixteenth and Seventeenth Centuries* (3 vols., 1834–39), which rested upon extensive research in the Vatican archives, and his studies on the history of Germany that brought him world fame. The first of these was the highly provocative *German History in the Age of the Reformation* (1839–47), a work supported by copious documentation from the proceedings of the Reichstag. An only less significant opus was Ranke's *Prussian History* (3 vols., 1852–61). While all of Ranke's mature narratives achieved a felicitous wedding of art and science, his Reformation and Prussian histories are noteworthy for their character portraits, lofty rhetoric, erudition, and keen analyses of the interrelationship of ideas and environment.

Philosophy: The Sequel to Kant

Germany's profound influence over higher thought in the period 1800–1860 was largely due to the immense reputation of Kant and his three great successors—Fichte, Hegel, and Schopenhauer. After Kant, German philosophy consciously strove, as did Goethe in literature, for an integral synthesis of mind and matter. Fichte, K. C. Krause (1781–1832), J. B. Herbart (1776–1841), and J. C. Fries (1773–1843) strove to found Kantian-idealist, unifying systems.

Fichte, the son of a Saxon ribbon maker, was the foreloper of romantic philosophy. Among his more important philosophic works were *Über den Begriff der Wissenschaftslehre (Concerning the Concept of the Theory of Philosophy*, 1794) and *Die Bestimmung des Menschen (The Destiny of Man*, 1800). The theory of epistemology of this savant, who was successively professor at Jena and Berlin, embraced the proposition that reality is but the symbol of thought and that all mental activity is stimulated by the transcendental ego. He maintained that all philosophy could be reduced to a struggle between dogmatism (materialism) and idealism. Fichte insisted that all knowledge has its beginning in a solipsist indulgence of the self-ego expressed in terms of an irresistible impulse to action. His devotion to epistemological and practical unity also led him to exalt duty. For him spiritual peace and self-regard can only be attained when the individual's natural impulses are governed in a civilized way by the conscience he inherits from the Infinite Ego or World Spirit.

Fichte's law of development, modified by Hegel, sired Marxian dialectical materialism. Fichte postulated an eternal process by which recurring syntheses of the Self-Ego and the external Non-Ego take place. The former he called the thesis, and the latter, the anti-thesis. Each synthesis becomes in time a new thesis and the starting point for another struggle ending in a composition of opposites.

Perhaps the most important interpreter of the romantic mentality was Friedrich Wilhelm von Schelling (1775–1854), successively professor of philosophy at Jena, Würzburg, and Berlin and the creator of the "philosophy of identity."

Schelling was certain that nature in all of its infinite variety was but the expression of the Divine Spirit. In an early work, *System des Transzendentalen Idealismus (Systems of Transcendental Idealism*, 1800), he hypothecated a communion between man and nature or mind and matter. He argued that these categories constituted so unstable a duality that they must be basically identical. After 1804 Schelling moved away from his philosophy of identity toward mysticism. He then came to embrace the belief, set forth in two pietistic works, *Philosophy and Religion* (1804) and *Untersuchungen über das Wesen der menschlichen Freiheit (Inquiries into the Essence of Human Freedom*, 1809), that God, love, and atonement were the primal realities of the cosmos.

Philosophy: Hegel

The task Hegel accomplished in his time was almost as impressive as those achieved by Thomas Aquinas or Christian von Wolff in theirs. Hegel shaped nineteenth-century thought to such a degree that no later philosophy could escape coming to grips with his system.

In several ponderous works, such as *Die Phänomenologie des Geistes (The Phenomenology of the Mind*, 1807), *Wissenschaft der Logik (Science of Logic*, 3 vols., 1812–16), and *Grundlinien der Philosophie des Rechts (Fundaments of a Philosophy of Law*, 1821), Hegel expounded a philosophy that was at once idealist and rational. He invested the cosmos with an Infinite Spirit (the Absolute or *Logos*), who was not the creator of reality but embraced all being and mind. Indeed, like the pantheists, Hegel believed that in a profound sense reality and thought are the same. He regarded ideas and objective concretions as merely modes of the *Logos*, which were subject to universal laws.

Although Hegel's syncretic philosophy was as unscientific as Schelling's, it discovered in causality the key for which philosophers since Leibniz had been searching: every force in the universe is profoundly dependent upon and in turn conditions every other. Expressed in historical semantics, each stage of society originates in the womb of its predecessor. Mind and reality are always evolving toward ever higher planes of consciousness of the Infinite Idea. He described the genetic process as the "dialectic," a triadic concept that had been suggested by Fichte's antithetic method. One of Hegel's more obvious yet provocative ideas was that it is in the prime of an institution or a civilization that decline, which leads to negation, sets in. He was convinced that every category of mind and reality—law, morality, religion, art, politics—evolves continuously, in keeping with the triadic dialectic, toward higher phases of the Divine Idea. From this standpoint all human history is but the story of the succession of dominant states endowed with ever greater resources of strength and culture. Romantic nationalists inferred from this that German civilization would be the next dominant one to emerge.

Philosophy: Schopenhauer

Whereas Hegel had sought in mind the ultimate reality, Arthur Schopenhauer (1788–1860), a bachelor and a despondent recluse, believed it lay in will. Schopenhauer's lucid and logical idealistic constructions were exceedingly difficult to demolish. Like his predecessors, he tried to deduce all things from a primal principle. Consequently he was always haunted by the fact that he could never satisfactorily explain how conflict and union could be engendered by the same universal *Logos*. In his two main works, *Die Welt als Wille und Vorstellung (The World as Will and Idea*, 1819) and *Über den Willen in der Natur (Concerning Will in Nature*, 1836), he set forth the view that the universe was structurally pure Idea, and nothing but ideas exist. He agreed with Fichte that mind itself was but a mode of will, which is the motivating force of all activity. The individual manifestation of will is but an alienation of the World Will, the original phenomenon *(Urphänomen)*. The progenitor of all late nineteenth-century philosophies of gloom and cataclysm, Schopenhauer was obsessed with sorrow and suffering, which he attributed to a conflict of individual wills in a bitter, unremitting struggle for existence. Obviously Schopenhauer heavily influenced Nietzsche and Spengler, but he also anticipated the thinking of Charles Darwin as respects natural selection. Schopenhauer's conviction that there is more misery than happiness in the world gave him a reputation for pessimism that sharply diminished his influence over an emerging optimistic society.

The Arts:
Architecture and Sculpture

After the lofty flights of German architecture in the baroque and rococo periods, little of surpassing worth was accomplished in stone and marble in the romantic era. Perhaps the most impressive monument of the Restoration was the Glyptothek at Munich, but this structure, one of the first public museums of art in Germany, was done in the classical, Ionic style (1816–30). Destroyed in World War II by Allied bombardment, it was later rebuilt. For the rest, most of the town halls and churches that were erected after 1806 were neo-Gothic edifices, neither original in conception nor in harmony with the idiom of a dawning industrial age.

Only one sculptor of European distinction was active in this period—Johann Gottfried Schadow (1764–1850). Rector and later director of the Berlin Academy of Fine Arts, Schadow, who was the father of another noteworthy sculptor (Rudolf, 1786–1822) and a painter (William, 1789–1862), is best remembered for his Victory Quadriga that stands on top of Berlin's *Brandenburger Tor*, his statue of Frederick the Great in Stettin (Szczecin), and a monument to Blücher in Rostock.

The Arts: Painting

Although no German painter of the romantic era is as well-known as Eugene Delacroix or Sir Thomas Lawrence, Germany's contemporary achievement in fresco and canvas was of higher quality than is commonly supposed.

German romantic painting was influenced by Italian models, media, and techniques, especially fresco. The most talented German frescoists belonged to a group called the "Nazarenes." Among them were: Peter Cornelius (1783–1867), who executed the marvelous wall paintings in the Munich Glyptothek and also illustrated Goethe's *Faust*; Julius Schnorr von Carolsfeld (1794–1872), who painted murals in Berlin and depicted themes from the *Lay of the Nibelungen* on the walls of the festal hall of King Ludwig's palace in Munich; and Alfred Rethel (1816–59), who commemorated Charlemagne in frescos on the *Rathaus* walls in Aachen.

The harbinger of the cult of sentimentality and feeling in canvas painting was Philipp Otto Runge (1777–1810), a north German who worked chiefly in Dresden and Hamburg. The most important portraitist and landscapist since Mengs, the imaginative Runge surpassed all German contemporaries in the romantic employment of symbolism and dreamlike mystery as well as in his philosophic-integrative approach to the world. Two other very successful romantic portraitists were William von Schadow, a professor at the Berlin Academy, and the Viennese Anton Einsle (1801–71), who gradually evolved into an exponent of Biedermeier art. Among the better romantic landscapists were the Tirolian Joseph Anton Koch (1768–1839), who painted much in the Alps and environs of Rome; Ferdinand G. Waldmüller (1793–1865), who depicted village life and bucolic scenes in Austria; Karl Rottmann (1797–1850), who painted twenty-three landscapes for the new Pinakothek in the Hofgarten in Munich for Ludwig I; and Carl Spitzweg (1808–85).

A transitional figure between late romantic and Biedermeier art, Spitzweg ranked as one of Germany's two best artists of the middle years of the nineteenth century. He was a fabulous colorist and a·felicitous interpreter of life's idyllic moments. Examples of his sensitivity to light are his "Cornfield"—a soft, greeny-gold, summer landscape, and the convivial, woodland "Picnic."

The second excelling master of the romantic style was Kaspar David Friedrich (1774–1840), who, like von Schadow and Runge, was a north German. A haunting colorist, Friedrich captured on his canvases the solitude of nature or, as in his celebrated "Wreck of the Hope," the despair and helplessness of man in the face of elemental natural forces. Like Spitzweg and Constable of England, Friedrich constantly experimented with light, the master necromancer, and was fond of depicting nature under changing atmospheric conditions. Like his peerless contemporary, the Englishman J. M. Turner, Friedrich assisted at the advent of French impressionism.

The years between 1830 and 1848 saw the gradual replacement of romantic by Biedermeier art. This vogue, so reminiscent of classic Dutch painting, attested to the social influence of the rising bourgeoisie. Household and business scenes, rustic and urban sports, swimming parties, card games in house and inn, and ordinary street scenes supplanted sylvan solitudes and poetic landscapes. Ludwig Richters (1803–44), Jakob Munk (1810–85), and Moritz von Schwind (1804–71) achieved success in the new middle-class genre, but it was Adolph Friedrich Menzel (1815–1905), well-known for his woodcuts and lithographs, who was the main oracle of Biedermeier art.

The Arts:
Romantic Instrumental Music

In instrumental music Germany continued to enjoy the European ascendancy that had been hers since Haydn's prime. Although the mood in symphonic and chamber music changed from the classical to the romantic and then to the realist, German leadership in instrumental composition persisted.

The transition from classical to romantic norms was exemplified in the symphonies and sonatas of Beethoven, although the moonflower of European romanticism was, of course, Frédéric Chopin (1810–49). In Germany the instrumental compositions of Weber, Schumann, Mendelssohn, and Schubert were suffused with romanticism. The knell of the lyric-sentimental era was sounded with Schubert's C Major and "Unfinished" symphonies, which reverted to classical models. Yet, so impressive was the bequest of the apostles of romanticism that their spirit continued to haunt the compositions of Johannes Brahms, Richard Wagner, and Richard Strauss, all of whom worked in a predominantly materialistic age. The realists and the relativists of the second half of the century never quite succeeded in driving rhapsodic and poetic music into permanent exile.

Standing at the threshold of the century like a great obelisk was Ludwig van Beethoven (1770–1827). A prosperous native of Bonn, Beethoven went in 1792 to live permanently in Vienna. There he studied under Schenk, Haydn, Salieri, and Albrechtsberger and patterned his style upon that of Clementi and Cherubini, the chief exemplars of Italian instrumental style. Although Beethoven eventually lost his hearing, his musical output, especially his piano concertos and symphonies, were of such surpassing quality as to put the whole world of music under his spell.

The genius of Franz Peter Schubert (1797–1828), a native Viennese, flowered early under the influence of models such as Haydn, Cherubini, and Beethoven. A product of the Viennese-Italian school, Schubert was perhaps the last of the incontestable magicians of music before Richard Wagner. Yet it is a fact that Schubert was unappreciated while he lived.

A prodigal melodist, Schubert brought the *lied* (song) to perfection. Before his death at thirty, he wrote more than six hundred *Lieder*, none of them labored or smacking of the lamplight. Some of his songs, deeply redolent of the German *Volksgeist*, such as "Gretchen at the Spinning Wheel," "The Erlking" (which he wrote when he was only eighteen), "Heather Rose," and his great song cycle, "The Beautiful Miller's Girl," were among the most graceful and spirited ever written. In addition, it should be noted that some of his sonatas, string quartets, and symphonies (especially the "Unfinished" and the C Major) bear comparison with the best work of Beethoven or Haydn.

The remaining chief romantic instrumental composers were Felix Mendelssohn-Bartholdy (1809–47), Baron Carl Maria von Weber (1786–1826), and Robert Schumann (1810–56). Mendelssohn, the grandson of the great Talmudic scholar and philosopher Moses Mendelssohn, was born into an actively intellectual family. At eighteen he wrote the enchanting overture to the *Midsummer Night's Dream*, and he early attained international fame. Although his balanced craftsmanship in one sense transcended mere style, his talent for melody and sentiment, which was revealed in songs, quartets, sonatas, and symphonies, nonetheless made Mendelssohn one of the most elegant representatives of the romantic idiom. Weber is chiefly remembered as the creator of German romantic opera, although he also composed chamber music, concertos, sonatas, overtures, waltzes, and variations—all in a lilting, sensuous vein. Schumann was a professor of music in Leipzig and the husband of the eminent musician Clara Wieck. A master of chromatic piano effects and bewildering rhythmic patterns, Schumann is especially noted for his *Paradise and Peri*, which was the finest secular oratorio of the era.

The Arts: Opera

German romantic opera before Wagner was inferior to and never as popular as Italian. Weber, Meyerbeer, and Kreutzer could not compare with Donizetti, Rossini, Bellini, and Verdi. The first distinctly romantic opera to be written in Germany was Beethoven's *Fidelio* (1805), which, however, was marred by a maladroitness in the interweaving of voice and orchestra. Weber carried opera to a higher level with his *Das Waldmädchen (The Witch of the Woods*, 1800) and *Oberon* (1826), but his most important contribution to this genre was *Der Freischütz (The Free Marksman*, 1826). This opera, which treated of love and charmed bullets, ensnared the audience in a skein of superstition and fancy and marked the final emancipation of this art form from Italian models. Meyerbeer (Jakob Beer, 1791–1864) was a comet who early (1826) left the German orbit to dwell in Paris, where he wrote a string of dramatic, historical operas.

After Weber, hundreds of operas were written by conductor-composers. Such works, called *Kapellmeister* operas, although robustly Germanic rather than imitative of the Italian style, are now justly forgotten. The most significant of these composers were: Konradin Kreutzer (1780–1849), who wrote thirty operas of which only one, *The Night Camp of Granada* (1834), is still staged; Otto Nicolai (1810–49), the director of the Berlin royal opera, who successfully combined old *Singspiel* with Italian opera buffa in *The Merry Wives of Windsor* (1849); Albert Lortzing (1801–51), the composer of *Tsar and Carpenter* (1837) and *Undine* (1845), an opera based on E. T. A. Hoffmann's tale; and Friedrich von Flotow (1812–83), whose chief work was the melodramatic *Martha* (1844), which includes Moore's sadly beautiful "Last Rose of Summer."

Chapter 28

THE ECONOMY

Preindustrial Germany

Until the 1860s Germany was far more a nation of savants, poets, and peasants than of captains of industry. Still chiefly a grain-exporting country, Germany was the breadbasket of western Europe. Yet her agriculture was relatively backward, being characterized by hand labor and low per-capita production. Her rural population was hidebound by tradition, subject to paralyzing controls by landlords and communes, unenlightened as to scientific methods of operation, and still largely defenseless against hunger and disease. Peasants could not protect their crops against blight, insects, and cutworms; their livestock, in the absence of veterinary science, against decimating diseases such as swine fever, sheep-foot rot, hoof and mouth, and anthrax; or themselves and their families against epidemics or even debilitating tides of dysentery and typhus which summer after summer swept over the villages.

For more than half the nineteenth century, Germany limped a long way behind Britain on the road to industrialization. Lacking capital reserves, which seemingly had vanished along with the great, private, south German banking families of the age of Charles V, Germany was at a grave disadvantage in modernizing transportation and mechanizing industry. The banking system was weak and decentralized. There was no central bank such as the Bank of England or the Bank of France, which could have controlled the issuance of currency and stabilized it or, by judicious discount policies toward commercial banks, have released substantial credits to industry. What capital was invested in internal improvements, the construction of canals, steamships, and railroads, or the purchase of machines, such as the steam engine, spinning jenny, water frame, mule, reaper and locomotive, came from abroad, mainly from England and France. Not only were there in Germany no vast mining and metallurgical combines such as those of Seraing in Belgium or Le Creusot in France, but there was practically no heavy machinery-manufacturing industry at all, and mining operations had scarcely progressed beyond the pick-and-shovel stage.

Not till close to the midcentury mark did a range of mammoth forces bring Germany to the end of the long ascendancy of the agrarian life. Then the joint stock company and the limited liability corporation destroyed the domination over industrial production that had been exercised by the cottage artisan and the master-owned, urban handicraft enterprise. After 1848 advances in many directions promised to transform Germany's economy: the destruction of the seigneurial and communal system, the opening of vast reserves of cheap fuel in the form of coal from deeper mines in the Ruhr, foreign loans, the contributions of science, and the revolution in transportation. The German Gulliver then, sensing its power, soon broke the bonds of backwardness.

Peasantry and Land:
The Continuing Agrarian Economy

The first half of the nineteenth century saw the establishment of a personally free peasantry, extensive transfers and parceling of land, and a sharp increase in the number of petty farm owners. This period also saw the onset of a drift, to become pronounced after 1850, of the rural population to the towns. Yet prior to midcentury there was no radical change in the economic face of Germany, which remained overwhelmingly peasant-aristocratic. In 1850 more than 70 percent of the population, 24.5 million out of a total of 35.4 million, still lived in communities of less than 2,000 inhabitants or on the farms. Some 60 percent of the people were still engaged in rural pursuits, although domestic industry was by then in virtual eclipse. The rural population was distributed in relatively uniform density throughout Germany, but concentration was slightly heavier in the older than in the newer parts.

Peasantry and Land:
Status of the Peasant
Before Napoleon

In the eighteenth century the condition of the peasants of western and southern Germany had not differed markedly from that of their French cousins. It is true that there was less peasant proprietorship in Germany than in France, but an analogous economic autonomy had been achieved by the peasant of the older regions of Germany as he had commonly come to enjoy either free, hereditary tenure *(Erbuntertänigkeit)* or life tenancy. Landlords in old Germany had had only lax control over their tenants or had confined themselves wholly to collecting rents *(Zins)*. The prevailing immobility of the peasantry had been less the consequence of the patrimonial regime than of immemorial custom and of the traditional organization of the rural population into communes *(Gemeinde)*, where councils of elders exercised fiscal and administrative control over them and the land.

In Mecklenburg, Pomerania, Pomerelia, and eastern Germany, where the land was sandy and less productive than in the older regions, farming could be conducted profitably only on larger tracts than the 15–50 acres average holding west of the Elbe. In eastern Germany 40 percent of the farms comprised more than 250 acres, and many Junker-owned estates were capitalistically operated *Latifundia*. Before Stein's ministry the peasants had still been nailed to the clod, and serfdom *(Leibeigenschaft)* had widely obtained. The landlords had exercised an authority over their peasants as broad as it was generally harsh. Whether tenants or household serfs, most of the rural population had been required to discharge excessive, unremunerated labor on their lords' demesnes. Virtually devoid of significant property rights, the trans-Elbean serfs had subsisted in static corporal bondage, their position closer to the downtrodden Ukrainian serfs than to the propertied and relatively independent peasants of southwest Germany.

Peasantry and Land:
From Agrarian Reform to Reaction

Important changes were made in Germany's heterogeneous agrarian pattern by the Prussian Land Law of 1794, the Code Napoléon, the various state constitutions, and the Stein-Hardenberg reforms of 1807, 1811, 1816, and 1821. As a result, the communal grip over common lands was broken, and woodland, waste, and pasture were parceled out among the peasants; serfs were ostensibly personally freed throughout Germany; estates were subdivided, and the principle of unrestricted sale or exchange of real property was recognized; peasant holdings were consolidated; and all services and renders to landlords were abrogated against indemnification.

However, hopes for establishment of a numerous proprietary peasantry were dashed by the Prussian edict of May 29, 1816. This law, while favoring the economic independence of the upper and middle strata of the peasantry, did nothing for the poorest and most numerous stratum. Unless a peasant paid a minimum tax and possessed draft animals for farming, he could not become a freeholder. Many patrimonial arrangements therefore continued in force, and supervision by the landlords over a considerable percentage of the peasants remained unimpaired until 1848. The effect of this edict was also to force the marginal peasant to sell his land.

Although emancipation of persons was decreed in Bavaria, Württemberg, and Hesse between 1811 and 1820, the whole concept of peasant freedom was allowed to lapse in many smaller states. Seigneurial and judicial authority of lords over peasants was widely restored, and generally speaking the emancipation movement hardly progressed much beyond personal mobility for a majority of peasants. The lords commonly opposed all efforts of the land-hungry peasants to become proprietors. They, in turn, denounced redemption payments, personal trammels (where they existed), and surviving instances of seignorial control over the land (*Grundherrschaft*) and judicial authority over the peasants (*Gerichtsherrschaft*). Except perhaps in Thuringia and Baden, where reimbursement for estate labor (*Robot* or *Frondienst*) was an important source of peasant income, the agrarian masses reviled the existing rural system.

Peasantry and Land:
Hard Times

A system that was barely tolerable in times of prosperity became insupportable in a period of falling agricultural prices or near-famine. Then peasants often rioted, pillaged manor houses, hacked at Jews and usurers, or reverted to mere banditry. Agrarian unrest was at its worst in the years 1806–10 because of the British blockade; 1815–16 when, because of foreign postwar competition, there was a drastic deflation of farm prices; 1824–25 and 1839–40 when there were bad harvests; 1845–46 when the high caloric yield potato crop, on which the people and livestock depended, failed disastrously; and in 1847 when there were general depression and serious peasant raids on seignorial property. At such times marginal peasants, unable to make ends meet, sold out and either sought cash wages in the towns or emigrated to America.

More could have been done to tide the peasants over hard times if easy credit had been available to them. But this was not possible until the 1860s, when farmers' cooperative banks, modeled after Friedrich Reiffeisen's Rhenish Loan Society, were widely established at least in west Germany.

Peasantry and Land:
Toward a Free, Land-Owning Peasantry

Because of the political fragmentation of Germany, which ruled out any universal agrarian law, the progress of the peasantry toward full emancipation and unrestricted ownership of land was piecemeal. Nevertheless, step by step the peasantry advanced legally and economically. By 1836 copyholders in Prussia who had elected under the decree of 1811 to pay quit-rents over a period of twenty-five years had completed installment payments and received clear title to two-thirds of the acreage they had been tilling. The number of new peasant proprietors in Germany steadily mounted. For the country as a whole, almost three times as many landowners were reported for the years 1821–48 as for the decade before 1820. By 1848, too, the great bulk of all village common lands had been transferred from the communes to individuals. Feudal *Grundherrschaft* was totally abolished in Hanover in 1831 and unlimited freedom of movement *(Freizügigkeit)* was granted the peasant.

Nevertheless the putrefying remains of the seignorial system persisted here and there until the Revolution of 1848. The aristocracy managed to fight a successful delaying action in many areas, especially in Austria where the reforms of Joseph II had long since vanished into thin air. In this agricultural museum of Europe, peasant dues and obligations were about as onerous as they had been in the days of Maria Theresa.

The Revolutions of 1848 completed the emancipation of the peasantry in all parts of Germany and Austria. Unrestricted freedom of movement and unqualified right to acquire and dispose of landed property were conferred upon all peasants without distinction. In Austria, all disabilities were abolished at a cost of one-third the value of the peasant's renders and services. The balance of the value was defrayed in equal shares by state and landlord. Peasants were allowed to retain the entirety of their holdings provided they redeemed them through installment payments extending over more than a generation. Diminished, "poverty" allotments were given to tenants who wished to avoid all payments.

In Germany proper there were states, such as Württemberg, where lords were indemnified by the government, and other states, such as Bavaria, where they lost all claims to peasant renders and services without receiving any compensation. In Prussia the edict of March 2, 1850, abrogated for the poorest servile peasants all remaining feudal rights, dues, and services without further indemnification. Heritable leaseholds were converted into fee simple. With this decree the last piers of the seigneurial social order collapsed, and the Prussian squires had no alternative but to make the transition as graciously as they could from *Grundherrschaft* with its feudal revenues to *Gutsherrschaft*, or capitalist dependence upon profits from the cash sale of crops. A further effect of the Prussian reforms was to augment the percentage of small landholdings. After 1850 about 53 percent of all the arable was in farms of between 19 and 189 acres. Until the 1870s the small farm heavily preponderated in all the lands west of the Elbe. One reason for this was that in most German states it was forbidden by law to consolidate holdings into mammoth estates.

Peasantry and Land: Agricultural Progress

During the greater part of the nineteenth century agriculture remained the most conservative sector of the German economy. Except in Prussia after 1807, larger estates were generally subject to entail and not disposable save with the consent of all members of the proprietary family. The four-course system (wheat, spring barley, fodder, and some root-plant), which involved the elimination of fallow, prevailed. The principal alternative was the older three-field system with fallow. Scientific fertilizing techniques were not employed, and night soil was still extensively and often exclusively used. As opposed to the English and Danish hedgerow and enclosure system, which featured operations by an individual owner, German farmers were attached to the open-field system and communal cultivation.

After 1815 the face of German agriculture slowly began to change. New staple crops were widely cultivated, especially sugar beets and potatoes. The potato substantially improved the physical appearance of Germans and promoted more economic utilization of small tracts of land. The Restoration Era saw the introduction on a wide scale of heavy plows, while the sickle supplanted the scythe. As a result harvest time was reduced. On the larger estates, especially east of Elbe, increasing capital was invested in new implements and machines and in the refinement of operational techniques in connection with production for a cash market.

In the early nineteenth century significant studies in agriculture, agronomy, soil chemistry, and animal husbandry were undertaken by Albrecht Thaer (1752–1828), a professor at the University of Berlin, and by his disciples (Koppe, von Thümen, Schönleutner, and von Schwerz). Of greater consequence were the contributions of Friedrich Wöhler (1800–1882), professor of chemistry at Göttingen, and the celebrated Justus von Liebig (1803–73), who taught chemistry at Giessen and, after 1852, at Munich. Wöhler was the first to synthesize an organic compound (urea, 1828), and his *Outline of Organic Chemistry* (1840) helped lay the foundation for the science of organic chemistry. Liebig, who on occasion collaborated in research with Wöhler, did fundamental work on the constitution of uric acid and the composition of organic matter. He gave farmers a better understanding of the causes of soil exhaustion and of the value of nitrogen-fixing plants as contrasted with natural humus. His experiments with artificial fertilizers were the prelude to the establishment of the modern chemical fertilizer industry. His most important work in print was *Organic Chemistry in its Application to Agriculture and Physiology* (1840).

The summary effect of these various improvements and discoveries was to increase and diversify the gross national agricultural product. More food and better diets led to an improvement in the health and physical appearance of the German people and to a gradual increase in height. What was most important, agricultural progress, supplemented by that in medicine, soon led to a decline in the infant mortality rate, a rise in the birth rate, and an extension of the average life expectancy.

Towns and Industry: Early Nineteenth-Century Towns

The fact that in 1815 Germany lagged industrially far behind England, France, and Belgium had its effect upon urban development. Because German production had not been mechanized to any marked degree and most of the industrial product still came from domestic and cottage handicraft workers, the nature and function of German towns in the post-Napoleonic era differed little from those in Luther's day.

More people dwelt in small towns than in big cities. In fact, only five German cities in 1820 had more than 60,000 residents. The two largest were Hamburg and Berlin, the latter having in 1830 about 200,000 inhabitants. Whereas the smaller towns were fairly evenly distributed throughout Germany, those with between 5,000 and 20,000 souls were located mainly in the river valleys or in the Ruhr, Siegerland, Saar, Bavaria, or north of the central uplands. Apparently the greatest density of urban population was either along the Rhenish axis or in a belt running laterally from Duisburg to Dresden.

Before the towns could become seats of an industrial culture, much spade work had to be done. Technical schools *(Realschulen)* had to be established and emphasis put on instruction in mathematics, finance, business, technology, and science. Chambers of commerce and industry and fraternal association of merchants and manufacturers had to be founded. Needed also were a large reservoir of cheap wage labor, uniform weights and measures, a common currency, more credit and investment capital, and elimination of internal tolls and tariffs.* City streets had to be paved and sidewalks built.** Transportation by river, road, and rail had to be improved and expanded. Finally, phases of production had to be rationalized and mechanized.

---

*In 1800 at least 33 tolls had to be paid on the Main River between Bamberg and Mainz, and 14 on the Elbe between Magdeburg and Hamburg.

**Even Berlin did not acquire its first sidewalks until 1824.

Towns and Industry:
Prelude to Industrialization

After 1815 a predominantly guild and domestic handicraft system was increasingly challenged by the "putting out" *(verlegen)* system and relatively large-scale capitalist enterprise. Beginning with the foundation of Cologne's chamber of commerce in 1802, trade and industrial associations were established in older Germany to promote the modernization of industry and influence governments to liberalize economic relations and abolish internal tolls and customs.

Industrialization penetrated Germany from the west, appearing first of all in the Ruhr and Rhine valleys and spreading only a generation later to Saxony and Silesia. Capitalist and factory methods of production developed first in Duisburg, Gelsenkirchen, Mulhouse, Essen, Dortmund, Bochum, Krefeld, Cologne, Düsseldorf, and neighboring Westphalian towns. Prussian laws of 1810–11 authorizing free industrial enterprise had greatly aided this development.

In the period 1815–48 reaction never achieved complete ascendancy over the Prussian bureaucracy. Although there was in post-Napoleonic Prussia, as in other German states, a retreat to medieval economic corporative concepts, a Prussian law of May 30, 1820, accorded free, competitive enterprise equal status with the guilds. Bureaucrats such as Karl von Maassen, Friedrich von Motz, Johann Albrecht Eichhorn (1779–1856), and Peter Christian Beuth (1781–1853) toiled to found the Zollverein, which was the cardinal factor in the development of German capitalism. The Prussian Trade Ordinance of January 17, 1845, further encouraged the emerging system of free enterprise. At the same time, however, this law prohibited trade unions and political associations of workers and sought to perpetuate eighteenth-century corporative-protective notions, such as responsibility of the employer for training and educating apprentices. Finally, the law of 1848 regularized and systematized the network of chambers of commerce that had formed throughout the kingdom, and the law of May, 1851, at last recognized the unrestricted right of private entrepreneurs to regulate their own production and sales. By the early 1850s the factory system had become fairly common in the kingdom, mechanization of production was beginning to be ubiquitous, and the fundament of industrial power had been laid.

Austrian conditions were less favorable to the development of capitalism. Despite the existence of appreciable reserves of raw material, ore, and investment capital, there was in the Habsburg empire, as in most Catholic states, powerful opposition to the factory system. It was widely believed that the new methods of production would destroy the worker's pride in the quality of his product, depopulate the countryside, and corrode the family. Government officials generally opposed the introduction of machines in cities and insisted on rigid surveillance of factory production. However, Metternich was at least interested in reorganizing the imperial customs system, and he tried to switch the focus of trade from north Germany to the Austrian-dominated Adriatic, objectives that would inevitably encourage the rise of free enterprise. While utterly failing to achieve his aim of an Austrian-controlled German customs union, Metternich did lend support to bureaucratic efforts to liberalize the Danubian monarchy's economy by building factories, importing skilled foreign workers and technicians, and opening technical secondary schools *(Realschulen)* and polytechnical institutes *(Hochschulen)*. However, the Catholic Church, guilds, and conservative ministers, who frowned on the pauperism and mammonism that attended the early stages of industrialization, offered such stout opposition to the advent of capitalism that it made but little progress in the Austrian Empire.

Elsewhere in central Europe the first wave of liberal decrees was succeeded after 1815 by a backwash. The guilds were generally rehabilitated, and it was not until the 1850s that freedom of enterprise was widely established in the Germanies.

Towns and Industry:
Influences Favoring Industrialization

Despite the presence of manifold obstacles, positive factors were operating to bring Germany to the portals of a capitalist age. Among the more obvious were the following: (1) the drastic reduction in 1803–6 of the number of sovereign German states, which resulted in the elimination of a multiplicity of currencies, weights and measures, and tariffs; (2) Napoleon's continental system, which encouraged sugar beet culture and the chemical industry as well as the regional industrialization of Saxony and Thuringia; (3) edicts and laws emancipating the serfs and reducing the size of peasant holdings, which had the effect of greatly swelling the reservoir of urban wage-labor; (4) the importation of British, French, and Belgian investment capital to modernize production and establish the mechanized factory system in Germany; (5) the revolution in science and technology; (6) the development of deep-pit coal mining in the Black Belt of the Ruhr and the opening of new coal mines in the Saar, which made available large reserves of cheap fuel; (7) the abolition of internal customs in Prussia and the establishment of the Zollverein; (8) the foundation of trade associations and chambers of commerce, culminating in the unification of the latter in Prussia and Bavaria by 1848; (9) the gold strikes of 1848–51 in the United States and Australia, which vastly stimulated production by increasing the volume of circulating medium; and (10) improvements in transportation resulting from the dredging of rivers and harbors, digging of east-west canals connecting major rivers, and construction of all-weather highways and railroads.

Towns and Industry:
Sluggish Progress

When fragmented Germany arrived at the midcentury mark she still had a long road to travel before she could compete profitably with England, which in most key areas of production had a lead of at least a generation. Germany remained an overwhelmingly agricultural and handicraft country. Her exports were principally raw materials and grain. Only 3.5 percent of her population as yet dwelt in cities of over 50,000 inhabitants. Concentration and fusion of industrial plants had made but little headway, and domestic markets plagued with a variety of state currencies still operated on a mixed cash and kind basis. Per capita production of the growing German labor force was considerably less than that of the British, even though after 1847 the former worked on the average of twelve hours a day to the British ten. Finally, the dearth of machines in Germany was reflected in high costs and relatively low productivity and in an inability to embrace free trade. When England, confident of her long lead, went over to free trade in 1846, the German Customs Union balked at following suit. The best the union could do was to authorize certain reciprocal low tariff trade agreements, as with the Dutch, while in some respects, as in the case of sugar, textiles, bar iron, and rails, import duties were sharply increased. Not free trade, but the Austrian high tariff of 1838 and the protectionism advocated by Friedrich List, seemed to be the proper nostrum for Germany's budding, mechanized industries.

In the main categories of output—textiles, coal, iron, and steel—Germany in 1850 still lagged far behind England. German cloth merchants of Elbefeld, Saxony, and the upper Rhineland were even yet struggling to rid themselves of hand spindles and looms at a time when British competitors possessed numerous spinning jennies and power looms. The steam-powered textile mill, which had put in its first appearance in Germany in 1822 at Chemnitz, was until 1840 still rare. In 1850 Germany possessed 9 million powered spindles, but that was still only a third of Britain's total. The coal-mining industry was even more backward. The first steam engines had been installed in German mines in 1820, and deep-pit mining began in the Ruhr in the late 1830s. German coal output soon forged ahead of that of France but trailed a long way behind that of Britain. In 1841 Germany as a whole was producing only 6.7 million tons, of which 4.5 million were mined in Prussia. By contrast, Britain's output was 49 million tons, representing four-fifths of the world's coal production. Not until the 1850s did German output begin to zoom. Similarly, low output and high production costs plagued the German iron and steel industry until midcentury. Although the country had fairly large deposits of ore in the Siegerland, Eiffel, Saxony, and Upper Silesia, the iron masters were hamstrung by lack of capital and machines and by dependence upon charcoal for fuel, as well as by the persistence of outmoded techniques of production and a multiplicity of small operators.

Not until the 1840s did coke begin to drive charcoal out of the smelting process in Germany. After the first modern, coke-fed blast furnace *(Hochofen)* was installed by the Trupacher firm in the Siegerland in 1843, it was clear that coke would be "king." In 1847 the cheaper *Hochofen* method for producing tough wrought-iron was introduced in Mülheim in the Ruhr, from whence it spread throughout the whole region. In 1850 the Friedrich Wilhelmshütte plant in the Ruhr converted to the coke-fired blast furnace, the biggest firm as yet to do so. However, as late as 1855 the output of French pig iron from coke-fired blast furnaces still surpassed the combined product of the sixty-odd coke and all the charcoal furnaces of Germany. Moreover, German output was still only a tenth that of the United Kingdom.

Another portentous advance was made when the first puddling plant was built at the Rasselstein mines in 1824. This revolutionary process produced pig iron by heating and stirring it in the presence of oxidizing agents, which reduced production time by six-sevenths. Puddling furnaces soon displaced the older bloomeries in Germany. No further revolution overtook the German iron industry until the much more rapid English Bessemer process was introduced in the 1860s.

In Saxony, Nassau, Silesia, Mark, the Siegerland, and the Saar, corporative combination promoted advances in the iron industry. The merger in 1855 of the French firm of Charles Detillieux et Cie. with the Belgian-owned Phoenix Mining and Metallurgical Company at Eschweiler created an early colossus. The Detillieux-Phoenix, with its iron mines, puddling and rolling mills, modern foundries, refineries, railroad facilities, and a work force of 6,000 employees, was the largest and best-integrated iron producer in Germany. Other predominantly foreign-owned mining and metallurgical giants operating in Germany by the mid-fifties were the Anonym Gesellschaft für Bergbau and Zinkfabrication zu Stolberg and the Societé de la Vieille-Montagne, which had roots and branches in three countries. The mainly or wholly German-owned, integrated enterprises were neither as ramifying in their operations nor as heavily capitalized as these firms. However, some of the most promising of the all-German companies were the Krupp ("cannon king") firm at Essen, the Hermannshütte in Hörde, the Hörder Bergwerks-und Hüttenverein, the Gelsenkirchener Bergwerks A. G., and Gustav Mevissen's Kölner Bergwerksverein. These new coal, iron, and steel complexes, chiefly located in the Ruhr, carried forward the rationalization and mechanization of German heavy industry to a point where it could in the foreseeable future compete with that of the English and French.

Towns and Industry:
Railroad Construction

The country's first railroad line went into operation in 1835 between Nuremberg and Furth. In 1839 two more, from Dresden to Leipzig and from Berlin to Potsdam, were opened. In the meantime, in 1837 the locomotive manufacturing firm of August and Johann Borsig had been founded at Oranienburger Tor in Berlin. Under the influence of List's book, *The National System of Political Economy* (1841), which argued for state construction of railways, a railroad boom developed in central Europe. By 1849 Germany possessed a web of more than 3,500 miles of trackage, compared with a European total of 14,000 miles. Her trackage, chiefly governmentally owned and employing Prussian-built Borsig locomotives, had by then come to surpass that of France by 1,500 miles. With a population of 35.5 million out of a European total of 274 million, Germany in 1850 contained one-quarter of the continent's trackage. This underlined the possibility that Germany might pose a military threat to France and the balance of power.

Towns and Industry:
The Threshold of Industrial Might

Seemingly by 1848 Germany was still an industrially retarded country largely dependent upon foreign countries for capital, machines, technical skills, and managerial experience. Because of lack of capital, multiple currencies, confusing patent laws, timidity of German investors, and absence of world markets for exports, vast reserves of natural resources—coal, iron, copper, and zinc—went virtually undisturbed. Yet in spite of this, the future of the German economy was promising. Not only the volume of food output but the entire gross national product was increasing faster than the nation's population. By 1840 German gross industrial product had risen to 57 percent of that of France, whereas forty years earlier it had only amounted to 32 percent, and to 38 percent that of Britain as compared with 26 percent in 1800. Between 1800 and the Revolution of 1848 Germany's production also increased 25 percent faster than that of either France or Britain.

Towns and Industry:
Condition of the Working Class

The boom period that developed after 1848 might have begun a decade earlier if the wretchedly underpaid but industrious German workers had had more purchasing power. Unfortunately their condition was even worse than that of the English proletariat and only a little better than the Irish and Russian. The English could point proudly to the ameliorative factory laws of 1833, 1842, and 1844, the Poor Laws of 1834 and 1847, adoption of external free trade, the repeal of the Corn Laws in 1846, and the Ten Hour Act of 1847 for women and children. But in traditionally paternalistic Germany nothing of the kind had yet been achieved.

Between 1820 and 1847 real wages in Germany had declined as the cost of living had steadily risen. Workers were still often paid in kind and compelled to toil an average of thirteen hours a day without governmental protection and sometimes without even Sunday rest. The gruesome exploitation of child labor (which constituted 10 percent of the work force) was an important feature of an excessively exploitative system that wore out even strong men and made them unmarketable at the age of forty. Employers, battling fierce external competition, paid barely enough to reproduce the labor power of their employees. Trade unions were banned. Women, whose nimble fingers and lower cash requirements commended them to factory owners, had often to supplement their meager income with prostitution and were driven to drink.

Factory and protectve inspection laws were either nonexistent or ignored in the Germanies. The Prussian law of March 9, 1839, had limited the workday of children under sixteen to ten hours and had forbidden employment of children under ten, but the law was a dead letter almost from the outset. Similar legislation had been enacted in Bavaria and Baden, where factory inspectors were actually appointed in 1840, but entrepreneurs flouted the laws and got away with it.

Before the Revolutions of 1848–49 Germany possessed no effective system of factory inspection, and Prussia until 1853 had no such system at all.

During the years 1844–47 the German workers moved from the penumbra into the umbra of misery. A two-year business recession swelled the numbers of unemployed and destitute. Prices rose on common necessities, while real wages declined ominously. At the same time, failure of the potato crop caused near famine conditions in certain areas. The domestic weavers of Silesia, the heroes of Hauptmann's celebrated play, were the first element of the German public to react to these conditions by violence. Long the object of inhuman exploitation, goaded by low piecework wages, crushed by taxes, and driven to the wall by the competition of Polish weavers and machines, the Silesian weavers rose in protest in 1844 in Langebielau, Peterswalden, and around Breslau but, at small cost of life, were speedily suppressed.

To darken the somber social picture, a growing percentage of the German labor force was being alienated from the land. Consequently a diminishing number of workers was able to supplement wages with income from the sale of farm produce or from cottage handicrafts. Under these circumstances, many toilers came to blame their misery upon avaricious capitalists. For the workers the *Rechtsstaat* and free enterprise were rapidly becoming empty shibboleths. A small but increasing number of toilers was beginning to hearken to the red cock of social revolution, which by late 1847 was crowing lustily.

Chapter 29

THE REVOLUTIONS OF 1848

Causes

The rise of mass democracy and the welfare state in the twentieth century has entailed a radicalization of earlier interpretations of the origins of the German Revolutions of 1848. Before the Great Depression it was the fashion among historians to attribute the coming of the revolts to the agitation of the liberals and the pressure of a constitutionally minded bourgeoisie. However, with the publication in 1930–31 of Veit Valentin's two-volume *Geschichte der deutschen Revolution* a leftist perspective on the causes of the uprisings won support in the Western world. Valentin disparaged the revolutionary sincerity of the liberals, contending that all they wanted was a comfortable compromise between autocracy and democracy. He suggested that the origins should be sought rather in mass discontent, which, however, focused workers' attention upon political solutions of a moderate, democratic nature. By vigorously advocating broader freedom and more security, moreover, the German workers put themselves in opposition to the state and dug a moat between themselves and the ruling order.

With the emergence of the Marxist "People's Democracies" after World War II, much more attention was given, especially by East European historians, to a putative working class role before and during the Revolutions of 1848. They sought the cause in the misery of the masses, which pushed the country toward a violent solution of class antinomies, and they castigated the German bourgeoisie for sabotaging the democratic-socialist demands that the workers had presented to the National Assembly in Frankfurt.

Post-World War II Western scholars, while usually conceding the importance of working-class grievances, do not recognize the plight of the masses as the main cause of the revolutions. These historians have emphasized that the German workers, who were as yet far from being a consolidated proletariat accustomed to think in terms of "class struggle," were in no position to stage a revolution. Most Western scholars still incline, as did L. B. Namier in his *The Revolution of the Intellectuals* (1946), to the traditionalist interpretation. They ascribe preponderant importance in the crisis to the parliamentarians, political professors, and intellectuals.

In the most comprehensive midcentury study of the question, Jacques Droz *(Les Révolutions Allemandes de 1848,* 1957) has cogently argued that the troubles of 1848 were the result of the interplay of many sociological forces: the despair of a brutally exploited and partly organized working class which yearned to break the bonds that held it in servitude to capital; the universal and irresistible demand for the foundation of some kind of unified German state; and the widespread determination, shared by both middle and lower classes, to demolish absolutist, corporative, and seigneurial obstacles to personal freedom. While Droz sees the economic crisis of 1845–47 as a contributing factor, he rejects any description of the revolutions as a class war between a bourgeoisie and proletariat. Rather, the capitalists aspired to join forces with the workers to compel by nonviolent means the grant of political and constitutional liberties on a national plane.

The modern Marxist view that the events of 1848–49 constituted a social revolution that failed only because of bourgeois betrayal is untenable. For such a revolution to have been the order of battle three preconditions would have had to be present: (1) a degree of political consolidation such as had been achieved in England, France, Russia, and the United States, which would have provided in a national capital a commanding height from which the whole country could be controlled; (2) a class-conscious proletariat bent on the forcible overthrow of the nobility and the seizure of power either on behalf of the middle class or the workers; and (3) a militant and independent bourgeoisie that owned the key sources of wealth and instruments of production.

None of these conditions existed in the Germanies in 1848. Political polycentrism still raised formidable barriers to economic growth and industrial consolidation. As for the proletariat, it was still mainly a vision in the minds of Marxists. In connection with the third point, there had never been a German social upheaval comparable to the English revolutions of 1647 and 1688 or the French of 1789–93 and 1830, because the German bourgeoisie had since the Thirty Years' War been a dependent element nourished by favors and commissions from numerous territorial courts, where the landed aristocracy arranged the economic orchestration. In a situation in which the towns were subservient to the wishes of the middle class and the latter aspired only infrequently to be anything more grandiose than provisioner *(Hoflieferant)* to the court or commercial adviser to some ducal government, class revolution was out of the question. Clearly, in 1848 the objective requirement of an overriding class conflict existed no more for the bourgeoisie versus the aristocracy than for the workers against the capitalists.

The relatively weak but nationalistically minded German middle class posed no serious threat to the monarchical constitution, which it only wanted to liberalize. Furthermore, the bourgeoisie feared mass violence more than it loved political power. The emerging captains of industry—the Krupps of Essen, Beckeraths of Crefeld, von der Heydts of Elberfeld, and Hansemanns of Aachen—had a mortal fear of Jacobinism, and they exercised a restraining influence on hotheaded, progressive intellectuals. The fact is the German capitalists were prepared in case of a typhoon to seek haven with the ruling establishment rather than risk drowning in the turbulent deep of the "general will."

The driving force in the revolutions was mainly furnished by the urban working class. Nothing could be further from the truth than to say that the movement of 1848 was wholly incited by the intelligentsia. But while the workers were not uninfluenced by the Communist Manifesto, which appeared in February, 1848, and by the German Communist League, such influences were exercised in the direction of a bourgeois, not a proletarian revolution. The maximalists who urged a workers' insurrection for seizure of power by themselves were few and almost without mass support. The main Communist League leaders—Karl Marx, Friedrich Engels, Heinrich Bauer, Stephan Born, Karl Schapper, and Joseph Moll—thought the idea of a proletarian conquest of power under existing conditions fantastic. They recognized in the situation of March–April, 1848, nothing more than a developing middle-class revolution.

During the troubles of 1848, the German working class, torn by individualism and buffeted by profoundly seated but vague social aspirations, was entirely unable to develop the discipline and self-sacrifice that are preconditions of success in rebellion against the ruling establishment. At best, the artisans and craftsmen were capable only of unplanned, desultory uprisings of local dimension, and this incapacity was, in the end, fated to wreck the revolutionary prospects of the bourgeoisie. Economic misery drove the workers to sporadic acts of violence and furnished the mass momentum of the German revolutions, but the pyrotechnics of mob rage were without issue. Crippled by internecine strife among the many leagues and associations that contended for their allegiance, the workers had little choice but to leave direction of the "revolution" to the liberals, who preferred the gradualist approach to democracy.

After the first few months when the futility of demonstrations and barricades had become apparent, the "revolution" subsided, broad and sluggish as a lowland river, into a mere drift toward unification and reform. The idea of a "bourgeois revolution" supported by the insurgent masses was relegated to the limbo. The next phase came in the fall of 1848 when the workers themselves abandoned the reform movement. The apostasy of the toilers was followed by that of the middle class, which drifted back into alliance with nobility and bureaucracy. Thereafter, it proved impossible to realize any one of the cardinal aims of the "revolution."

The fact is the revolutions were premature. They would not have occurred except for the February republican uprising in Paris. That event swept aside for a time the age-old timidity of the German bourgeoisie, who feared to be overborne by the Jacobins in the crisis. To think, however, that in February, 1848, Germany really was on the verge of an autochthonous social revolution is to mistake the fifth for the ninth month of pregnancy.

Scope of the Revolutions

In response to the news of the Paris uprising the first acts of overt defiance were committed, as in the Peasants' Rebellion of 1525, in the Schwarzwald and Odenwald. There the peasants broke into the mansions of the landlords, abused them, and burned the title deeds to real property. A "fear," reminiscent of the *grand peur* of 1789, swiftly spread from the countryside to the towns in Baden, the Palatinate, and Württemberg. At Heidelberg, Mülheim, Breisgau, Neckarbishofsheim, and Wiesbaden, roving mobs shattered store windows and looted shops, hanged supposed malefactors in effigy, attacked Jewish moneylenders, destroyed machines, and damaged factories. Generally speaking, such sporadic outbursts achieved little of enduring value but did drive the middle class into an alliance with the rulers.

The governments of most smaller states quickly yielded to demands for constitutional reforms, trial by jury, and freedom of speech and assembly. Bourgeois leaders were not infrequently introduced into state ministries, as in Hanover, Hesse, Saxony, and Bavaria. This encouraged the illusion that the middle class was being permanently subsumed into the ruling establishment. Perhaps the broadest concessions were made in Bavaria where the king's mistress, Lola Montez, had been forced into exile and Ludwig I, before abdicating, had recognized the capital principle of ministerial responsibility to the *Landtag*.

Despite the fact that by the end of March little blood had been shed in Germany, each class read into recent events a vindication of its conviction that central Europe was on the eve of far-reaching political changes. There was little appreciation of the deeper fact that the fate of Germany, and for that matter of central Europe, turned only upon the hinges of events in Berlin and Vienna. These capitals commanded the resources and power of two states that had by 1848 waxed to such degree that no other in Germany could hope to lead an independent existence in their shadows. Not surprisingly the German Revolutions were basically a tale of three cities, the third being the Germanic capital, Frankfurt, where the representatives of the nation met in St. Paul's church *(Pauluskirche)*. In these centers the grand questions of empire, imperialism, democracy, and constitutionalism were decided.

It took only a little more than a year to complete the trajectory of the German Revolution. Vaulting like an arrow in flight from March through early summer, the revolution, having failed to find a target, fell to the ground. The period of gathering monarchical reaction then continued until April, 1849, when, with his rejection of the National Assembly's offer of the crown of a united Small Germany, Frederick William IV figuratively broke the fallen arrow. As with the French Thermidorean Reaction, there was a last desultory challenge from the left. During the summer of 1849 the Revolution again pressed forward—in Baden, the Rhineland, and Württemberg—but this movement, like Babeuf's Society of Equals of 1795–97, was confined to the lower classes, who were abandoned by the bourgeoisie. By late fall of 1849 the workers had in the main either turned their backs upon revolt or had been suppressed. By then Bohemia and Lombardy-Venetia had been pacified and the sword struck from the hand of Hungarian nationalism. A miracle not less stunning than that which in 1762 had saved the Hohenzollerns had befallen the Habsburgs. By the close of 1849 Austria's undiminished sway had been restored throughout the empire. A sequel to the collapse of the revolutions was the irresolute effort of Frederick William IV to brush aside the Deutscher Bund and organize a united monarchical Germany under Prussian tutelage.

Events in Berlin

From March 6 to 15, 1848, various workers' associations in Berlin had held meetings and petitioned the crown for such reforms as the creation of a ministry of labor and a militia and stricter regulation of factory owners and usurers. Incensed by the ministry's refusal to grant even these modest demands, the workers turned toward the communists (Born, Moll, Gottschalk, Schapper, and Willich), who hoped for a middle-class seizure of power. When news of the outbreak of fighting in Vienna reached Berlin on March 16, barricades were erected in the streets. On the eighteenth the king had issued a proclamation from the Tiergarten in which he conceded most of the opposition's demands: withdrawal of troops from the city, a written constitution, and a reorganization of the confederation. Although the king had coupled this proclamation with an order to his troops not to fire on civilians, a massacre of 230 demonstrators, innocent bystanders, and children occurred that very day. Discouraged by the disintegration of Habsburg authority, Frederick William IV had no choice now but to identify himself with the popular cause. The terrified monarch appeared on the nineteenth on the palace balcony overlooking the forecourt to pay tribute and make obeisance to the slain, who were laid out on litters on the flagstones below.

On March 21 the king, abandoned by his brother William (who had fled to England), issued a new proclamation. Frederick William promised that "for the salvation of Germany" he would fulfill the hopes of all patriots by merging Prussia with the nation. As he rode through the streets of Berlin on that day, draped with black, red, and gold—the colors of the *Burschenschaften*—he was hysterically cheered by the fickle crowd.

Two things saved the Hohenzollern dynasty from overthrow in those March days: the revolutionary insincerity of the Prussian bourgeoisie and the seemingly conciliatory attitude of Frederick William IV. Beyond these things lies the more rational explanation that the dynasty had a record of impressive successes in war and diplomacy. Sustained thus by history and deceit, Frederick William managed to retain his grip on the throne until it stopped rocking. In late March he appointed a ministry headed by the liberal-Rhenish industrialists Ludolf Camphausen and David Hansemann, promised that a constitution would be drafted by May by an all-Prussian assembly, and even implied that he would not shrink from a military solution of the unification problem. Simultaneously he organized an unofficial cabinet or camarilla consisting of Count Dohna, General von Rauch, Leopold von Gerlach, Edwin von Manteuffel, and others, to provide a conservative counterweight to the Camphausen ministry.

The workers, no less than the bourgeoisie, were bought off with small coin. Although labor was given no voice in the new government, a decline in unemployment, the establishment in April of a Prussian Central Union for the Well-Being of the Working Class, and gradual revival of order and prosperity played their parts in pacifying the workers. Turning their backs upon the communists, they listened increasingly to moderate leaders, such as Gustav Schlöffel and Friedrich Held, for whom law and state took precedence over the rights of man.

The liberal Camphausen-Hansemann ministry tried to restore the bourgeois-toilers' alliance. The Prussian ministers persuaded the king to convene a royal constituent assembly. This first popular representative body in Prussian history was elected by universal and equal manhood suffrage. The deputies, who assembled on May 22, subsequently hammered out a democratic constitution, while the nobility fought a tenacious delaying action.

By the coming of autumn the scales were beginning to tip again in favor of reaction. On September 10 a moderately conservative ministry under General von Pfuehl was appointed. Power was now fast slipping away from the liberals, and they could only have retained power for a time if a desperate war against Russia or Austria could have been launched. Yet, for the king that was unthinkable. War would have involved him in a struggle with his Russophile and aristocratic officer corps, which was the mainstay of the Hohenzollern monarchy. Besides this, the king was jealous of his absolute command over the military and would on no account permit the people's representatives to pry into that arcanum. The truth is, he was beginning to heed circles that were advising him to strike a mighty blow against the party of revolution. This was urged by the camarilla, the reactionary jurist Friedrich Stahl (1802–61), the generals, and Ernst Ludwig von Gerlach (1795–1877), founder of the conservative Kreuzpartei (Cross Party) and its organ, the *Kreuzzeitung*.

After Gustav von Struve's rebellion in Baden had collapsed in the autumn and the counterrevolution in Austria had won out by November 1, the Prussian conservatives acted.

On November 2 Frederick William dismissed the mildly conservative von Pfuehl ministry and appointed the staunchly authoritarian Count Friedrich von Brandenburg minister-president and the brilliant Count Otto von Manteuffel minister of the interior. The king's henchman, General Wrangel, entered Berlin with 13,000 troops, established martial law and censorship, suppressed the bourgeois militia, and, without shedding blood, dissolved the Prussian Assembly on December 5. The disorganized opposition, including the leftist parliamentarians—Waldeck, Jacoby, Stein, and d'Ester—did not think of taking to the streets to oppose the *Staatsstreich*.

On the same day the monarch tried to repair the damage to his prestige by granting a "constitution." Although repudiating popular sovereignty, this instrument conceded a lower house elected by universal suffrage. On the other hand, the constitution gave the king an absolute veto over all legislation and invested him with extensive emergency powers.

The Miracle of the House of Habsburg

In Vienna public animus against absolutism was sharper than almost anywhere else. Fortunately for the crown, it possessed in Metternich an antediluvian symbol that could be sacrificed without material loss—a kind of lightning rod that could draw off most of the revolutionary voltage, for all social elements anathematized Metternich's outworn system.

The Viennese workers were worse off than their Berlin cousins. The former lived in vermin-infested tenement houses in densely populated, offal-littered districts like Mariahilf. The numerous homeless had often to sleep in the sewers, where they had to battle the rats. Privation, hunger, and unemployment made the Viennese workers acutely class-conscious. They were prepared to defend their illegal organizations tooth and nail against the police and their despised *agents provocateurs*.

The Viennese intelligentsia also had its clubs. These were of a literary-cultural nature, such as the Friends of Light and the German Catholics. However, the middle-class movement in Vienna aimed not at revolution but an alteration of the political system. Basically all this meant was the dismissal of Metternich, who for a generation had been "Horatio at the Bridge," fighting all the forces of reform.

On March 12 the more bellicose students of the University of Vienna took the initiative for reform. They staged a large protest meeting at which demands were aired for dismissal of the chancellor, abolition of the censorship, fair and public trials of political prisoners, and convocation of a constituent convention for the whole Empire. When troops tried to disperse the demonstrators, a battle royal commenced. In the end, however, Ferdinand I had to dismiss Metternich.

The fall of Metternich on March 13 seemed to open the sluice gates of hope all over the Austrian Empire. On the eighteenth fighting broke out in Milan. There ensued the famous "Five Days" *(Cinque Giornale)* of confrontation between Lombard Italian nationalists and Austrian authorities. The Lombard rebels under Carlo Cattaneo soon forced General Radetsky to withdraw his forces from Milan and the fortresses of the Quadrilateral (Verona, Legnano, Peschiera, and Mantua). Meanwhile Daniele Manin hoisted the flag of the Republic of St. Mark's in Venice on March 22, and again the Austrian troops retreated from a major Italian city. In vain did the emperor seek to check strong centrifugal forces in the Empire by promising autonomy to the minorities within it. Piedmont-Sardinia's answer was war. By May, 1848, it was no longer a question of reform but of the existence of the Habsburg monarchy.

Inside Vienna neither Metternich's departure nor the establishment of national workshops appeased the working class. Rightist and centrist elements of the middle class may have been lulled by governmental promises, but labor organizations were radicalized by unemployment and the outbreak of a cholera epidemic that cut like a reaper through the filthy streets of the poorer districts of Vienna. On May 15, 1848, a second uprising broke out. Intimidated, the emperor summoned a new ministry, headed by the aged Baron Wessenberg, who promised to convene a constituent assembly. Nevertheless, the situation continued to deteriorate. Ten days later a petty bourgeois Committee of Public Safety gained control in the capital.

In late June an unexpected cold front moved in. The European counterrevolution scored its first major triumph when on June 16 Prince Windischgrätz bombarded and occupied Prague, where a convention of united Slavs of all Habsburg dominions had been going through futile gestures. Then during the infamous "June days" (June 21–23) the workers of Paris were dealt a decisive, bloody defeat. On July 24 General Radetzsky smashed the army of Piedmontese king

Carlo Alberto at Custozza, forcing him to clear Lombardy and sign an armistice. Josef Jellačić, ban of Croatia and fugleman of the non-Germanic empire-loyalists, meanwhile marched against Hungary.

Despite the unfavorable turn of events, the Austrian revolutionaries were at first undaunted. The constituent assembly began its sessions on July 22. It registered two permanent achievements: establishment of the equality of all citizens before the law, and completion of the emancipation of the peasantry from all patrimonial controls by their landlords.

By September the counterrevolution in Europe and the Germanies was gaining momentum. An unbridgeable chasm had opened between the middle class and the workers. Working-class riots in Frankfurt were suppressed in September, while Struve's proclamation at Lörrach, Baden, of a German republic on September 21 was followed by its swift suppression. Riots in Cologne led to the imposition of martial law and suspension of reformist journals. In September, too, Jellačić led an army against the Hungarian freedom-fighters. Finally, on October 16 rioting Berlin workers were beaten down with considerable loss of life by the bourgeois civil guard.

The democratic workers of Vienna met their Waterloo at the end of October, when the worker-controlled social revolutionary municipal council, which had usurped the position formerly held by the Committee of Public Safety, was suppressed. Then on October 31 the armies of General Windischgrätz and Ban Jellačić stormed Vienna and hoisted the black and yellow flag over St. Stephan's again. A massacre of rebels ensued.

Immediately thereafter a brilliant nova appeared in the Habsburg sky. Prince Felix zu Schwarzenberg (1800–52), a grand seigneur by birth and an Epicurean by profession, was appointed chancellor (1848–52) by Emperor Ferdinand as almost his last official act before abdicating on December 2. It was not suspected that the profligate Schwarzenberg possessed exceptional abilities. But if ever a man rose to the responsibility of high office in time of crisis it was he. With justice he has been called "the last great Austrian," for it was Schwarzenberg who commanded the tide of nationalism to roll back and consummated the "miracle of the House of Habsburg." When he entered office, Emperor Franz Josef (1848–1916) was only eighteen years old and the Austrian Empire was cracking in every joint. The finely tempered, intrepid Schwarzenberg fought off all the forces of decomposition and lived just long enough to celebrate the last major victory of the continental empire over the nation-state.

Schwarzenberg's ministerial declaration of November 27 ostensibly pandered to the reform party. The statement pledged to establish "without reserve" a real constitutional monarchy and to preserve the free communes and equality of all citizens before the law. Encouraged by these gilded words, the Austrian *Landtag* proceeded to draft the Kremsier Constitution, which provided for a limited monarchy, bicameral legislature, civil equality, and a disestablished church.

The Kremsier Constitution never had a chance. On the day it was published (March 4, 1849), it was suppressed by Schwarzenberg, who slyly substituted his own instrument, the Stadion Constitution. Highly centralist and absolutist, this document conferred upon the emperor an unqualified veto and alarming emergency powers. The legislative competence of the parliament, or Reichsrat, and its power to vote taxes were circumscribed. At the same time a single free-trade area for the empire was instituted, the peasants were emancipated from the last semifeudal disabilities, and all citizens were accorded freedom of movement. These things and the customs union were lasting fruits of the Austrian Revolution of 1848. However, when there was no longer need to temporize with the reformers, the Stadion Constitution was replaced with the Sylvester's Day Patent of December 31, 1851, which dismissed the prospect of a parliament and revived autocratic government in the Habsburg Empire.

In view of Schwarzenberg's identification with reaction, a new German confederation including Austria was, after March 4, 1849, no longer a practical alternative to the *kleindeutsch* plan of unification under Prussian leadership. On the other hand, Prussia's involvement in a second war with Denmark in March over Schleswig-Holstein injured Hohenzollern prestige everywhere. The British and Russians even threatened naval action against Prussia. Frederick William IV, in particular, was so intimidated by the Russian frown that he signed an even less satisfactory armistice than that of Malmö with Copenhagen. Prussia's faux pas aided Schwarzenberg. Knowing that Russia and England had been antagonized, that Bohemia and most of northern Italy had meanwhile been pacified, and that revolution within Austria had been scotched, he felt that the pulse of the empire was returning to normal. He was therefore sanguine enough to reject on May 16 Berlin's presumptuous proposal that, in return for an Austro-Prussian alliance and an all-German guarantee of the territorial integrity of the Habsburg Empire, Vienna assent to the formation of a Prussian-dominated German federation without Austria.

The final act in the restoration of Habsburg authority was suppression of the Hungarian revolution. Russia, fearful that the Magyar revolt might spread to her own precincts, sent an army into Hungary in the summer of 1849. Collaborating with Croatian Ban Jellačić's forces, the Russian General Paskievich smashed all resistance and on August 13 compelled Kossuth, Déak, and Görgei, the main rebel leaders, to surrender. With this egregious demonstration of the antirevolutionary policies of Nicholas I, Prussia's hopes of changing the status quo by uniting Germany in 1849–50 were buried.

Fiasco in Frankfurt:
The National Assembly

Until March, 1849, Austria's chancellors were tormented by the fear that the king of Prussia would ally himself with the revolutionary National Assembly that was sitting in Frankfurt am Main. However, the assembly lacked even a single army division, and since it could not hope for Prussian military support, the Austrian government had nothing to fear.

In the spring of 1848 a preliminary parliament, preponderantly of south German monarchical liberals, had met in Frankfurt. It had adopted the black, red, and gold flag of the *Burschenschaften* and authorized the election, on the basis of universal manhood suffrage, of a constituent national assembly. That assembly, comprising nearly 600 deputies, met on May 18 in St. Paul's church in Frankfurt. The extreme left had boycotted the elections, and only a few Austrian delegates had been returned. Although various shades of political opinion were represented in the National Assembly, the moderate constitutional liberals possessed a strong majority. However, this group soon split into a right and left. The former, by far the stronger, was called the *kleindeutsch* or Gotha group and was led by Heinrich von Gagern, Christian von Dahlmann, Jacob Grimm, and Moritz Arndt. The left comprised the democrats and was led by Robert Blum. Gagern was elected president of the assembly, and Archduke Johann von Habsburg was chosen chairman of the all-German provisional council. When in August a ministry under Prince Leininger was formed, the Austrian constitutionalist Anton Ritter von Schmerling (1805–93) was given the portfolio of the interior.

The comic opera theatrics of the Frankfurt assembly become clear, as Frank Eyck has pointed out, when it is reflected that it lacked all military sanction to compel obedience to its directives. Moreover, the secondary state rulers would hardly have voluntarily consented to being "mediatized" by a legislature that acknowledged the sovereignty of the people. The Frankfurt harlequinade was already the jest of all Germany when in September the radical democrats, who were led by Struve and Hecker, invaded the *Pauluskirche* and hoisted the red flag. The ease with which this uprising was suppressed did not strengthen the assembly because the reactionary tide was now setting in.

The Assembly and the Malmö Peace

It helped undermine the prestige of the Frankfurt assembly that it had been unable to dissuade the king of Prussia from signing the Treaty of Malmö with Denmark in August.

Both Britain and Russia desired a strong Germany that could check a resurgent and expansionist France, but their beneficent attitude toward the unification of Germany was chilled by suspicion of German designs on the duchies and moral support for the restoration of Poland. In the case of Schleswig and Holstein, the expulsion of Danish troops by Prussian forces in response to a declaration by the duchies on March 24 that they wanted to become part of a united Germany antagonized Tsar Nicholas I, who feared that Germany might be reaching out for control of the Sound. Neither Russia nor England believed that Prussian military intervention in the Elbe duchies was necessary to promote the unification of any part of Germany. Faced with the hostility of all great powers, Frederick William IV was obliged to sip the hemlock. Bowing to a Russian demarche, he signed an armistice on August 26 with Denmark at Malmö, but it was not until 1852 that the Treaty of London recognized the Elbe duchies as autonomous.

As a result of the Schleswig-Holstein confrontation, Prussia earned the rebuffs of the powers. Palmerston, who privately had believed that a Prussian-dominated Germany "would be the best solution and a solid barrier between the great Powers of the continent,"* was permanently alienated. Finally German nationalists were compelled to see that Europe was momentarily practically opposed to German unification. While the inability of the Frankfurt assembly to dissuade Prussia from "betraying" the duchies impaired the assembly's prestige, what really deprived it of all credit was a growing awareness that the deputies had aroused foreign hostility where none had existed by making annexations the opening gambit in the political game. By setting its heart upon a foreign policy goal that involved the complex of European power interests and the Final Act of 1815, the assembly majority had ruined prospects of unification. The assembly majority never understood that unification could be achieved only on condition of neutrality of the Great Powers and that this had its territorial price.

The Last Straw

After the triumph of reaction in Berlin and Vienna, the National Assembly, terrified at prospects of forcible dissolution, led a despondent existence. In March, 1849, it thought to find a way out of its embarrassment by passing the ball to the king of Prussia, who had embarked upon a struggle with Austria for mastery of Germany. On March 28 the assembly adopted a pro-Prussian, albeit democratic, constitution. It excluded Austria and the Tirol from a proposed federal empire and established a national bicameral legislature, whose upper chamber was to represent the states and be elected in part by their diets and whose lower chamber was to be elected by universal, secret, manhood suffrage. The king of Prussia was to be hereditary emperor of the Germans. Then, by a margin of forty-two votes Frederick William IV was offered the crown of a German empire on March 12.

In spite of the fact that the assembly's *kleindeutsch* constitution received the hesitant endorsement of twenty-eight states, the king on April 28 disdainfully rejected the crown. The king's decision had been influenced by several things: his personal fear of Russian displeasure; a disinclination to risk civil war in which most German states would be against Prussia; and the opposition of his ministers and the conservative Kreuzpartei (Cross Party). While Frederick William IV certainly wanted to unite much of Germany under Prussia, it was possible for him, like the White Queen, to believe six impossible things before breakfast: Austria must consent to her own execution; the crown must be freely proffered by the princes rather than the people's representatives; and the ministry must be responsible to the emperor of Germany, not parliament.

The Frankfurt assembly now disbanded, and its deputies went home under the stigma of failure and impracticality. Obviously the National Assembly had never understood very well that neither the aims of its *grossdeutsch* nor its *kleindeutsch*

*Quoted in A. J. P. Taylor, *The Struggle for Mastery in Europe, 1848–1918* (Oxford, 1957), p. 37.

wing could be achieved except with the support of conservative forces and on their terms. Nor had the deputies understood that after August, 1848, it would for long be impossible to unite Germany. The Powers had come to oppose the project irrespective of whether the assembly opted for Austria or Prussia.

From the standpoint of the middle class it would have been better had the Revolution never occurred. The German bourgeoisie did not soon recover from its humiliation. For the remainder of the century it lacked all self-confidence. As a domesticated class, the bourgeoisie henceforth sought refuge in the *Rechtsstaat* rather than try to conquer independent power in the state. The bourgeoisie allowed actual authority to slip back into the hands of nobles and princes. Not only did the middle class not improve its position as a result of the gamble of 1848–49, but, as a result of sharp encounters between it and the workers, it conjured up a class conflict where virtually none had ever existed before. Many toilers thereafter embarked upon a bitter struggle against the "capitalist exploiters."

PART IX
FORGING THE SECOND EMPIRE

Chapter 30

PRUSSIA'S LAST YEARS

OF TUTELAGE, 1850–1862

The Bequest of the Revolutions of 1848

Despite all ostensible failure, the Revolutions of 1848 made impossible a complete return to pre-March conditions. In 1850 Europe stood trembling at the threshold of a populist age. The twilight of the nobility was a time of awakening for the masses. If the postrevolutionary German synthesis was slanted to conservative principles, it was nonetheless a first step in the direction of democracy. Notwithstanding all concessions to reaction, the postrevolutionary German states system was overwhelmingly constitutional. There were only two exceptions to the rule—Austria and the two Mecklenburgs.

The emergence of constitutional government in Prussia was a major dividend from the Revolutions. The minister-president (1850–58), Baron Otto von Manteuffel (1809–82), was not a supporter of personal absolutism, for he defended the autonomy of his ministry against all but minimal interference by the king. Manteuffel's ideal was bureaucratic, not despotic, authoritarianism. An aristocratically dominated Prussian diet also strove to limit the royal prerogatives. Triumphant Prussian conservatives might trample upon earlier democratic legislation, but there was no wholesale return to rule by monarchical caprice. The new order had come to stay in Prussia. Its hallmarks were a written constitution, a legislature, a quasi-independent ministry, and parliamentary control over the civil budget.

Conservatism won its first major victory in Prussia when on May 30, 1849, a new constitution replaced universal suffrage with an inequitable three-class electoral system. This grouped voters in categories depending upon their liability for payment of taxes. A majority of seats in the House of Representatives (Abgeordnetenhaus) henceforth went to the wealthy minority who paid the highest taxes. On January 31, 1850, a further reactionary revision of the constitution was adopted. This time the militia *(Bürgerwehr)* was abolished, while civil control over the army was rendered illusory by the assignment of supreme command to the king. The upper chamber was transformed into an appointive and hereditary House of Peers (Herrenhaus). But at least the purview of the lower house was extended to reviewing military appropriations.

Elsewhere in the Confederation, except in Mecklenburg (which remained without a constitution until 1918), constitutionalism likewise survived the conservative counteroffensive. In Bavaria, Minister-President Freiherr Ludwig von der Pfordten (1811–80) and the liberals in the *Landtag* continued to advance sluggishly along reformist paths until at least 1854 when laming conflicts in the diet, as well as King Maximilian's ultraconservatism, obstructed further progress. In Baden the conservatives, aided by Prussian troops, beat down the reformers but were unable to destroy the constitution. In Saxony the fundamental law of November, 1848, was repealed, but all this meant was that she reverted to the less progressive constitution of 1831. In Hesse-Cassel Frederick William I and his minister Hassenpflug, despite bitter opposition from Friedrich Oetker and the liberals in the *Landtag*, withdrew the progressive constitution of 1831 and replaced it with the less popular one of April 13, 1852. Württemberg also reverted to an earlier fundamental law, that of 1819. In Hesse-Darmstadt the reactionary minister Dalwigk was able to substitute a bicameral for a unicameral legislature and impose a three-class system of voting upon the electorate, but here, too, constitutionalism survived. In Hanover, a conservative constitution was adopted on August 1, 1866, but reforms continued to be introduced under the auspices of Stüve and Windthorst, ministers of blind King George V.

Alone of all the larger states, Austria chose to live without a constitution. The St. Sylvester's Day Patent of 1851 had abolished parliamentary government. It was replaced by the Bach bureaucratic system, named for the new chancellor, Alexander von Bach (1813–93). The Bach system was characterized by centralism and police oppression, which put Austria out of step with the secondary German states, whose support she needed now more than ever. In the end, the system, narrowly Germanophile, alienated the Slavic and Magyar minorities and even isolated Austria from the European community. When reactionary Turkey promulgated the Hatti-Humayn (Rescript) of 1856, confirming the equality of all citizens and promising extensive reforms, Austria and Russia were left as the last European asylums of eighteenth-century autocracy.

Consequences for the Bourgeoisie

The great gains from the Revolutions of 1848—equality of all persons before the law, freedom of person and movement, freedom of assembly and of speech—redounded principally to the benefit of the bourgeoisie. In the future that class, possessing a vested interest in the state, became patriotic and domesticated, refusing to conceive the problem of power in terms of class war. The retreat of the bourgeoisie to the haven of the *Rechtsstaat* was partly due to concessions that had been made to capitalism by the several state governments. It was also due to the economic upsurge of the 1850s, which left the middle class apathetic to all issues save material gain and disposed it slavishly to follow the lead of the ruling establishment in foreign and military policy. In Prussia, at least, there emerged by tacit agreement a working arrangement between nobility and bourgeoisie: the aristocracy would run the government, army, and diplomatic corps but promote political unification and the economic interests of the middle class; the latter would dominate production, commerce, and banking but support the traditional structure of authority.

The endemically timid, if not pusillanimous, character of the German middle class, exemplified but recently in the Revolution, is the main explanation of the political retardation of Germany in the nineteenth century. This habit of self-effacement accounts for the nation's inability to develop unqualified parliamentary government and ministerial responsibility. The Prussian constitution of 1850, the North German of 1866, and the Imperial (Reich) of 1871 were all fundamentally royal grants, which derailed government of and by the people. The collusion of the middle class with the aristocracy condemned the popular tribunes in the future Second Empire to sterile criticism of a government that, in spite of advanced social legislation, was in some ways to remain an anachronism surviving from the days of enlightened despotism.

The Humiliation of Olomouc

In 1850 Berlin framed a policy that was to make of Prussia the horse and Austria the rider for two generations. Temporarily shelved during the period of unification *(Reichsgründung)* and the ensuing *Gründerzeit* time of promotion and economic expansion, this diplomatic policy was picked off the scrap heap of history in 1879. Then it was refurbished and made the leitmotif of German foreign planning until near the end of World War I. The policy committed Germany to the defense of the territorial integrity of the Habsburg empire against both Russian expansion and Slavic nationalism. Germany's bondage to Vienna was to grow more hopeless with every decade.

After the Frankfurt assembly had failed to achieve unification along liberal lines, the king of Prussia tried to do it along conservative ones. On March 20, 1850, he organized the Erfurt Union, to which eventually twenty-eight more states formally adhered. The union covenant did not confer the title of emperor upon Frederick William IV but invested him with broad executive powers over the proposed federation. This displeased the proudly particularist Bavarian premier, von der Pfordten, and the Saxon foreign minister, Count Friedrich von Beust (1809–86). In late February they suddenly upset Frederick William's plans by organizing a middle German Union comprising Bavaria, Saxony, and Baden. In view of the fact that Württemberg and Denmark also opposed Prussian ascendancy, the Erfurt Union was doomed unless the king chose to lead a crusade against Austria. That the Hamlet of Berlin could not summon the resolution for this was obvious to all. Therefore, the Powers could be excused if they were amused at the unrealistic opéra bouffe of the congress of the Erfurt Union, which met in May at the invitation of the Prussian minister Joseph Maria von Radowitz (1797–1853).

Before Schwarzenberg lowered the axe on the union, he called a meeting of the Bundestag, which was legally still extant. To Frederick William the world looked black, but he deemed it expedient for Prussia to attend. Schwarzenberg next contrived to isolate the king and wrest the sword from his nerveless hand. The former, on October 28, 1850, secured from Russia a promise that if Prussia opposed action by the *Bund* to pacify Hesse (whose elector had appealed for help against his turbulent subjects), the tsar would give all moral support to Austria. Further, in the event of war between her and Prussia over the Elbe duchies, Russia would militarily aid Vienna. The British attitude was also discouraging to Frederick William.

England refused to regard the issue as one between constitutionalism and autocracy but merely thought it another round in the endless battle of the eagles for the mastery of Germany. London's patience had been sorely tried by recent Prussian aggression against Holstein, and now the British would do nothing to rescue Berlin from the consequences of its imprudence.

Schwarzenberg credited the king of Prussia with neither the strength nor the will to fight over Hesse. A Frederick the Great might have chosen Hesse as precisely the place in which to entrap the Austrian armies, but Frederick William IV had none of his genius. In the German poker game of November, 1850, clubs were trump, and these, Schwarzenberg knew, were all in Austria's hand. Prussia was too weak to fight, would have all major German states against her, and would be forced to reckon with the probability of an Austro-Russian alliance. Besides all this, the king had already revealed the weakness of his hand, for on November 2 he had replaced the bellicose Radowitz at the foreign office with the compromise-minded Manteuffel, who also headed the ministry.

Manteuffel was the one-eyed man in the kingdom of the blind. He dimly perceived that confronted with a menacing Russia and a deceitful France, Prussia had to give in to an Austria that was prepared to fight for the confederation. When, therefore, Vienna sent an ultimatum to Berlin to comply with the orders of the Bundestag as respects Hesse, Manteuffel sadly went to Canossa. He had no alternative in view of the fact that the king, the camarilla, and most of the high army brass were determined to preserve the friendship of Russia.

At Olomouc (Olmütz) in Bohemia on November 26, 1850, Prussia conceded most of Schwarzenberg's demands. She abandoned the Erfurt Union and acquiesced in the restoration of the *Bund* under Habsburg presidency, which in effect meant thrusting Germany under the claws of the Austrian eagle. The only pill Prussia refused to swallow was the demand, which Schwarzenberg let drop, that Austria's non-German territories be included in the confederation. Then on May 16, 1851, Prussia signed another convention with Austria, guaranteeing all their possessions against external or revolutionary threats. This provision was valueless to Prussia, which was in no danger.

The Honeymoon and the Customs Cloud

Almost from the outset the Austro-Prussian shotgun marriage was troubled by many disputes. These were aired in the diet of the *Bund*. Dominating all others was that related to the efforts of Schwarzenberg and the Austrian minister of commerce, Baron Karl Ludwig von Bruck (1798–1860), to build a Habsburg-dominated customs union. However, Schwarzenberg's death (April 5, 1852) ruined all efforts to destroy the Zollverein, and there was nothing for Austria to do but sign a six-year trade agreement in February, 1853, with Prussia. On April 14 the Zollverein treaties were renewed for twelve more years. On the other hand, Prussia had not been able to free itself from the political tutelage of Austria, and the trade dispute had left behind an ominous residue of irritation and Hohenzollern-Habsburg rivalry.

The Crimean War: A Turning
Point in German History

The repercussions of foreign policy decisions taken in the 1850s were to prove decisive for the outcome of the struggle for the mastery of Germany. These decisions affected the whole field of Austro-German relations.

Animated by the obsession that Russian aggrandizement in the Balkans and at the Straits would be the death of the Habsburg empire, Count Karl von Buol Schauenstein (1797–1865), Schwarzenberg's successor in the years 1852–59, riveted his attention upon a project for forming a consortium of the western powers and Austria against Russia. This contravened the Germanic postulates of the Bach system and made it impossible to maintain the time-tested entente of the three conservative powers.

That Austria was being compelled by emerging capitalist competition to penetrate an area that lay astride the path of Russian expansion toward Constantinople was her misfortune, not her fault: Austria had neither a vast hinterland in which to spread out nor an overseas empire to exploit. Nevertheless, by assigning imperialist aims top priority, she unwittingly cleared the arena for a new alignment of powers that was to deal the coup de grace to the Habsburg empire.

It had been a grave error for Schwarzenberg to have insisted upon his pound of flesh at Olomouc. He had acted as if Austria would never need a friend tomorrow. Prussia's humiliation had been needlessly thorough, and it would have been naïve for Vienna to expect her now to aid her blackmailer in a war against Russia. On the other hand, if the Russian drive to the Straits were to be forcibly opposed by Austria, she could not afford to run the risk of a flank attack by a vengeful Prussia, whose officer corps favored alliance with the Romanov empire. Buol barely managed to extort a purely defensive alliance (April 20, 1854) from Prussia. Even this was only possible because Frederick William IV and his legislature were convinced the Russians would not attack in the Balkans. In any case, the Prussians had inserted an escape clause in the convention: their narrowly delimited obligations were to become *nul et non avenu* if Austria made an alliance with any western power. Austria herself tore up the pact with Prussia when on December 22, 1854, an Austro-French convention was signed, envisaging military cooperation in both the Near East and Italy. It has been argued that behind this maladroit move lay an immoral plan to force Prussia to disgorge Silesia, restore Saxony, and cede the Rhineland to France. If this is so, Buol deserves an honored place in the Hohenzollern Valhalla. Whatever the truth respecting the Rhineland, it is clear that Vienna's act relieved Prussia of any obligation other than neutrality for the rest of the Crimean War.

This was, in fact, the advice given to his king by Otto von Bismarck-Schönhausen (1815–98), Prussia's representative at the Bundestag in Frankfurt. From having been a vociferous supporter of the conservative Austro-Prussian alignment in 1850–51, Bismarck had by 1854 done an about-face. He may have done so because of his personal contempt for the Austrian plenipotentiary to the Bundestag, Freiherr Prokesch von Osten, whom he reviled as an "Armenian" and a "mouse-trap peddler" and believed capable of every oriental treachery that had ever been conceived and some that hadn't. More probably Bismarck had by 1854 discovered that Manteuffel's Olomouc agreement had sacrificed Prussia's vital interests. Whatever the reason, Bismarck had formed the conclusion that the Crimean War afforded a rare opportunity to cut the apron strings that tied Berlin to Vienna. The Prussian diet concurred with this view. Thus, when Buol on December 15, 1855, threatened to join the war of England, France, and Piedmont-Sardinia against Russia unless she accepted Allied terms, Prussia stood aside and let things take their course.

It may be that in forcing the tsar to end the war, which he did on February 1, 1856, Buol was guided by other than Balkan considerations, such as the liberation movement in Italy. Nevertheless, the tsar judged Austria to be an ingrate, whereas he concluded that Prussia's attitude throughout the war had been correct.*

Vienna had managed by her myopic policy to incur the enmity of the one power that had consistently favored maintaining the status quo in central Europe and had been prepared to fight to prevent German unification. By alienating Russia, Vienna prepared the way for a diplomatic revolution. Within a decade it was appreciated that Austria had not lost the Austro-Prussian War of 1866 at Königgrätz but at the Ballhaus in Vienna in 1855.

The War for Italian Unification

By late winter of 1858–59 it had become apparent to all that in the Austro-Italian controversy Buol had led the Danubian monarchy into a cul-de-sac. In the rapidly deteriorating relationship with Piedmont-Sardinia, Austria had found herself without a supporter. Napoleon III, who was determined to revise the settlement of 1815, had entered a virtual alliance with Piedmont-Sardinia on July 20, 1858, at Plombières. Later, France signed a pact on March 3, 1859, with Russia, which guaranteed the former and Piedmont-Sardinia Russia's moral and diplomatic support.

Sometime earlier, in October, 1858, Prince William of Prussia had become regent for his brother Frederick William IV, whose health and mind had broken under the weight of the crown. The king had been pursuing a Franco-Russian orientation nurtured by desire for revenge on Austria. Notwithstanding this, William sought to initiate a pro-English policy that would lead Prussia back to western Europe. On the other hand, he was certainly troubled by the reflection that this line would antagonize Russia. This dilemma was dimly reflected in the foreign policy of the king's minister, Count Alexander von Schleinitz (1807–85).

When on April 29, 1859, Austria declared war on Piedmont-Sardinia, Prince William announced his readiness to save Austria from France, the ally of Turin.

---

*Some Prussian statesmen, such as Moritz A. von Bethmann-Hollweg and Count Robert von der Goltz, had been pro-Allied during the Crimean War, but the camarilla and army had been strongly pro-Russian, while the ministry and diet had been neutral.

His price,. however, was supreme military command in the Deutscher Bund. Although Vienna was unwilling to pay so high a premium, she took care not to dash William's hopes. She continued to dangle the carrot of de facto supremacy in Germany before the Prussian hare until the preliminaries of Villafranca (July 11, 1859) ended the war and made it no longer necessary.

When William came to see how he had been tricked, he junked his Anglophile policy and set his course toward the Muscovite star. During October he met Alexander II at Breslau. There William promised neutrality in the event of a war involving Austria. In return Russia agreed to protect Prussian territory against a French attack in the west. Although he refused to allow Prussia to be integrated in any Franco-Russian alliance system, William had at Breslau apostasized from the Austro-Prussian entente of 1851. Vienna was now isolated.

Austro-Prussian Rivalry Again

Schwarzenberg and Buol-Schauenstein showed far less regard than Metternich had for the fiction of joint control of Germany. The Austrian plenipotentiary to the Bundestag was under orders not to yield any essential part of Habsburg power over Germany, despite the fact that Austria's German population only amounted to 8 million as compared with 17 million for Prussia and an equal number for the aggregate of all other states in the *Bund*. The Viennese regime was, of course, convinced that domination over Germany was needful to Austria's great power status. In addition, this hegemony was imperative for the Germanizing policies that Bach was then imposing on the ethnic minorities of the Habsburg Empire. In its conservative policy, the government in Vienna was sustained to some degree by the fact that the middle states had come to view a mild domination as a shield against the harsher threat Prussia posed to their independence.

Bismarck's task was to forestall any further consolidation of Austrian ascendancy over Germany. In this he was aided by the plain fact that Prussia's population was just "too fat to allow Austria the latitude she needed." He could also count on the middle states to oppose any reorganization of the confederation that would strengthen Austrian control. Bismarck knew that they regarded the Habsburg-Hohenzollern rivalry as necessary to their survival. But he himself had come round to the view, hardened by daily confrontations in Frankfurt, that Austria and Prussia "rob each other of breath."

Bismarck was at this stage a rock-ribbed conservative who was averse to opening the sluice gates of nationalism and democracy. He was not then a *German* statesman but only a *Prussian* seeking the aggrandizement of the Hohenzollern kingdom. In his pursuit of purely dynastic aims he was encouraged by fellow conservatives in the camarilla—the brothers Gerlach (Leopold and Ludwig), Hans Hugo von Kleist-Retzow (1814–92) of the *Kreuzzeitung*, Stahl, and the Pomeranian minister Count Carl von der Groeben.

Most of the issues debated in the Bundestag were unimportant, but Bismarck managed to inflate them. The most consequential to come up in the 1850s was the proposal to strengthen the competence of the chamber. In the debates at Frankfurt Bismarck constantly maneuvered to subvert the executive power of the confederation because it was exercised by Austria. He was strongly supported in this by middle-state plenipotentiaries, particularly by the Bavarian premier, Baron Ludwig von der Pfordten.

From this wholly negative policy aiming at the hobbling of the confederation, Bismarck gradually retreated. By 1857 he had evolved into an advocate of the consolidation of Germany. He had concluded that the nation demanded a resolute step in that direction and that if Prussia would not lead her down that road the fickle masses would fall away from the Hohenzollern monarchy and subrogate the republican for the dynastic house flag.

Meanwhile, middle-class liberals founded the National Society (National-verein) in September, 1859. Captained by Victor von Unruh, Rudolf von Bennigsen, Johannes Miquel, and Hermann Schulze-Delitzsch, the Nationalverein was backed by industrial tycoons such as Adolf Hansemann of the Diskontogesellschaft, Gustav von Mevissen of the Deutscher Handelstag (Chamber of Commerce), Count Henckel von Donnersmarck, H. H. Meier, and Bismarck's own financial adviser, Gerson Bleichröder. Bismarck's connections with the world of industry and finance have led the most recent scholarship to aver, with some exaggeration, that his political aims were a derivative of his economic. According to this view, Bismarck was disposed to work to organize a new class foundation for Hohenzollern authority—a coalition of Junkers and capitalists.

The regent, Prince William, had no taste for Bismarck's unifying dreams, but because the former appreciated the latter's instrinsic worth, the regent decided to put him upon ice until he needed him for quite other purposes. Accordingly, Bismarck was sent to the embassy in St. Petersburg, where his mission from 1859–62 was to cultivate the Russian connection.

Prussian Politics and Army Reforms

With the emergence of capitalism and gradual revival of middle-class strength in Prussia, a potentially strong opposition developed in the *Landtag*. As a consequence, the regent was obliged to replace Manteuffel with the mildly progressive Prince Anton von Hohenzollern Sigmaringen. Meanwhile, a group of moderate Catholic deputies leagued with the conservative left, led by Moritz von Bethmann-Hollweg (1795–1877), to support the Liberal party in its fight to achieve the *Rechtsstaat*. The rising importance of the bourgeoisie and their industrial towns was reflected in the November, 1958, elections to the Prussian *Landtag*, when the Conservatives won only 29 out of 329 seats in the House of Representatives and 17 out of 166 in the House of Lords. Unfortunately, however, the Liberals almost at once broke into a number of factions.

More significant than the elections of 1858 was the military reorganization that ensued in Prussia. The appointment of Albrecht von Roon (1803–79), a conservative, to the ministry of war, and the replacement of the unimaginative reactionary General von Reyher by Helmuth von Moltke (1800–91) as chief of the general staff, inaugurated a new military era in Europe. Moltke, a military genius of fifty-three, was a highly cultured, brilliant, and humane individual possessed of a bold and independent spirit. He soon disabused the war ministry of the illusion that the general staff would continue in subservience to it as in Reyher's time. On the other hand, no friction developed between Roon and Moltke, because their basic military aims coincided.

To strengthen and improve the army in every way was the regent's constant preoccupation. Prince William supported Moltke's plan to rearm the infantry with the breech-loading needle gun and the plan of Roon and Moltke to popularize the military by reintroducing conscription on a three-year service basis. Regent, minister of war, and general staff stood behind the bill of 1860 to increase the number of line regiments and strengthen the officer corps, accelerate mobilization, incorporate the territorial reserve *(Landwehr)* into the standing army *(Heer)* for training under professional officers in barracks, and eliminate the comfortable system of substitutions that had long sapped the patriotism of the rich. Specifically the bill increased the peacetime strength of the army to 190,000 effectives.

Although the Liberals wanted to retain the old territorial reserve, whose recruits spent the better part of each year in civilian life, there did exist a certain basis for cooperation between opposition and government. The dream of pre-March liberalism had been to substitute for the professional army a superficially trained militia. William I, Roon, and Moltke, for their part, were actually proposing to democratize the army by creating a people's military establishment *(Volksheer)* based on universal conscription. And in fact, almost all the Liberal leaders hailed the temporary law of 1861, for they considered the conscript army *(Kommissarmée)* as a ''great guarantee of freedom.'' Their objections centered rather on the three-year term of service in the army that the law contemplated. They felt that it would involve unnecessarily high expenses, and they also feared that the government would exploit an unduly long service period to transform the army into a school of conservatism and militarism. Beyond these suspicions, the Progressive leader, Karl Twesten, (1820–70) clearly perceived that the government was aiming at removing the army from the surveillance of the *Landtag* and making it a pliant tool in the hands of an autocratic monarch. Demanding ''decisive measures to restore public confidence in the Prussian state,'' Twesten thenceforth made himself the scourge of the military camarilla and of divine-right monarchy.

The constitutional showdown was rendered unavoidable by the *Landtag* election of December 6, 1861. In it the Liberals, especially their left wing, which on June 8 had organized as the German Progressive party (Deutsche Fortschrittspartei), won a big majority. The Progressives alone won 109 seats.

The Constitutional Struggle

By early 1862 the discussion over the reorganization of the army had become a constitutional struggle. A majority of deputies of the several Liberal factions had accommodated themselves, for the sake of the union of army and people, to the idea of a three-year service term, but the Progressives would concede no more than two years' service for line regiments. The Progressives perceived that if the Conservatives gained control of the conscript army, the military state was unavoidable, and the dream of *Rechtsstaat* would never materialize. Consequently, the Progressive leaders—Twesten, Hermann Schulze-Delitzsch, the physiologist Rudolf Virchow, and the historian Theodore Mommsen—set their sights on a much more important objective than a two-year service bill. They aimed at exploiting the debate over the army bill of February, 1862, to establish a parliamentary army in Prussia.

While the military budget of 1861 had narrowly and on a temporary basis been approved, that for 1862, to support the three-year army bill, encountered the stiffest opposition. This was heightened by the circumstance that the Liberals gained again in the elections of May, 1862. William (king since 1861) flew into a towering rage and privately meditated abdicating rather than eat the pie the *Landtag* was baking for him.

The Advent of Bismarck

The most recent scholarship believes that Count Otto von Bismarck-Schönhausen, who was to become the king's champion, was helped into the saddle by German capitalism. This view sees Bismarck as being forced upon a hesitant monarchy by an alliance of the military-aristocratic stratum (represented by Manteuffel and Roon) and the industrial and commercial elements, all of whom favored a *Kleindeutschland*.

In 1862 Bismarck was forty-seven—tall, erect, and built like an ox. He was a Renaissance condottiere type, forceful and truculent. Upon entering his career as a public servant he had said: "I will make only music that I like or none at all."* The distrust he aroused was profound. Some regarded him as a cheap gambler, others as a clown, and still others as a glib phrasemonger. Almost everyone regarded him as an unsullied reactionary. But this he was not. So far from being a true-blue Junker, Bismarck was descended on his mother's side from middle-class urban officials and only on his father's side from an old noble family of the Mark. Bismarck combined a farmer's instinct with a businessman's realism, strength with flexibility, tenacity with adaptability, conscience with casuistry, and, not least of all, a mastery of the chiseled sentence with a capacity for low invective.

None of the estimates of him did him justice. All were oversimplifications. Illustrative of this was the fact that the sophisticated Jewish writer, attorney, and leader of a national socialist working-class movement Ferdinand Lassalle, who was drawn to Bismarck, thought he was to be distinguished from the garden variety of *Kreuzzeitung* politician only by the fact that he was baroque, his most baroque notion being that German unity could be built on a reactionary foundation. Yet Bismarck confused Lassalle by borrowing the latter's main political

---

*Quoted in Erich Eyck, *Bismarck* (Zurich, 1941), I, 30.

plank and becoming the first European statesman to advocate universal manhood suffrage. Furthermore, he harbored scant sympathy for the king's obdurate adhesion to outmoded absolutism, for Bismarck feared that William might end by discrediting monarchy and destroying all prospect of establishing Prussian hegemony over Germany.

The appointment of Bismarck (minister-president of Prussia, 1862–90) to the chancellery on September 24, 1862, presupposed his unconditional readiness to implement the king's military program even at the expense of flouting the constitution. Although several ministers, including the finance minister, von der Heydt, sympathized with the parliamentary opposition, the king, Roon, and Bismarck were not likely to allow a folio of paper to stand in their way. They rationalized their resolve, moreover, by pointing to Article 109 of the constitution, which stipulated that taxes, excises, and customs duties must be collected whether or not the diet approved the budget. Echoing his master's assertion that the army was the ward of the king, Bismarck rejected the constitutional provision that all appropriations must have the assent of both houses of the *Landtag*. Instead, he declared that the government was not bound by fundamental law or statutes in army matters and that the competence of the legislature was limited to approving the budget.

Actually, however, Bismarck was no unyielding wall of diorite. He covertly made overtures to the opposition in the House of Representatives. He was privately prepared to abandon the three-year service concept if thereby he could split the Liberals and rally a parliamentary majority behind a forward foreign policy, to which he gave priority over internal policy aims. His whole purpose was to subordinate the constitutional to the diplomatic issue. Yet, nothing is further from the truth than that Bismarck was resolved to proceed with the reorganization of Germany in complete disregard of parliament. He knew, better than any continental statesman of his time, that he could not be right, in a parliamentary age, against a legislative majority. Hence he angled from the beginning for its support. It is in this light that we must ponder his notorious, misleading declaration of September 30, 1862, in the Abgeordnetenhaus while speaking in support of the 1863 budget: "Not through speeches and majority decisions will the grand questions of the day be decided . . . but by blood and iron."

Chapter 31

THE STRUGGLE FOR MASTERY OF GERMANY

Enmity toward Bismarck

Bismarck's first year in office was no bed of roses. He was sufficiently identified with aggressive methods already to have made many enemies and few friends. Numerouse observers, horrified at his display of lust for power, cynicism, and reprehensible tactics, prophesied a violent end for him. His "blood and iron" speech of September 30, 1862, only aroused new hostility. All Germany trembled at his words: "Germany does not look to Prussia for liberalism but for might. The borders of Prussia are not conducive to a sound political existence." Twesten, Vincke, Waldeck, Simson, and Gneist and many other *Landtag* deputies were angered. The historian Heinrich von Treitschke (1834–96), whose devotion to Prussia and the Hohenzollerns none could doubt, thought that the malice of the chancellor's maiden speech in the budget committee was "only surpassed by its absurdity."

The mere summoning of Bismarck to the chancellery had gravely weakened Austro-Prussian friendship and had distressed every devotee of peace, for it was expected that he would regiment Russia and France against the Danubian monarchy. It was also believed that to enlist French aid in his campaign against Vienna he would not hesitate to alienate the Rhineland to Napoleon III. Consternation over Bismarck's course grew when it was reported in December that he had warned the Austrian Ambassador Károlyi that unsatisfactory relations between Prussia and Austria could lead to war unless the latter renounced all claims to control over north Germany.

No one remembered Bismarck's call of January, 1862, for universal, direct elections, except perhaps Lassalle and his tiny group of working-class followers, when the chancellor in the autumn plunged Prussia deeper into a constitutional crisis. He chose to ignore the fact that the Abgeordnetenhaus had rejected the government's budgetary proposals. Armed only with the assent (114 votes against 44) of the archaic Herrenhaus, Bismarck resolved to carry on the financial operations of the state in defiance of the constitution. His seemingly inexhaustible capacity for tactlessness, surpassed only by his resourcefulness, was further demonstrated when in December he implied that all Zollverein member states must become economic satellites of Prussia or be expelled.

Never were great deeds preceded by more inauspicious beginnings. The consensus by late 1862 was that with low cards in his hand, Bismarck could not last long in the international poker game. Clearly, his history as chancellor in 1862–63 was one of underestimation. However, Bismarck gradually succeeded in tipping the scales in his favor by according primacy to foreign affairs *(Primat der Aussenpolitik)*. In that field he had acquired almost unrivaled experience at Frankfurt, St. Petersburg, and Paris. After the successful Danish war, the opposition to Bismarck continued numerous but less articulate. Finally, after Prussia's victory over Austria in 1866, the opposition practically threw in its hand. The consummate skill and the mental agility with which Bismarck had by then led Prussia over the ice fields and crevasses of international politics awakened universal admiration, even secretly among his worst enemies.

The Play Begins

Bismarck's early diplomacy did not sharply deviate from that of his predecessor in the foreign office, but the prospects had improved. Bernstorff had also sought to destroy the Franco-Russian alliance of 1859, win French friendship, and isolate Austria. But whereas he had dreamed of a Franco-Prussian alliance, Bismarck, for all his cordiality toward St. Petersburg, neither then nor later wished to call in a foreign power to put the German house in order. The chancellor's sky was relatively free of thunderheads. Britain was distracted by the American civil war and would not be a significant quantity in European power politics for some years to come. Italy was grateful to Prussia for her stand during the Risorgimento. France and Russia had grown mutually suspicious. To top it all, the Franco-Russian alliance received a jolt when Thouvenel was replaced at the Quai d'Orsay in October, 1862, by the pro-Polish Drouyn de Lhuys, who was persona non grata in tsarist eyes. Thus Bismarck's foreign policy was not the gamble it might have seemed at first. No major power was prepared forcibly to oppose a Prussian reorganization of Germany. Austria stood alone.

At this juncture the Polish Rebellion of 1863 furnished Bismarck with an opportunity for a Russo-Prussian entente that proved decisive for the future of Germany. Like St. Petersburg, Berlin judged the Polish insurrection to be a threat to its vital interests. The whole eastern annexationist structure built by Frederick the Great was imperiled. Bismarck was convinced that the loss of Posen and West Prussia would be for Prussia "a death blow." Conversely, the Polish imbroglio might very well provide him with the very club he needed in order to intimidate the opposition in the *Landtag* and repel Austria.

The Alvensleben Convention of February 8, 1863, negotiated by Russian Foreign Minister Prince Gorchakoff and General Gustav von Alvensleben, pledged Russia and Prussia to cooperate in the suppression of the Polish rebels. The pact brought the Russian government the backing it needed to defy European opinion and denounce the Franco-Russian entente of 1859. From Bismarck's standpoint the Alvensleben Convention had the added merit of suppressing rumors of a Franco-Prussian-Russian alliance, which would have brought too many cooks into the German kitchen. Bismarck welcomed the revival of Prussia's traditional amity toward Russia, but beyond that he would not go. Indeed, he specifically admonished William I against complying with a Russian request that the Triple Alliance of Münchengrätz and Berlin (1833) be revived.

The Fürstentag

In 1861 the Danubian monarchy turned its back on the Bach system and set its course toward compromise with the bourgeoisie. Under the guidance of the mildly progressive new minister of the interior, the jurist Baron Anton Ritter von Schmerling (1805–93), constitutional government had taken form in Austria. Franz Josef's February Patent (1861) drastically modified the conservative-aristocratic October Patent of 1860, restored fundamental law, and established a German-dominated bicameral legislature. The lower house was to be elected in keeping with a four-class system of voting that favored landlords, merchants, and towns and was given limited control over the imperial debt and budget. These concessions put Austria in better position to compete with Prussia for the support of secondary state progressives and to launch a program for reform of the *Bund* to the prejudice of Prussia.

The Austrian trial balloon was launched in the summer of 1863 at the suggestion of Schmerling and of Ludwig Maximilian von Biegeleben, the chancellery's referent for German affairs. In the Austrian-sponsored Princes' Diet (Fürstentag), which met at Frankfurt on August 16, there was a majority in favor of a reorganized confederation that would embrace the Habsburg crown lands and stand guarantor of the integrity of the Austrian Empire. However, the assent of the secondary state delegates to the elaborate Austrian plan was made to depend upon Prussian approval. Meanwhile, Bismarck, whose acumen was put to its first real test, persuaded William I to boycott the Frankfurt meetings, and this doomed the Austrian project.

At the diet the princes made their assent to the Austrian reform proposals contingent upon Prussian approval. However, on September 22 Bismarck declared that Prussia could not associate herself with a proposal that pandered primarily to dynastic interests. In a *beau geste* to Ferdinand Lassalle and his working-class followers, Bismarck said it would be better to elect a representative national assembly on the basis of universal manhood suffrage.

What Bismarck was proposing was that a popular assembly should draft a constitution for a Germany in which, for the first time in history, Austria would have no place. One school of historians, of which A. O. Becker is but one of the latest of a long line of apologists for Bismarck, has stressed the chancellor's pacific intent, contending that from the beginning he wanted to unify Germany without war. Yet to this writer the facts seem to indicate that as early as 1863 Bismarck was ready to launch an armed crusade against Austria if she stood in his way. The Austrian foreign office in the Ballhaus appears to have concluded that Bismarck was perfectly capable of waging war if he were convinced Austria was isolated. In December, 1862, as a matter of fact, Bismarck had demanded recognition of Prussia's supremacy in northern Germany, failing which, he implied, Austria would have to reckon with an eventual decision by bayonets. When asked whether he did not flinch at assuming responsibility for civil war, the chancellor had blandly replied: "Where 'must' begins, fear ends."

By playing the card of mass opinion, Bismarck outtrumped Austrian constitutionalism. The slim margin by which the Habsburg program was defeated at the Fürstentag on January 22, 1863, buried the last chance for a *grossdeutsch* state. A dejected Austria drew back in alarm from the abyss toward which Biegeleben had been leading her. The emperor now transferred his favor to the conservative foreign minister, Count Bernhard von Rechberg (1806–99), a firm advocate of rapprochement with Prussia. A developing confrontation with Denmark, which involved all German states, seemed to offer opportunity for an entente with Berlin. Franz Josef, who was animated by deep, Germanic instincts and yearned for reconciliation, grasped at this straw.

Yet, was it not already too late for such expedients? Would not an Austro-Prussian entente be only a *pis aller*? Considering Prussia's increased prestige, resulting from the Fürstentag, was it not prudent to ask how long the Wilhelmstrasse would be content to play second fiddle in the German house?

The Quarrel with Parliament

From the outset Bismarck had believed that the road to victory in the constitutional struggle lay over the diplomatic ridge. His initial, "blood and iron" speech before the *Landtag* was essentially an effort to divert the opposition from internal issues by beating the drum of expansionism. Yet the positive results of his diplomacy only gradually became apparent. In the meantime, the internal contest mounted in intensity.

In January, 1863, Bismarck, with Roon's blessing, introduced a new military bill that fixed the active army's numerical strength at 1 percent of the population and appropriations at a specific rate per soldier. The effect of the bill was to withdraw from the House of Representatives all control over the military. The bill was hounded to its death, however, by the watchdogs of liberalism—Unruh, Sybel, Schulze-Delitzsch, Ludwig Loewe, and Benedikt Waldeck. In the ensuing struggle between the House and Bismarck, the latter achieved only limited success.

What fundamentally was at stake in the four-year feud between crown and parliament was not the government's responsibility to the diet but the capacity of both merely to cooperate. Bismarck charged that the House was derelict in its constitutional duty and was in a fair way to endanger the external security of the kingdom by refusing it funds. Resolved that the state machinery should not cease to function for even a minute, lest a fatal embolism develop, Bismarck now invented the theory of the "constitutional gap" *(Lückentheorie)*: if the Abgeordnetenhaus failed to discharge its assigned duties, the executive would have to fill the gap and carry on the vital functions.

Simultaneously with his struggle with the legislature, Bismarck waged a silent war against liberal influences in the judiciary and bureaucracy. The new minister of the interior, Count Friedrich zu Eulenburg (1815–81), warned civil servants that obedience and allegiance to the crown must be their first thought. Eulenburg left no doubt on the score that he was prepared to use the axe on recalcitrant officials. This admonition was not without a certain ennervating effect upon the parliamentary opposition inasmuch as there was no separation of powers in Prussia and many civil servants held seats in the lower house. In defiance of the tradition of judicial integrity, Bismarck tried to influence the political views of judges.

He also wielded the censor's club with vigor. A vaguely worded edict of June 1, 1863, authorized the suppression of any newspaper that continued, after appropriate warning, to print material imperiling the general welfare. Most editors were so intimidated by this threat alone that they surrendered to Bismarck.

On September 2 the king dissolved the chamber. Bismarck now decided to court the masses. Like the Bonapartist he secretly was, he coveted an alliance between nobles and workers, an aim that attracted to him the socialist leader Lassalle (1825–64), the founder of the *kleindeutsch* General Association of German Workers. Unfortunately Lassalle had but few followers, and, in any case, the Prussian three-class voting system all but prevented the election of a block of Lassallean working-class deputies.

In the elections of October 20, 1863, to the Abgeordnetenhaus the various Liberal factions did well, winning 258 out of a possible 350 seats. The Conservatives, due to governmental pressure and the appeal of the social program of their left wing (led by Hermann Wagener), increased their mandate from 10 to 36. The Liberals, accordingly, felt just strong enough to reject the press edict, army bill, and military appropriations for 1864. Beyond this they neither dared nor cared to go. Not only had the elections demonstrated that the Liberal tide had already crested. More consequentially, there was, as even the East German historians Rolf Weber and Ernst Engelberg have admitted, no longer any cogent economic reasons for an irreconcilable conflict of class interests between the Prussian aristocracy and bourgeoisie. The fact is that the bourgeoisie were disposed in worst case, as in 1848–49, to effect a working arrangement with the government and the Junkers, who were by then catering to middle-class requirements and transforming their own economic base in a capitalist sense, rather than ally with the inconsequential proletariat, whose class interests were sharply anticapitalistic.

The Danish War

Bismarck's refusal to adopt the nationalists' program in the dispute with the Danish king over Schleswig and Holstein at first deprived him of some of his few remaining friends. It also earned him the enmity of Crown Prince Frederick and his wife, Victoria, who was the daughter of Britain's queen. It was only later, when Prussia had won the game, that Bismarck began to climb the greased pole of popularity.

The intricate problem of the Elbe duchies was a consequence of the Danish law of royal succession. Frederick VII, last of the Oldenburg line, had no male heirs. This caused no difficulty in Denmark where a woman could succeed to the throne, but it did in Schleswig and Holstein, where only male succession was legal. To avoid any recurrence of the Danish aggression of 1848 that might provoke an uprising in the duchies and war with Germany, the Great Powers held a conference in London. The resulting Protocol of 1852 decided that feminine succession would also apply to Schleswig and Holstein. At the same time the Duke of Augustenburg, who had claims to the duchies, was bribed to relinquish them. However, the German Confederation never endorsed the protocol.

In 1863 the Danish king again tried to incorporate Schleswig into Denmark. On July 9 the German Bundestag demanded that he abandon his intent. When Christian IX of Glücksburg mounted the Danish throne in November, he allowed himself to be crowned duke of Schleswig-Holstein. On the same day Frederick of Augustenburg, son of the prince who had figured in 1852, proclaimed himself lawful duke of the provinces on the supposition that his rights could not be alienated by his father. Now the Germans had a symbol for which to fight.

For Bismarck the whole matter came at the wrong time. His hands were full with the struggle over the Fürstentag. He neither cared for the rights of the population of Schleswig-Holstein nor sympathized with schemes for their integration with the *Bund*. Certainly he did not intend to aid the revival of the expiring confederation by giving it a territorial transfusion. However, once the Danish question moved into the limelight, Bismarck sought, as a Prussia statesman, to turn it to the advantage of his kingdom.

In the race for the Elbe duchies Bismarck handled all the powers with the dexterity of a master charioteer. To London he posed as a pious disciple of the sanctity of treaties; to St. Petersburg, the right arm of the tsar in chastising the Poles; to Paris, the paladin of German nationalism; and to Vienna, the sheet anchor of conservatism. Bismarck's ostensible adhesion to the London Protocol neutralized the majority of the bellicose Palmerston's cabinet. Bismarck also contrived to forestall any restoration of the Anglo-French Crimean alliance. He divined that Napoleon III thought, as his foreign minister did not, that France would gain from a German nationalist victory and not condemn a Danish-German war. Bismarck counted on the fact that Napoleon III was furious with Palmerston for not supporting the French plan for a European conference on major issues. Bismarck also appreciated that Russia's attitude during 1863 would be governed by the exigencies of suppressing the Polish rebellion. As long as Bismarck whistled a dynastic tune and urged an Austro-Prussian solution of the problem of the Elbe duchies he knew he had nothing to fear from Russia. His most admirable performance, however, was his handling of Austria. He made it appear to the profoundly conservative Franz Josef that only the intervention of Berlin and Vienna on behalf of the duchies could prevent a popular uprising there. Out of fear of this alternative, the emperor was induced to endorse the Augustenburg cause, which was popular with the German people. When Franz Josef agreed to ally with Prussia to achieve a mutually agreeable solution, Bismarck knew the game was won. The Powers would think twice before attacking all the German eagles. It only remained to provoke Denmark to declare war.

Waiting for the adversary to strike the first blow required patience and fortitude. All Germany was storming toward a showdown with Denmark. Even the Prussian *Landtag* could not understand why the chancellor endlessly procrastinated. Bismarck's Italianate diplomacy was in those days so opaque that Württemberg and Bavaria even meditated mobilizing against Austria and Prussia if they would not march against the Danes. However, at the end of December the pot began to boil. Saxon and Hanoverian troops moved into the duchies. When on January 16, 1864, Prussia and Austria finally sent a joint ultimatum to Denmark demanding that the rights of Schleswig-Holstein be respected, the Danes answered (as Bismarck knew they would) with a declaration of war.

Using 43,000 troops to Austria's 28,000, Prussia dominated military operations. The decisive engagement was the capture of the fortified point of Düppel on April 18 by the octogenarian Prussian General Wrangel. Thereafter, only Britain could have saved the Danes. Instead, Palmerston decided on June 24 to let them sink. When the British proposed to Copenhagen that an armistice be signed, the Danes, infuriated, rejected the notion. Then the Prussians proceeded to occupy all Jutland, and it was all over but the shouting. Peace was made in Vienna on October 30. Denmark was obliged to cede jointly to Austria and Prussia the Elbe duchies and tiny Lauenburg.

Actually an effort had earlier been made at a conference in London to find a solution more acceptable to the Powers. Prussia had agreed to the Augustenburg accession instead of joint annexation of Schleswig and Holstein. However, Bismarck had been unable to persuade Prince Frederick, the claimant, to assent to two conditions: control over the Kiel canal between the North Sea and the Baltic, and integration of the duchies' armed forces with those of Prussia. When it appeared that the prince positively refused to settle for half a loaf, Bismarck resolved he should have none; so he took the lead at London in dropping the protocol. Along that path the rights of the people of the duchies, for which the German states had fought, were irretrievably lost.

Prussia's rise to dominance began with the Danish War. The preparedness of the kingdom had been decisively demonstrated, the king's army reform brilliantly vindicated, and the efficiency of the Bismarck-Roon-Moltke team proven. At the same time the diplomatic intermezzo acquainted the world with Bismarck's virtuosity. The war upset the balance of power, marked the end of Anglo-French amity, and landed Britain for two generations in the bog of isolation. Lastly, Schleswig-Holstein advanced the German problem from the wings of the stage into the limelight and revived Austro-German rivalry in its worst form.

The Gastein Convention

Once the war was over, the Austrian alliance was of no more use to Bismarck. He prepared to substitute for it a policy of annexing the duchies and of making Prussia paramount in Germany. It would, however, have been ingenuous of him to have openly charted a course leading to hostilities with Austria. William I would never have tolerated that. Nevertheless, a metallic hardness henceforth tempered Bismarck's conversations with the Austrian ambassador. The chancellor showed himself in all respects disagreeable. He even refused the slightest concession to Vienna in respect of admitting Austria into the Zollverein.

It soon appeared that Rechberg had unwittingly been buttering Prussia's bread instead of Austria's and hadn't even been thanked by Bismarck. On October 23 Emperor Franz Josef reluctantly replaced Rechberg at the foreign office with Count Alexander von Mensdorff-Pouilly (1813–71). He and his referent for German affairs, Freiherr von Biegeleben, discarded the policy of the open hand for that of the mailed fist. Once again, as in Schwarzenberg's time, Austrian diplomats assiduously cultivated the secondary states, while the atmosphere between Berlin and Vienna crackled with wintry invectives.

Bismarck's plan in early 1865 was to force Austria to acknowledge Prussian supremacy in north Germany or provoke Vienna to declare war. To his categorical demands respecting the Elbe duchies was added a new one on February 22—cession of Sonderburg. Austria thought the Prussian bill was too high, and most of Germany shared this view. Bismarck, however, only tightened the screws while carefully calculating the emperor's capacity to absorb insults.

By May Bismarck had reached the conclusion that war was ineluctable. He was, however, opposed in this estimate by the court and the ultraconservatives (led by Edwin von Manteuffel and Gerlach), who feared lest war with Austria would unchain revolution and end by destroying the monarchical principle everywhere. For his part, Bismarck refused to commit himself to any specific line of policy, least of all to strike war from his lexicon. In keeping with his method of exhausting all positions on the organ, he made overtures to France and Russia. He thereby discovered that Napoleon III did not object to Prussia's annexing the Elbe duchies provided the Danish part of Schleswig was accorded self-determination. When it appeared that Bismarck was succeeding in stripping Austria of every potential ally, even the conservatives rallied to his program, and Germany moved closer to war.

Emperor Franz Josef was too frightened to blow into Tieu's trumpet. So once more he sued for an honorable alternative. His transitory success in August at Wildbad-Gastein was mainly due to the fact that France had not yet decided to remain neutral in the event of hostilities.

With the French bird still in the bush, Bismarck had to appear conciliatory toward the Austrian plenipotentiary, the conservative Count von Blome, when they conferred at Gastein. During the talks, Bismarck joked, drank copiously, was loquacious and confiding, and managed to lose huge sums at cards to Blome without batting an eye (probably because the chancellor intended to charge his losses to the Prussian treasury). After purchasing the tiny duchy of Lauenburg, Bismarck assented to Blome's proposal which not only discarded the provisional condominium in the Elbe duchies but also Austria's original hope for an independent Schleswig-Holstein. Without regard to the rights of individual claimants or of the German Confederation, the administration of Schleswig was assigned to Prussia, while that of Holstein went to Austria. William I was delighted with Bismarck's handiwork: as a result of the agreement of August 14 he had brought home booty without drawing the sword. All Europe recognized that the Gastein Convention had been a victory for Bismarck, and William I made him a count.

It was Bismarck's guiding principle that civil war would be admissible only if Prussia could not by diplomacy overcome the obstacles Austria put in the way of Hohenzollern hegemony over north Germany. It was axiomatic to his thinking that Prussia must never undertake an ill-considered or aggressive war in opposition to Europe. Since, however, he reckoned with Austrian obstructionism, he felt that war in 1866 was probable. That he was right in supposing that the military solution, painful though it might be, was the only feasible road to unification is a time-honored thesis that has recently been repeated by Karl Faber. Believing that the suturing of Germany by Prussia would alone correspond to the economic imperatives of the dawning capitalist age, Bismarck after Gastein conceived his main task to be to insure that the Powers would do nothing to rescue the Habsburg empire. An ancillary task would be to encourage (up to a point) paralyzing nationalist divisions within the Austrian Empire.

The Web Draws Closer

In the broadest sense, it is true that, by comparison with Bismarck's policy, Austria's was vacillating. Yet, if we put the chancellor's policy under the magnifying glass, it loses rather than gains in definition. He had no blueprint for establishing Prussian hegemony over, much less unifying, Germany. To most of the questions respecting restructuring of the country and the diminution or absorption of Nassau, Hesse-Cassel, Hesse-Darmstadt, Brunswick, Anhalt, Hanover, Saxony, and the Saxon duchies, he had no glib answer. For him, everything depended on how the cards fell.

Austrian diplomacy was both greedy and indecisive. The reactionary first minister, Count Richard von Belcredi (1823–1902), believed that a moderately pro-Prussian policy would free Austria to suppress the rebellious Hungarians and restore her dominion over Italy. Yet Belcredi never offered the one thing—command over the armies of the German Confederation—that might have reconciled William I to the role of junior partner and driven a wedge between him and Bismarck. Belcredi's illusions were nourished by Blome and Moritz Esterhazy, minister without portfolio, both of whom believed that Bismarck was loyally conservative and concerned primarily with internal affairs. Confusion in Vienna was, however, compounded by the circumstance that the Prussophobes Biegeleben and Max von Gagern, undersecretary for foreign affairs, had been retained in an ostensibly Prussophile government.

After Gastein, Franz Josef came to regard Bismarck as an inveterate disturber of the peace. The emperor no longer believed in the chancellor's blandishments or the conservative platitudes that were always on his lips and had reluctantly reached the conclusion that Bismarck in the Prussian chancellery meant war. In the end the emperor's suspicions were confirmed when Austrian cryptographers deciphered an intercepted secret telegram from Bismarck to the Prussian ambassador in Florence, asking whether Italy was ready to march against Austria.

In October, 1865, Bismarck set about insuring the neutrality of Europe as the prelude to kicking Austria out of the German house. On the fourth, Bismarck met Napoleon III at the resort of Biarritz. There the chancellor outlined a policy in accordance with which Prussian expansion would stop at the Main, Austria be excluded from Germany, the two parts of Prussia be united by annexation of intervening territory, and a North German Confederation be founded under Berlin's direction. Bismarck stressed the community of interests between France and Prussia, their common task of reorganizing Europe, and suggested that the French "sphinx" might find compensation in the transfer of Venetia to disgruntled Italy. As for Austria, she was to be encouraged to seek her fortune along the lower Danube, where she must conflict with Russia. Because Bismarck's program appealed to the quixotic Napoleon, who fancied himself the arbiter of Europe, the chancellor did not have to make rash promises. He merely implied vaguely that he would not object if Napoleon reached for the Rhenish wine while William I was devouring the Holstein oyster. No precise commitment was made by the French emperor either, but Bismarck was nonetheless right in inferring that he had secured the neutrality of France. In view of excellent Prusso-Russian relations and the immobility of Britain, only one thing more remained to be done: Italy had to be ensnared into promising the second front that Moltke felt was needed to insure victory over Austria and her expected German allies.

After Gastein, Bismarck never gave another thought to the wishes of the people of Schleswig-Holstein, who favored union under Prince Frederick. By January, 1866, he had virtually decided on war, and there is no reason to give credence to his remark in December of that year to the Austrian ambassador that "I wish we had shot the deer together."* Meanwhile, Belcredi heeded Biegeleben's advice to reject all Prussian interference in Holstein, and the bulk of the secondary states backed Austria.

Vienna's ultimate blunder was to reject an Italian offer of a billion lire for Venetia. Bismarck instantly perceived his opportunity and thrust his sword into the chink in Austria's armor. With the blessings of Napoleon III, he concluded an alliance with Italy on April 8, 1866. By its terms Italy promised to declare war on Austria if before the lapse of three months hostilities had begun. This treaty violated the constitution of the *Bund*, set the tombstone over the hopes of the Austrian peace party, and removed the last obstacle to the greatest political revolution in German history.

Although Italy's defiant attitude toward Austria brought decisive reinforcements to the Prussian war hawks, Bismarck still faced a difficult task. He may have succeeded in splitting the Nationalverein and sown dissension in the Liberal party, but he was still opposed on almost all counts by a majority of deputies in the *Landtag*. He was still basically unpopular (being at this time the target of attempted assassination), and he had hopelessly antagonized Saxony, Hesse-Cassel, and Hanover. Finally, he was rapidly losing his influence in Munich, where Baron von der Pfordten was about to side with Austria.

Prussia was the first to mobilize and the first to order her troops to march. When Austria proposed on June 1 that the question of hereditary succession in Holstein be decided by the diet in Frankfurt, Bismarck responded by dispatching troops

---

*Heinrich Ritter von Srbik, *Deutsche Einheit, Idee und Wirklichkeit vom Heiligen Reich bis König-grätz* (Munich, 1935–42), IV, 386.

to the duchy. Yet it was only when the Prussian emissary, Karl von Savigny, proceeded to lay Bismarck's plan for a unified Germany without Austria before the diet that Vienna picked up the gauntlet. Her emissary then proposed that the seven non-Prussian army corps of the *Bund* be mobilized. This motion was adopted on June 14 by a vote of 9 to 5. To this the Prussian delegate rejoined, the *Bund* had just destroyed itself.

The Prussian "Blitzkrieg" of 1866

While Austria had struck a defensive posture throughout, it is nonetheless certain, as C. W. Clark proved, that the Belcredi-Esterhazy government, no less than Bismarck, wanted war. Under Biegeleben's baleful influence, the Viennese ministry discovered in the possible conquest of Silesia compensation for expected loss of Venetia. Convinced that in that Italian province Austria had something that would keep France neutral, the Belcredi ministry on June 12 negotiated a secret treaty with her. The pact stipulated that Venetia would be transferred to Italy, Austria would not oppose an independent Rhineland, and that, in consideration of these things, France would not join Austria's foes. Assured of the armed aid of most of the German middle states, Austria now faced the impending struggle with Prussia with equanimity.

War began when the secondary states rejected Bismarck's ultimatum of June 15, demanding they disarm and eject Austria from Germany. Although the Austrian army was numerically much larger, the Hohenzollern was better trained and commanded, more aggressive, and equipped with the murderous needle gun. The Austrians spoiled their chance of victory at the outset by sending their best general, Archduke Albert, against the Italians, while the defeatist Ludwig von Benedek, a Hungarian commander from the Ordnance Department and an expert on Italian terrain, was put in charge of the main armies in Bohemia.

The impatient Italians, bent on seizing what had already been guaranteed them by all parties, were ignominiously defeated by Archduke Albert at Custozza on June 24. However, Austria, whose allies had been virtually knocked out, met her Waterloo on July 3 in one of the biggest battles of the century—Sadowa (Königgrätz). Despite the fact that he enjoyed the advantages of terrain and numbers (220,000 against 120,000 Prussians), Benedek was beaten, with a loss of 45,000 effectives, by Crown Prince Frederick William of Prussia. Sadowa, not Sedan in 1870, was the real turning point in nineteenth-century German history. At Sadowa the prestige of the Prussian army was established. In that hour it began to cast its shadow over the civil government. Simultaneously Bismarck's fame was made. Benedek's defeat was, as Moltke had predicted, tantamount to winning the war, for now the way to Vienna lay open. After July 3 the heart went out of the anti-Prussian coalition, which was defeated in two more encounters in the middle of the month. On July 16 the Prussians entered Frankfurt and suppressed the moribund Deutscher Bund. The city was annexed to Prussia, but the population, as Werner Frauendienst has made clear, was treated less harshly by Bismarck than has formerly been supposed. Thereafter, the Prussian general staff could look forward to a triumphal march through Vienna.

However, Bismarck had other plans. The newer scholarship (Jedlicka, Wandruszka) has confirmed the fact that he neither aimed at the destruction of the Danubian monarchy nor the annihilation of its army. He was acutely aware that the Franco-Prussian entente was only tolerated by French public opinion (which, according to R. Buchner, had recently conceived Prussophobe sentiment), in expectation of territorial indemnification. While the Prussian officers, dominated by the concept of total war that Clausewitz had advanced, dreamt of extensive annexations in Bohemia and Saxony, Bismarck had been mainly concerned over the possibility of French intervention and, to lesser degree, the need to work out terms such as would not leave Austria, which was German in blood and culture, permanently embittered. Bismarck understood that Napoleon III, who had only wanted to tip, not destroy, the balance of power in Germany, had been dismayed by the magnitude of Prussia's triumph. Accordingly, Bismarck hastened to solicit Napoleon's mediation of the conflict now that there was nothing to mediate. The emperor was amenable on condition that Prussia restrict herself to annexations in north Germany not to exceed lands inhabited by more than 4 million persons and that the line of the Main River be the southern boundary of the Prussian sphere of influence.

The star of lasting fame was rising for Bismarck. However, much depended upon the speed and adroitness with which he negotiated a rational peace with the foe. His position in the Prussian *Landtag* was the strongest it had ever been. If he had not pursued a popular nationalist policy, it had at least been demonstrably nationalist. Accordingly, the Liberals were beginning to grab hold of his coat tails. In the elections of June 26 and July 3, 1866, they had campaigned on a foreign policy plank endorsing Bismarck's unprecedented achievements. The recalcitrant Progressives had experienced a sharp defeat at the polls. The combined mandates of the Liberals and Progressives in the *Landtag* now numbered only 148. The Conservatives, whose representation skyrocketed from 38 to 142, had emerged as the strongest party. However, they were divided on the revolutionary implications of Bismarck's program, and only their left, the Free Conservative group, led by Ernst Ludwig von Gerlach (1795–1877), followed Bismarck unreservedly.

The wind in his sails, Bismarck now carried off an extraordinary piece of legerdemain. He persuaded the *Landtag* to grant him (230 to 75) an Indemnity Bill, which ex post facto legalized all the arbitrary measures he had taken in recent years to finance government operations. In return he conceded that his actions had in fact been unconstitutional.

Nikolsburg and Bismarck's New Policy

On July 26 Bismarck and Count Károlyi, the Austrian minister, signed the Preliminaries of Nikolsburg. Bismarck had promised Napoleon III he would respect the territorial integrity of the Habsburg Empire. Indeed, he could not afford to do otherwise, in spite of pressure from the king and his generals, for the skies over Europe had grown much darker since Sadowa. Accordingly, Austria was obliged to cede only Venetia, which she had already done in the agreement of July 5 with France, and pay an indemnity of only fifteen million dollars. The separate peace treaties subsequently signed with Baden, Württemberg, Bavaria, and Saxony were also governed by moderation and due regard for territorial integrity. Even Saxony, that hardy annual weed in Prussia's back yard, did not lose a leaf.

Nevertheless, Bismarck got all he wanted. Austria was excluded from Germany, which now for the first time lay at the feet of the Hohenzollerns. Austria agreed to dissolution of the German Confederation and to the formation of a North German Confederation under Prussia's aegis, and a South German, the members of which would be free to ally themselves individually with the north. With Austria's assent, Schleswig-Holstein was annexed by Prussia on condition of prior plebiscite (which was never held) in North Schleswig. The vaguest clause in the Treaty of Nikolsburg dealt with the Prussian annexations north of the Main, which constituted a devastating assault upon legitimacy, notwithstanding Professor Hans Rothfels' brief for the chancellor's respect for tradition and the rights of German states. In insisting upon joining the two wings of Prussia, Bismarck proved to be more annexationist than the king or the Conservatives. He must therefore shoulder responsibility for having constructed the Second German Empire upon a faulty foundation. Having appeased France with vague allusions to compensations in the Rhineland and Saar, Bismarck proceeded on August 17 to annex Hesse-Cassel, Hanover, Nassau, Frankfurt, and part of Hesse-Darmstadt. All this was confirmed in the final Treaty of Prague (August 23).

Among the innumerable Bismarck scholars many—notably Franz Schnabel, Erich Eyck, A. J. P. Taylor, and Otto Pflanze—have said that it was a calamity for Europe that Bismarck drove Austria out of Germany and created an empire that put might above right and was a transparent mask for Prussian tyranny. The inference is that an alternative solution in which Austria would have remained part of Germany would have obviated a policy of Balkan imperialist penetration and a resulting war with Russia. To this author, however, it seems likely that any kind of German union that embraced Austria would ultimately have exerted heavy pressure on the whole Balkan peninsula and have antagonized Russia, as did Nazi Germany in the 1930s.

Without unduly detracting from the credit that Bismarck deserves for his manly restraint toward Austria, it can be said that he made a virtue of necessity. He needed Vienna's friendship in order to avert a Franco–South German–Austrian combination against Prussia at a time when Britain and Russia preferred neutrality. Although Bismarck believed reconciliation would ultimately win out over revenge sentiments, he was too much of a realist to think a dynasty that for centuries had dominated central Europe would now completely mortify its pride. Indeed, he even found confirmation for his forebodings in October, 1866, when his archenemy, the former prime minister of Saxony, Count Friedrich von Beust, became Austro-Hungarian foreign minister.

Bismarck did not generally indulge in premature threats. However, an unfortunate outburst shortly after Sadowa, when he threatened France with war if she continued to insist on compensation in the Rhineland (Ambassador Benedetti was demanding at least the frontiers of 1814, i.e., Saarbrücken and Landau, plus some Rhenish territory) for her neutrality, stunned Napoleon III. For the emperor was already dismayed that he had been shunted to the sidelines by Sadowa and that not he, but Bismarck, was remaking the map of Europe. From then on, the Parisian milieu was neither as frivolous nor as incurably optimistic as Offenbach had just portrayed it in his *La Vie Parisienne* (1866). The stupefying suddenness of the Prussian victory sobered France and prompted her to look for new friends. This complicated Bismarck's task. The longer the French hunger for territorial compensations went unsatisfied, the more hostile she became toward Prussia. That the French boil was not allowed to burst until Bismarck was ready was due less to his patience than to Napoleon's vacillation. On the other hand, it is undoubtedly true, as Ludwig Reiners and Rudolf Stadelmann aver, that Bismarck's Austrian policy helped mollify passions in Vienna and blocked the formation of a military alliance in 1866–67 that would have shattered his hopes.

Chapter 32

INTERLUDE: THE NORTH GERMAN

CONFEDERATION

The "Bismarck Boom"

Success is a paint that gilds the darkest deeds. Early in 1866 the idea of civil war had been repugnant to most Germans, and the Prussian government had been widely criticized for allegedly harboring nefarious war aims. When, however, Bismarck with surprising speed surmounted every barrier to Prussian dominance over Germany, the Liberals flocked to his standard.

In the *Landtag* the constitutional struggle was relegated to an inferior plane by Rudolf Haym, Otto Michaelis, and the historians Max Duncker, Heinrich von Sybel, and Heinrich von Treitschke. They perceived in the chancellor's program of internal and external consolidation something vastly more important for the nation and, of course, the bourgeoisie. Captains of industry, such as the Rhenish tycoons Gustav Mevissen and Hermann Baumgarten, gave Bismarck and his minister Rudolf von Delbrück the major credit for the euphoria that had come to envelop Prussia and wondered why the business community had taken so long to see the light.

Shortly after the *Landtag* elections of the summer of 1866, twenty-four of the most nationalistic Liberals and Progressives in the House of Representatives, including Twesten, Eduard Lasker, Johannes Miquel, Max von Forckenbeck, and Rudolf von Bennigsen, declared the time had come to back rather than buck Bismarck. The following winter Bennigsen organized the National Liberal party. This party, based upon big business, approved the Bismarckian order of priorities of deeds above ideals and soon became the principal grouping in the North German Reichstag. Because the National Liberals, with broad popular support cutting across all class lines, gave cardinal emphasis to the perennial German problem, they, in effect, postponed arrival of responsible government in Germany for several decades.

For his part, Bismarck did what he could to unite all moderate men behind him. He had rightly divined that the masses cared more for unity than freedom and that they would turn their backs not only upon the *gross deutsch*, petty bourgeois, and proletarian Federation of General Workers' Associations (Verband deutscher Arbeitervereine), which was led by Sonnemann, Staudinger, Liebknecht, Lange, and Bebel, but also upon the People's party (Deutsche Volkspartei) and the Progressive leaders—Virchow, Jacoby, Ziegler, Waldeck, Hoverbeck, Mommsen, and Schultze-Delitzsch. To achieve an heterogeneous mass support, Bismarck offered universal manhood, equal and secret suffrage; immunity of Reichstag deputies from arrest or prosecution; security of the Reichstag from arbitrary dissolution; and systematic rationalization and integration of the economy. Bismarck was clearly ranging himself with the reformers and constitutionalists.

Bismarck's methods, ever more refined, disarmed many opponents. He preferred never to take a position by frontal assault if it could be outflanked or infiltrated. He cared little for consistency but much for results. Earlier than most conservatives, he came to understand that absolutism really *was* dead and that crown and nobility could retain a commanding position only by grace of the bourgeoisie and workers.

That Bismarck now sought the nationalization of the Hohenzollern monarchy did not signify that he had ceased to believe that "only the kings make revolution in Prussia"* or that unification would have to come from a "revolution from above." Nationalization of the monarchy did not even imply that he was ready to invite National Liberals to join his ministry. All it meant was that Bismarck thought the time for undiluted Conservative rule was over. Bismarck's most adroit overture toward the moderate deputies was the previously mentioned indemnity bill. This rallied the Free Conservatives to his side and enabled the bulk of the Liberals to enter the national camp through the back door. However, it was the creation of the North German Confederation (Norddeutscher Bund) that tore the veil from the eyes of the nobility; for the first time they realized that a monarchical and Prussianized Germany could be achieved with Bismarck's methods, whereas that had been impossible with those of Frederick II or Stein.

The North German Constitution

The North German Confederation, a product of *Machtpolitik*, gratified the masses without, however, satiating their appetite for unification and centralism. Bismarck had offered the public less than it wished, not merely out of concern for France and Austria but for the liberties of the larger secondary states and their traditional sovereignty.

The constitution of the North German Confederation was mainly Bismarck's handiwork. Some wit called the new *Bund* a "union of a dog with its fleas." But persiflage aside, the Bismarckian creation was more than a device for extending Prussian power over northern Germany. The constitution was also a system of adroit checks and balances designed to quell Austria's hostility, allay French suspicions, conciliate Saxony, and prepare the South German states for painless absorption by Germany. The constitution represented a delicate equiponderation between *Recht* and revolution, conservatism and liberalism, liberalism and democracy. If it compelled the princes to surrender territory and part of their sovereignty, it also represented an alliance of the dynasts to check liberalism and socialism. Bismarck achieved the illusion of popular government without giving power to the masses. He achieved a mosaic of *Machtpolitik*, Prussianism, nationalism, states' rights and populism. His constitution neither united Germany nor subjected it to a Conservative-military tyranny. The attribution of substantial sovereignty and extensive residual rights to the states of the confederation held the "Prussian party" in check.

Bismarck felt that to found a German Empire before the nation had been mili-

*Bismarck, *Die gesammelte Werke* (Berlin, 1924–35), VIII, 459.

AREA INCORPORATED IN NORTH
GERMAN CONFEDERATION IN 1871
TO FORM GERMAN EMPIRE

NORTH GERMAN CONFEDERATION
AND GERMAN EMPIRE

AUSTRIA-HUNGARY

PRUSSIA

tarily galvanized by some great crusade was to put the cart before the horse. A German Kaiser in 1867 would have been emperor of only North Germany. He would probably have been a monarch responsible to parliament, and his exalted office and prerogatives might too sharply have circumscribed the rights of other princes. Into the constitutional brew, therefore, Bismarck stirred generous quantities of particularism. Member states were largely left to operate under their own laws. Even the diets of some annexed principalities, such as Hanover, Hesse-Cassel, and Nassau, were allowed to persist but with diminished competence. Saxony was left in essential command of its army. The Bundesrat (Federal Council), or upper chamber, which represented the sovereign states of the North German Confederation, was made strong, yet not so strong that it could settle all differences between members. Residual powers left to the component states were more numerous than those delegated to the central government, and in the former alone was recognized the right of direct taxation. Still, no state might pursue an individual foreign policy, maintain a wholly independent army, or wage its own war.

Prussia's control over North Germany was insured by the strength of the presidency and chancellorship and by her role in the Bundesrat. Among the broad powers of the king of Prussia as president were supreme command of the armies of the confederation and the right, with approval of the Bundesrat, to prorogue the Reichstag. The position of the chancellor, as it developed, was so strong that Bismarck concluded he alone must fill the post. The chancellor was to be appointed by the president to whom he was responsible, and he could not be compelled by parliament to resign. The chancellor was to preside over a ministry, chosen by him from the higher bureaucrats of the realm, rather than from among the leaders of parliament, and the ministers, who were only the lieutenants of the chancellor, were personally accountable to him. With the authorization of the president, the chancellor was to conduct foreign relations, negotiate treaties of commerce, conclude alliances, and declare war. No bill could become law without his signature.

Opposing the executive power was a relatively weak bicameral legislature. It was hobbled with artfully contrived checks and balances, for Bismarck wanted no parliament to which Prussia, no less than the secondary states, would be unconditionally subject. The looseness of the North German Confederation was a safety valve for the pressure of Prussian ambitions.

The Bundesrat, which represented the sovereign German states, afforded Prussia its main lever in the Confederation. Of a total of 43 votes, Prussia controlled 17. Her nearest rival, Saxony, had 4. Mecklenburg, Brunswick, and Schwerin had 2, and all other states each had but 1 vote. Since a constitutional amendment required a two-thirds vote (28), Prussia's voice was decisive.

Bismarck had early discarded an original impulse to create a lower house in which half the deputies would be elected from the topmost tax-paying stratum of the population. As finally adopted, the constitution provided for elections to the Reichstag on the basis of secret, universal manhood suffrage, with representation in proportion to a member state's population.

While the Reichstag never enjoyed independent legislative power and its control over the purse was a joke, the assent of the House was nonetheless required before a bill submitted by the ministry or Bundesrat could become law. An early amendment of the constitution increased the power of the Reichstag by according it the right to reject trade and diplomatic treaties. The privilege of sitting in the House was, moreover, accorded to civil servants and ministers of state. Finally, the decision, reached after a tug-of-war in the Bundesrat, to remunerate Reichstag deputies enabled working-class candidates to run for parliament and eventually deprived the Reichstag of the exclusively upper-class composition it would otherwise have had.

By the constitution, the central government was empowered to operate more directly in internal matters than had been the case with the former Bundestag. Although the absence of a central supreme court was a lacuna in the tensile constitutional structure, the unusual strength of the executive was a guarantee of the supremacy of the nation over the states. Despite all deference to a traditional particularism, which was necessary to elicit cooperation of the princes and state governments, Bismarck kept in mind long-term, unifying goals.

The Military Budget

Nowhere else in the North German Confederation was the line between Bismarck and Rousseau drawn as sharply as it was in the military sphere. Fundamental law conferred on the Reichstag power to approve or reject all terms of the civil budget every third year. However, military expenses constituted 99 percent of the total budget, and these were beyond the competence of the Reichstag to increase or reduce. For example, in 1868 the total of all ordinary expenditures amounted to 207,500,000 marks, of which 206,225,000 were allocated to army and navy and were exempt from Reichstag surveillance. Legislative control over the residual civil budget was even qualified by the stipulation that where the central government's income from excise taxes, customs, post, and telegraph was insufficient to cover operating expenses a deficit contribution could be levied upon the member states.

One of Bismarck's signal parliamentary victories had been to fix the size of the army initially for at least five years and model it upon the Prussian. The strength of the North German military was set until December 31, 1871, at 1 percent of the population of the confederation as of 1867. Quotas levied on member states were to be proportionate to their populations. In keeping with Bismarck's wish for an ironclad military budget, each state's liability for military support was till 1871 fixed at 225 talers (1 taler equals 3 gold marks) per soldier. The army, whose commander-in-chief was the president of the North German Confederation, was to consist of draftees who were to serve three years in the line, four with the active reserve, and five, finally, in the territorial reserve. The size of the army expressed as a percentage of the whole population was to be reviewed by the Reichstag every ten years. In the meantime the parliament was to have no supervision over the military or appropriations for it.

This was a bitter pill for the Reichstag to swallow. Without control of the army budget, the lower chamber was only a debating society. To save its reputation the Reichstag was forced to fight a historic struggle with autocracy over the issue of parliamentary control of the army and military finances. That struggle outlasted the North German Confederation and nurtured the growth of German socialism.

The Birth of the Dual Monarchy

Since the history of Germany now comes to diverge from that of Austria, only passing reference may here be made to the impact of the defeat of 1866 upon the Habsburg Empire. Only by transforming it into a dual monarchy, in which the Magyars were given parity with the Germans, was dissolution avoided. By the Compromise, or *Ausgleich*, of 1867, which was approved by the Magyar leader Franz Déak, the Danubian polyglot was reorganized and Habsburg authority gravely weakened. The *Ausgleich* divided the lands of the empire between Austria and Hungary. West of the Leitha and north of the Carpathians the Germans dominated a Slavic majority, while east of the Leitha and south of the mountains the Magyars also ruled over a Slavic majority subject to the kingdom of Hungary. The main link between the two parts of the Dual Monarchy, or Austria-Hungary as it came to be called, was the head of the House of Habsburg who ruled as emperor in Austria and as apostolic king in Hungary. Whereas in time of crisis the emperor could issue emergency decrees on his own authority without assent of the Austrian Reichsrat, in Hungary no royal decree possessed validity unless countersigned by the prime minister, who was responsible to the parliament in Budapest.

Under the *Ausgleich*, Austria and Hungary were largely independent of each other. After June, 1867, they pursued joint policy and pooled their resources only as respects three matters: foreign affairs, military affairs, and finances affecting both. Recommendations on these matters were made by parliamentary delegations of sixty members from each state, sitting alternately in Vienna and Budapest but possessing no legislative power. Affairs of joint concern to Austria and Hungary were regulated by treaties, all of which had a duration of ten years, subject to renewal. When the compromise was renewed in 1877, it was on terms even more favorable to Hungary. After the *Ausgleich*, Austria's first prime minister was Count von Beust, an opponent of trialism (equality of Slavs, Magyars, and Germans) and an advocate of German supremacy within the Empire. In Hungary the first prime minister was Count Julius Andrássy.

Despite parliamentary and constitutional trappings, both Austria and Hungary possessed undemocratic polities, the latter more than the former. In each the lower chamber was elected by direct but not universal or secret suffrage. In Austria the franchise was for long based on a four-class system of voting that favored the nobility and bourgeoisie. In ultra-reactionary Hungary, ruled by great landed magnates, even the Magyar lower classes, not to mention the ethnic minorities, were disenfranchised.

Because trialism was rejected in 1867 and in 1870–71, both Austria and Hungary were plagued by steadily growing minority unrest and conspiracies. At times the nationality conflict completely paralyzed the government. Two things resulted from this: the administrations of the Dual Monarchy became increasingly autocratic and ineffective, and the great powers came to regard her as a cow which they could milk until ready to butcher her. This was the future that Bismarck had unwittingly constructed for the creation of the Habsburgs.

The Lesser States and the Confederation

If Prussia's acendancy over the North German Confederation was imperfect, it was because Bismarck did not want to scare the South German states before unification was accomplished. He did not believe in the possibility of an enduring South German Confederation and intended that sooner or later—as the National Liberals were expecting—Prussia would fill the vacuum that had developed south of the Main. However, he dared not advertise his grand design.

Pending events that might congeal the critical mass, Bismarck bound the states of the South German Confederation by individual treaties of alliance *(Schutz- und Trutzbündnisse)* to the North German Confederation. He made it clear that the acceptance of such treaties by Baden, Hesse-Darmstadt, Württemberg, and Bavaria was a substitute for extensive Prussian annexations in South Germany. The cause of national consolidation was also served by the circumstance that all the South German armies were remodeled along Prussian lines and were to be put under command of the king of Prussia in wartime. Another powerful impetus to amalgamation was given by the common German Criminal Code and by the creation of central agencies and a parliament for the Zollverein.*

Popular opposition to union with the North German Confederation was pronounced but by no means universal in South Germany. In predominantly Protestant Baden the government was in the hands of unionist National Liberals. On the other hand, in mainly Protestant Württemberg anti-Prussian sentiment steadily increased as a result of the financial burdens originating with the *Schutz- und Trutzbündnis*. Although Hesse-Darmstadt's prime minister, Karl F. Dalwigk, favored a *grossdeutsch* solution, the very influential Primate Archbishop Emmanuel von Ketteler (1811–77) of Mainz favored a *kleindeutsch*. In Bavaria Ludwig II and von der Pfordten had resisted union, but the latter's successor, Prince Chlodwig zu Hohenlohe-Schillingsfürst (1819–1901), did not. The Bavarian Patriots, a predominantly Catholic party that cherished the independence of the Wittelsbach kingdom, fought Bismarck stubbornly and in two *Landtag* elections (May and October, 1869) succeeded in defeating Hohenlohe and achieving an absolute majority in the diet. The Patriot's success was a *cauchemar* for Bismarck, for it threatened to pull down the rising edifice of the German federation.

That South German fears of Prussia were not entirely without foundation was

---

*The non-Prussian states had a two-thirds majority in the Bundesrat of the Zollverein, although they possessed only 14 million out of a total German population of 35 million.

illustrated by Hanover's fate. After 1866 when it was incorporated into Prussia, Bismarck methodically stamped out all vestiges of the earlier British connection and drove from office everyone suspected of democratic views. The personal fortune of the Hanoverian Welf king was confiscated by the Prussian government. This "Guelph fund" was popularly labeled the "reptile fund." It was primarily used by the chancellor to finance bribes for political purposes.

Composition of the North German Reichstag

On April 16, 1867, the Reichstag, which had been elected on February 12, approved by a vote of 230 to 53 the amended, final draft of Bismarck's constitution. The opposition consisted of Progressives, Catholics, Poles, and two Social Democrats (Bebel and Liebknecht). The new parliament consisted of 297 deputies, the great majority from privileged social strata and almost half of them aristocrats.

The largest block of deputies belonged to the National Liberal party, which had cast the die for Bismarck. Against its 79 deputies, the Old Liberals had only 27, and the Independent Liberals, 15. The pro-Bismarckian Free Conservatives had 40 mandates, but the Progressive party had paid for having been more right than the public by losing all but 19 seats. On the other hand, Bismarck's popularity was insufficient to turn the scales decisively against the Old Conservatives, who retained 59 Reichstag mandates and still dominated the Prussian *Landtag*. All told, there was a block of 186 Reichstag deputies upon whom the chancellor, under certain conditions, could rely, while a motley opposition comprised 111.

Bismarck and the Generals

As the "iron chancellor" moved into the ascendancy in Berlin, the importance of the royal military camarilla (privy cabinet) rapidly waned. After 1865 the camarilla exercised almost no influence on governmental policy. Minister of War Roon, seeking to diminish the political role of the generals, had arranged that the then animating spirit of the camarilla, the politically ambitious General Edwin K. von Manteuffel (1811–85), be "exiled" to the governorship of Schleswig. Without Manteuffel's drive, the camarilla became lethargic and docile. Thenceforth only the general staff might conceivably have served the purposes of aspiring Caesars. Fortunately for the state, however, Moltke evinced a clammy disinterestedness as to political issues, and he dominated the staff.

Few things contributed more to the success of Bismarck's federal and internal policies than Moltke's lack of political ambition. The subordination of Germany's greatest nineteenth-century military genius to Bismarck was even more decisive for the course of German history than that of Garibaldi to Cavour in Italian history. The chief of the Prussian general staff was strictly concerned with professional matters and the successful conduct of military operations. He believed it was wholly the responsibility of the civil government to see to it that when hostilities were unavoidable, battle should be joined under optimum diplomatic conditions and with maximum popular support. Provided that victory arising out of war be utilized to the reasonable advantage of the fatherland, Moltke saw no cause for the professional soldier to encroach upon the sphere of the statesman. In his time, therefore, the military posed no threat to the supremacy of the Prussian civil government. Contrariwise, his perspective denied the civil government proper control over the armed forces. To Moltke's mind, the technical complexity of modern ordnance, logistics, and tactics in an era of total war made it inadvisable that civil government interfere with conduct of hostilities by the generals. This attitude was to have serious consequences for the Second German Empire. Moltke's spectacular battlefield victories, meanwhile, were a title to respect. They enabled Moltke to build a veritable "state within a state." Against its rampart the Liberals, who were toiling to establish the principle of civilian control over the armed forces, could make no headway. Their inability to do so was a tragedy of modern German history.

The almost mutual exclusiveness of civilian and military authority in Prussia in the 1860s suggests that whatever Prussia's guilt for the wars of 1866 and 1870–71 may have been, virtually none of it can be attributed to the military. The general staff under Moltke never sought to impose a line of action upon Bismarck. Yet, on the other hand, in the Franco-Prussian War the general staff was resolved that the civil government would not again, as in 1866, be informed of the war plan or be allowed to interfere with its execution. After 1866 Bismarck was accorded little knowledge of the Prussian war plan and did not even take part in the conferences of the camarilla, which were held under the chairmanship of General Hermann von Tresckow, although Roon did. A heavy veil was being lowered over the eyes of the chancellor by the generals whose support he needed.

Bismarck and Napoleon III

After 1866 Prussian hegemony was still a tender shoot, which stood at the mercy of the Powers. Nothing decreed that France, Austria, Britain, Russia, and Italy would remain aloof or would not confederate to humble the Hohenzollerns. Bismarck's cabinet diplomacy after 1866 was based on recognition of this situation.

As A. O. Meyer and Otto Becker have averred, Bismarck had good reason to hope that Napoleon III would not forcibly oppose unification. Few reports can be as specious as the canard that Bismarck (as August Bebel charged in the Reichstag) had deliberately charted a course of war with France, the "hereditary foe," so as to draw the South German states into a new empire. Bismarck may have been a stern disciplinarian, but he was quite consistently a man of continence and a deep sense of responsibility who would not frivolously risk the nation's whole political capital on one turn of the wheel. The findings of many scholars—among them Leopold von Muralt, Hans Rothfels, W. Mommsen, Gerhard Ritter, Becker, A. O. Meyer, Lawrence Steefel, Maximilian von Hagen, and Walter Bussmann, all of whom aided in the post-World War II Bismarck renaissance—corroborate this.

It was less the imperatives of unification or Bismarck's guile than Napoleon III's failures and the decline of France that drove the French Empire down the road to war with Prussia.

After the failure of France to annex Hessian or Rhenish territory in 1866, Napoleon's foreign policy, as directed by Rouher, his factotum, aimed at securing compensation in Luxemburg, Belgium, or the Near East. But the emperor had no luck, and disaster steadily dogged his footsteps.

The main result of the French effort to acquire a foothold in the Rhineland was to encourage the formation of general alliances between Prussia and the South German states. With those in his pocket Bismarck could have answered French importunities with war, and with every prospect of victory. The Prussian army was twice as big as the French; the former's esprit was much better; Austria-Hungary would probably remain neutral; and both Russia and Italy were friendly toward Berlin. Yet it did not occur to Bismarck to exploit that nonrecurring opportunity for the sake of unifying Germany in a twinkling.

Bismarck was always loath to reach for the battle axe. He was one of the few great modern statesmen who did not strive so much to create as to exploit events. A peerless improvisor, he often relied for success upon a mixture of patience and acumen. Although in his lifetime he committed some bad errors, he possessed a capability for consistently astute reactions, which often dismayed his adversaries and so undermined their self-confidence as to force them to make some reckless move. Yet he was not a maximalist even when the prey was under his claw. Although occasionally guilty of scurrilous methods, Bismarck at the peace table and in peacetime was one of the most moderate statesmen ever.

Lest we become the dupes of Bismarck's virtues, we must remember that he was anxiously awaiting the slow parturition of a united Germany. He knew that in 1867 the fetus was only in its seventh month. Moreover, the extremely delicate South German position argued against external complications. As Bismarck saw it, it was his duty to save Napoleon III from an act of folly that might not only mean war but destroy the prospects of a natural solution of the unification problem.

The Luxemburg Bait

Bismarck realized how badly Napoleon III needed some success to restore his tarnished prestige-image. The chancellor would have been only too happy to have paid France off for past services out of someone else's pocket—say Turkey's. He even tried to promote this in 1867, but France demurred. Bismarck regretted the narrowing of choice to western Europe. Yet he was prepared to pension off Napoleon III, as one would a cast-off mistress, provided the price were not exorbitant. Napoleon pointed suggestively to the grand duchy of Luxemburg, which belonged to King William III of the Dutch Netherlands but was part of the German Customs Union. Bismarck could not have cared less. He was merely at pains to explain to the Count de Benedetti, the strident French ambassador, that he (the chancellor) would interpose no obstacles to French purchase of the grand duchy provided that it be done cautiously without publicity or arousing German opinion.

Some historians have argued that Bismarck's tepid encouragement of Benedetti was insincere and that the former was privately counting upon the resistance of Europe, specifically Britain, and the pusillanimity of the Dutch king to block French expansionist designs. The fact is, however, that Bismarck hoped Napoleon would be able to get away with the boodle. The chancellor's big worry was lest the thief in the night awaken the watch dog, whose barking would compel the master of the North German house to put up a risky show of defense. Considering the temporary primacy of internal objectives for Bismarck at this time, it is plain that he could not afford to be compromised in the eyes of the German public.

In the Luxemburg affair Napoleon III showed himself to be a cheat and, what was worse, a bungler. Rather than see Luxemburg slip into the North German Confederation, William III was disposed to sell the grand duchy to France for 10 million francs. To the Dutch king's question whether Prussia had given prior assent to the withdrawal of the German garrison, Napoleon replied "yes," which was not the case. Then he compounded his error by publishing the secret negotiations over Luxemburg. Germany soon was in an uproar.

An enraged Bismarck was hard put to it to forestall a conflict, but like a superbly trained lion he suppressed his savage instincts and merely bared his claws. In December, 1866, he spoke menacingly of Luxemburg as being German and of its future as a matter of grave concern to all Germans. He hinted at a rupture but in the meantime brought pressure to bear on William III to withdraw his consent to the sale. At the same time Bismarck strove to form a European front against France. When England gave her pledge, deceitful though it turned out to be, to join the other Great Powers in their resolve to fight, if need be, to preserve Luxemburg's independence, Napoleon III drew back in alarm. When, finally, Bismarck, banging on all the keys of the piano, published the secret alliances with the South German states and seemingly gave war sentiment free rein, Napoleon's retreat turned into a rout.

If the French emperor had only been able to win over Vienna, there might have been a different outcome. Revenge sentiment certainly poisoned the Viennese atmosphere, and Bismarck despised Chancellor von Beust. The Prussian is reported to have said that when he assessed the capability of an adversary he generally first subtracted his vanity; when he did that with Beust there was nothing left. Yet, the fact is, Prussian policy toward Austria did not reflect this personal animus, and Bismarck did not let it destroy the conciliatory achievements of Nikolsburg and Prague. On the other hand, Beust tried to seduce Napoleon III with proposals to pursue the Balkan chimera but was cool to his suggestion that Silesia be grabbed by the Austrians while the French occupied the Rhineland. Although Napoleon was figuratively left at the altar, Bismarck tried to help him save face. Now that the independence of the grand duchy of Luxemburg was no longer endangered, the chancellor promised early withdrawal of the Prussian garrison. With a moderate diplomatic triumph assured, Bismarck frowned upon those back home who were beating the war drum.

In the Luxemburg episode Bismarck perceived that a conflict had arisen between the techniques of secret diplomacy and the will of the nation. Consequently he dropped the former like a hot potato. Nothing is so illustrative of his evolution from a rock-ribbed Prussian Conservative to a German statesman as his readiness to cooperate with the Reichstag in handling the crisis. He swiftly changed course and scudded before the wind without becoming panicky or abandoning hope of reaching peaceful waters. Although he worked with all tools at building a national fatherland, including traditional secret diplomacy, Bismarck realized that the day of popular sovereignty had dawned: a statesman could no longer be right or, what is more, effective in flagrant opposition to the will of the people.

Although Bismarck successfully maneuvered to avert war, the Luxemburg episode ushered in the winter of distrust in Franco-German relations. The temperature plunged sharply and remained below normal for the rest of the century.

After 1867 Napoleon ceased to be a champion of German unification and searched only for territorial salve with which to heal his wounds. Franco-Prussian amity was dead, and war must come sooner or later. France suddenly became aware that a new foe was coming to replace her olden ones. The government of the Second Empire perceived that the Prussians alone barred the way to French eastward expansion. Conversely, the conviction was widespread henceforth in Germany that France was the villain in the drama and that she would be the chief beneficiary of a divided central Europe. Had not Napoleon III himself said that if the South German states joined the North German Confederation, French guns would go off by themselves? It is probable that after the Luxemburg crisis the articulate elements of German society in their majority believed that the unification of Germany might be greatly accelerated through a national crusade against the "hereditary foe."

The Fox and the Grapes

Having failed to obtain Luxemburg, the French fox drew the conclusion that he could not reach the grapes without standing on an ally's shoulders. It was thenceforth his constant preoccupation to persuade the Austrians to help. From August 18, 1867, until at least May, 1869, sporadic attempts were made to forge this alliance. To achieve it, no stone was left unturned, the Empress Eugénie even going so far as to attire herself plainly when in the company of the Austrian empress Elizabeth so that the latter's beauty might sparkle alone. Yet every stratagem failed. France was unable to break out of the isolation into which she had drifted.

Beust thought the French project of a dual alliance was defective on several counts, but, on the other hand, his counterproposal was no more palatable to Napoleon III. The Saxon dreamt of a quintuple alliance among Britain, France, Austria-Hungary, Italy, and Turkey against Russia, with spoils for all allies in the Balkans and Near East. He reckoned that if the alliance came into being it would impale Prussia on the horns of a dilemma. If she came to despotic Russia's aid, she would certainly alienate the South German states and use up her credit with the Liberals. If, however, Prussia remained neutral, she would forfeit Russia's friendship and next time stand alone.

Beust's plan lacked the strength of simplicity. It crumbled when Bismarck paid court to the tsar and threatened Britain with a Russian alliance that would endanger her interests in the Middle East. Bismarck enjoyed a spectacular press in London, and his threat had the desired result, not least because Napoleon's designs on Luxemburg and Belgium vexed England.

The attempts of Napoleon III to revive the fortunes of the Second Empire by permitting extensive parliamentary reforms in 1869–70 could not substitute for external success, which alone passed as specie in France. Lacking the support of his people, Napoleon III had reached the point where he must hazard a diplomatic gamble. Given existing imperatives in France and the yearning for unification in Germany, the general peace was henceforth at the mercy of an incident—or of Bismarck, who would have to decide whether he could reject a conflict that arguably served a higher national purpose than peace did.

It was also a problem whether the French Empire could turn the other cheek again. Paris had attributed its failure to acquire control of the Belgian railways at least partly to Bismarck's malice. Even Ollivier, the new liberal French premier, who was a friend of peace, agreed that another rebuff from Prussia would mean war and that firmness was the only policy.

Chapter 33

THE CRUCIBLE

The Hohenzollern Candidature

It was Spain, rather than Bismarck, that originated the candidature that caused the Franco-Prussian War in 1870. In February it became known that the Spaniards some months earlier had offered their throne, rendered vacant by a revolution in 1868, to Prince Leopold von Hohenzollern-Sigmaringen, a South German aristocrat with a pedigree reaching back to the flood. The Hohenzollern-Sigmaringen family had split off from the Anhalt-Brandenburg line not less than six hundred years earlier. Despite this and the fact that Leopold was distantly related to Napoleon III, the Hohenzollern candidature was unacceptable to the French government. French public opinion saw in the Spanish offer only a Bismarckian scheme to put France in a vice, as in the time of Charles V.

Throughout the crisis the chancellor treated the candidature as a strictly private affair between a sovereign German prince and the Spanish Cortes. Nevertheless, almost from the outset the chancellor pushed the candidature for all it was worth, knowing it was repugnant to the French. He maneuvered as clandestinely as an underground river. Both Anton von Hohenzollern-Sigmaringen and his son Leopold were indisposed to accept the offer, and William I also disapproved. Nonetheless, in March, 1870, Bismarck persuaded them all to endorse the candidature. He argued convincingly from the dynastic, economic, and nationalist standpoints that a Hohenzollern on the Spanish throne would be an increment of strength for Prussia and would stimulate both monarchical and nationalist sentiment in Germany. He later stated in his *Gedanken und Erinnerungen*, which casts very little light on his diplomacy at this time: "I did not fail to calculate all the possible consequences from the point of view of our interests. . . . An element friendly to us in the Spanish government would have been an advantage which . . . there appeared to be no reason to reject *a limine*, unless the apprehension that France might be dissatisfied was to be allowed to rank as one."*

On June 19 a Spanish emissary telegraphed to Madrid that Leopold, with the assent of the king of Prussia, had accepted. The fact leaked out prematurely, and by July 1 it was known on every street in Paris. By the fifth the atmosphere in the Chamber of Deputies was explosive. The foreign minister, Duke Agénor de Gramont, a belligerent character who had experienced many disappointments during the eight years he had served as ambassador to Vienna, now hungered for a triumph as a cat does for fish. He declared before the deputies on July 6 that Leopold's acceptance would compromise the interests and honor of France. Gramont vindicated Bismarck's judgment of him that he was "the most stupid man in

---

Bismarck, Reflections and Reminiscences, ed. by T. S. Hamerow (New York, 1968), pp. 178–79.

Europe'' when, instead of lodging his complaint with Madrid, he summoned his countrymen ''without hesitation or weakness'' to defy Prussia. A few days after Gramont had thereby burned his bridges behind him he wrote to Benedetti, the French ambassador to Prussia, that if the candidature were not withdrawn at once war would instantly follow, ''and in a few days we shall be on the Rhine.''

War might still have been averted if Gramont had only been satisfied with the substance of victory and let the shadow go. But the reckless, disquieting French search for some spectacular compensatory triumph at Prussia's expense, such as could have consolidated the hold of the Bonapartist dynasty over France, is the most arresting feature of the diplomatic drama of 1870. William I, perceiving that he had been right all along to oppose the candidature, had counseled his cousin Anton to instruct his son to retract. On July 12 it became public knowledge that Leopold had done so. Nevertheless, unappeased by Prussia's severe humiliation, Gramont instructed Benedetti to demand that the candidature never be renewed. This the importunate ambassador did at Ems, where the king was taking the cure. William I politely declined to comply. He could only point out that he had no control over relatives who were not even his subjects, and indicated that in view of the withdrawal of the Hohenzollern candidature he had nothing more to say to the French ambassador. Bismarck's confidential agent reported the substance of the Ems conversations in a telegram to Berlin together with royal authorization to the chancellor to publish all or part of it as he saw fit.

As is now well known to scholars, Bismarck's account in his *Memoirs* of how he received the dispatch on the evening of July 13 and then made judicious emendations to it calculated to provoke France to war is pure fable. It is impossible to give any further credence to the chancellor's fanciful story of how his gloomy and despairing war hawk colleagues, Moltke and Roon, who were dining with him that evening, were suddenly transported with joy when they realized that Bismarck's artful changes had ensured hostilities and thus saved the situation. The suspicions of Max Lenz and Hans Delbrück before 1933 that the Bismarckian story of how he engineered the war was sheer dramatic invention have in recent years been confirmed. On the basis of the research and writings of William L. Langer (1961), J. Dittrich (1962) and Josef Becker (1971) it has become clear that the richly embroidered story was all theatrics on Bismarck's part. Neither in the former secret Prussian state archives nor in those portions of the Friedrichsruh *Nachlass* of Bismarck which in 1971 were transferred from the Friedrichsruh family archives to the Federal German archives at Koblenz is there any evidence of such a dispatch that was altered in Bismarck's handwriting.

The fact of the matter is that, as Egmont Zechlin and J. Dittrich have insisted, Bismarck until the spring of 1870 had continued to hope that France would not oppose the peaceable and gradual evolution of the German nation towards unification, and that he did not, in view of the mounting resistance of South German public opinion, believe until early July that a military solution of the problem, even when practicable, was desirable. However, it became apparent to Bismarck by the spring of 1870 that the new "Liberal Empire" of Émile Ollivier had no intention of permitting the peaceable consolidation of the German nation, and with that flash of realization the whole diplomatic game changed. For weeks before July 12 the Ollivier-Gramont government had been harping publicly on the shame of the Hohenzollern candidature and had, accordingly, embarked upon a course that assumed the risk of war. By early July Bismarck had reached the conclusion that the French official attitude had now made hostilities unavoidable. The conversations of Benedetti with King William I changed nothing in the picture. Ollivier needed no "doctored" Ems dispatch to indulge the emotionally provocative cry: "They have shown our envoy the door!" The war party in Paris, headed by the Empress Eugénie and Gramont, had been irresponsibly sowing general hysteria for weeks. It was only a logical matter of reaping the whirlwind when on July 19 the French government declared war against Prussia.

It is unlikely that Bismarck had initially wanted to set a trap for Napoleon III. It is equally doubtful that Bismarck meant to capitalize on the candidature to provoke France to a declaration of war. Before World War II it was often asserted that between 1866 and 1870 Bismarck changed his views on the desirability of war: while he had not wanted it in the Luxemburg affair, the alleged improvement in intra-German relations had by 1870 removed his last reservations and caused him to welcome a showdown with France. Against this argument it may be categorically affirmed that the gulf between North and South Germany had widened rather than narrowed. A host of conflicts had risen to plague the advocates of unification. Turbulent, particularist crosscurrents may actually have tempted Napoleon III to exploit Bismarck's difficulties and strike while the iron was hot. Furthermore, if Bismarck had really wanted war, an incomparably more popular pretext was at hand in the petition of Baden for admission to the North German Confederation. Accommodation of this by the Reichstag would have been a flagrant breach of the promise to France to respect the Main River boundary. Finally, if Bismarck *had* joined the war hawks in early 1870 he would surely not have allowed the Hohenzollern candidature to drag on so long as to deprive the Prussian army of the element of surprise. From every standpoint, the candidature, involving as it did neither vital German interests nor honor, was a less desirable casus belli than Luxemburg, Belgium, or Baden.

Specific War Guilt

Views on Franco-Prussian War guilt have changed somewhat in the twentieth century. They have evolved from the notion that the French declaration of hostilities was a legitimate response to Prussian provocation, through a later consensus of almost equally divided guilt, to the currently prevailing opinion that, notwithstanding Prussian ambitions, France was predominantly responsible for the outbreak of war. After all, as Lawrence Steefel has said, only the French declaration of hostilities made it reality.

Undeniably, a Hohenzollern prince on the throne of Spain would have shifted the balance of power against France. Consequently, Bismarck must be censured for relentlessly insisting upon the candidature. However, his aims did not pass beyond a certain improvement in Prussia's overall international position. In other words, he only pursued a diplomatic stratagem calculated to compromise France and weaken her power of action (Alexander Scharff). On the other hand, Napoleon III "was prepared to have recourse to all offensive means" (Bruno Gebhart); the Empress Eugénie and the secretive Gramont wanted to provoke war with Prussia (A. J. P. Taylor); and, in the last analysis, consummation of Napoleon's scheme for an offensive triple alliance of France, Austria, and Italy would have resulted in a shift in the balance far more dangerous than that which Bismarck contemplated.

The blame that Prussia must bear was mainly a consequence of Bismarck's miscalculations—the most serious of his career. He grossly underestimated the force of German nationalism in 1870 and overestimated Napoleon's fear of Prussia. The chancellor also erred in the belief that the candidature would provoke a grave internal crisis in France and that Napoleon III, plagued by revolutionaries and bereft of a single ally, would not fight. The fact was, however, that except for Benedetti's effrontery the whole episode would have ended in a serious diplomatic defeat for Bismarck.

German Military Victory

The French armies were beaten with speed and finesse. They could blame their fate upon French isolation, the foe's numerical and technical superiority, and the fact that for the first time in history the German nation and all its states fought as one.

Divided into three army groups—a northern commanded by Crown Prince Frederick William, a central by Prince Frederick Charles, and a southern by Count Leonhard von Blumenthal—the German forces were opposed by two French army groups—a northern under the emperor and General Bazaine, centered around the fortress city of Metz, and a southern under Marshal Mac Mahon. Irreparable disaster overtook the French in mid-August when in the battles of Mars and Gravelotte Moltke cut Bazaine's supply lines and forced his troops to retire to Metz. When Mac Mahon's relief army came up from the south, it was encircled on September 2 at Sedan. Bazaine, meanwhile, was obliged to surrender his entire army. Among the prisoners was Napoleon III himself.

The Second Empire was then swiftly overthrown and replaced on September 4 by a government of "national defense." Thereafter France fought a revolutionary war as in 1792. This time, however, she did not prevail, because the Germans had a better grand idea for which to die. By September 18 the German armies began the siege of Paris. Strassburg capitulated on September 27, and Metz fell a month later, when the French lost 6,000 officers, 173,000 men, and immense stores of ordnance. By the time the Germans began on December 27 to bombard the "city of light'' with heavy artillery, they had carried everything before them—at Beaune-la-Rolande, Loigny, Chateaudun, Beaugency, Le Mans, Montbéliard, Dijon, St. Quentin, and Belfort. The inadequately trained French levies, numbering almost 2 million, had proved to be no match for German conscripts and reservists.

After a month's bombardment, Paris surrendered on January 28, 1871. Thereafter, the French elected a national assembly that chose the historian and diplomat Adolphe Thiers as chief of state. With him the Germans signed a preliminary peace on February 26, followed by the final Treaty of Frankfurt am Main on May 10, 1871.

Bismarck's Wartime Diplomacy

France's predicament was hopeless in the absence of a European system of opposing alliances. Any remote possibility that a triple alliance might have rescued France had been dashed by Napoleon himself. His misguided defense of Rome and the papacy against the kingdom of Italy had only earned him its rebukes, culminating in 1870 in the annexation of the Eternal City and termination of French influence in the peninsula. The only other plank to which Napoleon III might have clung was war in the Near East, but this was adroitly forestalled by Bismarck, who mediated between Russia and Britain.

Throughout the Franco-Prussian War the sympathies of Europe were predominantly with Germany, and Bismarck toiled to keep them that way. The Italians applauded the nationalist aspirations of the German people and did nothing to embarrass their erstwhile ally. Nothing French diplomacy did could alter that fact. England, too, was enthusiastic over the German victories, for Napoleon III had too often twisted the lion's tail. Not until Bismarck presented France with the demand for Alsace and part of Lorraine did the British government experience a ripple of apprehension. Austria-Hungary, of course, hoped for a French victory, which would have forestalled absorption of the South German states and erased some of the humiliation of 1866. Yet Vienna did not dare aid France as long as Russian troops menaced the Habsburg rear. Tsar Alexander II would have liked to arrange a conciliatory peace between the combatants, and he toyed with the idea of guaranteeing the integrity of Austria-Hungary for a price. However, Austria-Hungary was reluctant to let the Russians fish in the Balkans, and Vienna's military preparations alarmed the tsar. Thus it is, in keeping with the findings of W. E. Mosse, not surprising that when news of the first great German victories reached St. Petersburg the Russian government dropped all idea of a European solution of the war.

Bismarck was perfectly aware that old friendship and past services would not be enough to insure Russian neutrality. He therefore informed the "tsar liberator" on August 24 in mellifluous tones that if Russia would only endorse Prussian annexation of French territory, Russia could rely upon Berlin's support for any revision the tsar might unilaterally make to the Treaty of Paris. On September 8 the Russian foreign minister Gorchakoff specified abrogation of the Black Sea disarmament clauses, and the chancellor readily assented. Thereafter the success of Russia's Near Eastern course depended upon Prussia's benevolent neutrality in any controversy with Britain. St. Petersburg could not afford to jeopardize that neutrality by flirting with France.

When on November 15 the Russians finally tore up the Treaty of Paris, Bismarck kept his promise despite his master's displeasure. Britain, for whom a Franco-British alliance was repugnant, was accordingly forced to rely upon Bismarck to moderate Russian demands. The chancellor, for his part, successfully played the role of "honest broker," and the Near Eastern situation was not allowed to deteriorate to the point where it might have brought comfort to France. In the Treaty of London of March 13, 1871, the Black Sea clauses, which shackled Russian power, were abrogated. So it was that when Bismarck presented his annexationist bill to France, the Russians, grateful for the chancellor's services in the Near East, interposed no more demurrer than did the British.

The Last Triumph of the Civil over Military Power

The dual civil and military command, which was to contribute to the undoing of the Second German Empire, had its origins in the Franco-Prussian War. From the beginning of the shooting, Moltke insisted upon wartime supremacy of the military over the state. He demanded that the civil authorities abstain from interference in the conduct of a war which he, in keeping with the prescription of Clausewitz, was bent on waging till the resistance of the foe had been completely broken and his armies annihilated. Acceptance of this viewpoint by the Prussian government would have sacrificed the fruits of patient diplomacy to operational imperatives and maximalist mob demands. For Bismarck, for whom responsible policy was an imperative, this was unthinkable.

Inasmuch as Bismarck's diplomacy was oriented to the attainment of ends more or less susceptible of endorsement by the Great Powers, a peace had to be made that would not provoke the intervention of a third party, which might be the case if France lay prostrate. Moltke thought just the opposite, arguing that France must be smashed before an armistice was concluded. So tense did relations between the two men become that the general would not even acquaint Bismarck with military plans and developments. What was most objectionable was Moltke's irritating habit of communicating directly with General Trochu, the nominal head of the French government of national defense. Such communications were established without foreknowledge, much less assent, of the Prussian foreign office. Arguably Moltke was guilty of having violated the constitution and ought to have been court-martialled. But who would treat a Caesar thus?

Bismarck eventually won his contest with the military. On January 25, 1871, the king deprived Moltke of the prerogative of conducting negotiations personally with Trochu and gave Bismarck the right to be heard in discussions affecting the conduct of military operations and the conclusion of an armistice. While the generals were not deprived of all influence upon war aims, Bismarck had managed for the last time in Prussian history to assert the supremacy of the civil over the military.

Birth of a Nation—in Spirit

If the bitterly Prussophobe patriots in Bavaria could have won the South German Liberals as confederates against the Junker-dominated Hohenzollern kingdom, there might have been a different issue to constitutional developments in 1870–71. As it was, the Liberals had been won for Bismarck's grand objective and were impatient only at the snail's pace with which he inched toward unification. Having abandoned particularism, formerly their sanctuary against Prussian aggrandizement, the Liberals could not now wait another year for Germany to be made. Again, as in 1848, Bennigsen, Miquel, and Lasker urged precipitate solutions. During the debates in the Reichstag over the admission of Baden to the North German Confederation, National Liberal leaders had publicly warned Bismarck that continued inactivity would compel them to forsake him. During the Hohenzollern candidature episode they had constantly wailed that he had missed the boat.

On July 19, the day France declared war, almost all Germany, including the bulk of the radical workers, rallied to Bismarck. In the Reichstag debate on war credits on July 19–21 even some of the ultramontane Centrist leaders, such as August Reichensperger (1808–95), rallied to the national cause. Other Catholics, who in their hearts could not approve the war, bit their tongues in silence. This was the case with Ludwig Windthorst (1812–91) and Hermann von Mallinckrodt (1821–74), who with Reichensperger were cofounders of the Center party. As Lothar Gall has shown, they were influenced by the fact that there was already strong sentiment in South Germany and in the Catholic press for a nationalist and annexationist outcome of the Franco-Prussian confrontation. The only two deputies to abstain from approving war credits were the Social democratic Workers' leaders Wilhelm Liebknecht (1826–1900) and August Bebel (1840–1913), who rejected the war as being a purely dynastic feud. However, they represented a minority even within their own party. On July 20 the Reichstag with near unanimity approved 120 million talers of extraordinary military credits.

Baden offered its army at once to William I. In Württemberg King Charles Alexander (1818–1901) and his minister Friedrich Varnbüler (1809–89) swam with the current and ordered mobilization, while the *Landtag* voted the war credits unhesitatingly. In Hesse-Darmstadt Grand Duke Ludwig III (1848–77) and his minister Baron Reinhard von Dalwigk (1802–71), both Prussophobes, waited in vain for some military miracle. When the French failed in produce one, they sadly bowed to popular clamor and joined the crusade. The great wind of chauvinism carried everything before it. In Bavaria the ''Patriots,'' who advocated armed neutrality, were overwhelmed by the masses and the Progressives. Premier Count Otto von Bray-Steinburg (1807–99), a staunch supporter of Bavarian independence, soon became convinced that the Schutz und Trutz alliance left the government no room for evasion. On July 20 the Bavarian *Landtag*, including the Catholic deputies, voted 101–47 to approve war credits and without formal declaration put Bavaria in the war.

Except for the Welf followers of the dethroned king of Hanover, all German states and peoples were for the first time since the Middle Ages galvanized for a common purpose. The military victories that were soon won made a Second German Empire appear to be the reward of general sacrifice.

The Role of Alsace-Lorraine in Unification

In the eyes of German patriots it was not enough to transform South Germans into nationalists by involving them in war with the "hereditary enemy." It was essential to a broader union that all German states share the booty. If they had to defend it against a vengeful France, they would stand together. This was the viewpoint of the German press, and whether or not it was manufactured by the chancellor, it definitely influenced him.

Bismarck showed scant interest in the type of government in France. He would have recognized any government that was prepared to cede Alsace to the German Empire. Actually, privately Bismarck did not covet Metz and the *pays Messin*. He feared to introduce "too many Frenchmen into the German house." However, the public demand for eastern Lorraine and the argument of the general staff that Metz was an indispensable bastion against a possible future attack forced him toward the larger annexation. There was the argument, too, that both Germanic Alsace and French Lorraine had been part of the Holy Roman Empire and that the victors in 1815 had been too lenient in leaving the whole strip in question in French hands. Nothing so serves to underline that this was the national sentiment in Germany as the fact that the loudest editorial voice favoring the annexation of Alsace-Lorraine was that of the Catholic journal, the *Kölnische Zeitung*.

Birth of a Nation in Fact

Only the fever that attended the French surrender of more than 80,000 men at Sedan on September 2 overcame the strong reservations of the South German princes respecting the future of their dynasties and the forfeiture of sovereignty. On that day, however, Baden took the lead. Minister Julius Jolly (1823–91) began talks with Bismarck to erase the line of the Main. Dalwigk in Hesse-Darmstadt soon followed with his own independent discussions. These talks were protracted but ended with glowing results on November 15 when Baden and Hesse-Darmstadt both signed treaties of union with the North.

Bavaria still hesitated, and Bismarck insisted on treating her with kid gloves. He opposed Crown Prince Frederick William's recommendation to use force upon an ally that had just fulfilled its wartime military obligations. More probably he did not want to thrust the Prussian king back upon Reichstag and public for support, for this would have vitiated his fundamentally monarchical, conservative policy.

Count Bray's last chips were on the Austrian card. When that failed him, he forsook his dream of a South German Confederation allied with the North German and Austria-Hungary. Meanwhile, the fantastic King Ludwig II (1864–86) had altogether compromised his minister's position by accepting a 300,000 mark bribe from Bismarck's "Reptile Fund" on consideration that Ludwig nominate William I to be German emperor. Lacking the supporting linesmen that would have been provided by a South German front, Bray settled on November 23 for concessions that were more apparent than real. The unionist agreement stipulated that Bavaria would retain domiciliary authority over its citizens and control over its army and military finances in peacetime and be entitled to permanent membership on the Bundesrat Committee of Foreign Affairs.

In Württemberg Baron Hermann von Mittnacht (1825–1909) had come to power with a popular mandate to take the kingdom into a German empire. He signed a preliminary convention with the North German Confederation on November 25. Mittnacht set as conditions Stuttgart's control over posts and telegraph, railroad, and appointments of officers in the Württemberg army. Bismarck also promised Mittnacht, as he had Bray, that a German empire would seek a military alliance with Austria-Hungary.

Ratification of the treaties of union by Hesse-Darmstadt, Baden, and Württemberg took place smoothly in December. In Bavaria, however, the irreconcilable wing of the Patriots, led by the historian Joseph Jörg (1819–1901), assailed the pact on the ground that it sacrificed state sovereignty. Unfortunately for him, the pope pulled the rug out from under the Patriots by advising Bavarian Catholics to endorse the *kleindeutsch* treaty, while even Emperor Franz Josef publicly approved of it. In the vote on union, taken in the Bavarian *Landtag* on January 21, 1871, the required constitutional two-thirds majority was obtained (102 to 48). Thereupon, the Reichstag voted (195 to 32) to admit all the supplicants. Meanwhile, on January 18, 1871, the traditional date of the coronation of Prussia's kings, William I, having been persuaded by the princes to accept the imperial crown, had been proclaimed German emperor *(Deutscher Kaiser)* in the Hall of Mirrors at Versailles.

In retrospect, the Second German Empire would seem to have been the achievement of a "sacred union" of the princes and all the classes. Supported by as impressive a political combination as any in modern times, Bismarck was able to erase the errors of 1848–49 and heal the long-existing lacerations of the national spirit. However, as he himself confessed to his wife, the exertions had left him utterly exhausted, used up, and enveloped by a Faustian world-weariness.

The Treaty of Frankfurt

The Franco-Prussian Treaty of Frankfurt of May 10, 1871, was not a draconic treaty. Considering that French opposition to Bismarck's grand objective, unification, had been broken, there seemed no reason for imposing limitations upon the size of the French army. Instead, Bismarck strengthened the new French chief of state, Adolphe Thiers, against the revolutionaries by reducing the war indemnity from six to five billion francs and promising to withdraw occupation forces from the northeastern departments as soon as it was paid. Bismarck also left Belfort in French hands.

Politically a mistake, the annexation of Alsace-Lorraine was from the military standpoint justifiable. In German hands fortress Metz cancelled out French-held Verdun and Belfort. The Franco-German border was in consequence so strengthened and stabilized that thereafter no successful offensive in that area from either east or west was possible. A moderate settlement by comparison with Tilsit (1807), Frankfurt conferred military security upon both signatories and left France, whose sovereignty was unimpaired, with ample opportunity for reconstruction and revival in every department of life.

PART X

GERMANY'S SECOND AGE OF ASCENDANCY

Chapter 34

YEARS OF EUPHORIA: 1860–1914

Emergence of an "Economic Mentality"

In the latter half of the nineteenth century Germany underwent far-reaching economic changes and an accompanying psychological metamorphosis that thrust her into an imperialist struggle for world power against greater empires than her own. Germany ceased to be a nation of "poets and dreamers," the despair of her underprivileged masses and the sport of Europe's statesmen and generals.

For many reasons German trade and industry had embarked upon a course of dynamic expansion and spiraling increases in the gross national product, which generated a popular climate of euphoria. By the eve of World War I Germany had become the strongest and most ambitious power in the Old World. She was also the proudest and noisiest about her accomplishments. Most Germans glowed at the thought of the fatherland's social legislation, scientific and technological progress, educational system, rising real wages, formidable military and naval might, blossoming overseas empire, mounting imports and exports, mushrooming mercantile marine, and vast industrial strength.

A milieu of profits and amenities, familiar to all societies that attain advanced industrialization, conditioned the prevailing outlook in late nineteenth-century Germany. All of her spectacular material progress had ended by conferring upon her people the highest standard of living in Europe. The nation, by and large, was prepared to sacrifice any supposed blessings that derived from cultivating intangible values for the sake of quantitative improvement in income and purchasing power. Highly competitive, aggressive habits of thought laid hold on the dominant social classes. All the canons and influences of a maturing Economic Age conspired to manufacture a mind that was preoccupied, not with the growing spiritual impoverishment of the nation, but with the "economic wonder" that was the modern German story.

A small and steadily dwindling corps of intellectuals, wedded to the values of a dying past, fought these tendencies. In his book *The Will to Power*, for example, Friedrich Nietzsche castigated the cult of the economic man and foretold the triumph of decadence and chaos as a consequence of man's absorption with things instead of ideals. He rejected the preposterous notion that the Franco-Prussian War had confirmed the superiority of German culture and lamented that England and the USA, with their apotheosis of materialism, had become archetypes for Germany. Similarly, the economist Werner Sombart wrote in 1913 that Germany was competing with the USA for "the distinction of being the highest embodiment of the capitalistic spirit." Jacob Burckhardt, William Dilthey, Ernst Troeltsch, and Oswald Spengler were no more sanguine than Nietzsche or Sombart. Dilthey complained to a friend in 1887 of the apostasy from religion, which was leading Germany at breakneck speed toward catastrophe. The other critics bemoaned the lack of individuality in German literature, the absence of grand conceptions and "monumentality" in almost all the plastic arts, the rarity of great musicians and the decline of German philosophy.

Inevitably, the attempts of the idealists to reconsecrate Germany to earlier purposes and effect a new spiritual synthesis failed. The fruits of applied science—a spate of labor-saving inventions and techniques—nurtured an ebullient optimism that smothered the gloomy prophecies of savants and artists. While they wailed about impending doom, the masses hailed a dawning utopia. Once again a deep rift developed in the national soul.

The common man had a vision "of the future and all the wonders that would be." He believed that a time was soon to come when technology would release him from eternal toil, when the masses would be lapped in plenty, and when a rational distribution of wealth would usher in a social democratic order. This sanguine viewpoint was embraced by all the trade unions. It encouraged the practical, when not theoretical, rejection of the Marxist class struggle and revolutionary seizure of power by the proletariat. By 1914 the bulk of the workers and their prime champion, the Social Democratic party, largest in the Empire, looked forward confidently to a not-too-distant day when the aims of labor would be achieved within, not upon the ruins of, the existing order.

It is not surprising that the proletariat, no less than the bourgeoisie, ridiculed the moribund kingdom of culture. Molded by the capitalist form, geared to the methods of assembly-line production, alienated from their own individuality, and transformed into marketing statistics, the German masses forsook ennobling sentiments. They came to put their trust in the alchemy of production, which would ultimately fill everyman's pot with gold. To the "soul" of the Age of Faith, and the "intellect" of the Age of Reason, succeeded the "product" of the Economic Age.

Growth of Population and Towns

The German economic wonder was powered by an exploding population which in the period 1845–1914 increased almost 100 percent from 34,300,000 to 67,790,000. Most of this increment redounded to the benefit of towns and cities. Whereas in 1871 only 36 percent of the total population (41,058,792) lived in towns of more than 2,000 inhabitants, in 1914 almost 66 percent of the population of the Reich did. By then, too, one out of every four persons was living in a metropolis, as compared with only one out of twenty-five in 1871. The number of great cities, meanwhile, had increased from eight to eighty-four. Germany's population may not have grown so rapidly as the Russian, but it is significant that the German rate of increase was eight times that of the French.

Causes of Industrial Growth

Among the factors that aided German industry in the later nineteenth century, three should be stressed. First, there was the passage of centralizing, standardizing, and liberating legislation for commerce and industry. Second, there was the rationalizing, combining, and cartelizing of corporations to lower costs of production, increase earnings, and encourage accumulation of investment capital. Finally, there were huge reserves of coal, mainly in the Ruhr, and of iron, concentrated primarily in the Saar-Lorraine area.

Other factors helping in lesser degree to promote German commercial and industrial development were: the war indemnity, which was largely used to prime the economic pump; the symbiotic relationship between government and industry in the Reich; the application of scientific techniques to all phases of production but especially to the tool and die industry; development of transportation; application of new methods for smelting iron ores with high phosphoric content, such as those of Lorraine; protective tariffs; acquisition of colonies, which were a source of inexpensive raw materials; opening of foreign markets; chemical discoveries; successes in basic electrical research and the initiation of urban electrification; rising national income; growth of a huge labor reserve; pacifying social insurance and graduated income tax laws; and, finally, a long international peace during which industrial expansion proceeded at an amazing pace.

Slow Beginnings

As the Chinese proverb goes, even a journey of a thousand miles begins with a step. The twelve years following the Revolutions of 1848 were for many German firms a time of troubled beginnings. Severe competition from abroad and the lack of protective tariffs forced entrepreneurs to take extraordinary risks and operate on slim margins of profit. However, in the 1860s the competitive position of German enterprise, especially the metal industry, rapidly improved. This was partly due to the introduction of the Bessemer converter process for making cast steel from Swedish iron ore with low phosphoric and sulphuric content, and, later in the decade, of the somewhat superior Siemens method of manufacturing steel by directing a jet of burning gas and air onto molten iron in an open hearth. These developments augmented production in the key steel industry and brought wage increases to many workers.

Hard work, ingenuity, and initiative all played their part in the German economic wonder. By 1870 the masses were decidedly better fed and housed and enjoyed more amenities than had been the case before 1848. Despite the continued existence of perennial poverty corners, such as Silesia, Pomerania, and Mecklenburg, the standard of living was rising.

Decline of the Agricultural Way of Life

Although dwarfed by gains in commerce, industry, and banking, German agriculture also registered significant progress in the late nineteenth century. By 1871 tenant farming had practically ceased to exist, and peasant proprietorship had become the rule at a time when tenantry was normal in Britain. A distribution of common lands among the farmers, moreover, had increased the total arable under cultivation in Germany. This, coupled with the introduction of mechanized seeding, harvesting, and weeding and the employment of artificial fertilizers, enabled farmers to produce more with fewer man-hours of labor. As a result, for example, production of grain and potatoes doubled between 1870 and 1914. By World War I Germany led the continent in potatoes and rye and was the second producer of oats and the fourth in the aggregate of all crops. For the century as a whole the gross agricultural output probably tripled. Nevertheless, by the last quarter of the century the long agricultural way of life was approaching its end. While local wars had forced produce prices steadily upward in the third quarter, the German peasant was exposed, from 1875 to 1914, to heavy competition from low-cost producers in Russia, China, Argentina, Uruguay, and Australia. As a result, there were drastic drops in crop prices in 1876–80, 1895–98, and 1913–14. German farmers were repeatedly caught in a pincers by low crop prices, high costs of production, and soaring prices for machinery and manufactured end-items. By 1913 80 percent of the arable was in uneconomically small farms of 280 acres or less. Millions of small operators, especially in North Germany and Trans-Elbea, where there were many huge estates, could not stand the pace of competition. A time came when the little fellow discovered that his income was less than the interest payments on money he owed. Then he abandoned the field for the town, where seemingly the wave of the future rolled.

In 1879 Bismarck embraced protectionism principally out of regard for the malingering state of agriculture. Yet Bismarck's tariff did not so much redound to the benefit of agriculture as of industry. The Caprivi bilateral trade treaties and tariffs of 1893–94 also failed to restore agriculture, which in the final decade of the century had entered a phase of chronic illness. When finally in 1903–4 something more tangible was done for the countryside by the Bülow government and higher protective tariffs were imposed upon almost all agricultural imports, it soon became plain that the prime beneficiaries of the ameliorative legislation were the big landlords, whose support Bülow needed for his naval building program. Thus little or nothing was done by the governments of the Second Empire to maintain a healthy balance between town and country and prevent the depopulation of rural areas. In the last years of peace the center of gravity of the labor force shifted ever more rapidly from farm to factory. By 1895 half of Prussia's population and 60 percent of Germany's derived its living directly from trade and industry. In 1907 more than 66 percent of the nation's gainfully employed worked in these sectors. By then the combined gross product of commerce and industry was double that of agriculture and forestry.

Milestones of Industrial and Commercial Growth

In July, 1869, the Prussian *Landtag* legislated complete freedom of enterprise for the kingdom, abolishing the last remnants of corporative, guild, and restrictive labor controls. In 1871 this law was extended to the whole German Empire with a resulting momentous stimulus to capitalism. Thenceforth, not the strength of her army nor the primacy of her educational system, but the mighty expansion of her trade and industry furnished the fundament upon which Germany built her aspirations of world power.

Phenomenal growth was reflected in the basic coal, iron, steel, chemical, electrical, and railroading industries.

Between 1870 and 1914 Germany moved ahead in the production of coal at a faster clip than any other nation. Production and financing had early been facilitated by the formation in 1862 of the Coal Producers' Association and by several important mergers, such as those in the Borsig (1857) and the Roman mines (1860). Between 1846 and 1867 Prussian output of coal increased from 3 million metric tons to 18.5 million. In the Second Empire era the coal industry made even more rapid progress under such entrepreneurs as Guido Prince Henckel von Donnersmark (1830–1916), August Thyssen (1842–1926) and his son Fritz (1873–1948), Emil Kirdorf (1847–1938), who headed the German Coal Syndicate, Hugo Stinnes (1870–1924), the Duke von Ujest (all operating in the Ruhr), and the Silesian magnate Heinrich Prince von Pless (1833–1907).

Whereas in the years 1850–60 Germany's production of coal was only half that of France, less than half that of Belgium, and only one-twentieth that of Britain, by 1873 German output was double the French and Belgian and a quarter of the British. In the years 1871–1913 German coal output increased from 29.4 million metric tons to 191.5 million, more than sixfold, while the production of lignite (brown coal) increased ninefold. Most of this output came from the Ruhr and Saar, with much smaller amounts coming from Bavaria, Silesia, and the Zwickau mines of Saxony. By 1914 Germany was mining a combined total of 281 million metric tons of anthracite and lignite. She was on the verge of overtaking Britain's 287,410,000 tons of 1913. By utilizing more efficient techniques of production and forming huge centralizing syndicates, such as the Rheinisch-Westfälisch Kohlen-Sindicat, the Gelsenkircher Bergwerke, and the vast Stinnes conglomerate, which amalgamated river and oceanic transportation, power plants, factories, and coal and iron mines, Germany was able in this period to achieve a rate of increase of production that was two and one-half times that of Britain.

An analogous sixfold increase of output was recorded between 1871 and 1914 in the iron industry. Production soared from less than 4.5 million metric tons of ore in 1871 to 28.7 million in 1913. For pig iron the figures were 1.6 million tons in 1871 and 14.8 million in 1910, a ninefold increase—still almost 13 million tons behind USA output but greater than Britain's. The chief sources of ore in Germany were in Silesia, Hanover, Thuringia, the Rhenish Siegerland, Bavarian Amberg, and, after 1871, Lorraine.

In the manufacture of steel Germany achieved primacy in Europe by 1910, when the Reich's product (13.7 million metric tons) almost doubled that of Britain. For the period 1886–1912 Germany increased steel production by 1,435 percent, the most impressive rate of any major power. By comparison, French output increased 693 percent, Britain's (which was second in Europe) 754 percent, and the USA's 910 percent. In an age of steel the meteoric rise of the German iron and steel industry bade fair to confer upon the Second Reich military preponderance in Europe and make of France and Britain superannuated states. However, it was also a fact that, by 1914, the might of the German metallurgical industry had come to surpass the strength of the Reich and was in a fair way to compromise it.

The upsurge of the German iron and steel industry was due most particularly to such things as: the acquisition of 700 million tons of ore reserves in Lorraine; application of the more efficient Thomas-Gilchrist process for removing phosphoric impurities from ore; the beneficent effects after 1879 of protective tariff legislation, which insured German producers a monopoly over the domestic market; accelerated development of railroad construction, which increased the national trackage from 11,500 kilometers in 1860 to 61,000 in 1910, as compared with 38,000 for Britain, 49,500 for France, and 70,000 for vast Russia; the rapid expansion of the mercantile marine, which by 1914 boasted 2,100 steamships of 4.4 million gross registered tons (mainly concentrated in the hands of two shipping companies—Albert Ballin's Hamburg-Amerika, or HAPAG, line and Hermann Meier's North German Lloyd); and, finally, the centralization and concentration of production through cartels and syndicates, which eliminated the effects of competition within the industry and, in the absence of antitrust legislation, conferred upon German producers a very strong position in world markets. Analogous organization and amalgamation to that which had been achieved in the French iron and steel industry by Schneider of Le Creusot and Wendel of Lorraine through the Comité des Forges and in the Russian through Prodamet was carried out in the Second Reich by the moguls of the Ruhr and Saar—Alfred Krupp, Friedrich Alfred Krupp, and Gustav Krupp von Bohlen und Halbach, Hugo Stinnes, August and Fritz Thyssen, Emil Kirdorf, Karl Freiherr von Stumm-Halberg ("King Stumm of Saarabia"), and Prince Guido Henckel von Donnersmark—and by Count Philipp von Colonna in Silesia.

In other areas of heavy industry Germany by 1914 had also achieved a commanding position. The potash, potassium, and metallurgical alloy industries all blossomed under the Second Reich. The German machinery industry stood in the world's front rank, as did also the German optical industry. In chemicals the basic theoretical work of Liebig, Kekulé von Stradonitz (1829–96), and August Wilhelm von Hofmann (1818–92) was the fundament upon which Friedrich von Bayer (1825–80) erected the firm of Bayer and Company and Carl Duisberg (1861–1935) helped organize the mammoth I. G. Farben cartel. By 1914 Germany had achieved absolute domination of the world's synthetic dye industry, producing about 85 to 90 percent of the global output. An electrochemist from Karlsruhe, Fritz Haber (1868–1934), achieved the synthetic production of ammonia in 1908–9 and therewith laid the basis for German primacy in the nitrate and munitions industries. Invention of a light internal combustion engine by Gottlieb Daimler (1844–1929) and Friedrich Benz (1834–1900) gave Germany a headstart in the youthful automotive industry. The extraordinary progress of the Second Reich as respects the manufacture of electrical parts and equipment and in electrical engineering was to no small degree due to pioneer work done by Werner von Siemens (1816–92) and Emil Rathenau (1838–1915). The former invented the electric dynamo and founded Siemens and Halske of Berlin. This company in 1903 merged with the rival Schuckert Company to form Siemens-Schuckert Werke, A. G. Rathenau founded the General Electric Company (Allgemeine Elektrizitätsgesellschaft or AEG) in 1883, and it promptly bought up the right to manufacture Edison's incandescent bulbs. Last, Robert Bosch (1861–1942), engineer and industrialist, founded Bosch Company of Stuttgart, which was to attain European leadership in the production of magnetos and automotive parts.

Foreign Trade

The late nineteenth-century metamorphosis in the economic structure of Germany destroyed her former self-sufficiency. Despite a tripling of her agricultural output in the course of the century and the fact that she still led Europe in the production of rye and potatoes and was second in oats in 1913, Germany was being thrust by industrialization and urbanization into dependence upon imports for at least dairy products, barley, and fodder. To maintain her high living standard without these imports would have necessitated doubling or tripling her pasturage and arable.

Momentous economic changes were reflected in the composition of Germany's foreign trade. Before 1860 the bulk of her imports had consisted of semifinished and finished goods. Exports had mainly been grain, potatoes, sugar, meat, wool, dairy products, wine, and vegetable oils. Between 1880 and 1913 the value of imports rose from 2,844 million Marks to 10,770 million, and of exports, from 2,977 million to 10,097 million Marks. Of the imports, foodstuffs in 1913 comprised 38.2 percent, raw materials 34 percent, semifinished goods 18.1 percent, and manufactured or processed end items only 9.7 percent. Of the exports in 1913, foodstuffs comprised only 12 percent, raw materials 13.4 percent, semifinished goods 10.7 percent, and manufactured items 63.9 percent. Within fifty years the emphasis had reversed itself: the bulk of Germany's exports on the eve of World War I comprised iron, steel, coal, textiles, machinery, electrical equipment, optical goods, dyes, and chemicals.

The Role of the Banks

To support German commercial and industrial growth a ramifying network of joint-stock banks sprang up. After 1860 it became increasingly plain that only a few of the very largest industrial enterprises, such as those of Hartmann, Borsig, Henschel, and Krupp, disposed sufficient funds to finance their mechanization and expansion. Almost all other firms urgently needed major financing, which could alone be supplied by joint-stock banks. Especially great sums of capital were required in the iron, coal, steel, railroad, machine, and construction industries. Millions of small investors put their capital in the new joint-stock banks of deposit and issue, the first of which had been founded in 1848 by Gustav von Mevissen (1815–99). These made available both long- and short-term credits to German business.

The joint-stock banks took the initiative too in founding or promoting the consolidation of industrial and mercantile limited liability companies *(Aktiengesellschaften*—A.G.)*, with the result that from 1870 to 1873 some 859 such companies were formed, a figure that was almost triple the number that had been founded during the preceding twenty years. The new banks were a major factor in the cartelization of large-scale industry.

Gradually the world of German finance-capitalism came to be overshadowed by four great commercial banks: the "four D's"—the Deutsche Bank, Dresdner Bank, Darmstädter Bank, and the Diskonto Gesellschaft. In 1875 the Prussian Bank was transformed by act of the Reichstag into the Reichsbank and put at the apex of the pyramid. The Reichsbank, which helped Germany to go onto and remain on the gold standard, was designated a central bank for the issue of a uniform currency. Eventually twenty-seven institutions surrendered to it their rights to print legal tender. The Reichsbank also served as a banker's bank by discounting commercial paper belonging to the joint-stock banks.

Rising Living Standards

The economic euphoria of the era of the Second German Empire may best be documented by the rise in real personal income. The promising portents of the period 1848–1870 were abundantly realized in the years 1871–1914. Total real individual income rose from a little under fifteen billion to almost fifty billion marks. With the steady rise in the purchasing power of the consumer, the living conditions of the lowest strata of society exhibited substantial improvement, especially in the period 1890–1913, and a greater percentage of persons than ever before was elevated to the middle class and middle income levels. By 1913 most Germans were living in tolerable circumstances, and the rich were more numerous and affluent than ever. About 85 percent of the German population in that year enjoyed an income of from 1,000 to 3,000 marks per annum. With the highest living standard of any major European power and with prospects of becoming a great welfare state, the Germany of 1913 was in reality further from social revolution than she had been in 1848.

The Role of Government

During the age of imperialism German big business achieved an organic connection with the ruling establishment. For reasons of state the imperial government came to regard industry as the "fair-haired boy" of the national family. The government was acutely aware of the facts that bourgeois support of the political order had become the deciding element in exorcising the specter of proletarian revolution and that industrial expansion would bring rising real wages and material benefits to the working class, which would attach it more firmly to the state.

Bismarck's efforts to extend the powers of the central government were strongly motivated by economic considerations. He never doubted that the basis of military and political strength was economic. In a powerful central government, the iron chancellor espied the stairway to economic ascendancy in Europe. He therefore labored to extend the constitutional prerogatives of the imperial government and concentrate novel powers in the hands of the ministries of the central chancellery (Reichskanzleramt). Under the presidency of Rudolf Delbrück (1817–1903), a champion of free trade, the chancellery, until its dissolution in 1878, was the auxiliary of finance-capitalism in the most critical phase of its development.

In the Second Empire the central government was the coadjutor of trade and industry. The Reich government never adopted any antitrust legislation that could have obstructed concentration of capital or cartelization of business. On the other hand, the central government experimented with state ownership of a range of enterprises and monopolized telegraphic, postal, and telephonic services, deriving more than half its income from its capitalist ventures, which included operation of many railroad lines.

Imperial legislation often aided German business. In 1873 the Imperial Railroad Bureau was established to improve transportation. In 1873, too, Germany joined England on the gold standard, while in 1874 the Reichsbank was founded. By 1878 the mark had been standardized and individual regional currencies had been suppressed. In 1877 the German Supreme Court (Reichsgericht), domiciled in Leipzig, was established. In 1879 the Reichstag standardized rules of civil and criminal procedure and defined the competence of the hierarchy of courts. In 1879–80 the Reichstag passed protective tariffs that sharply stimulated mining and manufacturing. In 1880 Bismarck assumed the portfolio of Prussian minister of commerce and, with it, personal responsibility for the economic wellbeing of Germany. After 1884, in response to pressure by the bourgeois German Colonial Society (Deutsche Kolonialgesellschaft), Bismarck began the systematic acquisition of overseas colonies. Under his successor, Chancellor Leo Caprivi, the central government passed new protective tariff legislation (1893–94), which, at the expense of agriculture, made Germany the leading industrial power in Europe. The creation of an Imperial Naval Office in 1889 and the construction after 1898 of a high-seas fleet were initiatives that were undertaken solely in response to pressure from the mercantile and industrial class, which clamored for protection of its overseas markets, sources of raw materials, and growing merchant marine. The twelve-year reciprocal trade treaties that were negotiated with Germany's neighbors during the Caprivi era lowered tariffs upon wheat, rye, and cattle with the result that the price of foodstuffs sank on the domestic market, which pleased both capital and labor. The construction of the Kiel Canal, which connected the North and Baltic seas, was undertaken in 1895. Not least of all, the purposes of German business were served by the adoption in 1900 of a great, uniform civil code.

Even the social reforms of the post-Bismarckian period were expressions of the government's procapitalist policies. The purpose of the chief exponents of these reforms, Hans Freiherr von Berlepsch (1843–1926), who was Prussian minister of commerce, and Count Arthur von Posadowsky-Wehner (1845–1932), who was the imperial secretary of the interior under Count von Bülow, was to harness labor and capital in the same span in order to generate vast economic and military potential. This is not to deny German statesmen the reputation of being humane and honestly concerned over the poor, weak, infirm, and aged. Nevertheless, it is a fact that in the thinking of the bureaucracy there was a clear connection between social reform and the *Machtstaat*.

The Caprivi-Berlepsch government surpassed Bismarck's in its advocacy of social welfare legislation. The former instituted industrial courts for arbitrating disputes between labor and capital (1890); secured passage of a Sunday holiday law in 1891 and legislation that limited and regulated child and female labor, defined harmful occupations, protected employees in them, and increased the authority of factory inspectors; and generally sought to eliminate the worst instances of capitalist exploitation. However, in 1894 when Prince Hohenlohe-Schillingsfürst became chancellor, a change of imperial policy toward the workers set in. Berlepsch resigned in 1896, and the government was free to indulge a brief "hate campaign" against the socialists. This so-called Battle Policy *(Kampfpolitik),* which for a time contemplated a *Staatsstreich* against the Social Democratic party (SPD), ended in electoral defeat for the reactionaries and in the adoption of Posadowsky-Wehner's conciliatory measures. In 1901 government-sponsored, low-cost housing projects were initiated. In 1900 and 1903 the accident and sickness insurance program was expanded, and in 1903 child labor in home industries was prohibited. In 1907, when Posadowsky-Wehner resigned from the ministry of the interior, new social legislation was passed. Then, finally, under prodding from the Social Democrats, the Reich government in 1911 adopted a comprehensive social insurance code, the most equitable and generous in the world at the time. The code consolidated and systematized the whole network of sickness, disability, accident, and old age insurance and increased benefit payments. By such measures, Bismarck, Berlepsch, and Posadowsky-Wehner, in effect, nationalized the Marxian SPD and transformed it into a loyal reform movement and coefficient of capitalist power.

Governmental Omissions and Failures

The German government was unprepared to cope with all the dangers generated by the frenzied tempo of industrialization. The imperial ministers intemperately gave lopsided emphasis to untrammeled expansion of industry and trade and to higher rates of increase of the gross national product. In so acting, they neglected to control and moderate the rate of growth for the good of the state. An overheated economy ought periodically to have been cooled by manipulating credit and rediscount rates, modifying tariff laws, and by other regulatory devices. A more prudent ministry would have been concerned to achieve a better balance among production, self-sufficiency, foreign trade, financial resources, and military-naval prowess. Care should also have been taken not to assume liabilities, such as both a high-seas fleet and a first-class army, which surpassed the state's resources. Nor should Germany's government have allowed her to slip into dependence upon foreign imports and markets to such degree that she became critically vulnerable to blockade in wartime.

The hectic thrust and strident noise that attended German industrial and commerical expansion created problems of the first magnitude that eventually destroyed the Empire. These might conceivably have been anticipated if the federal government had in proper time devised controls over speculation, construction, and excessive production. Likewise, a healthier society might have developed if the ministry had fostered more economic self-sufficiency by subsidizing agriculture, animal husbandry, and extensive chemical research in fertilizers, fodders, and substitute raw materials.

Instead, German production was permitted, even encouraged, to attain a tumorous growth. This had pathological effects upon the state as a whole. By 1913 the national wealth, which a generation earlier had limped far behind that of Great Britain, had reached 300 billion marks, as compared with the latter's 280 billion and 170 billion for France.

The federal government footed a not-inconsiderable part of the bill for this rash development. Partly because of this, the state was obliged to struggle under a public debt that mounted between 1890 and 1904 from one to three billion marks and upon which interest payments were far higher than in Britain or France. Increasing fiscal difficulties led the imperial government to seek new sources of revenue within the Reich, which provoked social unrest, or in the Near East, which antagonized the Russians, French, and British. It is more than likely that general war might still have been years away in 1914 had Germany not pushed feverishly and ostentatiously to compete with Britain and France as a world economic power.

Chapter 35

CULTURAL CHIAROSCURO

The Emergence of a Materialist Culture

After 1850 an increasingly large number of intellectuals repudiated the romantic and religious perspective in favor of the materialistic and realistic. Attention was focused upon the objective world of phenomena, physical life, and society. Acceleration of the capitalist revolution in Germany progressively alienated people from the basic goods of nature. Neither the squalid, urban proletariat nor the profit-grubbing middle class had much time to commune with creation or even had any real affinity for it. In an era when rural life was in decline, peasants and landlords, who were the most conservative elements, could offer only a negative, bovine resistance to the new craze for practicality.

In an atmosphere of unprecedented change, when the old ways of doing and thinking seemed hopelessly ineffectual and irrelevant, the conflict of generations became acute. German thought became more chaotic than it had been since Luther's time. Positivist, materialist, mechanistic, and scientific schemas, generally originating abroad with August Comte, Charles Darwin, Karl Marx, and Herbert Spencer, warred with native neo-Kantian, Hegelian, and romantic schools of thought for possession of the German mind.

In this clash of values, which was fundamentally a battle between art and science, articulate opposition to a materialist *Weltanschauung* was usually confined to humanist scholars, such as Wilhelm Dilthey, Count von Keyserling, Jakob Burckhardt, Paul de Lagarde, Friedrich Nietzsche, Rainer Maria Rilke, Richard Wagner, Hoffmann von Fallersleben, Julius Langbehn, Ricarda Huch, Stefan George, Moeller van den Bruck, and Oswald Spengler. All these critics admonished against the pernicious vulgarization of taste, denigration of aesthetics, and emasculation of individuality that capitalism had allegedly wrought.

It is hyperbole to adduce a deterioration in certain areas of thought as evidence of the decay of the whole. True, levels of accomplishment in some fields in this period were lower than had been the case in the eighteenth century or the romantic age. This was the case with philosophy and aesthetics. The accomplishments of later nineteenth-century thinkers, such as Nietzsche and Ludwig Wittgenstein, assuredly did not surpass those of Kant, Fichte, and Hegel. It may even be argued that poetry and art, and to a lesser extent prose, were corrupted by the influence of latter day modes of expression and by the glorification of wealth and power, or that the tyranny of psychoanalysis and scientific atomism was detrimental to art and literature. Yet, for every discipline that malingered during the epoch of the Second Empire, two flourished in its rich soil. Instrumental music, opera and operetta, the dance, mathematics, all the social and natural sciences, and Biblical studies, fructified—some as never before.

Materialism and *Machtpolitik*, so far from ruining German culture, conferred upon the educational system of the Second Reich a reputation for excellence that sent many an American to study at the leading German universities. The many-faceted success of the Second Empire was a brilliant that mocked the gloomy pictures painted by Julius Langbehn *(Rembrandt als Erzieher* or *Rembrandt as Educator)* or by a Moeller van den Bruck *(Die Deutschen* and *Kulturgeschichte)* of a mechanistic and spiritually degraded Germany that was facing cultural break-down. Not until the collapse of 1918 was a sable pessimist, Oswald Spengler (1880–1936), able to influence the thinking of a large section of the public with his funereal *Untergang des Abendlandes (Decline of the West*, 2 vols., 1918–22*).*

Literary Realism

As creative output in all fields immeasurably broadened in the second half of the century, romanticism and subjectivism, which are the modes of the individ-ualist, gave way to objectivism and positivism. Idealism came to be looked upon only as the opiate of an escapist who wished to ignore the harsh facts of life in an industrial society. For the realists, romanticism was endemically contemplative, incapable of generating an activist devotion to any of the great causes of the day. Somewhat contradictorily, however, literary realists were devotees of a cult of insensitivity and emotional detachment. They aspired to depict things, not as they might be at their best, but as they are at their sordid worst. The style had been set by great French masters—Flaubert, Maupassant, and Zola—and was imitated in Germany by a legion of hacks who dwelt morbidly and wearisomely upon ail-ments of the existing social order, while toiling to suffuse art with stultifying practicality. Of a mediocre field of exponents, the most significant were the Swiss epic poets Gottfried Keller (1819–90) and Conrad F. Meyer (1825–98), and the German Victor von Scheffel (1826–86) of Munich.

Neoromantic and Symbolist Poetry

Among those who carried the woodland melodies of romantic poetry into a bourgeois world was Theodor Storm (1817–88) of Schleswig-Holstein. He wrote melancholy poems, sonnets to the somber beauty of his native dunes and marsh-lands. Another was Paul von Heyse (1830–1914), a Berlin-educated writer of verse, dramas, and novelettes, who was patronized by the king of Bavaria. Heyse wrote nearly perfectly structured narrative and lyric poetry. His monumental masterpiece was *Die dramatische Dichtungen (Dramatic Poetry*, 38 vols., 1864–1905),* and he was the first German man of letters to be awarded the Nobel Prize for literature (1910). Also belonging to the cohort that transcended the wooden world of realism was Theodore Fontane (1819–98). Editor of the *Kreuzzeitung* between 1860 and 1870 and thereafter for twenty years the dramatic critic for the *Vossische Zeitung*, Fontane was better known for his novels than his verse. Never-theless, he was accounted one of the finest ballad writers of the century (e.g., *Balladen*, 1860, and *Jenseits des Tweed* or *The Other Side of the Tweed*, 1860). Others who defied the *Zeitgeist* were Baron Detlev von Liliencron (1844–1909) of Schleswig-Holstein, a composer of colorful verse, whose rhetoric was vigorous and lucid, and the lyric poet and playwright Hugo von Hofmannsthal (1874–1929), who also composed libretti for five operas by Richard Strauss.

Toward the turn of the century a new star, brighter than any of the aforementioned, appeared in the literary firmament. Rainer Maria Rilke (1875–1926) was possibly the greatest German poet since Goethe. An inner, religious light illumines Rilke's poetry. Artist and sculptor as well as poet, he was influenced by the French and Belgian symbolists—Baudelaire, Mallarmé, Verlaine, and Maeterlinck— but surpassed them in the precision and chiseled beauty of his verse. Drenched in pious revery, the esoteric prewar poetry of Rilke, often relating to his native Bohemia, included *Das Stundenbuch (Book of Hours,* 1905*), Die neue Gedichte (New Poetry,* 1907–8*)*, and the long narrative poem, *The Manner of Love and Death of Cornet Christoph Rilke* (1909).

In the last quarter of the century the decadent, sensuous, and shimmering verse of Charles Baudelaire *(Les Fleurs du Mal,* 1857*)* was widely imitated in the German Empire. At the end of the century poetry entered the symbolist stream. Stefan George (1868–1933), a Hessian who had translated *Les Fleurs du Mal*, emerged as Germany's chief exponent of aesthetic eroticism. He wrote rarified, frangible verse—"art for art's sake"—primarily for a coterie of kindred Pre-Raphaelite spirits. His trilogy *Pilgerfahrt (Pilgrimage,* 1890–95*)* revealed an aristocratic philosophy, preoccupation with total form, and novel punctuation.

The Realist Novel

In prose, too, the progression after midcentury was from romanticism through realism and naturalism to symbolism. Inspired by French and Russian masters, this line of development unfortunately gradually alienated the masses from higher literature and created the need for vulgar, "pulp" fiction.

Realist literature delineated character and situation with dispassionate objectivity. One of the earliest realist novelists was Karl Gutzkow. With his *Die Ritter vom Geiste (Knights of the Spirit,* 9 vols., 1850–52*)* he gave a powerful impetus to objectivism and apostasized from the romanticism of his youth. Similarly, Theodor Storm abandoned the romanticism of his *Immensee* (1850) period and entered the mainstream of continental literature with novels such as *Beim Vetter Christian (At Cousin Christian's,* 1874*), Carsten Curator* (1878), and *Die Söhne des Senators (The Senator's Sons,* 1880*)*, all pitiless analyses of contemporary society. Realistic tales of merit were also written by Detlev von Liliencron, Gottfried Keller, C. Meyer, Arno Holz (1863–1919), and the authoress Ricarda Huch (1864–1947). Holz is best remembered for the intensely austere sketches in *Papa Hamlet* (1889), while the historical narratives of Meyer and Huch had wide vogue. Mention must also be made of Paul von Heyse for his finely polished analytical novels and for having done for the German short story with his *Deutscher Novellenschatz (Treasury of German Short Stories,* 24 vols., 1870–76*)* what Balzac and Maupassant had done for the French.

Naturalism and Afterwards

In the late 1870s and the 1880s naturalism, the child of realism, celebrated its brief prime. Naturalism was socially more involved than its parent had been and, as Vernon Lidtke has shown, often crusaded arm in arm with socialism against an unjust order. Conceptually, however, the new cult was inexcusably rigid. Its demimondaines, prostitutes, and grisettes were all stereotypes. Practically oblivious of plot, action, or even character development, the new style focused on segments of life in the raw and served up human tragedies that had neither beginning nor end.

More than any German contemporary Theodore Fontane was the master of the frank and often prurient dialogue peculiar to naturalism. His pioneer novels *The Adulteress* (1882) and *Effi Briest* (1895), which dealt with emotional instability and illicit love, brought Fontane lasting fame. In other novels Fontane made invidious comparison between bourgeois society and a genteel aristocratic order of the past.

Even before naturalism crested, German writers abandoned socialism and began to seek inspiration in the symbolist works of French avant-gardists, in Nietzsche's doctrine of the will to power, and, somewhat later, in Freudian psychoanalysis. To be sure, this quest generated an attitude that was not less critical of the world but was no longer mainly dominated by class prejudices.

Ranking with Rilke, von Hofmannsthal, George, and the Viennese physician and man of letters Arthur Schnitzler (1862–1931) as one of the most caustic critics of the spiritual emptiness of Second Empire society, was the fiercely democratic Heinrich Mann (1871–1950). Scion of an old Lübeck merchant family, he wrote devastating satires upon the contemporary milieu, such as *Der Untertan (The Subject*, 1914*)* and the trilogy *Das Kaiserreich (The Empire*, 1914–25*)*. He also dealt successfully with the theme of devouring sexual desire, as in his world-famous *Professor Unrat* or *Der blaue Engel (The Blue Angel,* 1905*)*.

Heinrich Mann's brother Thomas (1875–1955) was destined to eclipse him. Thomas became the most profound German novelist of the twentieth century. His chief prewar narratives offered a penetrating critique of middle-class culture, which was mollified by a prognosis of future regeneration: *Buddenbrooks* (1901), *Tristan* (1903), *Der Tod in Venedig (Death in Venice,* 1913*)*, and *Tonio Krüger* (1914).

Drama

In drama, as in prose, the historical materialist view held sway for a span of years. The Marxist approach in literature postulated that the complex of economic relationships in any given epoch determines the whole social and cultural mosaic and accordingly focused attention upon the plight of the whole working class rather than the individual.

The ascendancy of mediocrity among German realist playwrights was typified by Friedrich Hebbel (1813–63). He delineated tawdry characters in sordid, erotic settings but because his plays were too intellectual to please the public they were soon forgotten.

Higher quality work was achieved in the naturalist era, especially by the socialistic Hermann Sudermann (1857–1928) and Gerhard Hauptmann (1856–1942), both of whom followed in the footsteps of Zola and Ibsen. The East Prussian Sudermann, an able craftsman who was active in Berlin, pioneered in the writing of drab, amoral plays, such as *Die Ehre (Honor*, 1889*)*, *Die Heimat (Homeland*, 1893*)*, and *Sodom's Ende* (1890), which often had an anti-Christian and anti-bourgeois bias. The Silesian Hauptmann was probably the finest dramatist since Schiller. His plays usually ponder the problems of society and the modern family without presuming to offer a prognosis. His two finest dramas were *Vor Sonnenaufgang (Before Sunrise*, 1889*)*, which treated the impact of alcoholism upon a degenerate family, and *Die Weber (The Weavers*, 1892*)*, which explored the grievances of the Silesian weavers in their rebellion of 1844. Later Hauptmann experimented with symbolism and the subliminal in *Hanneles Himmelfahrt (Hannele's Ascent to Heaven*, 1893*)*, where the heroine is only a child, *Die versunkene Glocke (The Sunken Bell*, 1896*)*, and the occult, macabre *Und Pippa tanzt (And Pippa Dances*, 1906*)*.

Austria produced no dramatist of the first rank in the realist era. The best was possibly Ludwig Anzengruber (1839–87). He, like Keller, was preoccupied with the bigotry and shallowness of rural life, of which he painted a somber picture in his *Der Pfarrer von Kirchfeld (The Pastor of Kirchfeld*, 1870*)* and *Das vierte Gebot (The Fourth Commandment*, 1878*)*.

In Germany symbolist techniques were most successfully adopted by Hofmannsthal, who stood under the influence of Maeterlinck but surpassed him in craftsmanship. After having established a reputation for neoclassical and neoromantic drama, Hofmannsthal wrote *Der Tod des Tizians (Death of Titian*, 1892*)* and *Der Tor und der Tod (The Gate and Death*, 1894*)*, plays that combined a naturalist indifference to plot and character development with symbolist dialogue and mood.

Art

One of the most important contenders for the mantle of Caspar D. Friedrich was Carl Spitzweg (1808–85), who painted with spontaneous sensitivity and realism scenes from everyday life. A fairly good genre portraitist and depicter of peasant life in the Alpine forelands was Wilhelm Leibl (1844–1900), who had studied with Courbet in Paris. Max Liebermann (1847–1935) painted realistic studies of the little people of his milieu, as in his "Country Tavern in Bavaria," "Woman Plucking Geese," and "The Hog Market." By contrast, the romantic tradition found at least one major devotee in an alien age in Hans Thoma (1839–1924), who painted Wagnerian operatic scenes on the walls of Neuschwanstein castle for Ludwig II.

The impressionists were more important than the realists in German painting of this era. The great French impressionists—Manet, Renoir, Monet, and Dégas—heavily influenced Menzel, Böcklin, Corinth, and Slevogt. Adolf Menzel (1815–1905) tried without much success to introduce the new style to the stolid Germans, but Arnold Böcklin (1827–1901), Lovis Corinth (1858–1925), and Max Slevogt (1868–1932) were better able to catch the French impressionists' vision of limpid colors and tremulous light. Nevertheless, German canvases of this genre were commonly marred by chromatic homogeneity and an opaqueness of objects. Best of the foregoing group, Slevogt, a master of the elegant portrait (e.g., "The White Ariadne") understood the secret of dissolving volume into light.

The tension and neurosis that characterized the *fin du siècle*, aggravated by the preoccupation of science with the subatom, fostered an interest in inner structural values. About 1904–5 a group of artists founded a new school at Dresden. Called Die Brücke (the bridge), this school broke with impressionism and founded expressionism in central Europe.

Taking their inspiration from van Gogh, Ensor, Seurat, and Munch, the German expressionists emphasized the highly subjective and abstract or stylized use of forms and symbols to depict reality. Franz Marc (1880–1916), who was killed in World War I, was widely admired for his expressionistic treatment of the animal kingdom. More important than he were the subjectivist artists of Der Blaue Reiter (Blue Horseman) school that was founded by Kandinsky and Klee in Munich around 1911. Like the romanticists of an earlier day, these expressionists also sought the evanescent "blue flower," but they hoped to discover it, somewhat improbably, in the abstract components of nature. Eventually the school absorbed the best talent of Die Brücke. Among the Blue Horsemen were Alexander Kanoldt (1881–1939), the Russian-born Vassily Kandinsky (1866–1944), and Paul Klee (1879–1940), who was a surrealistic anatomist of frangible, dreamlike themes. Perhaps the most famous of the Blauer Reiter school was Oscar Kokoschka (1886–), a versatile Austrian designer, poet, dramatist, and painter. Kokoschka's richly textured landscapes and portraits are among the most captivating expressionistic efforts of the century.

In architecture two styles, neo-Gothic and neo-Classical (or neo-Renaissance), competed for supremacy, but neither was able to regenerate German building. The most impressive examples of the neo-Classical were the Reichstag building and the Lessing Theater, both in Berlin. However, it was not until the advent of steel and glass construction that German architecture again began to influence Western tastes. Then, functional structures were designed by the innovative Peter Behrens (1868–1940), who pioneered the way for Gropius and the Bauhaus school.

Music

In instrumental music Germany maintained her olden sway throughout the century, while in opera she made her most important contributions since Mozart's time. After the Franco-Prussian War Germany also ennobled the operetta, a new and lilting art form, when the sparkling Johann Strauss (1825–99) displaced Jacques Offenbach as king of melody. Germany's ascendancy in music was not only due in part to the widespread private ownership of pianos, wind and stringed instruments, and transcriptions, but also to the fact that virtually every town of any importance in the land had its own concert hall and opera house and to the fact that opera and symphony were subsidized by state governments.

Germany's last great "classical" composer was the Hamburg-born Johannes Brahms (1833–97). An intellectual and philosophic composer who spent his mature years in Vienna, Brahms developed an extraordinary polyphonic technique. He wrote four great symphonies, overtures, intermezzi, sonatas for violin and piano (of which instrument he was a master), quartets, quintets, *Lieder*, chorals (such as his "German Requiem"), chamber music, dances, and rhapsodies.

Two other important instrumental composers were Anton Bruckner (1824–96) and Richard Strauss (1864–1949). Bruckner, an Austrian professor at the Conservatory in Vienna, composed numerous chorales, masses, and nine symphonies. The Bavarian-born Strauss, who was successively director of the state operas at Munich, Berlin, and Vienna, in his earlier period wrote much string and orchestral music and developed the symphonic poem, a new genre that Liszt had introduced to Germany. In his second period Strauss's chief contribution was to program music. Thus, during the years 1887–1904 he composed *Macbeth* (1887), *Tod und Verklärung (Death and Transfiguration*, 1887*)*, *Till Eulenspiegels lustige Streiche (Till Eulenspiegel's Merry Pranks*, 1895*)*, and *Also sprach Zarathustra (Thus Spake Zarathustra*, 1897*)*. After 1904 Strauss was mainly preoccupied with directing and writing operas, a form in which he was inferior to Wagner. Among his operas, all of which were replete with harmonic innovations, diatonic experiments, and frequent dissonance, were *Salomé* (1905), *Der Rosenkavalier* (1911), and *Die Frau ohne Schatten (The Woman without a Shadow*, 1919*)*.

The chief secondary composers were Franz Liszt (1811–86), Hugo Wolf (1860–1903), and Gustav Mahler (1860–1911). Liszt, an incorrigible philanderer—he had three children by the Countess d'Agoult (pseudonym Daniel Stern) and also entered into a liaison with the Princess Sayn-Wittgenstein—was a world-famous Hungarian pianist, whose daughter, Cosima, became Wagner's second wife. Liszt is remembered primarily for his difficult Hungarian rhapsodies, piano transcriptions, and symphonic poems. Wolf also strove to give new dimensions to instrumental music. His best achievements were symphonic poems, *Lieder*, and Hispanic, neobaroque-style chamber compositions. Mahler, a Bohemian Jew and director of the Viennese Court Opera (1897–1907), wrote ten symphonies, many songs, and orchestral music. Featuring extended solo passages, Mahler's works were another effort to discover new tonal media of expression. Arnold Schönberg (1874–1951), an Austrian Jew who worked in both Vienna and Berlin until 1933, penetrated much further into the wastelands of atonality, for he detested the shimmering web of neoromanticism in which Wagner had enmeshed German music. Schönberg's string sextet *Verklärte Nacht (Radiant Night*, 1899*)* and *Gurrelieder (Cooing Songs*, 1913*)* were his farewell to the chromatic scale. Thereafter he experimented with the tradition-breaking "twelve-tone scale."

Probably of much greater importance to the world was the champagne music of Johann Strauss, director of the Vienna Court Dance Orchestra. His waltzes are among the most melodic dance music ever written—glittering melodies to which, it may be imagined, Bach, Haydn, Beethoven, Mozart, and Brahms waltzed in heaven. Strauss also wrote the imperishable operettas *Die Fledermaus (The Bat*, 1874) and *Eine Nacht in Venedig (A Night in Venice*, 1883). In the music of Strauss Germany possessed an art form that gilded her gray industrial society and intoxicated the Western world.

The towering figure of late nineteenth-century music was Richard Wagner (1813–83). No German since Mozart made such a profound contribution to the development of opera. One may forgive this sickly, psychotic, histrionic, insufferably conceited, chauvinistic, anti-Semitic, and unscrupulous man all of his sins for the sake of his musical wizardry. For many, this intensely Germanic composer was the paramount instrumental composer since Beethoven.

Wagner already insured in three of his earliest music dramas—*Der fliegende Holländer (The Flying Dutchman*, 1843) and the medieval *Tannhäuser* (1845) and *Lohengrin* (1850)—that realism would never be able to exorcise German lyricism. In them he had exhibited melodic magic and a unique ability to integrate voice, orchestra, drama, and spectacle into an organic whole. The great operas of the *Ring of the Nibelungen (Das Rheingold*, 1854; *Die Walküre* or *The Valkyries*, 1856; *Siegfried*, 1857–68; and *Götterdämmerung* or *Twilight of the Gods*, 1869–74) were a conscious attempt by Wagner to glorify his country's past. All of his operas, including the erotic *Tristan and Isolde* (1857–59), which was based on the love story by Gottfried von Strassburg, and his profound, religio-philosophic *Parzifal* (1877–82), represented in their aggregate a titanic effort to create a shining myth of old Teutonic culture. Although there was much dross in Wagner's compositions, he achieved an orchestral texture, range of modulation, and a tonal beauty, augmented by the device of a recurring, symbolic melody (leitmotif), that were unique in musical history.

Philosophy

Positivism had little effect upon Germany, but the economic determinism of Marx and the natural determinism of Darwinism had great influence. The main champion of this trend in the Reich was, however, not a philosopher, but the celebrated Ernst H. Haeckel (1834–1919), a Darwinist professor of biology at Jena. In his *Riddle of the Universe* (1890) he expounded a "monist," agnostic *Weltanschauung* that stressed the material genesis of creation and the basic chemical unity of all matter. By applying the principle of selection in accordance with biological laws and mechanistic imperatives, he flattered himself that he had demolished the idea of divine design and rendered the notion of a "moral order" irrelevant.

Inasmuch as business, armies, and science—all practical things—enjoyed a strong hold on the German mentality in the late nineteenth century, philosophy lost face. In an age of exceptional concrete achievements and a milieu of optimism, the "gloomy" discipline until about 1890 passed into temporary decline. The public, no less than Karl Marx, lost patience with it.

Although idealism was perpetuated in many a pedestrian treatise by neo-Hegelians, such as Rudolf Lotze (1817–1881) and Rudolf Eucken (1846–1926), it was not until the rise of the neo-Kantian Marburg school, associated with Ernst Cohen (1842–1918) and Paul Natorp (1854–1924), that philosophy experienced a modest revival. A number of professors from south of the Main, notably Wilhelm Windelband (1848–1915) and Heinrich Rickert (1863–1936), aided the revival. They stressed the cardinal epistemological importance of inner experience, revelation, and intuition. A divergent system, at once more materialistic and historical, was elaborated by the intellectual historian Wilhelm Dilthey (1833–1911) and the Berlin philosopher Edmund Husserl (1859–1938). They directed attention to the dynamic, terrestrial forces of social and national evolution, which were the architects of mind and institutions. This perspective, whose remote progenitor was Herder, came to be called "historicism."

Incomparably the brightest comet to flash across the philosophic firmament in late nineteenth-century Germany was Friedrich Nietzsche (1844–1900). Not so much a formal metaphysician as an artist who daubed his pages with greeny-gold rhetoric, Nietzsche entranced his readers with the necromancy of poetry and imagery.

In his works, which were profoundly antidemocratic, Nietzsche differentiated, not between right and wrong, but between the morality of the strong and the weak. Nietzsche scorned Christianity as being "effeminate" and a "religion of slaves" and had no use for its ethics. In his main works *(Ecce Homo, Thus Spake Zarathustra, Beyond Good and Evil, The Will to Power*, and *The Genealogy of Morals)*, all of which were written in the 1880s, Nietzsche apotheosized the superior intellect of a hypothetically wholly enlightened and uninhibited superman *(Übermensch)* of the future. Nietzsche's notion of life as a raw struggle for power was patently influenced by capitalist imperatives and the Darwinian survival of the fittest. His emphasis upon the individual as a law unto himself and his denunciation of decadence, coupled with his faith in the regenerative potentiality of will power, led him to condone almost any kind of rebellious thinking or behavior of his day. He anticipated the findings of Heidegger, Sartre, and Freud and influenced symbolists, existentialists, expressionists, and elitists of every kind. Especially did his oriental rhetoric and Zarathustra's Magian speech entrance symbolists, abstractionists, and all who were in rebellion against the "hypocrisy" of the established order. In his prevision of a surpassing leadership above morality, which would make its own laws and govern the lives of the masses, Nietzsche influenced the development of Fascist and Nazi thought.

Chapter 36

THE GOLDEN CALF: THE SCIENCES

The Mental Climate

The restoration of German science, which commenced about 1830, was conditioned by the rise of industrial capitalism. The technologically oriented and practical German bourgeoisie were especially interested in applied science, which held promise of mechanical advances and chemical discoveries that could be translated into profits. At the same time, the great universities—especially Göttingen, Berlin, Bonn, Jena, Halle, Heidelberg, Tübingen, Erlangen, and Würzburg—provided the laboratory facilities and funding for fundamental research, and the territorial governments sympathetically financed it all. As the century wore on, the general public, heavily propagandized and indoctrinated by the middle-class press, conceived a passion for everything relating to science or what passed as science. Whereas in the eighteenth century the cult of reason had captured the imagination of the nobility and intelligentsia, "scientism" had by 1870 come to hypnotize all classes in Germany. Sustained by a universal enthusiasm, the physical and biological scientists achieved things by 1914 which for significance surpassed anything that had ever before been accomplished by Germans in those fields.

Mathematics and Physics

The advances in mathematics in the first half of the nineteenth century were the prelude to the revolutionary discoveries in physics in the period 1870–1914.

Germany's greatest mathematical physicist of the century was Karl Friedrich Gauss (1777–1855), professor at Göttingen. He made important contributions to astronomy and mathematics, expounding the mathematical theory of electricity, utilizing symbols and equations to interpret properties and potentialities of electricity, and formulating a general theory of mutually attracting forces. Wilhelm Weber (1804–91), who worked with Gauss investigating terrestrial magnetism, developed an absolute system of expressing magnetic and electrical units in terms of length, mass, and time. Weber also propounded a magnetic theory (1854) that foreshadowed the electron-orbit concept of Ernest Rutherford. One practical fruit of Weber's work was his invention of an electromagnetic telegraph. Georg Simon Ohm (1787–1854) studied the relationship between the intensity of a current and the resistance to it in a circuit, and he established the practical unit of resistance (ohm) for measurement of the amount of work needed to transmit an electromotive force from one point to another. The mathematical physicist Georg F. Riemann (1826–66) explored the potentialities of non-Euclidian geometry and advanced the line of symbolic calculus that led ultimately to the theory of relativity. Hermann Ludwig Helmholtz (1821–94), a versatile genius who was professor variously of physiology, anatomy, and physics at a number of universities including Berlin after 1871, not only invented the ophthalmoscope, but formulated the principle of the conservation of energy (1847) and defined the principle of energy of an electrostatic system. All the foregoing scholars regarded power and matter as the essential realities of the universe, thereby, incidentally, lending strong support to current materialist-deterministic philosophies.

Optics and Astronomy

Hardly less important than the progress made in mathematical physics was that achieved in optics and astronomy. In Königsberg in 1838 astronomy for the first time vaulted the local planetary system, when Friedrich Wilhelm Bessel (1784–1846), the director of the city's observatory, calculated the distance of the nearest fixed star (61 Cygni) as about 25 billion miles from our sun. Joseph von Fraunhofer of Munich (1787–1826) was the first to detect the dark lines in the solar spectrum and scientifically to study the spectra of the stars and planets. Fraunhofer devised finer and more exact instruments too—the micrometer, heliometer, and improved telescopes. His studies on the prismatic dispersion of light and the measurement of light waves ushered in an era of the chemical analysis of the universe. Following in his traces, Gustav Robert Kirchoff (1824–87) in 1860 formulated the principle of spectrum inversion, by which light from celestial sources of energy can be diffracted and its components arranged in order of their respective wave lengths for study on a spectograph. By applying the well-known Doppler principle in connection with spectrum analysis, Kirchoff was able to determine the direction and velocity of movement of the stars. Suddenly the cosmos received a spatial extension that vastly exceeded anything that had been entertained in the past and the way was open for the promulgation of startling new theories.

The Organic Sciences

Germany's discoveries in the natural sciences were hardly less important than in the physical. Between 1833 and 1835 Matthias Schleiden (1804–81), professor of botany at Jena, identified the nucleus as an essential part of the cell and discovered the phenomenon of its division. In 1838 Theodor Schwann (1810–82), working in Liège, identified the ovum as a cell and shortly afterward asserted that the entire animal or plant organism consists of cells or waste products thereof. Schwann was the first to expound a systematic theory of the cell and the first to establish the basic fact that the life of any individual cell is dependent upon that of the organism as a whole.

Cytology now made rapid progress. Karl W. Nägeli (1817–91), Swiss-born professor of botany at Munich, propounded the micellar theory, which related plant growth to the molecular process and affirmed that viable cells issue from cellular division. Robert Remak (1815–65) made important contributions to histology. The brilliant Rudolf Virchow (1821–1902), who was director of the Berlin Pathological Intitute and was also after 1862 a member of the Prussian *Landtag* and between 1880 and 1893 a Progressive deputy in the Reichstag, founded the science of cellular pathology about 1850. Author of a six-volume *Special Pathology and Therapy* (1858–76), Virchow proved that not only healthy cells, but also tumorous and cancerous ones, divide and reproduce themselves. The Estonian immigrant Karl Ernst von Baer (1792–1876) was the first to advance the germ layer theory, which hypothecated that various vertebrate organs are derived from the germ layer by process of morphological differentiation. Finally, the Hertwig brothers (Oscar, 1849–1922; and Richard, 1850–1937), who worked respectively in Berlin and Munich, significantly broadened and refined the germ layer theory.

Comparable advances were made by German scientists in human physiology and embryology. Von Baer discovered the human ovum and described the complete embryological cycle of the chick in his influential book *Concerning the Embryonic Development of Animals* (2 vols., 1828–37). The basic role of spermatozoa in the reproductive process was identified in the 1840s by Rudolf von Kölliker (1817–1905), a Swiss-born histologist at the University of Würzburg, while the well-known German anatomist and physiologist Rudolf Wagner (1805–64) was the first to detect the germinal zone in the human ovum. Remak advanced our knowledge of the sympathetic nervous system and made important discoveries in embryology. Ernst Wilhelm von Brücke (1819–92) also did fundamental research on the nervous system, and he broadened our understanding of the physiology of the circulation of blood. The trailblazer in the field of experimental physiology was Emil Du Bois-Reymond (1818–96), who was a pupil of Johannes Müller. Du Bois-Reymond investigated the vasomotor system, metabolic processes, the nervous and muscular systems, and electrophysiological responses in animals. Wilhelm von Waldeyer-Hartz (1836–1921), who was primarily an anatomist, achieved fame for his research on ovaries and the histology of the nervous system. Karl Ludwig (1816–95) investigated the relationship between the circulatory and nervous systems and furthered many fields of physiology. Finally, the aforementioned Virchow did fundamental work in hematology, investigated pathological conditions of the blood, advanced the study of thromboses and embolisms, and founded the world-famous Pathological Institute in Berlin.

Among the scientists who made straight the paths of Darwin in Germany were Gegenbaur, Müller, and Haeckel. The anatomist Karl Gegenbaur (1826–1903) was the first to apply the hypotheses of organic evolution to human and vertebrate anatomy. Fritz Müller (1821–97) was the first to enunciate *(For Darwin*, 1864*)* the biogenetic idea that in developing organisms ontogeny recapitulates phylogeny. Ernst Heinrich Haeckel (1834–1919), a professor at Jena, was the most aggressive continental champion of the theories of Darwin, as set forth in *The Origin of Species* (1859) and *Descent of Man* (1871). In two highly influential works, *Natürliche Schöpfungengeschichte (The Natural History of Creation*, 1868*)* and *Anthropogenie oder Entwicklungsgeschichte des Menschen (Anthropogeny or the Evolutionary Development of Man*, 1874*)*, Haeckel cogently argued for Darwin's view that one species is derived or descended from another by natural selection and that man himself is a derivative from some prehistoric creature of the anthropoid group.

Speculation as to whether acquired characteristics could be transmitted was ended by August Weismann (1834–1914), a professor at Freiburg, who denied that they could be inherited and thus influence natural selection. More original than Gegenbaur, Müller, or Haeckel was Gregor Johann Mendel (1822–84), a botanist and an Augustinian abbot at Brünn (Brno). Mendel's statistical analyses of the results of tedious experiments with hybridization led to the discovery in 1865 of the law of hereditary transmission of physical characteristics by the pairing and separation of dominant and recessive genes. His findings were widely publicized a generation later by the Dutch scientist De Vries. Mendel's discoveries, coupled with the mutation theory of De Vries, explained, as Darwin had been unable to do, the origin of new species.

Bacteriology and Medicine

The main advances in bacteriology and immunology did not come until after the discovery by Karl Weigert (1843–1905) of a practical method of staining microorganisms (1871). The next big step was taken by the famous Robert Koch (1843–1910), a physician and professor at the University of Berlin and the director of the Institute of Infectious Diseases. Koch was the first to isolate pure cultures of pathogenic microorganisms, notably the anthrax bacillus and the Asiatic cholera bacillus. He investigated sleeping sickness, the bubonic plague, and malaria. However, his greatest triumph was to isolate the tubercle bacillus, which was a basic step in the modern therapy of tuberculosis. Paul Ehrlich (1854–1915), a Silesian-born bacteriologist, helped develop the science of immunology. He, too, worked on tubercle bacilli, but his most important achievement was to demonstrate in 1891 that certain vegetable proteins caused the production of antitoxin when injected into the bloodstream. At about the same time Emil von Behring (1854–1917), conjointly with the Japanese bacteriologist Kitazato, discovered the antitoxin for diphtheria (1890). Ehrlich went on to standardize the antitoxin for this dread disease and thus helped to save the lives of countless thousands of children who would normally have perished from it. Behring's development of bovovaccine for the immunization of cattle against tuberculosis and Ehrlich's serum therapy for syphilis were other noteworthy achievements of German bacteriology. For their discoveries Koch, Ehrlich, and von Behring were all awarded Nobel prizes. Finally, mention must be made of August von Wassermann (1866–1925), a scientist at the Koch Institute and later of the Kaiser Wilhelm Institute in Berlin, who devised a simple test for the detection of syphilis.

One of the most remarkable discoveries of the century, benefiting medicine, dentistry, and industrial technology, was made in 1895 by Wilhelm Roentgen (1845–1923), professor of physics successively at Strassburg, Giessen, and Würzburg. He found that radium bombarded by a high-velocity stream of electrons produces an invisible electromagnetic ray, the X- or Roentgen ray. His discovery that atoms were composed of a host of subatomic particles was to have even more revolutionary consequences. He, too, received the Nobel prize.

Chemistry

The first significant German precursor of modern chemistry was J. B. Richter (1762–1807). He formulated the law of reciprocal proportions, according to which each element possesses a "combining weight" which governs its combination with any other element. This discovery was the prolegomenon not only to Dalton's atomic theory of matter but also to the establishment of the atomic weights of elements by Gay-Lussac and Avogadro. The end of this line of inquiry was the drafting in the 1860s of the periodic table of elements by Julius Lothar Meyer of Tübingen (1830–95) and the Russian chemist Mendeleyev, working independently of each other.

Not until Justus von Liebig (1803–73) established his chemical laboratory at Giessen did Germany pass into the vanguard of chemical research. In the middle years of the century, Friedrich Wöhler (1800–82), Robert W. Bunsen (1811–99), and Rudolf J. Clausius (1822–88) made significant contributions to this science. Wöhler produced synthetic urea; Bunsen, who had invented the burner named after him and had helped develop the technique of spectrum analysis, discovered a number of rare elements and demonstrated the properties of magnesium; and Clausius explained the phenomenon of electrolysis and in 1857 formulated the kinetic theory of gasses. A further important advance was made in 1877 by Ludwig Boltzmann (1844–1906), who altered the accepted kinetic-molecular theory by demonstrating its connection with thermodynamics. Boltzmann also helped found the science of statistical mechanics and prepared the way for a revolutionary electronic and solid-state physics of the mid-twentieth century.

From the technological standpoint a vast new manufacturing field was opened up by the brilliant German professor of chemistry at Bonn, Friedrich August Kekulé (1829–96). He solved the problem of the basic structure of organic compounds and established the valence (quadrivalency) of carbon. On the basis of his findings, he was able to diagram the structural arrangement of atoms within molecules, notably of the symmetrical, hexagonal, benzene ring (C_6H_6). This accomplishment was fundamental to the foundation of the German aniline (synthetic) dye industry. Finally, there was Fritz Haber (1868–1934), director of the Kaiser Wilhelm Institute of Chemistry in Berlin, who in 1909 was able to produce colorless synthetic ammonia. His process for manufacturing it was to be of great importance to the German munitions industry in World War I.

The Initial German Contribution
to Modern Nuclear Physics

Germany's contribution to the origination of the idea of the essential unity of energy and matter, space and time, and acceleration and gravitation was enormous. Beginning with the diverse experiments of Roentgen, Michelson, and

Morley, a line of thought was inaugurated that ended by significantly modifying Newtonian celestial mechanics. Heinrich Hertz (1857–94), a professor of physics at Bonn, demonstrated the existence of high-frequency, electric or electromagnetic waves that pass through the cosmos with the velocity and characteristics of light itself. In 1883 the Austrian physicist Ernst Mach (1838–1916) propounded a new definition of mass and coordinated it with force and acceleration to arrive at a quasi-relativistic system. Hertz and Mach concluded that force and energy are arbitrary abstractions and change with the perspective of the observer. A host of non-German physicists—among them H. A. Lorentz, Clark Maxwell, Frederick Soddy, Ernest Rutherford, Niels Bohr, and J. J. Thomson—meanwhile, gave direction to these findings.

One of the greatest scientific discoveries of the last five hundred years was made by the originator of the quantum theory, Max K. Planck (1858–1947) of the University of Kiel. About 1900 Planck established the fact that, contrary to the assumptions of classical physicists, matter does not radiate energy continuously but both emits and absorbs radiation in minute, discrete amounts, which he called "quanta." From this postulate Planck deduced the "universal (Planck's) constant," which expressed the ratio of the energy of an individual quantum of radiation to its frequency. Planck's law of radiation (1901), by equating the energy of a quantum of light to its frequency multiplied by the mathematically determinable Planck's constant, relegated to limbo the classical notion of light as a continuous series of waves.

It was above all Albert Einstein (1879–1955), a German Jew, who dislodged the keystone of the arch of classical physics. Successively professor at the universities of Zurich, Prague, and Berlin, Einstein electrified the scientific world in 1905 by enunciating the special theory of relativity, following it in 1916 with the general theory of relativity. The special theory was developed by meditating upon heavenly bodies moving relative to each other at a constant velocity. Einstein's basic postulate was that everything in the universe is in motion but must be considered with relationship to the observer. His theory recognized the classic three dimensions of the universe but added a fourth—his celebrated "space-time continuum." For the Newtonian principle that every object in the universe attracts every other in direct proportion to its mass, Einstein substituted the relativistic idea that a heavenly object is, in fact, a geodesic in a curved space-time continuum.

Psychology

Revelations about the mysteries of the mind captivated the public hardly less than did the great contemporary discoveries in the biological and physical sciences.

The two dominant figures in German psychology in that period were Wilhelm Wundt (1832–1920) and Sigmund Freud (1866–1939). The former, who was a professor at Leipzig, was the founder of the experimental and physiological school of psychology. With him the organic, biological bases of the psyche were the terminative factors in behavior. Freud, a Viennese physician and psychologist, discovered an arresting new dimension. Ignoring the axiomatic relationship between mind and body that Wundt had postulated in his *Physiological Psychology* (1872), Freud, like Nietzsche, pioneered in the identification of an occult, indeterminate dimension of the human mind. Freud demonstrated that man was less governed by either reason or organic processes than he was by a demoniacal irrationalism. During his years as professor of neuropathology at Vienna (1902–38), Freud gradually abandoned the therapy of hypnosis and initiated treatment of psychopathic conditions by means of the uninhibited association of a patient's dreams, ideas, and memories. Of enormous importance to many domains of knowledge, Freud's most important books (prewar: *The Interpretation of Dreams*, 1899; and *Concerning Psychoanalysis*, 1910) focused public attention upon what had formerly been unmentionable. To Nietzsche's will power, Freud counterposed an overpowering sexual drive (libido) as the strongest impulse of life. His emphasis upon the importance of long-repressed desires as the key to an understanding of aberrant behavioral patterns made possible fruitful discoveries in many fields and, with both salutary and questionable consequences, removed a range of social taboos.

Historiography

German historical studies, which had earlier been stimulated by Niebuhr, Böck, Savigny, Raumer, Ranke, and Burckhardt, received a new impetus from the *Reichsgründung*. The renaissance of public interest in the national past was symbolized by the founding of a large number of national and regional historical journals, above all the *Historische Zeitschrift* (1859–), which was edited by Heinrich von Sybel. At the same time, much attention was bestowed upon the compilation and editing of source material, e.g., the *Monumenta* for German medieval history, the Reichstag records of the Holy Roman Empire, the *Corpus inscriptionum latinarum*, and the *Regesta pontificum romanorum* for the medieval papacy.

Highly original research in Greek history was conducted by Johann Gustav Droysen (1808–84), Ernst Curtius (1814–96), and the Swiss Jakob Burckhardt (1818–97). Droysen's work on Greek history was eclipsed by his *kleindeutsch* studies, while Burckhardt's four-volume history of Greek civilization was destined to be less influential than his study of the Italian Renaissance.

One of the most learned German historians of the late nineteenth century was Theodor Mommsen (1817–1903), a scholar of world mark, whose name is usually mentioned only with those of Ranke and Burckhardt. Following in the paths blazed by Niebuhr, Mommsen devoted much of his life to restoring ancient Latin texts and writing the history of the Roman Republic.

The field of church history, fortified by compilations by Paul Kehr from the Vatican archives and from canon law, commanded the attention of Ignaz von Döllinger (1799–1890) of Tübingen, Heinrich Denifle (1844–1905), and Ludwig Pastor (1854–1928). For years Döllinger was the champion of Catholic historiography, but he was excommunicated for refusing to accept the doctrine of papal infallibility enunciated by Vatican Council I in 1870. Denifle wrote sympathetically and extensively about the history of Catholicism and the medieval papacy, as did also the Rhenish ultramontane, Johannes Janssen (1829–91), author of the *History of the German People at the Close of the Middle Ages* (8 vols., 1875–91). Ludwig Pastor wrote an immense vindication of the historic role of the papacy, *History of the Popes since the Middle Ages* (16 vols., 1886–1933), which was based on newly opened sources in the Vatican archives.

Much attention was, of course, devoted to economic, cultural, and intellectual history. The most conspicuous success in exploring an auxiliary field would seem to have been achieved in economic history. Here Karl W. Nitzsch (1818–80) wrote studies on the economy of the Roman Republic; Gustav Schmoller (1838–1917) explored the development of guilds and small industry in the European era and argued that economic institutions had a determinative influence upon political power; the Heidelberg professor Max Weber (1864–1920) traced the development of the bourgeois *Weltanschauung* back to the dogmatic values of Calvinism; and Werner Sombart (1863–1941) in his *Modern Capitalism* (3 vols., 1902–28) analyzed the historical materialist evolution of contemporary socioeconomic forms.

The contours of German cultural history were most thoroughly explored by Karl Lamprecht (1856–1915) and Gustav Freytag (1816–95). Lamprecht, a professor at Leipzig, wrote a vast nineteen-volume *German History* from the standpoint of the impact of the mind and ideals upon political and social developments. Freytag was one of the best nationalist writers of the day. His panoramic tapestry depicting the hegira of the German nation—*Bilder aus der deutschen Vergangenheit (Scenes from Germany's Past*, 5 vols., 1852–66*)*—was praised by Jakob Grimm and Heinrich Treitschke for its spiritual and literary qualities.

Of capital importance in defending the *Reichsgründung* was the Prussian school of historiography. This school, which conceptually extolled concrete, differentiated knowledge and experience and rejected abstract values and absolute truths as either imaginary or incomprehensible to the popular mind, derived its seminal philosophy from Herder's *Volksgeist*. The school's perspective, which was labeled historicism, made possible, as Georg Iggers has emphasized, a close spiritual bond between its representatives and the Prussian monarchy and the Second Reich. The main luminaries of the Prussian school was Droysen, Maximilian Duncker (1811–86), Ludwig Häusser (1818–67), Heinrich von Sybel (1817–95), and Heinrich Treitschke (1834–96). All of these men regarded the Second Empire as the first grand political act in the history of the German nation since Hohenstaufen times. The school had only scorn for the anticonsolidationist, confederative view of the Christian democrat Konstantin Frantz (1817–91).

Notwithstanding their adulatory appraisal of the Hohenzollern accomplishment, the main historians of the Prussian school were distinguished scholars. Droysen had already achieved fame with a *History of Hellenism* (2 vols., 1836–45), but his masterpiece was his *History of Prussian Policy* (14 vols., 1855–86). Duncker, who was successively Brandenburg state archivist and historiographer, was also a student of antiquity, but he served the fame of Prussia by editing the state papers of the Great Elector and the correspondence of Frederick the Great. Häusser wrote widely on the Reformation, Frederick the Great, the French Revolution (to which he was typically hostile), and recent German history. Sybel, who stood close to Bismarck and derided the policies of the medieval emperors, was a student of the Crusades, the impact of the French Revolution upon Europe, and recent German history. His monument was *Die Begründung des Deutschen Reiches unter Wilhelms I (Founding of the German Empire under William I*, 7 vols., 1889–94), an encomiastic work that was not exempt from distortions. Sybel was also the first scholar to conduct a history seminar in Germany. More famous than any of the foregoing was Treitschke, professor at Heidelberg and Berlin and member of the extreme right wing of the National Liberal party. An antisocialist, anti-Semitic, and Francophobe politician who was an impassioned admirer of Bismarck, Treitschke is best known for his magisterial, elegant, but highly subjective *German History in the Nineteenth Century* (5 vols., 1879–94), which, however, did not go beyond 1848.

On the eve of World War I the shadow of Bismarck still cast a long shadow over German historiography. The nationalist and historicist traditions were especially strong at the universities of Heidelberg and Berlin, where Max Lenz, Erich Marcks, Max Weber, Erich Brandenburg, Gustav Schmoller, Otto Hintze, and Hermann Oncken lectured. Virtually the whole German historical profession was convinced that the Bismarckian creation had been a constructive and moral act, the chancellor's foreign policy objectives were perfectly susceptible of vindication, the structure of the Wilhelmine state was fundamentally sound, and the Second Empire was a *Rechtsstaat*. Friedrich Meinecke (1862–1954), the doyen of the profession in the early twentieth century and the author of the humanistic-philosophical *Weltbürgertum und der Nationalstaat (Cosmopolitanism and the National State*, 1907), perpetuated the convictions of the Prussian school.

PART XI
FROM EUROPEAN TO WORLD
POWER, 1871–1914

Chapter 37

THE MOLDING OF THE SECOND EMPIRE

The Federative State

It is an exaggeration to aver, as do many historians, that in the process of unifying Germany Prussia devoured it. Despite the preponderance of Prussia, which embraced almost two-thirds of the country's population, Bismarck was hostile to the bourgeois demand that the polycentrist legacy be thrown overboard. The constitution of April 16, 1871, which was based upon that of the North German Confederation, conferred upon the German Empire (Deutsches Reich) a markedly federative character. The document recognized the sovereignty of the component states and free cities over their own internal affairs.

In general, the bourgeoisie opposed the perpetuation of states' rights. Liberal deputies in the Reichstag demanded immediate broadening of the work of centralization. Strongest of the parties to emerge from the elections of 1871 (119 mandates out of a grand total of 382), the National Liberal party provided in the Second Reich the main parliamentary impetus to the enlargement of the competence of the imperial government at the expense of the states.

The German Empire comprised twenty-five states, four of which were kingdoms, six grand duchies, five duchies, seven lesser states, and three free cities. In addition, Alsace-Lorraine was designated an imperial territory *(Das Reichsland)* and put under the direct control of the emperor. Apart from broad internal autonomy as respects such matters as administration, justice, banking and finance, schools, internal improvements, police, and church-state relations, each component imperial entity retained its own diplomatic representation both at the several German courts and abroad. Although the German emperor (kaiser) exercised supreme command over the armed forces of almost all German states, troop contingents were organized on a particularist basis and Bavaria was again permitted to wield supreme command over its contingent in peacetime. Another factor limiting the power of the Reich government was the fact that under the constitution it possessed insufficient means of raising revenue, so that the imperial chancellory was forced to depend in part upon matricular financial contributions from the states.

Because the lower house of parliament, the Reichstag, possessed neither real power nor control over the executive branch, Prussia was insured a dominant position in the federal empire. Given the authoritarian nature of the Prussian state, this meant the king could be the determinative factor in imperial politics.

Under the constitution Prussia's interests were amply protected in the Bundesrat. The delegates, who were like emissaries in that they were not elected but appointed, were answerable to their respective state governments. This circumstance gave the king of Prussia a commanding position in the Bundesrat. Prussia possessed or controlled (with the votes of Waldeck and Alsace-Lorraine) 21 out of a total of 61 representatives, and 14 were enough to block any constitutional amendment. Similarly it was extremely difficult to pass any bill without the assent of Prussia.

Other factors, too, contributed to the strength of the hegemony of Prussia over the Reich. Except for a short interval, the positions of both Reich chancellor and Prussian minister-president were held by Bismarck until 1890. Constitutionally, the chancellor was the only policy-making minister in the central government; all others were subordinate to him. A very strong chancellor was responsible, however, not to the Reichstag but to the kaiser alone. The Reichstag could not overthrow the chancellor by a vote of no-confidence. While both chambers possessed the veto over bills, all government-sponsored proposals were introduced in the Bundesrat, which was presided over by Prussia. The Reichstag was empowered neither to reduce nor increase appropriations in money bills, all of which had to originate with the imperial government. If the power of the emperor over internal imperial affairs was weak, it was considerable over foreign and military matters. He enjoyed the constitutional right to make treaties, either with or without the assent of the Bundesrat, and if Germany were invaded he could, on his own authority, declare war. In peacetime he exercised supreme command over the German armed forces, except for the Bavarian contingent, and in wartime he theoretically wielded supreme command over all armed forces.

If Prussian tutelage was so long tolerated by the German people it was because only a few put the requirements of freedom and equality above the need for security. The authoritarian, "Prussian militaristic" features of the regime, which were tirelessly criticized by Progressives and Social Democrats, were forgiven by most Germans for the sake of the social, economic, legal, and military advantages associated with the Bismarckian creation.

Centralizing Tendencies

Occupancy of the chancellorship by the domineering Bismarck was a pledge of cautious continuation of centralizing tendencies in the Reich. In the contest of centralism *vs* particularism Bismarck held high trumps. Unlike the situation in Prussia, where the collegial ministerial principle obtained, the only responsible minister of the crown in the Reich was the chancellor. This made it possible to concentrate federal power in one man's hands. No strong states' rights alliance was ever organized against Bismarck, for none was possible without Prussian support. Consequently the nationalization of Germany, like its unification, was carried out from above, and only ineffectual opposition developed. In the Reichstag, the "me too" attitude of the key National Liberal party was a replica of its stand during the *Reichsgründung*. Backed by the National Liberals and Free Conservatives (Reichspartei), which is to say by an "unholy alliance" of the upper bourgeoisie and the Junkers, Bismarck enjoyed the support of "the establishment" for his continuing "revolution from above."

Since Bismarck's expertise was in neither law nor economics, much of the actual unifying work was carried on by Rudolf von Delbrück (1807–1903), the able president of the imperial chancellery (Reichskanzleramt). His office exercised control over a range of departmental secretaries whose competence extended to justice, railroads, postal system, trade and industry, banking and currency, and finance. Until his departure from office in 1876 over the protectionist issue, Delbrück adroitly shepherded Germany along the road to consolidation, even at the expense of violating the spirit of the constitution. The assumption of broad responsibility by Delbrück was rendered the more necessary in view of the fact that Bismarck during these years was often very ill and had to absent himself from Berlin for months on end seeking the replenishment of his physical energies at spas or at his estates of Varzin and Friedrichsruh.

Arrogating to the imperial chancellory practically every function born of novel economic, financial, or administrative exigencies, Delbrück persevered with those great standardizing and unifying measure that have already been mentioned. In the Prussian government he enjoyed the cooperation of Otto von Camphausen (1812–96), the vice-president of the state ministry and minister of finance, but he too resigned over the tariff issue (1878). In the Reichstag Delbrück had the aid of the diminutive, razor-tongued Eduard Lasker (1829–84), a tireless champion of the *Rechtsstaat*. A great admirer of Bismarck, Lasker had seceded from the Progressive party and joined the National Liberals. One of their four principal spokesmen (Bennigsen, Miquel, and Forckenbeck were the others), Lasker toiled both in the Reichstag and Abgeordnetenhaus to extend imperial legislation to cover the civil law of all Germany. A recognized authority on jurisprudence, Lasker helped create a unified court system and common civil and criminal procedures for the empire. No other political leader did so much to promote the centralizing schemes of Bismarck.

The centralizing machinery devised by the Reichskanzleramt functioned smoothly as long as it avoided the reefs of deficit. Unfortunately, the French war indemnity was swiftly used up, and the depression that began in 1873 cut sharply into the revenues of almost all German governments. The imperial administration soon found that the few sources of income available to cover operating costs—domainal lands, excise taxes, posts and telegraph, certain railroads, and proportionate matricular contributions by the hard-pressed states—were insufficient in a time of spiraling costs. Bismarck had thought to be able to purchase all private and state-owned railroads, which would have opened up a huge source of revenue to the imperial railway department, but the Bundesrat shot down that idea.

Beginning in 1877 there were eight successive annual imperial deficits. Bismarck simply had to find new sources of money, but at the same time the state governments were clamoring not only for relief from matricular contributions but succor from the central government. Bismarck was ready to oblige the states, because he felt that the allocation of federal funds to them would bind them to the empire with hoops of gold. Meanwhile, his recipe for making the central government financially independent was protectionism.

Unfortunately the revenue yielded by the new duties fell short of expectations. None of the immediate goals Bismarck hoped to achieve through protectionism was realized. On the other hand, his whole internal program was endangered by the tariff issue. Abandonment of free trade led Delbrück to resign, and this entailed the breakup of the imperial chancellery into departments under secretaries of state responsible to Bismarck. The tariff alienated and rent asunder the National Liberal party and undermined the chancellor's popularity, causing him thenceforth to be mordantly suspicious of parliaments. Ironically, he was now forced increasingly to seek support from the formerly execrated Center. Since this party was incurably particularist, Bismarck was in no position after 1878 to progress further with his unifying measures.

Administrative Reform in Prussia

As in the Reichstag, so in the Prussian legislature, the Conservative party fought a determined rearguard action against the Liberal majority. But, in Prussia the retreat of the Conservatives, who were fortified by the three-class electoral system and the respect of the peasants for landlords, was less conclusive. Nevertheless, during the critical struggle over the Prussian County Administrative Reform Bill of 1871 Conservative strength was sorely tested.

The administrative problem of Prussia's eastern provinces, where serfdom had endured longest, consisted in the fact that after emancipation the authority of the county directors *(Kreisdirektoren)* had been sharply impaired where it had not actually disappeared. Self-government, modeled after that in the towns, had cropped up in the villages and counties, and no longer did landlords dominate the county councils and diets.

The Conservatives fought the County Administrative Reform Bill because it threatened to inter them as a class and deprive them of their reason for existence. The tensions engendered by the bill were in fact so great that they split the party in Prussia. However, the law, as finally passed in December, 1872, offered little ground for the exaggerated fears of the landed gentry. Local landlords lost their police power forever, but the new sheriffs *(Amtsvorsteher)*, who were appointed by the provincial president *(Oberpresident)* on the basis of ability and for specified terms of office, were also noblemen and, besides, exercised broader geographic jurisdiction than the former county directors had. To be sure, the gentry were now outnumbered in the county assemblies *(Kreistage)* by peasant and urban deputies, but the peasants remained deferential to their former patrons and usually followed their advice in voting in the assemblies. Bourgeois influence in the latter was minimized by a law of 1872, which excluded from the rural counties *(Landkreise)* towns of more than 25,000 population. Likewise, the Provincial Administrative Law of 1875 imparted to the provincial diets, which were to be elected by the county assemblies, a definitely conservative cast.

When the dust stirred up by the administrative reforms subsided, the landed nobility came to realize that its power had been by no means demolished. Appreciating that their services had been neatly channelized as a result of their altered roles, the aristocrats continued to shape the life of the Prussian countryside until 1918. About a third of the Conservative deputies in the *Landtag* concluded, upon reassessment of their opposition to the reforms, that it had been pointless. In 1876 this minority of some forty-five deputies bolted the party and formed the pro-Bismarckian, New Conservative party.

The Septennats

Fundamental to the thinking of Bismarck, Roon, and Moltke was the proposition that control of the army must rest with the emperor rather than the Reichstag. The chancellor deemed it expedient to work with the legislature as long as it did not oppose him on vital matters. Control of the army was one of these. Bismarck would have resigned rather than countenance a parliamentary army. In his eyes, this would have been tantamount to placing the defense of the empire in the hands of a hydra-headed command that was notoriously torn by factionalism and was subverted by leftist antimilitarist views.

The government's army bill of 1874 precipitated a furious debate. The bill was intended to replace the "iron law of 1867," which, expiring in 1871, had been renewed for another three years. Bismarck, who was in this matter instinctively supported by the bulk of the nation, was resolved to defeat all attempts to impose annual parliamentary review of the size of the military establishment and its budget. In the Reichstag the Free Conservatives and National Liberals sided with him. The latter were prepared to accept the chancellor's view of the army as sacrosanct because they feared the "black peril" of the Catholic international and the "red" of the Socialist International.

Bismarck had wanted to deprive the Reichstag of all surveillance over the military and its budgetary needs, but the intensity of the opposition, which consisted of the left wing of the National Liberals under Lasker, the Center, and the Progressives, forced him to concede a right of review every seven years. Thereupon the left Liberals and Progressives abandoned the struggle, which, however, was continued by the Center and a handful of Socialists.

In its amended version the Army Law of 1874 provided for a fixed, peacetime military strength of a little more than 401,000 men and for automatic allocations of money to finance the military for seven years. The law, called the Septennat, insured the perpetuation of the "king's own army." The dangers of parliamentary interference were minimized by the circumstance that, inasmuch as the duration of a parliament was three years, only every second Reichstag could review the government's military estimates and collaborate in revisions to army strength.

In the years following adoption of the Septennat the military cabinet under chairmanship of General E. L. von Albedyll and the general staff under Moltke conspired to free the army from almost all civilian control. Specifically and immediately the purpose of Moltke was to emancipate the general staff from tutelage to the minister of war (General von Kameke). Bismarck himself offered no serious objection to the gradual removal of the army from virtually all civilian control, although his failure to do so was, far more than the annexation of Alsace-Lorraine, the carcinogen from which the Second Reich was to die.

The result of the capitulation of the Reichstag in 1874 and again on the occasion of the renewal of the Septennat in 1880, when the size of the army was raised to a fixed quota of 427,000 men, was that the officer corps succeeded in retaining autonomous control over the army. This meant that the nobility had managed to preserve one of the commanding heights in the state. While it is by no means probable that a middle-class state possessing Germany's geopolitical liabilities would not also have maintained a large army, it is undeniable that the victory of authoritarianism in the matter of the Septennat gave to the Second Empire its characteristic drill-sergeant aspect. Last, as a result of loss of control by the Reichstag over the army and virtually the entire civil and military budget, Germany's progress toward a genuine parliamentary system was retarded, so that it was not till almost the eve of World War I that the deputies finally sighted the spires of political democracy.

Bismarck's Confederates in Parliament

In the early parliaments of the German Empire the institutions of the Reich were forged with the support mainly of the National Liberal party, the oracle of the great industrial and commercial capitalists. This party, possessed of a mass following, collaborated with the Free Conservatives (Reichspartei) to give to the Second German Empire hybrid vigor. Clearly the new Germany was from its birth never simply the private preserve of the Junkers and the army.

Very probably the comradeship between Bismarck and the National Liberals would have been more pronounced and less of a duel had it not been for the advent in 1873 of a depression which, commencing with crashes on the Viennese and New York stock exchanges, cast its pall over central Europe for almost five years. Taut tempers and sharpening antagonisms were mirrored in the controversy over the punitive censorship law of 1874. The National Liberals, who were confronted with an assault upon one of the fundamental freedoms that formed part of their political confession, fought the press law, but the best they could do was defeat the penal provisions of the bill.

During most of the 1870s the National Liberals dominated the Reichstag. This party had abandoned its original goal of middle class hegemony and found its way to fruitful cooperation with Conservative statesmen. The National Liberals also exerted a powerful attraction upon the Progressives. Disgusted with the sterility of their own party, men like Karl Twesten (d. 1870), Hans Victor von Unruh (1806–86), and Eduard Lasker bolted the Progressives and joined the National Liberals. There they found themselves in the company of a unique galaxy of spirit and talent—leaders such as the historian Treitschke, the former publicist Ludwig Bamberger (1823–99), and the famous jurist Rudolf von Gneist (1806–95).

Captained by four men above others—Bennigsen, Johannes Miquel, Eduard Lasker, and Max von Forckenbeck (1821–92), the National Liberal party grew like a green bay tree. In the elections of 1871 it won 29 percent of the vote cast and returned 119 deputies of a total of 382 to the Reichstag. In the elections of

1873 the party scored an even greater triumph, when 155 of its deputies stormed into the Reichstag. Correspondingly powerful in the Prussian Chamber of Deputies, the party increased its representation there between 1871 and 1873 from 123 to 178. But serious internal divisions over protectionism and the Anti-Socialist Law soon split the party. It secured only 127 Reichstag mandates in the elections of 1877, and 98 in those of the summer of 1878. Even worse days lay ahead in the 1880s for the Liberals. By the end of another decade the party had forfeited much of its mass following and had become almost exclusively the shield of big business.

The other pier of Bismarck's post-Frankfurt ministerial bridge was the Free Conservative party (Reichspartei). Though it embraced many able administrators, jurists, and statesmen, it was much smaller than the National Liberal party. The Free Conservatives were led by the Bavarian Prince zu Hohenlohe-Schillingsfürst, Freiherr von Roggenbach, and Bernhard von Bülow (1849–1929). As some wit remarked, the Reichspartei "was the party of has-been ministers and of those who wanted to be." The progressive-minded Rhenish, Silesian, and New Mark landlords, who composed the leadership of the party, had escaped the doctrinaire limitations of Prussian particularism. Inordinate admirers of Bismarck, the Free Conservatives were as attached to his moderate nationalism as an oyster to its bed. In numbers of deputies they about equaled the Progressives in both Reichstag and Prussian Abgeordnetenhaus. In the turbulent years 1877–78, when the Liberals were splitting, the Reichspartei attained the zenith of its strength, increasing its popular vote by 86.3 percent and its Reichstag mandate from 33 to 58 deputies.

At this early stage in the economic development of the Reich, big business and large-scale agriculture were as yet too undeveloped and unorganized to exercise paramount influence upon the grand policy of the Reich government. Also, tensions in the National Liberal party were too paralyzing and the servility of the Free Conservatives too marked to warrant acceptance of the hypothesis of the primacy of domestic policy *(Der Primat der Innenpolitik)*. Neither vested capitalist nor class interests could as yet challenge the dominance of foreign policy in national affairs; and that policy was still principally elaborated in keeping with the autonomous prescriptions of Bismarck, the last great practitioner of cabinet diplomacy.

The Conservative Opposition

After the fight over the Prussian County Administrative Reform bill of 1872, the Conservative party split, its parliamentary mandate dropped from 54 (1871) to 21 (1874), and it was without important influence for some years. Not till the National Liberals split did the Conservatives, reorganized in 1876 as the German Conservative party, revive. In the Reichstag elections of 1878 they won 59 mandates, and soon thereafter they regained control of the Prussian *Landtag*, which they retained until 1917.

Judged by the quality of party leadership, these gains were more than the German Conservative party deserved. Apart from Ernst Ludwig von Gerlach (1795–1877), the leaders of the party were mediocrities such as Kleist-Retzow and Count Voss, whose names are today forgotten. Retardatives in the popular growth of this party into the 1880s were: its attachment to an outmoded peasant-aristocratic order; an unalterable predilection for particularism (i.e., Prussia above Germany); continuing hostility toward Bismarck's consolidationist, centralizing policies; an obscurantist Protestant, antisecular, and anti-Semitic *Weltanschauung*; and a reticence to aid in economically transforming Germany into a major industrial and a world power.

After 1878 the Conservative party again became a potential ally of the ministry. The Conservatives had come to recognize that the Second Empire was there to stay and that only through collaboration with, or command of, the government could the party hope to promote the interests of its Junker and peasant constituents. For some years after 1878 the Conservatives entered into combinations with the Center, the Reichspartei, and some twenty-seven dissident National Liberals to provide Bismarck with his majorities. The Conservatives' abandonment of sterile opposition entailed a shift to the right in the center of gravity of the Reichstag, where it remained until World War I.

The "Kulturkampf"

Sharper than the struggle over the first Septennat but less grave in its consequences was the cultural battle *(Kulturkampf)* that was waged by the secular governments of Germany against the Catholic church. The campaign did not originate with Bismarck. However, once it commenced, he pretended that there existed a vast Catholic conspiracy against the state, and he summoned all patriots to rally to its defense.

In a deeper sense, Königgrätz and Sedan had been defeats for the Catholics. These battles buried all chance of a *Grossdeutschland*, in which Catholic Austria would have been a counterweight to predominantly Protestant Prussia, or of a constitution that would have conferred autonomy upon the Roman Catholic Church. After the *Reichsgründung* the Catholics composed only 35 percent of the population of the Empire as compared with 52 percent of that of the old Deutscher Bund.

On January 21, 1870, the First Vatican Council in Rome affirmed in its *schema de ecclesia* the cardinal importance of Church control over education. Then on April 24 the council promulgated the celebrated Decree of Papal Infallibility. Carried against the votes mainly of German and Austrian prelates, the decree evoked sharp criticism not only from German secular authorities but also from the distinguished ecclesiastical historian Ignaz von Döllinger of the University of Munich. He and several Munich priests were excommunicated in 1871 for refusing to accept the decree. They thereupon organized the "Old Catholic" opposition to the decisions of Vatican Council I.

While it is by no means easy to divine all of Bismarck's motives in launching the *Kulturkampf*, it is certain that he wanted to attach the National Liberals and Progressives to his unifying policies. He was counting upon the animus in both parties toward Pope Pius IX, who in 1864 had published the anti-Liberal and anti-capitalistic *Syllabus of Errors* in the papal encyclical *Quanta Cura*. By fanning class dislike for "reactionary" Catholic social philosophy, Bismarck hoped to soften Progressive opposition to his program and also reduce the National Liberals to his will. He further aimed at coordinating the restive Poles of Prussian Posen and Pomerelia with the German cultural structure and linguistically assimilating them for reasons of security. It would serve Bismarck's purposes to maneuver the Poles, who opposed the Liberal program of state control over the schools, into an untenable subordination to a foreign power—the papacy. Another goal was to attack the Catholic clergy with a view to advertising Germany's support of the Russian government, which since 1863 had been crossing swords with Rome and whose cooperation was needed if a continental system such as the old League of Münchengrätz of 1833 was to be reestablished. The *Kulturkampf* could also be used to dot the "i" in the isolation of Catholic France and to discourage prospects of a Franco-Russian alliance. Last, a cardinal aim of the chancellor was to destroy the confessional, particularist, and antifederal Center party, which was an obstacle to his internal program.

The origins of the Catholic Center party lay in the medieval Christian ideals that had earlier been preached by Novalis, Görres, and Adam Müller. In the era of the *Reichsgründung* these notions were perpetuated by the Jesuit Theodor Meyer and, more particularly, by Baron Wilhelm Emmanuel von Ketteler (1811–77), who was archbishop of Mainz, and Ludwig Windthorst, who had founded the People's Association for Catholic Germany (Volksverein für das Katholische Deutschland). At Ketteler's suggestion, the Center had been organized in the winter of 1870–71, and its main organ, the *Germania*, had begun publication. The new party was an omnibus for diverse movements opposed to the growing might of Prussia. In the Reichstag the Center was led by Windthorst, Mallinckrodt, and August and Peter Reichensperger. This confessional party strove to correct the worst injustices of laissez faire economics, defend the interests of the common man, and maintain civil rights against authoritarian government. The Center naturally also championed the parochial school system and specifically Catholic interests.

Unlike the Social Democratic Labor party, the Center never had to struggle upward from obscure beginnings. It entered the Reichstag of 1871 with 58 deputies, and the Prussian *Landtag* with 57 (out of 432). To this strength of the Center, which was mainly concentrated in the Rhineland and Westphalia, must be added 23 Poles and Danes who also opposed the consolidative policies of Bismarck.

Windthorst, the chief centrist leader, was a *grossdeutsch* Guelph from Hanover, whose resentment for Prussia was matched only by that of Liebknecht. Although only a little man, Windthorst had the heart and head of a lion. A master of irony and satire, he commanded a marvelous flow of rhetoric and was deadly in debate. But what really made him exceedingly dangerous in Bismarck's eyes was that he was a fanatic: he believed everything he said and did not know the meaning of compromise. He acted upon the chancellor's nerves like a man beating a drum in a sick room. Bismarck said of him: "Everybody needs someone to love and someone to hate. The good Lord has made my life complete, for I have my wife to love and Windthorst to hate."*

It was the Bavarian delegation that first introduced into the Bundesrat (November, 28, 1871) punitive legislation (the so-called pulpit paragraph) against clergymen who abused their immunities and the sacred Mass to assail the secular government. It is true that the Prussian minister-president had already dissolved the Catholic section of the ministry of culture in July and transferred Catholic affairs to the Lutheran section, but it was not till the Bavarian initiative that Bismarck fired his first salvo against the Catholic minority in Prussia.

In March, 1872, against the opposition of Kleist-Retzow and the Conservatives, the Prussian *Landtag* passed Bismarck's bill to establish state supervision over all schools in the kingdom. Thereupon, Bismarck directed the minister of the interior, Count Friedrich zu Eulenburg (1815–81), to proceed more vigorously against the Catholic Polish autonomous movement. Meanwhile in January Adalbert Falk, a doctrinaire jurist who was wholly subservient to Bismarck, had been appointed minister of culture.

A hail of anti-Catholic laws followed in the Reich and in Prussia and other states. The Reichstag passed a law on June 11, 1872, authorizing dissolution of the Jesuit order and expulsion of its members from Germany. Relations with the Vatican were severed. In May, 1873, the so-called May or Falk Laws were passed in Prussia. These stipulated that all clergymen must be citizens of Germany, have studied for at least three years in one of its universities, passed state examinations in a range of subjects, and received from the Prussian government confirmation of their parish or episcopal appointments. Schools were put under state inspection, and all religious congregations, except nursing orders, were dissolved. Civil marriage was made mandatory. Violators of the "Falk Laws" were to be deprived of civil rights and/or imprisoned. Recalcitrant bishops were to forfeit their state endowments. Subsequently the Reichstag on February 6, 1875, made civil marriage obligatory throughout the Reich.

While at the *Länder* level some states, such as Oldenburg, Saxony, and Württemberg, were hardly involved in the *Kulturkampf*, others were profoundly affected. In Baden the banner-bearer of the secular offensive against the clericals was Julius Jolly (1823–91), who was minister of the interior. In Hesse the struggle was also acute. The Catholics were encouraged by the leadership of Ketteler, but the government tried to break opposition with the five "April laws" of April 23, 1875, patterned on the "May Laws" of Prussia. In Württemberg, on the other hand, the secularizers, led by Minister von Mittnacht and the National Liberals, were frustrated by King Charles (1864–91) and his Queen Charlotte, who were

---

*Johannes Ziekursch, *Politische Geschichte des neuen deutschen Kaiserreiches* (Frankfurt a. M., 1925), I, 229.

unsympathetic to Bismarck's centralizing schemes. The *Kulturkampf* made little headway in Württemberg, and the kingdom remained relatively tranquil throughout the national crusade. In Bavaria, where the contest with the Church had already been bitter in the late 1860s, it was not until 1874 that, as a result of a ministerial reshuffle, the *Kulturkampf* began to abate. Nevertheless, symptomatic of continued bad feelings was the fact that the see of Freiburg im Breisgau was left vacant for fourteen years (1868–82).

During the *Kulturkampf* thousands of persons were fined, deprived of their civil rights, or imprisoned; yet from year to year the mass following of the Center waxed, and by 1878, with 92 deputies, it had become the strongest party in the Reichstag. By then the chancellor realized that he had failed to destroy the Center, split its mass following from it, or even to set Center and papacy against each other. The struggle with the Church had left behind it a bitterness that had needlessly complicated Bismarck's larger tasks, and he must have sensed that he had committed a monumental error.

The Liquidation of the Church-State Feud

In 1878, when the National Liberal party began to break away from the ministerial alliance and Bismarck became involved in a battle of annihilation against the Socialists, he began to have second thoughts about the Center. When, therefore, Pope Pius IX was succeeded in that year by Leo XIII, Bismarck made overtures to the papacy. A "Blue-Black-Block" of Conservatives and Centrists, replacing the Liberal-Free Conservative constellation, seemed to Bismarck to offer a suitable basis for the less liberal policies he now contemplated adopting. Soon the chancellor began to circulate the fiction that not he personally, but Falk, had been responsible for the *Kulturkampf*. When Leo XIII showed himself to be amenable to compromise without even insisting upon the abrogation of the "Falk Laws," Windthorst, dismayed by such an attitude, called the pope's action "a shot in the back."

Negotiations with Rome were, nonetheless, difficult and tortuous. They were complicated by the circumstance that irreconcilables dominated the Center, National Liberal, and Progressive parties. In 1880 the pope acceded to the principle of secular surveillance of the clergy. For his part, Bismarck made a conciliatory gesture by introducing a bill in the Reichstag to mitigate the worst asperities of the "Falk Laws" and apply them less strictly. Yet the first real thaw in Church-state relations did not begin until 1885. Then the Prussian government and Pope Leo XIII arranged a series of ad hoc compromises on the occupancy of the bishoprics of Cologne, Münster, Hildesheim, Ermland, and Posen. In 1886, to the chancellor's gratification, the pope accepted and cleverly discharged an invitation to mediate the Caroline Islands dispute between Spain and Germany. When in 1886–87 the demagogic chauvinism of the French minister of war, Boulanger, seemed to threaten Germany with a possible two-front war, Bismarck decided the time had come to liquidate the whole *Kulturkampf*.

Although Leo XIII had, in response to Bismarck's request, enjoined the Center to support the new Septennat during the Franco-German crisis, that party ignored the exhortation. Consequently, in 1887 Bismarck exploited the situation to dissolve the Reichstag and order new elections. These brought solid gains to the National Liberals and Free Conservatives but left the Center's representation (98) virtually unchanged. Bismarck now no longer needed the support of the Center to pass the Septennat. Nevertheless, this unpredictable party voted with the majority to accept the army bill on April 22, 1887. A week later the Prussian *Landtag* ended the hue and cry against the Catholic minority and largely dismantled the Falk system. For Windthorst, however, bread without jam was unacceptable. His group in the Center party refused to accept anything less than complete repeal of the obnoxious laws. Other states, meanwhile, followed the Prussian initiative. Then reconciliation with the Holy See proceeded smoothly.

While the honors in the *Kulturkampf* were divided, Bismarck and Germany lost more than they gained. It is true that the chancellor showed great acumen in engineering the liquidation of the dispute. It is true also that the papacy had been obliged to recognize the civic obligations of clergymen and that there persisted a residue from the "Falk Laws"—state supervision of the schools, enregistration of clergymen with and supervision by secular authorities, civil marriage, and the anti-Jesuit law. Yet, in a larger sense Bismarck failed.

He did not succeed in destroying the Center or even in drawing it permanently into collaborating in the tasks of government. The *Kulturkampf* accentuated the denominational schism that had been inherited from the Reformation and caused German Catholics to detest Prussia and mistrust the Reich. The distrust was strongest in the least well-integrated territories of the Empire—Posen and Alsace-Lorraine. Although the Church-state confrontation in Germany was only one facet of a European-wide secularizing movement, the *Kulturkampf* nonetheless damaged the Reich's prestige abroad. Finally, by lending encouragement to Bavarian particularism, the struggle with the clericals bequeathed Germany a chronic ailment that both in 1919 and 1923 almost destroyed Bismarck's masterpiece.

Chapter 38

IMPERIAL POLITICS: 1878–1887

Bismarck's Authoritarian Leanings

Endowed with the spirit of an absolutist and the heart of a gamecock, Bismarck was really out of his element in the parliamentary state. Had it not been for his incomparable mastery of the spoken word, infinite resourcefulness in debate, and his successes in foreign affairs, which often intimidated the opposition, it is likely that at an early date he would have lost control of the Reichstag. Then he would surely have turned against it and ridden the royal prerogative. However, the chancellor preferred not to dispense with the Reichstag if he could manipulate it, because it was, after all, his own brainchild and formed an essential element in his plan to interweave the institutions of Prussia and the Empire. Moreover, while stubbornly insisting on making his own music, Bismarck knew that he needed a Greek chorus to generate public empathy for his solo performance.

Bismarck schemed incessantly to reduce the power and integrity of every party that threatened to become an independent force. He was always tempted to destroy any political leader who set himself in opposition to fundamental imperial policy, which is to say to his own. Desiring a docile legislature, which he was never quite able to achieve, Bismarck did not feel the need to train statesmen to succeed himself. Thus, the laws of 1878–79, which transformed the office of the chancellery into a national ministry of the interior and enlarged the competence of the Reich ministers, did not enhance their individual importance but merely lengthened the shadow the great man cast over Germany. Since there was room in his government only for rubber-stamp bureaucrats, it could be predicted with certainty that his less able successors would be challenged by the Reichstag with ever-increasing prospect of success.

Seldom was Bismarck able to force the party leaders to bow their proud necks. Many of them—Windthorst, Bamberger, Lasker, Richter, Miquel, Bennigsen, Forckenbeck, and Bebel—were not only extremely capable men, but they also enjoyed strong popular backing. Their annoying intractability simply fed on Bismarck's major internal defeats—the *Kulturkampf* and the anti-Socialist campaign.

Although in the struggle against the Catholics Bismarck had tasted defeat, he had managed to compromise the libertarian principles of the National Liberal party by enlisting it for a policy of persecution. Since, however, that party, with 130 mandates, was still the strongest in the Reichstag after the elections of January, 1877, Bismarck decided to beat the National Liberals into submission with the tariff bludgeon.

As a result of the depression of the mid-1870s, big business no longer believed in the free-trade policies of the National Liberal leaders. In 1876–77 the executive committee of the Central Association of German Industrialists (Zentralverband deutscher Industrieller) petitioned Bismarck to adopt a protective tariff. The chancellor decided to comply and even offered Rudolf von Bennigsen (1824–1902), a key National Liberal spokesman, a chance to come into the ministry on a new protectionist platform, but he declined.

Bismarck hoped, by adopting a moderate protective tariff, to encompass a broad range of aims: (1) strengthen the hard-pressed Junkers, whose agricultural produce needed protection against competition from cheap Russian and Polish grain; (2) fortify the class-political position of the Conservatives, who were both landowners and principal struts of the monarchical-authoritarian society of the Reich; (3) augment the competitive potential of German heavy industry in world markets; (4) replenish the imperial treasury with customs receipts and thereby eliminate the need of the central government to rely upon proportionate matricular contributions from the states; (5) abolish direct taxes except for those imposed on the wealthiest segments of the population; (6) provide funds for financing a comprehensive social insurance system; and (7) humble and perhaps split the National Liberal party, with a view to clearing the road for a basically more promonarchist, Bismarckian, and conservative parliamentary combination. The chancellor reckoned on a bloc of big industrialists, Catholic agrarian Centrists, and Junker Conservatives to back his new national system. Such a parliamentary constellation promised to give him greater latitude than ever before.

Precisely because Bismarck knew it would be imprudent and perhaps impossible at this late date to govern without strong parliamentary backing, he was obliged to soft-pedal the *Kulturkampf* and restore the independence of the Catholic and Evangelical Lutheran churches. Only on such bases could the Center and Conservative parties be cajoled into supporting his new conservatism. The transition to neoauthoritarianism was extremely delicate. It demanded all of Bismarck's unquestionable talent. Delbrück, the free trader, and other unsympathetic ministers, such as Camphausen, Eulenburg, and Aschenbach, had to be dropped. Bismarck, finding no suitable minister of trade and commerce available to replace Aschenbach, took over the office himself and plunged into the study of economics with diligence. At the same time Bismarck* retained the offices of chancellor, foreign minister, and Prussian minister president. Until 1890 he managed to juggle these four portfolios, even though his powerful constitution had grown noticeably weaker and his body was often in such pain as to necessitate his absence from Berlin for weeks on end. Simultaneously, he had to cope with a court cabal, which, headed by Crown Prince Frederick William and his English wife, Victoria, allied itself with the Progressives and the National Liberals against him.

The Fight over Bismarck's
National Financial System

Many years earlier a Prussian diplomat had remarked that for Bismarck political parties were merely relay horses that he rode to the next station. By 1878 the postillion had reached his next station and was ready to change horses. In that

---

*He was, however, aided by his son and confidant, Count Herbert von Bismarck (1849–1904), who was titular secretary of state for foreign affairs from 1886 to 1890.

year the parliamentary campaign to win acceptance of Bismarck's new, unified, financial system began. The key to his success was the dissolution of a hostile Reichstag. A second attempt on the life of the 81-year-old William I, which left him gravely wounded, evoked general indignation with radicalism and provided the pretext for the chancellor to dissolve the Reichstag. In the elections of the summer of 1878 the two Conservative parties scored such a success that their combined mandates surpassed those of the declining National Liberals by seventeen. Bismarck now had the options of forming an all-Conservative-National Liberal majority or a Conservative-Centrist. With the former, he was able to ram through the Reichstag in October, 1878, the Anti-Socialist Law. With the latter majority he secured acceptance of his protective tariff bill.

From May through July, 1879, Bismarck's adjutant in the Reichstag, the Free Conservative Wilhelm von Kardorff (1828–1907), was busy forging a governmental tariff majority aggregating more than 200 deputies, consisting of 87 Centrists, 75 Free Conservatives and Conservatives, 27 National Liberal dissidents, and a handful of Independents. On July 12, 1879, the tariff bill cleared the last hurdle in the Reichstag and became law by a majority of one hundred votes, the Socialists, Progressives, and the bulk of the National Liberals opposing.

From the moment the Center genuflected before Bismarck's financial system that party could no longer be treated as an enemy of the Empire. Nevertheless, this did not mean that the Center would also have to desert states' rights. Feeling that the imperial government would be dangerously strengthened at the expense of the states if it were permitted to retain the vast revenues that would accumulate from the new protective tariffs, especially on iron, grain, tobacco, and sugar, the Center proposed and secured the adoption of the Franckenstein Proviso or Amendment to the tariff bill. This amendment set a maximum of 130 million marks to the revenues that the federal government might annually retain from customs and tobacco tax receipts and authorized the allocation among the states of any surplus above that figure. Inasmuch as the maximum was insufficient to finance the operating expenses of the imperial government, the Franckenstein clause insured its continued dependence upon matricular contributions from the states. This interposed a formidable obstacle to any scheme to forge a unitary German Empire.

Rocked to their foundation by Bismarck's oblique attack, the National Liberals were almost destroyed in the fighting. Not only did a small group on the right wing of the party defy discipline in July, 1879, to vote for the tariff and increased tobacco taxes, but a year later the entire left wing of the party, under leadership of Lasker and Bamberger, seceded because allegedly the majority of the party still hoped to compose differences with Bismarck.* This secession ended the day of the parliamentary dominance of the National Liberal party.

For the imperial ministry the consequence of the battle over the tariff and excise taxes was the departure of the remaining liberal-minded ministers and their re-

---

*This allegation found corroboration in the fact that during the fight over the tariff Bennigsen had offered Bismarck National Liberal support for his financial system if the chancellor would at least accord to the Reichstag the right to exercise annual control over duties on coffee and taxes on salt.

placement with Conservatives (von Puttkamer, culture; von Ballhausen, agriculture; and Bitter, finance), who for some years thereafter enjoyed a virtual monopoly over the imperial and Prussian governments. These changes had the consequence of briefly reviving the contest of earlier days between aristocracy and middle class for the political mastery of Germany.

Meanwhile, despite passage of the tariff bill, Bismarck's unitary financial concept was rebuffed. He had hoped to find the money to finance expanding governmental operations and the military Septennat of 1880 in customs receipts, income from the state tobacco monopoly, and increased yield from indirect taxes. However, in the fall of 1881 both the Prussian House of Representatives and the Reichstag voted against Bismarck's fiscal proposals, and the ensuing Reichstag elections did not bring him his hoped-for majority. While the vacillating Center increased its strength to 98 deputies, the Conservatives experienced a drop from 115 to 77 mandates, and although the National Liberals lost 43 of their 98 seats, the Liberal Secessionists increased their mandates from 31 to 59, and the new Liberal Union (Liberale Vereinigung) of the diminutive Lasker won 47. These were heavy blows for Bismarck, whose health was at this time poor, for he had not yet found Dr. Schweninger, who was to prolong his life by fifteen years. Sick in body and well-nigh desperate, Bismarck meditated a coup d'état. The temptation to suppress the Reichstag gained ever stronger attraction for him in the last decade of his chancellorship. To his mind, unconstitutional government seemed the only refuge of aristocratic-bureaucratic policy if it was serious about wanting to preserve its independence from intemperate popular pressure.

The Rise of German Socialism

Bismarck's aversion to public criticism was cynically demonstrated in connection with his efforts to suppress the German Socialist movement, whose meteoric rise was an harbinger of the age of democracy. Because of a ban imposed by law of July 13, 1854, on radical political organizations, it was not possible until the eve of the Danish War for any group to engage in Social Democratic organizational or agitational work in the German states. In effect it was left to the democratic bourgeois parties (Progressive and German People's parties) to defend workers' interests, and to liberal and Catholic agencies to organize labor for cultural purposes.

The first important organizer of a popular socialist movement in Germany was Ferdinand Lassalle (1825–64), a Jewish attorney of Breslau. A believer in Ricardo's iron law of wages and an advocate of governmentally aided cooperative consumers' and producers' associations, Lassalle was the first great champion of the German working class. Lassalle's thinking about politics was permeated with an Hegelian respect for the state, a Treitschkean love of country, and a Marxist antagonism toward the middle class. Lassalle was not alone in urging the working class to organize for political and social reform independently of the bourgeois Liberal parties. Friedrich Wilhelm Fritzsche (1825–1905), a cigar-maker, and

Julius Vahlteich (1839–1915), a shoemaker, were in the early 1860s demanding that in all workers' associations priority be given to political as compared with cultural education and that the proletariat should be organized into a great national vehicle for social reform.

In response to the stirring appeal of Lassalle on March 1, 1863, there was founded on May 23, 1863, in the Leipzig General German Workingmen's Association (Der Allgemeine Deutsche Arbeiterverein or ADAV) an organization of preponderantly Prussian membership. The Leipzig convention adopted a militant program that exhorted the masses to independent political action without reliance upon middle-class parties, and it called for establishment of a unified, democratic state. Also demanded were universal, equal, and direct manhood suffrage for all German states, cabinet responsibility, parliamentary control over the armed forces and the military budget, graduated income and inheritance taxes, and equal opportunity for all.

Despite his fiery speeches, Lassalle was not a revolutionary but a reformer and a nationalist. As Wilhelm Liebknecht rightly charged, Lassalle favored an alliance with the monarchy and did his best to come to terms with Bismarck and the Conservatives. The rank and file of the General German Workingmen's Association were devoted to him beyond reason, for he had done what no one else had ever done before—founded a German workers' party. Because of this, the masses were prepared to forgive him his autocratic behavior, and he had a real chance of capturing the revolutionary element in the country. Unfortunately he threw his brilliant prospects away in a duel (August 31, 1864) over a girl for whom he did not really care a fig. His untimely death cleared the way for a far greater working-class leader than himself.

Division and fragmentation overtook the tiny socialist movement after Lassalle's death. His association split in two in 1866. The larger succession organization was headed by Johann Baptist von Schweitzer (1833–75), a Catholic aristocratic socialist, who had been elected president of the ADAV in 1864. During the Austro-Prussian War Schweitzer's following supported Prussia and the *kleindeutsch* solution and after 1867 sought to use the North German Confederation to advance the interests of the workers through political unification, on the assumption that it must precede democracy.

East German historians, such as Horst Bartel, Rolf Dlubek, Reinhard Beike, and Gustav Seeber, have insisted that the Social Democratic Labor party (Sozialdemokratische Arbeiterpartei or SDAP), which was founded at Eisenach in 1869, was the first independent revolutionary workers' party. However, the viewpoint of West German historians, such as Gerhard A. Ritter, Werner Conze, Hermann Heidegger, and Suzanne Miller, that the SDAP, which had been founded by the master turner August Bebel and the Hessian journalist Wilhelm Liebknecht, was neither socially homogeneous nor decisively revolutionary appears to accord better with the facts. Bebel and Liebknecht, who were also members of the proletarian and petty bourgeois Federation of German Workers' Associations (Verband deutscher Arbeitervereine) and cofounders of the democratic Saxon People's party, neither wanted to exclude petty bourgeois democrats from the SDAP nor eliminate the gradualist approach to the democratization of Germany. Moreover, Bebel at least, after the Second Empire had been founded, was prepared to pursue the tactic of the parliamentary conquest of power in a "class state."

During the Franco-Prussian War before the proclamation of the French Republic on September 4, 1870, the Lassalleans regarded the conflict as one for the defense of Germany against the aggression of Napoleon III. They also believed the war would promote the unification of the nation. Accordingly, the Lassalleans approved the request of the North German Confederate government for war credits. Liebknecht and Bebel, on the other hand, regarded the war as a dynastic one, and on their own initiative, without the backing of their party, abstained from voting the war credits. After September 4, when it became plain that Prussia would insist upon the cession of Alsace and eastern Lorraine, both the Lassalleans and the Social Democrats argued that the war had changed into one of conquest. On this supposition, they rejected the government's next request for war credits.

After 1871 the Eisenach and Lassallean socialists began to draw together, because the issues of unification and war, which had earlier divided them, had receded into history. The coming of the depression of 1873 argued strongly for union of all socialist forces.

At the unionist convention in Gotha in 1875 the two parties fused as the SDAP and adopted a joint program that was more Lassallean than Marxist in tenor. The Gotha program repeated most of the demands of the earliest program of the ADAV, while adding freedom to organize trade unions, the legislation of social reforms, and the establishment of a "free people's state." The program stressed that these aims were to be achieved by legal means. No mention was made of historical materialism, seizure of power through insurrection, or dictatorship of the proletariat. To Marx's chagrin, Lassalle had triumphed from beyond the grave. Bebel, convinced that the unity of the working class was more important than doctrinal purity, had gone his independent way. The practical Gotha program influenced the whole later development of German Social Democracy. It determined that the workers' party would become the principal reformist agency within the Reich and that the party would seek its future in the state rather than upon its ruins. The political direction given at Gotha enabled Bebel and other socialist leaders to unfold a fruitful activity in the Reichstag, extending over a generation, which was to be a cardinal factor in raising the German working class to the highest standard of living in Europe.

With each succeeding Reichstag election the socialist movement gave Bismarck increasing concern. The mandate of the Socialists increased from two seats in 1871, representing 3.19 percent of the votes cast, to nine in 1874 and 6.78 percent of the electorate. The depression helped the united Socialists to achieve a brilliant success in the January, 1877, elections to the Reichstag. The party polled 493,000 votes (9.13 percent of the electorate) and returned twelve deputies. At that time the Socialist Labor party had revealed itself as especially strong in Saxony, Thuringia, and Schleswig-Holstein but still weak in the Rhineland and South

Germany. The party had become a national force, controlling forty-one larger and thirty-three smaller newspapers throughout Germany. However, as the new party gained popularity, the Conservative and Liberal elements took alarm and went over to an attack against organized socialism, and numerous party leaders, including Liebknecht and Bebel, were sentenced to prison in the 1870s.

The Anti-Socialist Law, 1878–90

By 1878 a sorely troubled Bismarck was thinking of taking decisive legislative action against the German Socialist Labor party. He seized upon an attempted assassination of William I on May 11, 1878, by a depraved non-Socialist to try to bludgeon the Reichstag into passing a severe anti-Socialist law. Although the National Liberals once again compromised their principles by endorsing Bismarck's draconic measures, the proposal was defeated. However, on June 2, 1878, a second attempt to assassinate the 81-year-old kaiser, by a fuzzy-minded, non-Socialist intellectual, so gravely wounded the emperor as to necessitate a temporary regency. Knowing that the nation would no longer temporize with terrorism, Bismarck exploited the kaiser's disability and dissolved the Reichstag. In the elections of July–August, 1878, the Socialists received 437,000 votes (7.5 percent of the electorate) and only nine mandates. They had lost 56,000 votes or about 11.3 percent of their 1877 voting strength—their first serious setback.

With an intimidated Reichstag at his beck, Bismarck secured passage of a new anti-Socialist bill. His majority comprised mainly Conservatives and National Liberals. The law was to be valid for eighteen months but was subsequently renewed at intervals until 1890, when Emperor William II allowed it to lapse. The law dissolved the Social Democratic Labor party's national organization; forbade Socialist meetings, processions, debates, and festivities; authorized seizure of party journals and provided fines or imprisonment for their publishers; and empowered state authorities to impose martial law. Although Bismarck did not think the law was harsh enough, inasmuch as it did not prevent Socialist candidates from running for the Reichstag, the provisions were enforced with severity in Prussia by the minister of the interior, Robert von Puttkamer (1828–1900), whose spies were everywhere.

Not the suppression but the radicalization of the socialist movement was the most important consequence of the Anti-Socialist Law. At the first congress of the exiled party, held at Wyden in Switzerland in 1880, it was unanimously voted to delete from the Gotha program the phrase that had compelled party members to limit their opposition to the government to "all *legal* means." In 1883 at Copenhagen the party was ostentatiously declared to be a revolutionary party that no longer looked to parliaments for attainment of its goals. Notwithstanding appearances, however, there was never a time even in this "heroic phase" of the history of the German Social Democratic party when powerful Lassallean reformist tendencies were subdued by the putatively militant Marxist leadership.

Persecution, practical difficulties, and threatening bankruptcy could not prevent the party from increasing its mandate between 1881 and 1884 from 13 to 24, or from 6.12 percent to 9.1 percent of the electorate, which was slightly more than in 1877. In 1887, a year of war scares, the Social Democrats received only 11 mandates but polled more than 750,000 votes, or 10.12 percent of the electorate. The passing of war fever improved the prospects of the antimilitarist socialist movement. In the ensuing elections of 1890 it scored a noble triumph. What in that year was renamed the Social Democratic party of Germany or SPD (Sozialdemokratische Partei Deutschlands), an organization affiliated with the Second International of Working Men's Associations, now received 1,427,298 votes and obtained 35 mandates in the Reichstag. Thereafter the SPD had the largest mass following of any German party.

In view of the fact that in 1890 the SPD had won the support of one out of every five voters, young Kaiser William II (1888–1918) decided, in spite of his profound antipathy for Marxism, to let the Anti-Socialist Law lapse and permit the SPD to operate legally. Seemingly another major defeat for Bismarck's domestic policies, the struggle against the SPD had personally ruined the chancellor, for the rift that developed between Bismarck and his impetuous and headstrong imperial master over the expediency of continuing the Anti-Socialist Law was a main factor in the chancellor's dismissal.

Bismarck's Social Insurance Legislation

In view of the Socialists' sharp defeat in the Reichstag elections of 1881 and the reaction evoked in Germany by the assassination of the "tsar liberator," Alexander II, in 1881, Bismarck thought that the German workers would now dance the monarchical waltz and abjure Socialist leadership.

Bismarck had long meditated espousing protective social insurance legislation, and now he considered the time was ripe for a great initiative that would steal the thunder of Bebel and Liebknecht. Whether or not Bismarck's social insurance laws were merely a political stratagem, it is impossible to deny the significance of legislation that for the first time anywhere in history established a state-controlled insurance program against major calamities that beset the poor. In late nineteenth-century Germany there was increasing recognition of the responsibility of the state to protect the workers against capitalist abuses. A number of thinkers—Rudolf von Gneist, Friedrich Lange, Archbishop von Ketteler, Adolph Kolping, Adolf Stöcker, Gustav Schmoller, and Lujo Brentano—sought to revive the humanitarian and paternalistic spirit of the past. Lange (1828–75) and Brentano (1844–1931) were the founders of academic socialism (*Kathedersozialismus*) and the Social Policy Association (Verein für Sozialpolitik), which included many professors and advocated government initiative for the solution of major social problems.

Bismarck's Prussian socialism never went beyond insurance against ill health, accidents, old age, and invalidity. Because he never really sympathized with proletarian economic objectives such as the six-day workweek, shorter hours, factory inspection laws, and higher real wages, Bismarck fought like any employer against the one type of program whose implementation would have cut deeply into the SDAP's mass following. For this reason Bismarck did not succeed in detaching the proletariat from the Social Democratic party. Yet had it not been for the National Liberals, Freisinnige, and Centrists, who opposed radical protective measures, Bismarck would have established a more comprehensive social insurance system, including an imperial department of social insurance.

The first piece of social welfare legislation—the Health Insurance Act—was enacted in 1883. Authorizing sick pay benefit payments to insured during the first thirteen weeks of absence from work, the act stipulated that two-thirds of the premiums were to be paid by the workers and one-third by employers. The administrative officers of the health insurance bureaus were to be elective, and this enabled the SPD and trade union leaders to gain control of at least one type of provincial agency.

After three years of hard fighting, the ministry in 1884 rammed the Accident Insurance Law through the Reichstag. This act was mainly designed to support insured workers who due to injury were temporarily off their jobs for more than thirteen weeks. Premiums were to be wholly defrayed by employers. Benefit payments up to two-thirds of the wage were provided from the fourteenth week of inactivity onward. In 1886 accident compensation was extended to agricultural day laborers.

Bismarck's last insurance law, providing old age and total disability benefits to virtually all workers at the age of seventy, was passed in 1889. In this, his greatest social monument, the principle of governmental contributions was admitted with respect to pensions, but the bulk of costs was to be defrayed in equal shares by workers and employers. Provincial (state) agencies under the supervision of the federal government were to be responsible for administering the law.

Conservatives, National Liberals, and Center had combined to provide the requisite legislative majority to enact these epochal laws, which diminished the insecurity that haunted millions. The Socialists opposed—not out of principle, of course, but in consideration of details of the legislation. By these laws Bismarck was able to prove that the Conservative imperial government was vitally interested in protecting the people against economic exploitation and the hardships of infirmity and disability. Bismarck demonstrated that a semiauthoritarian monarchy could pioneer in social legislation of prime significance. Moreover, in the long run Bismarck's palliatives largely reconciled the masses to the imperfections in the German political system. His social achievements served to confirm the truth, as Franz Schnabel has pointed out, that Prussian nineteenth-century thought was basically shaped by the view of Humboldt, Fichte, and Hegel that meaningful freedom for the individual citizen can exist only within and not beyond the state.

Clearly the contention that under Bismarck the Second Empire was progressively alienated from Western civilization is a questionable generalization that is rendered all the more dubious by the fact that it was probably invented to rationalize the failure of Germany in two great twentieth-century wars. Actually, however, in most of his major initiatives—establishment of universal manhood suffrage, military conscription, and a centralized imperial administration, the codification of national law, enunciation of the rule of law *(Rechtsstaat)*, institution of civil marriage and divorce, secularization of education and subordination of the church to the state, strengthening of executive power, adoption of a protective tariff system, attempts to nationalize transportation and communications, and the introduction of social insurance—Bismarck was the pacemaker of the Western world and the foreloper of the twentieth-century state.

Believers in an antinomy between Germany and European civilization in the Bismarckian era must seek corroboration for their questionable view in the occult realm of half-truths, where the responsible historian ought not to follow. All that may honestly be said is that the political modernization of Germany did not keep abreast of its economic and social progress, but that, in spite of this, Bismarck's ameliorative legislation encouraged nationalist and reformist attitudes among the masses that insured their loyalty to the state in World War I.

The Dilemma of the
Middle-Class Parties

In the 1880s the German middle-class parties had a very real choice to make between democracy and defense. If the middle-class parties had chosen to fight for total democracy, they could probably have achieved an ad hoc working alliance with the Socialists and attracted many Centrist deputies. Such a block would have commanded a huge majority in the Reichstag but would have run the grave risk of so weakening the Reich as to court general war with prospects of defeat and dismemberment. On the other hand, if the middle-class parties had chosen to rally to Bismarck's para-authoritarian system, this would have traduced the meaning of liberty in Germany and alienated the masses from the bourgeoisie. Confronted with this dilemma, which the ideologically revolutionary-oriented SPD escaped, the liberal parties all placed duty to country above democracy. This was not especially hard for them, considering that they had never been enthusiastic about the social democratic state.

Middle-Class Politics in the
Early 1880s

After the tariff issue had destroyed Bismarck's Free Conservative-National Liberal majority in the Reichstag, the chancellor was never again able to build so durable a legislative support. During the last decade of his chancellorship, Bismarck was obliged to pilot the government down a river of shifting sand bars. During the years 1881–86, at least two-thirds of the Reichstag was generally hostile to him. Inasmuch as the Center, though gradually conciliated by the liquidation of the *Kulturkampf,* remained an undependable ally for Bismarck, he could really only count upon Free Conservatives, Conservatives, and the National Liberal rump for the implementation of his grand policies. The fact that this combination represented a minority in Reichstag and nation led the chancellor to dwell upon desperate measures, such as a coup d'état, to retain absolute control over the state.

In August, 1880, the leftists in the National Liberal party, who called themselves Secessionists, bolted the parent organization over the tariff issue. Led by Max von Forckenbeck, Franz von Stauffenberg, Eduard Lasker, Ludwig Bamberger, and Theodor Barth (the editor of the progressive *Die Nation*), the Secessionists also included men of cultural mark, such as the historian Theodor Mommsen. They merged on March 15, 1884, with the Progressive party, which was led by Richter, Julius Lenzmann, and Albert Hänel, to form the Freisinnige or Independent Liberal party. Its chief was the diminutive atomic pile, Eugen Richter (1838–1906). Of him, the distinguished novelist Theodor Fontane wrote that of all Reichstag deputies Richter "most closely approached Bismarck in knowledge, wit, unaffectedness and pugnacity." Richter campaigned for freedom of enterprise, abolition of protective tariffs, ministerial responsibility, civil liberties, and the acquisition of colonies. As Gustav Seeber has abundantly shown, the fraternization of Freisinnige leaders with heavy industry and banking and commercial circles, instead of working-class leaders, rendered illusory any hope that the Independent Liberals would ever become serious foes of the existing social order.

Both the Anti-Socialist Law and the Septennat of 1880 were passed by a Reichstag that was reacting to the continuing wave of terrorism in Europe and to the critical position that Germany found itself in vis à vis France and Russia at that time. Bismarck's victories in this respect were due in no small part to the National Liberals, who, led by Miquel, now disposed of only one third of their strength of 1876 and were reduced to a party of heavy industry.

The new Septennat replaced that of 1874 (eighteen months ahead of time); it fixed the peacetime strength of the German army at 427,000 (an increase of 26,000) until 1888, maintained the three-year conscript service requirement, and stressed more intensive and accelerated training of reservists. This military establishment, answerable to no civil agency, could be used as a bludgeon by king and chancellor to compel compliance with governmental policy.

Although Bismarck did not share the formulation of grand policy with the middle class, he continued to the very end to enjoy the support of big business. Throughout the later history of the hybrid Wilhelmine Empire the split in the bourgeois parliamentary bloc, representing a potentially revolutionary class in what was still basically an aristocratic-authoritarian state, condemned Germany to political backwardness.

The elections of 1881 were a jolt to Bismarck in more ways than one. His parliamentary support was reduced to about a third of the Reichstag. The rump National Liberal party and the Reich party both suffered severe losses. The Secessionists, who had parted ways with Bismarck, received fifty mandates—about the same as were accorded the National Liberals. The Center emerged with 98 deputies to become the balance wheel of parliament. This defeat was tantamount to the frustration of one of Bismarck's cardinal aims, to increase indirect taxes and put customs receipts wholly at the disposal of the central government. All the parties that had opposed the further growth of a leviathan state had triumphed.

By the time the elections of 1884 rolled around, Bismarck had to some degree repaired his fences. His prestige had been augmented by Germany's successful transition of the diplomatic crises of the years 1878–81, the revival of the League of Three Emperors, Italy's adhesion (1882) to the Austro-German Alliance of 1879, inauguration of a German colonial policy, and formulation of a national social insurance program. In 1884 the rightist current was unmistakable in Prussia and increasingly apparent in the Reich. In the former, Puttkamer was vigorously sweeping all progressive elements from the Prussian administration and government. Conservative-monarchist elements had virtually come to monopolize the state apparatus, while in the Prussian Abgeordnetenhaus, elected on the basis of the inequitable three-class system, no Social Democrat was heard, the progressive factions were reduced to impotence, and a triple social alliance of Conservatives, National Liberals, and Center held the ring. All of these developments found their reflection in the antileftist composition of the national Reichstag of 1884. As a result of the elections the Conservatives increased their combined mandate by 50 percent, while the Center, which was protectionist and had come to support many of Bismarck's economic and military policies, remained the strongest party. The National Liberals polled a larger vote than in 1881 by grabbing hold of Bismarck's coattails.

There had been only one chance to stem the returning tide of Bismarckian conservatism, and that was a slim one. Had the bourgeois progressive elements joined hands with the Socialists on a common democratic platform, things might have turned out differently. If the Freisinnige had worked for the repeal of the Anti-Socialist Law, a modus operandi might have been achieved with the Socialist party, and it might have been possible to fight with success against the Bismarckian compromise and the military state. What is more, under the spell of such an agreement, it is likely that the semireformist Socialist party would have succumbed to revisionism and nationalism earlier than it in fact did. These prospects were dashed because the Freisinnige rejected the class struggle and scorned to join hands with a movement which, to its mind, threatened the existing social order and security of the state.

A result of the refusal of the Independent Liberals to abandon their consortium with the finance capitalists, who themselves kept company with industrialists and Junkers, was the shattering defeat of the Freisinnige in the elections of 1884. While 24 Socialist deputies were returned to the Reichstag, the Independent Liberals received only 67 mandates.

Bismarck's Last Victory

In 1886–87 a war scare, provoked by the bellicose Boulanger, the minister of war in France, caused the German people once again to scurry for protection under Bismarck's cloak.

Exploiting Boulangism with its revanchist threat of an offensive Franco-Russian alliance, Bismarck in 1886 introduced into the Reichstag a year and a half ahead of time a new Septennat, which was to run till 1894. It envisioned a peacetime military strength of 468,000 (1 percent of the population), amounting to an increase of 41,000 troops. Despite a great forensic effort by Bismarck, the Septennat was rejected by the Reichstag in January, 1887. New elections, under the circumstances, would yield him a much more obliging legislature. Therefore, he dissolved the Reichstag in January, 1887.

In the ensuing elections Bismarck, an adept at parliamentary politics in a country where parliament was not the decisive factor, carried off a triumph—the last of his career. He campaigned on the slogan: "Better an imperial than a parliamentary army." He had persuaded the three "government parties"—Conservatives, National Liberals, and Center—to form an electoral *Kartell* that should offer a common candidate in each constituency. Since by law only candidates who emerged in first or second place on the first ballot might compete in the run-off *(Stichwahl)* election, the *Kartell* held forth the prospect of victory for Bismarck.

Although the popular majority of the Socialist party remained about the same, its mandate, owing to inequitable apportionment, dropped from 24 to 11. The Freisinnige lost more than half their seats, declining to 32. Their future was dark indeed, for they had fallen between both stools, democracy and authoritarianism. Despite the fact that Bismarck's *Kartell* polled a little less than a popular majority, the Center kept its 100 seats, the National Liberals gained 48, and the Conservative party picked up 15 more, giving the chancellor the absolute majority he needed. Then the Septennat was adopted.

While Bismarck has been accused of cynically exploiting the Boulangist war threat to achieve a smashing victory of the government over the left, this was not his main aim. It was only a means to an end, for Bismarck was always first of all a statesman and only secondarily a politician. He acted in the crisis as a responsible custodian who was seeking to strengthen his country in the most menacing international situation since the Franco-Prussian War. He would have been derelict if he had not dissolved the Reichstag and sought to broaden popular support for what he regarded as vitally necessary military measures. Nor can it be seriously maintained that the chancellor or his son Herbert (who had recently been appointed foreign minister) invented the war scare of 1886–87. A reviving France, resentful of Germany, was beginning to court with success an alienated Russia. For the first time since 1859 a Franco-Russian alliance was a distinct possibility. Can Bismarck be censured for taking all precautions in the face of a threatening tornado?

Chapter 39

THE PERSONAL REGIME OF

WILLIAM II, 1888–1900

"One Foot in the Grave"

Nothing is more astonishing than the rapidity with which Bismarck within only three years lost command of Germany. In 1887, seemingly, he stood at the very pinnacle of his power. Having just snatched the Reinsurance Treaty with Russia from the wreck of the League of Three Emperors and having scored a diplomatic victory over Boulangist France, Bismarck remained, after a quarter of a century at the helm, the indispensable pilot. Due to his extraordinary skill, Germany was still the nexus of a system of alliances and alignments that extended even to isolationist Britain, whereas France was entering her eighteenth year in the diplomatic wilderness. On the domestic front the elections of 1887 had made it possible for the government's *Kartell* to dominate the Reichstag for some years to come.

Nevertheless, Bismarck was a colossus with feet of clay. His position after 1887 was far from secure. His marvelous system of external controls and balances was beginning to crumble, particularly in the east. Between 1887 and 1890 the temperature of Russo-German relations plummeted and entered the frigid zone, while sharp divisions between Czechs and Austrians made the Dual Monarchy an ally of doubtful value. There was also tension within the *Kartell*. The right wing of the Conservative party, strongly Lutheran, was coming to regard the Centrists as "Greeks bearing gifts," and the National Liberals stood ready to refight the battles of the *Kulturkampf* at a moment's notice. In particular they were prepared to resist any demand of the Center party to indemnify the Roman Church for losses incurred as a result of the battle with the state. Nor were the Conservatives comfortable in their alliance with the National Liberals, who disquieted them with agitation for reduction of duties on grain. Added to these woes, Bismarck was aging fast. It was even rumored that he was entering senility. Finally, the German Jupiter's future was put in jeopardy by the expectation that two new emperors would ascend the throne in swift succession, neither of whom was sympathetic to Bismarck's policies, both of whom chafed under the chancellor's strong hand. Bismarck had now to live with the fear that at any time he could be humiliatingly dismissed by an emperor whose prerogatives he had erected into the hypostasis of the German constitutional system.

On March 9, 1888, the aged William I died, and his son, who had waited a lifetime on the steps of the throne, mounted them on the eve of his own death. Frederick III, "the emperor of ninety-nine days," was fatally afflicted with cancer of the larynx and shortly after his accession could no longer speak. Heavily influenced by his domineering wife, Victoria, daughter of England's queen, Frederick III was so pro-English in all things that Bismarck, whose malice for the couple had long poisoned their lives, spoke derisively of the new kaiser as *Fried-*

rich der dritte, Friedrich der Britte ("Frederick III, Frederick the Briton"). Considering the unquenchable hatred that the strong-willed empress bore Bismarck, it is certain that had Frederick III lived he would soon have dismissed him.

The Character of William II

When in 1888 William II ascended the throne he was twenty-nine. Bismarck was seventy-three. The kaiser was very popular with all classes. Endowed with high intelligence and abundant energy, William's mind played on the surface of many fields of thought, and, although he really only knew the first lines of everything and the second of nothing, he passed as one of the most cultivated monarchs of his day. Mystical, brilliant, fiery, and unstable, he moved across the European sky like a comet. A person given to startling sallies, indiscreet tirades, and fustian, William II was the *enfant terrible* of international politics. Holstein said that he had more instinct for the theater than politics, and certainly the kaiser had a compulsive craving for limelight and applause. Gravely deficient in the essential qualities of the statesman, which are reason and restraint, he was, in moments of forensic intoxication, often carried away by his own eloquence. Yet his speech did not commonly mirror his thought. Where circumstances or his advisers did not permit him to fall captive to his rhetoric, he often showed himself to be perceptive, continent in aims, and devoted to the general peace.

The Circumstances of Bismarck's Dismissal

William II held a strong hand in the showdown with the aged Bismarck. The latter, though approaching senility, was reluctant to relinquish any of his power. The kaiser had managed to detach most of the princes from the chancellor, who also found it difficult to retain the allegiance of his own ministers. Some of them, including Holstein, had already deserted the sinking ship. Whereas Bismarck agitated for the extension of the Anti-Socialist Law when it came up for renewal in 1890 and even advocated strengthening it, William II sought to curry popular favor by opposing Bismarck on both counts. Avid of popularity, William II had strongly supported the Old Age and Invalidity Act of 1889 and now courted the masses with promises of factory protective legislation that would fill lacunae not covered by the social insurance laws. Bismarck, on the other hand, did not sympathize with legislation that regulated hours or conditions of labor. He foolishly defended workers' "morality" against the corruptions of excessive "leisure time."

By 1890 Bismarck had lost the support of key persons in the government or the emperor's retinue—Philipp zu Eulenburg, Fritz Holstein, and Alfred von Kiderlen-Wächter. While young William II was busying himself with detaching ministers from Bismarck, the latter was being assailed from the rear by Baron von Hammerstein, the editor of the *Kreuzzeitung*. In addition, the eastern horizon had become impermissibly dark due to a financial and commercial vendetta between Germany and Russia, for which Bismarck was partly responsible. Not least of the factors that figured in Bismarck's dismissal was the kaiser's alarm at this swift deterioration in Russo-German relations.

Bismarck thought to throw off ballast by proposing to surrender the minister-presidency, while retaining the chancellorship with its control over Bundesrat and foreign relations. But such concessions were in vain. William II stubbornly opposed the extension of the Anti-Socialist Law. A diversionary effort by Bismarck to lift the crossfire by proposing a large increase in the size of the army collapsed. It was too late to buy the friendship of William II with such coin.

Bismarck's "last Mohican" was the electorate. Unfortunately for him, the kaiser's social welfare proclamations and his "New Course" had brought about a tremendous swing to the left. In the elections of February 20, 1890, almost two-thirds of all votes went to the opposition. The *Kartell*'s strength dropped from 220 to 135 mandates in a Reichstag of 397 deputies, the National Liberals and Free Conservatives each losing more than half their seats. The Center party and the Freisinnige both made gains, but, as has been noted, the most impressive showing was that of the SPD. All told, it was a shattering defeat for Bismarck, who now saw the specter of ruin before his watery eyes.

Perhaps Bismarck's position would not have been irremediable had the kaiser supported him, because the chancellor was not by fundamental law dependent upon the good graces of the Reichstag. But William II, who had made up his mind to drop the old pilot, read into the election results a plebiscitary indictment of Bismarck. The kaiser, supported by the new chief of the general staff, the politically ambitious Count Alfred von Waldersee (1832–1904), summoned the chancellor to him on March 15, 1890. Three days later Bismarck tendered a carefully prepared apologia, which was his letter of resignation. His departure from the helm evoked general rejoicing throughout the land! *Sic transit gloria mundi*.

Bismarck's Successors

None of the four succeeding chancellors was able to throw Bismarck's javelin. Each of them—General Count Georg Leo von Caprivi (1831–1901), who served from 1890 to 1894, Prince Chlodwig zu Hohenlohe-Schillingsfürst (1819–1901), who was chancellor from 1894 to 1900, Prince Bernhard von Bülow (1849–1929), foreign minister since 1897 and chancellor from 1900 to 1909, and Theobald von Bethmann-Hollweg (1856–1921), chancellor from 1909 to 1917—was either too inexperienced or too ineffectual to keep Germany at the top of the diplomatic greased pole. Accordingly, each of these leaders left behind him a minus in the cardinal area of a statesman's activities. By 1914 the cumulative external liabilities incurred by these men had grown so great as to invite war.

It made little difference to the international community that each of Bismarck's four successors was a sincere friend of peace. More important was the fact that none of them knew how to preserve it. Having abandoned Bismarck's policy of limited liability, they were unprepared to take, while there was still time, the calculated risks that could alone have forestalled general war. Thus, Germany, lapped in the treasures she had won in the wars of the *Reichsgründung* and in the prosperity associated with her industrial upsurge, was viewed by the world as a retired highwayman, too fond of his possessions and comfort to undertake dangerous excursions. A time came by 1914 when, in spite of all burnt offerings the chancellors had brought to the altar of peace, war could be avoided only by paying an altogether exhorbitant blackmail.

The Caprivi Honeymoon

The chief importance of Caprivi's term in office is that externally and internally it was one of departures, generally for unknown parts. The "New Course" that William II personally charted was as uncertain as it was unintentionally perilous. In external affairs the kaiser's policy was one of peace at any price, which is to say a policy of drift. Its tombstone was the Franco-Russian alliance. In internal affairs the wavering "New Course" corroded the infrastructure of the state, for it ate at the foundations of the nobility and the quasi-authoritarian constitution. At the same time the kaiser's policy strengthened the left.

William II was Caprivi's shirt of Nessus. The kaiser never understood that a minister must be consistent and true to his own character. As one modern scholar put it, William II

> vacillated not only from week to week, but literally from day to day. He had to do with two ministers, whose policies moved along diametrically opposed paths. Botho Eulenburg steered towards a coup d'état . . . Caprivi unconditionally rejected a coup and any policy that would lead to it. Only one of these two policies could be that of the Kaiser. But today he was for one, and tomorrow for the other, and on the third day for a mixture of both . . .*

Caprivi tried to rally the workers behind throne and government. Desiring to emancipate himself from the parties of the right, he had to formulate a compromise strategy that would offer something to all classes. Indeed, if he were to satisfy the emperor, he had no alternative. Contradictorily enough, however, the kaiser had wanted to retain the rump *Kartell* as the plinth of the government and was not sympathetic to Caprivi's flirtation with the Center and the Freisinnige. Yet, if Caprivi's hopes of acquiring adequate parliamentary backing for protective labor legislation were to be realized, he had to court the left. William II, who wanted to have his cake and eat it too, came to resent Caprivi's show of independence. But as long as he was successful, the kaiser tolerated him.

Encouraged by the socially minded captain of industry Baron Carl Ferdinand von Stumm-Halberg (1836–1901), and aided by the recently appointed minister of trade Hans Freiherr von Berlepsch (1843–1926), who was a great believer in protective legislation, Caprivi persuaded the Reichstag to pass the celebrated labor law of June 1, 1891. This act was the most important piece of paternalistic

---

*Erich Eyck, *Das persönliche Regiment Kaiser Wilhelms II* (Zurich, 1948), pp. 95–96.

legislation of its kind that had ever been enacted in Germany. The law forbade, with minor exceptions, all work on Sunday, as well as employment of children under thirteen years of age. It also established six hours as the maximum work day for adolescents of thirteen and fourteen years, and ten hours for those from fourteen to sixteen. An eleven-hour work day was authorized for women; the Bundesrat was empowered to set hours for men in exceptionally hazardous or exacting employment. Voluntary labor courts were to be set up. These, which afforded labor and management the opportunity of amicably settling their disputes, were such a success that a law of 1904 made them mandatory for all larger towns. Taken in context with the Old Age and Invalidity Insurance Law of 1889, Caprivi's protective social legislation conjured up a vision of the welfare state and inaugurated the consolidation of the lower classes behind the Wilhelmine state. Despite the revolutionary program adopted by the SPD at its Erfurt Convention in 1891, reformist sentiments now began to compete with revolutionary Marxism in the party.

Caprivi's policy of taking account of the legitimate claims of all social strata was illustrated in a number of other initiatives. He restored the confiscated Welf money ("Reptile Funds") to the state of Hanover. He indemnified the Catholic Church to the tune of 16 million marks for funds the state had withheld from it during the *Kulturkampf*. He also extended the hand to the Center when he accepted the "little military bill" proposed by Windthorst and Count von Ballestrem. Made law on June 28, 1890, this increased the army by 18,000 men while reducing the term of service for more than half the recruits from three to two years. The Prussian minister of finance, Johannes Miquel, assailed the real property and excise taxes, which provided the Prussian government with most of its revenue, and secured adoption of an income tax act. This law, which followed those already enacted in Baden, Saxony, and other German states, relieved the landlords of burdensome real property taxes while accommodating workers' demands for an income tax statute that would provide exemptions for incomes below 900 marks per annum. Finally, Caprivi sought to consolidate the Poles behind Prussia. His minister of education, Count Robert von Zedlitz-Trütschler (1837–1914), suppressed discriminatory legislation against the Polish language, rights, and customs in the trans-Oder area, and in 1891 Caprivi's government extended state credits to needy Polish farmers. Zedlitz-Trütschler also countenanced the appointment of Dr. von Stablewski to the archepiscopal see of Posen and Gnesen, which had formerly been occupied only by German bishops.

Spreading depression during 1890–93 gave Caprivi still another opportunity to galvanize bourgeoisie and proletariat behind the government. From 1891 to 1894 Caprivi negotiated commercial treaties with foreign states. The pacts, while not basically altering the protectionist basis of the German tariff system, provided for a reduction of duties on imports of cattle and agricultural products in return for reciprocal concessions upon German industrial exports. His agreements, which were negotiated on the basis of the mutual interests of the countries involved, aimed at both lowering the price of bread and cereals to the German working class and at opening up broader continental markets for German manufactured end-items. The agreements, which turned out to be an important factor in the revival of German industry and the achievement of economic paramountcy in Europe, were applauded by most of the Reichstag parties. Only the Conservatives and their landholding Bavarian allies in the Center stood opposed. These elements, which eventually organized themselves into an Agricultural Association (Bund der Landwirte) in 1893, encouraged Bismarck to attack Caprivi in an effort to break the developing alliance between bourgeoisie and proletariat and restore the old bourgeois-conservative basis of imperial politics.

While Caprivi's trade policies were more popular than those of Bismarck, there can be no doubt that their effect was to sacrifice agriculture to commerce and manufacturing. Although Caprivi's minister of agriculture, the very wealthy Pomeranian, Wilhelm von Heyden-Cadow, set up provincial agricultural offices that tried to mitigate the damage done to the rural areas by the trade treaties (especially with Russia), the farm bloc, captained in the Reichstag by Count Hans von Kanitz-Podangen and Wilhelm von Hammerstein, was not to be reconciled. It continued to introduce bills that would have required state support of grain prices at minimal levels and governmental resale of grain imports at rates to be fixed by a central agricultural bureau. At the same time, the Conservative party, spurred on by Count Julius von Mirbach, adopted in 1893 the Tivoli Program, whose central point was the demand for a return to a protective agrarian policy. This was supported by the two great national farmers' organizations, the newly founded Bund der Landwirte, led by Berthold von Ploetz auf Doellingen, and the older Deutscher Bauernbund (German Farmers' Union), which was led by Kanitz Podangen. The agrarians kept up a massive barrage in the press, especially the *Deutsche Tageszeitung*, the organ of the Bund der Landwirte. In the end the Kaiser bowed to the agrarians. In the fall of 1894, Caprivi and von Heyden-Cadow were both dismissed. This cleared the way for a return to protectionism and brought closer a momentous rapprochement between Junkers and industrialists. Along this road shortly the global ambitions of the Pan German and Navy Leagues were to approach realization.

Caprivi's Fall

The Caprivi government suffered two critical defeats in 1892–93, which disposed the kaiser to abandon it.

As a result of the furor which Caprivi's bill for the strengthening of the confessional character of the Prussian public schools evoked throughout the kingdom in 1891, three ministers resigned, the minister of education was dismissed, and Caprivi himself eventually had to surrender his post as minister-president, although retaining that of Prussian foreign minister. Caprivi's replacement at the head of the Prussian government in 1894 by Count Botho zu Eulenburg (1831–1912), cousin to the kaiser's confidant, Prince Philipp zu Eulenburg (1847–1921), marked the beginning of a permanent separation of the governments of Prussia and the Reich. A consequence of the debate over the school bill was that a good part of Caprivi's conciliatory work was destroyed and the Center's latent hostility toward the Wilhelmine state was revived.

Depressed by growing public disenchantment, Caprivi also tasted defeat over the bill of 1893. The Reichstag shot down his proposals to strengthen the military, and the chancellor dissolved parliament and called for new elections. Held under the thunderclouds of a Franco-Russian military pact and an economic depression, the elections of June, 1893, returned no governmental majority. Caprivi was now forced to construct his parliamentary majority from issue to issue from such bits and fragments as the Poles, Danes, and Alsatians. By a slim majority the government's momentous army bill became law on July 15, 1894. It increased the standing army by 84,000 men, allocated huge new sums for armaments, reduced the service term from three to two years, and authorized the Reichstag to review the military budget once every five, instead of seven, years.

No one was especially impressed with this, Caprivi's last modest victory, for he had alienated the Conservatives and the Bavarian farmers by his lower agricultural duties, the Center by his school bill fiasco, and the National Liberals by refusing to endorse a new Anti-Socialist law. Nor had Caprivi's protective labor legislation persuaded the SPD to collaborate with the ministry. At the same time, Miquel and Botho zu Eulenburg were undermining Caprivi's position with William II, and in South Germany Freiherr von Mittnacht, minister-president of Württemberg, was campaigning against the chancellor.

Meanwhile the assassination of Sadi Carnot, president of France, in June, 1894, caused the aristocracy and bourgeoisie to howl for stern antirevolutionary measures such as Bismarck had advocated. William II now retreated, as he always did when anyone bared his teeth at him. Under strong agrarian and Conservative pressure to drop Caprivi, the emperor vacillated. Ultimately he decided to throw the liberal chancellor to the wolves and retain Botho zu Eulenburg, the authoritarian. Although it proved impossible to keep Eulenburg, Caprivi's fall accentuated the growing personal nature of the Wilhelmine state. In defiance of the wishes of the Reichstag, William II now sounded the bugle for a new assault upon the "revolutionary" left.

Hohenlohe and the Growth of the Kaiser's Power

Contrary to expectations, Caprivi's successor was not Botho Eulenburg but the 75-year-old former minister-president of Bavaria and governor of Alsace-Lorraine, Prince Chlodwig zu Hohenlohe-Schillingsfürst (1819–1904). He was too old and infirm to hold high office and had said so. Nevertheless, he was appointed imperial chancellor, Prussian minister-president, and for a short time also foreign minister, a formidable combination of offices. William II had been urged to appoint General Count Alfred von Waldersee (1832–1904), the pugnacious former chief of the general staff (1888–91), but this would have entailed a break with the Reichstag. Since the kaiser, neither then nor later, had any stomach for a real fight, he was pleased to have the docile and pacific Hohenlohe as his foil in the Reichstag.

Although William II would have preferred a wholly reactionary ministry, Hohenlohe, for whom the kaiser feigned inordinate respect, said the Reichstag wouldn't tolerate it. In this stand he was supported by several ministers. So the kaiser decided to bide his time. Meanwhile he was pressed almost daily by his close friend Philipp zu Eulenburg ("Phili") to restore every actual or presumed prerogative Hohenzollern kings had enjoyed in the age of despotism. William II, whose political notions were as fuzzy as they were luminous, dreamt of turning back the clock and ruling solely with support of the Conservatives. However, Hohenlohe objected, for he valued the confidence of the Center and National Liberals and was dubious about the wisdom of a *Kampfpolitik* against the left.

The fundamental irresolution of William II was revealed in connection with the attempt of the minister of the interior, Ernst von Köller, to force a new anti-socialist law upon the country. This measure would have made it a punishable offense to assail marriage, the family, property, the state, or its institutions or custodians. The bill was valiantly opposed by Freiherr von Berlepsch and a majority of the state ministers and finally in 1895 was rejected by the Reichstag. Having failed in this gambit legally to suppress the left and fearing that dissolution of parliament would entail a new and dangerous conflict with the masses, the emperor toyed with plans for a *Staatsstreich*. Waldersee and the minister of war, General Heinrich von Gossler, favored a coup.

One by one the ministers, including Berlepsch, who disagreed with the kaiser were released and replaced by reliable reactionaries. Finally, in 1897 the last frontal monarchical counteroffensive was launched. Hohenlohe, unable to resist the kaiser's expostulation, assented to the removal of all remaining state ministers who disagreed with William II. Indeed, Hohenlohe even agreed to his own eventual replacement by the new secretary of state for foreign affairs, Count Bernhard von Bülow, an adroit but malicious manipulator of parties whose ace in the hole was that he knew better than any one else how to flatter the emperor. If the personal regime the kaiser had inaugurated in 1896 had lasted, it would have halted evolution toward responsible government in Germany. Fortunately it did not. Within a dozen years the kaiser's authority was to be reduced to a negligible factor.

Civilian Abdication of Control
over the Military

For a few years after 1897 William II bestrode Germany, the chancellorship dangling from his saddle. Paradoxically, however, the degree of separation of civil from military authority had never been so dangerous. The power of the general staff had waxed greatly in the past decade under Waldersee and Count Alfred von Schlieffen (1833–1913), who succeeded him as chief (1891–1905). A man of less versatility and cosmopolitan interests than Waldersee, Schlieffen possessed a professional "tunnel vision" extraordinary for its narrowness of concentration. Working closely with the ministers of war, especially the brilliant Verdy du Vernois, he strengthened the army while freeing the general staff from all civil surveillance.

Nothing so blatantly confirms the judgment of Martin Kitchen and Karl Demeter that the officer corps had by the close of the century gradually come to isolate itself from the nation and the Reichstag as the fact that Schlieffen was free to devise an operational plan that could utterly compromise the work of the statesmen. Schlieffen, on the basis of the Franco-Russian alliance, assumed as neither Moltke nor Waldersee could, that a two-front war was inevitable. Dispensing with Waldersee's concept of mounting a massive attack initially against Russia upon the outbreak of war, Schlieffen worked out a plan between 1897 and 1905 that contemplated first defeating France before the German army would be swung around to smash Russia. After 1902, as both Gordon Craig and Gerhard Ritter have shown, Schlieffen's operational concept envisaged that immediately upon the beginning of hostilities the right wing of the German armies in the west, which was to be seven times as strong as the left wing holding Alsace, would advance through Belgium (violating its neutrality) and northern France. The plan involved the calculated risk that Britain, whose prowess was still sharply discounted by the general staff, would be drawn into the war by the invasion of Belgium. That this plan could ever have succeeded is doubted by the best recent scholarship. On the other hand, nothing is so certain as that the Schlieffen Plan gravely mortgaged Germany's future. It made certain that she would have to fight against three first-class powers simultaneously. That this plan could ever have become a talisman for the army and nation is a commentary on how far Germany had wandered from the unified policy of Frederick the Great.

Founding the German High Seas Fleet

Among the few new departures associated with the Hohenlohe era was the enactment of ambitious naval laws. These laid the fundament of a high seas German fleet. In view of the deleterious consequences of this for Anglo-German relations, it would seem that the decision to build a modern navy with offensive capabilities was another colossal blunder.

Plans for the expansion of the German navy had been formulated since 1889. In 1895 the Kiel Canal was opened, linking the Baltic and North Seas and affording Germany's modest fleet greater maneuverability. By 1897 William II was ready for a big leap forward. He aspired to be the founder of a great German navy. He swept unimaginative time-servers from the Imperial Naval Office (Reichsmarineamt) and put it under the command of a brilliant organizer, the 48-year-old Rear Admiral Alfred von Tirpitz (1849–1930). Tirpitz, who like many rightist leaders was an Anglophobe, dreamt of making the Reich a major naval power. He was, however, opposed at the outset by Hohenlohe, the High Command of the

Army (Oberste Heeresleitung or OHL), and the Junkers. Tirpitz' main support came from the mercantile and industrial bourgeoisie, whose eyes were focused upon world markets, colonies, and *Weltmacht*, especially from such middle-class organizations as the Wehrverein (Defense Association), Alldeutscher Verband (Pan-German League), the Deutsche Kolonialgesellschaft (German Colonial Society), and the Zentralverband deutscher Industrieller.

Tirpitz was planning to build a risk navy—a fleet so strong that Britain, even with her "two-power standard" navy, would fear to attack it and would prefer to sue for Germany's friendship instead. The kaiser had wanted an even stronger fleet—one comprising 28 new and 12 old battleships, which would exceed the combined strength of France and Russia; but after an alarmed Reichstag had cut the government's naval estimates sharply, Tirpitz countered with a memorandum that was to have a decisive influence upon the course of modern history. He suggested in June, 1897, to the Kaiser that a less expensive, smaller, but more heavily armed coastal defense navy could be built in shorter time than the one envisaged by William II. Tirpitz proposed a navy of only 19 battleships, 12 large cruisers, 30 smaller ones, and 8 coastal armored vessels.

The Naval Bills and the Reichstag

The antimilitaristic agitation of the fast-growing Social Democratic party, meantime, was causing the emperor to ponder the advisability of a military dictatorship. However, when the Saxon and South German princes warned that a coup could destroy the Empire and when Philipp zu Eulenburg, Bülow, and the Conservatives all sounded the alarm, William II swiftly sheathed his sword. He then decided to govern through an oligarchy of Hohenlohe, Köller, Eulenburg, Miquel, Waldersee, Tirpitz, Bülow, and Holstein. The kaiser embarked upon a policy (identified with the organizing efforts of the minister of the interior, Miquel) of consolidating behind the oligarchy all-important vested interests. The enemy, he declared, was on the left. The success of this policy of political concentration *(Sammlungspolitik)* with the aim of combatting the Socialists as foes of the country *(Vaterlandslosengesellen)* and winning Reichstag approval of Tirpitz's naval plans absolutely depended upon an expansion of Miquel's concentration of parties *(Sammlung)* to include the nationalist elements of the Center.

It was not an easy thing to bring the Center and the anti-Catholic parties, with their sharply opposing economic interests, into the same span again. However, the Center was decisively influenced by the argument that only a positive move on its part could exorcise the threat of military dictatorship. For a consideration—concessions to the agrarian interests—the Centrist leaders Dr. Peter Spahn (1846–1925), Count Georg von Hertling (1834–1919), Karl Bachem (1858–1945), and Count Franz von Ballestrem agreed to form a bloc with the Conservatives and National Liberals, support Hohenlohe in the 1898 elections, and back the naval bills. The defection of the bulk of the Center from the parliamentary opposition made possible the continuation of constitutional government in Germany, but it also enabled the Reich to embark upon battleship diplomacy *(Schlachtflot-tenpolitik)* and a course of global power policies *(Weltmachtpolitik)*, which threatened to disturb Britain's commanding position on the seas, in world markets, and in the colonial regions.

During the winter of 1897–98 Tirpitz' risk navy bill rapidly won popular support. The propaganda of the newly founded Navy League (Flottenverein) was not only joyously repeated by Friedrich Krupp and the Saar moghul Karl Freiherr von Stumm-Halberg, but by some of the country's most eminent scholars, such as Ulrich von Wilamowitz-Moellendorff, Lujo Brentano, Otto Gierke, Adolf Wagner, Max Weber, Hans von Delbrück, and Gustav Schmoller. The government continued to gain ground in the Centrist camp by allocating funds for cultural and educational programs in Catholic areas and by concessions to Alsace-Lorraine and the Polich provinces of Prussia, while the middle class was courted with a rain of government contracts, relaxation of credit, a uniform law code, and a moratorium on further protective factory legislation. The Reichstag majority was also influenced by mounting animosity for a Britain that was entering upon war with the Boers and by national pride in the acquisition of the Palau, Caroline, Mariana, and Marshall Islands in the Pacific.

The opposition in the Reichstag, led by Bebel and Richter, objected to the huge costs (400 million Marks) of Tirpitz' naval program and to the indirect taxes proposed to finance it. Even more, they objected to the fact that the naval bill removed fleet appropriations and control over the size of the fleet from the competence of the Reichstag. Nevertheless, sustained by mounting Anglophobia, the bill became law on March 26, 1898. It authorized funds for building 17 battleships and 35 cruisers, of which 7 of the former and 9 of the latter were to be constructed before 1905. Britain replied by proclaiming her determination to lay down two keels for every one laid by the Germans.

A Second Naval Law, which passed the Reichstag in 1900, fundamentally altered the original defensive concept of the First Naval Law, doubled the size of the fleet, and greatly increased the monetary burden on the masses. Since, as Eckart Kehr and his disciples (Helmut Böhme, Dirk Stegmann, and Volker Berghahn) have pointed out, the support of the naval laws came chiefly from an alliance between heavy industry (the Zentralverband deutscher Industrieller) and the landed nobility (represented by the Bund der Landwirte), and since the ruling classes had rallied behind Miquel's *Sammlungspolitik,* the campaign for an offensive capability navy was also an aspect of the defensive political strategy against the democratizing threat posed by the Social Democratic party.

The Advent of Bülow (1900–1909)

The Navy Law and the Anti-Strike bill of 1899, which would have made it a punishable offense to incite workers to go out on strike, ruined whatever credit the reputedly moderate Hohenlohe still had with the masses. When the Anti-Strike bill was rejected by the Reichstag on November 20, 1899, a howl of jubilation went up from the Socialists and all the trade unions. Hohenlohe was by then a used-up man. Even the Conservatives and National Liberals felt that he was overdue for retirement. Accordingly, in October, 1900, he was given his walking papers by William II. Eulenburg, meanwhile, arranged for the appointment of the suave secretary of state for foreign affairs, Bernhard von Bülow, as Hohenlohe's successor in the chancellorship and Prussian minister-presidency.

With Hohenlohe's departure it certainly seemed that the once brilliant chancellorship had passed into eclipse. Responsible government appeared to be further away than ever. The emperor had just carried off an impressive victory over the Reichstag in the matter of the Naval Law and had now elevated to the command of the Reich a mere sycophant. However, the occultation had not engulfed the Reichstag. The kaiser had already gone as far as he dared down the road of personal absolutism but had failed to destroy the independence of the legislature. As long as the representatives of the people had a national tribune, the imminent possibility continued to exist that the Reichstag, rather than the emperor, would ultimately decide whether a chancellor should stay or go.

Chapter 40

THE INDIAN SUMMER OF

AUTHORITARIANISM: BÜLOW TO

BETHMANN, 1900–1914

The *Obrigkeitsstaat* in 1900

When Bernhard von Bülow became chancellor in 1900 Germany's prestige was at its acme. If Bismarck's successors had not been able to maintain the diplomatic ascendancy of the Reich over Europe, other factors, seemingly, had offset that failure. The preceding decade had been a time of marvelous growth in trade and the gross national product, as well as of improvement in the German standard of living. The general euphoria was heightened by acquisition of a farflung colonial empire, development of a high seas fleet, and brilliant achievements in science, technology, and the liberal arts. Bülow felt the wind in his sails, and it is no wonder that he sensed no compulsion to alter the foundations of the imperial government.

Not until the eve of World War I did the sun of the authoritarian state *(Obrigkeitsstaat)* begin slowly to slip toward the horizon. Not until then did it become clear that the balance of power had critically shifted against the Reich and that all of its accomplishments were in jeopardy. Until the beginning of hostilities, demands for the complete democratization of the Empire and Prussia were not taken seriously. The nation was too self-satisfied. In spite of a certain ponderous progression toward virtual ministerial responsibility to the Reichstag, authoritarian monarchy remained, at least in theory, unshaken. At the same time, the inequitable three-class electoral system persisted in Prussia. Nevertheless, most Germans were convinced that their government was more stable and less susceptible than those of France or Britain to the emotional pressure of the masses. Germans generally cherished the strict rule of law *(Rechtsstaat)* and looked with scorn upon the tsarist police state or with condescension upon the ''corrupt'' government of France.

From the standpoint of all democrats it remained until 1918 the great tragedy of German government that the executive branch would never acknowledge its responsibility to the Reichstag. Until 1917 no chancellor or imperial minister was even selected from the Reichstag. No combination or coalition of parties was committed to support the chancellor, who rather negotiated for composite support from case to case. Until 1918, moreover, the Bundesrat retained its power of veto over legislation originating with the Reichstag, which, in effect, meant that ultimately the government of Prussia held the mace of power.

In spite of the foregoing, historians have usually exaggerated the negative role of the Reichstag. While it is true that it lacked the sanction of sovereignty and was helpless to oust a chancellor or an imperial ministry, it gradually came to exercise considerable influence over lawmaking. Despite all constitutional limitations upon its competence to alter money bills, the Reichstag was respected by all chancellors from Caprivi to Bethmann-Hollweg. No chancellor was prepared flatly to defy the will of the people's representatives or thought seriously of resorting to a military coup to force his way.

For its part, the Reichstag was also disposed to temporize. There was in the pre-1914 Reichstag neither cause nor inclination on the part of any major party to pursue a desperado program. The domesticated German middle class had no cause to risk confrontation with a government that catered to its economic needs, besides which the liberal parties believed that in a test of strength the army would cleave to the monarchy. The SPD was also already half-convinced that its goals could be attained within the framework of the existing order. Finally, the papacy had pacified the Center by making peace with the Reich. Under the circumstances it was entirely possible for the ministry and Reichstag to cooperate and strive for an equipoise of social forces. The executive and legislative branches of government gradually came to understand their symbiosis. From the realization of interdependence was born the dream of a people's monarchy.

Bülow's Domestic Program

The shrewd but shallow Bülow, who came to the chancellorship from the foreign ministry, chose to concentrate upon external affairs. Along this line, where he fancied himself an expert, he led Germany step by step into deepening isolation. The Naval Laws of 1898 and 1900, which launched the Reich on the waves and balefully influenced her foreign policy until 1914, forced Bülow to give chief attention to foreign affairs. The "risk navy" and a sudden Anglophobia, to which Germans succumbed as a result of the Boer War, were liabilities that to Bülow justified his leaving all but the most critical internal matters to his imperial secretary of the interior, Count Arthur von Posadowsky-Wehner (1845–1932).

If Posadowsky-Wehner was able to realize a broad program of social reform and national consolidation during his term, this was because in the first five years of Bülow's ministry the government did not feel itself acutely threatened by any power. This was due mainly to three things: Russian imperialist aggression in the Far East promised to involve Russia in war with Japan and paralyze the former's alliance with France; Anglo-French relations were for some years troubled as a result of the Sudanese Fashoda incident of 1898; and Britain was distracted by the Boer War. Conversely, Germany collaborated in 1900–1901 with the Great Powers to suppress the Chinese Boxer Rebellion. Under cover of these developments the Bülow ministry was able to make considerable progress toward the social betterment, economic growth, and spiritual unification of the German nation. For fifty years to come Germany was not to enjoy an era of good feelings comparable to that which was generated by the domestic program of Posadowsky.

If the first six years of Bülow's ministry were characterized by an unprecedented spirit of cooperation between government and Reichstag, this was because

Bülow and Posadowsky had from the outset held out the open hand to all parties and the clenched fist to none. Not only was Hohenlohe's *Kampfpolitik* repudiated, but the social policies of Berlepsch were revived and expanded with a view to reconciling the Socialists to the existing order. Although Bülow sought his main support in a combination of Conservatives and Center, called the ''Blue-Black Bloc,'' he constantly urged his ministers to seek to broaden this basis into majority parliamentary backing.

Labor had been pleased when in 1899 Posadowsky-Wehner had secured the repeal of the law prohibiting the federation of unions and associations. Now, determined in this auspicious hour not to play the sleeping hare to Bebel's tortoise, Bülow negotiated with Reichstag leaders for their assent to measures that were calculated to transform the class struggle into a wedding of the bourgeoisie and the proletariat. In this he was encouraged especially by the Center and by the National Social League (Nazional-sozialer Verein), which had been founded in 1895 by Friedrich Naumann (1860–1919), a socially and democratically oriented Protestant clergyman who preached class cooperation. Meanwhile, Posadowsky-Wehner, buttressed by wide popular support, obtained passage of laws providing for more comprehensive accident insurance (1900), making industrial arbitration courts obligatory for all towns with more than 20,000 inhabitants (1901), extending the benefits of sickness insurance (1903), prohibiting child labor in domestic handicraft industries (1903), and guaranteeing payment of an ample honorarium to Reichstag deputies (1906).

If Bülow and Posadowsky thought that a program of social reforms would tempt the electorate away from the Social Democratic party or cause it to forswear its anticapitalist line, the veil was torn from their eyes by the elections of 1903 when Naumann's National Social party, whose aim was to blur class lines, went down to defeat. At the same time the Social Democratic party polled a quarter of the electorate (3 million votes), the largest for any party. As the second most numerous faction, the SPD marched into the Reichstag with 81 deputies.

Nevertheless, Bülow was not totally discomforted by this turn of events. He entertained considerable respect for the integrity and good will of the Socialist leaders, who, he knew, were *politiques* rather than visionaries. Bülow was fully aware, moreover, that the real Socialist parliamentary tactic had become one of cooperation with the imperial ministry wherever that could demonstrably advance workers' interests. Nor did he for a moment believe in the reality of a revolutionary threat from the left. If anything, he privately welcomed a strengthening of the parliamentary left if this would undercut the authority of the kaiser, in whose loyalty he, privately, had no confidence.

The End of the Honeymoon with the Left

To achieve *Weltmacht*—a place in the sun—an imperial high seas fleet was imperative. To construct it, however, Bülow was critically dependent upon agrarian support. With the backing only of the National Liberals and some Conservatives

Bülow would have had to fight an uphill struggle against a Reichstag majority. Accordingly, he resolved to bribe both the landed gentry and small farmers with a tariff that would shield them from foreign competition. When Caprivi's ten-year bilateral trade treaties expired in 1903, the Bülow ministry proposed higher duties on agricultural and livestock imports. The new "green" policy was supported in the Reichstag now by a combination of Conservatives, National Liberals, and Center party deputies. Outside it was backed by the Bund der Landwirte, Deutscher Bauernbund, All-deutscher Verband, Tirpitz' Flottenverein, and the financially strong Zentralverband deutscher Industrieller, all of which had been toiling to promote a new modus operandi between landowners and bourgeoisie. The new trade treaties negotiated between 1904 and 1905 not only raised agricultural duties but gave added protection to domestic manufactures. As a result, trade continued to expand and the gross national product to rise under Bülow's regime. What is more, the government appeared to be firmly ensconced on a three-legged stool, whose legs were the Conservatives, National Liberals, and Centrists. Indeed, Bülow's ingenious policy even aimed at a national rather than a mere ruling-class *Sammlung*, such as Eckart Kehr, G. Röhl, and V. Berghahn have detected. Bülow hoped to add a fourth leg to his governmental stool by rallying the working class around a popular monarchy, a nationalist foreign policy, a bourgeois-democratic fleet, and a radical tax program. He had as much chance of reconciling all the divergent interests behind these symbols as of squaring the circle.

Eventually it was finances upon which Bülow's omnibus program foundered. The imperial government was confronted with a mounting deficit, while by 1904 its total indebtedness had skyrocketed to three billion marks—triple the figure of 1890. Faced with the dilemma of soaking the rich or milking the poor, Bülow reluctantly proceeded to do both. His minister of the treasury, Freiherr von Stengel, suggested an inheritance tax on land and real property, higher excise taxes on tobacco and beer, and indirect taxes upon freight and transportation. The inheritance tax, expected to be the first direct federal tax, had the enthusiastic endorsement of the SPD and some Independent Liberals, but the indirect taxes, which would bear heaviest upon the underprivileged, ran up against stonewall resistance from the former. In the end the Reichstag approved only reduced indirect taxes insufficient to cover the federal deficit. The imperial ministry then brought in a bill to finance increasing costs of administering the growing colonial establishment, but the Center and SPD torpedoed this measure too. Blocked at every turn in the quest for solvency, the chancellor dissolved the Reichstag on December 13, 1906, thereby throwing down the gauntlet to the Center and the left and ostentatiously writing finish to the period of temporization.

Thenceforth Bülow sought solace from those elements that had built the Empire—the Junkers and bourgeoisie. Pursuing a narrower bloc policy, he came to rely upon a combination of Conservatives, National Liberals, Independent Liberals (Freisinnige Vereinigung), and Populists (Freisinnige Volkspartei) and coquetted no more with the Center and SPD.

Bülow's Fall

Bülow was very much closer to becoming a parliamentary chancellor in 1906–9 than any of his predecessors had ever been. Seemingly he was on the verge of substituting popular sovereignty for monarchical hegemony when he was overthrown on a minor issue.

In 1906 the position was that Bülow's obvious foreign policy failures had largely cost him his master's confidence, while the chancellor's abandonment of much of the Posadowsky social welfare program had brought down on him the wrath of the SPD. In addition, a law of 1907 authorizing expropriation of Polish lands in Prussian Posen and encouraging the Germanization of Prussia's eastern provinces hopelessly alienated the Polish contingent in *Landtag* and Reichstag. In spite of this and other music in the minor key, Bülow managed to wring a personal success of sorts out of the Reichstag elections of 1907. Fought on the issue of foreign and colonial affairs, the elections were a sharp defeat for the anti-imperialist Socialists and a victory for the ruling front behind *Weltmacht* and *Weltpolitik*. The Socialists returned only 43 deputies and polled something less than 29 percent by comparison with 1903, when the SPD had garnered 31.7 percent of all votes cast. However, the Bülow offensive against the left was not the absolute victory it seemed to be because in 1908 the SPD finally breached the ramparts of the Prussian House of Representatives and secured its first seven mandates out of a total of 443. Meanwhile, Bülow could stretch his wings and crow, for his unstable bloc of Conservatives, Free Conservatives, and National Liberals had emerged from the elections of 1907 with a Reichstag majority of 203 out of 397. This freed him from immediate dependence upon the Center's 103 deputies or upon the Freisinnige factions. Furthermore, it encouraged him to think in terms of dismantling the kaiser's personal regime and of reforming the fundamental law. Bülow appeared to be on the verge of realizing the remark he had once made in jest: "I shall die a liberal."

The continuing deficit demolished his dream castles. Although the national debt amounted to four billion marks and the budget was in the red, the government was disinclined to end the costly competition with Britain in the construction of capital (dreadnought) ships. Consequently there was nothing for Bülow to do but go cap in hand before the Reichstag with another request for increased excise taxes, especially on brandy, and an inheritance tax on land. The latter provided for a graduated levy rising to a maximum, however, of only 4 percent on inheritances of 75,000 marks or more. In exempting all bequests of less than 10,000 marks, the bill left nine-tenths of all devised real property tax-free. Nevertheless, Bülow suspected that the nobility would fight the measure on principle, since land was the fundament of its political power. The chancellor managed to clear the first hurdle when in the fall of 1908 his tax proposals were approved by the Bundesrat, which, while wanting to leave direct taxes to the states, understood the urgent need for new imperial revenues.

At this juncture Bülow came within an ace of a tremendous victory arising out of the kaiser's indiscretions in foreign affairs. In an interview he had given to a reporter of the London *Daily Telegraph*, printed on October 28, 1908, William II was represented as saying that while majority opinion in Germany was Anglophobe he personally had restrained anti-English tendencies in Germany during the Boer War and had even supplied the British general staff with the operational plan that insured an English victory over the rebels. Although undoubtedly Bülow had seen the text of the interview in advance of publication, the malodorous effect of this article was such as to enrage German public opinion, lash the Reichstag deputies to attacks upon the kaiser, and compromise him to the extent that as of the end of 1908 his personal regime was a thing of the past. Bülow was determined to exploit this nonrecurring opportunity for constitutional purposes. For once in his life, Bülow had the temerity to admonish the kaiser (interview at Potsdam of November 17, 1908) against a repetition of such impulsive utterances. Bülow used the occasion to extort from William II a signed pledge that he would in the future, for the sake of the unity and stability of national policy, respect the limits of his constitutional prerogatives. Bülow was on the verge of setting in train an action that might well have revolutionized the German political system when the Reichstag stabbed him in the back.

On June 24, 1909, by a vote of 195 to 187 his tax bill was rejected by a combination of Poles, Conservatives, and Centrists, who collectively were called the "Blue-Black Bloc." The Conservative party must bear the brunt of the responsibility for the adverse vote. Led by the able orator Ernst von Heydebrand und der Lasa (1851–1924) the Conservatives put Junker economic interests above maintenance of Bülow's bloc. The Poles had even less reason to vote against the measure. They were simply avenging themselves for the expropriation law of 1907, which had really been a blessing in disguise for Posen. The action of the Conservatives and Poles threw imperial finances into chaos and destroyed Bülow's Conservative-Liberal *Kartell*.

After June 24, Bülow had three alternatives open: carry on the government in opposition to the Reichstag majority, dissolve parliament and call for new elections, or resign. If Bülow had been less an aristocrat, he might have played to the populace by choosing the second course and fighting a campaign on a platform of universal electoral reform. On the other hand, had the chancellor appealed to the Reichstag minority, which represented twice as many voters as did the majority parties, the kaiser might have retreated, as he so often did when the public joined the hue and cry. But the debonair Bülow was not constituted of the stuff of martyrs. Rather he chose to genuflect before his master. Bülow resigned on July 19, 1909, and was paid off with the highest honor which it was within the competence of the emperor to bestow—the brilliant-studded Order of the Black Eagle.

Although Bülow had in the hour of decision backed away from the cause of democracy, he had nonetheless inaugurated a political precedent of great importance. By resigning when he lost the support of the parliamentary majority, he had intentionally broken with the German constitutional tradition and turned his back on the precedents established by Bismarck and his successors. Like Walpole in 1742, Bülow had taken the first step toward cabinet government.

The Chancellor of the "Diagonal"

Bülow's successor, Theobald von Bethmann-Hollweg (1856–1921), was not a Junker but was of bourgeois antecedents. Nevertheless, he was, like all of his predecessors, a corbel of the existing social order. An admirable professional bureaucrat and minister of the interior, Bethmann-Hollweg was completely without experience in foreign affairs. Highly educated, refined, and diligent, he was not a fighter by nature. He was therefore not the man to concentrate power in his hands and dominate emperor and generals. Although he was occasionally capable of exceptional civil courage, he lacked the capacity for decision. When he was appointed chancellor, his good wife, aware of his limitations, exclaimed: "What a calamity for Germany!"

The key to the character of this solid, conscientious, *Biedermeier* statesman was his moderation. An ornament of the ruling establishment, Bethmann-Hollweg was not averse to liberal solutions; he favored some electoral reforms yet feared to allow the potentially intemperate masses to dominate policy-making. An advocate of social welfare measures, he nevertheless had no intention of undermining the fundament of aristocratic-bourgeois direction of Germany. Conceiving his duty to be to represent the whole nation and all classes, Bethmann-Hollweg felt unable to pursue any other policy than that of the "diagonal." The aim of this latitudinarian line was to find a platform on which the largest number of political parties and the bulk of the electorate could stand. He wrote of this policy: "The policy of the diagonal is one that is exposed to attacks from both flanks" and "has always from situation to situation to hunt for supporters"; it "lacks the luster which . . . is generated by a policy of excess."*

Highly cultivated and of a contemplative, artistic nature, Bethmann was no politico. Lacking both Bülow's sophistry and talent for manipulating men, the new chancellor was more honorable and ingenuous than his predecessor. He resisted a policy of outright imperialism, such as the National Liberals were coming to espouse, and he disapproved of the Conservatives' wishes to suppress the radical progressive and Social Democratic elements in society. But if Bethmann was less bold and sly than Bülow, the new chancellor was also more pessimistic as to Germany's future and more maladroit in the implementation of governmental policy. All his life a sincere friend of peace who enjoyed the confidence of foreign statesmen who would give it to no other German leader, Bethmann was fated to be maneuvered into a desperate position the only egress from which was a great war that destroyed the Empire he served and the social order of which he was an ornament.

---

*Theobald von Bethmann-Hollweg, *Betrachtungen zum Weltkriege* (Berlin, 1921), II, 34–35.

Bethmann-Hollweg's Pluralistic Policies

Impatient of extremist utterances, Bethmann always preferred compromise to confrontation. Unfortunately for him, however, the leaders of the Conservatives, the Free Conservatives, and the right wing of the Center party, which normally supported his government, were determined to combat the progressive internal measures by which Bethmann hoped to placate the parliamentary left. At the same time the proimperialist upper bourgeoisie made life difficult for the chancellor. In spite of this crossfire, Bethmann-Hollweg managed to drag the country across the threshold of the welfare state. His government successfully piloted the passage of such measures as a capital gains tax law, liberalization of the Industrial Code, and adoption of an Imperial Social Insurance Code. The first, which fell most heavily upon the business and landowning elements, was a conciliatory gesture to the SPD as compensation for the objectionable tax statute of 1909 which, while increasing excise taxes on the poor, had eliminated the popular inheritance tax. The Industrial Code was amended in 1911 to permit reduction of hours of work in most branches of industry, improvement of working conditions, control of hazards to life and limb in factories, and higher wages for domestic handicraft manufacturers. The Imperial Insurance Code of 1911 consolidated all earlier social insurance laws and applied them to all strata of the population, while establishing uniform rules and procedures for the payment of accident, sickness, invalidity, and old-age benefits. Finally in 1913, poor relief, which until then had been the responsibility of the states, was improved and standardized on a national basis. All of these measures helped make the German standard of living the highest in any major European country.

In two important respects, however, progress was blocked. Reapportionment of Reichstag seats was one of them. It was supported by the chancellor but foundered under the attacks of the Conservative leader, the Junker Oskar von Normann-Barkow, and the Centrist Peter Spahn. The Blue-Black Bloc also obstructed any effort to reform or eliminate the notorious three-class Prussian electoral system, even though electoral laws had already been democratized in Bavaria, Saxony, Baden, and Mecklenburg. In the end, the Prussian *Landtag* would adopt in February, 1909, only a compromise measure that abolished indirect voting but left representation in the House of Representatives almost as disproportionate as ever. Thus, in Prussia the Conservatives disposed of 46 percent of the mandates in the Abgeordnetenhaus as compared with less than 15 percent in the Reichstag, and the SPD, already the largest party in Germany, was awarded less than 2 percent of the seats in the Prussian House of Representatives. Notwithstanding all agitation by the parties of the left in favor of secret, direct, equal, and proportionate representation, Prussia remained saddled until the end of World War I with a system that accorded, on the basis of paid taxes, equal numbers of mandates to each of three artificial classes, the first comprising 3.8 percent of the electorate, the second 13.8 percent, and the third 82.4 percent.

The defense program of the government elicited broad support from the public, which recognized that the nation's growing population, increasing isolation, and exposed geographic position made imperative a strengthening of the military establishment. A series of moderate army bills had by 1912 brought the peacetime force up to 544,000 men. Then in 1913 the government, in response to the urging of the minister of war, General Josias von Heeringen (1850–1926), who at long last had been alarmed by the Balkan Wars, persuaded the Reichstag to authorize a peacetime force of 870,000 men. Only the Socialists, Poles, and Alsatians opposed the bill. France and Russia countered by augmenting their own military establishments so that by June, 1914, France, which had only two-thirds the population of Germany, was maintaining a peacetime army of 920,000.

In the absence of a promise of British neutrality, the German government, which for a decade had conceded only modest increases in manpower to the army, was resolved that the ground forces must forthwith be strengthened. The effect of the naval bills of 1906 and 1908 had been to accelerate the construction program and offer the prospect that by 1917 Germany would have fifteen more capital ships than had been authorized by the law of 1900. But after failure of the Anglo-German naval conversations of 1912, naval appropriations were reduced. A projected third battle squadron was restricted to cheaper ships of pre-Dreadnought design, and the original "Tirpitz-Plan" was otherwise altered. By contrast, the army budget bill of 1912 sharply increased outlays for the ground forces.

Bethmann-Hollweg courageously refused to permit the transfer of the burden of financing armaments to the poorer strata. Instead he fought for and obtained higher probate fees on bequests and a new defense tax on real and personal property (including that belonging to reigning princes) having a value in excess of 100,000 marks. However, no imperial income tax was ever passed, and the combined burden of indirect taxes fell more heavily upon the masses than taxes upon wealth and property weighed upon the affluent.

Alsace-Lorraine

In contrast to the disappointing failure of electoral reform in Prussia, significant steps were taken in the direction of popular government and educational improvement in Alsace-Lorraine, or the Imperial Territory (Reichsland), as it was called. Yet no plebiscite had ever been held in the annexed territories; and, in spite of the fact that the Alsatian population, at least, was overwhelmingly German and used German in daily intercourse, all efforts of the Reich authorities to win over the peoples of the Imperial Territory by material concessions had failed.

The capital blunder of the German government was not immediately to make of Alsace-Lorraine a federated and coequal state of the Empire. Instead, from 1871 until 1879, the Reichsland was in one way or another administered from Berlin under direct supervision of kaiser, chancellor, and Bundesrat. Although during that time efforts were made to Germanize the provinces, justice was dispensed without discrimination, and administration was characterized by probity and a genuine concern for the well-being of the inhabitants.

By the law of July 4, 1879, the entire administration of the Imperial Territory was transferred from Berlin to Strassburg, and a governor responsible to the emperor was appointed. Self-government was denied the provinces, and all laws affecting them had to be approved by the Bundesrat. From 1879 to 1885 a high standard of administrative efficiency and a Christian sense of social responsibility prevailed under Field Marshal Edwin von Manteuffel, the first governor. However, the Boulangist hysteria in France and the war scare of 1886–87 evoked sympathetic Germanophobe demonstrations in the Imperial Territory, and Manteuffel's successor, the Bavarian Prince Hohenlohe-Schillingsfürst, had to resort to mildly repressive measures.

Despite setbacks, the process of Germanization made headway. The bonds between Alsace (but not Lorraine) and the Reich were strengthened by the founding of the University of Strassburg, educational and eleemosynary institutional building programs, and the grant of access to the Rhenish commercial arterial system. After 1878 the liquidation of the *Kulturkampf* in Germany, which stood in happy contrast with the aggressive policies of the French Ferry regime toward the clergy, pleased Alsatian Catholics.

In 1911, finally, the Reichsland was accorded a constitution. But the population did not consider a bicameral provincial legislature and representation in the Reichstag the same as autonomy. Aggrieved that the governor was still empowered to veto legislation, the natives rejected the instrument. Antagonism developed between governor and legislature, and, as a response to the development of an Alsatian separatist movement, French were discriminated against in the Reichsland. The imperial government took punitive measures against demonstrators, and passions continued to mount until the winter of 1913–14. Then an ugly incident took place in the Alsatian town of Zabern when Colonel von Reuter, commander of the 99th Infantry Regiment, which was stationed there, took twenty-nine civilians into custody illegally. This confrontation became a cause célèbre throughout Germany. The Reichstag took the part of the inhabitants, while the Reich government supported the army. Local revulsion toward Germany was such that in July, 1914, with war threatening, martial law was imposed on Alsace-Lorraine.

The Socialist "Empire"

In the course of a long and heated struggle with the ruling classes, the Socialist party of Germany had by 1912 grown into a tightly knit and strictly disciplined mass organization that elicited the secret admiration of all other parties. The Social Democratic party of Germany (SPD) had what the other socialist parties of Europe were still striving for—unity, organization, leadership, and popularity. Entrenched in the strongest state of the continent and closely associated with the Free Trade Unions and the consumers' movement, the SPD was by 1912 unquestionably the foremost section of the Second International. As early as 1900, the eminent historians Hans Delbrück and Theodor Mommsen, realizing the party's great strength with the masses, had admonished against any further attempts to destroy it.

By 1912 the SPD's following was virtually coextensive with the German proletariat, and the party's membership identical with the political organization of
the workers in towns and cities. The secret of the SPD's success was that it was
the only really democratic, mass party in Germany. The fact is that the bourgeois
parties and the Rhenish industrialist and Bavarian landholding elements of the
Center party had by their records demonstrated that neither liberalism nor Catholicism should be confused with democracy.

After the repeal of the Anti-Socialist Law in 1890 the SPD experienced a phenomenal growth. Commanding 1.5 million voters and 35 Reichstag deputies,
the now legalized SPD constituted for the first time a real threat to the existing
order. That threat was seemingly accentuated when in 1891 an allegedly revolutionary program drafted by Karl Kautsky (1845–1938) was adopted at the
party's Erfurt Convention.

For some years after 1890 the SPD preserved what is best described as a jelly-
fish organization. The aim was to keep the party formless and slippery so that it
could not be seized upon by the authorities in the event of reversion to a governmental *Kampfpolitik*. There were in the 1890s no well-knit party organization,
party statutes, rules of procedure, lists of members, or fixed dues. The communal
cells enjoyed maximum freedom. It was in this permissive atmosphere that the
revisionist challenge to revolutionary Marxist tactics was first launched.

The SPD did not develop marked cohesion until after 1900 when all laws against
political associations were finally repealed. By 1912 a corporate, monolithic
structure, which may be described as "Bebel's Shadow Empire," had been constructed. From a loose, amorphous mass, the party had become a tightly mortised
pyramid of mass power. Its growing popular support was reflected in electoral
statistics. In 1893 the party polled 1,790,000 votes (23.28 percent of those cast)
and returned 44 deputies to the Reichstag; in 1903, 3,010,771 votes (31.7 percent) and 81 deputies; and in 1912, after a setback in the depression year 1907,
4,250,324 votes. In this last triumph better than every third voter (34.8 percent
of the electorate) cast his ballot for the SPD, and the party returned 110 deputies,
the largest for any Reichstag faction. Similarly impressive results were obtained
by the SPD in elections for the state diets and communal council in the decade
before World War I. Only in the Prussian *Landtag* was the party hobbled by an
archaic franchise and held to only 10 seats out of 231.

The SPD's 836,000 dues-paying members were mainly drawn from the Free
Trade Unions (Bund der freien Gewerkschaften), which themselves had in 1914
about 2.5 million members. In the party, women constituted an increasing per-
centage of the membership, rising from 6 percent in 1908 to 14.4 percent in 1913.
The main cadres of the SPD were located in Hamburg, Leipzig, Breslau, Lübeck,
Frankfurt am Main, Berlin, and the towns in Thuringia and the Ruhr. Greater
Berlin alone had 111,000 members, as much as the total of all South Germany,
where the Social Democratic party was weak.

By the eve of World War I the SPD had become an important capitalist enterprise. It had 20 million marks invested in business and 11,000 persons on the
payroll. The party owned and operated 94 newspapers, more than 95 percent of

which appeared six times weekly. Among them was the *Vorwärts*, the party's central organ. In addition there were party journals, such as the woman's liberationist *Die Gleichheit*, the humorous *Der wahre Jakob*, and the Marxist theoretical review *Die Neue Zeit*, which was edited by Kautsky.

It was ironic that the SPD, which in 1912–14 had the voting support of a third of the nation, still exercised control over no branch of the German or Prussian governments. The party was virtually without direct influence on the formulation and implementation of ministerial policies. Socialist leaders were discriminated against everywhere and excluded from all significant administrative, military, or judicial posts. A Socialist, it was said, could not even be a night watchman in imperial Germany.

The Victory of Reformism and Nationalism in the SPD

After the close of the "heroic period" and the adoption in 1891 of the Marxist Erfurt Program, the Social Democratic party was gradually transformed in the course of daily agitation from an ostensibly revolutionary organization into a broad popular movement which by 1914 was content to work for reform and democracy within the Wilhelmine state.

In 1891 a right-wing opposition emerged in the SPD. The Bavarian Socialist deputy in the Reichstag George von Vollmar (1850–1922) denied, in his "El Dorado" speeches, that the SPD was or ought to be a party of class struggle. Vollmar contended that more sensible than a policy of waiting for an economic breakdown, war, and the overthrow of capitalism would be one that strove for limited, practical objectives the cumulative attainment of which would facilitate a natural transition to socialism. The overwhelming majority of the party rejected his theses. However, the spectacular upsurge in the 1890s of German production and real wages contradicted Marx's prognosis that an increase in productivity would lead to a reduction of the value of all labor power. When the posthumous third volume of Marx's *Capital* (1894) failed to resolve this paradox, many German Socialists concluded that Marx had been wrong. Thereupon, Eduard Bernstein (1850–1932), the former editor of the *Sozial-Demokrat*, in 1896 launched a campaign for revision of the party's ideology, which, as Erich Matthias has maintained, was a Kautskyite interpretation of Marxism. Bernstein, who was subjected to bitter attacks by Bebel, Kautsky, and Rosa Luxemburg, published in 1899 the first systematic Socialist critique of Marxism: *Die Voraussetzungen des Sozialismus und die Aufgaben der Sozialdemokratie* (Eng. trans., *Evolutionary Socialism*, 1909). In this work he contended that the end was nothing, the movement everything: day-to-day trade union agitation and parliamentary activity would so alter the existing order that it would "organically grow into socialism." Bernstein's assault upon doctrinaire revolutionary thought provoked the most violent polemic in prewar socialist history, one that assumed European dimensions. Into it Mehring, Luxemburg, Plekhanov, Lenin, Antonio Labriola, Jules Guesde, and Jean Jaurès were all drawn.

Although revolutionary ideology formally triumphed at every Socialist convention before 1912, only a tiny minority on the extreme left of the SPD (Luxemburg, Karl Liebknecht, Clara Zetkin, Franz Mehring, Karl Radek, and Anton Pannekoek) really persevered in the insurrectionary approach to power and absolutely rejected the duty of defense of country.

Curiously enough the center of the SPD, whose leader was Bebel and whose theoretician was Kautsky, agreed with the left that class antagonisms were steadily intensifying and expected crises of mounting magnitude. But in view of the retarded political development of Germany, the centrists decided that the fight for political democracy must be their grand aim. They defined social revolution as the abolition of German military autocracy and Wilhelmine "absolutism." Theoretical agreement between the left and center that the immediate goal of the proletariat must be the conquest of power by the latter long obscured the basic difference in spirit between them. Nevertheless, the center gradually lost its appetite for the class struggle, tended to lose sight of ends, became more engrossed in the day-to-day workers' movement for social amelioration, and finished by following the right into apostasy from armed revolution. After 1906 the left, not the right, was the real opposition within the party. After the Chemnitz (1912) and Jena (1913) party conventions, when a very large majority buried theoretical revisionism once and for all, the bulk of the party membership embraced a practical reformist and nationalist program. From that time onward there was serious danger that the revolutionaries would secede.

The decision of the SPD on August 4, 1914, to rally 'round the flag was foreshadowed by the Socialist posture toward the defense bill of 1913. The party had always opposed every military appropriation bill in the past but in 1913 reversed itself and for the first time voted for one. The reason was that this budget bill contained tax clauses that were popular with the masses, in particular a broadened inheritance tax. In an attempt to save the public from new taxes for the army and navy, the SPD, while rejecting increases in troop strength, felt obliged to endorse outlays for the defense of country.

Ominous, too, was the defeat of a resolution in favor of the general strike, which was introduced at the Jena convention (1913) by Rosa Luxemburg (1870–1919). The strike, which she described as "the strongest pulse of the revolution and at the same time its most powerful impulse," was rejected 333 to 142. By this action the class struggle was interred, and the sun set on proletarian internationalism.

The triumph of reformism and nationalism within the SPD was due to many things—the sensational growth of the party, the increasing wealth of the SPD, the rapid development of the Free Trade Unions, the retardation of proletarian class consciousness in Germany. Most of all it was due to the emergence of an elemental patriotism in the heart of the worker. Months before the great war broke out, this irresistible force was moving like a river of lava, thrusting aside and crumpling Socialist international loyalties.

PART XII

DIPLOMATIC OVERTURE AND THE FIRST

GERMAN WAR, 1871–1918

Chapter 41

THE LONG PEACE

The Diplomacy of the Satiated State

After the defeat of France in 1870–71 military ascendancy in Europe passed to Germany for the first time in centuries. The world was curious to see how the Reich would employ its paramountcy.

La Rochefoucauld once wrote that "we need greater virtue to sustain good than evil fortune." It would be hard to find a better illustration of this maxim than the continence with which Bismarck for twenty years after 1871 conducted German foreign policy. Until he resigned in 1890 he acted on the premise that Germany was a satiated state with no more territorial claims in Europe. He therefore strove to preserve the continental status quo and resisted all domestic pressures to aggrandize the Second Empire. Out of regard for British sensitivity, he was even reluctant to acquire overseas colonies. It is plain that he had no wish to risk his architectonic creation in a war of aggression that must have called down upon the unstable Reich a coalition of powers.

To maintain the Treaty of Frankfurt Bismarck employed all his remarkable knowledge of men and rare diplomatic skill. He reasoned that peace was secure only if he could erect a durable dam against the French spirit of revenge. France was not to be dismembered or destroyed, only isolated. For two decades he managed to keep her from finding a major continental ally; yet he encouraged her to seek compensation abroad for the loss of Alsace-Lorraine. This does not mean that Bismarck thought that time and sympathy would heal the wound Germany had dealt to French pride. Actually, he believed that France was irreconcilable and would toil in season and out to discover opportunities to turn the tables on Germany. For this reason, Bismarck believed he must applaud every step that France took toward radical republicanism because this might prejudice the chances of her suit for a partner in monarchical Europe. Bismarck pursued a policy of limited liability that at all costs avoided provoking a coalition of the major powers against the fledgling Reich. The piers of the peace system that he laboriously erected were good relations with isolationist England and entente with conservative Russia. As long as the tsarist empire was linked with his system, war was unlikely. If, at the same time, Austria-Hungary could be associated with the Russo-German bloc, war was impossible. In a Europe dominated by five great powers, Germany would be with the majority. Accordingly, the iron chancellor toiled to revive the Triple Entente of Münchengrätz.

Bismarck's masterpiece was to bring Vienna and St. Petersburg into a League of Three Emperors. In persuading them to an arrangement that was basically inimical to their disjunct imperialist interests in the Balkan peninsula, Bismarck eliminated a dangerous powder keg. However, only an orderly division of the Turkish boodle offered hope of even a transient modus operandi between Austria-Hungary and Russia. Only thus could they be dissuaded from fighting over Turkey's Balkan bones and blaming their misfortunes on Germany.

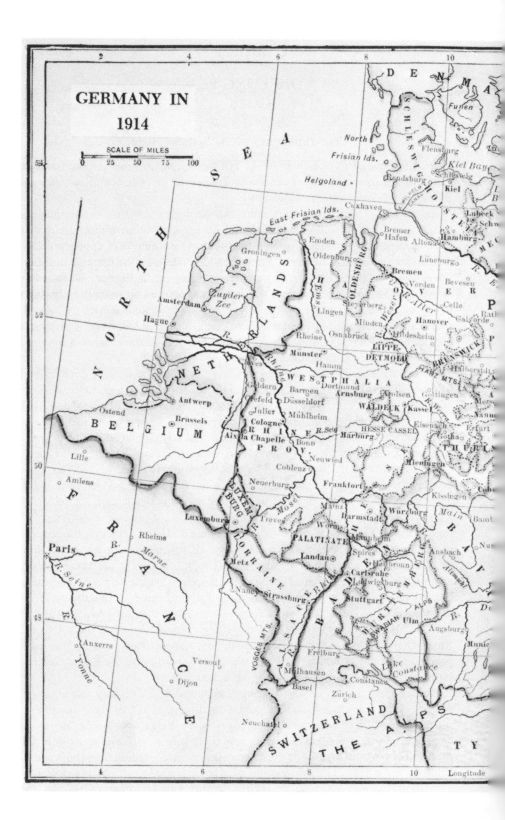

**GERMANY IN
1914**

SCALE OF MILES

0   25   50   75   100

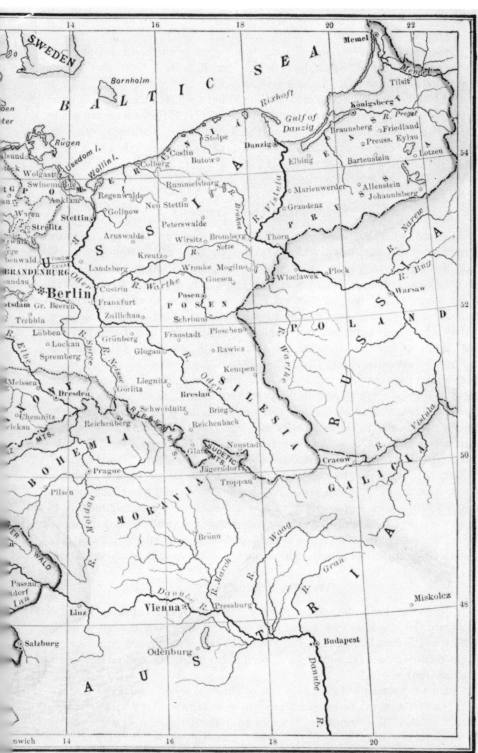

The wizard of the Wilhelmstrasse was right when he predicted that the great war would arise out of "some damn thing in the Balkans." Inexorably, events demonstrated that the fatal flaw in Bismarck's peace system was not the acquisition of Alsace-Lorraine, for France could not have been reconciled to a German peace anyway, but the lack of a first-class antagonist in the Balkans against whom Austria-Hungary and Russia could have formed an enduring alliance. Bismarck must have viewed the southeastern horizon with deepening pessimism after 1877, for he sensed that a system of mutually opposing grand alliances, which is to say abject failure, awaited him at the end of the Balkan road.

The League of Three Emperors

Inasmuch as the Treaty of Frankfurt had put no limitations upon the size of the French army, Germany had to reckon with the possibility of resumption of hostilities, because less than 1 percent of the French population was prepared to accept the permanence of its eastern frontiers. The peace of the continent "would remain at the mercy of an incident"—unless France was unable to exploit it when it came. Therefore, while France went about reconstructing her political and financial system, reorganizing her army, and discharging her war indemnity in two instead of four and one-half years, Germany used the breathing spell to insulate her from all potential allies.

Bismarck took out insurance in the form of a triple entente with Austria-Hungary and Russia. Since mutual suspicion between them ruled out a triple alliance, Bismarck eschewed alliance with either one of them. What emerged from the meetings of Bismarck, Gorchakov (Russia), and Count Gyula Andrássy (Austria-Hungary) in 1872 and of William I, Franz Josef, and Alexander II in 1873, therefore, was only a conservative consortium—the League of Three Emperors (Dreikaiserbund), which was formed on June 6, 1873. The league's avowed purpose was to maintain the peace against subversive influences, and it provided for consultations among the signatories in case of a threatening rift among them or of danger of war. Despite grave weaknesses, deriving from rivalry among the signatories, the league was a deterrent to an Austro-Russian conflict. Had this ramshackle triple entente persisted, there probably would have been no world war.

The War Scare of 1875

In 1875 increases in the number of French infantry staff and battalion officers awakened German fears of a war of revenge. While Bismarck did not seriously believe in a French attack, he decided to capitalize on the French Army Law to frighten Paris so that she would not be tempted to strengthen her military establishment further.

Orders were issued forbidding the sale of horses to foreign purchasers, a measure usually taken in a period preparatory to war. Then on April 8 a provocative article, entitled "Is War in Sight?" appeared in the Berlin *Post*. It was followed by a general discussion in the German press, especially in the alarmist *Kölnische*

Zeitung, of the prospects for a French offensive. The French became very frightened, and Bismarck relented. He sent a calming dispatch to the German ambassador in Paris, but too late. The French foreign minister Decazes had stirred up Russia, which now sent a demarche to Berlin. Fortunately Bismarck was able to allay the suspicions of the tsar and his foreign minister Gorchakov. Thereafter, the whole "war in sight" crisis faded away. Yet it had ended with a setback for Germany, for Gorchakov had artfully made it seem that only Russian intervention had forestalled general war. Henceforth, Bismarck knew that Germany would have to reckon with a strong France and the disturbing possibility that under certain conditions Russia might switch partners.

The Balkan Crisis, 1875–78

The first League of Three Emperors foundered upon the Balkan Wars of 1876–78 and Austro-Russian rivalry.

The year 1875 was one of general crisis for the Ottoman Empire. The Bosnian Serbs and the Bulgars, both of whom were oppressed by their Turkish masters, rose up against them. Bismarck feared that the Russian government, influenced by the Pan-Slavs, would exploit Turkish embarrassment to make a grab for the Straits. Reckoning with the probability that the League of Three Emperors might decompose over Russia's Balkan ambitions, Bismarck tried to broaden his system by linking Britain with it. He suggested in January, 1876, Anglo-German cooperation for the maintenance of peace in the Near East, or at worst, for partitioning the Ottoman Empire, in which case Britain would get Egypt. However, Prime Minister Disraeli wished only to break the connection between Austria-Hungary and Russia and was not to be had for Bismarck's purposes.

On July 1, 1876, the pot began to boil. Serbia and Montenegro declared war against Turkey, and Russia had to come to an immediate understanding with Austria-Hungary. In the secret convention of Reichstadt of July 8, 1876, both parties agreed to preserve the integrity of Serbia and Montenegro or, in case of Turkish defeat, to divide the spoils: Austria-Hungary would get the bulk of Bosnia-Herzegovina, while Russia would get all of Bessarabia, the mouth of the Danube, and parts of Asiatic Turkey.

A shattering Turkish defeat of the Serbs in late July invited Russian intervention to save the Slavic cause. Bismarck was now confronted with a Russian demand for reimbursement for neutrality during the Franco-Prussian War. St. Petersburg put the question whether in the event of war with Turkey, the chancellor would not restrain Austria-Hungary, which was allegedly anxious to annex Bosnia-Herzegovina, from attacking Russia. Bismarck parried the question, intimating that Germany could not take sides, but he admonished Russia that he could not permit any action that would undermine the integrity of the Habsburg monarchy. For the rest, Germany wished Russia well: she had Berlin's blessing for limited expansion at the expense of Turkey.

A vexed Russia was once more obliged to sue at the Viennese counter. On

January 15, 1877, by the Convention of Budapest she bought the neutrality of the Dual Monarchy at the price of Bosnia-Herzegovina. No compensation for Serbia was stipulated, while, on the other hand, Greece was to be enlarged (with the idea of blocking Serbia from the Aegean), and Constantinople was to be made into a free port. Bent on achieving her imperialistic aims in the Balkans, Russia now obstreperously thrust aside all restraints—including the London Protocol of March 31, 1877, pledging all powers to disarm and work for a peaceable solution of the problem of the Balkan Christians and the fact that Turkey and Serbia had on March 1 already concluded a status quo peace. A reckless Russia declared war on the Ottoman Empire on April 24, 1877. Although all the initial battles in the war were won by the Allies, the Turks managed to win an important engagement at Plevna, the consequence of which was that a portion of the Ottoman Empire in the Balkan peninsula was preserved until the eve of World War I. The Russians were persuaded to sign an armistice, which was followed on March 3, 1878, by the Treaty of San Stefano.

San Stefano provided for what was in the eyes of most of the powers of Europe an impermissible extension of Russian power in a direction that compromised the security of the eastern Mediterranean. The convention established a greater Bulgaria, under a Christian prince, with frontiers coterminous with the ethnically Bulgarian population. This meant that Serbia was to be blocked from the Aegean Sea. The independence of Rumania was recognized, and the Dobrudja was ceded to it in return for the cession of Bessarabia and the mouth of the Danube to Russia, and permission militarily to occupy Bulgaria for two years.

Whereas Russia had gotten most of what she had coveted, Austria-Hungary had come away empty-handed. The Treaty of San Stefano, therefore, tossed an apple of discord into Austro-Russian relations. By demolishing the League of Three Emperors, moreover, the Russians imparted a fluidity to European diplomacy, which pleased both England and France because it made new combinations possible. The sinister policy of the Austro-Hungarian foreign minister Count Gyula Andrássy and the bellicose threats of Lord Beaconsfield (Disraeli) against Russia imperilled Bismarck's entire diplomatic system. The situation was rendered more difficult by the fact, which has been demonstrated by W. N. Medlicott, that although Bismarck's chief concern was the maintenance of the general peace, Disraeli was mainly preoccupied with a brash effort to recapture from Germany the diplomatic leadership of Europe. In the end Bismarck found a way out of the swamp by proposing that a continental congress be convened at Berlin. There, the English and the Austrians drew together, to the alarm of Bismarck. They reached an understanding on June 6, 1878, to oppose San Stefano and force Russia to disgorge some of her spoils.

The Treaty of Berlin

The Treaty of Berlin of the summer of 1878 confirmed the independence of Serbia, Montenegro, and Rumania and the earlier dispositions respecting Dobrudja and Bessarabia. However, only northern Bulgaria, between the Danube and the Balkans, received autonomy under a Christian prince. Southern Bulgaria, or Eastern Rumelia as it was called, was returned to Bulgarian sovereignty but given self-administration. The most ominous part of the settlement was that touching on Bosnia-Herzegovina. The province was left under Turkish suzerainty but accorded autonomy under the joint supervision of Austria-Hungary and Russia, subject to military occupation by Habsburg troops. Article 25 of the treaty recognized Austria-Hungary's right eventually, with the approval of the great powers, to annex the disputed area.

At Berlin Germany increased her prestige by ostensibly playing the Olympian role of a disinterested arbiter or, as Bismarck expressed it, an "honest broker" *(ehrlicher Makler)*. Disraeli and Salisbury, whose avarice was directed to Cyprus and Egypt, were very much surprised that Bismarck lodged no territorial bill for his mediatory services. However, the legend of Germany's irenic impartiality at the Congress of Berlin does not comport with the facts. Out of a strong determination to forestall any Austro-English alliance, Bismarck was prepared to pare the claws of the Russian bear. The Treaty of Berlin, as a result, compromised the ambitions of Russia and publicized the isolation of the tsarist empire.

Alexander II and Gorchakov blamed Bismarck for their fall from the summit of San Stefano. Since the chancellor had summoned the congress that thrust Russia into the bear pit again, the charge was not without justice. The restoration of Macedonia and Saloniki to Turkish sovereignty was intended to block the southward expansion of either Bulgaria or Serbia, which, it was feared, would entail further Russian penetration of the Balkans. Finally, while Bismarck would have shed only crocodile tears over the Ottoman Empire if its Balkan possessions had been partitioned between Austria-Hungary and Russia, he saw in the end that there was really no alternative to the containment of the Romanov empire. He knew that if Vienna were convinced that that was Bismarck's Near Eastern policy, Austria-Hungary would be disposed to cultivate the friendship and military support of Germany.

The Austro-German Alliance of 1879

The question has often been raised by historians: why, when all is said, did the iron chancellor choose Austria-Hungary rather than Russia in 1879? Of a range of several answers the most cogent is that to have opted for Russia would have put Germany in a minority where she might have been opposed by a combination of France, Britain, and Austria-Hungary. Beyond this, there were other considerations: strong ethnic and cultural ties bound Germany to Austria-Hungary; Bismarck felt a moral compulsion to compensate the latter for her defeat in 1866 and for her failure at the Congress of Berlin to acquire any territorial annexations to counterbalance those achieved by Russia; the breakdown of the Dreikaiserbund had exposed Austria-Hungary to a double danger from Russia and irredentist Italy; and it would be impolitic to incur British animosity by openly supporting Russia. In any case, Bismarck could not believe that Russo-German relations were dead for good. Once Gorchakov left the Russian foreign ministry, it was very likely that Russia, realizing how much Bismarck had procured for her at Berlin, would gravitate back to the conservative alignment of Münchengrätz.

The secret Austro-German Alliance of October 7, 1879, negotiated by Bismarck and Andrássy, was the cornerstone of the system of mutually opposing alliances that was to develop in pre-World War I Europe. Renewable at the end of five years, the pact's manifest intent was defensive. It was to conserve the territorial integrity of the Habsburg Empire. Each signatory pledged itself to come to the military aid of the other in the event of attack by Russia, or to be benevolently neutral in case of an attack by a third power (such as France or Italy), unless the latter were militarily aided by Russia, when the Austro-German alliance would be invoked against both of them. Bismarck's whole purpose had been to prevent an Austro-Russian conflict and to fortify the dwindling security of the Dual Monarchy until Russia could be cajoled back into the conservative camp. However, a time would come when it would be clear that the pact had committed Germany less to the aid of Austria-Hungary against direct attack by Russia than to maintaining the integrity of the Habsburg Empire against the South Slav nationalists, who were being encouraged by Russian Pan-Slavism. What Bismarck did in 1879 was to revive a perilous *grossdeutsch* guarantee, which had been rejected in 1848–49, to defend the non-German territories of the Dual Monarchy against whatsoever aggressor.

The Second League of Three Emperors (1881)

For many months after 1879, when Russo-German relations were ice-locked, Bismarck held out hope that the League of Three Emperors would be restored. In this he was scarcely supported by Vienna, which much preferred an alliance with Britain, Russia's archfoe. However, as the octogenarian Gorchakov wandered into senility and the more conciliatory Nicholas Giers took charge of the Russian foreign office, the sun rent the clouds in the east. At the same time the advent of the more pacific Gladstone to power in London brought the collapse of the Anglo-Austrian alliance project and left the Austro-Hungarian foreign minister, Haymerle, with no alternative but to follow Bismarck's advice.

The League of Three Emperors was revived on June 18, 1881, for three years. Renewed in 1884, it finally lapsed forever in 1887. The second Dreikaiserbund, like the first, was born under an unlucky star. Freighted from the outset with mutual suspicions, it was much weaker than the entente of a decade earlier. The new convention divided the Balkans into an eastern or Russian and a western or Austro-Hungarian sphere of influence. Blessing was given to Austria-Hungary for the annexation of Bosnia-Herzegovina at some appropriate time in the future, while the Germanic powers agreed not to oppose a union of Eastern Rumelia with Bulgaria. The pact thus recognized the fait accompli by which in 1881, as a result of a treaty between the government of Vienna and the Obrenovich dynasty in Belgrade, Serbia became the virtual satellite of Austria-Hungary in return for a blank check to Russia to make of a moderately enlarged Bulgaria a protectorate too. For the rest, the convention of the Dreikaiserbund pledged the signatories to nothing more belligerent than benevolent neutrality in the event any of them became involved in war with a fourth power and to concert their actions in case of any threat to the status quo in the Balkans.

The Triple Alliance of 1882

Despite the second League of Three Emperors, relations between Berlin and Vienna, on the one hand, and St. Petersburg on the other, continued relatively tense. The protective tariffs of 1879 had unavoidably had a point against Russian grain and livestock, while Russian troop concentrations at the Polish border could not have been directed at anyone other than Austria-Hungary and Germany. So pessimistic was Bismarck by early 1882 that he reached the conclusion that any decisive improvement in Russia's financial situation would mean war for Europe. Fortunately for the peace, Germany was still Russia's main banker and St. Petersburg could not have operated the government for two years on end without German loans.

Despite the détente in Franco-German relations, which had resulted from German support of French ambitions in Tunisia and in Southeast Asia, Bismarck resolved in 1882 to bring Italy into the Austro-German Alliance. The Secret Triple Alliance Treaty of May 20 was valid for five years. Renewed regularly down to 1912, the treaty stipulated that Germany and Austria-Hungary would aid Italy militarily in the event of a French attack upon her, while Italy would come to the support of Germany if she were attacked by France. In the event of war among the powers of the League of Three Emperors, however, Italy promised no more than benevolent neutrality.

From Italy's standpoint the convention promised decisive support in case competition with France over Tunisia and Mediterranean trade should lead to war. From Germany's viewpoint, the Triple Alliance was a fetter on Russia. The pact offered a certain guarantee against formation of a Franco-Russian offensive alliance, a possibility with which Bismarck from this time forth had to reckon. While the Triple Alliance made it unlikely that France would jump into the abyss, Bismarck believed that a Russia faced with imminent revolution would be even less inclined to take the field against an overwhelming combination, which might embrace Germany, Austria-Hungary, Serbia, Italy, Turkey, Rumania, and Britain. Notwithstanding, Bismarck had really tried to avoid the appearance of provoking Russia. That was the beauty of the convention of 1882. The Triple Alliance would not become operative in the event of war between the signatories of the League of Three Emperors pact unless France simultaneously attacked Germany. No matter how one looks at the Triple Alliance, it was for Bismarck a deterrent to Russian military excursions and a contribution to the general peace of Europe.

Because Tsar Alexander III was seized by steadily growing hatred for Germany, Bismarck was driven in spite of himself to support every initiative that might strengthen Austria-Hungary. He had not wanted it that way, for he had always been more partial to Russia than to the Danubian monarchy, for which he privately entertained contempt. Nevertheless, he instinctively aligned the Reich with the powers that were most likely to oppose revisionism through war, whether in Alsace-Lorraine, the Balkans, or at Constantinople.

Except for British procrastination, Bismarck's new perspective might have led to an Anglo-German alliance. But when the British foreign secretary, Salisbury, finally did respond with mild interest to Bismarck's feelers, it was too late. The elections of 1880 brought Gladstone, a Liberal and a foe of European entanglements, to the prime ministry, and hopes of a diplomatic marriage evaporated.

Germany's Colonial Adventure

Acquisition of colonies had never been important to a chancellor whose gaze was directed to the army and Europe. If they involved any threat to his peace system, colonies were unacceptable. Of course, he was aware of the fact that the German public was jealous of the colonial "success" of France and Britain, and he was not altogether unsympathetic to the arguments of the merchant class that overseas territories would provide Germany with cheap sources of raw materials, markets for surplus production, and safety valves for excess population. However, the pursuit of *Weltmacht* never really appealed to Bismarck, for it would augment the risks of German foreign policy and distract the government from the cardinal mission of defending the settlement of 1871.

In 1884 the deterioration of relations between London and St. Petersburg over rivalry in Afghanistan and the Straits afforded Bismarck the opportunity of showing England on which side its bread was buttered. Desirous of strengthening the perilously weak connection with Russia, Bismarck launched a colonial initiative designed to rub the British lion's hair the wrong way.

In that year Germany established protectorates over Southwest Africa, Togoland, and the Cameroons. In 1885 the Reich also acquired East Africa, which had been opened up by Carl Peters' Association for German Colonization, the northern part of New Guinea, and the Bismarck Archipelago in the Pacific. By his initiative in Africa, Bismarck had thrown a monkeywrench into a planned Cape-to-Cairo axis of British colonial power, had broken the British monopoly over central African trade, and encouraged the French to try to forge an east-west axis joining the western Sudan and Djibouti, both of which they already controlled. As a consequence of this seeming display of malice, Anglo-German relations took a turn for the worse. However, Bismarck sedulously avoided giving the appearance of wishing to make an irrevocable choice between Britain and Russia. In any case, difficulties with France and a new estrangement from Russia were soon to compel Germany to abandon her brief colonial advance.

The Franco-German Crisis of 1886–87

In 1885 France turned her back upon the policy of good relations with Germany that had characterized the past decade. Ferry's schemes for the conquest of Indo-

China had met with an humiliating check at the hands of the natives, and the hour of the revanche camp, which was headed by Paul Déroulède, Georges Clemenceau, and General Boulanger, seemed to have struck. Henceforth France would avert her eyes from Asia and concentrate upon building up her army, finding allies, and recovering Alsace-Lorraine. When General Boulanger, a revanchist, became minister of war in the Freycinet cabinet in January, 1886, and shortly afterward a seven-year army law was adopted with a view to modernizing the French army and increasing it to over 700,000 effectives, Bismarck suddenly realized that he, no less than Ferry, had been duped by the colonialists. The chancellor lost all interest in unfurling the German flag over the earth. Henceforth his map of the world was in Europe.

Unfortunately for the chancellor, the Balkan brew just then poisoned Austro-Russian relations. In September, 1885, Eastern Rumelia had torn up the Treaty of Berlin and declared itself part of Bulgaria. In 1886 its prince, the anti-Russian von Battenberg, was overthrown, and the question of succession to the Bulgarian throne became the issue that wrecked the Dreikaiserbund. During the Balkan crisis Bismarck refused to accommodate the demands of London and Vienna that Germany join them in opposing any new Russian military action in the Balkans. By having the courage to say no, Bismarck managed to salvage Russian esteem from the wreck of the League of Three Emperors.

With his rear ostensibly protected, Bismarck on January 11, 1887, delivered a strong speech in the Reichstag. Supporting the new Septennat, which was passed on March 11 and which set total army strength at 468,409 noncommissioned officers and men, Bismarck underlined his fear of revanche, even though he was reasonably sure that it had not gained control over the Freycinet government. Once again, as in 1875, Bismarck poured oil on the waters by disclaiming any intention of launching a preventive war.

Although Bismarck genuinely feared that revenge sentiments might eventually undermine the peace, he probably exaggerated the peril so that he might intimidate the Socialists and secure the requisite army increases. He knew that France in 1887 was not basically war-minded, that Boulanger (who was driven from office in May) had the support neither of his own ministerial colleagues nor of the popular majority, and that if the contrary were the case France could still not attack because she lacked a continental ally. Out of consideration for Britain, Freycinet's government would not support Russia's imperialist ambitions at the Straits. In any case, Bismarck managed to outbid the French for Russia's hand. His Reinsurance Treaty (Rückversicherungsvertrag) of 1887 put Russia beyond French reach for yet a few years.

The Last Train to St. Petersburg

For Bismarck there was grave need for some kind of extension of the German system of alignments to compensate for lapse of the Dreikaiserbund. The Mediterranean and Black Sea agreement of March 24, 1887, among Britain, Italy, and Austria-Hungary for the maintenance of the status quo in those areas did not fill the bill. Yet this *pis aller* at least linked Great Britain with the Triple Alliance and interposed another barrier to war between the Habsburgs and Romanovs. At the same time Bismarck toiled to clear the track to St. Petersburg. On June 18, 1887, he succeeded in concluding with the Russian foreign minister the three-year Reinsurance Treaty. Its purpose was less to restrain Austria-Hungary from attacking the eastern colossus than to perpetuate the isolation of France. But from whatever perspective the Reinsurance Treaty is viewed it must be admitted that it was a skillful contribution to the peace.

By the secret clauses of the treaty Russia's predominant interest in Bulgaria was recognized, and the signatories agreed to consult with each other before effecting any change in the Balkan territorial status quo. A top secret supplementary protocol, whose contents did not become known until recent times, flagrantly contradicted the terms of the Austro-German Alliance of 1879 and the spirit of the Mediterranean Entente of 1887. This supplement pledged Germany to look with benevolence upon the attainment of Russian aims at the Straits and Constantinople. In return Russia agreed to be neutral in case of a French attack upon Germany.

By keeping a foot in each of the opposing camps—the Russian and the Anglo-Austrian—Bismarck hoped to tame their aggressive instincts and thereby relieve Germany of having to honor her promises of aid in futurity. That the various pacts to which Germany was a party were in contradiction with each other is unquestionable. In effect Bismarck had in one set of treaties pledged the Reich to protect Balkan properties which in another convention he deliberately mortgaged to the aspiring thief.

Bismarck had associated so many powers with Germany that no alliance against her was possible. The real beauty of his opaque grand policy and "mania for secret alliances," however, lay in the fact that the agreements he contracted cancelled each other out. Thus, in the Reinsurance Treaty the promise of German support to Russia was worthless: if she moved against Constantinople she would come up against the British navy and simultaneously expose the long, unprotected Balkan flank of the Russian army to Habsburg attack.

The Russophile policy of Bismarck and his son was deplored by Friedrich von Holstein (1837–1909), an influential councilor in the foreign office. While the older view (Krausnick) that Holstein was a determined opponent of the iron chancellor can no longer be supported in light of the evidence adduced by Norman Rich, Werner Frauendienst, and Günther Richter, which shows Holstein to have been just as proarmy, anticolonial, and suspicious of England as Bismarck, the councilor did question the wisdom of pandering to Russia. With a myopia that he shared with the SPD he wrote in December, 1886: "Instead of flattering Russia, we ought to stand up to her. . . ."* He was to have his way within two years: the economic interests of the German ruling classes, which were coming into

---

*Normal Rich and M. H. Fisher (eds.), *The Holstein Papers* (Cambridge, 1957), II, 325.

sharp conflict with those of the Russian aristocracy and bourgeoisie, asserted the primacy of internal policy, involved the Reich in an economic and financial feud with Russia, and forced the government to make a fateful choice between her and Austria-Hungary.

Bismarck's last two years in office were the most tragic of his career. In them occurred the one irreversible loss that was to put a blight upon Germany's future for a century to come: Russia was progressively alienated. Between 1888 and 1890 many things muddied the waters of Russo-German relations: the tsar's hatred of Germans, the contempt of both Frederick III and William II for the Russians, closer friendship between Berlin and Vienna, attempts by German financial circles to depress the price of Russian securities, pogroms against the Jews in Russia, new Russian prohibitions against the acquisition or inheritance of Baltic and Polish lands by Germans, constant agricultural tariff war, suspension of German financial credits to the tsarist government, and, finally, the flotation of a French loan of 500 million francs to substitute for customary German loans to finance the operations of the tsarist empire.

The Reinsurance Treaty did not long survive Bismarck's resignation. Despite the fact that Giers, who disagreed with Alexander III, was anxious to renew it, the treaty was allowed to die on the vine by William II, Caprivi, and Holstein. That the willful kaiser, who took the lead in this matter, could capriciously have allowed the Russian bass to slip his hook before he had securely netted the English eel is the measure of his incompetence. It was becoming clear that Germany's future was now in the hands of a vainglorious dilettante.

Chapter 42

GERMANY'S LOSS OF PREPONDERANCE,

1890–1908

The "New Course" in Diplomacy

The Caprivi era was a watershed in European history. Before 1890 all the rivers of continental diplomacy merged in the sea of German hegemony. After that date they moved, at first uncertainly but later with fearful speed, toward the more turbulent deep of French ascendancy. For years, authoritative instances in Germany could not recognize that the great divide had been passed. One reason for this was the inelastic judgment of German diplomats respecting Anglo-Russian antagonism. They persisted in the fatuous belief, long after evidence to the contrary was in their hands, that hostility between England and Russia was a permanent feature of the international landscape. The corollary of this notion, which ignored the axiom that there are no everlasting enmities among states, was that Anglo-German amity would always be able to dampen Russia's aggressive instincts even if Paris and St. Petersburg should form an alliance. Because Britain possessed no major continental ally, the Germans reasoned further, she would be forced to sue at their counter. This would leave the Reich, just as in Bismarck's time, in the European majority. The kaiser and his ministers did not abandon this delusion until the bell tolled for the fatherland.

What was to make the German diplomatic position irremediable, in that it shifted the balance of power against the Reich, was the defection of Great Britain from what had lately been the "quadruple entente." The *refroidissement* that was to develop between London and Berlin was the result of the decision taken by the kaiser to achieve a position of power for the Reich outside Europe. To explain Britain's estrangement it is not necessary to hypothecate a concerted and extravagant effort on the part of the German government after 1890 to achieve world dominance. The alienation of the English can be adequately accounted for by the German repulse of feelers for an Anglo-German entente over Asia and the Near East. Such an agreement might decisively have mollified the irritation that the English were experiencing as they contemplated the growth of German power in many ways.

The tasks the German government set the nation exceeded its capability. The mission of founding a global economic and colonial dominion *(Weltmacht)* in a world that had already been partitioned among the great naval powers involved such a commitment of resources and great risks that the task could only have been accomplished with the assent of Great Britain. Germany's statesmen never understood that they must court the British, and not the reverse. Not to have drawn from the collapse of Germany's Russian policy the conclusion that, regardless of risk of war with the tsarist empire, the fatherland must align itself with Britain was the capital error of the diplomacy of the "New Course."

The Franco-Russian Alliance

By 1890 formulation of the foreign policy of the Reich had fallen into the hands of Baron von Holstein, a mole rather than a statesman. First councilor of the foreign office since 1878, Holstein exercised preponderant influence over the framing of external policy from 1890 until 1906. Taciturn, publicity shy, rarely seen in public, working endlessly in his gloomy office to perforate mountains of dispatches, Holstein owed his power to a remarkable memory, infinite knowledge of detail, prodigious industry, and a talent for intrigue that he mistook for diplomacy. To the very end, he held the confidence of the kaiser by invariably deferring to his will. However, Bismarck, who had a low opinion of Holstein, once wrote on his dossier: "fit only for the cellar." His addiction to deceit and the delight he took in sowing mistrust among others had corrupted his spirit. That such a man, who had a normal appearance but the "moral character of a hunchback," should have attained so powerful a position is in itself an indictment of the personal regime of William II.

Holstein and the emperor took an ostentatious step away from Russia on July 1, 1890, when an Anglo-German treaty was signed. By that convention Germany limited her ambitions in East Africa and surrendered Zanzibar to Britain in exchange for the island of Helgoland in the North Sea. In 1891, when the Triple Alliance was renewed, the tsar, who exaggerated its threat and resented Caprivi's tariff policy, decided not to wait any longer. In August a Franco-Russian political agreement was therefore signed; and exactly two years later, after protracted negotiations between French and Russian general staff officers, a secret Franco-Russian military alliance was ratified by the tsarist government. When in January, 1894, the French government did likewise, the tombstone was placed on Bismarck's diplomacy.

By the Franco-Russian alliance republican France and the despotic tsarist empire agreed upon specific measures in the event of war with Germany and Austria-Hungary, or in case of war between France and the Italo-German combination. In either case, France was to put in the field 1.3 million troops for offensive operations against Germany, while Russia was to commit from 700,000 to 800,000 against the Reich and an equal number against Austria-Hungary if she should become a belligerent.

In the absence of a Russian disposition to fight for Alsace-Lorraine or of a French for the sake of Constantinople, it can be said that the alliance was still essentially defensive. Its aim was to enhance the security of the signatories and end their isolation. However, a feature of the convention fraught with peril to the peace was that authorizing joint military staff conversations. These soon led to the dovetailing of operational planning, which eventually brought about such concord between the French and Russian war plans as to tie the hands of the diplomats and predetermine that when hostilities came they would be European-wide. The provision for staff conversations largely negated the virtues of civilian control over the army in France. Furthermore, the obvious aim of the joint staff discussions, which found no counterpart in the terms of the Austro-German treaty of alliance, was to confront Germany with a two-front war.

Deteriorating Anglo-German Relations

After 1894 the great fact of international relations was that a balance of power had been restored in Europe. Approximately equally strong armies faced each other in opposing camps. After that year France stood a fair chance of winning a continental war. Bismarck's criticism, appearing in the *Hamburger Nachrichten,* of the German government's shortsighted Russian policy was justified to the hilt. William II, Holstein, and Count von Kiderlen-Wächter had all grossly underestimated the danger of a two-front war. These policy-makers had allowed Russia to slip out of the German planetary system. Henceforth, logic demanded that if the peace were to be preserved Germany must substitute Great Britain for Russia as an ally. No strengthening of the German military establishment alone was likely to be sufficient to fill the lacuna left by the loss of Russia.

The overtures to England that filled the years 1890–95 were aimed at persuading her to join the Triple Alliance so that Britain would under no circumstances embrace the French courtesan. Unfortunately German diplomats were unwilling to make the tangible concessions that might have made the British comfortable in the camp of the Central Powers. Thus the kaiser's personal efforts to knit Anglo-German friendship were only a little more effective than his "Willy to Nicky" correspondence with Nicholas II. William II appeared each summer from 1889 to 1895 at the regatta and royal yacht club at Cowes, where he fawned on Queen Victoria, his grandmother, showered fulsome praise on his vain uncle, the prince of Wales, and strove by smiles and promises to win the royal ministers to the concept of an Anglo-German alliance, which Holstein was meanwhile covertly sabotaging.

All the while, however, Anglo-German rivalry in the economic and colonial spheres was cancelling out whatever salutary effects the kaiser's blandishments at Cowes might have had. There was, for example, cause for friction between the two powers in west Africa (Cameroons to Lake Chad), New Guinea, Walvis Bay, Uganda, and Rhodesia and in the Samoan Islands. Also, Holstein in 1894 offended the British by rejecting Salisbury's proposal to partition the Turkish Empire.

Hohenlohe's appointment to the chancellorship only led to a further erosion of Germany's diplomatic position. He was a novice at foreign affairs, and his greatest successes were of a negative order, resulting from his capacity for procrastination. His secretary of state for foreign affairs, Adolf Marschall von Bieberstein (1842–1912), although clever and experienced, was, on the other hand, perpetually undecided as to what course to pursue and, in any case, lacked the will to overcome Holstein's tenacity. The latter had become a determined advocate of *Weltmachtpolitik*; he believed that England, friendless as she was, needed German support and therefore could not afford to deny the Reich its just place in the imperialist hierarchy.

While German policy floundered aimlessly, the Jameson raid against the Transvaal in December, 1895, almost wrecked Anglo-German relations. It so incensed the kaiser that he spoke heatedly to Hohenlohe and his principal admirals of mobilizing the naval infantry and sending troops to the South African Republic (Transvaal). Hohenlohe was stunned at the implications of such a rash step and brought pressure on William II to content himself with an idea that had either originated with him or Holstein, namely to dispatch a congratulatory telegram (January 3, 1896) to President Krüger for having repelled Jameson's men and preserved the independence of the Transvaal. The kaiser's Krüger telegram, the dullest of all the weapons his hand had reached for, was, as J. David Fraley has explained, Hohenlohe's contribution to the preservation of the peace. Of course, the Krüger telegram neither helped the Boers nor hindered the British. It was, as a matter of fact, a faux pas of a very serious order, for it revealed the instability of the kaiser, led him by way of compensation to launch a great naval building program, and fired public opinion in Britain as nothing else had since the Crimean War. Only the Ethiopian defeat of the Italian army at Adowa on March 1, 1896, which foreshadowed an Anglo-French contest for the Egyptian Sudan, dissuaded the Court of St. James from trying at this juncture to reach an understanding with France. A deep wedge had been driven between the British and German people. This wedge, which could not be eliminated even as a result of the coldly correct, neutralist posture struck by the Wilhelmstrasse during the ensuing Boer War, affords a psychological explanation for the popularity of the dream of a great German battle fleet.

The Mürzsteg Agreement of 1897

At the beginning of 1897 Robert Gascoyne-Cecil, marquis of Salisbury, Britain's prime minister and foreign secretary, made it clear that Britain was no longer interested in the Mediterranean Entente of 1887. Deprived of English support, Austria-Hungary felt obliged to make overtures to the Russians for an agreement to preserve the status quo in the Balkans. The Russians, preoccupied with vast East Asian projects, felt they would benefit from shelving the Balkan problem for the time being. Accordingly, an agreement to keep the peace in the peninsula was signed on May 5, 1897, with Vienna. The so-called Mürzsteg Pact relieved the pressure on Europe for a decade by diverting Russia's attention to East Asia. At the same time the Mürzsteg pact promoted peace in western Europe inasmuch as France, in the absence of Russian military aid, could make no move to recover Alsace-Lorraine. All of this, however, was acceptable to Paris at the time because she was preoccupied with colonial adventures in Africa.

The Rebuff to Russia

The appointment in June, 1897, of Bernard von Bülow as secretary of state for foreign affairs brought German *Grosse Politik* more closely under the emperor's surveillance. Bülow's appointment was tantamount to the subordination of every consideration of German politics to global power and a great high seas fleet.

The kaiser, who was heavily under the influence of Mahan's *Influence of Sea Power in History*, disparaged continental defense and completely underestimated the need to neutralize Russia. Neither did he see that the pursuit of *Weltmacht* might end by so antagonizing Britain as to leave Germany in the minority in Europe.

The idea that it was far better for Germany to preserve neutrality in the Anglo-Russian feud led Bülow and Holstein to reject Russian overtures for German support at Constantinople in return for aid in constructing the Berlin-to-Baghdad railway. They couldn't see why they had to buy St. Petersburg's blessing, since nobody, including the Turks, opposed the German project except Russia, which was alarmed at the prospect of German economic penetration of the Ottoman Empire.

This rebuff to Russia was unnecessary and cost Germany more than it was worth. Russia was driven into the arms of France and was led to take rash steps. Thus, the Delcassé-Muraviev agreement of 1899, supplementing the Franco-Russian Treaty of 1893–94, transformed it, as respects the Balkans, from a defensive into a potentially offensive instrument. This pact was the first major diplomatic stroke of Théophile Delcassé, the French foreign minister, who was an implacable foe of Germany. Delcassé was persuaded to enter the pact with Muraviev not merely to protect France's very substantial investment in the Balkan states but also, according to at least one recent scholar (Christopher Andrew), because of a fantastic fear that Germany harbored a determined design to dominate the Mediterranean Sea. The agreement terminated the brief détente between France and Germany that had been achieved by Delcassé's predecessor, Gabriel Hanotaux. The Delcassé-Muraviev supplement was only the first of three shining diplomatic victories achieved by Delcassé.

London's Last Flirtation with Berlin

The years 1898–1901 constitute a milestone in British foreign policy and in the history of the balance of power. Britain in those years appears finally to have reached the conclusion that she could no longer afford to carry on with an isolationist policy. Having decided to embrace one of her three principal antagonists, she approached Germany first. This may have been because Joseph Chamberlain, colonial secretary and the dominant personality in Salisbury's cabinet, favored an alliance among Teutonic people in preference to one with Latins. There was also the consideration that while Anglo-German relations had slightly improved since 1896, Anglo-French were fast reaching a crisis.

While Salisbury was the first to evince a desire for an understanding with Germany (July 31, 1897), it was the British colonial secretary who strove more vigorously for an alliance with the Reich. Actuated by bitter hostility toward Russia, Chamberlain formally proposed to the German ambassador, Count von Hatzfeldt, on March 29, 1898, a defensive alliance among Britain and the Triple Alliance states: if Germany would presently support England in China, Egypt, and elsewhere, Britain would fight alongside of Germany if she were attacked at some later date.

In the ensuing negotiations, which dragged on until December, 1901, against a background of increasing Anglo-German industrial, commercial, and imperialist rivalry, Berlin procrastinated. In the judgment of the most recent scholarship (Stegmann, Schenk, Wehler, Böhme, Puhle, and Berghahn) Germany must bear the greater responsibility for the breakdown of the talks. Holstein and Bülow temporized out of both internal and external considerations. A fragile alliance between agrarian Conservatives and industrialist National Liberals, which later dissolved over the issue of tax and fiscal reform (Witt and Puhle), had in 1900 definitely decided in favor of building a battle fleet, whose offensive-defensive capability could not but cool Britain's ardor for an entente with Germany. Externally Bülow and Holstein wanted at all costs to avoid treading upon the Russian corns. Moreover, Bülow stressed that an agreement confined to colonial areas would be of exiguous value to the Reich, which had to have iron-clad guarantees of the integrity of her European boundaries. Behind the expressions of carping distrust uttered by Bülow and Hatzfeldt was the worry that alliance with England would brand Germany as Russia's foe. The German government could only risk leaving that impression, with the fell consequences it might entail, if the British government and parliament unequivocally promised to defend Germany against an anticipated Franco-Russian military reaction to the pact.

In later discussions it became apparent that Chamberlain did not necessarily represent the views of his colleagues in the cabinet and that Balfour also doubted whether the projected treaty would win the support of the majority in parliament. The fact is that neither the British prime minister nor the chancellor really desired an alliance. When Bülow discovered that Salisbury was also reticent, he backed away from the whirlpool with relief, believing that his prudence had saved the peace of Europe. In reality, his timidity, inspired by a genuine devotion to the peace or by considerations of class politics, deprived Germany of preponderance in Europe.

All that Germany extracted from the conversations of 1898–1901 was a trivial colonial agreement over Portugal's African colonies. The Anglo-German treaty of August 30, 1898, provided for extending a joint loan to Portugal, and a secret supplement to the pact pledged the signatories to resist intervention by a third power if the partition of the Portuguese African empire should become necessary. Due, however, to British suspicions of German intentions, the Portuguese loan was subsequently floated solely in London. This acted like a cold shower upon Anglo-German relations.

In the meantime a crisis had been reached and passed at Fashoda in the Egyptian Sudan. On September 19, 1898, Marchand voluntarily retreated before the forces of Kitchener, which was tantamount to French surrender of the Sudan to the British. Delcassé's *beau geste* was calculated not only to cool the ardor of Chamberlain and Balfour for an Anglo-German entente but to pave the way for a diplomatic revolution of the first order. Henceforth Britain was freed of the fear of having to face both France and Russia simultaneously. The value of German friendship sharply declined in London, where, in any case, there was profound resentment against the Germans for their Naval Law of 1898 and their sympathy for the Boers.

In spite of the emperor's dramatic efforts, Anglo-German friendship was at long last dying. Not a year passed by that did not see new occasion for resentment of parvenu Germany. From every standpoint, except perhaps a mutual interest in containing Russia, the two countries had reached the parting of the ways. It was not so much that the points of friction between Germany and England were of capital importance. In retrospect many of them—such as the Samoan Islands, the open door in China, and atrocities in the Boer War—must seem trivial. Rather it was that Bülow and Holstein were unwilling to identify themselves with the British quarrel with Russia, a fact that stands in awkward contradiction with the Kehrite thesis of the primacy of internal policy, which in this context should mean (Hans-Ulrich Wehler) that Germany's eastern policy was determined by the heavy industrialists who were bent on forcing their way into the Russian market and by the Junkers who were resolved to keep cheap Russian grain out of Germany at any price. Actually, the architects of German foreign policy felt that the British weren't offering anything half so valuable as Russian good will. Consequently, the reticence of Bülow and Holstein prompted England, who was searching for a partner, to lend an ear to the French suit.

It adds to the tragedy of German diplomacy that Bülow's great "no" was inspired by a sincere desire to preserve the peace of Europe, which he believed would be jeopardized if he turned his back upon Russia. Nevertheless, the wisdom of so ambivalent a foreign policy is open to question. Downing Street was surely flirting with revolutionary alternatives to the status quo. Bülow and Holstein probably exaggerated the risk of war associated with the British initiative. In any case, it is clear that to reject the British suit was tantamount to excluding from the German range of options a hypothetical war that the Reich would probably have won, for the sake of an unstable peace that it could no longer maintain.

The "Entente Cordiale" and Germany

Between 1902 and 1904 the scales tipped visibly against Germany. On June 30, 1902, the Franco-Italian Prinetti Agreement was reached, which committed Italy to strict neutrality in the event France became involved in war. Bülow, who was married to an Italian and owned a villa in Rome, disparaged the importance of the pact, saying that he did not mind if Italy had a dance with another partner. However, the Prinetti Agreement initiated Italy's apostasy from the Triple Alliance, which she had only just renewed two days before. Fearing a possible Anglo-German conflict, Rome wanted to be certain she would not have to fight the British navy.

On April 8, 1904, the marquis of Lansdowne, a proponent of amity with France who back in 1900 had succeeded Salisbury at the foreign office, negotiated an

Anglo-French entente cordiale. This blockbuster, which exposed the fallacy of Holstein's conviction that British imperialism would be forced permanently to depend upon the good will of Germany, pledged the signatories to settle all remaining issues that divided them. The core of the agreement was a French surrender of interest in Egypt, a country that had already been lost to the British, and a British promise to support a French sphere of influence in Morocco, a country that had yet to be won. The two signatories had their eyes averted from Europe when they entered this entente cordiale. For the English the main value of the agreement was to protect their rear in Africa and the Mediterranean in case of war with Russia. For the French the pact exorcised the possibility of a global war between the Anglo-Japanese and the Franco-Russian alliance blocs.

Delcassé worked cunningly during the Russo-Japanese War to dissuade Britain from attacking Russia. With Japan's victory (Treaty of Portsmouth, 1905), the way was suddenly opened for the formation of a startling new combination of Britain, France, and Russia. A strange scenario began to take shape when the English encouraged the French to violate, in spite of all Delcassé's pious denials, the open door policy in Morocco and trample on German, if not Spanish, interests. If the Germans should energetically oppose a French takeover in Morocco, Paris would invoke the *casus* of the entente. In aligning Britain with France and ranging the latter with the European majority, the Anglo-French entente pushed Europe closer to the abyss.

From Morocco to Algeçiras

For some time after the signing of the Anglo-French entente, the Germans pinned their hopes upon a falling-out between England and France. This was an illusion in a class with earlier hallucinations that had afflicted German diplomacy, such as that Russia would never ally with republican France, or that imperialistic England was permanently dependent upon German good will.

Germany's stand in the Moroccan crisis of 1905 was juridically and ethically proper, but diplomatically stupid. It was folly for the German government to persist with a line that must strengthen the bonds between Paris and London. The risk for Germany was particularly great because she had only sixteen battleships compared with Britain's forty-six and France's twelve, and Germany could no longer count upon the support of the Italian navy.

Bülow and Holstein now worked to convene an international conference on Morocco. While the ostensible aim of German foreign policy was to preserve the open door in Morocco, the larger purpose was to achieve a diplomatic victory over France. Specifically the German government hoped to force the French premier to throw the dangerous Delcassé to the wolves. Believing that the Russians were too weak to fight and that in the crisis the British would confine themselves to mere diplomatic support of France, Bülow did not hesitate to confront her with the possibility of war. When it appeared that not even the British were inclined to rescue Delcassé with a declaration of armed aid, Premier Rouvier dropped him from the cabinet on June 6, 1905. The kaiser chortled and made Bülow a prince.

The raucous jubilation of William II over the discomfiture of France and England was, of course, only the braying of an ass. Bülow's victory turned out to be a hollow one. It persuaded the entente partners, both of whom were incensed at the kaiser's surprise appearance in Tangiers on March 31, 1905, that German obstructionism could not be overcome without the aid of a militarily strong Russia.

Meanwhile William II tried, on his own initiative, to spirit Russia out of the arms of France. On July 25, 1905, he met Nicholas II near Björkö in the Gulf of Finland and signed a convention with him, which stipulated that if one of the signatories were attacked by a European power, the other would come to its aid on the continent. Unfortunately, this pact, as the Wilhelmstrasse pointed out to the kaiser, was worthless to Germany, for it did not obligate the Russians to attack India—the only place a diversion might help. Aghast at the Tsar's naiveté, Count Lamsdorff, the Russian foreign minister, pointed out the fundamental incompatibility of the Björkö convention with the Franco-Russian alliance. By excluding a Franco-German war from the applicability of the Björkö agreement, Lamsdorff relegated it to the circular file. In the meantime Bülow, who was at odds with Holstein on the value of the pact, submitted his resignation but was dissuaded from his intent by the histrionic kaiser, who threatened to commit suicide if his chancellor left.

The Moroccan Conference, for which Germany had pressed, met in Algeçiras in January, 1906. Of all the powers that attended the meetings, only Austria-Hungary supported the German position. Even Italy, a member of the Triple Alliance, stood opposed. Algeçiras simply blatantly advertised the fact that on top of the loss of Russia and England, post-Bismarckian German diplomacy had not even been able to hold on to Italy. Furthermore, Rouvier now showed himself to be determined to accept no more humiliations at the hands of the Reich. In the end, Germany was obliged to accede to the unfavorable Act of Algeçiras of April 7, 1906, which, while establishing certain international controls over Morocco, gave France a stronger position there. Algeçiras exposed the growing isolation of the Central Powers. Holstein thought the time had come to leave the ship that he had done so much to scuttle, and he submitted his resignation on April 5, 1906.

Forming the Triple Entente

The Russian defeat by Japan and the destruction of the Russian navy were not the only factors that prompted England to seek reconciliation with the tsarist empire. Equally important were the inauguration of a new era in naval warfare and the beginning of really lethal competition on the seas with Germany. In 1906 the first English dreadnought was commissioned. Faster than any capital ship afloat and boasting heavier armament, disposing of ten large-caliber guns instead of the usual four, the new type battleship, paradoxically, threatened to end the long era of British naval supremacy. All existing battleships were now obsolete.

The Germans, who had never had a first-class navy, might now benefit most of all from the changeover. Their only disadvantage was that the Kiel canal was not big enough to accommodate the dreadnoughts. Any British complacency on that score, however, was dispelled when in May, 1906, the Reichstag adopted a new naval act. This law simultaneously authorized the widening of the canal and the construction of the first dreadnoughts.

Assurances that the German navy was being built for commercial reasons failed to allay British fears. England had only just succeeded in 1904 in persuading France to abandon further capital ship building. Now Britain's two-power naval standard and insular security were seemingly endangered from a new quarter. This estimate, generally entertained in the British Isles, led naval officers to contemplate the desirability of a "Copenhagen" (i.e., a preventive attack) upon the German fleet while it still could be done. The same view impelled Downing Street to make a choice between naval supremacy and the preservation of the moribund Turkish Empire. There being no doubt as to which the government would choose, it followed logically that a British policy aim of demonstrated value would eventually have to be abandoned. Anglo-Turkish friendship was obviously an insuperable obstacle to Anglo-Russian entente, which would consolidate British dominion over the oceans.

This analysis heartened the sly Alexander P. Izvolsky, Russia's new foreign minister (1906–10). His task, as he saw it, was to liquidate his predecessor's ill-fated program in the Far East and find compensation in the Balkans. To this end he required British support against Turkey and Austria-Hungary. In enlisting that aid, Izvolsky did what no one since Nesselrode had come even close to doing—namely, persuade the British to abandon their historic Near Eastern policy. The efforts of the Russian foreign minister were at this time facilitated by the unwillingness of the kaiser, Bülow, and Tirpitz to reduce their naval building program.

The newer historical scholarship sees in the Anglo-Russian understanding of August 31, 1907, which divided Persia into spheres of influence and excluded Afghanistan from the Russian, not so much an "encirclement" of Germany *(Einkreisungspolitik)* as her elimination from the concert of world powers. Despite pressure of Britain's first sea lord, Sir John Fisher, for a preemptive strike against the German fleet, there can be no doubt that the British government in 1907–8 was mainly animated by considerations of a defensive nature. The mere fact that British diplomacy continued till 1911 to strive for an agreement with Berlin over naval construction proves this. Nevertheless, pending such an agreement, Britain had certainly embarked upon an enterprise fraught with the gravest peril for European peace.

It must not be forgotten that Russia's prime objective was to free her Asiatic rear so that she could focus upon a forward policy in the Balkans. It was axiomatic to Russian thinking that British assent to that policy was the guarantee of its success. The newer scholarship errs when it discounts the fact that France was just then giving top priority to building up her ground forces in Europe and to aiding Russia to restore her military strength through massive loans, or that the British badly needed Russia to divert Germany's attention and resources from the North Sea and the building of a navy. Clearly, any considerable improvement in Russia's military posture must complicate life for the Central Powers and impose a laming division of resources upon future eastern and western theaters of war. Finally, it must be averred that the web around the Central Powers was intentionally drawn closer when on June 8, 1908, King Edward VII and some of his ministers met Tsar Nicholas and their counterparts at Estonian Reval and urged the Russian government to do everything possible to fortify tsarist armed forces by land and sea. From Reval dates the existence of an encircling Triple Entente and the hopelessness of the German diplomatic position. Henceforth, in a world dominated by eight great powers, the Reich could in a showdown count upon the support of only one.

Izvolsky's Aims

Soviet scholars have sought to modify the older portrait of Alexander P. Izvolsky as the Lucifer of prewar tsarist diplomacy. Brezhnev era historians refuse to seek the key to Izvolsky's policies in either personal ambition or malice. Rather they see him as the perplexed practitioner of a diplomacy that owed its vagaries less to caprice than preoccupation with placating warring factions in both Duma and government, which were out to destroy him.

This estimate, even if true, is essentially *nihil ad rem* as respects Izvolsky's war guilt. The fact is, the Russian minister-president, Peter Stolypin, had to restrain his foreign minister from dangerous expedients to which his ambition, no less than the auspicious external situation, impelled him. It is specious to deny that Izvolsky's provocative initiatives and personal grievances, to which he sacrificed national policy, pushed Europe a good deal closer to the whirlpool. After the formation of the Triple Entente, Izvolsky turned his attention to securing compensation in the Balkans for losses incurred in the war with Japan. He sought first to achieve this through direct negotiations with Vienna. When this failed, he conceived the perilous plan of detaching Germany from Austria-Hungary and isolating her. When this also failed, Izvolsky became a man with a grudge. He then espoused a policy involving even greater risk—a militant advance of Pan-Slavism in the Balkan peninsula. This course, continued by his successor, Sergei Sazonov (foreign minister, 1910–16), helped bring on the Balkan Wars of 1912–13.

Chapter 43

THE FAILURE OF DIPLOMACY, 1908–1914

The Buchlau Agreement

As early as January 27, 1908, Izvolsky made his first gambit in a game whose ultimate objective was Russian control over the Straits and Constantinople. Izvolsky declared Austria-Hungary had broken the Mürzsteg Agreement of 1897 by planning to build a railway through the Sanjak of Novi Bazar to Saloniki. He then arranged an historic meeting with the Austro-Hungarian foreign minister, Count Aloysius Aehrenthal (1906–12). At this conference, which took place on September 16, 1908, at Bohemian Buchlau (Buchlov), Austria-Hungary agreed to support the opening of the Straits to Russian warships in return for a Russian pledge to restrain Bulgaria, Montenegro, and Serbia when Vienna should proceed to annex Bosnia and Herzegovina.

The trouble came when the Dual Monarchy annexed the territories before Izvolsky had been able to win French and British approval for the new regime at the Straits. When the British secretary of state for foreign affairs (1905–16), Sir Edward Grey, demurred to his scheme, Izvolsky perceived that he had reckoned without his host—London, the real overlord of the Near East. As a result, he conceived an undying hatred for Aehrenthal, whom he blamed for it all, and this resentment henceforth completely poisoned Austro-Russian relations.

Izvolsky now sought to offset Vienna's fait accompli by encouraging Serbia to clamor for compensation in return for countenancing Habsburg annexation of Bosnia and Herzegovina. Serbia, which since the palace revolution of 1903 in Belgrade had been a Russian satellite, gladly complied. Meanwhile, during 1909 Izvolsky was importunate in his demands upon Germany. He insisted that she mediate between Austria-Hungary and Serbia or summon a European conference to review the Bosnian annexation. Success in either respect would manifestly augment Russian prestige in the Balkans. Fearing that if Germany left Austria in the lurch the former would lose its last dependable ally, Bülow replied to Izvolsky that the Reich would neither put pressure on the Dual Monarchy nor abandon her. Convinced that Russia was still too weak to go to war, Bülow informed Izvolsky on March 21 that if he persisted in his demands, Germany would "withdraw and let events take their course." Left out on a limb, the Russian, who had been unable to elicit tangible support from London or Paris, was obliged to advise Serbia to drop her demands.

During the crisis Germany had tried to weaken the Triple Entente. However, neither Germany nor Austria-Hungary cared to push the affair to war. Vienna knew that since the Russo-Japanese treaties of June 13 and July 28, 1907, Russia's rear was protected. Austria-Hungary, therefore, contented herself with digesting Bosnia and Herzegovina and building a railway, to which Turkey agreed on February 26, 1909, through the Sanjak of Novi Bazar to the Aegean. For her part, Serbia had temporarily to adjust to an arrangement which, if left to stand, would be the end of her dream of a kingdom of the South Slavs. From the Buchlau crisis, clearly, the South Slav nationality problem, upon which Bernadotte E. Schmitt laid cardinal emphasis in his analysis of the origins of the war, emerged in its ugliest form. Henceforth the very existence of the Habsburg polyglot empire was at stake. By deciding for peace in 1909, Austria-Hungary missed her last opportunity to solve the Serbian problem on her own terms.

The Potsdam Agreement

After Buchlau, Europe breathed a sigh of relief and intensified preparations for the next trial of strength.

Various attempts were made to repair the damage done in 1909. Bethmann and Alfred von Kiderlen-Wächter (1852–1912), deputy secretary of state for foreign affairs (1908–10, foreign minister, 1910–12), tried to achieve a political agreement that would entail a détente with Britain. They attached the greatest importance to obtaining her pledge of neutrality in a continental war. For its part, the Asquith-George government was endeavoring to win Germany's assent to a naval agreement that would limit the size of its navy or at least slow down the tempo of construction, which under the German Naval Law of 1908 was to be four dreadnoughts for the span 1908–11 and two each year thereafter. In another direction, the new Russian foreign minister, Sergei Sazonov (1910–16), who had replaced Izvolsky when he had been transferred to the Paris embassy, inspired in Berlin hopes of improved Russo-German relations. Also, in February, 1909, Kiderlen negotiated a new understanding with France over Morocco, which recognized French political preponderance in return for establishing a Franco-German economic condominium over the country.

Nevertheless, even in fairly tranquil times the position of the Central Powers steadily crumbled. Thus, in October, 1909, Italy drew further away from her olden allies by entering into the Racconigi Agreement with Russia. By this pact Russia engaged to indulge Italian ambitions in Tripoli and Cyrenaica, which must serve to embroil Italy with Turkey, the friend of the Central Powers. In return, the Italians agreed to regard with benevolence Russia's ambitions at the Straits. Racconigi exerted a baleful influence over the peace of the Balkans forasmuch as Izvolsky, who had been mortally affronted by Aehrenthal, was working persistently but covertly to humiliate the Central Powers.

After Izvolsky's departure for Paris, Bethmann-Hollweg made a determined effort to achieve a Russo-German agreement, which should weaken the Franco-Russian alliance and revive European confidence. Nicholas II and Sazonov met with William II and his ministers at Potsdam in early November, 1910, where Sazonov was assured orally that even if Austria-Hungary were to entertain aggressive designs in the Balkans, which was not the case, Germany would not support them. Sazonov in turn promised the Germans that Russia would never join England in any conspiracy against Germany. Neither side reduced its respective promise to writing, for in that case each would have been compromised with its friends. By a later, written Potsdam Agreement of August 19, 1911, Germany recognized the Russian sphere of influence in Persia, while St. Petersburg withdrew its opposition to the construction of a Berlin-Baghdad railway and agreed to build a Teheran-Khanikin line that would link the former with the Persian railway system.

The Second Moroccan Crisis

While Russo-German relations were improving, German relations with France and England were taking a turn for the worse. In April, 1911, the French, in violation of the Algeçiras Act, dispatched troops to rebellious Fez. Anxious not so much to preserve the independence of Morocco as to secure territorial compensation for Germany's assent to the consolidation of the French African Empire, Kiderlen-Wächter took a firm stand. On June 26 the German cruiser *Panther* was dispatched to Agadir, a Moroccan port close to Gibraltar. The German foreign office followed this admonition with a demand for a piece of the French Congo, which was subsequently rejected by the French. Britain, fearing that the Germans were trying to obtain a naval base at Agadir, which was not the case, rallied to the support of France. The chancellor of the exchequer, Lloyd George, made an inflammatory speech at the London Mansion House, which cemented the already close political and military ties between London and Paris and intemperately warned Berlin that peace at the price of Britain's humiliation would be intolerable.

Notwithstanding British bluster and the indignant assaults of the German press upon Kiderlen for his "weak" line, he achieved a compromise settlement on November 4, 1911. By it Germany surrendered all interest in Morocco in return for some 100,000 square miles of worthless territory in the Congo. He had rescued the peace from the imbroglio but had in a larger sense catastrophically failed. He had been guided throughout the crisis by foreign policy considerations and had not been demonstrably influenced by capitalist or imperialist circles (A. Vagts and Wolfgang Mommsen). Kiderlen's cardinal objective in the Moroccan altercation had been at long last to liquidate this issue, which he believed stood in the way of an Anglo-German rapprochement. In this assumption he abjectly erred.

Although Kiderlen had succeeded, seemingly, in intimidating France and Bethmann had combatted the mounting bellicosity of the imperialists and the general staff and had labored to allay British fears regarding German intentions, the second Moroccan crisis ended disastrously for the Reich. Its sequel was not a new era of Anglo-German friendship but the commencement in July, 1911, of Anglo-French joint ground force operational planning for possible war with the Central Powers. The sky darkened further when in November, 1912, the general staff agreements were confirmed in an exchange of letters between Sir Edward Grey and the French ambassador, Paul Cambon. Thus, it may be averred that although Germany was morally and legally right as respects the cause of Moroccan independence, she contributed to a new deterioration of the diplomatic climate through her gruff response to French aggression.

Meanwhile, even before the new Moroccan treaty had been signed, Italy clawed at the peace. She exploited the commotion occasioned by the Moroccan tension to stage her own little side show. On October 24 she encashed the Racconigi blank check by pouncing on Tripoli and commencing a war against Turkey, Germany's partner, that dragged on through most of 1912.

The Last Chance for a Naval Agreement

Prospects for a peaceful settlement of the cardinal continental issues that divided the Great Powers were further diminished when Anglo-German attempts to reach a naval and neutrality agreement definitely broke down in 1912. The English were alarmed at the frenzied tempo of German naval construction. Although it was deliberately exaggerated for political purposes by the lord of the Admiralty, the German building program was actually pretty formidable, as has been noted. Fearing that she might soon lose preponderance in dreadnoughts, Britain pressed for an agreement limiting German naval construction in return for colonial concessions. For its part, the Wilhelmstrasse was anxious to have a political understanding with Downing Street, which would diminish Germany's liabilities in any two-front war.

The way was prepared for top-level conversations by contacts between Albert Ballin, director of the Hamburg-America Line, and his English banker friend, Ernest Cassell. At length Sir Edward Grey sent Richard Burdon, Viscount Haldane, the secretary of state for war, to Berlin, but Haldane had no power to make the sort of agreement the Germans contemplated.

Bethmann wanted the British to give a promise of neutrality in the event of war, regardless of how it arose. In return for such a pledge he was prepared to accept a slower tempo of capital ship construction and a ratio in dreadnoughts more favorable to Britain. Unfortunately, the chancellor reckoned without the kaiser, naval ministry, or military camarilla, all of whom at this time were incensed by the recent naval agreement between England and France by which the French Atlantic fleet was to be transferred from Brest to Toulon, while the British Mediterranean squadron was to be moved to the North Sea and English Channel, where it would have the mission of covering the denuded northern coast of France. Friends of a German navy wondered how Britain could henceforth claim she was uncommitted and remain neutral in a continental war. In any case, the kaiser was furious, and he telegraphed the German ambassador in London, Metternich, that the English action was being regarded back home as a belligerent act and would be answered by a new navy law and perhaps mobilization. Bethmann was alarmed by these irresponsible utterances and threatened to resign if the kaiser did not stop meddling in foreign affairs. William II yielded.

Meanwhile, at the negotiating table the British refused to offer anything half as valuable as they asked. Haldane offered no more than a lame declaration that England would not join any combination directed toward aggression against Germany—a worthless formula to the Wilhelmstrasse. When the Reichstag replied with the naval act of 1912, which while compromising the "Tirpitz-Plan," nevertheless authorized three additional dreadnoughts for 1913–1917, Grey decided to break off negotiations as inoffensively and courteously as possible.

Although the naval talks had run into the sand, this was not allowed to stand in the way of a superficial improvement of Anglo-German relations. Bethmann took to heart the injunction of Kiderlen-Wächter (who died on December 30, 1912) that "good relations with England are incontestably one of the most worthy goals of German policy." During the Balkan crisis of 1912–13 Bethmann cooperated with the British government to pacify the Balkans or localize the war, and in 1914 the British and German governments confirmed the détente in their relations by signing an agreement over the Berlin-to-Baghdad railway. France took undue alarm lest Germany detach Britain from the Triple Entente and considered whether it were not better to fight now rather than when the Triple Entente lay in wreckage.

Bethmann-Hollweg's Moderation

Shortly before his death, Kiderlen advised the pacific Bethmann not to let Austria drag Germany into a war with Russia unless the latter launched a direct attack. This view, which was a further aberration from the policies of Bülow and Holstein, suffered from the most serious error a diplomat can make: to assume that there is an alternative when none exists.

The intelligent but indecisive Gottlieb von Jagow (1863–1935), who was secretary of state for foreign affairs from 1913 to 1916, and Chancellor Bethmann-Hollweg believed that they could organize an international fire brigade that could extinguish any diplomatic blaze. With them the diplomatic deterrent took precedence over a military deterrent. Bethmann and Jagow were especially scrupulous about avoiding new provocations of France and England, mainly because the chancellor was a true friend of peace. Neither he nor his ministers were guided by the Pan-German League, whose members, financially powerful even if few in number, were clamoring to twist the lion's tail. While the German government still hungered for world power, it did not wish to antagonize the British.

That the cautious Bethmann-Hollweg fully realized the gravity of Germany's predicament was revealed in a speech before the Reichstag in 1912. Hypothecating a war in which the Reich would be forced to attack an arrogant France, Bethmann averred that in such case she would have the support of Russia and doubtless of England too, "whereas for our allies the *casus foederis* will not arise, and we shall have to beg for their aid or neutrality."[*] It is impossible to impugn the integrity of a chancellor who declared that he could not be responsible for creating that kind of situation.

The Coming of the Balkan Wars

In 1912 Sazonov, acting through the Russian ministers at Belgrade and Sofia, organized a Balkan League. Properly described by the French Premier Poincaré (who, however, endorsed it) as "an instrument of war," the Balkan League treaty

---

[*]Quoted in G. P. Gooch, *Before the War Studies in Diplomacy* (reprint, New York, 1967), II, 234.

was designed so that the alliance could be turned against either Turkey or Austria-Hungary. It also strengthened Russia's hold on Serbia and Bulgaria. Poincaré, who himself favored a strong Russian policy in the Balkans, assured Sazonov that if Germany intervened in case of hostilities there, France would automatically honor her obligations toward Russia under the convention of 1893–94. In September, 1912, the French premier and foreign minister confirmed this blank check to Russia.

Despite attempts of Germany to forestall hostilities, Montenegro on October 8, 1912, declared war on Turkey, which was just then defending itself against Italy's assault on Tripoli. However, Sazonov and Poincaré soon took fright and drew back from the brink of general war, toward which Europe was rushing. They joined Bethmann, Kiderlen, and Grey in an effort to localize the conflict. However, by then Greece had joined the Balkan allies, all of whom were determined to aggrandize their territory. In a situation where the existence of not only the Ottoman Empire but the Dual Monarchy was jeopardized by Balkan nationalist aims, Count Leopold von Berchtold (1863–1942), the new foreign minister of Austria-Hungary (1912–15), hesitated and, in the end, did nothing.

The whole bent of the diplomacy of the Wilhelmstrasse and the Austro-Hungarian foreign ministry at the Ballhausplatz during the First Balkan War was to solicit the cooperation of Russia to preserve the status quo in the peninsula. Bethmann and Berchtold counted on the support of Sazonov, for whose probity they entertained respect. Yet Sazonov was all quicksand and offered no firm basis on which to build the peace. It is true that in 1912–13 he was averse to taking the risk of a general war and that he warned Bulgaria and Greece not to reach for Constantinople. Yet, on the other hand, he encouraged every Serbian or Montenegrin action that was calculated to weaken Austria-Hungary and block her access to the Balkans. Sazonov was also conscious of the fact that the Russian army was stronger than in 1908–9 and that Russia could now rely upon the armed support of both France and Britain.

The Extent of German Support to Austria

Faced with militant Serbian expansionism, the Viennese government feared that conspiratorial South Slav organizations, such as the Black Hand (Narodna Odbrana) and Union or Death Society (Ujedinjenie ili Smrt), would be able to drive Belgrade into a war to liberate all South Slavs from Austria-Hungary.

Before his death, Kiderlen-Wächter attempted to force the Dual Monarchy to strike a purely defensive posture. He had admonished Vienna that the *casus foederis* would only arise in case of direct attack by Russia and that German armed support would depend on how the war broke out. Kiderlen was quite evidently trying to restrain his country's ally.

Notwithstanding German hesitancy, Berchtold knew that if he were to insist that Austria-Hungary's vital interests were to ensnare her in a war with Russia, Germany could not stand aside and allow her one dependable ally to be destroyed. Kiderlen said as much in his address to the Reichstag on November 28, 1912, and

William II and Bethmann-Hollweg shared his conclusion that in a life-and-death struggle Germany would have to rally to the defense of the Dual Monarchy so that Germany would not have to fight alone at a later time. However, they all urged Vienna to act with extreme caution, and the kaiser even disapproved any Austrian advance into Serbia. His worst nightmare was that the Reich would become involved in a two-front war in which England would support France and Germany would be pitted in a struggle for existence against three great powers.

Although the ambassadors' conference in London, which met in the winter of 1912–13, recognized the independence of Albania, the Serbs, encouraged by Russia, occupied Djakova and Dibra. Sazonov warned the Austrians that if they tried to expel the Serbs the Russian army would be mobilized. Berchtold backed down and on February 13, 1913, conceded the two towns on condition that the Serbs evacuate the rest of northern Albania. Further, when in April–May, 1913, the Montenegrins seized Scutari, it was awarded to them by the Powers.

Meanwhile, Turkey was defeated by the Balkan allies and her hegemony in the peninsula was destroyed. Then in late June Bulgaria attacked Serbia and Greece, inaugurating a second Balkan war. The Treaty of Bucharest (August 10, 1913) sealed the defeat of Bulgaria and the transfer of Macedonian territory claimed by her to both Greece and Serbia. Subsequently a disappointed Bulgaria drifted away from its Russian moorings and moved toward the Central Powers. Rumania, on the other hand, passed into the Russian orbit, inasmuch as she had obtained the Dobrudja with Sazonov's blessing.

The Second Albanian Confrontation

During the second Albanian crisis Russia was mortified. She never subsequently forgave Austria-Hungary, preferring to pull the Habsburg Empire down into the grave with her.

Serbia's appetite grew with the eating. In the autumn of 1913, with Russian encouragement, she again violated Albanian territory and the London Convention guaranteeing its integrity. Throughout the Balkan Wars Bethmann-Hollweg and von Jagow had consistently tried to apply the brakes on Vienna. But this time the provocation was too much. With prior knowledge and the sympathy of the German government, Berchtold dispatched an ultimatum on October 18, 1913, demanding that the Serbs withdraw within eight days from Albania. Inasmuch as the English could not imagine themselves fighting in so bad a cause, there was nothing for the Russians to do but advise Belgrade once again to strike its colors, which it did. This second humiliation of Serbia within four years at the hands of Austria-Hungary was widely interpreted as a *coup de pied* to Russia, which indignantly added the memory of it to its stock of grievances against the Habsburg monarchy.

After the Balkan Wars an almost unbearable strain in relations between Russia, on the one hand, and Germany and Austria-Hungary, on the other, developed. In recent times a number of Soviet historians (e.g., V. I. Bovykin, I. V. Bestuzhev, and P. N. Efremov) have shown that the rapidly growing industrial bourgeoisie and the big landlords who had adopted capitalistic methods had become bitterly Germanophobe and were vigorously agitating in the press and through a variety of commercial and governmental agencies for the transformation of the Triple Entente into a Triple Alliance, whose aim would be to smash the Teutonic dam that had been erected against the Russian imperialist drive in the Near East. So successful was Germanophobe pressure that by the beginning of 1914 anti-Germans controlled the general staff (General Yanushkevitch) and the ministerial council (including the chairman, the formerly pro-German Goremykin).

Having failed in earlier direct approaches to both Austria-Hungary and Turkey and having also failed to obtain control of the Straits in a local war, the Russian government in secret ministerial council meetings in St. Petersburg on December 31, 1913/January 13, 1914, and February 8/21 now pondered under what conditions its grand goals could be accomplished. At these conferences a majority of ministers, including the formerly cautious Sazonov, reached the conclusion that Constantinople and the Straits could no longer be won except in a general war and that such a war was inevitable. While it was agreed that Russia needed more time to prepare for a European war, no one expressed the desire to avoid it, and there was a consensus on the score that the dissolution of the Ottoman Turkish Empire, which was thought to be imminent, would bring the great war at once. There was reason for confidence in the fact that Russia was both militarily and diplomatically in a stronger position than she had been since the days of Napoleon I.

The German government also drew grim lessons from the Balkan Wars: if Russia should ever feel compelled to mobilize against Austria-Hungary in support of Serbia, Germany would have to stand by the Dual Monarchy no matter how the war arose, or the Reich would have to stand alone in the next European crisis. The tragedy of the whole situation was that the controlling ministers in Russia, Austria-Hungary, and Germany (not to mention Serbia) all thought that war was inevitable. Berchtold may have striven to confine it to a mere campaign against troublesome Serbia, but the kaiser, Bethmann, Jagow, and Lichnowsky, the German ambassador to London, were convinced that hostilities would be global. Sazonov, too, felt that the war would be worldwide: Britain would surely come in, even though in peacetime she might, in response to the antimilitarist pressure of English labor, resist the signing of a formal alliance.

Seized with a sense of impending doom, European governments strove frantically to strengthen their military establishments. The German Army Act of March, 1913, brought the peacetime force up to a total of 748,000, while the French Army Law of the fall of 1913 enabled metropolitan France, with only two-thirds the population of Germany, to keep 750,000 men under arms. Extensive reorganization of the Russian army in 1913–14 gave it a peacetime strength of 3,220,000.

Russo-German Friction

During the winter of 1913–14 Germany, which had considerable financial investments in the Ottoman Turkish Empire, sought to repair her prestige in Constantinople, which had suffered from the Italo-Turkish War. At the invitation of the Sublime Porte the Reich sent General Liman von Sanders to reorganize the Ottoman army. Since he was given the supreme command in Constantinople, the Russians, who descried in that a political aim, objected vigorously. Ultimately the Wilhelmstrasse retreated under this pressure and requested Liman's transfer to other headquarters in Turkey, and apparent calm was restored in the Near East. Nevertheless, because Pan-Slavism and the Germanophobes were steadily tightening their hold on Russian policy, Germany's services in the Liman affair were swiftly forgotten, and she was subjected to almost daily assaults by Russian newspapers. On the other hand, German official fears of Russian intentions were heightened by the startling report of February 24, 1914, which was made by the chief of the German general staff, Helmuth von Moltke the Younger (1848–1916), regarding massive Russian military preparations.

Nothing did so much to fan animosity between the Russian and German public as the press war in the first half of 1914. It orchestrated military preparations and drowned out the pacifying efforts of true conservatives in both countries. The newspaper feud was already several months old when a sensational article, under the signature of a St. Petersburg correspondent, appeared in the *Kölnische Zeitung* without the government's foreknowledge. This article, dated March 2, 1914, predicted that Russia would be ready for war with Germany by 1917, a view that synchronized with the conclusions in Moltke's report. The article set off a panic on the St. Petersburg stock exchange. The German ambassador, von Pourtales, was dismayed. Although he grabbed for the flute, he was unable to calm Sazonov. Meanwhile, the officially controlled St. Petersburg newspaper, the *Birshevija Vjedomosti*, stridently boasted that in the future the Russian army would play an "active" rather than a defensive role. A reading of this article caused William II to conclude that "without the slightest doubt Russia is preparing war against us systematically."

Throughout the spring the press feud was fed by mutually hostile economic measures. It reached a crescendo in June, 1914, after Jagow had failed to propitiate the Russians. On June 13 a highly incendiary article, written at the instigation of the Russian minister of war, General Sukhomlinov, appeared in the *Birshevija Vjedomosti*. Coming at a time when Germans were depressed at the news of highly secret Anglo-Russian naval conversations, the article stated that the time required for mobilizing the Russian army had been reduced from fifteen to ten days and that the annual Russian draft contingent had just been raised from 450,000 to 580,000. The numerical strength of that army (3,220,000) was "so vast that no other nation has ever equalled it." In conclusion the writer urged France to be firm about putting 770,000 men in the field and maintaining the Three Year Service Law: "Russia is ready. France must be too." It should not be a matter for surprise that confronted with such steely resolution and the prospect of a militarily increasingly strong Russia, General von Moltke and some elements in the Conservative and National Liberal parties began seriously to press the government to seize some desirable opportunity to wage a preventive war against the Franco-Russian camp.

Serbia's Guilt

No serious scholar has ever contended that the origins of World War I are to be sought solely in the plot that resulted in the assassination of the Archduke Franz Ferdinand, heir to the Habsburg throne, and his wife, on June 28, 1914, at Sarajevo in Bosnia. Underlying animosities, tensions, rivalries, treaty commitments, fears in several capitals that continuation of peace would result in a deterioration of the diplomatic position, and, above all, staggering armaments had prepared the way for the final trial of strength. All parties to the grand alliance game were more or less guilty of bringing on World War I. However, the Serbian government was probably more immediately culpable than any other except, possibly, Austria-Hungary. Serbia's guilt consists in deliberately encouraging South Slav nationalist agitation that aimed at destroying the Dual Monarchy. The latter's crime, on the other hand, was, after much vacillation and in the face of a critical attitude of the Hungarian government, to decide upon the chastisement of Serbia because she posed a mortal threat to the polyglot empire.

Doubt no longer exists that the Serbian premier, Pašić, had been kept informed of the conspiratorial operations of the Black Hand organization and of the Union or Death Society, including the plot hatched by them against the archduke (J. Remak). Although motivated by not wholly ignoble nationalist aims, the Serbian government was an accomplice before the fact, for the premier did nothing to warn the government of Austria-Hungary of the precise nature of the plot to assassinate Franz Ferdinand when he came to Bosnia.

The "Blank Check" to Austria-Hungary

William II was outraged by the assassination because Franz Ferdinand and his wife were his personal friends. The kaiser's indignation was fanned by the circumstance that the aged Franz Josef had already suffered many stark family tragedies, including the assassination of his own wife.

Until June, 1914, the government of Bethmann-Hollweg had striven to repair relations with Great Britain and had not seriously thought of trying to achieve any of its grand policy aims by war (W. J. Mommsen). However, from the outset of the Serbian crisis Germany in fact renounced her freedom of decision. Between July 3 and 5 Bethmann and William II agreed that a nearly isolated Germany had no alternative but to stand by Austria-Hungary if Russia attacked, and assurances to this effect were transmitted to Vienna on July 6 through official channels. A long risk of general war was taken with this step. However, neither kaiser nor chancellor thought it likely that the *casus foederis* would arise. It is, the Fritz Fischer school notwithstanding, certain that William II, Bethmann, and Jagow knew from Sir Edward Grey's flat warning of December, 1912, that in the event a European war arose out of the Balkans, England would positively come to the military aid of France and Russia. But Bethmann was fairly sure that Russia was not ready for war and would not rally to Serbia's aid. Moreover, while not expecting British neutrality in wartime, Bethmann counted upon Downing Street to aid him to find a diplomatic solution of the Balkan problem short of general war.

Still, the decision to authorize an Austrian punitive campaign against Serbia did carry with it the risk of swift escalation, and the German "blank check" was a departure from Bethmann's earlier consistently cautious policy. His hesitant decision to change course can only be explained by the fact that his position vis-á-vis his internal foes had eroded. Faced with the demands of the war hawks for a preventive assault against Russia, the assurance to Vienna of support in a local war was the minimal concession that could avert Bethmann's dismissal. A chancellor who was under heavy parliamentary attack for his allegedly pro-English and otherwise spineless foreign policy was banking on the correctness of General von Moltke's estimate that Russia would not be ready for war until 1917. If Bethmann held on to the chancellorship, general war might be avoided; if he succumbed to internal pressure, Moltke, Tirpitz, and the war party would surely have their way. Bethmann believed that the Austro-Serbian confrontation would find Britain working to preserve the peace and demonstrate that a diplomatically insecure Russia was less belligerent than Moltke thought it was. Bethmann was gambling on the test case, it is true, but, given his whole past, pacific policy, it is unlikely that even in the event of failure of the test he would without a struggle capitulate to the war party in Germany.

Meanwhile, the kaiser, who regarded the Serbs as "a gang of criminals," on July 17 unconditionally confirmed the original promise of support to Vienna. In his message he declared that he recognized the necessity for Austria-Hungary to defend herself against heavy pressure on her southern frontiers and the attempts of Pan-Slavism to destroy her.

The Last Act

In the crisis of late July, 1914, Habsburg diplomacy again demonstrated its propensity for arriving one day too late. Wishing for incontrovertible evidence of official Serbian complicity in the assassination, Berchtold procrastinated until world opinion was no lnger overwhelmingly sympathetic to Franz Josef and considerations of material interest had turned many nations against Austria-Hungary. When it was too late for Vienna to have its way without paying an exorbitant price, Berchtold dispatched an ultimatum to Serbia on July 23. The Wilhelmstrasse, which had largely been kept in the dark as to his intentions, was only inadequately briefed on this note. Nevertheless, for Russia's and Bethmann's benefit, the Ballhaus did disclaim any intention of annexing Balkan territory.

In the first three weeks of the month Bethmann's main idea had been to enlist England's aid in localizing a Balkan war. However, toward the end of July he began to fear that his earlier estimate as to what Russia would do had been in serious error, and he began to lose his confidence in his ability to box the war in the Balkans. Above all, he was haunted by the conviction that England would enter any continental war shortly after it had commenced. Reports of Anglo-Russian naval conversations and of the blank check that Poincaré and Viviani had just given Sazonov on their visit with him in St. Petersburg from July 20 to 23 convinced the German chancellor that if the guns went off it was probable that the conflict would immediately escalate and that Germany and Austria would shortly have four powers to contend with, while Italy and Rumania would remain on the sidelines. It was unnecessary to postulate Britain's entering the war to honor her commitments to her entente partners; the mere implementation of the Schlieffen Plan, Bethmann knew, was calculated to evoke a British declaration of war in defense of Belgium. A dejected Bethmann now acceded to an urgent Russian request that Germany mediate between Austria-Hungary and Serbia. The success of this effort presupposed that all powers would refrain from further measures that might precipitate hostilities. Neither Austria-Hungary nor Russia did.

On July 28 Austria-Hungary rejected Serbia's reply as evasive and recalcitrant. The kaiser, on the other hand, who was deeply concerned to preserve the general peace, was prepared to see in the Serbian note a complete accommodation of Vienna's demands. Nevertheless, Berchtold and Franz Josef took the plunge. On July 28 Austria-Hungary declared war on Serbia and commenced bombardment of Belgrade. Sazonov declared that Vienna had set Europe aflame.

Although Bethmann was fast falling prey to a fatalistic pessimism, he still clung to a flotsam of hope: as long as the armies of Austria-Hungary did not proceed beyond the border city of Belgrade and Vienna abjured annexationist aims, the peace might still be saved. The German chancellor now cast reserve aside and strongly admonished the Ballhaus against any immoderate action. On both July 29 and 30 he warned Berchtold that he absolutely declined to allow the Dual Monarchy "wantonly and in disregard of our advice to drag Germany into a conflagration in which England is against us and we should be two powers to four."*

While Bethmann, at Russia's request, was earnestly trying to persuade Vienna to accept mediation and only temporarily occupy Belgrade, the tsar sabotaged the German initiative and took the one step that could destroy the peace of the world. Despite secret assurances tendered to Sazonov on July 29 that Germany agreed that Vienna make concessions to Serbia, Nicholas II on the same day approved Sukhomlinov's demand for total mobilization. In response to impassioned appeals by William II, the tsar late on the same day rescinded the mobilization order; but on July 30 at 6:00 P.M., under excruciating pressure from Sazonov and the Russian generals, he reissued the order.

In the meantime the Habsburg government had assented to the proposal for mediation but, to the bewilderment of the friends of peace, continued to insist that Serbia must accept Austria's demands *in toto*. In any case, the Austrian acceptance came too late to save the peace. Russian mobilization had for a genera-

---

German Documents on the Outbreak of the War, ed. by Count Max Montgelas and Walter Schücking, II, Doc. 396, Bethmann-Hollweg to Tschirschky; see also G. P. Gooch, *Before the War Studies in Diplomacy* (N.Y., 1967. Reprint), II, 279; and Immanuel Geiss (ed.), *Julikrise und Kriegsausbruch 1914* (Hanover, 1964), II, Docs. 793, 380.

tion been regarded as the agreed signal for the commencement of general war. Now, Germany simply could not afford to wait, for almost all other military establishments that might be involved (including the British navy) were already under partial or total mobilization. Russian mobilization against Austria-Hungary represented the *casus foederis* for Germany; Germany's mobilization against Russia would be the same for France; and French involvement must raise the question whether Britain could honorably expose the denuded French coast to German naval attacks.

Late on July 30 the German government demanded that Russia halt mobilization within twelve hours. The following day, failing satisfactory response, Germany, the last power to take steps preparatory to mobilization, proclaimed a state of threatening danger of war *(drohende Kriegsgefahr)*. The same day Austria-Hungary commenced mobilizing her armies facing Galicia. On the afternoon of August 1 the German ambassador to Russia, von Pourtales, after urging Sazonov in vain to revoke the mobilization order, delivered the declaration of war. Next an ultimatum was dispatched to Paris. She replied that France "would act in accordance with her interests." Germany responded with a declaration of war on her, too. Here the exigencies of the Schlieffen Plan forced Germany to act swiftly in the west before wheeling her manhood around to deal the coup de grace to the giant in the east. Italy, meanwhile, declared neutrality. On August 2 German troops invaded Luxemburg. When Brussels refused free passage on the third, the German army, following a modified version of the Schlieffen Plan, which spared the Netherlands, invaded Belgium. Britain then sent an ultimatum to Berlin, followed by a declaration of war at midnight on August 4.

By dawn of August 5 the ring was closed, and one of the greatest and least justifiable wars in history had begun. Both Bethmann-Hollweg and Lord Grey understood its deeper significance from the outset: a proud civilization, with an aristocratic-bourgeois patina, was about to expire.

Germany's Guilt

The question of German guilt for the coming of the war has been the subject of heated debate ever since Leon Trotsky published the incriminating secret treaties reposing in the Russian imperial archives. On the basis of the later voluminous serial publications by most of the belligerent governments, a majority of serious students of the war guilt question *(Kriegschuldfrage)* came to reject the exclusive indictment that had been brought against the Central Powers in Article 231 of the Treaty of Versailles. The revisionist view, represented by such scholars as William Langer, Erich Brandenburg, Hermann Oncken, Sidney B. Fay, Georges Michon, and Alfred von Wegerer, was more commonly accepted by historians than the view, associated with Bernadotte Schmitt and Pierre Renouvin, that stressed the paramount guilt of the Central Powers.

Until 1959 the prevailing attitude was that the German government had worked as conscientiously as any to avert war. Two generations of scholars had, in the main, concluded that: (1) Germany had sincerely striven to localize the conflict in the Balkans until Russian mobilization took the initiative out of the hands of the statesmen; and (2) German foreign policy in the July crisis was neither dominated by a resolve to break up the Triple Entente nor to wage war for the sake of territorial gain or economic preferment. "The long time dominating view outside Germany," wrote Erich Eyck in 1948, "that William II and his ministers consciously steered towards World War is today everywhere abandoned."*

In 1952 the first volume of Luigi Albertini's three-volume study of the origins of the war appeared, challenging this traditionalist view and reasserting the cardinal war guilt of Germany. Between 1959 and 1961 the first systematic attempt since World War II by a major German historian to demolish the eclectic view of German war guilt appeared. On the basis of new archival materials, Fritz Fischer of Hamburg University concluded that the main influence on German official prewar and wartime foreign policy had been monopoly capitalism and that the government, far from having entertained moderate aims, pursued from beginning to end expansionist objectives. Fischer and his disciples ascribed aggressive motives to virtually every major decision taken by the German government between 1913 and 1918 and redirected the attention of students of the question of war guilt to the economic interests that allegedly dictated Bethmann's foreign policy. In a range of publications from 1959 to 1969 Fischer argued that Bethmann predicated his crisis diplomacy on the conviction that Britain would remain neutral in a continental war and that consequently Germany and Austria-Hungary would be able to initiate hostilities with the overriding objective of destroying the Triple Entente and slamming Russia back further east.

A Fronde of German historians, led by Gerhard Ritter, Wolfgang Steglich, Egmont Zechlin, Golo Mann, Andreas Hillgruber, Eberhard von Vietsch, and Wolfgang Mommsen did not hesitate to set about demolishing Fischer's central theses. These in return received support from Klaus Wernecke and Immanuel Geiss and Fischer's doctoral students. Scholars in the Soviet Union, France, the USA, and Australia were drawn into the increasingly acrimonious dispute. In the end, most West German historians repudiated Fischer's extremist theses and reaffirmed the traditional view of the basic probity, moderation, and pacific inclinations of Bethmann-Hollweg. Soviet historians, such as W. I. Salov, V. M. Khvostov, P. N. Efremov, and I. V. Bestuzhev, mindful that the Fischer perspective compromises the Leninist proposition of the equal guilt of all imperialist nations, have recently played heavily in the center of the keyboard again. On the other hand, the East German historians Fritz Klein, Kurt Stenkewitz, Willibald Gutsche, and Joachim Petzold stress that Germany's ruling classes were more responsible than those of other countries for the catastrophe.

The most recent scholarship (von Vietsch, W. J. Mommsen, Egmont Zechlin, Konrad Jarausch, Dieter Groh), which rests upon unpublished embassy reports, personal papers *(Nachlässe)*, and the diary of Bethmann's confidant, Kurt Riezler,

---

Das persönliche Regiment Wilhelms II (Zurich, 1948), p. 781.

exculpates Bethmann from a lust for territorial accessions or hegemonial world power, as well as from a conscious desire to plunge Europe into general war for whatsoever purpose. His "blank check" to Austria-Hungary was inspired, as Zechlin has affirmed in harmony with the older scholarship, by dark fears of a growing encirclement and of future Russian domination of Europe, rendered more terrifying as a result of a developing Anglo-Russian alliance, discussions for the formation of which Grey had falsely denied. Contrary to Fischer, Geiss, Pogge-Strandmann, and Wernecke, William II and Bethmann were certain that England would enter any continental war, if only to prevent Germany from crushing France. On the other hand, ironically, a declaration of British neutrality would only have played directly into the hands of Moltke and the war party in the Reich and probably would have frustrated Bethmann's efforts to block hostilities.

Although Bethmann counted upon Britain's aid to keep the general peace, he was at pains to avoid any overt action that might provoke a Russian attack. Nevertheless, he *did* take a calculated risk in July. Hard-pressed by his internal foes and weary of the losing struggle to maintain the peace of Europe, Bethmann compromised with the war hawks by accepting the suggestion of the "blank check" to Vienna. He did so, believing that, as in 1909 and 1913, Russia, enjoying minimal encouragement from England, would not fight.

If the support Bethmann gave to Berchtold irritated the Russian government, France's "blank check" of late July to Russia antagonized the Central Powers. Nor is there any evidence that the French government ever retracted its endorsement of Russia's provocative course or endeavored to bridle St. Petersburg. For her part, Russia enormously increased tensions by encouraging Serbian nationalist agitation and backing Belgrade to the hilt. Above all else, it was Russia's impetuous mobilization when Vienna was beginning to be accommodating that put the match to the European powder keg. As respects Great Britain, she was a member of a Triple Entente, which, as P. J. V. Rolo has affirmed, had become an anti-German combination and was on the way to becoming a Triple Alliance. Her naval conversations with Russia in 1914, which Grey denied, weakened Bethmann's position against the war party in Germany. Britain's decision to go to war in 1914 was in no case solely a reaction to the German invasion of Belgium but, as has recently been argued by Samuel R. Williamson, was strongly influenced by the Anglo-French Entente and the military staff talks.

Chapter 44

GERMANY'S FIRST WORLD WAR

The Odds Against Victory

Throughout the war the scales were tipped heavily against the Central Powers. Although Germany, Austria-Hungary, Turkey, and Bulgaria had the advantage of operating along interior lines and had superiority in artillery fire, their combined population and military strength were much less than those of the Entente. By the close of 1914 the Central Powers, with a combined population of 137 million Europeans, had 136 divisions, while the Entente had 256 million Europeans and 199 divisions. Whereas Germany had 27 dreadnoughts and the Central Powers a total of 35 older battleships, the Entente had 44 dreadnoughts and 71 older ships of the line. In cruiser and destroyer strength Entente supremacy was even greater. The vast superiority of the Entente and Allied Powers in manpower, war materiel, and food steadily increased as more nations joined their camp.

In 1914 Germany possessed a field army of 2 million men, backed up by 3.8 million reservists. Whereas the 87 German divisions in the west fought well, the armies of Austria-Hungary, which totaled 49 divisions, were sapped by internal nationality conflicts and handicapped by language barriers. The French army, which was as zealous as the German, comprised 62 divisions at the outset, but each was slightly larger than a German division. The Russian field army was vast, numbering 114 divisions, but although its soldiers were capable of extreme endurance, they were led by generally incapable commanders and were hamstrung by munitions shortages. The British army, a highly trained professional corps in 1914, numbered only seven divisions, totaling 125,000 men. As the fighting progressed Germany by the spring of 1916 increased her combat forces to 4.5 million, France (with a smaller population) to 3.5 million, and Russia to 6 million. After introduction of compulsory military service, Britain increased her army by 1916 to 66 divisions, or 2.7 million troops. The largest external reenforcements of Allied strength came from the entrance of Italy into the war in the spring of 1915 and the USA in the spring of 1917. Only the collapse of tsarist Russia in March, 1917, enabled the Central Powers to replenish their depleted reserves on the Western Front and kindle the hope that France might still be beaten before the American tidal wave arrived.

In view of the odds, a protracted war of attrition had to be avoided by the Central Powers. Without command of the seas, which would have insured a flow of war materiel and food, Germany must either shatter the foe at the outset, or the Central Powers would either be starved out or bled to death. These unspeakable alternatives to a blitzkrieg go far to explain the almost mystical reliance of the German nation upon the Schlieffen Plan. All eyes were riveted on the 66-year-old chief of the general staff, Helmuth von Moltke, bearer of his uncle's illustrious name.

The First Battle of the Marne

No battle of World War I was as decisive as the First Battle of the Marne, fought on the Western Front between September 5 and 12, 1914. If Germany had won that battle, the war would have been over within a few months. As it was, the successful French defense determined that the conflict would be long, sanguinary, and exhausting.

Gerhard Ritter has demonstrated that the modified Schlieffen Plan not only envisioned the assumption of enormous risks but posed very nearly insuperable technical and logistical difficulties. The demands it made exceeded Germany's war capability. Although the implementation of this plan brought the condemnation of almost the whole civilized world down upon Germany's head, there is no good reason to think that it could successfully have been executed even if Moltke had not modified it.

The initial object of the plan was to achieve the defeat of the French by circumventing their strong fortress system of Epernil-Nancy-Verdun-Belfort and the wooded terrain of the Ardennes. This was to be done by a German invasion of Belgium, but not the Dutch Maastricht appendix. The success of the plan postulated an irresistably strong German right wing, which was to wheel through Belgium and northeastern France, enveloping Paris as it went, driving the French armies before it until they were shattered in a great battle west of the Vosges and their remnants flattened up against the German left wing under Bavarian Crown Prince Rupprecht. The beauty of the plan was that Rupprecht's forces were to be left intentionally weak so as to draw the French out from their fortresses and invite them to attack Alsace. In this way the revolving-door concept would inexorably be brilliantly realized. Unfortunately for the Germans the aging and ailing Moltke deprived the Schlieffen Plan of its subtlety. He not only weakened the German right by dispatching two army corps to the succor of hard-pressed East Prussia, but he also strengthened Rupprecht's army.

While Moltke must bear ultimate responsibility for the loss of the First Battle of the Marne, considerable blame must also be assigned to the commander of the German First Army, the 68-year-old, irascible General von Kluck. He led the extreme right wing of the German armies, which was to be the hammerhead of the whole wheeling movement. Although his troops had the greatest distance to traverse, he disobeyed orders to remain in echelon with General von Bülow's Second Army. In the hope of outflanking the French left wing, Kluck deliberately moved forward too rapidly in spite of the exhaustion of his troops and the lack of reinforcements that never came. He thus allowed a fatal gap to develop, amounting to a two days' march, between his army and Bülow's and rendered his own position untenable. Thereupon, the French, who had already suffered 300,000 casualties in a ghastly attack upon Rupprecht's forces along the Vosges, counterattacked and brought the German advance to a standstill. The Battle of the Marne was over, and the Schlieffen Plan had failed. Germany had now to fight the protracted two-front war she had long dreaded. Moltke correctly assessed the situation when on the morrow of the Battle of the Marne he wired the kaiser: "Sire, we have lost the war!"

Trench Warfare in the West

After the Battle of Ypres in Belgium in early November, 1914, open warfare ended in the west until the summer of 1918. The opposing armies were deadlocked. Operations bogged down and were characterized by extreme immobility, the massing of huge concentrations of troops and guns on a narrow sector, ear-splitting artillery barrages in support of infantry going "over the top" in the face of a hail of machine gun bullets, and insane offensives for the conquest of a few square miles of desolate terrain and blasted villages. Life on the Western Front was for most combatants an endless nightmare, punctuated by orgies of bloodshed. Soldiers lived like moles in a labyrinth of vermin- and rat-infested trenches, in which they froze in the winter and baked in the summer or through which they swashed in mud and water. Between opposing multiple rows of trenches lay a shell-pocked "no man's land," mournful as the surface of the moon. In this area between the lines ran parallel skeins of twisted telephone cables and miles and miles of protective barbed wire entanglements secured on twisted iron stakes. Artillery and the machine gun lorded it over the battlefield until September, 1916, when the British inaugurated the era of armor by introducing the tank in the Battle of the Somme. Although, in general, German artillery preponderated, the French possessed an unsurpassed gun in the 75 mm. recoiling field piece, which, where it was present in sufficient numbers, gave them a ballistic advantage over the Germans.

Gallantry and idealism inspired the fighting men of both sides at the outset but gradually gave way to cynicism, brutality, depravity, and mutiny as the armies of the belligerents sustained ever more appalling and senseless losses. In many a contest on the Western Front during 1914 and 1915 the killed and wounded exceeded 100,000, as in the first and second battles of Ypres, and the engagements in the Champagne, and at Artois and Loos. In the Champagne campaign of May–June, 1915, the French lost 100,000 men, the Germans 178,000. Yet such losses paled beside those yet to come in the vast Battle of Verdun.

Open Warfare in the East

A wilderness of space on the Eastern Front made a continuous, fortified line an impossibility. There the war was one of movement, of outflanking operations and grand-scale encirclements, involving the capture of hundreds of thousands of prisoners at a time and the conquest of thousands of square miles of territory.

In August, 1914, the Austrians had launched an ill-fated offensive on the Galician front, but the German Eighth Army, under General von Prittwitz, remained on the defensive in East Prussia, pending the outcome of the campaign for France. However, when two Russian armies under Generals Rennenkampf and Samsonov converged upon East Prussia from the east and south, Moltke, losing his nerve, reenforced Prittwitz at the expense of the right wing of the western armies. On August 22 General Erich Ludendorff (1865–1937), a brilliant strategist, was sent to the Eastern Front as chief of staff to the aging General Paul von Beneckendorff and von Hindenburg (1847–1934). When the Germans counterattacked on August 26, Samsonov's army was swiftly separated from that of Rennenkampf and hacked to pieces at historic Tannenberg between August 27 and 30. Samsonov, heartbroken, went into the woods and shot himself. A few days later, on September 9, the Germans shattered Rennenkampf's army at the Masurian Lakes in East Prussia and captured 300,000 prisoners.

Mid-September found the Russians back at the San River. Yet they still held Galicia east of Przemysl as a result of their victory over the Austro-Hungarian armies under Archduke Frederick and General von Hötzendorff. Although the Austrian setback was eclipsed by the spectacular German triumph over the Russians, the melancholy truth could not be hidden that the armies of the Central Powers, despite 677,000 casualties, had failed to break out of the iron ring of the Entente. The Germanic territories had become a beleaguered fortress.

Falkenhayn's Chance

The ailing Moltke was replaced in mid-September by the Prussian minister of war, the energetic and domineering General Erich von Falkenhayn (1861–1922), who was also chief of the general staff. He tried frantically to rescue the Schlieffen Plan and outflank the Allied left in Flanders. Antwerp was captured by the Germans, but in October their advance in the Ostend-Ypres sector was checked by British and Empire troops, while the Belgians, who opened the sluice gates, turned the battlefield into a sea of mud. Subsequently Falkenhayn launched a whole series of attacks in Flanders but without positive results. Thereafter he decided to abandon the Schlieffen concept entirely. The German armies in the west were ordered to remain on the defensive throughout 1915, while Falkenhayn divided his attention between driving the Russians out of Poland and persuading the tsar's government to negotiate a separate peace.

A factor determining Falkenhayn to make his main effort in the east was the entry of the Ottoman Empire on the side of the Central Powers on November 1, 1914. In Berlin the authorities now envisaged the consolidation of all the lands from the North Sea to Persia into a huge dike that would cut Russia off from the Allies. The only obstacle to this plan was Serbia; the only menace Britain. She, all during 1915, tried desperately, but without success, at the Dardanelles and Gallipoli to open a supply corridor to southern Russia.

While the British were running into stone-wall Turkish resistance, Falkenhayn tried for a knockout blow against Russia. He sent the Eleventh Army under Field Marshal von Mackensen to aid Ludendorff and Hindenburg. In May, 1915, the Germans stove a deep hole in enemy lines in Galicia and proceeded to drive the Russians back rapidly so that by the end of the year all Poland and Lithuania were under German and Austrian occupation. They had taken 300,000 prisoners, and

Falkenhayn had won a magnificent victory, but the Russians had not hoisted the white flag. On the other hand, in October Bulgaria had been influenced by the course of battle to cast her lot in with the Central Powers. Counteracting this had been the fact that Italy had entered the war on the Allied side in May, 1915 and a third front had thus been opened. After Italy's plunge, the German shortage of manpower revealed itself as more acute, for the new diversion for Austria-Hungary only put a heavier burden upon the German armies in Poland.

Falkenhayn counted upon the steadily weakening Russian morale to bring him the separate peace he needed. By fall of 1915 it was open knowledge that the tsarist army was scandalously short of guns and ammunition, that men in rear battalions had often to wait for those in the front lines to be shot down so that they could pick up the latter's rifles, and that defeatism was spreading among the masses. To convince the tsarist government of the hopelessness of its position, Falkenhayn resolved to smash Serbia, eliminate the Balkan theater of war, and erect an impenetrable land blockade against the Romanov Empire. Falkenhayn also aimed at relieving hard-pressed Austria-Hungary, clearing the Berlin-to-Constantinople railway line, and keeping Turkey in the fray. After Bulgaria's belligerency had been duly purchased with territorial promises, the axe fell on Serbia. German, Austrian, and Bulgarian armies launched converging attacks that overwhelmed the Serbs, who retreated through the mountains of Albania, where thousands of them died from exposure in the bitter cold. Subsequently thousands of Montenegrin troops were captured, and the German and Austrian troops drove to the Greek frontier.

Even these impressive victories failed to induce the Russians to sue for peace. Falkenhayn at length had no alternative but to try once again for victory in the west. This he vaguely hoped to do by attacking at some point of critical importance that the French would have to defend even if they bled to death doing it. If a mortal defeat could be inflicted upon the French, the English, Falkenhayn thought, might realize the folly of persevering in support of their ally.

Still in occupation of extensive tracts of Belgian and French soil, the Germans were in a position to call the time of attack and take the initiative from favorable ground. Falkenhayn selected Verdun, the key to the defenses of eastern France and the historic road from the east to Paris. The Battle of Verdun was one of the longest and bloodiest in all history. It commenced on February 21, 1916, and lasted till the following December 15. The Germans are said to have lost 615,000 men; and the French and British combined, nearly as many. There is some doubt in the minds of military experts whether Falkenhayn was not striving to achieve a Cannae, a battle of annihilation, rather than wear the defenders down. If this were, in fact, his aim, his best chance came in March when the Germans mounted a massive drive across the Forges River, a tributary of the Meuse. After denting the French lines 2½ miles, the attackers were drowned in blood on Mort Homme hill. After that there was no more chance for a Cannae, for both the British and Russians were about to mount offensives to relieve Verdun. Nevertheless, the Germans advanced doggedly in a series of limited pushes prepared by short but intensive bombardments. On June 7, when Fort de Vaux fell, Verdun was in sight. But by then the weary Germans had shot their bolt.

At this juncture the Russians, under the able General Brusilov, passed over onto a general offensive on a 300-mile front. With 130 divisions against 42 for the Germans (under Prince Leopold of Bavaria) and Austrians, the Russian armies between July 3 and August 8 advanced from 40 to 85 miles from Khust to Czernowitz. At terrific cost to themselves the Russians bagged 400,000 prisoners. It was Russia's last great effort of the war. Brusilov had forced Falkenhayn to detach troops from the western theater and send them to the aid of the reeling Austrians. Russian successes also persuaded Rumania to enter the war on August 27 on the side of the Allies, but too late to make a critical difference in the outcome of the battle on the Eastern Front. The Brusilov offensive also toppled Falkenhayn, who was demoted. He had grossly underestimated the recuperative powers of the Russian army. In late August, 1916, he was replaced as chief of the general staff by Hindenburg, who took Ludendorff with him to the Western Front. Last, the great Russian thrust was a major factor in turning the tide at Verdun, for it coincided with the very heavy but less successful British relief offensive on the Somme, which began on July 1. Together, the Russians and British made it possible for the French to slug their way back again and regain almost all the ground they had lost around Verdun. However, from the Russian standpoint the Brusilov offensive was a Cadmean victory. Before it ground to a sickening halt in October, it had cost the Romanov Empire a million casualties and pushed it down the chute of revolution.

The Fall of Rumania and
the Romanov Empire

Instead of coming to the support of Brusilov, Rumania concentrated its effort on the conquest of Transylvania. Although the Rumanians easily penetrated the Carpathian passes, German divisions were soon rushed eastward through Hungary to meet the new threat. General Falkenhayn's Ninth Army collaborated with a conglomerate force of Germans, Bulgarians, and Turks under General Mackensen to humble the Rumanians. In a brilliant campaign commencing on September 30 the armies of the Central Powers swept over the Rumanian plain and forced the Danube. On December 5 Falkenhayn entered Bucharest in triumph. Three weeks later all Rumania, save Moldavia, had been occupied by the forces of the Central Powers.

Ever since the appointment of Hindenburg and Ludendorff to the general staff on August 29, 1916, the reality of political power had been gravitating into their hands. Although they promised that they would win the war not by diplomacy but on the battlefields, the prospects of victory were actually remote. The German armies in the west had been terribly battered and wearied by their Herculean efforts at Verdun and on the Somme during 1916, and esprit was declining dangerously. All during the autumn and winter of 1916–17, therefore, the general staff took steps to substitute a strategy of minimal for maximal objectives. One of the most formidable defense lines in the whole history of warfare was built—the Siegfried-Stellung, known to the Allies as the ''Hindenburg Line,'' which ran from Arras in the British sector to a point just north of Soissons in the French.

The pessimistic implication of these preparations was hidden by the collapse of imperial Russia. Overwhelmed by 6 million casualties and crippled by incurable munitions and food shortages, the Romanov regime was finally overthrown on March 12, 1917, by the workers of Petrograd. Although the first Russian Revolution did not eliminate Russia as a military factor or lead at once to a separate peace with the Central Powers, it encouraged the hope in Germany that the strategy of Ludendorff and Hindenburg would ultimately bring general victory. Clearly, the eastern jaw of the Allied vice on Germany was cracking. What was not appreciated in jubilant Berlin was that the ensuing democratization of Russia would influence the United States of America to enter the war less than a month later.

The War at Sea

Despite their crushing numerical naval superiority, the British and French fleets were unable to destroy the German High Seas Fleet in any Trafalgar-like battle. From the outset, Admiral Jellicoe's fleet was in complete command of the Channel and North Sea. The naval balance was tipped even more heavily against the Germans when on August 29, 1914, Admiral Beatty's squadron sank several light cruisers in Helgoland Bay. But thereafter, the German High Seas Fleet remained until May, 1916, bottled up in the Jade, protected by the big guns of Wilhelmshaven.

In the face of crushing Allied naval superiority, the few German cruisers that were on the seas when war broke out could only prey on enemy commerce. The most famous of them, the *Emden*, was destroyed in the Indian Ocean on November 9, 1914. Admiral Count von Spee's small flotilla, including the cruisers *Scharnhorst* and *Gneisenau*, did manage to batter a British cruiser squadron that autumn, but several battle cruisers soon hunted Spee down and sank four of his vessels off the Falkland Islands on December 8. That ended even moderate-scale surface operations by Germany until the Battle of Jutland.

In hope of annihilating a British squadron that had been lured out, the German High Seas Fleet, under Vice Admiral Reinhard Scheer (1863–1928), sailed from the Jade on May 31, 1916, into waters west of Denmark (Jutland). There Scheer stumbled onto the British Grand Fleet that had just been concentrated in the North Sea. Grand Admiral Jellicoe succeeded in putting his ships between Scheer and his base, but in the ensuing engagement the British sustained a grave tactical defeat, for they lost three battle cruisers, three cruisers, eight destroyers, and 6,784 men, while the Germans lost one battleship, one battle cruiser, four light cruisers, five destroyers, and 3,079 men. However, Jutland was a strategic victory for the Allies inasmuch as the German fleet, which escaped under cover of night, did not sally forth from its anchorage again for the rest of the war.

In the absence of opportunities for grand-scale engagements between armadas,

each side strove to inflict maximum damage upon the economy and civilian population of its adversary. This game was played with garish arrogance by the Allies,
whose surface ship captains were under orders to seize practically all oceanic
freight that might be of comfort to the foe, and stealthily and brutally by the Germans through offensive submarine (*Unterseeboot*, U-boat) action.

From the outset of hostilities the British arbitrarily extended the scope and definition of contraband to include goods that had never been put in that category by
the Declaration of London in 1909. That document, to which most of the naval
powers of the world had subscribed, aimed at mitigating the asperities of war for
civilians by recognizing categories of conditional contraband (e.g., food, fodder,
fuel, and clothing) and "free" articles, comprising most raw materials and cotton,
which were not liable to seizure at sea. Although the Germans unreservedly accepted the Declaration of London, the British parliament had never ratified it.
Instead, as the war progressed, Britain elevated maritime nihilism to a system.
She progressively extended the meaning of contraband until it was made to cover
virtually everything of actual or presumed value to the foe. Nevertheless, the
British never succeeded in imposing anything more than a "paper blockade"
upon the Central Powers, because they could be provisioned from Scandinavia
through the Baltic, which Germany dominated, or from Switzerland, or, for a
time, through the ports of neutral Italy.

When, in violation of the canons of maritime law, the British on November 3,
1914, declared the North Sea a military area in which all neutral craft would be
liable to search and seizure, the Germans responded on February 4, 1915, by
launching a submarine offensive against the United Kingdom. The Germans were
also acting in retaliation for the fact that enemy merchant vessels were frequently
armed and often flew a neutral flag. The German declaration proclaimed the waters
around the British Isles a war zone in which enemy or neutral ships were liable
to be sunk without warning, which meant without regard to the lives of crews or
passengers. The worst casualty of the submarine war was the sinking of the British
liner *Lusitania* on May 7, 1915, which, however, was carrying a heavy shipment
of ammunitions for the Allies (at the time staunchly denied). The *Lusitania* was
torpedoed with the loss of 1,198 lives, 128 of whom were American.

In the blockade tournament the Allies enjoyed vastly superior resources, so
that the Germans were at a great disadvantage. Tirpitz had flagrantly neglected
the undersea naval arm. As a consequence, German submarines were too small
and flimsy, too few in number, and had too short a cruising radius to starve out the
British. In June, 1915, the Germans had only 40 U-boats, and in April, 1916, no
more than 52, of which only 18 were in operation at one time. At its height, the
underwater fleet comprised only 148 units. In the course of the war Germany lost
199 submarines to enemy action, including mines and depth charges.

Nevertheless the innovative submarines inflicted huge losses upon Allied shipping before the British in the spring of 1917 found a way to nullify the menace by
using warships to convoy merchant vessels to the British Isles. At the peak of the
submarine offensive the Irish southwestern coastal approaches became a cemetery
for Allied freighters and even passenger liners. In the fearful three months follow-

ing commencement of "unrestricted" submarine warfare on January 31, 1917, about 2 million tons of Allied and neutral shipping were sent to the bottom. The British alone suffered the loss of 470 vessels. Yet, in the end the submarine campaign not only failed to force the British to hoist the white flag but was the main factor that impelled the United States to abandon an uncertain neutrality and declare war (April 6–7, 1917).

On June 5, 1915, and May 4, 1916, the German government, fearful of the repercussions of the submarine offensive on neutral opinion, had ordered a relaxation of operations. If, thereafter, passenger ships continued occasionally to be torpedoed, this did not form part of any systematic official policy. Chancellor von Bethmann-Hollweg was, however, under the heaviest kind of pressure from the general staff, admiralty, and Reichstag majority to resume unrestricted submarine warfare. After the Allies ignored his December, 1916, peace note, Bethmann found it all but impossible to resist a demand that had the backing of the majority of a desperate German people. Perceiving that renewal of the submarine offensive would both give Wilson the pretext he was seeking to bring the USA into the war and at the same time hoist Ludendorff and the military to supreme power in the Reich, Bethmann-Hollweg fought manfully against the inevitable. Since, however, he could not promise the German nation an honorable peace from an enemy that was resolved to fight the war *à outrance*, he authorized (but under formal protest) resumption of unrestricted submarine warfare, to become effective on January 31, 1917.

The Western Front in 1917

In 1917 the Germans stood on the defensive in the west while waiting with baited breath for the Russian surrender. The construction of the Hindenburg Line made possible an effective holding operation with minimal losses, which nevertheless were more than Germany could tolerate. After inflicting a fearful artillery battering upon the Germans, the Allied forces mounted a major attack around Arras and Soissons in mid-April. The objective of the French General Nivelle, who was an exponent of limitless offensive action, was Laon. However, the Hindenburg Line withstood the heaviest kind of bombardment, and, for the sake of a gain of five miles of mud, the British in the Arras sector lost 150,000 killed and wounded.

Unwilling to abandon the offensive, Nivelle now ordered one of the most massive assaults in French military history. The Second Battle of the Aisne, which was joined on April 16, forced the Germans to commit 36 of their remaining 52 reserve divisions. French gains were miniscule. However, the effort, which cost the French another 100,000 men, led to Nivelle's replacement by the defense-minded Henri Pétain as field commander-in-chief. Nivelle's attack, moreover, caused a breakdown of discipline in the French army, for in May mutiny spread to 54 divisions, as a result of which more than 20,000 soldiers were court-martialled.

The unreliability of the French army now caused the British to shoulder a disproportionately large part of the burden in the west. They tried to keep the Germans under pressure by attacking, on June 7 at Messines Ridge and again in mid-July at Passchendaele near Ypres. Although the British hardly dented the German lines, casualties on both sides were staggering, reaching a combined total of 500,000 troops. Subsequently in the Battle of Cambrai the British introduced the armored tank and temporarily effected a deeper penetration at less cost than any the Allies had achieved till then. But the British exhausted their reserves in the initial attack, and almost all territory won was regained by the Germans in a counteroffensive. Then followed the appalling Third Battle of Ypres from mid-July to mid-November, which the British and Empire troops carried against the Germans with virtually no French support. In this campaign, fought in one vast bog of mud, the British lost 240,000 men. German losses were possibly even higher—260,000. Meanwhile, the French at Verdun in August and at the Chemin des Dames ridge in October erased some of the salients in the Hindenburg Line.

In October, 1917, fortune turned her wan smile upon the German Reich for the last time. Italy almost collapsed, and the Russian provisional government was so artfully undermined by the Bolsheviks that it was overthrown by Lenin and Trotsky on November 7.

General Otto Below's Fourteenth German Army, operating in the Julian Alps in the upper Isonzo River area, dealt a staggering blow to the Italians in the Battle of Caporetto (October 25–November 2). The Germans, supported by the Austrians, penetrated 80 miles to the Piave River, bagged 275,000 prisoners of war and huge quantities of war materiel. The Italian armies were only narrowly rescued by French and British divisions in November.

The annexationist Russian provisional government, which chose to ignore the popular clamor for peace, had launched a last, forlorn offensive against the Austrians. General Brusilov had driven the Germans and Austrians back across the old Galician battlefields in early July, but when they had counterattacked under the brilliant General Hoffmann, Ludendorff's old aide, the Russian front had broken like thin ice. By September the Russian armies were mutinous, the Germans had taken Riga, and Kerensky's government, discredited by military defeats and an attempted coup by Kornilov, was stumbling toward the grave.

Since 1915 the Germans had been using the threat of revolution to help persuade the tsarist government to desert its allies. Russian revolutionaries had been subsidized by the Reich ministry. Finally, in April, 1917, it transported the archrevolutionary Lenin from Switzerland through Germany to Russia. The accession of Lenin to power on November 7, 1917, was the prelude to attainment of official German policy objectives in the east.

Brest-Litovsk

In December the Bolsheviks proceeded to redeem their peace pledge to the Russian people. Plenipotentiaries of Germany and Austria-Hungary met with the Russians at Brest-Litovsk on December 20. The latter proposed a settlement on the basis of "no annexations and no indemnities," a formula that had been endorsed by a majority in the Reichstag. The foreign minister of Austria-Hungary (1916–18), Count Ottokar Czernin (1872–1932), who responded for the Central Powers' delegation, agreed to the Bolsheviks' proposal on condition that all other belligerents accept it also as the basis for a negotiated general settlement. When the Allies ignored the invitation to join the peace conference, the arch-annexationist Ludendorff, who was now the dominant political and military authority in Central Europe, demanded that Russians cede all Poland, Courland, Latvia, Esthonia, Finland, and the Ukraine. Although the bulk of the territory that was to be surrendered was not marked for outright annexation by Germany or Austria-Hungary, there can be no doubt that the areas mentioned were to be reduced to satellites of the two great Central Powers. Considering the dissolving state of the Russian army and the fact that the German armies had occupied Kiev in early March, the Bolshevik government had no alternative but to sign on March 3, 1918, the Treaty of Brest-Litovsk.

By the Treaty of Brest-Litovsk Russia lost 62 million people and 1,267,000 square miles of territory, embracing a third of her arable, the bulk of her coal and iron mines, and a third of her factories. All German parties, except the two Socialist, endorsed the treaty. The Left Socialists or USPD (Unabhängige Sozialdemokratische Partei Deutschlands—Independent SPD) denounced it as a militaristic *Diktat* and rejected it absolutely. The Majority Socialists (SPD) admitted that this was true. However, while conceding that the policy of force in the east was contrary to the interests of the nation, "which require lasting, pacific relations and friendship between the German and Russian peoples," the SPD recognized that the adamant attitudes of the French, British, and American governments left the German authorities with virtually no alternative but to terminate the war in the east. Consequently the SPD merely abstained from the voting on the treaty.

The "Friedenssturm" of 1918

Ludendorff now resolved to win a decisive victory on the Western Front while the yawning gaps in the British armies had not yet been filled, American forces had not yet landed in sufficient numbers to break the Hindenburg Line, and German planes were inflicting more casualties upon the population of London than the earlier Zeppelin dirigibles had. Between March 21 and July 17, 1918, Ludendorff, with practically the whole fighting manpower of the fatherland at his back, embarked upon a gamble with the fate of Germany.

Supported by huge numbers of troops from the east, the Germans on the opening day of the so-called peace offensive *(Friedenssturm)* enjoyed numerical superiority on the Western Front for the first time since the early days of the war. They had 194 divisions to the Allied 173, both sides at reduced strength. In five stupendous assaults during those four months—against the British between Arras and La Fère and against the French along the Somme, again against the British on the Lys, against the French between Soissons and Reims, against the Allied salient around Amiens and Château-Thierry, and, finally, at Reims—the Germans usually had the advantage of surprise and fought with valor and even skill. Paris was subjected to sporadic bombardment with long-range guns, and at one time (June 3) the Germans were again within 55 miles of it along the Marne. Nevertheless, the offensive was a boulder rolled into the sea. Ludendorff's generalship was not worthy of the colossal sacrifices he demanded of his troops. Repeatedly, as after March, when a significant penetration had brought the German tide to the outer defenses of Amiens or after May 27 when his armies had won considerable ground between Soissons and Reims, Ludendorff showed unaccountable reluctance to exploit brilliant initial successes. He husbanded his dwindling reserves like a miser nearing bankruptcy. Had he been more daring, the Germans might conceivably have achieved a breakthrough in March or April.

Ludendorff's last push, around Reims beginning July 15, was a catastrophe for the Germans. At the outset they lost all their tanks to French artillery and were stopped cold. It was the last great effort of the Reich, for in the *Friedenssturm* she had suffered a million casualties and had nothing more to give.

Meanwhile, the Allies had established a united command under Generalissimo Foch, and Austria-Hungary had been virtually knocked out of the war when on June 15 the Italians won a major victory on the Piave. American troops were appearing in the battle lines (notably at Château-Thierry in connection with Ludendorff's last offensive) in greatly increased numbers, and Germany was henceforth left to face the waxing strength of the foe alone. Plans for Ludendorff's sixth assault—Case Hagen—were scrapped when on July 18 the French commenced the first in a series of major and almost continuing counteroffensives that by November 11 overran all of the defenses of the Hindenburg triple line and forced the Germans back to the Ardennes, Sedan, Mons, and Ghent. During that time over a million American troops had come to reenforce the Allied counteroffensive. Nevertheless, in spite of shortages of munitions, guns, and artillery and an air force that numbered only 2,600 first-line planes to 3,300 for the British air force alone, the Germans conducted their retreat with great skill. The disparity of forces—217 Allied to 193 German and 4 Austrian divisions—was by the time of the Armistice not sufficiently great that the Allies could have delivered a knockout blow. But Ludendorff had fallen prey to hysterical fears. The war lord who in March had been positive that he could win the peace on the battlefield and had evinced no sympathy for defeatists, on September 29 pleaded with the government for an armistice within forty-eight hours! As he had earlier exaggerated the country's war capability, he now underestimated it, for his armies still stood everywhere on enemy soil. However, when the mythical heroes of Tannenberg were revealed to have feet of clay, the heart went out of the German nation. With the same impulsive, childish trust they had shown toward Hindenburg and Ludendorff, the German masses now fixed upon Wilson. They looked to the man of the Fourteen Points as to a savior who would lead a contrite world to a conciliatory peace.

Chapter 45

WAR AIMS AND THE HOME FRONT

Formation of the "Burgfrieden"

In early August, 1914, the German people were convinced that they were fighting a fundamentally defensive war and that they could not afford simply to wait until their enemies invaded the Reich. This viewpoint had the endorsement of the nation's most distinguished intellectuals, 93 of whom signed a memorandum to that effect. Among the signatures were those of Franz Liszt, Max Planck, Hermann Sudermann, Paul Ehrlich, Wilhelm Roentgen, Wilhelm Wundt, and Karl Lamprecht. The German Social Democratic party likewise renounced all thoughts of general strike or armed seizure of power. Abandoning its recent caustic criticism of the government's support of Austro-Hungarian policy in the Balkans, the SPD locked arms with the rest of the nation in an unprecedented civil peace *(Burgfrieden)*. In an hour of emotional empathy William II declared that he no longer recognized classes, parties, or interests, but only Germans.

The Triumph of Nationalism in the SPD

All during the July crisis the SPD had toiled with vigor and courage to compel the German government to keep the peace. Aware of the indifference of the SPD to the fate of the Dual Monarchy, all other sections of the Socialist Second International looked to the German for leadership in opposing the war. Disillusionment settled on the International when, however, the SPD reversed its attitude because of the Russian mobilization. The overwhelming majority of German Socialists rationalized their action with the argument that the enormity of the Russian provocation relieved the party of any duty save national defense, a duty which, in the face of a Russian attack, the SPD had never in its history denied. The Socialist rank and file did not even wait for its leaders after July 31. In the hectic hours following news of Russian mobilization, arguments that Germany dared not sit with hands folded until Russia's vast reserves of manpower cut through the country's feeble eastern defenses dispelled scattered objections everywhere.

Bethmann-Hollweg was, moreover, a real obstacle to Socialist opposition to the war. The Socialists believed that he was a sincere opponent of war and esteemed his honest record as chancellor. For his part, Bethmann-Hollweg did not wish to paralyze the war effort at the outset by needlessly suppressing the Socialist movement.

In the caucus of the Reichstag SPD group on August 3 one of the two party chairmen, Hugo Haase (1863–1919), adhered to the old revolutionary line and opposed the grant of war credits to the government. However, Eduard David (1863–1930), foreign policy expert of the SPD, held the majority in his palm. Most comrades agreed with him that the SPD could not stand aside in a crusade to liberate the Russian masses from despotism, that a Russian victory would set back the cause of the European working class, and that if the SPD left Germany in the lurch at such a time the party could kiss good-bye to its future political prospects. By a vote of 78 to 14 the Socialist deputies decided to vote for the war credits. Voting cut across prewar revisionist lines. Eduard Bernstein and Hugo Haase sided with Karl Kautsky and Karl Liebknecht in opposing. Karl Legien brought the support of the Free Trade Unions to the Socialist majority. Ultimately, however, all deputies bowed to the dictates of Reichstag group discipline, and on August 4 the SPD deputies announced in the lower house their unanimous support of the national war effort to achieve "the aim of security." Without a dissenting vote, the Socialist Reichstag bloc approved the war credits. From then until the spring of 1917 the majority of the party did not abandon hope that Bethmann-Hollweg would be able to achieve the conciliatory peace for which the European working class yearned.

War Aims

Extremely few were the German citizens who were prepared in 1914 to believe that the officials of the Reich had deliberately planned a general war out of desire for annexations or world power. It was believed that a fundamentally defense-minded Bethmann-Hollweg had given way only when it appeared that to rein the general staff any longer was to sacrifice Austria-Hungary and compromise the territorial integrity of Germany.

Two generations after World War I most historians have come to reject the thesis of the Fritz Fischer school that from beginning to end of the war all German governments pursued with astonishing continuity and determination a coordinated, graduated program of insatiable war aims, the attainment of which would confer upon the Reich paramountcy in Europe and the world. Most historians, inspired by the thinking of Gerhard Ritter, Walter Bussmann, Egmont Zechlin, E. von Vietsch, W. J. Mommsen, and Hans Herzfeld, found it difficult to lend credence to a view, unsupported by conclusive evidence, that ascribed aggressive motives to every important act or decision of the German government from 1913 to 1918. The notion of a continuity of German war aims is the result of a misunderstanding of the German predicament and of the possibilities open to the Reich government.

A memorandum of September 9, 1914, signed by the chancellor and unearthed by Fischer, is cited as proof that the German government from the outset of the war harbored the extravagant aim of achieving security in both east and west "for all imaginable time." To this end, the chancellor is supposed to have committed himself to the decisive weakening of France and to breaking Russian domination over the peoples of the western border states. The weakening of France was to be consummated—surely ineffectually if Bethmann were to confine himself to these terms—by annexing the iron ore fields of Briéy in Lorraine and by imposing a high war indemnity on France, possibly also by seizing Belfort and the western slopes of the Vosges. As respects Belgium, the memorandum spoke of annexing Liège and Verviers and adding a strip of Belgian Luxemburg to the Duchy of Luxemburg, which in its turn would be admitted to the Reich as a federal state. Beyond this, the memorandum spoke of reducing Belgium to economic and military vassalage to Germany. Nothing specific was said in the document respecting annexations in the east.

If this program had been seriously entertained and consummated by the German government it would have produced a momentous shift in the European balance of power. But so also would the realization of the war aims of England, France, and Russia, which, to judge by the secret treaties among them, were even more voracious than those of the "September Program." They envisaged the utter destruction of the Dual Monarchy, the confiscation of the German colonial empire, subtraction of Alsace-Lorraine and the Rhineland from the Reich, the annexation of West Prussia, Posen, and Silesia to Russian Poland, and the establishment of Russian control over the Straits and at Constantinople (Tsargorod). The "September Program" was never anything more than an impulsive effusion evoked by the jubilation that attended the German onrush toward the Marne and the initial titanic victories over Russia. These war aims harmonized neither with Bethmann's record of temperance, nor his desire for a lasting peace, nor even his known reluctance to introduce any more Slavs or Frenchmen into the German house.

It was not long before Bethmann reverted to his customary caution. By October, 1914, mindful of Moltke's gloomy message from the Marne, he was already principally concerned with extricating the fatherland from the quagmire into which she had stepped. A year later the chancellor had no more use for the formula of "securities and guarantees." After the grand campaigns on the Eastern Front failed to knock Russia out of the war in 1915, Bethmann lost hope of peace through victory. Thereafter he gave top priority to persuading Russia to sign a separate peace, and to this end he was prepared, at the slightest sign of a Russian willingness to negotiate, to drop annexationist war aims in the east. In the fall of 1915 he even offered to approve Russian control over the Straits and was ready to retrocede all or nearly all of occupied Poland to the Romanov Empire.

Although Bethmann entertained no territorial aims before the outbreak of war, once it began he probably would have welcomed modest territorial accessions: Briéy in France and, in the east, up to a line from Mitau to Vilna and the Narev River. Yet, as Werner Conze, Egmont Zechlin, Wolfgang Steglich, Karl-Heinz Janssen, and Hans Herzfeld have all persuasively argued, Bethmann-Hollweg would never have allowed rectifications of the border to stand in the way of a status quo peace and amicable postwar relations with France and Russia. Unfortunately, the war aims of the enemy left him very little latitude for a peace of understanding.

An old-fashioned, moderate nationalist, rather than a Pan-German or advocate of the extravagant annexationist program of the Zentralverband deutscher Industrieller, Bethmann pursued a policy that cut diagonally across the war aims of special interest groups and parties. As eclectic as he was philosophical, the chancellor was destined to conduct, with insufficient popular support, Germany's last stand against military dictatorship. It would have helped the cause of civil government if he could openly have renounced annexations and large indemnities. But it was the fatal weakness of his position that he could never point to a concrete Allied interest in negotiations, which would have justified this.

The Polish Riddle

In the knotty question as to what to do with Poland after the armies of the Central Powers had overrun that land in 1915 and expelled the Russians, the chancellor was at first against taking steps to organize an independent "Congress Poland." Only gradually, as hopes for separate peace with Russia dimmed, did Bethmann-Hollweg come to accept the idea, subject, of course, to the condition that Poland would seek protection from Germany.

The project of an "independent" Poland was popular with the German people, who wished to drive Russia back farther east. The SPD, for example, wanted to emancipate the Poles from tsarism, while the Center party wished to detach Polish Catholics from Orthodox Russia. Ludendorff, Falkenhayn, Hindenburg, and the military governor of German-occupied Poland, General von Beseler, had their eyes focused upon an "independent" Poland as a reservoir of troops for prosecuting the war against Russia. They disregarded the danger that a new center of Polish nationalism would pose for Austrian Galicia and Prussian Posen. Bethmann disapproved the generals' project because it would hopelessly alienate Russia. Nevertheless, the chancellor had finally to strike his colors because he could offer no evidence that the tsarist government was disposed to make a separate peace. On November 5, 1916, Poland, the first of the succession states to be created in World War I, came into being with the blessings of the German and Austro-Hungarian governments. The new state, formed without the cooperation of the Poles, was given an eastern boundary running along the line Kovno-Grodno-Brest-Litovsk.

Failure of the German Peace Note of
December 12, 1916

Bethmann-Hollweg still hoped to thwart the arch-annexationists. He pinned great hopes upon his peace note to the foe to participate in negotiations for a conciliatory settlement. Unfortunately, the German invitation, dated December 12, 1916, was silent as to specific terms. In any case, it was ignored or rejected by all of the Entente governments, which were bent on eliminating the Reich as a great power. The German note also irritated President Woodrow Wilson, who had been planning to mediate in lieu of his election promise to hold a peace conference. The American initiative elicited an unsatisfactory response in Allied capitals, where the governments were privately determined to fight on *à outrance* for annexationist aims contained in the secret treaties they had signed with each other. These aims committed them to the substantial reduction of the German land area, the dismemberment of Prussia, the destruction of the German colonial empire, and the Balkanization of central Europe. These purposes were not, of course, revealed to Wilson, for the aim of the Entente was not to find the way to a negotiated peace but to bring the USA into the war. For its part, the Reich government couched its reply to Wilson in guarded language, which led him to conclude that Germany would not renounce her designs on either Belgium or French Briéy.

The most tragic consequence of the failure of the December peace initiatives was the chancellor's capitulation on January 9, 1917, under protest, to the demands of the Army High Command *(Oberste Heeresleitung* or *OHL)* for unrestricted submarine warfare. Bethmann was also finally obliged on April 23 at the Kreuznach conference of the OHL to endorse, again under strong protest, its annexationist program in the east. This embraced territories reaching almost to Riga and Bukhovina, and stipulated detachment of the Ukraine from Russia.

By late April Bethmann-Hollweg was a lost man, abandoned by all. Nevertheless, he persisted in his view that the extravagant schemes of the Supreme Command could be achieved only if Germany were in position to dictate the peace, which was impossible. With this the kaiser concurred, but he had long since forfeited the controlling authority that had been assigned him under the constitution.

Governmental Coordination of the Economy

Germany was caught by surprise in 1914. She had not intended war. When she blundered into it, few Germans thought it would be a long one. This was all radically changed, however, when the German armies were decisively checked in the First Battle of the Marne. Many hopes were then laid to rest. As trench warfare consumed all forms of war materiel at an appalling rate, it became evident that the victor in the struggle would prevail only after he had utterly worn down the adversary and bled him white. The vast, prolonged battle of attrition into which the war swiftly developed determined that the German government would be obliged to exercise stringent controls over the nation's resources and manpower. State intervention in the affairs of labor and business was rendered the more imperative as the impact of the British blockade upon the Reich's military and civilian population became ever more severe. The nation was exposed to privation and acute shortages of resources, while the blockade destroyed German commerce and foreign investments. By contrast, the Entente countries had easy access to the inexhaustible bread basket and armory of the USA.

In the face of steadily mounting shortages of food, oil, rare metals, rubber, cotton, fertilizers, and nitrates, the German people fought on doggedly because they were convinced that the war had been thrust upon Germany. Taught to cherish the old Teutonic virtues of valor, perseverance, and *Nibelungentreue,* they displayed an ingenuity, industry, and talent for organization that enabled the Reich to hold off the concentrated might of almost all the civilized nations of the earth for four years.

The process of industrial combination and concentration was accelerated by the war. While remaining private, business became bigger than ever. However, it was subject to a system of autarchic governmental controls. Olden concepts that centered on freedom of individuals and enterprise were sacrificed to the exigencies of history's biggest war. The whole productive mechanism was transformed into a war economy *(Kriegswirtschaft)*, which operated under the direction of a myriad of local boards and bureaus subordinate to higher echelons of authority.

The most powerful of the national emergency agencies was the Strategic War Materiel Office (Kriegsrohstoffabteilung or KRA). This office was responsible for the procurement and distribution, in keeping with government-assigned priorities, of all strategic war materials. The KRA was also charged with promoting the discovery or invention of substitutes *(Ersatz)* for natural products that could not be obtained. More than any other German, Walter Rathenau (1867–1922), the president of German General Electric (AEG) and chairman of the KRA, was the architect of the country's war economy. Among those who rendered him valuable aid were Gustav Krupp von Bohlen und Halbach (1870–1950), who was lord of the vast Krupp-Essen munitions works, and Carl Duisberg of I. G. Farben chemical company. Krupp's "smithy" *(Waffenschmiede)* in the Ruhr was the mainstay of the army, producing huge quantities of cannon and artillery shells. Krupp produced such spectaculars as the stubby "Big Bertha" 98-ton howitzer and the enormous "Paris cannon," a tapered gun that fired 230-pound shells 80 miles. Krupp also delivered a fleet of 148 submarines to the German navy. Duisberg's I.G. Farben company produced the synthetic nitrates and other chemicals that were the life's blood of the war machine. Rathenau accomplished his assigned mission to such degree that by the spring of 1915 the most critical shortages of raw materials had been overcome, and the German war machine was no longer in danger of grinding to a halt.

A second office of controls was the War Food Office (Kriegsernährungsamt or KEA). The KEA established maximum prices for foodstuffs, supervised operations of local price control boards, assumed responsibility for the success of the rationing system and for the production of *Ersatz* foodstuffs, and arranged the distribution of comestibles. Karl Helfferich (1872–1924), imperial minister of finance (1915–16) and of the interior (1916–18), headed the KEA.

Despite the heroic exertions of KEA officials, hunger gained an ever tighter stranglehold on the German people. Due to the blockade the average caloric intake dropped by 1916 to three-fifths the normal of the average person and to 800 calories below recognized minimal requirements. The shortages extended to fats, grain, meat, milk—in fact, to almost every staple foodstuff. A disastrous potato crop failure in 1916 led to the substitution of the turnip as the mainstay of the daily diet. During the dread "turnip winter" of 1916–17 the average caloric intake dropped to about 1,000 per day, and starvation stalked the towns of Germany. While hundreds of people were dying from submarine attacks, hundreds of thousands of Germans, most of them in the very young, old, or infirm categories, were dying from the effects of the blockade.

Not till the incredible expenditures of materiel and lives in the battles of the Verdun and Somme sectors in 1916 was it found necessary to regiment labor.

On December 5, 1916, the National Auxiliary Service (Vaterländische Hilfsdienst) was established. Under the supreme direction of Ludendorff, the Hilfsdienst was directly supervised by Helfferich. It was empowered, where advisable, to assign jobs to males (but not females) between the ages of 17 and 60. Boards, on which sat representatives of both management and labor, were set up in each district to coordinate manpower requirements and direct the allocation of labor. No worker having been assigned a job was free to change employment without the consent of his employer and the National Auxiliary Service. The great bulk of the working force, with the tacit approval of the Free and Christian Trade Unions, was thus frozen for the duration. Although women were not subject to the jurisdiction of the National Auxiliary Service, they volunteered in large numbers to aid production of munitions and other military end items. Their unprecedented invasion of industry was a capital feature of the war economy.

In spite of the rationalization and standardization of industrial production and the coordination of manpower and resources on a national scale, it proved impossible to correct inequities or abuses effectively or combat profiteering in the wartime economy. The government was plagued with monetary inflation and black markets. It was unable to hold the line on wages, hours, or prices. Moreover, in the absence of really total controls over the nation, it was not possible to stop workers from going out on mass economic strikes such as those that occurred in the Berlin munitions factories in January, 1918, and in the Upper Silesian mines the following July.

The German war effort, which cost over 150 billion marks, was primarily financed by printing paper and by internal loans. Foreign credit was in extremely short supply, and Germany's assets abroad were largely confiscated by belligerent Allied governments. Loan banks *(Darlehenskassen)* were established in the various regions of the Reich at the behest of Helfferich. The Reichsbank was allowed to suspend payment in gold and substitute paper collateral for specie reserves, which enabled the bank to extend a much greater volume of credit to governmental agencies. However, twice as much money was realized by the sale of federal bonds as was acquired through these loans. In both cases, payment for the cost of the war was deliberately transferred to future generations rather than discharged in taxes by the generation that fought the war.

The Socialists and the Conduct of the War

The Social Dmeocratic party (SPD) majority, which was led by Fritz Ebert (1871–1925), Philipp Scheidemann (1865–1939), and Eduard David, blamed the international "capitalist-imperialists" for the war but admitted that the class-dominated German government must bear a share of the war guilt. In the first year of hostilities the famous "Scheidemann Peace" formula was calculated to allay criticism from the left wing of the party. That concept did not contradict the popular aim of peace through victory but did demand that there be a freely negotiated settlement, not just a "Tilsit Peace," between victors and vanquished. Like Bethmann-Hollweg, Jagow, and Zimmermann, the SPD leaders were opposed to extensive annexations and the subjugation of alien peoples.

Gradually, however, a group that did not trust the government's war aims came to oppose war credits. It was led by Hugo Haase, Georg Ledebour (1850–1947), Bernstein, and Kautsky. From early 1915 this group, which was separated from the majority by purely tactical and not ideological differences, exerted pressure upon the party to foreswear all annexations and indemnities.

Further to the left of this group stood a small cohort of extremists who drew the most uncompromising revolutionary conclusions from Marxist teachings. This group, which wanted to turn the World War into a series of civil wars for the overthrow of capitalists and landlords, comprised Karl Liebknecht (Wilhelm's son, 1871–1919), the party historian Franz Mehring, and the brilliant but sardonic Polish Jewess, Rosa Luxemburg (1870–1919).

The first major breach of Socialist Reichstag group discipline came over the issue of war credits. On December 2, 1914, Liebknecht cast the sole opposing vote against the military finance bill in the Reichstag. Although nobody else ventured to do likewise, Liebknecht had nonetheless been supported in party caucus by seventeen comrades. From this time on, the left wing of the SPD, sustained by the party's central organ *(Vorwärts)* and the *Leipziger Volkszeitung*, grew rapidly. Liebknecht's induction into the army in January, 1915, and Luxemburg's imprisonment on February 18 hobbled the left but did not bring its subversive activities to a halt.

Soon the *Bergfrieden* itself came under attack as a substantial group of SPD Reichstag deputies prepared to resume the class struggle. On March 18, 1915, when the radicals tried to cut military appropriations by half, some 35 out of 104 Socialist deputies followed Karl Liebknecht into open opposition to the party's official war credit policy. The left had lost confidence in Bethmann-Hollweg, whom it now charged with flirting with avowed annexationists. In the summer of 1915 the left circulated brochures among the workers, denouncing annexations and affirming the independence of nations. The Socialist minority, under the leadership of Hugo Haase, Kautsky, Bernstein, and Liebknecht, grew rapidly during 1916, and by Easter of 1917 it parted ways with the majority. The leftists had already been excluded from all SPD organizations when on April 6, 1917, at the Gotha Convention the Independent Social Democratic party (Unabhängige sozialdemokratische Partei Deutschlands or USPD) was founded. It declared its opposition to the war as one of conquest and expressed its determination to achieve the complete democratization (but not the early socialization) of Germany.

Many historians have affected to see in the Socialist minority's secession a great stride along the road to democracy. This is a specious judgment. As we now know, Haase's act, undignified by genuine principled differences with the majority, was a major factor in the ruin of the democratic idea in the era of the First German Republic. Haase's act heralded a fateful split in the German proletariat, which in time became permanent and prevented Socialists and Communists from uniting to oppose the Nazi grasp at power.

Independent Socialist efforts at a peace completely devoid of annexations, indemnities, or subjugation of alien peoples filled the summer of 1917. This campaign suffered a serious setback, however, when the Allied governments turned a cold shoulder toward the International Socialist Conference that met in Stockholm at that time. The Allies merely regarded German Socialist participation in the conference as proof of a growing war-weariness and ignored the conference formula of a peace of forgiveness.

The Political Crisis of July, 1917

The Reichstag in July, 1917, launched two conceptually related offensives. The one was to democratize the polity, bury authoritarianism, and elevate the middle class to seniority in a new bourgeois-aristocratic ruling establishment. The other was to put the legislature on record as favoring a conciliatory peace. Assuming the remote possibility of Allied approval of these initiatives, the second had no prospect of success without the prior attainment of parliamentary responsibility.

By early July a general govement was under way to "dump" Bethmann. This was the common denominator that united diverse parties. Bethmann's opposition to unrestricted submarine warfare and to the Kreuznach annexationist program of April, 1917, had incurred the enmity of the High Command. The chancellor's diagonal policy and his flirtation with the National Liberals incurred the censure of the Conservatives. His opposition to war *à outrance* and advocacy of a peace of understanding alienated the National Liberals. On the other hand, the USPD charged the chancellor with equivocation and deceit in his endorsement of a "Scheidemann Peace." The Majority Socialists no longer believed that Bethmann knew the way out of the morass into which Germany had slipped. Finally, even the Center had lined up with the chancellor's foes.

It was the leader of the left wing of the Center, Matthias Erzberger (1875–1921), who administered the coup de grace to Bethmann. He had once been a fiery Pan-German and, as a director of the Thyssen firm, had advocated the seizure of the Longwy-Briéy mines. However, by 1917 he had evolved into a foe of submarine warfare and a champion of a conciliatory peace. On both counts he had supported the chancellor, and this had involved him in conflict with the right wing of the Center, whose spokesman was Peter Spahn. However Erzberger had now become disillusioned with the luckless Bethmann-Hollweg, whom he blamed for the failure of peace initiatives and for yielding to the OHL's Kreuznach program. Erzberger's approval in early July of the Socialists' peace resolution draft was the initial act in a grave constitutional crisis.

Encouraged by Erzberger's stand, Ludendorff and Hindenburg on July 12 handed in their resignations in a move to force the chancellor's resignation, for which they ought by rights to have been court-martialed. When Bethmann found himself with the support of only the Progressive party, his "last Mohican," he resigned on July 14. In doing so, he disregarded the fact that the kaiser still basically supported him and that under the constitution the chancellor could be removed by no other authority.

The Reichstag crisis was the symptom of the resumption, after two generations, of the middle-class struggle for power. A new coalition of Center, Progressives, and SPD Majority, representing substantial elements of bourgeoisie and working class, sponsored the conciliatory Reichstag Peace Resolution of July 19, 1917. This combination was later to become the bulwark of the Weimar Republic. At the same time a shift also occurred in the National Liberal party. Gustav Stresemann (1878–1939), leader of its left wing and a prominent figure in the Central Association of German Industrialists, had on July 9 approved the overthrow of Bethmann. Because Stresemann and the National Liberal majority refused to forsake annexations, their agreement with Erzberger extended only to removal of the chancellor and the displacement of the politically bankrupt aristocracy by the bourgeoisie as arbiters of Germany's destiny.

The Reichstag Peace Resolution, which called for "a peace of understanding and the permanent conciliation of nations," was adopted by parliament by a vote of 212 to 126. The opposition consisted of the Conservative, National Liberal, and Independent Socialist parties. The USPD rejected the resolution because it did not flatly renounce annexations and was not linked with a demand for democratization. The Allied governments were confirmed in their suspicion that it was worthless by the reservation with which Dr. Georg Michaelis, the new chancellor (July–November, 1917), had hedged his endorsement of it. Michaelis, a former Prussian food commissioner without broader diplomatic or political experience, had told the Reichstag that the aims of the government, which embraced the "security of the boundaries of the German Empire for all time," were "capable of realization within the scope of your resolution *as I interpret it*" (italics mine). The enemy press merely portrayed the gesture as the foreloper of German surrender, choosing to ignore the important fact that the Reichstag had put itself on record as the first parliament of any belligerent to repudiate the notion of a harsh peace.

It was the irreparable blunder of the German Reichstag that it put the cart before the horse. The Peace Resolution might not have been barren of positive results had it followed rather than preceded the establishment of parliamentary responsibility in the Reich. Thoroughgoing political reform would have maneuvered the Allied governments into a position where they would have been obliged to accept conciliatory terms or be held up to the odium of their own working classes. But by assigning priority to the resolution rather than the conquest of power, the Reichstag majority only aided the disciples of Allied victory.

The proponents of middle-class democracy had failed to exploit the constitutional crisis to impose their candidate on the state and achieve parliamentary responsibility. Paralyzed by a split on the nature of the peace, the bourgeois bloc had allowed political victory to elude it. Consequently the chancellorship had fallen to Ludendorff's man, Michaelis, who privately confessed that his apodosis to the Peace Resolution had been deliberately inserted to allow the OHL to make whatever kind of peace it wanted. From then on, the Supreme Command (which meant Ludendorff) shaped the official policy of the Reich along militaristic lines. The German bourgeoisie had written another chapter in its unedifying history.

To the Bitter End

Michaelis and the man who succeeded him on November 2, 1917, the Centrist reformer Count Georg von Hertling (1843–1919), and the successive foreign ministers, Richard von Kühlmann (1873–1948) and Admiral Paul von Hintze (1864–1941), all took refuge under the field grey army cape of Ludendorff. Under his lash the government accepted the Treaty of Brest-Litovsk, which caused the Allied peoples to fear that in the event of a German victory in the west they would be subjected to a similarly draconic peace. Brest-Litovsk removed the last reservations of the Allies against fighting on until the OHL and kaiser should be overthrown. The Russian treaty encouraged Wilson, in particular, to connive at the subversion of the German imperial government. His Fourteen Points were, from one standpoint, the opening gambit in his strategy of German revolution.

In the spring of 1918 Ludendorff worked to engineer the association with or the "attachment" to Germany of the Baltic areas and the Ukraine, which had seceded from Russia. While the German people waited with bated breath for the outcome of the OHL's *Friedenssturm* in the west, Ludendorff encouraged the "United National Council" of the Baltic peoples to request personal union of Lithuania and Courland with the Reich and permanent German military protection for Livonia and Esthonia. During the summer of 1918 Ludendorff grasped for the Ukraine. He engineered a coup d'état that brought to power the reactionary hetman Skoropadsky, who now, in contravention of the desire of the Little Russians, signed an agreement that made of the Ukraine the military and economic cornerstone of German imperialism in southeastern Europe.

After the collapse of the *Friedenssturm* and the commencement of the final Allied counteroffensive in the west, the OHL was gripped by defeatism. When Austria requested peace terms on September 15, Ludendorff concluded that "the military situation could only grow decidedly worse." At the end of September the man who had always insisted that Germany could achieve peace through victory was suddenly seized with panic, for the Bulgarian capitulation had exposed the underbelly of the Central Powers. Hysterical fears gripped many Germans; the middle-class press was now urgently demanding creation of a "peoples" government; and Ludendorff declared on September 29 that the army could not wait forty-eight hours for an armistice.

Ludendorff had concluded that only drastic changes in the government could now alter world opinion toward Germany. Thinking that perhaps not even the Socialists would have the courage to force such changes, he, on his own initiative, arranged to transfer power at long last to the Reichstag. Hertling was forced to resign and the progressive-minded Prince Max of Baden (1876–1929) was appointed by the emperor, who on September 30 announced that he desired to draw the people into more effective participation in government. This was the beginning of responsible parliamentary government in Germany. A little later, on October 15, equal and direct suffrage replaced the three-class system in Prussia.

With the appointment of Max of Baden, power was suddenly thrust into the hands of the middle class and the representatives of the moderate workers—the same elements that had not known what to do with it in 1848. No one had thought that so sudden and catastrophic a collapse of the old regime was possible. The masses were almost completely taken by surprise. As it turned out, Ludendorff's action was the initial move of the German Revolution.

The Abdication Crisis

Despite the arbitrary selection of a chancellor who had not been proposed by the Reichstag majority, Max's cabinet, installed on October 4, enjoyed the support of that majority. On the other hand, despite the presence of two Majority Socialists—Philipp Scheidemann and Gustav Bauer—in the new cabinet, it could not be said that the government was exclusively one of fresh or democratic talent. It seemed that if Germany were finally to be democratized, a prince must take the lead.

The liberal government of Prince Max requested an armistice of Wilson, offering to lay down its arms in return for peace based upon his Fourteen Points and "Four Particulars." In a series of notes, commencing with his reply of October 8, Wilson expressed the belief that the present government was not sincerely democratic but was only a façade behind which the OHL still ruled Germany.

For some weeks the German people refused to see in Wilson's demands an offensive against the monarchical structure of the Reich. But Wilson's note of October 16 eliminated doubt. It contained a virtual ultimatum drastically to change the government. This set in train a movement to renovate the Reich. Ludendorff was replaced in the supreme command by General Wilhelm Groener (1867–1939). Fritz Ebert and Hugo Haase, speaking in the Reichstag, denounced the personal regime of William II, and on October 24 the Majority Socialist Gustav Noske (1868–1946) invited the emperor to make the "great gesture" and give up the throne. The middle class joined the hue and cry when on the twenty-fifth the *Frankfurter Zeitung* demanded abdication. This marked the beginning of the end for William II.

Abdication was rendered imperative also by the deteriorating internal situation. The revolutionary Spartacist group, headed by Rosa Luxemburg and Karl Liebknecht, which aimed not merely at overthrow of the monarchy but also of the bourgeoisie and their "Social Democratic hirelings," was drawing the whole left wing of the USPD—Ledebour, Barth, and Richard Müller—into a united front. In Berlin the revolutionary trend was pronounced. The only alternative to revolution and civil war was rapidly coming to be the abdication of the kaiser. A question that had originally been raised by an impatient rank and file in both Socialist parties and had been rendered urgent by Wilson's notes was made imperative by the presumed threat of Bolshevist revolution in Germany.

On November 3 mutiny broke out among the sailors of the Kiel naval base when the High Seas Fleet had been ordered, without the knowledge of Prince Max, to steam out and engage the British in a "do or die" action. On the fifth, with the red flag flying in the northern port cities and uprisings spreading to south Germany, the non-Socialist members of the cabinet tried desperately to strengthen Ebert and Scheidemann against the extremists. It was now generally recognized that the SPD was the kaiser's last chip. The question was whether Majority Socialist influence over the masses could be restored in such pandemonium. If the forces of insurrection were to gain the upper hand, the impression might be given that Germany was on the brink of dissolution, and the Allies would exploit her misery to impose on her a worse treaty than Tilsit. The Allies could be expected to do the same if Germany were to follow the extremists into the Bolshevist camp.

On November 6 Wilson's fourth note was made public, which revealed that England and France had, with reservations as to freedom of the seas and war indemnities, accepted the Fourteen Points as the basis for the peace. On the same day Groener brought word from the front that the army would have to hoist the white flag if it didn't obtain an armistice by the ninth at the latest, for it was now a race between armistice and mutiny.

In the meantime the pressure in the steam boiler was mounting to an alarming level. Everywhere in the cities of Germany the rank and file of workers and soldiers were taking things into their own hands, guided, if at all, only by local Socialist leaders. On November 7 a spontaneous mass movement compelled the establishment of the Bavarian Republic under the leadership of the Independent Socialist Kurt Eisner (1867–1919).

On the morning of Germany's sham revolution, November 9, 1918, Berlin, under Majority Socialist control, was still loyal to the Reich government. However, a strike had been called for that day by the USPD. The masses now streamed into the streets, and the soldiers in the urban garrisons were joining them. Bauer and Scheidemann felt that they must now abandon ship, and they resigned. Meanwhile, Prince Max, to forestall the announcement from some soap box of the emperor's deposition, informed the press on his own initiative that William II had decided to step down, that the crown prince had renounced his rights of succession, and that a regency council would be formed. Max recommended the former saddle maker and the then Majority Socialist chairman, Fritz Ebert, as *imperial* chancellor and the last bulwark of the monarchy. Before the sun set, nevertheless, the first German republic had been proclaimed, and all the crowns of Germany had fallen with a thud.

After 1918 the upper middle class enjoyed dominant authority in Germany, and the roles of nobility and bourgeoisie were reversed. The transfer of power that had been begun in July, 1917, was ostensibly completed in October–November, 1918, without a French-style revolution. The Socialists were the midwives in this easy parturition of the bourgeois republic. What had proven to be impossible in 1848–49 now seemed child's play in 1918.

The capitalists could not immediately seize the heights of power in the republic. They had, for appearances' sake, to ally themselves for a short time with the leaders of the working class. To defend themselves against social revolution, the upper bourgeoisie had to hide themselves behind Socialist skirts. Only after the turbulence of the masses had subsided did the political spokesmen of the capitalists or their junior partners, the aristocrats, themselves occupy commanding posts in the state. However, in the ostensibly middle-class Weimar Republic the bourgeoisie were destined never to exercise an exclusive control comparable to that which the nobility had in the aristocratic-peasant age of German history. It was not merely that the former had not driven the nobility from the bureaucracy, judiciary, and officer corps of the army; it was also that the common man had become a political factor that could no longer be ignored. The restive, insensitive, and sometimes hysterical masses were to be the decisive factor at every critical juncture in the Weimar Republic's life.

PART XIII
BETWEEN THE WORLD WARS, 1918–1939

Chapter 46

BIRTH OF AN UNWANTED REPUBLIC

The "Sham" Revolution

Actually no genuine social revolution occurred in November, 1918. The complex events of November 9 and 10, which forced the proclamation of the democratic republic and the organization of an all-Socialist national executive—the Council of People's Representatives (Rat der Volksbeauftragten)—were not the fruits of a planned insurrection. Rather, they were the spontaneous expression of universal fear, fear of the turbulent ultraradicals, fear of the malice of the foreign foe, and, perhaps above all, fear of Russian bolshevism. There was no wholesale transfer of power in the state. Despite the presence of certain objective preconditions for a social revolution in Germany, the upper middle class did not exploit them to liquidate the aristocracy or even to constitute a bourgeois interim government. For their part, the representatives of the SPD and USPD, who filled all the seats on the council, never seriously contemplated the expropriation of the nobility or the bourgeoisie. The council made no effort to nationalize the key instruments of production, confiscate the big landed estates, or eliminate monarchist elements from the bureaucracy, judiciary, or army.

Only the Spartacists and their USPD left confederates were animated by a true revolutionary spirit. But except perhaps in Berlin they had no chance of seizing power. The public knew instinctively that this would entail civil war, Entente occupation of all Germany, and the wreck of the economy.

In the confused sequel to the death of the Second Reich it was the Majority Socialists who had the principal hand in restoring order to Germany and piloting her away from Bolshevist shoals back to an anchorage in the west. On November 10 Fritz Ebert, the leading member of the six-man Council of Peoples Representatives,* compacted with Hindenburg and General Wilhelm Groener for the attainment of three objectives: safeguarding the return of almost five million soldiers from across the Rhine; maintaining order against the rabble; and preserving the essential territorial unity of the Reich. This agreement with the army brought the endorsement of the bulk of middle class to the SPD-USPD council. Proletariat, Supreme Command, and bourgeoisie thus combined to block all prospects of founding a genuine socialist republic.

The achievements of the government Socialists in stabilizing Saxony, Bavaria, and Germany itself by gaining control over most of the workers' and soldiers' councils *(Räte)* were impressive. But they were the more remarkable when it is considered that the Armistice, signed on November 11, 1918, at Compiègne,

---

*The other members were Philipp Scheidemann (SPD), Otto Landsberg (SPD), Hugo Haase (USPD right), Wilhelm Dittmann (USPD right), and Emil Barth (USPD left).

had badly tarnished the reputation of the all-Socialist Council of People's Representatives. The severity of the terms belied the expectation that a democratic Germany would receive conditions harmonizing with the Fourteen Points and Four Particulars. It was obvious that Clemenceau and Foch did not need unconditional surrender, because with Allied occupation of the Rhineland and corridors in depth on the right bank of the Rhine they had all the security pledges they required. German rightists inveighed against the folly of a policy that had disarmed the Reich and pawned its territories without securing compensations. Even the Independent Socialist newspaper, the *Leipziger Volkszeitung*, admitted that by comparison the terms of the Treaty of Brest-Litovsk were mild.

There was in the Armistice one provision that aided the Majority Socialists in their fight against the revolutionaries. The Allies had promised to victual Germany, which remained under blockade, provided there was urgent need and that public order prevailed. Thus the Allies helped bolster the teetering Council of People's Representatives and deterred it from flirting with Soviet Russia. By consequence, the council adopted an unnecessarily antagonistic attitude toward Moscow that harmed Germany by depriving her of the only possible external support she might have enjoyed against the malice of the victors.

During November and early December the whole governmental and conservative press vigorously exploited Allied hostility toward the *Räte*. Claiming that the Allies identified them with soviets, the stabler elements of German society launched a counterrevolutionary offensive for the convocation of a national constituent assembly and the establishment of parliamentary institutions. The masses were persuaded to substitute stability and industrial recovery for the goal of socialism and became convinced that the early meeting of the National Assembly would promote these ends. That the SPD committed an historic error in discarding all thought of the nationalization of the key instruments of production when the huge majority of the German people would have supported such a program may not be doubted. But the SPD had bound its own hands at the outset of the "Revolution" by entering into compromising alliances with army and bourgeoisie.

Only in Berlin had a serious purge of the old imperial officials been attempted, and that had been the work of the Independent Socialist-dominated executive council *(Vollzugsrat)* of workers' and soldiers' deputies. Asked by the Independents to make a clean sweep of the remnants of the old bureaucracy in the central government too, the Majority Socialists replied that they preferred to leave purges and economic reforms up to the National Assembly. In reaching this decision, the Majority Socialists adjourned the struggle against the big capitalists and Prussian landlords, who remained basically hostile to the republic till its dying day. By omitting to appease the just demands of the masses for the expropriation of the Junkers and manufacturing and service industry magnates, the Majority Socialist ministers deprived the republic of badly needed popular support. Never again was the government able to ensconce itself in the affections of its citizens. What they later did in its defense was done out of fear of a worse alternative.

The Blunder of the USPD

In a time of milling mobs and political murders, the All German Congress of Workers' and Soldier's Councils opened its sessions in Berlin on December 16. The Majority Socialists controlled 288 of the 489 delegates, which showed that the SPD had regained domination over the proletariat. The congress approved (400 to 50) elections for January 19, 1919, to a national constituent assembly. The *Räte* also adopted an antimilitary "Hamburg Program" calling for the democratization of the army but left the matter to what would be, when elected, a predominantly non-Socialist constituent assembly.

The "Revolution" now rushed swiftly toward its denouement. The USPD had waged a fight for the democratization of the officer corps and the elimination of its influence over the council from the first day of the republic. This had led gradually to a polarization of all public opinion. Here it must be affirmed that implementation of the USPD's military policy would assuredly have run long risks, especially at the hands of the Allies and the Poles, but the policy actually pursued by the Council of People's Representatives ran greater. The reactionary military caste proved to be of small value to the republic. The ultimate fate of Germany could not have been worse if there had been no army at all.

The suppression of a sailors' mutiny was the pretext for the departure of the Independent Socialists from the council. On December 27 Haase, Dittmann, and Barth left the provisional government because they objected to the fact that the SPD had used the army to suppress the uprising. Simultaneously the Independent Socialists resigned from the ministries of Prussia, Baden, and Württemberg.

That the Independents committed a grave mistake is clear. Their decision deprived the government of much-needed strength in negotiations with the Allies and excluded from the central ministry the very elements that offered the best pledge for a complete break with the old military autocracy. Furthermore, the split in the ranks of Socialism alienated many followers and left policy formation to the Majority Socialists. The latter were thrust back for support upon the capitalists and the generals, and that ruined prospects for an orderly transition to social democracy. Worst of all, the USPD's action revived the prestige of the military and provoked the Spartacist uprising.

Spartakus Unfurls the Red Flag

On December 30, 1918, the extreme left wing of the USPD, the "Spartacists," seceded from the party and established the German Communist party (Kommunistische Partei Deutschlands or KPD). On January 5 a revolutionary manifesto was published in both the USPD central organ, *Die Freiheit*, and the Communist journal, *Die Rote Fahne*, denouncing the "Ebert-Scheidemann tyranny." The next day Spartacist rank-and-file elements raised the standard of revolt and dragged along their hesitant leaders, Liebknecht, Luxemburg, and Paul Levi (1883–1930).

By January 13 regular army men and conservative, volunteer Free Corps youths, acting on orders from the SPD minister of defense, Gustav Noske, and the army commander, General Reinhardt, had smashed the rebellion in Berlin and mopped up insurgents who had simultaneously raised the red flag in Bremen, Hamburg, Brunswick, Leipzig, Oldenburg, Munich, and the Ruhr. While the central government had every right to defend itself against irresponsible and rebellious elements in the streets, it must be censured for employing troops that were known to be hostile to both the workers and the republic. The legacy of "Spartacist Week" was deep-seated, permanent hostility between radical and moderate sections of the German working class. The bloody murders of Liebknecht and Luxemburg during the January uprising were followed by counterrevolutionary assassinations of Kurt Eisner, the minister president of Bavaria, and Hugo Haase, the leader of the USPD right. Nothing did so much to aid the Nazi conquest of power as this river of blood that came to divide the German working class. Spartacist Week and two subsequent blows that were dealt the Communists and left Independents in Berlin in March and in Munich in April–May crippled the revolutionary movement and left it enfeebled until 1923. An historic shift of political opinion toward the right now set in. This shift was not to halt until every department of government had again more or less fallen under the influence of social elements that had dominated the Second Empire.

Elections to the National Assembly

The January elections to the Constituent Assembly brought brilliant gains to both Majority and Independent Socialist parties, but the KPD black-balled the balloting. The combined Socialist vote (SPD—37.82 percent; USPD—7.6 percent) was 45.4 percent of the total, as compared with an SPD vote in 1912 of 34.81 percent. The SPD in 1919 received 11,509,100 votes and 165 mandates, while the USPD received 2,317,500 and 22 seats. The nearest rivals, the Center and Democratic (formerly Progressive) parties, respectively received only 19.67 percent and 18.55 percent. The Center returned 91 deputies, and the Democrats 75.

Despite tremendous success, the combined forces of SPD and USPD had not been able to capture a majority of the electorate, for their composite strength had declined since the high-water mark of radicalism in November. The non-Socialist vote in January, 1919, outweighed the Socialist 16.4 million to 13.7 million. Accordingly, under the rules of the democratic game, a coalition had to be formed with at least two bourgeois parties. Since the USPD absolutely refused to countenance collaboration, the SPD was obliged to form a government with the only other parties whose allegiance to the republic was above doubt—the Center and the Democratic.

The conservative and rightist bourgeois parties constituted what for some years to come must be described as a disloyal opposition. These elements comprised the German National People's party or DNVP (Deutsch-nationale Volkspartei), which had been the Conservative party, and the German People's party or DVP (Deutsche Volkspartei), formerly the National Liberal party. Although heavy industry supported both parties, the landlords, army, aristocracy, and many peasants felt more comfortable in the DNVP, whereas middling industrialists and merchants clustered in the DVP.

The Socialists surrendered power too early. In fighting to break the power of the *Räte*, the SPD committed the blunder of convening the National Assembly before popular policies, such as expanding civil rights, purging the bureaucracy, nationalizing key industries, shortening hours of labor, breaking up big estates, and abolishing the old officer corps, could be implemented. In the prematurely summoned National Assembly the Socialists were in a minority. They were forced to compromise in every field in order not to alienate progressive bourgeois elements upon whose votes they believed themselves dependent. This tactic of accommodation cost the Socialist parties much support, for many workers concluded that power had practically been handed back to the nobility and the capitalists. A ministry was formed, which rested upon a tripod of Majority Socialist, Center, and Democratic parties—the so-called Weimar Coalition. This was destined to be the main support of the republic. In the new government Fritz Ebert was president and Philipp Scheidemann chancellor. Foreign affairs were conducted by Count Ulrich von Brockdorff-Rantzau (1869–1928), while the defense portfolio went to Gustav Noske.

The Weimar Constitution

The constitution, adopted by the National Assembly on July 31, 1919, against 75 opposing votes, was mainly the handicraft of Hugo Preuss (1860–1925), a jurist and the minister of the interior. The Weimar Constitution, whose name recalled a court of the Enlightenment, was the most democratic the world had ever seen. Women were given the vote and equal rights with men, while the state was charged with a range of eleemosynary and educational responsibilities.

A strong federal rather than a unitary state was established. At the risk of perpetuating the conservative bureaucracies and judiciaries, the *Länder*, including huge Prussia, were preserved. The supremacy of the central government was guaranteed by the circumstance that although it shared concurrent powers with the states, it was empowered to veto their laws and impose its will in every case of doubt. Where the national government did not choose to insist upon paramountcy, a wide range of powers was left to the *Länder* governments.

The bicameral legislature comprised an upper house, called the Reichsrat, or Federal Council, and a Reichstag. The former comprised representatives of the states. It was no longer dominated, as its predecessor had been, by Prussia, and it held only a suspensive veto over bills passed by the lower chamber. The Reichstag, elected on the basis of proportional representation, was the supreme legislative body of Germany, except where the people directly intervened, as in the case of the initiative *(Volksbegehren)* or the referendum *(Volksentscheid)*.

The president, who was popularly elected by direct franchise of both sexes, was endowed with exceptional powers. Not only could he appoint or dismiss the chancellor and his cabinet, as well as many other important officials, but he could also dissolve the Reichstag and, in case of disagreement between the upper and lower chambers, employ the pocket veto to kill a bill. He could also use a suspensive veto over an act passed by the Reichstag. Under Article 48 of the constitution the president was also empowered to proclaim martial law in time of grave emergency and with the assent of the Reichstag exercise a vaguely limited dictatorial authority. In the hands of a foe of democracy this authority was one day to subvert the republic.

The constitution further provided for a judiciary, which at the lower and middle levels served both the Reich and the *Länder*. The national supreme court (Reichsgericht) also acted as a supreme court of cassation for each *Land*. Disputes between *Länder* were decided by a special high tribunal, the Staatsgerichtshof. It did not, however, possess the power of reviewing the constitutionality of laws passed by Reichstag or legislatures of the component states of the republic.

The End of the Räte

During the early months of 1919, while Germany was still heaving with commotion, the USPD was drawn into more revolutionary channels by its growing left wing under Ernst Däumig (1866–1922) and by the hypnotic example of the KPD, now under Paul Levi's leadership. The revolutionaries pinned their hopes on the workers' and soldiers' councils and advocated that the *Räte* should be incorporated in the constitution. The councils, however, experienced steadily declining popularity as a result of the decisions of the *Räte* congress of December, the convocation of the National Assembly, the work on the drafting of the Weimar Constitution, and the failure of Spartacist Week. In March new general strikes, which did not receive the support of the major trade unions with their four million members, were suppressed by Free Corps fighters. These strikes turned out to be the funeral pyre of the *Räte*. Their sequel was the disarmament of the revolutionary workers.

In mid-April Noske's storm troopers crushed the Bavarian conciliar government in Munich. In a bloody struggle the Bavarian capital was retaken from the minority-supported soviet government, whose establishment had been inspired by the example of the proclamation of the Hungarian Soviet Republic on March 20, 1919. On May 3, 1919, the Majority Socialist government of Johannes Hoffmann was restored to power. In the reign of terror that ensued, about seven hundred persons were executed. The Bavarian government was forced to dissolve its autonomous army, a relic from the Bismarckian past, and the *Land* was bound more closely to the Reich. On May 10, Noske's Free Corps men smashed the similarly radical regime in Leipzig, Saxony.

By mid-May the national government was firmly in the saddle everywhere in the Reich. At the same time reactionary paramilitary units had been encouraged by counterrevolutionary strokes against the *Räte* and the ultras. Under governmental protection, a considerable number of anti-Socialist paramilitary organizations auxiliary to the 1-million-man Reichswehr cropped up all over Germany.

The existence of all these units was especially rationalized by the need to protect the eastern frontiers against the Red Army or the Poles.

The Treaty of Versailles

While the blockade continued in force and German soldiers were held as prisoners of war on enemy soil, the Big Three fashioned the peace settlement behind a veil of mystery in Paris. No German delegate was invited to the Paris conference because no Talleyrand was wanted. After having been held virtually incommunicado in a Paris hotel for two weeks, the German delegation, headed by Count von Brockdorff-Rantzau, was finally admitted to the Hall of Mirrors at Versailles, where once the German Empire had been proclaimed. On May 7 the text of the peace treaty was given the vanquished, who had no advance information as to its contents but were required within two weeks to make observations and counterproposals to a document of 440 articles (in French) that had taken an army of diplomats more than four months to draft.

In response to Clemenceau's ominous words, "The hour for a heavy reckoning has come," Brockdorff-Rantzau rose to tell the peace delegates: "In their hearts the German people will resign themselves to their hard lot if the bases of the peace, as mutually agreed upon, are not destroyed. A peace that cannot be defended before the world as a peace of justice would always evoke new resistance. No one could sign it with a clear conscience, for it could not be carried out. No one could venture to guarantee its execution, though this obligation is implied in the signing of the treaty."*

The Treaty of Versailles was, in spite of all apologia, a dictated peace. Written solely by the victors in a city that was a superheated crucible of war passions, the treaty reflected popular hysteria. Although less harsh than the treaties of Tilsit or Brest-Litovsk, Versailles had been written in peacetime and was in important particulars a violation of the spirit of the Fourteen Points and Four Particulars, that is, the contractual basis on which the vanquished had agreed to lay down their arms. On the other hand, the Treaty of Versailles preserved the basic unity of Germany and left it the means by which it could reconstruct its economic and political power.

In the retributive clauses of the peace treaty the Germans read a litany of all the supposed or alleged crimes that Germany or Prussia had committed against their neighbors since 1772. They read that the kaiser and his top generals were to be tried before an international war crimes tribunal. The clauses by which all of Germany's colonies were confiscated were predicated on the postulate of German "inhumanity" toward their native populations. German colonies were in the future to be administered as mandates by the principal Allied Powers subject to supervision by the Mandates Commission of the newly established League of Nations. The Germans, of course, were denied any mandates.

Although the French had not prevailed over Anglo-American objections with

---

*Luckau, Alma, *The German Delegation at the Paris Peace Conference* (1941), Doc. 29.

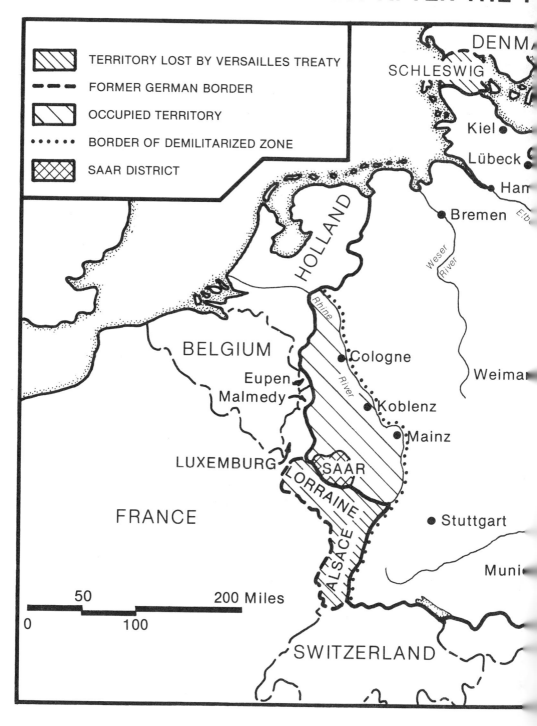

GERMANY AFTER THE T

TERRITORY LOST BY VERSAILLES TREATY

FORMER GERMAN BORDER

OCCUPIED TERRITORY

BORDER OF DEMILITARIZED ZONE

SAAR DISTRICT

DENM

SCHLESWIG

Kiel

Lübeck

Han

Bremen

Elb

Weser River

HOLLAND

Rhine River

BELGIUM

Cologne

Weima

Eupen
Malmedy

Koblenz

Mainz

LUXEMBURG

SAAR

LORRAINE

FRANCE

ALSACE

Stuttgart

Muni

50   200 Miles

0   100

SWITZERLAND

MEMELLAND

Baltic Sea

Memel River

Danzig

EAST PRUSSIA

WEST PRUSSIA

Oder River

POSEN

Vistula River

Warsaw

POLAND

erlin

UPPER SILESIA

CZECHOSLOVAKIA

Danube River

Vienna

Budapest

AUSTRIA
(**Anschluss** Prevented)

HUNGARY

their demand for the separation of the Rhineland from Germany, the Reich nonetheless lost more than 13 percent of its territory and some 6.5 million citizens. Germany was forced to cede to France, without plebiscite, Alsace-Lorraine and proprietary rights in the coal mines of the Saar. Germany had also to agree to: the administration of the Saarland by the League of Nations until 1935, when a plebiscite was to be held to determine the future allegiance of the area; the demilitarization of the Rhineland; and the construction of no fortifications within a 50-kilometer strip on the right bank of the Rhine. The Rhineland was to be occupied by Allied soldiers for fifteen years, but staged withdrawals of troops were to take place as Germany fulfilled her treaty obligations. Minor compensatory cessions of territory (Eupen and Malmédy) were made to Belgium. Germany also ceded, subject to plebiscite, northern Schleswig to Denmark. In spite of the fact that overwhelming majorities of the German and Austrian peoples desired the union of their two countries *(Anschluss)*, this was not permitted. On the other hand under the terms of the treaty Germany had to cede West Prussia (Pomerelia) and almost all of Posen (Poznania) to Poland, and Memel to Lithuania. In addition, plebiscites were to be held in certain areas of East Prussia and in Upper Silesia to determine whether those regions should be transferred to Poland. Danzig, which was 95 percent German, was made a free city under a high commissioner appointed by the League of Nations. The Elbe, Oder, Danube, and Niemen rivers were internationalized, and Czechoslovakia was given free zones in the ports of Stettin and Hamburg. Naturally, Germany was also required to repudiate the Treaty of Brest-Litovsk.

Under the disarmament clauses, Germany was permitted an army (Reichswehr) of only 100,000 men but no general staff. A provision calculated to block any rapid buildup of a pool of reservists was that obligating enlisted men to serve twelve years, and officers twenty-five. The largest component in the German navy was to be six 10,000-ton cruisers. Germany was forbidden to manufacture or possess military planes, tanks, heavy artillery, submarines, or poison gas. In addition to cash reparations in foreign currencies, Germany had also to make reparations in kind—to deliver an enormous quantity of raw materials, rolling stock, lorries, livestock, and war materiel. Reparations, which were inadmissible at international law, were rationalized on the basis of Article 231 of the treaty, which postulated the moral turpitude and sole war guilt of Germany and Austria-Hungary.

The precise limits of Germany's reparations liability were to be established by a Reparations Commission, which was dominated by France. This commission was to arrange for the amortization of the whole amount within thirty years. Included were to be payments for all damage to property of Allied civilians and compensation for all loss of life by German military action. Also included in the bill was the unprecedented item, inserted at the insistence of Lloyd George and Woodrow Wilson, of pensions for widows and orphans of Allied and Associated personnel slain in the war. While Germany was waiting for the Reparations Commission to fill in the amount on this blank check, an initial payment of 20 billion marks (5 billion dollars) was to be made by May 1, 1921.

The Treaty of Versailles was basically unenforceable because almost every

German condemned it. It left behind it a residue of hatred that was directed not only against the victors but also against a state that would bow to such terms. Incontrovertibly, the Allies made a serious mistake when they put such murderous ammunition in the hands of the foes of the Weimar Republic.

Acute dismay over the Treaty of Versailles was universal in Germany. Where even the Marxist SPD rejected the treaty, what hope was there that the bourgeois majority would reconcile itself to fulfillment? The ministry itself was deadlocked 7–7 over acceptance, but Scheidemann himself stood opposed, asking gloomily: "What hand would not wither that signed such a treaty?" Since however, there was virtually no support for resuming hostilities, there was nothing for the German government to do in the end but go mournfully to Canossa. On June 19 Scheidemann resigned, and a government of acceptance, comprising only the SPD and Center, was formed under the Socialist Gustav Bauer (1870–1944). This ministry, supported by the National Assembly, gave its conditional approval to the treaty, while rejecting "every responsibility for the consequences that might ensue." When the Allied Powers rejoined with a demand for unconditional and instantaneous acceptance, the Bauer government had to yield on June 23. With the support of an assembly majority comprising only SPD, USPD, most Centrists, and some Democrats, the Bauer ministry promised to fulfill the treaty "as far as it can be carried out." In choosing this road, the German people proclaimed their affinity for the west and turned their backs upon a possible alternative Russian orientation.

The Russians and the End of the USPD

Confronted with the unquestionable military domination of Europe by France, which was then building a *cordon sanitaire* against Soviet Russia, the German government decided not to estrange Paris and London or risk war with Poland by coquetting with Moscow. From 1918 to 1921, therefore, the bridge between Berlin and the Russian capital fell into desuetude. Not until the government of Soviet Russia shelved the Trotskyite thesis of "permanent revolution" and inaugurated the New Economic Policy in 1921 was it possible to restore Russo-German relations, which had been severed in July, 1918, when Count von Mirbach, the German ambassador to Russia, was assassinated in Moscow.

Meanwhile, during the era of foreign intervention in Russia, many Germans were disgusted by French demands that Germany participate in the blockade against her. "Almost in the same breath," wrote Gustav Noske, "Germany was ordered to battle stations against Russia and insulted because German soldiers wanted to participate in the fight against Bolshevism."* The Weimar government was being impelled by this behavior and other things—the extension of the Allied blockade to German waters, occupation of right-bank Rhenish cities by the French, and Polish attacks upon Silesia—to reappraise its eastern policy.

The reconciliation with Russia was delayed, however, by the split that de-

---

*G. Noske, *Von Kiel bis Kapp* (Berlin, 1920), p. 181.

stroyed the USPD in October, 1920, at Halle, where the bulk of the party, led by Ernst Däumig, Richard Müller, Ernst Thälmann (1866–1944), Curt Geyer, and Wilhelm Pieck (1876–1960), decided to accept the notorious "Twenty-One Demands" of the Comintern's Central Committee. The USPD left joined the KPD, transforming it into a mass party, whereas the USPD right (minority), under Wilhelm Dittmann (1874–1954) and Artur Crispien (1875–1946), found its way back sluggishly into the SPD. At the joint convention of the United Social Democratic party in September, 1922, at Nuremberg a prowestern program was adopted. Hermann Müller (1876–1931), Crispien, and Otto Wels (1873–1939) were elected cochairmen of the joint central committee. Henceforth, the SPD, convinced of the sterility of irresponsible criticism, became the greatest champion of the republic.

The Kapp Putsch

The steady retreat from radicalism that marked the autumn and winter of 1919–20 was accelerated by the trial of Erzberger, the national minister of finance. Whereas the reactionary Helfferich was exonerated of charges of libel and slander against Erzberger, the latter was convicted of tax evasion and obliged to resign. His departure was a harsh blow for the young republic. The very next day, March 13, 1920, the counterrevolutionary Kapp putsch began.

The coup, led by the Pan-German nationalist Wolfgang Kapp (1858–1929), was the first attempt of the Old Guard to overthrow the Weimar Republic. The putsch came at a time of serious monetary inflation and Polish incursions on German soil. The conspirators enjoyed very considerable support among reactionaries and paramilitary organizations, and especially from General Walter von Lüttwitz, the monarchistic commander of the First Army district in Berlin.

Kapp's *Staatsstreich* was a failure almost from the start. When the rebellious Ehrhardt Brigade, with swastikas painted on many helmets, marched on Berlin, the civil servants and administrators joined hands with the trade unions to stage Germany's first and only general strike. Paradoxically the Reichswehr refused to defend the government against other Reichswehr units seeking to topple it. General Walter Reinhardt (1872–1930), the chief of the army command, and Noske, the minister of defense, wanted to suppress the putsch. However, to the latter's astonishment General Hans von Seeckt (1886–1936), the stern, monocled chief of the troop office *(Truppenamt)* and, to all intents, army chief of staff, demurred, declaring that *"Reichswehr does not fire on Reichswehr."* Seeckt's defiance encouraged army units in Mecklenburg, Wilhelmshaven, Pomerania, Silesia, and Kiel to join Kapp and Lüttwitz. Nevertheless, the general strike and the refusal of Reichsbank officials to make funds available to the rebels sealed their fate.

After the attempted coup, Noske, who had been charged by Scheidemann with intimacy with reactionary Free Corps personnel, was dismissed. He was succeeded in the defense ministry by Dr. Otto Gessler (1875–1955), a Democrat, who remained at that post until 1928, helping Seeckt to strengthen the Reichswehr and establish its neutralist position in the state.

Although the Kapp putsch did not destroy the republic, the Hoffmann Majority Socialist government in Munich was a casualty. At the insistence of paramilitary forces, a bourgeois-aristocratic regime was organized by the antidemocratic Bavarian People's party. Thereafter it proved impossible to prevent the proliferation of reactionary and National Socialist cells in Bavaria.

Toward the end of March, 1920, the third Weimar Coalition government took office. The new chancellor was the stolid Socialist Hermann Müller, who had been Brockdorff-Rantzau's successor as minister of foreign affairs. This time, too, the USPD refused to enter a cabinet of the "hirelings of capitalism." Meanwhile, on March 29 the Socialist government of Paul Hirsch fell in Prussia and was replaced by a Weimar Coalition ministry headed by the Social Democrat Dr. Otto Braun (1872–1955). A genial giant of a man, Braun was ably assisted by his party comrade Carl Severing (1875–1952), who became his minister of the interior. The Prussian Weimar Coalition government was thereafter the citadel of the republic. Braun resolutely clung to the minister-presidency of the largest German state until 1932, imparting to it an altogether novel reputation for democracy.

The Middle Class Recaptures the Government

The Reichstag elections of June 6, 1920, revealed that the prestige of the republic was already in decline. The parties of the Weimar Coalition, especially the SPD, suffered serious losses. Whereas in 1919, 37.9 percent of the electorate had voted Majority Socialist and only 7.6 percent had cast for the USPD, in 1920 the SPD polled 21.7 percent and the USPD 17.8 percent. The SPD suffered a drop from 11,509,100 to only 5,614,456 votes. Nor does this tell the whole story. Although the USPD vote had risen from 2,159,653 to 4,895,317, making it the second strongest political party, the combined vote of SPD, USPD, and KPD accounted for only 3.6 percent more of the electorate than had the SPD alone in 1919. Moreover, the KPD (2 mandates) and a majority of the USPD (81 mandates) bitterly opposed the policies of the SPD. Thus, it is clear that as early as June, 1920, very nearly a majority of the German people were dead set against the existing polity.

The elections to the first Reichstag of the Weimar Republic boded ill for democracy. The parties of the Weimar Coalition (Democrats, 45 deputies; Center, 68; and SPD, 112) henceforth disposed somewhat less than an absolute majority in the Reichstag. There now set in a retrograde phase lasting eight years, during which formation of policy was at first decided by the progressive elements of the middle class, then later by the strongly nationalist and antidemocratic upper bourgeoisie and landlords.

Withal, the influence of the SPD over the German Reich had not been eliminated. The middle class and the generals soon discovered that the only kind of regime that the Allies would tolerate must at least have the tacit support of the SPD. Without it, moreover, no cabinet dedicated to defend the republic and fulfill the treaty could survive.

Further Decline of the Prestige of the Republic

The autumn of 1920 was a period of anxious waiting—the doldrums before the Reparations Commission announced the total liability of Germany. Meanwhile, the recommendations of the Reparations Commission precluded any real change for the better in Franco-German relations; Polish brigandage in Upper Silesia made impossible any genuine friendliness between Berlin and Warsaw; and relations with Soviet Russia had further deteriorated.

The true hopelessness of the German position was revealed at the Paris reparations conference (January 24–30, 1921) where the English again, as at Spa (July 15–16, 1920), joined hands with the French to paint a schedule of German payments that totaled 226 billion gold marks, along with a variable levy of 12 percent annually on the value of Germany's exports for the next forty-two years. All German parties pronounced these decisions impractical and in contravention of Article 233 of the peace treaty, which had promised a fixed reparations settlement. But the impracticality of the London and all previous reparations demands attested not merely to vindictiveness on the part of Britain and France, but to folly, which was worse. Such fiats were simply ludicrous because the transfer of such huge payments in kind was quite impossible unless Germany enjoyed a decidedly favorable balance of trade. It was not widely understood in Allied countries that the achievement of such a balance would make of Germany a far more serious business rival of Britain, and to much less extent of France, than the Wilhelmine Reich had been before the war, and that acute German industrial competition must generate unemployment in the victor states.

When the Allies rejected the German counterproposals to the Paris decisions, Marshal Foch was ordered to occupy Düsseldorf, Ruhrort, and Duisberg, while the Allies seized the German customs. By late April the Fehrenbach government had failed to secure the mediation of the USA, and the plight of the Weimar Republic grew worse.

At the end of April, 1921, the Reparations Commission lodged a new and final demand upon Germany for a greatly reduced sum of 132 billion gold marks, leaving the government until only May 11 to reply. The note also reiterated an earlier demand for surrender of the entire gold reserve of the Reichsbank to the Banque de France.

While Germany weighed the acceptance of this "London ultimatum" against the alternative of French occupation of the Ruhr, the industrial heart of Germany, the Poles deliberately moved to set aside the results of the plebiscite of March 20, 1921, in Upper Silesia. The returns, which had been made public on April 23, had yielded an impressive majority for Germany despite the fact that the inter-

Allied commission, dominated by France, had inserted electoral qualifications designed to swell the Polish vote. Although this industrially indivisible province ought now to have reverted to Germany, the Poles launched a military attack on Silesia on May 3.

At that moment Germany was confronted with a unique crisis in her history, when she was simultaneously threatened with the loss of both the Ruhr and Upper Silesia. The crisis precipitated the fall of the Fehrenbach-Simons government. Since a government of rejection was a manifest impossibility, the fourth cabinet of the Weimar Coalition was formed on May 9. The new government was headed by a Centrist, Josef Wirth (1879–1956), who was a friend of organized labor. Walter Rathenau was the new minister for reconstruction.

The Republic without Republicans

After Wirth's Weimar Coalition government had in mid-May, 1921, mustered a modest Reichstag majority for the London ultimatum, the apostasy from the republic began to assume grave proportions. The memory of every one of its sins, real or invented, was revived. It was recalled that Hindenburg had once before a Reichstag committee maliciously accused the very parties that in 1921 governed Germany of having in November, 1918, stabbed the German army in the back *(Dolchstosslegende)*. Now, the loss of the better part of Upper Silesia (finalized in the spring of 1922) and the indisposition of the Allies to help revive German credit came as a windfall to the internal foes of the republic. They charged that the parties that had plunged the dagger in the nation's back in 1918 had also failed to awaken Allied sympathy for the amelioration of the treaty or of reparations. All through 1921 the columns of the *Kreuzzeitung, Tägliche Rundschau, Deutsche Allgemeine Zeitung,* and other reactionary journals were daily filled with invectives against everything that the Weimar creation stood for. Leading supporters of the republic were proscribed by such militant counterrevolutionary groups as the Orgesch (Organisation Escherich), the Organisation Consul (Org C), and the paramilitary Stahlhelm, to mention only the strongest and most numerous of these formations. On August 26, 1921, the Org C succeeded in assassinating Erzberger, which cleared the way for the recapture of control over the Center party by the antirepublican landed gentry. Then in June, 1922, an unsuccessful attempt was made on the life of Scheidemann with prussic acid. Ebert, Bernstein, and many other prominent champions of the republic were all marked for assassination. A veritable white terror was sweeping over a country that was seething with indignation at the "inglorious" policies of the Weimar Coalition.

Chapter 47

FROM COERCION TO CONCILIATION,

1923–1928

Poincaré and the Policy of Force

Hopes that Wirth's policy of fulfillment would soften French hearts were dashed when in January, 1922, Raymond Poincaré again became premier at the head of a chauvinistic "sky-blue" cabinet, which enjoyed the support of a *bloc national* in the Chamber of Deputies. The French had regarded with alarm the growing inclination of the English to agree with John Maynard Keynes, the brilliant author of *The Economic Consequences of the Peace* (1919), in his judgment that reparations schedules were too severe. The French were also vexed that the peace treaty (1921) between Germany and the USA omitted mention of war guilt and resented demands of the USA that France repay the 40 billion francs she owed her. The French, meditating the fearful material losses they had sustained during the war, rallied to Poincaré, who promised to make the *boche* pay to the hilt and was prepared to pursue a policy aiming at the destruction of the very unity of Germany.

When in the fall of 1921 Wirth's appeal for an international loan was rejected by English financiers, while the Reparations Commission insisted upon reduced but still huge reparations payments of 720 million gold marks and 1.45 billion marks in kind for 1922, Wirth was forced to warn that Germany might not be able to meet her January and February payments. Poincaré, however, cared nothing for conciliating Germany. He wanted to use reparations as a hammer with which to fracture the German state. In its extremity the Wirth government, to the consternation of many, played the Russian trump card and almost spoiled the French game.

The Treaty of Rapallo

After Wirth had formed his second cabinet in the autumn of 1921, based solely upon the Center and the USPD but enjoying SPD parliamentary support, the chancellor and Rathenau had tried in vain to dissuade the French from their dire purpose. Failing in that, they decided to adopt a new policy toward Soviet Russia. That in doing this they contemplated the development of an aggressive policy toward the western powers is untrue, because financial and military resources were lacking for such a tactic.

Despondent over the loss of Upper Silesian resources, which Wirth considered a worse blow than all the rest of the territorial clauses of the Treaty of Versailles put together, the chancellor and his ministers concluded that the Allies had shown absolutely no appreciation for the efforts of German ministers to fulfill the treaty even at the risk of their lives. Wirth and Rathenau had come to see in amity with Soviet Russia a reprimand to the western powers.

Negotiations for a Russo-German military understanding had commenced in the spring of 1921. A special section for Russian affairs (Sondergruppe R) had at that time been established within the Reichswehr ministry. At the same time Baron Adolf von Maltzan of the eastern division of the foreign office and General Hans von Seeckt exerted heavy pressure upon Wirth to demolish the wall that separated Germany and Russia. While Rathenau was moving heaven and earth to impress the English and French with Germany's need for relief, Maltzan and the Reichswehr negotiated at Christmas, 1921, the main outlines of a Russo-German agreement that would enable Germany to circumvent in minor particulars the disarmament clauses of the peace treaty. Simultaneously negotiations were conducted for resumption of relations with Russia. Basically the two agreements, taken in context, provided for German aid to the Russian economy in the form of loans and technical aid in return for ordnance for the Reichswehr and the privilege of using military training facilities in Russia.

Contrary to the earlier opinion of scholars, Wirth was at all times aware of the exact nature and progress of the Russo-German talks (Gatzke). However, there is no documentary corroboration for the charges that the ideologically Catholic and strongly prowestern chancellor wanted to revenge himself on the Entente by adopting an eastern orientation (Goerlitz) or, what would have been more offensive, by allying Germany with Communist Russia (Hilger and Freund).

Meanwhile Rathenau, who enjoyed exceptional personal prestige abroad, persuaded the Allies to send diplomats and financial experts to meet with the Germans at a conference in Genoa in April. Unfortunately, the chances for an accommodation were prejudiced when the Reparations Commission lodged a demand that before May 31, Germany submit a plan to increase taxes on her economically depressed citizens by 60 billion marks. An indignant Reichstag, on March 30, 1922, approved (248 to 81 with 43 abstentions) rejection of the new ultimatum. It was the first time since the Armistice that a German government had said "no" to an Allied order.

When the Genoa conference convened on April 10, German hopes were at once dashed. Reparations and discussion of the peace treaties were excluded from deliberations. Poincaré had defiantly absented himself from the sessions, and the French delegation adamantly opposed admitting Germany to the League. The German delegates thereupon grasped the hand the Russians had been extending to them. On Easter Sunday, April 16, at the seaside resort of Rapallo the first negotiated postwar peace treaty was signed. The Germans had been impelled to this act by resentment at French obduracy and out of fear that the French and English were, in any case, about to sign a separate agreement of their own with Russia, which would restore the prewar encirclement of the Reich.

The Treaty of Rapallo was not conceived aggressively. Whatever the politically ambitious Seeckt's aims may have been, the dominant elements in the German civil government all flatly opposed any serious military adventure. The notion that the treaty contained secret military clauses has, moreover, long since been refuted by historians (Rothfels, Kochan, Laqueur, Helbig, Gatzke, etc.). It simply provided for reestablishing diplomatic and commercial relations between Germany and Russia and for a mutual waiver of Russian claims to war reparations and claims for indemnification of German citizens whose property had been nationalized by the Soviets. Nevertheless the treaty had important results. It was the first successful flight of the German eagle since the war, and it ended the isolation of both Germany and Russia, reduced pressure on the eastern frontier, exorcised the Polish threat, and restored Russia to the family of nations. It also opened the way for a modest collaboration between the two countries: Seeckt now sent tank troops and fighter pilots to be trained in Russia, while Russian officers such as Tukhachevsky and Zhukhov came to Berlin to study German methods of training. When all is said, however, the Treaty of Rapallo did not effect a diplomatic revolution, nor did it reestablish for the German government the *Primat der Aussenpolitik*. For that, both a strong army and a genuinely sovereign German state were lacking.

Aftermath of Rapallo

In June, 1922, the richest parts of Upper Silesia were formally incorporated into Poland, and on the fourteenth the White Terror reached its first pitch. Following a rabid attack on the Jewish Rathenau by Helfferich in the Reichstag, the former was murdered by Org C men. Wirth's continuing prowestern orientation and French hostility inflamed all German chauvinistic and reactionary organizations—among them the DNVP, the National Socialist party (Nationalsozialistische Deutsche Arbeiterpartei or NSDAP), the racist Deutsch-Völkisch party, Gustav von Kahr's (1862–1934) antifederalist Bavarian People's party, and paramilitary groups, including the Einwohnerwehren, Operland, Werwolf, and the NSDAP's Sturmabteilung or SA (storm troopers).

In this time of peril the German People's party and the Communist party temporarily rallied to the defense of the state. The DVP agreed in July, 1922, to form a "working fellowship of the constitutional middle" with the Center and Democrats, while the KPD, under orders from the Kremlin, put its Rote Front Kämpferbund (Red Front Battle Organization) into the fight against reaction. Also, in Prussia, meanwhile, Otto Braun had succeeded in broadening his cabinet by taking the DVP into what came to be known as the Great Coalition (SPD, Democrats, Center, and DVP). By such shifts as these, White Terrorist hopes that the reviled "Jewish-Catholic-Socialist state" would be overthrown were for the moment frustrated.

The German republic was saved at a price. Few decisions in its history can have been more baleful in the long run than that which prompted the SPD, at first on the *Länder* level and then in the Reich government, to collaborate with the DVP. The latter never had been, nor was in 1922, a genuinely democratic or even a truly republican party. The defense of the republic in which the DVP now indulged amounted to no more than a transient tactic. The prowestern left-wing leader Gustav Stresemann (1878–1929) was under perpetual attack from the party's right wing, which ultimately by 1930 came to prevail. Under the circumstances, the DVP, which was closely identified with economic interest groups, was prevented from contributing anything positive to the cause of democracy.

Occupation of the Ruhr

Since the SPD was not yet ready to enter a national cabinet of the Great Coalition, the Wirth government, its credit entirely dissipated, resigned in the autumn of 1922. It was succeeded by a government of economic and financial experts from among the middle bourgeois parties, headed by Dr. Wilhelm Cuno (1876–1933), the director-general of the Hamburg-Amerika steamship line. Cuno was soon called upon to meet the Franco-Belgian military occupation of the Ruhr, which began January 11, 1923.

It was a little thing that Poincaré seized upon as pretext for the invasion of the Ruhr—a default in the matter of delivering 140,000 telegraph poles. He insisted that the Germans were plotting to defraud the French of just reparations, and his reaction was out of all proportion to the triviality of the failure.

For the next seven and one-half months (until September 26, 1923) the German people, encouraged by their government, staged a campaign of passive resistance to the French and Belgian invaders. The population of the Ruhr sabotaged the occupation, and what came close to being a general strike paralyzed all important services in the area. The French fired on recalcitrant workers, causing many deaths, and French courts sentenced resistance leaders, including Alfred Krupp, to long prison terms. One saboteur, Leo Schlageter, who was executed in May by the French, was later regarded as a martyr by the Nazis.

During many months of disorder, pillage, and sabotage in the Ruhr, the French position was: first unconditional submission, then negotiations. Although the German position was the reverse, the Ruhr industrialists did not cleave to this line. Their dependence upon global markets gradually caused their fervor to abate. The workers were still willing to make any sacrifice for the fatherland, but by summer the Ruhr industrialists and bankers, encouraged by Cuno and Hugo Stinnes (1870–1924), head of the mighty Stinnes conglomerate, had signed agreements with their French counterparts. This was tantamount to abandoning passive resistance.

Cuno was as much to blame as the French for the misery that had engulfed Germany. Abjuring the wise fulfillment policy of his predecessors, he had allowed the dangerous confrontation with France to persist over a difference of only 8 billion gold marks—the gap between the German offer of May 2 and the figure proposed by Paris. Eventually ever sharper attacks upon Cuno by the Socialists and trade unionists forced him to resign on August 11.

The deepening economic crisis and the depletion of trade union treasuries, meanwhile, impelled the masses in more radical directions. As the lust for violence grew, the ranks of the anticonstitutional parties began to swell ominously. In the summer of 1923 an exodus from the SPD to the KPD took place. It is just possible that Arthur Rosenberg was right when he said that at some point in the course of that year the bulk of the proletariat was pro-Communist. However, in view of the fact that the Kurt Brandler–Ernst Thälmann leadership of the KPD dangled from strings manipulated by the Kremlin, the German Communists at no time posed a real revolutionary threat.

Stresemann's Great Coalition

Because of the gravity of the crisis, the SPD, against the opposition of 47 of its deputies, entered a bourgeois government of the Great Coalition. This ministry, organized on August 12, 1923, by Gustav Stresemann (1878–1929), the leader of the DVP, comprised DVP, Center, Democratic party, and SPD. The Stresemann government had been thrown together hastily to rescue Bismarck's handiwork. In that hour the French were striving to detach the Rhineland, radical leftist governments controlled Thuringia and Saxony, and in Bavaria the racists were girding for a stroke against the republic. Fearful of the immediate future, the SPD put heavy pressure on Stresemann to liquidate at once the calamitous policy of passive resistance.

From the outset of his ministry, Stresemann realized that Germany could expect no aid from England and that his country, which had lost the struggle, must now negotiate. In hopes of being able to save the Ruhr and the Rhineland, he commenced with an offer to pledge the entire remaining portion of Germany's industrial wealth as guarantee that the reparations schedules would be met. Inasmuch as the French rejected this and a second offer by Stresemann, the chancellor was ultimately obliged to kowtow. With the mark virtually worthless and the life's savings of millions of Germans wiped out by inflation, Stresemann announced on September 26 that passive resistance was over, and bayonets had won.

In the autumn of 1923 the focus of power within the German People's party began to shift away from Stresemann toward the right. An anti-Marxist virus was raging through the capitalist stratum, and big business was howling for the head of the Socialist finance minister, Rudolf Hilferding (1877–1940). His proposals for sharply increased taxes upon large incomes and property and his resistance to demands to abolish the eight-hour work day alienated the bourgeoisie. The Kahr-Knilling regime in Bavaria, in particular, demanded that the Socialists be dropped from the ministry and a wholly bourgeois-landlord government be constituted. Stresemann was obliged to let Hilferding go on October 6, but the Socialists remained one of the legs of his ministry. Although heavy industry now put its candidate, Dr. Hans Luther (1879–1962) into the ministry of finance, the SPD chose to collaborate with this more markedly middle-class government because it seemed to be the only alternative to rightist dictatorship backed by the Reichswehr. Stresemann's second ministry, in which the chancellor continued to be his own foreign minister, was pledged to open negotiations with the Entente as soon as possible, try to make reparations deliveries, and secure the evacuation of the Ruhr.

A most dangerous precedent was set on October 13, 1923. Under threat of dissolution, the Reichstag adopted by a vote of 316 to 34 an enabling act that conferred emergency powers upon the government. This act was to be used solely for purposes of stabilizing the currency and defending the republic against coups from the right or the left. Care had been taken that whenever the Reichstag desired, the act would instantly lapse. Nevertheless, it was a serious blunder to transfer ultimate authority, even if only temporarily, from a Reichstag, where the democratic forces were still strong, to a ministry where they were considerably weaker.

A little more than a week later the Socialists discovered their mistake. Toward the end of October the Reichswehr, acting under orders from Defense Minister Gessler, marched into Saxony and Thuringia and forcibly deposed the constitutionally elected SPD-KPD coalition "workers' governments." The SPD was also incensed that Stresemann should have used the slogan of "stabilizing finances" as a bludgeon with which to beat down social-welfare legislation and the gains the working class had scored since 1918. When events in Bavaria confirmed suspicions that Stresemann preferred relations with racists and reactionaries to coalition with the socialists, the SPD left the cabinet on November 2.

On November 8 the Hitler-Ludendorff "beer hall" putsch took place in Munich. Encouraged by the questionable internal and military policies of both the Reich and Bavarian governments, the conspirators staged a comic opera scene in the *Hofbräuhaus*. Adolf Hitler (1889–1945), a low-born, histrionic Austrian who had served in the German army in the war and had been awarded the iron cross, had scraped together drifters, ne'er-do-wells, reactionaries, and racists into the National Socialist (Nazi) party. With its support he had, on November 8, forced the reactionary Bavarian minister president, Gustav von Kahr (1862–1934), and the rebellious General von Lossow to join himself and Ludendorff in their attempt to establish a military dictatorship. The putsch, which collapsed with bloodshed within twenty-four hours, exposed the nature of the Bavarian regime for which Stresemann had put the country in jeopardy. Having forcibly expelled the popularly elected leftist coalition governments in central Germany, the chancellor had declined to use the military against the refractory and illegal regime in Bavaria because that might have driven the Bavarians to secede from the Reich. Stresemann's decision illustrated the class prejudice of his now wholly bourgeois ministry.

On November 23 Stresemann was abandoned by the racists and nationalists because of his "lenience" toward the Marxists. When he resigned, the conservative Centrist jurist Wilhelm Marx (1863–1946) formed a new government that featured the nonparty man Luther at finance and Stresemann at the foreign office. Marx's ministry rested upon a coalition of the DVP, Bavarian People's party, Center, and Democratic party. The SPD now retreated to the loyal opposition for four years.

It was hard to determine whether the Marx government commanded strong support in the country. It had been four years since parliamentary elections. Since then almost every party had undergone profound transformation. Nevertheless, the middle class in November, 1923, thought it still too risky to hold new elections. Therefore, the ruling powers contented themselves with reshuffling a crooked deck.

The Dawes Plan

The first months of 1924 brought auspicious changes in western Europe. On January 21 the British Conservatives were defeated and a reformist Socialist, Ramsay MacDonald, became prime minister. This promised to take the edge off Poincaré's intransigence and contribute to the pacification of the continent. At the same time, the collapse on February 17, 1924, of the French-supported separatist regime in the "autonomous Rhenish Palatinate" betokened the end of French "black-jack" tactics. Poincaré's encouragement of Rhenish and Bavarian separatism had stoked the fires of revenge in Germany, which had ended by alienating many French voters. The latter, moreover, were coming to believe that the Ruhr invasion was to be blamed for the depreciation of the franc.

As chancellor, Stresemann had proved to be impossible because of his reactionary mentality. As foreign-minister, he turned out to be a wizard. The convention he signed with England in 1924 was the first in a long string of modest successes. It provided for the reduction of German export taxes, levied under the Reparations Recovery Act of March, 1921, from 26 percent to 5 percent ad valorem. German trade and industry were the beneficiaries. Meanwhile, international committees that had been established in November, 1923, had prepared the Dawes Plan. Submitted to Germany in April, 1924, the plan provided for a more practical, but still onerous, amortization schedule. Reparations payments were to begin with 1 billion marks and rise until by 1928–29 they reached 2.5 billion. Germany was to be helped to make her first payment with a largely American-financed loan that almost equalled the first reparations installment. The plan was a repudiation of Poincaré's retributive policy, for the perspective was now no longer that the Reich should pay but how much it could afford to.

Before the Dawes Plan could go into effect, it had to be accepted by a two-thirds majority in the Reichstag and be endorsed by the French government. The latter followed automatically after Éduard Herriot's conciliatory leftist Cartel came to power in France in May. The Dawes Plan did not pass until August, because of the rapidly growing strength of the Nationalists, who for long had opposed it as a species of debt slavery.

The Reichstag elections of May 4, 1924, revealed that the electorate had polarized. Both extremes had gained at the expense of the middle parties. The Nationalists had not only taken the November beer hall fiasco in their stride but, on a purely negative foreign policy platform, polled 35 percent more votes than in 1920 and sent 96 deputies into the lower house. The National Socialist Freedom party had won almost 2 million votes and 32 mandates in spite of the fact that its leader, Adolf Hitler, was then roosting in the prison of Landsberg am Lech. The KPD had climbed to fourth rank, polling 3.7 million votes—a 700 percent increase over 1920—and had returned 62 deputies to the Reichstag. The SPD had lost 71 of its 171 mandates. Counting the support of 10 independent rightists, the DNVP had emerged as the strongest party in the republic!

The aggregate strength of the antidemocratic parties now comprised 243 out of 472—a majority. Having neglected to renovate the bureaucracy and judiciary or democratize the army, and having early lost the chancellorship, the democratic camp was now thrust back upon the defensive. The sands were, in fact, running out for the "abandoned" republic. In 1925 its foes even captured the presidency. Probably it was only the economic recovery, which began in 1924, that postponed the overthrow of the Weimar regime. A euphoria began to rise in Germany, which sapped the vigor and support of all parties that flourished on acute discontent.

By the summer of 1924 even the DNVP was forced to see that improvement of Germany's general position was a hard fact and that sabotage of the Dawes system would simply be regarded by the public as a wrecking tactic. In the key debate over the railroad bill, therefore, the leadership of the party instructed its Reichstag deputies that they might vote at their discretion and in disregard of party discipline. This insured acceptance of legislation needed to implement the Dawes Plan regardless of the unalterable opposition of the KPD and the racist groups.

No radical departure from the Versailles regimen, the Dawes Plan nevertheless inaugurated an era of economic normalcy. For the first time the Reich could now turn its energies wholly toward economic reconstruction. Germany no longer had to fear an unheralded French attack, and the Ruhr ceased to be a "pledge" for reparations payments. France abandoned her encouragement of Rhenish and Bavarian separatism, and by 1925 the last phase of French troop withdrawals from the Ruhr had been accomplished. Not only had an era of conciliation been inaugurated in foreign affairs, but the Nationalists' completely negative attitude toward the republic had been compromised. These gains were not without their price, which was the financial dependence of Germany upon continued American short-term loans and prosperity.

Recovery

In 1923 Germany suffered financial collapse. In the course of the most devastating currency depreciation in the nation's history the mark had declined in value from 65 to the dollar in April, 1921, to 6,600,000,000,000 to the dollar in mid-November, 1923. Merchandise began to disappear from market and acute shortages developed. Meanwhile, a handful of entrepeneurs made fantastic profits by financing undertakings with short-term loans, then repaying on maturity with paper money of sharply reduced value. On the other hand, practically everyone whose capital had been in liquid assets, such as bonds, treasury notes, debentures, securities, mortgages, or savings accounts, lost everything. While the few made huge fortunes, the many went bankrupt. At length, however, the mark was stabilized on November 15, 1923, at 1,000,000,000 paper marks to one of gold. The government's action provoked a new wave of business failures because corporations were now obliged to repay depreciated paper debts in hard money.

There was a transitional period during which a rentenmark, which was secured only by the value of German industry and agriculture, was used for payment of public debts to all agents under contract to the government. Then early in 1924, before arrival of the Dawes loan, the Reichsbank was empowered to issue new notes, which, unlike rentenmarks, passed as legal tender. Finally, the Reichsbank founded the Gold Discount Bank to aid in obtaining credits in foreign currencies and in hitching the mark to gold. A last step in the reconstruction of the German monetary system was taken on August 30, 1924, when the reichsmark (RM), with a value of .238 dollars, was made the basis of the currency.

Monetary stabilization brought a retreat from extremism. The efforts of the Communists and Nazis to keep alive the fire of hatred now fell on wet straw. In the Reichstag elections of December 7, 1924, the National Socialist party, crippled by the secession of the Great German People's group, lost 14 of its 32 mandates and for some years thereafter ceased to be a serious factor in politics. The KPD, too, suffered losses. The DNVP gained slightly (from 96 to 103 mandates), but this may have been due to having jumped on the Dawes bandwagon. The big winner was the SPD, which increased its Reichstag representation to 131 to become the strongest party once more. However, in the Prussian *Landtag* elections, held on the same day, the Communists and Nationalists made modest gains.

For the next five years, governments headed successively by Wilhelm Marx, Hans Luther, and the Socialist Hermann Müller, discharged Germany's scheduled reparations payments under the Dawes Plan. At the same time German business boomed for the first time since 1914. As the loans came trooping gaily in from Wall Street, the public ignored the blusterings of the extremists and put its nose to the grindstone. Industry was revitalized, retooled, and rationalized. Civil aviation (Junkers, Heinkel, Dornier, Focke-Wolf, and Willy Messerschmitt's Bavarian Aircraft companies) was born, while Erhard Milch (future co-architect of the Luftwaffe) helped organize the state-controlled Deutsche Lufthansa (German Airlines).

The whole infrastructure of the nation was transformed. Schools, hospitals, playgrounds, theaters sprang up. Prewar levels of production were in most cases surpassed by 1926. The 1914 level of exports was reached in 1929, and the next year the rebuilt German merchant marine attained a tonnage that almost equaled that of 1913. Thus, in spite of all pejoratives hurled at the Versailles Treaty, the territorial losses of 1919 and 1921 proved to be no more ruinous for Germany than the loss of Alsace-Lorraine had been for France in 1871.

Whereas commercial credit was eased for entrepeneurs and cartels, and syndicates and conglomerates were encouraged by the federal law of 1923, the bourgeois Weimar governments were not nearly so magnanimous toward the workers. Although the constitution had conferred upon the central government supervisory power over labor relations, this authority was not used to improve the economic position of the workers. The advance in real wages during the years 1924–29 was minuscule by comparison with that in corporative profits and capital gains. Furthermore, very few of the objectives of the SPD, as announced in its Berlin platform of 1924—income and corporative tax reform, establishment of public ownership of the key industries, government regulation of business, the eight-hour day, and expansion of the social insurance system—elicited any kind of ministerial support.

The Conservatives Capture the Presidency

Neither the revolutionaries nor the counterrevolutionaries rocked the boat in the brief interval between the end of the Ruhr occupation and the beginning of the Great Depression. The Communists, intimidated by the rightward swing of Stalin, had ceased to believe in or work for world revolution. The German Nationalists, basking in affluence, no longer felt the urgency of a monarchical restoration. Nobody paid much attention to the ravings of the racists, and Hitler's book *Mein Kampf (My Struggle)* was ridiculed as *Mein Krampf* (My Cramp) by an indifferent public. No great divide was reached during these five years, and foreign policy was but a pale reflection of the general desire for stability.

On February 10, 1925, the 47-year-old Hans Luther became chancellor. A sympathizer with the DVP right, he formed the most reactionary cabinet yet—comprising DVP, Center, and, for the first time, the DNVP, all economic interest agents rather than true political parties. Eighteen days later President Ebert died. He had made important contributions to the well-being of Germany. Without trumpet blast or display he had toiled daily in his stuffy office, with its old furniture and two windows, at the pedestrian task of building a democratic society and restoring the good name of Germany. The reactionaries, who had seen in him the incarnation of the execrated republic, had never forgiven him. Upon his death, they nominated one of their own, General von Hindenburg, to succeed him.

In the run-off presidential election of April 25, 1925, Hindenburg, the simpleminded monarchist and militarist, defeated the joint candidate of all the defenders of the republic, Wilhelm Marx. By a vote of 14.6 million to 13.7 million the reactionaries stormed the last stronghold in the state, which till then had eluded their grasp. Yet, if the Communists had not thrown their votes away upon Ernst Thälmann, there might have been a different story to tell.

The Treaties of Locarno and Berlin

During the years of "normalcy," the chief successes of Stresemann's policy were the Locarno treaties and the admission of Germany to the League Council. Stresemann achieved these things in the face of opposition from the KDP, DNVP, and elements of his own party. Externally, Soviet Russia tried to demolish the western orientation, while the Allied Control Council constantly harped upon alleged breaches of the disarmament clauses.

The Locarno treaties, the product of the joint efforts of Stresemann and the leftist French premier, Éduard Herriot, were Germany's response to a specific threat to her. The Allies had refused on January 5, 1925, to evacuate the first, or Cologne, zone of the Rhineland. Stresemann feared that this was the prolegomenon to a new Anglo-French entente. To prevent this and secure the staged military evacuation of the Rhineland, which was the precondition of total German sovereignty, the foreign minister decided to sue at the French counter without further delay. It was his good furtune that the Labor government in Britain had been overthrown, because Ramsay MacDonald had preferred collective security to the regional approach. If he had remained prime minister he would probably have supported the Geneva Protocol of 1924, which envisaged branding any nation an aggressor that refused or repudiated an arbitration settlement. Along that road France would not have been obliged to evacuate the Rhineland, and Germany might not have been admitted to the League Council so soon.

Stresemann shrewdly stressed the security aspect of his proposed tripartite pact rather than evacuation of the Rhineland. He understood that, failing an Anglo-French alliance, some other form of guarantee of the permanence of the eastern frontiers of France could alone induce her to surrender what amounted to an initial operational base in Germany in case of war. Stresemann was encouraged in his efforts at direct agreement with France and Belgium by the evidence that Great Britain was reluctant to ally with France and much preferred another solution of the security problem. Internally, however, Stresemann had to cope initially with cross fire from Seeckt and the DNVP, who feared that a western convention might harm relations with Russia.

Intimidated by Stresemann's vague admonition that the alternative to a western security pact would be a Russo-German entente, the British and French grasped his proffered hand. On October 15–16, 1925, a nonaggression pact was negotiated in the Locarno-Ascona area of the Swiss Ticino by Stresemann, British Foreign Secretary Austin Chamberlain, and French Foreign Minister Aristide Briand. The pact "finalized" existing frontiers among France, Belgium, and Germany, which implied Germany's definite renunciation of Alsace-Lorraine, and perpetuated the demilitarized status of the Rhineland. Britain and Italy stood guarantors of the treaty. Supplementing it were arbitration agreements providing for amicable settlement of disputes among the contracting parties as well as among Germany, Poland, and Czechoslovakia. Among the latter powers there was no recognition of permanent frontiers, and no security pact was signed. In the delicate negotiations that were characterized by much less cooperation and amity than was formerly supposed (Jon Jacobson), Briand's eye was on the British guarantee of French security, and Stresemann's was on the termination of Allied occupation of German soil and a compromise on disarmament.

Neither Stresemann nor any other German foreign minister until 1970 dared to recognize the finality of the German-Polish border. This has caused some historians to insist that Stresemann was pursuing a potentially aggressive policy in the east and that the German government did not regard the Reichswehr merely as a defensive weapon. From the short-range viewpoint this assessment is an exaggeration. Yet it remains a question whether Stresemann would have been prepared in fifteen years or so to have solved the Polish problem by force. When, during the winter and spring of 1924–25 the Marx-Stresemann government agreed with Moscow on the desirability of "driving Poland back," the Weimar ministry was formulating an aim that was in principle to enjoy the adherence of every government from that of Marx to Kurt Kiesinger. On the other hand, as Hans Gatzke has shown, Stresemann's aims in the east were purposely left vague in 1924–25 and he did not contemplate any action to expel the Poles from former German territories. Rather, in a far more devious approach to his ultimate goals in the east, he sought to solicit a moral indictment by Britain and the USSR of the injustice of Germany's frontier with Poland. Beyond this, he hoped more tangibly, as has cogently been argued by Helmut Lippelt, to strengthen Germany's international position, demote the German-Polish border to secondary importance, weaken Poland's ties with France, and build up a revisionist bloc to counterbalance the hitherto crushing hegemony of France in Europe.

Although the DNVP sabotaged Stresemann's treaties when it withdrew from the government on October 23, 1925, the Reichstag, recognizing in them victory in both west and east, accepted them in November by a vote of 275 to 183. When Reichsrat and president also approved Locarno, the way was open to the admission of Germany to a permanent seat on the Council of the League of Nations. Meanwhile, Stresemann could argue that since Locarno had greatly augmented French security there was no longer reason for continued occupation of the Rhineland.

In October, 1925, Germany moved to calm Russian apprehensions respecting Locarno by negotiating a new treaty with Moscow. The Treaty of Berlin, signed on April 24, 1926, pledged the signatories to friendship and nonaggression for five years and obligated Germany to oppose any anti-Russian action undertaken by the League of Nations. Germany also promised to refuse transit rights to French troops seeking to aid Poland, which contributed to the growing isolation of that country. Since the Treaty of Berlin secured Germany's eastern frontier in the event of war with France, the Reichstag approved the pact with only three dissenting votes. France countered by allying with Rumania.

From Luther to Müller

The negative attitude of the Nationalists toward Locarno necessitated the formation of a second Luther ministry (January 26, 1926). The new government rested on another bourgeois combination, which was tacitly tolerated by the SPD. When in the spring Luther's government foundered over a dispute involving the national flag, another Wilhelm Marx ministry, a replica of Luther's, succeeded in May. It remained in office till the end of 1926, when the Nationalists were brought back into the government again.

Luther and Marx achieved certain successes in foreign affairs. Germany's admission in 1926 to a permanent seat on the League Council and the rejection (with approval of England and France) of Poland's bid for permanent status on the council amounted not merely to international recognition of the conciliatory policy of the German Republic but to defeat and isolation for Poland (J. Spenz, Lippelt, and M. Gilbert). Stresemann might now conclude that a main obstacle in the way of frontier revision in the east had been removed. Amicable general talks between Stresemann and Briand at Thoirry near Geneva on September 17, 1926, were followed by the withdrawal on January 31, 1927, of the Allied Military Control Commission from German soil and transfer of supervision of disarmament to the League. Then, on August 27, 1928, Germany signed, along with fourteen other powers, the Kellogg-Briand (Paris) Pact, outlawing war as an instrument of policy.

To a degree Stresemann was embarrassed by the activities of the Reichswehr and the armaments industry. Gessler relieved the pressure on him somewhat by pressing successfully for the dismissal of General von Seeckt from the *Heeresleitung* (1926) and his replacement by General Wilhelm Heye (1869–1946). Unfortunately Gessler, himself, was obliged to resign on January 28, 1928, because of the malfeasance of a subordinate in the Reichswehr ministry and because the Reichswehr itself had been under caustic attack for many months from Scheidemann and his Socialist colleagues.

One of the first duties of the democratically minded General Wilhelm Groener (1867–1939), who was appointed to succeed Gessler as minister for the Reichswehr, was to review Germany's eastern military policy. Renewed Polish incursions in Silesia caused him to strengthen the recently organized Border Defense *(Grenzschutz)*. On the other hand, Groener was far less inclined than the Reichswehr officers or than German iron, steel, and armaments manufacturers to extend more aid to the USSR to equip the Red army or augment Soviet military production. Stresemann, Luther, and Marx were even more opposed. Thus, the German government torpedoed a trade agreement that the Krupp firm entered into to furnish the Russians with steel and artillery, and in early 1930 pressure was brought to bear on Rheinmetall to repudiate the contract it had just signed with the USSR. The army chief, General Hammerstein-Equort (1878–1943), who succeeded Heye, was more responsive to Russian blandishments. However, Hammerstein's view was to elicit only rejection from Chancellor Hermann Müller and Foreign Minister Julius Curtius (1877–1948), who opposed entering into any arrangements that might delay Allied withdrawal from the Rhineland or disrupt adoption of the Young (reparations) Plan.

Plainly, none of the discussions that the Weimar government or the Reichswehr quietly conducted with Soviet Russia seriously undermined the Treaty of Versailles. Although the German government was generally aware of all important negotiations, it never gave unhesitant support to any of them. At all times the government set decided limits to Russo-German military collaboration. National civil authorities were not only steadfastly prowestern in their thinking and sympathies, but they sincerely feared that a truly mighty Russian army, trained and equipped by the Weimar Republic, might one day end by attacking it.

Elections of 1928

A long dispute over the school system led to the withdrawal of the Center party ministers from the government and to the return of the Socialists to power. In the elections of May 20, 1928, the only important victors were the SPD and the KPD. The former, swollen by an interval of prosperity, achieved its biggest success since 1919. It increased its popular vote by more than 1.2 million over that of 1924 and its Reichstag mandates from 131 to 152. The KPD, which had been under orders from the Comintern to pursue a united front with the Socialists in equivocal support of democracy and attacks upon the reactionary Reichswehr, increased its vote by 300,000 and its representation in the Reichstag from 45 to 54. All the other parties, including the Nazis, suffered losses. The antirepublican DNVP lost 25 mandates and retained only 78 deputies. The Nazis, repudiated by the electorate, were almost extinguished, retaining only 12 seats.

The Socialist leader Hermann Müller was now called upon by Hindenburg to form a new coalition government. Müller's ministry comprised representatives from the German People's party, Center, Democratic party, and the SPD. Coming to power on June 28, 1928, under auspicious circumstances, this government was destined to be the last genuinely parliamentary one in the history of the First German Republic.

Chapter 48

THE STRANGE DEATH OF THE

WEIMAR REPUBLIC

The Flight from Moderation

A momentous shift toward the right set in in all bourgeois and conservative parties during 1928. Dissatisfaction with performance in the spring elections, a deteriorating balance of international payments, overproduction, resentment of the Young Plan, and the onset of ominously high unemployment even before the Great Depression promoted a grim contest for power in the DNVP, DVP, and Center. At the same time the Democratic party, a pier of the republic, was decomposing. Parallel with these developments, the KPD, in consonance with the decisions taken by the Sixth Congress of the Third International in 1928, adopted a more hostile position toward the defenders of the state, especially the SPD, than at any time since 1920. A new polarization of public opinion was taking place. This boded ill for a regime that had not yet rid the nation of the shackles of reparations or achieved any serious modification of the peace treaty.

In July the relatively temperate leader of the DNVP, Count Kuno von Westarp (1864–1945), resigned the chairmanship of the party. He had been unwilling to endorse the intemperate language that his colleagues of the Nationalist right wing employed against the Young Plan. His successor was the industrial tycoon Alfred Hugenberg (1865–1931), who hated the republic with all his heart. His rise to dominance in the DNVP provoked a minor secession of some of its deputies in January, 1930. Under Hugenberg's guidance the party began to coquette with conspiracy against the state and entered a confederacy with the Nazis in 1930, which made Adolf Hitler appear respectable to the nobility and bourgeoisie.

With the death of Stresemann on October 3, 1929, the right wing of the German People's party, which had always had reservations about collaborating with the anticapitalist SPD, assumed the leadership of the DVP. Thereafter, the DVP, a party of steadily dwindling popular support, moved toward a dissolution of first the Great Coalition in the Reich and then of the multiparty system itself.

Gravity within the Center party also shifted toward the right in 1928–29. To the leadership of a Stegerwald, who had stood close to the Christian Trade Unions, and a Wilhelm Marx, who had held the balance between the party ultras, now succeeded the conservative papal supporter, Monsignor Dr. Ludwig Kaas (1881–1952), and his floor leader in the Reichstag, Heinrich Brüning (1885–1970). Both of these men had been sharp critics of Stresemann's policy of fulfillment and had toyed with the idea of forming an interparty conservative front against socialism. Behind them stood a number of influential Catholic bishops, among them some, like Cardinal Faulhaber of Munich (1869–1952), who were actually foes of the republic. The strengthening of contacts between the Center party, on the one hand, and conservative landed and business interests, on the other, subverted the mutual confidence that had sustained the Great Coalitions in both the Reich and Prussia.

The flirtation of the center with the right was the more serious in that it came at a time when mass support of the Democratic and the People's parties was evaporating into thin air and the Communists were denouncing the Socialists as "social fascists." The conduct of the Centrist leaders helped to demolish the democratic party system.

Young Plan and Depression

The Young Plan of 1929, named after Owen Young, the American chairman of the reparations commission that drafted it, was mainly important for the stimulus it unintentionally gave to the radicalization of German public opinion. The plan provided for the amortization of Germany's reparations liability over a period of 59 years. Annuity payments were to begin at 1,675 million Marks and rise to almost 2,000 million in 1937–38, when they were to run until 1965–66 at about 1,708 million annually, and thereafter until 1988 at around 2,400 million annually. The Young Plan payment schedules were 17 percent lower than those of the Dawes Plan. Nevertheless, the former postulated two things for success: continued foreign loans and prolonged German prosperity.

The Young Plan, adopted on March 11, 1930, was Stresemann's last achievement. All external Allied controls over the Reichsbank and railroad were dissolved, and the Rhineland was now entirely freed of occupying troops. The ultras, however, objected that these concessisons were illusory, for they did not make the German government master in its own house. The reparations debt would still constitute a heavy mortgage upon German production and revenue for the next two generations. To his detractors, Stresemann was always seeing violins hanging from heaven, but the trouble was they had no strings and their sounding boards were cracked.

Harping on the theme of betrayal of eternal German interests, the DNVP and the NSDAP joined hands in November, 1929. The working arrangement had the support of the president of the Reichsbank, Dr. Hjalmar Schacht (1877–1970). The Hugenberg-Hitler-Schacht Fronde proposed a "Law against the Enslavement of the German People," which they called the "Freedom Law." It repudiated the war guilt clause and declared that Germany would pay no more reparations. When the proposal obtained more than 4 million signatures, it was submitted by popular initiative to the Reichstag, which rejected it. Then the measure was submitted to a plebiscite. In a campaign that was remarkable for passion and defamation the Freedom Law went down to defeat, receiving only 6 million of the 21 million votes needed to make it the law of the land. Nevertheless, the campaign brought the NSDAP once again into the limelight, garish though it may have been, and introduced Hitler to men of great wealth and influence on the right.

Even before the New York Stock Exchange crash of October 23–24, 1929, the German economy had begun to stagnate. Automation and rationalization coupled with a decline in exports combined to bring about a dangerous level of unemployment in the winter of 1928–29, when 2.4 million were jobless. A general decline in world agricultural prices, provoked in part by Russian "dumping," also helped diminish the purchasing power of German consumers. This left manufacturers with mounting inventories and falling earnings. Although unemployment sank again in the summer of 1929, it began to skyrocket when the Wall Street bankers' panic hit Germany. In a twinkling the fundament of German prosperity and reparations capability collapsed, because American short-term loans were recalled. Suddenly it became clear that Stresemann's castles had been built on air.

Hilferding, Müller's finance minister, was unable to cope with the situation. In the typhoon that engulfed the nation the Socialists had no ready panacea. Faced with a situation where large strata of the public were pauperized for the second time in the history of the republic, the government coalition could formulate no fiscal or taxation policies that might have saved the economy. When in December, 1929, the antirepublican Schacht refused to lend Reichsbank money to the state unless the Müller ministry increased taxes and decreased outlays for social purposes, the government was set on the inclined plane of insolvency.

The Crucial Fight over Social Insurance

During the winter of 1929–30 the rightist parties waged a campaign against exorbitant governmental expenditures, which, crystallized in a demand for reduction of unemployment insurance benefit payments, forced Hilferding's resignation from the finance ministry. The SPD countered this campaign by proposing an increase of one-half of 1 percent (3.5 to 4 percent) in unemployment insurance premiums, with employers and employees each underwriting an increase of one-fourth of 1 percent. The DVP insisted that the line should be held at 3.5 percent and that the government should either defray the increased costs of operating the unemployment insurance program or reduce annuity payments to the jobless.

Ostensibly it was on this issue, where the gap that separated the coalition parties was only one-half of 1 percent, that the Müller ministry was overthrown. From this circumstance historians have argued that the SPD ought to have been more accommodating, since there was no feasible parliamentary alternative to government by the Great Coalition. Although this argument is valid, it should be pointed out in fairness to the SPD that it and the trade unions were alarmed at the increasing ascendancy of reaction in the Center, DVP, and DNVP and the threat of a capitalist dictatorship.

To the extent that the Socialist leaders took this heroic stand in defense of working-class interests, they remained, as Erich Matthias has affirmed, the staunchest champions of German parliamentary democracy. But to the degree that Socialist tactics in 1930 were still conditioned by outmoded Marxist postulates, the SPD was prevented, as Karl Dietrich Bracher has averred, from exhausting all possibilities of rescuing the national Great Coalition. As it turned out, the fall of Müller's ministry on March 27, 1930, brought an end to parliamentary government. Henceforth for the remainder of the life of the moribund republic, no other combination of parties could command the support of a majority in the Reichstag.

Brüning and the Presidential Dictatorship

At the suggestion of the politically ambitious General Kurt von Schleicher (1882–1934), an official in the Defense Ministry, Hindenburg commissioned the bourgeois leader of the Catholic Center, Heinrich Brüning, to form a new government. Brüning, who had the appearance of the white rabbit in _Alice in Wonderland_, put together a ministry solely of DVP, Center, and Democratic party members that had only minority support in the Reichstag. Under the circumstances, he accepted Hindenburg's advice to govern by presidential fiat. This was tantamount to the resumption of authoritarian government in Germany. That the public tolerated this dangerous augmentation of executive power shows the lengths to which people are prepared to go in stormy times to obtain resolute leadership.

When Brüning failed to secure parliamentary approval of his requests for higher taxes on middle and upper incomes, reduced unemployment insurance annuity payments, and higher tariffs on agricultural produce, Hindenburg resorted to his presidential emergency powers. In doing so, he deliberately violated the constitution. Article 48 was to have been employed only in case of an armed attack or a revolt against the republic. Even then, government by decree was to terminate on demand of the Reichstag. Brüning, of course, promised that the government would not abuse Article 48 but would have recourse to it only in cases where a deadlocked Reichstag was unable to discharge its constitutional responsibilities. Thus, presidential dictatorship was established in Germany, which was to afford a first precedent for Hitler. Hindenburg and Brüning were resolved, almost in defiance of the country, to pull it out of the worst of all economic swamps. Neither had the ability to manage the task or even looked as if he did. Hindenburg, at 83, was already wandering in the mists of senility, while Brüning altogether lacked the charisma that makes people believe one can perform miracles.

Brüning was temporarily spared because neither the Nationalists nor the Socialists had made up their minds to overthrow his ministry. The decision of the Nationalists, in disregard of Hugenberg's demand, to tolerate Brüning while refusing to endorse his specific measures led to the dissolution of the working arrangement between the DNVP and the NSDAP. An incensed Hitler went his own megalomaniacal way for more than a year, trying by obstructionism in the Reichstag and assaults and murders in the streets, which were perpetrated by the Nazis' _Sturmabteilung_ (SA), to make orderly government an impossibility.

The street fights, violence, and killings practiced by the SA and the Stahlhelm (Steel Helmet) paramilitary organization of veterans headed by Franz Seldte (1882–1947) mounted as unemployment rose. By June, 1930, there were more than 3 million jobless, of whom only two-thirds received unemployment benefits or poor relief. But it was not so much unemployment as the deficit that preoccupied Brüning. As a strictly orthodox financier, he was determined to balance the budget by devising new taxes and effecting economies. He did not seriously consider increasing the national debt by creating jobs for the destitute. His thought was to raise unemployment insurance premiums on management and labor from

3.5 to 4.5 percent. His worst mistake, however, was the failure to stamp out the paramilitary organizations of armed hoodlums. This omission left in the hands of the terrorists the sledgehammer with which they were soon to shatter the republic.

The September, 1930, Elections

Brüning also seriously erred when he dissolved the Reichstag on July 18, 1930, two days after it had rejected his fiscal proposals by a vote of 256 to 193. The predominantly left-centrist, republican Reichstag had two more years to run. By then, conceivably, the worst of the depression would be past, and the Nazis, who in 1930 were making alarming gains, would have passed their peak and entered upon decline. Unfortunately Brüning, hoping for a majority to support his fiscal policies, called elections at a time when his adversaries were flexing their muscles and he himself could point to no successes.

The Nazis, confident of victory, waged an aggressive fight. They promised jobs to the industrial workers, relief to the peasants, and better earnings to the bourgeoisie. They castigated the Jews, thereby ingratiating themselves with the traditionally anti-Semitic agricultural element, and they flayed the Socialists and Communists, which gratified the middle class. They denounced international-finance capitalism, which pleased many radical workers. And they rang the changes on the Treaty of Versailles and pilloried France, which appealed to almost everyone.

The National Socialist German Workers' party was not confined to any one class or religious confession and so could claim that it was more thoroughly German and populist *(völkisch)* than was any other party. Hitler, who had only the fuzziest idea of economics, offered a dozen panaceas to cope with the depression, many of them in conflict with each other. But that did not matter. What the masses saw behind his melodramatics, paranoiac shouting, and Nietzschean apotheosis of sheer will power, were vigor, resolution, and courage.

In the September, 1930, elections the NSDAP vote skyrocketed from 800,000 in 1928 to 6.5 million. The Nazi mandate in the Reichstag increased from 12 to 107. Brüning's hopes for a good showing by the newly organized Conservative People's party and the German State party (a derivative of the Democratic party) were wholly disappointed. All of the middle parties suffered further attrition. Most of the apostates went over to the Nazis or the Communists. The KPD, which had attacked all parties, increased its vote from 3.25 million to 4.25 million and its Reichstag representation from 54 to 77. The SPD lost only 500,000 voters, dropping from 153 to 143 mandates.

Not only did the new Reichstag offer Brüning no majority; it was far less viable than its predecessor, for it now contained 200 deputies who were hostile to the republic.

No Bed of Roses

Brüning was obliged to continue the presidential dictatorship. He had no alternative, for the warring political parties threatened to tear the state asunder and the depression was steadily deepening. The authoritarian regime served the interests mainly of the capitalist-managerial and large landowner classes. Nevertheless, the Socialists decided to tolerate Brüning as preferable to Hitler. With the decision of the SPD in October, 1930, not to challenge the principle of rule by emergency decree, German parliamentary democracy was doomed.

A second jolt was dealt the economy when in May, 1931, the Oesterreichische Kreditanstalt collapsed. On July 13, 1931, the Darmstädter und National-Bank (DANAT) closed its doors—with devastating consequences for business, banks, and the German stock exchanges. President Hoover's moratorium on all international debt payments (June, 1931) had little immediate salutary effect upon the German economy, but the government was kept solvent as a result of a RM 485 million loan from the central banks of England and France and an agreement not to recall short-term loans to Germany for six months. Nevertheless, export trade and business earnings catastrophically plummeted, and unemployment continued to mount till by 1932 it was 6 million and mass purchasing power had largely dried up. The formation of an Austro-German customs union, proposed by the Wilhelmstrasse in March, 1931, might have helped stimulate central European trade. But the French feared a *Zollverein* would be the prelude to *Anschluss*. In any case, Brüning's customs union was shot down by the World Court in the summer of 1931. All the while, meantime, the leaders of the Nazi Reichstag group—Hermann Göring (1893–1946), Paul Joseph Goebbels (1897–1945), Gregor Strasser (1892–1934), and Wilhelm Frick (1877–1946)—were making life unbearable for the chancellor. Clad in their brown-shirted uniforms, the Nazi deputies daily defamed him and had the effrontery to pose as the champions of the rights of the legislature against the executive dictatorship.

Brüning's efforts to enlist Hitler's support for the government's reparations policy at least until Hindenburg could be reelected also backfired, for Hitler now sensed the approaching opportunity to destroy democracy by its own methods. On October 11, 1931, he somewhat reluctantly entered into a front with the right wing of the DNVP at a big demonstration in the Harz Mountains town of Harzburg. However, Hitler's vanity was ruffled at Harzburg by the circumstance that Hugenberg and Seldte's *Stahlhelm* stole the show. The confederacy with the Nationalists and their industrialist backers, such as Kirdorf, Thyssen, and Voegler, which in 1933 was to carry the Nazis to power, was temporarily dissolved by the Nazi high command on February 22, 1932. On that day Goebbels announced that Hitler would be a candidate for the Reich presidency. Hugenberg's Nationalists, disgusted, temporarily forsook the *Führer*.

The NSDAP Girds for Victory

In 1930 Hitler had taken firmer control of his party. He had beaten down a developing internal revolt led by Otto Strasser, Ernst Röhm (1887–1934) and the pro-Russian Nazi element. Otto had been expelled from the party but continued to assail the growing rightist tendencies of Hitler, Göring, and Goebbels. While Göring had undertaken a minor purge of the SA, Hitler had proceeded thereafter to build up a new paramilitary organization, the SS (Schutzstaffeln) or Security Squadron, which would be more loyal than the intractable SA.

The Nazi national command or RL (Reichsleitung) now made a big effort to streamline administration, develop new affiliated organizations, make inroads into the farming and industrial elements of the population, and increase party membership. The RL bombarded the veterans' organizations with propaganda; the SA was subjected to intensive reeducation; the National Socialist Student Union was amalgamated with the Hitler Youth (Hitler Jugend or HJ) under Baldur von Schirach and directed to include children 10 to 14 years old, hitherto exempt; the League of German Girls (Bund deutscher Mädel or BDM) was founded; women's auxiliary cells *(Frauenschaften)* were organized in every district *(Gau)* and linked with the SA; and leadership schools *(Reichsführerschule)* were established for the indoctrination of party cadres. Bureaus for Race and Culture were established by Goebbels in every *Gau*. Meanwhile, under the lash of gutter language used daily in the Nazis' central newspaper, *Völkischer Beobachter*, and Goebbels' *Der Angriff*, many people in every town and hamlet were herded into Hitler's movement.

The Presidential Election

In March, 1932, Hitler was, against his judgment, persuaded to run against Hindenburg for the presidency. Brüning, who grossly underestimated the Nazi threat, had suggested that Hindenburg's term of office simply be extended by vote of the Reichstag. Hitler, however, had countered with the demand for Brüning's dismissal and the holding of new Reichstag elections.

Despite tremendous exertions by Hitler, who flew everywhere and spoke to every sort of audience during the campaign, he lost the election of March 13. The legend of Tannenberg was still sufficient to carry the octogenarian field marshal to victory, Yet, Hindenburg's margin fell short of a majority. This would not have been the case had the Communists not run their own candidate, Thälmann, or if the *Führer* had not made substantial inroads into the middle-class electorate. In the run-off election, which was fundamentally a plebiscite on Nazism, Hindenburg prevailed with 19.4 million votes to 13.4 million for Hitler and 3.7 million for Thälmann. Hitler gnashed his teeth but consoled himself with the malicious remark that Hindenburg was 83, while he, Hitler, was only 48 and could wait.

Papen as Chancellor

Still riding the crest of popularity, the Nazis in the April, 1932, elections in the *Länder* of Bavaria, Anhalt, Hamburg, Württemberg, and Prussia scored impressive successes. In Prussia, for example, the party won 162 out of 420 possible seats in the House of Deputies. These *Länder* elections put the finish to democratic government in the German states.

On May 30 Brüning was obliged to resign. Since the sole basis of his power had been the support of the president, Brüning had no alternative when he lost

Hindenburg's confidence. Although Brüning may be criticized for having consorted with authoritarian rightists, coddled the Nazis, and imposed a finance-capitalist dictatorship, he had, it must be conceded, never abandoned hope that when the depression was over, parliamentary government would be restored in Germany. He had also belatedly (April 13, 1930) promulgated a decree suppressing paramilitary organizations.

At Brüning's suggestion, Hindenburg named Colonel Franz von Papen (1879– 1969) chancellor. A very conservative, aristocratic Centrist, Papen built a cabinet of generals and Hugenberg nationalists, including Schleicher as minister of Reichswehr, which was so reactionary that it repelled even the DNVP. Nevertheless, luck smiled on Papen at the outset. The Lausanne Reparations Conference reached an agreement (never ratified) in June providing for the extension of the moratorium on reparations payments until 1935 and abrogating Germany's entire liability except for a single reparations payment of $714 million to be paid in bonds in 1935. Papen was also appointed commissioner for Prussia by Hindenburg, and the former proceeded on July 20, 1932, with all nonchalance to dismiss the Braun-Severing caretaker Great Coalition government and preempt all Prussian posts.

The coup of July 20 was a brazen stroke against the Socialists at a time when trade union treasuries were so empty that a general strike was deemed impractical. No other single act since the commencement of the presidential dictatorship did so much to condition the public to the tyranny of force. Even the national supreme court failed the republic. On October 25 it ruled that the arbitrary dismissal of the Prussian ministers did not contravene fundamental law. Before then, Papen had replaced every democratic bureaucrat in Prussia with a reactionary.

Almost the first act of Papen was to dissolve the Reichstag. His game was to built a strong anti-Marxist front. The Nazis, thriving on the depression, scored a spectacular triumph in the election of July 31, as Papen knew they would. The NSDAP returned 230 deputies to the Reichstag. NSDAP and DNVP (37 mandates) together now commanded a little more than 43 percent of the electorate. The Center and Bavarian People's party gained slightly, but the DVP and the State party were virtually extinguished. The SPD's mandate dropped from 144 to 133, and that party emerged from an election for the first time since 1912 as only the second-strongest party. The KPD booked solid gains, increasing its mandate from 77 to 89, mainly at the expense of the SPD. Together, the avowedly antirepublican parties—the NSDAP and KPD—disposed of an absolute majority of deputies in the new Reichstag. Thus, Papen is to be blamed for an initiative that virtually terminated parliamentary government in Germany.

Although the voters had jumped like fish into the Nazi frying pan, Hitler could not form an exclusively National Socialist ministry. If he were to take power legally, he would have to join forces with the DNVP, a course advocated by Gregor Strasser, Wilhelm Frick, Alfred Rosenberg, and Göring. However, Hitler himself continued to insist that he alone must be chancellor.

Papen made still another overture to the Nazis. He repealed the prohibition on SS and SA, while continuing in force that against the Communists' Red Front formations. Nevertheless, he was unable to seduce the Nazi Reichstag faction and so was forced to continue the regime of emergency decrees. Papen would not yield the chancellorship to Hitler, because he distrusted the Nazis and deplored their unorthodox financial ideas. Papen, rebuffed by Hitler, now bet upon an ebb in the tide of Nazi fortunes, for the depression seemed to have hit bottom even though in the fall of 1932 there were 6 million who were still unemployed. Papen felt that if the *Führer* continued to pursue the adamant policy urged by Göring and Göbbels, he would alienate many of his followers.

By confronting the Nazis with evidence of their declining popularity, Papen calculated that he could compel them to enter a coalition government as junior partners of the Nationalists. When the Reichstag, presided over by Göring, voted to repeal an emergency decree, Papen dissolved the house. In the elections of November 6 the Nazi vote declined from 37.3 percent to 33.1 percent of the electorate, and their mandate dropped from 230 to 196 out of a total of 584. In almost all districts Nazi strength waned. By contrast, the KPD won 17 percent of the national vote and 37.7 percent of the ballots in Berlin. The Reichstag mandate of the KPD rose from 89 to 100. The only other party to gain was the DNVP, which increased its representation in the Reichstag from 37 to 52. However, the Nazi-Nationalist combination, disposing of 248 deputies, was still supported by less than a majority of (42 percent) of the electorate.

The Last Non-Nazi Cabinet

The November elections only demonstrated the stark isolation of Papen. Having no support outside the DNVP, he was now obliged to submit his resignation. Since Hitler was unable to form a majority cabinet either, Hindenburg on December 3 made overtures to the moderate parties by appointing General Kurt von Schleicher (1882–1934) chancellor. When Göring refused to cooperate with him, Gregor Strasser warned Hitler that if the NSDAP persisted in its exclusivist course, the whole Nazi movement would disintegrate.

Schleicher strove to steer a middle course between capital and labor. He fought high prices on foodstuffs and coal, opposed further wage cuts, and generally solicited the support of the SPD and the Socialist wing of the NSDAP, which he needed to survive. If he could have turned this trick, Schleicher would have been able to restore government by legislative majority. Unfortunately, Hitler anticipated him and removed Strasser from his posts in the NSDAP before he could challenge Hitler's control over the party. Unfortunate for Schleicher, too, was the fact that the Socialists were suspicious of his connections with the Reichswehr and the Nazis.

A despondent Schleicher resigned on January 28, 1933. Before then Hitler, deeply worried over party finances and the decline of his movement, had, with Hindenburg's consent, proposed to Papen and the representatives of big business that the Harzburg Front be reactivated. At the famous meeting between Hitler and the industrialists on January 4, 1933, at the home of the Cologne banker Curt von Schroeder, the Rhenish-Westphalian heavy industrialists (Kirdorf, Thyssen, Flick, Voegler, Schacht, Knepper, Buskuehl, Kellermann, Springorum, Tengelmanns, and Gattineau) underwrote the bulk of the Nazis' election debts.On January 30, 1933, Hindenburg perfidiously appointed Hitler chancellor, allegedly to exorcise "the Communist menace." The fact remains, however, that the president had broken his promise never to put him at the helm. Assuredly, Hindenburg was one of the "gravediggers" of the Weimar Republic.

The Burial of the Republic

Hitler's ministry rested on a coalition of the DNVP and NSDAP. Ostensibly a constitutional government, it, like its immediate predecessors, did not command a Reichstag majority. However, pressure and terrorism rectified this within five weeks. In the cabinet the Nazis held only three of the eleven posts. One of the most important, that of foreign affairs, was to be held till 1938 by the career diplomat Konstantin von Neurath (1873–1956). Notwithstanding their seeming numerical weakness in the ministry, the Nazis, by reason of their vast popular support, dominated the government. Hitler's position, moreover, was fortified further when Hindenburg appointed as Reichswehr minister Werner von Blomberg (1878–1946), the one general who in 1933 was already a disciple of Hitler.

From the outset of the Hitler ministry, his Nationalist colleagues were so intimidated as to subvert what remained of their integrity and independence. A fanfare of giant Nazi demonstrations, torchlight processions, displays of SA might, bombastic speeches, and daily acts of violence in the streets terrorized the Nationalist ministers.

In mid-February the Nazis moved swiftly to consolidate their hold on Germany. Three aims were attained in swift succession: the suppression of civil liberties that had survived the presidential dictatorship, the destruction of an independent Prussian bureaucracy, and the destruction of the KPD. In late February many newspapers were suppressed. Göring, meanwhile, purged the Prussian civil service and filled hundreds of posts with Nazis. On February 22 he swamped the Prussian police force by pouring 50,000 deputies into it. Four-fifths of them were SA and SS men. Albert Grzesinski, Berlin's chief of police, saw the handwriting on the wall and fled to Switzerland. Göring then proceeded with impunity to harry the enemies of the regime by beatings, killings, and destruction of property.

There was much heated talk about a workers' general strike and of police resistance to the Nazis, but nothing came of it. On February 24 Thälmann urged the SPD to form a combat front with the Communists against the Nazis, but the Socialists thought his price, which was abject submission to Moscow, too high. While the Marxist parties were milling aimlessly, the pretext to smash the KPD materialized, or rather, as seems to be corroborated by recent evidence, was manufactured by the Nazis. On the evening of February 27 the Reichstag building was set afire and gutted. The KPD was blamed, and some of its leaders, including the Reichstag deputy Ernst Torgler, were taken into custody for future trial. Thereafter thousands of Communist party members were arrested in a determined effort to cripple, then destroy the entire weak-willed left.

The day following the Reichstag fire, February 28, Hitler promulgated, under cover of Article 48, an Emergency Decree for the Protection of Nation and State and another against treason to the fatherland. The significance of these decrees, which had their dictatorial precedents in Hindenburg's unconstitutional acts and in the *Staatsstreich* of July 20, 1932, was to deprive the people of the vestiges of freedom and even the right of appeal to the courts from the tyranny of force. Since the armed uprising and the proposed joint KPD-SPD general strike had till then failed to materialize, there was no more hope that it ever would. By February 28, too, all hopes that internal tensions in cabinet or NSDAP would tear either or both asunder had turned out to be illusory.

Hitler reaped the first fruits of his offensive in the elections of March 5, 1933, when he converted the regnant coalition from a minority into a majority government. The elections were dominated by Nazi physical and psychological terrorism. Nazi storm troopers and symbolism flooded the country. The uniformed and booted SA and SS men moved past the polling booths in clanking and menacing formation, carrying revolvers, black metal swastika standards surmounted by silver wreaths and eagles, and red banners with the hooked cross *(Hakenkreuz* or *swastika)* in a white circle. Yet in spite of all intimidation, almost a third of the voters (30.6 percent) cast ballots for either the SPD or KDP. The SPD, with 7,180,000 votes (18.3 percent) received 120 Reichstag mandates, losing only one, while the KDP, with 1,132,000 votes (12.3 percent) retained 81 mandates in spite of the punitive measures that had been taken against its leaders. Except for the Center (73 mandates) all moderate-rightist parties suffered further attrition. The DNVP and NSDAP sucked up more of the middle-class rank and file. The DNVP polled more than 3.1 million votes (8 percent) and received 52 mandates. The Nazis polled 17,277,328 votes and won 43.9 percent of all cast. NSDAP and DNVP together now controlled 340 Reichstag seats and were backed by 51.9 percent of the electorate.

The last scene in the tragedy of the republic was the acceptance of an Enabling Act *(Gesetz zur Behebung der Not von Volk und Reich)* on March 23, 1933, by a Reichstag from which the KPD had been forcibly excluded. The enabling measure, which proposed to confer upon the chancellor the right to make laws and conclude treaties without the assent of either house and without regard to constitutional limitations upon executive power, needed a two-thirds majority in both chambers to become law. Hitler overcame the qualms of the Center, the chief obstacle to passage, by assuring its leader, Dr. Kaas, that the government would respect the rights of Church, Reichstag, and judiciary. Since the alternative to acceptance was thought to be a reign of terror, the Center scuttled the republic. Of the parties present in the Reichstag, only the SPD had the courage to defend, at least by legal means and public protest, the memory of the *Rechtsstaat*. The courage the Socialist floor leader, Otto Wels (1873–1939), displayed in the Reichstag on that day, when he denounced Hitler's aims, redounded to the glory of German Socialism but was completely ineffectual.

The Center must bear a heavy responsibility for casting the decisive vote legitimizing Nazi tyranny. Had the Center opposed Hitler on March 23, he would have been hard put to obtain the required two-thirds majority and could not have pretended that he had legally been given supreme power in accordance with democratic forms.

After March 23 it was no longer possible for the bureaucracy or the courts to contest the validity of any of Hitler's acts. Despairing of the possibility of effective opposition to the Nazis, many persons from all walks of life joined the exodus from Germany. Among them were the Socialist leaders Wels, Braun, and Dittmann. On the other hand, many stayed on, not simply out of inertia or weariness but often out of moral conviction that it was their duty to do what they could for their countrymen in distress. Some of these heroic spirits later joined the resistance movement.

Reflections on the
Fall of the Republic

There has been much speculation on the causes of the fall of the First Republic. Although many diagnoses have been made and massive studies, such as those by Karl D. Bracher, Erich Matthias, and Rudolf Morsey, have been devoted to the problem, no glib answers have found scholarly acceptance. Nazism was no more a derivative of Wilhelmine authoritarianism or of a perennial German will to world conquest than de Gaullism was the natural derivative of Bonapartist despotism or than Stalinism was just one more manifestation of the imprint the Tartaric occupation left on Russian character.

A multitude of things, some of them domestic, others linked to global developments, accounted for the strange death of the Weimar Republic. To begin with, we may ask ourselves whether without the Treaty of Versailles, the departure of the kings, the split in the proletariat, politicization of the masses, the decay of democracy in Europe after World War I, and the ruin of the middle and lower strata of the population in 1923 and again in the Great Depression, the republic would have died.

High on the list of causes of the successful Nazi *Machtergreifung* must be, as G. W. Hallgarten and Gustav Stolper have said, the depression and the attendant resolve of corporative capitalism to defend itself by all means against the threat of Communist revolution. Emulating the Italian experience of 1922, key German industrialists compounded with Hitler on January 4 and February 20, 1933, to perpetuate by unconstitutional means the dominance of big business and destroy the KPD. Long meditated by the Hugenberg wing of the DNVP and the right wing of the DVP, authoritarian government first became possible as a result of the general despair generated by the Great Depression. Brüning and Papen sought, under cover of a "presidential dictatorship," to save the half-ruined capitalists from having to make serious financial sacrifices to rescue the unemployed. Wholly subordinating political considerations to economic, Brüning inaugurated unconstitutional government by deliberately excluding the SPD from the government, although he knew that only a ministry of the Great Coalition would enable the Reichstag to discharge its responsibilities. For its part, the Reichstag made it possible for a ruthless dictator to strip it of every remnant of power by simply failing to set limits, when it was still possible to do so, to the emergency powers of the president.

As the depression deepened, class ties swiftly superseded traditional party loyalties. Public opinion rapidly polarized, and parliamentarism came to be regarded as anachronistic. This, in turn, made an integrative, democratic policy illusory. Large numbers of people now indulged in mordant criticism of the party-state as being controlled by an hierarchy of superannuated "time-servers" and apostles of outmoded ideologies, who were unresponsive to the demands of the hour. The failures of that party-state in foreign affairs were then, more than ever, held against it. As Bracher has said, the "immobility, slowness and irresolution of parliamentary government" drove a majority of voters into the activist, anti-legalistic movements, whose leaders peddled toxic nostrums.

The SPD and KPD have been subjected to extremely harsh criticism by the historical profession. Of course, in the broadest sense the SPD must be censured for not having taken at the outset of the republic the long risk of democratizing the officer corps and the Reichswehr ministry. When it finally did launch an offensive against the Reichswehr, it came, as G. A. Caspar and Wolfgang Sauer have insisted, woefully late. On the other hand, it is a singular distortion to contend, as Wilhelm Ersil, Gerald Freund, and Alfred Bornhardt have, that the SPD was a willing accomplice to the militarization of Germany, which facilitated the triumph of the Nazis. As has been affirmed, the SPD may justifiably be charged with having failed in 1918–20 to bring the proletariat into one span when, as Berlau, O'Boyle, and Kollmann have stressed, the party failed to nationalize the key industries. It may also be said that the SPD erred in allowing itself to be maneuvered into being virtually the only political party to defend the Weimar Republic until the bitter end. In doing so, the Socialists dissociated themselves from the mass majority, which wanted to replace Weimar with a more radically oriented regime. Yet if, as Bracher alleges, the Socialists were unable to put themselves at the head of the angry masses, it was not because the SPD adhered to outworn shibboleths of class warfare but precisely because it did not implement them. In a time of rapid polarization of public opinion, the SPD erred in failing to identify itself closely with broad, revolutionary minded elements among the lower classes. What was needed was an activist program for a united working class. If such a program, backed by a Socialist-Communist Front, could have been devised, it might well have driven the Nazis wholly to the right. A resulting exclusive association of the NSDAP with big business and Junker interests might have destroyed its appeal. As it was, the SPD was too profoundly influenced by the democratic reformist tradition to see that in the twilight of the First Republic the alternative was not between democracy and dictatorship but between two types of dictatorship—a Nazi or a Marxist. The imperatives of a national revolution were far more categorical at the end than at the beginning of the Weimar Republic.

Assuming that the republic could not have been saved, the SPD ought to have led the attack upon Brüning's ministry, which was the red carpet to capitalist dictatorship, and campaigned for the socialization of the economy. This would have sapped the following of the NSDAP, which had grown rapidly only because of the irresolution and indirection of the Communist and Socialist parties. Instead, by temporizing with Brüning, the SPD bucked the elemental force of radical populism, which was battering at the foundations of the existing order.

In spite of the allegations of court historians of Communist Europe that the KPD had made sincere overtures to the SPD for a united front and, on February 28, 1933, for a general strike, the facts are otherwise. The KPD had been systematically indoctrinated with an anti-Socialist animus. In setting impossible conditions for united action, the German Communists, who had accepted the *Diktat* of the Sixth Congress of the Comintern, consciously split the workers. Nothing, in fact, contributed so much to make straight the Nazi seizure of power as this lamentable split in the proletariat. Of only lesser significance was the fact that in a time of crisis neither the SPD nor the KPD was a genuinely revolutionary party any more.

However, if we magnify the guilt of the SPD and KPD, do we not in inverse proportion reduce that of the reactionaries? Is it not true that the cynical indifference of capital toward the unemployed and destitute revealed that heavy industry assigned top priority to protecting its vested interests? Did not the pretense of a presidential dictatorship and the *Staatsstreich* of July 20, 1932, teach Hitler how the constitution could legally be interred? Upon Hindenburg's shoulders, similarly, must rest dishonor for having elevated to supreme power a man who was the deadly foe of the state, which the president had sworn to uphold. Papen's action reauthorizing the SA and SS in June, 1932, set an incubus on the chest of the expiring republic, while his deliberate disregard of the Reichstag, which he entered only once while in office, was a blow to parliamentarism. As for the Reichswehr, successively commanded by Schleicher, Hammerstein, and Blomberg, it also buried the republic, not by any overt act but, as Ritter, Craig, Carsten, and Sauer have made clear, by striking a neutralist posture toward the battling forces and refusing to do its plain duty, which was to defend the state. Permeated with reactionary ideas, the Reichswehr chose to fight neither for nor against the Nazis. Consequently, inasmuch as the Marxist parties were indisposed to make a revolution, the extreme right was free to stage a counterrevolution.

Chapter 49

THE THIRD REICH, 1933–1939

Nazi Aims

The Nazi leaders spoke of the events of 1933 as constituting a "Second Revolution." Actually, however, this was a distortion. There was no wholesale expropriation of the upper classes or transfer of economic power to either proletariat or state. Hence, within the accepted meaning of the word there was in Germany in 1933 no social revolution. Rather there were the beginnings of a comprehensive process of concentration of all political power and thought control in the hands of a single party, whose demoniacal genius was Adolf Hitler. To an even greater extent than had been the case in Bolshevist Russia or Fascist Italy, the Nazi party based itself upon an uprooted, radicalized, and vengeful mass of humanity. With its support, the party proceeded from the morrow of the *Machtergreifung* with astonishing resolution, speed, and violence, not to digest Nazi gains but to remake the entire country in the National Socialist image. Above all else, the *Führer* aimed at achieving two things: (1) the rapid merger of the German nation, including all public and private agencies and organizations, with the Nazi party; and (2) the restoration of the economic and military power of Germany to a point that would permit the overthrow of the Versailles system, the establishment of the hegemony of the Third Reich over Europe, and the pursuit of *Weltmacht*.

In their stress upon "leadership" the Nazis broke with the whole Western historical tradition. Hitler repeatedly castigated the concepts of individuality, rights of man, Christian dignity, and the *Rechtsstaat*. For these he substituted the irrational idea of the spiritual unity of a collective community *(Volksgemeinschaft)* in which the entire nation was loyally to accept his prescriptions. The preternatural emphasis he put upon authoritarianism corresponded to a profound desire on the part of a desperate people, mired in a grave economic crisis, for resolute guidance. What distinguished the Third Reich from the *Ständestaat* and the historic German states system was the absence of a moral obligation of the *Führer* to the classes and the orientation of responsibility solely from the bottom up. Hitler had no thought of burning himself out for the sake of the fatherland, but he expected it to sacrifice itself for him. From this perverted, egotistical perspective on the role of authority derived a disregard for law, custom, canon, and usage. These trammels, which in the past had set limits to the will of rulers, no longer embarrassed Hitler.

That the *Führer* was able to persuade the nation to put its neck under his foot was partly due to the fact that he so skillfully identified himself with what was believed to be the overriding purpose of Germany—the restoration of its power. For the consummation of this end almost all corporative elements of German public life were prepared to follow him. To the incarnation of purpose must be added Hitler's other assets: his commonplace ways, ordinary language, emotionalism, implicit belief in everything he said, an indomitable will, but, above all, his mastery, amounting to genius, of the technique of the tirade. In haranguing the masses, it was not what he said but how he said it that counted:

> As an orator Hitler had obvious faults. The timbre of his voice was harsh, very different from the beautiful quality of Goebbels's. He spoke at too great length; was often repetitive and verbose; lacked lucidity and frequently lost himself in cloudy phrases. These shortcomings, however, mattered little beside the extraordinary impression of force, the immediacy of passion, the intensity of hatred, fury, and menace conveyed by the sound of the voice alone without regard to what he said.*

The *Gleichschaltung*: **Phase I**

Except for the army, which Hitler feared most, the occupation of Germany was carried out with lightning speed. Shortly after convocation of the Reichstag in Potsdam on March 21, 1933, Papen was driven from the Prussian minister-presidency and replaced by Göring. He completed the swift subversion of the prorepublican Prussian police. In April most other *Länder* police were brought under SA appointees. The political police of Bavaria fell under the SS, whose tsar was Heinrich Himmler (1900–1945). On April 7 a network of national commissioners *(Statthalter)* was established to appoint and direct the *Länder* ministers. Finally, on January 30, 1934, all state governmental powers were transferred to the Reich, thereby creating the first unitary totalitarian polity in German history. In the meantime the Reichstag had by the November, 1933, elections been reduced to the level of an Augustan Senate, richly compensated but ineffectual. Also parallel national and Prussian ministerial portfolios had each, except for finance, been joined in the hands of a single minister. In May, 1933, the president of the Reichsgericht, Erwin Bumke, became Hitler's disciple. Thereafter the whole legal profession was swiftly coordinated under direction of the National Socialists, Hans Frank (1900–1946) and Wilhelm Frick (1877–1946). A decree of May 12 disbarred Jewish attorneys and removed Jewish judges from the bench. To all these changes, Hindenburg, apathetic and befogged, gave his blessing. Then, in May, 1933, the Free Trade Unions, 4.5 million strong, and the Christian Trade Unions (600,000 members) were dissolved and replaced by the compulsory German Labor Front (Deutsche Arbeitsfront) under Robert Ley (1890–1945). Henceforth the workers were deprived of the right to strike or negotiate wage contracts, which were drawn up by appointed labor trustees. For the loss of their rights the workers were consoled with a mess of pottage—paid vacations, free shows, and sport spectacles, which were provided through the "Strength Through Joy" *(Kraft durch Freude)* program.

In late June, 1933, the final assault upon the party system was launched. On June 22 the SPD was outlawed, and its funds and property were confiscated by the Reich government. On June 27, Hugenberg having earlier departed from the

---

*Alan Bullock, *Hitler, A Study in Tyranny*, rev. ed. (New York, 1962), p. 373.

ministry, the DNVP dissolved itself. On July 14 the NSDAP was proclaimed the sole political party of Germany. Shortly afterward, all other remaining political parties obligingly committed hara-kiri. In November the last of the surviving independent paramilitary formations, the Stahlhelm, followed the parties into discard.

The job of liquidating all independent thinking was entrusted to Dr. Paul Joseph Goebbels, the silver-tongued, sly product of many universities, a cynic and a brute, who was even more spiritually than physically deformed. As Reich minister of propaganda, culture, and enlightenment, the club-footed Goebbels regimented press, radio, and public speakers with a view to reducing all individuals to subservience to the state. He was aided by the state police or Gestapo (Geheime Staatspolizei), which was initially dominated by Göring but later put under the savage Himmler. Systematic attacks were organized against all forms of art or thought that were considered to be un-German, Jewish, or degenerate.

Only a tiny minority tried by word or deed to stem the Nazi steamroller. Most people thought only of the positive things Hitler was doing—the reduction of unemployment, the improved earnings of big business, the increased volume of sales, the laws guaranteeing to farmers minimum plots and hereditary rights in them, the halt to reparations payments, and the end of street fights between paramilitary organizations. Hitler's stock went up, too, when in the autumn of 1933 he announced plans for construction of a belt of concrete superhighways *(Autobahnen)* around the Reich. So ubiquitous was the support that he garnered with these developments that even so venerable a biblical scholar as Ildefons Herwegen, abbot of Maria-Laach, came over to the Nazi camp. Not even the Socialists were entirely immune to Hitler's seductive powers, for in May, 1933, the bulk of the Reichstag SPD group decided to endorse his "pacific" foreign policy utterances. While covert opposition to the Nazis naturally persisted in certain quarters, it was held in check by the knowledge that persons disloyal to the regime usually lost their jobs and found it very difficult to obtain others.

Nor were the theatrical and musical worlds immune to Hitler's magnetism. The eminent playwright Gerhard Hauptmann, the world-famous conductor Wilhelm Furtwängler, the operatic genius Richard Strauss, and the famous pianist Wilhelm Backhaus lent their prestige to the *Gleichschaltung* of German musicians and composers. Apart from the many intellectuals who emigrated, there were, of course, even more who, remaining behind, refused to cooperate with the Nazis. Among this group were Hermann Oncken, Gerhard Ritter, Ricarda Huch, Werner von Heisenberg, Max Planck, Karl Jaspers, Karl Barth, and Friedrich Meinecke. However, after all allowances are made for integrity or courage, it must be affirmed that by early 1934 the vast majority of German people in all walks of life had come to tolerate the Nazi regime.

Church and State

At first the two great churches of Germany—Catholic and Evangelical (Lutheran)—offered little or no opposition to the Third Reich.

In the summer of 1933 the Catholic hierarchy came to terms with the Nazi government. In hopes of protecting Catholic liberties from secular infringement and of avoiding a new *Kulturkampf*, Pope Pius XI instructed Cardinal Eugenio Pacelli (later Pius XII) to conclude a concordat with Hitler's Germany, which was signed on July 20 in Rome in the presence of Bishop Konrad Gröber of Freiburg, Dr. Kaas, and the future Pope Paul VI, Giovanni Montini. The concordat secured the secrecy of the confessional, freedom of worship, immunities of the clergy, episcopal privilege to transmit pastoral letters to the faithful, and the right to found or maintain Catholic schools. On the other hand, many religious organizations were to be dissolved and the clergy was prohibited from interfering in any way with political affairs.

Hitler sabotaged the concordat from the outset. Soon some prelates began to attack the assumptions of Nazism. In the autumn Cardinal Pacelli encouraged critics by writing antagonistic articles in the *Osservatore Romano*. The Roman Church began to object to Hitler's racist ideas and to Nazi removal of Catholic non-Aryan clergymen from Church offices. Similarly, the Church did not look indulgently upon Nazi theories of eugenics or the law of July 25 authorizing the sterilization of the physically unfit.

At Advent, 1933, the once antirepublican Cardinal Michael von Faulhaber (1869–1952) of Munich delivered a series of sermons denouncing racism and Nazi attacks upon the Judaic-Christian heritage. Catholic relations with the government steadily deteriorated during the winter of 1933–34. On March 26, 1934, Clemens August von Galen (1878–1946), bishop of Münster, assailed the Nazis for their attacks upon Christian dogma. State and Catholic Church were now on the verge of open war for the first time since the *Kulturkampf*. Within a short time thousands of priests were being brought to trial and sentenced to prison or concentration camps *(Konzentrationslager* or KZ). On August 20, 1935, the German Catholic hierarchy sent a long letter of protest to Hitler, which he ignored. Then on March 14, 1937, Pope Pius XI, at the urging of the German prelates, issued the provocative *Mit brennender Sorge (With burning Anxiety)*. Composed in Rome by Faulhaber, the encyclical was read in all Catholic churches on Palm Sunday. It accused the government of Germany of deliberately sabotaging the concordat by falsifying or circumventing its provisions and rejected the notion (affirmed by the government on February 13, 1937) of the supremacy of state over church.

The prewar record of the Catholic Church respecting both the Jews and Hitler's aggressive foreign policy is less satisfactory. Neither in 1934, when Jews were deprived of all civil rights, nor in 1938 when the first great pogrom was launched against them, did the Church come to their aid. Many priests individually protested against Nazi inhumanity and were sent to concentration camps or executed for their temerity, but the hierarchy remained silent. The sympathy and help of the bishops and abbots were confined to their own flock or to Catholic non-Aryan victims of the regime.

The Catholic hierarchy, heavily influenced by the pro-Nazi Archbishop Gröber, did not oppose Hitler's methodical destruction of the Treaty of Versailles or Germany's invasions of Austria or Czechoslovakia. In fact, on each of these occasions there were even some episcopal congratulations of Hitler. Finally, when the Wehrmacht (armed forces) invaded Poland, Catholic prelates in a collective pastoral letter exhorted the faithful to do their duty for the fatherland and prayed God that German arms might be blessed with victory.

Similarly the great majority of the Lutheran community adjusted swiftly to the "New Order" and subsequently never abandoned it. In that respect the record of the Evangelical Church was less edifying even than the Catholic. When on June 29, 1933, Pastor Ludwig Müller (1883–1945), Hitler's coadjutor, was made Reich bishop and given control of the Evangelical Church League, the Lutherans did not protest. Only after his regimen turned out to be repressive and subversive of Christian doctrine did a small oppositional group develop, toward the end of 1933. Called the "Confessing Church" (Bekennende Kirche), it was led by the 41-year-old pastor of the Berlin-Dahlem congregation, Martin Niemöller 1892–). The Confessing Church was also vigorously supported in its denunciations of Müller's autocracy by the young Dietrich Bonhoeffer (1906–45), an instructor in theology at the University of Berlin, who was later martyred by the Nazis, and by Karl Barth (1886–1968), an internationally known Calvinist professor of theology at Bonn.

Meanwhile Müller had organized a pro-Nazi "German Christian" movement within the Evangelical Church, and by January 27, 1934, the entire Lutheran episcopate was ready to take the oath of loyalty to Reich and *Führer*. In July, 1935, the Lutheran community accommodated itself to the severe procuratorship of Hans Kerrl (1887–1941), the new Reich minister of ecclesiastical affairs. However, at least one Lutheran bishop, Otto Dibelius (1880–1967), a member of the Confessing Church, flatly rejected the domination of church by state. Unfortunately, the Confessing Church, torn by internal dissension, broke up in 1937, and some of its leaders, such as Bonhoeffer, were sent to concentration camps.

On the Jewish question and Hitler's aggressive foreign policy, it is unlikely that the attitude of the great majority of the Evangelical clergy and laity differed from that of the Catholics. Only a small number of Protestants and Catholics, it is clear, actively opposed the Hitlerite regime. Nevertheless, in many a church in Germany today there is a plaque commemorating some local minister or priest who personally refused to compromise his beliefs and was executed for them.

The Rapprochement with the Army

Of all the centers of potential opposition to Hitler, the most difficult to conquer was the army. The aristocratic traditions of the officer corps and its great technical knowledge were formidable obstacles to the coordination of the Reichswehr by the NSDAP. Hitler made deep inroads into the military establishment and morally corrupted many generals and flag officers, but there always remained in the officer corps an ineradicable residue of opposition to his plans of conquest.

After January 31, 1933, Hitler moved swiftly to invest the main citadel of independent power in the Reich. Ex-captain Göring, who had been a member of Baron von Richthofen's "flying circus" in World War I and was soon to be made a general, was put in charge of building an air force (Luftwaffe) that was to be separate from army and navy. In October, the government ordered many anti-Nazi army officers to retire. In December the hostile chief of the army, Hammerstein-Equort, was obliged to step down and make way for the unpolitical General Werner Freiherr von Fritsch (1880–1939), who offered no opposition to Hitler's plans to coordinate the Reichswehr. Meanwhile Blomberg, who sympathized with Hitler, was made a colonel general and given command over all three branches of the service, and the Reichswehramt was renamed the Wehrmachtamt (Department of Defense) to accommodate the emergence of a navy and an air force.

The generals and admirals moved ever closer to Hitler in the winter of 1933–34. Many were impressed when Hitler took Germany out of the League of Nations in the fall of 1933 and when on January 26, 1934, he concluded a ten-year non-aggression pact with Poland, which weakened the French alliance system. The Wehrmacht was elated at Hitler's plan to triple the size of the army by the end of 1934 and provide for a respectable navy and air force. The officer corps also gravitated toward the *Führer* because it came to regard him as a rampart against a "second revolution."

At this time Ernst Röhm and his deputy, Karl Ernst, leaders of the SA, were openly speaking about the need for a new revolution. Schleicher and Gregor Strasser sympathized with their dissatisfaction with Hitler's social moderation and their demand for more restraints upon big business and the great landlords. Röhm also advocated that all Reichswehr personnel be recruited from his SA, which would immediately coordinate the army and destroy the exclusiveness of the officer corps. The big industrialists, landlords, generals, and admirals all feared Röhm and the Nazi left wing. So also did Röhm's rivals in the party—Rudolf Hess (1894–   ), Göring, Himmler, Heydrich, and Bormann. Even Hitler resented Röhm's vaulting ambition. In any case the generals could no longer view with equanimity the nemesis of the SA, a privileged political army of more than 2.5 million men.

Unable to appease the SA leader, Hitler compounded with Blomberg, Fritsch, and the naval chief, Admiral Erich Raeder (1876–1960), on April 11, 1934, on the cruiser *Deutschland* to proceed draconically against the SA and the Nazi left. On May 16 many other officers endorsed the Deutschland Pact.

Destruction of the Nazi Left

Hitler delivered his blow against "permanent revolution" on the weekend of June 30–July 1, 1934, the so-called night of the long knives. He demonstrated to perfection that he had carefully studied Stalin's methods of crushing opposition within one's own party and the army. On Hitler's orders a savage purge was carried out, mainly in Berlin and Munich, as a result of which an indeterminate number of army men, SA chiefs, and personal foes of Hitler, Göring, and Himmler—possibly as many as 1,000—were shot. Röhm, who refused to commit suicide, was riddled with bullets at the Stadelheim prison in Munich, while Kahr,

Lossow, von Bredow, Gregor Strasser, and Schleicher and his wife were among those slain by SS men. Papen was spared only because he enjoyed Hindenburg's protection. Fritsch and Lieutenant General Ludwig Beck (1880–1944), the new chief of the Truppenamt had, according to Walter Goerlitz, been kept in ignorance of the nature of the shootings, while Blomberg, Reichenau, and Walter von Brauchitsch (1891–1946), the commander of the 1st Army District, strove to suppress murmurs of disapproval among the officer corps and hold the ship of state to its course. As for Hitler, he merely vindicated the purge by claiming he had acted as "the supreme tribunal of the German people."

The "night of the long knives" destroyed the power of the SA forever, but the SS soon threatened to take the place of the SA as a potential rival of the army. Comprising only Aryans of unquestionable loyalty to Hitler, the black-shirted SS troops were beloved by him. This was especially true of the SS-Leibstandarte, Hitler's own praetorian guard. Numbering 52,000 in 1933, the SS was to attain a strength of 350,000 by 1939 and double that by 1945. Hitler equipped the SS with heavy weapons, including artillery, and even dreamt of building, to the dismay of his generals, the postwar German army entirely around the Waffen-SS, the elite fighting corps of the SS.

The generals also took alarm at the growth of Himmler's empire. By mid-1936 this crafty, ruthless, but unquestionably capable organizer had, as chief of the German police in the Reich ministry of the interior, gained dominion over SS, police, and Gestapo. Through his lieutenant, Richard Heydrich (1904–42), Himmler also indirectly controlled the political police or SD (Sicherheitsdienst, "security police"). By 1938 he had become the second most important person in Germany.

Hitler Subverts the Officer Corps

Hitler took a first step toward the *Gleichschaltung* of the officer corps on August 2, 1934, the day of Hindenburg's death. Having decided to abolish the presidency, Hitler exacted an unprecedented oath of allegiance from all armed forces personnel, not to the state or the constitution, but to himself personally. Had the oath been refused, Hitler's prestige must seriously have been impaired. Ever afterward, this oath to *Führer* and chancellor stood like a barrier that for many senior officers barred the paths of reason and patriotism, preventing them from joining the resistance movement.

On March 16, 1935, Hitler fulfilled his second major promise to the soldiers when he took unilateral action to abrogate the military clauses of the Treaty of Versailles. Seizing upon Franco-Italian negotiations for an entente and upon the current French army bill extending the service term from one to two years, Hitler proclaimed that universal military conscription was being restored for all men between 18 and 45. He also promised that the Reichswehr would be expanded to 12 corps and 36 divisions (550,000 men).

By 1935 Hitler had achieved such a string of external and internal victories that the officer corps entertained no thought of leading a national opposition to his "New Order." The plebiscite of January 13, 1935, in the Saar, when 90 percent of its electorate voted to restore the area to the Reich, as well as Hitler's declaration of rearmament, convinced many of the last "doubting Thomases." For three years thereafter the officers turned away from politics and were content to devote their energies to the expansion of the Wehrmacht.

In March, 1935, important organizational changes in the armed forces were effected. The office of Reichswehr minister was renamed Reich War Ministry and was assigned formal control over all three branches of the armed forces. A new high command of the army (Oberkommando des Heeres or OKH) replaced the _Heeresleitung_, while the Truppenamt was transformed into the general staff of the army (Generalstab des Heeres). The latter organization, responsible to the supreme commander of the army (Fritsch), was headed by the conservative General Ludwig Beck (1880–1944), one of the nation's best strategists and noblest spirits. With his aid the Wehrmachtakademie was opened in October, 1935, for training future general staff officers. On the other hand, Generals Werner von Fritsch and Beck were mainly responsible for the fact that Field Marshal Göring's farsighted proposal to build a strategic bombing force was rejected and that a cautious perspective of coordinated employment of infantry, tanks, artillery, and tactical aircraft was adopted instead.

A general's concupiscence at long last put the supreme command of the Wehrmacht in Hitler's palm. On January 12, 1938, von Blomberg, chief of the Reich War Ministry and the first officer in the land, married Fräulein Grühn, a whore. Göring, covetous of Blomberg's position, transmitted details of her past to General Wilhelm Keitel (1882–1946), head of the director's staff of the armed forces, who passed them on to Hitler. At the same time documents allegedly proving that Fritsch, a possible successor to Blomberg, was a homosexual were also forwarded to the _Führer_. While Fritsch was probably guiltless of a charge that might more truthfully have been leveled at Göring and was acquitted by a military court, Hitler wanted to see both Blomberg and Fritsch framed, not with the design of elevating Göring to command of the Wehrmacht but of seizing control himself.

On February 4, 1938, Hitler brought his coup to fruition. He ordered major changes in the chain of command. A new office, the supreme command of the armed forces (Oberkommando der Wehrmacht or OKW), was established under the obsequious Keitel. His staff _(Wehrmachtführungsstab)_ was to be independent of Beck's army general staff. Fritsch was replaced by General Walther von Brauchitsch as chief of the army, while Hitler himself took over the war ministry. Similarly, at the foreign office Konstantin von Neurath was replaced by the former champagne salesman and ambassador to Britain, Joachim von Ribbentrop (1893–1946). For the first time in 150 years supreme civilian and military authority in Germany had been joined in the hands of one person—ironically, a civilian.

Autarky

All forms of _Gleichschaltung_ would ultimately have failed the Nazis had it not been for the success with which the Hitlerite regime combatted unemployment. This definitely attached the bulk of the German people to his cause. While Hitler cannot be credited with having singlehandedly licked the depression, which receded on a worldwide front during his first two years in office, he adopted certain measures that accelerated reemployment in Germany. Among these were: constructing public facilities, air fields, barracks, party offices, and *Autobahnen*; a high protective tariff that helped revive industry; the utilization of hand labor instead of machines on works projects and farms; and, of course, rearmament and military procurement, which provided jobs and withdrew hundreds of thousands of men from the labor market to serve with the Wehrmacht. The Nazis also waged the fight against unemployment by encouraging females to retire from wage jobs and by excluding Jews from all public service positions. In 1935 obligatory military service for one year (increased in 1936 to two) and mandatory labor *(Arbeitsdienst)* where there was already a manpower shortage significantly lowered the level of unemployment. Whereas there had in January, 1933, been 6 million jobless, there were 2.3 million in December, 1934, 1.8 million in 1935, and only 200,000 in 1938.

A range of factors decided Hitler to set Germany the goal of industrial and agricultural self-sufficiency. Dwindling gold reserves in the Reichsbank, high protective tariffs abroad, sequestration of foreign assets, the "blocking" of debts to foreign creditors, an aggressive foreign policy, and the enormous exigencies of rearmament combined to drive the Third Reich, whose resources were strictly limited, toward autarky. Pending the day when the German people would, in Hitler's words, "swim in plenty," the Nazi government instituted far-reaching controls over capital and labor.

The establishment of Ley's Labor Front (DAF) was but the first step toward the goal of the corporative economy. On January 20, 1934, a Law for the Organization of National Labor deprived the workers of the right to strike or bargain collectively. The whole personnel of each firm or shop was to constitute a community *(Betriebsgemeinschaft)*, organized in accordance with the principle of capitalist leadership paralleling that of Nazi leadership in the state.

Early in 1934 Hitler began to construct a Fascist-type corporative economy in Germany. Kurt Schmitt was given authority to create, merge, or dissolve all industrial enterprises and appoint or dismiss all directors and executives. The law of March 14, 1934, organized business into twelve great corporations and thirty-two subgroups. Each embraced all capitalists, managers, and workers in a given field or industry and was hierarchically organized. Ultimate responsibility in every case rested with the Reich minister of economics (successively Schmitt, Schacht, and Walter Funk). By overcoming the class struggle through establishment of a community of "blood" and purpose among "Aryans," Hitler hoped to achieve a simulacrum of that egalitarian society the NSDAP had promised to create.

Big business was vexed by Nazi bureaucratic schemes for predetermining profits and volumes of sales, allocating raw materials and quotas of production, and, after 1935, imposing strict wage and price controls. Government competition in the automotive and metallurgical industries incensed many private entrepreneurs. They resented the fact, too, that in the Third Reich private property enjoyed no legal immunities and could be commandeered for purposes that served the "interests of the people." Businessmen instinctively distrusted the aggregate of devices altering the old free market economy and subjecting wealth to heavy taxes. On the other hand, however, it is a fact that, despite individual defections of capitalists such as Hjalmar Schacht (1939), big business did not pass over to the opposition against Hitler, because economically the capitalists were the main beneficiaries of the corporative state.

In 1936 a Four-Year Plan for the attainment of specific production goals was instituted. Drafted with the help of the NSDAP's economic expert, Wilhelm Wagener, the plan was administered by Göring. It facilitated the achievement of moderate increases in heavy industrial production but only limited ones in consumer's goods. Lacking the direction and technical support that would have been supplied by a genuine central planning agency, the Four-Year Plan yielded comparatively unimpressive results and was handicapped by lack of thoroughgoing coordination and by the syphoning off of corporative profits by the state.

In the period 1933–38 the German national income doubled, but wages and salaries increased by only 50 percent. Profits rose more rapidly. On the other hand, there was a modest improvement in the workers' earnings and standard of living, which reconciled them to the loss of liberty. By the late 1930s the workers were fully employed and eating three square meals a day. For this they paid in the hard coin of bondage. They had lost the right to strike or bargain collectively, were subject to maximum wage controls, were often paid on a piecework basis, were heavily taxed and inadequately housed, and could change jobs only with difficulty. By 1939 the "pass book" *(Arbeitsbuch)* system, instituted in 1934, had become universal. Workers were registered at national labor exchanges and were required at all times to have a pass book on their person. By this device and the "Strength through Joy" movement the worker was regimented and exposed even in his spare time to continuous scrutiny by the authorities.

The bulk of the capital created by the frantic exertions of an indoctrinated labor force was channelized into rearmament, for the grand goal of Nazi planning was to augment production for the sake of the Wehrmacht. In the years 1934–38 military expenditures rose almost ninefold: RM 2 billion in 1934; RM 5.8 billion in 1936; and RM 17.2 billion in 1938. By 1939 the revenues of the Reich government were grossly inadequate to meet the needs of the voracious Wehrmacht, and the national debt, amounting to RM 30 billion (five times that of 1933), was approaching a point where the solvency of the state was in question. As a consequence of Hitler's repudiation of part of that debt in 1939, Hjalmar Schacht resigned the presidency of the Reichsbank and was succeeded by the more pliant Walter Funk.

Agriculture

The Nazis also coordinated agriculture. The law of 1933 (Erbhofgesetz) had recognized the hereditary character of farms up to approximately 320 acres and stipulated that the normative holding of about 25 acres was indivisible and in-alienable. Although this provision ostensibly protected the small farmers against loss of their land and seemed to be a reversion to the old concept of *Bauernschutz*, it also in effect nailed the peasants to the clod as in the Middle Ages. While it is true that by 1939 the Nazis had broken up many of the entailed estates of the east-ern provinces, very little of this acreage found its way into the hands of small homesteaders. In many cases the Junkers were able, by proving socially bene-ficial operation, to avoid expropriation.

In 1933 all farmers, tenants, agricultural day laborers, and large-scale land-lords were grouped together into a National Food Estate (Reichsnährstand), headed by Hitler's agricultural oracle, Walter Darré (1895–1953). He and his staff improvised methods for restraining operators from rationalizing and mech-anizing the productive process until unemployment disappeared. While the state imposed iron controls over all farm properties, it also arranged for low-interest loans and generous credits to small operators and reduced their taxes. At the same time the state both fixed and subsidized prices and set production quotas. In spite of Darré's efforts, agricultural production did not materially increase between 1932 and 1937, and by 1938 it was feeding only 6 percent more people than in 1928. Farm income rose between 1933 and 1938, but in terms of percentage of the national income it remained static, while the indebtedness of small farmers increased.

Hallmarks of the Nazi Economy

Nazi autarky exhibited a number of curious features. In the first place, it is an error to think that the entire system of controls was operated by the party. Rather, it was the bureaucracy, oftentimes nearly exempt from NSDAP interference, that molded and superintended the economy. Most of the key positions in the control apparatus went not to the "Old Fighters" of the party but to professional civil servants or post-1933 NSDAP recruits. This circumstance retarded any economic revolution, leaving heavy industry in command of the principal instruments of production. Small wonder that many old-line Nazis were bitterly disillusioned with the failure of the "revolution." Furthermore, there was in the Third Reich an intimate relationship between political leaders and big businessmen. Many Nazi leaders became corporation directors or managers, while capitalists were often made the heads of government agencies.

Unusual by the standards of the free market was manipulation of international trade. The government of the Third Reich controlled all foreign commerce. Gold and dollar deposits had to be paid into the Reichsbank, while all German payments to foreign creditors had to be deposited with clearing offices in blocked reichsmark accounts. Creditors might use them for the purpose of buying German products, but such funds could not be exported. German international trade proceeded by the devices of clearing offices, blocked RM accounts, or simple barter aggree-ments. Foreign creditors, obliged to take payment in Reichsmarks or German goods, found themselves increasingly embarrassed as Germany devoted more and more of her industrial capacity to military hardware, leaving only a dwindling range of consumers' items they might purchase. Two of the many European states that had clearing arrangements with the Reich, Yugoslavia and Rumania, eventually demanded payment in foreign currencies for their exports.

The Prewar Treatment of Jews

Nothing the Nazis did in the history of the Third Reich is so likely to earn them the lasting opprobrium of posterity as their treatment of the Jews. No other element of German society was so systematically isolated and persecuted. Even a Communist of "Nordic" blood could theoretically be rehabilitated, but there was no hope for the Jew. The Nazis, preoccupied with euthenics and the ethnic improvement of German stock, regarded the Jew as a "subhuman" *(Unmensch)*, whose assimilation by the "Aryan" Germans was unthinkable.

Discriminatory acts against Jews characterized the "New Order" from the outset. Jews were expelled in 1933 from the civil service, bar, judiciary, and diplomatic corps. Subsequently they were driven from all the free professions. An insidious anti-Semitic campaign of defamation was organized by Himmler, Streicher, Goebbels, Göring, and the chief of the SS, the quarter-Jew Reinhard Heydrich. The SS Central Office for Race and Settlement maintained files on all persons in Germany of Jewish extraction. Similarly the SS subsidiary Association for Germanism Abroad (Verein für das Deutschtum im Ausland, or VDA), under Hans Steinacher, kept files on all Jews residing in German communities external to the Reich.

A first general boycott of Jewish stores and business houses was staged in April, 1933. In May it was followed by the burning of books by Jewish authors, and in July a government decree authorized physicians in certain cases to perform involuntary sterilization operations upon persons of "tainted stock" *(Erbkranker)*. In 1933 there were still about 500,000 Jews in Germany. However, by 1939, in spite of the increment of more than 185,000 Jews when Austria was annexed, their number had dwindled, as a result of emigration, to 275,000. Leading Nazis, such as Heydrich and Göring, favored the attainment of the "racial purity" of the German nation by either encouraging or forcing the Jews to emigrate from the Reich.

The plight of the German Jewish community drastically worsened in September, 1935, when at the Nuremberg party rally Hitler promulgated further discriminatory decrees, depriving Jews of citizenship and civil rights and forbidding them to display the national flag, marry Germans, or hire Aryan employees of female sex unless they were over forty-five. In general, a nation that saw in the Jew the international Marxist, the Shylock who extorted usurious rates of interest from his debtors, and the symbol of international finance capitalism that had enslaved Germany after World War I, did not object to these measures.

Subsequently to the Nuremberg Decrees a succession of new laws completely insulated Germany against Jews. Every door that led to gainful employment was soon closed to them. Then in 1938 their position sharply deteriorated again. As a consequence of the assassination of a German official in the Paris embassy by a 17-year-old Jewish youth, a pogrom was launched against the Jews of Germany on the night of November 9–10, 1938, the so-called night of glass, or *Kristallnacht*. The Reich government subsequently even imposed a fine upon the whole German Jewish community to indemnify non-Jews for any property damage caused by the pogrom. Thereafter, Jews were forbidden to enroll at higher schools and universities or to buy or acquire land or real estate. Jews had also to carry special identification cards, and, as a crowning indignity, prominently display the Star of David on their apparel. Finally, on January 30, 1939, Hitler warned that in the event of war he would destroy all the Jews of Europe. Subsequently the way was prepared for the "final solution" of the Jewish problem by the transfer of virtually supreme authority over the Jews to the vicious Himmler.

Chapter 50

PRELUDE TO THE SECOND GERMAN WAR

Hitler's Early Diplomacy

Hitler's maiden performance on the diplomatic stage was accompanied by dulcet music. His initial foreign policy utterances of March 21 and May 17, 1933, stood in disarming contrast with his threats in *Mein Kampf* or his fulminations just before the *Machtergreifung*. At least two steps taken by him in his first months in office encouraged the belief that he would respect international law. On May 15 the Reich government renewed the Treaty of Berlin of 1926 with the USSR, in spite of the ideological antagonism between the two regimes. The Russo-German pact of 1933 pledged the signatories to neutrality in the event of an attack on either of them by a third power and was to run until December 31, 1945! Second, the Four Power Pact of June 7, 1933, among Britain, France, Italy, and Germany committed the signatories to cooperate for the preservation of peace. These two conventions were generally viewed by foreign statesmen as a continuation of the east-west pacificatory diplomacy inaugurated at Rapallo and Locarno. For Hitler, however, the new pacts were sand in the eyes of foreign foes, which would enable the Nazis to throttle all opposition within the Reich while accustoming Europe to think in terms of the equality of Germany. Hitler believed that general acceptance of the principle of parity would lead the Great Powers to resign themselves at the very least to large-scale German rearmament and the rectification of the borders of the Reich where they mocked self-determination and were not conducive to German security.

Although Hitler wanted no early war, it was not long before he was again hurling pejoratives at the "foreign oppressors" of Germany. After July, 1933, his foreign policy utterances were once more sprinkled with attacks upon the peace treaty. He gave tangible expression to the national complaint by taking Germany on October 14, 1933, out of the League. Yet, it was not until 1936 that Hitler overtly violated his pledge not to revise the status quo save in accordance with international law and procedures sanctioned by Article 19 of the Covenant of the League of Nations.

The Pact with Poland

In the winter of 1933–34 Hitler blew up the bridge to Russia. In December he rejected Soviet Russian overtures to conclude a pact guaranteeing the territorial integrity of Lithuania, Latvia, and Esthonia without their consent. The Soviet demarche might, as Gustav Hilger and Jan Librach inferred, have been a scheme of Stalin's to forestall a future Russo-German war by partitioning Poland and the Baltic states. But Hitler either did not believe in Stalin's reliability or was attracted by other foreign policy objectives. On the one hand, the evasion of Stalin's ruse would permit Hitler to unite the German people behind Nazism in a common hatred of Soviet Communism. On the other, a Polish-German rapprochement, resulting from Polish vexation at the fact that France had signed the Four Power Pact, might end by dislodging the keystone of the arch of the French eastern alliance system and at the same time intimidate those Reichswehr generals who favored the Russian orientation. Accordingly, Germany on January 26, 1934, entered into a ten-year nonaggression pact with Poland. This did not mean, however, that Germany was waiving her claims to her lost eastern territories, nor that Poland was about to divorce France.

While the Polish action impelled Paris to seek new allies to strengthen her military hegemony, Hitler could claim, howsoever hypocritically, that all of the treaties his government had concluded were aimed at conciliating Germany's neighbors and promoting international cooperation. Yet he had already set off the alarm bell in Paris. Henceforth the French government strove feverishly to inaugurate a diplomatic revolution that should bring either Italy or the USSR into a grand alliance to contain the Third Reich.

The Murder of Engelbert Dollfuss

The French, who rightly feared that Hitler intended eventually to go to war, found confirmation for their fears in the attempted Nazi putsch of July 25, 1934, in Vienna, when the Austrian Chancellor Dollfuss was assassinated by Nazi agents whose aim was to subvert Austrian independence and prepare the way for *Anschluss*. Hitler had planned not merely the elimination of Dollfuss but also the replacement of all the members of his cabinet by Nazi puppets. If this had happened, Mussolini, who had mobilized his army at the Brenner Pass, would have challenged Hitler.

The Austrian chancellor had virtually been the ward of the Italian dictator Benito Mussolini (*il Duce*, 1883–1945), who had labored to build a combination of Italy, Hungary, and Austria to block *Anschluss*. Mussolini had formed a low opinion of Hitler when they had met in Venice in June for the first time and was perfectly ready to chastise the beer-hall barker if he encroached on Italian preserves. Subsequently to the July assassination, Mussolini strengthened his ties with Austria and Hungary. On September 27, 1934, Italy joined France in reaffirming their resolve to defend Austria. In this mutual disposition of France and Italy toward a security pact lay Europe's first opportunity to prevent a second German war. It was only a question whether France and Britain would pay Mussolini's blackmail, which, in retrospect, seemed relatively small.

Stresa: The Lost Opportunity

Instead of playing the Italian card at once, the French foreign minister, Louis Barthou, sought French security in the east. When his proposal for an eastern Locarno was rejected by Germany, which would under no circumstances fight on behalf of the Soviet Union, and by Poland, which would not allow Red army troops upon Polish soil, Barthou approached Moscow with the proposal for a treaty of mutual assistance. Stalin and the Soviet foreign minister, Maxim Litvinov, were just then plucking on the string of collective security. Therefore, they were amenable to Barthou's proposal. But a Franco-Russian alliance would alienate Mussolini and cause him to reorient his foreign policy.

Barthou was well on the way to achieving his alliance with Moscow when on October 9, 1934, he was assassinated at Marseilles. His successor, Premier and Foreign Minister Pierre Laval, much preferred a combination of Britain, France, and Italy supported by Poland, Hungary, and the Little Entente. This, however, would be hard to achieve in view of deepening French naval rivalry with both Britain and Italy. Nevertheless, on January 7, 1935, Laval succeeded in concluding a colonial agreement with Italy. While France made only inconsequential actual territorial concessions in Africa, Laval appears to have given the *Duce* vague assurances that he would not oppose Italian designs upon Ethiopia (Abyssinia). Here, however, it was the British who were unwilling to pay the price for an entente. An Italian east African colonial empire would have transected Britain's Cape-to-Cairo commercial axis. Furthermore Ethiopia had already virtually become a British satellite. The return of the Saar to Germany on March 1 and Hitler's decision of February 26 to build a military air force and of March 16 to establish a 36-division army of 550,000 men certainly demonstrated the urgent need for a triple alliance against the Reich. Unfortunately, a meeting at Stresa April 12–14 of Flandin, Laval, the mortally ill Prime Minister MacDonald, and his foreign secretary, Sir John Simon, with Mussolini yielded only sonorous platitudes. The British, obviously, were not much interested in pursuing Laval's concept of containing Germany. Their moderate attitude toward the Third Reich was governed by their wish to avoid antagonizing her at a time when Italy was preparing to twist the lion's tail in Africa and England's air force was utterly incapable of defending the homeland.

At Stresa the three powers declared that they were ready to act in unison to defend Austrian independence, but Britain parted company with Italy over Ethiopia and inferentially rejected any new partition of Africa. Because the MacDonald–Simon government regarded Mussolini as a greater threat than Hitler to their empire, the Stresa Front was stillborn. Unfortunately the British failed to appreciate that opportunity was knocking at their door, for at that time Hitler believed Mussolini's Ethiopian escapade had the blessing of the British government, and Italo-German relations were frigid (Fritz Kuhn). As G. L. Weinberg and James Dugan have made plain, the Wilhelmstrasse opposed Italy's African policy. It seems not to have occurred to the British cabinet that a disgruntled Mussolini might seek solace at Hitler's *Bierstube*.

The logical sequel to the repulse of Italy was, from the French standpoint, the Russian alliance. Laval reluctantly signed the pact with Moscow on May 2, 1935. Britain was irritated, if not dismayed, by this step. She countered by striving for a modus vivendi with Germany and on June 18 signed a naval pact with her. In allowing Germany to quadruple the size of her fleet, London was indubitably influenced by the memory of the costly Anglo-German naval race that had poisoned relations with Berlin before World War I. Furthermore, Simon hoped to persuade Hitler to sign an air pact with Britain.

For the *Führer* June 18, 1935, was "the happiest day" of his life. The naval pact of that date permitted Germany to build up to 35 percent of Britain's surface fleet strength, which was 420,000 tons as compared with the 144,000 tons conceded by the Treaty of Versailles. Germany might also build up to 45 percent of the submarine strength of Britain but was to be bound by no ratio to the French surface or submarine fleets. Henceforth the Reich was not even bound by the 35,000-ton limitation to which the naval powers had agreed in 1922 at the Washington Naval Conference. Having already begun construction of the 26,000-ton battleships *Scharnhorst* and *Gneisenau*, Germany shortly proceeded to lay the keels for the 45,000-ton *Tirpitz* and *Bismarck*, which would outgun anything afloat. Of additional value to Hitler was the fact that Britain had been detached from the ring of his enemies and now the maritime powers would be unable to enter into an anti-German naval agreement (C. Bloch).

Britain's Myopia

In the summer of 1935 Anglo-French relations were badly strained. If the British public were convinced the French had encouraged Italy to attack Abyssinia, the French were embittered by the Anglo-German naval agreement, which had given the green light to German rearmament and made a shambles of the French security system. An enraged Laval felt that he was being forced to desperate expedients—a line of action that would lead him to compete with Britain in domesticating the Third Reich. The Italians, for reasons of their own, spoke of English duplicity and drove deeper the wedge between England and France. Soviet Russia accused Britain of having apostasized from collective security.

An astute German diplomacy could have exploited this contretemps for the benefit of the Reich. However, the foreign minister, Baron Konstantin von Neurath (1873–1956), and the chief of the foreign office, Ernst von Weizsäcker (1882–1951), neither of whom coveted the whole pie, were not permitted to develop a realistic policy. Hitler's aim, cast in iron and unbending, was still the mastery of Europe (H. A. Jacobsen).

In spite of his vaulting ambitions, it is a mistake to think that Hitler possessed a master plan or a timetable for the accomplishment of specific territorial objectives. It is also dubious to argue, as has the revisionist historian A. J. P. Taylor, that the *Führer* was only a vulgar improviser who had no clear idea of where he was headed and that consequently successive British prime ministers, especially Arthur Neville Chamberlain (1937–40), may be excused for trying to do business with him. Such a judgment ignores Hitler's dream of conquering eastern Europe and his conviction that he was a superman endowed with the will to achieve the impossible.

A consistent underestimation of Hitler and an overestimation of Mussolini, no less than imperialistic greed, kept the British from collaborating with France and Italy to build a genuinely effective security system, which could only be done outside the impotent League of Nations. The British belatedly tried to retrieve their error when in December Sir Samuel Hoare, the foreign minister, concluded a pact with Laval in Paris, partitioning Abyssinia and giving half of it to Italy. Unfortunately the chicken was already in Mussolini's vest. It is barely possible that if the British public, incensed at the Hoare-Laval pact, had not forced the British government to repudiate it, the peace of Europe could still have been rescued. Yet it may also have been too late, because by the close of 1935 Mussolini, driven by English intransigence, was preparing, as George Baer has shown, to embrace Hitler, whom he detested. There were now only two alternatives open to Britain: either join France in strengthening the Franco-Russian mutual assistance pact or reconcile herself to making bigger concessions to Germany than London was disposed to make to Rome. This latter course would open the way for a new *Drang nach Osten* and a German war against first Poland, then Russia.

Restoration of German Sovereignty in the Rhineland

As late as May 21, 1935, Hitler had still proclaimed his devotion to peace and the Locarno treaties. However, when the French chamber of deputies ratified the Franco-Russian military alliance on February 27, 1936, Hitler claimed that by their violation of the spirit of the Locarno treaties the French had released Germany from further obligation to observe them. Then on March 7, 1936, Hitler demonstrated the bankruptcy of the Franco-Russian Alliance. Against the advice of several of his generals, he sent a few battalions into the Rhineland to symbolize peaceful German reoccupation. Very probably, as Alan Bullock thinks, they were under orders to withdraw if they encountered a French invading force, and the view must be rejected that it is a myth that the German troops would in that event have automatically been withdrawn.

In the Rhineland occupation Hitler took long risks. He gambled that the French army, which was unprepared for war, would not be mobilized. He gambled that the French, disillusioned with offensive strategy, had reconciled themselves to the defensive and would fight only if the Germans attacked the Maginot Line, which ran along their eastern border from Belfort to Montmédy. And he gambled that neither the British nor the Russians would march to aid the French. His intelligence service had told him that Britain had virtually no ground forces that she could commit to a continental war. He was also aware that Franco-Russian relations had deteriorated, due both to the savage purges that had begun in the USSR and to the fact that the French bourgeoisie and officer corps were, in their hostility toward communism, sabotaging the Franco-Russian Alliance of May 2, 1935. Furthermore, Hitler reasoned that the Sarraut-Flandin government was only a caretaker ministry that would undertake no military action but merely mark time until the April general elections. Last, the *Führer* believed the British had been neutralized by the Anglo-German naval pact, while Italy had been alienated from Britain and France as a result of the League's imposition of sanctions in punishment for the invasion of Abyssinia.

In the weeks following March 7, 1936, the French dissipated the advantages that would have accrued from prompt retaliation. A Polish offer to march against Germany if France did likewise was rejected. When the British lamely hinted to Ribbentrop, the Nazi ambassador in London, that they expected a German contribution to the restoration of confidence, Hitler knew he had carried off his bluff: Britain could be placated with small bribes. In this assumption he was, indeed, correct. Both Baldwin and Eden had warned Flandin that British military assistance would not be forthcoming if the French army invaded the Rhineland.

In his note of March 31 to London and Paris Hitler emptied a bag of petty gifts into the laps of the French and British. He professed his desire to cooperate in the work of reconciliation, promised neither to reinforce German forces already stationed in the Rhineland nor move them closer to the French and Belgian frontiers for at least four months, and he offered to sign a 25-year nonaggression pact with France and Belgium, and an air pact with Britain guaranteeing that in a future war her cities would be spared bombardment by German planes.

From the German standpoint, Hitler's peace proposals were a huge success. They evoked sympathetic responses from the western democracies, especially Britain, where Foreign Secretary (1935–38) Anthony Eden thought Hitler's plan deserved careful study. To Germany's presumptuous armed challenge the western powers had opposed only an assortment of conciliatory suggestions in April and May and the starry-eyed project of a revitalized Concert of Europe that would include the Third Reich. Having alienated Italy and discouraged Belgium, Poland, and the Soviet Union, the French had ended by carrying the train of British foreign policy. Yet all of Britain's principal ministers and the leader of the parliamentary opposition had professed in varying degree faith in Hitler's fundamentally pacific intentions and in the prospect that a general agreement could be negotiated with him. Inasmuch as the Popular Front ministry of Léon Blum, which took office in France in June, also displayed a conciliatory attitude toward the Reich, Hitler, whose vaticinations had been vindicated, merely continued to ply Paris and London with endless memoranda while Germany rearmed in all haste.

The upshot of negotiations in the spring and summer of 1936 was that Germany had managed to elude Anglo-French efforts to enmesh her in a web of collective security. Instead, the Third Reich went its fateful way. For the sake of world opinion Hitler pretended that because the existing order favored the French and Russians, the entrance of Germany into the system of pacts proposed by Paris would only obstruct attainment of equality by the Reich. The real significance of what had taken place in 1936, however, was that France had lost the bridgehead into Germany that a demilitarized zone had given her. An important deterrent to war had fallen away.

In the twilight of French ascendancy it was imperative for Paris to turn back the clock by exerting the national might decisively in some one direction. The time for lackadaisical recourse to ponderous formalities under the League covenant was past. France could no longer be secured that way. The tragedy of the "gravediggers" of the Third Republic is that although basically they understood all this, they had allowed the myopic British to persuade them that dusk was dawn.

The Growth of the Nemesis

With the peaceful recovery of the Rhineland began the legend of Hitler's infallibility. His success worked like a magnet upon Italy and Japan and caused Belgium to revert in 1936 to neutrality. For some time Hitler had been delivering coal and other raw materials to Mussolini, aiding him to circumvent League sanctions in the Abyssinian war. Now Hitler and Mussolini cooperated to help Franco win the civil war in Spain (1936–39). In September, on the occasion of the first official visit of *il Duce* to Berlin, the "Rome-Berlin Axis" was formed. On November 25 Japan, which feared war with Soviet Russia over Manchuria, concluded an Anti-Comintern Pact with Berlin. While technically it was only a convention to combat world communism, the *Führer* discovered in it a means of conjuring up the naval might of Japan so as to keep the British neutral. On November 6, 1937, Italy joined the Anti-Comintern combination, transforming it into a triple entente against the USSR.

The farces of nonintervention in the Spanish Civil War and American neutrality strengthened Hitler's hand. While France, Britain, and the USA hid their moral bankruptcy behind the screen of a "hands off" policy, Hitler and Mussolini, both adherents of the Non-Intervention Agreement, supplied Franco with war materiel and sent "volunteers" to help strangle the government of the Spanish republic.

Between 1935 and 1937 a diplomatic revolution had taken place. Germany had rearmed and in August, 1936, even reintroduced the two-year military service requirement. She had reoccupied the Rhineland and detached Italy from France. Above all, Hitler had forged a triple entente, which, as was the case with that of Delcassé in 1904, made general war a probability. But all of these things were only *vin ordinaire* to Hitler. It was now possible for him to reach for the champagne—the 12 million Germans who lived outside the Reich but proximate to it.

The decline in Soviet prestige, due to the Great Purge, was a major factor in the growing power of the Third Reich. Indeed, as E. H. Carr has suggested on the basis of fragmentary evidence, the Nazis (in particular Heydrich) seem to have furnished Soviet authorities with documents—whether authentic or forged it is not yet possible to say—that established the collusion of Red army senior officers with their Reichswehr counterparts for the purpose of assassinating Stalin and forming a Russian government that would resume cooperation with Germany. If this is true, it can only be concluded that Hitler was seeking to defame the USSR in Western eyes and compromise the German officer corps so that he could bend it to his will.

Such was the disarray in which Europe found itself in the autumn of 1937 that the *Führer* decided to proceed with the annexations of Austria and the Sudeten areas, which were inhabited by 3 million Germans who lived in a horseshoe strip around Bohemia. The notorious Hossbach Memorandum, in which Colonel Hossbach summarized Hitler's statements of November 5, 1937, in conference with Blomberg, Raeder, Fritsch, Keitel, and Brauchitsch, is evidence that to achieve

Anschluss aims in Austria and Czechoslovakia the *Führer* was prepared to risk a European war. Hitler did not believe in the myth of collective security, and he was, as the newer scholarship has proved, correct in discounting the military preparedness of Britain and France. He was convinced that without strong air defenses or an expeditionary force Britain would not seriously concern herself over the fate of Czechoslovakia. He was almost certain, too, that France, paralyzed by class conflict and disillusioned with Soviet Russia, did not even have a war plan for the invasion of Germany and hence would balk at coming to the defense of the Czechs.

The Hossbach Memorandum does not in itself confirm that Hitler wanted an early general war. Yet taken in context with his dream of an east European empire, the reorganization of the Wehrmacht and the memorandum are circumstantial evidence of Hitler's hostile intentions. They lend considerable color to the thesis of John Wheeler Bennett, H. M. Robertson, Rudolf Eucken, G. L. Weinberg, and Christopher Thorne that Hitler had embarked upon a conspiracy against the peace of the world.

Anschluss

Before the Czech roast was ready, the Austrian soup suddenly boiled over. On July 11, 1936, Austria's Chancellor (1934–38) Kurt Schuschinigg had been obliged to sign a pact with von Papen that ostensibly had insured Austria's independence but had conceded so much economically and diplomatically to the Reich as plainly to foreshadow *Anschluss*. Even so, Hitler had not ceased to nibble at the agreement, and Austro-German relations had steadily deteriorated down through January, 1938. Despite evidence to the contrary, Schuschnigg still hoped to improve Austro-German relations. For this reason he accepted Hitler's invitation to come to Berchtesgaden on February 12, 1938. At the "eagle's nest" Schuschnigg was subjected to one of Hitler's marathon tirades and presented with the demand that full freedom of political action be accorded the Austrian Nazis and that their leader, Dr. Artur Seyss-Inquart (1892–1946), be appointed minister of the interior.

The Hossbach Memorandum notwithstanding, Hitler was privately anxious to achieve union without having to invade a German country and believed *Anschluss* without war was possible. On the strength of British assurances of November 19, 1937, that London was ready to countenance the peaceful revision of Versailles as respected Austria, Czechoslovakia, and Danzig, Hitler's hopes soared. His elation knew no bounds when Mussolini, too, told him that he would not oppose *Anschluss*.

Schuschnigg now had recourse to a ruse. On March 9 he summoned all Austrians over twenty-four to vote on Sunday, the thirteenth, on the question whether they preferred a free Austria. Hitler was taken by surprise. Knowing that a very heavy majority would probably endorse independence, Hitler cast the die. The Wehrmacht was ordered into Austria on the night of March 11–12, where it was jubilantly hailed by Cardinal Innitzer of Vienna and most Catholic prelates. Since most of the countryside was already under Nazi control, Schuschnigg realized the futility of resistance and ordered the armed forces not to oppose the Germans. Thereafter, Hitler stuck an edelweiss in his lapel, put Schuschnigg in prison, and appointed Seyss-Inquart chancellor of what was soon to become the German Ostmark (Austria). The Austrian army was amalgamated with the Wehrmacht, and Germany was increased by the addition of 7 million new citizens. She also acquired access to the middle Danubian waterway. Most ominous was the fact that now Bohemia was caught in the jaws of a nutcracker.

The Revival of Military Opposition

After *Anschluss* Hitler assured his worried officers that he had no intention of attacking Czechoslovakia. But many of them no longer believed his words. In 1938 a military resistance movement gradually took shape. A number of senior officers—Generals von Fritsch, von Hammerstein (retired), Wilhelm Adam, Franz Halder, Erwin von Witzleben, Georg Thomas, Karl von Stülpnagel, Erich Hoepner, Ludwig Beck, and Admiral Canaris (chief of the counterintelligence, or *Abwehr*, of the OKW)—now believed that Hitler was planning a European war and began to plot his overthrow.

The military conspiracy, led by Beck, chief of the army general staff, gathered momentum when, in May, Hitler signed the operational directive Case Green, which contemplated a forcible solution of the Sudeten question by October 1. Rumors on May 20 that Nazi troops were concentrating along the Czech frontier acted like an alarm in the night upon London, Paris, and Prague. Although Prime Minister Chamberlain and French Premier (1938–40) Édouard Daladier did not think Germany would attack so soon after *Anschluss*, the Czechs mobilized and Britain and France were obliged to assure them of their support. When Hitler insisted that the rumors of a German invasion had all been a false alarm, which at that time was the case, the crisis blew over.

When on May 30 the German generals heard from Hitler that he was resolved to strike Czechoslovakia on October 1, they established contact with Carl Goerdeler's civil resistance movement and laid plans to prevent the *Führer* from forcing Germany into what would be a disastrous two-front war. The keenly intelligent Beck, who was inspired by a strong sense of moral responsibility to God and nation, concerted with many of his colleagues, as well as with the resistance leaders Goerdeler and Schacht, to try to persuade the senior officers to resign in a body. Although von Brauchitsch, the commander of the army, privately sympathized with Beck, he vacillated and, out of loyalty to the oath he had taken to Hitler on August 2, 1934, finally rejected Beck's last memorandum of July 16, 1938. Being unable to convince von Brauchitsch, Beck forthwith resigned (August 18). He was succeeded by General Franz Halder (1884–1972), a Bavarian Protestant who had long secretly opposed the Nazis and who was to become a main leader of the military conspiracy against Hitler in World War II.

Meanwhile in Czechoslovakia the German party of Sudetenland, which was led by the former Nazi schoolteacher Konrad Henlein (1898–1945), was loudly demanding that the Czech government accept the Sudeten German Carlsbad Program of April 24, 1938. This would have accorded comprehensive autonomy to the 3.5 million Germans who ringed Bohemia and permitted a plebiscite on whether the Sudetenland should be ceded to Germany. Under the leadership of their president (1935–38), Edward Beneš, the Czechs, however, steadfastly refused to comply with Henlein's demands. Finally, the British intervened to compel compromise. Lord Runciman, who had gone to Prague on August 3, persuaded Prime Minister Hodza to make a generous offer to the Sudeten Germans on September 7. But it was far too late to appease Hitler with half a loaf.

To block implementation of Case Green on October 1, Halder, Beck, and Hans Gisevius plotted to overthrow Hitler on September 30. Since this could be done only if Britain and France firmly opposed him, the generals sought to elicit a British promise of support for their aims. Major Erwin von Kleist-Schmenzin, a conservative landowner, was dispatched to London, but unfortunately neither Chamberlain nor Eden would receive him. Even those who would, including Vansittart and Churchill, gave him no encouragement. Similarly, a parallel attempt by the counselor of the embassy in London, Theodor Kordt, to elicit a British declaration that a German attack upon Czechoslovakia would mean general war was refused by the foreign office. The fact is that the British government, apprised by the general staff of the army that the country was not prepared for war, preferred to rely on Hitler's words.

Although the French government was ostensibly more bellicose than the British, Daladier, the premier, would not take the irrevocable step without allies. He had been thoroughly scared by General Vuillemin's report earlier in the year as to the current strength and capabilities of the Luftwaffe. Daladier was, moreover, restrained from doing anything "rash" by his appeasement-minded foreign minister Georges Bonnet, who opposed reviving the Russian alliance.

The Munich Sellout

Whatever slim chance of success the German generals' plan may have had was destroyed at Munich in late September by Britain and France. In an atmosphere of extreme tension, aggravated by Hitler's histrionic performance at the party convention in Nuremberg, Chamberlain thought it best for the mountain to go to Mohammed. On September 15 he flew to Berchtesgaden, and on September 22 to Bad Godesberg to confer with Hitler to find the formula for giving him what he wanted without war. Beneš, who had been prepared to cede some land, had been put under pressure by the British and French to be even more accommodating. However, when Chamberlain was confronted on the twenty-second with the demand for *immediate* cession of the Sudetenland, he was staggered.

The following week was one of wild alarms. The Czech army was mobilized at once, the French army began partial mobilization on September 24, and the British fleet was mobilized on the twenty-eighth. Throughout the week of crisis the attitude of Soviet Russia was equivocal. Despite vague intimations that she would aid Czechoslovakia if the latter denounced Germany, at no time did the USSR assure Prague that the Red army would come to the defense of the Czechs regardless of what the French did. The most recent scholarship has concluded that it is a myth that Soviet Russia would have fought Germany singlehandedly over Czechoslovakia. Indeed, the chaos sown in the Soviet state and army by the Great Purges would not have permitted Stalin to take such a risk. On the other hand, the government of the USSR might well have honored its treaty obligations toward the Czechs if France had marched to their aid first. As things stood, however, Stalin was quite sure that Daladier would leave Czechoslovakia in the lurch and there would be no *casus foederis* for the USSR.

On September 29 Mussolini pulled the powers back from the brink. At his suggestion, Daladier, Chamberlain, Hitler, and the *Duce* met on the thirtieth in Munich. The "tragic" agreement that they signed there was not, from the British viewpoint, a ruse to gain time so as to fight with better prospects of victory later but, as Martin Gilbert and Richard Gott have convincingly argued, simply to avoid war entirely. Moreover, Chambelain believed (Raymond J. Sonntag) that Hitler in his saner moments would, like other chiefs of state, try to avert war.

The Munich Agreement authorized Germany to annex areas of Czechoslovakia that were inhabited by German majorities, the transfer to be effected in stages between October 1 and 10. It had compounded the misery of Beneš and Prime Minister Hodza that Poland and Hungary had also militarily threatened to increase their territorial blackmail of Czechoslovakia.

Munich was the first step in a preconceived, long-range project for the conquest of *Lebensraum* in the east (C. R. Cole, F. M. Hinsley, K. Eubank, and H. R. Trevor-Roper), not merely the attainment of a traditional policy aim by traditionalist diplomatic means. With the Czech border fortifications in his hand and the Czech army (which on paper possessed more divisions than the German) demoralized by the "betrayal" of its country, Hitler could look forward to the early disintegration of the Czechoslovakian rump and the planning of either a Polish-German attack on the Soviet Union or an assault with Russian blessings on Poland. Not the least sorrowful aspect of the Munich settlement was that the four-power pact swiped the ground out from under the German resistance movement. To the mortification of the generals, Hitler had again demonstrated the correctness of his intuition that the West would not fight. If only Hitler had fallen victim to an assassin in 1938, he probably would have gone down in history, as Joachim Fest has asserted in his massive biography of the Nazi leader, as "one of the greatest German statesmen."

Czechoslovakia's Dismemberment

Having opted for Germany, Britain and France now hoped, as Soviet historians maintain, that Hitler would next move against isolated Russia. But to embark on its conquest Hitler had first to destroy Czechoslovakia and then Poland or win the latter to an alliance. As Gerhard Weinberg has shown, Hitler was less interested in the Sudeten question than in the strategic-operational dividends that would accrue from shattering Czechoslovakia. He had no intention of honoring his promises to Chamberlain. Actuated by unprecedented, preposterous dreams of *Lebensraum* in the east, he soon showed himself to be the pathological liar and martial opportunist Alan Bullock has depicted him to be.

In spite of the fact that Hitler, no less than Britain, France, Poland, and Italy, guaranteed what was left of Czechoslovakia after Poland had been awarded Teschen, and Hungary all southern Slovakia (November 2, 1938), Hitler prepared to violate his pledge. He plotted to use Slovakia, which had been granted autonomy on October 7, as the gunpowder to blow up the rump Czech state. On November 26 he told his generals to prepare an operational plan to defeat France, because he knew that he was on the brink of taking a long risk that might provoke war with the western powers.

Incensed at the collusion between the Slovakian Tiso administration and the German Nazis, the Prague government on March 9 deposed Tiso, arrested leading Slovakian separatists, and proclaimed martial law in Slovakia. Hitler exploited the parting of the ways between the Czechs and Slovaks to summon President Hácha and Foreign Minister Chvalkovsky to Berlin. There on the night of March 14 they were so tongue-lashed by Hitler and intimidated with threats of aerial bombardment of Prague that they collapsed.

While this was going on, the Wehrmacht invaded Bohemia and Moravia on the morning of March 15. The following day a triumphant Hitler proclaimed from the Hradčany that they were now protectorates of the Reich. Subsequently Hungary occupied more Slovakian territory and all of Ruthenia, while what was left of Slovakia became a German satellite. A week later Hitler forced Lithuania to retrocede the Memel territory.

In a twinkling the Munich settlement had been relegated to the circular file, and a stunned Britain and France abandoned appeasement. Italy, too, was indignant at Hitler's acts, which has led Walther Hofer to advance the untenable thesis that Hitler was pushing Germany into isolation again. Such a view does less than justice to Hitler's slyness. He knew that Mussolini had uttered his *jacta est alea*. From top secret contacts, too, the *Führer* was convinced that the Soviet Union was on the verge of abandoning its collective security policy. At the same time, negotiations were in progress for a military alliance between Germany and Japan.

Hitler's calculations regarding Italy proved to be correct. On April 8, 1938, she invaded Albania and further antagonized all champions of the 1919 settlement. On May 23 Italy signed the Pact of Steel with the Reich, by which the former promised unconditionally to come to the military support of the latter in the event of an unprovoked French attack. Japan, however, eluded the Nazi trap. Tokyo's offer of March 22 of a five-year alliance against the USSR, subject to the condition that Japan would not have to fight in Europe, was unacceptable to Hitler. Similarly, a more liberal offer by Prime Minister Hiranuma on May 4 was rejected, and a compromise offer by him on June 5 was sabotaged by the Japanese military. When, finally, Germany plunged Europe into war, it was without any assurance of Japanese support. No alliance between Berlin and Tokyo was signed until September, 1940—after the collapse of France.

The signing of the Pact of Steel did not, of course, mean Italy was prepared to march at once with Germany against France and England. Indeed, during the German-Polish crisis of 1939 Mussolini and Ciano did everything they could to bring about a mediation of the dispute and defer war at least until 1942. That the *Duce* was hoodwinked by the *Führer* there can be no doubt. Mario Toscano, Ivone Kirkpatrick, Elizabeth Wiskemann, and D. C. Watt have proved, on the basis of the German documents and Count Ciano's diary, that until August 11, 1939, Mussolini was left in the dark concerning Hitler's imminent attack. When the information was at length conveyed to him through Ciano, Mussolini was "horrified" at Hitler's treachery.

The Suit for Russia's Hand

There had already been a grave deterioration in German-Polish relations in 1939 when the government of the USSR took the initiative to achieve a rapprochement with the Third Reich. The Munich Pact had seemingly given Hitler the green light to begin his assault upon Russia, with the aim of securing *Lebensraum*, and dismemberment of Czechoslovakia had opened the Balkans to Germany. Stalin had cause to tremble when on October 24, 1938, Ribbentrop proposed to Foreign Minister Joséf Beck of Poland a general settlement in return for merely the cession of Danzig and laying a German-controlled railroad and *Autobahn* through the Polish Corridor. By the close of March, 1939, the German tide appeared to be lapping dangerously at Stalin's feet.

The Soviet government now realistically sought to deflect the German threat by playing the trump card of the partition of eastern Europe. Hitler became aware of the warmer wind from the east when on March 10 Stalin stated his belief to the eighteenth congress of the Communist Party of the Soviet Union (CPSU) that the Reich would refuse to act as hireling for the West in war against Russia.

After the liquidation of Czechoslovakia, Britain and France swung the tiller around. On March 31 Britain guaranteed the territorial integrity of Poland, and France did likewise two weeks later. On April 13 similar pledges were given to Rumania and Greece. An analogous pledge was given on May 23 to Turkey but was confined to the case of a Mediterranean war. As respects Poland, obviously, Anglo-French promises of military aid were worthless, for the western states had no way to send troops to her.

Until the commitments to Poland Hitler's eastern policy had been contradictory and even becalmed. He had been disinclined to attack Poland in 1939 unless unusually favorable circumstances warranted it. The Anglo-French guarantee roused the *Führer* from his torpor and to that extent accelerated the coming of war. On April 3 he finally ordered the Wehrmacht to prepare for an attack on Poland by no later than September 1.

Meanwhile, the Soviet government took the first step toward a major change in policy. On April 17 the Russian ambassador in Berlin, Merekalov, confided to Nazi state secretary Baron von Weizsäcker that "ideological differences . . . did not have to prove a stumbling block" and there was no reason why Russo-German relations could not be normalized and "become better and better." Taking the cue, Hitler on April 28 denounced the German-Polish Non-Aggression Pact of 1934 and the Anglo-German Naval Pact of 1935. At the same time he lodged a formal demand with Warsaw for Danzig and extraterritorial communications across the Corridor. On May 3, significantly, Litvinov was replaced as Soviet foreign minister by Vyacheslav Molotov. This was tantamount to an advertisement of Stalin's formal, but not necessarily final, abandonment of collective security.

From early April onward it was a basic assumption of Soviet diplomacy that Hitler would attack Poland unless a grand coalition dissuaded him, but that such an alliance could not be built without the aid of the Red army. The Soviet government reasoned that it could legitimately ask as the price of military support of the West the abrogation of the Treaty of Riga of March, 1921, respecting cessions of parts of White Russia and the Ukraine to Poland.

By mid-April England and France had begun the trek to Canossa. On April 15th France offered a new alliance to the USSR. This was solely for the contingency of war over Poland or Rumania. From then on, Allied discussions with Soviet Russia proceeded at a leisurely pace without making much headway until the end of July. Howsoever much the British and the French desired an alliance with Soviet Russia, it was always the weakness of their position that they were unable to demonstrate a willingness on the part of Poland, or even Rumania, to admit passage of the Red army or the establishment of Russian military bases on their soil. Both Poland and Rumania feared for the territories that they had detached from Russia in her weakest hour. Because of this factor Soviet diplomats decided that there was more likelihood that a political agreement could be reached between Russia and Germany than with the western democracies.

The western powers could not seriously have believed in the possibility of a triple alliance because they never sent a cabinet minister to Moscow to negotiate. For some strange reason they elected to give Stalin offense by sending a mere sectional chief, rather than the British foreign minister, or, as was the case with the Munich agreement, the prime minister. When, finally, Molotov on July 27 demanded that military staff conversations begin at once, Britain and France had the effrontery to dispatch another low-level mission, not by plane, but by boat. When the military delegation arrived in Moscow after six days en route, it resumed the old haggling but could make no progress in the face of Polish obduracy.

The Russo-German Nonaggression Pact

Considering the improbability of alliance with the West, the Russians signed a trade treaty with the Germans on August 19. The Kremlin then requested that a high-ranking German plenipotentiary be sent to Moscow by August 26–27. Hitler, who by now despaired of detaching England from France, asked that the date be moved up to the twenty-third. Stalin assented. On that day Ribbentropp flew to Moscow and that very night signed the historic nonaggression pact. This pledged the signatories to neutrality in the event of attack upon either by a third power. A secret codicil provided for the division of eastern Europe into two spheres of influence. Esthonia, Latvia, and Poland to the east of the Narev-Vistula-San line were to be in the Russian sphere, and the special interest of the USSR in Bessarabia was recognized. The German sphere was to comprise Lithuania, including Vilna, and western Poland.

Soviet Russia could have prevented the war but wished to save its skin or at least buy time in which to rearm. Stalin calculated that a protracted war of attrition between the Reich and the western powers would leave the USSR in the position of arbiter of Europe. Britain, too, could have blocked war. But she reviled Soviet Russia and was insincere in her negotiations for an alliance with the USSR. Accordingly, the British government neglected to bring the requisite pressure to bear on Warsaw to accommodate Moscow's demands. As for France, she had no confidence in the Red army. Nor could she bring herself to abandon all her old client states in eastern Europe. Yet that was the price of alliance with the USSR. Thus, by irresolution or inflexibility each of the members of the later Grand Alliance against Germany contributed to the coming of World War II.

That Hitler could once again have been pulled back from the abyss was possible but unlikely. He was determined, as Klaus Hildebrand has recently reaffirmed, to have his east European *Lebensraum*, sooner or later. However, it is a fact that even after August 23 Hitler vacillated. The Anglo-Polish Mutual Assistance Treaty of August 25 alarmed him. He momentarily wavered between two alternatives: invasion of Poland, which on August 28 he definitely set for September 1, and a spectacular but purely diplomatic victory that would temporarily put the military solution on ice. In an effort to retain the latter alternative should it suit him in the twelfth hour, Hitler formally renounced all claims to Alsace-Lorraine and directed Göring to approach Downing Street with less objectionable demands on Poland, which the British should ask Warsaw to accept. Eden indicated that Britain might mediate on that basis, and Hitler, thinking he had nothing to lose from that, demanded that the Poles send a plenipotentiary to Berlin before midnight of August 30. Halder's diary and other circumstantial evidence indicate, however, that Hitler's Polish policy hung by a thin, taut thread. Hitler was in a state of feverish emotional stress, and the slightest show of Polish opposition or even hesitancy would have caused the thread to snap.

Although Poland had decided to resist, she could not help herself because two cannibal countries were both out to devour her. On August 30 Poland responded to Germany's last summons by mobilizing. This provoked Hitler to cast the die. At dawn on September 1 he ordered the Wehrmacht to commence the invasion of Poland at once. Mussolini's last-ditch attempt to arrange another Munich-style conference for September 5 encountered sympathy from Chamberlain and the French foreign minister, Georges Bonnet, but Daladier, who had at last restored the word "honor" to his vocabulary, insisted that the Germans must withdraw from Poland before talks could begin. Hitler, however, had opened the doors of Janus. For a man of destiny such as he, they could not be closed again until victory or death.

PART XIV
WORLD WAR II AND AFTERMATH

Chapter 51

THE TIDE OF NAZI CONQUEST,

1939–1942

Reaction of the German Public to War

When Hitler ordered the Wehrmacht to assault Poland on September 1, 1939, there was little rejoicing in Germany. Chauvinistic demonstrations were discouraged by the fact that people were still too stunned by the reverberations of the Russo-German Pact and because memories of the suffering and defeat in World War I were still too vivid. It did not add to the general enthusiasm that from the outset Germany found herself one power against three, for England and France had declared war on September 3. On the other hand, the Axis partner, Italy, was pouting in surly neutrality. Even more than the public, the German generals had trepidations regarding the enormous task Hitler had set them. It was a source of dissatisfaction, too, that Hitler had issued the two basic operational directives for the Polish campaign without taking his senior officers into consultation. Finally, everyone knew that the Reich was outnumbered in population and troops, was deficient in raw materials, was vastly inferior to France and Britain on the seas, and was vulnerable to a hunger blockade. Unlike the situation in August, 1914, few Germans believed the war would be a short campaign. Most of them dwelt gloomily on the probability of another long and bloody war of attrition. The most that can be said is that Hitler's trump card of August 23 had temporarily silenced serious opposition in the Reich.

The Balance of Forces

From the beginning to the end of the second German war of the twentieth century the Allies enjoyed numerical superiority on land and sea, while they were at a disadvantage only in the air and then but for a short time. Germany's mainly conscript ground forces numbered in September, 1939, approximately 103 divisions of all kinds. France had 108, although her population was less than that of the Reich. The discrepancy in naval strength was enormous. At this time Germany no longer possessed a high seas fleet. She had only 2 battleships (the *Scharnhorst* and *Gneisenau*), 3 pocket battleships (the *Admiral Scheer, Admiral Graf Spee,* and *Deutschland*), 2 heavy cruisers (the *Hipper and Blücher*), 6 light cruisers, 22 destroyers, 35 coastal submarines, 27 larger, high seas submarines, and about 70 lesser craft. The French fleet alone was twice as strong (except for submarines) as the German. The British enjoyed crushing superiority, with their 12 battleships, 3 battle cruisers, 6 aircraft carriers, 15 heavy cruisers, 49 light cruisers, 185 destroyers, 57 submarines, and a host of lesser craft. On the other hand, the Luftwaffe, despite failure to expand rapidly, was still the most advanced air fleet in Europe, comprising 4,333 aircraft, of which 2,700 were combat planes, including 1,180 light bombers, 771 fighters, and 336 Stukas (dive bombers). Among the best German craft were the Henkel 111, Junker (Stuka) 87, Dornier 17, and the Messerschmitt 109 fighter. There were as yet no jet planes in the Luftwaffe, but a more serious deficiency was the lack of heavy bombers and fighter escorts, which attested to an underestimation in command circles of the importance of strategic air operations.

The Polish Campaign

The war against Poland was the first Nazi blitzkrieg. Although plagued by shortages of materiel, the Wehrmacht crushed a nation of 35 million in about three weeks. At the outset the Polish air force was destroyed on the ground by the Luftwaffe. Poland was invaded from three sides by the Germans, and her economic and industrial power, which was mainly concentrated in the west, was overrun in the first days of fighting. It made the task of the Wehrmacht easier that the Poles had also to guard against an attack from the Red army. Decisive for the outcome of the campaign was the big qualitative and quantitative margin enjoyed by the attackers as respects fighting men, armor, artillery, motorized units, and tactical air support, and the superiority of the superbly trained, long-term German officer corps.

While inaction characterized the Western Front, four German armies slashed into Poland with such force that by September 17 the issue was no longer in doubt. Almost all of Poland's archaic fortresses had fallen, and the British and French had been of no direct help. Poland's cavalry had been slaughtered and her armies had been shattered. Warsaw had been bombarded with artillery and by light bomber aircraft. On the seventeenth the Red army was ordered to invade in the east and occupy those areas of Poland that had been allotted on August 23 to the Soviet sphere of influence. By the third week of September Polish civil officials were racing the generals for asylum in Rumania. After Warsaw fell on September 27, it was all over. The Germans had achieved their first wartime conquest at the minimal cost of 11,000 dead and 30,000 wounded.

On September 28 Stalin and Molotov met Ribbentrop in the Kremlin and drafted a supplement to the pact of August 23. The Soviet dictator indulged in blackmail, for the Red army had done none of the fighting. Soviet Russia now received a full half of Poland together with its principal oil resources. At the same time Lithuania was transferred to the Soviet zone of influence. In return, territory east of the line agreed upon in August—Lublin, Lodz, and part of the province of Warsaw—was left to the mercy of the Nazis. Some Polish territory was annexed, but the bulk of the German share was organized as the semi-independent governor-generalcy of Poland with capital at Krakow. Thenceforth Germany was obliged to station large numbers of troops along an imperiled Russo-German frontier, because all Europe east of the Vistula had now fallen under the Russian shadow. The restoration of Russia in eastern Europe to the territorial position she had enjoyed toward the end of the reign of Peter the Great was the price Hitler paid for banishing the phantom of a two-front war. The only other important advantage he derived from the treaty was a promise by the Russians that they would deliver grain and raw materials to Germany, which would mitigate the asperities of the British blockade.

The "Phony War" in the West

After Britain and France had rejected Hitler's offer of October 6 to participate in a general peace conference, the Western Front from Basel to Luxemburg for many months remained completely immobile. There were no attacks, and casualties were minuscule. This condition of "twilight war" or "phony war" continued till the spring of 1940 when the Wehrmacht was finally hurled against the Allied lines.

Hitler would have preferred to attack France in the autumn of 1939. As early as September 27 he had, in fact, set November 12 as the date for implementing Case Yellow, the operational plan for the invasion of the Low Countries and France. He was concerned to prevent any concentration of superior Allied strength on the continent. However, Brauchitsch pointed out that the weather would probably be unfavorable in November for tactical air support of advancing ground troops, and armor might be bogged down in mud. Hitler reluctantly gave in and, after long hesitation, postponed the blow until May.

Originally General Keitel, head of the OKW, and his taciturn operational chief of staff, General Jodl, had favored a modified version of the Schlieffen Plan. However, General Erich von Mannstein elaborated a brilliant alternative during the dull months when France was extending her Maginot Line along the Belgian border and bringing pressure to bear on Brussels to allow French armies to take up positions along the shorter Maas-Antwerp line. Mannstein's plan called for a strong armored penetration of the impassable Ardennes, a massive strike at the Sedan anchor of the original Maginot Line, and a daring thrust from there to the Abbéville area at the Somme estuary. It was this concept that was executed in the spring of 1940.

The Norwegian Campaign

Relations between Germany and the USSR narrowly survived the "winter war" that the latter commenced against Finland on November 30, 1939. Although the German people sympathized with the plucky Finns, the Nazi government rigorously pursued a policy of nonintervention. This really decided the fate of Finland. After months of inept operations by the Red army, it finally broke through the defenders' Mannerheim line. Thereafter, the Helsinki government felt that it could not afford to wait for the arrival of military aid that had been promised by London and Paris, and Finland capitulated on March 12, 1940.

Alarmed at this new extension of Soviet influence, Hitler drafted plans for the conquest of Norway and Denmark. At the same time, the British government strove to provoke a German attack upon Denmark and Norway with the aim of forcing the Wehrmacht to spread its forces dangerously thin. Without the consent of Norway, the British began to mine its coastal waters on April 8, 1940.

Hitler had planned to invade both countries. He needed Norwegian ports and submarine berths to enable him to break the British blockade. Control over western Scandinavia would also protect the right flank of the Wehrmacht when it commenced the contemplated campaign against France. As early as March 1 Hitler had issued the directive Case Weser-Exercise for the occupation of Norway and Denmark. On April 1 he ordered that the invasion be carried out on April 9. On the night of April 8–9 the Luftwaffe delivered a diversionary blow at the British naval base at Scapa Flow. The next day Denmark was smothered and occupied without resistance. Simultaneously Norway was struck by land, sea, and air. German parachutists secured most of the key points in the country before nightfall. The whole aerial-amphibious operation was a spectacular success, carried out, as Churchill conceded, with faultless planning and precision.

The Norwegians, however, bitterly opposed the Germans from the outset. A small Anglo-Polish expeditionary force was landed at Namos and Andalsnes in northern Norway but, after several weeks of aimless operations, was ingloriously withdrawn. During the evacuation the British lost the aircraft carrier *Glorious*, two cruisers, and nine destroyers. Decisive for the outcome of the campaign had been the superior strength of the Luftwaffe, which ruled the Norwegian skies. King Haakon and his government fled to London, and the Nazis installed a puppet regime in Oslo under Major Vidkun Quisling, whose name thereupon became the universal synonym for traitor. With Norway's iron deposits under Nazi control and her long, indented coastline available for U-boat operations against the British, Hitler could now proceed to implement Case Yellow, the operational plan for the invasion of the Low Countries and France.

The German Effort on the Seas

Throughout the war Germany was the underdog in the maritime war. She had no high seas fleet, and even as late as December, 1941, she had only 90 submarines, which was far below the necessary minimum of 300 for decisive success.

At the commencement of hostilities German submarines caught a considerable number of British and French merchant ships returning to their home ports. These ships had largely been unarmed and could not defend themselves against the submarines. Almost at once, however, the English revived the World War I escort system of accompanying destroyers, cruisers, and airplanes. At the same time most merchantmen were refitted with guns and armaments, and a decline in sinkings ensued.

German construction of submarines during 1939–40 proceeded only slowly, partly because of conflicts between the High Command of the Navy (Oberkommando der Kriegsmarine—OKM) and Admiral Doenitz, who was a champion of unrestricted U-boat operations. At the same time the construction of Junker 88 attack planes, which were to be used for patrolling the waters around the British isles and sinking shipping, also proceeded sluggishly, so that deliveries could not be expected before the autumn of 1940 at the earliest. Meanwhile, German vessels and such planes as could be detached for the work mined the English coast in the winter of 1939–40 with novel magnetic-type devices. Until the secret of their operation was discovered, they proved extremely effective.

In early 1941 there were only 6 German submarines operating along the main Allied shipping routes at any one time. By the end of the year the U-boat fleet had grown from an initial 57 to 100 but was grossly inadequate to its mission. Nevertheless during 1942 the Allies lost 900 ships, totaling more than 6 million gross tons to German U-boats, which was for Allied shipping the most catastrophic year of the war. In total, 7,706,000 tons of vessels were lost from all causes in that year. However, in 1943 only 2,579,000 tons were sunk by submarines, and in 1944 only 773,000. Between 1939 and 1945 the Allies lost more than 21 million tons of shipping to mines, U-boats, aircraft, and enemy surface action. On the other side of the ledger the British alone seized 9 million tons from various European countries by March, 1941.

The big submarine success of 1942 might have been even greater had Doenitz' advice to stress U-boat action against Britain been heeded earlier. Not until the defeat of the German Sixth Army at Stalingrad did the *Führer* turn his ear to Doenitz, whom he then appointed supreme commander of the navy. In 1943, as a consequence, 300 submarines were built, but this came too late to turn the tide. By then the vast superiority of the combined American, British, and French navies had cancelled out the advantages of submarine wolf-pack tactics that in 1942 had reaped so rich a harvest. Radar, depth charges, and improved armaments conspired to blunt the underwater offensive. Moreover, Britain was building vessels faster than they were being sunk, while German submarine sinkings were at only half the rate of World War I. Last, on April 28, 1943, the U-boat fleet sustained a crushing blow when 41 submarines were lost in a running battle with a west-bound convoy between Newfoundland and Iceland. Thereafter, the main ocean lanes between North American and European ports became secure. Moreover, no German snorkel submarine was ever able to duplicate the victory of the daring U-boat commander who on October 14–15, 1939, had penetrated Scapa Flow harbor and sunk the battleship *Royal Oak*.

For a time German pocket battleships sank a number of Allied merchantmen in the South Atlantic and Indian oceans. The *Graf Spee* sank 50,000 tons of shipping before she was disabled, trapped by a British squadron, and then scuttled in La Plata estuary by her captain, who ended by shooting himself (December, 1939). After September, 1940, when the US government released 50 over-age destroyers to Britain for convoy duty, the Allies' surface warship preponderance became ridiculous. Nevertheless, in May, 1941, German men-of-war sent to the bottom off Greenland the biggest ship in the British navy, the *Hood*. One of the attackers, the battleship *Bismarck*, was subsequently sunk in the Atlantic after a 1,700 mile chase by a British squadron. Germany's largest battleships, the juggernaut *Tirpitz* and *Scharnhorst*, also came to grief. The former was sunk in a Norwegian harbor; the latter was shattered by British bombs in 1942.

The Collapse of France, 1940

F. Lee Benns and Mary Elisabeth Seldon, EUROPE: 1939 to the Present, Revised Edition, © 1971 by Meredith Corporation. Reprinted by permission of Prentice-Hall, Inc., Englewood Cliffs, New Jersey.

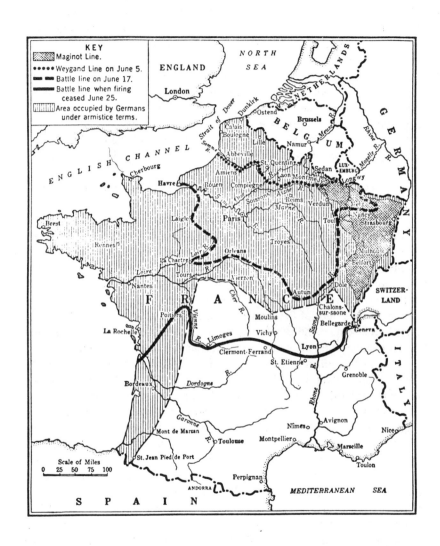

The Fall of France

Disregarding the chill skepticism of his generals, Hitler proceeded in the winter of 1939–40 with the drafting of Case Yellow, the plan for the assault upon the combined ground forces of France, Britain, and the Low Countries. He was about to execute the most brilliant blitzkrieg in modern history.

On May 10, 1940, Winston Churchill replaced Chamberlain as British prime minister, and on the same day Hitler launched his offensive in the west. For him the tide was at the flood. His rear seemed so secure at the time that only 7 divisions were entrusted with the defense of the eastern frontiers. Soviet Russia had signed trade agreements with Germany on October 24, 1939, and February 11, 1940, and the imports of cereals, oil, cotton, and phosphates from the USSR were trooping in. Italy, too, was on the verge of honoring her obligations under the Pact of Steel.

Utilizing the Mannstein operational concept, which balanced enormous risks against disabling surprise, Hitler assigned the great bulk of 10 panzer divisions, including 1,000 heavy tanks, not to the right wing but to the center. The delicate task of forcing the Maas between Dinant and Sedan and breaking the hinge of the Maginot Line was given to Field Marshal Gerd von Rundstedt (1875–1953) and his Army Group A. Although the OKW and OKH contemplated an advance through both the Netherlands and Belgium, the beauty of Mannstein's plan was that, if successful, the German motorized and armored salient from the Ardennes and Sedan to the mouth of the Somme would cut off the British and the bulk of the French defenders, who would be moving up to take positions in Belgium.

Contrary to the rules of warfare, the attackers did not enjoy numerical superiority. They possessed an offensive force of 72 divisions with 47 in reserve, while the "West Wall" along the Rhine was guarded by 17. The French opposed with 96 divisions, including 32 in reserve and 22 garrisoning the fortresses. To these must be added 10 serviceable British divisions (9 of which were in Belgium), 22 Belgian, and 8 Dutch divisions. The attackers had no more tanks than the defenders but disposed theirs better, grouping them into 10 panzer divisions, most of which were under command of General Ewald von Kleist. In the air alone the Germans had numerical superiority, disposing of 3,500 combat planes, compared with a combined force of 1,200 for the French and British.

The attack proceeded with the precision of a computer. At the outset, highly trained parachutist and glider troops captured the great Belgian fortress of Eben Emael on the Prince Albert Canal. By May 15 the Dutch Netherlands capitulated. Nobody, not even the OKW, was prepared for the incredible speed with which the army advanced. Hitler could not believe his success, and he, who had been confident at the outset, began to spy all manner of phantoms. Meanwhile, the armored columns of Kleist and General Heinz Guderian (1882–1954), the tank expert, dislocated the French defense by smashing through the wooded Ardennes and gliding over the northern French plain. The columns reached the mouth of the Somme by May 20. Guderian had been ordered to halt and consolidate, but he disobeyed. What had failed for Kluck in World War I succeeded brilliantly for Guderian. By May 24 the Germans, turning northward from Abbéville, had reached Calais.

At this point 1 million Dutch and Belgian troops had been defeated, the British Expeditionary Force had been entrapped, and three French armies had been cut off from their country. Whether Hitler now intended, as was urged by Göring, to destroy the pocketed foe by air, whether Kleist and Guderian were reluctant to commit their armor to the treacherous dunes around Dunkirk, or whether Hitler, who hoped for peace with England, perceived in an arranged escape of its army the opportunity to detach Britain from France cannot be said with certainty. After the war General von Rundstedt averred that it was the *Führer* who had interrupted the course of operations at the "decisive moment" because he hoped for a negotiated peace with England.

At the end of May Mussolini informed Hitler that Italy was about to enter the war. Before this took place, however, the bulk of the British Expeditionary Force and substantial elements of the French army, collectively more than 350,000 troops, had by June 4 been evacuated under British air and naval cover from Dunkirk and transported to England. All heavy equipment and 30,000 Britons were left in German hands.

On June 5 the *Wehrmacht* began the second phase of its western campaign. A Schlieffen wheeling offensive was launched south of the Somme with the aim of driving the French army against its Maginot Line in the east. On June 10, sensing a monumental German victory, Italy finally entered the war, and on the 14th the Germans entered Paris. The next day, as the invaders raced towards Verdun, the Reynaud ministry resigned, giving way to a government under the hoary Marshal Henri Pétain. On June 16 invincible Verdun fell. France was by then in a state of incredible turmoil: refugees by the millions streamed along all open roads. Pétain requested an armistice, and on June 22 it was signed (theatrically) in the same railroad carriage at Compiègne where the Germans had signed the armistice in 1918.

For France the Armistice was a harsh blow. She had to submit to the occupation of almost two-thirds of her soil, including the most populous and the main industrial areas, except for Lyons and Marseilles. All of the Channel and Biscayne coasts fell under German control. The government of Chief of State Pétain and Premier Pierre Laval was obliged to move to Vichy, the new capital of unoccupied, southern France. Tribute money amounting to 400 million francs a day was levied on the French, whose soldiers were to remain prisoners until the general peace. The French navy was to be demobilized and interned in French home or colonial ports. However, on July 3 British warships staged a "Copenhagen" on the French fleet. Most of its battleships at Mers El-Kebir, Oran, and Dakar were damaged or destroyed. The very next day a furious Vichy government severed relations with England.

Meanwhile, between June and August, 1940, the USSR was annexing the three Baltic states, Bukhovina, and Bessarabia. Soviet Russia thereby acquired territories which in their aggregate area vastly exceeded the permanent gains Germany contemplated in western Europe. Following occupation of those lands by the Red army came a reign of terror and atrocities. Hitler, incensed at Soviet perfidy, in October ordered German troops to occupy Rumania and "protect it."

The First German Defeat:
The Battle of Britain

Having failed to persuade the British to make separate peace, an angry Hitler decided to invade the British Isles. Most flag officers were stunned by the idea, for Germany lacked the warships and landing craft to carry out the project. Nevertheless Göring pressed him to proceed. The air marshal believed that the Luftwaffe was capable of destroying the Royal Air force (RAF) and, neutralizing the British navy, would be able to gain command of the Channel.

On July 22, 1940, the OKW was directed to prepare Operation Sea Lion, the plan for invading Britain. In view of the presumed demoralization and weakness of her defense forces, only 25 assault divisions were to be utilized. What the OKW did not know, however, was that in 1939, according to recent disclosures by the former chief of British air intelligence, British intelligence agents had in 1939 stolen a German encoding machine ("Enigma") in Poland, devised from it another decoding machine ("Ultra"), and knew in advance not only the details of Sea Lion but of most other major moves the OKW was to plan against England and for Italy and North Africa.

Before the invasion of Britain could begin, the RAF had to be cleared from the skies. This might just possibly have been achieved if Göring had concentrated solely on that. However, since his strategic purpose was not clear, he alternated his attacks between British planes on the ground and airfields one time and cities the next. In the end he fell between both stools. A main reason for his failure was that he had earlier rejected the prediction of the Italian air force General Douhet that the next war would be decided by strategic aerial bombardment, and Göring had consequently neglected to build the requisite heavy bombers.

The Battle of Britain began in July, 1940, and lasted till November. Estimates of comparative strengths vary widely, but it is probable that the attackers enjoyed a slight numerical edge. However, after the war Air Marshal Albert von Kesselring (1885–1960) averred that Germany had had only 900 fighter planes to Britain's 1,700 and had had no four-engined long-range, heavy bombers at all. Whatever the truth may be, the British had the advantage of radar, whose high-frequency radio wave transmitter-receiver system enabled the defenders to track attacking planes.

For three weeks after August 23 Field Marshal Göring used more than 700 bombers and fighters daily in a relentless effort to crush the RAF. By September 1 he began to experience his first doubts. Sorely worried, he then ordered the bombing of Coventry and Liverpool-Birkenhead in an effort to terrorize the British public. On September 7, allegedly in retaliation for the first British raid on

Berlin, the Germans, with inadequate means, began the blitz of London, which raged for weeks. By the tenth Britain had lost more than 300 planes, and the Germans 400. The assault reached a crescendo on the fifteenth when the attackers lost 60 planes. By then half the total German fighter-bomber force had been sacrificed. Yet Britain, which had fought back with great valor, was as far as ever from bending its stiff neck. Lacking a strategic bomber force, the Luftwaffe could inflict casualties but *not* win the Battle of Britain. The raids cost 23,000 civilian lives and continued into December, but Hitler spoke ever less about Sea Lion. Henceforth he sought to compensate for his defeat by trying to induce Franco to seize Gibraltar, but the *Caudillo* was too foxy.

North Africa and the Balkan Campaign

Upon Italy's entrance into the war, the Balkans and Africa were also drawn into it. On October 28 Mussolini, not to be denied his share of the pie, mounted a maladroit attack from Albania upon Greece. In Africa, meanwhile, British forces in Egypt under General Wavell penetrated 500 miles into Italian Libya in December, 1940. Loyal to Mussolini, Hitler resolved to rescue him in both areas. In February, 1941, a German *Afrikakorps* was organized and put under the command of General Erwin Rommel (1891–1944). Its mission was to restore the Italian position in north Africa. However, in the see-sawing tank battles of 1941 Rommel, the so-called desert fox, was unable permanently to drive the British out of Libya, much less capture Cairo, because Hitler never made available to him sufficient tanks, men, or materiel to accomplish that.

During the autumn of 1940 the OKH conceived an operational plan for the destruction of Soviet Russia. To minimize the risks of the gigantic invasion Hitler contemplated, he signed a pact with Italy and Japan on September 27, 1940. While officially the Tripartite Pact was not directed against the USSR but was designed to deter the USA from taking further belligerent steps, its real purpose was to link Japan more closely with the western theater of hostilities. Nevertheless, the impact of this convention was to deflect Japan's gaze away from Russia's maritime provinces toward Indochina and the East Indies. The pact confronted the Empire of the Rising Sun with such formidable tasks that she was obliged on April 13, 1941, to take out insurance in the form of a nonaggression treaty with the USSR. Ironically, this freed Russia's rear and made it possible for her to survive the massive German attack.

Meanwhile, the British had sent military aid to the Greeks, and the RAF, operating from Greek bases, made life miserable for the Italian navy. Hitler realized that the British had to be cleared from the Balkans. On March 25, consequently, he arranged with Yugoslavia for the transit of German troops. But unexpectedly, on March 29, the Belgrade government was overthrown by the army and replaced by a pro-Soviet regime. Hitler was beside himself with anger, and he resolved to break Yugoslavia. On April 17 Yugoslavia capitulated. Meanwhile German armored columns had sliced to Saloniki. Despite brave resistance, the Greek army surrendered on April 23. By then the Germans had taken 550,000 prisoners in the Balkan campaign. As of April 23 the British began evacuating some 43,000 of their troops to Crete, while on April 27, the Germans took possession of Athens. Finally, on May 20 the Germans commenced their assault upon Crete, which they occupied by means of the world's first glider-borne invasion. After ten days of fighting, the British forces were withdrawn under cover of the Mediterranean fleet.

By early June, 1941, the whole Balkan peninsula, except Bessarabia, lay under the *Führer*'s hand. Rumania, Slovakia, Hungary, and Bulgaria all adhered to the Tripartite Pact, and their forces were, in effect, integrated with the Wehrmacht. In the north, Finland stirred with new hope for recovery of the lands she had lost to the USSR in the "winter war." Now that Hitler's Scandinavian and Balkan flanks were secure, the men in the Kremlin did not have to ask for whom the bell tolled.

Case Barbarossa

Immediately after the fall of France, as Alan Clark avers, Hitler began to weigh the advisability of attacking Russia. On July 31, 1940, he confided to his generals that he contemplated an offensive against Russia. He seems to have reasoned that the British could still be knocked out of the war by depriving them of all possibility of securing the USSR as an ally.

Although in the fall of 1940 Hitler signed the Tripartite Pact and thereafter sought to win Slovakian, Hungarian, Rumanian, and Bulgarian adherence to it, he was prepared to postpone indefinitely the attack on Soviet Russia if he could persuade Stalin to stir up trouble in India or Persia. When Molotov visited Berlin on November 12, Ribbentrop urged the advantages of a penetration of the British sphere of influence in the Middle East and sought to elicit a Soviet endorsement of the Tripartite Pact. However, Molotov was indifferent to the argument that Germany had freed the Russian rear by making it possible for Japan's forces to be sent southward. Molotov retorted that he was less interested in the Arabian Sea than the Mediterranean. Foreign Minister Molotov not only stressed Russia's cardinal interest in the Straits, Turkey, and the Balkans but the displeasure of Stalin with the presence of German troops in Finland, Rumania, and Bulgaria. However, Molotov's demands were ignored.

Although after the Balkan campaign, Russo-German friendship was a corpse awaiting formal interment, Stalin continued to try to deflect German wrath by punctually making the deliveries that had been agreed upon in treaties with the Reich. At the same time he ordered the Red army to begin a buildup in the west. Recent historians (Tippelskirch, Greiner, Seraphim, Wright, and Higgins) reject the view that Stalin was deliberately preparing an offensive against Germany, insisting that Soviet military dispositions were purely defensive. This comports with logic, for the Red army was still weak and the Russians had been warned by the British of the impending German attack. The most effective defensive move made by Stalin, however, was the nonaggression pact of April 13, 1941, with

Japan. This released several Soviet armies from the maritime provinces in Asia and was decisive for the entire European war.

The operational plan of the OKH for attacking the USSR contemplated employing 180 divisions. The plan, which was ready by early December, aimed at capturing Moscow, the transportation and industrial hub of the country. Hitler and the OKW, however, decided to postpone the siege of Moscow until Leningrad had fallen and the Donetz metallurgical complex and Caucasian oil fields had been taken. This altered plan was dubbed Case Barbarossa. Formally endorsed on December 18, it was to be the source of acute friction between Hitler and most of his generals, except Keitel and Jodl, because the failure to drive hard and fast against Moscow cost Germany the war.

The most stupendous conflict the world had ever seen began very late in the year—on June 22, 1941, the anniversary of the date on which Napoleon had begun his ill-fated campaign of 1812. The Nazi offensive was handicapped from the start by the brevity of the Russian summer and the fact that many German generals had a presentiment of doom, stemming from the memory that Russia had been for centuries the "graveyard of empires." Beyond this, no German general was psychologically prepared for the fact that after the initial colossal battles of encirclement in White Russia and the Ukraine, the Red army would be able so quickly to replace its staggering losses in manpower with Asiatic levies.

The Russian Campaign: Phase I

Spearheaded by armored and motorized formations, the invading German armies comprised 153 divisions, of which 19 were armored. They were divided into a northern group under General Ritter von Leeb, a central under General Fedor von Bock, and a southern under von Rundstedt. Marching on the Wehrmacht's flanks were the Finns in the north and the Hungarians and Rumanians in the south. The front extended from the Arctic to the Black Sea. Ultimately 9 million men were to be locked in combat in this titanic war.

Stalin's later asseveration that his defensive strategy postulated the need to trade space for time is belied by the fact that almost the entire first-line troops of the Red army were encircled in the initial battles along the frontier. These triumphs, which entailed fearful Russian losses, led Hitler on July 4 publicly to boast that the Russians had lost the war. There followed other tremendous victories in August and early September—the Battle of Kiev and, what was perhaps the most stupendous victory of all time, the twin Battles of Vyazma-Briansk, when the Germans encircled the Russian troops east of the Pripet marshes and captured more than 660,000 prisoners. Yet, in the eyes of the German army's general staff, the Battles of Vyazma-Briansk were Hitler's greatest mistake of the campaign in the east—another "Battle of the Marne," tantamount to loss of the war for Germany.

Army Commander Brauchitsch and his Chief of Staff Halder had advised Hitler against engaging in this battle and had urged him to concentrate instead on taking Moscow. However, Hitler was afraid of repeating Napoleon's mistake. Furthermore, he was anxious to achieve mastery over the Baltic and Gulf of Finland. Therefore, he even took away some of Bock's armor to strengthen Leeb's siege of Leningrad. Confident that total victory was in sight, Hitler also cut off the re-supply of tanks for the Eastern Front.

Meanwhile, Leeb had no luck before Leningrad. Continuously resupplied from across Lake Ladoga, the city defied all efforts to starve it out. At the same time the southern armies under Rundstedt sustained a check in the Ukraine. After having stormed to the bend of the Dnieper, he sent an advance column into Rostov, only to be expelled on November 29 by Red army units. Furious with Rundstedt, Hitler abruptly relieved him of his command. This precipitated a crisis of confidence in the OKH. Brauchitsch and Leeb resigned. Bock was soon dismissed. Then, with unsurpassed vanity and folly, Hitler on December 19 assumed personal command of the army!

By October, German armored units had pushed to within fifteen miles of Moscow, which at the time, unknown to Bock, was practicaly undefended. However, he lacked the tanks to take the city and, in any case, one of the worst winters in living memory was bringing the Wehrmacht to a halt.

By the close of 1941 the Germans had taken 3 million prisoners and had killed 2 million Russian soldiers. Yet the Red army had not been crushed. Numbering 200 divisions in July, it mushroomed to 400 by January, 1942. Parallel with this revival, the Soviets built a largely new industrial empire in the Urals and western Siberia. Moreover, since August, 1942, the USSR, allied with Britain since July 12, 1941, had been receiving American lend-lease military aid through Murmansk and Persia.

Meanwhile, to the satisfaction of Stalin, the scales of attrition began to tip against the Third Reich as a result of the unneutral attitude of the USA. In March, 1941, President Roosevelt had persuaded Congress to pass the famous Lend-Lease act, by which an initial $1.3 billion credit for acquisition of war materiel was put at the disposal of England and France. American belligerent gestures had followed thick and fast thereafter—the occupation of bases in Greenland and Iceland, naval patrols as far as 1,000 miles from the American east coast, and the grant of fifty "over-age" destroyers to Britain. Then on August 14, 1941, Roosevelt and Churchill had promulgated the Atlantic Charter on the British cruiser Prince of Wales, which dedicated the USA and Britain to the destruction of Nazi Germany and foreshadowed the early entrance of the USA into the war. Finally, on December 7, 1941, the Japanese staged a surprise attack upon the American fleet at Pearl Harbor, making the war global. At the same time, British armies in north Africa recaptured Tobruk. Encouraged by these developments, the Red army counterattacked in December and retook Rostov on the Don.

Hitler's Second Offensive in the East

Ribbentrop's suggestion that the Reich open peace negotiations with Soviet Russia in the winter of 1941–42 and concentrate upon building up the "West

Wall'' was rejected by Hitler. This left the German forces to suffer the ravages of a Russian winter, for which they had not been prepared. Nevertheless, when the mud hardened in the spring, they began a second vast offensive, but this time from positions far to the west of their maximum penetration the year before. Now, Moscow was no longer in danger, its garrison having been heavily reinforced. The Wehrmacht, on the other hand, could mount a major offensive on but one of the three eastern sectors. For economic reasons, Hitler chose the southern.

In the spring of 1942 German morale was still at safe levels, because the invaders had inflicted extremely heavy casualties upon the Russians. The Red army had lost 4 million prisoners, whereas German casualties by the end of the winter had amounted to no more than 1.1 million killed, wounded, and captured, and the Wehrmacht had survived the worst season without catastrophe. It helped German esprit, too, that 35 divisions of Hungarians, Rumanians, and Italians had been sent to support the spring offensive. Finally, it was widely believed by German officials that Soviet Russia would not be able to replace the lost breadbaskets of White Russia and the Ukraine, or the latter's industrial plant.

In March, 1942, Hitler told his generals that the coming summer would see the utter annihilation of the Red army. To counter Russia's production of 600 tanks a month, he had ordered substantial increases in the delivery of tanks to the Eastern Front. The initial attack of 1942 was on the great naval base of Sevastopol in the Crimea. A collateral assault was launched on those Red army units that had been pocketed in the peninsula farther to the east, where Kerch fell on May 16. In the meantime the Russians had sought to expand the area they had reconquered in their winter counteroffensive. On May 12 they launched a bloody but unsuccessful assault northeast and south of Kharkov. Five days later the Germans countered with their own summer offensive. Before long, parts of 27 Soviet divisions and 14 armored brigades were entrapped west of the Donetz, 240,000 Russians taken prisoner, and more than 2,000 guns and 1,250 tanks captured. Nevertheless, at that price the Red army had managed to disrupt Hitler's timetable for reaching the Volga and seizing the oil of the Caucasus.

In late June and July five German armies, supported by Italian, Rumanian, and Hungarian auxiliaries, tried to annihilate the foe in a tremendous trap in the bend of the Don River. Despite heavy losses, however, Marshal Timoshenko did not allow his men to be pocketed between the Donetz and Don but withdrew the bulk of them to relatively safe positions north and south of Stalingrad (now Volgagrad). Storming swiftly eastward the German armies now separated into two spearheads. One, the Sixth Army, supported by only one tank corps, pushed toward the great rail and road hub of Voronezh on the north and the key Volga city of Stalingrad on the south. The second, the Seventeenth Army, supported by two tank armies, advanced southward toward the Caucasus. In pursuing this debatable strategy, the OKW aimed at achieving two things: first, gain control of the oil resources and facilities in the Baku-Maikop-Grosny-Batum area of the Caucasus, not only with the purpose of refueling Germany's motorized and tank divisions but of denying the Red army the oil without which it must disintegrate;

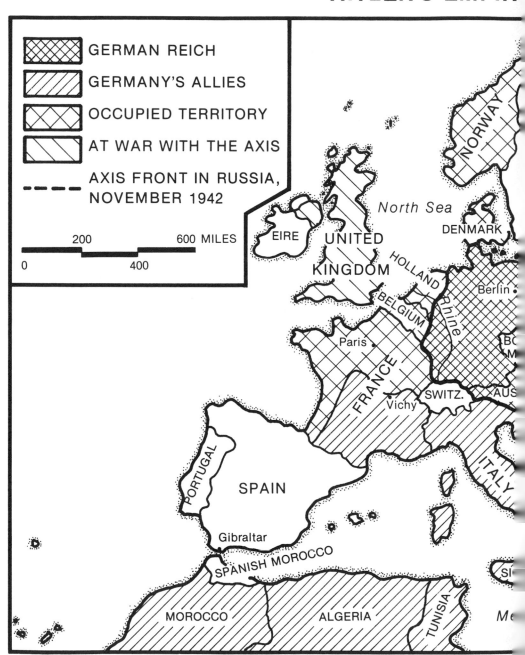

GERMAN REICH

GERMANY'S ALLIES

OCCUPIED TERRITORY

AT WAR WITH THE AXIS

AXIS FRONT IN RUSSIA,
NOVEMBER 1942

200   600 MILES

0   400

EIRE   UNITED

KINGDOM

NORWAY

North Sea

DENMARK

HOLLAND

Rhine

BELGIUM   Berlin

Paris   BO
M

FRANCE

Vichy   SWITZ.   AUS

PORTUGAL

SPAIN

ITALY

Gibraltar

SPANISH MOROCCO

MOROCCO   ALGERIA   TUNISIA

SI

Me

ITS ZENITH, 1942

and, second, take Stalingrad and Astrakhan and then, moving northward along the Volga, roll up the left flank of the Red army and come up behind Moscow.

The Russian armies reeled beneath the weight of the vast German attack, but the attackers failed to achieve any one of their goals. In the Caucasus the drive made impressive headway in July and August. However, it soon became necessary to reinforce General Paulus' Sixth Army with trucks, tanks, and fighter squadrons at the expense of the Seventeenth Army. The latter soon ground to a halt around Maikop, never reaching Baku and Batum.

The Battle of Stalingrad

Although the decisive battle of the Russo-German war had been that of Moscow in 1941, the Battle of Stalingrad was for Soviet Russia the turn of the tide. Never afterward could the Wehrmacht crush her.

General Paulus' Sixth Army was handicapped in its offensive against Stalingrad because the Germans, having failed to capture Voronezh, were unable to cut off the flow of supplies from Moscow to the city on the Volga. Furthermore, heavy attacks by the Red army to the north had necessitated the transfer by the Germans (with salutary results) of large quantities of war materiel from the Ukrainian to the Leningrad-Schlüsselberg, Vyazma, and Voronezh sectors. Unfortunately for Paulus, it was he who had to pay in badly needed military hardware for the defensive victories of the Wehrmacht elsewhere.

In the fight for Stalingrad the casualties on both sides were staggering. By the beginning of October the Germans and Rumanians had drawn a semicircle around the city. The month before, General Halder had strongly objected to the impermissible cost of the whole operation. His dismissal by Hitler led to an intensification of the efforts of the resistance movement to slay Hitler before he destroyed Germany.

Meanwhile, the Germans bombarded Stalingrad by plane and with long-range artillery. After it had been reduced to rubble, the Germans entered and commenced hand-to-hand fighting from house to house. Three times they cut through to the river but were hurled back. Supported by heavy artillery firing from the east bank, constantly resupplied, and reinforced by Asiatic levies ferried across the river, the Soviet garrison fought on doggedly till at last massive relief arrived.

Before commencement of the Russian counteroffensive at Stalingrad, the Germans suffered significant reverses in Africa. Field Marshal Rommel had been forced to retreat from Egyptian El Alamein to Tobruk and Bengasi and finally, on January 23, 1943, to yield Tripoli to Montgomery's Empire forces. Meanwhile, major Allied forces under General Eisenhower had occupied French Morocco and Algeria on November 7. Simultaneous destruction of French warships at Oran by the Allies had provoked an infuriated Hitler to retaliate by occupying all of Vichy France and Corsica.

Field Marshal Zhukov's counterattack began on November 19. Although concerted attacks from north and south swiftly closed a pincers on the German Sixth

Army, Paulus could probably have extricated his diminishing army from the trap if Hitler had not insisted that he fight on to the last man. The collapse of the supporting Italian Eighth Army on December 18 and of the Hungarian Second Army on January 15 (the day the siege of Leningrad was broken) left Paulus with no alternative but to surrender. The end came on January 31, 1943, when he surrendered what was left of his army—220,000 out of an original 1.5 million. The psychological blow to Hitler was indescribable. After Stalingrad he never smiled again.

Chapter 52

THE YEARS OF TORMENT, 1943–1945

Hitler's Empire

At its greatest scope the Nazi empire comprised 250 million people and three-fifths of Europe. This vast area was not, however, uniformly coordinated because of the exigencies of total war. Varying treatment was accorded subject states. Some countries, such as Luxemburg and Denmark, which had offered minimal resistance to the aggressors, were dealt with leniently. Their citizens, regarded as Aryans, were even encouraged to become German nationals. Other states, such as Bulgaria, Rumania, Hungary, Slovakia, and Croatia, were for a period accorded considerable independence. Holland, Norway, Denmark, and, of course, Italy, were allowed to retain their own civil governments and administration subject, except for Italy, to supervision by Nazi commissars. Unoccupied France was permitted to retain its own government under Chief of State Henri Pétain and Premier Pierre Laval. Although the Nazis had initially regarded the French with contempt, the former endeavored to cultivate better relations with the latter after the British raids of July, 1941, on French ports. However, senseless, forced deportations of French laborers and vicious SS reprisals for acts of sabotage thwarted these diplomatic efforts. Only a small minority of Frenchmen became genuine collaborators. In Belgium King Leopold kept his throne and stayed in Brussels for the duration. The Nazis considered him a valuable gage to command the obedience of the Belgians. In addition, the Nazis sought to win over the Flemish by favoring them in their age-old feud with the French Walloons. In both Belgium and the Dutch Netherlands many high officials were permitted to keep their posts. Although the Dutch found it hard to forgive the Nazis for the bombing in May, 1940, of Rotterdam, the former were treated by the latter as first cousins and given relatively considerate treatment.

For the Slavs the Nazis reserved their most bestial mien. Bohemia-Moravia and Poland, temporarily designated as protectorates of the Reich, were pricked down for early absorption by it and for resettlement by Germans. The ultimate fate of Poland was foreshadowed by the wartime surgery the Nazis performed on her. The Reich annexed Upper Silesia, the Wartheland, West Prussia, Danzig, Suwalki, and Białystok, pushing Germany's frontiers to the farthest point eastward in history. South of Austria, Germany annexed Slovenia. East of Poland lay the Baltic and Russian territories under German occupation and administered by Alfred Rosenberg (1893–1945) as minister for eastern occupied territories. East of White Russia and the bulk of the Ukraine lay the domain of the eastern army command (*Ob-Ost*), its operational base in the USSR. In most of the annexed areas many of the natives were dispossessed of their property or driven out and replaced by *Volksdeutsche*, i.e., Germans who in 1939 had resided beyond the borders of the Reich.

As the requirements of a war of attrition mounted, the need for more thoroughgoing control over foreign labor reserves became obvious. The protection of the German armies in France, Belgium, Poland, Yugoslavia, and Russia and the suppression there of sabotage and civil disobedience became increasingly difficult as the indigenous population came to realize that the tide was turning against the Wehrmacht. The desperate Nazis sought to cope with mounting unrest by greatly expanding the operations of their police machine. The Gestapo, SS, and Heydrich's SD (Sicherheitsdienst or Security Service) were all strengthened and ordered to proceed more ruthlessly. After 1943 all this vast, infernal network, including a huge elite army (the Waffen SS), functioned under the mailed fist of Himmler. Having replaced Frick as Reich minister of the interior, Himmler had become one of the troika, with Hitler and Speer, that ruled the Nazi empire in its time of agony and impending ruin.

The Solution of the
Jewish and Slavic Questions

Hitler's goal was not the launching of a European crusade against Soviet Communism, but the destruction of Poland and Russia. Communism had never been anything more than a straw man for him. He would have struck at any Russian state, of whatever ideological orientation. What he really was after was *Lebensraum* (living space) for a projected 100 million Germans. To this end, Hitler admitted that he was prepared to exterminate 30 million Slavs and all the Jews of eastern Europe.

While there were shootings of underground partisans *(Maquis)* and hangings of hostages in France and Belgium, it was in the east wing of the Nazi house of horrors, where the Slavs and most Jews dwelt, that man's inhumanity to man was most revolting. In the Protectorate of Bohemia-Moravia over a million Czechs were forcibly deported to Germany to work, while, by contrast, less than 100,000 were deported from Alsace. When "hangman Heydrich" was assassinated in Prague on May 26, 1942, Oswald Pohl, the chief of the SS central office of economics and administration, caused scores of Czech intellectuals to be executed, the village of Lidice razed to the ground, and 172 of its male inhabitants shot. Alfred Rosenberg had tried to capitalize upon the historic hatred of the Ukrainians for the Great Russians by organizing a nationalist Ukrainian army under Stephan Bandera and Andrew Melnik. However, Rosenberg was overridden by Hitler and Himmler. They were thinking of the expulsion of up to 85 percent of the inhabitants of Poland, White Russia, and the Ukraine. Having no other aim than the creation of *Lebensraum* for German settlers, the Nazis missed the opportunity to proclaim an independent Ukrainian state. Similarly, Hitler scorned to turn the proprietary ambitions of the White Russian and Ukrainian peasants to his advantage. Instead of dissolving the collectives and paving the way for the restoration of the lands to individual peasants, he did no more than concentrate them on huge state farms, where they were treated like serfs by Nazi overlords. Actuated by an inexpressible contempt for the Slavs, whom Goebbels labeled a "herd of animals," the Nazi authorities applied the same repressive measures in the Ukraine that they had in Poland. Hitler thereby turned the natives from neutrals into foes and partisans who harassed the occupation forces and pinned down substantial numbers of German military personnel and police.

Scores of thousands of Ukrainians and White Russians were forcibly deported to Germany to work in the factories or were put in concentration camps, where they died like flies from disease, starvation, or exposure. The Reich commissioner for the Ukraine, Erich Koch, instituted a savage reign of terror against the whole populace. The result was that the morale of the Slavic Army for the Liberation of Russia, which had been organized by General Vlassov after his capture by the Germans in 1942, was undermined. Koch's subordinates, working in collaboration with SD leaders, covered the Ukraine with cairns of corpses. Great numbers of saboteurs, partisans, and suspects were arbitrarily executed by SD Special Readiness Detachments *(Einsatztruppen)*. Among the most zealous butchers were Otto Ohlendorf, chief of *Einsatz* Detachment D, which killed 80,000 persons by means of firing squads and portable gas vans, and Erich Naumann, chief of *Einsatz* Detachment B, which executed more than 50,000. Fortunate were those who were merely deported to Germany to join Fritz Sauckel's foreign labor force.

The Nazis soon abandoned the ideas of Göring and Heydrich of resettling Jews in other parts of the world or in restricted areas of eastern Europe. Hitler personally decided that in any case the Slavic Jews were to be destroyed. Because Jews had usually been confined by tsarist law to the so-called pale (White Russia, Poland, and the western Ukraine), most of them still resided there in 1941, especially in Poland. There the Nazis established the ghastly extermination centers—Auschwitz (Oswiecim), Treblincz, Maidanek, and Palszov—where, under the direction of the notorious SS Death's Head Units *(Totenkopfverbände)*, victims were flogged, tortured in a variety of diabolical ways, or executed.

These camps, even more horrible than their counterparts in Germany (e.g., Dachau, Flossenburg, Belsen, and Buchenwald), were the end of the road for most eastern Jews. At the overall direction of Eichmann, the head of the Jewish division of the Gestapo, millions of them were taken from the ghettos and herded into these centers where they toiled and lived on starvation rations until their turn to be liquidated. For many the "final solution" of the "Jewish question" was to be shot or hanged. But for vastly more it was the steam vapor blockhouse or gas chamber, in which they were crowded together and exterminated in twelve to twenty minutes with steam, carbon monoxide or, later in the war, Zyklon B gas.

Estimates by recent specialists of the number of Jews who were executed center between 4.2 million and 4.6 million. The figure used by the postwar Nuremberg Tribunal was 5,721,800. In no case can the number of slain have been less than 4 million out of a total 1939 Jewish population of 9.2 million. Many more Jews died from privation or mass slaughter, as in April–May 1943, when those of the Warsaw ghetto rebelled and 50,000 of them were slain by machine gunning and bombardment. By 1945 the total European Jewish population had been halved.

The magnitude of the Nazi crime against the east European Jews was unique in history. Yet it is clear that the great majority of Germans were unaware of the killings in the concentration camps. Nor were the Nazis the only ones to indulge in bestialities. On a much smaller scale, the experienced Russians probably massacred thousands of Polish soldiers, whose corpses were found in a mass grave in April, 1943, at Katyn near Smolensk. Nor should it be forgotten that after the Nazi collapse in 1945 the Slavs rose up against the Germans who had been residing in the east, often for generations. The world was then treated to a new bloodcurdling spectacle—the mass deportations and executions of millions of civilians.

The Onset of Total Economic War

Because Hitler had banked on blitzkrieg, he had until 1943 neglected to mobilize fully the manpower and resources of his vast empire or adequately equip the Wehrmacht. Inasmuch as German armaments in 1939 surpassed those of any other country and considerable reserves of war materiel had been accumulated, German military production and the allocation of scarce raw materials from 1939 to 1941 was allowed to remain in relatively uncoordinated, and even chaotic, condition (B. A. Carroll).

When the concept of swift victories achieved by lavish consumption of tanks, artillery, and oil over strictly limited periods was finally discarded in 1942, instances of duplication in economic authority were ended, and a novel austerity was introduced into the lifestyle of top Nazi officials.

It was now found necessary to draw upon the experience of the *Kriegswirtschaft* of World War I, for the setbacks of the Wehrmacht in Russia brought home the realization that hostilities would be protracted. During 1942 mounting Allied bombings of rolling stock and industrial plants, increasing shortages due to blockade, and the drain on manpower and materiel resulting from the Russian campaign gradually forced Hitler to accommodate his undisciplined mentality to total planning.

In January, 1942, a start was made. The dormant ministry for armaments and munitions was summoned to activity, and the economic branch of the OKW was denied any authority over it. The armaments ministry was accorded plenary powers to augment production of every strategic item. Then on February 7, 1942, the architect Albert Speer (1905–) was appointed head of this ministry, and on March 21 Hitler decreed the subordination of the requirements of the German economy to the production of armaments, giving Speer virtually dictatorial powers over the economy. The inexperienced Speer was to become the Rathenau of World War II. He was to overcome the production and armaments crisis that at the end of 1941 was as critical as it had been in 1915. A multiplicity of agencies responsible till then for these matters—Robert Ley's Labor Front, Göring's Four-Year Plan, George Thomas' economics and armaments office of the OKW, Walter Funk's ministry of economics, the German Industry Association under Wilhelm Zangen—all fell under Speer's surveillance. He was nominally put under Göring but actually operated independently of anyone save Hitler. As respects manpower, Speer was aided by the sinister Fritz Sauckel (1894–1946), a *Gauleiter* from Thuringia, who was appointed minister for allocation of labor and was held accountable to Hitler alone. Between Speer and Sauckel were to develop fundamental differences as to how to recruit industrial labor: Speer favored the full utilization of German, especially female, labor power, while Sauckel, who prevailed because he had the support of Hitler and Himmler, favored the importation of foreign workers.

The War Economy at its Peak

Speer was able to eliminate most of the snags in armaments production. Six months after taking office, the production of guns had risen by 27 percent, tanks by 25 percent, and ammunition by 97 percent. By the close of 1942 total armaments production had climbed 56 percent. In 1942–44, despite massive Allied bombing, production rose spectacularly. By mid-1944, when decline set in, the production of tanks had increased by 500 percent, while overall armaments output had risen from an index of 98 for 1941 to 322 by July, 1944. In 1944 alone, 130 infantry and 40 armored divisions were completely re-equipped with weapons. However, Allied air raids so depleted Germany's petroleum stocks that many tanks and motor vehicles were stranded for lack of fuel.

Part of Speer's achievement was due to the exploitation of foreign labor, which by 1944 comprised about a fifth of the work force in wartime Germany. Already by the end of 1942 Sauckel had conscripted a total of 3.6 million foreign workers. By the fall of 1944 that number was 4.5 million. An additional 500,000 foreigners volunteered to work in Germany. On the home front, Sauckel in January, 1943, decreed total mobilization of all civilian men between 16 and 65 and (with less success) of women between 17 and 45 years of age. Without noticeably increasing the cost of production, the Speer-Sauckel economic dictatorship managed by mid-1944 to double the output of labor.

It was, of course, impossible through any display of managerial genius to make Germany economically self-sufficient. She remained dependent upon imports from all over Europe—petroleum, wolfram, manganese, nickel, oil, copper, iron ore, pyrites, rayon, and hemp. In many respects, however, Speer was able to meet Germany's needs through rationalizing domestic production, as in the case of rubber, coal, nitrates, potash, cement, and electric power. Foodstuffs were mainly furnished by France, Hungary, Poland, and the White and Ukrainian Soviet republics.

Disproportionately heavy emphasis was given to the production of armaments. The result was that consumer goods were grievously neglected during the war. By 1944 the index of production in the latter category had sunk to only 87 as compared with a 1939 base of 100. On the other hand, the vast sums spent on armaments production caused the national debt to rise almost tenfold from 1939 to 1945, from RM 40 billion to RM 400 billion. The financial insolvency of the government of the Third Reich was by early 1945 common knowledge.

Speer's planning enabled the Reich to elude the worst consequences of the blockade. His efforts were the cardinal factor in the maintenance of a wartime average food consumption that was only slightly less than that for the year 1938–39 and considerably better than in World War I. By 1943 Germans were receiving between 2,400 and 2,500 calories on the average per day, as compared with an immediate prewar level of 2,700–2,800. This was maintained till the final nine or ten months of the war, when as a result of the loss of France and the Slavic farmlands, the caloric average dropped to about 2,000 per day. Then the luxury restaurants closed, and hunger stalked every part of Germany.

Air Raids on the Reich

Germany's basic disadvantage in the years after the USA entered the war was that in no major category of production could she even remotely compete with the combined capability of the Grand Alliance against the Reich. The discrepancy was particularly acute in aircraft production. Already in the spring of 1942 the American output alone was 3,000 planes a month. In the final year of the war the German fighter plane output, though greatly increased since 1940, was only about 13,000 craft a year.

Commencing on May 30, 1942, with the first 1,000-plane RAF bomber attack upon a major German city (Cologne), urban centers and strategic targets were subjected to steadily intensifying aerial bombardment. Communications, transportation, ball-bearing plants, plane factories, dams, synthetic rubber or nitrate plants, refineries, and research stations were blasted. On May 17, 1943, the RAF hit the hydroelectric stations of the Ruhr and temporarily destroyed their largest dam, the Möhne.

As was the case with the Luftwaffe's offensive against London, Allied aerial blows were sporadic and shifted capriciously from one type of target to another. If attacks by the US Eighth and Fifteenth Air Forces had been continuous upon hydroelectric facilities and dams, aircraft plants, or upon ball-bearing factories, such irreparable damage could have been dealt the Reich that the war would have been shortened by many months. As it was, tanks, planes, and weapons continued to flow from German factories almost to the bitter end. Meanwhile, by October, 1943, the Germans began a patchwork dispersion of their industrial plants to the villages or to towns in the east and southeast, where they were less likely to be bombed. This materially reduced production losses due to air attacks.

So mighty were the combined attacks of the RAF Bomber Command and the US Tactical and Strategic Air Forces that by late 1944 the German cities were half-destroyed. Without much rhyme or reason, one city after another was reduced to rubble in vast bombing raids employing high explosive and incendiary bombs. Apart from dwellings, the loss of cultural values, churches, and works of art was beyond belief. After the 10-ton bomb was introduced in March, 1945, US Flying Fortresses wreaked more destruction upon German cities in an hour's time than the Luftwaffe had during three months of pounding London in 1941. Berlin and Worms sustained ten times the destruction that had been visited upon either Plymouth or London. While it is impossible for any truly religious person to justify indiscriminate bombing of defenseless civilians in saturation raids that were among the most culturally destructive and savage episodes of history, it is a fact that if the aerial attacks had concentrated solely on the big cities, systematically reducing them one by one, the Germans would have been forced to hoist the white flag sooner. As it was, the civilian population was able to adjust to the horrors of sporadic mass attacks.

One of the most gruesome and least justifiable air raids of the war was that against Dresden, the "northern Florence." In the triple strike by Lancasters and Flying Fortresses on February 14–15, 1945, on the Saxon capital, British bombers alone dropped 650,000 incendiary bombs. About 135,000 persons died in this senseless assault, among them thousands of refugees from eastern Europe. Although the Dresden casualty figures were far greater than those from the conventional bombing of Tokyo (83,000 deaths) on March 9–10, 1945, and the atomic bombardment of Hiroshima (71,379) on August 6, 1945, the terror attack failed to provoke popular rebellion in Germany. The people, confronted with the Allied policy of unconditional surrender (announced in February, 1943, by Roosevelt and Churchill), remained fundamentally loyal to the fatherland because they believed that the foe had left them no alternative.

The Great Retreat in Russia

Hitler's absolute unwillingness even to consider a timely retreat to the bluffs on the west banks of the Dnieper led to quarrels with his generals. Henceforth, the relationships of the *Führer* with the officer corps were envenomed. Hitler increasingly ignored the advice of Jodl, Kurt Zeitzler (Halder's successor as army chief of staff), and Walter Warlimont, who was the later deputy chief of operations staff of the OKW, and was accessible only to the pliant Keitel. After the debacle at Stalingrad almost all capital decisions were made by Hitler alone. The "great dictator" was disposed to retire moodily more and more to his Berlin underground bunker, remote from almost everyone except Keitel, Goebbels, Speer, Eva Braun, Martin Bormann (his personal secretary), and Hans Lammers (chief of the chancellery). There, in isolation, a taciturn and despondent Hitler unrealistically moved immense masses of troops on war maps. After February, 1943, the *Führer*, wholly preoccupied with military plans, left the governance of the Reich to Speer, Himmler, and Goebbels.

On July 5, 1943, the Wehrmacht launched the "no-quarter" attack, Operation Citadel, in the Orel area, but it collapsed within two weeks. The Russians then counterattacked and thereafter maintained with huge concentrations of artillery a constant, massive pressure on their foe, dealing him one staggering blow after another. From July through November the Soviet generals—Malinovsky, Vatutin, Koniev, Tolbukhin, Rokossovsky, and Zhukov—retook Orel, Kharkov, Taganrog, Bryansk, Smolensk, Kremenchug, Perekop, Dnepropetrovsk, Gomel, and Zhitomir. Yet the Russians neither entrapped nor broke the front of the Ger-

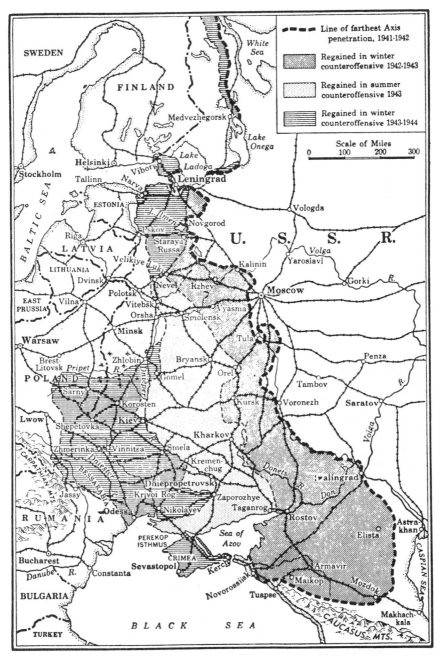

THE RUSSIAN COUNTEROFFENSIVES OF 1942–1944

F. Lee Benns and Mary Elisabeth Seldon, EUROPE: 1939 to the Present, Revised Edition, © 1971 by Meredith Corporation. Reprinted by permission of Prentice-Hall, Inc., Englewood Cliffs, New Jersey.

man army. Its retreat was conducted in good order and much more adroitly than that of Napoleon's Grand Army.

In the opening counterattacks the Russians badly shook eight German armies lying between Smolensk and the Crimea. By the end of August the most significant cities of the Donetz basin had fallen to the Russians, and by September 25 they pulled up along the Dnieper between Zaporozhie and Dniepropetrovsk. Behind the broad river the Germans tried frantically to rest and regroup their weary forces. Thus far the retreat, though extensive, had not been turned into a rout. The Russians had failed to effect any major breakthrough.

However, in late September, in defiance of Hitler's orders to stand their ground at whatsoever cost, the German armies were obliged to evacuate Smolensk and Roslavl, the scenes of their first stupendous victories over the Red army in 1941. By October, 1943, the Germans, without permitting their lines to be turned or irremediably broken, had retired on a broad front to a line formed by the Pronya and Dnieper rivers as far south as Zaporozhie and thence to Melitopol north of the Sea of Azov.

At this time the Russians passed from their summer to their winter offensive. Backed by seemingly endless reserves, they at last punched a gaping hole between the German Central and Southern Army Groups. The way to Poland was open. In the latter part of 1943, the Red army also cracked the German lines at Melitopol and reached the isthmus of Perekop. At the same time, in hard fighting they effected landings on the Kerch peninsula and reconquered the Crimea. By January, 1944, the whole southern Ukraine, the intended fabulous *Lebensraum* of the "Thousand Year Reich," had been evacuated by the exhausted and impoverished German armies. The Russians then stormed forward toward the Pruth and Sereth rivers into Rumania.

Twice before, Hitler had rejected advice, as when Rundstedt and Halder had advocated capturing Moscow. Now Hitler, by obstinately insisting upon a rigid defensive strategy, blighted all hope of retaining any part of Russia. Moreover, it was clear to all save the *Führer* that Case Barbarossa had turned out to be a complete disaster. Mussolini, Ribbentrop, and the Japanese government all pressed Hitler to sign a separate peace with the USSR, but he would not hear of it, knowing in his heart it was too late for such shifts.

The Italian Front

In the winter of 1942–43 the forces of Field Marshal Rommel, which had retreated to the Mareth line, were amalgamated with those of Field Marshal von Arnim in Tunisia. The destruction or surrender of the entire force, trapped between the British in Libya and the Americans in Algeria, was only a matter of time. Despite an initial German victory at the Kasserine Pass in February , 1943, in which the Americans lost 100 tanks, the Mareth line was shattered in March. On May 13, 1943, with no hope of reinforcement or resupply, Arnim surrendered at Cap Bon. By then the Afrika Korps had lost 250,000 killed or captured in the Tunisian retreat. With the collapse of Axis resistance in Africa, the Mediterranean was open from one end to the other to Allied shipping and operations.

The Allies next tried to slash at the "soft underbelly" of the Axis. The US Seventh and British Eighth armies landed in Sicily on July 22, 1943, and swept the German defenders back to the peninsula. There ensued a monarchical coup in the course of which the Fascist Grand Council deposed Mussolini on July 25 and theoretically transferred supreme power to King Victor Emmanuel III. In September a renovated Italian government, headed by Marshal Pietro Badoglio, unconditionally sued for an armistice, declared war on Germany, and claimed to be a cobelligerent of the Allies. Meanwhile, Mussolini was imprisoned but was subsequently freed in a daring German parchutist exploit. He was brought to northern Italy, where he proclaimed the Italian Social Republic but afterward was obliged to live as Hitler's vassal.

Between July 25 and the first Allied landings in Calabria on September 2, the Germans had managed to repair some of the damage to their cause and slam shut the southern gate to the Reich. They had reestablished military control over northern and central Italy and swiftly replaced Italian military units, now considered unreliable, in all occupied Mediterranean lands. All Axis forces in Italy had been put under command of Field Marshal Albert Kesselring, one of the ablest field commanders on either side during the war. Finally, a defense line had been set up south of Naples.

Although the Allies effected landings at Salerno below Naples, they made little headway in the drive on Rome. Making use of the strong natural defenses around the 1,500-year-old Benedictine monastery of Monte Cassino, which the Americans eventually demolished, the Germans pinned down the foe for nine months after the initial landings. After Monte Cassino was finally taken, Kesselring pulled his force back north of Rome, inasmuch as the OKW decided not to expose its religious and art treasures to destruction. Meanwhile, Anglo-American troops that had landed on the Anzio shore thirty miles south of Rome on January 22, 1944, broke the German lines around the beachhead in late May. At last, on June 4 the Americans, under General Mark Clark, entered the "eternal city." Despite possession of Rome, however, it was never subsequently possible for Allied troops to break or encircle Kesselring's army, which, fighting with skill and stubborn valor, took maximum advantage of mountainous terrain and the narrowness of the peninsula. Although during the remainder of the war the Anglo-American armies inched northward through the Appenines to reach the Po Valley, Kesselring was able to hold substantial parts of northern Italy until the very end.

The Second Front in the West

In response to Stalin's oft-repeated demands, a plan to open a real second front was adopted by the Allies, when Roosevelt, Churchill, and Stalin met at Persian Teheran on November 28–December 2, 1943. Although Churchill would have preferred an invasion of Austria through Trieste and the Lyubliana Gap, Operation Overlord was approved. This plan envisioned an invasion of northern France, supplemented by a second landing on her South coast. Stalin promised, for his part, to distract the Wehrmacht from Overlord by launching a huge new offensive toward Poland and Hungary.

Supreme command of the invading armies in the west was conferred upon the American General Eisenhower, and it was decided to land on the coast of Normandy rather than farther east where the coastal defenses were stronger. Vast amounts of materiel, planes, munitions, lorries, landing craft, and escort vessels were assembled preparatory to the invasion. Two artificial harbors were constructed out of sunken hulls to serve the disembarkation until the Allied armies could conquer the heavily fortified ports of Cherbourg and Le Havre, and a thousand precautions were taken by the invaders.

The Allies enjoyed crushing superiority, and once the landings had succeeded, the rest was a foregone conclusion. The invading forces, the bulk of which was American, comprised 86 divisions: 36 stationed in England, 40 in America, and 10 others in Italy. The Allied air fleet committed to the invasion comprised 3,112 bombers, 5,049 fighter planes, and 5,000 other escort and transport planes. The Allies enjoyed a superiority of planes in the ratio of 28 to 1 over the German defenders.

Confronting the attackers were badly demoralized, defeatist German troops, whose units were often under strength as a result of transfers to the Eastern Front. Harassed by French resistance forces, the Wehrmacht divisions in the west were commonly watered down with teen-age conscripts and men too old for combat duty.

German coastal defenses, the so-called "Atlantic Wall," were of varying strength, being weakest in the south, somewhat better in Normandy, and strongest at the Pas de Calais. The man upon whom the brunt of the invasion was to fall was Field Marshal Rommel, whom Hitler had entrusted with the manning of the "Atlantic Wall" from Brest to Holland. Rommel took orders from Rundstedt, who had been restored to favor and was then supreme commander of all armies in the west. Although Rommel had taken every precaution to interpose obstacles to the invaders, he was hampered by lack of troops and planes with which to smash the invasion on the beachheads. Yet he believed that the war would be lost if the invasion were not speedily crushed precisely there, and so he wanted to hold all his motorized and armored reserves just behind the coastal area. He believed that the landings would come on the Norman coast.

The thinly spread defenders comprised only 59 under-strength divisions, of which 17 were normal infantry units and 10 were armored. These divisions were organized into Rommel's Army Group B for the area north of the Loire River, and Army Group G, under General Blaskowitz, for the area from the Loire to the Pyrenees, as well as a 19th Army (21 divisions) defending the Mediterranean coast. The Luftwaffe, which was supposed to be the eyes and claws of the defense, was wholly inadequate to its tasks, comprising as it did only 319 planes. Motorized and armored reserves consisted of ten under-strength divisions, of which two were in the Paris area subject only to direct orders from Hitler.

On June 5, 1944, the day before the invasion, the German Supreme Command, according to General Warlimont, "had not the slightest idea that the decisive event of the war was upon them."* The warning that reconnaissance planes might have given never came. When the landings did take place on the sixth (D-Day), Jodl committed an irreparable blunder that destroyed any remote chance there may have been of throwing back the invaders. Believing that the main landings would come not in Normandy but to the east of it, he refused to commit the armored and mobile reserves of Army Group B until 250,000 enemy troops had landed and it was too late to throw them back into the sea, even if the defenders had had the strength to do so. Hitler also blundered: when Rommel finally realized that the Normandy landings represented the main Allied punch and begged the *Führer* for troop and armor reinforcements, Hitler would not agree to detach anything from the 15th Army farther east. Nor would he permit a prudent retreat from the 1,200 miles of coastline the German armies were forced to defend in the face of ruinous aerial attacks.

Despite unexpected resistance from one German infantry division in the Cotentin peninsula, the Allies swiftly won the battle of the Normandy beaches. Hitler dallied almost twelve hours, until it was too late to make a difference, before releasing to Rommel the two armored divisions in the Paris area. The Luftwaffe meanwhile was driven from the skies. Within three days, 250,000 Allied troops had been set ashore. If any possibility of a concentrated counterattack by heavily outnumbered German forces had existed, it evaporated as a result of the grievous attrition inflicted by General Montgomery in the protracted battle for Caen in eastern Normandy.

The Americans finally stormed out of the Cotentin peninsula at Avranches in late July and then fanned out swiftly over all northwestern France. By late August, Paris had fallen with only minor fighting, and all south France had also been freed by Allied forces coming up through the Rhone Valley. Rundstedt was now replaced by Marshal von Kluge, for the former's dream—to inflict a crushing defeat upon the invaders in a great armored battle deep in the heart of France—had never descended from the clouds.

The Attempt of July 20, 1944, on Hitler's Life

The German resistance movement, which had already made several abortive attempts on Hitler's life, was encouraged by Allied successes in France. During the years of Nazi diplomatic and military triumphs after Munich, the opposition's prospects had malingered. Yet the leaders of the movement, which centered on the civilian Carl Goerdeler and General Franz Halder, had not despaired, and it had never dissolved.

A serious retardative upon the growth of the opposition was not merely Hitler's

---

*Walter Warlimont, *Inside Hitler's Headquarters, 1939–45* (New York and Washington, 1964), p. 422.

spectacular successes but also the circumstance that Hitler kept very meticulous files on all of his major officials, noting all their vices and significant indiscretions. With this club over their heads, many persons who might otherwise have thrown their lot in with the opposition were obliged to hold their silence. Allied adoption of the Casablanca formula of unconditional surrender further discouraged resistance to the Nazi government, giving hesitant German officers a good reason for putting oath to *Führer* and duty to fatherland above eternal principles of morality.

Under the circumstances, the marvelous thing about the July 20, 1944, conspiracy was, as Gerhard Ritter has said, that "it penetrated to the topmost places in army and government and that it remained secret in spite of the fact that almost all the higher headquarters and staff officers eventually became to some degree aware of the planned coup d'état."* Most of those associated with the German resistance—among them leaders such as Halder, Trescow, Olbricht, Canaris, Oster, Beck, Witzleben, Stülpnagel, and Stauffenberg (for the military) and Goerdeler, Mierendorff, Ritter, Leuschner, Leber, Popitz, and von Hassell (for the civilians)—were inspired by a hatred for Nazi immorality and inhumanity. But they were also motivated by a desire to save Germany from complete disaster by a timely stroke against the government.

Carl Goerdeler was the liaison man between all the groups—military, civilian, religious, labor—linked with the conspiracy. While he was at all times "the white-hot center" of the resistance movement, valuable services were provided by Beck and Halder, as well as Admiral Canaris' office of counterintelligence *(Abwehr)* in the OKW.

The conspirators had already been compromised as a result of the removal of Canaris and Hans Oster from the *Abwehr*, when the plot of July 20, 1944, turned into a fiasco. Although the bomb planted by Colonel Claus Stauffenberg in Hitler's headquarters exploded and killed a number of staff officers, Hitler was again almost miraculously spared. The plot disastrously failed, and a wave of suicides and executions followed. Beck, Rommel, and General von Kluge (supreme commander in the west) all took their own lives. General Fromm immediately executed Olbricht and Stauffenberg. Goerdeler was arrested and ultimately executed on February 2, 1945. Perhaps as many as 5,000 more were summarily shot or sentenced to death by the People's Court, which was presided over by the infamous Roland Freisler (later providentially killed by a falling beam during an air raid). Ironically even the toadying General Fromm was later shot on charges of cowardice.

The resistance movement failed to shorten the war, as would have happened if Hitler had been slain. Yet the conspirators did not sacrifice themselves wholly in vain. On this point all major scholars of the movement, from Hans Rothfels to Peter Hoffmann and Hans Reichhardt, are agreed. The plotters advertised to all the world that Germany was not a monolith and that its love of humanity, morality, and religion had not been extirpated by the Nazis. To have demonstrated this at a

---

*G. Ritter, "Die Wehrmacht und der politische Widerstand gegen Hitler," in *Lebendige Vergangenheit* (Munich, 1958), p. 199.

time when Allied armies had not yet set foot on German soil entitles the resistance leaders to the reverence of posterity.

The Collapse of the Third Reich

In the late summer of 1944 the Allied armies tore great chunks of territory from Hitler's empire. By early September all France and most of Belgium had fallen to the British and Americans. The Germans had been obliged to retreat in the west to a line along the Dutch rivers and canals and to the Siegfried Line along their own border.

Yet it was no parade of roses for the British and Americans. An English attempt to vault the Dutch Waal and Rhine by parachute landings at Arnhem and Nijmegen disastrously failed. The Americans speared through to Aachen in late September but were held up for months by stubborn resistance in the Jülich area. On November 23 Strassburg and Metz fell. Then on December 16, 1944, Rundstedt, who had been reappointed supreme commander in the west, launched a surprise counterattack, the last one of the war. The so-called Battle of the Bulge (Bastogne) resulted from a German drive through the Ardennes toward Antwerp. The offensive, supported by 24 divisions, of which 10 were armored, was thrown back by the Allies after a week of heavy fighting in which the Germans lost 120,000 men and 600 tanks. Thereafter the Allies, with vastly superior numbers and fire power, pressed toward the Rhine, crossing it on March 7, 1945, at Remagen.

In the east, Finland, which had been isolated for months from German aid, was forced to hoist the white flag on September 19. In July the Red army enveloped the Baltic states and by October 5 cut off Riga. On the central Russian sector the Red army punched gaping holes in German lines in White Russia and forged deep into Poland. Lvov (Lemberg) was taken, and by late July the Russians had pulled up before Warsaw, where oddly enough they waited until the Germans had crushed General Bor's Polish uprising before storming the city on January 17, 1945. The German Vistula Army Group, which Hitler had put under the command of Himmler (!), now retreated back to the Oder before the armies of Generals Rokossovsky, Zhukov, and Koniev.

On the southern Russian sector the Germans were driven from the Ukraine and Bessarabia. The Red army entered Rumania. The Antonescu regime was overthrown. The king signed an armistice on September 13 and later declared war on Germany. A coup opened the gates of Sofia to the Red army, and Bulgaria signed an armistice with the Soviet Union on October 28. Under the circumstances the German armies were obliged to evacuate Greece and Yugoslavia. While millions of Germans who had resided in east-central and Balkan Europe were fleeing westward, Stalin's hand closed upon all that vast area by the fall of 1944.

With the occupation of the Ruhr and Upper Silesia by the Allies, the last powerful industrial sinews of the Reich were cut, and collapse followed swiftly. Having taken Saxony in mid-April, the Red army encircled Berlin and reduced what was left of it with rockets and artillery. On April 13 the armies of Generals Malinovksy and Tolbukin took Vienna.

During the April hand-to-hand and house-to-house fighting in Berlin, Hitler and Eva Braun, the whole Goebbels family, and Martin Bormann hid, like vermin, in the chancellery bunker. The psychologically broken Hitler had lived to rejoice at the news of Roosevelt's death (April 12) and even to observe a last, gloomy birthday on April 20. Till almost the end, Hitler, now ignored or mocked by most German authorities, hoped desperately for some such miracle as had saved Prussia in 1762. However, when a German relief force failed to break the Russian ring of fire, Hitler ordered the nation to turn Germany into a funeral pyre. He dismissed Himmler and Göring for having tried to negotiate peace and appointed Admiral Doenitz dictator. Then on April 30 Hitler—an unkempt and pitiful apparition—gave poison to Eva and shot himself. The Goebbels family also took their lives, but Bormann seems to have fled. Aides burned Hitler's body, whose charred remains allegedly were later discovered by the Russians.

The Third Reich came to an end on May 7–8, 1945. At Reims, Jodl and Keitel unconditionally surrendered. A similar surrender was made in Berlin to the Russians on May 8. At that time the Wehrmacht was still in occupation of Norway, Denmark, Bohemia, Lithuania, Croatia, northern Italy, and the Aegean islands. But Germany itself had been overrun and its armies shattered. No such legend as the *Dolchstoss* myth of 1918 could be fabricated after 1945.

In Europe the guns were now silent after more than six years. About 45 million perished in the second German war, and 75 million had been wounded or maimed. German casualties alone totaled 7 million dead, of whom 3,450,000 had died in battle and 500,000 perished in air raids. An estimated 3.5 million civilians had died in the course of the great exodus from the Slavic lands.

This time Germany could not look for clemency to a Wilson and his Fourteen Points. She could only pray that the anti-Communist West would deal with her less severely than the Russians would, because it was in the interest of the British, French, and Americans to interdict the heart of Europe to Soviet Russian military might and Communist influences. This fragile hope was to be the fundament upon which most of Germany was to build an uncertain future.

Chapter 53

THE HOUSE DIVIDED

Negative Plans for Postwar Germany

The broad lines of policy toward defeated Germany had been laid down in a series of inter-Allied conferences during the war. The decisions taken were, however, of such a negative character or were so shrouded in ambiguity that it occurred to only a few that no real agreement had been reached among the Soviet Union, Great Britain, and the United States respecting postwar Germany. All of the decisions were reached by only three powers. Neither France nor Italy participated. As at Paris in 1919, policy was formulated solely by the Big Three in an arbitrary, often capricious, fashion, which was further away than ever from the spirit of the Wilsonian dictum of "open covenants openly arrived at."

All the tenebrous efforts of the Allied chiefs of state to frame a common policy toward Germany were flagrantly unrealistic. They ignored several elementary facts: World War II had ended the primacy of Europe in the world; every continental state except the USSR had been reduced to a military zero; the German glacis that for centuries had protected Europe against the Russian colossus had been leveled; and the exigencies of a global balance of power between the camps of the two superstates—the USA and USSR—precluded the restoration of a consolidated Germany.

Germany's fate was ominously foreshadowed at the Teheran Conference of November, 1943. Then Roosevelt and Stalin leagued to block Churchill's proposal for an Anglo-American invasion of the northern Balkans, which might have interdicted much of that area and of east-central Europe to the Russians. Churchill also failed to win approval for his plan to deal harshly with North Germany but to federate South Germany, Austria, and perhaps some non-German Danubian territory into a large new entity capable of defending the heart of Europe against Soviet imperialism. Roosevelt and Stalin prevailed instead with the concept of the Balkanization of all Germany no less than of the Danubian lands. The three conferees also agreed to deindustrialize Germany.

At Quebec in September, 1944, Roosevelt presented to Churchill a plan that had been drafted by his secretary of the treasury, Henry Morgenthau. By it Germany was to be transformed into a "cabbage patch." Churchill mildly objected that this would create a power vacuum in the heart of Europe into which Soviet imperialism would rush. Roosevelt, whose confidence in Stalin's noble intentions was marvelous to contemplate, belittled the Englishman's fears and sugarcoated the pill by offering Britain an occupation zone that would include Hamburg, Bremerhaven, and the Ruhr.

At the ensuing Moscow Conference of October, 1944, among American Ambassador Averell Harriman, Churchill, and Stalin, the Morgenthau Plan was unanimously endorsed. At the same time the Soviet dictator parried Churchill's efforts to forestall complete Russian control over Poland. Stalin won his approval for what was an abominable partition of the Balkans into Russian and Anglo-American spheres of influence.

The western powers had now collaborated to put all of eastern Europe from the Greek border to Finland under the Russian umbrella and had substituted Stalin for Hitler as the nemesis of the free world.

At the Allied Conference at Yalta in the Crimea, from February 4–11, 1945, Roosevelt, Churchill, and Stalin agreed to transplant Poland far to the west at the expense of Germany. The admonition of a sorely troubled Churchill against ''stuffing the Polish goose'' with so much German territory that she would die of indigestion went unheeded. A truncated Germany was divided into three (eventually four) zones of occupation. As respects indemnities, Stalin prevailed with his demand that 56 percent of twenty billion dollars in reparations from Germany should go to the USSR, with 22 percent of the balance to go to the USA and the UK, the remaining 22 percent to be shared by all the other Allied Powers. Stalin won out too with his demand that 10 percent of the reparations extracted from existing plant and assets in the western zones should be reserved for the Soviet Union and an additional 15 percent of reparations taken from the English and American zones should be allocated to Russia against payment in kind in coal, wood, zinc, and food from the eastern zone. No decision was reached at Yalta regarding the return of millions of German prisoners of war detained in Soviet Russia.

At the Potsdam Conference of July–August, 1945, President Harry Truman, Prime Minister Clement Attlee; and Stalin committed another alarming transgression against the principle of self-determination. All German territory, including the port of Stettin, lying east of a line running along the Oder and Neisse rivers was transferred to temporary Polish administration, pending conclusion of a final peace treaty with an acceptable German government. East Prussia was horizontally divided, Poland receiving the southern half and Soviet Russia the northern. The lands thus stripped from Germany amounted to considerably more than were taken from her after World War I. In time, the temporary territorial transfer, sanctioned by long military occupation, became so permanent a feature of European political geography that in 1972 the West German parliament reluctantly recognized the finality of the Oder-Neisse border.

By the Potsdam Agreement of August 2, 1945, all that remained to German sovereignty—about 138,000 square miles of territory (an area somewhat smaller than Montana)—was to be divided into four occupation zones to be assigned severally to Soviet Russia, Great Britain, France, and the USA. Of the 66 million people within the German land area in 1945, approximately 17 million living in 42,000 square miles of territory were placed under Russian occupation. The Soviets received a zone comprising the eastern third of Germany; the British a zone embracing northwestern Germany and the lower Rhenish provinces; the French received Alsace in full sovereignty and the usufruct of the Saar coal mines, as well as a zone comprising the Saar, the southern Rhenish provinces, the Black Forest, and southern Württemberg; and the Americans acquired a zone* embracing Bavaria, most of Württemberg, northern Baden, and Hesse-Darmstadt.

In view of pronounced ideological differences that separated the USSR from the western Allies, it was naive to expect that the victors would really be able to implement the provision of the Potsdam Agreement decreeing that Germany should be "treated as a single economic unit" and that her people should be accorded "uniform treatment" in all zones. An even greater mockery was the Potsdam affirmation that there must be "an orderly and humane transfer" to Germany of the many millions of Germans residing in eastern Europe.

The Condition of Postwar Germany

It was small comfort to the German people that the French and probably also the English nation had, as a result of the war, joined the Reich in the limbo of great powers. While misery likes company, the Germans were simply too miserable to enjoy it. After having experienced the most complete military defeat in her history, Germany was a shambles. Many of her cities had been more than half-leveled by bombs, and the housing shortage, complicated by the arrival of some 7 million refugees and millions more of displaced persons from outside the 1937 borders of the Reich, was acute. The unwelcome newcomers competed with the indigenous population in every vocation and profession, creating large-scale unemployment. Many people lived in utter penury; theft, larceny, and prostitution were commonplace. The judicial and educational systems had virtually collapsed, and administration had been dealt a staggering blow as a result of the ban upon former Nazi officials, who were virtually the only element of the population with the necessary governmental experience. Hundreds of thousands of prisoners of war were, meanwhile, grouped together in labor service companies and assigned to various military commands, which employed them on construction and other projects that, with more profit to the faltering economy, might have been carried out by German civilians. At the same time the occupying powers set about their insane design to deindustrialize the country, carting away its movable wealth, dismantling its plants, levying reparations upon current production, and in general striving to set the German economy back to where it had been in 1932.

The Early Years of Military Occupation

In the spirit of Potsdam, it was decided that Germany was neither to be unitary nor centralized. A supreme supervisory agency, the Allied Quadripartite Control Council, was established, to which was subordinated a Coordinating Committee that supervised most affairs of major importance in the four zones. Berlin was the

---

*In 1948 Bremen Land was also transferred to their zone.

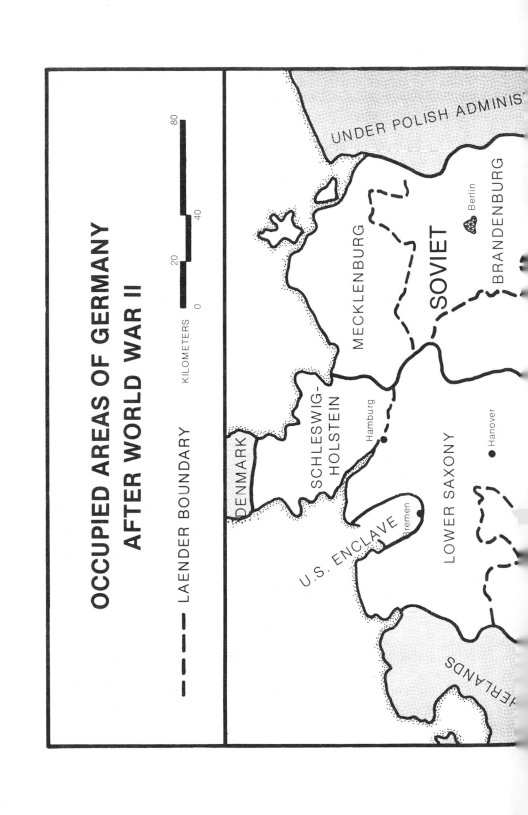

OCCUPIED AREAS OF GERMANY
AFTER WORLD WAR II

– – – LAENDER BOUNDARY

KILOMETERS

0   20   40   80

DENMARK

UNDER POLISH ADMINIST

SCHLESWIG-HOLSTEIN

MECKLENBURG

Hamburg

SOVIET

Berlin

BRANDENBURG

U.S. ENCLAVE

Bremen

LOWER SAXONY

Hanover

NETHERLANDS

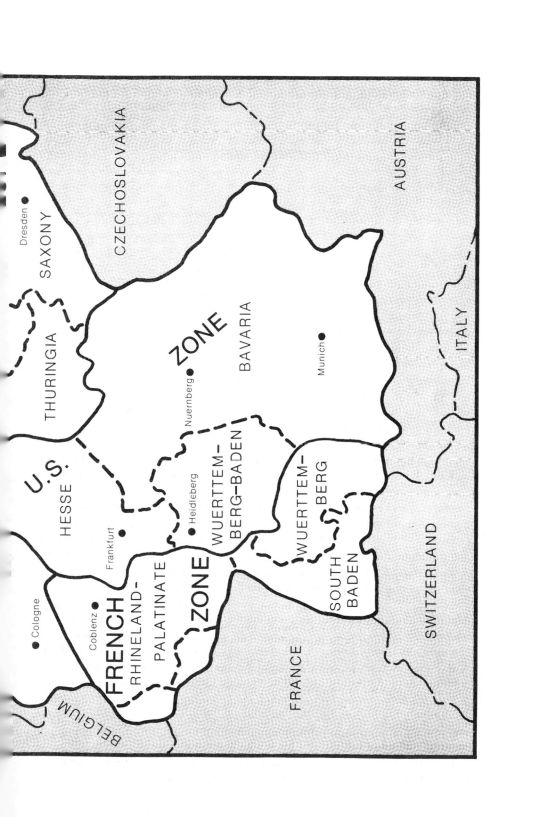

seat of a Quadripartite Kommandatura, which maintained order and implemented Allied policies in the four military sectors of the city. The Allied Control Council, which also sat in Berlin, endeavored to work out uniform procedures and policies for all Germany as respects labor, agriculture, finances, demilitarization, denazification, deindustrialization, and decentralization. Although the council issued more than 150 directives within less than three years, it proved impossible to achieve unity of approach among occupying powers that pursued conflicting aims.

Under the circumstances, there was from the outset of the occupation a tendency for each zone commander to govern his own area without much regard to the Control Council. This habit of independence of the military governors eventually completely lamed the Control Council. On March 20, 1948, it sank into complete desuetude when the Soviet Commandant walked out of a council meeting. This intemperate action prompted the governments of the USA, Britain, and France to establish without delay a single government for the three western zones. Indeed, it was high time, because there was no prospect of the conclusion of a peace treaty with Germany such as had been achieved on February 10, 1947, with Italy, Hungary, Rumania, Bulgaria, and Finland. Besides, the USSR was still extorting half a billion dollars in reparations annually from its zone, furiously milking the German cow at one end while the Western Allies, grown compassionate, were feeding it at the other with $700 million worth of aid each year. Finally, the Soviet's demand that Germany be reunited on a centralized basis was wholly unacceptable to France, if not to the USA and UK.

During the first phase of the occupation the highest German governmental unit was the *Land*. The first *Länder* were organized in the American zone in 1945 and included Hesse, Bavaria, and Württemberg-Baden. Each *Land* was permitted to have a minister-president and an assembly elected in keeping with democratic electoral practices. Subordinate to the *Länder* were the provincial *(Bezirke)* and county *(Kreise)* governments. The powers of state, provincial, and county governments were strictly limited and were superintended by zonal administrative and economic advisory councils, which were responsible to the military governor and ultimately to the ineffectual Control Council in Berlin. In 1946 comparable representative governments were set up in the British and French zones. The zonal commandants conserved their authority over the implementation of fundamental occupation policies and exercised a veto over any acts by *Land*, *Bezirk*, or *Kreis* governments that contravened the stated aims of the victor country in question. Nevertheless, representative institutions originating and corresponding with the will of the German people had by late 1946 been reestablished. Ultimately more power was deputed to the *Länder* governments in the American and French zones than in the British, but everywhere in these three zones the principle of popular sovereignty was enshrined in the constitutions adopted. Thus it was possible for Hesse to adopt a fundamental law that authorized the socialization of key industries. On the other hand, it is a question whether the arbitrary dissolution of Prussia in February, 1947, by act of the Allied Control Council would have been approved by the German electorate if its views had been solicited.

A beginning was made toward a new economic and political consolidation of limited nature when in January, 1947, the British and American zonal administrations were merged as "Bizonia." The new creation, which the French did not join until 1949, was accorded a single Bizonal Economic Council, whose powers were considerable from the outset but were expanded by a further directive of February, 1948.

Simultaneously with this first major step toward the restoration of a German state went attempts by the USA and Britain to revive the economy in their zones. As early as May, 1946, when relations with Soviet Russia had plummeted as a result of Churchill's Fulton, Missouri, speech, deliveries of reparations in kind from the western zones to the USSR were suspended. In early 1947 the American and British zonal commanders, wishing to put the German people back on their own economic feet, authorized an increase of steel production and other producers' goods in Bizonia.

The Russians were the first to abandon (1946) the concept of an agrarian Germany and to cease dismantling industrial plants and carting their equipment and machinery back to the USSR. By contrast, the western powers continued into 1947 with the absurd Morgenthau deindustrialization policies, which subverted Germany's will to produce and aggravated social distress. On the other hand, the USSR, while augmenting production in its zone, extorted reparations from current output long after the Allies had wholly repudiated the idea of reparations. Politically the USSR as early as mid-1946 turned its back upon decentralization in Germany on the premise that it would complicate the tasks of a "proletarian" assumption of power. The Kremlin, instead, devised plans for a unitary German state, whose fatherland front government would take its orders from Moscow. At the foreign ministers' conferences in London in September–October, 1945, and in Paris in April–July, 1946, Molotov rejected US Secretary of State Byrnes's offer of a four-power treaty respecting the decentralization and deindustrialization of Germany and demanded instead a unitary, consolidated Reich, but with reduced frontiers.

A first step toward Molotov's solution was taken by the Kremlin in the autumn of 1945. At that time twelve central departments, which were superior to the *Länder* governments, were established in the Soviet zone. Domiciled in Berlin, the department heads were to formulate and implement, without regard for *Länder* borders, uniform policies and procedures for a multitude of internal affairs. The twelve departments also served to transmit Soviet military control directives to all zonal municipalities.

Determined that an authoritarian socialism permeate every area of zonal life, the Soviet occupying authority promoted the fusion of the Social Democratic and Communist parties in the Russian zone to form the Socialist Unity party (Sozialistische Einheitspartei Deutschlands—SED). This party, under the leadership of Wilhelm Pieck (1876–1960) and Walter Ulbricht (1893–1973), was the pliant tool of Moscow and has ever since been the dominant political power in East Germany. Supported by the Red army, the SED achieved spectacular victories in successive "elections," which for monotony recalled the triumphs of the Nazis at the polls.

Denazification

During the occupation it was a relatively simple thing to dissolve all Nazi organizations, eliminate Nazi teachings from the schools, and prohibit all flags, insignia, or emblems that had been associated with the Third Reich. It was quite another matter to eliminate all former Nazis or collaborators from commanding positions in state and industry, because virtually all experienced industrial-executive, administrative, and judicial talent had served the Third Reich. Except for Nazis, there was an acute shortage of expertise in Germany.

Immediately following the end of the war it seemed natural that the canons of humanity and international law be vindicated by punishing those Nazi leaders who had most odiously transgressed them. Under the doubtful authority of Allied Control Council Law No. 10, which pretended to provide a uniform legal basis for the prosecution of German war criminals, hundreds of military denazification courts were established in the four zones. No attempt was made, of course, to bring war criminals of other nationalities to justice, but various categories of Nazis were defined and many Germans were arraigned for alleged war crimes, crimes against humanity, and complicity in aggression. Without universally recognized legal authority or any precedent in the body of the law of nations, the victors sat in both prosecution and judgment upon the civilian and military leaders of the vanquished country.

The greatest show trial was that which was staged in Nuremberg in 1945 and 1946, when twenty-two of the surviving capital figures of Hitler's "New Order" were prosecuted before the International Military Tribunal. Only three defendants—Papen, Schacht, and Hans Fritsche—were acquitted. Twelve were sentenced to death, ten of whom were hanged: Keitel, Jodl, Sauckel, Ribbentrop, Frick, Frank, Seyss-Inquart, Streicher, Kaltenbrunner, and Rosenberg. Göring managed to hide a capsule of poison and committed suicide in his cell. Martin Bormann, who had been sentenced to death in absentia, was never aprehended. Funk, Hess, and Raeder were given life, while Neurath, Doenitz, Speer, and Schirach received sentences of from 10 to 20 years in prison.

Between 1947 and 1949 twelve more war-criminal trials were staged at Nuremberg but under American, rather than international, auspices. During 1949 military courts at Nuremberg and Landsberg sentenced fifteen more leading Nazis to death, but by January, 1951, twelve of these sentences were commuted. Defendants had been charged with performing odious medical experiments on concentration camp inmates, practicing euthanasia killings and wholesale genocide, shooting hostages and civilians, and through the SS *Einsatz* units systematically destroying 2 million persons. On April 14, 1949, twenty-one lesser criminals, including Weizsäcker, Nazi press chief Otto Dietrich, and Reich chancellery chief Hans Lammers, as well as industrialist Alfred Krupp von Bohlen and Halbach, were given sentences of up to 20 years by the Nuremberg Tribunal. Meanwhile, under authority of the Allied Control Council, military tribunals had also been established in the other zones. By late 1950 some 3.5 million persons (7.5 percent of the population) had been brought to trial. Many petty offenders had been given stiff sentences, while major criminals had been able to confound justice or were mildly punished. Long after the military tribunals had closed shop, German courts arraigned wartime offenders until the mid-1960s, despite the fact that in May, 1949, the death penalty was abolished in western Germany.

Formation of the Federal Republic of Germany

During 1947 and 1948 the developing "cold war" between the Soviet Union and the western powers compelled a reappraisal of American, British, and French policies in Germany. It came to be understood in the western capitals that all the ancient outposts against expansion of Russian influence into the heart of Europe had been yielded without firing a shot. Yet the rugged Russian bear had not changed his ways. The Kremlin was in the act of developing a Communist offensive in Europe that was destined to be of greater world-historic consequence than that which Nazi Germany had launched. The hour was fast approaching when a grand coalition against the USSR would have to be formed. Among the milestones along the road to that goal were the Truman Doctrine (March 12, 1947) in support of the independence of Greece and Turkey; the Marshal Plan (June 5, 1947) for the stabilization of Europe's economy; founding of the western-oriented Organization of European Economic Cooperation (OEEC) to receive European Recovery Program funds; and the formation in 1948 of the Western Military Union. Concomitantly the Western Allies altered the mission of their armies in Germany from implementing the Potsdam Agreement and the articles of surrender to restoring and strengthening the defenses of old Europe against Soviet aggression.

Prior to 1948 all *Länder* government proposals to form a West German state had been rejected by the military governors. In that year, however, a Parliamentary Council was allowed to convene. Having adopted the olden republican black, red, and gold flag, the council elected a president and proceeded to draft a Basic Law *(Grundgesetz)*, which should serve the state until such time as a constitution for a reunited Germany could be promulgated. The Basic Law reflected the opposition of all major parties to the idea of a centralized political structure. It was thought that such a polity would violate German constitutional traditions and possibly also facilitate the task of a Communist conquest of power. Instead, there was established a federated republic of eleven states—Baden-Württemberg, Bavaria, the Saar, Bremen, Hamburg, Hesse, Lower Saxony, the Rhineland-Palatinate, North-Rhine-Westphalia, Schleswig-Holstein, and Berlin. However, the status of the Saar was open to question, and the four occupying powers objected to admitting Berlin because that would have contravened international treaties. The victors merely acceded to an arrangement by which the delegates from Berlin might sit in the federal parliament but without voting rights.

The Basic Law of the Federal Republic of Germany (Bundesrepublik Deutschland) went into effect on May 23, 1949. A subsequent statute of September 21, 1949, affirmed the superiority of Allied occupation directives. Meanwhile, the French, British, and American occupying authorities dissolved their respective military governments. In recognition of the altered relations between the Allies and the Bundesrepublik, supervisory powers of the zonal commanders-in-chief were transferred to three high commissioners—one for each region of national responsibility. The US, British, and French high commissioners also jointly exercised the overall responsibilities of their respective governments as regards the Federal Republic through an Allied High Commission for Germany (HICOG), subordinate to which were numerous committees and subcommittees whose task it was to coordinate Allied policies until the time should come to abolish occupational authority. The Allied High Commission finally expired when the Contractual Agreements were signed in 1952 with the West German government in Bonn.

The Berlin Air Lift

While the integration of West Germany into the OEEC helped the movement for federation, it was accelerated even more by the Russian blockade of Berlin and the reform of the currency of the western zones.

In late January, 1948, the Soviet zonal authorities began an attempt, which was to continue until May, 1949, to sever all road, rail, and canal traffic to and from Berlin. Russia aimed at expelling the western occupation forces from the city by showing that they were holding an untenable position surrounded by a Red sea. The Kremlin hoped to be able to facilitate the total absorption of Berlin by the eastern zone. However, efforts to freeze and starve out the population and military forces in western Berlin failed because the US Air Force mounted a massive airlift that greatly mitigated the effects of the blockade. An average of 5,500 tons of food, fuel, and supplies were flown into the western sectors daily by American transport planes. After a perilous US–Soviet confrontation in June, 1948, the Russians no longer interfered with the air lift. Eventually they abandoned the blockade altogether, and a Four-Power Agreement on Berlin was signed on May 5, 1949.

In the meantime the unified municipal government of Berlin had disintegrated, and a separate regime was established in the eastern sector under Soviet military protection. The first mayor of East Berlin was Friedrich Ebert, Jr., the Communist son of the Weimar Socialist president. The western sectors responded by organizing their own municipal governments under the overall lord mayoralty of the Socialist Ernst Reuter.

The Currency Reforms

By June, 1948, the old reichsmark had become so inflated that it constituted a serious obstacle in the way of German economic recovery. The Western Allies decided that it was time to create a new currency regardless of losses to millions of plain people. Although the Germans had little to do with initiating the currency reform, its success was insured by the cooperation of the able Christian Democratic economic director of Bizonia, Ludwig Erhard (1897–   ). In June the Deutsche mark (DM) appeared. Simultaneously all price and wage controls from the Nazi period were abolished and a free market was restored.

The currency reform did not at first ameliorate the lot of the common people. Although prices rose for the first eighteen months after the reform, unemployment increased, due in part to the continuing influx of refugees, and wages tended to remain stationary. Nevertheless, the introduction of the Deutsche mark accomplished a number of things essential to revival. Production doubled within six months, profits climbed steeply, and a new crop of millionaires sprang up. The DM drew forth large quantities of goods that had disappeared from store counters during the "bad" money era. An increased volume of trade was now insured between West Germany and foreign lands.

West Germany, into which Marshal Plan (ECA) aid began to pour in December, 1948, took on a veneer of prosperity. Offshore procurement orders, generated by the Korean War, were placed in West Germany, causing industrial production to rocket. By 1952 the world was speaking of a German "economic wonder." Neither the SPD nor the German Federation of Labor (Deutscher Gewerkschaftsbund—DGB) cared to dampen the capitalistic euphoria. It was realized that mass strikes would only obstruct recovery and the reduction of unemployment. Meanwhile, however, the jobless, whose number had grown from 760,000 in 1948 to 2 million in early 1950, were largely sustained by hope and the dole. Increased tax receipts enabled the Bonn government to support the unemployed and destitute with welfare programs of such scope as to reconcile them to the inequities of the German "miracle."

Immediately following the cue of the western zones, Soviet-occupied Germany initiated its own currency reform. It also adopted a Deutsche mark (DM, or ostmark). The regrettable refusal of eastern and western zones to cooperate in currency reform led to complete economic bifurcation, paralleling the political cleavage of Germany.

Establishment of the German Democratic Republic

When in 1947 Soviet authorities concluded that it would not be possible to put "Humpty Dumpty" together again in the near future, steps were taken to build an east German state, distinct from West Germany. Simulated elections to a People's Council *(Volksrat)* were staged, to which delegates from authorized parties and organizations were returned. Then on October 22, 1948, the *Volksrat* submitted the constitution it had drafted to the Soviet military commander, who approved it. Then in the spring of 1949 elections were held to the Third People's Congress. The SED influenced voters to support the regime. Pressure was applied through the Anti-Fascist Democratic Block and such Socialist-Communist organizations as the Free German Youth (FDJ), the Free Trade Union Federation (FDGB), the Democratic Women's League (DFD), and the Cultural League.

The Congress of May 30, 1949, adopted the constitution for an indivisible Deutsche Demokratische Republik (German Democratic Republic or GDR). The first government of the republic was organized on October 11. The old Communist Wilhelm Pieck was elected first (and only) president of the GDR; Otto Grotewohl (1894–1964), a cofounder of the Weimar Republic, became minister-president; and Walter Ulbricht, a Communist cofounder of the SED, was made one of three deputy minister-presidents, a position that disguised the enormous power he was soon to wield. The Soviet Military Government was simultaneously transformed into a Soviet Control Commission—still, however, under Marshal Zhukov.

The parliamentary elections of May 15, 1950, advertised how far the Soviet *Gleichschaltung* had proceeded in East Germany. With a crushing majority, which amounted to 99.7 percent of the electorate, the new government was endorsed. Not until 1955 did the Soviet high commissioner relinquish supreme responsibility for diplomacy, defense, support of Soviet occupation troops, and certain other matters. Although ostensibly the highly centralized East German state was ultra-democratic, its entire political superstructure was really manipulated in an authoritarian manner by the SED.

The legislative branch of the GDR consisted initially of two chambers: an upper or Länderkammer, which, theoretically representing the *Länder*, actually possessed negligible powers and could only retard but not reject bills; and a popularly elected Volkskammer (People's Chamber), comprising 400 voting deputies and 66 nonvoting ones to represent Berlin. The bicameral parliament was distinctly inferior in importance to the minister-president, who himself was overshadowed by the first secretary of the SED, Walter Ulbricht.

Centralizing pressures mounted until all pretense at compromise with the particularist legacy of German history was finally abandoned on July 23, 1952, when the *Länder* and their diets were abolished and their functions transferred to fourteen provincial *(Berzirk)* administrations answerable directly to the central government.* The Länderkammer, however, persisted until December 8, 1958, when it was also abolished.

The Government of the Bundesrepublik

The Basic Law *(Grundgesetz)* of the Bundesrepublik Deutschland (Federal Republic of Germany or FRG) contained a bill of rights but provided for no clear separation of the legislative from the executive branch. The *Grundgesetz* estab-

---

*The fourteen *Bezirke* were: Leipzig, Rostock, Magdeburg, Schwerin, Suhl, Gera, Cottbus, Halle, Potsdam, Frankfurt, Dresden, Neu-Brandenburg, Erfurt, and Chemnitz.

lished a weak president but a strong chancellor, who, collectively with his cabinet, was to be responsible to parliament. Reflecting the federal nature of the West German state was its bicameral legislature (Bundesversammlung). This comprised an upper chamber (Bundesrat) of 38 members, representing the *Länder* diets, and a lower house, the Bundestag, of 402 deputies, who were to be elected by universal and secret suffrage. The custodian of the *Grundgesetz* was the federal supreme court (Bundesgericht), which was to be domiciled at Karlsruhe, Baden. Amendments to the Basic Law had to have the assent of two-thirds of the membership of both chambers.

The federal parliament enjoyed both exclusive and concurrent legislative powers. The former, upon which the *Länder* were forbidden to encroach, extended to such matters as defense, foreign policy, currency, coinage, customs, nationally-owned rail and air transport lines, and immigration. The central government shared power concurrently with the *Länder* governments with respect to a broad range of social, economic, and fiscal affairs, certain areas of transportation and communication, and civil and criminal law. In case of conflict between a *Land* and the federal government, federal law, in accordance with article 31 of the *Grundgesetz*, was to prevail. Where a *Land* opposed an order of the central government, the latter was empowered by Article 37 to compel compliance. Finally, the president of the Bundesrepublik was given no such plenary emergency powers as had been conferred upon the president of the Weimar Republic by virtue of Article 48 of its constitution.

Elections to the lower house or Bundestag were to be conducted in accordance with an electoral system that was a compromise between the concepts of single-member constituency and proportional representation. In keeping with this method, the Bundestag elections of August 14, 1949, yielded marked disparities in apportionment but near parity between the petty bourgeois and working class SPD (131 seats) and the nonconfessional Christian Democratic Union (Christlich-Demokratisch Union—CDU) and its Bavarian affiliate, the Christian Social Union (Christlich-Soziale Union—CSU), which collectively obtained 139 mandates. However, if a simple single-member plurality electoral law had prevailed in the FRG, the SPD would have suffered a serious defeat in 1949. Among the other political parties— the German party (Deutsche Partei—DP), Federation of Expellees and Victims of Expropriation (Bund der Heimatvertriebenen und Entrechteten—BHE), Bavarian party (Bayerische Partei—BP), the KPD, and the liberal-bourgeois Free Democratic party (Freie Demokratische Partei—FDP)—the FDP had the largest following. It had won 52 mandates in the Bundestag as compared with only 15 for the KPD, which was destined to be outlawed in 1956. On September 12, 1949, the Bundesversammlung elected Professor Theodor Heuss (1884–1963) president of the Federal Republic. Three days later the Catholic Dr. Konrad Adenauer (1876– 1964), chairman of the CDU, was elected chancellor by a very slim Bundestag majority (202 to 200).

The two giant parties, the SPD and CDU/CSU, had collaborated to adopt an electoral law that would insure their political hegemony and, by eliminating all but a few parties, impart stability to the state. By federal law a party had to poll 5 percent of the national ballots to secure representation in the Bundestag, and 10 percent in a *Land* election in order to acquire mandates in a *Landtag*. This electoral device had the effect of pushing the Federal Republic toward a two-party system. The number of political parties tended to diminish from election to election. The BHE barely managed to clear the 5-percent hurdle in the national elections of 1953 and fatally tripped in those of 1957. By 1961 the hurdles had eliminated all but three contestants—the SPD, CDU/CSU, and FDP.

In retrospect it must be said that 1949 was a major turning point in German history. It was the year of the definitive ideological bifurcation of the country. The adoption of the East German constitution and the West German Basic Law not only violated the Potsdam concept, which was to treat Germany as a decentralized unit, but postponed to a distant future any prospect of a peace treaty with the whole German nation. On the other hand, the cold war had compelled Washington and Moscow to adopt policies that aimed at the speedy legal reestablishment of the sovereignty of East and West Germany and a recognition of their coequality with the other states in their respective camps. It was only a matter of a few years before the Federal Republic and the GDR would both be rearmed and integrated respectively with NATO and the Warsaw Military Alliance system. Then for the first time in modern history the battle line between opposing alliances would run through the heart of Germany.

Toward Sovereignty for the FRG

For many years reunification was of cardinal importance to the Bundesrepublik. However, that goal proved to be impossible of consummation. Chancellor Adenauer would neither accommodate the GDR by compromising his principles nor by promising that in the event of general war a reunited Germany would be neutral. The Federal Republic's secondary aims—full sovereignty over all West German territories—was much easier to attain.

The Occupation Statute of September, 1949, assigned ultimate supervision over a broad range of affairs, including reparations, demilitarization, denazification, police, the coal and iron industries, and foreign relations, to the USA, France, and the UK. This authority was to be exercised conjointly by the zonal commanders and the new Allied High Commission for Germany (HICOG). This latter agency exercised responsibility for implementing and enforcing the directives of the Allied Control Council. HICOG operated through both the Bonn and *Länder* governments, any of whose enactments it was empowered to review. The three zonal high commissioners—John J. McCloy (USA), Brian Robertson (UK), and André François-Poncet (France)—sat in the Petersburger Hof across the Rhine from Bad Godesberg.

Meanwhile, the growing acerbity of the cold war hastened the day of German equality. A grand anti-Soviet alliance came into being by stages. On March 17, 1948, Britain, France, and the Benelux countries (Belgium, the Netherlands, and Luxemburg) formed the defensive Pact of Brussels. After the Communist takeover in Czechoslovakia and the commencement of the Berlin blockade, the USA on April 4, 1949, concluded an alliance with eleven other nations (the Brussels Pact states, Italy, Portugal, Denmark, Norway, Iceland, and Canada), which came to be known as the North Atlantic Treaty Organization (NATO). Then following the formation of the Council of Europe (May 5, 1949), the USA organized a Mutual Defense Assistance Program (MDAP), whose object was to rearm Europe mainly at American expense. At the same time Supreme Headquarters, Allied Powers in Europe (SHAPE) was organized outside Paris under the supreme command of General Eisenhower (SACEUR).

The long Berlin crisis finally provoked the US high commissioner on October 8, 1950, to warn the Soviet Union that the Western Allies would consider any attack upon West Berlin or the territory of the Federal Republic as an attack upon themselves that would be answered with appropriate military measures. As the Soviet Union was perceptibly switching the focus of her expansionist drive to Korea and the Far East, the Allies now pressed an ideological offensive against the eastern European block. On December 22, 1950, the western powers formally demanded free elections under international control as the proper solution of the German problem. The Soviet Union countered by insisting on reunification first. At the Washington Conference of Foreign Ministers September 10–14, 1951, the western diplomats, influenced by the Korean War, declared that a democratic Germany must be integrated into the European community and be accorded full equality. Adenauer's government, strongly supported by an electorate that had during the Nazi period been indoctrinated with anti-Communist sentiments, wholeheartedly acclaimed this revision of Allied thinking. To merge the Federal Republic with western Europe, Adenauer was even willing, in contravention of the Basic Law, to rearm and make significant contributions of troops and aircraft to the European Army that French Foreign Minister Pleven had proposed in October, 1950. In 1951 the Bundesrepublik joined France, Italy, and the Benelux countries in the European Coal and Steel Community (ECSC), which pooled the coal and iron reserves and related industrial plant of the six member states.

Mainly to promote the military security of old Europe, Britain and the USA pressed for early restoration of full sovereignty to the FRG. On March 6, 1951, a federal foreign ministry was created and accorded responsibility for all West German consulates. On the seventh the Kommandatura for the western sectors of Berlin promulgated a revised Occupation Statute for the city, reducing the supervisory powers of the military authorities. On May 26, 1952, the Treaty of Germany (Deutschland Vertrag) was signed. It abrogated the Occupation Statute for the FRG, dissolved HICOG, authorized exchanges of ambassadors with West Germany, and, except for the status of Allied forces stationed there and international implications of the division of the country, recognized the sovereignty of the government in Bonn. The capstone to these endeavors was set when on May 27 the Europen Defense Community Treaty (EDC) was signed in Paris, stipulating a German contribution of twelve ground divisions and 1,350 aircraft and crews to a European army.

Although the SPD was willing to see the Basic Law eventually amended to permit rearmament of the Federal Republic, the SPD would have preferred to try once more for a modus vivendi with the USSR, which had on March 10, 1952, submitted to the western powers the draft of a treaty with Germany that offered a new solution of the German problem. Fearing that a rearmed West Germany allied with NATO could undermine the whole structure of Russian hegemony in Europe, Stalin as one of his last major initiatives offered to agree to the reunification of Germany and the creation of a German military establishment exempt from international surveillance. However, his assent to this was to be on one condition: that a united Germany enter into no military alliances and observe permanent neutrality. The prospect of an independent, militarily strong, united Germany was rejected by the Bundestag for the reason that it had no confidence in the probity of the Soviet government and believed that an isolated Germany could not defend itself against the Red army. While the Adenauer regime was choosing German disunity, western integration, and NATO, the US Secretary of State Dean Acheson on August 2 and 28 repeated the admonition of October 8, 1950, that any attack upon the territory of the Federal Republic of Germany would be considered an attack upon all the Allies.

During 1952 the German Democratic Republic, feeling that reunification was a dead issue, began to dig a broad moat between itself and the FRG. A long-range attempt was launched to block almost all intercourse and traffic between East and West Germany. GDR authorities again harassed traffic between the western sectors of Berlin and the FRG and made a major effort to halt the exodus of GDR citizens to the west by establishing a five kilometer no-man's land running from the Baltic to the Czech border. Despite the vigilance of sentries, refugees continued to slip across the strip to the west. By the close of 1954 a total of 2 million persons had escaped to the FRG.

Believing that German rearmament would make impossible the reunification of the country, SPD leaders tried in 1953 to block ratification of the Contractual Agreements of May 26–27, 1952. Although the SPD brought suit before the Bundesgericht to have the agreements declared a violation of the constitutional prohibition against armaments, the issue was not to be decided by the courts but by the Bundesversammlung. Adenauer felt that he could circumvent a judicial decision if he could persuade two-thirds of the members of each house to approve a constitutional amendment authorizing rearmament. This he was able to do as a result of the September elections, which increased the CDU/CSU's percentage of the popular vote from 31 percent to 45.2 percent while that of the SPD remained static. Thereafter, it was relatively easy for Adenauer to muster the necessary two-thirds majority. The amendment was approved by a vote of 346 deputies against the Socialists' 151. This cleared the way for endorsement by the government of the FRG of all military treaties submitted to it by the Allies. In March, 1954, the Bundesversammlung approved the EDC Treaty.

Allied plans for integrating West Germany in a European defense system received a temporary setback, however, on August 30, 1954, when, to the general amazement, the French National Assembly rejected the EDC Convention. This development encouraged the Malenkov-Molotov government, which had come to power in Moscow after Stalin's death, to make new proposals for the solution of the German question, but, in view of the outcome of the recent West German elections, these were ignored by Bonn.

The Allies now moved swiftly to incorporate the Federal Republic, one way or another, into their military system. They accepted the FRG into Western Union (an outgrowth of the Brussels Alliance) by means of the Paris Treaties of October 19–23, 1954. At that time Bonn agreed to certain limitations upon West Germany's sovereignty, including renunciation of all atomic, biological, and chemical weapons, and assented to permanent supervision of its military establishment by the Brussels Powers. The Paris Treaties also assured the Federal Republic of Germany the support of all her European allies in the event of attack. The Allies recognized the Bonn government as the sole legitimate spokesman of the German nation in international affairs. With respect to the Saarland the Paris Treaties stipulated, subject to approval of the diet of the region, that it be politically independent but economically tied to France. However, this was opposed by the Saarlanders, who rejected the Paris Treaties in October, 1955, and eventually won unrestricted admission to the FRG in 1957. Taken all in all, the Paris Treaties were an expression of European confidence in Adenauer's government. Yet reunification was further away than ever.

Pursuant to the denigration of Stalin in Russia, a thaw began in Soviet relations with the western states. On January 25, 1955, Moscow declared that the state of war with Germany was at an end. Acknowledging the existence of two Germanies, the Soviet government announced it was ready to extend formal diplomatic recognition to the FRG. The following May the USSR signed a state treaty with Austria. In return for independence and the withdrawal of Soviet troops she pledged permanent neutrality. The refusal to Austria of the privilege of contracting alliances or of the stationing of foreign forces on her soil underlined the fact that the Kremlin still hoped that the German problem could be solved along similar lines. In the summer of 1955 Chancellor Adenauer exploited the thaw in the Kremlin's policy to pay a state visit to Moscow and reestablish diplomatic relations with the USSR. Nevertheless, at the summit conference in Geneva on July 18–23, 1955, the western chiefs of state insisted that the solution of the German question must be prefaced by free, all-German elections, which would serve not only the interest of the German nation but European security as well.

By the autumn, Russia's unrequited courtship of the West was engendering a new freeze in Moscow. The admission of the Federal Republic into NATO in

September evoked the expected counterblast from the Kremlin. The Soviet high commissar's office was abolished, and the German Democratic Republic was accorded control over its internal and external affairs. This was but the prolegomenon to the integration on January 28, 1956, of the armed forces of the GDR into the Warsaw Alliance, which had been established on May 14, 1955. Thenceforth the political division of Germany was cast in iron.

Chapter 54

THE FEDERAL REPUBLIC OF GERMANY

The Adenauer Boom

The economic revival of the Federal Republic of Germany was the main factor in restoring a European balance of power in the 1950s. West Germany's industrial recovery, engineered within the framework of European cooperation, promoted restoration of her prestige and military power. A strong Bundesrepublik facilitated the defense of western Europe against Soviet ground attack. No less than the American deterrent, the strengthening of the FRG and its integration with the Atlantic Alliance persuaded the USSR to exchange a policy of westward expansion for one that aimed at preserving the status quo. In this way the German economic wonder *(Wirtschaftswunder)* made a major contribution to the peace.

A system of free enterprise tempered by Christian concern was among the most powerful stimuli to West Germany's economic recovery. Once the currency reform of 1948 and the influx of modest ERP (Marshall Plan) aid had helped prime the pump, it was of cardinal importance to the economic revival that a milieu of free competition be restored in the FRG. No other form of industrial organization—corporative, nationalized, or state-controlled—could facilitate the economic recovery of West Germany so quickly.

Two men—the Christian Democratic Union (CDU) economic expert, Ludwig Erhard, and the federal minister of finance, Fritz Schäffer—were mainly responsible for building what came to be called the "social market economy" *(Soziale Marktwirtschaft)*. Their idea was to reestablish in West Germany a system of free, capitalist enterprise, to break up the big cartels and syndicates, and thereby increase opportunities for smaller firms. Erhard tried to indoctrinate management and capital with a sense of social responsibility toward the workers. He also encouraged the cooperation of management and labor in making operating decisions through the device, instituted in 1946, of the *Mitbestimmungsrecht*, or right of codirection.

Many other factors helped stabilize the economy. Abundant harvests augmented rural purchasing power and stimulated demand for manufactured goods. Rapid growth in foreign currency reserves and a relatively high percentage of annual capital reinvestment in plant expansion helped restore world confidence in the German banking and industrial communities. The punctuality with which Bonn paid off its foreign indebtedness, including the bulk of that incurred by the Third Reich, founded the international credit of the Federal Republic. It also so fortified the mark that by 1972 it had become the strongest monetary unit in Europe. The influx of millions of immigrants and expellees into West Germany augmented the labor supply and held wages to relatively low levels, thereby giving to German exporters a big advantage in international trade. The absence during the first seven years of the FRG of a conscription law and a federal army also contributed to maintain a big reservoir of cheap labor. Furthermore, German industry

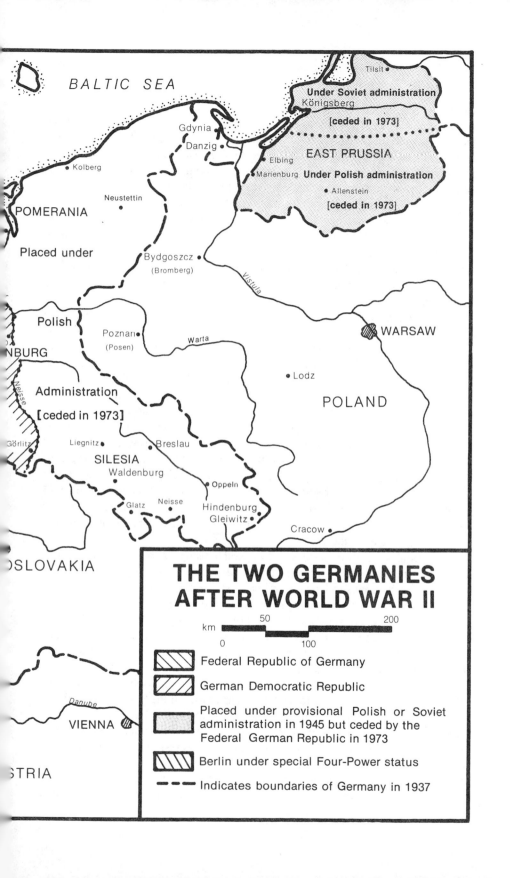

BALTIC SEA

POMERANIA

Placed under

Polish

NBURG

Administration

[ceded in 1973]

Görlitz Liegnitz• •Breslau

SILESIA
Waldenburg

Glatz Neisse

Kolberg

Neustettin

Bydgoszcz•
(Bromberg)

Poznan•
(Posen)

Warta

•Oppeln

Hindenburg
Gleiwitz•

Gdynia•
•Danzig

Elbing•
•Marienburg

Tilsit•

Under Soviet administration
Königsberg

[ceded in 1973]

EAST PRUSSIA

Under Polish administration

•Allenstein

[ceded in 1973]

Vistula

WARSAW

•Lodz

POLAND

•Cracow

OSLOVAKIA

Danube

VIENNA

STRIA

THE TWO GERMANIES
AFTER WORLD WAR II

km ▮▮▮▮ 50 ▮▮▮▮ 200

0   100

▨ Federal Republic of Germany

▨ German Democratic Republic

▨ Placed under provisional Polish or Soviet
administration in 1945 but ceded by the
Federal German Republic in 1973

▨ Berlin under special Four-Power status

– – – Indicates boundaries of Germany in 1937

recommenced production after 1945 with almost wholly new plant and machinery, which enabled manufacturers to operate at low costs. The huge demand of the German people for housing and all manner of consumer goods, amenities, and labor-saving devices, likewise fuelled production. Demand was also generated by offshore procurement contracts between occupying forces and German firms and by occupation-army personnel and their luxury-loving wives.

As a result of these and other factors the rate of industrial growth of the FRG during the Adenauer era exceeded that of any other Western state, being around 10 percent per annum, which was double that of the USA and close to that of the Soviet Union. As early as 1952 production was already almost 150 percent above that of 1936, and by 1963 it had increased by 283 percent over 1950. Per capita output had also registered substantial gains, and unemployment had virtually been wiped out.

The percentage of the total population that made its livelihood from agriculture or forestry declined from 17.9 percent in 1939 to 5.6 percent in 1960. This was due to such things as the subtraction of the east German agricultural lands from the GDR, mechanization of agriculture, high costs of farm machinery, and the inefficiently small size (less than•thirteen acres) of the average farm.

The industrial upsurge eventually yielded a gross product that the hungry demands of the domestic market could not absorb. West German exports mounted swiftly until by 1960 the FGR had become the second exporting country of the world, accounting for 10 percent of the total exports. Furthermore, an excess of exports over imports, which characterized much of the period 1949–75, gave West Germany a preponderantly favorable balance of trade. This imparted greater strength to the mark so that by March, 1961, it had to be revalued upward by 4.75 percent. In 1971, when the dollar was in unprecedented difficulties, the Brandt government of the FRG allowed the mark to float upward to attain an even higher exchange level against the dollar.

After initial demands for food, clothing, and housing had been satisfied, investmend concentrated, often with spectacular results, upon mainly or wholly new industries, such as plastics, nylon and polyester textiles, automobiles, gasoline and oil distribution, television, tape recorders and cassettes, middle-sized computers, antibiotic pharmaceutics, etc. Although after World War II steel was of declining importance, the Federal Republic was by 1962 the third largest steel producer in the world. In shipbuilding West Germany had come to surpass every country save the United Kingdom and Japan. In volume of exports of machinery, mechanical devices, tools, heavy electrical equipment, and optical products, the FRG was by 1977 second only to the USA. The glories of the Hanse and HAPAG, too, were revived in the Lufthansa, West Germany's global airline.

Although by 1977 the Federal Republic, which had attracted capital investments, had become one of the foremost industrial powers, her new-found prosperity had not been achieved without heavy cost. Her cities, which had swallowed up some of the best arable land, had lost much of their former beauty. Automotive traffic and concrete expressways encroached upon the palaces, guild halls, and charming half-timbered houses from a statelier past. High-rise office and apartment buildings dwarfed the churches that had once imparted an ineffable symmetry to the urban landscape. Cities became more dangerous, noisier, and dirtier and were enveloped in a pall of smoke and smog.

The condition of the workers, though much improved by the late 1970s, still left much to be desired as respects wages, housing, inflation, and equalization of tax burdens. It is true that a social insurance system, which was an improvement over that of the First Republic, had been established and that the federal government had in 1952 passed a "Law for the Equalization of Burdens," which proposed to transfer over a period of thirty years special tax proceeds to refugees and persons who had incurred serious material loss during the war. The *Länder* governments had also enacted analogous legislation. Nevertheless, the gap between the rich and poor grew with alarming speed, dismaying friends of true democracy. The garish affluence of the super-rich seemed the more insupportable in that they were often former high-ranking Nazis, their offspring, or their industrial co-adjutors. All too frequently the chief beneficiaries of the German miracle were persons who had earlier run the nation into the mire.

The Revival of the Ruhr

If the Allies had really been serious about reducing Germany to a "cabbage patch" they ought to have deprived it of the Ruhr. This area normally produced 93 percent of the coal, 77 percent of the iron, and 75 percent of the steel of the area of the Federal Republic. By 1960 the coal output of the Ruhr accounted for half the total product of the European Coal and Steel Community (ECSC).

After the war the cartels and syndicates into which the industries of the Ruhr had been grouped were dissolved. Yet the reality of power was largely rescued by the establishment of a new pattern of interlocking directorates and managerial alliances. To these were added, in the late 1960s, diversified conglomerates in which the key figures were members or agents of the families that for three generations had controlled the wealth of the Ruhr.

The public was often deceived as to the real substance of power in the Ruhr because some of the juggernauts of the Nazi era—such as the vast Vereinigte Stahlwerke (United Steel Works), Otto Wolff A. G., the Flick combine, the Reichswerke, A. G., and the mastodontic Krupp Reinhausen Steel Works—were, like the I. G. Farben dye trust of Frankfurt, never restored to their former owners. Yet the managers were seldom engulfed in the ruin. Most of them soon contrived to recoup both wealth and prestige and found new enterprises or rebuild the old ones under new names. The Gutehoffnugshütte mining company, Ilsederhütte, Klöcknerwerke, Mannesheim, Mannesmannröhrenwerke, Krupp Essen, Gelsenkirchener Bergwerksverein, and Thyssensche Gas und Wasserwerke soon spread themselves out in the Ruhr again as in a conquered land. Wilhelm Roellen of the Thyssen Company continued to be a directing factor in this utilities firm. Wilhelm Zangen, former head of the Third Reich's Association of Industrialists, and Walter

Rohland, former chairman of the board of United Steel, figured prominently in the operations of Mannesmannröhrenwerke and other metallurgical firms in the postwar era. Alfred Krupp von Bohlen und Halbach, after having spent five years in prison to expiate his aged father's crimes against humanity, built up, with the aid of the brilliant Berthold Beitz, a wholly new diversified European industrial empire. When in 1968 he voluntarily dissolved his conglomerate, his fortune, amounting to more than DM 4 billion, made him the richest capitalist in Europe.

While the olden ruling families of the Ruhr regained their dominant positions in postwar German industry, they never quite recovered their monopolistic stranglehold on the nation's economy. In general, because of substitution of oil and electricity for coal, the construction of pipelines, the growth of automotive transportation, and the building of high-speed throughways, industry in the FRG was less regionally concentrated than it had been under the First Republic or the Third Reich.

Nevertheless, the Ruhr figured above all other German mineral regions in the production of iron, coal, and steel. If by 1959 the ECSC had attained an output of more than 260 million metric tons of coal, 63 mmt of steel, and 247 million kilowatt hours (as compared with the Soviet Union's 330 mmt, 60 mmt, and 264 mkwh respectively), this was due in large part to the Ruhr, which by 1955 had been freed from all shackling production quotas.

The Autocrat and Europeanism

Konrad Adenauer, who had become chancellor of the FRG at the ripe age of 73, had only two main ideas, but, from the standpoint of the western powers, both of them were right. They were to integrate the FRG with free Europe and make the former industrially and militarily a strong partner of the western powers. On the other hand, his policy toward the USSR was unelastic and basically negative. The adamant attitude of this subtle practitioner of *Realpolitik* was largely responsible for the continuing division of the continent. Adenauer pursued positive external aims with increasing vigor but somewhat less success in his third term in office (1957–61) than in either of his first two (1949–53, 1953–57).

Because Adenauer assigned primacy to foreign policy aims, he was disposed to neglect social legislation. His most important venture in that area was his pension law of 1957. On the other hand, despite a relatively unimpressive rate of increase of workers' real wages, he did not scruple to spend large sums of money to aid underdeveloped countries. Between 1950 and 1961 the FRG contributed no less than 20 billion marks to foreign aid.

Adenauer's quiet, unemotional, determined nature and his earlier relative anonymity served the requirements of the Federal Republic for commonplace but shrewd leadership. *Der Alte* (The Old Man) was an unmalleable Catholic from Cologne who, though often high-handed, was guided by Christian moral precepts. During his fourteen years as chancellor (1949–63) he manipulated the Bundestag as one would a well-trained dachshund. As his political strength waxed from election to election, he evolved what came to be called ''chancellor democracy,'' a mode of governance that was stultifying for administrative or legislative talent. When in the October 1957 elections the CDU/CSU achieved a majority of 43 in the Bundestag, the semiauthoritarian character of Adenauer's personal regime became clearer than ever. Surrounded by mediocre ministers, opposed by a Socialist chairman (Erich Ollenhauer) of modest abilities, and served by a parliament that danced to the tune the CDU fiddled, its chairman, Chancellor Adenauer, was until his eighty-eighth year the uncrowned king of the Federal Republic.

Adenauer, like Bismarck, attached prime importance to foreign policy and during at least two of his three ministries campaigned vigorously for a united Little Europe. He linked the FRG to a broad range of western organizations and United Nations agencies and put the capstone to his western orientation when Bonn signed the Rome Accords on March 25, 1957. By these treaties the FRG helped found the European Economic Community (EEC) or "Common Market" and the Atomic Energy Community (EURATOM). Within the Common Market, which embraced the six nations of the ECSC, internal customs barriers were gradually to be dismantled. The Atomic Energy Community was intended to serve as a clearing house for exchange of nuclear information and as an agency to coordinate nuclear research in the EEC area.

Until 1955 Adenauer alone or with the advice of Dr. Walter Hallstein (1901–   ), the later chairman of the executive commission of the EEC, framed West German foreign policy. Adenauer's first actual foreign minister was Dr. Heinrich von Brentano (1904–1964). He served in that capacity from 1955 to 1961. Taking his cue from Hallstein, Brentano declared the Federal Republic of Germany would not enter into diplomatic relations with any state (except the USSR) that formally recognized the GDR. By the close of the 1960s the Hallstein Doctrine was much eroded, and between 1971 and 1974 the other main foreign policy position of the Adenauer government—that the Bonn government alone was legitimate and it was therefore impermissible to negotiate with GDR as a legal equal—was also relegated to the scrap heap of history.

Brentano's foreign policy greatly aided the restoration of the Saar to West Germany. The Franco-German Saar Agreement of October 27, 1956, abrogated the Saar Statute of 1954 and paved the way for establishment of the Federal Republic's unimpaired political sovereignty over the area (January 1, 1957) and then, on condition that French industry be accorded special access rights, of full proprietorship over the mines and factories of the Saar (July 5, 1959). Rapport between Bonn and Paris became even more cordial when General Charles de Gaulle became president of France in 1958. Only later did clouds appear upon the horizon, when divergencies in the European policies of de Gaulle and US President John F. Kennedy confronted Adenauer with having to make a choice.

The Triumph of Revisionism in the SPD

By the close of the 1950s Adenauer's Europeanism had come to enlist the qualified support even of the SPD. At its Bad Godesberg convention (November 13–15, 1959), that party at long last experienced its "Damascus." In its two preceding programs (Erfurt, 1891, and Görlitz, 1925) the SPD had endorsed and clung to the doctrines of Marxism. Now, however, a new group of reformers, reminiscent of the Vollmarists and revisionists of the years before World War I, rose to banish once and for all the contradiction between the practice and theory of the SPD. Professor Carlo Schmid (1896–   ), Fritz Erler (1901–   ), who was the party's military expert, Herbert Wehner (1906–   ), the former Communist who had become the Social Democratic party's foreign policy authority, and the English-speaking urbane lord mayor of West Berlin, Willy Brandt (1913–   ), contended (as had Vollmar and Bernstein in Wilhelmine imperial times) that the El Dorado of the masses was to be sought within existing society. Under their pressure, a majority of the delegates at Bad Godesberg adopted the Third Program of the SPD. This recognized that the party was a synchretic national party and no longer just a workers' organization and that it was duty-bound to defend the democratic order. The Third Program put the SPD on record as endorsing the Social Market Economy and free enterprise as long as genuine competition existed but as favoring public ownership where monopoly or insolvency made this necessary. For the first time the SPD abandoned its opposition to rearmament and NATO. This change of tune strengthened the government's western orientation. On the other hand, the program rejected the idea of stationing chemical, biological, or nuclear weapons, or even nuclear shells without warheads, on German soil. The Bad Godesberg confession of faith in the West was not, as the SPD had warned, intended to preclude a search for new avenues toward reunification through détente and collective security pacts. Evidently the idea of the first postwar Social Democratic party chairman, Kurt Schumacher (1895–1952), that the proper way to cement East and West Germany together was through cooperation with the USSR, had never died.

Schumacher's concept was given a new lease on life as a result of the relaxation that was setting in between the governments of the USA and USSR. People were forgetting the lamentable impression that Premier Khrushchev had made in November, 1958. At that time he had demanded that Berlin be made a free, demilitarized city and that a general peace treaty with the Germanies be immediately concluded on pain of transfer to the GDR of all Soviet responsibilities respecting access to and protection of Allied rights in Berlin.

In 1959 the unobtrusive Erich Ollenhauer (1901–1963), who had been chairman of the SPD since 1952, visited Moscow and brought back with him a proposal that had originated with Adam Rapacki, the Polish foreign minister. The Rapacki Plan proposed a phased reunification of Germany. At the same time it suggested that a nuclear-free "disengagement" zone be formed to comprise Germany, Poland, Czechoslovakia, Hungary, and neutral Austria, and that from this area all foreign forces be withdrawn. The buffer states would be privileged to maintain their own strictly limited military establishments but would be expected to withdraw from NATO and the Warsaw Alliance. Although there was strong liberal support for this "Deutschland Pact," and the FDP even evolved a similar concept, the whole idea was adamantly opposed by the US Secretary of State, John Foster Dulles, and, consequently, by Adenauer.

Chronically suspicious of Soviet Communism, the chancellor regarded the Bundesrepublik as rather in the light of a shining rampart defending European culture against eastern barbarism. Adenauer not only refused to recognize the German Democratic Republic but also steadfastly rejected the finality of the Oder-Neisse frontier with Poland and would not even enter into any treaty of indemnification with Poland such as the FRG had signed with Israel. If he had sanctioned the resumption of relations with the USSR, it had only been because she was one of the four occupying powers with which the FRG would have to negotiate. Considerably less interested in the unification of Germany than in its integration with the western alliance system, the Old Man turned a cold shoulder to all schemes of disengagement. Neither he nor his second foreign minister, Gerhard Schröder (1911–), was prepared to move toward détente with eastern Europe, because they feared this might imperil the chancellor's grand design of the "Europeanization" of the Bundesrepublik.

The Moribund Adenauer Regime

In 1960 it seemed to many that it was high time for the Old Man to retire. The SPD and FDP had found increasing reason to criticize his autocratic, intolerant, and undemocratic behavior. It was charged that he had exploited his coalition partners, the DP and BHE, simply to obtain the requisite two-thirds majority with which the Basic Law was amended to permit rearmament, and, having achieved that, had cast them aside like discarded mistresses. A glimmer of hope had shone when, upon the retirement of the beloved President Theodor Heuss, in 1959 Adenauer had announced his own candidacy for the presidency. However, when he learned that Ludwig Erhard would succeed him as chancellor, Adenauer retrieved his hat from the ring. Many party colleagues who had impatiently waited for Adenauer to relinquish power were now alienated from him. Dr. Erich Mende (1916–), who had succeeded Dr. Reinhold Maier as chairman of the FDP in 1960, now flayed the chancellor for having built a one-party monopoly over the government. The Catholic autocrat was vulnerable on other counts too. His relations with the Kennedy-Rusk administration were much cooler than had been those with Eisenhower and Dulles. The strong position of the FRG within NATO, whose central European land forces were commanded by German general Hans Speidel (1897–), elicited grave misgivings in both the SPD and a divided FDP, where it was suspected that the Old Man's military policy was a formidable obstacle to reunification of the country. The fact that the FRG's intelligence service (Bundesnachrichtendienst or BND) was headed by Reinhard Gehlen (1902–), Hitler's chief of intelligence on the Eastern Front, also made Adenauer's government vulnerable to East German criticism. Finally, the building of the Berlin Wall by the GDR in 1961, splitting the city in two, symbolized in graphic manner the failure of the *Deutschland* policy of the "chancellor of the Allies."

In the federal elections of 1961 the CDU/CSU lost its absolute majority in the Bundestag. Renewed confrontation between the two superpowers, arising out of a reconnaissance flight of an American U-2 over Soviet territory, brought welcome sympathy for the Old Man. At the same time, he was supported by the Federal Association of German Industrialists and by all who gave priority to the unification of Europe above that of their country.

Despite these advantages, the CDU/CSU combination in 1961 polled only 45.3 percent of the votes compared with 50.2 percent in 1957, and it lost 28 seats in the Bundestag. The SPD reaped the reward of its metamorphosis at Bad Godesberg, for it attached to itself important segments of the middle class without alienating the German Federation of Labor. The SPD garnered 20 percent more votes than in 1957 and won 36.2 percent of the popular vote in 1961, securing an additional 21 mandates in the lower house, The FDP, on the strength of its assault upon the Adenauer ministry, was able to increase its percentage of the ballots from 7.7 percent in 1957 to 12.7 percent in 1961. For the rest, the elections confirmed the trend toward a three-party system. The DP and BHE, having failed to obtain the required 5 percent of the total vote, were eliminated from the Bundestag. Prosperity also destroyed the prospects of the neo-Nazi Socialist Reich party (SRP).

The grave Berlin crisis in 1961 and the ensuing deterioration in Russo-American relations would have justified forming a national bipartisan government in the FRG. However, the CDU/CSU shut the door on the SPD and formed a ministry only with Mende's FDP, which in the meantime had cynically forgotten its election promises.

The Last Year of the "Reign"

Coinciding with the onslaught of a business recession came an unsavory confrontation with the press, which compromised the ministry. When on October 8, 1962, Rudolf Augstein's tabloid *Der Spiegel* blamed Franz Josef Strauss (1915–), the militant minister of defense, for the state of "inadequacy" of Germany's military preparations, Augstein's offices in Bonn and Hamburg were raided and he himself was clapped into prison. This action endangered the freedom of the press. Public opinion was incensed at the arbitrary methods of the administration. The SPD seized upon the whole affair to discredit Strauss, who was both the architect of the Bundeswehr and the chairman of the Bavarian CSU. He was rebuked for having argued that the West Germany army should be equipped with nuclear-tipped missiles subject to control by American forces. The upshot of the *Spiegel* affair was that Adenauer was obliged on November 5, 1962, to drop Strauss and the state secretary for defense, Hopf.

At the height of the scandal the FDP ministers all resigned so as to facilitate formation of a new government without Strauss. On December 11, 1962, the perpetual chancellor's last government, again a CDU/CSU–FDP combination, was formed on condition that he resign by early 1964. Adenauer began his last ministry with a parliamentary majority of only eight. In his own party 49 deputies opposed him.

The last year of Adenauer's chancellorship passed under the cloud of a mild business recession. Furthermore, the population of the Bundesrepublik was now weary of the incessant alarms and excursions of grand politics and yearned for a new foreign policy that could really pacify Europe. It seemed to a growing percentage of the West German electorate that it was naïve to expect either the USSR or Poland to assent to the creation of a united Germany that would be allied with NATO. Many West Germans believed it was high time for some new approach to the whole *Deutschland* problem, which Adenauer was conceptually incapable of initiating.

In the last year of his chancellorship Adenauer uncertainly vacillated between the USA and France. Although he was reluctant to encourage de Gaulle to develop his nuclear *force de dissuasion* for fear that it might provoke an American military withdrawal from Europe, he nonetheless permitted the French president, for whom he felt an aristocratic affinity, to drive a wedge between Bonn and Washington. Adenauer was not exactly hostile to de Gaulle's views that for the present Great Britain should be excluded from the Common Market and that the military and political integration of Little Europe was premature. The entente Adenauer entered with de Gaulle on January 22, 1963, compromised the chancellor's earlier policy in that it seemed he was now sabotaging European union and destroying the only justification for his long opposition to Soviet proposals to reunite Germany.

A détente in Soviet-American relations in the late summer of 1963, following the tense Cuban nuclear missiles confrontation (October 22–28, 1962), encouraged the West German foreign minister, Gerhard Schröder, to devise a policy that was in important essentials at variance with Adenauer's. In the fall of 1963 the US Senate approved the nuclear test-ban treaty with the Soviet Union, and in October President Kennedy authorized the sale of a large volume of surplus wheat to the USSR. Schröder now joined the USA and Britain in opposing de Gaulle's Common Market policies, which seemed to be based solely on resentment over the British naval victory at Trafalgar. Schröder also sought to counteract the debilitating consequences for NATO of de Gaulle's Third Force notion of an independent continental bloc, as opposed to a Little United Europe, which would hold the balance between the USA and the USSR. Although Schröder, a wandering star between two constellations, failed to bring the FRG wholly within the Anglo-American field of gravitation again, he nonetheless pulled much support away from his chief.

Adenauer was finally forced to resign on October 15, 1963. The obese, cigar-smoking Ludwig Erhard, a North German Protestant and a right-wing Christian Democrat, was elected the second chancellor of the Bundesrepublik. He was endorsed by a vote of 279 out of 499 in the Bundestag. Adenauer, meanwhile, was reelected chairman of the CDU in March, 1964, and in the elections of September, 1965, was returned as a deputy from Bonn to the Bundestag, although he was then nearly 90.

At the time the Old Man stepped down from the chancellorship the FRG was in a fundamentally strong financial position. The mild recession of 1962–65 had not seriously weakened the economy. West Germany had, moreover, been rebuilt on firm liberal foundations, neo-Nazism was at low ebb, and revolutionary Marxism had become virtually extinct in the Federal Republic. Except for classroom and school construction, housing was no longer a serious problem. Conscription had been reintroduced, and the federal defense forces (Bundeswehr) had grown to embrace a ground force of 325,000 men, a reserve of 250,000, a Luftwaffe of 250,000 crewmen and pilots, and a navy of 400 vessels. Not least of all, by 1963 German science and technology had regained the respect of the world.

Yet the picture was not without its chiaroscuro. The darker areas included: increasing crime, delinquency, and insecurity of life and property in the cities; preponderantly low money wages (in 1963, 78 percent of all workers were still earning less than DM 800, or $210 per month); an infant mortality rate that was double that of the Dutch and the Swedes; a traffic accident death rate that was triple that of the USA; continuing decentralization of an undemocratically structured and uncoordinated educational system; continuing shortages of teachers, class-rooms, learning resources, and funds for education in all *Länder;* and the absence of an enthusiastic commitment of the electorate to the principles of democracy, which in the public mind were widely connected with an empty civic ritualism.

Erhard's Chancellorship

Embarrassed by a recession, Erhard's administration was not one of new de-partures. In fact, his easy-going, conversational, simplistic approach to policy-making did not elicit the respect and strong loyalties that a bold program requires.

Erhard liberalized and democratized the chancellorship. He also revived close relations with Britain. But he discovered no new paths to reconciliation between eastern and western Europe. Although in his time the FRG increased its trade somewhat with Soviet satellite lands and signed promising trade agreements in 1963 with Poland and Hungary, Erhard was unable to usher in a genuine détente because he evinced less than good faith in international affairs.

Thus, in the course of 1964 it was revealed that the Erhard government had been supplying Israel, which was at war with its Arab neighbors, with arms for some years past. It was also disclosed that the Bundesrepublik had promised to deliver 150 tanks in 1964 to Tel Aviv. Colonel Nasser of Egypt reacted sharply to these revelations and threatened to retaliate by recognizing the GDR. There-upon the Federal Republic broke its promise to Israel, whose wails were heard around the world. Shortly afterward, SED chairman Walter Ulbricht visited Cairo and pledged the GDR to lend Egypt DM 400 million, whereupon the Bundes-republik severed diplomatic relations with the United Arab Republic, which was to be for some years to come within the Soviet orbit. Presently, thirteen Arab states responded by recognizing the GDR and severing diplomatic (but not commercial) relations with the FRG. Unwilling to destroy her lucrative trade with the Arab world, the FRG did not invoke the Hallstein Doctrine against the offenders. Never-theless, the whole affair confirmed the fact of a German diplomatic syndrome. Plainly the FRG was so preoccupied with national reunification that it was still pursuing a foreign policy that was a neurotic expression of its *Deutschlandpolitik*.

Erhard's efforts to placate the Russians were equally maladroit. In March,

1966, he sent a conciliatory note to the Kremlin, but in public appearances he continued to brandish the mace of cold war. On the one hand, he practically ignored the signs that a USSR, whose relations with the People's Republic of China were as bad as they well could be, was desirous of détente with the western powers. And on the other, Erhard made no move to make treaty arrangements or establish diplomatic relations with Rumania or Poland, which were then exhibiting a modest independence from Moscow. At most, Erhard worked for only limited improvement in relations with the GDR, hoping that reunification would come from such seed. Specifically, Foreign Minister Gerhard Schröder believed that multiplying contacts between the GDR and FRG might lead to the liberalization of the East German regime.

Erhard and Schröder, annoyed at de Gaulle's attitude toward NATO and opposition to admitting Britain to the Common Market, were unwilling to go as far toward building bridges to eastern Europe as he was. de Gaulle had long since recognized the finality of the Oder-Neisse frontier and had given ample evidence that France believed the German problem was one for Europeans, not Americans, to solve. By contrast, Erhard's ministry still subordinated the German question to American global strategy and patriotically scorned to follow the French president in writing off the trans-Oder-Neisse territories.

Despite sharp criticism of the foreign policies of the FRG, attention was focused in the September 19, 1965, elections to the Bundestag upon domestic issues, such as economic inequities, the educational system, an unbalanced tax structure, and family allowances for parents with three or more children. Since none of these things was vital to the state, the electorate unenthusiastically endorsed the Erhard ministry. The CDU/CSU barely increased its mandate in the Bundestag from 242 to 245, the SPD increased its to only 202 seats, and the FDP declined from 67 to 49. Since the CDU/CSU was still able to dominate the three-ring political circus, a new coalition government of CDU/CSU was constituted.

Notwithstanding the victory of the Christian Democrats, signs multiplied that the electorate was coming to embrace the view that the old diplomatic orthodoxy must be swept out of the foreign office, as, indeed, Schröder seemed to be hinting. Following a double defeat of the CDU in North-Rhine-Westphalia and Hesse in the *Länder* elections of 1966, demands for a new approach to the *Deutschland* problem, coupled with troubled relations with France and a serious industrial slowdown, forced Erhard to give way to a Great Coalition government. It comprised the CDU/CSU and SPD. A former administrator of the Third Reich (but never a Nazi), the suave minister-president of Baden-Württemberg and Christian Democratic leader, Dr. Kurt Georg Kiesinger (1904–   ), became chancellor. The Socialist Willy Brandt was foreign minister and Franz Josef Strauss was finance minister in the new cabinet.

Forging a New *Ostpolitik*

Kiesinger and Brandt were faced with a novel situation arising out of the fact that the Soviet Union was approaching military parity with the USA. The two superpowers henceforth seemed to have no alternative to the policy of peaceful coexistence that Khrushchev had once preached. They became increasingly preoccupied with negotiations to ban the spread of nuclear weapons, limit strategic arms, restrict the number of antiballistic missile sites, and achieve a balanced mutual reduction of forces in Europe. In an atmosphere of mutual fear, if not respect, the USA and USSR allowed neither the Vietnamese War, the Israeli-Arab War of June, 1967, nor the Soviet invasion of Czechoslovakia in August, 1968, to jeopardize the general peace. Thus, there appeared to be diminishing logic to the stubborn hostility between FRG and GDR.

Meanwhile, de Gaulle pressed Bonn to recognize the finality of the eastern boundary of the GDR. The Frenchman urged the Kiesinger government to drop the fiction that the GDR was "middle Germany" and the trans-Oder-Neisse lands were "East Germany." He implied, too, that it had been an error for Adenauer to have abandoned Germany's historic role of the "state of the middle" for one of exclusive integration with the Atlantic Alliance. Such criticisms led the Kiesinger-Brandt government to conclude that Adenauer's uncompromising policy would have to be replaced by one that made Germany a bridge rather than a wall between East and West.

The precondition to détente, seemingly, was abandonment of certain anachronistic principles: (1) the East German people must be encouraged to overthrow their Communist regime; (2) reunification must precede any East-West political agreement; (3) the FRG was the only legal spokesman for the whole German people; and (4) the matter of sovereignty over Polish and Soviet administered lands east of the Oder-Neisse must be decided by a final peace settlement with a united Germany. A starting point for bilateral German discussions would be to concede the economic and political stability of the GDR, which could no longer be ignored.

Though driven by West German opinion to discard the *Deutschlandpolitik* of Adenauer and Erhard, Kiesinger would not contemplate an *Ostpolitik* without a quid pro quo. In return for as yet undetermined sacrifices, the chancellor hoped to pry open the doors of East Berlin and the GDR to liberalizing influences. Kiesinger's first gambit was to abandon the Hallstein Doctrine. In January, 1967, the FRG formally recognized the autonomy-minded Rumanian government of Ceaucescu. A year later diplomatic relations were established with Yugoslavia. In August, 1967, the FRG even tried unsuccessfully to resume diplomatic relations with Czechoslovakia.

The Kiesinger-Brandt *Ostpolitik* was a step-by-step affair. Numerous minor contacts were to pioneer the way to improvement of FRG-GDR relations, which must then promote the peace of all Europe. What Kiesinger did not appreciate was that his new *Ostpolitik*, delineated in his statements of December, 1966, and February, 1967, disturbed more than pleased the Kremlin, which contemplated with concern any loosening of the ties of the GDR with the Warsaw Alliance and the Soviet-sponsored Council for Mutual Economic Assistance (COMECON). When it became clear that Kiesinger was not prepared to renounce claims to the trans-Oder-Neisse lands, the Kremlin launched a smear campaign against his government, which was charged with being revisionist, tolerant of neo-Nazi movements, and dominated by militarist-industrialist interests. As a case in point the Russians castigated the National Democratic party (NPD), a grouping of former Nazis and right-extremists who were led after March, 1967 (until 1971), by Adolf von Thadden (1921–   ) and were bitterly anti-Soviet. In recent *Länder* elections in Hesse, Bavaria, Schleswig-Holstein, and Lower Saxony the NPD had won from 5.8 percent to 8.8 percent of the votes and by 1968 had a following of a million electors. The Kremlin also complained that the FRG was trying to subvert the special status of Berlin. Consequently traffic between it and the FRG was again curtailed.

The First Socialist Government of the FRG

During 1967 and most of 1968 the sporadic intra-German dialogue failed to produce results. Both sides were obdurate. Kiesinger would not recognize the sovereignty of the GDR or the finality of the Oder-Neisse boundary, while the chairman of the Council of Ministers of the GDR, Willi Stoph (1914–   ), insisted upon both as well as the admission of the two Germanies to the UN. Still, there were grounds for some optimism. The FRG had virtually scrapped the Hallstein Doctrine and had entered upon a low-keyed dialogue with the GDR, which for its part no longer insisted upon a precedent formal recognition. From those talks had at least issued on December 8, 1968 a trade agreement, which envisaged progressive increases in the volume of goods exchanged.

When in 1969 Heinrich Lübke retired from the presidency of the FRG, the *Bundesversammlung*, defiantly convening in West Berlin, voted 512 to 506 to elect the Social Democratic jurist, Dr. Gustav Heinemann (1899–1976), as the third president. The Christian Democrat, Gerhard Schröder, was narrowly defeated. Then in the September 28 elections to the Bundestag, the SPD and the NPD were the big gainers. The former, led by Willy Brandt, polled 14,000,000 votes or 42.7 percent of all cast (39.3 percent in 1965) and increased its mandate from 202 to 224 deputies. The NPD polled 1,500,000 votes (4.3 percent of the total), doubling its showing of 1965, whereas the newly legalized German Communist Party (now the DKP) was, in spite of subsidies from the East German SED, a negligible factor. The mandate of the CDU/CSU dropped from 245 to 242, but that of the FDP fell from 49 to 30. When the SPD and FDP formed their so-called "social-liberal coalition," the Bundestag on October 21, 1969 approved the fifty-five-year-old Brandt as chancellor by a vote of 251 to 235. He was the first Social Democratic chancellor in nearly thirty years.

Brandt shortly took an historic, but debatable, step toward conciliating eastern Europe. He held summit talks with Willy Stoph, while the foreign minister of the FRG, Walter Scheel (1919–   ), Mende's replacement as chairman of the FDP, opened negotiations with the USSR for a "no force" convention and with Poland for a comprehensive political and trade agreement. The first fruits of Brandt's *Ostpolitik* were a non-aggression pact signed with the USSR on August

12, 1970 and a treaty with Poland on December 7, 1970. The former treaty led to a tripling of the volume of trade between the FRG and the USSR by 1976 and led the then president of the FRG, Walter Scheel, to say in Moscow in November 1975 that the pact had served the interests of both countries very well. The latter treaty pledged the FRG to relinquish all claims to territories east of the Oder-Neisse boundary. This Bonn-Warsaw political agreement was to be complemented by 1974–1975 by five additional treaties, all directed to the progressive normalization of relations between the FRG and Poland and to the increase of economic and technical cooperation between them. The agreements of 1975 provided for the emigration of up to 125,000 Germans living in Poland to the FRG, the grant of a loan of one billion D-marks at low interest rates to Poland, and the settlement of complex pension fund and accident claims of their respective citizens against each other. While by 1977 reconciliation had not actually been achieved, long steps had been taken towards the restoration of mutual respect.

Back in the FRG, however, there was no agreement as to the worth of the Bonn-Warsaw treaty of December 7, 1970, even though it was reluctantly ratified by the Bundestag on May 17, 1971. Territories that had been acquired by Brandenburg-Prussia before 1772 east of the Oder-Neisse were lost, seemingly, forever. Nevertheless, this gift to Poland was regarded by Brandt and Scheel not merely as a recognition of a *fait accompli* but as reparation for an injustice done and as a constructive contribution to détente and the peace of Europe. Taken in context with the "no force" agreements with the Soviet Union and the GDR, this voluntary alienation of ancient German lands amounted to a withdrawal to approximately Germany's eastern boundary in the tenth century.

Following the initial treaties with Poland and the USSR, the FRG signed a Treaty on the Basis of Relations with the GDR on December 21, 1972. This pact guaranteed unimpeded access to West Berlin from the FRG and aimed at promoting freer movement of persons between it and the GDR. To the disappointment of the Bavarian State Government, which argued that the treaty contravened provisions in the *Grundgesetz* relating to reunification, the West German supreme court on July 31, 1973 upheld the Bundestag's decision of June 20 to endorse it (268 to 217). Karl Carstens (1914–   ), the new chairman of the CDU/CSU, and his parliamentary following remained unconvinced. They persuaded the Bundestag to adopt a resolution asserting that the treaties with Poland and the GDR did not affect the competence of a general peace conference to settle the Polish-German boundary question.

At the same time as the Basic German Treaty, a Quadripartite Convention was signed which defined the respective rights and obligations of the four occupying powers with respect to Berlin. It was asserted that this city of 2,000,000 people would continue to be governed by the *Grundgesetz* and in harmony with unalterable rights reserved to the American, British, and French governments. The Bundestag was banned from holding sessions in West Berlin, but the western military occupation (11,000 troops) was to continue unchanged, and the dividing wall was not to be demolished.

The foreign policy of the Brandt-Scheel government rested on the cornerstone of cooperation with the USA and NATO. Indeed this association was thought to be the necessary precondition for détente with the Soviet bloc. The chancellor and his minister of defense, Georg Leber (1920–   ), were quite certain that a continued US troops and nuclear weapons presence in Europe was exigent to the maintenance of a balance of power. The FRG now shifted the quest for peace from bilateral to multilateral negotiations. It advocated the convocation of an international East-West Conference on Security and Cooperation in Europe (CSCE), which, while in no way weakening the association of the FRG with its western partners, would promote a rapprochement between the two European blocs. While the *Ostpolitik* of the FRG was making further steps along the road of détente, signing treaties with Soviet Russia (1973), Rumania (1973), Hungary (1974), and Czechoslovakia and Poland (1975), the CSCE held its first session in Geneva in 1975 and its second in Helsinki in 1975. Among the representatives of the more than thirty-five nations who attended were those from all COMECON countries, as well as from France and the USA. At the Helsinki conference of the CSCE the delegates affirmed their respect for human rights, fundamental freedoms, and international law and recognized the principle of self-determination.

The government of the FRG hoped to be able to link the CSCE to the SALT talks on limitation of strategic offensive weapons and to the conversations, which opened in Vienna in 1973, aiming at the attainment of militarily mutual balanced force reductions (MBFR). Here the viewpoint of the Brandt government and its successor, the Schmidt ministry, was that political and military security are inseparable, that the fundament of MBFR must be a global, neighborly renunciation of force, and that the liberation of Europeans from fear of war presupposed reduction of armaments and the preservation of a balance of power. Neither CSCE nor MBFR was construed by the FRG as altering or curtailing in any way the rights and responsibilities of the four victor powers towards the Germanies or as finalizing the bifurcation of the country or of its frontiers. Nor did either CSCE or MBFR in any way prejudice the buildup of the Bundeswehr, which, the Bundestag unanimously decided in January 1975, was to be supplemented by a civilian reserve that together with the regular uniformed forces was to attain by 1978 a combined strength of at least 465,000 men organized into 36 brigades.

Of even greater importance than détente or conciliation of East and West was the consolidation of free Europe. It was in fact the cardinal aim of the social-liberal ministries to promote the coordination of all major policies of the European Community (EC, formerly EEC). To this end Brandt urged giving greater authority to both the European Parliament at Strassbourg and the newly formed committee on European Political Cooperation. Bonn also urged European cooperation in drafting a joint energy plan, formulating anti-pollution measures, and in establishing a European regional monetary fund and a joint European floating currency (SNAKE) system. The comprehensive integration of western Europe promised finally to become a reality when in January 1976 in Rome and on July 12, 1976 in Brussels the heads of the nine member states of the EC agreed to hold the first direct, democratic election for the European Parliament in May 1978. The FRG with 62,000,000 of the 250,000,000 individuals in the European Community was to have 81 representatives (exactly the same number as for the UK, France, and Italy) out of a total of 410 anticipated seats in the Parliament.

Bonn also constantly urged the closer cooperation of OECD countries and the linkage of other countries with the European Community. The Ten Year Multilateral Development Concept of the FRG, which was promulgated on November 6, 1975, stressed above all the idea of global interdependence and a concerted campaign to narrow the per capita income gap between the industrialized and underdeveloped countries. Furthermore, in February 1975 a unique multilateral mutual aid agreement, the so-called Lomé pact, was concluded by the nine governments of the EC with forty-six Atlantic, Black African, Caribbean, and Pacific countries. The object was to aid them to find assured markets for their exports in Europe, while at the same time securing for the EC sources of energy and raw materials. A novel aim of the FRG in promoting this multilateral approach was to avoid any future North-South (white-black) confrontation. Beyond this, the FRG strove to encourage increased participation of underdeveloped nations in world trade and in international monetary and banking organizations. As expressed by the West German minister of foreign affairs, Hans-Dietrich Genscher (1927–   ), before the general assembly of the UN on September 24, 1975, the grand external aim of the FRG was to accord proper recognition to the great truth that

> for the first time mankind as a whole is moving towards a common future: either to survive together or to perish together, to prosper together or to decline together. The world as a whole lives under the iron law of interdependence: its parts cannot prosper unless the whole prospers.

The Brandt and Schmidt governments were agreed that the pursuit of an opposite policy of segregation, fragmentation, and confrontation would endanger the general peace and the status of Berlin.

Continuity under Helmut Schmidt

At the Hanover Convention of the SPD in April 1973 Brandt was reelected chairman by a vote of 404 out of 435 delegates. Subsequently in the elections of November 19 the SPD, benefiting from the reduction of the voting age to eighteen, won a landslide victory. SPD and FDP won a combined 54 percent of the vote and 272 mandates compared to 224 for the CDU/CSU. While the FDP increased its percentage to 8.4 percent of the vote, the two extremist parties, the NPD and DKP, both polled less than 1 percent of the total—in itself an accolade for the policies and achievements of the social-liberal alliance.

By the month of April 1974, Brandt could look back on almost as successful a domestic as a foreign policy. The FRG had been further democratized and made more responsive to the needs of the workers. New property and inheritance tax legislation favoring lower income persons was in the mill. Vested pension interests had been protected by law. Educational opportunities had been broadened on the secondary and university levels. Hospitalization for indefinite periods had been instituted under a modified national insurance plan. Pension rates, adjusted for increased costs of living, had risen by 19 percent from 1972–1974. Under the Freedom of Movement Guarantee in EC countries, all persons had been accorded the right to work anywhere in the EC area; accordingly, right-to-work permits had been extended to 2.7 million foreign workers in the FRG, while those who had held jobs for five years in the country had been given the right to stay on indefinitely. An Employee Representation Law had put teeth into codetermination *(Mitbestimmung)*. A second draft bill on codetermination which was not to be submitted to the Bundestag until March 1976 further humanized employer-employee relations. Codetermination was to be applied to all firms and corporations with more than 2,000 employees. Shop councils *(Betriebsräte)* were set up on which jobholders and shareholders had equal representation but on which the chairman was to be elected by the latter. Finally, a Formation of Property Act, which went into force on January 1, 1975, permitted workers to share in the firm's profits and develop vested property rights in the enterprises that employed them.

From the pinnacle of success Brandt plummeted in May 1974 into the abyss of disaster. Just as a new recession was beginning, Brandt's prestige was tarnished by the disclosure that an official in the chancellery, one Günter Guillaume, had been arrested on April 24 on charges of spying for the GDR. Brandt courageously accepted responsibility in the affair and on May 6 resigned the chancellorship. On May 15 Walter Scheel, the deputy chancellor, was elected the fourth president of the FRG. At the same time Helmut Schmidt (1918–   ), Brandt's minister of the interior, became chancellor. Hans-Dietrich Genscher was named foreign minister, while Leber was retained at the ministry of defense.

Schmidt chose to continue Brandt's policies but with diminishing success. Although the FRG and the GDR were both admitted to the UN in the fall of 1974, French President Valéry Giscard d'Estaing refused to cooperate fully with respect to either farm price-support measures in the EC or the regional monetary (SNAKE) system. Schmidt's life was further complicated by the gathering recession of 1974–1975, which was aggravated by the unavoidable transfer of $71.5 billion in 1975 and nearly $100 billion in 1976 from the western world to the petroleum exporting countries (OPEC).

Many of the monetary and economic accomplishments of the FRG—its relatively lower cost of living, stronger currency, and higher rates of employment than those of most west European countries—were compromised in 1974–1976 by spiraling prices, inflation, instability of exchange rates between SNAKE (EC) and dollar zones, plummeting security quotations, and more than a million unemployed and 500,000 partially employed. To combat the deepening recession of 1975–76 the Schmidt government pursued Keynesian economics, incurring a deficit in the public sector of the economy. Much money was invested in creating jobs and subsidizing firms that would offer permanent work to the unemployed.

Tax breaks and financial aid were accorded to energy-saving enterprises and operations. Money was ploughed into publicly sponsored housing programs, and family allowances for low income households were increased.. By early 1976 the West German economy was coming out of the deepest recession of the postwar period. By the fall the risks taken by the Schmidt government were beginning to pay off in a 29% rise in internal and external orders for German manufactured products as compared with 1975, and in a thriving shipbuilding industry. While employment was still 5 percent below the figure of mid-1975—due in part to the circumstance that there were 2.6 million foreign workers (10 percent of the work force) in the FRG—the real GNP had risen since June 1975 by 3.5 percent. The FRG had fully made up the losses inflicted by the recession. Through it all she had held consumer inflation to 7 percent or less, whereas Japan in 1974 had an inflation rate of 23, Italy 19, and Britain 17 percent. At the same time the value of the DM had increased in the first four months of 1976 by 6.5 percent, and in October by an average of another 3 percent against other currencies in the European joint exchange rate float (SNAKE) system. Moreover, mindful of its continuing surplus balance of payments, the Schmidt government magnanimously sought to help other countries back to recovery by systematically reducing that favorable balance from 25.1 billion D-marks in 1974 to only 7.5 billion by the start of 1977. In keeping with Bonn's desire to normalize relations between the FRG and the Soviet bloc and between the EC and COMECON, the Schmidt government had also since 1972 steadily increased its trade with Eastern Europe. By early 1977 the volume of that trade—the fastest growing component of the total trade of the FRG—had increased over 1967 by 380 percent.

Despite dangers posed by a Middle Eastern and an Angolan confrontation between the Soviet and American camps, the government of the FRG persisted in its conciliatory and altruistic foreign policy. Animated by an almost unequalled desire to promote freedom, universal respect for law, social justice, and a greater economic equality among nations, the Schmidt government continued to pursue a program that comprised the following features: détente; further integration and development of the EC; strengthening NATO; encouragement of SALT, CSCE, MBFR, and other multilateral discussions to fortify European security and restore reciprocal confidence; improvement of cooperation with OPEC countries with a view to recycling the vast petroleum currency surpluses that had gravitated into Arab hands; discovery of new sources of energy, such as by building by 1979 a European plant for production of enriched uranium to supply EC nuclear power stations; and assistance to underdeveloped "third world" countries in keeping with the realities of economic interdependence and the need to combat racial and political turbulence especially in Africa. However, while Defense Minister Georg Leber continued strongly to support the U.S. quest for MBFR, and while the NATO alliance remained the fundament of the foreign policy of the FRG, clouds began to darken German-American relations by the outset of 1977. This was in no way due to the termination of the formal agreements on financial measures to be undertaken by the FRG to offset costs of stationing U.S. troops in Germany. Rather it was due to the fact that Schmitt and Genscher openly refused to endorse the proposal by President Jimmy Carter and U.S. Secretary Cyrus Vance that the FRG oppose the further spread of nuclear technology. Schmidt assured the new U.S. administration that he would go ahead with the fulfillment of Germany's contractual obligations to supply nuclear technology to Brazil.

In the elections of October 3, 1976 it was apparent that the economic woes of the immediate past and the erosion of détente were taking their toll in popular support for the social-liberal coalition. In regional elections in 1975 and early in 1976 in West Berlin, the Saarland, North-Rhine Westphalia, Baden, and Württemberg, the CDU/CSU had registered significant gains. Indeed, by the opening of 1976 the CDU/CSU had 21 votes to 20 for the SPD-FDP coalition in the Bundesrat. Now in the national elections of October Schmidt's coalition barely managed to wrest victory from the jaws of defeat. The SPD received only 42.8 percent of the vote (compared with 45.9 in 1972), while the FDP won 7.9 percent (compared with 8.4 in 1972), yielding an aggregate of 50.5 percent of the votes cast. The CDU/CSU, marching under the banner of Helmut Kohl (1930–   ), the prime minister of the Rhineland-Palatinate, and of Franz Josef Strauss of the CSU, almost stole the show, winning 48.6 percent of the vote and emerging once more as the strongest single party in the FRG. The SPD now had 215 deputies in the Bundestag, the FDP 38, whereas the CDU/CSU had 243. Thus the Schmitt-Genscher coalition possessed an almost razor-thin majority of seven in the Bundestag. Retention of public confidence by the social-liberal coalition henceforth depended mainly upon the revival of world prosperity. And this in turn depended in an arcane way upon the problematic confidence of the American business and financial community in the economic policies of President Carter.

Chapter 55

THE GERMAN DEMOCRATIC REPUBLIC

Planning for a Socialist Future

In 1949 few observers in the West would have cared to bet that the German Democratic Republic (GDR) would survive a decade. Freighted with staggering reparations, high costs of military occupation, a predominantly agrarian economy, and a totalitarian government, the GDR, seemingly, could offer its citizens nothing but poverty and austerity. The Atlantic states contemplated the lackluster Soviet creation with frigid contempt and, believing that it had been built from the roof down, would have nothing to do with it. It was refused formal recognition by the entire free world, which referred to the GDR disparagingly only as the Soviet Occupation Zone or even just "middle Germany." Its early demise or overthrow was confidently predicted. Yet, in spite of these soothsayers, the GDR survived a disadvantaged childhood and waxed to robust maturity by the late 1960s. The principal explanation of this unexpected development lies in the progress of the GDR toward a socialist economy.

While the GDR's troika of Walter Ulbricht (first secretary of the SED), Wilhelm Pieck (president), and Otto Grotewohl (prime minister), aided by the existence of a large residuum of socialist sentiment dating from Weimar times, sought to pattern East Germany on the USSR, the transition of the former from Nazi autarky to Leninist socialism was obstructed by several factors. Down to 1953, 50 billion marks in reparations had been extracted from her substance. She had lost all the lands east of the Oder-Neisse border, including the mines and industrial plant of Upper Silesia. Her soil was minerally deficient. Occupation costs were high. A vast number of skilled workers had fled to the FRG. Her population of 17 million had to be supported in an area (42,000 square miles) that was a little smaller than Tennessee. And Poland and Czechoslovakia were fundamentally hostile to the idea of cooperating with any German state. On the other hand, the GDR possessed an asset of great importance. She professed to be a state whose social and political forms harmonized with the modern idiom. The theory of East German, as of all communist, government was that of a people's democracy, of unlimited popular sovereignty in an allegedly classless society, where distinctions based on race, sex, and privilege had ceased to exist.

Beginning in 1950 a series of five- and seven-year plans altered the face of East Germany. In that year, when the future looked bleak for the GDR, about 94 percent of the arable of a state that was 40 percent as large as the FGR was still privately owned. However, under the First Five-Year Plan the Junker estates were broken up. All holdings over 100 hectares (c. 240 acres) were confiscated without compensation and divided among the poorer peasants and agricultural laborers. In the process, the olden landlord-gentry was forever destroyed as a class. A decade later the petty farm proprietor, who had briefly succeeded the Junker, virtually followed him into the discard. Relatively big farms had always been the rule in eastern Germany, and it was soon discovered that small holdings were uneconomical.

Collectivization was carried out with far less dislocation than had been the case in the USSR in the 1930s. Agrarian collectives *(Landwirtschaftliche Produktionsgenossenschaften)* and, to lesser extent, state farms were set up wherever there had been a Junker estate. In 1955 on the eve of the Second Five-Year Plan (1956–60) only about 20 percent of the arable was as yet collectivized, but the nationalized and collectivized sector of agriculture was already producing about 80 percent of the gross product. By 1959, when the Second Five-Year Plan yielded to a Seven-Year Plan (1959–65), to parallel that which had been instituted in the USSR in 1957, collectives embraced more than 43 percent of the land under cultivation. By the end of 1960 that percentage had doubled. After that year, when collectivization finally became compulsory, the rate of increase of the gross agricultural product rose significantly. Moreover, collectivized and state farms, which in 1950 had produced only 12.6 percent of the product, were by 1966 accounting for 91.3 percent. By 1969–70, when recession had laid hold on the western world again, the food shortage that had once been a conspicuous feature of the drab lives of the citizens of the GDR had given way to a sufficiency, and in many cases an abundance, of foodstuffs.

The growth of national income and of the gross social product (GSP) in the GDR was fairly rapid in the 1950s, modest in the early 1960s, and remarkable after 1963. At that time a partially decentralized operational concept was introduced under the New System of Economic Planning and Direction, patterned after that which had recently been initiated in the USSR. In the period 1950–57 the East German gross social product doubled, and prices, taking 1950 as the base year, did likewise. The gross social product again doubled in the next decade, but prices by 1967 rose by only 75 percent. Inasmuch as the economic recovery of the German Democratic Republic started from a low level, the spectacular and erratic advances in the rate of increase of the gross social product in the 1950s are apt to be misleading. Nevertheless, when all allowances are made, the East German achievement was still impressive. Despite the exodus of laborers to the west, the GDR experienced in each of six years in the decade of 1950–60 more than a 9 percent annual rate of increase of the gross social product. A steep drop occurred after 1959, when the western world experienced a recession. Then the rate fell from 10.9 percent to 2.9 percent by 1962. However, with the introduction of the New System of Economic Planning, the GDR again surged forward, and by 1965 the rate of increase of the gross social product was once more above 7 percent.

From the outset of planning, more than 70 percent of the gross industrial product of the GDR came from nationalized enterprises, while in transportation, government-owned facilities accounted for 84 percent of all services. In 1950 the great bulk of nationalized industry was, however, concentrated in a few large towns: Magdeburg (230,000 people), Karl Marx Stadt (Chemnitz, 250,000), Halle (250,000), Dresden (400,000), Leipzig (500,000), and Berlin (1,190,000). Between 1950 and 1955 the nationalized sector of the industrial economy grew but modestly. At the expiration of the First Five-Year Plan nationalized industry was contributing 79 percent of the gross industrial product. In the period of the inter-rupted (1955–57/60) Second Five-Year Plan this percentage rose another 5.6 percent, but under the Seven-Year Plan (1959–1965) it only went up 1 percent because by then nationalization had been 94 percent accomplished.

After 1955 the steepest rates of climb were in electronics, optics, precision tools, chemistry, machinery, energy, and woodworking. However, the traditional sinews of heavy industry were not neglected. In the production of iron, for in-stance, the GDR in 1970 produced sevenfold what eastern Germany had in 1936, and in steel, fivefold. With only 23 percent of the land area of the Third Reich in 1937 and one-quarter of its population, the GDR by 1970 was producing more than all Germany had turned out in 1939.

The Agony of Reincarnation

For most people in East Germany the early 1950s were a time of suffering. The harshness of the new totalitarian regime, which mobilized resources and man-power to a degree never attempted even by the Nazis, weighed like an incubus on almost everyone. General embitterment was fed by many wrongs and by the government's determination to transmogrify the GDR. Landlords, industrial capitalists, and free enterprise were systematically eradicated. Almost all mass organizations and political parties were coordinated by the SED. States' rights and ancient political traditions were suppressed: the *Länder* were replaced by 14 provinces divided into 214 counties. Former Nazi professors, technicians, and scientists were rehabilitated and often favored above the few Jews in the GDR. The last vestiges of the confessional schools were erased and the public educa-tional system was gradually extended downward to embrace two-thirds of all children between three and six years of age. Endless, discouraging food shortages and wretched housing conditions persisted. *Vopos (Volkspolizei*—people's po-lice*)* tyrannized over the public, while the sullen hostility of the bulk of the popu-lace expressed itself in sabotage and emigration of between 12,000 and 15,000 persons monthly.

All of this protest against the iniquities of the regime was crystallized in the rebellion of June 17–18, 1953. What started as a demonstration by construction workers in East Berlin against low wages and increased production quotas swiftly mushroomed into an uprising against the government and spread to other parts of the country. In the larger cities factories, administration offices, and radio sta-tions were occupied by the rebels. But since they had no arms, they were soon suppressed by Soviet troops. Basically leaderless and without a plan, the insur-rection, unsupported by the western powers, was already breaking up before three Red army divisions and hundreds of tanks were sent into Berlin and Leipzig on the night of June 17–18. In the ensuing "show trials" about one hundred persons were convicted of high treason and executed, while an additional 1,200 were given prison sentences.

The uprising had the consequence that at least Ulbricht and Grotewohl confessed that certain errors had been made, and they promised to do better in the future. During the summer of 1953 the central committee of the SED was, however, purged of "defeatists," including Rudolf Herrnstadt, minister of public education and editor of the SED's central organ, *Neues Deutschland*. Wage raises, increased bonuses, and better housing were promised to persons in the lowest income brackets, and efforts were made to ameliorate the lot of the peasants. Still, when all is said, Ulbricht had no intention of compromising his Five-Year Plan by shifting emphasis from producer to consumer goods. A year after the uprising the regime abandoned the "New Course." By then most of the concessions made under duress had been rescinded.

Integration with the Eastern Bloc

Essential to the political rehabilitation of the GDR was its prior, voluntary acquiescence in the consequences of the Nazi defeat. Accordingly, one of the first major diplomatic initiatives of the GDR was to sign a treaty of cession and recognition with Poland. In defiance of the principle of international law, *pacta sunt servanda*, the two governments signed a convention at Görlitz on June 6, 1950, which set aside the Potsdam Agreement. The treaty with Poland affirmed that the Oder-Neisse border was the definitive frontier between the GDR and the Polish People's Republic, despite the fact that at Potsdam it had been designated "provisional." Poland, for its part, unilaterally recognized the government of the GDR to be the sole spokesman for all East Germans.

The German Democratic Republic was rewarded for signing away the eastern lands when on October 21, 1950, she was integrated into the Soviet economic bloc. In 1953 reparations payments were declared at an end, and shortly thereafter the Kremlin gave tacit assent to establishing an East German army. On March 25, 1954, the USSR formally recognized the GDR as a sovereign state, and it was admitted as an equal partner to the Council for Mutual Economic Assistance COMECON (est. 1949), a trading and commercial organization of Soviet satellites.

These concessions were adroitly exploited by the defense minister of the GDR, Willi Stoph (1896–   ), who on September 24, 1964, was to succeed Grotewohl as minister-president. Stoph prepared the way for the integration of the GDR in the Warsaw Alliance system. When on January 27–28, 1956, its Political Advisory Committee accepted East Germany as an ally, plans for a National People's army were implemented at once. At the same time an eighteen-month service, universal conscription system was established. Shortly afterward, an air force, comprising MIG 15 and 16 pursuit-type fighter planes and 200 older craft, was organized, and a small navy begun.* As of 1957 the two Germanies faced each

---

*Never formidable, the East German defense force consisted in 1970 of only 137,000 men, including 90,000 army personnel, 16,000 naval, and 31,000 air force.

other in armored array—the FRG allied with NATO, and the GDR with the Warsaw Powers. Once again the vision of a demilitarized Germany had proved to be a mirage.

The "Politics" of Totalitarianism

The Fourth Party Convention of the SED was held from March 30 to April 16, 1954. At this congress there was elected a new central committee, which in turn selected the small but powerful Politburo and Party Secretariat. A new party program was also endorsed. It was a virtual replica of that adopted by the CPSU at its fourteenth congress in 1952. The SED program affirmed that the central committee "will direct the work of the central governmental and social institutions and organizations. . . ."

The elections of October 17, 1954, to the Volkskammer and district legislatures *(Bezirkstage)*, as always, were conducted in the absence of secret suffrage and for the purpose of securing popular support of a "unity list," which had the endorsement of the government. Mandates were to be allocated among the component parties of the list—CDU, LDPD (Liberal Democrats), NDPD (National Democrats), and SED—in consonance with preapportioned percentages. Although voting was preceded by a lively campaign mounted by the Central Block of Anti-Fascist Democratic Parties and Mass Orgniazations,* the elections were a bad joke becuase their outcome was a foregone conclusion. Of all eligible voters, 96.41 percent cast ballots, and of these, 98.46 percent voted for the "unity list." Accordingly a second Grotewohl ministry, in which all portfolios except two were held by the SED, was formed on November 19, 1954.

Notwithstanding the show of unity, individual dissatisfaction was still widespread in East Germany, and it should be noted that at least one "mass organization," the East German Lutheran Church (Evangelische Kirche Deutschlands-Ost, EKD-O), led by Bishop Otto Dibelius (1880–1967), who dwelt in West Berlin, was at this time even more antagonistic to the Communist belief system than the Lutheran majority had been to the ideology and mystique of the Nazis.

The denigration of Stalin at the twentieth congress of the CPSU in February, 1956, did not materially impair the cult of personality as developed in the GDR around Ulbricht. His power survived the third party conference of the SED (March 24–30, 1956) and was not seriously shaken by either the uprising in Posen in June, 1956, the demonstrations in Warsaw and Breslau, or the abortive Hungarian revolution—all in the autumn of 1956. Ulbricht had already made anticipatory minor

---

*Among the mass organizations, virtually all of which were controlled by internal SED cells, were the Democratic Women's Federation (Demokratischer Frauenbund Deutschlands, DFD), the Federation of Free German Trade Unions (Freier Deutscher Gewerkschaftsbund, FDGB), the Peasants' Union for Mutual Aid (Vereinigung der gegenseitigen Bauernhilfe, VGB), the Association of People's Industries (Vereinigung Volkseigener Betriebe, VVB), the Union of Persons Persecuted by the Nazi Regime (Vereinigung der Verfolgten des Nazi regimes, VVN), the agricultural collectives (Produktionsgenossenschaften), and the Free German Youth (Freie Deutsche Jugend, FDJ).

concessions to the workers, such as a shorter work week, increased pension payments, and more and better housing. In early 1957 Ulbricht also emerged with undiminished authority from the debates over revisionism and national communism held at the Nineteenth Plenum of the Central Committee of the SED.

By 1958 Ulbricht had become the "Pooh Bah" of the East German "Titipu," for President Pieck, reelected in 1957, was powerless under the constitution, and Grotewohl was growing old and unimportant. The ostensibly stern but actually relatively elastic Ulbricht was not only chairman of the SED but virtually "Lord High Everything Else." In 1957 Ulbricht had silenced opposition within the SED, when in a series of trials the hostile, reform-minded Wolfgang Harich and his followers in the party's central committee were sentenced to prison. Ulbricht's hand had also been strengthened by the supplementary penal law of December 11, 1957, which made crimes against government and state, including defamation and mere hostile propaganda, punishable by confiscation of property and even death.

The years 1960–61, which brought enforced collectivization and a slackening in the rate of increase of the gross social product, carried Ulbricht to the zenith. In February, 1960, he was made chairman of the new National Defense Council (National-Verteidigungsrat), which endowed him with the authority of commander-in-chief. When President Pieck died in September, 1960, Ulbricht was designated chairman of the newly created central Council of State *(Staatsrat)*. This organ, intended originally to replace the office of the president, which was now abolished, became the main arm of the East German government.

Immediately after the Volkskammer elections of October 20, 1963, in which 99.25 percent of the electorate voted and 99.9 percent of the votes cast were given to the government's list, Ulbricht was reappointed chairman of the 24-member *Staatsrat*. His wheelhorse was the deputy chairman, Willi Stoph, an army general who had been minister of defense since 1956. On November 14 the Volkskammer conferred upon the *Staatsrat* vast interim authority to promulgate decrees having the force of law and made the council of ministers and supreme court responsible to the council of state.

In the SED, too, Ulbricht retained an iron grip on things. During 1963–64 a minor challenge to his authority was posed by industrial managers and technocrats. But they could not topple the stern Buddha and had to content themselves with the grant of broader latitude for stimulating production. For the remainder of the decade Ulbricht was the dominant force in East Germany.

East German Foreign Policy
in the Khrushchev Era

In all essentials the foreign policy of the GDR was still formulated in the late 1950s by the Kremlin. East Germany, situated on the great northern invasion route to Russia, remained the constant concern of Khrushchev and the Soviet council of ministers. More than twenty Red army divisions continued in occupancy of the GDR. Furthermore, Khrushchev was at pains to make periodic visits to Berlin-Pankow to reaffirm the close connection between the GDR and the USSR.

Through the turbulent years (1959–63) of the Berlin and Cuban missiles crises, the government of the German Democratic Republic insisted unalterably that recognition and a final peace treaty must precede unification. To these demands was shortly added another: the whole of Berlin must be declared a free city. Acceptance of the latter would have nullified the rights of the western powers in the metropolis and was therefore repugnant to them.

In early June, 1961, at his meeting with President John F. Kennedy in Vienna, Soviet Premier Khrushchev again urged the logic of recognizing the GDR, establishing a "free" Berlin, and concluding peace with the two Germanies. But all this, in the eyes of the western Big Three, was just another rock upon the talus. A note of September 27 from the GDR to the United Nations elicited no more sympathy. It proposed a general peace treaty as precondition to the confederation of the two Germanies in a nuclear, weapons-free, neutral state that would form part of a "disengagement" belt from Sweden to Austria.

In the years that followed, Ulbricht continued to seek a détente with the Bundesrepublik, without, however, sacrificing a single important piece in the chess game. The West read only hypocrisy into the East German approach because the Ulbricht regime kept up a sporadic harassment of interzonal border crossers and finally on August 12, 1961, completed its north-south "death strip" and its "death wall," which divided Berlin in twain. These and other hostile moves synchronized, it is to be noted, with a new deterioration in US–Soviet Russian relations.

Following the Cuban missiles crisis, President Kennedy concentrated upon the delicate but ultimately successful negotiations for a nuclear test-ban treaty with the USSR. Ulbricht, too, blew into the rusty flute of peaceful coexistence. On July 31, 1963, he advocated signing a system of nonaggression pacts between the NATO and Warsaw Pact countries and a "no-force" agreement between the GDR and FRG.

At this juncture, Ulbricht stood on the threshold of great accomplishments. The Seven-Year Plan and the New Economic System had revitalized the East German economy. Construction of the Berlin Wall and the "death strip," while viewed in the West as a propaganda victory for the free world, had enabled the GDR to husband its manpower resources and integrate better with the COMECON system. Having triumphed over all internal opposition and vindicated his innovations by increased production and improved living standards, Ulbricht saw the halo of canonization before his eyes. There lacked only international recognition of the GDR, which must be preceded by a formal peace treaty with the USSR.

In Moscow Ulbricht was unable to obtain the peace treaty he coveted, but on June 12, 1964, he came away with a twenty-year treaty of friendship and alliance, which guaranteed the territorial integrity of the GDR. This pact continued in force under Leonid Brezhnev and Andrei Kosygin, when in October, 1964, they became respectively first secretary of the CPSU and premier of the Soviet Union. With the conclusion of the alliance, Ulbricht became the first personage at the Soviet court of satellites.

Ulbricht's Balance Sheet

High on the list of achievements of this competent martinet were the economic strength and military security he had conferred upon the GDR. The increased rates of production and capital investment were evidence of the salutary effects deriving from the introduction of the methods of his system of New Economic Planning, while military potential had been augmented by the signing in early 1967 of mutual assistance pacts with Poland and Czechoslovakia.

Of course, the GDR was spiritually and intellectually still the kingdom of the blind, although by no means the incompetent. When all is said in favor of the accomplishments of the regime, certain ugly realities remained: there was no refuge from incessant propaganda against myriad, imaginary "enemies of the state" within and without; no honesty in reporting international news; no room for any scheme of thought other than the Marxist-Leninist; no approximate equality of income; and no escape from the universal tutelage of an elite of bureaucrats, technocrats, and commissars.

On the other hand, the Ulbricht government had built up respectable assets. By 1966 the average monthly wage in the GDR had climbed to more than two-thirds that in the FGR, a richer country. A new affluence, deriving from a more than 7 percent per annum rate of increase in the gross social product, was reflected in the spread of household amenities (such as washing machines and TV sets) among ever broader strata of the population. Women in East Germany played a larger role in industry and the professions than in West Germany. Rents in the GDR were low, as was common in Communist-oriented countries, averaging from 5 percent to 7 percent of the worker's monthly salary. Where admissions were charged for cultural and sports events, they were also low. Extremes of wealth and poverty were less acute than in the FGR. Unemployment was virtually a thing of the past. Taxes on lower income brackets were not so high as in the FGR. Although automobiles were still in short supply, foodstuffs (except fresh meat, coffee, tea, and cocoa) were cheap and abundant, because from 1959 to 1965 the volume of agricultural and dairy products had risen almost 50 percent. A comprehensive system of hospitalization and medical and dental care, the cost of which was borne by a centralized social insurance system that was more advanced than that of the Bundesrepublik, helped confer upon the East German public the second highest standard of living in Communist Europe. In a country where ballots decided nothing, the legal voting age had been lowered to eighteen as early as May, 1950. Although East Germany was officially atheistic and chairs of scientific atheism had been established in its universities, the church-state conflict had greatly abated as a result of the extension of governmental financial aid to both Evangelical and Catholic churches and official recognition that the church is a humane and utilitarian institution.

In no field of endeavor have the accomplishments of the Ulbricht regime been regarded as more modern and democratic than in education. The law of 1965 on the Unified Socialist Educational System proclaimed the duties of the individual to the state and of the schools to society. While strengthening state control over formal education, this law made it available to everyone without discrimination of any kind. Every child was guaranteed a free and uniform schooling from the *Volksschule* (or even from the nursery school) through the polytechnical school (eighth through the tenth grades). By lowering admissions standards and making scholarships very easy to obtain, the state modernized, democratized, and vulgarized the higher schools (*Gymnasien* and universities) to a revolutionary extent. In proportion to its population, there are in the GDR far more children attending nursery school and kindergartens and there are about 35 percent more university students than in the Bundesrepublik. By 1970–1972 the GDR was spending 24 percent more on education than was the FRG. On the other hand, the entire secondary and higher educational program was suffused with the Marxist-Leninist world outlook, and western books were in short supply in the libraries of the Democratic Republic.

By the late 1960s the churches, mass organizations, and "opposition" parties were all unmistakably loyal to the Ulbricht regime. This was demonstrated when, without ostensible intimidation, 99.93 percent of the ballots cast in the Volkskammer elections of July 2, 1967, were given to the SED-sponsored National Front, comprising the SED, NDPD, DBD, LDPD, and CDU. In April, Ulbricht was reelected first secretary of the SED, and on July 2 chairman of the *Staatsrat*. Willi Stoph was reelected president of the council of ministers, and Otto Winzer was named minister for foreign affairs.

During 1967 and 1968 important new fiscal and constitutional innovations were registered in the German Democratic Republic. The currency was overhauled, and both a national bank *(Staatsbank)* and a Bank for Industry and Trade were founded. On January 12, 1968, a penal code, to replace that of 1871, was adopted. It was designed to protect the socialist state. Eleven offenses against the public order were specified for which the death sentence might be imposed. Shortly thereafter, the *Volkskammer* adopted (March 26, 1968) a new constitution, which superseded the fundamental law of October 1949 and was subsequently amended on October 7, 1974. The new constitution stated that the GDR was a "socialist country with a socialist ownership of the means of production" and "a planned economy." Theoretically the *Volkskammer* was vested with supreme power and capital responsibilities, but actually the Council of State, supposedly its creature, was the *deus ex machina* of the state. The constitution guaranteed religious liberty, the right to work, equal pay for both sexes, and the right of all to education.

Détente with the Bundesrepublik

Ulbricht and Stoph were acutely aware of their failures to reunify Germany or establish trade relations between the GDR and either the EEC or the European Free Trade Association (EFTA), both of which were merged as the European

Community (EC) in 1972. On the eve of détente the GDR had embassies in only thirteen countries, all satellites of the USSR.

As early as 1964 Minister-president Stoph had come to realize that there was a limit to the economic and military dividends that could accrue from exclusive association with the Soviet bloc. By 1968 he had become convinced that no further sharp increments of power could be expected except as a result of bilateral limitations of armaments or the economic unification of Germany. Stoph's overtures to the West, of course, paralleled the odyssey the USSR had just commenced with destination either entente with Paris or accommodation with Washington and London.

The new constitution of the GDR heralded a diplomacy of peaceful coexistence. Article VI declared that the state "strives for a system of collective security in Europe and a stable and peaceful order in the world." It, in fact, echoed Chancellor Kiesinger's advertised wish for a step-by-step rapprochement between the two German states "until their unification can be achieved," adding that this must be on the "basis of democracy and socialism."

On August 20, 1968, the very day that the governments of the FRG and the GDR were to begin talks on the ministerial level, the Kremlin ordered units of the Red army, in cooperation with Polish, Hungarian, Bulgarian, and East German troops, to invade Czechoslovakia to overthrow the liberal Communist regime of Dubček and Svoboda. Not till the fall of 1969 was it possible for the western powers to forget East Germany's wrongful act. However, at this time the delay in the East-West German dialogue was not unwelcome in Moscow, where the wish for détente was weighed against the disadvantages of weakening the complex ties of the GDR with the Soviet bloc.

Even after the complicated machinery of détente had been set in motion by Poland's offer on May 17, 1969, to sign a treaty with the FRG on condition of recognition of the finality of the Oder-Neisse boundary, mutual suspicions impeded rapprochement between East and West Germany. Bonn was reluctant to extend *de jure* recognition to the GDR, while the latter feared the aims and influence of an allegedly growing military-industrial complex in the FRG.

When finally the Quadripartite Pact and the Treaty on the Basis of Relations between the FRG and the GDR had been implemented, Pankow could take a certain satisfaction in the fact that the visible political presence of the *Bundesrepublik* in West Berlin was to be reduced and in the permission given to the USSR to establish a consulate general in one of the western sectors. After traffic and transit details had been worked out, an unprecedented number of West Germans and West Berliners took advantage of relaxed controls to visit East Berlin and the GDR. Despite minor monetary obstacles interposed by the government of the latter, some 1,300,000 old age pensioners and around 3,000,000 West German tourists were able to visit parts of East Germany in 1975. Likewise, as a result of the Basic Treaty, trade between the two Germanies registered a modest but steady increase. An undoubted dividend that accrued to the GDR from détente was a considerable increase in the number of states that now extended formal diplomatic recognition to it. Not only many African and Asian countries but also all NATO states fell into line, Canada being the last NATO country to accord recognition (1975).

The GDR in the Mid-Seventies

In 1971 the fifty-nine-year-old Saarlander, Erich Honecker (1912–), who had made his way up from the chairmanship of the FDJ to membership in the Politburo of the SED, succeeded Ulbricht, who at seventy-eight had resigned his offices because of ill health. The new first secretary (after 1976, general secretary) of the Socialist Unity Party possessed but a pedestrian intellect but had always known on which side his bread was buttered. An unswerving supporter of Ulbricht and a strong believer in socialism and the permanent separation of the two Germanies, Honecker also never failed to seize an opportunity to advocate closer integration of the GDR with COMECON and unquestioning acceptance of the leadership of the European Communist movement by the Soviet Union. Harboring private reservations on détente, he covertly sabotaged in minor ways the Basic Treaty of December 21, 1972. The constitution of the GDR, which was amended under his direction in 1974, omitted all mention of any future unification of Germany. Under his direction the demarcation line ("death strip") and the Berlin wall, which had cut emigration from the GDR to a trickle, was extended and strengthened. By 1976 it embraced a 155-mile-long barbed wire fence, 80 miles of electrified wire fence, 120 miles of ditches, 190 miles of mine fields, 378 watch towers and bunkers, and numerous automatically triggered shrapnel guns.

Honecker was uncompromising in his thoroughgoing socialization of the East German economy. By 1977 the sector under individual control was negligible: 99.9 percent of all industry and services had been nationalized and agriculture was almost entirely collectivized. Skillfully steered by Honecker and his chief lieutenants, Willi Stoph (advanced to the chairmanship of the *Staatsrat* but in October 1976 demoted to the largely titular post of chairman of the Council of Ministers) and the Saxon-born Horst Sindermann (1915–), who was chairman of the Council of Ministers until he was elected in the fall of 1976 to the presidency of the Volkskammer, the GDR, in spite of all handicaps, became a relatively strong industrial country. By the spring of 1977, the GDR, with a population of only 17,000,000 and zero demographic growth and with a lack of almost all major natural resources except raw lignite, was experiencing an almost consistently high rate of growth. Even though her living standard was still about 25 percent lower than that of the FRG, the GDR under its successive five year plans had achieved an economic miracle *(Wirtschaftswunder)* of its own. As a result especially of the 1970–1975 plan the East German state had attained the highest standard of living in the Soviet bloc and in relation to its size had become one of the leading industrial countries of the world. In that five year span the national income had grown by 30 percent, and the GDR had increased its industrial productivity by 37 percent and since 1949 by more than eightfold. Of course, production of some raw materials and end items lagged or even declined, but advances in productivity were especially pronounced as regards electricity, pig iron, steel, cement, diesel motors, optical goods, and railway rolling stock. On the other hand, consumers' goods by 1977 still enjoyed only secondary priority, although foodstuffs had substantially increased. Internal and external trade showed gratifying increases, although the volume of combined imports and exports in commerce with COMECON countries was still double that with those outside the Soviet bloc. While the non-Communist world was wallowing in the slough of recession in 1974–1976 and often experiencing double-digit inflation, prices in the GDR remained stable or were in many cases deliberately reduced by from 7–30 percent, while wages rose in the 1970–75 period by one-third.

Addressing the ninth congress of the SED on May 22, 1976, Honecker announced that under the new plan for 1976–1980 some 20–22 percent more consumers' goods would become available, and some 750,000 apartments would be built or renovated. Because of the system of national price-support subsidies, prices were expected to remain stable. In his remarks before the congress, Premier Sindermann predicted that from 1976–80 the productivity of labor in industry would rise at least 30 percent, while the annual rate of growth of industrial production would continue at between 6.0 and 6.3 percent, as compared with a rate of 6.3 percent in 1974. Income was expected to rise by 24 percent by 1980. He also promised that while lignite would remain the most important indigenous source of energy the GDR would heavily invest in a joint East European energy development project. For his part, cognizant of the dwindling energy reserves of the world, Honecker appealed for an annual reduction in the consumption of energy by 2.8 to 3 percent.

Accompanying the fairly steady economic boom went the more complete integration of women into the work force. For example, by 1975 about 80 percent of women between the ages of fifteen and sixty were remuneratively employed. A five-day workweek was fairly uniform for all wage earners, and pension and invalidity benefit payments had been sharply increased. In 1969 the whole educational system had been broadened and democratized, and in 1975 the universal ten-year polytechnic school was substituted for the old elementary and secondary schools. The minimum school-leaving age was set at sixteen. However, many graduates would enter one of the seven universities or technological institutes (Rostock, Leipzig, Berlin, Greifswald, Wittenberg, Halle, Jena, and Dresden). A State Committee for Physical Education encouraged interest in competitive sports, one result of which was the astonishing performances of the East German Olympic teams at Munich (1972) and at Innsbruck and Montreal (1976), where they won a total of gold, silver, and bronze medals second only to that of the USSR.

A consequence of all these accomplishments and growth has been the emergence of a state where a theoretical egalitarianism flourishes, where there is neither racial nor sexual discrimination, where there are low rents and transportation costs and full employment, and where there are stable prices, few strikes, and relatively little major crime. Yet all is not gold that glitters. The GDR remains a police state with all the baseness that implies. A political autocracy still shackles thought and stultifies the soul. There, too, agriculture remains the stepdaughter of the economy, and the needs of the consumer are still subordinated to those of heavy industry. All too often the result is a monotonous uniformity and ineradicable drabness which impoverish the meaning of life.

Nor are the colors in the tapestry of East German existence likely to become much brighter as long as the GDR is shackled to the USSR. Yet these links were intentionally strengthened when on October 7, 1975, the two countries signed a twenty-five year Treaty of Friendship, Cooperation and Mutual Assistance. When Honecker affixed his signature to this pact in Moscow he pledged his country and his regime to be the unswerving advocate of the solidarity of the Communist community, as represented by COMECON and the Warsaw Alliance. Not only did Honecker and his foreign minister, Oskar Fischer, pledge long-term mutual coordination and harmonization of economic planning but they also accepted the permanence of existing European state frontiers. Above all, they hitched the East German chariot to the Russian war-horse. The treaty stipulated that in the event of an armed attack by a third state or any group of states upon one of the contracting parties the other would lend all military aid to its partner. This could mean East German involvement in a Middle Eastern or a Sino-Soviet war.

PART XV
THE CRISES OF GERMAN CULTURE

Chapter 56

ARTS AND SCIENCE

The Chaos of Thought
after the Armistice, 1918

War World I was a traumatic experience for a nation that had not lost a major war in a hundred years. The shock was augmented by the fact that Germany was for some years after 1918 treated as a pariah. All the gloomy prophecies of the heralds of doom—Langbehn, Stefan George, Wagner, Keyserling, Dilthey, Nietzsche, de Lagarde, Moeller van den Bruck, Rilke, and Spengler—seemed to have been vindicated by the collapse of the Second Empire. The magnitude of Germany's defeat would alone have sufficed to have enveloped the national mind in confusion. But the defeat was accompanied by destruction of the monarchies, the displacement of the nobility by the bourgeoisie, and the rapid rise of the common man. Political philosophy, mores, social values, and even styles were revolutionized on the grand scale as a result of the advent of a novel system of democratic beliefs.

It added to the chaos of values that not only had the French political model of 1875 been widely established east of the Rhine and in the Balkans, but the first avowedly all-workers' state in history had been established in Russia. Many Germans were obsessed with the thought that European, no less than German, hegemony had been overthrown. What would now become of a world that was no longer subject to the West? The pathological condition of the postwar German mind was also partly the result of the corrosion of the classical canons of art, music, science, thought, and literature.

Painting

As was the case with French, Italian, and British painting in the twentieth century, German art spun around in the cascade and whirlpools that mark the end of a civilization. The confused rise and fall of post-impressionism, symbolism, Dadaism, pointism, abstractionism, cubism, surrealism, futurism, and other "isms" only mirrored the universal disintegration of olden systems and truths. The intellectual individualism of existentialist philosophy, the demonic expressionism of modern literature, and the indeterminism of the new physics found their natural counterpart in a subjectivist-relativist anarchy of art.

Almost all German painters, including the Dresden *Brücke* ("bridge") group, could trace their new-found individualism back to Van Gogh, Cézanne, or Gauguin. However, the common ancestry was soon obscured by a variety of tendencies. German artists variously strove to dissolve reality into formless dreams, reduce it to geometric solid components, discover radical new media of expression without regard to beauty, or achieve a senseless, absolute "anti-art," the complement of their assault upon "convention."

The *Brücke* circle of Dresden artists was the first important twentieth-century school of German painting. Strongly influenced by the French Fauves ("wild ones")—Henri Matisse, Georges Rouault, Georges Braque, and André Derain, the *Brücke* brushmen cultivated clear, primitive, virile lines and a disquieting use of unmixed colors. The school's foremost representatives—Emil Nolde (1867–1956), Max Beckmann (1884–1950), and Oskar Kokoschka (1886–   )—were all destined for eminence. Nolde, who was of rugged peasant stock, was famed for the stark purity of his colors, especially in his still lifes. Nolde sketched expressionistic landscapes that were less visions than elemental experiences of earth and sky. Beckmann, who was driven into exile by the Nazis, evolved into a desperate expressionist whose paintings suggested nightmares but whose chief work, a Gothic triptych, *Departure* (1932–35), was a haunting symbolist indictment of Nazism. Kokoschka, a Danubian-Austrian, soon dissociated himself from any school of art, but became possibly the most important artist of the mid-twentieth century. Rejecting the flat, solid style and unmixed colors that had attracted him in his younger years, Kokoschka developed a highly unique, integrative technique that united the legacy of the past with the anxieties and mobility of the present. A master colorist of the format of Titian, Lorraine, and Renoir, Kokoschka painted opulent landscapes, such as those of the Isar and Linz. His triptych at the University of Heidelberg, the *Battle of Thermopylae,* stands as a monument on the grave of a dead civilization of which he was basically a spiritual part.

Der blaue Reiter ("the blue horseman") school of Munich brought German art into line with the subjectivist mood of the Weimar period. The Russian-born Wassily Kandinsky (1866–1944), the school's foremost representative, made war on the geometrical, objective world. He rejected linear depiction outright, striving to reduce reality to simple fundamentals expressed in terms of stark colors or abstract internal rhythms.

While in the Weimar period expressionism found staunch champions in Karl Schmidt-Rottluf (1884–1976), Willy Jaeckel (1888–1944), Hans Baluschek (1870–1935), and, of course, Kokoschka, it had to run stiff competition from Dadaism. Initially associated with the planless, confused canvasses of Marcel Duchamp, Dadaism invaded Germany from France. Max Ernst (1891–1976) collaborated with Hans Arp (1887–1966) to found the Cologne Dada group in 1919. Above all others, Ernst introduced the fantastic psychedelic style into Germany and pioneered in collage and frottage. Among the post-World War II painters who were still influenced by his tenebrous, magical style were Georg Meistermann, E. W. Nay, Willi Baumeister, and Fritz Winter. All of them appealed to the subconscious with dream themes and unrealistic colors.

Another influence that derived from France was cubism. It had begun its course under the influence of Picasso and Braque before World War II. The unrealistic geometrical forms and chaotic, angular and diagonal vagaries of cubist painting found German interpreters in Georg Grosz (1893–1959) and the part-Swiss Paul Klee (1879–1940) of the Dessau *Bauhaus*. Klee, who had worked in Dessau with Kandinsky and Feininger, was more successful than Grosz. Critics who affect to see in Klee's canvases a contrapuntal balance of imagination, line, and color regard him as one of the twentieth century's leading artists. Klee's ostensibly childlike, ideographic paintings, such as the famous *Twittering Machine*, prepared the way for the "naive" school, whose disciples (e.g., H. L. Spegg, Kurt Mühlenhaupt, Manfred Söhl, Klaus Riedel, Johann Riedel, Hilke Hendewerk, Lucie Frassa, and Sofia Erkens) strove to capture the public's favor with a primitive, imagist type of representation, at once grotesque and simplistic.

During the 1960s pop art, an omnibus plastic style that embraced all media and all creation beyond the traditional bounds of painting and architecture, made its way into Germany from New York. Many exhibitions were devoted to the new pop art. In the late 1960s and 1970s there followed new types of objective art, photo-realistic art, antiart, and kinetic art, most of which was spiritually impoverished, was avowedly in tutelage to science and technology, or even repudiated art as basically superfluous in a materialistic society. A good deal of it partook of the youthful spirit of rebellion that had been unleashed by student demonstrations in the USA and Paris in the late 1960s or by the invasion of Czechoslovakia in 1968 and the failure of the western powers to come to her aid. Among the exemplars of the recent antiexpressionistic, hard edge, or kinetic art, which devotes attention to minute detail and is inspired with a scientific-theoretical dialectic, are C. Boltanski, Gerhard Richter, Franz-Erhard Walther, Klaus Rinke, Werner Hilsing, and Hans Troekes. By 1977 the most active and prolific of the newer artists were gravitating toward Troekes and his *Die neue Gruppe* ("the new group").

Sculpture and Architecture

In the post-World War I era German sculpture lost its affinity for form and content. Talent sought simply to extract from its material its quintessence without regard to the accidents of externality. Influenced by Constantin Brancusi and the metallic "tubist" ideas of Fernand Léger, Germans such as Hans Arp and Bernhard Heiliger and the Austrian Fritz Wotruba created a plastic art that did not so much mold as it was molded by its medium.

Of course, there were always some sculptors who bucked the current or shot off in singular directions. Such was the case with Ernst Berlach (1870–1938), Wilhelm Lehmbruck (1881–1919), and Gerhard Marcks (1889–   ). The first two depicted in crude pseudo-Gothic style the drives and emotions of human beings who are molded by elemental forces beyond their control. Marcks, who came from Berlin, sought in some of the most powerful of modern German sculptured pieces to emphasize Spartan, purist, and stylized line.

Twentieth-century German architectural concepts had relatively marked influence upon the evolution of an international *Baustil* ("structural style"). One of the precursors of the glass-house architects of most recent times was Bruno Taut (1880–1938). However, it was Walter Gropius (1883–1969) whose ideas best synchronized with the vision of the great foreign pioneers of modernism—

Frank Lloyd Wright and the Dutchman Gerrit Rietveld. Gropius, the guiding star of the Dessau *Bauhaus* of composite art, developed a group of glass and steel structures both cubist and functional, admitting and reflecting light. Both in Germany and later in England, Gropius did more than any one else to spread the first global architectural style.

When Hitler came to power Gropius and another eminent *Bauhaus* colleague, Mies van der Rohe (1887–1969), emigrated to the USA, where they successfully continued their work. In the Third Reich their style went out of favor and was superseded by the grandiose, ponderous conceptions of Albert Speer. Similarly the sculpture of the Third Reich was dominated by the delineator of noble Nordic countenances, Georg Kolbe (1877–1947). Kolbe, who had been influenced by Rodin and had in his youth shown great promise, lent his art to racist ends. His mannerist figures were severe and simple in conception and for stylization recalled Egyptian sculpture.

A post-World War II Germany that was in urgent need of new buildings of all kinds was receptive to the "modern *(Baustil)* international style." Cubist, functional structures allegedly erected with regard to the composite requirements of urban living sprang up in every big city of the FRG or GDR. By the late 1960s German architects, infatuated with the potentialities of the twentieth-century *Baustil*, were striving to anticipate rather than follow urban developments. New composite apartment complexes, such as the Märkisches Viertel in Berlin, Hamburg-Osdorf, Frankfurt's northwest section, the Neue Vahr in Bremen, and Perlach in Munich are representative of the effort to accommodate a growing compression of population with conventional constructional materials assembled in unconventional manner. Among the later-twentieth-century exemplars of the international architectural style are Johannes Ludwig, Otto Bartning, Stefan Leuer, Olaf Gulbransson, Karl Band, and Siegfried Östreicher. Their efforts have also been extended by Dominikus Böhm, Emil Steffan, and O. Dörzbach to Catholic and Protestant church architecture, where lavishly ornamented, stained glass churches have been superseded by simple and even barren structures which for horizontality suggest clubhouses. However, the willingness of German religious communities to commission the building of plain or even austere edifices that are supposed to promote concentration upon the liturgy rather than decor has not filled the churches. Similarly, satisfaction with the mammoth, high-rise apartment and office buildings is far from general, for they blot out the hills and sky and sadden the soul. German architects have recently tried to counter this objection by building structures that take more imaginative advantage of terrain.

Music

All the spiritual torment and travail of the turbulent post-World War I era were reflected in the impoverishment and inconsonance of German expressionistic music. Rarely did the composer seek to charm with melody or rhapsodic waves of tonal color. Rather he often used shock treatment on his audience by developing greatly magnified intensities or cacophonous effects through the use of horns and percussion. The next step was atonality—complete disregard of symmetrical rhythmic patterns but with augmented friction and dissonance. While the Nazi interlude represented a break in this continuity, the music that was tolerated by Professor Peter Raabe's Reichsmusikkammer (National Chamber of Music) was, by contrast, only vapid, enfeebled, and retrograde. The only exceptions to the rule of mediocrity were the aging Richard Strauss (1864–1949), who in Nazi times composed *Die schweigsame Frau (The Silent Woman*, 1935) and *Daphne* (1938), and Carl Orff (1895–   ). Following World War II, composers sought to rebuild the bridge to the permissive Weimar era. They declared their emancipation from voice and lengthy melody and strove to achieve unemotional musical montages that only occasionally displayed diatonic tonal harmonies. In place of euphony or passion, German composers thenceforth stressed orchestral structure and horizontal counterpoint like that of the eighteenth century but without classical rhythms.

After World War I three German composers, above others, successfully spread the gospel of modern music: Arnold Schoenberg (1874–1951), Alban Berg (1885–1935), and Paul Hindemith (1895–1963). Schoenberg, a Viennese Jew who became a Catholic convert, attempted to revolutionize composition by eliminating tonality and keys and introducing a radical twelve-tone scale. His many abstract, atonal works were replete with unbearably tense, serial cacophony and bewildering rocketing and plummeting from one octave to another. Schoenberg left Germany after the Nazi seizure of power and resettled in Los Angeles. Berg, a student of Schoenberg, made his initial mark with his expressionistic opera *Wozzeck* (1925), which was based on Büchner's play *Woyzeck* (1837). When Berg's dodecaphonic atonal music, like that of Schoenberg, was banned from the Third Reich, Berg went to the USA, where he lived to write at least the twelve-tone opera *Lulu*. Hindemith was from every standpoint the most significant figure in post-World War I German music. Together with Kurt Weill, Ernst Krenek, and Hans Eisler, he founded the *Gebrauchsmusik* ("functional music") school. After his initial triumph, the song cycle *Das Marienleben (Life of Mary*, 1923), which involved a novel harmonic system with complex chords, came the expressionistic opera *Cardilla* (1926). After 1934 he became enamored of Renaissance and baroque melodies and increasingly apostasized from atonality. In true melodic tradition, in works such as the intensely Germanic *Mathis der Mahler (Matthias the Artist*, 1934) symphony, he united neoclassicist with neoromantic forms, while staying within the bounds of tonality. Having fallen under the displeasure of the Nazis, he left for America in 1939, where he spent the next thirteen years mainly as professor of musical theory at Yale. In 1952 he returned to Europe to become professor of musical theory at Zurich, where he wrote the opera about Kepler and Wallenstein, *Die Harmonie der Welt (Harmony of the World*, 1958), which exhibited his phenomenal mastery of polyphony.

Among other pioneers of the atonal dodecaphonic instrumental composition were: the two Viennese musicians Anton von Webern (1883–1945) and Karl-

Heinz Stockhausen (1928–   ), the latter of whom has written eleven operas and five symphonies; and the Dessau composer Kurt Weill (1900–50), whose opera, *Der Protagonist* (1926), won the acclaim of the critics. Weill also collaborated with Bertold Brecht to write the universally successful *Dreigroschenoper (Three-Penny Opera, 1928)*, which was based on Gay's *The Beggar's Opera* (1728). After emigrating from Germany in 1933 Weill eventually came to the USA, where he composed the music for many successful Broadway productions. More important than any of the foregoing and only a little less distinguished than Hindemith was Carl Orff. He wrote purely melodic, rhythmic, but primitivist percussion pieces, such as the ballet opera *Carmina burana* (1936) and the folklore operas *Der Mond (The Moon*, 1939*)* and *Die Kluge (The Wise Woman*, 1943*)*, or the thematically classical *Antigone* (1949).

Although after 1948 opera entered decline in the Germanies it still attracted the talents of a number of composers, among them Giselher Klebe (1925–   ), *Die Rauber (The Robbers*, 1958*)* and *Jacobowsky und der Oberst (Jacobowsky and the Colonel*, 1966*);* Berndt Zimmermann, whose *The Soldiers* (1965) may be the best German opera since *Wozzeck;* the older Werner Egk (1901–   ), a master of iridescent orchestral compositions and of nostalgic operas such as *The Irish Legend* (1955); Aribert Reimann (1936–   ), who is known for his requiem, *Wolkenloses Christfest (Cloudless Nativity);* and Mauricio Kagel, who has attempted to write an "anti-opera" entitled *State Theater* (1971), which endeavors to draw the audience into participation. In East Germany the most noteworthy operatic composer has been Paul Dessau (1894–   ), who has four operas to his credit, the latest of which *(Einstein)* achieved resounding success in 1974 in East Berlin. Of course the older, classic operas of the eighteenth and nineteenth centuries continued to have their devotees. The fact that Wagner continued to have considerable appeal in post-Hitlerian Germany was in some measure due to the original staging of his operas by his grandson Wieland Wagner (1917–1966), who for fifteen years before his death strove to make of Bayreuth the center of modern interpretations of Wagnerian opera. The emphasis given to staging at Bayreuth had marked influence upon the development of opera throughout the Federal German Republic, where by 1977 the tendency in production was more and more to transform opera into musical theater, a composite vehicle in which the accent was even more upon scenery and staging than upon voice.

Science

In 1914 Germans commonly stood in the foremost files in almost all fields of scientific research. The ensuing thirty-five years, which were often lean ones financially, witnessed a general decline in the volume, diversity, and importance of German scientific contributions.

After World War I it was not until the Dawes and other international loans began to arrive in the Weimar Republic that the laboratories again began to function normally. The years 1924–33 saw the revival of the Kaiser Wilhelm Institute in

Berlin and of the laboratories of the universities of Göttingen, Munich, Hamburg, Heidelberg, Marburg, and Tübingen, as well as those of such firms as A. E. G., I. G. Farben, and Bayer A. G. By 1932 German science was so far restored that the Nobel Prize in physics was conferred upon the 31-year-old Werner Heisenberg (1901–76) of the University of Würzburg, the youngest man ever to receive it.

Although the emigration after 1933 of about one-third of Germany's scientists had a debilitating effect upon basic research in the Third Reich, it would be wrong to exaggerate the degree of decline. Many first-rate scientists continued their research under Hitler. If Einstein, Lisa Meitner, and Wolfgang Pauli emigrated, others—Weiszäcker, Butenandt, Domagk, Hahn, Schrödinger, Strassmann, von Laue, Bayer, and Warburg—chose to remain behind.

During the Nazi era Nobel prizes were awarded to a number of German scientists: Erwin Schrödinger (1887–1961) for his work in quantum wave mechanics; the 36-year-old Adolf Butenandt (1903–   ), of the Kaiser Wilhelm (now Max Planck) Institute of Bio-Chemistry in Tübingen, for his pioneer research into the nature and properties of sex hormones; Gerhard Domagk (1895–1964), professor of chemistry at Münster, for epochal achievements in the field of sulfanilamide therapy; Otto Hahn (1879–1968), director of the Kaiser Wilhelm Institute for Physical Chemistry in Berlin, for having in 1939 been the first to split the uranium atom.

After World War II many eminent scientists were interned by the Allies for a time. However, by 1948 a number of savants, headed by Heisenberg and Max Born (1883–1970), took the lead in reestablishing the bombed-out and half-ruined scientific institutes and laboratories. Chief among those that were restored were the Max Planck Society for the Advancement of Science and the Endowed Association for German Science. Nevertheless certain types of research were long handicapped by foreign occupation, lack of funds, and either lack of interest or actual prohibitions. Not until 1961, when the 31-year-old R. L. Mossbauer of Munich received the Nobel Prize for his discovery of the effects of gravitational shifts, did West Germany again become competitive in science.

The era after World War I was a time of remarkable German contributions to the formulation of a new theory of the universe. Philipp Lenard (1862–1917), director of Heidelberg's Radiological Institute, was doing his Nobel-Prize-winning work on cathode rays. Max von Laue (1879–1962), of the University of Frankfurt, was discovering that crystals can diffract x-rays and was thereby paving the way for solid-state physics. Einstein of Zurich was working out those equations which, based on a theory of the union of space and time, were to demonstrate the curvature of space-time in proximity to matter, and he was developing his general theory of relativity, equally applicable to systems of uniform or accelerated motion. In 1918 Otto Hahn, of the Kaiser Wilhelm Institute for Physical Chemistry, was, in collaboration with Fritz Strassmann and Lisa Meitner, discovering protoactinium and doing pioneer research on elements beyond uranium. In 1919 Arnold Summerfeld of Munich was laying the foundations of dualistic, wave-particle mechanics. In the mid-1920s Wolfgang Pauli (1900–1958), Austrian physicist at Hamburg, was doing the basic work in nuclear magnetism that made possible the eventual discovery of the meson.

Among the German scientists of the Weimar era Heisenberg was second in importance only to Einstein as an architect of the new model universe that replaced the Newtonian. By 1925 Heisenberg had developed a purely mathematical quantum mechanics that brought to fruition the work of many predecessors. He had come to reject the contemporary view that the orbits of electrons were either regular or stable. In 1928 he discovered the origins of magnetic molecular fields and concluded that in a relativistic universe it was impossible to determine simultaneously with accuracy the position and velocity of a quantum. This principle of indeterminacy *(Unschärferelation)* led him to the belief that there were no certain points of departure or arrival, let alone movement, in the cosmos. This concept had an extraordinary impact upon modern outlooks in many fields of thought and can be regarded as the source of the notion that God has gambled with the universe. Schrödinger modified Heisenberg's theory by suggesting that the subatomic system was not a stream of particles but a continuous wavelike cloud of electrical quanta moving in irregular, often rosettelike, wavering orbits about the nucleus. Summerfeld of Munich subsequently modified Schrödinger's concept in the direction of erratic elliptical orbits. The culminating achievement of this progression in thought was Einstein's unitary or unified field theory (1929), a mathematically elegant synthesis of macrocosm and microcosm, of the phenomena of the space-time universe with those of the submaterial world. Einstein further refined his theory while working at the Institute for Advanced Studies in Princeton, New Jersey.

One consequence of this animated research and theorizing was Carl Friedrich von Weizsäcker's (1912–) conversion of hydrogen into helium (1938). Another was Hahn's demonstration of nuclear fission (1939). That Hahn's discovery did not lead to Germany's being the first to develop the atomic bomb was partly due to the fact that the humane Heisenberg would not adopt Houtmann's suggestion to build a uranium pile for military purposes.

While the physicists were reconstructing Newton's universe, advances were being made in mathematics by David Hilbert (1862–1943), professor at Göttingen, and by Kurt Gödel (1906–), the mathematical logician who in 1931 extended Heisenberg's law of uncertainty to mathematics. In the same year M. Knoll and E. Ruska built the first microscope to operate by means of a beam of electrons, thereby making possible direct observation of biological ultrastructures. In astronomy the Hamburg professor Weiszäcker formulated a revolutionary theory of the origins of the solar system, while the *Astronomische Gesellschaft* published valuable stellar catalogues, among them the AGK3 (1964), which described the proper motions of 180,000 stars.

In the biological sciences Otto Warburg (1883–1970), a recipient of the Nobel Prize in 1931, did outstanding work on metabolic cell processes and the catalyzing of oxidation. In 1934 Butenandt and Wintersteiner crystallized the sex hormone progesterone, and Butenandt succeeded in partially synthesizing it. Heberer and Schindewolf suggested exciting modifications to the theory of evolution. M. Künitz worked fruitfully with the crystallization of enzymes, while Heitz, Möbius, Moewus, and Hartmann made advances in botany.

One of the greatest chemical breakthroughs of the century was Otto Bayer's discovery in 1937 of polyurethane, a light polymer, which heralded the synthetic textile and plastic industry. Working for I. G. Farbenindustrie, K. Freudenberg made advances in stereochemistry. With financial aid from Farbwerke Hoechst, Mietsch and Klarer worked with Domagk for many years finally to evolve effective sulfanilomide drugs, among them Domagk's protonsil and Tb I.

All of this scientific research in many fields was greatly encouraged by the establishment in 1948 of the Max Planck Institute in Göttingen, with its physical scientific, chemical, and biological subdivisions and its daughter and affiliated institutions located in many German cities. Heisenberg was its first director. Dividing his time between administration and research, he was by the early 1970s coming ever closer to discovering that superb, clear formula that would in a single equation explain the harmonious workings of heaven and earth, which once Newton and Kepler erroneously thought they had conceived.

By the mid-1970s international recognition had been accorded to many contemporary German scientists, while the Federal Republic was itself helping to fund the research of scientists in many European countries. Thus, for example, in 1973 the FRG contributed 122 million Marks for the financing of research work by the European Organization for Nuclear Research in Geneva, an institution that among other tasks was trying to build a super proton accelerator 7 kilometers in circumference for experiments with high-energy and elementary particles. Among the myriad significant German scientists who were at work in the FRG by 1977 some of the most effective were Rudolf Scherhag, the first German since the war to receive the International Meteorological Prize; Victor Weisskopf in physics; Konrad Lorenz, director of the Max Planck Institute for Nautical Science, for his contributions in animal psychology; Hermann Schildknecht of Heidelberg for his research on the defense mechanisms of insects and plants; Karl Heinz Stegerwald for his invention of the Stegerwald gun or cannon, which, charged with kinetic energy, can by means of a beam of bundled electrons accomplish all manner of complicated jobs; and Wilhelm Mühlbauer of Munich, a surgeon who discovered a method of suturing with the aid of magnetic coils. Clearly, West German science, resting upon hundreds of comparable or only less important contributions, was by the later-1970s again marching in the front files of the international scientific army.

Chapter 57

HIGHER THOUGHT AND LITERATURE

The Twentieth-Century Anarchy of Values

All the doubts and anxiety that had been evoked by the orchidaceous growth of capitalism and the state before 1914 were aggravated by war and revolution in the twentieth century. By the time the cannon ceased firing in 1918 the optimism of the nineteenth century lay buried beneath a mountain of rubble. In the Weimar era scientific indeterminism, which was antipodal to Marxian determinism, sapped belief in absolutes and utopias. Freud's discoveries bewildered many by revealing that human behavior could not be charted by reason and objective science alone. The Great Depression caused millions of people to reject the economic postulates of rugged individualism and compounded the anarchy of thought that the German philosopher Ernst Cassirer (1874–1945) considered to be a chronic condition of the new age. During the span 1918–33 the wholesale repudiation of the "wisdom" of the past produced not only moods of somber fatalism but of hectic iconoclasm too. In place of the older unities was set a hydra-headed subjectivism, as indefinite in its message as it was depressing in its implication of the purposelessness of existence. The new pessimistic, nihilistic attitude, which is commonly associated with the transition from one civilization to another, was reflected in every chamber of German art and thought.

The erosion of European civilization, which had been charted in the cyclical-morphological philosophy of Oswald Spengler (1880–1936), was mirrored in the writings of many post-World War I German thinkers. It was to be found in the racism and *völkisch* mysticism of Alfred Rosenberg and Moeller van den Bruck, the revolutionary Marxist testament of Rosa Luxemburg, the relativistic "logical positivism" of the University of Vienna circle of philosophers (Ludwig Wittgenstein, Felix Kaufmann, Otto Neurath, Rudolf Carnap, and Hans Reichenbach), the expressionistic dicta of the theologian Paul Tillich (1886–1965), the "collective subconscious" analytic psychology of Carl Jung (1875–1961), and the Christian existentialism disseminated by neo-orthodox Protestant theologians such as Karl Barth (1886–1968), Emil Brunner (1889–1966) of Zurich, and Rudolf K. Bultmann (1884–1976). Most of all, scientific relativism was reflected in the anti-Christian existentialist philosophy of Karl Jaspers (1883–1969) of Basel and Martin Heidegger (1889–1976), who argued that there were as many varieties of truth as there are beings to conceive them.

Social Sciences

During the period of the Weimar Republic the humanistic and philosophical faculties of the major German universities of Germany were still dominated by conservative professors from the Second Empire, almost all of whom were nationalists and opposed to the new subversive or corrosive ideas. During the Nazi period the racist nationalism of Hitler and Rosenberg and the anti-individualist philosophy of their sympathizer Heidegger favored the psychological integration of the German nation. Whether or not Hermann Rauschning is justified in affirming in his *Revolution of Nihilism* (1939) that Hitler did not possess any integrative, constructive concept at all, the fact remains that the fall of the Third Reich dealt a blow to the German nationalist tradition.

After 1945 the statist views of the sociologist Max Weber and the historians Hans Delbrück, Hermann Oncken, Erich Marcks, Max Lenz, A. O. Meyer, Dietrich Schäfer, Adalbert Wahl, and Walter Kienast were shelved or, as in the case of Friedrich Meinecke and Gerhard Ritter, modified to suit the changing times. Not even the democratic views of Veit Valentin, Theodor Schieder, Johannes Ziekursch, Franz Schnabel, Hermann Kantorowicz, or Walter Goetz escaped attack. All these historians were presumably "tainted" by their endorsement of questionable features of the German past. The denigration of German nationalism was greatly aided by the rise of a monistic political philosophy in East Germany. Marxist ideologues did not miss an opportunity to shovel earth on the idea of a united Germany within a European community. East German historians, such as Werner Berthold, Fritz Klein, Karl Leidigkeit, Horst Bartel, and Leo Stern pilloried the Federal German Republic and vied with the Hamburg school of Fritz Fischer, Immanuel Geiss, and Werner Basler in linking the nationalist tradition with perennially "aggressive" and "militaristic" German policy aims.

In the Weimar era Sigmund Freud continued to make an important contribution to the stream of western culture. His profoundly philosophic *Die Zukunft einer Illusion (The Future of an Illusion,* 1927) and *Das Unbehagen in der Kultur (Uneasiness in Culture,* 1930) augmented his already great fame. Werner Sombart (1863–1941), the immensely erudite political economist, continued to explore socialistic alternatives to Marxism-Leninism. His *Modern Capitalism,* volume III (1928), was hailed as the most important critique of free enterprise since *Das Kapital.* Max Weber (1864–1920), the Heidelberg sociologist, died soon after the war, but his younger brother Alfred (1868–1958) was a cosmopolitan thinker who was destined to be regarded as the Nestor of German sociologists. Carrying on the tradition of Sombart, Franz Oppenheimer (1864–1943), and Ernst Troeltsch (1865–1923), Alfred Weber hypothecated that civilizations progress steadily upward, through crises, toward higher goals expressed in terms of syncretic patterns of basic experiences. His most influential work was his *Cultural History as Cultural Sociology* (1935), but the magnum opus of his old age was *Der dritte oder der vierte Mensch. Vom Sinn des geschichtlichen Daseins (The Third or Fourth Human Being. Concerning the Meaning of Historical Existence),* in which he affected to discover against a background of coequal races four basic historical types of man.

In historiography Friedrich Meinecke (1862–1954), the founder of intellectual history and author of the celebrated prewar *Weltbürgertum und Nationalstaat,* was the Thucydides of his day. In the Weimar period his best work was the widely read *Die Idee der Staatsräson in der neueren Geschichte (The Concept of Reason of State in Modern History*, 1924), which affirmed that *Realpolitik*, subject to ethical limits, had always been the method of grand politics. Meinecke's historical relativist philosophy found expression in another masterpiece, *Die Entstehung des Historismus (The Rise of Historicism*, 1936), which analyzed the extent to which the history of a given nation is governed by immutable laws peculiar to itself.

While none of the post-World War II German historians was in a class with Ranke or Theodor Mommsen, there were many able and prolific scholars. There was a greater outpouring of monographic literature than ever before, and much of it emphasized novel sociological, economic, and interest or pressure group approaches to an understanding of grand movements and policies. Among a large confraternity of historians some of the most influential were: Ludwig Dehio, Günther Franz, M. Braubach, Franz Schnabel, Johannes Bühler, A. Hauck, Karl D. Bracher, Friedrich Haselmayr, H. W. Bechtel, the emigré Erich Eyck, Golo Mann, Hans Herzfeld, P. E. Schramm, Friedrich Heer, Fritz Fischer, Rudolf Morsey, Michael Stürmer, Gerhard Ritter, and Gerhard A. Ritter.

When Meinecke died, the mantle of doyen of the profession fell upon the shoulders of Professor Gerhard Ritter (1888–1967) of the University of Freiburg i. Br., a savant whose works ranged over German history from late medieval to modern times. After the war Ritter, who had opposed Nazi Walther Frank's Reichsinstitut of History and had been a member of Goerdeler's Resistance Movement, undertook the thankless task of rehabilitating German nationalism. To this end was written his magnum opus, the *Staatskunst und Kriegshandwerk* (4 vols., 1954–68, translated as *The Sword and the Scepter*). Ritter's emphasis upon the gradual separation of military from civil power in the Second Reich and his defense of the moderate nature of the grand policy of Bethmann-Hollweg were the perspectives of a preeminently political historian. Ritter's approach and conclusions were rejected by Fritz Fischer (1908–   ) of the University of Hamburg. He and his students (Immanuel Geiss and Werner Basler) launched a heavy attack upon Ritter with the aim of establishing that economic and internal pressures were paramount influences upon the formulation of German foreign policy in the periods before and during World Wars I and II. The Hamburg school also sought to show that, as respects the nature and scope of German foreign policy and annexationist aims, there was a continuity between Bethmann, Ludendorf, and Hitler and that cardinal war guilt in 1914 must be assigned to the German government, concepts that have failed to gain unqualified or even sympathetic acceptance from historians such as E. von Vietsch, Karl D. Erdmann, Hans Herzfeld, Golo Mann, Wolfgang Steglich, and W. J. Mommsen. However, the unremitting debate over the Fischer theses, which continued even after Ritter's death, opened up fertile new historical approaches and revived the Kehrite hypothesis, applied to several phases of modern German history, of the primacy of domestic over foreign policy, a view that owed much to twentieth-century Marxist examples.

Philosophy and Theology

Ritter's colleague at Freiburg, Martin Heidegger (1889–1976), was the principal expositor of existentialism in Germany in the twentieth century. Heidegger, breaking with such traditionalist philosophers as Edmund Husserl (1859–1938) and Max Horkheimer (1895–1973), contended that the whole course of western metaphysics from Plato to Nietzsche had been in error, for the reason that it had concentrated upon the problem of becoming rather than being. Elaborating a functional and positivist philosophy, Heidegger summoned man to abandon passivity and pursue his conception of being in accordance with his own scheme of values so that he might impart meaning to his existence. Heidegger's message was most persuasively stated in his *Sein und Zeit (Existence and Being*, 1949*)* and later works such as *Vom Wesen der Wahrheit (The Essence of Truth)* and *What is Philosophy?*

Karl Jaspers (1883–1969), another existentialist, has had greater appeal than Heidegger because the former, unlike the latter, has admitted the collective guilt of the German people for the crimes of the Nazis. Sharing the common fund of beliefs that were harbored by Heidegger and the French existentialists Jean Paul Sartre and Gabriel Marcel, the Basel Professor Jaspers rejected the idea that there are universal truths and drew the conclusion, which encouraged license and hedonism, that in the end absolute death, failure, and futility await every individual. His gloomy ratiocination was most clearly presented in his *Von der Wahrheit (The Way to Wisdom*, 1951*)*.

In theology Karl Barth (1886–1968), a conservative thinker, has exercised noteworthy influence upon modern German Protestantism. Like Rudolf Bultmann and Paul Tillich, Barth was a neo-orthodox Christian existentialist. Because he believed as Søren Kierkegaard had, that man was hopelessly defiled by original sin and could achieve nothing, least of all salvation, without the help of God, Barth experienced difficulty in reconciling the image of insignificant man with the existentialist gospel of the efficacy of self. Heidegger, Jaspers, Bultmann, Tillich, and Barth, no more than Freud and Nietzsche, were able to lead the German people to paradise because they themselves did not know the way.

German Literature under Weimar

As the leading literary school of many during the Weimar Republic, expressionism tried to portray in manifold ways the conflict of the individual, of the "I" *(ich)*, with its environment and with the image of it that society has conceived. Expressionist writers rejected traditional forms, rules, terminology, and nomenclature as being no longer appropriate to the tasks of modern literature. They invented a new syntax, diction, symbolism, and manner of narration. Expressionist poems, plays, and novels put heavy demands upon the public, which had great difficulty comprehending their unorthodox syntax, orthography, diction, montages, abstractions, and morbid philosophizing.

Not till the late 1920s was the dominance of expressionism challenged. Then neorealism or objectivism *(Neue Sachlichkeit)* displaced it. Neorealists, often preoccupied with carnal sexual desires, closely examined the relationship of the individual to his milieu and his alienation from society and self. Inasmuch as postaristocratic society in Weimar Germany was basically bourgeois in *Weltanschauung*, this contrapuntal treatment of man and society involved either an implied or actual repudiation of middle-class mores.

Poetry and Drama

Expressionist poetry, which was no longer poetry in the conventional sense, was usually so abstruse as to have little appeal for the masses. What attractions it did have were generated chiefly from its absorption with sex or revolution. The expressionists had to their own satisfaction substituted a new deity for the Christian God, who had been destroyed by Nietzsche. Their deity was woman, the eternal ''she.'' Among the high priests of the new cult were: Richard Dehmel (1863–1920), a brilliant, passionate lyricist who in his *Aber die Liebe (And Yet, Love,* 1893) had done more than any other German poet to anoint sex with chrism; Stefan George (1868–1933), whose *Der Stern des Bundes (Star of the Alliance,* 1914) extolled feminine beauty and whose *Der Dichter in Zeiten der Wirren (The Poet in Times of Confusion,* 1921) and *Das neue Reich (The New Empire,* 1929) eulogized the spiritual ''mission'' of the German people and predicted the advent of a new people's state; and Rainer Maria Rilke (1875–1926), one of the finest poets in the history of the nation, who wrote piercingly beautiful, warmly mystical lyric poetry, such as his *Sonnets to Orpheus* (1923) and *Duino Elegies* (1912), that declared that the great transfiguring force in the human struggle against the materialist world is love.

Expressionist drama had been inaugurated in prewar years with Gerhard Hauptmann's *Und Pippa tanzt* (1906). The new vogue enjoyed the widest popularity of all dramatic styles in the Weimar Republic. The heir of Dostoevsky, Freud, and the French symbolists, expressionism was strongly encouraged by Max Reinhardt (1873–1948), founder of the Grosses Schauspielhaus (Great Theater) and director of the Berlin Deutsches Theater. He divided his attention between gorgeously staging the works of classical international masters and producing the plays of modern expressionists, such as Arthur Schnitzler (1862–1931), Richard Beer-Hoffmann (1866–1945), Hugo von Hofmannsthal (1874–1929), Fritz von Unruh (1885–1971), Walter Hasenclever (1890–1940), and Bertold Brecht (1898–1956).

Typical of expressionist drama were Hasenclever's *Jenseits (Beyond,* 1920) and *Gobseck* (1921). Perhaps Brecht was the most successful apostle of the new genre. The shocking language employed in his *Trommeln in der Nacht (Drums in the Night,* 1918–20) and his stark treatment of human bondage in his *Im Dickicht der Städte (In the Jungle of the Cities,* 1924), exercised considerable influence upon the development not only of German drama in the 1920s but of drama in the USA, to which he migrated in the 1930s.

The pacifist and egalitarian tendencies that distinguished the left wing of Weimar expressionism was typified in the plays of Georg Kaiser (1867–1945). His *Von*

Morgens bis Mitternachts (From Morning to Midnight, 1916*),* which indicted capitalistic materialism and militarism, was followed by his celebrated trilogy *Die Koralle—The Corral* (1917), *Gas I* (1918), and *Gas II* (1920)—which, with striking theatrical effects, delineated the inhumanity of an inequitable social order, and by his revolutionary-minded *A Day in October* (1928). In the late 1920s this relentless concern with social justice led to a brief reign of objective or factual drama *(Die neue Sachlichkeit),* a form exemplified by the plays of Hans Rehfisch, Max Rohr, and Paul Kornfeld. On the other hand, Fritz von Unruh exhorted his contemporaries in such pieces as *Heinrich von Andernach* (1925) to return to a deindustrialized, communal society.

The Novel through Two Wars

The extraordinary rise in literacy accompanying the advent of democracy, coupled with a vulgarization of taste, determined that the novel would be the most popular form of literature in the post-World War I era.

Among the most significant novelists who were carryovers from the Second Empire and in Weimar times worked in symbolist, psychoanalytical, or expressionistic media, the greatest were the Swabian Hermann Hesse (1877–1962) and the Lübeck-born Thomas Mann (1875–1955).

Hesse, who had suffered acute mental stress during the war and had been restored to health only by Jung's methods, wrote a series of psychoanalytical novels between 1915 and 1919. An avant-garde experimentalist who must be ranked with André Gide, Hesse in 1927 entered the wastes of surrealism with his *Der Steppenwolf (Wolf of the Steppes),* which was a novel of unusual intensity that minutely explored schizophrenia in the chaotic personality of the hero, Harry Haller. Hesse's impressionistic-symbolistic novel of medieval monasticism *Narziss und Goldmund (Narcissus and Gold Mouth,* 1930*),* remorselessly delineated the laws that govern the behavior of the psyche and the affinities of opposites. During the 1930s Hesse wrote progressively more pious poetry and philosophic prose in Switzerland. Hesse's genius was at length recognized universally when, on the strength of his last powerful novel, *Das Glassperlenspiel (The Game of Beads,* 1943*),* he was awarded both the Nobel and Goethe prizes.

Thomas Mann, like most German writers of the post-World War I period, turned his back upon the robust hero. Mann concentrated upon persons who were often physically or mentally ill but by nobility of character had in some measure been able to transcend terrestrial decay. The decomposition of the great German unities of the nineteenth century caused Mann to abjure the problems of society for knowledge of self. This quest for the unquenchable inner light that nourishes human hope imparted such depth and earnestness to Mann's novels that gradually he came to be recognized, while he yet lived, as the foremost German writer since Goethe.

For twelve years Thomas Mann toiled at penning the greatest masterpiece of the Weimar era—*Der Zauberberg (The Magic Mountain,* 1924*),* which earned him the Nobel Prize. *The Magic Mountain* was actually only a Swiss mountain near Davos, on the slope of which was a tuberculosis sanatorium where the plot of the novel unfolds, but symbolically the *Zauberberg* is the "proud tower" of European culture mortally stricken with disease. Like his popular brother Heinrich, whose trilogy *Das Kaiserreich (The Empire*, 1914–25) was then enjoying acclaim, Thomas evolved into a democrat and a republican. In all things less passionate and less given to hyperbole than Heinrich, Thomas Mann achieved a philosophic serenity that derived from his conviction that the consolation for death is the regeneration of life. He created intensely conscious exemplars of a rarified culture and symbolically depicted their pathetic struggle with mindless forces in their environment.

When the Nazis came to power, Thomas Mann, who was married to a Jewess, emigrated to the USA, where he wrote the mighty tetralogy about biblical Egypt and the soul's growing awareness of God—*Joseph und seine Brüder (Joseph and His Brothers*, 1930–36), as well as the sequel about Moses, *Das Gesetz (The Law*, 1944). After World War II Mann continued to write novels—among them *Doktor Faustus* (1947) and the picaresque, personalized *Das Bekenntnis des Hochstaplers Felix Krull (The Confessions of the Con-Man, Felix Krull*, 1954)— until his death in Switzerland at age eighty.

Standing considerably below Hesse and Thomas Mann was a range of lesser but not ignoble literary peaks. Franz Kafka (1883–1924), a tubercular Jew of Prague, purveyed a little of several nostrums—expressionism, symbolism, mysticism, and existentialism. His three powerful, controversial, unfinished novels— *Der Prozess (The Trial*, 1925), *Das Schloss (The Palace*, 1926), and *Amerika* (1927)—were posthumous publications noteworthy for their expression of infinite truths in finite but oftentime terrifying terms. Alfred Döblin (1878–1957) was an expressionist whose best works were the proletarian-oriented *Berlin, Alexanderplatz* (1929) and *Trilogie: November 1918* (1949–50). Erich Maria Remarque (1898–1970) gained world fame with his starkly realistic tale of a young German soldier whose ideals and life were sacrificed to war *(Im Westen nichts Neues, All Quiet on the Western Front*, 1929), but none of his later works matched his early achievement. Franz Werfel (1890–1945), a Jewish expressionist poet and dramatist from Prague, was a lifelong foe of war and later of Nazism. Among his best plays were the Mephistophelian *Der Spiegelmensch (The Mirror Man*, 1920), *Das Reich Gottes in Böhmen (God's Kingdom in Bohemia*, 1930), and his sentimental, comic drama *Jacobowsky and the Colonel* (1944). More important as a novelist, Werfel wrote the immensely popular tales *Die vierzig Tage des Musa Dagh (The Forty Days of Musa Dagh*, 1933) and *The Song of Bernadette* (Eng., 1941). Ricarda Huch (1864–1947), a lifelong resident of Italy and a better stylist than Werfel, was the leading female novelist of the first half of the century. Her epic biographies and historical novels, most of them written before the war, betrayed opulent and dynamic Renaissance influences. That she was also capable of writing critical, scholarly works was illustrated by her *Der grosse Krieg in Deutschland (The Great Thirty Years War*, 1912–14) and *Das Römische Reich deutscher Nation (The Roman Empire of the German Nation*, 1934). Hans Fallada (1893–1947) made an international name for himself with his depressing novel of everyday life in Germany after the big crash of 1929 *(Kleiner Mann, was nun?, Little Man, What Now?*, 1932). A foe of the Third Reich, Fallada during the Nazi era withdrew to a Mecklenburg farm, where he wrote a number of novels (e.g., *Wolf under Wölfen, Wolf among Wolves*, 1937; and the nostalgic *Damals bei uns daheim, At Home in Days Gone By*, 1942). After the war Fallada expressed a sense of collective guilt for Nazi crimes by writing chilling indictments in powerful novels such as *Der Alpdruck (The Nightmare*, 1947) and *Jeder stirbt für sich allein (Each One Dies for Himself Alone*, 1947). Last, Stefan Zweig (1881–1942), a cosmopolitan Viennese Jew and a lyric poet, dramatist, essayist, literary critic, and novelist rolled into one, achieved a worldwide audience with such finely embroidered historical novels as the realistic *Joseph Fouché* (1929), *Marie Antoinette* (1932), and *Maria Stuart* (1935). Zweig fled Germany in 1935 only to commit suicide in Rio de Janeiro in 1942.

After 1933 only a few novelists of international repute remained in the Third Reich and then usually in seclusion. Apart from Gerhart Hauptmann and Hans Fallada, literary figures who stayed on in Hitler's state were usually of second-rate stature, and their names are best forgotten. An exception to this judgment was Ernst Wiechert (1887–1950), who had already written important novels *(The Forest*, 1922; and *The Wolf of Death*, 1924) in pre-Nazi times. Hostile to the Hitlerite regime, Wiechert was eventually sentenced to five months in Buchenwald for his novel *Das einfache Leben (The Simple Life*, 1939). After the war his fame revived with the writing of two artistically constructed novels, *Die Herminkinder (The Hermin Children*, 1947) and *Missa sine nomine (The Mass without a Name*, 1950).

Early Post-World War II Literature

For some years after 1945 relatively little important literature emerged from a country that had been battered by bombs and artillery shells. However, Germany's high rate of literacy and lofty cultural heritage decreed that books must soon preempt the free time of the impoverished multitude. An organized initiative at rebuilding Germany's literary reputation was first made in Munich where Gruppe 47 (Group 47) brought together a coterie of novelists, who founded a journal, *Der Ruf (The Call)*, which stimulated general interest.

The first wave of post-1945 literature was mainly anti-Nazi or preoccupied with the recent war. With symbol and paradigm the philosophy and practice of Nazism were pilloried. In the posthumously published *Der Versucher (The Tempter*, 1954) Hermann Broch (1896–1951) created the demoniacal character of Ratti, a small-town "Hitler," whose demagogic powers enslaved his fellow men. Stefan Andres (1906–1970) wrote a powerful trilogy, *Das Tier aus der Tiefe (The Monster from the Depths*, 1949), which traced the rise and fall of another demagogue (The Norm), who wielded supreme authority in a wartorn Germany. A horrifying, graphic trilogy about the fate of the Wehrmacht on the eastern front *(Stalingrad,* 1946; *Moskau,* 1952; and *Berlin,* 1954) was written by the returned emigré Theodor Plevier (1892–1955).

As German literature revived, it came to exhibit the same antinomies that were splitting the land into Communist and anti-Communist camps. On the other hand, in neither East nor West Germany was there a discernible succession of literary movements. As in the 1920s, there was only cohabitation or conflict among many contemporary styles. Some novels, such as the trilogy *Fluss ohne Ufer (River without Banks,* 1949–61) by Hans Henny Jahnn, following the earlier example of Robert Musil's (1880–1942) *Mann ohne Eigenschaften (Man without Characteristics,* 1930–33), tended to be repositories of all the problems and aspirations of an irrational and expiring European civilization. Others, like Broch's *Death of Virgil,* broke with the remnants of traditional narrative and conversation and, while clinging to the old elegiac myths, substituted lyrical tableaus that were animated by timeless soliloquies.

East German literature, isolated from West German influences (except perhaps for the novels of Heinrich Böll), developed the traits of its Russian "big brother." Generally devoid of humor but granitic in conviction and unalterable in purpose, East German literature was until but very recently as drab as the streets of East Berlin and Leipzig were in the 1950s.

Poetry and Drama after Potsdam

Whereas East German poets, headed by the Bavarian-born Bertold Brecht, have been inspired by a Marxist-Leninist *Weltanschauung* that postulates the burial of capitalism by socialism, West German poets display a far less didactic approach. They have generally been at pains to salvage whatever *can* be from the lyric-cosmopolitan legacy of Goethe and Hölderlin. Whereas East German poets have regarded persons as mere determinist products of their environment, their West German confreres have stressed free will. Writers in the GDR have been less attracted by the ethereal and mystical than have been those in the FRG. The former have boasted of having discovered a new world of meaning, whereas the West Germans have too often been tormented by the suspicion that they are simply advocates of an expiring order in which liberation and revolt against rules substitute for creativity. These misgivings have been exemplified in the cultural perspective characterizing the poems of Peter Huchel (1903–   ) and Magnus Enzenberger (1929–   ).

While most West German poets, typified by Dagmar Nick (1926–   ) and Christoph Meckel (1935–   ), have enthusiastically embraced the grammatical idiom of our times, some poets have striven to invent a language that is less disturbing. Among these the most impressive are: Günter Eich (1907–   ), whose *Botschaften des Regens (Messages of the Rain,* 1955) recalls the poetry of the Minnesingers and whose *Ausgewählte Gedichte (Selected Poems,* 1960) betrays a radiant piety; Ingeborg Bachmann (1926–   ), who is celebrated for her mysterious *Anrufung des grossen Bären (Invocation of the Big Dipper*, 1956*)*; and Christina Busta (1915–   ), who is best known, perhaps, for her *Die Sternemühle (Mill of Stars*, 1959*)*.

East German drama experienced an early rebirth after World War II. This was because it was encouraged by the political authorities, who regarded drama as a propaganda medium. Brecht and his Theater am Schiffbauerdamm in East Berlin contributed strongly to this dramatic awakening. One of the products of the Brecht school of playwriting was Helmut Baierl. His plays *Die Feststellung (The Detection*, 1958*)* and *Frau Flinz* (1962) have enjoyed wide popularity in the GDR. However, in recent years the quality of East German drama has been mediocre. The most significant playwrights have been: Heinrich Müller *(Die Umsiedlerin, The Transplanted Woman*, 1960*)*, Gustav von Wangenheim *(Die vertauschten Brüder, The Brothers Who Exchanged Places*, 1960*)*, and Peter Hack *(Moritz Tassow*, 1965*)*.

In the Bundesrepublik plays have tended to pander increasingly to the popular craving for violence, eroticism, obscenity, occultism, and sensationalism. Among the most representative West German playwrights are Heinar Kipphardt (1922–), Martin Walser (1927–), and Günter Grass (1927–). Of these, Grass has the widest reputation. He is generally ranked with Böll as one of the two outstanding contemporary German authors. Grass wrote, among other plays, the provocative *Die Plebeier proben den Aufstand (The Plebeians Rehearse the Uprising*, 1966*)*. Kipphardt, mainly a comic dramatist, also won acclaim for his *In the Affair of J. Robert Oppenheimer* (1964). Walser, who is currently in the front rank of West German novelists, has also written a number of important plays, such as *Eiche und Angora* (translated as *The Rabbit Race,* 1962*)* and *Der schwarze Schwann (The Black Swan,* 1964*)*. Very recently Adolf Muschg, a Switzer, has won the applause of German audiences with his *Kellers Abend (Keller's Evening,* 1974*)*, and Gerlind Reinshager for *Die Sonntagskinder* (Sunday's Children, 1976).

The Recent Novel

For some years after 1945 stories about World War II were the rungs by which many an aspiring German novelist climbed to fame. Of this group, perhaps the best-known writer was Hans Helmut Kirst, whose trilogy *Null-acht fünfzehn (08:15*, 1954–55*)* was widely read.

Several West German novelists have in recent years sought to advertise their disillusionment with the dreary vistas of modern materialist society by means of emblematic animal or freak stories. Illustrative of this trend, not entirely free from Kafkaesque influences, have been: Hans Henny Jahnn's *Die Nacht aus Blei (The Night of Lead,* 1956*)*; Walser's *Halbzeit (Half-time,* 1960*)*; and Grass's popular dialectical-symbolist *Die Blechtrommel (The Tin Drum,* 1959*)*, which personified recent German history as a loathsome dwarf banging on a tin drum, and his *Hundejahre (Dog Years,* 1963*)*.

These West German authors and many more have not ceased to impugn the absence of standards, and the myths and casuistry of a crass world that worships wealth, condones degeneracy, and devours fictional *Kitsch* (junk). In the vanguard of this coterie stand Jahnn, Hans Magnus Enzenberger, Grass, Stefan Andres, Erich Kuby, Alexander Kluge, Uwe Johnson, Peter Härtling, Heinz Piontek, and Heinrich Böll, most of whom had been associated with Group 47. Of these, the most universally lauded is Heinrich Böll (1917–   ), who in 1972 won the Nobel Prize for literature and has been elected president of the International PEN Society. A Catholic Rhinelander of lowly origins who was wounded four times during World War II, Böll is an imagist and satirist whose oversimplified diagnoses of the pathological state of western society have recommended him to East German readers. Böll's novels recognize no martyrs—only fools who are condemned to defeat and sorrow. His works, which have been translated into numerous languages, include *Und sagte kein einziges Wort (And Uttered Not a Single Word,* 1953), *Ende eines Dienstfahrt (End of a Service Trip,* 1966), *Ansichten eines Clowns (A Clown's Views,* 1967), and one of his most recent and best, *Gruppenbild mit Dame (Group Portrait with Lady).*

None of West Germany's post-World War II writers compared for profundity and elegance with Thomas Mann or Hermann Hesse. Oftentimes they were handicapped by their identification with the idols of one or the other tribe in the cold war. Thus, Böll's rejection of power as the source of all evil and his somewhat too apodictic socialist perspective have invited informed criticism. On the other hand, the popularity of some authors has benefited from their strictures against the Communist camp. This is true, for example, of Grass in his recent play *Davor (In Front,* 1969) and Uwe Johnson in his *Das dritte Buch über Achim (The Third Book about Achim,* 1961) and *Zwei Ansichten (Two Viewpoints,* 1965).

While Böll, Grass, Johnson, and Walser have probably earned themselves permanent places in the history of German literature, it is too early to say the same for most other contemporaries. A possible exception may be Ingeborg Drewitz (1923–   ), the authoress of the novel *Städte (Cities,* 1970) and of many dramas and biographies, who has also served as vice president of the FRG branch of PEN. Schiller and Georg Mackensen prize-winners, such as Max Frisch, Günter Eich, Ernst Jünger, and Roderick Feldes (G. M., 1977), presently popular with West German readers, must still await the verdict of literary history.

In East Germany one of the most important novelists is Karl Mundstock (1915–   ). His finest work was *Die Stunde des Dietrich Conradi (The Hour of Dietrich Conradi,* 1958). However, Mundstock's qualitative output has been perceptibly lower than that of the doyen of East German literature, Arnold Zweig (1887–1968), who in the 1950s continued his post-World War I classic, the sociological Grischa saga, with *Der grosse Krieg der weissen Männer (The Great War of the White Races).* Most other East German authors were after 1945 preoccupied (as were Bruno Apitz, Eduard Claudius, Bodo Uhse, Willi Bredel, and Anna Seghers) with Nazi crimes and wartime tragedies. Typical of this horror genre was Seghers' novel *Die Toten bleiben Jung (The Dead Stay Young,* 1949).

However, in the 1950s many East German novelists radiated confidence in the socialist future of the GDR. Conversely, their fiction was often marred by an animus against the Federal Republic, which was libelled as the heir of the Third Reich. Illustrative of the East German propagandistic novel are Bredel's trilogy of a modern working-class family *(Die Väter, The Fathers*, 1941; *Die Söhne, The Sons*, 1947; and *Die Enkel, The Grandsons,* 1953); Claudius' *Von der Liebe soll man nicht nur sprechen (Speak Not of Love Alone,* 1957); and Segher's *Die Entscheidung (The Decision,* 1959).

Recently a refreshing humor has softened the austerity of East German literature. Manfred Bieler (1934–   ) has won international fame with his drolly satirical tale of the picaresque adventures of a German sailor during the war *(Bonifaz oder der Matrose in der Flasche, Boniface or the Sailor in the Bottle,* 1963). Fritz R. Fries (1935–   ) matched this with his laughable portrait of life in the East German Socialist never-never land *(Der Weg nach Oobliadooh, The Road to Oobliadooh,* 1964). Likewise, Hermann Kant, a *dozent* at East Berlin's Humboldt University, has written a witty, barbed novel, *Die Aula (The Assembly Hall,* 1965). While the works of Fries and Kant may have been influenced by Alexander Solzhenitsyn's critique of Soviet society, *A Day in the Life of Ivan Denissovitch* (1962), it is just as arguable that this disposition to smile at itself is proof of the growing maturity of East Germany.

CHRONOLOGICAL LISTS
OF RULERS

Germany under the Carolingians

768–814	Charlemagne, King of the Franks
800–814	Charlemagne, Emperor
814–840	Louis the Pious, Emperor
840–855	Lothair, Emperor
840–876	Louis (Ludwig), the German, King of the East Franks
855–875	Louis, Emperor
855–869	Lothair, King of Lorraine
875–881	Charles the Bald, Emperor
876–880	Carloman, King of Bavaria
876–882	Louis (Ludwig), King of Saxony
880–882	Louis, King of Bavaria
881–887	Charles the Fat, Emperor
884–887	Charles the Fat, King of Franks
887–894	Guido (Italy)
887–899	Arnulf, King of the East Franks
894–896	Lambert (Italy)
896–899	Arnulf, Emperor
899–911	Louis, the Child, King of the East Franks

Kings and Emperors of Medieval Germany

911–918	Conrad I of Franconia

The Saxon Dynasty

919–933	Henry I, the Fowler
933–973	Otto I, the Great
962–973	Otto I, first Emperor of the Holy (Roman) Empire
973–983	Otto II
983–1002	Otto III
1002–1024	Henry II

The Salian Dynasty

1024–1039	Conrad II
1039–1056	Henry III, the Black
1056–1106	Henry IV
1106–1125	Henry V
1125–1137	Lothair, the Saxon

The Hohenstaufen Dynasty

1138–1152	Conrad III
1152–1190	Frederick I Barbarossa

1190–1197	Henry VI
1198–1208	Philip (Hohenstaufen) of Swabia, Contender
1198–1208	Otto (Welf) of Brunswick, Contender
1208–1212	Otto IV (Brunswick), sole king
1212–1250	Frederick II, last Hohenstaufen emperor

Kings of Germany, 1246–1272

1246–1247	Henry Raspe
1247–1250	William of Holland
1250–1254	Conrad IV (Hohenstaufen)
1254–1257	Interregnum
1257–1272	Richard of Cornwall, Contender, double election
1257–1272	Alfonso of Castile, Contender, double election

Habsburg, Wittelsbach, and Luxemburg Emperors

1273–1291	Rudolf I, Habsburg
1292–1298	Adolf I of Nassau
1298–1308	Albert (Albrecht) I, Habsburg
1308–1313	Henry VII, Luxemburg
1314–1330	Frederick of Austria, Contender, double election
1314–1347	Ludwig of Bavaria, joint ruler with Frederick till 1330
1347–1378	Charles IV, Luxemburg
1378–1410	Wenceslas, Luxemburg
1410–1437	Sigmund, Luxemburg
1438–1439	Albert (Albrecht) II, Habsburg
1438–1439	Albert V, Luxemburg
1440–1493	Frederick III, Habsburg
1493–1519	Maximilian I, Habsburg

3. Hohenzollern Electors of Brandenburg (After 1618 also Dukes of Prussia)

1417–1440	Frederick I, Elector of Brandenburg and ruler of Bayreuth and Ansbach
1440–1470	Frederick II, "Iron Tooth"
1470–1486	Albert Achilles
1486–1499	John (Johann) Cicero
1499–1535	Joachim I
1535–1571	Joachim II
1571–1598	John George
1598–1608	Joachim Frederick
1608–1619	John Sigismund, Elector and Duke of Prussia
1619–1640	George William
1640–1688	Frederick William, the Great Elector
1688–1713	Frederick III, Margrave of Brandenburg, 1688–1713, and as Frederick I, King in Prussia, 1701–1713

4. Hohenzollern Kings of Prussia

1701–1713	Frederick I, King in Prussia
1713–1740	Frederick William I, King of Prussia
1740–1786	Frederick II, the Great
1786–1797	Frederick William II
1797–1840	Frederick William III
1840–1861	Frederick William IV
1861–1888	William I, became German emperor in 1871

5. German Emperors (and Kings of Prussia) 1871–1918

1871–1888	William I
1888	Frederick III
1888–1918	William II

6. Habsburg Emperors of the Holy Roman Empire in Early Modern Times

1519–1556	Charles V
1556–1564	Ferdinand I
1564–1576	Maximilian II
1576–1612	Rudolph II
1612–1619	Matthias
1619–1637	Ferdinand II
1637–1657	Ferdinand III
1658–1705	Leopold I
1705–1711	Joseph I
1711–1740	Charles VI
1742–1745	Charles VII (Wittelsbach) of Bavaria
	Maria Theresa was ruler of all Austrian crown lands from 1740–1769, and joint ruler with her son Joseph from 1765–1780
1745–1765	Francis I of Lorraine, husband of Maria Theresa
1765–1790	Joseph II of Habsburg-Lorraine
1790–1792	Leopold II of Habsburg-Lorraine
1792–1806	Francis II of Habsburg-Lorraine

In 1806 the Holy Roman Empire came to an end.

7. Emperors of Austria (Austria-Hungary after 1867)

1804–1835	Francis I (Francis II of the Holy Roman Empire)
1835–1848	Ferdinand I
1848–1916	Franz-Joseph
1916–1918	Charles I

GLOSSARY OF SELECTED
GERMAN WORDS AND TERMS

Abgeordnetenhaus House of Representatives of the kingdom of Prussia

Abwehr Counterintelligence; a section of the OKW under Admiral Canaris in the Third Reich

Adel Aristocracy, noble landowner or tenant

Aktiengesellschaft Joint stock company

Akzise Excises; inland revenue

Alldeutscher Verband Pan-German League

Alleinvertretungsanspruch The claim of the Federal Republic of Germany to be the sole authority entitled to represent the whole German nation

Allgemeiner Deutsche Arbeiterverein (ADAV) The General German Workingmen's Association, founded by F. Lassalle in 1863

Allmende Common lands, such as waste, meadow and woodland, on a medieval manor

Alod Small proprietary holding or free land; from Old German *Odal*, "all free"

Anschluss Union; specifically of Austria and Germany after 1919

Arbeitsdienst Mandatory labor in the Third Reich

Armer Konrad Pre-Reformation peasants' movement directed against landlords and nobles

Au Meadow

Aufklärung The Enlightenment

Aufsichtsstaat Paternalist state, exercising supervision over all subjects or citizens

Ausgleich Equalization or compromise on a basis of parity; specifically the Austro-Hungarian agreement of 1867, establishing a Dual Monarchy

Bach Brook

Baltikum Lands of the eastern Baltic area

Bauernschutz Protection of peasants, especially decrees or legislation protecting against expropriation or abuse of peasant rights

Bauhaus Modern school of design and architecture, founded in 1919 in Weimar by Walter Gropius; moved in 1926 to Dessau

Baustil Style of architecture

Befreiungskrieg German war of liberation fought against Napoleon in 1813

Bekennende Kirche The "Confessing Church," led by M. Niemöller, a Lutheran minister, during the Third Reich

Berg Mountain or hill

Betriebsgemeinschaft The aggregate of all personnel of a firm or factory in the Third Reich

Bezirk District or shire

Bezirkstag District diet

Blauer Reiter, Der The "Blue Horseman" circle of artists in Munich during the Weimar Republic

Blockflur Block of irregular arable in a single field; cultivated by an individual family; common in the east

Brücke, Die "The Bridge," a school of expressionistic art during the Weimar Republic; founded in Dresden; influenced by the French Fauves ("wild ones")

Bühel Hill

Bund der freien Gewerkschaften Federation of Free Trade Unions

Bund der Heimatvertriebenen und Entrechteten (BHE) League of Expellees and Disenfranchised in the Federal Republic of Germany

Bund der Landwirte Federation of Farmers in the Second Reich; mainly well-to-do or affluent landowners

Bund Deutscher Mädel (BDM) Federation of German Girls in the Third Reich

Bundesgericht Supreme Court of the FRG, domiciled at Karlsruhe

Bundesnachrichtendienst Intelligence Service of the Federal Republic of Germany

Bundesrat Federal Council or upper house of the legislatures of the North German Confederation (1866–70), Second Reich (1871–1918), and FRG (1949ff)

Bundesrepublik Deutschland (BRD) Federal Republic of Germany (FRG), 1949ff

Bundestag Diet of the German Confederation (1815–66); also the lower house of the FRG

Bundesversammlung Federal Assembly, or bicameral legislature of the FRG

Bundeswehr Defense Forces of the FRG

Bundschuh Peasant's clog or brogue; emblem of the insurgent peasants during the Reformation era

Burgfrieden(e) Civil Peace, especially among the political parties in World War I

Burgrecht Civic rights or code of a town

Burgward Fortified point or settlement protected by a castle

Burschenschaft German academic youth society of the early nineteenth century; pledged to the ideals of honor, freedom, and fatherland; federated nationally in 1818

Centralverband der deutschen Industrieller Central Association of German Manufacturers in Second Reich

Deutsche Arbeitsfront German Labor Front, headed by Robert Ley, in the Third Reich

Deutsche Brücke "German Bridge," the trading compound or emporium of the Hanse in Bergen, Norway

Deutsche Demokratische Republik (DDR) German Democratic Republic

Deutsche Handelstag German Chamber of Commerce

Deutsche Kolonialgesellschaft German Colonial Society in Second Reich

Deutscher Bauernbund German Farmers' Association (mostly smallholders) in the Second Empire

Deutscher Bund The German Confederation, 1815–66

Deutschland Vertrag The Treaty on Germany (May 26, 1952), abrogating the Occupation Statute for the FRG and dissolving HICOG

Diktat A dictate, specifically, dictated peace

Dispositionsfond Funds at the disposal of a ministry

Dolchstoss A dagger stab, specifically the alleged "stab in the back" administered by the German Socialists to the German armies toward the end of World War I

Dorf Village

Drang nach Osten Drive to the East

Dreibund The Triple Alliance of Germany, Austria-Hungary, and Italy (1882ff) in defense of the status quo of 1871

Dreifeldwirtschaft The medieval three-field system, comprising two cultivated fields and one fallow, alternating from year to year

Dreikaiserbund League of Three Emperors: of Austria-Hungary, Russia, and Germany (1873–78, and 1881–87)

Drohende Kriegsgefahr State of threatening danger of war

Einkreisungspolitik Policy of encirclement

Einsatztruppen Special readiness military detachments used by Nazis in the eastern occupied areas in World War II

Einwohnerwehr Inhabitants' Defense Organization; a paramilitary unit operating on the eastern frontier under the Weimar Republic

Erbhofgesetz Hereditary Farm Law of 1933, declaring farms of up to 320 acres hereditary and making normal-sized farms, averaging 25 acres, indivisible

Erbuntertänigkeit Hereditary dependent, bondsman status

Ersatz Substitute

Evangelische Kirche Lutheran Church

Fachwerk Half-timber (timber, lath, and wattle or daub) construction

Fahneneid Oath of allegiance to the flag; actually the oath of the German Reichswehr on August 2, 1934, to Hitler personally

Flottenverein Navy League in the Second Empire

Flur Arable land on a manor

Fraktur Pointed, ornamental style of Gothic writing

Frauenzimmer Lady, usually of quality

Freie Deutsche Jugend (FDJ) Free German Youth, in the German Democratic Republic

Freier Deutscher Gewerkschaftsbund Federation of Free German Trade Unions, in the GDR

Freiheit Freedom

Freizügigkeit Freedom to move about or settle wherever one wishes

Friedenssturm Peace offensive; Ludendorff's last offensive in the west in World War I

Frondienst Forced manual labor required of serfs by their lords; *corvée* or *Robot*

Fronhof Soccage copyhold; bondsman's cottage and land on which it was located

Führer Leader, especially Hitler

Fürst Prince

Fürstentag Diet of the Princes, specifically, that summoned in 1863 by Austria to reorganize the German Confederation

Fürstentum Principality, ruled over by an imperial prince

Gau A rural district; in ancient times the area occupied by a German tribe

Gauleiter District or regional leader in the Third Reich

Gefolgschaft Also *Gefolgswesen* or *Comitatus* (Lat.); an elite corps of young German warriors who in ancient times grouped themselves around a leader for defense and war

Gefolgswesen See *Gefolgschaft*

Geheime Haus -, Hof -, und Staatskanzlei Secret Dynastic, Court and State Chancery, or Foreign Office, of the Austrian court after 1742

Geheimer Staatsrat Privy Councillor

Geheimratsliberalismus Bureaucratic liberalism

Gemeinde Community, municipality

Gemeinfreie A free man

General Ober-, Finanz -, Kriegs -, und Domänendirektorium Supreme Fiscal, War and Domainal, or Central, Directory, est. in 1723 in the kingdom of Prussia

Generalkriegskommissariat General War Office or Commissariat of Brandenburg, est. by Frederick William, the Great Elector

Generalstab General staff

Gericht Court, tribunal
Gerichtsherrschaft Judicial authority of the lord of a manor
Gesamtstaat Organic, integrated state
Gesetz Law
Gestapo Abbreviated form of Geheime Staatspolizei, or the Nazi secret police
Gewanne Consolidated block of tenures in one field on a manor
Gleichheit Equality
Gleichschaltung Coordination, synchronization or unification in a leveling sense
Graf Count
Grafschaft County
Grenzschutz Border defense
Grossdeutsch Great German, meaning a Germany including Austria
Grosse Politik Grand (foreign) policy
Gründerzeit Period from 1871 to 1873 in Germany when many new, often highly speculative, companies were established
Grundgesetz The Basic Law (1949) of the Federal Republic of Germany
Grundherrschaft Manor, territorial domain
Gymnasium Classical type secondary school

Hakenkreuz Swastika; Nazi emblem derived from ancient India and the Near East
Hanse Hanseatic League of German and Baltic towns
Haushörige Domestic bondsman or serf
Hausmacht Lands and property belonging personally to a ruler, constituting the economic basis of his dynastic power
Heer Army
Herrengut A seigneur's private land on the manor, also called *Salland*
Herrenhaus Prussian House of Lords in the Second Empire
Herzog (-tum) Duke; duchy
Hitler Jugend (HJ) Hitler Youth
Hochschule University level institute or college
Höfisches Epos Courtly epic
Hofkammer Austrian court chamber
Hofkanzlei Court chancellery
Hofkriegsrat Austrian Council of War
Hörigkeit Serfdom, bondage
Hufe Fixed tenure of 60–100 acres
Hundertschaft A "Hundred," the basic unit of the German fighting force in ancient times; also the basic tribal juridical unit underlying the "Hundred Court"

Junges Deutschland "Young Germany"; a politically progressive society inspired by the ideals of Mazzini's Giovane Italia organization
Junker *"Jung Herr,"* or young lord; originally the son of a grand seigneur, later designated the proprietor of a large landed estate in eastern Germany

Kameralwissenschaft Science of political economy, differing from mercantilism mainly in that, in the German model, paternalist duties toward society are ascribed to government; cameralism
Kammer Chamber, court treasury, or legislature

Kampfpolitik Policy of combat

Kathedersozialismus Academic socialism

Kirchenvogt Bailiff or lay administrator of church property

Kleindeutsch "Small Germany," excluding the Austrian empire, under Prussian tutelage

Kleinstaaterei Condition of territorial fragmentation or polycentrism

Kogge Hanseatic merchant vessel, averaging 100 gross tons

Königtum Kingdom

Konzentrationslager (KZ) concentration camp

Kopfzins Capitation tax levied on bondsmen

Kraft durch Freude (KdF) "Strength through Joy"; the system of cultural, educational, and sports benefits and paid vacations conferred upon workers by the Nazi Labor Front

Kreis Circle, county, or district

Kreishauptmann County or district captain; an official in the Habsburg empire

Kreistag County or district diet of estates

Kriegsernährungsamt (KEA) German War Foods Office in World War I

Kriegsrohstoffabteilung (KRA) German Office of Strategic War Materiel in World War I

Kriegsschuldfrage The question of war guilt

Kriegs- und Domänenkammern War and domainal provincial treasury offices in Brandenburg-Prussia

Kristallnacht "Night of glass," November 9–10, 1938, when the Nazis conducted a pogrom against the German Jews

Krümpersystem A system of recruiting and training recruits for a short period of time prior to retirement to the reserve army; used by Prussia during the era of the War of Liberation (1808–13)

Kultur Civilization

Kulturkampf "Battle for Civilization"; the fight of the governments of Germany in Bismarck's time against the political influence of the Catholic clergy

Kurfürst Electoral prince

Länderkammer In the German Democratic Republic the Chamber of *Länder* or provinces, constituting the upper house of the legislature; suppressed in 1958

Landesding Sovereign assembly of all freemen in a German tribe

Landeshoheit Territorial sovereignty

Landrat County (rural) councillor

Landtag Diet of a principality or state

Landwirtschaftliche Produktionsgenossenschaft A collective farm in the German Democratic Republic

Langstreifenflur A long, narrow plowland or tenure, usually 4 by 40 rods

Lebensraum "Living space"

Lehensempfänger A vassal

Lehnsherr Overlord or seigneur

Leibeigene Bondsman or serf

Leitmotiv Dominant recurring theme or motive, as in Wagnerian opera

Lied Song or lay

Lückentheorie Bismarck's theory of a constitutional gap or omission, which justified

the Prussian minister-president in carrying on state operations in the absence of a budget
approved by the *Landtag*

Luftwaffe German Air Force

Lustschloss Pleasure palace

Machtergreifung Seizure of power

Machtpolitik Power politics

Machtvacuum A power vacuum

Märchen Tale or fairy story

Mark Unit of currency; also a march or frontier district between ancient tribes or bordering a foreign state

Markgraf Margrave or marquess; count of a march province *(Markgrafschaft)*

Markgrafsrhaft Margravate or march province, located near the frontier of the Empire

Markttag Seasonal fair

Meistersinger Master singer; late medieval tradesman or artisan composer and performer of poetry and music

Messe Mass; also fair

Minne Courtly chivalrous love

Minnelied Medieval courtly love song or poem

Minnesinger Knightly, aristocratic composer and singer of *Minnelieder*

Mitbestimmungsrecht Right of codetermination in a firm or factory, exercised by employees in the FRG

Mitgift Under ancient tribal law the possessions that a woman brought into her marriage and which she retained throughout life

Mitteleuropa Central Europe, specifically, a central European economic community under German domination

Nationalverein National Society, founded in 1859 to promote the unification of Germany on a *kleindeutsch* basis

Nibelungentreue Fidelity of the Nibelung dwarfs

Norddeutscher Bund North German Confederation (1866–71)

Oberkommando der Kriegsmarine (OKM) Supreme Command of the Nazi Navy, under Admiral Doenitz

Oberkommando der Wehrmacht (OKW) Supreme Command of the Armed Forces, under General Keitel, in the Third Reich

Oberkommando des Heeres (OKH) High Command of the Army in the Third Reich

Oberpräsident Lord lieutenant or administrator of a province

Oberste Heeresleitung (OHL) Army High Command in the Second Reich

Obrigkeitsstaat Authoritarian state

Odal Old German for ''land''

Ordenschule School run by a religious order

Ostmark East March, early designation for Austria

Ostpolitik Eastern policy

Pfaffengasse ''Priests' lane,'' or the Catholic Rhine River valley

Pflicht zur Hilfe mit Rat und Tat Obligatory conciliar and military aid, due the overlord from his vassal

Primat der Aussenpolitik Primacy of foreign policy

Putsch A *coup de main* or insurrection against the government

Rat der Volksbeauftragten Council of People's Representatives during the German Revolution of 1918

Räte Councils, specifically, of Workers' and Soldiers' Deputies, 1918–19

Realpolitik Realistic, unsentimental policy, esp. that of Bismarck

Realschule Nonclassical secondary school

Rechtsstaat A state or realm governed in accordance with customary or established law

Reformverein Reform Association; a *grossdeutsch* organization that aimed at founding a united Germany including Austria

Reich Empire, realm, or nation

Reichsbanner Schwarz-Rot-Gold "National Flag: Black, Red, Gold," a Social Democratic paramilitary organization in the Weimar Republic

Reichsdeputation Imperial Deputation, comprising electoral princes and a small number of other territorial rulers of the Holy Roman Empire, representing the Reichstag when it was not in session

Reichsdeputationshauptschluss A decree of 1803 of the Imperial Deputation of the Reichstag, authorizing extensive territorial changes in Germany

Reichsfürst A prince of the Holy Roman Empire, who was entitled to sit in the Reichstag in the Curia of Princes, or Second Estate

Reichsgericht Supreme tribunal of the Weimar Republic

Reichsgründung The foundation of the Second Empire

Reichshofgericht Supreme court of the medieval Holy Empire

Reichskammergericht Supreme Court of the Holy Roman Empire, 1495–1806

Reichskanzlei Imperial chancery or chancellery

Reichskanzler Imperial chancellor

Reichskanzleramt Office of the imperial chancellery under the Second Empire, 1871–78

Reichskreis Circle or department of the Holy Roman Empire in early modern times

Reichskrieg An imperial war

Reichsland The Imperial Territory, i.e., Alsace-Lorraine after annexation to Germany in 1871

Reichsleitung (RL) Supreme authority of the Nazi civil government of Germany

Reichsmarineamt Imperial Naval Office of the Second Empire

Reichsmark The mark (worth $0.238) of the Weimar Republic, adopted in 1924

Reichsnährstand National Food Estate, under Walter Darré, in the Third Reich

Reichsrat The Imperial Council of the Austrian Empire, 1860–1918; also the federal Council of *Länder* of the Weimar Republic

Reichsregiment Imperial government council of the Holy Roman Empire after 1500

Reichsstadt Free city of the Holy Roman Empire

Reichstag Imperial, federal, or republican legislature of Germany; the lower house of parliament, 1871–1918, 1919–33, and 1933–45

Reichswehr Armed forces of the Weimar Republic and the first years of the Third Reich

Rentenmark A mark issued by the Stresemann government in 1923, backed not by gold but by mortgages on all agricultural and industrial property in Germany

Reptilienfonds "Reptile Funds," money seized by Bismarck when in 1866 he confiscated the treasury of Hanover; used to advance the aims of Prussia

Rheinbund Confederation of the Rhine (1658–66, 1806–13)

Ritter Knight

Ritterorden Order of the Teutonic Knights

Rote Front Kämpfer Bund Red Front Battle Organization; a Communist paramilitary formation in the Weimar Republic

Rückversicherungsvertrag The Reinsurance Treaty between Russia and Germany, 1887–90

Sachlichkeit Objectivity, detachment

Schöffe Juror, juryman

Schultheiss Village mayor

Schutzstaffeln SS Defense Squadron, or Praetorian Guard of Adolf Hitler

Schutz- und Trutzbündnisse Defensive and offensive alliances signed between the North German Confederation and the governments of the South German states in 1866

Schwertbrüder Knights of the Sword of Livonia

Sendboten Missi dominici of Charlemagne's empire

Septennat The seven-year defense budget bill in the Second Empire

Sicherheitsdienst (SD) Security service (political police), under H. Himmler, in the Third Reich

Sippe Old Germanic clan or community of kinsmen

Soziale Marktwirtschaft Social market economy, sponsored by Ludwig Erhard in the early years of the FRG, stressing both free enterprise and governmental paternalism

Spartakusbund Spartacist League; the extreme left wing of the Independent Social Democratic party

Spiegel Specula or mirror; a kind of medieval commentary on or code of laws

Staalhof Trading compound and emporium of the Hanse in London

Staatsgerichtshof Special high court of the Weimar Republic empowered to decide disputes between *Länder*

Staatsministerium Ministerial council established in 1810 in Prussia, under Hardenberg's presidency

Staatsräson Raison d'état, reason of state

Staatsrat Privy council or council of state, as in the GDR

Staatsstreich Coup d'état

Stahlhelm "Steel Helmet," a paramilitary organization controlled by the German Nationalist People's Party (DNVP) in the Weimar Republic

Stamm Race, tribal grouping or clan in early German history

Stammesherzogtum Stem duchy; one of the original larger political-geographic divisions of early medieval Germany, corresponding to a major tribal confederate grouping

Stand (pl., Stände) Estate or estates of the Holy Roman Empire

Ständestaat A realm possessing representation by estates rather than constituencies

Statthalter National commissioner or governor

Steuerrat Tax councillor or fiscal agent who supervised the collection of excises in the towns of Brandenburg-Prussia

Sturmabteilung (SA) The brown-shirted paramilitary formations, led by Ernest Roehm of the Nazi party

Sturm und Drang "Storm and Stress" literary movement of the late eighteenth century

Treupflicht Oath of fidelity which a free German warrior took to a leader

Truppenamt Troop training office; the highest military authority in the Reichswehr after suppression of the general staff, following World War I

Tugendbund League of Virtue, a patriotic society during the era of the War of Liberation

Übermensch Superman

Unschärferelation The physicist Werner Heisenberg's principle of indeterminacy

Unterseeboot U-boat, submarine

Vaterländische Hilfedienst National Auxiliary Service, under Karl Helfferich, in World War I; controlled manpower other than armed personnel

Vaterlandslosengesellen Men without a country

Verband deutscher Arbeitervereine (VDAV) Federation of German Workers' Associations, founded in 1863 by bourgeois democrats and progressives

Verfassung Constitution

Vogt Advocate or administrator, superintending the estates or fiefs of a lay or ecclesiastical lord

Volk People, confederation of tribes, or nation

Völkerschaft Tribal confederation

Völkerwanderung Great migrations of the German tribal confederations, occurring mainly from the fourth through the sixth centuries

Völkisch Popular, especially in an ethnic sense

Volksbegehren Popular initiative

Volksdeutsche Germans dwelling outside the boundaries of the Reich in 1939

Volksentscheid Referendum

Volksepos Folk epic

Volksgeist Spirit or soul of a people or nation

Volksgemeinschaft National unity or community of the nation

Volksheer Militia

Volkskammer People's Chamber, lower house of the GDR until 1958, when it became the sole national legislative body

Volkspolizei VOPO's or People's Police of the GDR

Volksrat People's Council in the GDR

Volksschule Elementary or primary school

Volksverein für das katholische Deutschland People's League for Catholic Germany

Vollzugsrat Executive Council of Workers' and Soldiers' Deputies during the German "Revolution"

Waffen SS Nazi Armed SS, employed for combat in World War II

Wehrmacht Defense Forces of the Third Reich

Wehrverein Defense Association

Weiler Hamlet

Weltanschauung Philosophical outlook on life; also *Weltbild*

Weltpolitik World power policy, aiming at establishing the global importance of a state

Wiedertäufer Anabaptists

Wissenschaft Science, learning, or scholarship

Zeitgeist Spirit of the age

Zeitstück A work of art or literature that is an outgrowth of the times

Zollverein German Customs Union, primarily organized by the Prussian minister of finance, von Motz, and reasonably completed by 1834

Zunft Guild

BIBLIOGRAPHY

Sources and Aids

The sources for a thousand years of German history are vast. The main collections on medieval history alone—the *Monumenta Germaniae Historica* and the *Regesta imperii (Imperial Acts)*—run to hundreds of volumes. Manifestly in a survey such as this it would be inappropriate to list anything more than a few indispensable general guides to and collections of source materials. For the sake of brevity most memoirs, chronicles, and newspapers, as well as Latin sources, have been omitted.

The chief bibliography covering the sweep of German history is Friedrich Dahlmann and Georg Waitz, *Quellenkunde zur deutschen Geschichte*, an old work that has been revised many times. The tenth edition (Stuttgart, 1965–) is currently being published under the auspices of the Max Planck Institute for History in Göttingen. On a much more modest scale is Günther Franz, *Bücherkunde zur deutschen Geschichte* (Munich, 1951), which lists selected titles on German and Austrian history from earliest times to 1933. John C. Fout has compiled a bibliography of scholarly articles dealing with recent German history: *German History and Civilization 1806–1914* (Metuchen, N.J., 1974). A wide variety of treaties, memoirs, and correspondence is to be found in R. Oldenbourg, *Geschichtliches Quellenwerk*, ed. by E. Chudzinski, 10 vols. (Leipzig, 1931). Austrian sources from earliest years are listed in R. Charmetz, *Wegweiser durch die Literatur der österreichischen Geschichte* (Stuttgart, 1912). There is is a helpful collection of older and more recent treaties in K. Ploetz, *Konferenzen und Verträge*, 2 vols. (Bielefeld, 1953). A small number of translated documents will be found in Louis Snyder, *Documents of German History* (New York, 1958). The Commission for the History of the Parliamentary system and Political Parties publishes a list of all university monographs on modern German history: *Hochschulschriften zur neueren deutschen Geschichte*, ed. by Thilo Vogelsang et al. (1945–55; 1956–). The annual *Jahresberichte zur deutschen Geschichte* lists all newer studies relating to the period 1878–1945. Extensive bibliographies by period are also to be found in the major handbooks of German history, such as by P. Rassow, Bruno Gebhardt, and L. Just.

For the study of the German Middle Ages the student would do well to begin by consulting the general introduction that was written by Heinz Quirin: *Einführung in das Studium der mittelalterlichen Geschichte*, 2nd ed. (Braunschweig, 1961). By far the most important collection of sources on medieval German history was that compiled by Wilhelm Wattenbach: *Deutschlands Geschichtsquellen bis zur Mitte des dreizehnten Jahrhunderts*, 2 vols., which has been reedited by R. Holtzmann in 1938–43 and since then partly revised by W. Levison and Heinz Löwe. A more modest compilation is that by Max Jansen and Ludwig Schmitz-Kallenberg, *Historiographie und Quellen der deutschen Geschichte bis 1500*, 2nd ed. (Leipzig, 1914).

The Reformation Era has been the subject of a considerable number of bibliographical works. Source and secondary material relating to German renaissance humanism is contained in I. Irmscher (ed.), *Renaissance und Humanismus in Mittel- und Osteuropas*, 2 vols. (Berlin, 1962). The most comprehensive recent compilation of sources and literature concerning the religious schism in Germany has been the celebrated work by Karl Schottenloher (ed.), *Bibliographie zur deutschen Geschichte im Zeitalter der Glaubensspaltung 1517–1585*, 7 vols., 2nd ed. (Stuttgart, 1956–58). The distinguished historian Franz Schnabel has masterfully discussed the sources of the German Reformation for the years 1500–1550: *Deutschlands geschichtliche Quellen und Darstellungen in der Neuzeit*.

Vol. I: *Das Zeitalter der Reformation* (Berlin and Leipzig, 1931). An older and larger collection is that by Gustav Wolf (ed.), *Quellenkunde der deutschen Reformationsgeschichte*, 3 vols. (Gotha, 1915–23). Publication of a 55-volume American translation of Martin Luther's works has been in progress since 1955 at St. Louis and Philadelphia under the editorship of Jaroslav Pelikan and Helmut T. Lehmann. A selective German edition of Luther's works is Albert Leitzmann and Otto Clemen (eds.), *Luthers Werke in Auswahl*, 8 vols. (Berlin, 1930–35). For Zwingli the most exhaustive collection of writings and sermons is *Zwinglis Werke*, ed. by E. Egli and G. Finsler *(Corpus Reformatorum*, 88–100, 1963–   ). Lists of printed and manuscript documents relevant to the reign of the Emperor Charles V are to be found in Karl Brandi's memorable biography, *Karl V,* II: *Quellen und Erörterungen* (Munich, 1941).

The early modern proceedings and acts of some of the larger German states, such as Brandenburg-Prussia, Bavaria, Saxony, Württemberg, and Baden, as well as those of some of the smaller states, such as Jülich and Berg, have been assembled and published. The deliberations of the municipal councils of many of the larger cities were also published for specific periods, as were the debates of the Hanse diet down to the late sixteenth century. Few of these collections, however, were anything more than fragmentary or for broken series of years. The official and administrative acts for the larger German states have also been published. Typifying these collections are: O. Hintze, *Acta Borussica, Behördenorganisation: Die Behördenorganisation und die allgemeine Staatsverwaltung Preussens im 18. Jahrhundert*, 6 vols. (Berlin, 1894–1908); A. F. Riedel (ed.), *Codex diplomaticus Brandenburgensis, Sammlung der Urkunden, Chroniken und sonstigen Quellenschriften für die Geschichte der Mark Brandenburg und ihrer Regenten*, 36 vols. (Berlin, 1838–65); and Eugen Schneider (ed.), *Ausgewählte Urkunden zur württembergischen Geschichte, Württembergische Geschichtsquellen* (Stuttgart, 1911).

The history of Germany during much of the eighteenth century can be studied in the writings and correspondence of Frederick the Great. His most important works have been edited by G. B. Volz, *Werke Friedrich des Grossen*, 10 vols. (Berlin, 1913–14). The vast mass of Frederick's correspondence is in *Politische Correspondenz Friedrich des Grossen*, ed. by the Prussian Academy of Science, 46 vols. (Berlin, 1879–1939).

Lists of sources and secondary materials on Germany in the Napoleonic era are in Friedrich M. Kircheisen, *Bibliographie des napoleonischen Zeitalters* (Berlin, 1902). Metternich's papers and correspondence are in *Aus Metternichs nachgelassenen Papieren*, 8 vols. (Vienna, 1880–84), while his memoirs have been translated: *Memoirs of Prince Metternich*, 5 vols. (New York, 1880–82). Freiherr vom Stein's writings and letters have been newly edited by Walter Hubatsch and published as *Stein, Briefe und amtliche Schriften*, 8 vols. (Berlin, 1957–60). Selected sources and writings on the German Youth Movement and the campaign for unification are to be found in Hermann Haupt (ed.), *Quellen und Darstellungen zur Geschichte der Burschenschaften und der deutschen Einheitsbewegung*, 17 vols. (Berlin, 1910–40).

Hans-Joachim Schoeps has recently given us a new listing of nineteenth-century Prussian history sources: *Neue Quellen zur Geschichte Preussens im 19. Jahrhundert* (Berlin, 1968). H. Poschinger has compiled a collection of sources on Prussian foreign policy in the 1850s: *Preussens auswärtige Politik 1850–58*, 3 vols. (Berlin, 1902). For the years 1858–69, however, the indispensable diplomatic collection is E. Brandenburg, et al. *Auswärtige Politik Preussens 1858 bis 1871*, 10 vols. in 11 tomes (Berlin and Oldenburg, 1932–45). Bismarck's collected works have been published as *Die gesammelten Werke*, 19 vols. (Berlin, 1924–35), while Horst Kohl has edited the iron chancellor's political speeches: *Die politischen Reden des Fürsten Bismarck*, 14 vols. (Berlin and Stuttgart, 1892–95). Documents on both the internal and external policy of the Deutscher Bund, the German Empire, and the German states since 1918 and down to 1954 have been assembled by Johannes Hohlfeld (ed.), *Dokumente der deutschen Politik und Geschichte von 1848 bis zur Gegenwart*, 8 vols. (Berlin, 1951–54). A shorter collection of documents for the early and middle years of the nineteenth century is to be found in Harry Pross (ed.), *Dokumente zur deutschen Politik 1806–70* (Frankfurt a.m., 1963). An important recent collection of documents, not contained in the major German or French series, bearing upon the origins of the Franco-Prussian War, is Georges Bonnin (ed.), *Bismarck and the Hohenzollern Candidature for the Spanish Throne* (London, 1857).

A great deal of the political history of the Second Empire can be followed in the proceedings of the Reichstag: *Stenographische Berichte uber die Verhandlungen des Deutschen Reichstags, 1871–1918*, 325 vols. (Berlin, 1871–1918). For the sequence of events leading up to World War I the greatest official, documentary collection and the first to be published under the auspices of a former belligerent country is Albrecht Mendelssohn Bartholdy, Johannes Lepsius, and Friedrich Thimme (eds.), *Die grosse Politik der europäischen Kabinette, 1871–1914; Sammlung der diplomatischen Akten des Auswärtigen Amtes*, 40 vols. (Berlin, 1922–27). A selection of ocuments bearing more directly upon the immediate prelude to the war is to be found in translation in E. T. S. Dugdale (ed.), *German Diplomatic Documents, 1871–1914*, 4 vols. (London, 1928–31). The secret papers of the *éminence grise* of the German foreign office during the years 1890–1906, Friedrich von Holstein, have in recent years been edited by W. Frauendienst: *Die geheimen Papiere Friedrich von Holsteins*, 4 vols. (Göttingen, 1956–63), and a selection has appeared in translation: Norman Rich and M. H. Fisher (eds.), *The Holstein Papers*, 2 vols. (Cambridge, 1955–63).

The sources for the study of the history of the German working-class movement have very recently been assembled by historians of East Germany working under the auspices of the Institut für Marxismus-Leninismus beim ZK der SED: *Dokumente und Materialien zur Geschichte der deutschen Arbeiterbewegung* (East Berlin, 1967ff), and many documents concerning the history of the working class under the Empire and First Republic are to be found in the issues of the *Archiv für die Geschichte des Sozialismus und der Arbeiterbewegung*, ed. by Carl Grünberg, 15 vols., reprinted in Graz, 1965–66. The Institute for the History of the Parliamentary System and Political Parties has undertaken the publication of source materials relating to that theme, notably Eberhard Pikart and Erich Matthias (eds.), *Die Reichstagsfraktion der deutschen Sozialdemokratie, 1898–1918*, 2 vols. (Düsseldorf, 1966); and Quellen zur Geschichte des Parlamentarismus und der politischen Parteien. Part I: *Von der konstitutionellen Monarchie zur parlamentarischen Republik Der interfraktionelle Ausschuss, 1917–18*, 2 vols. (Düsseldorf, 1959), which contains the deliberations of the Reichstag's interparty committee during 1917–18.

The German Revolution and the Armistice provoked legislative investigations into the causes of the German defeat and ensuing upheaval. The results of the inquiry are in *Untersuchungsausschuss über die Weltkriegsverantwortlichkeit*, 4th series: *Die Ursachen des deutschen Zusammenbruches im Jahre 1918*, 12 vols. (Berlin, 1925–29). For aspects of the activities of the Workers and Soldiers Councils in the wake of the Revolution the student is advised to consult *Quellen zur Geschichte der Rätebewegung in Deutschland 1918–19*, 2 vols. (Leiden, 1968–70). Proceedings of the German Constituent Assembly, which founded the Weimar Republic, are in *Verhandlungen der verfassunggebende deutschen Nationalversammlung,* 6 vols (Berlin, 1920). The main source for the political history of the First Republic is, of course, the *Verhandlungen des deutschen Reichstags*, 1920–32, vols. 332–458 (Berlin, 1921–32).

For the diplomatic history of the period 1918–45 there are the published documents from the German foreign office archives. The English translation, covering the period 1933–41, has appeared under the title *Documents on German Foreign Policy*, Series C (Göttingen, 1933–36), 5 vols., and Series D (1937–41), 13 vols. Series E will cover the span 1942–45. Since 1966 the untranslated Series B (1925–33) of the *Akten zur deutschen auswärtigen Politik, 1918*–45 has been in course of publication. The appearance of the volumes in Series B and the projected Series A (1918–24) has proceeded very slowly.

Hitler's speeches are to be found in Count Raoul de Sales (ed.), *My New Order* (New York, 1941), Norman H. Baynes (ed.), *The Speeches of Adolf Hitler*, 2 vols. (Oxford, 1942), *Hitler's Table Talk, 1941–4* (London, 1953), and in Max Domarus (ed.), *Hitler: Reden und Proklamationen*, 2 vols. (1961–62).

For the study of the origins of World War II and the conduct of hostilities by the German government, an indispensable collection is the trial proceedings at Nuremberg, published as *The Trial of the Major War Criminals before the International Military Tribunal, Proceedings*, 23 vols. (Nuremberg, 1947–49). The record of the trials of other war criminals is to be found in *Trials of War Criminals before the Nuremberg Military Tribunals*, 14 vols. (Washington, D.C., 1951–53).

The immediate aftermath of 1945 has been the subject of two collections of source materials: J. Hohlfeld (ed.), *Dokumente der deutschen Politik und Geschichte von 1948 bis zur Gegenwart*, 6 vols. (Berlin, 1951–52); and K. Hohlfeld (ed.), *Deutschland nach dem Zusammenbruch 1945: Urkunden und Aktenstücke zur Neuordnung von Staat und Verwaltung sowie Kultur, Wissenschaft und Recht* (Berlin, 1952).

Essential for the study of the history of the Federal Republic of Germany are the legislative proceedings, which have been published as *Verhandlungen des Deutschen Bundestags. Sitzungsberichte* (Bonn, 1949–   ). The laws of the Federal Republic are published annually in the *Bundesgesetzblatt* (Bonn, 1949–   ), while those for the German Democratic Republic are published in the *Gesetzblatt der Deutschen Demokratischen Republik* (East Berlin, 1949–   ). The party conventions of the Socialist Unity Party (SED) take on an inordinate importance in the GDR, because it is basically a monolithic state. The SED proceedings at conventions have been published in successive *Protokolle dr Verhandlungen des Parteitages der Sozialistischen Einheitspartei Deutschlands* (East Berlin, 1949–   ), while the decrees and declarations of the central committee and politburo of the SED have been published since 1950 as *Dokumente der Sozialistischen Einheitspartei Deutschlands* (East Berlin, 1950–   ). The government of the GDR has also published annually collections of documents relating to its foreign policy: *Dokumente zur Aussenpolitik der Regierung der Deutschen Demokratischen Republik* (East Berlin, 1954–   ). There is no analogous West German publication.

Important collections relating to the foreign and Deutschland policies of the Federal Republic of Germany are to be found in *Dokumente zur Deutschlandspolitik*, prepared by E. Deuerlein, Series 3 (1955–58), 4 vols. (1961–71) and Series 4 (1958–66), 1 vol.– (1960–   ); and in H. von Siegler (ed.), *Dokumentation zur Deutschlandfrage. Von der Atlantik Charta bis zur Genfer Aussenministerkonferenz 1959* (Bonn, 1959). Documents concerning the expulsion of Germans from east-central Europe have been published in *Dokumentation der Vertreibung der Deutschen aus Ostmitteleuropa*, prepared by a commission headed by Theodor Schieder, 8 vols. (Bonn, 1953–61). On the Berlin question since World War II see W. Heidelmeyer and G. Hindrichs (eds.), *Dokumente zur Berlin-*

frage, 1944–66 (Munich, 1967). The US government has also published a collection of documents upon the German and Berlin questions: US Senate, Committee on Foreign Relations, *Documents on Germany, 1944–61* (Washington, D.C., 1961). On Germany's postwar eastern frontier, the student may wish to consult R. Goguel (ed.), *Polen, Deutschland und die Oder/Neisse/Grenze* (East Berlin, 1959), which is a publication of the Marxist Deutsche Institut für Zeitgeschichte, or G. Rhode and Wolfgang Wagner (eds.), *Quellen zur Entstehung der Oder-Neisse Linie in den diplomatischen Verhandlungen während des zweiten Weltkrieges*, 2nd ed. (Stuttgart, 1959).

Finally, the student's attention is directed to a few aids, such as the three great *Konversationslexika* of Herder, Meyer, and Brockhaus, and the vast biographical dictionary, *Allgemeine Deutsche Biographie*, 56 vols., covering the period 1875–1912, which has been supplemented for the years since 1912 by *Die grossen Deutschen: Deutsche Biographie* (1956–57). An even more recent biographical compilation for the years before 1917 is *Biographisches Lexikon zur deutschen Geschichte. Von den Anfängen bis 1917*, ed. by K. Obermann, et al. (1967). The Bavarian Academy of Science is also publishing a *Neue Deutsche Biographie* (Munich, 1953–).

The principal older journals devoted to German history in the German language were: the *Historische Zeitschrift*, which continues to be the cardinal journal in the field; *Preussische Jahrbücher, Deutsche Zeitschrift für Geschichtswissenwissenschaft*, and *Forschungen zur brandenburgischen und preussischen Geschichte*. The main Austrian journal has always been the *Mitteilungen des Österreichischen Instituts für Geschichtsforschung*. The leading modern German journal dealing with the medieval period is *Deutsches Archiv für Geschichte des Mittelalters*. Since World War II two new dominant journals have been founded: in East Germany the *Zeitschrift für Geschichtswissenschaft*, and in West Germany the *Vierteljahrshefte für Zeitgeschichte*. The most suitable historical atlas for the student is *Westermanns Grosser Atlas zur Weltgeschichte*, ed. by H. E. Stier and others (numerous recent editions).

General Literature

Bartmuss, H., et al. (eds.). *Deutsche Geschichte.* 3 vols. Berlin, 1965– .

Bechtel, Heinrich. *Wirtschaftsgeschichte Deutschlands*. 5 vols. Munich, 1951–56.

Boor, H. A. W. de and R. Newald. *Geschichte der deutschen Literatur von den Anfängen bis zur Gegenwart*. Munich, 1949.

Brandis, Klemens Graf zu. *Die Habsburger und die Stephanskrone*. Vienna and Zurich, 1937.

Brandt, O., A. O. Meyer, and L. Just. *Handbuch der deutschen Geschichte*. 5 vols. (Vol. III—2 sections; Vol. IV—3 sections). Constance, Marburg, and Frankfurt, 1954–68.

Bretholz, B. *Geschichte Böhmens und Mahrens*. 4 vols. Reichenberg, 1924.

Brunner, H.. *Grundzüge der deutschen Rechtsgeschichte*. 8th ed. Berlin and Leipzig, 1930.

Bryce, James Viscount. *The Holy Roman Empire*. rev. ed. London, 1963.

Bühler, Johannes. *Deutsche Geschichte*. 6 vols. Berlin, 1954–60.

Colombier, Pierre de. *L'art allemand*. Paris, 1950.

Dehio, Ludwig. *Geschichte der deutschen Kunst*. 4 vols., rev. ed. Berlin, 1919–34.

Dickinson, R. E. *Germany, A General and a Regional Geography*. New York, 1953.

Dietrich, Richard. *Kleine Geschichte Preussens*. Berlin, 1966.

Doeberl, Michael. *Entwicklungsgeschichte Bayerns*. 3 vols., 3rd ed. Oldenburg, 1928.

Ernst, Fritz. *The Germans and their Modern History*. Trans. by C. M. Pruch. New York and London, 1966.

Fischer, Otto. *Geschichte der deutschen Malerei*. Munich, 1943.

Flenley, Ralph. *Modern German History*. rev. ed. New York, 1968.

Franz, Günther. *Deutsche Agrargeschichte*. 5 vols. Stuttgart, 1963– . Only two volumes to date through the 18th century.

Frischauer, P. *The Imperial Crown: The Story of the Rise and Fall of the Holy Roman and Austrian Empires*. Trans. New York, 1939.

Gebhardt, Bruno. *Handbuch der deutschen Geschichte*. 4 vols., 9th ed. Stuttgart, 1970–72.

Giesebrecht, Wilhelm von. *Geschichte der deutschen Kaiserzeit*. 6 vols. Leipzig, 1855–95.

Görlitz, Walter. *History of the German General Staff, 1657–1945*. Trans. by Brian Battershaw. New York, 1953.

Gössmann, Wilhelm. *Deutsche Kulturgeschichte im Grundriss*. 2nd rev. ed. Munich, 1963.

Haller, Johannes. *The Epochs of German History*. Trans. and abridged. London, 1930.

Hantsch, H. *Die Geschichte Österreichs*. 2 vols., 3rd ed. Graz, 1951–62.

Hartung, Fritz. *Deutsche Verfassungsgeschichte vom 15. Jahrhundert bis zur Gegenwart*. 5th ed. Stuttgart, 1950.

Hauck, Albert. *Kirchengeschichte Deutschlands*. 5 vols., 9th ed. Berlin, 1958–59.

Heer, Friedrich. *The Holy Roman Empire*. Trans. by Janet Sondheimer. New York, 1968.

Henderson, E. F. *A Short History of Germany*. 2 vols., rev. ed. New York, 1937.

Hoffmann, Albert von. *Politische Geschichte der Deutschen*. 5 vols. Stuttgart, 1922–29.

Holborn, Hajo. *A History of Modern Germany*. 3 vols. New York, 1959–69.

Hubensteiner, Benno. *Bayerische Geschichte*. Munich, 1960.

Huber, Alfons. *Geschichte Österreichs*. 4 vols. Gotha, 1885–96. To 1648. Continued by O. Redlich, *Österreichs Grossmachtbildungen der Zeit Kaiser Leopolds I*, Gotha, 1921, and *Das Werden einer Grossmacht: Osterreich von 1700 bis 1740*, Leipzig, 1938.

Huber, Helmut. *Deutsche Verfassungsgeschichte*. 4 vols. 1957–69.

Jany, C. *Geschichte der königlich-preussischen Armee*. 5 vols. Berlin, 1927–37.

Kaindl, R. F. *Österreich, Preussen und Deutschland: Deutsche Geschichte in grossdeutscher Beleuchtung*. Vienna, 1926.

Kann, Robert A. *A History of the Habsburg Empire, 1526–1918*. Berkeley, 1974.

Kitchen, Martin. *A Military History of Germany from the Eighteenth Century to the Present Day*. Bloomington, Ind., 1975.

Kohn, Hans. *The Mind of Germany: The Education of a Nation*. New York, 1960.

Kretschmayr, H. *Geschichte von Österreich*. Vienna and Leipzig, 1936.

Löwenstein, Prince Hubertus zu. *The Germans in History*. New York, 1945.

Lütge, Friedrich. *Geschichte der deutschen Agrarverfassung vom frühen Mittelalter bis zum 19. Jahrhundert*. 4 vols. Stuttgart, 1967.

Malsch, Rudolf. *Geschichte der deutschen Musik*. Berlin, 1949.

Mann, Golo. *Deutsche Geschichte des 19. und 20. Jahrhunderts*. Berlin, 1958. Trans. as *History of Germany since 1789*. New York, 1968.

Marriott, J. A. R. and C. G. Robertson. *The Evolution of Prussia*. Oxford, 1946.

Martini, F. *Deutsche Literaturgeschichte von den Anfängen bis zur Gegenwart*. Stuttgart, 1960.

Mayer, F. M., R. F. Kaindl, and H. Pirchegger. *Geschichte und Kulturleben Deutsch-oesterreichs*. 3 vols. Vienna and Leipzig, 1929–37.

Meinecke, Friedrich. *Die Idee der Staatsräson in der neueren Geschichte*. Leipzig, 1925. Trans. as *Machiavellism: The Doctrine of Raison d'état and Its Place in History*. London and New Haven, 1957.

Mönch, Walter. *Deutsche Kultur von der Aufklärung bis zur Gegenwart*. Munich, 1962.

Nelson, Walter Henry. *The Soldier Kings: The House of Hohenzollern*. New York, 1970.

Offler, H. S., E. Bonjour, and G. R. Potter. *A Short History of Switzerland*. Oxford, 1952.

Orthbrandt, E. *Deutsche Geschichte. Lebenslauf des deutschen Volkes*. Laupheim, 1954.

Pinson, Koppel S. *Modern Germany: Its History and Civilization*. 2nd ed. New York, 1966. Chap. xxiii by K. Epstein.

Prutz, Heinrich. *Preussische Geschichte*. 4 vols. Stuttgart, 1900–1902.

Rassow, Peter. *Deutsche Geschichte im Überblick*. 3rd ed., ed. by Theodor Schieffer. Stuttgart, 1973.

Reinhardt, K. F. *Germany: 2000 Years*. 2 vols. New York, 1951.

Ritter, Gerhard. *Staatskunst und Kriegshandwerk. Das Problem des Militarismus in Deutschland*. 4 vols. Munich, 1954–1968. Trans. by Heinz Norden as *The Sword and the Scepter. The Problem of Militarism in Germany*. 4 vols. Coral Gables, Fla., 1969–73.

Robertson, J. G. *A History of German Literature*. rev. New York, 1961.

Rodes, John E. *Germany: A History*. New York, 1964.

Schmoller, Gustav. *Preussische Verfassungs-, Verwaltungs-, und Finanzgeschichte*. Berlin, 1921.

Schoeps, Hans-Joachim. *Preussen. Geschichte eines Staates*. Berlin, 1966.

Schramm, Percy E. *Denkmale der deutschen Könige und Kaiser*. Munich, 1962.

Simon, W. M. *Germany: A Brief History*. New York, 1966.

Spenle, J. E. *Der deutsche Geist von Luther bis Nietzsche*. Meisenheim, 1949.

Spindler, Max (ed.). *Handbuch der bayerischen Geschichte*. 3 vols. Munich, 1968–71.

Srbik, Heinrich ritter von. *Deutsche Einheit. Idee und Wirklichkeit vom Heiligen Reich bis Königgrätz*. 4 vols. Munich, 1935–42.

Stern, Selma. *Der preussische Staat und die Juden*. 7 vols. in 4 parts. Tubingen, 1971–75.

Tenbrock, Robert H. *A History of Germany*. Trans. Munich, 1968.

Treue, Wilhelm. *Deutsche Geschichte. Von den Anfängen bis zur Gegenwart*. Stuttgart, 1965.

Uhlirz, Karl and Mathilde. *Handbuch der Geschichte Österreichs und seiner nachbarländer Böhmen und Ungarn*. 4 vols., 2nd ed. Vienna, 1963–65.

Valentin, Veit. *The German People*. Trans. New York, 1946.

Vermeil, Eduard. *Germany's Three Reichs: Their History and Culture*. London, 1945.

Waddington, Albert. *Histoire de Prusse*. 2 vols. Paris, 1911–22.

Zoepfl, Friedrich. *Deutsche Kulturgeschichte*. 2 vols. Freiburg i. Br., 1929–30.

Literature by Era
A. Tribal and Medieval Times

Andreas, Willy. *Deutschland vor der Reformation*. Berlin, 1932.

Barraclough, Geoffrey. *Medieval Germany, 911–1250: Essays by German Historians*. Trans. 2 vols. Oxford, 1938.

———. *The Origins of Modern Germany*. Oxford, 1947.

Bayley, C. C. *The Formation of the German College of Electors.* Toronto, 1949.

Behn, Friedrich. *Römertum und Völkerwanderung.* Stuttgart, 1963.

Below, Georg von. *Der Deutsche Staat des Mittelalters.* Leipzig, 1914.

Brooke, Zachary N. *Lay Investiture and its Relations to the Conflicts of Empire and Papacy.* London, 1939.

Bullough, D. *The Age of Charlemagne.* London and New York, 1965.

Calmette, J. *Charlemagne, sa vie et son oeuvre.* Paris, 1945.

Clark, J. M. *The Great German Mystics: Eckhart, Tauler and Suso.* New York, 1949.

Cleve, Thomas C. van. *The Emperor Frederick II of Hohenstaufen: Immutator Mundi.* New York, 1972.

Dollinger, Philippe. *The German Hansa.* Trans. and ed. by D. S. Ault and S. H. Steinberg. Palo Alto, 1970.

Dopsch, Alfonso. *Herrschaft und Bauer in der deutschen Kaiserzeit.* Jena, 1939.

Ehrismann, Gustav. *Geschichte der deutschen Literatur bis zum Ausgang des Mittelalters.* 3 vols. Munich, 1918–35.

Fichtenau, Henri. *The Carolingian Empire.* Trans. and abridged. London, 1957.

Fisher, Herbert. *The Medieval Empire.* 2 vols. New York, 1969.

Günter, H. *Das deutsche Mittelalter.* 2 vols. Leipzig, 1936–39.

Hampe, Karl. *Germany under the Salian and Hohenstaufen Emperors.* Trans. by Ralph Bennett. Totowa, N.J., 1973.

Heimpel, Hermann. *Deutsches Mittelalter.* Leipzig, 1941.

Holtzmann, Robert. *Geschichte der sächsischen Kaiserzeit.* Munich, 1961.

Hugelmann, K.G. *Stämme, Nation und Nationalstaat im deutschen Mittelalter.* Würzburg, 1955.

Kantorowicz, E. *Emperor Frederick II.* London, 1931.

Kienast, Walter. *Deutschland und Frankreich in der Kaiserzeit, 900–1270.* Leipzig, 1943.

Koepp, Friedrich. *Die Römer in Deutschland.* Bielefeld, 1926.

Kötzschke, R. and W. Ebert. *Geschichte der ostdeutschen Kolonisation.* Leipzig, 1937.

Lintzel, M. *Die Kaiserpolitik Ottos des Grossen.* Munich, 1943.

Maschke R. *Das Geschlecht der Staufer.* Dresden, 1943.

————. *Der Kampf zwischen Kaisertum und Papstum.* Constance, 1955.

Musset, Lucien. *Les invasions: les vagues Germaniques.* 2 vols. Paris, 1965.

Pacaut, Marcel. *Frederick Barbarossa.* Trans. by A. J. Pomerans. New York, 1970.

Pfitzner, J. *Kaiser Karl IV.* Potsdam, 1938.

Pinder, Wilhelm. *Die Kunst der deutschen Kaiserzeit.* Leipzig, 1940.

Planitz, Hans. *Die deutsche Stadt im Mittelalter.* Cologne, 1954.

Santifaller, L. *Zur Geschichte des ottonisch-salischen Reichskirchensystems.* Vienna, 1954.

Schieffer, Theodor. *Winfrid Bonifatius und die christliche Grundlegung.* Freiburg i. Br., 1972.

Schlesinger, Walter. *Beiträge zur deutschen Verfassungsgeschichte des Mittelalters.* 2 vols. Gottingen, 1963–65.

Schramm, Percy. *Kaiser, Rom und Renovatio.* Leipzig and Berlin, 1929.

Sigmund, Paul E. *Nicholas of Cusa and Medieval Political Thought.* Cambridge, Mass., 1963.

Smidt, Wilhelm. *Deutsches Königtum und deutscher Staat während und unter dem Einfluss der italienischen Heerfahrten.* Wiesbaden, 1964.

Tellenbach, Gerhard. *Church, State and Christian Society at the Time of the Investiture Contest.* Oxford, 1940.

Thompson, E.A. *The Early Germans.* New York, 1965.

Thompson, James W. *Feudal Germany.* Chicago, 1918.

Waas, Adolf. *Der Mensch im deutschen Mittelalter.* Cologne, 1964.

B. From the Reformation to Westphalia, 1500–1648

Bainton, Roland H. *Here I Stand* (a life of Luther). New York, 1950.

———. *The Reformation of the Sixteenth Century.* New York, 1952.

Benesch, Otto. *German Painting from Dürer to Holbein.* Trans. H. S. B. Harrison. Geneva, 1966.

Bibl, Victor. *Maximilian II, der rätselhafte Kaiser.* Hellerau, 1929.

Borth, Wilhelm. *Die Luthersache (Causa Luther), 1517–1524: Die Anfänge der Reformation als Frage von Politik und Recht.* Lübeck, 1970.

Brandi, Karl. *Deutsche Geschichte im Zeitalter der Reformation und Gegenreformation.* 4th ed. Berlin, 1969.

———. *The Emperor Charles V.* Trans. by C. V. Wedgwood. London, 1939.

Brodrick, J. *Saint Peter Canisius.* New York, 1935.

Buchner, R. *Maximilian I: Kaiser an der Zeitenwende.* Göttingen, 1959.

Carsten, F. L. *The Origins of Prussia.* Oxford, 1954.

———. *Princes and Parliaments in Germany from the Fifteenth to the Eighteenth Century.* Oxford, 1959.

Denifle, P. *Luther und Luthertum.* 4 vols. Berlin, 1904–1906.

Dickmann, F. *Der Westfälische Friede.* 2nd ed. Münster, 1965.

Eberling, Gerhard. *Luther, An Introduction to His Thought.* Trans. by R. A. Wilson. Philadelphia, 1970.

Farner, Oskar. *Zwingli, the Reformer.* New York, 1952.

Fife, R. H. *The Revolt of Martin Luther.* New York, 1957.

Fischer-Galati, Stephen. *Ottoman Imperialism and German Protestantism, 1521–1555.* Cambridge, Mass., 1959.

Franz, Günther. *Der deutsche Bauernkrieg.* 2 vols. Munich, 1933, 1956.

———. *Der Dreissigjährige Krieg und das deutsche Volk.* 2nd ed. Jena, 1943.

Götz von Pölnitz, Freiherr. *Anton Fugger.* Tübingen, 1963.

Green, V. H. H. *Luther and the Reformation.* New York, 1964.

Hantsch, J. *Die Kaiseridee Karls V.* Graz and Vienna, 1958.

Hildebrandt, E. *Melanchthon: Alien or Ally.* New York, 1946.

Jedin, Hubert. *History of the Council of Trent.* 2 vols. London and New York, 1957–61.

Joachimsen, Paul F. *Die Reformation als Epoche der deutschen Geschichte.* Munich, 1951.

Kann, R. A. *Werden und Zerfall des Habsburgerreiches.* Graz and Vienna, 1962.

Koenigsberger, H. G. *The Habsburgs and Europe, 1516–1660.* Ithaca, 1971.

Lortz, Joseph. *Die Reformation in Deutschland.* 2 vols. Freiburg i. Br., 1948.

Mackinnon, J. *Luther and the Reformation.* 4 vols. London and New York, 1925–30.

Mann, Golo. *Wallenstein. Sein Leben erzählt.* Frankfurt am Main, 1971.

Manschreck, Clyde L. *Melanchthon: The Quiet Reformer.* New York, 1958.

Marius, Richard. *Luther.* Philadelphia, 1974.

Pages, G. *La Guerre de Trente Ans.* Paris, 1949.

Panofsky, E. *Albrecht Dürer.* 3rd ed. Princeton, 1948.

Pevsner, Nikolaus and Michael Meier. *Grünewald.* New York, 1958.

Rassow, P. and F. Schalk. *Karl V, der letzte Kaiser des Mittelalters.* Göttingen, 1957.

Repgen, Konrad. *Papst, Kaiser und Reich, 1521–1644.* Tübingen, 1962.

Ritter, Gerhard. *Luther, His Life and Work.* Trans. New York, 1963.

Ritter, Moritz. *Deutsche Geschichte im Zeitalter der Gegenreformation und des Dreis-sigjährigen Krieges 1555–1648.* 3 vols. Stuttgart and Berlin, 1889–1908.

Schwiebert, E. G. *Luther and His Times: The Reformation From a New Perspective.* St. Louis, 1950.

Spitz, Lewis W. *The Religious Renaissance of the German Humanists.* Oxford and Cambridge, Mass., 1963.

Steinberg, Sigfried H. *The Thirty Years War and the Conflict for European Hegemony.* Göttingen, 1967.

Tyler, Royall. *The Emperor Charles the Fifth.* London, 1956.

Watson, F. *Wallenstein, Soldier under Saturn.* New York, 1938.

Wedgwood, C. V. *The Thirty Years War.* 2nd ed. London, 1967.

Williams, Huntston. *The Radical Reformation.* Philadelphia, 1962.

C. *Westphalia to the*
Congress of Vienna, 1648–1815

Anderson, E. N. *Nationalism and the Cultural Crisis in Prussia, 1806–1815.* New York, 1939.

Andreas, Willy. *Das Zeitalter Napoleons und die Erhebung der Völker.* Heidelberg, 1955.

Arenberg, Prince J. E. *Les princes du St. Empire et l'epoque napoléonienne.* Brussels, 1951.

Barnard, F. M. *Herder's Social and Political Thought from Enlightenment to National-ism.* New York, 1965.

Bechtel, H. W. P. *Wirtschaftsgeschichte Deutschlands von Beginn des 16. bis zum Ende des 18. Jahrhunderts.* 2 vols. Munich, 1952.

Benedikt, E. *Kaiser Joseph II, 1741–1790.* Vienna, 1936.

Bernard, Paul P. *Joseph II.* The Hague, 1968.

Bibl, Victor. *Kaiser Joseph II: Ein Vorkämpfer der grossdeutschen Idee.* Vienna, 1943.

Bielchowsky, Albert. *Life of Goethe.* 4 vols. Berlin, 1905–1908.

Biro, S. S. *The German Policy of Revolutionary France, 1791–1797.* Cambridge, Mass., 1957.

Boehm, Max von. *Deutschland im achtzehnten Jahrhundert. Das Heilige Römische Reich Deutscher Nation.* 2 vols. Berlin, 1922.

Braubach, M. *Der Aufstieg Brandenburg-Preussens, 1649–1815.* Freiburg i. Br., 1933.

——— . *Prinz Eugen von Savoyen.* 5 vols. Vienna, 1963–65.

Bruford, W. H. *Culture and Society in Classical Weimar, 1775–1806.* New York, 1962.

——— . *Germany in the Eighteenth Century.* New York, 1935.

Brunschwig, H. *Le crise de l'état prussien à la fin du XVIII siècle.* Paris, 1947.

Buchwald, R. *Schiller.* 2 vols. Leipzig, 1937.

Cassirer, Ernst. *Die Philosophie der Aufklärung.* Tübingen, 1932. Trans. as *Philosophy of the Enlightenment,* New York, 1951.

Crankshaw, Edward. *Maria Theresa.* New York, 1970.

Dorwart, R. A. *The Administrative Reforms of Frederick William I of Prussia*. Cambridge, Mass., 1953.

——— . *The Prussian Welfare State before 1740*. Cambridge, 1971.

Droz, Jacques. *L'Allemagne et la révolution française*. Paris, 1949.

——— . *Le Romantisme allemand et l'État*. Paris, 1966.

Epstein, Klaus W. *The Genesis of German Conservatism*. New York, 1966.

Ergang, Robert. *Potsdam Führer: Frederick William I of Prussia*. New York, 1941.

Ermatinger, E. *Deutsche Kultur im Zeitalter der Aufklärung*. Potsdam, 1935.

Fauchier-Magnan, A. *The Smaller German Courts in the Eighteenth Century*. London, 1958.

Fay, Sidney B. *The Rise of Brandenburg-Prussia to 1786*. rev. ed. New York, 1964.

Feulner, A. *Skulptur und Malerei im 18. Jahrhundert in Deutschland*. Potsdam, 1929.

Ford, Guy S. *Stein and the Era of Reform in Prussia, 1807–1815*. Princeton, 1922.

Garland, H. B. *Lessing: The Founder of Modern German Literature*. New York, 1962.

Gaxotte, Pierre. *Frederick the Great*. Trans. from French. New Haven, 1942.

Gay, Peter. *Weimar Culture: The Outsider as Insider*. New York, 1968.

Gooch, G. P. *Frederick the Great: The Ruler, the Writer, the Man*. New York, 1947.

——— . *Germany and the French Revolution*. London, 1920.

Griewank, K. *Der Wiener Kongress und die europäische Restauration 1814/15*. 3rd ed. Leipzig, 1963.

Haas, Robert. *Die Musik des Barock*. Berlin, 1934.

Hausherr, Hans. *Hardenberg: eine politische Biographie*. Cologne, 1963

Heer, Friedrich. *Leibniz*. Frankfurt, 1958.

Hempel, Eberhard. *Baroque Art and Architecture in Central Europe*. Trans. Baltimore, 1965.

Henderson, Nicholas. *Prince Eugene of Savoy*. New York, 1964.

Hubatsch, Walter. *Das Zeitalter des Absolutisumus 1600–1789*, 2nd ed., Braunschweig, 1965.

Johnson, Hubert C. *Frederick the Great and his Officials*. New Haven, 1975.

Kahn, Robert A. *A Study in Austrian Intellectual History: From Late Baroque to Romanticism*. New York, 1960.

Koselleck, Reinhart. *Preussen zwischen Reform und Revolution: Allgemeines Landrecht, Verwaltung und soziale Bewegung von 1791 bis 1848*. Stuttgart, 1967.

Koser, Reinhold. *Friedrich der Grosse*. 4 vols., 7th ed. Berlin, 1921–25.

Kraehe, Enno E. *Metternich's German Policy*. Vol. I: *The Contest with Napoleon, 1799–1814*. Princeton, 1963.

Kretschmayr, H. *Maria Theresia*. 2nd ed. Leipzig, 1938.

Küntzel, G. *Fürst Kaunitz-Rietberg als Staatsmann*. Frankfurt a. M., 1923.

Langsam, Walter C. *Francis the Good, The Education of an Emperor*. New York, 1949.

——— . *The Napoleonic Wars and German Nationalism in Austria*. New York, 1930.

Meinecke, Friedrich. *Das Zeitalter der deutschen Erhebung, 1795–1815*. 3rd ed. Leipzig, 1924.

Meyer, R. W. *Leibniz and the Seventeenth Century Revolution*. Trans. by J. P. Stern. Cambridge, Mass., 1952.

Nidda, R. Krug von. *Eugen von Savoyen*. Vienna and Zurich, 1963.

Otruba, Gustav. *Die Wirtschaftspolitik Maria Theresias*. Vienna, 1963.

Padover, Saul K. *The Revolutionary Emperor Joseph II of Austria*. rev. ed. Hamden, Conn., 1967.

Paret, Peter. *Yorck and the Era of Prussian Reform, 1807–1815*. Princeton, 1966.

Petersdorff, Hermann von. *Der Grosse Kurfürst*. Berlin, 1939.

Philippson, M. *Der Grosse Kurfürst; Friedrich Wilhelm von Brandenburg*. 3 vols. Leipzig, 1897–1903.

Redlich, O. *Das Werden einer Grossmacht: Österreich von 1700–1740*. Vienna, 1940.

————. *Weltmacht des Barock: Österreich in der Zeit Leopolds I*. 4th ed. Vienna, 1961.

Reinhold, P. *Maria Theresia*. Wiesbaden, 1957.

Ritter, Gerhard. *Friedrich der Grosse: Ein historisches Profil*. 3rd ed. Heidelberg, 1954. Trans. as *Frederick the Great: A Historical Profile*. Berkeley and Los Angeles, 1975.

————. *Stein: Eine politische Biographie*. 2 vols., 3rd ed. Stuttgart, 1958.

Rössler, Helmuth. *Österreichs Kampf um Deutschlands Befreiung 1805–1815*. 2 vols., 2nd ed. Hamburg, 1940.

————. *Graf Johann Philipp Stadion: Napoleons deutscher Gegenspieler*. 2 vols. 1966.

Rudé, George. *Europe in the Eighteenth Century: Aristocracy and the Bourgeois Challenge*. New York, 1972.

Schevill, Ferdinand. *The Great Elector*. New York, 1947.

Shanahan, William O. *Prussian Military Reforms, 1786–1813*. New York, 1945.

Simon, Edith. *The Making of Frederick the Great*. London, 1963.

Simon, W. M. *The Failure of the Prussian Reform Movement, 1807–1819*. Ithaca, N.Y., 1955.

Solz, Walter. *Early German Romanticism*. Cambridge, Mass., 1929.

Srbik, Heinrich Ritter von. *Das österreichische Kaisertum und das Ende des Heiligen Römischen Reiches, 1804–1806*. Berlin, 1927.

————. *Metternich, Der Staatsmann und der Mensch*. 3 vols., 2nd ed. Munich, 1954.

Stadelmann, Rudolf. *Scharnhorst: Schicksal und geistige Welt*. Wiesbaden, 1952.

Stoye, John Walter. *Emperor Charles VI*. New York, 1962.

Streisand, J. *Deutschland von 1789 bis 1815*. East Berlin, 1959.

Treue, W. *Deutsche Geschichte von 1713–1806*. Sammlung Göschen, No. 35, 1956.

Tschuppik, Karl. *Maria Theresia*. Vienna, 1934.

Tuttle, Herbert. *History of Prussia to the Accession of Frederick the Great*. 4 vols. 1884–96.

Valjavec, Fritz. *Die Entstehung der politischen Strömungen in Deutschland, 1770–1815*. Munich, 1951.

Waddington, A. *Le Grand Electeur: Frédéric Guillaume de Brandebourg—sa politique extérieur*. Paris, 1905.

Wahl, Adalbert. *Über die Nachwirkungen der französischen Revolution, vornehmlich in Deutschland*. Stuttgart, 1939.

Wandruszka, A. *Leopold II*. 2 vols. Vienna, 1963–65.

Zacharias, Theodor. *Joseph Emanuel Fischer von Erlach*. Vienna, 1960.

Zottman, A. *Die Wirtschaftspolitik Friedrichs des Grossen*. Leipzig, 1937.

D. *1815–1914*

Anderson, E. N. *The Social and Political Conflict in Prussia, 1858–1864*. Lincoln, Neb., 1954.

Angel, Pierre. *Éduard Bernstein et l'évolution du socialisme Allemand*. Paris, 1961.

Bachem, Karl. *Vorgeschichte, Geschichte und Politik der deutschen Zentrumspartei 1815–1914*. 9 vols. Cologne, 1927–32.

Benz, Richard. *Die deutsche Romantik: Geschichte einer geistigen Bewegung*. Leipzig, 1937.

Berghahn, Volker R. *Der Tirpitz-Plan: Genesis und Verfall einer innenpolitischen Krisenstrategie unter Wilhelm II.* Dusseldorf, 1971.

————. *Germany and the Approach of War in 1914.* New York, 1973.

Bibl, Victor. *Metternich, der Dämon Österreichs.* Vienna, 1936.

Blum, Jerome. *Noble Landowners and Agriculture in Austria, 1818–1848.* Princeton, 1961.

Böhme, Helmut. *Deutschlands Weg zur Grossmacht, 1848–1881.* Cologne and Berlin, 1966.

Born, Karl E. *Staat und Sozialpolitik seit Bismarcks Sturz.* Wiesbaden, 1957.

Borries, Kurt. *Deutschland im Kreis der europäischen Mächte.* Stuttgart, 1963.

Bramsted, E. K. *Aristocracy and the Middle Classes in Germany.* 2nd ed. Chicago and London, 1964.

Brandenburg, Erich. *Die Reichsgründung.* 2 vols. Leipzig, 1916.

————. *Von Bismarck zum Weltkrieg: Die deutsche Politik in den Jahrzehnten vor dem Kriege.* 3rd ed. Reprint, 1967. Trans. as *From Bismarck to the World War: A History of German Foreign Policy, 1870–1914.* Delhi, n.d.

Bruck, Werner F. *Social and Economic History of Germany, 1888–1938.* Cardiff, 1938.

Carroll, E. M. *Germany and the Great Powers, 1866–1914.* New York, 1938.

Chickering, Roger. *Imperial Germany and a World without War: The Peace Movement and German Society, 1892–1914.* Princeton, 1976.

Clapham, Sir John H. *The Economic Development of France and Germany, 1815–1914.* Cambridge, England, 1936.

Clark, Chester W. *Franz Joseph and Bismarck.* Cambridge, Mass., 1934.

Conze, Werner. *Die Zeit Wilhelms II und die Weimarer Republik: Deutsche Geschichte 1890–1933.* Stuttgart, 1964.

———— and Dieter Groh. *Die Arbeiterbewegung in der nationalen Bewegung: Die deutsche Sozialdemokratie vor, während und nach der Reichsgründung.* Stuttgart, 1966.

Craig, Gordon. *From Bismarck to Adenauer: Aspects of German Statecraft.* Baltimore, 1958.

————. *The Politics of the Prussian Army, 1640–1945.* Oxford, 1955.

Demeter, Karl. *The German Officer Corps in Society and State.* Trans. New York, 1965.

Dittrich, J. *Bismarck, Frankreich und die Spanische Thronkandidatur der Hohenzollern.* Munich, 1962.

Droz, Jacques. *Les révolutions allemandes de 1848.* Paris, 1957.

Eyck, Erich. *Bismarck.* 3 vols. Erlenbach-Zurich, 1941–44. One vol. trans. *Bismarck and the German Empire.* London and New York, 1950.

————. *Das persönliche Regiment Wilhelms II.* Erlenbach-Zurich, 1948.

Eyck, Frank. *The Frankfurt Parliament, 1848–1849.* New York, 1968.

Findlay, J. H. *Hegel: A Re-examination.* London and New York, 1958.

Fischer, Fritz. *Krieg der Illusionen: Die deutsche Politik vom 1911 bis 1914.* Düsseldorf, 1969. Trans. as *War of Illusions: German Policies from 1911 to 1914.* New York, 1975.

Franz, Georg. *Kulturkampf: Staat und katholische Kirche in Mitteleuropa von der Säkularisation bis zum Abschluss des preussischen Kulturkampfes.* Munich, 1954.

Gay, Peter. *The Dilemma of Democratic Socialism: Eduard Bernstein's Challenge to Marx.* New York, 1952.

Göhring, Martin. *Bismarcks Erben, 1890–1945: Deutschlands Weg von Wilhelm II bis Adolf Hitler.* Wiesbaden, 1959.

Groh, Dieter. *Negative Integration und revolutionärer Attentismus: Die deutsche Sozial-*

demokratie am Vorabend des Ersten Weltkrieges. Frankfurt a. M., 1973.

Gutsche, Willibald. *Aufstieg und Fall eines kaiserlichen Reichskanzlers: Theobald von Bethmann-Hollweg 1856–1921: Ein politisches Lebensbild*. East Berlin, 1973.

Haas, Arthur. *Metternich, Reorganization and Nationality, 1813–1818*. Wiesbaden, 1963.

Hallgarten, George W. F. *Imperialismus vor 1914: Die soziologischen Grundlagen der Aussenpolitik der europäischen Grossmächte vor dem Ersten Weltkrieg*. 2 vols., rev. 2nd ed. Munich, 1963.

Hallgarten, George W. F. and Joachim Radkau. *Deutsche Industrie und Politik: Von Bismarck bis Heute*. Frankfurt am Main, 1974.

Hamerow, Theodore S. *Restoration, Revolution, Reaction: Economics and Politics in Germany, 1815–1871*. Princeton, 1958.

———. *The Social Foundations of German Unification, 1858–1871*. Princeton, 1969.

Haselmayr, Friedrich. *Diplomatische Geschichte des Zweiten Reiches von 1871 bis 1918*. 6 vols. Munich, 1956–64.

Heckart, Beverly. *From Bassermann to Bebel: The Grand Bloc's Quest for Reform in the Kaiserreich, 1900–1914*. New Haven, 1974.

Henderson, W. O. *The Zollverein*. Cambridge, England, 1938.

———. *The Rise of German Industrial Power, 1834–1914*. Berkeley, Cal., 1976.

Hillgruber, Andreas. *Bismarcks Aussenpolitik*. Göttingen, 1972.

———. *Deutschlands Rolle in der Vorgeschichte der beiden Weltkriege*. Göttingen, 1967.

Höfele, Karl H. *Geist und Gesellschaft der Bismarckzeit 1870–1890*. Gottingen, 1967.

Höhn, Reinhard. *Die vaterlandslosen Gesellen: Der Sozialismus im Licht der Geheimberichte der preussischen Polizei 1878–1914*. Vol. I: 1878–1890. Cologne and Opladen, 1964.

Howard, Michael. *The Franco-Prussian War*. London, 1961.

Hubatsch, Walter. *Die Ära Tirpitz: Studien zur deutschen Marinepolitik 1890–1918*. Göttingen, 1955.

Jarausch, Konrad. *The Enigmatic Chancellor: Bethmann-Hollweg and the Hybris of Imperial Germany*. New Haven, 1973.

Kaelble, Hartmut. *Industrielle Interessenpolitik in der wilhelminischen Gesellschaft: Centralverband deutscher Industrieller 1895–1914*. Berlin, 1967.

Kehr, Eckart. *Der Primat der Innenpolitik: Gesammelte Aufsätze zur preussisch-deutschen Sozialgeschichte im 19. und 20. Jahrhundert*. ed. by Hans-Ulrich Wehler. 2nd ed. Berlin, 1970.

Kiszling, R. *Fürst Felix zu Schwarzenberg*. Graz, 1952.

Klein, Fritz. *Deutschland, 1897/98–1917*. East Berlin, 1963.

Kosellek, Reinhart. *Preussen zwischen Reform und Revolution: Allgemeines Landrecht, Verwaltung und soziale Revolution von 1791 bis 1848*. Stuttgart, 1967.

Kröger, Karl H. *Die Konservativen und die Politik Caprivis*. Rostock, 1937.

Kuczynski, Jurgen. *A Short History of Labour Conditions in Germany 1800 to the present Day*. London, 1945.

———. *Darstellung der Lage der Arbeiter in Deutschland von 1789–1900*. 3 vols. East Berlin, 1961–1962.

Kumpf-Korfes, Sigrid. *Bismarcks "Drang nach Russland": Zum Problem der sozialökonomischen Hintergründe der russisch-deutschen Entfremdung im Zeitraum von 1878 bis 1891*. Berlin, 1968.

Kürenberg, Joachim (pseudonym for J. von Reichel). *The Kaiser: A Life of William II, last Emperor of Germany*. Trans. by H. T. Russell and Herta Hagen. London, 1954.

Lambi, I. N. *Free Trade and Protection in Germany, 1868–1879*. Wiesbaden, 1963.

Lenz, Max. *Geschichte Bismarcks*. Leipzig, 1922.

Lidtke, Vernon. *The Outlawed Party: Social Democracy in Germany, 1878–1890*. Princeton, 1966.

Löwith, Karl. *Von Hegel bis Nietzsche*. Trans. by David Green. Zurich and New York, 1964.

Macartney, C. A. *The Habsburg Empire*. New York, 1969.

Maehl, William H. *German Militarism and Socialism*. Lincoln, Neb., 1968.

Marcks, Erich. *Der Aufstieg des Reiches: Deutsche Geschichte von 1807–1871/78*. 2 vols. Stuttgart, 1936.

Medlicott, W. N. *Bismarck and Modern Germany*. London, 1965.

Meyer, Arnold O. *Bismarck. Der Mensch und der Staatsmann*. Stuttgart, 1949.

Meyer, Henry C. *Mitteleuropa in German Thought and Action, 1815–1945*. The Hague, 1955.

Mommsen, Wilhelm. *Bismarck: Ein politisches Lebensbild*. Munich, 1959.

Mommsen, Wolfgang. *Bethmann-Hollweg und das Problem der politischen Führung*. Cologne, 1967.

Morsey, Rudolf. *Die oberste Reichsverwaltung unter Bismarck 1867–1890*. Münster, 1957.

Mosse, W. E. *The European Powers and the German Question, 1848–1871*. New York and Cambridge, Eng., 1958.

N'aman, Shlomo. *Lassalle*. 2nd ed. Hanover, 1971.

Namier, Lewis. *The Revolution of the Intellectuals*. London, 1944.

Naujoks, Eberhard. *Bismarcks auswärtige Pressepolitik und die Reichsgründung, 1865–1871*. Wiesbaden, 1968.

Nichols, John Alden. *Germany after Bismarck: The Caprivi Era, 1890–1894*. Cambridge, Mass., 1958.

Nipperdey, Thomas. *Die Organisation der deutschen Parteien vor 1918*. Düsseldorf, 1961.

Noyes, P. H. *Organization and Revolution: Working Class Associations in the German Revolutions of 1848/49*. Princeton, 1966.

Oncken, Hermann. *Das deutsche Reich und die Vorgeschichte des Weltkrieges*. 2 vols. Leipzig, 1933.

——— . *Die Rheinpolitik Napoleons III 1863–1870 und der Ursprung des Krieges von 1870–1871*. 3 vols. Stuttgart, 1926.

Palmer, Alan. *Metternich*. New York, 1972.

Pflanze, Otto. *Bismarck and the Development of Germany: The Period of Unification, 1815–1871*. Princeton, 1963.

Price, A. H. *The Evolution of the Zollverein, 1815–1833*. Ann Arbor, Mich., 1949.

Puhle, Hans-Jürgen. *Agrarische Interessenpolitik und preussischer Konservatismus in wilhelminischen Reich 1893–1914*. Hanover, 1966.

Ramm, Agatha. *Germany, 1789–1919: A Political History*. London, 1967.

Rath, R. J. *The Viennese Revolution of 1848*. Austin, Tex., 1957.

Rauh, Manfred. *Föderalismus und Parlamentarismus in wilhelminischen Reich*. Düsseldorf, 1972.

Reiners, Ludwig. *Bismarck*. 2 vols. Munich, 1956–65 (to 1871).

Rich, Norman and M. H. Fisher. *Friedrich von Holstein: Politics and Diplomacy in the Era of Bismarck and William II*. Cambridge, 1965.

Richter, Werner. *Bismarck*. New York, 1965.

Ritter, Gerhard. *Der Schlieffen Plan: Kritik eines Mythos*. Munich, 1965.

———. *The Sword and the Scepter*, vols. I and II. Trans. from *Staatskunst und Kriegshandwerk*. Coral Gables, Fla., 1969–70.

Ritter, Gerhard A. *Die Arbeiterbewegung im wilhelminischen Reich*. Berlin, 1959.

Röhl, John C. *Germany without Bismarck: The Crisis of Government in the Second Reich, 1890–1900*. Berkeley, Cal. 1967.

Röhr, Donald G. *The Origins of Social Liberalism in Germany*. Chicago, 1963.

Rosenberg, Hans. *Grosse Depression und Bismarckszeit: Wirtschaftsablauf, Gesellschaft und Politik in Mitteleuropa*. Berlin, 1967.

Roth, Günther. *The Social Democrats in Imperial Germany*. Englewood Cliffs, N.J., 1963.

Schmidt-Volkman, Erich. *Der Kulturkampf in Deutschland 1871–1890*. Göttingen, 1962.

Schnabel, Franz. *Deutsche Geschichte im 19. Jahrhundert*. 5 vols. Freiburg i. Br., 1949–59.

Schoeps, Hans J. *Das andere Preussen. Konservative Gestalten und Probleme im Zeitalter Friedrich Wilhelms IV*. 3rd ed. Berlin, 1964.

Schorske, Carl E. *German Social Democracy, 1905–1917*. Cambridge, Mass., 1955.

Schottelius, Herbert and Wilhelm Deists (eds.). *Marine und Marinepolitik im kaiserlichen Deutschland 1871–1914*. Düsseldorf, 1972.

Schröder, Hans-Christoph. *Sozialismus und Imperialismus. Die Auseinandersetzung der deutschen Sozialdemokratie mit dem Imperialismusproblem und der "Weltpolitik" vor 1914*. Part I. Hanover, 1968.

Schwarzenberg, A. *Prince Felix zu Schwarzenberg, Prime Minister of Austria, 1848–1852*. New York, 1946.

Seeber, Gustav. *Zwischen Bebel und Bismarck*. East Berlin, 1965.

Simons, W. M. *Germany in the Age of Bismarck*. New York, 1968.

Sombart, Werner. *Die deutsche Volkswirtschaft im 19. Jahrhundert und im Anfang des 20. Jahrhunderts*. rev. ed. Stuttgart, 1954.

Stadelmann, R. *Moltke und der Staat*. Krefeld, 1951.

Steefel, Lawrence D. *Bismarck, the Hohenzollern Candidacy and the Origins of the Franco-German War of 1870*. Cambridge, Mass., 1962.

———. *The Schleswig-Holstein Question*. Cambridge, 1932.

Stern, Fritz. *The Politics of Cultural Despair: A Study in the Rise of Germanic Ideology*. Berkeley, Cal., 1961.

Stolper, Gustav, Karl Häuser and Knut Borchardt. *The German Economy, 1870 to the Present*. Trans. by Toni Stolper. New York and Chicago, 1967.

Stürmer, Michael (ed.). *Das kaiserliche Deutschland: Politik und Gesellschaft, 1870–1918*. Düsseldorf, 1970.

———. *Regierung und Reichstag im Bismarckstaat 1871–1880*. Dusseldorf, 1974.

Taylor, A. J. P. *Bismarck: The Man and the Statesman*. New York, 1955.

Tirrell, Sarah. *German Agrarian Politics after Bismarck's Fall*. New York, 1951.

Valentin, Veit. *1848: Chapters of German History*. London, 1940.

Vietsch, E. *Bethmann-Hollweg. Staatsmann zwischen Macht und Ethos*. Boppard am Rh. 1969.

Vogel, Barbara. *Deutsche Russlandpolitik: Das Scheitern der deutschen Weltpolitik unter Bulow, 1900–1906*. Gütersloh, 1973.

Vossler, Otto. *Bismarcks Sozialpolitik*. Darmstadt, 1961.

Wachenheim, H. *Die deutsche Arbeiterbewegung, 1844–1914*. Stuttgart, 1967.

Wahl, Adalbert. *Deutsche Geschichte von der Reichsgründung bis zum Ausbruch des Weltkrieges 1871–1914*. 4 vols. Stuttgart, 1926–1936.

Wehler, Hans-Ulrich. *Bismarck und der Imperialismus*. Cologne, 1969.

———. *Krisenherde des Kaiserreichs 1871–1918: Studien zur deutschen Sozial- und Verfassungsgeschichte*. Göttingen, 1970.

———. *Sozialdemokratie und Nationalstaat*. Würzburg, 1962.

Winkler, Heinrich A. *Preussischer Liberalismus und deutscher Nationalstaat*. Tübingen, 1964.

Wolter, Heinz. *Alternative zu Bismarck: Die deutsche Sozialdemokratie und die Aussenpolitik des preussisch-deutschen Reiches 1878–1890*, Berlin, 1970.

Zechlin, Egmont. *Bismarck und die Grundlegung der deutschen Grossmacht*. Stuttgart, 1930.

Zeender, J. K. *The German Center Party, 1890–1906*. Philadelphia, 1976.

Ziekursch, Johannes. *Politische Geschichte des neuen deutschen Kaiserreiches*. 3 vols. Frankfurt a. M., 1925–30.

Zucker, Stanley. *Ludwig Bamberger: German Liberal Politician and Social Critic, 1823–1899*. Pittsburgh, 1975.

E. From World War I to the Present

Anderle, Alfred. *Die deutsche Rapallo-Politik*. East Berlin, 1962.

Angress, Werner. *Stillborn Revolution: The Communist Bid for Power in Germany, 1921–1923*. Princeton, 1963.

Baumgart, Winfried. *Deutsche Ostpolitik 1918. Von Brest-Litovsk bis zum Ende des Ersten Weltkrieges*. Vienna and Munich 1966.

Ben Elissar, Eliahu. *La diplomatie du III Reich et les Juifs, 1933–1939*. Paris, 1969.

Bennett, Edward W. *Germany and the Diplomacy of the Financial Crisis*. Cambridge, Mass., 1962.

Berlau, Abraham. *The German Social Democratic Party, 1914–1921*. New York, 1949.

Besson, W. *Die Aussenpolitik der Bundesrepublik*. Munich, 1970.

Bewley, Charles. *Hermann Göring and the Third Reich: A Biography*. New York, 1962.

Birnbaum, Immanuel. *Entzweite Nachbarn: Deutsche Politik in Osteuropa*. Frankfurt a. M., 1968.

Boelcke, W. A. *Deutschlands Rüstung im Zweiten Weltkrieg*. Frankfurt am Main, 1969.

Bracher, Karl D. *Die Auflösung der Weimarer Republik: Eine Studie zum Problem des Machtverfalls in der Demokratie*. 4th ed. Villingen, 1964.

———. *The German Dictatorship: The Origins, Structure and Effects of National Socialism*. Trans. by J. Steinberg. New York, 1970.

———, Wolfgang Sauer, and Gerhard Schulz. *Die nationalsozialistische Machtergriefung*. 2nd ed. Cologne, 1962.

Bullock, Alan. *Hitler, A Study in Tyranny*. rev. ed. New York, 1971.

Carroll, B. A. *Design for Total War*. The Hague, 1968.

Carsten, F. L. *The Reichswehr and Politics, 1918 to 1933*. New York and Oxford, 1966.

Castellan, Georges. *L'Allemagne de Weimar, 1918–1933*. Paris, 1969.

Childs, David. *From Schumacher to Brandt: The Study of German Socialism, 1945–1965*. New York and London, 1966.

———. *Germany Since 1918*. New York, Evanston, San Francisco, 1970.

Clark, Alan. *Barbarossa: The Russian-German Conflict, 1941–1945*. New York, 1965.

Compton, James V. *The Swastika and the Eagle: Hitler, the United States and the Origins of World War II*. Boston, 1967.

Conway, J. S. *The Nazi Persecution of the Churches*. New York, 1968.

Conze, Werner. *Das deutsch-russische Verhältnis im Wandel der modernen Welt*. Göttingen, 1967.

Dahrendorf, Ralf. *Society and Democracy in Germany*. Trans. Garden City, N.Y., 1967.

Dallin, Alexander. *German Rule in Russia, 1941–1945*. London, 1957.

Deutsch, Harold C. *The Conspiracy against Hitler in the Twilight War*. Minneapolis, 1968.

Dönhoff, Marion Gräfin von. *Die Bundesrepublik in der Ära Adenauer*. Reinbeck bei Hamburg, 1963.

Dorpalen, Andreas. *Hindenburg and the Weimar Republic*. Princeton, 1964.

Dülffer, Jost. *Weimar, Hitler und die Marine: Reichspolitik und Flottenbau 1920–1939*. Düsseldorf, 1973.

Edinger, Lewis J. *Kurt Schumacher*. Stanford, 1965.

Edwards, Marvin L. *Stresemann and the Greater Germany, 1914–1918*. New York, 1963.

Elben, Wolfgang. *Das Problem der Kontinuität in der deutschen Revolution 1918–1919*. Düsseldorf, 1965.

Epstein, Klaus. *Matthias Erzberger and the Dilemma of German Democracy*. Princeton, 1959.

Erdmenger, Klaus. *Das folgenschwere Missverständnis: Bonn und die sowjetische Deutschlandpolitik 1949–1955*. Freiburg, i. Br., 1967.

Eschenburg, Theodor. *Die improvisierte Demokratie* (Weimar Republic). Munich, 1963.

———. *The Road to Dictatorship in Germany, 1918–1933*. Trans. by L. Wilson. London, 1964.

Eubank, Keith. *Munich*. Norman, Okla., 1963.

Eyck, Erich. *A History of the Weimar Republic*. Trans. by H. P. Hanson and R. G. L. Waite. 2 vols. Cambridge and Oxford, 1962–64.

Favez, Jean-Claude. *Le Reich devant l'occupation Franco-Belge de la Ruhr, 1923*. Geneva, 1969.

Feldman, G. D. *Army, Industry and Labor in Germany, 1914–1918*. Princeton, 1966.

Felix, David. *Walter Rathenau and the Weimar Republic: The Politics of Reparations*. Baltimore, 1971.

Fest, Joachim C. *Hitler*. Trans. by Richard and Clara Winston. Vintage Books ed., New York, 1975.

Fischer, Fritz. *Griff nach der Weltmacht; die Kriegszielpolitik des kaiserlichen Deutschlands 1914–1918*. Düsseldorf, 1961. Trans. and abridged as *Germany's Aims in the First World War*. New York, 1967.

Flechtheim, Ossip K. *Die Kommunistische Partei Deutschlands in der Weimarer Republik*. Offenbach, 1948.

Fraenkel, Heinrich and R. Manwell. *Goebbels: His Life and Death*, New York, 1960.

———. *Heinrich Himmler: Kleinbürger und Massenmörder*. New York, 1965.

———. *Hermann Göring*. Hanover, 1964.

Freund, Gerald. *Unholy Alliance*. New York, 1957. (German-Russian Relations, 1918–1926.)

Friedensburg, Ferdinand. *Die Weimarer Republik*. 2nd ed. Hanover, 1959.

Frölich, Paul. *Rosa Luxemburg: Her Life and Work*. Trans. by Edward Fitzgerald. New York, 1969.

Gangen, Welles. *The Muted Revolution: East Germany's Challenge to Russia and the West*. New York. 1966.

Gatzke, Hans W. *Germany's Drive to the West: A Study of Germany's Western War Aims during the First World War*. Baltimore, 1950.

Göhring, Martin. *Alles oder nichts: Zwölf Jahre totalitärer Herrschaft in Deutschland, 1933–1945*. 2 vols. Tübingen, 1966.

Goodspeed, D. J. *Ludendorff, Genius of World War I*. Boston, 1966.

Gordon, Harold J. *The Reichswehr and the German Republic, 1919–1926*. Princeton, 1957.

Görlitz, Walter. *Hindenburg: Ein Lebensbild*. Bonn, 1953.

Gropius, Walter. *The New Architecture and the Bauhaus*. Trans. by P. J. Shand. New York, 1937.

Grosser, Alfred. *Die Bundesrepublik Deutschland: Bilanz einer Entwicklung*. Tübingen, 1967.

Grosser, Alfred and Henri Menudier. *La vie politique en Allemagne fédérale*. Paris, 1970.

Grossler, Alfred. *Germany in our Time: A Political History of the Postwar Years*. Trans. by Paul Stephenson. New York, Washington, and London, 1971.

Grunberger, A. *A Social History of the Third Reich*. New York, 1972.

Haffner, Sebastian. *Failure of a Revolution: Germany 1918–1919*. Trans. by George Rapp, La Salle, Ill., 1973.

Hallgarten, George W. *Hitler, Reichswehr und Industrie*. Frankfurt a. M., 1955.

Hallgarten, G. W. F. and Joachim Radkau. *Deutsche Industrie und Politik: Von Bismarck bis Heute*. Frankfurt, 1974.

Halperin, S. William. *Germany Tried Democracy: A Political History of the Reich from 1918 to 1933*. New York, 1946, 1965.

Hanrieder, Wolfram. *West German Foreign Policy 1949–1963*. Stanford, 1967.

Heiber, Helmut. *Die Republik von Weimar*. 2nd ed. Stuttgart, 1968.

Heiber, Helmut. *Goebbels*. 1962.

Heiber, Helmut et al. *Deutsche Geschichte seit dem Ersten Weltkrieg*, I. Stuttgart, 1971.

Hildebrand, Klaus. *Vom Reich zum Weltreich: Hitler, NSDAP und Kolonialfragen 1919–1945*. Munich, 1969.

———. *The Foreign Policy of the Third Reich*. Trans. by Anthony Fothergill, Berkeley and Los Angeles, 1973.

Hillgruber, Andreas. *Hitlers Strategischepolitik und Kriegsführung 1940–1941*. Frankfurt a. M., 1965.

Hoegner, Wilhelm. *Die verratene Republik: Geschichte der deutschen Gegenrevolution*. Munich, 1958.

Hoffmann, Peter. *Widerstand—Staatsstreich—Attentat: Der Kampf der Opposition gegen Hitler*. Munich, 1969.

Hubatsch, Walter. *Der Admiralstab und die obersten Marinebehörden in Deutschland 1848–1945*. Göttingen, 1958.

———. *Hindenburg und der Staat*. Göttingen, 1966.

Hunt, Richard N. *German Social Democracy, 1918–1933*. New Haven, 1964.

Jacobsen, Hans-Adolf. *Nationalsozialistische Aussenpolitik 1933–1938*. Frankfurt a. J., 1968.

Jacobson, Jon. *Locarno Diplomacy: Germany and the West, 1925–1929*. Princeton, 1972.

Klein, Burton S. *Germany's Economic Preparations for War*. Cambridge, Mass., 1959.

Klein, Fritz (ed.). *Deutschland im ersten Weltkrieg*. 3 vols. East Berlin, 1968–69.

Kochan, Lionel. *Russia and the Weimar Republic*. New York, 1954.

Kotowski, Georg. *Friedrich Ebert; Eine politische Biographie*. 2 vols. Wiesbaden, 1963–68.

Kuczynski, Jürgen. *Darstellung der Lage der Arbeiter in Westdeutschland seit 1945*. 2 vols. East Berlin, 1965.

Kuhn, Axel. *Hitlers aussenpolitisches Programm: Entstehung und Entwicklung 1919–1939*. Stuttgart, 1970.

Kulski, W. W. *Germany and Poland: From War to Peaceful Relations*. Syracuse, 1976.

Laursen, Karsten and J. Pedersen. *The German Inflation, 1918–1923*. Amsterdam, 1964.

Lebovics, Herman. *Social Conservatism and the Middle Class in Germany, 1914–1933*. Princeton, 1969.

Lewy, Guenter. *The Catholic Church in Nazi Germany*. New York and Toronto, 1964.

Manchester, William. *The Arms of Krupp*. Boston and Toronto, 1968.

Maser, Werner, *Adolf Hitler: Legende, Mythos, Wirklichkeit*. Munich, 1971. Trans. as *Hitler: Legend, Myth, and Reality*. New York, 1973.

Mason, Herbert Molloy, Jr. *The Rise of the Luftwaffe: Forging the Secret German Air Weapon, 1918–1940*. New York, 1973.

Matthias, Erich and R. Morsey. *Das Ende der Parteien*. Düsseldorf, 1960.

Maurer, Ilse. *Reichsfinanze und Grosse Koalition. Zur Geschichte des Reichskabinetts Müller 1928–1930*. Bern, 1973.

Mayer, Arno J. *Politics and Diplomacy of Peacemaking: Containment and Counter-revolution at Versailles, 1918–1919*. New York, 1968.

McSherry, James E. *Stalin, Hitler and Europe, 1933–1939: The Origins of World War II*. Cleveland, 1968.

Meier-Welcker, Hans. *Seeckt*. Frankfurt a. M., 1967.

Meyer, Karl W. *Karl Liebknecht: Man without a Country*. Washington, 1957.

Miller, Susanne. *Burgfrieden und Klassenkampf: Die Deutsche Sozialdemokratie im Ersten Weltkrieg*. Düsseldorf, 1974.

Milward, S. *The German Economy at War*. London, 1965.

Mitchell, Allen. *Revolution in Bavaria, 1918–1919*. Princeton, 1965.

Morsey, Rudolf and K. Repgen. *Adenauer Studien*. Munich, 1971.

Mosley, Leonard. *On Borrowed Time: How World War II Began*. New York, 1969.

Mosse, George L. *The Nationalization of the Masses: Political Symbolism and Mass Movements in Germany from the Napoleonic Wars through the Third Reich*. New York, 1975.

Müller, K. J. *Das Heer und Hitler: Armee und nationalsozialistische Regime 1933–1940*. Bonn, 1969.

Nettle, Peter. *Rosa Luxemburg*. abridged ed. New York, 1969.

Nolte, Ernst. *Deutschland und der Kalte Krieg*. Munich, 1974.

O'Neill, Robert J. *The German Army and the Nazi Party, 1933–1939*. London, 1966.

Orlow, Dietrich. *The History of the Nazi Party, 1933–1945*. Pittsburgh, 1973.

Peters, Max. *Friedrich Ebert*. 2nd ed. Berlin, 1954.

Petersen, Jens. *Hitler-Mussolini: Die Entstehung der Achse Berlin-Rom 1933–1936*. Tübingen, 1973.

Peterson, Edward. *The Limits of Hitler's Power*. Princeton, 1969.

Pirker, Tho. *Die SPD nach Hitler: Die Geschichte der sozialdemokratischen Partei Deutschlands 1945–1964*. Munich, 1965.

Plessner, H. *Die verspätete Nation* (Weimar Republic). Stuttgart, 1959.

Poppinga, Anneliese. *Konrad Adenauer: Geschichtsverständnis, Weltanschauung und politische Praxis*. Stuttgart, 1975.

Pritti, Terence. *Willy Brandt: Portrait of a Statesman*. New York, 1974.

Pritzel, Konstantin. *Die wirtschaftliche Integration der sowietischen Besatzungszone Deutschlands in den Ostblock und ihre politischen Aspekte*. Bonn, 1965.

Rich, Norman. *Hitler's Aims*. Vol. I: *Ideology, the Nazi State, and the Course of Expansion;* Vol. II: *The Establishment of the New Order*. New York, 1973–74.

Ritter, Gerhard. *Carl Goerdeler und die deutsche Widerstandsbewegung*. Stuttgart, 1954.

Robertson, Esmonde M. *Hitler's Pre-War Policy and Military Plans, 1933–1939*. London and New York, 1963.

Roh, Franz. *German Art in the Twentieth Century*. Greenwich, Conn., 1968.

Rosenberg, Arthur. *The Birth of the German Republic*. London, 1932.

Ryders, A. J. *The German Revolution of 1918: A Study of German Socialism in War and Revolt*. Cambridge, Mass., 1967.

Schoenbaum, David. *Hitler's Social Revolution: Class and Status in Nazi Germany, 1933–1939*. Garden City, N.Y., 1967.

Schramm, P. *Hitler als militärischer Führer*. Frankfurt am Main, 1962.

Schulz, G. *Zwischen Demokratie und Diktatur: Verfassungspolitik und Reichsreform in der Weimarer Republik*. Vol. I: 1919–1930. Berlin, 1963.

Seaton, Albert. *The Russo-German War, 1941–1945*. New York, 1971.

Silberstein, Gerard E. *The Troubled Alliance: German-Austrian Relations, 1914–1917*. Louisville, 1970.

Smith, Jean Edward. *Germany Beyond the Wall*. Boston and Toronto, 1969.

Speer, Albert. *Inside the Third Reich*. New York, 1970.

Steglich, W. *Die Friedenspolitik der Mittelmächte 1917–1918*. Vol. I. Wiesbaden, 1964.

Stehkämpfer, Hugo, ed. *Konrad Adenauer: Festgabe*. Cologne, 1976.

Steinert, Marlis G. *Hitlers Krieg und die Deutschen*. Düsseldorf, 1970.

Stürmer, Michael. *Koalition und Opposition in der Weimarer Republik 1924–1928*. Düsseldorf. 1967.

Thimme, Annaliese. *Gustav Stresemann: Eine politische Biographie*. Hanover, 1959.

Thomson, Laurence. *The Greatest Treason: The Untold Story of Munich*. New York, 1968.

Trumpener, Ulrich. *Germany and the Ottoman Empire, 1914–1918*. Princeton, 1965.

Turner, Henry A. *Gustav Stresemann and the Politics of the Weimar Republic*. Princeton, 1963.

Volkmann, Hans-Erlich. *Die deutsche Baltikum-politik zwischen Brest-Litovsk und Compiègne*. Cologne, 1970.

Waidson, H. M. *The Modern German Novel*. London, 1959.

Weber, Hermann. *Die Wandlung des deutschen Kommunismus. Die Stalinisierung der KPD in der Weimarer Republik*. 2 vols. Frankfurt am Main. 1969.

——— . *Von der SBZ zur DDR 1945–1968*. Hanover, 1968.

Weinberg, Gerhard. *Germany and the Soviet Union, 1939–1941*. rev. ed. Leiden, 1972.

———. *The Foreign Policy of Hitler's Germany, 1933–1936*. Chicago, 1970.

Wettig, *Entmilitarisierung und Wiederbewaffnung in Deutschland. 1943–1955*. Munich, 1967.

Whaley, Barton. *Codeword Barbarossa*. Cambridge, Mass., 1973.

Wheeler-Bennett, J. W. *The Nemesis of Power: The German Army in Politics*. London, 1953; New York, 1964.

Wighton, Charles. *Adenauer: A Critical Biography*. New York, 1963.

Wiskemann, Elizabeth. *The Rome-Berlin Axis*. New York, 1949.

Zapf, W. *Wandlungen der deutschen Elite 1919–1961*. Munich, 1965.

Zimmermann, Ludwig. *Deutsche Aussenpolitik in der Ära der Weimarer Republik*. Göttingen, 1958.

INDEX